A Publication of the Law School Admission Council

The Official Guide to U.S. Law Schools

FROM THE PRODUCERS OF THE LSAT

Bantam Doubleday Dell

Published by
Bantam Doubleday Dell Publishing Group, Inc.
1540 Broadway
New York, New York 10036

The Law School Admission Council is a nonprofit corporation that provides services to the legal education community. Its members are 193 law schools in the United States and Canada.

Law School Admission Council fees, policies, and procedures relating to, but not limited to, test registration, test administration, test score reporting, misconduct, and other matters may change without notice at any time. To remain up to date on Law School Admission Council policies and procedures, you may obtain a new *Registration and Information Book*, or you may contact our candidate service representatives.

ISBN: 0-385-32340-9

ISSN: 0886-3342

Manufactured in the United States of America
Published simultaneously in Canada

June 1996

10 9 8 7 6 5 4 3 2 1

Table of Contents

How to Use This Book

The Official Guide to U.S. Law Schools is both a resource book for individuals seeking broad information about law school in general, and an up-to-date, detailed guide to the 178 ABA-approved law schools.

In the school profiles section, which comprises the bulk of this book, you will find several pages of information on each of the LSAC-member law schools in the United States. This information is provided by the individual schools each fall and includes current data on the school's admission process, programs of study, enrollment and student body, faculty, library and physical facilities, career services, financial aid, and more. We also offer a visual geographic guide to law schools across the country. We provide information on school and city populations on these pages as well. Most schools include an admission profile grid displaying information on the number of applicants and admitted students grouped by their LSAT scores and GPA numbers.

The first 13 chapters of the *Official Guide* are geared toward answering your questions if you are:

- considering a law school education after graduation from college;
- preparing to enter law school in the near future;
- thinking about law as a possible career choice; or
- contemplating a change from your current career.

The *Guide* gives answers to the most commonly asked questions regarding law as a career, preparation for and application to law school, the choice of a school to attend, and the financing of a law school education. Additionally, the *Guide* addresses the important issue of opportunities in law for minority men and women. Information can be found both within the individual school descriptions and, more specifically, in Chapter 7. This book also contains recent information regarding admission to the bar and job prospects, including useful statistics based on the experiences of 1994 law school graduates.

No guidebook on legal education can rightly claim to be a final authority on the many questions that the law school applicant will encounter. Whether you are choosing a school, selecting courses or other activities, or investigating career opportunities, you will be faced with decisions that, in the final analysis, will be yours alone to make. As you seek counsel from those who have been to law school, those who teach law school, those who admit students to law school, and those who successfully practice law, you are likely to meet strongly divergent viewpoints on the numerous points that concern you. Regarding various aspects of legal education, there is no single school of thought, but rather ongoing, vigorous discussion of numerous important issues. Your research will help you to make **informed** choices, which will increase your chances of success in meeting your own goals. We urge you to review carefully the information in this book and understand its limitations. Additionally, you should seek information from as many sources as possible, particularly from the law schools themselves. The information provided in this volume is one way to start.

Chapter 1: Being a Lawyer

Lawyers and Their Skills

Law practice is so diverse that it is not possible to describe the so-called typical lawyer. Each lawyer works with different clients and different legal problems. Ordinarily, certain basic legal skills are required of all lawyers. They must know:

- how to **analyze** legal issues in light of the existing state of the law, the direction in which the law is headed, and relevant policy considerations;
- how to **synthesize** material in light of the fact that many issues are multifaceted and require the combination of diverse elements into a coherent whole;
- how to **advocate** the views of groups and individuals within the context of the legal system;
- how to give intelligent **counsel** on the law's requirements;
- how to **write** and **speak** clearly; and
- how to **negotiate** effectively.

■ Analyzing

Lawyers must be able to determine the fundamental elements of problems. They spend much time discerning the nature and significance of the many issues in a particular problem. In every issue, the lawyer must study the relationship between each element in order to arrive at an answer, result, or solution.

■ Synthesizing

Lawyers must learn that because of the complexities of many issues and the number of laws either directly or tangentially relevant, they must be able to pull together in a meaningful, focused, cogent manner often large amounts of material.

■ Advocating

As an advocate, the lawyer's role is to represent his or her client's particular point of view and interests as vigorously as possible. The American judicial system assumes that equitable solutions will emerge from the clash of opposing interests. The success of this adversarial system of American law depends upon the talents and training of the lawyers who work as advocates within it. Lawyers must be able to use their advocacy skills to marshal evidence and present arguments as to why a particular outcome is desirable.

■ Counseling

Lawyers also spend a good deal of their time giving clients legal advice. Few ventures in the modern world can be undertaken without some understanding of the law. Through their knowledge of what the law involves, lawyers advise clients about partnerships, decisions, actions, and many other subjects. In many cases, the lawyer's role as a counselor serves as much to prevent litigation as to support it.

■ Writing and Speaking

Whether in the courtroom or the law office, lawyers must be effective communicators. If lawyers could not translate thoughts and opinions into clear and precise English, it would be difficult for the law to serve society. After all, the law is embodied in words, and many of the disputes that give birth to laws begin with language—its meaning, use, and interpretation. Litigation leads to written judicial opinions; congressional enactments are recorded as printed statutes; and even economic transactions must be expressed as formal, written contracts.

■ Negotiating

One of the lawyer's primary roles is reconciling divergent interests and opinions. When the parties to a proposed transaction disagree, the lawyer, acting as a facilitator, may be able to help them negotiate to a common ground. Although the client's interests are a lawyer's first priority, often those interests are served best after compromise and conciliation have paved the way to an equitable settlement. Because lawyers are trained to see the implications of alternative courses of action, they are often able to break an impasse.

Fields of Law

Lawyers are central figures in the life of a democratic country. They may deal with major courtroom cases or minor traffic disputes, complex corporate mergers or straightforward real estate transactions. Lawyers may work for giant industries, small businesses, government agencies, international organizations, public interest groups, legal aid offices, and universities—or they may work for themselves. They represent both the impoverished and the wealthy, the helpless and the powerful. Lawyers may work solo, in a small group, or in a large law firm.

About 72.9 percent of American lawyers are in private practice, most in small, one-person offices and some in large firms. Roughly 8.2 percent of the profession works for government agencies, 9.5 percent works for private industries and associations as salaried lawyers or as managers, 1.1 percent works for legal aid or as public defenders, and one percent is in legal education. (About 4.6 percent are retired or inactive.) Many lawyers develop expertise in a particular field of law. Large law firms that provide a full range of legal services tend to employ more specialists. The sole practitioner, who must handle a variety of problems alone, may have greater opportunity to work in several areas. Of course, there are lawyers in large firms who maintain general practices, and lawyers in one-person offices who concentrate on a particular legal issue. Both specialized and general practice can be rewarding. One offers the satisfaction of mastering a particular legal discipline, and the other the challenge of exploring new fields. Following are brief descriptions of selected areas of specialization, though there are many areas of the law that can rightly fall into more than one category:

■ Corporate Law

The corporate lawyer helps clients conduct their business affairs in a manner that is efficient and consistent with the law. The responsibilities of a corporate lawyer can range from preparing the initial articles of incorporation and bylaws for a new enterprise to handling a corporate reorganization under the provisions of federal bankruptcy law. Examples of other areas of corporate law practice include (but are not limited to) contract, intellectual property, legislative compliance, and liability matters.

■ Criminal Law

Criminal defense lawyers represent clients accused of crimes. Their public counterparts are the prosecutors and district attorneys who represent the interests of the state in the prosecution of those accused of crimes. Both types of criminal lawyers deal with fundamental issues of the law and personal liberty. They defend many of the basic rights considered crucial to the preservation of a free and just society.

■ Environmental Law

Environmental law is a relatively new area that was born out of widespread public and professional concern about the fate of our natural resources. Lawyers in this field may tackle legal and regulatory issues relating to air and water quality, hazardous waste practice, natural gas transportation, oil and gas exploration and development, electric power licensing, water rights, toxic torts, public land use, marine resources, and energy trade regulation. They may work directly for governmental agencies that address environmental problems or represent corporations, public interest groups, and other entities concerned about protecting the environment.

■ Family Law

Family, or domestic relations, law is concerned with relationships between individuals in the context of the family. Many lawyers who practice this kind of law are members of small law firms or are sole practitioners. They specialize in solving problems that arise among family members and in creating or dissolving personal relationships through such means as adoption or divorce.

■ Intellectual Property Law

Intellectual property law is concerned with the protection of inventors' rights in their discoveries, authors' rights in their creations, and businesses' rights in their identifying marks. Often, an intellectual property lawyer will specialize in a particular area of the law. For example, for those attorneys with a technical background, patent law is a way to combine one's scientific and legal background into one practice. A copyright attorney counsels authors, composers, and artists on the scope of their rights in their writings, music, sculpture, and even personal identities, negotiates contracts which will protect these rights, and litigates in court to enforce these rights. Additionally, in today's global economy, intellectual property issues are at the forefront of international trade negotiations and environmental treaties.

■ International Law

International law has grown significantly as a field of practice, reflecting the increasing interdependence of nations and economies. Public international law provides a limited range of job opportunities, particularly with national governments or international institutions or with public interest bodies. Immigration and refugee law also assumes increasing importance as more people move more frequently across national boundaries for business, tourism, or permanent resettlement. Private international law may offer more extensive employment opportunities, either through law firms or for corporations, banks, or telecommunications firms. Fluency in another language or familiarity with another culture can be a decided advantage for law school graduates who seek to practice in the international arena.

■ Securities Law

Securities law is an extremely complex area that almost always requires the services of a specialist. In the past, lawyers who acquired this specialty were involved with the formation, organization, and financing of corporations through securities such as stock. However, in recent years, such lawyers also have become involved in mergers, acquisitions, and corporate takeovers.

■ Tax Law

In the past 50 years, the importance and complexity of federal, state, and local taxes have necessitated a specialty in this field of law. It is one area of the law where change is constant. The federal Internal Revenue Code and its associated regulations are now several thousand pages in length. New statutes, court decisions, and administrative rulings are issued frequently, and the tax lawyer must be alert to these changes. Economic planning usually includes attention to taxes, and the tax lawyer often assists clients in understanding and minimizing their tax liabilities.

Chapter 2: Becoming a Lawyer

A legal education is both challenging and rewarding. You will develop your analytical, synthesizing, creative, and logical thinking skills, and you will strengthen your reading and debating abilities. A legal education is necessary to become a lawyer in the United States, but it is also excellent preparation for many other careers, both because of the framework for organizing knowledge it provides and the analytical approach it brings to problems. Many teachers, business people, and writers first obtained a legal education before pursuing careers other than law.

Juris Doctor Degree

ABA-approved law schools generally require three years of full-time study to earn the Juris Doctor (J.D.) degree. Schools with part-time programs require four years of part-time study to earn the J.D. degree. Most law schools share a common approach to training lawyers. However, they differ in the emphasis they give to certain subjects and teaching methods, such as opportunities for independent study, legal internships, participation in clinical programs, and involvement with governmental affairs.

Law school can be an intense, competitive environment. Students have little time for other interests, especially during the first year of law school. The ABA requires that no full-time student hold an outside job for more than 20 hours a week. Most schools encourage their students to become totally immersed in reading, discussing, and thinking about the law.

■ The First Year

The newness of the first year of law school is exciting for many and anxiety-provoking for almost all. Professors expect you to be prepared in class, but in most courses, grades will be determined primarily from examinations administered at the end of the semester or, at some schools, the end of the year. The professor may give little feedback until the final examination.

■ The Case Method Approach

The "case method" is what first-year law students are likely to find least familiar. By focusing on the underlying principles that shape the law's approach to different situations, you will learn to distinguish among subtly different legal results and to identify the critical factors that determine a particular outcome. Once these distinctions are mastered, you should be able to apply this knowledge to new situations.

The case method involves the detailed examination of a number of related judicial opinions that describe an area of law. You will also learn to apply the same critical analysis to legislative materials and scholarly articles. The role of the law professor is to provoke and stimulate. For a particular case, he or she may ask questions designed to explore the facts presented, to determine the legal principles applied in reaching a decision, and to analyze the method of reasoning used. In this way, the professor encourages you to relate the case to others and to distinguish it from those with similar but inapplicable precedents. In order to encourage you to learn to defend your reasoning, the professor may adopt a position contrary to the holding of the case.

Because this process places much of the burden of learning on the student, classroom discussions can be exciting. They are also demanding. However uninformed, unprepared, or puzzled you may be, you will be required to participate in these discussions.

■ The Ability to Think

The case method reflects the general belief that the primary purpose of law school is not to teach substantive law but to teach you to think like a lawyer. Teachers of law are less concerned about rules and technicalities than are their counterparts in many other disciplines. Although the memorization of specifics may be useful to you, the ability to be analytical and literate is considerably more important than the power of total recall. One reason for this approach to legal education is that in our common-law tradition, the law is constantly evolving and changing; thus, specific rules may quickly lose their relevance.

Law is more an art than a science. The reality lawyers seek in analyzing a case is not always well-defined. Legal study, therefore, requires an attentive mind and a tolerance for ambiguity. Because many people believe incorrectly that the study of law involves the memorization of rules in books and principles dictated by learned professors, law schools often attract those people who especially value structure, authority, and order. The study of law does **not** involve this kind of certainty, however; complex legal questions do not have simple legal solutions. Law professors rarely have the answers and they prefer to encourage students to develop their own responses to legal issues.

■ The Curriculum

As a first-year law student, you will follow a designated course of study that may cover many of the following subjects:

- **Civil procedure**—the process of adjudication in the United States; i.e., jurisdiction and standing to sue, motions and pleadings, pretrial procedure, the structure of a lawsuit, and appellate review of trial results.

- **Constitutional law**—the legislative powers of the federal and state governments, and questions of civil liberties and constitutional history, including detailed study of the Bill of Rights and constitutional freedoms.

- **Contracts**—the nature of enforceable promises and rules for determining appropriate remedies in case of nonperformance.
- **Criminal law and criminal procedure**—bases of criminal responsibility, the rules and policies for enforcing sanctions against individuals accused of committing offenses against the public order and well-being, and the rights guaranteed to those charged with criminal violations.
- **Legal method**—students' introduction to the organization of the American legal system and its processes.
- **Legal writing**—research and writing component of most first-year programs; requires students to research and write memoranda dealing with various legal problems.
- **Property law**—concepts, uses, and historical developments in the treatment of land, buildings, natural resources, and personal objects.
- **Torts**—private wrongs, such as acts of negligence, assault, and defamation, that violate obligations of the law.

In addition to attending classes, you may be required to participate in a moot court exercise in which you take responsibility for arguing a hypothetical court case.

After the first year, you will probably have the opportunity to select from a broad range of courses. Generally, you will take courses in administrative law, evidence, civil litigation, corporations, taxation, wills and trusts, commercial law, and family law before completing your degree. These universal courses are basic to legal education. Every law school supplements this basic curriculum with additional courses, such as international law, environmental law, conflict of laws, labor law, criminal procedure, and jurisprudence.

■ Opportunities to Practice What Is Learned

Legal education is primarily academic, in that students devote most of their time to mastering general concepts and principles that shape the law. Most schools offer a variety of professional skills courses as well. Law schools place less emphasis on matters such as legal drafting and law office management than on legal principles. However, a number of schools have programs designed to offer students direct experience in legal practice. These programs allow second- and third-year students to participate in court trials and appeals, render counseling, undertake legislative drafting, and do other legal work for academic credit. Schools differ in the range and variety of practical education they offer, but the trend toward integrating this experience with theoretical study continues to grow.

■ Extracurricular Activities

Student organizations greatly supplement classroom learning. Typically, these organizations are dedicated to advancing the interests of particular groups of law students, such as black, women, or Hispanic students; or to promoting greater understanding of specific legal fields, such as environmental or international law; or to providing opportunities for involvement in professional, social, and sports activities.

A unique feature of American law schools is that law students manage and edit most of the legal profession's principal scholarly journals. Membership on the editorial staffs of these journals, also called law reviews, is considered a mark of academic distinction. Selection is ordinarily based on outstanding academic performance, writing ability, or both, as discussed on page 19 of this book.

Bar Associations

Bar associations are membership organizations designed to raise the standards of the legal profession and to encourage professional unity. Each state has its own bar association. There are also a variety of national, state, local, and special-interest bar associations.

The largest national organization of attorneys in the United States is the American Bar Association (ABA), which sponsors a number of programs dealing with legal education, law reform, judicial selection, and professional responsibility. The ABA publishes the *Model Rules of Professional Conduct*, a set of regulations governing ethical standards in the practice of law. Attorneys who violate such standards are subject to censure, suspension, or disbarment by the state bar admitting authorities.

Many bar associations sponsor programs intended to broaden the availability of legal services and to familiarize the public with the legal profession. They also conduct extensive continuing legal education programs to help members update their skills and their knowledge of the law.

■ Admission to the Bar

To practice law in the United States, every lawyer must be admitted to a state bar. Standards for admission to state bars are regulated by each state and differ from state to state. In order to be admitted to the bar, most states require that candidates:

- Possess a law degree from an ABA-approved law school;
- Pass state examinations that test their knowledge of the law, skill in reasoning, and understanding of legal ethics and professional responsibility; and

- Show evidence of fitness to practice law, understanding of legal ethics, and sound character.

Lawyers may practice only in the state or states where they are members of the bar in good standing. However, many states will admit a lawyer to its bar if the lawyer has been admitted to the bar of another state and has practiced law actively for a certain number of years. This is known as reciprocity. States usually grant temporary bar admission for particular cases.

Many states have student practice rules that, in conjunction with students' academic programs, admit advanced law students who are under the close supervision of an admitted lawyer. A few states require law students to register with the board of bar examiners before graduation or, in some cases, soon after they're enrolled in law school, if they intend to practice in those states. So, if you're planning to attend law school, you should check the bar admission requirements for those states in which you may wish to practice after graduation.

Federal courts set their own standards for admission. The most basic requirement for federal district court admission is that the lawyer be admitted to the bar in the state in which the federal district is located.

A good source of information regarding bar admission requirements is the latest edition of the ABA's *Comprehensive Guide to Bar Admission Requirements*, which should be available in any law school library.

■ Bar Approval and School Selection

A number of law schools have not been approved by the American Bar Association. Some states permit graduates of these schools to take the bar examination or will admit to their bars one who has been admitted to the bar of another state (even though he or she graduated from a school not approved by the ABA), but most do not. Before you enroll in a law school not approved by the ABA, contact the bar admission authorities in your state for more information about the limitations that may result from obtaining a degree from these programs.

A few institutions offer correspondence courses purporting to provide a legal education. The ABA expressly disapproves of correspondence law courses. Correspondence law school graduates are not eligible to take the bar examination in any state except California, and even there only under special conditions.

Legal Education and Bar Admission Statistics

Year	Total J.D. Enrollment*	Total J.D. Women Enrollment*	First Year Enrollment*	Total LSAT Administrations	Est. ABA Applicants†	J.D. or LL.B Awarded*	New Admissions to the Bar*
1981-82	120,879	43,245	42,521	119,291	72,912	35,598	45,382
1982-83	121,791	45,539	42,034	112,125	71,755	34,846	42,905
1983-84	121,201	46,361	41,159	105,076	63,801	36,389	41,684
1984-85	119,847	46,897	40,747	95,563	60,338	36,687	42,630
1985-86	118,700	47,486	40,796	91,848	61,304	36,829	42,450
1986-87	117,813	47,920	40,195	101,235	65,145	36,121	40,247***
1987-88	117,997	48,920	41,055	115,988	74,938	35,478	39,918***
1988-89	120,694	50,932	42,860	137,088	82,741	35,701	46,528
1989-90	124,471	53,113	43,826	138,865	88,303	35,520	47,174
1990-91	127,261	54,097	44,104	152,685	94,026	36,385	43,286***
1991-92	129,580	55,110	44,050	145,567	91,954	38,800	54,577
1992-93	128,212	54,644	42,793	140,054	86,104**	39,425**	57,117
1993-94	127,802	55,134	43,644	132,028	84,574	40,213	N/A
1994-95	128,989	55,808	44,298	128,553	78,821	39,710	N/A

* Sources for these figures include ABA's *A Review of Legal Education in the United States*, Fall 1994.
** Revised figure.
*** Data was not complete for these years; this figure is lower than prior years.
† Numbers noted in this column include only current-year applicants.

Chapter 3: Preparing for Law School

Acquire a Well-Balanced Education

Students interested in legal study should get the most from their undergraduate education. A college education should stand on its own merits as preparation for a lifetime of active involvement in a diverse and changing society.

Admission committees are usually impressed by applicants who can convincingly demonstrate that they've challenged their thinking and reasoning skills in a diverse course of undergraduate study. Law schools prefer students who can think, read, and write well, and who have some understanding of what shapes human experience. Because a lawyer's work involves most aspects of our complex society, a broad liberal arts curriculum is the preferred preparation for law school.

Maintain a Rigorous Courseload

High academic standards are important when selecting your undergraduate courses. The range of acceptable majors is broad; the quality of the education you receive is most important. Undergraduate programs should reveal your capacity to perform well at an academically rigorous level. An undergraduate career that is narrow, unchallenging, or vocationally oriented is not the best preparation for law school.

Law school admission committees want to see how the courses you chose relate to one another, and they want a sense of how you rise to intellectual challenge, whether in the sciences, the liberal arts, the business curriculum, or elsewhere. In assessing how favorably a law school will view your application, you should examine your courses. Try to fit them into this sort of overview. To what extent can they be seen as part of a whole, and to what extent do the parts seem to coalesce intellectually?

The Pros and Cons of a "Prelaw" Major

Unlike the premedical curriculum that contains specific courses, some obligatory, there is no recommended set of prelaw courses. Law schools prefer that you reserve your legal study for law school and fill your undergraduate curriculum with broad, diverse, and challenging courses. Prelaw courses that introduce you to broad legal principles may present you with enough information to decide whether you want to continue with a legal education, but they are rarely taught with the same depth and rigor as actual law school courses. A prelaw curriculum that is designed to encompass a broad array of liberal arts courses, however, can be excellent preparation for law school. Be sure you know precisely what is meant by "prelaw" when choosing your undergraduate course of study.

Prelaw Advisors

Prelaw advisors at undergraduate institutions are a good source of information before and during the law school admission process. If you are considering law school, you should introduce yourself to a prelaw advisor as soon as possible. The advisor knows his or her school's course offerings quite well and will be able to direct you to courses that will better prepare you for law school. The prelaw advisor should also be quite helpful during the law school application process. Advisors have the latest information on the Law School Admission Test (LSAT), the Law School Data Assembly Service (LSDAS), and even on many law school requirements. In addition, they may be able to point you toward law schools that would be particularly well suited to your needs and interests.

If you are considering law school but are not currently enrolled in a university, you may be able to obtain counsel from the undergraduate prelaw advisor at the college from which you graduated. Most prelaw advisors will be happy to answer any questions you may have.

Chapter 4: LSAT and Other Criteria for Admission

How Law Schools Select Applicants

Almost everyone admitted to law school graduates. In fact, on average, less than 5 percent of law students drop out of school for academic reasons.

No concrete principles exist for predicting who will perform well in law school, so admission committees seek the most qualified from the pool of applicants. In order to be fair, schools rely heavily upon selection criteria that bear on expected performance in law school and can be applied objectively to all candidates. Law schools consider a variety of factors in admitting their students, and no single qualification will independently guarantee acceptance or rejection. However, the two factors that usually outweigh the rest are prior academic performance and the Law School Admission Test score.

The most difficult admission decisions are those regarding candidates who are neither so well qualified nor so deficient as to present a clear-cut case for acceptance or rejection. These applicants constitute the majority of the applicant pool at many law schools and are the candidates that most law schools spend the bulk of their time reviewing.

■ Criteria that May Be Considered by Law School Admission Committees

- LSAT score
- Undergraduate grade-point average
- Undergraduate course of study
- Graduate work, if any
- College attended
- Improvement in grades and grade distribution
- College curricular and extracurricular activities
- Ethnic/racial background
- Individual character and personality
- Letters of recommendation
- Written personal statement on the application
- Work experience or other postundergraduate experiences
- Community activities
- Motivation to study and reasons for deciding to study law
- State of residency
- Difficulties that you have overcome
- Precollege preparation
- Anything else that stands out in an application

The Law School Admission Test (LSAT)

All American Bar Association (ABA)-approved law schools and many non-ABA-approved law schools require that you take the LSAT. (On rare occasions, exceptions may be made for people with certain disabilities.)

The test consists of five 35-minute sections of multiple-choice questions, in three different item types. A 30-minute writing sample is administered at the end of the test. Four of the five sections contribute to the test taker's score. The fifth section typically is used to pretest new test items and to preequate new test forms. Law Services does not score the writing sample. Copies of the writing sample are sent to all law schools to which you apply.

Some schools place greater weight than others on the LSAT; still, low LSAT scores will hamper your chances for admission, particularly at the most competitive schools. Most law schools do make a genuine effort to evaluate your full credentials.

■ What the Test Measures

The LSAT is designed to measure skills that are considered essential for success in law school: the reading and comprehension of complex texts with accuracy and insight; the organization and management of information and the ability to draw reasonable inferences from it; the ability to reason critically; and the analysis and evaluation of the reasoning and argument of others.

The three item types in the LSAT are:

Reading Comprehension Questions
These questions measure your ability to read, with understanding and insight, examples of lengthy and complex materials similar to those commonly encountered in law school work. The reading comprehension items consist of passages of approximately 450 words, each followed by five to eight questions that test reading and reasoning abilities.

Analytical Reasoning Questions
These questions are designed to measure your ability to understand a structure of relationships and to draw conclusions about that structure. You are asked to make deductions from a set of statements, rules, or conditions that describe relationships among entities such as per-

sons, places, things, or events. They simulate the kinds of detailed analyses of relationships that a law student must perform in solving legal problems.

Logical Reasoning Questions
These questions are designed to evaluate your aptitude for understanding, analyzing, criticizing, and completing a variety of arguments. Each logical reasoning question requires you to read and comprehend a short passage, then answer one or two questions about it. The questions test a variety of abilities involved in reasoning logically and critically.

■ Your Score as a Predictor of Law School Performance

The LSAT, like any aptitude test, is not a perfect predictor of law school performance. The predictive power of an admission test is limited by many factors, such as the complexity of the skills the test is designed to measure and the unmeasurable factors that can affect students' performances, such as motivation, physical and mental health, or work and family responsibilities. In spite of these factors, the LSAT compares very favorably with admission tests used in other graduate and professional fields of study. (For additional information about the predictive value of LSAT scores, refer to Appendix G in the 1996-97 edition of the *LSAT/LSDAS Registration and Information Book.*)

■ Test Preparation

Most law school applicants familiarize themselves with test mechanics and question types, practice on sample tests, and study the information available on test-taking techniques and strategies. Though it is difficult to say when examinees are sufficiently prepared, very few people achieve their full potential without some preparation.

Law Services publishes a variety of materials to help you prepare for the LSAT.

The Official LSAT PrepTest

Each *Official LSAT PrepTest* contains a previously administered LSAT, an answer key, and a conversion table that helps you compute your score. The PrepTest allows you to prepare for the LSAT by simulating actual test conditions and checking your answers to see which question types you might need to practice. The disclosed tests are made available approximately six weeks after they are administered. *The Official LSAT Sample PrepTest* (the June 1991 test) is included as part of the *LSAT/LSDAS Registration and Information Book* which is available through the mail from Law Services, or at law school admission offices, undergraduate schools, and testing and counseling centers.

LSAT: The Official TriplePrep

Three PrepTests provide more practice than one, and buying three together in one book costs less than buying them separately. *TriplePrep—Volume 1* contains PrepTests II (October 1991 LSAT), IV (February 1992 LSAT), and V (June 1992 LSAT). *TriplePrep—Volume 2* contains PrepTests III (December 1991 LSAT), VI (October 1992 LSAT), and VII (February 1993 LSAT). *TriplePrep—Volume 3* contains PrepTests VIII (June 1993 LSAT), IX (October 1993 LSAT), and X (February 1994 LSAT). *TriplePrep* contains answer keys, writing samples, and score-conversion tables for all three PrepTests.

LSAT: The Official TriplePrep ***Plus*** *with Explanations*

This is the only official LSAC product that contains explanations for all three LSAT-item types. *TriplePrep* ***Plus*** also contains almost 50 previously administered writing sample prompts in addition to three complete PrepTests—XI (June 1994 LSAT), XII (October 1994 LSAT), and XIII (December 1994 LSAT). These PrepTests are also sold separately.

Candidates may order publications directly from Law Services by mail, or by telephone using a VISA, MasterCard, American Express, or DISCOVER. For further information, or to order publications, contact:

Law Services
Box 2400
661 Penn Street
Newtown, PA 18940-0977
215.968.1314

For further information about your LSAT score and on the question of taking the test more than one time, please refer to your *LSAT/LSDAS Registration and Information Book.*

Academic Record

Undergraduate performance is generally an important indicator of how someone is likely to perform in law school. Hence, many law schools look closely at college grades when considering individual applications.

Course selection also can make a difference in admission evaluations. Applicants who have taken difficult or advanced courses in their undergraduate study often are evaluated in a more favorable light than students who have concentrated on easier or less advanced subjects.

Many law schools consider undergraduate-performance trends along with a student's numerical average. Thus, they may discount a slow start in a student's undergraduate career if he or she performs exceptionally well in the later school years. Similarly, admission committees may see an undergraduate's strong start followed by a mediocre finish as an indication of less potential to do well in law school. Candidates are advised to comment on irregular grade trends in the personal statement section of the application.

Grade Conversion Table

LSDAS Conversion	Grades as Reported on Transcripts				
4.0 Scale	A to F	1 to 5	100-0*	Four Passing Grades	Three Passing Grades
4.33 4.00 3.67 3.50	A+ A A- AB	1+ 1 1-	98-100 93-97 90-92	Highest Passing Grade (4.0)	Highest Passing Grade (4.0)
3.33 3.00 2.67 2.50	B+ B B- BC	2+ 2 2-	87-89 83-86 80-82	Second Highest Passing Grade (3.0)	Middle Passing Grade (3.0)
2.33 2.00 1.67 1.50	C+ C C- CD	3+ 3 3-	77-79 73-76 70-72	Third Highest Passing Grade (2.0)	Lowest Passing Grade (2.0)
1.33 1.00 0.67 0.50	D+ D D- DE or DF	4+ 4 4-	67-69 63-66 60-62	Lowest Passing Grade (1.0)	
0.00	E and F	5	Below 60	Failure (0.0)	Failure (0.0)

*In some instances, a school's numeric grading scale might be converted differently than shown here.

Additional Admission Decision Factors

Most law schools consider more than academic records and LSAT scores when evaluating applicants. These factors are particularly significant after the preliminary review of an application.

Letters of Recommendation

The most effective letters of recommendation are those from professors who have known you well enough to write with candor, detail, and objectivity about your academic and personal achievements and potential. Work supervisors also can write in support of your application. Letters that compare you to your academic peers are often considered the most useful. Most schools do not consider general, unreservedly praiseworthy letters helpful. Some schools do not require letters at all, and some schools will not read letters of recommendation if they receive them.

Work Experience

Law schools want diverse, interesting classes, representative of a variety of backgrounds. A candidate who applies to law school several years after completing his or her undergraduate education, and who has demonstrated an ability to succeed in a nonacademic environment, is sometimes more motivated than one who continues his or her education without a break. In fact, only about 40 percent of law students enter directly from college.

Interviews

In general, interviews are not a part of the law school admission process. You are encouraged to visit law schools to gather information, and often an appointment with admission personnel will be a part of the visit. The purpose of your conversation with the admission staff will be informational rather than evaluative and will not become a part of your admission file. An occasional school will grant an interview, and some may even request it, but, in general, you should not count on an interview as a means to state your case for admission; this is best done in the personal statement.

Graduate or Professional Study

Prior success or failure in other graduate or professional school work, including other law schools, may also be a factor in the admission committee's decision. In any case, you are required to report such work to any law school to which you apply.

Minority Applicants

Almost all law schools have active recruitment programs for students who are members of minority groups to help ensure greater minority representation in the legal profession. Law schools strongly encourage minority applicants. (See Chapter 7 for further details on minority recruitment and enrollment.)

Your Personal Essay

Always remember that there is something special—something interesting—about you. Maybe you've had some experience, some training, or some dream that sets you apart from others. Law schools want to recruit men and women who are qualified for reasons beyond grades and scores. The essay or personal statement in your application is the place to tell the committee why you are special. Your application is definitely not the place to be falsely modest.

In general, your evaluation of actual experiences has more value to the committee than speculation about future accomplishments. Also, if you have overcome a serious obstacle in your life to get where you are today, by all means let the admission committee know about it. Any noteworthy personal experience or accomplishment may be an appropriate subject for your essay, as long as it is meaningful and interesting. Be sure to do more than just state it; describe what you are talking about briefly but concretely, and why it had value to you, whether it is a job, your family, or your upbringing. You are simultaneously trying to add information and create structure. **Be brief, be factual, be comprehensive, and be organized.**

You are a storyteller here. You want a living person—**you**—to emerge. The statement is your opportunity to become vivid and alive to the reader, and it is an opportunity to demonstrate your ability to write and present a prose sample in a professional manner.

Assessing Yourself Realistically

When selecting law schools to which you will apply, the general philosophy is that you should have a threefold plan: dream a little, be realistic, and be safe. Most applicants have no trouble selecting dream schools—those that are almost, but not quite, beyond their grasp—or safe schools—those for which admission is virtually certain. Applicants often have difficulty being realistic about their qualifications and their chances of being accepted at particular law schools.

Unquestionably, **the number one strategic error in law school admission is a candidate's failure to evaluate realistically his or her own credentials.**

■ Use Admission Profile Grids in this Book

Check your qualifications against the admission profile of the law schools to which you aspire. Most schools publish detailed statistics on how many applicants with a certain LSAT score and GPA are accepted. You can also find LSAT/GPA data grids, charts, and statistics in this book. You may use these data to help you determine where you should apply. Apply to those law schools whose student body profiles most closely match your personal profile. Those schools will be as anxious to accept you as you are to be admitted.

The school profiles contained in this volume should provide you with some of the information you'll need to help you make this decision. You should make your final decision only after reading the informational materials available directly from law schools.

■ Research Specific Law Schools that Interest You

Other sources of information include:

- **The school's admission office.** This is a good source for general information about your chances for admission . Do not hesitate to request admission counseling. Be sure to obtain current catalogs from each law school you are considering.
- **Your college or university prelaw advisor.** Your prelaw advisor can often provide you with reliable information about which law schools fit your personal

profile. He or she may also be able to tell you which law schools have accepted students from your school in the past and provide you with an overview of the admitted students' credentials. This is not to say that you should narrow your focus to only those law schools where others from your undergraduate school have been admitted.

- **Law School Forums.** The Law School Forums, organized by the Law School Admission Council, are excellent opportunities to talk with law school representatives from around the country in one central, urban location—usually a hotel exhibit hall. Recent forums have been held in Atlanta, Boston, Chicago, Houston, Los Angeles, and New York City. Forums are also being planned for Washington, DC, in the summer of 1996. In 1995, 160 of the 178 U.S. LSAC-member law schools participated in the forums, and 14,848 people registered as attendees. Because the costs of traveling to a number of law schools can be expensive, many prospective law students find the forums to be the most productive means of gathering information and making school contacts. Approximately 21.4 percent of the forum attendees traveled over 100 miles to get to a forum. Forum admission is free; for dates, times, and locations of 1996 Law School Forums, see the list toward the end of this book.

- **School representatives and alumni.** Take advantage of opportunities to talk with law school representatives and alumni. When you talk with alumni, remember that law schools sometimes change fairly quickly. Try to talk to a recent graduate or to one who is active in alumni affairs and therefore knowledgeable about the school as it is today.

- **School visits.** You can learn a surprising amount about a school from talks with students and faculty members. Many law schools have formal programs in which a currently enrolled student will take you on a tour of the campus and answer your questions. Such a first-hand experience can be quite valuable in assessing how you would fit into the school.

■ Keep Your Options Open

Flexibility is a key word in the law school admission process. Keep your options open. Even during the early stages of the admission process, you should continually reevaluate your prospects and prepare alternative plans. For example, don't set your sights on only one law school and one plan of action. You could severely limit your potential and your chance to practice law.

Chapter 5: Applying to Law School

Working With Law Services: Registering for the LSAT, Subscribing to the LSDAS

Law Services administers the LSAT and serves as a liaison for much of the communication between you and the law schools. You are expected to send your individual law school application **directly to each law school** to which you apply; however, your test scores, transcripts, and other academic information and biographical data are sent to the law schools through the Law School Data Assembly Service (LSDAS).

Comprehensive information about LSAT registration and LSDAS subscription is set forth in complete detail in the *LSAT/LSDAS Registration and Information Book*, published annually. This publication is available at no charge through Law Services or at any of 1,500 national distribution sites located on undergraduate campuses (principally prelaw advising offices and career centers) and at law schools. (Law Services operators will provide a list of distribution locations nearest your zip code; call 215.968.1001.)

You need not subscribe to the LSDAS at the same time you register for the LSAT, but doing so will simplify the process. Application deadlines for the law schools to which you apply dictate when you should subscribe to the LSDAS.

■ Planning Ahead for Law School Deadlines

Most law schools have a variety of application requirements and deadlines that you **must** meet to be considered for admission. If you are applying to a number of schools, the various deadlines and requirements can be confusing. It probably will be helpful if you set up a detailed calendar that will remind you of when and what you must do to complete an application.

You will also want to be sure you can make an LSAT score available to a law school before its application deadline. In registering for the LSAT, be sure to give yourself enough time to select a convenient testing location and prepare for the actual test.

Below is a chart listing all scheduled test administrations, including alternate dates for Saturday Sabbath observers, along with corresponding deadlines and fees.

LSAT Dates, Deadlines, and Fees (1996-1997)

All scheduled administrations of the LSAT, both for regular test takers and test takers who are Saturday Sabbath observers, are listed below along with their corresponding deadlines and fees.

Test Dates

▪ **Regular**	Monday, **June 10, 1996**	Saturday, **Oct. 5, 1996**	Saturday, **Dec. 7, 1996**	Saturday, **Feb. 8, 1997** Nondisclosed*	
▪ **Saturday Sabbath Observers**		Monday, **Oct. 7, 1996** Nondisclosed*	Monday, **Dec. 9, 1996** Nondisclosed*	Monday, **Feb. 10, 1997** Nondisclosed*	
▪ **Score Report mailed (approx.)**	**July 22, 1996**	**Nov. 18, 1996**	**Jan. 21, 1997**	**March 24, 1997**	
Deadlines	**Postmarked by**	**Postmarked by**	**Postmarked by**	**Postmarked by**	**Fees**
▪ **Regular Registration** US/Canada/Puerto Rico	**May 3, 1996**	**Aug. 30, 1996**	**Nov. 1, 1996**	**Jan. 3, 1997**	**$81**
Foreign	**April 26, 1996**	**Aug. 23, 1996**	**Oct. 25, 1996**	**Dec. 27, 1996**	
▪ **Late Registration by Mail** US/Canada/Puerto Rico	**May 4-10, 1996**	**Aug. 31-Sept. 6, 1996**	**Nov. 2-8, 1996**	**Jan. 4-10, 1997**	**$81** plus $49 late registration fee
▪ **Late Registration by Telephone** (215) 968-1001	**May 13-17, 1996**	**Sept. 9-13, 1996**	**Nov. 11-20, 1996**	**Jan. 13-17, 1997**	**$81** plus $49 late registration fee (VISA, MasterCard DISCOVER, and American Express only for telephone requests)
▪ **LSAT Registration Refunds** (partial only)	**June 17, 1996**	**Oct. 14, 1996**	**Dec. 16, 1996**	**Feb. 17, 1997**	**$36**

* Persons who take a nondisclosed test receive only their scores. They do not receive their test questions, answer key, or individual responses.

The Law School Data Assembly Service (LSDAS)

Nearly all LSAC-member law schools in the United States require applicants to subscribe to the LSDAS. Many nonmember law schools require this as well.

The LSDAS provides a means of centralizing and standardizing undergraduate academic records to simplify the law school admission process. The service organizes, analyzes, and summarizes biographical and academic information for law school applicants and subsequently prepares an LSDAS Law School Report to be sent within two weeks to all law schools from which a report request has been received.

If you subscribe to the LSDAS, every undergraduate, graduate, and professional school you have attended—including law school—must send an official transcript to Law Services. An official transcript is one that is signed, sealed, and sent by the registrar to Law Services. Do not send your own transcripts directly to Law Services; these will be returned to you unprocessed.

You may subscribe to the LSDAS by using the same registration form you use to register for the LSAT in the *Registration and Information Book*. This book also provides complete information on transcripts, LSDAS Law School Reports, and other LSDAS subscription information.

You will make the processes of registering for the LSAT and subscribing to the LSDAS much smoother if you take the time to read and understand all the information in your *Registration and Information Book*. Many applicants delay the processing of their registration forms because they have not followed all directions and have not filled out the forms correctly.

Information on LSDAS fees is as follows:

- **LSDAS subscription fee** 12 months of service (includes reporting to one law school requiring LSDAS) — **$82**
- **LSDAS Law School Reports** (ordered when you subscribe to LSDAS and pay the $82 LSDAS subscription fee) — **$8 each**
- **Additional LSDAS Law School Reports** (ordered after you subscribe to LSDAS initially) — **$10 each**
- **LSDAS subscription renewal** — **$49**

■ Fee Waivers for Law Services

Fee waivers are available for the LSAT, LSDAS, and TriplePrep **Plus** (see the *Registration and Information Book*). Fee waivers can be authorized by Law Services or LSAC-member law schools, which are listed in the *Registration and Information Book*. Fee waivers cannot be granted by financial aid offices of undergraduate institutions, non-LSAC -member law schools, or any other individual organization. See the *Registration and Information Book* or contact a law school admission office for details.

The Admission Process

Law school applicants can expect that the admission process will be quite competitive. Most law schools receive more than enough applications from highly qualified candidates, many of whom would be perfectly capable of completing a law school education. The dilemma for admission committees is that limited space and resources mandate the denial of admission to many of these candidates.

■ The Importance of Complete Files

Remember that law schools require complete files before making their decisions. A law school will consider your file complete when it has received your application form; LSDAS Law School Report (or LSAT Law School Report if the law school does not require the LSDAS); letters of recommendation (if required); any requirements unique to the particular school; and application fee.

■ Rolling Admission

Many law schools operate what is known as a rolling admission process: the school evaluates applications and informs candidates of admission decisions on a continuous basis over several months, usually beginning in late fall and extending to midsummer for waiting-list admissions.

At such schools, it is especially important for you to apply at the earliest possible date. The earlier you apply, the more places the school will have available. Most schools try to make comparable decisions throughout the admission season, even those that practice rolling admission. Still, it is disadvantageous to be one of the last applicants to complete a file. Furthermore, the more decisions you receive from law schools early in the process, the better able you will be to make your own decisions, such as whether to apply to more law schools or whether to accept a particular school's offer.

■ Applying to More than One School

The average applicant applies to 4.7 law schools. You should be sure to place your applications at schools representing a range of admission standards. Even if you have top qualifications, you should apply to at least one safety school where you are almost certain of being admitted. This is your insurance policy. If you apply to a safety school in November, and are accepted in January or February, you may be disappointed but not panicked if you are later rejected by your top choices.

■ The Preliminary Review of an Application

Applicants whose qualifications more than fulfill the school's admission standards are usually accepted during the first round of decisions. With some exceptions, candidates whose credentials fall below the school's standards are usually rejected. Full admission committees may never even get to examine these files.

Most applications are not decided upon immediately. They are usually reviewed in depth by a full committee that bases its admission decision on many facets of each application (see "How Law Schools Select Applicants," page 7). The length of time it takes the committee to review an application varies; consult the individual law schools to which you apply.

■ Waiting Lists

If you have strong qualifications, but you do not quite meet the competition of those currently being admitted at a particular law school, you may be placed on a waiting list for possible admission at a later date. The law school will send you a letter notifying you of its decision as early as April or as late as July.

It is up to you whether you wish to wait for a decision from a school that has put you on a waiting list or accept an offer from a school that accepted you at an earlier date.

Most schools rank students who are on the waiting list. Some law schools will tell you your rank. If a law school doesn't tell you, you might ask the admission office how many students have been placed on the waiting list.

■ Seat Deposits

Many law schools use seat deposits to help keep track of their new classes. For example, a school may require an initial acceptance fee of $100, which is credited to your first-term tuition if you actually register at the school; if you don't register, the deposit may be forfeited or returned partially. A school may require a larger deposit around July 1, which is also credited to tuition. If you decline the offer of admission after you've paid your deposit, a portion of the money may be refunded, depending on the date you actually decline the offer. At some schools, you may not be refunded any of the deposit.

The official position of the Law School Admission Council is:

> Except under early decision plans, law schools should permit applicants to choose among offers of admission as well as offers of scholarships, grants, and loans without penalty until April 1. Admitted applicants who have submitted a timely financial aid application should not be required to commit to enroll until notified of financial aid awards that are within the control of the law school.

Misconduct and Irregularities in the Admission Process

The Law School Admission Council has established procedures for dealing with instances of possible candidate misconduct or irregularities on the LSAT or in the law school admission process. Misconduct or irregularity is a serious offense with serious consequences. Misconduct or irregularity is the submission, as part of the law school admission process, of any information that is false or misleading. A finding of misconduct or irregularity does not require a finding of intent. Examples of misconduct and irregularities include, but are not limited to: submission of an altered or a nonauthentic transcript; submission of an application containing false or misleading information; submission of a fraudulent letter of recommendation; falsification of records for the purpose of applying to another law school; impersonation of another in taking the LSAT; switching of LSAT answer sheets with another; taking the LSAT for purposes other than law school admission; copying on, or other forms of cheating on, the LSAT; obtaining advance access to test materials; theft of test materials; submission of false information to the Law School Data Assembly Service (LSDAS); false statements or omissions of information requested on the LSAT/LSDAS Registration Form or on individual law school application forms; or falsification of transcript information, school attendance, honors, awards, or employment. A charge of misconduct or irregularity may be made prior to a candidate's admission to law school, after matriculation at a law school, or after admission to practice.

When alleged misconduct or irregularity brings into question the validity of the data about a candidate submitted to Law Services, the school may be notified of possible data error, and transmission of LSAT scores and LSDAS reports will be withheld until the matter has been resolved by the Law School Admission Council's Misconduct and Irregularities in the Admission Process Subcommittee. The Council and/or Law Services will investigate all instances of alleged misconduct or irregularities in the admission process in accordance with the *LSAC Rules Governing Misconduct and Irregularities in the Admission Process.*

A subcommittee representative will determine whether misconduct or an irregularity has occurred. If the subcommittee representative determines that a preponderance of the evidence shows misconduct or irregularity, then a report of the determination is sent to all law schools to which the individual has applied, subsequently applies, or has matriculated. Such reports are retained indefinitely.

In appropriate cases, and in accordance with the *Rules,* state and national bar authorities and other affected persons and institutions may also receive notification. Individual law schools and bar authorities determine what action, if any, they will take in response to a finding of misconduct or irregularity. Such action may include the closing of an admission file, revocation of an offer of admission, dismissal from law school through a school's internal disciplinary channels, or disbarment. Thus, a finding of misconduct or irregularity is a very serious matter. More information regarding misconduct and irregularity procedures may be obtained by contacting Law Services.

Chapter 6: Choosing a Law School

For some people, the choice of which law school to attend is an easy one. The most outstanding students will probably be able to go anywhere, and they will select the schools they perceive to be the most prestigious or which offer a program of particular interest. Others who need to stay in a particular area, perhaps because they have a family or a job they don't want to leave, will choose nearby schools and schools with part-time programs.

However, the majority of applicants will have to weigh a variety of personal and academic factors to come up with a list of potential schools. Then, once they have a list, and more than one acceptance letter, they will have to choose a school. Applicants should consider carefully the offerings of each law school before making a decision. The quality of a law school is certainly a major consideration; however, estimations of quality are very subjective. Factors such as the campus atmosphere, the school's devotion to teaching and learning, and the applicant's enthusiasm for the school also are very important. Remember that the law school is going to be your home for three years. Adjusting to law school and the general attitudes of a professional school is difficult enough without the additional hardship of culture shock. Don't choose a law school in New York City if you can't bear subway commutes, noise, and the fast pace. And, if you've lived your entire life in New York, can you face the change you will experience in Kentucky? You also may want to ask yourself if you are already set in an unshakable lifestyle or if you are eager for a new environment.

■ Applicants With Disabilities

If you are a student with a disability, you need not permit your disability to govern choices of where to further your education. You should decide which schools you are interested in attending, based on your interests and qualifications, regardless of disability.

Often law schools give weight to the fact that an applicant has successfully overcome obstacles to build a solid record of academic and professional performance. By law, schools are not permitted to ask about an applicant's disability status, except in very limited circumstances; thus whether or not you disclose on your application that you have a disability is entirely up to you.

The HEATH Resource Center can help you throughout the admission process. For more information on how to contact this organization, see page 39.

Ranking Law Schools

■ Law Schools and Reputation

Many people will tell you to apply to the schools that take students in your GPA and LSAT ranges, and then enroll in the best one that accepts you. Law school quality can be assessed in a number of ways.

There is a hierarchy of law schools based on reputation, job placement success, strength of faculty, and the prestige of the parent institution (if there is one). In fact, a study done at one university suggests that undergraduate students perceive schools not only in terms of a hierarchy but also in terms of hierarchical clusters. In other words, certain schools are grouped together in terms of equivalent quality and prestige. Also, there are books or magazine articles that assign law schools purported numerical quality rankings. According to the ABA:

> No rating of law schools beyond the simple statement of their accreditation status is attempted or advocated by the official organizations in legal education. Qualities that make one kind of school good for one student may not be as important to another. The American Bar Association and its Section of Legal Education and Admissions to the Bar have issued disclaimers of any law school rating system. Prospective law students should consider a variety of factors in making their choice among schools.[1]

Since there is no official ranking authority, you should be cautious in using such rankings. The factors that make up a law school's reputation—strength of curriculum, faculty, career services, ability of students, quality of library facilities, and the like—don't lend themselves to quantification. Even if the rankings were more or less accurate, the school's reputation is only one factor among many for you to consider.

■ What's in a Name?

While going to a "name" school may mean that you will have an easier time finding your first job, it doesn't necessarily mean that you will get a better legal education than if you go to a lesser-known law school. Some schools that were at their peaks years ago are still riding on the wave of that earlier reputation. Others have greatly improved their programs and have recruited talented faculty, but have not yet made a "name" for themselves. Of course, schools already considered excellent have a stake in maintaining their status.

Once admitted, many applicants elect to attend "name" schools. However, in making this decision you should consider a variety of factors, such as the contacts you may acquire at a school in the area where you hope to practice, the size of the school, and cost. The substantive differences between schools should be your focus when making this important choice rather than the school's reputed ranking.

■ The Parent University

About 90 percent of ABA-approved law schools are part of a larger university. The reputation of an undergraduate school may influence the reputation of the law school so you might want to investigate the college before committing to the law school.

In addition, there may be some advantages to attending a law school that is part of a university. Such law schools may have more options for joint-degree programs or for taking a nonlaw school course or two. They also may have more academic and social activities, campus theater groups, sports teams, and everything else that comes with university life. Perhaps most important, the university can act as a support system for the law school by providing a wealth of facilities, including student housing and support for career services.

■ National, Regional, and Local Schools

A **national** school will generally have an applicant population and a student body that draws almost indistinguishably from the nation as a whole and will have many international students as well. National schools also have the most information about employment opportunities across the United States. A **regional** school is likely to have a population that is primarily from the geographic region of its location, though many regional schools have students from all over the country as well; a number of regional schools draw heavily from a particular geographical area, yet graduates may find jobs all over the country. Generally speaking, a **local** school is drawing primarily on applicants who either come from or want to practice in the proximate area in which the school is located. Many local law schools have excellent reputations and compete with the national schools in faculty salaries, in research-supporting activities, and in resources generally. Check the school's catalog or talk with the admission and placement staff to get a clear breakdown on where their students come from and where they are finding jobs.

[1] The American Bar Association. *Policies of the Council of the Section of Legal Education and Admissions to the Bar and of the Accreditation Committee.* Indianapolis, IN: 1987, Statement 20, p. 18.

Evaluating Law Schools

The best advice on how to select a law school is to choose the school that is **best for you**. The law schools invest substantial time and effort in evaluating prospective students, and applicants should evaluate law schools with equivalent care. The following are some features to keep in mind as you systematically evaluate law schools. (Costs and other financial criteria are not included below; they are discussed in Chapter 8.)

Each listing in this *Guide* provides school-specific information in the following categories as well.

■ Enrollment/Student Body

The academic qualifications of the student body are important to consider. It's a good idea to select a law school where you will be challenged by your classmates. Use the admission profile grids in this book to check the LSAT scores and GPAs for the previous year's entering class. Try to select a school where your averages will not be significantly different from those of your fellow law students. This is especially true for those with high scores and high GPAs, who would do well at any law school. Because of the important role of student participation in law school classes, your legal education might not be as rewarding as it could be if you are not challenged by your classmates.

You might also inquire about the diversity of the student body. Are a majority of the students the same age, race, sex, and so on? Remember, differences among students will expose you to various points of view; this will be an important aspect of your law school education.

Find out how many students are in a typical class. Much of the learning in law school depends on the quality of class discussion. Small classes provide essential interaction; large classes and the Socratic method provide diversity, challenge, and a good mix of reactions, opinions, and criticism.

It is also important to find out the total number of students enrolled at the school. Not surprisingly, the larger law schools tend to offer a larger selection of courses. Of course, more doesn't always mean better, and no one student has time to take all the courses offered at a large school. However, if you think you want to sample a wide range of courses, you are apt to have more opportunity to do so at a law school with a large faculty.

Part of the law school learning experience takes place after class with fellow students and with members of the faculty. Check to see whether faculty and students are on campus for a substantial part of the day.

Larger schools may also offer more extracurricular programs, greater student services, and a larger library. However, faculties at smaller schools may be able to give students more attention, and students at smaller schools may experience greater camaraderie. The size of a school is a personal consideration. Some students thrive in large schools; others prefer a smaller student community. Ask yourself which kind of student you are.

■ Faculty

You will undoubtedly wish to assess the faculties of the law schools you are considering. School catalogs will give you some idea of the backgrounds of the full-time faculty—where they went to school, what specialties they have, and what they have published. If the catalog tells you only where degrees were earned, ask for more information. You may also want to check the latest edition of the AALS's *Directory of Law Teachers* available at law school libraries. It may help you to know that some of the faculty have interests similar to your own.

- **Is the faculty relatively diverse with respect to race, ethnic background, gender, degrees in other fields, and breadth of experience?** A faculty with diverse backgrounds will have various points of view and experiences. This diversity will enrich your legal education, broaden your own point of view, and help prepare you for the variety of clients you will work with after law school.

- **How many full-time professors teach how many students—that is, what is the faculty/student ratio?** Although some of the most prestigious law schools are famous for their large sections in the introductory courses, they also provide smaller classes, clinics, simulations, and seminars in advanced subjects. According to the ABA's *Standards and Interpretations*, it is not favorable to have a full-time faculty to full-time student ratio of 30 to one or more. (The ABA, for purposes of its calculations only, counts as "full-time" those teachers who are employed as full-time teachers on the tenure track or an equivalent, and who do not hold an administrative office. In addition, the ABA considers three part-time students equivalent to two full-time students.)

- **Are some of the teachers recognized as authorities in their respective fields through their writings and professional activities?** Law school catalogs vary widely regarding information about faculty. Some merely list each faculty member's name along with schools attended and degrees earned. Others may provide details about publications, professional activities, and noteworthy achievements, particularly when an individual is an authority in his or her field.

- **Are there visiting professors, distinguished lecturers and visitors, symposiums and the like at the schools you are considering?** Law school lectureship programs are a good means of presenting the knowledge and views of academics outside of the particular law school you attend.

■ The Library and Other Physical Facilities

Chances are you will spend more time in the library than anywhere else, so take stock of the place before you get there. There are five factors to consider when assessing a law school library: the quality of its holdings, cataloging methods, staff, and facilities; and the hours the library remains open.

Whether a library has 250,000 volumes or 2.5 million volumes tells you little about the actual usefulness of the library. It may have an unfathomable number of volumes, but many of them may be outdated, irrelevant, or not readily available to students. All ABA-approved law schools must maintain a library that has the research materials considered essential for the study of law. Beyond that, find out if the school has any special collections and whether it subscribes to a computerized legal research service such as LEXIS or WESTLAW. Also, find out how many copies of essential materials are available, particularly for large classes.

Even if the library has all the materials you need, you won't be able to get your hands on those materials if the cataloging is years behind. Find out about the quality of the library's professional staff. Is there an adequate number of reference librarians for the number of students and faculty being served? Is the staff helpful?

Be sure the library has an adequate number of comfortable seats with at least enough carrels to accommodate a reasonable number of students at any given time. There should also be conference rooms that students may use for group discussions.

Because you will need to spend much of your time in the library, make sure its hours will accommodate just about any schedule you might have. It should open its doors by the start of classes and remain open well into the night, with a professional library staff available to assist students.

■ Curriculum

The range and quality of academic programs is one of the most important factors to consider when choosing a law school.

Almost all law schools follow the traditional first-year core curricula of civil procedure, criminal law, contracts, torts, and property (see Chapter 2). Do not assume that all law schools have programs that suit your personal needs and special interests. If you don't have any specific interests in mind—and many beginning students don't—try to make sure the school offers a wide range of electives so that you will have many options. A thorough grounding in basic legal theory will enable you to apply the principles learned to any area of law to which they pertain.

In fact, you shouldn't overemphasize your search for specialties; most law students are not specialists when they graduate, nor do they need to be. Generally speaking, new lawyers begin to find their specialties only in the second to fifth years of their careers. A well-rounded legal education from a respected law school is the best preparation for almost any career path you take. The schools' catalogs and the descriptions in this book will tell you a good deal about academic programs. You may also wish to ask school representatives questions such as: Does the school offer a variety of courses, or is it especially strong in certain areas; what sizes are the classes; are seminars and small-group classroom experiences available; and are there ample opportunities for developing writing, researching, and drafting skills?

Beyond the content of law school courses, other academic program considerations may be of interest to you as a prospective law student.

■ Special Programs and Academic Activities

Joint-degree Programs

Joint-degree programs allow you to pursue law school and graduate degrees simultaneously. Almost every combination is available at some institutions. Among the more popular degrees are the J.D./ M.B.A. and the J.D./M.A. in such areas as economics or political science. For details, check individual school catalogs and Chapter 12 in this book (Key Facts About LSAC-Member Law Schools).

Master of Laws (LL.M.) Programs and Special-Degree Programs

Many law schools offer advanced degrees that allow students to take graduate-level law courses. The LL.M. degree is quite common and usually is tailored to individual interests. Some schools offer master of laws degrees with particular concentrations, such as a master of laws in taxation and master of comparative law. Students may enroll in LL.M. programs only after having received the J.D. degree.

A few schools also offer very specific, special-degree programs. Some of these specialties include a Doctorate in Civil Law, Doctor of Juridical Science, and Doctor of Jurisprudence and Social Policy. Finding out what types of advanced degrees a law school offers may help you determine the emphases of the school.

Part-Time and Evening Programs

Part-time programs may be offered either in the evening or the day. For the past 10 years, approximately 17 percent of law students have been enrolled in part-time programs. The conventional wisdom is that if you are financially able to attend law school full-time, you ought to do so.

Part-time programs generally take four years to complete instead of three years. If you wish to enroll in such a program, you may be limiting your options somewhat since less than half of the law schools offer part-time programs.

Clinical Programs and Moot Court Competition

Many law schools offer students authentic experiences as lawyers by involving them with clients and providing opportunities to rehearse trial advocacy in moot court competitions. It is important that students become adept at using interviewing, counseling, negotiating, and investigating skills.

The best clinical programs involve students in actual legal situations, simulations of such situations, or a combination of both, either at the school itself or in the community. Clinical programs at some schools offer a team-teaching approach; practical, professional skills are taught along with traditional classroom theory. In this manner, faculty can advise and work closely with students.

Law Reviews

Most law schools have a law review—a journal of scholarly articles and commentaries on the law. Writing for the law review of a school can be important to both your legal education and your career in law. Thus, evaluating the law review at a particular law school may be worthwhile when trying to choose the right school to attend.

Traditionally, student law review editors are chosen on the basis of academic standing—usually from the top 10 percent of the class—but writing ability may also be a criterion. Today, a growing number of schools select law review editors by holding a competition in which students submit a previously assigned writing sample to the current editorial board of the review. If you are on the law review, employers may assume you are either one of the brightest in your class, or an outstanding writer—or both.

If possible, check the law reviews of the schools you are considering. The character of the review may be a reflection of the character of the institution that supports it.

Order of the Coif

Many law schools have a chapter of the Order of the Coif, a national honor society for outstanding students. Students are elected to Coif on the basis of scholarship and character. Check to see if the schools you are considering include such a chapter.

Academic Support Programs

Programs for students who need or who are expected to need assistance with legal analysis and writing are offered by most law schools. Students are invited to participate in these programs on the basis of either their entering credentials or their demonstrated academic performance. This assistance may be offered in the summer prior to beginning law school, during the academic year, or both. The aim of academic support programs is to ensure that students have an equal opportunity to compete in law school. For further information about academic assistance programs, consult the admission office at the law school.

■ Student Organizations

You can also tell something about a law school's intellectual resources and its students by the number and range of student associations and organizations sponsored on campus. Many schools have chapters of the American Bar Association—Law Student Division; a student bar association; associations for minority groups, such as the Asian, Black, Hispanic, and Native American Law Student Associations; and associations based on religious affiliations. Some, but not all, schools sponsor an environmental law society, a gay and lesbian law student society, a legal assistance society, a postconviction assistance project, an ACLU group, a federalist society, a volunteer income-tax assistance program, a law student spouses' club, an international law society, a law and technology society, or a client-counseling society. Determine which associations are important to you and check individual law school catalogs to see which law schools offer what you need.

■ Career Services and Employment

One of the tests of a good law school is the effort the institution makes to help its students and graduates understand their career options and find satisfying employment. Planning a career in law requires students to integrate their legal education and personal goals in the context of the employment marketplace. Some students begin law school with a clear idea of how they expect to use their legal education (although they may change their minds along the way). Others are uncertain, or see a number of tempting possibilities. The career services office, faculty, and alumni/ae of the school are valuable resources in the process of understanding and selecting among the many opportunities available to lawyers.

The first role of the career services office is to educate students about career opportunities in all sectors, including government and public service, law firms of all sizes and specialties, corporations, and so forth. To accomplish such a task, a law school may arrange panel presentations, meetings with practicing lawyers in different fields, and a library of career information materials. Career services professionals also teach students job-search strategies, such as effective interviewing skills and employment research, and discuss students' individual interests, options, and presentation.

One of the most visible career services provided by many law schools is the opportunity to interview with employers on campus for summer and full-time jobs. Ideally, the recruiters should represent a broad range of legal options (small and large firms, government agencies, public interest groups, corporate law departments) and sufficient geographic diversity to meet your needs. Be aware that the number of recruiters at the law school does not necessarily reflect the range of options open to students.

In most schools, only a small percentage of the class gets jobs through on-campus interviewing. Therefore, it is important to investigate the additional support provided by the career services staff and the experiences of the school's students and graduates in finding jobs.

Career services offices are concerned about all students, not just those at the top of the class rankings. Most spend a great deal of time and effort working with students individually and marketing the school to potential employers in order to increase students' options.

Here are some questions you may want to ask about a school's career services:

- What programs does the school offer to introduce students to career options? Do they seem interesting, relevant, and timely?
- Are the career-counseling professionals accessible, respected, well-qualified, and supportive?
- Are the school's faculty and graduates involved in educating students about their career options?
- What types of employers, and how many, recruit on-campus each year? What are the average number of interviews and offers per student? What percentage of students obtain jobs through the on-campus interviewing process?
- What positions have graduates taken in recent years? What work do students do during the summers? In what locales do students and graduates work? Are these employment profiles changing?
- What are the average or median salaries for the school's graduates?
- What percentage of students have accepted positions by graduation; within six months of graduation?
- Does the school offer career counseling and information for its graduates?

Chapter 7: Opportunities in Law for Minority Men and Women

A Career in Law for Minority Group Members

The legal profession is cognizant of the minority exclusion and underrepresentation that has historically pervaded American society. The legal system, which greatly values and benefits from multicultural perspectives, acknowledges the importance of diverse legal representation.

Many minority men and women seek a career in law as a way to address social and political issues. A law career provides a singular opportunity to effect change both on an individual level—by representing the interests of a client—and on a global level—by setting policy or establishing a precedent in the governmental or business arenas.

Although minority participation in law school and the legal profession is increasing every year, more can and is being done to attract minority men and women to the profession. Outreach efforts by the legal system can and do counteract the shortage of minority lawyers. So does the realization on the part of minority men and women that law can be a rewarding and fulfilling career.

Acquiring a Legal Education

Individual law schools and legal organizations have worked hard to assure continued progress toward alleviating the historic shortage of minority lawyers. For example, the Law School Admission Council established a Minority Affairs Committee and appropriated $1.2 million to be used for projects designed to increase the number of minority men and women who attend law schools. The American Bar Association adopted a law school standard calling for specific commitments to provide full opportunities for members of minority groups. The Association of American Law Schools also requires that member schools provide full opportunities in legal education for minorities and has programs to increase the number of minority faculty.

A legal education can provide you with considerable opportunity. You will have spent approximately three years thinking critically, reading broadly, and debating forcefully, and these skills are worthwhile in most everything you do.

Admission to Law School

Admission to law school is competitive—sometimes very competitive. However, getting into law school may be less difficult than you expect. Because there are many law schools and varied admission standards, it is advisable for you to do sufficient research and be selective.

- Read and reread the information in this book and study law school catalogs.
- *Thinking About Law School: A Minority Guide* offers realistic tips on how to assess your chances for admission, select the right law school, and finance your legal education. It also includes personal accounts by law school graduates who represent the kind of ethnic diversity law schools seek to achieve. (The book is published by and available free of charge from Law Services.)
- Get advice from a prelaw advisor, an academic counselor, a minority affairs advisor, or a practicing lawyer.
- Find out more about the regional summer institutes sponsored by the Council on Legal Education Opportunity (CLEO). Contact information for CLEO can be found on page 39 of this book.

Let the law schools you have selected know that you are interested. Often a school will have a specific program, a minority organization, designated personnel, or a law student to provide assistance for minority applicants.

Don't be intimidated by the law school admission process. Many minority men and women have been surprised by how well their credentials served them in getting into law school. The schools take all aspects of candidates' applications into account when they evaluate them. Personal, social, and ethnic background are considered, as are undergraduate records, LSAT scores, and letters of recommendation. Interesting life experiences, as well as past employment experiences, also count.

For information on the number and percentages of specific minority students and specific minority faculty at ABA-approved law schools, consult the Key Facts for Minority Law School Applicants on the following pages.

Once You Are in Law School

Once you are in law school, you will encounter a difficult but manageable academic program. Very often minority student groups will advise, assist, and support newcomers. Most minority students perform successfully in law school; they are also able to make effective use of their law degrees, whether practicing law or following other career avenues.

The chart that follows is based on figures supplied by the majority of Law School Admission Council-member law schools in the fall of 1995. Not all schools use the same classifications for minority groups; as a compromise we are using the classifications defined at the end of this chart.

This information was reported by the schools in Fall 1995, thus the figures may have changed.	Total No. of Students (Full-time + Part-time)	Number and Percentage of Minority Students					Total No. of Minority Students	Total No. of Full-time Faculty	Number and Percentage of Full-time Minority Faculty					Total No. and % of Full-time Minority Faculty	No. of Part-time Minority Faculty	Total No. of Full-time Visiting Minority Faculty	% of Minority Students Receiving Scholarships or Grants	Average Amount Per Scholarship or Grant
		AI AN	A PI	B A-A	H L	Other			AI AN	A PI	B A-A	H L	Other					
University of Akron School of Law	635	5 0.8%	16 2.5%	18 2.8%	12 1.9%	-	51 8%	21	-	-	4 19%	1 4.8%	-	5 23.8%	3	-	-	-
Albany Law School	787	1 0.1%	52 6.3%	42 5.1%	33 4%	11 1.3%	139 16.9%	41	-	2 4.9%	2 4.9%	-	-	4 9.8%	4	-	71	$9,800
American University—Washington College of Law	1136	15 1.3%	100 8.8%	80 7%	62 5.5%	9 0.8%	266 23.4%	59	-	-	4 6.8%	1 1.7%	-	5 8.5%	12	2	40	$7,904
University of Arizona College of Law	454	11 2.4%	29 6.4%	18 4%	69 15.2%	-	127 28%	30	1 3.3%	-	-	2 6.7%	-	3 10%	3	-	60	$3,800
Arizona State University College of Law	476	27 5.7%	26 5.5%	27 5.7%	56 11.8%	-	136 28.6%	35	1 2.9%	-	1 2.9%	2 5.7%	-	4 11.4%	-	-	51	$5,633
University of Arkansas School of Law—Fayetteville	396	8 2%	4 1%	16 4%	4 1%	-	32 8.1%	35	-	-	3 8.6%	-	-	3 8.6%	-	-	50	$4,710
University of Arkansas at Little Rock School of Law	428	6 1.4%	7 1.6%	34 7.9%	9 2.1%	-	56 13.2%	24	-	1 4.2%	2 8.3%	-	-	3 12.5%	2	-	15	$5,387
University of Baltimore School of Law	1066	2 0.2%	21 2%	109 10.2%	8 0.8%	-	140 13.1%	45	-	-	4 8.9%	-	-	4 8.9%	9	-	80	$1,000
Baylor University School of Law	399	3 0.8%	8 2%	4 1%	36 9%	5 1.3%	56 14%	20	-	-	1 5%	-	-	1 5%	-	-	92	$1,350
Boston College Law School	829	6 0.7%	41 4.9%	54 6.5%	45 5.4%	-	146 17.6%	57	-	2 3.5%	5 8.8%	2 3.5%	-	9 15.8%	-	-	60	n/a
Boston University School of Law	1101	11 1%	105 9.5%	51 4.6%	65 5.9%	-	232 21.1%	57	-	1 1.8%	3 5.3%	1 1.8%	-	5 8.8%	5	1	53	$7,775
Brigham Young University—J. Reuben Clark Law School	468	7 1.5%	26 5.6%	5 1.1%	23 4.9%	4 0.9%	65 13.9%	33	1 3%	-	-	1 3%	-	2 6.1%	1	-	90	$2,500
Brooklyn Law School	1451	3 0.2%	119 8.2%	65 4.5%	56 3.9%	-	243 16.7%	65	-	1 1.5%	2 3.1%	1 1.5%	-	4 6.2%	6	-	114	$4,800
University at Buffalo, State University of New York School of Law	810	6 0.7%	38 4.7%	64 7.9%	33 4.1%	-	141 17.4%	39	-	-	3 7.7%	-	-	3 7.7%	2	-	30	$10,000
University of California at Berkeley School of Law (Boalt Hall)	861	12 1.4%	116 13.5%	76 8.8%	114 13.2%	-	318 36.9%	61	-	3 4.9%	2 3.3%	2 3.3%	-	7 11.5%	7	1	65	$1,500
School of Law, University of California—Davis	467	8 1.7%	78 16.7%	17 3.6%	55 11.8%	4 0.9%	162 34.7%	29	-	-	1 3.4%	2 6.9%	1 3.4%	4 13.8%	-	-	-	not available

University of California—Hastings College of the Law	1262	10 0.8%	197 15.6%	58 4.6%	109 8.6%	32 2.5%	406 32.2%	47	-	3 6.4%	4 8.5%	2 4.3%	3 6.4%	12 25.5%	12	10	71	$2,560
School of Law, University of California, Los Angeles	955	10 1%	194 20.3%	89 9.3%	138 14.5%	-	431 45.1%	74	-	1 1.1%	4 4.3%	5 5.4%	-	10 10.8%	1	-	-	-
California Western School of Law	796	8 1%	78 9.8%	25 3.1%	53 6.7%	7 0.9%	171 21.5%	46	-	1 2.2%	4 8.7%	2 4.3%	-	7 15.2%	-	-	76	$18,250
Capital University Law School	812	-	9 1.1%	46 5.7%	18 2.2%	-	73 9%	31	-	-	4 12.9%	-	-	4 12.9%	-	-	86	$3,000-$4,000
Benjamin N. Cardozo School of Law Yeshiva University	975	1 0.1%	53 5.4%	31 3.2%	36 3.7%	-	121 12.4%	46	-	-	2 4.3%	-	-	2 4.3%	-	-	-	-
Case Western Reserve University School of Law	724	1 0.1%	46 6.4%	56 7.7%	8 1.1%	-	111 15.3%	42	-	-	1 2.4%	-	-	1 2.4%	2	-	92	$11,000
Catholic University of America—Columbus School of Law	945	2 0.2%	47 5%	76 8%	19 2%	16 1.7%	160 16.9%	50	-	-	5 10%	1 2%	-	6 12%	4	-	-	-
Chicago-Kent College of Law—Illinois Institute of Technology	1224	3 0.2%	98 8%	67 5.5%	40 3.3%	6 0.5%	214 17.5%	75	-	-	4 5.3%	5 6.7%	-	9 12%	6	-	58	up to $17,950
University of Chicago Law School	545	1 0.2%	46 8.4%	46 8.4%	23 4.2%	-	116 21.3%	39	-	1 2.6%	3 7.7%	-	-	4 10.3%	2	3	76	-
University of Cincinnati College of Law	382	1 0.3%	8 2.1%	29 7.6%	7 1.8%	1 0.3%	46 12%	25	-	-	2 8%	-	-	2 8%	-	-	89	$5,000
Cleveland State University—Cleveland-Marshall College of Law	910	2 0.2%	26 2.9%	73 8%	21 2.3%	-	122 13.4%	34	-	1 2.9%	2 5.9%	-	-	3 8.8%	2	1	17	$900
University of Colorado School of Law	498	16 3.2%	17 3.4%	28 5.6%	44 8.8%	-	105 21.1%	35	-	1 2.9%	1 2.9%	2 5.7%	-	4 11.4%	5	-	83	$4,887
Columbia University School of Law	1060	5 0.5%	125 11.8%	102 9.6%	86 8.1%	-	318 30%	64	-	1 1.6%	6 9.4%	1 1.6%	-	8 12.5%	1	1	46	$10,330
University of Connecticut School of Law	628	2 0.3%	30 4.8%	44 7%	24 3.8%	-	100 15.9%	44	-	-	3 6.8%	1 2.3%	-	4 9.1%	1	-	34	$11,128
Cornell University Law School	568	7 1.2%	57 10%	35 6.2%	30 5.3%	-	129 22.7%	39	-	1 2.6%	3 7.7%	-	-	4 10.3%	-	-	62	$10,339
Creighton University School of Law	504	-	10 2%	14 2.8%	14 2.8%	-	38 7.5%	25	-	-	1 4%	-	-	1 4%	-	-	68	$9,849
Cumberland School of Law of Samford University	652	-	4 0.6%	48 7.4%	4 0.6%	-	56 8.6%	33	-	1 3%	3 9.1%	-	-	4 12.1%	-	-	80	$10,000
University of Dayton School of Law	484	-	10 2.1%	21 4.3%	11 2.3%	-	42 8.7%	27	-	-	2 7.4%	1 3.7%	-	3 11.1%	-	-	45	$5,450
University of Denver College of Law	1080	10 0.9%	40 3.7%	29 2.7%	67 6.2%	1 0.1%	147 13.6%	49	-	2 4.1%	2 4.1%	2 4.1%	-	6 12.2%	6	4	68	$8,000
DePaul University College of Law	1129	3 0.3%	30 2.7%	50 4.4%	62 5.5%	-	145 12.8%	51	-	1 2%	2 3.9%	1 2%	1 2%	5 9.8%	3	1	49	$6,395
Detroit College of Law at Michigan State University	715	2 0.3%	8 1.1%	66 9.2%	12 1.7%	-	88 12.3%	29	-	-	2 6.9%	1 3.4%	-	3 10.3%	6	1	-	n/a

This information was reported by the schools in Fall 1995, thus the figures may have changed.	Total No. of Students (Full-time + Part-time)	Number and Percentage of Minority Students					Total No. of Minority Students	Total No. of Full-time Faculty	Number and Percentage of Full-time Minority Faculty					Total No. and % of Full-time Minority Faculty	No. of Part-time Minority Faculty	Total No. of Full-time Visiting Minority Faculty	% of Minority Students Receiving Scholarships or Grants	Average Amount Per Scholarship or Grant
		AI AN	A PI	B A-A	H L	Other			AI AN	A PI	B A-A	H L	Other					
University of Detroit Mercy School of Law	763	1 0.1%	24 3.1%	94 12.3%	7 0.9%	-	126 16.5%	28	-	1 3.6%	4 14.3%	-	3 10.7%	8 28.6%	1	5	80	$2,000-$8,000
Dickinson School of Law	525	2 0.4%	13 2.5%	13 2.5%	16 3%	-	44 8.4%	27	-	1 3.7%	2 7.4%	-	-	3 11.1%	1	-	34	$6,400
District of Columbia School of Law	279	2 0.7%	11 3.9%	143 51.3%	11 3.9%	-	167 59.9%	19	-	-	6 31.6%	-	-	6 31.6%	-	-	59	$4,465
Drake University Law School	519	2 0.4%	13 2.5%	12 2.3%	13 2.5%	2 0.4%	42 8.1%	23	-	-	1 4.3%	-	-	1 4.3%	4	-	71	$10,687
Duke University School of Law	593	3 0.5%	29 4.9%	40 6.7%	13 2.2%	1 0.2%	86 14.5%	35	-	1 2.9%	2 5.7%	-	-	3 8.6%	10	-	-	$5,750
Duquesne University School of Law	643	1 0.2%	6 0.9%	49 7.6%	5 0.8%	-	61 9.5%	24	-	2 8.3%	2 8.3%	1 4.2%	-	5 20.8%	-	-	60	$6,000
Emory University School of Law	742	3 0.4%	38 5.1%	69 9.3%	27 3.6%	-	137 18.5%	40	-	1 2.5%	3 7.5%	1 2.5%	-	5 12.5%	3	1	30	$9,000
University of Florida College of Law	1170	4 0.3%	36 3.1%	154 13.2%	66 5.6%	-	260 22.2%	78	-	-	6 7.7%	2 2.6%	-	8 10.3%	-	-	44	$11,462
The Florida State University College of Law	621	5 0.8%	19 3.1%	68 11%	57 9.2%	-	149 24%	41	1 2.4%	-	2 4.9%	2 4.9%	-	5 12.2%	-	-	56	$10,395
Fordham University School of Law	1481	3 0.2%	104 7.0%	148 10.0%	129 8.7%	-	384 26%	61	-	1 1.6%	2 3.3%	1 1.6%	-	4 6.6%	-	10	54	$5,200
Franklin Pierce Law Center	398	2 0.5%	14 3.5%	6 1.5%	9 2.3%	-	31 7.8%	26	-	-	-	-	-	-	-	-	70	$14,200
George Mason University School of Law	696	3 0.4%	28 4%	32 4.6%	4 0.6%	-	67 9.6%	33	-	2 6.1%	2 6.1%	1 3%	-	5 15.2%	3	-	30	up to $6,500
George Washington University Law School	1528	2 0.1%	113 7.4%	171 11.2%	117 7.7%	-	403 26.4%	67	-	1 1.5%	6 9%	2 3%	-	9 13.4%	14	2	76	$7,000
Georgetown University Law Center	2024	16 0.8%	168 8.3%	224 11.1%	127 6.3%	-	535 26.4%	87	-	1 1.1%	8 9.2%	1 1.1%	-	10 11.5%	7	1	-	$6,000
University of Georgia School of Law	641	-	10 1.6%	68 10.6%	6 0.9%	3 0.5%	87 13.6%	42	1 2.4%	1 2.4%	2 4.8%	-	-	4 9.5%	-	1	52	$3,250
Georgia State University College of Law	631	5 0.8%	33 5.2%	95 15.1%	26 4.1%	6 1%	165 26.1%	40	1 2.5%	1 2.5%	3 7.5%	-	-	5 12.5%	6	-	1.9	$2,500
Golden Gate University School of Law	713	5 0.7%	101 14.2%	28 3.9%	66 9.3%	-	200 28.1%	35	-	3 8.6%	2 5.7%	2 5.7%	-	7 20%	14	-	17	$10,400
Gonzaga University School of Law	587	15 2.6%	37 6.3%	7 1.2%	24 4.1%	-	83 14.1%	33	-	-	1 3%	1 3%	-	2 6.1%	-	-	10	$2,500 to full tuition
Hamline University School of Law	590	7 1.2%	16 2.7%	25 4.2%	14 2.4%	7 1.2%	69 11.7%	29	1 3.4%	-	1 3.4%	-	-	2 6.9%	-	7	29	half or full

Harvard University Law School	1658	9 0.5%	186 11.2%	179 10.8%	75 4.5%	-	449 27.1%	105	2 1.9%	1 1%	13 12.4%	7 6.7%	-	23 21.9%	8	1	43	$7,258
University of Hawai'i at Manoa— William S. Richardson School of Law	241	2 0.8%	166 68.9%	3 1.2%	3 1.2%	-	174 72.2%	18	-	3 16.7%	1 5.6%	-	-	4 22.2%	9	1	-	-
Hofstra University School of Law	850	-	31 3.6%	58 6.8%	53 6.2%	-	142 16.7%	42	-	-	4 9.5%	1 2.4%	-	5 11.9%	-	-	68	$4,949
University of Houston Law Center	1018	10 1%	68 6.7%	45 4.4%	86 8.4%	-	209 20.5%	48	-	-	3 6.3%	4 8.3%	-	7 14.6%	-	-	20	$2,500
Howard University School of Law	443	1 0.2%	32 7.2%	360 81.3%	20 4.5%	-	413 93.2%	29	-	1 3.4%	22 75.9%	-	1 3.4%	24 82.8%	14	-	60	$7,500
University of Idaho College of Law	279	3 1.1%	9 3.2%	1 0.4%	14 5%	3 1.1%	30 10.8%	27	-	1 3.7%	-	-	-	1 3.7%	-	-	-	n/a
University of Illinois College of Law	623	-	50 8%	82 13.2%	35 5.6%	-	167 26.8%	39	-	-	3 7.7%	1 2.6%	-	4 10.3%	-	-	24	$8,040
Indiana University School of Law—Bloomington	620	2 0.3%	23 3.7%	70 11.3%	34 5.5%	-	129 20.8%	34	-	-	2 5.9%	-	-	2 5.9%	-	-	58	varies
Indiana University School of Law—Indianapolis	835	3 0.4%	26 3.1%	63 7.5%	13 1.6%	4 0.5%	109 13.1%	41	-	-	2 4.9%	-	-	2 4.9%	-	-	50	$3,000
University of Iowa College of Law	682	10 1.5%	47 6.9%	57 8.4%	35 5.1%	-	149 21.8%	49	1 2%	1 2%	3 6.1%	1 2%	-	6 12.2%	-	1	75	$5,150
The John Marshall School of Law	1161	6 0.5%	62 5.3%	56 4.8%	53 4.6%	23 2%	200 17.2%	54	-	-	3 5.6%	1 1.9%	-	4 7.4%	-	-	3	$2,000
University of Kansas School of Law	498	12 2.4%	8 1.6%	15 3%	28 5.6%	-	63 12.7%	29	1 3.4%	-	1 3.4%	2 6.9%	-	4 13.8%	-	-	75	up to $8,500
University of Kentucky College of Law	435	-	4 0.9%	31 7.1%	-	-	35 8%	28	-	-	2 7.1%	-	-	2 7.1%	1	-	94	at least tuition
Lewis and Clark, Northwestern School of Law	700	12 1.7%	49 7%	14 2%	30 4.3%	-	105 15%	29	-	-	1 3.4%	-	-	1 3.4%	-	-	-	-
University of Louisville School of Law	478	1 0.2%	17 3.6%	11 2.3%	3 0.6%	-	32 6.7%	27	-	-	2 7.4%	1 3.7%	-	3 11.1%	-	-	55	$5,565
Loyola University Chicago School of Law	769	3 0.4%	64 8.3%	48 6.2%	39 5.1%	20 2.6%	174 22.6%	34	-	-	3 8.8%	1 2.9%	-	4 11.8%	2	-	34	$2,350
Loyola Law School, Los Angeles, Loyola Marymount University	1396	16 1.1%	274 19.6%	79 5.7%	151 10.8%	-	520 37.2%	59	-	3 5.1%	5 8.5%	5 8.5%	-	13 22%	6	13	68	$10,832
Loyola University New Orleans School of Law	768	7 0.9%	26 3.4%	93 12.2%	60 7.8%	-	186 24.3%	36	-	-	5 13.9%	1 2.8%	-	6 16.7%	-	-	29	$4,440
University of Maine School of Law	280	5 1.8%	7 2.5%	3 1.1%	6 2.1%	-	21 7.5%	16	-	-	-	-	-	-	-	-	70	$3,000 to full tuition
Marquette University Law School	475	4 0.8%	25 5.3%	18 3.8%	23 4.8%	-	70 14.7%	23	-	-	1 4.3%	1 4.3%	-	2 8.7%	1	-	35	$500 to full tuition
University of Maryland School of Law	863	3 0.3%	61 7.1%	174 20.2%	23 2.7%	-	261 30.2%	54	-	1 1.9%	8 14.8%	-	-	9 16.7%	5	-	75	20% of need-based award

This information was reported by the schools in Fall 1995, thus the figures may have changed.	Total No. of Students (Full-time + Part-time)	Number and Percentage of Minority Students					Total No. of Minority Students	Total No. of Full-time Faculty	Number and Percentage of Full-time Minority Faculty					Total No. and % of Full-time Minority Faculty	No. of Part-time Minority Faculty	Total No. of Full-time Visiting Minority Faculty	% of Minority Students Receiving Scholarships or Grants	Average Amount Per Scholarship or Grant
		AI AN	A PI	B A-A	H L	Other			AI AN	A PI	B A-A	H L	Other					
McGeorge School of Law, University of the Pacific	1220	23 1.9%	135 11.1%	26 2.1%	80 6.6%	14 1.1%	278 22.8%	53	-	2 3.8%	1 1.9%	1 1.9%	-	4 7.5%	2	4	51	$1,000 to full tuition
The University of Memphis—Cecil C. Humphreys School of Law	464	-	2 0.4%	45 9.7%	1 0.2%	-	48 10.3%	22	-	-	1 4.5%	-	-	1 4.5%	3	-	94	$5,000
Mercer University—Walter F. George School of Law	408	1 0.2%	7 1.7%	38 9.3%	19 4.7%	-	65 15.9%	29	-	-	2 6.9%	-	-	2 6.9%	-	-	67	$9,042
University of Miami School of Law	1341	7 0.5%	40 3%	169 12.6%	217 16.2%	-	433 32.3%	54	-	-	4 7.4%	2 3.7%	-	6 11.1%	-	-	confidential information	confidential information
University of Michigan Law School	1159	18 1.6%	63 5.4%	105 9.1%	55 4.7%	-	241 20.8%	61	-	1 1.6%	5 8.2%	1 1.6%	-	7 11.5%	2	-	59	$7,300
University of Minnesota Law School	810	14 1.7%	59 7.3%	36 4.4%	21 2.6%	-	130 16%	43	1 2.3%	1 2.3%	3 7%	-	-	5 11.6%	1	5	50	$2,000 to full tuition
University of Mississippi School of Law	467	7 1.5%	8 1.7%	46 9.9%	5 1.1%	-	66 14.1%	25	1 4%	-	3 12%	-	-	4 16%	2	-	91	full tuition for residents
Mississippi College School of Law	385	3 0.8%	4 1%	20 5.2%	8 2.1%	-	35 9.1%	16	-	-	2 12.5%	-	-	2 12.5%	1	-	7	$11,400
University of Missouri—Columbia School of Law	462	4 0.9%	4 0.9%	31 6.7%	5 1.1%	-	44 9.5%	23	-	-	2 8.7%	-	-	2 8.7%	-	-	90	$4,200
University of Missouri—Kansas City School of Law	484	7 1.4%	7 1.4%	23 4.8%	12 2.5%	-	49 10.1%	29	-	-	3 10.3%	-	-	3 10.3%	1	-	59	varies
University of Montana School of Law	235	10 4.3%	2 0.9%	1 0.4%	2 0.9%	1 0.4%	16 6.8%	17	1 5.9%	-	-	-	-	1 5.9%	1	-	38	$1,278
University of Nebraska College of Law	415	2 0.5%	11 2.7%	10 2.4%	17 4.1%	-	40 9.6%	26	-	-	2 7.7%	-	-	2 7.7%	1	-	80	varies
New England School of Law	1097	8 0.7%	33 3%	37 3.4%	39 3.6%	16 1.5%	133 12.1%	40	-	1 2.5%	3 7.5%	-	-	4 10%	2	-	42	varies
University of New Mexico School of Law	335	34 10.1%	7 2.1%	9 2.7%	100 29.9%	-	150 44.8%	32	-	-	2 6.3%	6 18.8%	-	8 25%	7	2	46	$2,478
City University of New York School of Law at Queens College	458	1 0.2%	25 5.5%	79 17.2%	38 8.3%	8 1.7%	151 33%	40	-	6 15%	3 7.5%	7 17.5%	-	16 40%	7	-	-	-
New York Law School	1401	7 0.5%	95 6.8%	128 9.1%	98 7%	-	328 23.4%	52	-	2 3.8%	3 5.8%	3 5.8%	-	8 15.4%	-	-	38	$4,873
New York University School of Law	1275	-	125 9.8%	89 7%	86 6.7%	-	300 23.5%	95	1 1.1%	3 3.2%	9 9.5%	-	-	13 13.7%	4	-	-	-
University of North Carolina School of Law	696	8 1.1%	28 4%	76 10.9%	18 2.6%	-	130 18.7%	43	-	-	2 4.7%	-	-	2 4.7%	2	-	-	$2,600

North Carolina Central University School of Law	329	2 0.6%	-	170 51.7%	1 0.3%	-	173 52.6%	20	-	-	14 70%	-	-	14 70%	4	3	-	varies
University of North Dakota School of Law	217	5 2.3%	5 2.3%	1 0.5%	2 0.9%	-	13 6%	14	-	-	-	-	-	-	-	-	31	varies
Northeastern University School of Law	617	-	58 9.4%	54 8.8%	36 5.8%	-	148 24%	32	-	1 3.1%	4 12.5%	1 3.1%	-	6 18.8%	-	-	-	varies
Northern Illinois University College of Law	299	1 0.3%	9 3%	27 9%	22 7.4%	2 0.7%	61 20.4%	29	-	-	3 10.3%	1 3.4%	-	4 13.8%	2	-	32	varies
Northern Kentucky University—Salmon P. Chase College of Law	411	1 0.2%	6 1.5%	29 7.1%	3 0.7%	-	39 9.5%	19	-	-	2 10.5%	-	-	2 10.5%	7	-	-	varies
Northwestern University School of Law	606	1 0.2%	49 8.1%	48 7.9%	31 5.1%	-	129 21.3%	54	-	1 1.9%	4 7.4%	-	-	5 9.3%	9	-	76	varies
Nova Southeastern University—Shepard Broad Law Center	906	4 0.4%	3 0.3%	109 12%	118 13%	8 0.9%	242 26.7%	41	-	1 2.4%	4 9.8%	4 9.8%	-	9 22%	3	1	30	varies
Ohio Northern University—Claude W. Pettit College of Law	354	3 0.8%	3 0.8%	20 5.6%	8 2.3%	-	34 9.6%	19	-	-	1 5.3%	-	-	1 5.3%	-	-	50	$10,000
The Ohio State University College of Law	690	1 0.1%	25 3.6%	64 9.3%	17 2.5%	-	107 15.5%	35	-	1 2.9%	6 17.1%	-	-	7 20%	2	-	80	varies
University of Oklahoma College of Law	600	28 4.7%	19 3.2%	12 2%	13 2.2%	-	107 15.5%	35	-	-	2 5.7%	1 2.9%	-	3 8.6%	1	1	20	$3,500
Oklahoma City University School of Law	640	28 4.4%	15 2.3%	12 1.9%	14 2.2%	-	69 10.8%	32	2 6.3%	-	1 3.1%	-	-	3 9.4%	2	-	-	n/a
University of Oregon School of Law	478	8 1.7%	38 7.9%	15 3.1%	14 2.9%	-	75 15.7%	32	-	1 2.6%	3 7.9%	1 2.6%	-	5 13.2%	-	1	-	-
Pace University School of Law	803	3 0.4%	37 4.6%	46 5.7%	51 6.4%	-	137 17.1%	51	-	-	-	-	3 5.9%	3 5.9%	-	-	-	-
University of Pennsylvania Law School	742	2 0.3%	55 7.4%	67 9%	50 6.7%	-	174 23.5%	39	-	-	3 7.7%	-	-	3 7.7%	-	-	-	-
Pepperdine University School of Law	702	15 2.1%	81 11.5%	25 3.6%	53 7.5%	-	174 24.8%	33	-	2 6.1%	1 3%	1 3%	-	4 12.1%	-	-	100	$9,080
University of Pittsburgh School of Law	703	3 0.4%	24 3.4%	58 8.3%	9 1.3%	6 0.9%	100 14.2%	44	-	2 4.5%	5 11.4%	-	-	7 15.9%	3	1	60	$5,000
Quinnipiac College School of Law	795	6 0.8%	28 3.5%	28 3.5%	36 4.5%	-	98 12.3%	40	-	1 2.5%	1 2.5%	-	-	2 5%	1	-	-	varied
University of Richmond—T.C. Williams School of Law	481	3 0.6%	34 7.1%	48 10%	18 3.7%	16 3.3%	119 24.7%	25	-	2 8%	8 32%	-	-	10 40%	5	-	78	$4,809
Roger Williams University School of Law	472	1 0.2%	4 0.8%	12 2.5%	8 1.7%	6 1.3%	31 6.6%	26	-	-	1 3.8%	2 7.7%	-	3 11.5%	-	-	1	$3,000/year
Rutgers—The State University—School of Law—Camden	776	-	70 9%	66 8.5%	42 5.4%	-	178 22.9%	39	-	2 5.1%	4 10.3%	1 2.6%	-	7 17.9%	4	-	31	varies
Rutgers University School of Law—Newark	792	-	66 8.3%	109 13.8%	79 10%	1 0.1%	255 32.2%	39	-	1 2.6%	6 15.4%	-	-	7 17.9%	3	1	40	$2,000

This information was reported by the schools in Fall 1995, thus the figures may have changed.	Total No. of Students (Full-time + Part-time)	Number and Percentage of Minority Students					Total No. of Minority Students	Total No. of Full-time Faculty	Number and Percentage of Full-time Minority Faculty					Total No. and % of Full-time Minority Faculty	No. of Part-time Minority Faculty	Total No. of Full-time Visiting Minority Faculty	% of Minority Students Receiving Scholarships or Grants	Average Amount Per Scholarship or Grant
		AI AN	A PI	B A-A	H L	Other			AI AN	A PI	B A-A	H L	Other					
St. John's University School of Law	1118	2 0.2%	116 10.4%	77 6.9%	84 7.5%	-	279 25%	59	1 1.7%	1 1.7%	6 10.2%	2 3.4%	-	10 16.9%	-	-	82	$3,985
Saint Louis University School of Law	843	2 0.2%	35 4.2%	91 10.8%	25 3%	1 0.1%	154 18.3%	44	-	1 2.3%	3 6.8%	-	-	4 9.1%	-	-	90	$4,500
St. Mary's University School of Law	771	14 1.8%	22 2.9%	23 3%	197 25.6%	-	256 33.2%	31	-	-	1 3%	8 24.2%	-	9 27.3%	4	1	-	varies
St. Thomas University School of Law	521	3 0.6%	6 1.2%	55 10.6%	101 19.4%	-	165 31.7%	34	-	1 3.1%	3 9.4%	2 6.3%	-	6 18.8%	6	1	35	$6,000
University of San Diego School of Law	1110	16 1.4%	112 10.1%	18 1.6%	71 6.4%	-	217 19.5%	60	-	2 3.3%	3 5%	3 5%	-	8 13.3%	4	-	43	up to full tuition
University of San Francisco School of Law	687	5 0.7%	114 16.6%	20 2.9%	31 4.5%	-	170 24.7%	27	-	1 3.7%	2 7.4%	2 7.4%	-	5 18.5%	9	1	-	$5,000
Santa Clara University School of Law	882	10 1.1%	151 17.1%	47 5.3%	81 9.2%	36 4.1%	325 36.8%	35	-	2 5.7%	2 5.7%	1 2.9%	-	5 14.3%	3	2	70	$1,000-$18,650
Seattle University School of Law	887	31 3.5%	68 7.7%	32 3.6%	33 3.7%	16 1.8%	180 20.3%	41	-	-	2 4.9%	-	-	2 4.9%	4	3	35	up to full tuition
University of South Carolina School of Law	765	1 0.1%	12 1.6%	60 7.8%	7 0.9%	-	80 10.5%	44	-	-	3 6.8%	-	-	3 6.8%	-	-	30	$1,500
University of South Dakota School of Law	223	1 0.4%	-	3 1.3%	2 0.9%	-	6 2.7%	15	1 6.7%	-	-	-	-	1 6.7%	1	-	17	$6,168
South Texas College of Law	1249	3 0.2%	72 5.8%	87 7%	100 8%	-	262 21%	56	-	-	2 3.6%	1 1.8%	-	3 5.4%	2	-	79	$2,461
University of Southern California Law School	610	1 0.2%	90 14.8%	64 10.5%	84 13.8%	-	239 39.2%	49	-	1 2%	2 4.1%	-	-	3 6.1%	1	5	64	$10,736
Southern Illinois University School of Law	354	3 0.8%	23 6.5%	24 6.8%	13 3.7%	-	63 17.8%	24	-	-	2 8.3%	1 4.2%	-	3 12.5%	-	-	83	$3,675
Southern Methodist University School of Law	768	11 1.4%	51 6.6%	52 6.8%	60 7.8%	-	174 22.7%	41	-	1 2.4%	3 7.3%	3 7.3%	-	7 17.1%	-	1	-	$9,400
Southern University Law Center	324	-	-	205 63.3%	-	-	205 63.3%	28	-	1 3.6%	17 60.7%	-	-	18 64.3%	8	-	20	$4,000
Southwestern University School of Law	1207	13 1.1%	185 15.3%	70 5.8%	91 7.5%	-	359 29.7%	48	-	1 2.1%	3 6.3%	2 4.2%	-	6 12.5%	13	-	39	$6,152
Stanford University Law School	574	19 3.3%	63 11%	23 4%	73 12.7%	-	178 31%	45	-	-	4 9.3%	1 2.3%	-	5 11.6%	4	-	83	up to full tuition
Stetson University College of Law	680	6 0.9%	16 2.4%	38 5.6%	50 7.4%	4 0.6%	114 16.8%	33	2 6.1%	-	2 6.1%	-	-	4 12.1%	2	-	85	$1,000 to full tuition
Suffolk University Law School	1700	8 0.5%	63 3.6%	85 4.9%	55 3.2%	-	211 12.2%	61	-	1 1.6%	6 9.8%	3 4.9%	-	10 16.4%	-	-	-	-

Syracuse University College of Law	794	2 0.3%	81 10.2%	66 8.3%	38 4.8%	-	187 23.6%	41	-	1 2.5%	3 7.3%	-	-	4 9.8%	3	1	50	$4,725
Temple University School of Law	1185	5 0.4%	81 6.8%	153 12.9%	54 4.6%	-	293 24.7%	55	-	2 3.6%	8 14.5%	2 3.6%	-	12 21.8%	18	-	59	$1,540
University of Tennessee College of Law	480	4 0.8%	6 1.3%	44 9.2%	2 0.4%	-	56 11.7%	36	-	-	2 5.6%	-	-	2 5.6%	-	1	79	$8,541
The University of Texas School of Law	1468	4 0.3%	86 5.9%	98 6.7%	178 12.1%	2 0.1%	368 25.1%	72	-	1 1.4%	2 2.8%	3 4.2%	-	6 8.3%	8	-	79	$2,500
Texas Southern University— Thurgood Marshall School of Law	550	5 0.9%	16 2.9%	278 50.5%	118 21.5%	11 2%	428 77.8%	29	-	-	20 69%	4 13.8%	-	24 82.8%	11	2	15	$1,000
Texas Tech University School of Law	628	12 1.9%	7 1.1%	11 1.8%	61 9.7%	1 0.2%	92 14.6%	22	-	-	1 4.5%	1 4.5%	1 4.5%	3 13.6%	1	-	100	$2,033
Texas Wesleyan University School of Law	671	7 1%	9 1.3%	39 5.8%	56 8.3%	14 2.1%	125 18.6%	23	-	-	1 4.3%	-	-	1 4.3%	1	-	-	-
The University of Toledo College of Law	670	4 0.6%	9 1.3%	47 7%	20 3%	-	80 11.9%	37	-	-	2 5.4%	-	-	2 5.4%	2	-	55	$5,500
Touro College— Jacob D. Fuchsberg Law Center	794	1 0.1%	43 5.4%	104 13.1%	73 9.2%	-	221 27.8%	43	-	-	3 7%	-	-	3 7%	-	-	75	$1,000 to full tuition
Tulane University Law School	1014	4 0.4%	61 6%	103 10.2%	63 6.2%	20 2%	251 24.8%	58	-	1 1.7%	4 6.9%	1 1.7%	-	6 10.3%	3	-	45	$8,500
University of Tulsa College of Law	623	42 6.7%	18 2.9%	8 1.3%	7 1.1%	2 0.3%	77 12.4%	36	1 2.8%	1 2.8%	1 2.8%	2 5.6%	-	5 13.9%	-	-	22	$5,525
University of Utah College of Law	366	9 2.5%	26 7.1%	3 0.8%	19 5.2%	2 0.5%	59 16.1%	28	1 3.6%	1 3.6%	-	3 10.7%	-	5 17.9%	1	-	60	50% of residence tuition
Valparaiso University School of Law	482	2 0.4%	11 2.3%	35 7.3%	15 3.1%	3 0.6%	66 13.7%	21	-	-	2 8.3%	-	-	2 8.3%	1	-	65	$4,600
Vanderbilt University School of Law	550	2 0.4%	36 6.5%	51 9.3%	9 1.6%	-	98 17.8%	32	-	-	1 3.1%	-	-	1 3.1%	5	-	80	$8,500
University of Virginia School of Law	1152	3 0.3%	44 3.8%	119 10.3%	9 0.8%	-	175 15.2%	59	-	1 1.7%	4 6.8%	-	-	5 8.5%	2	1	48	$7013.09
Wake Forest University School of Law	464	6 1.3%	-	31 6.7%	6 1.3%	1 0.2%	44 9.5%	34	-	-	2 5.9%	-	-	2 5.9%	1	-	-	-
Washburn University School of Law	417	10 2.4%	22 5.3%	21 5%	24 5.8%	-	77 18.5%	27	-	2 7.4%	3 11.1%	2 7.4%	-	7 25.9%	-	-	56	$2,900
University of Washington School of Law	495	24 4.8%	94 19%	31 6.3%	38 7.7%	-	187 37.8%	45	-	-	3 6.7%	-	-	3 6.7%	-	-	50	$1,200
Washington and Lee University School of Law	374	3 0.8%	9 2.4%	33 8.8%	8 2.1%	3 0.8%	56 15%	35	-	1 2.9%	2 5.7%	-	-	3 8.6%	-	-	90	-
Washington University School of Law	622	5 0.8%	44 7.1%	55 8.8%	6 1%	-	110 17.7%	41	-	1 2.3%	2 4.5%	-	-	3 6.8%	-	-	-	-
Wayne State University Law School	747	4 0.5%	16 2.1%	75 10%	19 2.5%	-	114 15.3%	33	-	-	3 9.1%	-	-	3 9.1%	3	-	95	$2,200
West Virginia University College of Law	427	2 0.5%	5 1.2%	20 4.7%	4 0.9%	-	31 7.3%	28	-	-	1 3.6%	-	-	1 3.6%	-	-	17	$500 to $17,000

This information was reported by the schools in Fall 1995, thus the figures may have changed.	Total No. of Students (Full-time + Part-time)	Number and Percentage of Minority Students					Total No. of Minority Students	Total No. of Full-time Faculty	Number and Percentage of Full-time Minority Faculty					Total No. and % of Full-time Minority Faculty	No. of Part-time Minority Faculty	Total No. of Full-time Visiting Minority Faculty	% of Minority Students Receiving Scholarships or Grants	Average Amount Per Scholarship or Grant
		AI AN	A PI	B A-A	H L	Other			AI AN	A PI	B A-A	H L	Other					
Western New England College School of Law	741	2 0.3%	14 1.9%	27 3.6%	30 4%	-	73 9.9%	28	-	2 7.1%	1 3.6%	-	-	3 10.7%	4	-	33	$4,437
Whittier Law School	-	-	-	-	-	-	-	-	-	-	-	-	-	-	-	-	-	-
Widener University School of Law	1991	4 0.2%	20 1%	61 3.1%	22 1.1%	11 0.6%	118 5.9%	104	-	-	6 5.8%	1 1%	-	7 6.7%	6	-	36	$10,931
Willamette University College of Law	458	6 1.3%	28 6.1%	11 2.4%	9 2%	-	54 11.8%	27	-	-	1 3.7%	-	-	1 3.7%	-	-	27	$9,117
College of William and Mary School of Law	524	3 0.6%	17 3.2%	60 11.5%	9 1.7%	-	89 17%	30	-	1 3.3%	3 10%	-	-	4 13.3%	3	-	65	$1,907
William Mitchell College of Law	1068	13 1.2%	55 5.1%	46 4.3%	23 2.2%	-	137 12.8%	36	-	2 5.6%	1 2.8%	-	-	3 8.3%	12	-	42	$4,340
University of Wisconsin Law School	884	19 2.1%	26 2.9%	83 9.4%	61 6.9%	-	189 21.4%	49	1 2%	-	4 8.2%	1 2%	-	6 12.2%	-	-	50	$6,000
University of Wyoming College of Law	226	2 0.9%	2 0.9%	1 0.4%	8 3.5%	-	13 5.8%	14	-	-	-	-	-	-	-	-	25	$7,500
Yale Law School	573	2 0.3%	74 12.9%	64 11.2%	30 5.2%	-	170 29.7%	48	-	3 6.3%	3 6.3%	-	-	6 12.5%	-	-	-	n/a

Minority Key Facts

AI/AN American Indian/Alaskan Native
A/PI Asian/Pacific Islander (i.e., Chinese, Japanese, Korean, Vietnamese, etc.)
B/A-A Black/African American
H/L Hispanic/Latino (i.e., Mexican American, Chicano, Puerto Rican, etc.)
Other

Note: Enrollment figures listed in this Minority Key Facts chart may not directly correspond to figures listed on the Key Facts chart. The discrepancies are due to differences in enrollment definitions used by schools. For example, some schools include part-time as well as full-time students in their totals; others do not. Several schools included LL.M. candidates, dual-degree students, or other graduate students in their totals on one chart but not the other. For the most up-to-date and accurate figures, contact individual schools directly.

Chapter 8: Financing Your Legal Education

The Cost of a Legal Education

The cost of attending law school is a figure that includes tuition, fees, books, housing, and other living expenses for the academic year. It can vary significantly from one school to another. Tuition alone can range from a few thousand dollars a year to more than $20,000 per year. After adding in housing, food, books, and personal expenses, the figure *could* exceed $100,000 for a three-year law school education.

The cost of attending a particular law school is only one of the many factors you should consider in making your choice.

Financial Aid: A Student's Responsibility

The first step in applying for financial aid for law school is to complete the Free Application for Federal Student Aid (FAFSA), available from your college or university financial aid office or from the law school to which you are applying. The FAFSA is a need analysis tool developed by the U.S. Government, Department of Education. It asks for information about your income, assets, and other financial resources. The information you provide on the financial aid form will be used to compute how much you and your family should contribute toward your legal education. Most schools also require copies of annual federal tax returns to verify financial information; some schools also require students to fill out a supplemental form to be considered for institutional aid. Once the analysis is completed, the financial aid officer at the school can determine what types of aid you will need—such as scholarships, grants, loans, or work-study—to pay your law school expenses.

A newly revised brochure published by the Law School Admission Council, *Financial Aid for Law School: A Preliminary Guide*, is available at most law school financial aid offices. For complete and individualized information on financing your law school education, contact the financial aid office at the individual law school(s) to which you apply.

Determining How You Will Pay

There are three basic types of financial aid:

- **Scholarships, Grants, and Fellowships**—These types of awards, which do not have to be repaid, are given according to need and/or merit. *Their availability is quite limited*, and they are usually awarded by the law schools themselves. The law school's financial aid office can give you more information.

- **Federal Work-Study**—Federal Work-Study is a program that provides funding for students to work part time during the school year and full time during the summer months. Students sometimes may work on campus in a variety of settings or in off-campus nonprofit agencies. Additional information is available from any law school financial aid office.

- **Loans**—Education loans may be awarded directly by the school or through other private agencies. The largest student loan programs are funded or guaranteed by the federal government. Some are awarded on a need basis, while others are not need-based. Some types of loans will require a credit check. Student loans are usually offered at interest rates lower than consumer loans, and the repayment of principal and interest usually begins after the end of your educational program.

Debt Management

Approximately 80 percent of law school students rely on education loans as their primary source of financial aid for law school. An education loan is a serious financial obligation that must be repaid. Dealing with this long-term financial obligation can be made easier through the implementation of sound debt management practices—both while you are in law school and following your graduation.

■ Credit History

It is very important that you have a good credit history. In today's society, most students have already established a credit history through their repayment records as reported by financial institutions and major retail stores to national credit bureaus. Lenders refer to these credit bureau records to determine your credit worthiness. The credit bureaus report the amounts you borrowed or charged, your outstanding balances, and the promptness by which payments have been made. Failure to pay your financial obligations in a prompt and timely manner will jeopardize your eligibility for some education loans.

If you have been denied credit in the past—or if you even suspect a problem with your credit history—it is wise to get a copy of your credit report. Usually, you can obtain it from a credit bureau in your area. Contact the bureau in writing, giving your name, address, and social security number. You can expect to pay a nominal fee unless you have been denied credit recently, in which case the report may be free. Review your report carefully and clear up any problems you can. Keep in mind that it takes time—possibly months—to clear up errors or other problems, so do not wait until the last minute.

■ Loan Default or Delinquency

These two terms are often confused: **delinquency** occurs when you have begun repayment on a loan or other obligation and have missed one or more payment dates; **default** generally occurs when a delinquency goes beyond 150-180 days.

Delinquencies appear on credit records and may hinder you from qualifying for an education loan that requires a credit check. Defaults are even more serious and are likely to prevent you from successfully applying for federal financial aid as well as disqualifying you for most other educational loans. If you are in a default status, you must take steps to change your status if you wish to apply for a federally guaranteed loan for law school. Contact the servicer of your loan(s) for more information on this subject.

■ Planning Ahead: Repayment of Your Loan

Your income after law school is an important factor in determining what constitutes manageable payments on your education loans. Although it may be difficult to predict what kind of job you will get (or want) after law school, or exactly what kind of salary you will receive, it is important that you make **some** assessment of your goals for the purpose of sound debt management. In addition to assessing expected income, you must also create a realistic picture of how much you can afford to pay back on a monthly basis and maintain the lifestyle that you desire. You may have to adjust your thinking about how quickly you can pay your loans back, or how much money you can afford to borrow, or just how extravagantly you expect to live in the years following your graduation from law school.

Your education loan debts represent a serious financial commitment which must be repaid. A default on any loan engenders serious consequences, including possible legal action against you by the lender and/or the government.

There are alternatives available to you to lessen the burden of repayment following law school, including the Federal Consolidation Loan program. The financial aid office at your law school can advise you about repayment issues.

Chapter 9: Finding a Job

Employment Prospects

Because the number of practicing lawyers in the United States continues to increase, it may become more difficult for recent graduates to find jobs in some fields and in certain parts of the country. Opportunities will vary from locality to locality and among legal disciplines. Future lawyers may have to devote considerable time and energy to secure a first job that they consider acceptable. Competition for certain positions will continue to be intense, while opportunities in other fields may expand.

Future demand for people with legal training is almost impossible to predict. Demand for legal services is substantially influenced by the state of the economy. Rising caseloads in the nation's courts and continuing federal and state regulation suggest that the need for lawyers is growing. Whether this expanding need will match or fall short of the parallel growth in the number of practicing lawyers is a question no one can answer with certainty. Lawyers with outstanding academic credentials will continue to obtain desirable positions.

The legal profession itself may adapt to changing job markets by encouraging the entry of lawyers into relatively new fields of law, such as environmental law, intellectual property law, immigration law, and other fields. In addition, certain parts of the country are underrepresented by lawyers.

■ Career Satisfaction

A job search strategy requires careful self-assessment in much the same way as a school search strategy does. A legal career should meet the interests, abilities, capacities, and priorities of the individual lawyer. Career satisfaction is a result of doing what you like to do, and being continually challenged by it. It is up to you to determine what skills you are comfortable using, and to discern which skills are required in the specialties or types of practice you are considering.

■ Gathering Information

Take advantage of any programs and workshops offered by the career services office at your law school. (See page 20 for more on the role of the career services office.) Place your name on file in the office, and be sure to maintain contact with the staff even after you leave school.

The National Association for Law Placement (NALP) is an important source of information (see page 40 for details). This chapter includes a number of charts and graphs compiled by NALP that provide current information relating to employment of law school graduates.

■ Nonlegal Careers for Lawyers

Law-trained individuals pursue a wide variety of careers, and the skills discussed in the first section of this chapter provide excellent training for law school graduates who pursue directions outside the practice of law itself. Lawyers work in the media; as teachers of college, graduate school, and law school; and in law enforcement, public relations, foreign service, politics, and administration.

National Association for Law Placement (NALP) Employment Report and Salary Survey

■ Types of Employment

Data collected on employer types help us understand how new graduates are absorbed into various sectors of the economy. As in all prior years that NALP has collected data, the most common employment setting was that of private practice within a law firm. Of graduates known to be employed, 55 percent obtained their first job in a law firm. This represents a decline from the 57.1 percent for the Class of 1993 and the sixth year in a row that this percentage has declined from the high of 64.3 percent for the Class of 1988.

The second most frequent employment setting, accounting for 27.9 percent of employed graduates, was in public service. This total consisted of government (including the military) at 13.1 percent, judicial clerkships at 12 percent, and public interest at 2.8 percent. Government positions increased by 0.5 percentage points, as did public interest jobs. Business and industry, accounting for 12 percent of jobs, again showed a notable increase from the 1993 figure of 10.6 percent.

Types of Employment
Class of 1994*
(Six Months Post-J.D.)

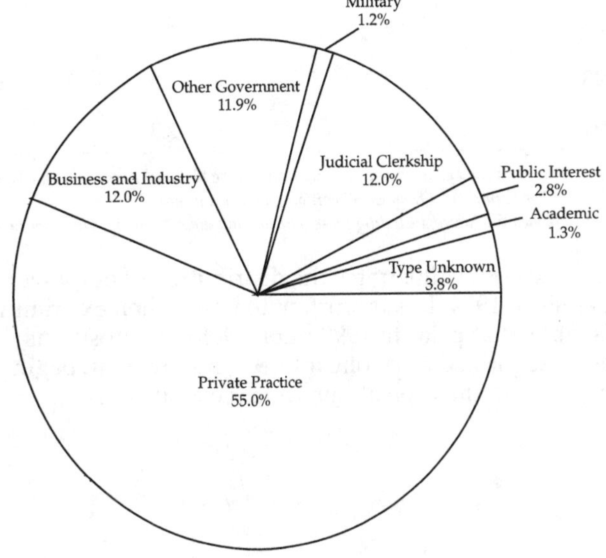

*Represents 75.5% of survey respondents

Twenty-one-year Comparison of Employment (by Field) of New J.D. Graduates*

Year	Employment Field					
	Academic	Public Interest	Business	Government	Clerkship	Private Practice
1974	3.5	5.3	9.7	18.5	8.4	51.9
1975	3.3	5.4	9.2	19.3	9.3	49.2
1976	3.3	4.9	9.6	18.5	8.7	50.4
1977	3.3	5.2	9.9	18.2	8.8	52.1
1978	3.4	5.8	10.4	17.0	8.7	51.8
1979	3.0	5.3	10.4	16.2	9.7	53.0
1980	3.0	4.2	10.8	15.5	9.9	54.0
1981	3.1	3.4	11.0	13.4	10.2	56.6
1982	3.0	2.9	10.4	12.1	10.6	57.5
1983	1.2	2.8	10.1	12.8	11.9	58.9
1984	1.8	3.3	11.1	12.2	10.5	58.9
1985	1.5	3.3	10.4	12.0	12.0	60.6
1986	1.6	3.0	9.0	11.8	12.1	62.3
1987	1.0	3.0	7.9	12.2	12.4	63.5
1988	1.0	3.1	6.9	12.0	12.7	64.3
1989	1.0	3.4	5.8	11.4	12.2	62.4
1990	0.8	2.1	6.9	13.7	12.7	62.9
1991	1.0	2.3	7.5	13.4	12.4	60.8
1992	1.1	2.4	8.9	13.4	12.4	59.0
1993	1.1	2.3	10.6	12.6	12.3	57.1
1994	1.3	2.8	12.0	13.1	12.0	55.0

Charts, tables, and copy adapted with permission from the National Association for Law Placement's Class of 1994 Employment Report and Salary Survey (ERSS).
**This chart has been revised from ERSS editions published prior to 1992 to include military employment within the government category across all years. Also, a more comprehensive base of employed graduates, including those with an "unknown" employer type, was used across all years.*

The table above illustrates the distribution of employer types since 1974. It is important to note, when examining this table, that prior to 1990 public defender positions were categorized as public interest employment; beginning in 1990, these positions were reclassified as government employment. In addition, prior to 1983, the academic category included those pursuing an advanced degree full-time.

■ Salary as an Employment Factor

The average starting salary for the class of 1994 was $44,149, and the median starting salary for the class of 1994 was $37,000. Both figures are up slightly from 1993. This salary reflects the fact that relatively more graduates continue to accept jobs in smaller firms and nonfirm settings.

Nearly half of all salaries were in the $25,001-40,000 range, and salaries of $30,000 and $35,000 were the most frequently reported. The data also show that the highest paying jobs were the exception rather than the rule: salaries of more than $70,000 accounted for just 8.8% of all salaries reported.

Median Starting Salaries* In:

	Private Practice	Business & Industry	Government
Atlanta	$58,500	$36,500	$35,900
Boston	$66,000	$43,000	$30,000
Chicago	$68,000	$44,000	$33,000
Dallas/ Ft. Worth	$53,000	$36,000	$33,300
Houston	$53,000	$50,000	$35,500
Los Angeles	$70,000	$45,000	$42,000
Minneapolis/ St. Paul	$46,000	$35,000	$34,500
New York City	$83,000	$52,000	$33,000
Philadelphia	$59,000	$40,500	$32,200
Washington, DC	$70,000	$42,500	$35,000

*Full-time jobs only

Full-Time Salary Median By Employer Type*

General Category	Legal Jobs Only	Nonlegal Jobs Only
Academic	$30,000	$36,000
Business/Industry	$42,000	$40,000
Government	$32,000	$36,000
Private Practice	$50,000	$28,500
Public Interest	$28,800	$26,000
All Types	$37,000	$40,000

*Based on 1994 Salary Data, full-time jobs only

■ Geography as an Employment Factor

Geographic considerations provide yet another perspective on the placement of new law graduates.

Jobs by City

The 20 cities with the largest number of jobs reported accounted for 40.6 percent of all jobs with a known location. Many of these 20 cities, listed in the table, correspond to the 20 largest cities in terms of population. Not surprisingly, New York City accounts for the largest number of jobs, just under 8 percent of the total. The three largest cities in the country as of July 1, 1992—New York, Los Angeles, and Chicago—continue to be major employment centers for new law graduates.

Seven of the 20 cities providing the most jobs, however, are not among the largest cities in the country. Some of these seven cities are older industrial cities that have been eclipsed in population by the rapidly growing cities of the south and west. Others are state capitals, where government job opportunities may be a factor.

Jobs by State

States vary widely in the number of jobs each provides, again reflecting the distribution of the total population. However, the top 10 states in terms of total reported jobs taken by law graduates have remained the same over the past six years, with New York and California consistently ranked first and second. Other states have fluctuated to varying degrees in their ranking.

Cities With the Largest Number of Jobs Reported

	City	Number of Jobs
1.	New York City	2,047
2.	Washington, DC	1,280
3.	Chicago	1,051
4.	Los Angeles	800
5.	Boston	533
6.	Houston	514
7.	Atlanta	440
8.	Philadelphia	430
9.	Minneapolis/St. Paul	406
10.	Dallas/Fort Worth	382
11.	San Francisco	357
12.	Miami	285
13.	San Diego	266
14.	St. Louis	251
15.	Indianapolis	210
16.	Baltimore	207
17.	Columbus, OH	197
18.	Austin	190
19.	Cleveland	186
20.	Sacramento	183

Jobs by Region

The distribution by region of jobs taken by law graduates reflects the overall distribution of population. Two regions, Mid-Atlantic and South Atlantic, dominated the job market, accounting for a plurality (41.1 percent) of the jobs for which a location was reported. The East North Central and Pacific states each accounted for about an additional 14 percent of jobs. The East South Central and Mountain states continued to provide the fewest jobs.

Place of Work versus Place of School

Comparing the locations of graduates' law school training with the location of their first job offers some insight into the way each geographic market attracts and absorbs graduates within that market. Some of the underlying factors at work are the supply and demand for new law graduates in each market, the perceived attractiveness of each market, and individual preferences.

Nationally, about three-quarters of graduates accepted jobs within the region where they attended law school. Only two regions, Mid-Atlantic and Mountain, were below this average: 56.2 percent of jobs in the Mountain region were taken by graduates from that region and 67.8 percent of jobs in the Mid-Atlantic region went to regional graduates. In contrast, about 86 percent of jobs in the West North Central and West South Central regions were obtained by regional graduates.

These percentages may reflect, in part, variations in each region's ability to attract new lawyers. There appears to be some correlation also between a region's supply of graduates and the extent to which employers hired from that supply.

States With Largest Number of Jobs Per State 1989-1994

Rank	1989	1990	1991	1992	1993	1994
1.	New York	New York	New York	New York	New York	New York
2.	California	California	California	California	California	California
3.	Illinois	Wash DC	Illinois	Pennsylvania	Texas	Texas
4.	Wash DC	Illinois	Wash DC	Illinois	Illinois	Illinois
5.	Pennsylvania	Texas	Pennsylvania	Wash DC	Pennsylvania	Wash DC
6.	Massachusetts	Pennsylvania	Texas	Texas	Wash DC	Florida
7.	Florida	Florida	New Jersey	Massachusetts	Florida	Pennsylvania
8.	Ohio	Massachusetts	Massachusetts	Florida	New Jersey	New Jersey
9.	Texas	New Jersey	Florida	New Jersey	Massachusetts	Massachusetts
10.	New Jersey	Ohio	Ohio	Ohio	Ohio	Ohio

Jobs and Graduates by Region*

	Region									
	New England	Mid-Atlantic	East North Central	West North Central	South Atlantic	East South Central	West South Central	Mountain	Pacific	Total
Graduates with Known Employment Status	2,947	5,178	4,841	2,338	6,811	1,359	3,034	990	4,255	31,753
Graduates with Known Job Location	2,304	4,188	3,921	1,929	5,232	1,179	2,410	784	3,196	25,145
Jobs Reported in Region	1,573	5,257	3,543	1,683	5,077	1,044	2,342	1,130	3,354	25,003
Graduates Staying in Region	1,243	3,562	3,005	1,453	3,812	857	2,015	635	2,668	19,250
Percentage of Jobs to Region Graduates	79.0%	67.8%	84.8%	86.3%	75.1%	82.1%	86.0%	56.2%	79.6%	76.6%
Percentage of Graduates Staying in Region	54.0%	85.1%	76.6%	75.3%	72.9%	72.7%	83.6%	81.0%	83.5%	76.6%
Supply/Demand Index	1.87	0.99	1.37	1.39	1.34	1.30	1.30	0.88	1.27	1.26

***U.S. Census Bureau Regions**

	Region	States Included
1.	New England	CT, ME, MA, NH, RI, VT
2.	Mid-Atlantic	NJ, NY, PA
3.	East North Central	IL, IN, MI, OH, WI
4.	West North Central	IA, KS, MN, MO, NE, ND, SD
5.	South Atlantic	DE, DC, FL, GA, MD, NC, SC, VA, WV
6.	East South Central	AL, KY, MS, TN
7.	West South Central	AR, LA, OK, TX
8.	Mountain	AZ, CO, ID, MT, NV, NM, UT, WY
9.	Pacific	AK, CA, HI, OR, WA

Chapter 10: Organizations You Should Know About

You may have questions concerning a variety of issues while you are applying to law school, once you are in law school, and even after you have your degree. The following organizations may provide you with the answers you need.

American Association of Law Libraries (AALL)

The American Association of Law Libraries exists to provide leadership in the field of legal information, to foster the professional growth of law librarians, to develop the profession of law librarianship, and to enhance the value of law libraries to the legal community and to the public. AALL members come from all sizes and types of libraries: the Library of Congress, legislative libraries, academic law libraries, law firm libraries, bar association libraries, county law libraries, court libraries, and law libraries in business and industry. The association publishes a scholarly journal, a monthly magazine (*AALL Newsletter*), and an annual directory and handbook (which includes a minority law librarians directory).

For more information, write to:

American Association of Law Libraries
53 W. Jackson Blvd., Suite 940
Chicago, IL 60604
312.939.4764

American Bar Association (ABA)

The American Bar Association is the national organization of the legal profession. It is composed principally of practicing lawyers; judges; court administrators; law teachers; public service attorneys; many nonpracticing lawyers who are business executives, government officials and so forth; and law students. Although the ABA does not have the power to discipline attorneys or enforce rules, the association leads by serving as the national voice of the profession.

The ABA, with about 350,000 members and 30,000 law student members, is the world's largest voluntary professional association. It serves a dual role as advocate for the profession and for the public. During the past decade, the association has initiated hundreds of programs addressing a wide range of public concerns. Response to these concerns is made possible by thousands of volunteers who contribute both time and money.

The Council of the Section of Legal Education and Admissions to the Bar of the ABA is identified by the U.S. Department of Education as the "nationally recognized accrediting agency for professional schools of law." The role that the American Bar Association plays as a central accrediting body has allowed accreditation to become national in scope rather than fragmented among the 50 states, District of Columbia, the Commonwealth of Puerto Rico, and other territories. Most admitting jurisdictions require applicants for admission to be graduates of law schools approved by the American Bar Association.

The ABA may be contacted for information on the accreditation of law schools and the role of lawyers in the legal profession:

Office of the Consultant on Legal Education
American Bar Association
Indiana University
550 West North Street, Third Floor
Indianapolis, IN 46202
317.264.8340

Association of American Law Schools (AALS)

The Association of American Law Schools was founded for "the improvement of the legal profession through legal education." It is an association of law schools that serves as the law teachers' learned society. The association requires quality teaching and scholarship of its 160 member schools.

The organization provides a range of services to law schools. Among them are professional development workshops and conferences for law faculty, facilitation of law faculty recruitment, publication of the *AALS Directory of Law Teachers*, and interpretation of the mission and needs of legal education as the principal representative to other national higher education organizations, the federal government, and learned societies.

The AALS may be contacted for specific information about the role of legal education in the profession:

Association of American Law Schools
1201 Connecticut Ave., NW
Suite 800
Washington, DC 20036-2605
202.296.8851

Council on Legal Education Opportunity (CLEO)

The Council on Legal Education Opportunity has a 28-year history of assisting economically and educationally disadvantaged law school applicants. Each year CLEO accepts approximately 120 applicants nationwide and places them through an intensive, six-week summer institute program that prepares them for the first year of law school. The institute is conducted each year, from early June through July, by five ABA-approved law schools. Faculty is comprised of law professors familiar with the first-year law curriculum and problems that first-year students often encounter. Students who are certified by the program are then eligible to receive scholarship funds upon immediate entrance into an ABA-approved law school. For some law school candidates, with marginal academic credentials, completion of the CLEO institute is a requirement for admission to law school. However, students who have already secured law school acceptance are also encouraged to apply.

For more information, write to:

Council on Legal Education Opportunity
1420 N Street, NW
Suite T-1
Washington, DC 20005

HEATH Resource Center

The American Council on Education operates the HEATH Resource Center, the national clearinghouse on postsecondary education for individuals with disabilities. HEATH can provide information about requesting disability-related accommodations, ascertaining the level of physical and programmatic access available at law schools, and thinking through disability issues surrounding the application process. A reprint of "Students with Disabilities and Law School" from the HEATH newsletter is available free by request.

For more information, write or call:

HEATH Resource Center
One Dupont Circle, NW
Suite 800
Washington, DC 20036-1193
202.939.9320 (in Washington)
800.54.HEATH (outside DC)
(Both numbers are Voice/TDD.)

Law School Admission Council

The Law School Admission Council (LSAC or Law Services) is a nonprofit corporation whose members are 193 law schools in the United States and Canada. It was founded in 1947 to coordinate, facilitate, and enhance the law school admission process. The organization also provides programs and services related to legal education. All law schools approved by the American Bar Association (ABA) are LSAC members. Canadian law schools recognized by a provincial or territorial law society or government agency are also included in the voting membership of the Council.

The services provided by Law Services include: The Law School Admission Test (LSAT); the Law School Data Assembly Service (LSDAS); the Candidate Referral Service (CRS); and various publications and LSAT preparation tools. The LSAT, LSDAS, and CRS are provided to assist law schools in serving and evaluating applicants. Law Services does not engage in assessing an applicant's chances for admission to any law school; all admission decisions are made by individual law schools.

The LSAC and Law Services exist to serve both the law schools and their candidates for admission. Last year, Law Services administered about 128,600 tests, and processed 176,650 transcripts, 397,250 law school report requests, and 508,000 law school reports.

For more information on the LSAT, LSDAS, and law school admission, write or call:

Law Services
Box 2000
661 Penn Street
Newtown, PA 18940-0998
215.968.1001

For information on minority opportunities in law, write or call:

Law Services
Minority Opportunities in Law
Box 40
661 Penn Street
Newtown, PA 18940-0040
215.968.1338

Law Services' World Wide Web site is located at http://www.lsac.org.

National Association for Law Placement (NALP)

The National Association for Law Placement is a professional organization of law schools and legal employers. NALP's mission is to provide information, coordination, and standards for fair recruiting for all of the participants in the legal recruiting process. NALP provides a forum for discussion of recruiting trends and problems among school and employer representatives; provides professional education and resources for law school career services professionals and legal employers, recruiting directors, and hiring attorneys; and conducts research on legal employment.

NALP publishes resource materials that assist students in making informed career choices. NALP publications are available through law school career services offices and may be ordered directly through NALP. However, NALP is not an employment agency, and does not offer specific job listings or maintain comprehensive employment statistics on attorneys other than recent graduates.

NALP believes that each law school offers unique programs and opportunities and, like the American Bar Association and the Law School Admission Council, does not rate law school or career services offices.

For further information, write or call:

National Association for Law Placement
Suite 325
1666 Connecticut Avenue, NW
Washington, DC 20009-1039
202.667.1666

Chapter 11: Prelaw Readings: Books of Interest

The following list of prelaw readings offers prospective law students an overview of selected classics and current titles in certain subjects: law school and legal education, the legal profession, biography, jurisprudence and legal issues, and financing a law school education. Some of these publications list sources for financial aid, but students will need to call or write the individual organizations for the most up-to-date information.

This list should not be construed as the official bibliography of Law School Admission Council; it is beyond the scope of this publication to provide any sort of definitive catalog of prelaw readings.

Some of these books have already withstood the test of time, and are as relevant today as when they were first written and published, generations ago. Examples are: Richard Kluger's *Simple Justice*—a rare glimpse into the private workings and deliberations of the Supreme Court; and Karl Llewellyn's *The Bramble Bush*—a classic study of how legal education shapes our legal institutions.

Some titles simply reflect the most current writing on the subjects listed above and are not necessarily recommended simply because they appear on this list. It will be up to you to search out the titles that pique your interest and make your own determination of their worth. The aim of our list is merely to give you a head start. We hope that those interested in pursuing legal studies will find the issues raised and the ideas discussed in these works helpful in making the decision to choose law as a career.

■ Law School and Legal Education

Barber, David H. *Winning in Law School: Stress Reduction.* 2d ed. Dillon, CO: Spectra, 1986.

Bay, Monica. *Careers in Civil Litigation.* Chicago: American Bar Association/Law Student Division, 1990.

Bell, Susan J. *Full Disclosure: Do You Really Want to Be a Lawyer?* Princeton, NJ: Peterson's Guides, 1989.

Bell, Susan J. *Interviewing for Success and Satisfaction.* Chicago: American Bar Association/Young Lawyers Division, 1989.

Calamari, John D. and **Joseph M. Perillo**, eds. *How to Thrive in Law School.* Pelham Manor, NY: Hook Mountain Press, 1984.

Carter, Lief H. *Reason in Law.* Boston: Little, Brown and Company, 1988.

Chase, William C. *The American Law School and the Rise of Administrative Government.* Madison, WI: University of Wisconsin Press, 1982.

Curry, Boykin, ed. *Essays That Worked for Law Schools: 35 Essays from Successful Applications to the Nation's Top Law Schools.* New York: Fawcett Book Group, 1991.

Deaver, Jeff. *The Complete Law School Companion: How to Excel at America's Most Demanding Post-Graduate Curriculum.* New York: John Wiley & Sons, 1992.

Delaney, John. *How to Do Your Best on Law School Exams.* 2d ed. Bogota, NJ: John Delaney Publications, 1988.

Directory of Law School Joint Degree Programs. 2d ed. Washington, DC: Federal Reports, Inc., 1991.

Dutile, Fernand N., ed. *Legal Education and Lawyer Competency: Curricula for Change.* Notre Dame, IN: University of Notre Dame Press, 1981.

Dworkin, Elizabeth, Jack Himmelstein, and **Howard Lesnick.** *Becoming a Lawyer: A Humanistic Perspective on Legal Education and Professionalism.* St. Paul, NM: West Publishing, 1989.

Farnsworth, Edward A. *An Introduction to the Legal System of the United States.* 2d ed. Dobbs Ferry, NY: Oceana Publications, 1983.

Gillers, Stephen, ed. *Looking at Law School: A Student Guide from the Society of American Law Teachers.* 3d ed. NAL/Dutton, 1990.

Goldfarb, Sally F. *Inside the Law Schools: A Guide by Students for Students.* 6th ed. New York: Plume, 1993.

Goodrich, Chris. *Anarchy and Elegance: Confessions of a Journalist at Yale Law School.* Boston: Little, Brown and Company, 1991.

Hegland, Kenney F. *Introduction to the Study and Practice of Law in a Nutshell.* St. Paul, MN: West Publishing, 1983.

Kaplin, William A. *The Concepts and Methods of Constitutional Law.* Durham, NC: Carolina Academic Press, 1992.

Kelman, Mark. *A Guide to Critical Legal Studies.* Cambridge, MA: Harvard University Press, 1987.

Legal Education and Professional Development — An Educational Continuum. Report of The Task Force on Law Schools and the Profession: Narrowing the Gap. Chicago: American Bar Association, Section of Legal Education and Admissions to the Bar, July 1992.

Llewellyn, Karl N. *The Bramble Bush: On Our Law and its Study.* rev. ed. Dobbs Ferry, NY: Oceana Publications, 1981.

Margulies, Sheldon and **Kenneth Lasson.** *Learning Law: The Mastery of Legal Logic.* Durham, NC: Carolina Academic Press, 1993.

Martinson, Thomas H., J.D., and **David P. Waldherr, J.D.** *Getting Into Law School: Strategies for the 90s.* New York: Prentice Hall, 1992.

Mayfield, Craig K. *Reading Skills for Law Students.* Charlottesville, VA: Michie Co., 1980.

Moliterno, James E. and **Fredric Lederer.** *An Introduction to Law, Law Study, and the Lawyer's Role.* Durham, NC: Carolina Academic Press, 1991.

Re, Edward D., and **Joseph R. Re.** *Law Students' Manual on Legal Writing and Oral Argument.* Dobbs Ferry, NY: Oceana Publications, 1991.

Roth, George. *Slaying the Law School Dragon: How to Survive—and Thrive—in First-Year Law School.* 2d ed. New York: John Wiley & Sons, 1991.

Simenhogg, Mark. ed. *My First Year As A Lawyer.* New York: Walker and Company, 1994.

So You Want to be a Lawyer: A Practical Guide to Law as a Career. Newtown, PA: Law School Admission Council, 1996

Stevens, Robert. Law School: *Legal Education in America from the 1850s to the 1980s*. Chapel Hill, NC: University of North Carolina Press, 1983.

Stover, Robert V. *Making It and Breaking It: The Fate of Public Interest Commitment During Law School*. Urbana, IL: University of Illinois Press, 1989.

Swygert, Michael I., and **Robert Batey**, eds. *Maximizing the Law School Experience: A Collection of Essays*. St. Petersburg, FL: Stetson University College of Law, 1983.

Turow, Scott. *One L.: An Inside Account of Life in the First Year at Harvard Law School*. New York: Penguin Books, 1978.

Vanderbilt, Arthur T. *Law School: Briefing for a Legal Education*. New York: Penguin Books, 1981.

Williams, Glanville. *Learning the Law: A Book for the Guidance of the Law Student*. 11th ed. London: Stevens, 1982.

Wydick, Richard C. *Plain English for Lawyers*. 2d ed. Durham, NC: Carolina Academic Press, 1985.

■ Legal Profession

Abel, Richard L. *American Lawyers*. New York: Oxford University Press, 1989.

Arron, Deborah. *Running From the Law: Why Good Lawyers Are Getting Out of the Legal Profession*. Berkeley, CA: Ten Speed Press, 1991.

Arron, Deborah. *What Can You Do With a Law Degree? A Lawyer's Guide to Career Alternatives Inside, Outside, and Around the Law*. Seattle: Niche Press, 1992.

Bailey, F. Lee. *To Be A Trial Lawyer*. New York: John Wiley & Sons, 1985.

Caplan, Lincoln. *Skadden: Inside the Business of Law in America*. New York: Farrar, Strauss & Giroux, 1993.

Carey, William T. *Law Students: How to Get a Job When There Aren't Any*. Durham, NC: Carolina Academic Press, 1986.

Couric, Emily. *The Trial Lawyers: The Nation's Top Litigators Tell How They Win*. New York: St. Martin's Press, 1988.

Delaney, John. *Learning Legal Reasoning: Briefings, Analysis and Theory*, rev. ed. Bogota, NJ: John Delaney Publications, 1987.

Epstein, Cynthia Fuchs. *Women in Law*. 2d ed. Urbana, IL: University of Illinois Press, 1993.

Foonberg, Jay G. *How to Start and Build a Law Practice*. 3d ed. Chicago: American Bar Association/Law Student Division, 1991.

Fox, Ronald W. *Lawful Pursuit: Careers in Public Interest Law*. Chicago: American Bar Association, Career Series, 1995.

Galanter, Marc, and **Thomas Palay**. *Tournament of Lawyers: The Transformation of the Big Law Firm*. Chicago: University of Chicago Press, 1991.

Glendon, Mary Ann. *A Nation Under Lawyers: How the Crisis in the Legal Profession is Transforming American Society*. New York: Farrar, Straus & Girous, 1994.

Greene, Robert Michael. *Making Partner: A Guide for Law Firm Associates*. Chicago: American Bar Association, Section of Law Practice Management, 1992.

Harrington, Mona. *Women Lawyers: Rewriting the Rules*. New York: Alfred A. Knopf, 1994.

Henslee, William D. *Careers in Entertainment Law*. Chicago: American Bar Association/Law Student Division, 1990.

Kelly, Michael J. *Lives of Lawyers: Journeys in the Organizations of Practice*. Ann Arbor: University of Michigan Press, 1994.

Killoughey, Donna M. ed. *Breaking Traditions: Work Alternatives for Lawyers*. Chicago: American Bar Association, Section of Law Practice Management, 1993.

Kronman, Anthony T. *The Lost Lawyer: Failing Ideals of the Legal Profession*. Cambridge, MA: Harvard University Press (Belknap Press), 1993.

Linowitz, Sol M., with **Martin Mayer.** *The Betrayed Profession: Lawyering at the End of the Twentieth Century*. New York: Charles Scribner's Sons, 1994.

López, Gerald P. *Rebellious Lawyering: One Chicano's Vision of Progressive Law Practice*. Boulder, CO: Westview Press, 1992.

Luney, Percy R., Jr. *Careers in Natural Resources and Environmental Law*. Chicago: American Bar Association/Law Student Division, 1987.

Mayer, Martin. *The Lawyers*. Westport, CT: Greenwood Press, 1980.

Moll, Richard W. *The Lure of the Law: Why People Become Lawyers, and What the Profession Does to Them*. New York: Penguin Books, 1990.

Munneke, Gary A. *The Legal Career Guide: From Law Student to Lawyer*. Chicago: American Bar Association Career Series, 1992.

Munneke, Gary A. and **William D. Henslee** *Nonlegal Careers for Lawyers*. Chicago: American Bar Association, 1994.

O'Neill, Suzanne B. and **Catherine Gerhauser Sparkman.** *From Law School to Law Practice: The New Associate's Guide*. Philadelphia: American Law Institute/American Bar Association Committee on Continuing Professional Education, 1989.

Shaffer, Thomas L. with **Mary M. Shaffer**. *American Lawyers and Their Communities: Ethics in the Legal Profession*. Notre Dame, IN: University of Notre Dame Press, 1991.

Shropshire, Kenneth. *Careers in Sports Law*. Chicago: American Bar Association/Law Student Division, 1990.

Speiser, Stuart M. *Lawyers and the American Dream*. New York: M. Evan and Co., 1993.

Stewart, James B. *The Partners*. New York: Simon & Schuster, 1983.

Thorner, Abbie Willard, ed. *Now Hiring: Government Jobs for Lawyers (1990-1991 edition)*. Chicago: American Bar Association/law Student Division, 1990.

Wayne, Ellen. *Careers in Labor Law*. Chicago: American Bar Association/Law Student Division, 1985.

■ Biography

Auchincloss, Louis. *Life, Law and Letters: Essays and Sketches*. Boston: Houghton Mifflin Co., 1979.

Baker, Leonard. *John Marshall: A Life in Law*. New York: Macmillan, 1974.

Barth, Alan. *Prophets with Honor: Great Dissents and Great Dissenters in the Supreme Court*. New York: Vintage Books, 1975.

Darrow, Clarence. *The Story of My Life*. New York: Charles Scribner's Sons, 1932.

Davis, Deane C. *Justice in the Mountains: Stories & Tales by a Vermont Country Lawyer*. Shelburne, VT: New England Press, 1980.

Davis, Lenwood G. *I Have a Dream: The Life and Times of Martin Luther King*. Westport, CT: Negro Universities Press, 1973.

Davis, Michael D. and **Hunter R. Clark**. *Thurgood Marshall: Warrior at the Bar, Rebel on the Bench*. New York: Birch Lane Press/Carol Publishing Group, 1993.

Douglas, William O. *Go East Young Man: The Early Years*. New York: Random House, 1974.

Douglas, William O. *Court Years, 1939-1975: The Autobiography of William O. Douglas*. New York: Random House, 1980.

Dunne, Gerald T. *Hugo Black and the Judicial Revolution*. New York: Simon & Schuster, 1977.

Frankfurter, Felix. *Felix Frankfurter Reminisces*. New York: Reynal & Co., 1960.

Goldman, Roger, with **David Gallen.** *Justice William J. Brennan, Jr.: Freedom First*. New York: Carroll & Graf Publishers, Inc., 1994

Griffith, Kathryn. *Judge Learned Hand and the Role of the Federal Judiciary*. Norman: University of Oklahoma Press, 1973.

Griswold, Erwin N. *Ould Fields, New Corne: The Personal Memoirs of a Twentieth Century Lawyer*. St. Paul, MN: West Publishing, 1992.

Gunther, Gerald. *Learned Hand: The Man and the Judge*. New York: Alfred A. Knopf, 1994.

Howe, Mark deWolfe. *Justice Oliver Wendell Holmes*. Cambridge, MA: Harvard University Press, 1957 (vol. 1), 1963 (vol. 2).

Jeffries, John, Jr. *Justice Lewis F. Powell*. New York: Scribner, 1994.

Kahlenberg, Richard D. *Broken Contract: A Memoir of Harvard Law School*. New York: Farrar, Straus & Giroux, 1992.

Lynn, Conrad J. *There is a Foundation: The Autobiography of a Civil Rights Lawyer*. Westport, CT: Hill & Company, 1978.

Marke, Julius J. *The Holmes Reader*. Dobbs Ferry, NY: Oceana Publications, 1964.

Mason, Alpheus. *Harlan Fiske Stone: Pillar of the Law*. New York: Viking Press, 1956.

Murphy, Bruce Allen. *The Brandeis/Frankfurter Connection: The Secret Political Activities of Two Supreme Court Justices*. New York: Oxford University Press, 1982.

Nizer, Louis. *Reflections Without Mirrors: An Autobiography of the Mind*. New York: Doubleday, 1978.

Noonan, John T., Jr. *Persons and Masks of the Law: Cardozo, Holmes, Jefferson, and Wythe as Makers of the Masks*. New York: Farrar, Straus & Giroux, 1976.

Pusey, Merlo J. *Charles Evans Hughes*. New York: Macmillan, 1951.

Rowan, Carl T. *Dream Makers, Dream Breakers. The World of Justice Thurgood Marshall*. Boston: Little Brown & Company, 1993.

Schwartz, Bernard. *Super Chief, Earl Warren and His Supreme Court—A Judicial Biography*. New York: New York University Press, 1983.

Simon, James F. *Independent Journey: The Life of William O. Douglas*. New York: Harper & Row, 1980.

Strum, Phillippa. *Brandeis: Beyond Progressivism*. Lawrence, KS, 1993.

Thomas, Evan. *The Man to See: Edward Bennett Williams, Ultimate Insider; Legendary Trial Lawyer*. New York: Simon & Schuster, 1991.

Urofsky, Melvin I. *Louis D. Brandeis and the Progressive Tradition*. Boston: Little, Brown and Company, 1981.

Westin, Alan F. *Autobiography of the Supreme Court: Off-the-Bench Commentary by the Justices*. Westport, CT: Greenwood Press, 1978.

White, G. Edward. *Earl Warren: A Public Life*. New York: Oxford University Press, 1982.

White, G. Edward. *Justice Oliver Wendell Holmes: Law and the Inner Self*. Oxford University Press, 1993.

Wigdor, David. *Roscoe Pound: Philosopher of Law*. Westport, CT: Greenwood Press, 1974.

■ Jurisprudence and Legal Issues

Ball, Milner S. *The Word and the Law*. Chicago: University of Chicago Press, 1993.

Bickel, Alexander M. *The Least Dangerous Branch: The Supreme Court at the Bar of Politics*. 2d ed. New Haven: Yale University Press, 1986.

Bickel, Alexander M. *The Morality of Consent*. New Haven: Yale University Press, 1975.

Bodenhamer, David J. and **James E. Ely, Jr.**, eds. *The Bill of Rights in Modern America*. Bloomington and Indianapolis: Indiana University Press, 1993.

Burns, James MacGregor, and **Stewart Burns**. *The People's Charter: Pursuing Rights in America*. New York: Alfred A. Knopf, 1991.

Cahn, Edmond. *The Moral Decision: Right and Wrong in the Light of American Law*. Bloomington, IN: Indiana University Press, 1955.

Cardozo, Benjamin N. *The Nature of the Judicial Process*. New Haven: Yale University Press, 1921.

Dershowitz, Alan M. *The Best Defense*. New York: Random House, 1982.

Dershowitz, Alan M. *Taking Liberties: A Decade of Hard Cases, Bad Laws, and Bum Raps*. Chicago: Contemporary Books, 1988.

Finkel, Norman J. *Insanity on Trial*. New York: Plenum, 1988.

Greenberg, Jack. *Crusaders in the Courts: How a Dedicated Band of Lawyers Fought for the Civil Rights Revolution*. New York: Basic Books, 1994.

Guinier, Lani. *The Tyranny of the Majority: Fundamental Fairness in Representative Democracy*. New York: Martin Kessler Books (The Free Press), 1994.

Howard, A.E. Dick. *The Road from Runnymeade: Magna Carta and Constitutionalism in America*. Charlottesville, VA: University of Virginia, 1968.

Irons, Peter. *The Courage of their Convictions: Sixteen Americans Who Fought Their Way to the Supreme Court*. New York: Penguin, 1990.

Irons, Peter and **Stephanie Guitton**, eds. *May It Please the Court: The Most Significant Oral Arguments Made Before the Supreme Court Since 1955* [audiocassette]. New York: New Press, 1993.

Kairys, David, ed. *The Politics of Law: A Progressive Critique*. New York: Pantheon Books, 1982.

Kirk, Russell. *The Roots of American Order*. Malibu, CA: Pepperdine University Press, 1981.

Kluger, Richard. *Simple Justice: The History of Brown vs. Board of Education and Black America's Struggle for Equality*. New York: Alfred A. Knopf, 1976.

Konefsky, Samuel J. *The Legacy of Holmes and Brandeis: A Study in the Influence of Ideas*. New York: DeCapo Press, 1974.

Lee, Rex E. *A Lawyer Looks at the Constitution*. Provo, UT: Brigham Young University Press, 1981.

Lewis, Anthony. *Gideon's Trumpet*. New York: Random House, 1964.

Lewis, Anthony. *Make No Law: The Sullivan Case and the First Amendment*. New York: Random House, 1991.

MacKinnon, Catharine A. *Only Words*. Cambridge, MA: Harvard University Press, 1993.

Pfeffer, Leo. *Religion, State and the Burger Court*. Buffalo, NY: Prometheus Books, 1984.

Pound, Roscoe. *Law and Morals*. South Hackensack, NJ: Rothman Reprints, 1969.

Rehnquist, William H. *The Supreme Court: How It Was, How It Is*. New York: Quill Press, 1987.

Rosenberg, Gerald N. *The Hollow Hope: Can Courts Bring About Social Change?* Chicago: University of Chicago Press, 1991.

Savage, David. *Turning Right: The Making of the Rehnquist Supreme Court*. New York: John Wiley & Sons, 1992.

Schwartz, Bernard. *A History of the Supreme Court*. New York: Oxford University Press, 1992.

Shapiro, Fred R. *The Oxford Dictionary of American Legal Quotations*. New York: Oxford University Press, 1993.

Shapiro, Joseph P. *No Pity: People with Disabilities Forging a New Civil Rights Movement*. New York: Random House, 1993.

Simon, James F. *The Antagonists: Hugo Black, Felix Frankfurter and Civil Liberties in Modern America*. New York: Simon & Schuster, 1989.

Sobol, Richard B. *Bending the Law: The Story of the Dalkon Shield Bankruptcy*. Chicago: University of Chicago Press, 1991.

Spence, Gerry. *With Justice for None*. New York: Penguin, 1990.

Stone, Geoffrey R., Richard Epstein, and **Cass R. Sunstein**, eds. *The Bill of Rights in the Modern State*. Chicago: University of Chicago Press, 1992.

Sunstein, Cass R. *Democracy and the Problem of Free Speech*. New York: The Free Press, 1993.

Treanor, Richard Bryant. *We Overcame: The Story of Civil Rights for Disabled People*. Falls Church, VA: Regal Direct Publishing, 1993.

Tribe, Laurence H. *God Save This Honorable Court: How the Choice of Supreme Court Justices Shapes Our History*. New York: Penguin/Mentor, 1986.

Tushnet, Mark V. *Making Civil Rights Law: Thurgood Marshall and the Supreme Court, 1936-1961*. New York: Oxford University Press, 1994.

Unger, Roberto M. *Knowledge and Politics*. New York: The Free Press, 1984.

van den Haag, Ernest, and **John P. Conrad.** *The Death Penalty: A Debate*. New York: Plenum, 1983.

Westin, Alan F. *The Anatomy of a Constitutional Law Case: Youngstown Sheet & Tube Co. v. Sawyer*. New York: Columbia University Press, 1990.

Williams, Patricia J. *The Alchemy of Race and Rights*. Cambridge, MA: Harvard University Press, 1991.

Wishman, Seymour. *Anatomy of a Jury*. New York: Penguin, 1987.

■ Financing Law School

The Black Collegian's Guide to Graduate and Professional Fellowships for Minority Students. 5th ed. New Orleans, LA: The Black Collegian, 1994.

Cantrell, Karen and **Denise Wallen**. *Funding for Law: Legal Education, Research and Study*. Phoenix, AZ: Oryx Press, 1991.

Cassidy, Daniel. *The Graduate Scholarship Book: The Complete Guide to Scholarships, Fellowships, Grants, and Loans for Graduate and Professional Study*. 2nd ed. National Scholarship Reference Service, Prentice-Hall, 1990.

Johnson, Willis L. *The Big Book of Minority Opportunities: Directory of Special Programs for Minority Group Members.* Garrett Park, MD: Garrett Park Press, 1995.

Financial Aid for Minorities in Business and Law. Garrett Park, MD: Garrett Park Press, 1995.

Kirby, Deborah M., ed. *Scholarships, Fellowships, and Loans: 1994-1995.* 10th edition. Detroit: Gale Research, Inc.

Schlachter, Gail Ann. *Financial Aid for the Disabled and Their Families, 1994-96.* San Carlos, CA: Reference Service Press.

Schlachter, Gail Ann. *Directory of Financial Aids for Minorities, 1993-95.* San Carlos, CA: Reference Service Press.

Schlachter, Gail Ann. *Financial Aid for Veterans, Military Personnel, and Their Dependents, 1993-95.* San Carlos, CA: Reference Service Press.

Schlachter, Gail Ann. *Directory of Financial Aids for Women, 1993-95.* San Carlos, CA: Reference Service Press.

Williams, Franklin A. and **Mark Fischer.** *The Law Student's Guide to Scholarships and Grants.* New York: Scovill, Paterson, Inc., 1994.

This information was reported by the schools in Fall 1995, thus the figures may have changed. The reader is cautioned against making direct comparisons of complex information limited to chart form. Be sure to go beyond the table, indeed beyond the two-page descriptions that follow, if you wish to inform yourself adequately about a particular school. Symbols and footnotes are explained on the last page of this chart.	Fall 1995 Enrollment/Student Body				Faculty		Programs										Library		Tuition				Miscellaneous				
	Full-time	Part-time	Percentage of Women	Percentage of Minority	Total full-time	Total part-time	Part-time	Evening division	Total credits from required classes	Total credits required to obtain J.D.	Joint degrees offered	Graduate law study available	Transferable summer courses offered	Summer matriculation for first-year students	Midyear matriculation for first-year students	Academic Support Programs offered	Number of full-time staff	Number of volumes and equivalents	In-state, full-time	Out-of-state, full-time	In-state, part-time	Out-of-state, part-time	Application fee	Application deadline for fall admission	Financial aid application deadline	Official Guide page number	Grid included with narrative school description
ALABAMA																											
The University of Alabama School of Law	565	-	42	12	30	33			36	90	•					•	7	338,916	$3,440	$7,286	-	-	$25	3/1	03/01	-	
Cumberland School of Law of Samford University	652	-	36	8.6	33	25			53	90	•	•	•	•		•	13	210,000	$15,698	$15,698	-	-	$40	5/1	3/1	-	•
ARIZONA																											
Arizona State University College of Law	476	-	47	29	35	12			40	87	•		•			•	17	340,000	$3,950	$9,978	-	-	$35	03/01	03/01	-	•
University of Arizona College of Law	454	-	46	28	30	18			39	85	•	•	•			•	14	353,260	$3,950y	$9,978y	-	-	$35	03/01	03/01	-	•
ARKANSAS																											
University of Arkansas School of Law—Fayetteville	396	-	40	8	35	10			44	90	•	•	•				5	220,000	$3,374	$7,286	-	-	-	04/01	05/01	-	•
University of Arkansas at Little Rock School of Law	272	156	44	13.2	24	13	•	•	50	87	•		•			•	13	240,000	$3,477y	$7,605y	$136h	$308h	$40	04/01	05/01	-	•
CALIFORNIA																											
University of California at Berkeley School of Law (Boalt Hall)	861	-	50	37	61	85			31	85	•	•				•	12	650,000	$8,800	$16,500	-	-	$40	02/01	03/02	-	•
School of Law University of California—Davis	467	-	50	34.7	29	12			33	88						•	16	383,634	$8,796	$16,495	-	-	$40	02/01	03/01	-	•
University of California—Hastings College of the Law	1262	-	47	32.2	47	68			34	88	•					•	19	563,260	$9,588	$17,287	-	-	$40	02/15	02/15	-	•
School of Law, University of California, Los Angeles	955	-	50	45.1	74	22			35	87	•	•				•	26	500,000	$8,782	$16,481y	-	-	$40	01/16	-	-	•
California Western School of Law	796	-	47	21.5	46	26			45	89			•		•	•	14	231,293	$18,250	$18,250	-	-	$45	04/01	03/20	-	•
Golden Gate University School of Law	469	244	51	28.1	35	100	•	•	54	86	•	•	•		•	•	12	200,000	$16,965	$16,965	$11,115	$11,115	$40	04/15	03/01	-	•
Loyola Law School, Los Angeles, Loyola Marymount University	982	414	44	37.2	59	48	•	•	43	87	•					•	30	393,083	$18,634	-	$12,532	-	$50	02/01	03/02	-	•

McGeorge School of Law, University of the Pacific	886	334	45	23	53	60	•	•	53	88	•	•	•			•	21	400,000	$16,400	$16,400	$9,714	$9,714	$40	d 05/01 e none	none	-	•
Pepperdine University School of Law	702	-	48	24.8	33	49			57	88	•		•			•	30	252,000	$19,870	$19,870	-	-	$50	03/01	05/01	-	•
University of San Diego School of Law	763	347	43	19.5	60	40	•	•	48	85	•	•	•	•		•	19	375,000	$18,120	-	$12,860	$610u	$35	02/01p	03/02p	-	•
University of San Francisco School of Law	567	120	51	24.7	27	58	•	•	48	86	•		•			•	12	264,797	$17,810	$17,810	$635u	$635u	$40	04/01	03/01	-	•
Santa Clara University School of Law	660	222	50	36.8	35	40	•	•	45	86	•		•			•	18	234,893	$18,482	-	$13,503	-	$40	03/01	03/01	-	•
University of Southern California Law School	610	-	45	39	49	32			34	88	•					•	21	340,000	$21,200	$21,200	-	-	$60	02/01	02/15	-	•
Southwestern University School of Law	838	369	49	29.7	48	39	•	•	52	87			•			•	20	364,000	$18,220	$18,220	$11,576	$11,576	$50	06/30	06/03	-	•
Stanford University Law School	574	-	45	31	45	53			26	86	•	•					9	436,000	$22,350	-	-	-	$65	02/15	03/15	-	•
Whittier Law School	451	204	51	35	34	12	•	•	38	87			•		•	•	14	230,000	$18,000	-	$10,800	-	$50	03/15	06/1F	-	•
COLORADO																											
University of Colorado School of Law	498	-	45	21	35	34			45	89	•		•			•	8	325,000	$4,394	$14,630	-	-	$40	02/15	asap	-	•
University of Denver College of Law	800	280	45	13.6	49	38s	•	•	47	90	•	•	•			•	8	291,839	$16,895	$16,895	$10,900	$10,900	$45	03/01	02/15	-	•
CONNECTICUT																											
Quinnipiac College School of Law	565	230	36	12.3	40	21	•	•	53	86	•	•	•		•	•	6	293,309	$15,960	$15,960	$665	$665	$40	rolling	04/01	-	•
University of Connecticut School of Law	432	196	48	15.9	44	41	•	•	36	86	•	•	•			•	17	416,819	$9,972	$21,030	$348c	$734c	$30/$45	03/01	03/01	-	•
Yale Law School	573	-	45	29.7	48	57			24	82	•	•					47	800,000	$21,660	-	-	-	$60	02/15	03/15	-	•
DELAWARE																											
Widener University School of Law	1383	608	42	5.9	104	89	•	•	51	87	•	•	•			•	40	530,000	$15,900	$15,900	$11,925	$11,925	$60	05/15	-	-	
DISTRICT OF COLUMBIA																											
American University—Washington College of Law	286	87	61	23	59	100	•		34	86	•	•	•			•	9	386,354	$20,640	$20,640	$725ch	$725ch	$55	03/01	03/01	-	•
Catholic University of America—Columbus School of Law	694	251	45	17	50	80	•	•	32	84	•		•			•	17	252,000	$19,600	$19,600	$705ch	$705ch	$55	03/01	03/01	-	•
District of Columbia School of Law	253	26	52	60	19	6	•	•	54	85			•			•	7	175,000	$7,000	$14,000	$250ch	$500ch	$35	04/01	05/30	-	
Georgetown University Law Center	1526	498	45.8	26.4	87	166	•	•	31	83	•	•	•			•	68	822,686	$21,280	$21,280	$725c	$725c	$60	02/01FT 03/01e	03/01	-	
George Washington University Law School	1310	218	45	26.3	67	185	•	•	32	84	•	•	•			•	29	454,752	$20,360	$20,360	$710c	$710c	$55	03/01	-	-	•
Howard University School of Law	443	-	56	93.2	29	17			30	88	•	•	•			•	17	250,000	$11,100	$11,100	-	-	$60	04/30	04/01	-	•
FLORIDA																											
University of Florida College of Law	1170	-	42	22.2	78	9			34	88	•	•	•		•	•	27	558,000	$3,400	$10,775	-	-	$20	2/1F 5/15S	4/1F 7/1S	-	•
The Florida State University College of Law	621	-	45	24	41	7			35	88	•		•			•	18	375,000	$3,608	$11,250	-	-	$20	02/15	04/01	-	•
University of Miami School of Law	1093	248	43	32.3	54	76	•	•	76	88	•	•	•				13	425,783	$19,928	$19,928	$14,706	$14,706	$45	03/08	03/01	-	
Nova Southeastern University—Shepard Broad Law Center	880	26	43.4	26.7	41	51	•	•	34	87	•		•			•	9	278,789	$17,990	$17,990	$14,500	$14,500	$45	03/01p	03/01	-	•
St. Thomas University School of Law	521	-	37	31.7	34	27			49	90			•			•	16	233,834	$16,300	$16,300	-	-	$40	04/30	03/01	-	

This information was reported by the schools in Fall 1995, thus the figures may have changed. The reader is cautioned against making direct comparisons of complex information limited to chart form. Be sure to go beyond the table, indeed beyond the two-page descriptions that follow, if you wish to inform yourself adequately about a particular school. Symbols and footnotes are explained on the last page of this chart.	Fall 1995 Enrollment/Student Body				Faculty		Programs										Library		Tuition				Miscellaneous				
	Full-time	Part-time	Percentage of Women	Percentage of Minority	Total full-time	Total part-time	Part-time	Evening division	Total credits from required classes	Total credits required to obtain J.D.	Joint degrees offered	Graduate law study available	Transferable summer courses offered	Summer matriculation for first-year students	Midyear matriculation for first-year students	Academic Support Programs offered	Number of full-time staff	Number of volumes and equivalents	In-state, full-time	Out-of-state, full-time	In-state, part-time	Out-of-state, part-time	Application fee	Application deadline for fall admission	Financial aid application deadline	Official Guide page number	Grid included with narrative school description
Stetson University College of Law	680	-	53	16.8	33	34			55	88	•		•	•	•	•	17	325,000	$18,175	$18,175	-	-	$45	03/01	03/01	-	•
GEORGIA																											
Emory University School of Law	742	-	38	18.5	40	38			39	88	•					•	22	300,000	$19,600	$19,600	-	-	$45	03/01	03/01	-	•
University of Georgia School of Law	641	-	43	14	42	18			33	88	•	•	•			•	20	457,672	$2,988	$8,270	-	-	$30	03/01	03/01	-	•
Georgia State University College of Law	401	230	48	26	40	27	•	•	44	90	•		•			•	6	249,219	$2,870	$8,502	$1,886	$5,406	$10	03/01	05/01	-	•
Mercer University—Walter F. George School of Law	408	-	40	15.9	29	24			54	90	•		•			•	13	265,000	$16,443	$16,443	-	-	$45	03/01	03/01	-	•
HAWAII																											
University of Hawai'i at Manoa—William S. Richardson School of Law	241	-	49	72.2	18	26			42	89	•					•	10	234,551	est. $5,000	est. $12,000	-	-	est. $30	02/16	03/01	-	•
IDAHO																											
University of Idaho College of Law	279	-	42	10.8	27	3			32	88						•	10	161,085	$3,260	$8,640	-	-	$30	02/01	02/15	-	•
ILLINOIS																											
Chicago-Kent College of Law—Illinois Institute of Technology	889	335	47	17.5	75	74	•	•	39	84	•	•	•			•	28	500,000	$17,950	$17,950	$12,950	$12,950	$40	04/01	04/01	-	•
University of Chicago Law School	545	-	40	21.3	39	28			40	105	•	•					24	575,000	$21,210	$21,210	-	-	$60	-	04/01	-	
DePaul University College of Law	807	322	46	12.8	51	70	•	•	40	86	•	•	•			•	26	330,000	$16,195	$16,195	$10,308	$10,308	$40	04/01	03/01	-	•
University of Illinois College of Law	623	-	40	27	39	35			38	90	•	•	•			•	6	643,058	$5,000	$14,136	-	-	$30	03/15	03/15	-	•
The John Marshall School of Law	819	342	41	17.2	54	136	•	•	41	90	•	•	•		•	•	22	280,000	$15,750	$15,750	$11,550	$11,550	$50	03/01	-	-	
Loyola University Chicago School of Law	580	189	51	22.6	34	120	•	•	43	86	•	•	•			•	17	300,000	$17,628	$17,628	$13,216	$13,216	$45	04/01	03/01	-	•
Northern Illinois University College of Law	291	8	44	20.4	29	14	•		38	85	•					•	12	225,000	$5,057	$9,329	$178ch	$356ch	$35	05/15	03/01	-	•
Northwestern University School of Law	606	-	45	21.3	54	114			32	86	•	•				•	31	604,300	$20,128	-	-	-	$60	02/01	03/16	-	

Southern Illinois University School of Law	354	-	41	17.8	24	8			47	90	•		•			•	19	320,000	$4,934	$12,942	-	-	$25	-	-	-	•
INDIANA																											
Indiana University School of Law—Bloomington	620	6	44	20.8	34	19	•		38	86	•	•	•	•		•	9	560,000	$5,099	$14,027	$164c	$452c	$35	-	03/01	-	•
Indiana University School of Law—Indianapolis	574	261	46	13	41	17	•	•	53	90	•		•	•		•	23	410,000	$5,110	$13,020	$3,791	$9,660	$35	03/01	-	-	•
University of Notre Dame Law School	563	-	38	16	28	25			63	90	•	•	•			•	20	354,000	$18,420	$18,420	-	-	$45	03/01	03/01	-	
Valparaiso University School of Law	432	50	47	14	21	20	•		49	90			•			•	8	245,699	$14,630	$14,630	$8,025	$8,025	$30	04/15	04/01	-	•
IOWA																											
Drake University Law School	502	17	38	8.1	23	24	•		45	90	•		•	•		•	5	250,000	$15,200	$15,200	$525	$525	$35	03/01	03/01	-	•
University of Iowa College of Law	682	-	44	22	49	4			35	90	•	•	•	•		•	26	806,534	$4,660	$12,876	-	-	$20	02/01	03/01	-	•
KANSAS																											
University of Kansas School of Law	498	-	41	13	29	9			45	90	•		•	•		•	9	325,000	$3,712	$8,590	-	-	$40	03/15	03/01	-	•
Washburn University School of Law	417	-	42	18.5	27	32			34	90			•		•	•	17	280,000	$5,712	$8,624	$204ch	$308ch	$30	03/15	03/15	-	•
KENTUCKY																											
University of Kentucky College of Law	435	-	34	8	28	24			34	90	•		•			•	13	350,000	$4,440	$12,040	-	-	$25	03/01	04/01	-	•
University of Louisville School of Law	366	112	48	7	27	15	•	•	44	90	•		•			•	14	244,700	$4,470	$11,820	$3,740	$9,860	$30	02/15	-	-	•
Northern Kentucky University—Salmon P. Chase College of Law	224	187	40	9.2	19	40	•	•	61	90	•		•			•	6	238,027	$4,540	$11,894	$191sh	$497sh	$25	05/15	02/01	-	•
LOUISIANA																											
Louisiana State University Law Center	677	-	46	8	33	11			39	97	•	•	•				8	552,426	$1,961	$4,271	-	-	$25	02/01	03/01	-	•
Loyola University New Orleans School of Law	553	212	46	24.3	36	41	•	•	76	90	•		•			•	17	244,315	$16,905	$16,905	$11,455	$11,455	$20	-	-	-	•
Southern University Law Center	324	-	43	63	28	10			75	96			•			•	17	366,085	$3,088	$6,288	-	-	-	03/31	04/15	-	
Tulane University Law School	1014	-	43.3	25	58	58			31	88	•	•	•			•	19	501,000	$21,286	$21,286	-	-	$45	05/01	02/15	-	•
MAINE																											
University of Maine School of Law	273	7	46	7.5	16	7			42	89	•		•			•	12	280,000	$7,920	$15,720	-	-	$25	02/15	02/01	-	•
MARYLAND																											
University of Baltimore School of Law	624	442	48	13.1	45	79	•	•	39	90	•	•	•			•	18	265,000	$3,317	$5,812	$275h	$455h	$35	04/01	04/01	-	•
University of Maryland School of Law	611	252	49	30.2	54	57	•	•	38-39	85	•		•			•	25	360,000	$8,137	$14,872	$6,050	$11,099	$40	02/15	03/15	-	•
MASSACHUSETTS																											
Boston College Law School	829	-	46	17.6	57	54			39	85	•					•	10	340,000	$20,180	$20,180	-	-	$50	03/01	03/01	-	•
Boston University School of Law	1101	-	47	21	57	78			29	84	•	•				•	26	500,000	$19,420	$19,420	-	-	$50	03/01	04/01	-	•
Harvard University Law School	1658	-	41	27.1	105	53			30	82	•	•				•	95	1,847,567	$20,500	$20,500	-	-	$65	02/01	03/01	-	
New England School of Law	651	446	46	12.1	40	62	•	•	42	84			•			•	17	260,000	$12,650	-	$9,526	-	$50	03/15	04/15	-	•
Northeastern University School of Law	617	-	64	24	32	29			48	99	•		•			•	14	260,496	$18,825	$18,825	-	-	$55	03/01	03/01	-	•
Suffolk University Law School	1023	709	51.5	12	61	76	•	•	52	84	•		•			•	28	300,000	$16,580	$16,580	$12,436	$12,436	$50	03/01	03/01	-	•
Western New England College School of Law	461	280	48	10	28	29	•	•	42	88			•			•	13	317,000	$13,890	$13,890	$10,416	$10,416	$35	raf	04/01	-	•

This information was reported by the schools in Fall 1995, thus the figures may have changed. The reader is cautioned against making direct comparisons of complex information limited to chart form. Be sure to go beyond the table, indeed beyond the two-page descriptions that follow, if you wish to inform yourself adequately about a particular school. Symbols and footnotes are explained on the last page of this chart.	Fall 1995 Enrollment/Student Body				Faculty		Programs										Library		Tuition				Miscellaneous				
	Full-time	Part-time	Percentage of Women	Percentage of Minority	Total full-time	Total part-time	Part-time	Evening division	Total credits from required classes	Total credits required to obtain J.D.	Joint degrees offered	Graduate law study available	Transferable summer courses offered	Summer matriculation for first-year students	Midyear matriculation for first-year students	Academic Support Programs offered	Number of full-time staff	Number of volumes and equivalents	In-state, full-time	Out-of-state, full-time	In-state, part-time	Out-of-state, part-time	Application fee	Application deadline for fall admission	Financial aid application deadline	Official Guide page number	Grid included with narrative school description
MICHIGAN																											
University of Detroit Mercy School of Law	763	-	45	16.5	28	29	•	•	45	90	•		•			•	10	190,000	$13,500	-	$5,400	$5,400	$50	04/15	03/01	-	•
Detroit College of Law at Michigan State University	409	306	36	12.3	29	35	•	•	60	85			•			•	6	200,000	$485c	$485c	$485c	$485c	$50	04/15F	03/15	-	•
University of Michigan Law School	1159	-	43	20.8	61	44			31	83	•	•		•		•	45	750,000	$15,814	$22,026	-	-	$70	02/15	-	-	•
Thomas M. Cooley Law School	55	1685	32	11	49	100	•	•	74	90					•	•	34	341,000	$465c	$465c	$465c	$465c	$100	-	-	-	•
Wayne State University Law School	548	199	46	15.3	33	34	•	•	35	86	•	•	•	•		•	12	500,000	$6,290	$13,580	$3,420	$7,308	$20	03/15	04/23	-	•
MINNESOTA																											
Hamline University School of Law	590	-	50	12	29	44			34	88	•		•			•	34	220,000	$13,808	$13,808	-	-	$30	05/15	-	-	•
University of Minnesota Law School	810	-	45	16	43	72			32	88	•		•			•	28	800,000	$8,228	$14,124	-	-	$30	03/01	03/15	-	•
William Mitchell College of Law	578	490	49	13	36	85	•	•	56	86		•	•			•	17	200,000	$14,460	$14,460	$10,500	$10,500	$35	04/15	03/15	-	•
MISSISSIPPI																											
The University of Mississippi School of Law	465	2	36	14.1	25	5			55-58	90	•		•	•		•	13	263,000	$3,096y	$7,018y	-	-	$20	03/01	03/01	-	•
Mississippi College School of Law	385	-	36	9	16	21			44	88			•			•	4	220,000	$11,650	$11,650	-	-	$25	05/01	05/01	-	•
MISSOURI																											
University of Missouri—Columbia School of Law	462	-	38	9.5	23	10			57	89			•			•	13	288,000	$7,368	$14,538	-	-	$40	-	03/01	-	•
University of Missouri—Kansas City School of Law	471	13	45	10	29	32	•		52	91	•	•	•			•	7	255,000	$7,606	$14,747	$4938y $271ch	$9528y $526ch	$25	rolling	-	-	•
Saint Louis University School of Law	561	282	42	18.2	44	15	•	•	36	88	•	•	•			•	9	450,000	$16,000	$16,000	$11,950	$11,950	$40	03/01	04/01	-	•
Washington University School of Law	622	-	40	18	44	68			35	85	•	•	•				17	518,694	$19,380	$19,380	-	-	$50	03/01	03/01	-	•
MONTANA																											
University of Montana School of Law	235	-	40	7	17	11			69	90	•					•	5	127,352	$5,090	$10,252	-	-	$60	03/15	03/01	-	•

NEBRASKA																										
Creighton University School of Law	484	20	44	8	25	39	•		39	94	•		•			•	14	223,123	$13,610	$13,610	$455ch	$455ch	$40	05/01	04/01	-	•
University of Nebraska College of Law	415	-	40	10	26	19			45	96	•		•			•	10	323,969	$3,402	$8,748	-	-	$25	03/01	03/01	-	•
NEW HAMPSHIRE																										
Franklin Pierce Law Center	398	-	36	12	26	28			39	84	•	•	•			•	9	194,000	$14,200	$14,200	-	-	$45	04/01	-	-	•
NEW JERSEY																										
Rutgers—The State University—School of Law—Camden	600	200	45	23	39	56	•	•	34	84	•		•			•	20	380,000	$8,550	$12,305	$313	$471	$40	03/01	03/01	-	•
Rutgers University School of Law—Newark	549	243	44	32.2	39	45	•	•	31	84	•		•			•	9	404,424	$8,488	$12,243	$313c	$471c	$40	03/01	03/01	-	•
Seton Hall University School of Law	992	375	45	20	51	97	•	•	46-48	85	•		•			•	26	315,595	$17,160	$17,160	$13,100	$13,100	$50	04/01	05/15	-	•
NEW MEXICO																										
University of New Mexico School of Law	335	-	52	45	32	28			42	86	•		•			•	16	346,000	$2,984	$10,012	-	-	$40	02/01	03/01	-	•
NEW YORK																										
Albany Law School	751	36	48	17	41	38	•		30	87	•		•			•	17	470,000	$17,795	$17,795	$13,346	$13,346	$50	03/15	-	-	•
Brooklyn Law School	986	465	43	16.7	65	87	•	•	34	86	•		•	•		•	21	450,000	$18,600	$18,600	$13,950	$13,950	$50	-	03/01	-	•
University at Buffalo State University of New York School of Law	810	-	46	17.4	39	32			34	82	•		•			•	20	310,000	$6,100	$10,750	-	-	$50	02/01	03/01	-	•
Benjamin N. Cardozo School of Law Yeshiva University	975	-	47	12.3	46	76			34-35	84			•	•	•	•	7	385,000	$18,100	$18,100	-	-	$60	04/01 Ma,Se	04/15 Ma,Se	-	•
Columbia University School of Law	1060	-	43	30	64	40			32	83	•	•				•	44	935,357	$23,178	-	-	-	$65	02/15	03/01	-	•
Cornell University Law School	568	-	40	23	39	18			32	84	•	•	•			•	22	550,000	$21,135	$21,135	$21,135	$21,135	$65	02/01	03/15	-	•
Fordham University School of Law	1129	352	42	26	61	145	•	•	45	83	•	•	•			•	10	450,000	$20,499	-	$15,399	-	$60	03/01	03/01	-	•
Hofstra University School of Law	850	-	41	16.7	42	24			45	87	•		•			•	21	440,000	$19,454	$19,454	-	-	$60	04/15	05/15	-	
City University of New York School of Law at Queens College	456	2	52	33	40	18	•		66	91						•	12	221,692	$3,225s	$4,840s	$240c	$375c	$40	03/15	7/1	-	•
University at Buffalo State University of New York School of Law	810	-	46	17.4	39	32			34	82	•		•			•	20	310,000	$6,100	$10,750	-	-	$50	02/01	03/01	-	•
New York Law School	911	490	43	23	52	74	•	•	34	86	•		•			•	22	395,000	$18,570	$18,570	$13,930	$13,930	$50	04/01	-	-	•
New York University School of Law	1275	-	46	24	95	97			37	82	•	•	•				60	912,000	$22,144	-	-	-	$65	02/01	05/01	-	
Pace University School of Law	474	329	47	17.1	51	40	•	•	40	90	•	•	•			•	10	300,000	$18,210	-	$13,710	-	$55	03/15	02/01	-	
St. John's University School of Law	827	291	38	25	59	20	•	•	61	85	•		•		•	•	8	440,000	$19,000	-	$14,250	-	$50	03/01	04/01	-	•
Syracuse University College of Law	787	7	43	23.6	41	40	•		39	87	•		•			•	20	346,246	$18,720	$18,720	$819ch	$819ch	$40	04/01	03/01	-	•
Touro College—Jacob D. Fuchsberg Law Center	464	330	40.7	27.8	43	12	•	•	41	87		•	•			•	22	338,000	$17,350	-	$13,600	-	$50	05/01	05/01	-	
NORTH CAROLINA																										
Campbell University—Norman Adrian Wiggins School of Law	316	-	40	11	20	15			70	90	•		•				7	156,342	$13,500	$13,500	-	-	$40	03/31	-	-	
Duke University School of Law	593	-	40	14.5	35	63			30	84	•	•		•			23	477,000	$21,200	$21,200	-	-	$65	01/15	01/15	-	•

This information was reported by the schools in Fall 1995, thus the figures may have changed. The reader is cautioned against making direct comparisons of complex information limited to chart form. Be sure to go beyond the table, indeed beyond the two-page descriptions that follow, if you wish to inform yourself adequately about a particular school. Symbols and footnotes are explained on the last page of this chart.	Fall 1995 Enrollment/Student Body				Faculty		Programs										Library		Tuition				Miscellaneous				
	Full-time	Part-time	Percentage of Women	Percentage of Minority	Total full-time	Total part-time	Part-time	Evening division	Total credits from required classes	Total credits required to obtain J.D.	Joint degrees offered	Graduate law study available	Transferable summer courses offered	Summer matriculation for first-year students	Midyear matriculation for first-year students	Academic Support Programs offered	Number of full-time staff	Number of volumes and equivalents	In-state, full-time	Out-of-state, full-time	In-state, part-time	Out-of-state, part-time	Application fee	Application deadline for fall admission	Financial aid application deadline	Official Guide page number	Grid included with narrative school description
University of North Carolina School of Law	696	-	46	18.7	43	47			39	86	•		•			•	21	408,000	$2,243	$12,396	-	-	$55	02/01	03/01	-	•
North Carolina Central University School of Law	239	90	54	52.6	20	5	•	•	65	88	•					•	10	101,649	$1,825	$10,439	$1,825	$10,439	$30	04/15	02/01	-	
Wake Forest University School of Law	473	-	40	9.5	34	29			41	89	•		•				13	250,000	$16,600	$16,600	-	-	$50	03/15	05/01	-	•
NORTH DAKOTA																											
University of North Dakota School of Law	217	-	50	6	14	11			33	90							9	230,000	$3,848	$8,074	-	-	$35	04/01	05/01	-	•
OHIO																											
University of Akron School of Law	452	183	39.8	8	21	23	•	•	44	88	•		•			•	10	233,867	$6,623	$11,330	$5,175	$8,852	$35	-	-	-	•
Capital University Law School	476	336	43	9	31	46	•	•	42	86	•	•	•			•	11	225,000	$14,663	$14,663	$8,987	$8,987	$35	05/01	04/01	-	•
Case Western Reserve University School of Law	666	58	42.3	15.3	42	55	•		33	88	•	•	•			•	29	342,630	$18,300	$18,300	$763ch	$763ch	$40	04/01	5/01	-	•
University of Cincinnati College of Law	382	-	46	12	25	26			35	88	•		•				24	354,562	$6,570	$12,768	-	-	$35	04/01	03/01	-	•
Cleveland State University—Cleveland-Marshall College of Law	571	339	43	13	34	31	•	•	46-56	87	•	•	•	•		•	-	380,000	$6,541	$13,082	$251sh	$502sh	$35	03/01	03/01	-	•
University of Dayton School of Law	484	-	40	8.7	27	31			36	87	•		•			•	11	215,000	$15,668	$15,668	-	-	$40	05/01	03/01	-	•
Ohio Northern University—Claude W. Pettit College of Law	355	-	34	9.6	19	19			54	87	•		•			•	11	240,000	$19,290	$19,290	-	-	$40	-	-	-	•
The Ohio State University College of Law	690	-	43	16	35	20			39	91	•		•			•	20	615,000	$5,860	$13,980	-	-	$30	03/15	03/01	-	•
The University of Toledo College of Law	455	215	41	12	37	15	•	•	40	87	•		•			•	14	285,000	$6,158	$11,672	$4,362	$8,268	$30	03/15	04/01	-	•
OKLAHOMA																											
University of Oklahoma College of Law	600	-	40	12	35	19			40	90	•		•			•	25	296,358	$3,274	$10,216	-	-	$50	03/15	03/01	-	•
Oklahoma City University School of Law	425	215	37	10.8	32	33	•	•	43	90	•		•			•	5	230,000	$12,245	$12,245	$7,900	$7,900	$35	08/01	03/01	-	•

University of Tulsa College of Law	473	150	36	12.4	36	23	•	•	42-44	88	•		•			•	15	265,000	$14,100	$14,100	$9,400	$9,400	$30	-	-	-	•
OREGON																											
Lewis and Clark, Northwestern School of Law	514	186	43	15	29	52	•	•	35-40	86	•	•	•			•	-	410,000	$15,625	$15,625	$11,000	$11,000	$50	03/15	02/15	-	•
University of Oregon School of Law	478	-	49	16	32	6			40	85	•		•			•	12	340,000	$8,000	$13,190	-	-	$50	04/01	03/01	-	•
Willamette University College of Law	458	-	39	11.8	27	17			37	88	•		•			•	13	261,200	$15,400	$15,400	-	-	$40	04/01	02/01	-	•
PENNSYLVANIA																											
Dickinson School of Law	521	4	47	8	27	58	•		41	88		•	•			•	14	374,800	$13,900	$13,900	$450ch	$450ch	$50	03/01	02/15	-	•
Duquesne University School of Law	299	344	42	9.5	29	44	•	•	34	87	•		•				16	200,000	$12,215	$12,215	$9,201	$9,201	$50	04/01d	05/01e	-	
University of Pennsylvania Law School	741	1	40	23.5	39	57			34	89	•	•					80	560,000	$22,097	$22,097	-	-	$60	02/01	-	-	•
University of Pittsburgh School of Law	697	6	41	14	44	30	•		53	88	•					•	13	300,000	$10,491	$16,241	$10,491	$16,241	$40	03/01	03/01	-	•
Temple University School of Law	802	383	46	25	55	152	•	•	38	83	•	•					10	468,178	$7,800	$14,314	$6,240	$11,452	$50	03/01	03/01	-	•
Villanova University School of Law	690	-	47	16	41	34			45	87	•	•				•	23	432,000	$17,200	$17,200	-	-	$75	01/31	-	-	•
Widener University School of Law	1383	608	42	5.9	104	89	•	•	51	87							40	530,000	$15,900	$15,900	$11,925	$11,925	$60	05/15	-	-	
PUERTO RICO																											
Pontifical Catholic University of Puerto Rico, School of Law	309	151	48	0	20	17	•	•	82	94	•		•				14	168,387	$3,570s	-	$2,520s	-	$25	04/15	09/22Se 01/26Ja	-	
Inter American University School of Law	354	294	0	0	30	16	•	•	62	92		•	•				-	167,995	$8,480	-	$6,360	-	$25	03/31	-	-	-
University of Puerto Rico School of Law	317	208	57	0	33	23	•	•	70	92			•				10	275,064	$2,623	-	$1,713	-	$15	02/16	04/15	-	•
RHODE ISLAND																											
Roger Williams University School of Law	294	178	39	7	26	4	•	•	54	90	•		•			•	12	165,000	$16,050	$16,050	$12,305	$12,305	$60	05/15	n/a	-	
SOUTH CAROLINA																											
University of South Carolina School of Law	765	-	39	10	44	25			45-47	90	•		•			•	5	326,000	$6,168	$12,224	$256ch	$503ch	$25	02/15	04/15	-	•
SOUTH DAKOTA																											
University of South Dakota School of Law	223	-	36	3	15	2			44-45	90	•		•			•	7	171,833	$84ch	$208.50ch	-	-	$15	03/01	-	-	•
TENNESSEE																											
The University of Memphis—Cecil C. Humphreys School of Law	438	26	41	10.3	22	22	•		56	90	•		•			•	13	258,242	$3,582	$8,978	$152h	$386h	$10	02/15	04/01	-	•
University of Tennessee College of Law	480	-	48.3	11.7	36	17			45	89	•		•			•	18	365,000	$3,564	$8,958	-	-	$15	02/01	02/14	-	•
Vanderbilt University School of Law	550	-	38	17.8	32	33			33	88	•						18	329,060	$19,750	$19,750	-	-	$50	02/01	03/01	-	
TEXAS																											
Baylor University School of Law	399	-	37	14	20	40			76	120	•	•	•	•	•	•	4	160,940	$9,758	$9,758	-	-	$40	03/01	05/31	-	•
University of Houston Law Center	811	207	40	20.5	48	95	•	•	35	88	•	•	•	•		•	24	400,000	$4,959	$8,836	$4,869 135ch	$8,384 260ch	$50	02/01	-	-	•
St. Mary's University School of Law	771	-	47	33.2	33	49			47	90	•		•			•	-	267,600	$470h	-	-	-	$45	03/01	03/31	-	•
South Texas College of Law	853	396	40	21	56	40	•	•	41	90			•		•	•	24	317,000	$13,800	$13,800	$9,400	$9,400	$40	03/01	05/01	-	•

This information was reported by the schools in Fall 1995, thus the figures may have changed. The reader is cautioned against making direct comparisons of complex information limited to chart form. Be sure to go beyond the table, indeed beyond the two-page descriptions that follow, if you wish to inform yourself adequately about a particular school. Symbols and footnotes are explained on the last page of this chart.

	Fall 1995 Enrollment/Student Body				Faculty		Programs										Library		Tuition				Miscellaneous				
	Full-time	Part-time	Percentage of Women	Percentage of Minority	Total full-time	Total part-time	Part-time	Evening division	Total credits from required classes	Total credits required to obtain J.D.	Joint degrees offered	Graduate law study available	Transferable summer courses offered	Summer matriculation for first-year students	Midyear matriculation for first-year students	Academic Support Programs offered	Number of full-time staff	Number of volumes and equivalents	In-state, full-time	Out-of-state, full-time	In-state, part-time	Out-of-state, part-time	Application fee	Application deadline for fall admission	Financial aid application deadline	Official Guide page number	Grid included with narrative school description
Southern Methodist University School of Law	741	27	43	22.7	41	3	•		33	90	•	•	•			•	20	467,503	$18,848	$18,848	-	-	$45	modified rolling	05/01	-	•
The University of Texas School of Law	1468	-	41	25	72	72			39	86	•	•	•			•	36	887,828	$5,560	$12,000	-	-	$65	02/01	03/31	-	•
Texas Southern University—Thurgood Marshall School of Law	550	-	46	80	29	19			68	90			•		•	•	6	300,000	$1,950	$3,750	-	-	$40	rolling	05/01	-	•
Texas Tech University School of Law	628	-	37	15	23	11			55	90	•					•	15	250,000	$135ch	$260ch	-	-	$50	02/01	-	-	•
Texas Wesleyan University School of Law	349	322	42	18.6	23	15	•	•	35	88			•			•	5	137,000	$370c	$370c	$370c	$370c	$50	rolling	n/a	-	
UTAH																											
Brigham Young University—J. Reuben Clark Law School	468	-	30	14	33	26			32	90	•	•				•	21	380,000	$4,600	$6,900	-	-	$30	02/15	05/01	-	•
University of Utah College of Law	366	-	43	16	28	37			36	88	•	•	•			•	23	271,000	$4,516	$10,116	-	-	$40	02/01	02/15	-	•
VERMONT																											
Vermont Law School	470	-	45	10	35	22			42	84	•	•	•			•	12	200,000	$17,325	$17,325	-	-	$60	02/15	02/15	-	•
VIRGINIA																											
George Mason University School of Law	375	321	38	10	33	24	•	•	v	90			•			•	10	300,000	$7,084	$17,920	$253sh	$640sh	$35	03/01	-	-	
Regent University School of Law	348	-	29	8	16	15			67	90	•		•			•	10	290,000	$13,800	$13,800	$445ch	-	$40	04/01	07/15	-	•
University of Richmond—T.C. Williams School of Law	476	5	48	25	25	65	•		35	86	•		•	•			14	230,000	$16,100	$16,100	$800ch	$800ch	$35	01/15	02/25	-	•
University of Virginia School of Law	1152	-	39	15	59	55			27	86	•	•				•	26	734,500	$10,290	$18,694	-	-	$40	01/15	02/01	-	•
Washington and Lee University School of Law	374	-	40	15	35	11			37	85						•	25	317,500	$15,250	$15,250	-	-	$40	02/01	03/01	-	•
College of William and Mary—School of Law	524	-	49	17	30	34			36	90	•	•	•			•	19	325,000	$6,076	$16,324	-	-	$35	03/01	02/01	-	•
WASHINGTON																											
Gonzaga University School of Law	575	12	37	14	33	10	•		58	90	•		•			•	11	200,215	$520c $16,120y	$520c	$520c	$520c	$40	03/15	05/01	-	•

Seattle University School of Law	721	166	46	20.3	41	24	•	•	45	90			•	•		•	18	320,776	$15,330	$15,330	$12,775y	$12,775y	$50	04/01	03/01	-	•
University of Washington School of Law	495	-	48	37.8	45	25			84q	135	•	•	•				32	450,000	$4,800	$12,000	-	-	$50	01/15	02/28	-	•
WEST VIRGINIA																											
West Virginia University College of Law	418	9	49	7.3	28	12	•		52	93	•					•	11	215,000	$4,122y	$10,634y	$231ch	$593ch	$45	02/01	03/01	-	•
WISCONSIN																											
Marquette University Law School	475	6	41	14.7	23	35	•		43	90	•		•			•	14	238,148	$15,310	$15,310	$581c	$581c	$35	04/01	03/01	-	•
University of Wisconsin Law School	816	68	45	21	49	-	•		60	90	•	•	•			•	10	400,000	$5,211	$13,488	$218c	$563c	$38	02/01	03/01	-	•
WYOMING																											
University of Wyoming College of Law	226	-	42	6	14	3			52	88	•					•	6	174,000	$3,427	$7,819	-	-	$35	04/01	02/15	-	•

Key Facts Abbreviations and Footnotes

•	yes	ch	per credit hour	h	per hour	nr	nonresident	raf	rolling application deadline for fall admission	s	per semester	v	varies
-	not available	d	day(s)	hr	hour(s)	p	priority deadline			Se	September	y	per year
asap	as soon as possible	e	evening(s)	Ja	January	q	per quarter credits			sh	per semester hour		
c	per credit	F	Fall semester	Ma	May	r	resident	S	Spring semester	u	per unit		

Chapter 13: Geographic Guide to Law Schools in the United States (by region)*

New England

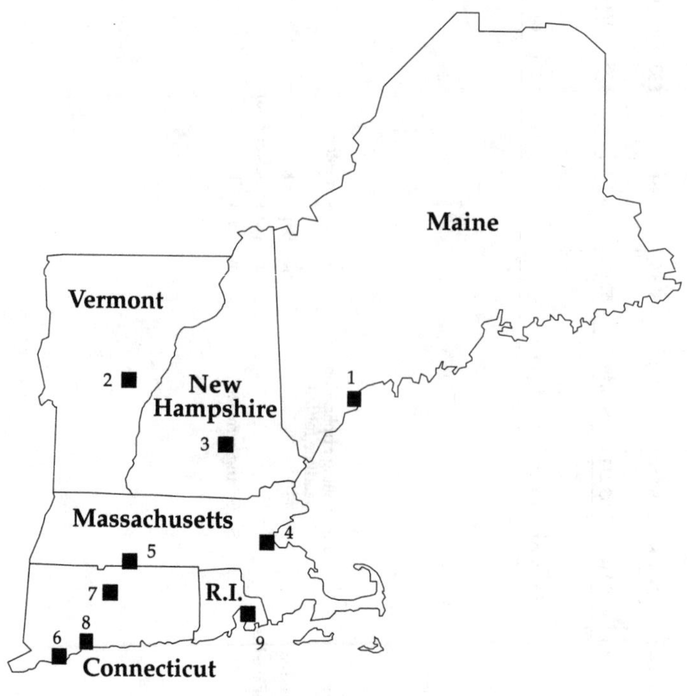

Maine

1. **Portland—Population: 64,358**
   University of Maine—Enrollment: 273/7

Vermont

2. **South Royalton—Population: 2,500**
   Vermont Law School—Enrollment: 470/NA

New Hampshire

3. **Concord—Population: 36,006**
   Franklin Pierce—Enrollment: 398/NA

Massachusetts

4. **Boston—Population: 574,283**
   Boston College—Enrollment: 829/NA
   Boston University—Enrollment: 1,101/NA
   Harvard (Cambridge, MA)—Enrollment: 1,658/NA
   New England—Enrollment: 651/446
   Northeastern—Enrollment: 617/NA
   Suffolk—Enrollment: 1,023/709
5. **Springfield—Population: 156,983**
   Western New England College—
   Enrollment: 461/280

Connecticut

6. **Bridgeport—Population: 141,686**
   Quinnipiac—Enrollment: 565/230
7. **Hartford—Population: 139,739**
   University of Connecticut—Enrollment: 432/196
8. **New Haven—Population: 130,474**
   Yale—Enrollment: 573/NA

Rhode Island

9. **Bristol—Population: 21,625**
   Roger Williams—Enrollment: 294/178

"Enrollment" represents the numbers of total full-time/total part-time students unless otherwise indicated. NA stands for "Not Applicable."

*Population information is derived from the U.S. Bureau of the Census, Population Division, Washington, DC. Data is accurate as of the 1990 Census. City populations reflect the number of people residing in the city proper, not the metropolitan area which would include outlying suburbs as well. Donald P. Racheter, director of the prelaw program at Central University of Iowa, also contributed data for these regional maps.

Northeast

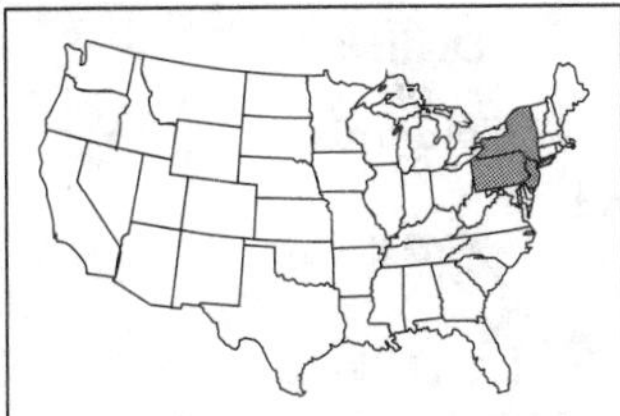

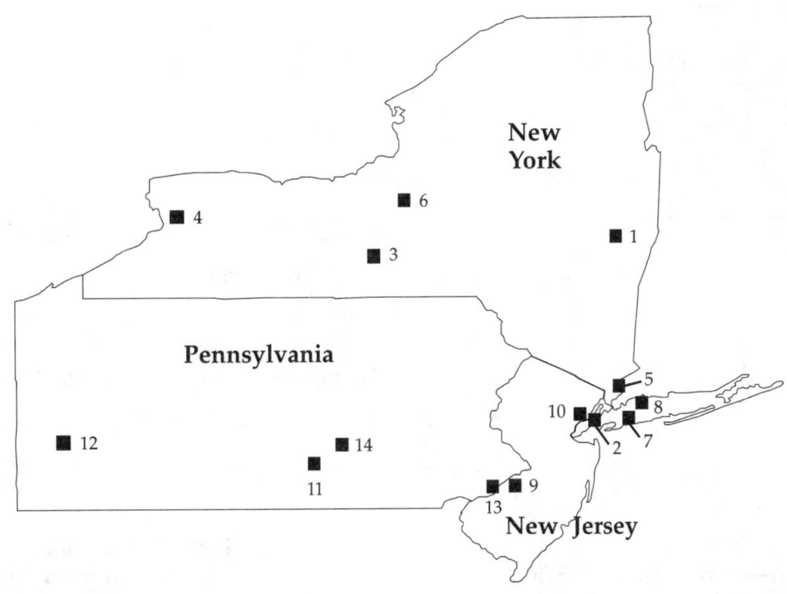

New York

1. **Albany—Population: 101,082**
   Albany—Enrollment: 751/36
2. **New York City—Population: 7,322,564**
   Benjamin N. Cardozo—Enrollment: 975/NA
   Brooklyn—Enrollment: 986/465
   Columbia—Enrollment: 1,060/NA
   Fordham—Enrollment: 1,129/352
   City University of New York—Enrollment: 456/2
   The New York Law School—Enrollment: 911/490
   New York University—Enrollment: 1,275/NA
   St. John's University (Jamaica, NY)—Enrollment: 827/291
3. **Ithaca—Population: 29,541**
   Cornell—Enrollment: 568/NA
4. **Buffalo—Population: 328,123**
   University at Buffalo—Enrollment: 810/NA
5. **White Plains—Population: 48,718**
   Pace—Enrollment: 474/329
6. **Syracuse—Population: 163,860**
   Syracuse—Enrollment: 787/7
7. **Hempstead—Population: 725,639**
   Hofstra—Enrollment: 850/NA
8. **Huntington—Population: 18,243**
   Touro—Enrollment: 464/330

New Jersey

9. **Camden—Population: 87,492**
   Rutgers–Camden—Enrollment: 621/155
10. **Newark—Population: 275,221**
    Rutgers–Newark—Enrollment: 549/243
    Seton Hall—Enrollment: 992/375

Pennsylvania

11. **Carlisle—Population: 18,419**
    Dickinson—Enrollment: 521/4
12. **Pittsburgh—Population: 369,879**
    Duquesne—Enrollment: 299/344
    University of Pittsburgh—Enrollment: 697/6
13. **Philadelphia—Population: 1,585,577**
    University of Pennsylvania—Enrollment: 741/1
    Temple—Enrollment: 802/383
    Villanova (Villanova, PA)—Enrollment: 690/NA
14. **Harrisburg—Population: 52,376**
    Widener—(see Delaware—Midsouth region)

Midsouth

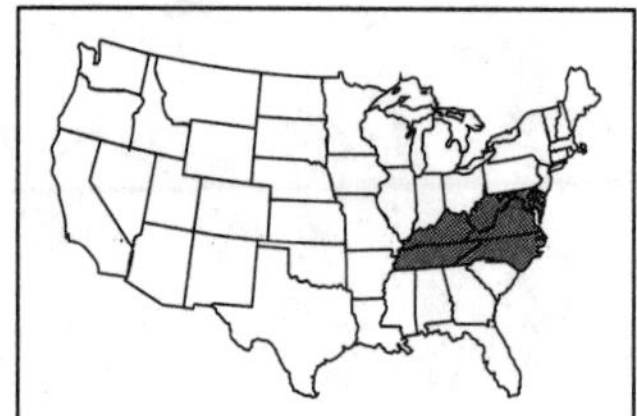

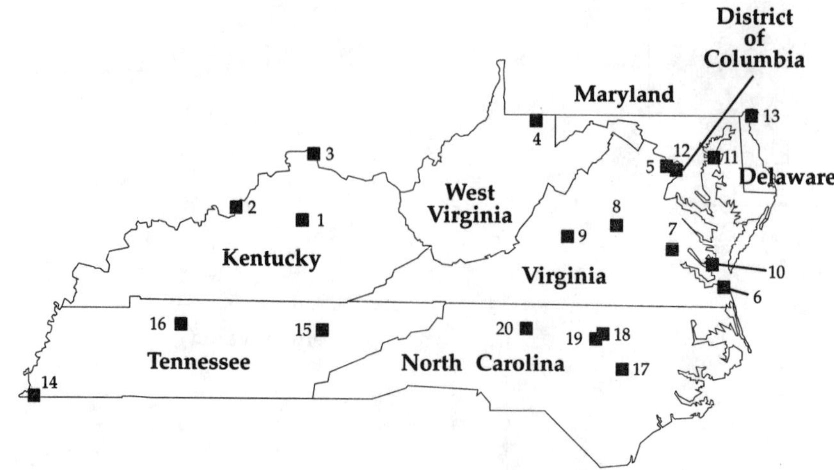

Kentucky

1. **Lexington—Population: 225,366**
   University of Kentucky—Enrollment: 435/NA
2. **Louisville—Population: 269,063**
   University of Louisville—Enrollment: 366/112
3. **Highland Heights—Population: 4,223**
   Northern Kentucky University—
   Enrollment: 224/187

West Virginia

4. **Morgantown—Population: 25,879**
   West Virginia—Enrollment: 418/9

Virginia

5. **Arlington—Population: 170,936**
   George Mason—Enrollment: 375/321
6. **Virginia Beach—Population: 393,069**
   Regent—Enrollment: 348/NA
7. **Richmond—Population: 203,056**
   University of Richmond—Enrollment: 476/5
8. **Charlottesville—Population: 40,341**
   University of Virginia—Enrollment: 1,152/NA
9. **Lexington—Population: 6,959**
   Washington and Lee—Enrollment: 374/NA
10. **Williamsburg—Population: 11,530**
    College of William and Mary—Enrollment: 524/NA

Maryland

11. **Baltimore—Population: 736,014**
    University of Baltimore—Enrollment: 624/442
    University of Maryland—Enrollment: 611/252

District of Columbia

12. **Washington, DC—Population: 606,900**
    American—Enrollment: 286/87 (First-year class)
    Catholic University of America—
    Enrollment: 694/251
    District of Columbia—Enrollment: 253/26
    Georgetown—Enrollment: 1,526/498
    George Washington—Enrollment: 1,310/218
    Howard—Enrollment: 443/NA

Delaware

13. **Wilmington—Population: 71,529**
    Widener—Enrollment: 1,383/608

Tennessee

14. **Memphis—Population: 610,337**
    University of Memphis—Enrollment: 438/26
15. **Knoxville—Population: 165,121**
    University of Tennessee—Enrollment: 480/NA
16. **Nashville—Population: 488,374**
    Vanderbilt—Enrollment: 550/NA

North Carolina

17. **Buies Creek—Population: 2,085**
    Campbell—Enrollment: 316/NA
18. **Durham—Population: 136,611**
    Duke—Enrollment: 593/NA
    North Carolina Central—Enrollment: 239/90
19. **Chapel Hill—Population: 38,719**
    University of North Carolina—Enrollment: 696/NA
20. **Winston-Salem—Population: 143,485**
    Wake Forest—Enrollment: 470/NA

Southeast

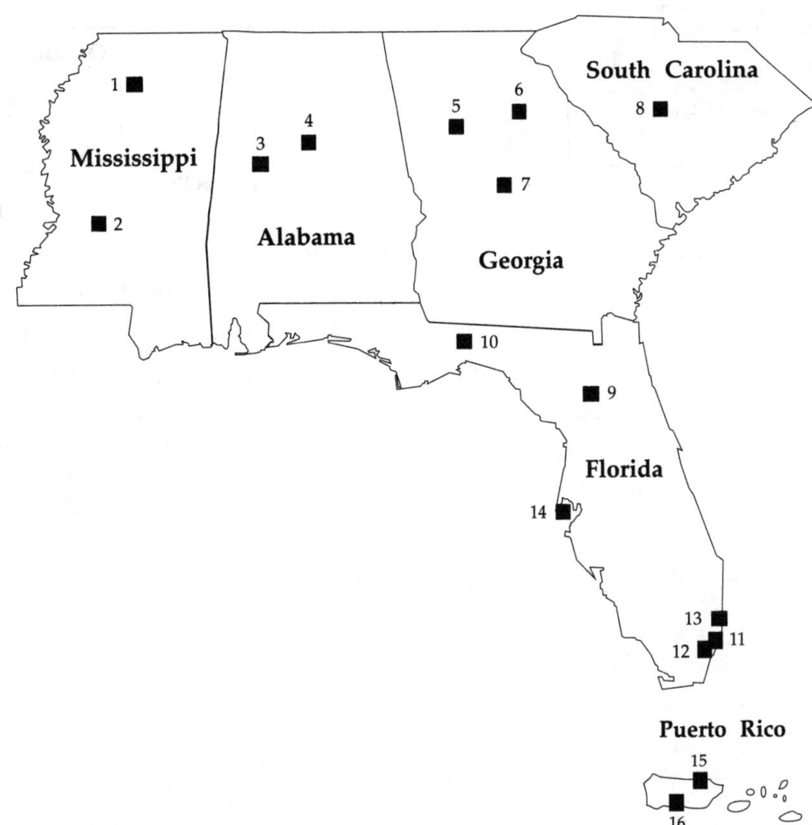

Mississippi

1. **Oxford—Population: 9,984**
   University of Mississippi—Enrollment: 465/2
2. **Jackson—Population: 196,637**
   Mississippi College—Enrollment: 385/NA

Alabama

3. **Tuscaloosa—Population: 77,759**
   University of Alabama—Enrollment: 565/NA
4. **Birmingham—Population: 265,968**
   Cumberland School of Law–Samford University—Enrollment: 652/NA

Georgia

5. **Atlanta—Population: 394,017**
   Emory—Enrollment: 742/NA
   Georgia State—Enrollment: 401/230
6. **Athens—Population: 45,734**
   University of Georgia—Enrollment: 641/NA
7. **Macon—Population: 106,612**
   Mercer—Enrollment: 408/NA

South Carolina

8. **Columbia—Population: 98,052**
   University of South Carolina—Enrollment: 765/NA

Florida

9. **Gainesville—Population: 84,770**
   University of Florida—Enrollment: 1,170/NA
10. **Tallahassee—Population: 124,773**
    Florida State—Enrollment: 621/NA
11. **Miami—Population: 358,548**
    St. Thomas—Enrollment: 521/NA
12. **Coral Gables—Population: 40,091**
    University of Miami—Enrollment: 1,093/248
13. **Ft. Lauderdale—Population: 149,377**
    Nova—Enrollment: 880/26
14. **St. Petersburg—Population: 238,629**
    Stetson—Enrollment: 680/NA

Puerto Rico

15. **San Juan—Population: 437,745**
    Inter American—Enrollment: 354/294
    University of Puerto Rico—Enrollment: 317/208
16. **Ponce—Population: 187,749**
    Pontifical Catholic University—Enrollment: 309/151

South Central

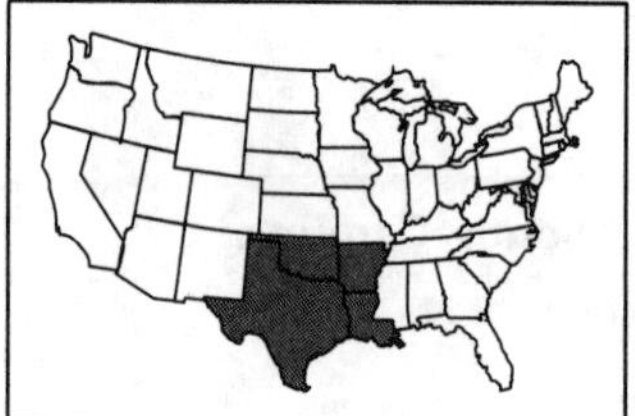

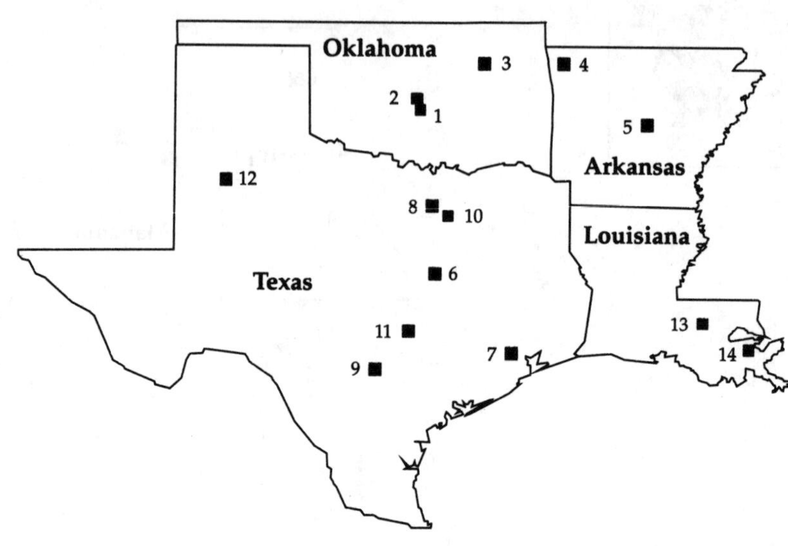

Oklahoma

1. **Norman—Population: 80,171**
   University of Oklahoma—Enrollment: 600/NA
2. **Oklahoma City—Population: 444,719**
   Oklahoma City—Enrollment: 425/215
3. **Tulsa—Population: 367,302**
   University of Tulsa—Enrollment: 473/150

Arkansas

4. **Fayetteville—Population: 42,099**
   University of Arkansas–Fayetteville—Enrollment: 396/NA
5. **Little Rock—Population: 175,795**
   University of Arkansas–Little Rock—Enrollment: 272/156

Texas

6. **Waco—Population: 103,590**
   Baylor—Enrollment: 399/NA
7. **Houston—Population: 1,630,553**
   South Texas—Enrollment: 853/396
   University of Houston—Enrollment: 811/207
   Texas Southern—Enrollment: 550/NA
8. **Irving—Population: 155,037**
   Texas Wesleyan—Enrollment: 349/322
9. **San Antonio—Population: 935,933**
   St. Mary's—Enrollment: 771/NA
10. **Dallas—Population: 1,006,877**
    Southern Methodist—Enrollment: 741/27
11. **Austin—Population: 465,622**
    University of Texas–Austin—Enrollment: 1,468/NA
12. **Lubbock—Population: 186,206**
    Texas Tech—Enrollment: 628/NA

Louisiana

13. **Baton Rouge—Population: 219,531**
    Louisiana State—Enrollment: 677/NA
    Southern—Enrollment: 324/NA
14. **New Orleans—Population: 496,938**
    Loyola–New Orleans—Enrollment: 553/212
    Tulane—Enrollment: 1,014/NA

Mountain West

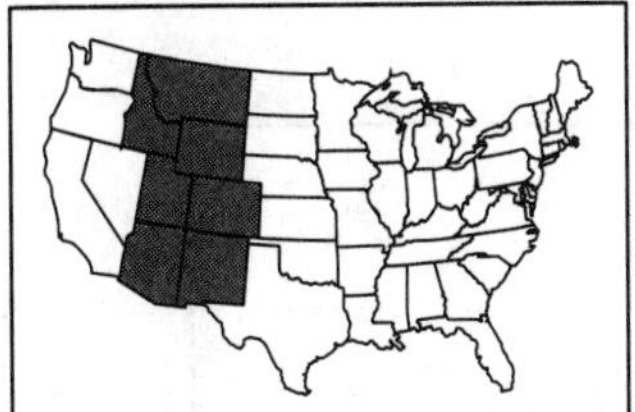

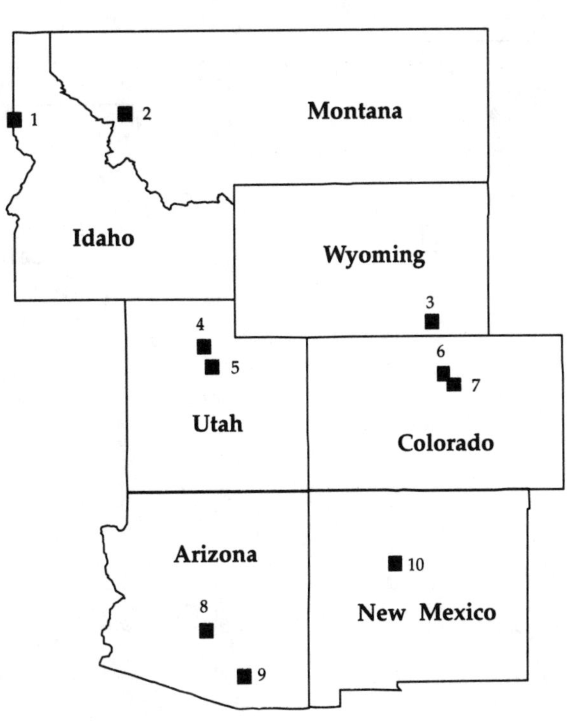

Idaho

1. **Moscow—Population: 18,519**
   University of Idaho—Enrollment: 279/NA

Montana

2. **Missoula—Population: 42,918**
   University of Montana—Enrollment: 235/NA

Wyoming

3. **Laramie—Population: 26,687**
   University of Wyoming—Enrollment: 226/NA

Utah

4. **Salt Lake City—Population: 159,936**
   University of Utah—Enrollment: 366/NA
5. **Provo—Population: 86,835**
   Brigham Young—Enrollment: 468/NA

Colorado

6. **Boulder—Population: 83,312**
   University of Colorado—Enrollment: 498/NA
7. **Denver—Population: 467,610**
   University of Denver—Enrollment: 800/280

Arizona

8. **Tempe—Population: 141,865**
   Arizona State—Enrollment: 476/NA
9. **Tucson—Population: 405,390**
   University of Arizona—Enrollment: 454/NA

New Mexico

10. **Albuquerque—Population: 384,736**
    University of New Mexico—Enrollment: 335/NA

Far West

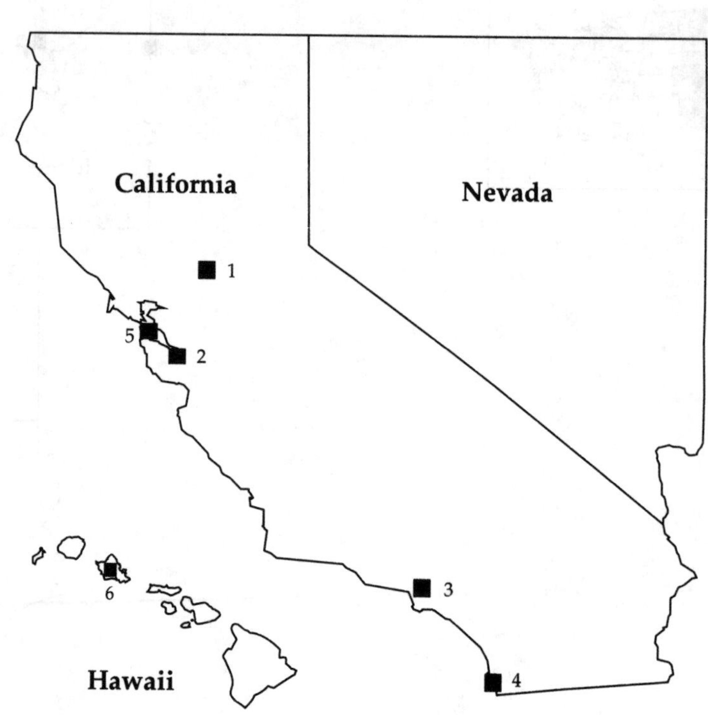

California

1. **Sacramento—Population: 369,365**
   University of California–Davis (Davis, CA)—Enrollment: 467/NA
   McGeorge—Enrollment: 886/334
2. **Santa Clara—Population: 93,613**
   Santa Clara—Enrollment: 660/222
3. **Los Angeles—Population: 3,485,398**
   University of California–Los Angeles—Enrollment: 955/NA
   Loyola–Los Angeles—Enrollment: 982/414
   Pepperdine—Enrollment: 702/NA
   University of Southern California—Enrollment: 610/NA
   Southwestern—Enrollment: 838/369
   Whittier—Enrollment: 451/204
4. **San Diego—Population: 1,110,549**
   California Western—Enrollment: 796/NA
   University of San Diego—Enrollment: 763/347
5. **San Francisco—Population: 723,959**
   University of California–Berkeley (Berkeley, CA)—Enrollment: 861/NA
   University of California–Hastings—Enrollment: 1,262/NA
   Golden Gate—Enrollment: 469/244
   University of San Francisco—Enrollment: 567/120
   Stanford (Stanford, CA)—Enrollment: 574/NA

Hawaii

6. **Honolulu—Population: 365,272**
   University of Hawai'i—Enrollment: 241/NA

Northwest

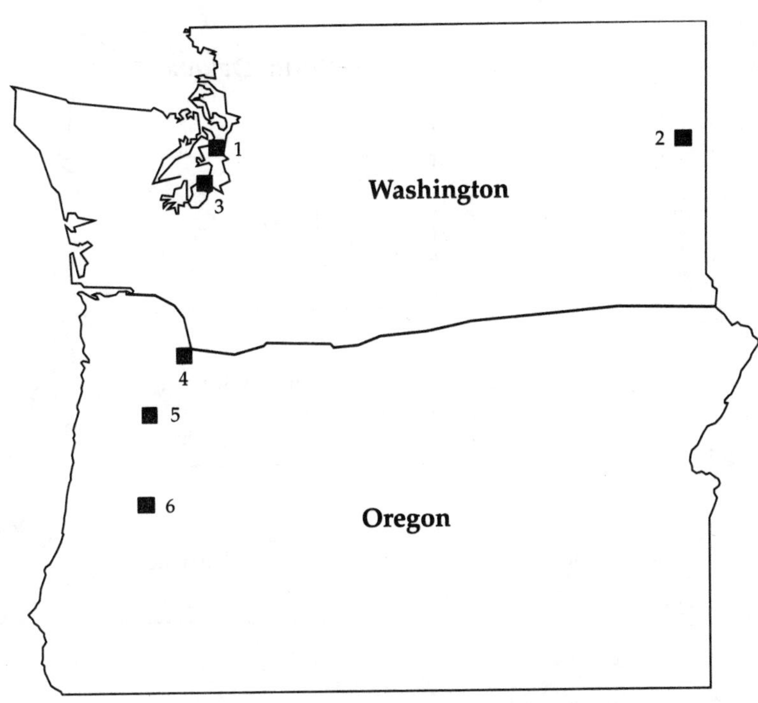

Washington

1. **Seattle—Population: 516,259**
   University of Washington—Enrollment: 495/NA
2. **Spokane—Population: 177,196**
   Gonzaga—Enrollment: 575/12
3. **Tacoma—Population: 176,664**
   Seattle University—Enrollment: 721/166

Oregon

4. **Portland—Population: 437,319**
   Lewis & Clark—Enrollment: 514/186
5. **Salem—Population: 107,786**
   Willamette—Enrollment: 458/NA
6. **Eugene—Population: 112,669**
   University of Oregon—Enrollment: 478/NA

Midwest

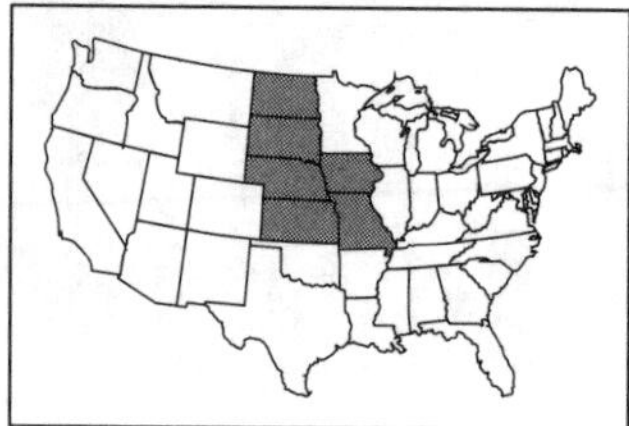

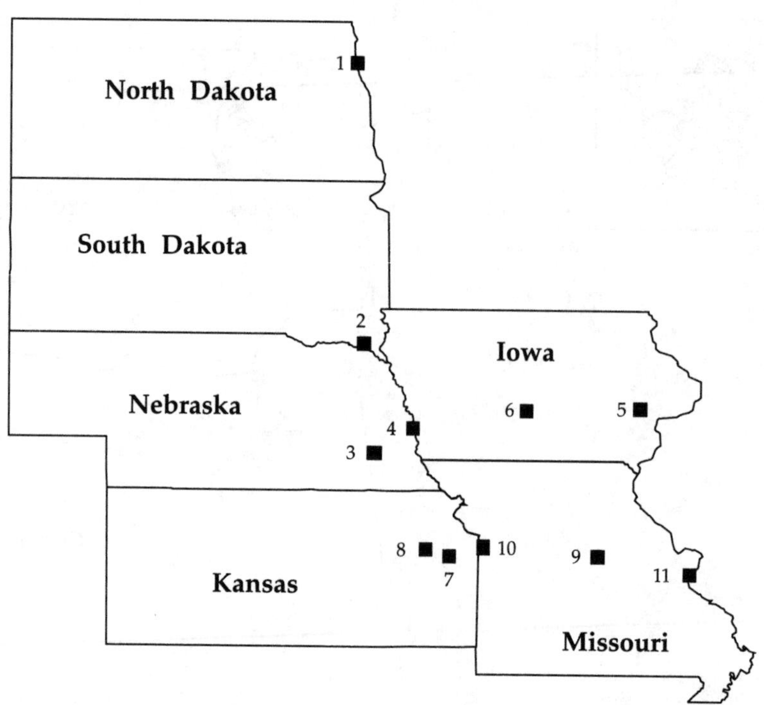

North Dakota

1. **Grand Forks—Population: 49,425**
   University of North Dakota—Enrollment: 217/NA

South Dakota

2. **Vermillion—Population: 10,034**
   University of South Dakota—Enrollment: 223/NA

Nebraska

3. **Lincoln—Population: 191,972**
   University of Nebraska—Enrollment: 415/NA
4. **Omaha—Population: 335,795**
   Creighton—Enrollment: 484/20

Iowa

5. **Iowa City—Population: 59,738**
   University of Iowa—Enrollment: 682/NA
6. **Des Moines—Population: 193,187**
   Drake—Enrollment: 502/17

Kansas

7. **Lawrence —Population: 65,808**
   University of Kansas—Enrollment: 498/NA
8. **Topeka—Population: 119,883**
   Washburn—Enrollment: 417/NA

Missouri

9. **Columbia—Population: 69,101**
   University of Missouri–Columbia—Enrollment: 462/NA
10. **Kansas City—Population: 435,146**
    University of Missouri–Kansas City—Enrollment: 471/13
11. **St. Louis—Population: 396,685**
    St. Louis—Enrollment: 561/282
    Washington University—Enrollment: 622/NA

Great Lakes

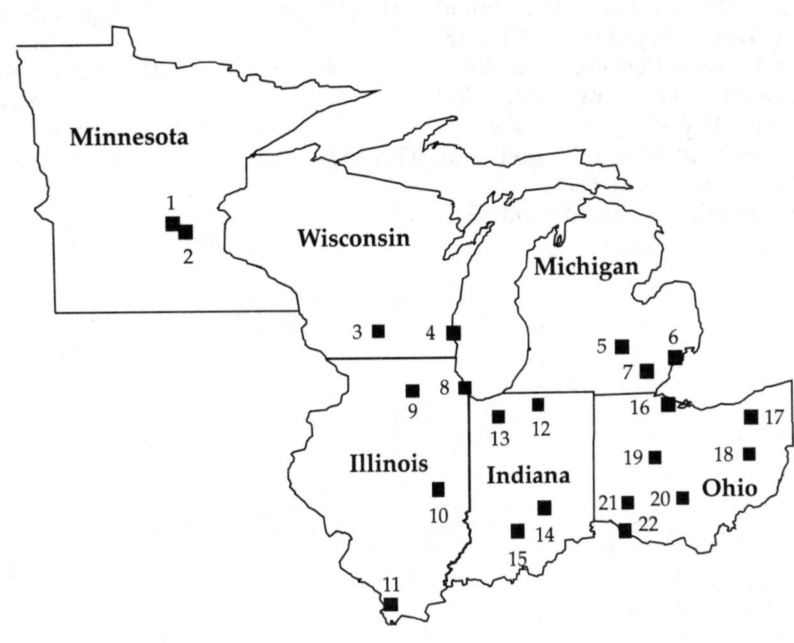

Minnesota

1. **Minneapolis—Population: 368,383**
   University of Minnesota—Enrollment: 810/NA
   William Mitchell—Enrollment: 578/490
2. **St. Paul—Population: 272,235**
   Hamline—Enrollment: 590/NA

Wisconsin

3. **Madison—Population: 191,262**
   University of Wisconsin—Enrollment: 816/68
4. **Milwaukee—Population: 628,088**
   Marquette—Enrollment: 475/6

Michigan

5. **Lansing—Population: 127,321**
   Thomas M. Cooley —Enrollment: 55/1,685
6. **Detroit—Population: 1,027,974**
   Detroit College of Law—Enrollment: 409/306
   University of Detroit, Mercy—Enrollment: 763/NA
   Wayne State—Enrollment: 548/199
7. **Ann Arbor—Population: 109,592**
   University of Michigan—Enrollment: 1,159/NA

Illinois

8. **Chicago—Population: 2,783,726**
   University of Chicago—Enrollment: 545/NA
   Chicago-Kent—Enrollment: 889/335
   DePaul—Enrollment: 807/322
   John Marshall—Enrollment: 819/342
   Loyola-Chicago—Enrollment: 580/189
   Northwestern—Enrollment: 606/NA
9. **DeKalb—Population: 34,925**
   Northern Illinois—Enrollment: 291/8
10. **Champaign—Population: 63,502**
    University of Illinois—Enrollment: 623/NA
11. **Carbondale—Population: 27,033**
    Southern Illinois—Enrollment: 354/NA

Indiana

12. **South Bend—Population: 105,511**
    Notre Dame—Enrollment: 563/NA
13. **Valparaiso—Population: 24,414**
    Valparaiso—Enrollment: 432/50
14. **Indianapolis—Population: 731,327**
    Indiana–Indianapolis—Enrollment: 574/261
15. **Bloomington—Population: 60,633**
    Indiana–Bloomington—Enrollment: 620/6

Ohio

16. **Toledo—Population: 332,943**
University of Toledo—Enrollment: 455/215
17. **Cleveland—Population: 505,616**
Case Western Reserve—Enrollment: 666/58
Cleveland State—Enrollment: 571/339
18. **Akron—Population: 223,019**
University of Akron—Enrollment: 452/183
19. **Ada—Population: 5,413**
Ohio Northern—Enrollment: 355/NA
20. **Columbus—Population: 632,910**
Capital—Enrollment: 476/336
Ohio State—Enrollment: 690/NA
21. **Dayton—Population: 182,044**
University of Dayton—Enrollment: 484/NA
22. **Cincinnati—Population: 364,040**
University of Cincinnati—Enrollment: 382/NA

Chapter 14: LSAC-Member Law School Descriptions

The descriptions that follow were prepared by each law school under editorial and formatting guidelines provided by Law Services. The schools were encouraged to use the bulleted lead-ins to each section for quantitative data that did not require a narrative explanation, and to use the descriptive text to provide details on the unique features of the school. Most schools also include admission profiles that illustrate admission prospects based on a combination of LSAT score and GPA.

The purpose of this book is to provide a brief introduction to the programs, facilities, and admission requirements of each ABA-approved law school. For a balanced view of each law school, it is important not only to look at all of the elements included in each school's description on these pages, but also to obtain the catalog and admission materials of each school that interests you. The data in the school descriptions and admission profiles are for the 1995-96 academic year unless otherwise noted, and represent full-time, day programs unless otherwise noted.

There are factors that may not predict law school performance but may otherwise affect an admission decision. Many law schools give special admission consideration to members of minority and disadvantaged groups because traditionally they have been underrepresented in the legal profession. Footnotes to the admission grids generally will note any special information about the composition of the applicant pool.

Please Note:

- Unless otherwise indicated, bulleted details in the school descriptions under the heading "Enrollment/Student Body" refer to the 1995 first-year class. The rest of the details under this category refer to the total student body of the law school.
- **Full-time** students are those registered for the number of units that would constitute a full-time load to complete the J.D. in the normal three-year period.
- **Part-time** is anything less than the above.
- **Range of first-year class size** is the range from the smallest first-year class section to the largest. This differs from the size of the entire first-year class.
- **Total full-time faculty** represents permanent faculty appointments teaching full time.
- **Total part-time faculty** represents part-time and adjunct appointments.
- **Total credits from required classes** are nonelective courses needed to obtain the J.D.

University of Akron School of Law

Office of Admissions
Akron, OH 44325-2901

Phone: 216.972.7331 or 800.4.AKRON.U; Fax: 216.258.2343

■ Introduction

The University of Akron was founded in 1870 and is a public higher education institution. The Akron Law School was founded in 1921 and merged with the University of Akron in 1959. Since 1921, this school has graduated over 4,700 lawyers.

The School of Law is accredited by the American Bar Association and is a member of the Association of American Law Schools and the League of Ohio Law Schools. Graduates are eligible to take the bar exam in every state.

Located in Northeast Ohio, Akron is approximately 45 minutes south of Cleveland.

■ Enrollment/Student Body

➧ 1,621 applicants ➧ 719 admitted first-year class 1995 ➧ 239 enrolled—166 day and 73 evening ➧ 635 total (all students—day and evening) in fall 1995 ➧ 8% minority enrollment in fall 1995 ➧ 39.8% women enrollment in fall 1995 ➧ 23 states & 3 foreign countries represented ➧ 98 undergraduate schools represented ➧ 71 majors represented ➧ average age—day, 26; evening, 32 ➧ age range—day, 22-47; evening, 22-53

■ Faculty

➧ 54 total ➧ 21 full-time ➧ 33 part-time or adjunct

■ Library

➧ over 230,000 volumes & equivalents ➧ 5 full-time librarians ➧ library seats 261 ➧ library hours: Mon.-Fri., 8:00 A.M.-11:00 P.M.; Sat., 9:00 A.M.-6:00 P.M.; Sun., NOON-11:00 P.M. ➧ Legal Trac CD-ROM ➧ Wilson Disk CD-ROM ➧ CIS Master File CD-ROM ➧ Federal Government Depository ➧ Interactive Video Disk material ➧ Computer-Based Education Terminals ➧ LEXIS ➧ NEXIS ➧ WESTLAW ➧ Internet ➧ OhioLINK

OhioLINK, an online public-access catalog system, connects the library by daily courier service to seven other Ohio law schools, all state universities in Ohio, plus two major private universities. Any item available for check-out at any member library may be requested online. When this system is completed, over 20 million items will be listed and the holdings of seven of the nine Ohio law schools will be included. These systems are also accessible via home computer.

Materials for conducting research on federal law and the law of every state are available. Group study rooms are also available, some equipped with VCRs/TVs, others with interactive video. A major addition, doubling the law library size was completed in 1989.

■ Physical Facilities

Three connected main buildings house the School of Law. The school is within close walking distance to an Ohio Court of Appeals, the Summit County Court of Commons Pleas, the Federal Courthouse, and many administrative agencies. This convenient location proves to be beneficial for students working at these offices.

■ Curriculum

➧ 88 semester credit hours required to graduate ➧ 3 year or 2 1/2 year full-time, day J.D. program ➧ 4 year or 3 1/2 year part-time, evening J.D. program ➧ joint degrees available; J.D./M.Tax; J.D./M.B.A.; and J.D./M.P.A. ➧ students admitted to start in fall only ➧ fall semester begins in mid-August

The first-year curriculum is traditional. Courses include a wide range of substantive courses suited to developing the analytical skills essential to lawyering. Private and public law, judicial and legislative process, and research and writing are all subsumed in this curriculum. A comprehensive writing program designed to enhance students' skills in exposition, drafting, and argumentation is an integral part of the curriculum.

Four tracks are offered—Litigation, Business, Tax, and Ohio Bar/Required. Other interesting courses of study include Law and Genetics, AIDS Law, Media Law, Sports and Entertainment Law, Labor Law, Real Estate Law, International Law, and more.

■ Special Programs

Akron has a longstanding tradition of winning regional competitions in both the American Trial Lawyers Association and American Bar Association Mock Trial Competitions. On the national level, Akron's ATLA trial team has placed second several years in a row.

A variety of opportunities for clinical training are offered. Students can experience the actual practice of law in a variety of supervised settings. Programs offered include: Trial Litigation Clinic, Appellate Review, Clinical Seminar, and Inmate Assistance.

■ Admission

➧ Bachelor's degree from accredited college or university required ➧ No application deadline ➧ LSAT, LSDAS required ➧ median GPA—3.12 ➧ median LSAT score—153 ➧ application fee—$35

Applications for fall admission begin arriving in September and October. While decisions are made when files are complete, most decisions are made beginning December/early January. Although an applicant's LSAT and undergraduate GPA are important indicators of academic preparation and motivation, the Admissions

Committee also considers: nature and the difficulty of major; ascending/descending grade trends; graduate work/degrees (if any); extracurricular activities while a student; LSAT writing sample; work experience; community activities; personal achievements/obstacles; letters of recommendation, and personal statement.

■ Tuition and Financial Aid

- *in-state tuition—full-time, $6,623; part-time, $5,175*
- *out-of-state tuition—full-time, $9,979; part-time, $7,790*
- *additional expenses—books, $400 to $500; on-campus housing, $3,844 (fall & spring semesters)*
- *FAFSA required (file early)*

All first-year students are automatically considered for full or partial scholarships based on merit and diversification of class. Merit and need-based loans available. File FAFSA early.

■ Housing

Many options are available. For more information, contact On-Campus Housing at 216.972.7800 or Off-Campus Housing at 216.972.6936.

■ Career Planning and Placement

The six-month, post-graduation employment survey, of which 82.4 percent of our 1994 graduating class responded, was 93.7 percent. Each year nearly 1,000 prospective employers seek applications from Akron law students and alumni for clerkships, internships, externships, and permanent employment.

Applicant Group for the 1995-1996 Academic Year

University of Akron School of Law
This grid includes only applicants who earned 120-180 LSAT scores under standard administrations.

LSAT Score	3.75 +		3.50 - 3.74		3.25 - 3.49		3.00 - 3.24		2.75 - 2.99		2.50 - 2.74		2.25 - 2.49		2.00 - 2.24		Below 2.00		Total	
	Apps	Adm	Apps	Adm	Apps	Adm	Apps	Adm	Apps	Adm	Apps	Adm	Apps	Adm	Apps	Adm	Apps	Adm	Apps	Adm
160 - 180	1	1	5	5	15	15	5	5	9	9	14	13	11	10	3	1	2	1*	65	60
154 - 159	13	13	24	23	28	28	53	52	45	43	67	55	32	16	16	5	4	2*	282	237
15 0- 153	14	14	39	37	72	70	92	86	95	58	56	19	23	3	13	1	5	2*	409	290
145 - 149	19	13	33	20	64	29	109	29	102	24	62	8	34	2	17	2	3	2*	443	129
120 - 144	6	0	24	1	40	0	67	0	69	0	62	0	61	0	28	0	15	0*	372	1
Total	53	41	125	86	219	142	326	172	320	134	261	95	161	31	77	8	29	7*	1571	716

Apps = Number of Applicants
Adm = Number Admitted
Reflects 96.9% of the entering class applicant pool.
*Represents foreign-educated applicants; no GPA available.

The University of Alabama School of Law

Box 870382
Tuscaloosa, AL 35487-0382

Phone: 205.348.5440

■ Introduction

The University of Alabama School of Law is located on the main university campus at Tuscaloosa. Founded in 1872, the law school has served the state and the nation as the training ground for leaders of the legal profession, business, and government. The curriculum is traditional but broad, with Alabama law emphasized only in a few elective courses. The school has a national reputation for excellence in teaching although the faculty is also committed to scholarly research and writing. The school is accredited by the ABA and AALS.

■ Enrollment/Student Body

➧ *930 applicants* ➧ *295 offers first-year class 1995*
➧ *193 enrolled first-year class 1995* ➧ *565 total full-time*
➧ *12% minority* ➧ *42% women*
➧ *17 states & foreign countries represented (all offers)*
➧ *78 degree-granting schools (all offers)*

■ Faculty

➧ *63 total* ➧ *30 full-time* ➧ *33 part-time or adjunct*
➧ *11 women* ➧ *4 minority*

■ Library and Physical Facilities

➧ *240,116 volumes & 98,740 equivalents* ➧ *library hours: weekdays, 7:30 A.M.-MIDNIGHT; Sat., 9:00 A.M.-10:00 P.M.; Sun., 10:00 A.M.-MIDNIGHT; varies during holidays*
➧ *LEXIS* ➧ *NEXIS* ➧ *WESTLAW* ➧ *DIALOG*
➧ *OCLC* ➧ *Alabama on disc* ➧ *7 full-time librarians*
➧ *library seats 562*

In January 1978, the school moved into the new Law Center building, a spacious structure located on a 27-acre tract on the east side of the campus. The building has been acclaimed as one of the nation's finest educational facilities. The Law Center's library provides students, faculty, attorneys, and other users with a substantial research collection of Anglo-American and international legal materials.

■ Curriculum

➧ *Academic Support Program* ➧ *90 credits required to graduate* ➧ *degrees available: J.D.; J.D./M.B.A.; M.C.L.*
➧ *semesters, start in Aug.*
➧ *range of first-year class size—96-Section I, 97-Section II*

■ Special Programs

The clinical program, under the supervision of the faculty, enables law students to gain valuable practical experience in interviewing clients, preparing cases, and participating in courtroom presentations. The joint degree program enables students to earn the J.D./M.B.A. (Master of Business Administration). The LL.M. in taxation is awarded to qualified graduates of accredited law schools upon completion of 24 graduate hours. The M.C.L. (Master of Comparative Law) degree is offered to a limited number of international lawyers.

■ Admission

➧ *Bachelor's degree required* ➧ *application deadline—March 1; Feb. 1 for M.C.L. applicants*
➧ *LSAT, LSDAS required* ➧ *median GPA—3.40*
➧ *median LSAT score—156* ➧ *application fee—$25*

A student must obtain a bachelor's degree at an accredited institution before enrolling but may apply during the senior year. Applicants must register for and take the LSAT, preferably no later than the December before enrollment, and subscribe to LSDAS for transcript analysis. Transcripts must show all schools attended and include at least three-fourths of the hours needed for graduation. Students are admitted only for the next immediate fall semester and only for full-time study. Application materials are available in September each year. Students are encouraged to submit applications early. The committee considers all information available about an applicant; however, the LSAT score and undergraduate GPA are by far the most important. Other factors considered include honors, activities, work experience, difficulty of undergraduate course of study, trends in academic performance, leadership ability, writing ability, and the applicant's personal statement. Admission decisions will also be influenced by the law school's commitment to racial, ethnic, cultural, economic, and geographic diversity. Special programs and support are available to members of minority and other diversity groups. Written letters of recommendation are not required. Personal interviews are usually not recommended.

Summer school is open to students who have completed the first year of law school (including students in good standing at other law schools), and graduation can be accelerated one semester by summer coursework. The full-time faculty of 30 is comprised of graduates of leading American law schools.

■ Student Organizations

Student organizations represent diverse interests. They include: Black Law Students Association, Environmental Law Society, Trial Advocacy Association, Association for Women and the Law, International Law Society, American Civil Liberties Union Tuscaloosa/University Chapter, and Christian Legal Society.

■ Activities

A broad range of student activities adds to the students' law school experience. *The Alabama Law Review*, published three times a year and edited by students, devotes substantial space to national issues as well as issues of relevance to Alabama. Three additional publications involve student participation: *The Journal of the Legal Profession*; the *Law and Psychology Review*; and the *American Journal of Tax Policy* (American College of Tax Fellows).

The law school's moot court, international moot court, and trial advocacy teams have won national honors in recent years. The Student Bar Association (SBA) provides several student services and sponsors a variety of academic and social activities.

■ Expenses and Financial Aid

➽ *tuition & fees—resident per semester, $1,720; nonresident per semester, $3,643* ➽ *estimated additional expenses—$500 books, first-year* ➽ *scholarships available* ➽ *minority scholarships available* ➽ *financial aid available; Family Financial Statement required; March 1 priority deadline*

The great majority of the students enrolled in the School of Law finance their legal education through loans, savings, earnings, and/or contributions from their families. Scholarships are awarded to approximately 25 percent of the first-year students. Scholarship recipients are identified on the basis of their applications for admission, and scholarship applications are unnecessary. Scholarships are sometimes renewable during the second and third years, often depending upon funding availability, the student's need, and whether the recipients maintain stated levels of academic achievement. Limited law school scholarship funds are available to assist extremely needy students. Applicants who have been admitted to the first-year class and who believe they qualify for these need-based scholarships should apply, using the form supplied by the School of Law and available upon request, not later than May 1 preceding the anticipated enrollment. Scholarship applications are generally required for renewal of law school scholarships. Aidis also available for law students from the university's Financial Aid Office. Further information can be obtained by writing to Director of Student Financial Services, The University of Alabama, Box 870162, Tuscaloosa, AL 35487-0162. Phone: 205.348.6756.

■ Career Services Program

The Career Services Program is designed to assist all students in their efforts to find employment. Extensive on-campus interviewing occurs.

The office has an excellent Career Resource Library. Seminars are presented on résumé writing, interviewing techniques, and job-search techniques to help students refine their job-search skills. Panel discussions are scheduled, and job fairs are supported as part of the Career Services Program.

■ Housing

The university maintains residence halls and apartment units for students. Off-campus housing is also available. For information, students may write to the Office of Housing and Residential Life, The University of Alabama, Box 870399, Tuscaloosa, AL 35487-0399.

Admission Profile Not Available

Albany Law School

80 New Scotland Avenue
Albany, NY 12208

Phone: 518.445.2326

■ Introduction

Albany Law School, founded in 1851, is one of the nation's oldest law schools. This midsize Law School is part of Union University, which includes Union College, Albany Medical College, and Albany College of Pharmacy. The Law School, while part of the university, has its own governing board.

Albany Law School, a member of the AALS, is fully accredited by the ABA and the New York State Department of Education. The policies of the school are in full compliance with Title IX of the 1972 Education Amendments.

The City of Albany is located 150 miles from New York City and 160 miles from Boston. Albany is an exceptional laboratory for the study of law. Long established here are the agencies of state government, the legislature, executive offices, and the state's highest court, the Court of Appeals. Through programs at the Law School and positions available in state government, the Albany Law School student has the opportunity to participate in those processes.

■ Enrollment/Student Body

➽ 1,705 applicants ➽ 914 admitted first-year class 1995 ➽ 265 enrolled first-year class 1995 ➽ 751 total full-time ➽ 36 total part-time ➽ 17% minority ➽ 48% women ➽ 28 states & foreign countries represented ➽ 203 undergraduate schools represented

Nearly 20 percent of our students completed their undergraduate studies five or more years before starting their legal education, and almost half of our students graduated from college at least one year prior to entering law school.

Additionally, 46 percent of the class entering in the fall of '95 were women and 21 percent were people of color.

■ Faculty

➽ 79 total ➽ 41 full-time ➽ 38 part-time

Diversity characterizes the Albany Law School faculty. The 41 full-time professors, clinical and legal research and writing instructors possess law degrees from 24 different law schools, including Harvard, Yale, Columbia, Stanford, New York University, Northwestern, St. John's, Howard, Georgetown, and Oxford University. In addition, 38 adjunct professors enrich the curriculum with their expertise in specific practical areas of the law.

■ Library and Physical Facilities

➽ 470,064 volumes & equivalents ➽ library hours: Mon.-Thurs., 8:00 A.M.-MIDNIGHT; Fri., 8:00 A.M.-10:00 P.M.; Sat., 9:00 A.M.-9:00 P.M.; Sun., 10:00 A.M.-MIDNIGHT ➽ LEXIS ➽ NEXIS ➽ WESTLAW ➽ DIALOG ➽ VU/TEXT ➽ WILSONLINE ➽ 7 full-time librarians ➽ library seats 490 ➽ 54 personal computers available for student use

In 1986 the Schaffer Law Library, one of the finest law libraries in the country, was added to Albany Law School. In addition, a new moot courtroom, a gymnasium, student lounge, and open-air courtyard complement the law school complex.

■ Curriculum

➽ Academic Support Program ➽ 87 credits required to graduate ➽ 118 courses available ➽ 20 clinical options including a wide range of externships ➽ degrees available: J.D./M.B.A.; J.D./M.P.A.; J.D. ➽ terms start in Aug. only ➽ range of first-year class size—25-88

An "Introduction to Lawyering" course offers a unique year-long case simulation that combines legal writing, clinical methodology, and professional skills development designed to introduce first-year students to what lawyers do and how the legal system works.

Students may select electives after the first year from a variety of areas including business organizations, constitutional law, environmental law, family law, government administration and regulation, international law, intellectual property, labor law, and taxation.

■ Special Programs

Clinical Legal Studies provides opportunities for upperclassmen to work and study for credit. They offer students a chance to view the legal system first hand and to begin participating in that system as professionals. Students may choose to participate in the AIDS Law Clinic, Disabilities Law Clinic, Family Violence Litigation Clinic, the Litigation Clinic, or the Placement Clinic which includes Albany County District Attorney's Office, Environmental Protection Bureau, U.S. District Court, U.S. Court of Appeals, NYS Supreme Court, Legal Aid Society, NYS Assembly, Prisoner's Legal Services and the U.S. Attorney's Office. Additionally, students may choose an externship. There are over 30 public law offices in which to work and study as externs.

The Government Law Center (GLC) was established in 1978 to facilitate multidisciplinary study and research in government and the problems facing the government; to introduce students to policy analysis and to public service; and to provide a resource to government in the resolution of specific problems. The GLC sponsors conferences, symposia, and seminars on a wide range of topics.

■ Admission

➽ Bachelor's degree required ➽ application deadline—March 15 ➽ applicants encouraged to apply early ➽ LSAT, LSDAS required ➽ median GPA—3.12 ➽ median LSAT score—153 ➽ application fee—$50 ➽ students with exceptional academic credentials may apply if 90 semester hours are successfully completed in a regionally accredited institution

An Admissions Committee, consisting of four full-time faculty members, reviews all parts of all applications. Albany Law School does not participate in any type of screening process whereby applicants are automatically accepted or denied. The Committee attempts to select a highly qualified and diverse student body and, therefore, takes many factors into consideration, including LSAT scores, previous scholastic achievement, employment experience, socioeconomic status, minority status, recommendations, and any exceptional circumstances pertaining to the applicant. Evaluative interviews are not part of the admissions process. Rather, applicants are encouraged to submit a written statement detailing all information that might be relevant for an admissions decision.

A small number of transfer students are usually admitted to the second-year class based on superior academic performance.

■ Student Activities

Students at Albany Law School are provided with opportunities to participate in educational, as well as social, activities. *Albany Law Review* is published four times a year. The *Albany Law Journal of Science & Technology* is a student publication dedicated to the development of the law as it relates to the sciences and the effect technology has upon society. Nationwide moot court competitions help students develop their legal research and advocacy skills. In addition, students can become involved in numerous organizations. The recently renovated gymnasium also provides students with an opportunity to participate in a variety of organized intramural athletic programs.

■ Expenses and Financial Aid

➽ *tuition & fees—$17,900, full-time; $13,451, part-time* ➽ *merit scholarships awarded on the basis of UGPA and LSAT score* ➽ *diversity scholarships awarded to students with unusual backgrounds including minorities* ➽ *need-based grants from $1,000 to $5,100 per year*

Part-time employment is available. More than 85 percent of the students receive federal, state, or law school monies. Financial aid applicants must submit the FAFSA form and Albany Law School Request for Financial Assistance, a copy of their 1995 Federal Income Tax form, and financial aid transcripts from all postsecondary institutions attended. Prospective students should file the FAFSA as soon after January 1 as possible regardless of whether or not an admissions decision has been received. Accepted applicants with a FAFSA on file in the Financial Aid Office will receive an estimate of their eligibility for all types of aid.

Most students live off-campus in moderately priced, privately owned housing. The Admissions Office maintains a listing of available accommodations. Additionally, a dormitory houses 84 law students in single rooms.

■ Career Services

The Career Planning Office provides career information and assistance to all students and alumni. Panels, workshops, and individual consultations are offered. Students can participate in on-campus and off-campus recruitment programs. Statistics from the past few years show an employment rate of over 94 percent for graduates.

Applicant Group for the 1995-1996 Academic Year

Albany Law School
This grid includes only applicants who earned 120-180 LSAT scores. If multiple LSAT scores are earned, placement on the grid is determined by the highest score.

LSAT Score	GPA: 3.75 +		3.50 - 3.74		3.25 - 3.49		3.00 - 3.24		2.75 - 2.99		2.50 - 2.74		2.25 - 2.49		2.00 - 2.24		Below 2.00		No GPA		Total	
	Apps	Adm	Apps	Adm	Apps	Adm	Apps	Adm	Apps	Adm	Apps	Adm	Apps	Adm	Apps	Adm	Apps	Adm	Apps	Adm	Apps	Adm
175 - 180	1	1	0	0	0	0	0	0	0	0	0	0	0	0	0	0	0	0	0	0	1	1
170 - 174	0	0	0	0	0	0	1	1	0	0	0	0	0	0	0	0	0	0	0	0	1	1
165 - 169	2	2	2	2	9	9	7	6	5	5	2	2	1	1	0	0	0	0	1	1	29	28
160 - 164	8	8	22	22	35	35	26	24	25	25	16	15	11	7	4	3	0	0	1	1	148	140
155 - 159	14	14	49	49	91	91	87	85	74	63	38	20	8	2	4	1	0	0	2	2	367	327
150 - 154	19	19	60	59	111	89	126	80	76	30	60	19	29	4	4	1	1	0	5	4	491	305
145 - 149	9	7	30	16	67	20	84	20	78	18	36	5	21	1	10	1	1	0	6	4	342	92
140 - 144	6	1	15	4	21	7	29	4	48	3	31	1	18	0	13	0	1	0	4	0	186	20
135 - 139	1	0	2	0	4	0	20	0	12	0	19	0	11	0	5	0	0	0	3	0	77	0
130 - 134	0	0	1	0	3	0	6	0	8	0	3	0	4	0	3	0	0	0	1	0	29	0
125 - 129	0	0	0	0	1	0	1	0	2	0	0	0	1	0	2	0	0	0	0	0	7	0
120 - 124	0	0	0	0	0	0	0	0	0	0	0	0	0	0	0	0	0	0	0	0	0	0
Total	60	52	181	152	342	251	387	220	328	144	205	62	104	15	45	6	3	0	23	12	1678	914

Apps = Number of Applicants
Adm = Number Admitted

	APPS	ADM
Applicants with only 10-48 LSAT scores earned under standard administrations	2	0
Applicants with no LSAT	25	1

American University—Washington College of Law

4400 Massachusetts Avenue, N.W.
Washington, DC 20016

URL: http://www.wcl.american.edu/pub/wcl.html
Phone: 202.274.4101

■ Introduction

The American University's Washington College of Law offers opportunity for the study of law in the center of the nation's legal institutions. The law school is minutes from downtown Washington, but at the same time offers the facilities and ambiance of a true campus environment in one of the city's most beautiful residential neighborhoods.

Founded in 1896 by two women, the law school is national in character. It is committed to the development of the intellectual abilities and practical skills required to prepare lawyers to practice in an increasingly complex and transnational world. The school is noted for the accessibility of faculty and administration to its students.

■ Enrollment/Student Body (First-Year Class)

➽ *5,100 applicants* ➽ *1,800 admitted* ➽ *373 enrolled*
➽ *286 total full-time* ➽ *87 total part-time* ➽ *25% minority*
➽ *61% women* ➽ *35 states & 4 foreign countries represented*
➽ *173 undergraduate schools represented*

■ Faculty

➽ *159 total* ➽ *59 full-time* ➽ *100 part-time*
➽ *42 women* ➽ *17 minority*

■ Library and Physical Facilities

➽ *386,354 volumes & equivalents* ➽ *library hours: Mon.-Thurs., 8:00 A.M.-2:00 A.M.; Fri., 8:00 A.M.-MIDNIGHT; Sat., 9:00 A.M.-MIDNIGHT; Sun., 10:00 A.M.-2:00 A.M.*
➽ *LEXIS* ➽ *WESTLAW* ➽ *9 full-time librarians*
➽ *library seats 623*

The American University's Washington College of Law will move into the long awaited new building by the end of 1995. The new law school is located at 4801 Massachusetts Avenue, less than one-half mile from the main campus. This new state-of-the-art facility allows an unparalleled opportunity not only to house all of the law school's programs under one roof, but also to develop a structure which will prepare lawyers for practice in the twenty-first century.

The new two-story library is the heart of the complex. It is approximately two and one-half times the size of the existing facility and seats over 600 students. Approximately half of the total seats will initially be equipped with data ports so a student can plug in a portable computer and have access to all Internet and campus wide research databases. The library collection includes European Community and U.S. Government depositories and the Baxter Collection in International Law. The library was recently designated as the repository for the National Equal Justice Library, which will be an archive of primary and public-defender programs. Students also have access to the university's library, the Library of Congress, specialized agency libraries, and other area law libraries to which the school is electronically linked.

■ Curriculum

The law school offers full-time and part-time programs leading to the J.D. degree, which is awarded after satisfactory completion of 86 credit hours, 34 of which are prescribed. All degree candidates must also fulfill an upper-level writing requirement. The Socratic method is the basic form of instruction in the first year. Its purpose is to develop the skills of critical analysis, provide perspectives on the law and lawyering, and deepen understanding of fundamental legal principals. In the Legal Method program, basic legal research and writing skills are taught to groups of 14 students by practicing attorneys and upper-level assistants. In the second and third years, students elect a course of study drawing from advanced courses, seminars, independent research, externships, and clinical programs. Students are exposed to a variety of teaching processes by the law school's distinguished full-time faculty of 59. Other specialized courses are taught by eminent Washington lawyers widely recognized as experts in their fields in the private and public sectors.

■ Special Programs

While many of the advanced courses take place in a traditional classroom setting, a variety of other innovative teaching modes is available to enhance research skills and provide professional training. The Washington College of Law Practicing Law Center enjoys a national reputation for clinical education. Second-year students may participate in the Public Interest Law Clinic; third-year students may develop their lawyering abilities in the Criminal Justice Clinic, the DC Civil Litigation Clinic, the International Human Rights Clinic, the Tax Clinic, or the Appellate Clinic. The Women and the Law Program includes a clinical component in which students represent indigent women in the District of Columbia courts. This program also offers several public-education projects each year, and is designed to integrate women's legal studies into the overall curriculum and to heighten awareness about legal issues affecting women.

Complementing its outstanding curriculum in International Law, the university offers a combined J.D./M.A. in International Affairs with the School of International Service. Combined-degree programs also include a J.D./M.S. with the School of Justice, and a J.D./M.B.A. with the Kogod College of Business Administration. Graduate study is available leading to the LL.M. degree in International Legal Studies.

The externship program places upper-level students in many regulatory and administrative agencies in the city. Field components, taken simultaneously with a seminar, include such areas as security and commodities markets regulation. The Program for Advanced Studies in the Federal Regulatory Process, offered each summer, provides an intensive analysis of the federal regulatory process through lectures and optional field placements in a myriad of federal agencies and nonprofit organizations.

■ Admission

➽ *Bachelor's degree from accredited college or university required* ➽ *application deadline—March 1* ➽ *rolling admission, early application preferred* ➽ *LSAT, LSDAS required* ➽ *application fee—$55*

Applicants to the law school are admitted on the strength of their entire academic and related records. The faculty admission committee gives primary emphasis to the undergraduate record, LSAT scores, and other major accomplishments and achievements, whether academic, work-related, or extracurricular. The benefits the school derives from racial, ethnic, cultural, and geographical diversity among its students are considered in admission decisions. Members of disadvantaged and minority groups are encouraged to apply. Admission to the law school is highly competitive, and operates on a rolling admission basis, so early application is strongly encouraged.

■ Student Activities

The *Law Review*, the *Journal of International Law and Policy*, the *Administrative Law Journal*, and the *Journal of Gender and the Law* are edited and published by students selected on the basis of scholarship and creative research. The Moot Court Board sponsors intraschool competitions for first-year and upper-level students, and selects representatives for a number of interschool competitions, including the National Moot Court Competition. Other student activities include active chapters of the Black Law Students Association, the Women's Law Association, the Environmental Law Society, the Hispanic Law Student Association, the Asian Pacific American Law Student Association, the National Lawyers Guild, the Federalist Society, the Lambda Law Students Association, and many other student groups.

■ Expenses and Financial Aid

➽ *tuition & fees—$19,550; part-time, $725/credit* ➽ *fees—full-time, $340; part-time, $224* ➽ *estimated additional expenses—$11,565 (room, board, books)* ➽ *need-based scholarships available* ➽ *FAFSA form due by March 1; Need Access diskette due by Feb. 15 for scholarships*

The Office of Career Services provides individual assistance to students on career counseling and the techniques of job searching. The office arranges for both on- and off-campus recruitment for summer and permanent legal positions, and participates in a variety of hiring consortia. Graduates from 1994 report employment in the following areas of practice: private practice, 37.2 percent; business and industry, 12.8 percent; government, 19.17 percent; judicial clerkships, 20.03 percent; public interest, 7.4 percent; other, 3.4 percent. A majority of the law school's alumni practice in the Washington, D.C. metropolitan area; however, its graduates can be found in every state and many foreign countries.

Applicant Group for the 1995-1996 Academic Year

American University—Washington College of Law
This grid includes only applicants who earned 120-180 LSAT scores under standard administrations.

LSAT Score	GPA 3.75 +		3.50 - 3.74		3.25 - 3.49		3.00 - 3.24		2.75 - 2.99		2.50 - 2.74		2.25 - 2.49		2.00 - 2.24		Below 2.00		No GPA		Total	
	Apps	Adm	Apps	Adm	Apps	Adm	Apps	Adm	Apps	Adm	Apps	Adm	Apps	Adm	Apps	Adm	Apps	Adm	Apps	Adm	Apps	Adm
175 - 180	0	0	0	0	2	2	0	0	0	0	0	0	0	0	1	1	0	0	0	0	3	3
170 - 174	1	1	5	5	4	4	11	11	7	7	5	5	1	0	0	0	0	0	0	0	34	33
165 - 169	12	12	34	34	42	40	46	46	40	38	22	15	10	4	3	1	1	0	2	0	212	190
160 - 164	42	40	150	146	231	216	196	159	112	46	57	12	31	5	5	0	2	1	7	6	833	631
155 - 159	82	74	264	195	363	164	302	92	165	33	103	14	33	5	9	0	3	0	12	4	1336	581
150 - 154	50	19	171	51	294	52	280	46	198	18	94	6	53	1	18	0	0	0	16	2	1174	195
145 - 149	33	7	71	7	149	20	156	11	157	8	92	2	50	1	19	0	4	0	10	1	741	57
140 - 144	8	1	24	3	56	3	84	5	83	3	68	0	57	1	21	0	3	0	14	3	418	19
135 - 139	0	0	9	0	23	1	28	0	35	0	37	0	32	0	17	0	4	0	17	1	202	2
130 - 134	1	0	3	0	4	0	7	0	11	0	9	0	11	0	5	0	2	0	3	0	56	0
125 - 129	0	0	0	0	1	0	1	0	2	0	6	0	3	0	0	0	0	0	4	0	17	0
120 - 124	0	0	0	0	0	0	0	0	0	0	0	0	1	0	0	0	0	0	0	0	1	0
Total	229	154	731	441	1169	502	1111	370	810	153	493	54	282	17	98	2	19	1	85	17	5027	1711

Apps = Number of Applicants
Adm = Number Admitted
Reflects 98% of the total applicant pool.

University of Arizona College of Law

Tucson, AZ 85721

URL: http://www.law.Arizona.edu/~law/
Phone: 520.621.3477

■ Introduction

The University of Arizona College of Law was founded in 1915, is the oldest law school in Arizona, and has a rich and distinguished history. The college is an integral part of the University of Arizona, one of the nation's leading research institutions. The College of Law has a national reputation for providing its students a high quality education in a collegial, friendly, and intellectually challenging atmosphere. The College of Law is located in Tucson, an environmentally beautiful and culturally rich city of 720,000, which is home to an active legal and judicial community. The college is approved by the ABA, and has been a member of the AALS since 1931.

■ Enrollment/Student Body

➧ 2,090 applicants ➧ 415 admitted first-year class 1995 ➧ 153 enrolled first-year class 1995 ➧ 454 total full-time ➧ 28% minority ➧ 46% women ➧ 40 states & foreign countries represented ➧ 150 undergraduate schools represented ➧ 3% persons with disabilities

The students of the College of Law bring varied work and life experiences to the College. The average age of students entering in the fall of 1995 was 27; with 25 percent of the class age 30 or above, and 16 percent of the class holding graduate degrees.

■ Faculty

➧ 56 total ➧ 30 full-time ➧ 18 part-time or adjunct ➧ 15 women ➧ 5 minority

With a ratio of 15 to 1, the college has one of the most favorable student-faculty ratios of any American law school. Many members of the faculty are nationally recognized legal scholars. Five members of the faculty hold endowed chairs. Six faculty members with national and international reputations from other university departments hold joint appointments in the college of law.

■ Library and Physical Facilities

➧ 353,260 volumes & equivalents ➧ library hours: Mon.-Thurs., 7:00 A.M.-11:45 P.M.; Fri., 7:00 A.M.-10:00 P.M.; Sat., 8:00 A.M.-8:00 P.M.; Sun., 9:00 A.M.-11:45 P.M. ➧ LEXIS ➧ NEXIS ➧ WESTLAW ➧ OCLC ➧ DIALOG ➧ 7 full-time librarians ➧ library seats 353

The College of Law occupies a modern building, which is fully wheelchair accessible, with outstanding classroom, library, and conference facilities. The Arizona State Supreme Court convenes annually at the college and hears arguments on a variety of cases. The library, housing a major research facility, is one of the foremost legal research facilities in the Southwest. There is an expanding foreign law collection emphasizing Latin American law and an International Commercial Law Center within the library. The library houses computer terminals and a student computer laboratory equipped with the most modern technology.

■ Curriculum

➧ Academic Support Program ➧ BRIDGE (a week-long prelaw program for minority and disabled enrollees) ➧ 85 credits required to graduate ➧ 80 courses available ➧ degrees available: J.D.; J.D./Ph.D. (Economics, Philosophy, Psychology); J.D./M.A. (Economics); J.D./M.B.A.; J.D./M.P.A. ➧ an LL.M. Program in International Trade Law began in fall 1994 ➧ semesters, start in Aug.

The college has committed substantial faculty resources to the development of research and writing skills. Each first-year student meets in a section of approximately 25 students in one of the first-semester courses. In addition to the substantive course material, the student receives rigorous instruction in legal research and writing. Students must also complete a special writing seminar during the second or third year.

After completing the first-year requirements, students have considerable flexibility in considering second- and third-year coursework. The college offers a rich variety of courses taught by nationally recognized faculty, including courses in Business and Corporate Law, Securities, Employment Law, Criminal Law, Constitutional Law, Remedies, International Law, Tax, Wealth Transfer (Estates and Trusts), Indian Law, Environmental Law, Legal History, Water Law, and a wealth of Trial Advocacy offerings.

Students may choose clinical courses offered in criminal and civil law, participating in classroom instruction and field placements in a variety of settings.

In addition, the college sponsors several Congressional internships and internship programs with the Navajo, Pascua Yaqui, White Mountain Apache, and Tohono O'Odham tribal governments.

The course of study leading to the J.D. degree is normally completed in six semesters of resident study; a cumulative average of 2.0 (C) is required to graduate.

■ Admission

➧ Bachelor's degree required ➧ application deadline—March 1, rolling admission Dec. through May, early application preferred ➧ LSAT, LSDAS required ➧ median GPA—3.40 ➧ median LSAT score—162 ➧ application fee—$35

Admission to the College of Law is very selective. There are two ways to be admitted to the College: through the Presumptive Admission process and through the Admission Committee. In the Presumptive process, all applicants are initially ranked according to an index score combining undergraduate grade-point average and LSAT score in a formula. Some applicants are then admitted primarily based upon their index rankings.

In the Admission Committee process, a portion of those students who are not admitted on the basis of their index score in the presumptive process are selected for further consideration by the Admission Committee. In making decisions, the Admission Committee considers all relevant personal information, including graduate education; nature of undergraduate experience; distinctive ethnic or cultural backgrounds; unusual work and travel experience; unique talents, interests, accomplishments; special personal goals; extracurricular activities; substantial community service; or other circumstances such as personal or family responsibilities. The college is very committed to enrolling students who bring diverse perspectives to the college and the legal profession and encourages applications from minority, disadvantaged, and disabled candidates and candidates who bring varied life experiences to the educational process. Students begin their studies in the fall only and must have completed an undergraduate degree from an accredited four-year college. The deadline forcompleted applications, including transcripts, LSAT scores and two letters of recommendation is March 1. Applicants must take the LSAT no later than the December prior to the year of expected enrollment. A waiver of the fee is available when requested and explained in writing and substantiated by a financial aid award letter or a tax return.

■ Student Activities

The *Arizona Law Review* and *The Arizona Journal of International and Comparative Law* are well-known, student-operated and student-edited scholarly journals on current legal problems. The law school newspaper, *The Arizona Advocate*, serves as a voice for student and faculty opinions on a variety of issues. A new journal, *The Journal of Psychology, Public Policy & Law* is of special interest to concurrent degree students. The students in the moot court program participate in national and state appellate advocacy competitions.

The student body is self-governing through the Student Bar Association. Students also participate in making law school policy by serving as voting members of student-faculty committees. There are a variety of law student organizations and outstanding scholarship is recognized by membership in the Order of the Coif.

■ Special Programs

The College of Law cooperates with other colleges at the University of Arizona and offers joint J.D./Ph.D. programs in philosophy, psychology, or economics; a J.D./M.A. program in economics; a J.D./M.B.A. program; and a J.D./M.P.A. Other concurrent degree programs are available by special arrangement. In the fall of 1994, the college began offering a 24- unit LL.M. program in International Trade Law.

■ Expenses and Financial Aid

➧ *tuition & fees—full-time residents, $3,950 (annually); nonresidents, $9,978 (annually)* ➧ *estimated additional expenses—$11,800 (room, board, travel, books, misc.)* ➧ *scholarships available: need-based & merit-based; tuition waivers* ➧ *minority scholarships available: Graduate Minority Fellowships, Cordova Scholarships, cash awards* ➧ *financial aid available* ➧ *FAFSA required—due March 1*

The cost of living in Tucson is relatively modest.

Applicant Group for the 1995-1996 Academic Year

University of Arizona College of Law
This grid includes only applicants who earned 120-180 LSAT scores under standard administrations.

LSAT Score	3.75 +		3.50 - 3.74		3.25 - 3.49		3.00 - 3.24		2.75 - 2.99		2.50 - 2.74		2.25 - 2.49		2.00 - 2.24		Below 2.00		No GPA		Total	
	Apps	Adm	Apps	Adm	Apps	Adm	Apps	Adm	Apps	Adm	Apps	Adm	Apps	Adm	Apps	Adm	Apps	Adm	Apps	Adm	Apps	Adm
175 - 180	0	0	1	1	0	0	1	1	0	0	0	0	0	0	0	0	0	0	0	0	2	2
170 - 174	0	0	2	2	5	5	4	4	7	4	1	1	1	1	0	0	0	0	0	0	20	17
165 - 169	14	14	27	24	33	29	33	24	18	12	10	7	6	3	0	0	0	0	1	1	142	114
160 - 164	48	29	78	41	109	47	73	19	51	14	28	5	12	1	2	0	1	0	0	0	402	156
155 - 159	55	12	113	14	128	11	111	13	66	6	32	2	11	1	5	0	0	0	2	0	523	59
150 - 154	36	7	80	4	113	10	91	8	80	5	31	1	17	1	8	0	2	0	8	0	466	36
145 - 149	9	1	33	0	58	1	51	2	44	2	37	0	16	1	12	0	1	0	4	0	265	7
140 - 144	1	0	8	0	22	0	33	0	26	0	16	0	19	0	6	0	2	0	2	0	135	0
135 - 139	0	0	5	0	10	0	12	0	16	0	17	0	5	0	4	0	5	0	4	0	78	0
130 - 134	0	0	0	0	1	0	2	0	3	0	5	0	0	0	3	0	2	0	1	0	17	0
125 - 129	0	0	0	0	0	0	1	0	0	0	1	0	0	0	1	0	0	0	0	0	3	0
120 - 124	0	0	0	0	0	0	0	0	1	0	0	0	0	0	0	0	0	0	0	0	1	0
Total	163	63	347	86	479	103	412	71	312	43	178	16	87	8	41	0	13	0	22	1	2054	391

GPA column groups as above.

Apps = Number of Applicants
Adm = Number Admitted
Reflects 98% of the total applicant pool.
This grid is to be used as a general guide only. Qualitative factors, including each candidate's personal statement, letters of recommendation, and life experiences, play an important role in the evaluation process.

Arizona State University College of Law

Box 877906
Tempe, AZ 85287-7906

URL: http://aspin.asu.edu/provider/law/index.html
Phone: 602.965.7896

■ Introduction

The College of Law is located on the campus of the Arizona State University in Tempe, a suburb of Phoenix. Established in 1966, the law school was accredited by the AALS and ABA in 1969. In the fall of 1992 the college celebrated its 25th anniversary and the accomplishments it has achieved in a relatively short time.

■ Enrollment/Student Body

➧ *2,087 applicants* ➧ *383 admitted first-year class 1995*
➧ *149 enrolled first-year class 1995* ➧ *476 total full-time*
➧ *29% minority* ➧ *47% women*
➧ *36 states & foreign countries represented*
➧ *153 undergraduate schools represented*
➧ *1995 entering class, 81% resident, 19% nonresident*

■ Faculty

➧ *47 total* ➧ *35 full-time* ➧ *12 part-time or adjunct*
➧ *10 women* ➧ *4 minority*

■ Library and Physical Facilities

➧ *340,000 volumes & equivalents* ➧ *library hours: Mon.-Thurs., 7:00 A.M.-MIDNIGHT; Fri., 7:00 A.M.-10:00 P.M.; Sat., 8:00 A.M.-10:00 P.M.; Sun., 10:00 A.M.-MIDNIGHT*
➧ *LEXIS* ➧ *WESTLAW* ➧ *6 full-time librarians*
➧ *library seats 590*

Armstrong Hall, a modern, air-conditioned structure, is architecturally designed for the special functions of legal education. Among its features are classrooms with seating on elevated tiers to facilitate dialogue between professors and students; the Willard H. Pedrick Great Hall, seating 400, which serves not only as a courtroom, but also as a location for campus events; and a trial courtroom which is equipped to permit videotaping of trials and other advocacy exercises to facilitate instruction in litigation techniques. Armstrong Hall houses a legal clinic, providing easy access for law student interns.

The John J. Ross—William C. Blakley Law Library is housed in a dramatic and functional new building that opened in August 1993. The collection includes growing special collections in the areas of international law, Indian law, Mexican law, and law and technology. The library has a thirty station computer lab, as well as LEXIS and WESTLAW rooms each containing ten stations, 27 meeting and study rooms and a microforms facility.

■ Curriculum

➧ *Academic Support Program* ➧ *Law School Clinic, Prosecutor Clinic, Externship Programs*
➧ *87 units/credits required to graduate* ➧ *85 courses available* ➧ *degrees available: J.D.; J.D./M.B.A.; J.D./M.H.S.A.; J.D./Ph.D Justice Studies*
➧ *fall semester starts in Aug., spring semester starts in Jan.*
➧ *range of first-year class size—35-140*

The College of Law awards the J.D. degree following a three-year course of study. The first year consists of a required curriculum. In the following years, the student selects from a wide number of legal courses, including small-group seminars, clinic internships, independent and interdisciplinary study, and a trial practice program. Many students also choose to enhance their theoretical classroom knowledge with the practical experience of an externship. The college offers a variety of externship opportunities with agencies and governmental offices.

■ Center for the Study of Law, Science, and Technology

The Center for the Study of Law, Science, and Technology was established in 1984 in response to the increasing number of social and legal questions arising out of new scientific and technological development in areas such as computers, communications, medicine, genetics, space technology, and nuclear power.

The center conducts research, engages in curricular development, sponsors papers and conferences, and brings visiting scholars to the law school. The College of Law co-edits the *Jurimetrics Journal*, a quarterly journal of the ABA Section of Science and Technology.

■ Clinical Programs

The College of Law offers a variety of clinical courses. In the Law School Clinic students gain experience in interviewing, legal research and writing, fact investigation, discovery, pretrial procedure, and oral advocacy in the courtroom. Students may be assigned to a variety of civil matters. Prosecutor Clinic interns prosecute misdemeanor charges in city courts in Tempe and neighboring communities.

■ Indian Legal Program

The Indian Legal Program (ILP) at the Arizona State University College of Law actively recruits American Indian students and promotes Indian legal education in the course curriculum. The ILP also seeks to provide public service to American Indian tribes and tribal governments.

The ASU College of Law student body currently includes students from 18 different American Indian tribes.

■ Student Activities

The Student Bar Association sponsors numerous activities including lectures and social events. Second- and third-year students publish a professional law review, *Arizona State Law Journal*. Students also direct the moot court program and participate in national and international moot court competitions. In addition, law students publish a newspaper, *Devil's Advocate*, and have formed such independent organizations as Women's Law Student Association, Chicano/Latino Law Students Association, American Indian Law Students, Asian Law

Students Association, legal fraternities, and a chapter of the Black Law Students Association. Many students participate in pro bono activities including the Volunteer Income Tax Assistance program and the Homeless Legal Assistance Project. Students also serve as voting members of several College of Law committees.

■ Admission

➻ *Bachelor's degree required from an accredited institution* ➻ *application deadline—March 1* ➻ *LSAT, LSDAS required* ➻ *median GPA—3.40* ➻ *median LSAT score—159* ➻ *application fee—$35*

With approximately 14 applicants for each place in the first-year class, admission to the College of Law is highly selective. Such varied factors as the undergraduate education, LSAT score, trend of college grades, course-selection patterns, quality and grading patterns of undergraduate institutions, work or other nonacademic experience, and cultural or socioeconomic background are considered in the admission decision.

Transfer applications will be considered on a space-available basis for students with excellent records.

Students who are members of minority groups are encouraged to apply. The College of Law has a vital diversity admission policy, a policy to which the college is enthusiastically committed. Students from diverse cultural, ethnic, and racial backgrounds enrich the educational experience of all students and faculty and ultimately increase the number of minority lawyers in the country.

■ Expenses and Financial Aid

➻ *tuition & fees—full-time resident, $3,950 per year; non-resident, $9,978 per year* ➻ *estimated additional expenses—$7,000 (living expenses, books/9-month academic year)* ➻ *scholarships available: merit & need based* ➻ *minority scholarships available* ➻ *financial aid available*

■ Placement

The law school Placement Office provides assistance to students and alumni seeking employment. Placement services include a computerized job line and bulletin board of job openings, a resource library, an alumni mentor program, and workshops on résumé writing, interviewing, and research techniques. Special-interest workshops are offered on various topics such as clerkship positions and public interest law opportunities. The Placement Office also arranges for on-campus interviews with law firms and governmental agencies.

Applicant Group for the 1995-1996 Academic Year

Arizona State University College of Law

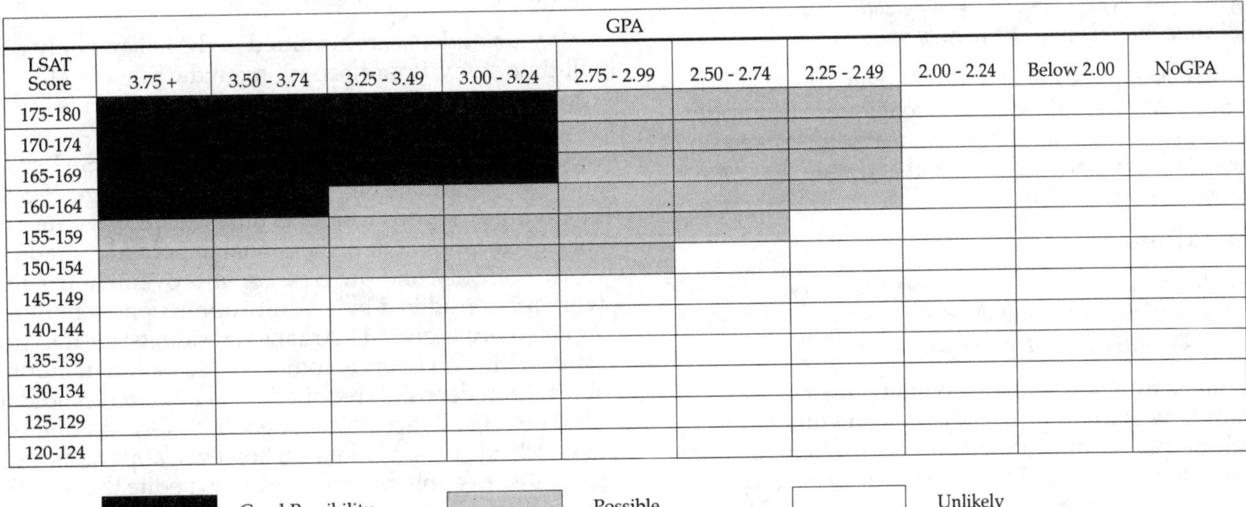

University of Arkansas School of Law—Fayetteville

Robert A. Leflar Law Center
Fayetteville, AR 72701

Phone: 501.575.3102

■ Introduction

The University of Arkansas School of Law is located on the main university campus at Fayetteville, a city of 49,000 in Northwest Arkansas. The School of Law was established in 1924 and has continuously sought to provide high quality legal education in a university community. In 1926 the School of Law was approved by the ABA, and in 1927 the school became a member of the AALS.

■ Enrollment/Student Body

➡ 824 applicants ➡ 340 admitted first-year class 1995 ➡ 140 enrolled first-year class 1995 ➡ 396 total full-time ➡ 8% minority ➡ 40% women ➡ 35 states & foreign countries represented ➡ 102 undergraduate schools represented

Although 80 percent of the students are Arkansas residents, others are from every part of the United States. Since the school has no undergraduate course prerequisites, the academic backgrounds and nonacademic experiences of students are varied.

■ Faculty

➡ 45 total ➡ 35 full-time ➡ 10 part-time or adjunct ➡ 11 women ➡ 3 minority

■ Library and Physical Facilities

➡ 220,000 volumes & equivalents ➡ library hours: Mon.-Thurs., 7:00 A.M.-MIDNIGHT; Fri., 7:00 A.M.-10:00 P.M.; Sat., 9:00 A.M.-10:00 P.M.; Sun., 1:00 P.M.-MIDNIGHT; 107 total hours ➡ LEXIS ➡ WESTLAW ➡ Legislate ➡ 5 full-time librarians ➡ library seats 346

The library is expanding at a rate of over 10,000 volumes a year. Students are trained in the techniques of computer-assisted legal research as well as in the traditional research methods. The law library is a federal and state depository for government documents.

■ Curriculum

➡ 90 credits required to graduate ➡ 102 courses available ➡ degrees available: J.D.; J.D./M.B.A. ➡ semesters, start in Aug. ➡ range of first-year class size—30-70

The primary function of the University of Arkansas School of Law is to prepare lawyers who will render the highest quality of professional service to their clients, who are interested in and capable of furthering legal process and reform, and who are prepared to fill the vital role of the lawyer as a community leader. The school offers a full-time, three-year program leading to the J.D. degree. The degree is conferred upon satisfactory completion of 90 semester hours, including 44 hours of required courses. The first-year curriculum is required. A broad selection of elective second- and third-year courses is available. Students who have completed the first year of law school may earn up to 12 semester hours of credit in summer school, and graduation can be accelerated one semester by summer coursework. The School of Law offers a joint J.D./M.B.A. program with the College of Business Administration. If a student is accepted into both programs, a maximum of six hours of approved upper-level elective law courses may be used on duplicative credit toward the M.B.A. degree and a maximum of six hours of approved graduate courses in business administration may be used as duplicative credit toward the J.D. degree. The Graduate Program in Agricultural Law provides opportunities for advanced study, creative research, and specialized professional training in this rapidly developing area of law. The program is designed to prepare a small number of carefully selected attorneys as specialists in the legal problems of agricultural production, distribution, and marketing. Applicants for admission as candidates for the Master of Laws (LL.M.) in Agricultural Law must have earned a J.D. or LL.B. degree from a fully accredited law school. The applicant must have demonstrated a high degree of academic excellence as evidenced by high academic standing, law review membership, or other educational or professional achievement indicating potential for success in graduate study.

■ Admission

➡ B.A. required ➡ application deadline—April 1, rolling admission, early application preferred ➡ LSAT, LSDAS required ➡ median GPA—3.18 ➡ median LSAT score—153

First-year students are admitted in the fall and only for full-time study. Prior to enrolling in the School of Law, applicants must have completed all requirements for an undergraduate degree from an accredited four-year college. Admission is based on the applicant's LSAT score and undergraduate GPA. In a small percentage of cases involving Arkansas residents only, additional criteria such as vocational or professional experience, graduate work, ethnicity, and progressive improvement in college work are considered by a faculty admissions committee. A preference is given to Arkansas residents; for the current status of this preference, contact the school. A nonrefundable tuition deposit is required of all admitted candidates. The law school's application deadline is April 1 of the year in which admission is sought; however, applicants are requested to apply by January 1 to expedite the selection and notification process. Applicants must take the LSAT no later than February. Applications completed after April 1 will be considered only on a space-available basis.

■ Housing

Housing for single students is available in campus dormitories; apartments are also available for married students. Applicants should write to the Housing Office,

University of Arkansas, Fayetteville, AR 72701. A variety of private off-campus housing is available in Fayetteville and surrounding communities, within easy commuting distance of the law school.

■ Student Activities

The *Arkansas Law Review* is a legal periodical published quarterly by the students of the School of Law in cooperation with the Arkansas Bar Association. Candidates for the *Review* are selected on the basis of scholarship and writing ability. Students in their second and third years are encouraged to compete in an intramural moot court competition, and Arkansas students participate in national moot court competitions. The University of Arkansas School of Law also participates in the ABA Law Student Division Client Counseling Competition. The law school operates a legal aid clinic providing counseling and representation for university students and indigent persons seeking legal assistance. An Arkansas Supreme Court Rule permits senior law students, upon certification and under supervision, to appear in court on a no-fee basis. The Student Bar Association sponsors a variety of academic and social activities. All students are also eligible for membership in the Law Student Division of the Arkansas Bar Association. Three of the largest national legal fraternities, Delta Theta Phi, Phi Alpha Delta, and Phi Delta Phi, maintain active chapters at the school. The Women's Law Student Association was organized to provide an opportunity for women to discuss and work with common professional interests and problems. Members of the Arkansas Chapter of Black Law Students Association work as a collective body to inform black students of the availability and advantages of a legal education, to promote the academic success of black law students at Arkansas, and to increase the awareness and commitment of the legal profession to the black community.

■ Expenses and Financial Aid

➽ *tuition & fees—full-time resident, $3,374; nonresident, $7,286*
➽ *scholarships available* ➽ *minority scholarships available*

Students are expected to make sufficient financial arrangements for the first year of study without the necessity of seeking employment. All law students are required to be full-time students. All financial aid in the form of Perkins Loans (formerly NDSL), higher education loans, and work-study grants is processed by the University of Arkansas Office of Student Financial Aid, University of Arkansas, Fayetteville, AR 72701. A limited number of law school-administered scholarships are available to entering students. Applications are distributed following fall registration in August.

■ Career Services

The law school maintains a Career Services Office with a full-time, highly qualified director and staff to assist and advise students and graduates. Services offered by the office include: on-campus interviews for permanent and summer employment; individual career counseling sessions; workshops and handbooks regarding résumé preparation, interviewing skills and techniques, and job searches; panels of lawyers who present programs on a variety of topics; a bi-monthly jobs bulletin; and, a comprehensive placement library. The office also maintains employment and salary statistics.

Applicant Group for the 1995-1996 Academic Year

University of Arkansas School of Law—Fayetteville
This grid includes only applicants who earned 120-180 LSAT scores under standard administrations.

	GPA																				
LSAT Score	3.75 +		3.50 - 3.74		3.25 - 3.49		3.00 - 3.24		2.75 - 2.99		2.50 - 2.74		2.25 - 2.49		2.00 - 2.24		Below 2.00		No GPA		Total	
	Apps	Adm	Apps	Adm	Apps	Adm	Apps	Adm	Apps	Adm	Apps	Adm	Apps	Adm	Apps	Adm	Apps	Adm	Apps	Adm	Apps	Adm
175 - 180	0	0	0	0	0	0	0	0	0	0	0	0	0	0	0	0	0	0	0	0	0	0
170 - 174	1	1	1	1	0	0	1	1	0	0	0	0	0	0	0	0	0	0	0	0	3	3
165 - 169	0	0	1	1	0	0	3	3	1	1	3	3	1	1	0	0	0	0	0	0	9	9
160 - 164	5	5	6	6	6	6	17	17	10	10	7	7	3	1	0	0	0	0	3	3	57	55
155 - 159	7	7	22	22	23	23	31	27	29	21	16	5	8	0	4	1	1	0	2	1	143	107
150 - 154	12	10	19	12	44	29	46	23	43	22	35	3	10	1	3	1	2	0	4	0	218	101
145 - 149	10	7	21	9	35	13	51	15	29	1	25	0	9	1	4	0	1	0	2	0	187	46
140 - 144	3	2	11	2	21	4	14	1	25	1	25	3	11	0	8	0	1	0	4	0	123	13
135 - 139	0	0	5	1	5	0	6	0	7	0	4	0	11	0	6	0	1	0	2	0	47	1
130 - 134	0	0	1	0	0	0	2	0	4	0	4	0	3	0	2	0	0	0	0	0	16	0
125 - 129	0	0	0	0	1	0	1	0	1	0	2	0	0	0	0	0	0	0	0	0	5	0
120 - 124	0	0	0	0	0	0	0	0	1	0	0	0	0	0	0	0	0	0	0	0	1	0
Total	38	32	87	54	135	75	172	87	150	56	121	21	56	4	27	2	6	0	17	4	809	335

Apps = Number of Applicants
Adm = Number Admitted
Reflects 98% of the total applicant pool.

University of Arkansas at Little Rock School of Law

1201 McAlmont St.
Little Rock, AR 72202-5142

Phone: 501.324.9439

■ Introduction

The School of Law is one of seven colleges and schools that form the University of Arkansas at Little Rock. The School of Law is located in the heart of metropolitan Little Rock, approximately six miles from the main campus of the university. The law school enrolls 428 students out of a total UALR enrollment of 11,035.

UALR is fully accredited by the North Central Association of Colleges and Schools. The law school is approved by the ABA and is a member of the AALS.

■ Enrollment/Student Body

➠ 576 applicants ➠ 262 admitted first-year class 1995 ➠ 128 enrolled first-year class 1995 ➠ 272 total full-time ➠ 156 total part-time ➠ 13.2% minority ➠ 44% women ➠ 19 states & foreign countries represented ➠ 102 undergraduate schools represented

■ Faculty

➠ 37 total ➠ 24 full-time ➠ 13 part-time or adjunct ➠ 12 women ➠ 5 minority

■ Library and Physical Facilities

➠ 240,000 volumes & equivalents ➠ 99 library hours/week ➠ LEXIS ➠ NEXIS ➠ WESTLAW ➠ DIALOG ➠ Lois & Case-Base ➠ 5 full-time librarians ➠ library seats 378

In August 1992, the School of Law moved to the new law center building. This 140,000-square-foot building is next to MacArthur Park, a 40-acre expanse of greenery, ponds, and gazebos. The five-story atrium library houses conference rooms, open and private carrels, and a reading room, as well as computer labs offering word processing, instructional software, legal research databases, and internet access.

■ Curriculum

➠ Academic Support Program ➠ 87 credits required to graduate ➠ 101 courses available ➠ degrees available: J.D.; J.D./M.B.A. ➠ semesters, start in Aug. ➠ range of first-year class size—27-83

The School of Law offers a program of legal education in both day and evening divisions. The day division operates a full-time program, with an average courseload per semester of 15 hours. A full-time student will normally complete the course of study in three years. The average courseload per semester in the part-time evening program is 10 hours; the maximum load is 11 hours. The part-time course of study is normally completed in four years. The first-year curriculum is prescribed.

■ Special Programs

The School of Law is noted for its practice skills programs in the upper years. All students are required to enroll in a course in trial advocacy conducted in the law school's trial courtroom. Additionally, students may enroll in other classroom courses with a clinical emphasis and participate in the school's legal clinic. An Arkansas Supreme Court Rule permits senior law students, upon certification and under supervision, to represent clients in civil and criminal cases. Students enrolled in the clinic represent indigent clients under the supervision of law school faculty members. The School of Law offers a joint J.D./M.B.A. degree with the UALR College of Business Administration.

■ Admission

➠ Bachelor's degree required ➠ application deadline—April 1 (strictly enforced) ➠ LSAT, LSDAS required ➠ median GPA—3.14 ➠ median LSAT score—152 ➠ application fee—$40 ➠ rolling admission, early application preferred

The School of Law enrolls 125 to 135 students each year. At least 80 percent of the entering students are Arkansas residents. The majority are selected on the basis of LSAT scores and undergraduate GPAs, while approximately 40 percent are selected by using additional criteria, such as letters of recommendation, work experience, graduate education, extracurricular activities, evidence of strong motivation and maturity, ethnicity disadvantages, underrepresentation of minorities in the legal profession, and diversity of backgrounds. Nonresident students are selected on the basis of LSAT scores and undergraduate GPAs.

A specific prelaw curriculum is not required. The School of Law subscribes to the comments found in the introduction to this handbook. Each applicant must hold a degree from an accredited college or university. Prospective applicants should contact the Admissions Office as early as possible for details about admission requirements. Students are enrolled only in the fall. Application for admission should be made as early as possible during the school year preceding the date of desired admission and must be completed by April 1 of the calendar year of desired admission.

■ Housing

UALR does not maintain student residence halls for law students; however, numerous private quarters are located within easy commuting distance of the law school.

■ Activities

Law students participate in the many activities generally available at larger law schools. The *UALR Law Journal*, a scholarly publication edited by students at the law school, publishes student notes and comments as well as articles by noted legal educators, judges, and practicing attorneys. A special feature is the Annual Survey of Arkansas Law. A number of prominent speakers are brought to the School of Law each year. The School of Law participates in the national trial advocacy competitions and several appellate moot court competitions. All students may become members of an active student bar association, and advanced students are eligible for membership in the Law Student Division of the Arkansas Bar Association. The Arkansas Bar Association and the School of Law were among the first such institutions in the country to establish this type of student-practitioner relationship. Membership is also available in the Law Student Division of the ABA. Students are represented on some faculty committees and are represented by elected students, who have a vote, at all general faculty meetings. The School of Law has many other student organizations, including the Black Law Students Association, Federalist Society, Community Outreach Opportunity League, Christian Legal Society, Environmental Law Society, and units of Phi Alpha Delta, Delta Theta Phi, and Phi Delta Phi legal fraternities.

■ Expenses and Financial Aid

➽ *full-time tuition—resident, $3,477.50/year; nonresident, $7,650/year* ➽ *part-time tuition—resident, $136/credit hour; nonresident, $308/credit hour* ➽ *average part-time tuition—resident, $3,178/year; nonresident, $6,962/year* ➽ *estimated additional expenses—$350/semester (books)* ➽ *scholarships available* ➽ *financial aid available* ➽ *application for Federal Student Aid due May 1*

A growing number of scholarships are available to second- and third-year students who demonstrate financial need and possess a strong academic record. The School of Law participates in the Federal Family Education Loan programs (subsidized and unsubsidized Stafford Loans) and Federal College Work-study programs. Short-term student loans are also available. The School of Law requires that applicants for financial aid complete the Free Application for Federal Student Aid, and applicants anticipating financial aid should complete this form. Requests for financial assistance should be addressed to Director of Student Financial Services, UALR, 2801 South University, Little Rock, AR 72204. Phone: 501.569.3130.

■ Career Services

The law school maintains an active Career Services Program within the Office of Student Services. The objectives are: (1) to assist students in defining and exploring career goals, (2) to increase students' awareness of effective job search strategies, and (3) to serve as the liaison between students and alumni and potential employers, allowing the opportunity for mutual consideration for employment opportunities. Career Services provides workshops on job search strategies, including networking, résumé writing, and interviewing preparation. The office also makes available current position openings, locally and statewide, as well as nationally and internationally; hosts employers for on-campus interviews and provides a résumé referral service to employers. Career Services also provides a number of resources, including WESTLAW and LEXIS access, allowing individuals to explore career possibilities and employment opportunities.

Applicant Group for the 1995-1996 Academic Year

University of Arkansas at Little Rock School of Law
This grid includes only applicants who earned 120-180 LSAT scores under standard administrations.

LSAT Score	GPA 3.75 +		3.50 - 3.74		3.25 - 3.49		3.00 - 3.24		2.75 - 2.99		2.50 - 2.74		2.25 - 2.49		2.00 - 2.24		Below 2.00		No GPA		Total	
	Apps	Adm	Apps	Adm	Apps	Adm	Apps	Adm	Apps	Adm	Apps	Adm	Apps	Adm	Apps	Adm	Apps	Adm	Apps	Adm	Apps	Adm
175 - 180	0	0	0	0	0	0	0	0	0	0	0	0	0	0	0	0	0	0	0	0	0	0
170 - 174	0	0	0	0	0	0	0	0	1	0	0	0	0	0	0	0	0	0	0	0	1	0
165 - 169	2	2	1	1	1	1	2	2	1	0	1	1	3	3	0	0	1	1	0	0	12	11
160 - 164	6	5	6	5	1	1	5	5	3	2	2	2	2	1	1	1	0	0	4	3	30	25
155 - 159	7	7	10	10	12	12	13	12	12	11	10	5	3	2	4	2	0	0	1	1	72	62
150 - 154	10	9	13	12	25	19	25	19	40	17	22	12	6	2	4	1	2	1	1	0	148	92
145 - 149	7	6	18	11	21	13	29	10	23	11	16	5	9	2	7	2	1	0	2	0	133	60
140 - 144	3	1	3	2	7	1	12	2	20	0	21	1	17	1	6	0	0	0	1	0	90	8
135 - 139	0	0	2	1	4	0	8	0	7	0	9	0	7	0	7	1	1	0	2	0	47	2
130 - 134	0	0	0	0	1	0	3	0	4	0	5	0	6	0	5	0	0	0	2	0	26	0
125 - 129	0	0	0	0	0	0	1	0	1	0	0	0	0	0	0	0	0	0	0	0	2	0
120 - 124	0	0	1	0	0	0	0	0	1	0	0	0	0	0	0	0	0	0	0	0	2	0
Total	35	30	54	42	72	47	98	50	113	41	86	26	53	11	34	7	5	2	13	4	563	260

Apps = Number of Applicants
Adm = Number Admitted
Reflects 97% of the total applicant pool.

University of Baltimore School of Law

1420 North Charles Street
Baltimore, MD 21201-5779

E-Mail: lwadmiss@ubmail.ubalt.edu
URL: http://www.ubalt.edu/www/law
Phone: 410.837.4459, Fax: 410.837.4450

■ Introduction

The University of Baltimore is one of eleven institutions in the University of Maryland System. It offers upper-division, graduate, and professional academic programs through the Yale Gordon College of Liberal Arts, the Robert G. Merrick School of Business, and the School of Law. Among its resources devoted to public interest research and analysis of contemporary issues are the Hoffberger Center for Professional Ethics, the Center for Business and Economic Studies, and the Schaefer Center for Public Policy. The School of Law is accredited by the American Bar Association and is a member of the Association of American Law Schools. It is located in Baltimore, near state and federal courts, the attractions of the Inner Harbor, and Oriole Park at Camden Yards.

■ Enrollment/Student Body

➽ 2,294 applicants ➽ 848 admitted first-year class 1995 ➽ 313 enrolled first-year class 1995 ➽ 184 total full-time in first year class 1995 ➽ 129 total part-time enrolled first-year class 1995 ➽ 13.1% minority ➽ 48% women ➽ 19 states & Washington, DC represented ➽ 121 undergraduate schools represented

■ Faculty

➽ 124 total ➽ 45 full-time ➽ 79 part-time ➽ 37 women ➽ 10 minority

■ Library and Physical Facilities

➽ 265,000 volumes & equivalents ➽ library hours: Mon.-Fri., 8:00 A.M.-MIDNIGHT; Sat. & Sun., 9:00 A.M.-MIDNIGHT ➽ LEXIS ➽ WESTLAW ➽ CARL (electronic card catalog servicing the University of Maryland library system as well as the university libraries of California, Colorado, and Hawaii) ➽ 18 staff members ➽ library seats 158

Ten dedicated terminals for computer-assisted legal research systems are available for use by law students and faculty, and library staff members provide training in the use of LEXIS and WESTLAW. In addition, the library's two computer labs are open to law students during library hours.

■ Curriculum

➽ Academic Support Program ➽ 90 credits required to graduate ➽ 105 courses available ➽ degrees available: J.D.; J.D./M.B.A.; J.D./M.P.A.; J.D./M.S. in Criminal Justice; LL.M. in Taxation; J.D./LL.M.; J.D./Ph.D. in Policy Sciences ➽ semesters, start in Aug.

■ Special Programs

Areas of Concentration—The School of Law has introduced an innovative curriculum designed to better prepare its students for the transition from law school to the practice of law and for law-related careers. This goal is achieved by starting with a range of traditional substantive and skills courses with special emphasis on analysis, writing, research, and advocacy skills. Upper-level students may combine other traditional substantive courses with courses required for recognition of a concentration in a particular field of law.

The option of earning recognition for a concentration will involve the student in a sequence of courses of increasing depth and will assist the student in developing more complex professional skills. Students are encouraged to take a variety of courses to prepare themselves to be capable practitioners, but they are also counseled and encouraged to obtain an in-depth knowledge of one or more of the following areas of concentration: Business Law, Criminal Practice, Environmental Law, Estate Planning, Family Law, General Practice, Intellectual Property, International and Comparative Law, Litigation and Advocacy, Public Interest Law, Real Estate Practice, and Theories of the Law.

Center for International and Comparative Law—promotes the study and understanding of international and comparative law and of the political and economic institutions that support the international legal order. The Center sponsors research, publication, teaching, and the dissemination of knowledge about international legal issues, with special emphasis on environmental law, human rights, intellectual property, and international business transactions.

Clinical and Advocacy Programs—Professional development is enhanced through clinics in which students represent individuals and organizations in litigation and transactional matters. These programs enable students to develop lawyering skills and professional responsibility in the context of live client practice. Clinical experiences include the Appellate Advocacy Clinic, Civil Practice Clinic, Environmental Justice Project, Criminal Practice Clinic, and Family Law Clinic.

■ Student Activities

Through participation in student organizations, law students explore specific fields of practice, enhance professional skills, enjoy social and athletic activities, and contribute to community projects. The Office of Student Affairs provides personal counseling and academic advising as well as coordinating accommodations for disabled students requesting assistance.

Law reviews, journals, and other periodicals give students an opportunity to hone their skills in research, analysis, and writing. The *University of Baltimore Law Review, The Journal of Environmental Law*, and *The Intellectual Property Law Journal* are scholarly publications offering in-depth analyses of relevant legal issues of current concern to practitioners and judges. *The Law Forum* specializes in articles that trace developing trends in the law.

■ Admission

➽ Baccalaureate degree required ➽ application deadline—April 1 ➽ rolling admission, complete files before April 1 advised ➽ LSAT required (score no more than 3 years old) ➽ LSDAS required ➽ median GPA—3.15 ➽ median LSAT score—153 ➽ application fee—$35

The School of Law has established an admission policy designed to obtain a diverse and well-qualified student body. In evaluating applicant files, the Admissions Committee places primary emphasis on the Law School Admission Test score and the cumulative undergraduate grade-point average; in most cases, a combination of these elements will be sufficient for the admission decision.

The committee also considers, in close cases, nontraditional factors that may be relevant in determining an applicant's ability to succeed in law school. It seeks to include persons of diverse racial, ethnic, and cultural backgrounds. It considers such factors as the difficulty of the undergraduate field of study, graduate degrees, and other indicators not susceptible to measurement by traditional academic criteria, such as demonstrated ability to overcome adversity, individual achievement, motivation, work experience, and character. Applicants should discuss fully in a personal statement any such factors they wish the committee to consider in evaluating their applications. Interviews are not part of the process; however, frequent group information sessions are scheduled throughout the year.

■ Expenses and Financial Aid

➽ full-time tuition & fees, per semester—in-state, $3,317; out-of-state, $5,812.50 ➽ part-time, per credit hour—in-state, $275; out-of-state, $455 ➽ additional expenses for fees at registration range between $200 and $425 each semester, depending on number of credits and division ➽ eligibility for limited scholarship aid based on merit and need

The Office of Financial Assistance administers federal, state, and institutional loan programs. First-year students and transfer students seeking financial assistance should apply for financial aid when they submit the application for admission, but no later than April 1 for the fall term.

■ Housing

The university's Student Activities Office assists in locating suitable accommodations near the university and offers a roommate referral service.

■ Career Services

The Career Services Center is dedicated to assisting law students in articulating, developing, and attaining their professional goals. The CRC provides career counseling, offers a broad array of programs and workshops, maintains an extensive resource library, and is online with both LEXIS and WESTLAW.

A survey of the 1994 graduating class discloses that 86 percent of those responding to the survey were employed within six months of graduation.

Applicant Group for the 1995-1996 Academic Year

University of Baltimore School of Law
This grid includes only applicants who earned 120-180 LSAT scores under standard administrations.

	GPA																					
LSAT Score	3.75 +		3.50 - 3.74		3.25 - 3.49		3.00 - 3.24		2.75 - 2.99		2.50 - 2.74		2.25 - 2.49		2.00 - 2.24		Below 2.00		No GPA		Total	
	Apps	Adm	Apps	Adm	Apps	Adm	Apps	Adm	Apps	Adm	Apps	Adm	Apps	Adm	Apps	Adm	Apps	Adm	Apps	Adm	Apps	Adm
175 - 180	0	0	1	1	1	1	0	0	0	0	0	0	0	0	0	0	0	0	0	0	2	2
170 - 174	0	0	1	1	0	0	1	1	0	0	0	0	0	0	0	0	0	0	0	0	2	2
165 - 169	0	0	0	0	3	3	3	3	5	5	4	1	2	0	1	1	0	0	0	0	18	13
160 - 164	4	4	15	15	16	16	29	28	28	26	24	16	13	4	3	2	1	0	1	1	134	112
155 - 159	15	13	38	38	85	80	78	73	69	50	62	21	23	4	8	0	3	1	2	0	383	280
150 - 154	20	19	64	58	109	69	125	73	124	46	72	17	49	10	17	1	2	0	5	1	587	294
145 - 149	13	8	37	18	76	21	112	23	116	12	82	8	53	3	15	2	4	0	5	0	513	95
Below 144	6	1	24	5	56	4	100	5	119	5	105	2	96	0	55	1	11	0	18	0	590	23
Total	58	45	180	136	346	194	448	206	461	144	349	65	236	21	99	7	21	1	31	2	2229	821

Apps = Number of Applicants
Adm = Number Admitted
Reflects approximately 98% of the total applicant pool.

Baylor University School of Law

P.O. Box 97288
Waco, TX 76798

E-Mail: law_support@baylor.edu
URL: http://www.baylor.edu/baylor/Departments/acad/law/Welcome.html
Phone: 800.BAYLOR.U. or 817.755.1911

■ Introduction

Baylor University School of Law is a private, ABA-approved law school and is a member of the American Association of Law Schools. Formally organized in 1857, Baylor Law School is the oldest law school in Texas. The School of Law is located on the campus of Baylor University in Waco. The Waco metropolitan area has nearly 200,000 residents and is located midway between Dallas and Austin.

Baylor Law School stands today at the forefront of practice-oriented law schools nationally. Consistent with Baylor's traditional mission of preparing students to be outstanding practicing attorneys, our academic program has been developed to achieve three basic objectives. First, our curriculum assists students in developing the intellectual and analytical skills necessary to practice law. Second, our curriculum exposes students to the fundamental legal doctrine and values necessary to function as competent and literate professionals, while also offering students an opportunity for more specialized study in areas of interest. Third, our curriculum offers all students skills training in advocacy (including both trial and appellate advocacy), planning, negotiating, counseling, legal writing, and legal research.

■ Enrollment/Student Body

➽ 746 applicants ➽ 257 admitted first-year class 1995
➽ 59 enrolled first-year class, fall 1995
➽ 399 total full-time ➽ 51 minority ➽ 148 women
➽ 29 states & foreign countries represented
➽ 130 undergraduate schools represented

■ Faculty

The strength of Baylor Law School is its faculty. Faculty members hold degrees from the finest law schools, colleges, and universities throughout the United States.

■ Library and Physical Facilities

➽ 160,940 volumes & equivalents ➽ LEXIS ➽ NEXIS ➽ WESTLAW ➽ DIALOG ➽ OCLC ➽ automated online card catalog ➽ 4 full-time librarians

The law school is located in the center of the university campus. The M.C. and Mattie Caston Law Library is designed to provide ample small rooms and areas for study. IBM compatibles and Macintosh computers are available in two of the library's computer rooms to serve student research and word processing.

■ Curriculum

➽ Academic Support Program ➽ 120 quarter hour credits required to graduate ➽ 84 courses available
➽ degrees available: J.D.; J.D./M.B.A.; J.D./M.Tax; and J.D./M.P.P.A. ➽ quarters, start in Aug., Nov., Feb., & May
➽ range of first-year class size—30-70
➽ 7 areas of concentration

Baylor Law School offers students the opportunity to obtain a concentrated course of study in one or more of seven areas of interest—general civil litigation, business litigation, business planning, criminal practice, estate planning, administrative practice, and health care law. Focused study builds upon the foundational theory and doctrine of the first two years and culminates in an experience that allows students to perform specialized lawyering tasks under the direct supervision of accomplished lawyers.

In conjunction with Baylor University's Hankamer School of Business, the law school offers two joint degrees—J.D./M.B.A. and J.D./M.Tax. Baylor Law School also offers a J.D./M.P.P.A. in conjunction with the Political Science department.

In recognition of the importance of writing skills, Baylor Law School has a Legal Analysis, Research, and Communication course that focuses on teaching students these skills. Throughout the first year of law school, students receive instruction from full-time professors who are experts in legal analysis and communication.

■ Individual Attention

Baylor Law School has a target student population of 410. This smaller size allows for all students to be active participants in class. There is room for each student to participate in extracurricular activities, including moot court, mock trial, negotiation, and client counseling competitions at the intraschool and interscholastic level. The legal research and writing program is designed to give students intensive, small-group instruction with generous feedback.

One of the distinctive features of the school is that professors maintain unrestricted hours for student consultation. They are actively involved in all intraschool and interscholastic competitions. Every professor is available for lending advice and guidance in all academic and other matters of concern to students.

■ Flexible Calendar

The school year at the law school is divided into four quarters. A full curriculum is offered during each quarter, enabling a student to graduate in as little as 27 months. After completing the first three quarters, a student generally may elect at any time during the year to take time off from their legal studies to pursue a clerkship, internship, or other program to allow the student to apply the principles and skills developed in school. Full-time study is required. Evening classes are not offered.

■ Admission

➽ three entering classes ➽ fall application deadline—March 1 ➽ spring application deadline—Nov. 1
➽ LSAT, LSDAS required ➽ median GPA—3.48
➽ median LSAT score, fall 1995—160
➽ application fee—$40 ➽ reapplication fee—$20
➽ summer application—Feb. 1 ➽ spring application—Nov. 1

The law school accepts beginning students for the fall, spring, or summer quarter. Prior to enrollment, a student must either have an undergraduate degree from an accredited college or university or 90 hours of theory work from an accredited college or university.

The law school considers such factors as the Law School Admission Test score, the undergraduate grade-point average, work experience, demonstrated leadership potential, cocurricular and extracurricular activities, academic performance trends, undergraduate major, caliber of undergraduate school, graduate school attendance and performance, racial and ethnic background, circumstances of particular disadvantage, and any other relevant information submitted by the applicant.

■ Student Activities

Each year, Baylor student teams enter several interscholastic mock trial, moot court, negotiation, and client counseling competitions. A number of regional and national championships have been won in recent years by the law school.

The *Baylor Law Review* gives outstanding students an opportunity to develop legal-writing ability. Baylor Law Review candidates are selected on the basis of academic performance or through a writing competition. The Student Bar Association, affiliated with the Law Student Division of the ABA, is the student government in the law school. Three national legal fraternities have active chapters at the law school and sponsor an array of activities. Other student organizations include the Environmental Law Society, the Civil Rights Society, the Christian Legal Society, the International Law Society, the Asian Society, the Black Law Student Association, the Hispanic National Bar Association Student Division, the Texas A & M Club, and the Women's Information Network.

■ Expenses and Financial Aid

➽ tuition & fees—$10,164 ➽ academic and merit scholarships available (ranging from amounts equal to 1/3 to full tuition) ➽ minority scholarships available (ranging from amounts equal to 1/3 to full tuition) ➽ financial aid available: Texas Tuition Equalization Grant, Perkins Loans, Baylor Revolving Loans, Stafford Loans, Law Access Loans, supplemental loans, and College Access Loans

Merit scholarships are available for entering students based upon their undergraduate GPA and LSAT results. Scholarship grants are awarded for the first three quarters in which a student is enrolled. Entering students eligible for academic merit scholarships will be notified in their acceptance letter of the amount of the scholarship being awarded. No action by the student is necessary for first-year scholarships.

■ Career Services

The law school's Career Services Office is directed by an attorney and acts as a liaison between employers and law students. In addition, the facilities of the University Career Services Office are available to law students. Employment interviews are conducted by prospective employers throughout the year, although most interviewing takes place during the fall. Law firms, corporations, courts, and other employers normally visit the law school each year for the purpose of hiring both full-time associate positions and law clerkships or other temporary employment.

Applicant Group for the 1995-1996 Academic Year

Baylor University School of Law
This grid includes only applicants who earned 120-180 LSAT scores under standard administrations.

GPA

LSAT Score	3.75 +		3.50 - 3.74		3.25 - 3.49		3.00 - 3.24		2.75 - 2.99		2.50 - 2.74		2.25 - 2.49		2.00 - 2.24		Below 2.00		No GPA		Total	
	Apps	Adm	Apps	Adm	Apps	Adm	Apps	Adm	Apps	Adm	Apps	Adm	Apps	Adm	Apps	Adm	Apps	Adm	Apps	Adm	Apps	Adm
175 - 180	0	0	0	0	0	0	0	0	0	0	0	0	0	0	0	0	0	0	0	0	0	0
170 - 174	3	3	2	2	0	0	0	0	3	3	0	0	1	1	0	0	0	0	0	0	9	9
165 - 169	7	7	9	9	9	9	7	7	5	5	2	2	1	1	0	0	0	0	0	0	40	40
160 - 164	12	12	35	33	31	31	21	20	14	13	4	3	3	0	0	0	0	0	0	0	120	112
155 - 159	30	29	66	63	64	34	44	22	24	7	15	3	7	0	2	0	1	0	2	1	255	159
150 - 154	25	19	57	34	49	9	58	10	41	3	21	1	15	0	1	0	0	0	2	0	269	76
145 - 149	7	2	16	3	32	1	31	1	33	1	17	1	8	0	1	0	0	0	1	0	146	9
140 - 144	3	0	4	0	15	0	15	0	15	0	13	0	10	0	3	0	3	0	0	0	81	0
135 - 139	1	0	2	0	2	0	6	0	4	0	10	0	6	0	3	0	3	0	0	0	37	0
130 - 134	1	0	0	0	2	0	1	0	2	0	2	0	2	0	0	0	0	0	0	0	10	0
125 - 129	0	0	0	0	0	0	0	0	1	0	0	0	1	0	0	0	0	0	0	0	2	0
120 - 124	0	0	0	0	0	0	0	0	0	0	0	0	0	0	0	0	0	0	0	0	0	0
Total	89	72	191	144	204	84	183	60	142	32	84	10	54	2	10	0	7	0	5	1	969	405

Apps = Number of Applicants
Adm = Number Admitted
This grid reflects 92% of Baylor Law School's total application pool. This grid also reflects each of Baylor's three entering classes. Not reflected on this grid are applicants who applied for admission to more than one quarter during the 94-95 application year.

Boston College Law School

Office of Admissions
885 Centre Street
Newton, MA 02159

URL: http://www.bc.edu/bc_org/avp/law/lwsch/Index.html
Phone: 617.552.4350

■ Introduction

Since its founding in 1929, Boston College Law School has earned a national reputation for educational excellence and the highest standards of professionalism while fostering a unique spirit of community among its students, faculty, and staff. The diverse curriculum is designed to help students develop the skills and knowledge needed to adapt successfully to changes in society and the legal profession. Boston College Law School is located on an attractive 40-acre campus in Newton, Massachusetts, just minutes from downtown Boston. It is fully accredited by both the American Bar Association and the Association of American Law Schools, and has a chapter of Order of the Coif, the prestigious national law school honorary society.

■ Enrollment/Student Body

➽ 6,077 applicants ➽ 1,126 admitted first-year class 1995 ➽ 280 enrolled first-year class 1995 ➽ 17.6% minority ➽ 46% women ➽ 40 states & foreign countries represented ➽ 200 undergraduate schools represented

■ Faculty

➽ 111 total ➽ 57 full-time ➽ 54 part-time or adjunct ➽ 21 women ➽ 9 minority

■ Library and Physical Facilities

➽ 340,000 volumes & equivalents ➽ library hours: Mon.-Thurs., 8:00 A.M.-MIDNIGHT; Fri., 8:00 A.M.-11:00 P.M.; Sat., 9:00 A.M.-10:00 P.M.; Sun., 10:00 A.M.-MIDNIGHT
➽ LEXIS ➽ NEXIS ➽ WESTLAW ➽ DIALOG
➽ 10 full-time librarians ➽ library seats 550
➽ member, New England Law Library Consortium

All academic, administrative, library and service facilities, including a new library facility which opened in January 1996, are accessible to disabled persons.

■ Curriculum

➽ Academic Support Program ➽ 85 credits required to graduate ➽ 110 courses available
➽ degrees available: J.D.; J.D./M.B.A.; J.D./M.S.W.
➽ semesters, start in the fall
➽ range of first-year class size—30-145
➽ semester abroad at the University of London

The faculty of Boston College Law School strongly believes in the importance of a general legal education designed to enable graduates to adapt to the changing demands of law practice. Areas of particular focus include constitutional law, business law, dispute resolution, environmental law, family law, international law, sports and entertainment law, and clinical programs.

In the first year, all students take traditional courses including Civil Procedure, Constitutional Law, Contracts, Property and Torts, as well as Legal Research and Writing and an innovative skills course titled Introduction to Lawyering and Professional Responsibility. More than 100 courses offered in the second and third years are elective.

■ Clinical Courses

The Law School is committed to making clinical experiences available to all students who desire them. Present clinical programs offer a variety of subject matter and experiential opportunity. The **Urban Legal Laboratory** is an externship program of individually designed placements with judges, government agencies, public-interest organizations, and law firms in the greater Boston area. At the **Boston College Legal Assistance Bureau** (LAB), students assume responsibility for representation of indigent clients in civil cases.

Criminal Process offers the opportunity to prosecute or defend criminal cases in state court. The **Attorney General Law Clinic** provides a placement in the Massachusetts Attorney General's office and the **Judicial Process** course includes clinical placement with a specific Superior Court justice.

■ Student Activities

Selected students may participate in the following writing programs: *Boston College Law Review; Boston College Environmental Affairs Law Review; Boston College International and Comparative Law Review; Boston College Third World Law Journal*; and the *Uniform Commercial Code Reporter-Digest*.

Boston College Law School supports several annual competitions that help students develop writing, courtroom-advocacy, and client-counseling skills. Over the years, Boston College has performed extremely well in the regional and national competitions, which are judged by faculty, state and federal judges, and practicing attorneys.

The Law School also has a number of student groups reflecting both personal and professional concerns.

■ Admission

➽ Bachelor's degree from accredited college or university required ➽ application deadline—March 1
➽ LSAT, LSDAS required ➽ application fee—$50
➽ rolling admission
➽ median GPA (admitted students)—3.55
➽ median LSAT score (admitted students)—165

The Law School has no minimum cutoff either for GPA or LSAT. Academic achievement and LSAT scores are extremely significant, but work and professional experience, college extracurricular activities, the quality of recommendations, and the personal statement also play an important role in decision making.

In evaluating GPA, class rank as well as courses taken are considered. If the LSAT has been taken more than once, scores are averaged unless a compelling reason is presented for considering a particular score. Less weight is given to the LSAT if the applicant has a history of poor standardized testing.

The personal statement is reviewed with the objective of finding diverse, well-rounded individuals. When an applicant is accepted, a tuition deposit is required, the details of which accompany the acceptance letter.

■ Minorities and Affirmative Action

Boston College Law School strongly encourages applications from qualified minority, disabled, or other students who have been socially, economically, or culturally disadvantaged. Each applicant is evaluated in an effort to ensure that all relevant credentials are favorably considered. The Law School has been very successful both in admitting minority and special students, and in retaining them to graduation. Both academic support and minority student mentor programs are available.

■ Expenses and Financial Aid

➽ *full-time tuition & fees—$20,180* ➽ *estimated additional expenses—$11,000 (room, board, books, health insurance)*
➽ *need-based financial aid available*
➽ *FAFSA and Needs Access forms required*

All financial aid is processed through the university's Office of Financial Aid and the Law School Admissions Office. The Financial Aid Office administers federal and private loan programs, the College Work-Study program, and the major Presidential and Law School Scholarship programs. The Law School has also developed a Public Interest Loan Assistance program providing financial assistance to graduates taking lower-paying positions in government, nonprofit corporations, and legal services programs.

All applicants wishing to be considered for financial aid must submit the processed FAFSA (Free Application for Federal Student Aid) and the Needs Access form to the Boston College Office of Financial Aid, Lyons Hall 201, Chestnut Hill, MA 02167 by March 1.

■ Housing

Housing assistance is provided through the university's Office of Off-Campus Housing. Applicants seeking resident assistantships should write the University Housing Office, Boston College, Chestnut Hill, MA 02167.

■ Career Services

The Office of Career Services is dedicated to helping students make the transition from law student to employed professional. Both students and alumni may avail themselves of a wide range of career planning services.

The range of opportunities for graduates spans virtually the entire spectrum of legal practice. Each year more than 1,000 prospective employers solicit applications from Boston College law students. In 1994-95, government agencies, corporations, and public-interest organizations from 27 states visited the campus. Approximately 90 percent of graduates are employed either prior to or within several months of graduation. The nearly 8,600 alumni are presently practicing in 48 states and a number of foreign countries.

Applicant Group for the 1995-1996 Academic Year

Boston College Law School
This grid includes only applicants who earned 120-180 LSAT scores under standard administrations.

	GPA															
LSAT Score	3.75 +		3.50 - 3.74		3.25 - 3.49		3.00 - 3.24		2.75 - 2.99		Below 2.75		No GPA		Total	
175 - 180	3	2	5	5	5	5	6	3	2	0	2	1	0	0	23	16
170 - 174	19	18	33	28	53	40	20	8	13	6	6	1	2	2	146	103
165 - 169	79	76	173	155	180	116	108	30	43	12	30	8	5	3	618	400
160 - 164	175	110	408	207	446	108	234	25	91	11	53	5	15	5	1422	471
150 - 159	209	29	530	41	559	24	436	26	237	10	147	7	16	2	2149	139
140 - 149	41	2	111	9	192	7	205	7	166	2	149	5	9	0	888	32
Below 140	3	0	14	0	16	0	34	0	30	0	71	0	8	0	127	0
Total	529	237	1274	445	1451	300	1043	99	583	41	458	27	87	12	5425	1161

Apps = Number of Applicants
Adm = Number Admitted
Reflects 99% of the total applicant pool.

Boston University School of Law

765 Commonwealth Avenue
Boston, MA 02215

Phone: 617.353.3100

■ Introduction

Located in Boston, Massachusetts, overlooking a beautiful stretch of the Charles River, Boston University School of Law boasts a 125-year history of outstanding legal education. The school is committed to giving its students the broadest possible exposure to the practice and theory of law. Students graduate with a deep understanding of legal rules and principles, enriched by insights from related disciplines such as economics, philosophy, and history, and with strong analytical and practical skills that lay the foundation for a challenging and satisfying legal career. Boston University School of Law is located in one of the country's most vital intellectual and cultural centers. As a result, the school offers students a wide range of opportunities both inside and outside of class that make for a memorable law school experience.

■ Enrollment/Student Body

➧ 4,700 applicants ➧ 1,694 admitted first-year class 1995 ➧ 371 enrolled first-year class 1995 ➧ 1,101 total full-time ➧ 21% minority ➧ 47% women ➧ 61 states & foreign countries represented ➧ 279 undergraduate schools represented

■ Faculty

➧ 135 total ➧ 57 full-time ➧ 78 part-time or adjunct ➧ 40 women ➧ 11 minority

■ Library and Physical Facilities

➧ 500,000 volumes & equivalents ➧ library hours: Mon.-Thurs., 8:00 A.M.-11:30 P.M.; Fri., 8:00 A.M.-10:00 P.M.; Sat., 9:00 A.M.-9:00 P.M.; Sun., 10:00 A.M.-11:30 P.M. ➧ LEXIS ➧ NEXIS ➧ WESTLAW ➧ DIALOG ➧ 10 full-time librarians ➧ library seats 830

■ Curriculum

➧ Academic Support Program ➧ 84 credits required to graduate ➧ 172 courses available ➧ degrees available: J.D.; J.D./M.B.A. (Law & Management & Health Care Management); J.D./M.P.H.; J.D./M.S. (Law & Mass Communications); J.D./M.A. (Law & Preservation Studies; International Relations); LL.M. (American Banking Law, International Banking Law, Taxation, American Law) ➧ semesters, start in Aug. or early Sept. ➧ range of first-year class size—90-97

During the first week, minority and first-year orientations introduce law students to the study of law. Most of the first-year curriculum is required. Constitutional Law is required in the second year. In the second and third years, the school offers a wide variety of courses and seminars in advanced areas. Legal ethics is taught throughout the curriculum and in a special intensive program.

Concentrations are available in Business Organizations and Finance Law, Environmental Law, Health Care Law, and Intellectual Property.

■ Law, Technology, and Innovation

Situated in an important high-technology area, the school offers a rich array of courses in the rapidly growing area of law, technology, and innovation, including offerings in patent law, copyright, trademark, computer law, communication law, art law, entertainment law, and environmental regulation and toxic torts. In addition, the school offers concentration in intellectual property and a dual J.D./M.S. degree in Mass Communication, and houses the Center for Law and Technology, which explores the frontier of current technology issues.

■ Health Law

Home of the Center for Law and Health Sciences and the American Society of Law and Medicine, the school is well-known for its strong health law curriculum, distinguished health law faculty, a concentration in health care law and two health-related dual degree programs. The school's extremely broad selection of courses, together with health-related offerings in the School of Public Health, comprise one of the most comprehensive health law curricula in the country. In addition, those students who qualify have an opportunity during their second and third years to work for the internationally prestigious *American Journal of Law and Medicine.*

■ International Law, Environmental Law, and Clinical Programs

The School of Law also has special strengths in international and environmental law. The school offers a strong, and rapidly expanding, curriculum in each of these two areas, study abroad programs with Université Jean Moulin in Lyon, France, Oxford University, England, and Tel Aviv University, Israel as well as a dual J.D./M.A. degree in International Relations.

The school is known for some of the finest clinical offerings in the country. The student can choose from among nine different programs covering practice in the civil, criminal, and alternative dispute resolution areas. With ties to Greater Boston Legal Services and other organizations, these programs offer actual practice experience under the close supervision of a dedicated and highly accomplished group of full-time clinical faculty.

■ Admission

➧ Bachelor's degree required for admission ➧ application deadline—March 1 ➧ LSAT, LSDAS required ➧ median GPA—3.44 ➧ median LSAT score—162 ➧ application fee—$50

The Admissions Committee places primary emphasis on an applicant's cumulative undergraduate grade-point average and score on the LSAT. The committee also takes into account other factors, such as marked and sustained improvement in undergraduate grades, outstanding leadership ability, significant postgraduate experience, and motivation for law study. Letters of recommendation also can be very important.

■ Student Activities

Approximately one-third of upper-division students have an opportunity for professional writing experience by participating in one of six law journals. These include: *Boston University Law Review, Annual Review of Banking Law*, the *American Journal of Law and Medicine, Boston University International Law Journal*, the *Public Interest Law Journal*, and *Probate Law Journal*.

The School of Law also encourages students to become active in student organizations. Reflecting our students' diverse interests and backgrounds, there are a number of active student organizations, including: The American Bar Association/Law Student Division; the Asian American Law Students Association; American Inns of Court; the Black Law Students Association; the Battered Women's Advocacy Project; the Civil Liberties Union; the Communication, Entertainment, and Sports Law Society; the Environmental Law Society; the Film Society; the Gay, Lesbian, and Bisexual Caucus; the Hispanic American Law Students Association; the International Law Society; the Japanese Law Society; the Jewish Law Students Association; Law and Business Society; Legal Follies; the Married Law Students Association; Phi Alpha Delta Legal Fraternity; Public Interest Project; South Asian Law Students Association; Student Bar Association; SBA Yearbook; the Technology, Engineering, and Science Law Association; Voice for Choice; and Women's Law Association, as well as various sports clubs.

Upper-class students may participate in the intramural appellate moot court competition. Teams also compete in the National Moot Court, National Appellate Advocacy, Jessup International Law, Benton Information and Privacy Law, Wagner Labor Law, and Kaufman Securities Law moot court competitions.

■ Expenses and Financial Aid

➧ *tuition & fees—$19,676* ➧ *estimated additional expenses—$11,840* ➧ *tuition grants available, primarily need-based* ➧ *minority scholarships: Martin Luther King Fellowships include tuition, fees, living expenses* ➧ *financial aid available; Profile, FAFSA & school of law financial aid application due April 1, parental data required on all forms*

■ Career Services

The Office of Career Planning and Placement actively assists students and alumni/ae in securing employment. Each year more than 500 law firms, government agencies, public interest organizations, and corporations from all regions of the United States recruit law students for summer and permanent positions through visiting, nonvisiting, off-campus, and Massachusetts Law School Consortium recruitment programs. The office maintains a comprehensive career resource library, provides career counseling and job listings, and sponsors career panels and interview workshops.

Over the past three years, approximately 86 percent of graduates reporting employment have secured positions or enrolled in an advanced-degree program within six to nine months of graduation. First-year and second-year law students have been similarly successful in securing summer employment.

Applicant Group for the 1995-1996 Academic Year

Boston University School of Law
This grid includes only applicants who earned 120-180 LSAT scores under standard administrations.

LSAT Score	3.75 +		3.50 - 3.74		3.25 - 3.49		3.00 - 3.24		2.75 - 2.99		2.50 - 2.74		2.25 - 2.49		2.00 - 2.24		Below 2.00		Total	
	Apps	Adm	Apps	Adm	Apps	Adm	Apps	Adm	Apps	Adm	Apps	Adm	Apps	Adm	Apps	Adm	Apps	Adm	Apps	Adm
175 - 180	3	3	0	0	1	0	2	2	2	2	1	1	0	0	0	0	0	0	9	8
169 - 174	12	11	24	23	27	27	19	17	14	13	4	3	4	2	0	0	0	0	104	96
163 - 168	60	59	124	121	173	167	141	136	74	69	25	16	11	4	3	1	1	1	612	574
157 - 162	125	116	345	296	410	259	291	100	140	32	55	6	21	2	6	0	2	0	1395	811
151 - 156	96	38	243	21	337	40	300	22	168	7	64	2	35	1	6	0	0	0	1249	131
145 - 150	28	6	101	6	156	5	170	5	130	6	53	1	27	0	18	0	2	0	685	29
139 - 144	11	1	36	1	54	0	86	0	68	0	48	0	21	1	9	0	2	0	335	3
133 - 138	0	0	5	0	5	0	21	0	15	0	16	0	11	0	9	0	1	0	83	0
127 - 132	1	0	0	0	1	0	4	0	5	0	3	0	3	0	1	0	1	0	19	0
120 - 126	0	0	0	0	0	0	0	0	0	0	0	0	0	0	0	0	1	0	1	0
Total	336	234	878	468	1164	498	1034	282	616	129	269	29	133	10	52	1	10	1	4492	1652

GPA column groups as above.

Apps = Number of Applicants
Adm = Number Admitted
Reflects 98% of the total applicant pool.

Brigham Young University—J. Reuben Clark Law School

340 JRCB
Box 28000
Provo, UT 84602-8000

E-Mail: wilcockl@lawgate.byu.edu
URL: http://wwwlaw.byu.edu
Phone: 801.378.4277

■ Introduction

Brigham Young University, J. Reuben Clark Law School, located in Provo, Utah (about 50 miles south of Salt Lake City), is an integral part of the largest private university in the United States on the basis of full-time student enrollment. Brigham Young University is sponsored by The Church of Jesus Christ of Latter-day Saints (Mormon Church) and has a present enrollment of 27,000 students from all 50 states and more than 70 foreign countries. The Law School is fully accredited by the American Bar Association and is a member of the Association of American Law Schools.

■ Enrollment/Student Body

➽ 718 applicants ➽ 236 admitted first-year class 1995 ➽ 140 enrolled first-year class 1995 ➽ 468 total full-time ➽ 14% minority ➽ 30% women ➽ 42 states & foreign countries represented ➽ 71 undergraduate schools represented

■ Faculty

➽ 59 total ➽ 33 full-time ➽ 26 part-time or adjunct ➽ 10 women ➽ 3 minority

■ Library and Physical Facilities

➽ 380,000 volumes & equivalents ➽ library hours: Mon.-Fri., 7:30 A.M.-9:30 P.M.; Sat., 8:00 A.M.-11:00 P.M. ➽ LEXIS ➽ NEXIS ➽ WESTLAW ➽ RLIN ➽ Nortis ➽ 8 full-time librarians ➽ library seats 550

The law building is designed to accommodate 500 students. By August 1, 1996 an addition of 39,000-square-feet will be added to the library. In addition to the law library facilities, the law building contains nine classrooms, three seminar rooms, rooms for group study, a four room interviewing complex, a television studio, a student commons area, and ample space for student organizations and activities.

The law library provides public access by computer terminal to over 150 other institutions' card catalogs on the Research Library Information Network (RLIN) and is equipped with both WESTLAW and LEXIS, computer-assisted legal research databases, which are available for student access. There are personal computers and related printers located in the library that are exclusively for student use. The personal computers are interfaced with the Law School's main computer and are capable of the full range of computer applications from word processing to legal research and data management.

■ Curriculum

➽ Academic Support Program ➽ Tutorials; Legal Writing Class ➽ 90 credits required to graduate ➽ 98 courses available ➽ degrees available: J.D.; J.D./M.B.A.; J.D./M.P.A.; J.D./M.A.C.C.; J.D./Ed.D.; J.D./M.O.B.

The Law School is operated on a semester basis. The fall semester runs from approximately the third week in August until the third week of December. Winter semester begins the first week in January and runs until the fourth week in April. The first-year course of study is prescribed and consists of approximately 15 hours per semester. A broad selection of elective courses and seminars is available in the second and third years. The law school offers a tutorial program for all students at no cost.

■ Special Programs

The Law School, in combination with the graduate school of the university, offers joint J.D./M.B.A., Master of Public Administration, Master of Accountancy, and Master of Organizational Behavior degrees. The Law School provides clinical opportunities for students by means of well-developed simulated clinical programs in both civil and criminal matters and by extensive pro bono and externship experience with government and other not-for-profit agencies. A number of innovative curricular and cocurricular programs are being used by the faculty and students: Family Law Society, Natural Resources Law Forum, Government and Politics Legal Society, the International and Comparative Law Society, Negotiations Forum, and American Trial Lawyers Association

■ Admission

➽ Bachelor's degree required ➽ application deadline—Feb. 15 ➽ LSAT, LSDAS required ➽ median GPA—3.60 ➽ median LSAT score—160 ➽ application fee—$30

Students are admitted only in the fall semester and only for full-time study. Applications, which are processed on the basis of college work completed to date, may be made at any time after the beginning of the fall semester of the year preceding admission. College grades and the LSAT score are significant but not exclusive determinants of admissibility. The required written recommendations and personal statement are of significant influence.

■ Student Activities

Law schools have traditionally offered important additional training to a limited number of students through participation on a law review. The objective of the cocurricular programs offered at the J. Reuben Clark Law School is to make law review-quality experience available to a much larger number of students by extending its principles to more categories of activity. Comparable standards of excellence in research, writing, and editing are presently offered in four activities: *Journal of Public Law*, Board of Advocates, *Brigham Young University Education and Law Journal*, and the *Brigham Young University Law Review*.

■ Expenses and Financial Aid

➽ *tuition & fees—full-time, $4,600 and $6,900; part-time, $255 per semester hour* ➽ *estimated additional expenses—$9,300 (room & board, textbooks and supplies, personal expenses, transportation)* ➽ *scholarships available* ➽ *merit- and need-based minority scholarships available* ➽ *financial aid available: Federal Student Financial Aid, within 30 days of acceptance to the BYU Law School*

■ Career Services

Placement is regarded by the faculty as a matter of highest priority. A full-time law career services director, a full-time assistant, a full-time secretary, and one part-time employee are assigned to work with students and alumni in finding permanent and part-time employment in the legal profession and summer clerkships. Over 50 law firms, government offices, and businesses recruit regularly at the law school while over 100 other employers work closely with the Career Services Office in arranging field interviews. Types of employment by the 1994 graduating class include private practice (55 percent), business (15 percent), government including judicial clerkships (23 percent), and other areas (7 percent). Job locations include Intermountain West (62 percent); East, South, and Midwest (6 percent); Pacific Coast and Hawaii (22 percent).

Applicant Group for the 1995-1996 Academic Year

Brigham Young University—J. Reuben Clark Law School

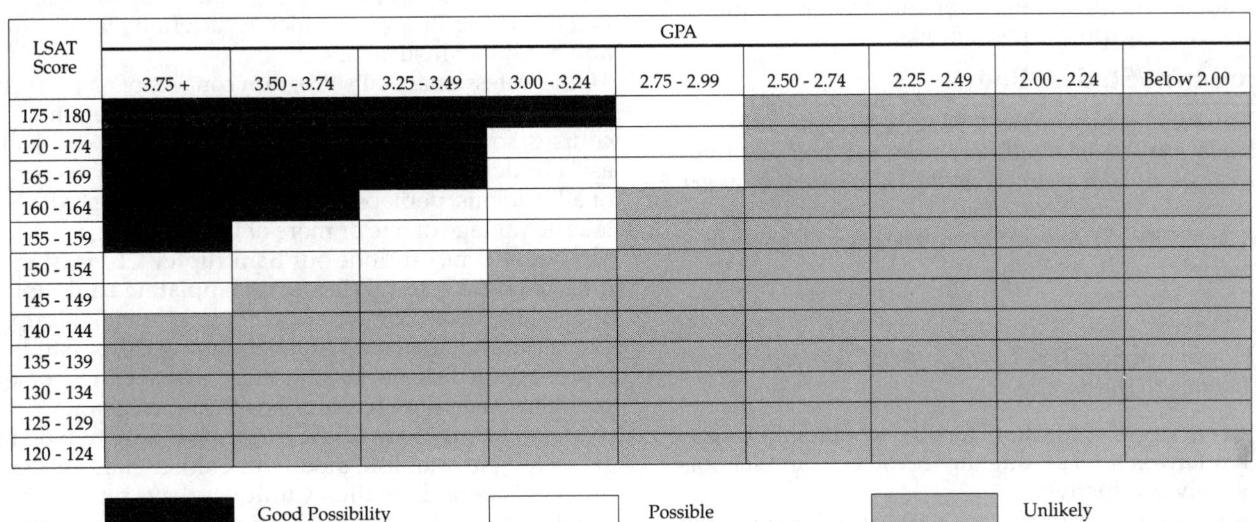

Brooklyn Law School

250 Joralemon Street
Brooklyn, NY 11201

Phone: 718.780.7906

■ An Environment for Learning

Brooklyn Law School, a private, independent institution established in 1901, is flanked by the Brooklyn Heights Historic District and the Brooklyn Civic Center. Built up with grand mansions, stately rowhouses, diminutive carriage houses, and handsome educational and religious institutions, the Heights reflects what our city was like at the turn of the century. Lush gardens and almost-secret mews and tree-lined back streets make the Heights one of the most tranquil and beautiful neighborhoods of New York City. The school itself looks out over the U.S. District Court, the New York State Appellate Division Court, the State Supreme and Family Courts, and the City Civil and Criminal Courts. Within easy walking distance are the U.S. Attorney's Office, Kings County District Attorney's Office, Legal Aid Society, and numerous city, state, and federal governmental agencies. Just a few minutes away are Wall Street and its array of financial, legal, and corporate institutions.

■ Enrollment/Student Body

➠ *467 enrolled first-year class 1995 (278 full-time, 189 part-time)* ➠ *986 total full-time* ➠ *465 total part-time* ➠ *18.8% minority (first-year)* ➠ *44.2% women (first-year)* ➠ *22 states, the District of Columbia, & 15 foreign countries represented* ➠ *171 colleges and universities represented* ➠ *56 majors*

■ Faculty

➠ *65 full-time, almost 37% female* ➠ *87 part-time* ➠ *21/1 student/faculty ratio*

A recent survey of law school faculty scholarship ranked Brooklyn Law School among the top 50 U.S. law schools for scholarly productivity.

Recently, two of our professors were appointed by the American Law Institute, one to serve as Reporter for the Restatement of the Law of Suretyship, the other as Co-Reporter for the Restatement of the Law of Torts (Third): Products Liability; they are among the very few faculty members from outside the ranks of the most highly rated national law schools to be so honored. Yet another professor has been named Reporter to the Advisory Committee on Federal Rules of Evidence.

■ Library and Physical Facilities

➠ *over 450,000 volumes & equivalents* ➠ *over 1,000 periodicals* ➠ *LEXIS* ➠ *NEXIS* ➠ *WESTLAW* ➠ *DIALOG* ➠ *10 full-time librarians* ➠ *library seats 650 (approximately)*

Fall 1993 saw the opening of an 85,000-square-foot addition to our main building, enough room for a 50 percent expansion of our library, including 3 reading rooms, 25 study rooms, 6 conference rooms, 2 computer research centers, a computer training/word processing center, and wired carrels and tables to accommodate laptop computers. Also housed in the building are multi-use classrooms wired for computer-assisted instruction, a new student center and dining hall, a conference/reception center, and increased space for faculty and student organization offices.

■ Curriculum

➠ *nearly 150 electives in 10 clusters, including criminal law, litigation, economic regulation, international law, and public interest law* ➠ *6 joint-degree programs* ➠ *range of first-year class size—15-125*

The core of the first-year curriculum is a Seminar Section Program that provides groups of 30-32 day students with a small-class experience in a substantive, required course during the first semester. This allows professors to depart from the standard lecture/Socratic dialogue format and to build a substantial skills training component into the course. This program is augmented by our first-year Legal Writing Program, which is taught by 9 full-time and 8 adjunct instructors.

Our Professional Skills Program consists of an extensive array of in-house and extern clinics and simulation courses; so much so that in a recent article we were hailed as "a leader in the field." By graduation, nearly 60 percent of all students, perhaps 75 percent of full-time students, take advantage of one or more of these offerings.

In-house clinics include our **Bankruptcy Clinic** (students interview and counsel clients contemplating bankruptcy and, where necessary, represent the debtor in Bankruptcy Court through final discharge); **Elderlaw Clinic** (students represent aged clients in connection with a variety of legal problems, including benefits, health and consumer matters); **Family Law Clinic** (students represent individuals seeking to establish, modify, or enforce child support orders); **Federal Litigation Clinic** (students represent clients in federal court); **Legislation and Law Reform** (students research, develop, and implement legislative initiatives for the New York State Law Division Committee); **Post Conviction Advocacy Clinic** (offering students the opportunity to work on a variety of criminal cases at the post-conviction stage); and **Prosecutor's Clinic** (students prosecute misdemeanor cases in Brooklyn Criminal Court).

Extern clinics include **Civil Practice** (students assigned to assist attorneys in a variety of settings in federal, state, and city agencies—past placements include the S.E.C., U.S. Attorneys Office for both the Southern and Eastern District, and the New York State Attorney General's Office, as well as Legal Aid Society and Legal Services offices); **Criminal Practice** (students work in the office of either of the U.S. Attorneys, one of the District Attorneys, Victim Services Agency, or the Legal Aid Society); **Mediation Clinic** (the conceptual framework, range of application and normative constraints on nonjudicial processes—negotiation, mediation, and arbitration) and **Judicial Clerkship Clinic** which, in the past three years, has averaged 140 placements annually, including (again an average) 45 at the Federal level. Seven **simulation courses** focus on discrete skills or on the application of certain skills to a particular area of practice, all in the context of prepared problems and case files.

■ Admission

➻ average applicant volume 1993-95—3,815 ➻ average admittance rate 1993-95—34% ➻ Bachelor's degree required ➻ fall semester admission for entering class ➻ no application deadline; rolling admission favors early filing ➻ LSAT, LSDAS required ➻ application fee—$50 ➻ median full-time LSAT/GPA (1993-95)—158/3.31

■ Housing

Brooklyn Law School has six residence halls in historic Brooklyn Heights, offering affordable housing just a few blocks from the Law School for a limited number of students.

■ Career Center

With five attorney-counselors comprising one of the largest placement offices in the New York metropolitan area, the Career Center is able to offer unusually comprehensive services to students and alumni. The Center emphasizes individualized counseling, including assistance with résumé/cover letter writing, interviewing skills, networking techniques, as well as career planning generally. The professional staff believes that maximizing the marketability of the School's students/graduates through an emphasis on job search skills and realistic career strategies is the linchpin of a successful placement program. Individual counseling is supplemented with skills workshops and panel discussions. An active public service program, encompassing both traditional public interest as well as government service, is led by an attorney-counselor with several years of public interest practice. Of equal priority is an aggressive job development program supplementing a substantial on-campus interviewing program and computerized job listing service. Employment rates have been very high. The average employment rate (six months after graduation) for the classes of 1990-94 was 87 percent.

■ Special Programs

The school's **Center for the Study of International Business Law** trains lawyers to function in a global environment, shaping international law and business policy. Our curriculum offers over 20 courses in the business law field, several of which focus on international and comparative law. The center sponsors a Fellowship Program and, with the cosponsorship of Queen Mary & Westfield College of the University of London, biennially hosts a symposium in London and New York on international business issues.

In 1985, Brooklyn Law School established the **Edward V. Sparer Public Interest Fellowship Program** which has provided substantial stipends to students who have served as legal interns in nearly 70 public interest law offices nationwide. It also sponsors forums that bring prominent scholars, lawyers, and public policy advocates to the school to discuss current issues in public interest law.

An effective approach to maximizing our students' learning potential is a comprehensive **Academic Success Program** offered during the first year. The program consists of an early-start summer legal process course and a series of outreach programs conducted during the first two semesters.

Applicant Group for the 1995-1996 Academic Year

Brooklyn Law School
This grid includes only applicants who earned 120-180 LSAT scores under standard administrations.

GPA

LSAT Score	3.75 +		3.50 - 3.74		3.25 - 3.49		3.00 - 3.24		2.75 - 2.99		2.50 - 2.74		2.25 - 2.49		2.00 - 2.24		Below 2.00		No GPA		Total	
	Apps	Adm	Apps	Adm	Apps	Adm	Apps	Adm	Apps	Adm	Apps	Adm	Apps	Adm	Apps	Adm	Apps	Adm	Apps	Adm	Apps	Adm
175 - 180	0	0	1	1	0	0	0	0	0	0	0	0	0	0	0	0	0	0	0	0	1	1
170 - 174	2	2	1	1	2	2	3	3	2	2	0	0	0	0	0	0	0	0	0	0	10	10
165 - 169	4	3	10	10	13	13	24	23	13	12	7	7	1	1	2	0	0	0	0	0	74	69
160 - 164	21	20	42	41	85	85	76	75	51	51	38	37	11	9	8	4	2	0	4	3	338	325
155 - 159	42	41	99	98	129	107	147	90	108	74	49	34	15	11	7	3	4	1	7	7	607	466
150 - 154	32	27	114	75	171	88	202	52	157	42	113	21	58	7	19	2	6	0	16	3	888	317
145 - 149	21	9	75	26	102	35	181	10	147	6	106	3	56	0	26	0	9	0	16	0	739	89
140 - 144	11	0	31	1	58	1	89	1	94	0	83	1	58	0	16	0	7	0	15	0	462	4
135 - 139	3	0	11	0	17	0	40	0	60	0	52	0	36	0	26	0	3	0	15	0	263	0
130 - 134	0	0	7	0	6	0	13	0	22	0	16	0	18	0	16	0	4	0	6	0	108	0
125 - 129	0	0	0	0	2	0	2	0	4	0	6	0	2	0	3	0	0	0	1	0	20	0
Total	0	0	0	0	0	0	0	0	0	0	1	0	0	0	0	0	1	0	0	0	2	0
	136	102	391	253	585	331	777	254	658	187	471	103	255	28	123	9	36	1	80	13	3512	1281

Apps = Number of Applicants
Adm = Number Admitted
Reflects 98% of the total applicant pool.

University at Buffalo, State University of New York School of Law

Admissions Office
O'Brian Hall, Amherst Campus
Buffalo, NY 14260
Phone: 716.645.2061

■ Introduction

The University at Buffalo School of Law is the only law school in the SUNY system. The school provides a comprehensive curriculum similar to that of other major state law schools, while at the same time affording students a broad range of curricular options and special programs. The Buffalo model of legal education emphasizes the study of law in its social context, and a large number of interdisciplinary courses and programs support this emphasis. Close connections are maintained with other departments in the university, and dual and joint-degree programs are encouraged and supervised through the Baldy Center for Law and Social Policy.

■ Library and Physical Facilities

➧ 310,000 volumes & equivalents ➧ LEXIS ➧ NEXIS ➧ WESTLAW ➧ DIALOG ➧ LRS ➧ QL

The school is housed in John Lord O'Brian Hall, a seven-story building completed in 1973. O'Brian Hall is located on the Amherst Campus of the University at Buffalo, which is one of the four university centers of the SUNY system. The classrooms, library, offices, and study space for the law school are in carpeted rooms which provide bright and comfortable work places. The library contains a major collection of periodicals and public documents; has an extensive collection of microfilms, audiovisual equipment, and materials; and is a depository for U.S. government publications.

The Amherst Campus provides recreational and cultural space including two theaters, chamber music, and concert halls, a ceramics and art center, and athletic facilities in a new 10,000-seat fieldhouse.

■ Curriculum

➧ Academic Support Program ➧ 82 credits required to graduate ➧ two semesters and summer session

Instruction is offered in two semesters from late August to May and in a summer session from mid-May to mid-July. Six full-time semesters, or five full-time semesters plus two summer sessions, are required for graduation. A part-time program allows students to spread their work over eight semesters.

The first-year program includes instruction in civil procedure, contracts, constitutional law, criminal law, legal research and writing, property, and torts (civil wrongs).

These are the standard subjects in the first year of all American law schools. In addition, the first year affords an introduction to aspects of the social and economic context of the legal system and to legal institutions and processes.

Beyond the first year, students are required to complete 54 semester credit hours of work. One course is required (federal taxation, three credit hours), and each student must complete one seminar or other approved writing course (three credit hours). The balance of the upper-division program is elective, and students may choose from a full spectrum of survey and advanced courses covering the main fields of public and private law, from a very rich selection of seminars and small group courses in special or emerging areas of law study and research, and from clinics and simulations devoted to professional skills training.

■ Special Programs

The school offers special programs emphasizing interdisciplinary study and applications of law. The clinical program is distinguished in that the skills training is coordinated with substantive law courses to give students theoretical understanding of practical issues. The program allows students to serve clients and conduct research and fieldwork in such areas as economic development, mental health law, occupational safety and health law, school and education law, and international protection of human rights.

The school also has an extensive joint-degree program, which permits students to earn credit toward a master's or Ph.D. degree and the J.D. In recent years, the most active joint-degree programs have been with political science, management, philosophy, sociology, and economics. Special programs can be arranged with other departments. The interdisciplinary programs of the school are administered by the Baldy Center for Law and Social Policy. The center provides fellowship awards for outstanding J.D./Ph.D. students, offers advice and assistance to all joint-degree candidates, and supports interdisciplinary research and curriculum development.

The Legal Methods Program is a first-year program for students who are educationally disadvantaged. Based on the recognition that quantitative measurements of success in law school are not infallibly reliable predictors, the Admissions Committee reviews these applications for other signs of achievement that portend success in law school. Tutorial assistance in substantive courses is provided as well as intensive writing assignments given in the LMP and in the research and writing course. Correspondence regarding the program should be directed to Aundra Newell, Associate Dean for Admissions and Student Services.

■ Admission

➧ application deadline—Feb. 1 ➧ LSAT, LSDAS required

The school has no specific undergraduate course prerequisites. The school admits first-year students only in the fall semester; application materials are available the preceding September.

Transfer with advanced standing is open to students who have successfully completed one year of work in an ABA-accredited law school.

■ Student Activities

Law student extracurricular activities are managed by law students through an elected representative body, the Student Bar Association. SBA-sponsored activities include lectures and special education programs, coordination of student participation in law school governance, and social events for students and faculty. Other student organizations include the Moot Court Board, which sponsors mock appellate practice competitions; *The Opinion*, the student newspaper; the *Buffalo Law Review*, a professional journal edited by students; and special interest groups such as the Asian Law Students Association (ALSA), the Latin American Law Students Association (LALSA), the Black Law Students Association (BLSA), the Native American Law Students Association (NALSA), the Association of Women Law Students, and the National Lawyers Guild.

■ Expenses and Financial Aid

- *tuition & fees—resident, $6,100; nonresident, $10,750*
- *estimated additional expenses—$4,000-$5,000*

New York state residents are eligible for the Tuition Assistance Program (TAP) and State University Supplemental Tuition Awards (SUSTA). Students are eligible for Perkins (formerly NDSL) and federally insured loans offered through the New York State Higher Education Assistance Corporation (NYSHEAC). TAP and SUSTA are based on need.

For more information, write to the Financial Aid Office, 232 Capen Hall, North Campus, Buffalo, NY 14260.

■ Housing

Limited housing for single students is available in the new dormitory complex. A wide range of private apartments is available. Write to the University Housing Office, Richmond Quadrangle, University at Buffalo, Amherst Campus, Buffalo, NY 14261.

■ Career Services

The school's Career Development Office (CDO) guides students in career selection and serves as a liaison between students and prospective employers.

In addition to providing services for third-year students, the CDO Office also aids first- and second-year law students in conducting their summer job search.

In recent years, over 90 percent of the eligible graduates in a class have been employed in legal work within nine months of graduation. New York and the northeastern states, as well as Washington, DC, are the most common locations for SUNY at Buffalo graduates. The southeastern, midwestern, and western states have also attracted graduates to such cities as Chicago, Miami, Detroit, and Los Angeles.

To obtain additional information, please contact the Assistant Dean of CDO, School of Law, O'Brian Hall, Amherst Campus, Buffalo, NY 14260.

Applicant Group for the 1995-1996 Academic Year

University at Buffalo, State University of New York School of Law
This grid includes only applicants who earned 120-180 LSAT scores under standard administrations.

GPA

LSAT Score	3.75 +		3.50 - 3.74		3.25 - 3.49		3.00 - 3.24		2.75 - 2.99		2.50 - 2.74		2.25 - 2.49		2.00 - 2.24		Below 2.00		No GPA		Total	
	Apps	Adm	Apps	Adm	Apps	Adm	Apps	Adm	Apps	Adm	Apps	Adm	Apps	Adm	Apps	Adm	Apps	Adm	Apps	Adm	Apps	Adm
175 - 180	0	0	0	0	0	0	0	0	0	0	0	0	0	0	0	0	0	0	0	0	0	0
170 - 174	0	0	0	0	3	3	1	1	2	1	1	1	0	0	0	0	0	0	0	0	7	6
165 - 169	5	5	4	4	9	9	11	11	5	5	2	2	1	1	2	1	0	0	0	0	39	38
160 - 164	11	11	21	21	27	27	35	33	23	17	12	8	6	4	1	0	1	1	1	1	138	123
155 - 159	21	21	45	45	62	58	60	38	46	29	30	15	10	3	3	1	0	0	4	3	281	213
150 - 154	24	23	44	39	74	45	72	27	65	19	42	7	24	8	6	1	5	1	4	4	360	174
145 - 149	6	6	22	13	50	19	48	17	59	11	26	5	11	1	8	2	3	3	0	0	233	77
140 - 144	2	1	10	5	18	6	20	3	39	4	22	1	12	0	7	0	2	0	6	1	138	21
135 - 139	2	1	3	0	5	0	15	0	18	0	16	0	11	0	7	0	0	0	2	0	1196	1
130 - 134	0	0	0	0	2	0	4	0	4	0	6	0	3	0	2	0	0	0	0	0	2392	0
125 - 129	0	0	0	0	0	0	1	0	1	0	1	0	0	0	3	0	1	0	0	0	7	0
Total	71	68	149	127	250	167	267	130	262	86	158	39	78	17	39	5	12	5	17	9	1303	653

Apps = Number of Applicants
Adm = Number Admitted

University of California at Berkeley School of Law (Boalt Hall)

220 Boalt Hall
U.C., Berkeley, CA 94720-7200
Phone: 510.642.2274

■ Introduction

Boalt Hall is located on the campus of the University of California at Berkeley. The campus is surrounded by wooded, rolling hills, and the city of Berkeley, which has a long history as one of America's most lively, culturally diverse, and politically adventurous cities. The surrounding San Francisco Bay Area offers culture, entertainment, and natural beauty without rival, much of which is accessible by BART (the Bay Area Rapid Transit system). All of Northern California, with its great variety of cultural and recreational opportunities, is within easy reach. Boalt Hall is one of the world's leading institutions of legal education and research. The school is a member of AALS and is approved by the ABA.

■ Enrollment/Student Body

➽ 4,798 applicants ➽ 848 admitted first-year class 1995 ➽ 266 enrolled first-year class 1995 ➽ 861 total full-time (no part-time) ➽ 37% minority ➽ 50% women ➽ more than 50 states & foreign countries represented ➽ 82 undergraduate schools represented

The academic backgrounds and nonacademic experiences of Boalt Hall students are varied, and there is a substantial representation of various graduate and professional degrees. An advanced graduate (LL.M.) program admits 20-25 students annually from foreign countries.

■ Faculty

➽ 61 full-time ➽ 85 part-time or adjunct ➽ 33 women ➽ 15 minority

■ Library and Physical Facilities

➽ 650,000 volumes & equivalents ➽ 12 full-time librarians ➽ LEXIS ➽ NEXIS ➽ WESTLAW ➽ INNOPAC ➽ MELVYL

The law library's collection includes the Robbins Collection of Ancient, Canon, and Ecclesiastical Law, and extensive special collections on comparative and international law, natural resources, and the environment. The law library is linked by computer to the collections at other national law schools and to the combined university library holdings that number more than seven million volumes. The late Chief Justice Earl Warren, an alumnus of the school, designated the law library as a depository for U.S. Supreme Court records and briefs, and it is also a selective official depository of U.S. government documents. The library maintains a photocopying service and IBM and Macintosh PCs for student word processing.

A studio apartment complex is reserved for law students. The university also maintains limited housing for students who are married or who have children. Most law students live in rented apartments or houses in the area.

■ Admission

➽ Bachelor's degree required ➽ application deadline—Feb. 1, early application strongly preferred ➽ LSAT, LSDAS required ➽ median GPA—3.70 ➽ median LSAT score—168 ➽ application fee—$40, fall admission only

Applications are evaluated primarily in terms of undergraduate academic work and LSAT score. Applicants are encouraged to include in their personal statement a discussion of their exceptional accomplishments, prior employment, graduate study, or any other special characteristics, including nonacademic experiences, talents, and ambitions. Two letters of recommendation submitted with the application are advised. December is the last acceptable test date to meet the February application deadline, and repeated LSAT scores are averaged. Admission is highly selective; approximately 20 applications are received annually for each place in the first-year class. Some decisions are made as early as January, and the bulk of decision letters are mailed by May. Early application is advised.

■ Student Activities

Students edit and publish nine legal periodicals—the *African-American Law and Policy Report*, the *Asian Law Journal*, the *Berkeley Journal of Employment and Labor Law*, the *California Law Review*, *Ecology Law Quarterly*, *High Technology Law Journal*, the *International Tax and Business Lawyer*, *Berkeley Women's Law Journal*, and *La Raza Law Journal*.

Participation in moot court is compulsory for first-year students; advanced students may participate in voluntary moot court and in honors competitions. Other activities include the Boalt Hall Student Association, the Boalt Hall Women's Association, the Berkeley Law Foundation, International Law Society, National Lawyers' Guild, and many student cultural and affinity groups.

Student activities and educational programs are enriched by the activities of the Earl Warren Legal Institute, an interdisciplinary law-related research and public service unit of the university.

■ Curriculum

➽ Academic Support Program ➽ 85 credits required to graduate ➽ more than 175 courses available ➽ semesters, start in Aug. ➽ range of first-year class size—30-100

An orientation program introduces new law students to the school and to legal learning at the beginning of the fall term. The first-year curriculum is prescribed. Upon completion of the first year, simulation-based courses are available in legal interviewing, legal counseling, legal accounting, and legal document drafting and are taught by teams of lawyers from Bay Area law firms. Boalt Hall also offers the following clinical programs that are integrated with substantive courses— Disability Rights; Immigration and Asylum Appeals; Environmental Law; Domestic Violence; and The Berkeley Community Law Center. Interested students may be placed for a full semester as law clerks to federal and state judges or with public interest, government, and private lawyers.

■ Special Programs

Concurrent-degree programs that allow students to earn the J.D. and a master's degree in another field in four years have been established with the following departments of the university—Asian studies, business administration, city planning, economics, international and area studies, journalism, public policy, and social welfare, as well as doctoral programs in economics and legal history. In addition, students may arrange concurrent programs with other campus departments.

Combined-degree programs are available with the Fletcher School of Law and Diplomacy at Tufts University or with the John F. Kennedy School of Government at Harvard University. Unique among American law schools is the graduate program in Jurisprudence and Social Policy, an interdisciplinary legal studies program leading to the Ph.D. that requires no prior legal training, and which also may be earned concurrently with a J.D.

Boalt Hall's concentration programs include Environmental Law; International and Comparative Legal Studies; Law and Technology/Intellectual Property; and Traditionally Disadvantaged Groups.

■ Expenses and Financial Aid

➽ *tuition & fees—full-time resident, $8,800, nonresident, $16,500* ➽ *estimated additional expenses—$10,532*
➽ *need-based financial aid available*
➽ *FAFSA form for need analysis due*
➽ *deadline for priority consideration—March 2*

All financial aid is need-based and each package may consist of grants-in-aid, Perkins and Stafford loans, and work-study funds for continuing students. Nonresidents may become residents after one year if appropriate steps are taken and if certain eligibility requirements are met. All fees are subject to change without notice.

■ Career Services

The Boalt Hall Career Services Office serves as a resource for Boalt Hall students, alumni, and prospective employers. It operates one of the largest on-campus recruitment programs in the country; provides opportunities for part-time, summer, and full-time legal positions; and maintains extensive files on a wide variety of positions available throughout the nation. The career services staff announces career counseling, résumé workshops, and programs on opportunities for traditional and nontraditional law careers.

Applicant Group for the 1995-1996 Academic Year

University of California Berkeley School of Law (Boalt Hall)
This grid includes only applicants who earned 120-180 LSAT scores under standard administrations.

LSAT Score	3.75 +		3.50 - 3.74		3.25 - 3.49		3.00 - 3.24		2.75 - 2.99		2.50 - 2.74		2.25 - 2.49		2.00 - 2.24		Below 2.00		No GPA		Total	
	Apps	Adm	Apps	Adm	Apps	Adm	Apps	Adm	Apps	Adm	Apps	Adm	Apps	Adm	Apps	Adm	Apps	Adm	Apps	Adm	Apps	Adm
175 - 180	38	38	30	29	25	18	9	2	3	0	0	0	1	0	0	0	0	0	0	0	106	87
170 - 174	91	85	126	91	85	24	21	1	16	2	6	0	4	0	0	0	0	0	8	7	357	210
165 - 169	235	168	340	102	187	13	83	7	35	2	13	0	3	0	1	1	0	0	21	10	918	303
160 - 164	245	86	352	25	272	18	122	10	69	3	34	2	10	1	2	0	2	0	18	3	1126	148
155 - 159	126	12	217	17	207	18	137	4	77	2	36	1	12	0	4	0	2	0	26	2	844	56
150 - 154	63	7	108	5	154	11	100	3	69	1	45	0	16	0	9	0	3	0	23	0	590	27
145 - 149	26	0	55	0	74	0	64	0	57	0	31	0	18	0	10	0	2	0	26	0	363	0
140 - 144	4	0	14	0	30	0	39	0	47	0	34	0	20	0	10	0	2	0	20	0	220	0
135 - 139	0	0	7	0	14	0	12	0	19	0	17	0	10	0	8	0	2	0	10	0	99	0
130 - 134	1	0	1	0	7	0	8	0	2	0	7	0	4	0	3	0	0	0	4	0	37	0
125 - 129	0	0	0	0	0	0	1	0	2	0	5	0	2	0	1	0	1	0	0	0	12	0
120 - 124	0	0	1	0	0	0	0	0	1	0	0	0	0	0	0	0	0	0	1	0	3	0
Total	829	396	1251	269	1055	102	596	27	397	10	228	3	100	1	48	1	14	0	157	22	4675	831

GPA

Apps = Number of Applicants
Adm = Number Admitted
Reflects 97% of the total applicant pool.

School of Law, University of California—Davis

Admissions Office
Davis, CA 95616-5201

E-Mail: admissions@lawadmin.uc.davis.edu
URL: http://kinghall.ucdavis.edu
Phone: 916.752.6477

■ Introduction

The School of Law at the University of California, Davis, was founded in 1965. It is accredited by the American Bar Association and is a member of the Association of American Law Schools. The school has a chapter of the Order of the Coif, the national honor society. The law building, King Hall, was named for Dr. Martin Luther King, Jr., in recognition of his efforts to bring social and political justice to disadvantaged peoples.

The Davis campus is 20 minutes from Sacramento and an hour-and-a-half from San Francisco, within easy reach of the major recreational areas of the Sierra Nevada, Lake Tahoe, and the Mother Lode. The campus occupies 3,600 acres within the college town of Davis, where the small-town, friendly atmosphere is a welcome change from the distractions and stress usually associated with more urban environments.

The close proximity to the state capitol and the Bay Area provide both social and political stimulus necessary for a well-rounded educational experience. The campus also offers a full range of graduate and professional programs.

■ Enrollment/Student Body

➧ 3,004 applicants ➧ 712 admitted first-year class 1995 ➧ 136 enrolled first-year class 1995 ➧ 467 total full-time ➧ 34.7% minority ➧ 50% women ➧ 120 undergraduate schools represented

■ Faculty

➧ 41 total ➧ 29 full-time ➧ 12 part-time ➧ 9 women ➧ 4 minority ➧ 1:16 faculty student ratio (full-time faculty only)

■ Library and Physical Facilities

➧ 383,634 volumes & equivalents ➧ library hours: Mon.-Thurs., 8:00 A.M.-10:00 P.M.; Fri., 8:00 A.M.-5:00 P.M.; Sat., NOON-5:00 P.M.; Sun., NOON-8:00 P.M. ➧ LEXIS ➧ NEXIS ➧ WESTLAW ➧ MELVYL ➧ 4 full-time librarians ➧ library seats 348

The law school and library are housed in the same building, one of the more modern on campus. It has moot courtrooms, a pretrial skills laboratory, an instructional computer laboratory, study carrels, Law Review quarters, lounges, an infant care co-op, offices for student organizations, and is comfortably accessible to disabled students. Every law student has a key to the building and may use the facilities around the clock.

The law library has an open-stack system. All students are assigned to carrels, and books can be charged to carrels. Areas of specialization include international law, comparative law, environmental law, water law, and intellectual property law. The library is a federal and California documents depository and has an extensive collection of California and federal government documents.

■ Curriculum

➧ Academic Support Program ➧ 88 credits required to graduate ➧ 128 courses available ➧ degrees available: J.D.; J.D./M.B.A.; J.D./M.A. ➧ semesters, start in Aug. ➧ range of first-year class size—25-70

During the first year at King Hall, students study six basic areas of the law—civil procedure, constitutional law, contracts, crimes, property, and torts. In a major departure from tradition, one of these courses is taught in small sections of 25-30 students. The first year also includes a week-long introductory course and courses in legal research and writing. Second- and third-year programs are elective, except for a course on professional responsibility and a legal writing requirement. Courses may be selected within broad areas of concentration such as administration of criminal justice, business and taxation, civil litigation, estate planning and taxation, labor and employment law, environmental law, public interest law, and transnational studies.

■ Special Programs

Second- and third-year students have the opportunity to work under the supervision of practicing lawyers in clinicals in immigration law, environmental law, tax law, employment relations, public interest law, prison law, and criminal justice administration.

King Hall has an integrated civil rights curriculum including a substantive course in civil rights law, a civil rights litigation skills seminar, and a clinic representing indigent persons in civil rights cases. Students participating in the King Hall Civil Rights Clinic are certified to appear in federal court where they provide representation to people who would otherwise have no counsel and gain first-hand experience in constitutional litigation.

First-year students engage in oral argument as a part of the required legal research and writing course. This provides basic preparation for participation in the formal Moot Court program which emphasizes appellate advocacy skills. The program includes an honors competition and a series of regional, national, and international competitions.

Our moot court and trial competition teams have each advanced to the final rounds of the National Moot Court Competition and the National Mock Trial Competition in the last four years. We have also won other state, regional, and national competitions.

Skills courses cover the major elements of both litigation and nonlitigation practice. These include pretrial skills (interviewing, counseling, document drafting) negotiation and alternative dispute resolution, as well as introductory and advanced trial practice courses.

Students in the Public Interest Law Program receive a special certificate after completing 150 hours of public interest legal service. They take a selection of specialized courses and devote 25 hours to enhancing public interest law programs.

■ Admission

➽ *Bachelor's degree or equivalent from college or university of approved standing required* ➽ *application deadline—Feb. 1*
➽ *rolling admission, early application encouraged*
➽ *LSAT, LSDAS required* ➽ *median GPA—3.46*
➽ *median LSAT score—162*
➽ *application fee—$40 (waivers available)*

Undergraduate grades and LSAT score form the foundation of the admission evaluation. The Admission Committee seeks students of diverse backgrounds. Consideration is given to ethnic and economic factors, advanced studies, significant work experience, and extracurricular and community activities. An applicant's maturity, capacity to grow, and commitment to law study are also major considerations. Multiple LSAT scores will be averaged. Admission Information Sessions are held at King Hall in October, November, December, and January. Law student guided tours can be arranged by contacting the Admission Office.

■ Cocurricular Activities

The student-run *Law Review* publishes four issues, including a single-topic symposium issue. The members of the *Law Review* are selected through a writing competition open to all.

The Law Student Association coordinates law student activities. Students sit on the student-faculty Educational Policy, Faculty Appointments, and Admission Committees. Other active organizations include the International Law Society, Environmental Law Society, Student Lawyers for the Arts, Women's Caucus, and Asian, Black, Christian, Jewish, La Raza, native American, and Filipino Law Student Associations.

■ Expenses and Financial Aid

➽ *tuition & fees—residents, $8,796; nonresidents, $16,495*
➽ *estimated additional expenses—$9,662 (room, board, books)*
➽ *some need-based scholarships available*

Although grant monies are limited, the School of Law Financial Aid Office administers all nationally recognized aid programs, such as Stafford Loans, Perkins Loans, and Work Study, and participates in the new Federal Direct Student Loan Program. University student loans and grants are also available. Financial aid applications must be submitted by March 1 of the year in which admission is sought. Applications are accepted after that date, but are considered only after timely applications.

■ Housing

A wide variety of housing is available but it is advisable to begin seeking preferred accommodations early. The university maintains on-campus apartments for married students and Leach Hall for single graduate students. Students desiring on-campus housing should apply well in advance of the April deadline.

■ Career Services

The law school maintains an active Career Services Office to help students secure permanent positions and summer work, as well as part-time or temporary employment during the academic year. Career counseling and résumé consultation are available to all students. Approximately 100 employers use the facilities of the office to interview Davis law students on campus. Special career workshops are scheduled throughout the year to provide students with employment information and to help them develop techniques useful in their job search.

Applicant Group for the 1995-1996 Academic Year

School of Law, University of California—Davis
This grid includes only applicants who earned 120-180 LSAT scores under standard administrations (98% of the total applicant pool).

GPA

LSAT Score	3.75 +		3.50 - 3.74		3.25 - 3.49		3.00 - 3.24		2.75 - 2.99		2.50 - 2.74		2.25 - 2.49		2.00 - 2.24		Below 2.00		No GPA		Total	
	Apps	Adm	Apps	Adm	Apps	Adm	Apps	Adm	Apps	Adm	Apps	Adm	Apps	Adm	Apps	Adm	Apps	Adm	Apps	Adm	Apps	Adm
175 - 180	1	1	1	1	1	1	3	3	1	1	0	0	1	0	0	0	0	0	0	0	8	7
170 - 174	6	6	20	20	19	17	10	9	13	6	6	3	2	1	0	0	0	0	1	1	77	63
165 - 169	34	31	67	63	68	56	48	27	28	7	11	1	3	0	0	0	0	0	5	2	264	187
160 - 164	75	65	161	117	217	87	96	18	68	5	29	3	10	0	1	0	2	0	11	6	670	301
155 - 159	59	26	159	41	194	24	144	15	92	4	24	0	12	0	2	0	3	0	20	1	709	111
150 - 154	45	7	122	6	122	6	128	5	75	1	48	0	16	0	10	0	3	0	13	0	582	25
145 - 149	21	1	42	1	67	0	69	1	46	0	28	0	24	0	8	0	0	0	14	0	319	3
140 - 144	3	0	15	0	29	0	34	0	43	0	30	0	16	0	10	0	1	0	13	0	194	0
135 - 139	2	0	4	0	7	0	8	0	21	0	12	0	9	0	4	0	2	0	4	0	73	0
130 - 134	1	0	1	0	7	0	2	0	3	0	5	0	4	0	2	0	2	0	1	0	28	0
125 - 129	0	0	0	0	0	0	1	0	1	0	0	0	3	0	0	0	0	0	0	0	5	0
120 - 124	0	0	0	0	0	0	0	0	0	0	0	0	0	0	0	0	0	0	0	0	0	0
Total	247	137	592	249	731	191	543	78	391	24	193	7	100	1	37	0	13	0	82	10	2929	697

Apps = Number of Applicants
Adm = Number Admitted

University of California—Hastings College of the Law

200 McAllister Street
San Francisco, CA 94102

URL: http://www.uchastings.edu
Phone: 415.565.4623

■ Introduction

Since its founding in 1878 as the University of California's first school of law, Hastings College of the Law has been at the center of the legal community in the West. In addition to pursuing legal practice that covers the entire spectrum of law, Hastings graduates sit as judges on the California bench by a 3-to-1 margin over any other law school.

Located in San Francisco's Civic Center, Hastings provides students unparalleled access to legal institutions. The California Supreme Court, California Court of Appeals, and the U.S. Court of Appeals for the Ninth Circuit are nearby. Two blocks away is City Hall, as well as superior and municipal courts. With its central location and strong community links to many of the Bay Area's multicultural neighborhoods, Hastings offers students an educational experience that is virtually unlimited in its breadth and diversity.

■ Enrollment/Student Body

➽ 5,281 applicants ➽ 1,505 admitted first-year class 1995 ➽ 416 enrolled first-year class 1995 ➽ 1,262 total full-time ➽ 32.2% minority ➽ 47% women ➽ 58 states & foreign countries represented ➽ 119 undergraduate schools represented

Many students come to Hastings from other career experiences. Though student ages range from 20-55, there are a significant number of students over 30; the average age of Hastings students is 27.

■ Faculty

➽ 108 total ➽ 47 full-time ➽ 68 part-time or adjunct ➽ 37 women ➽ 12 minority

■ Library and Physical Facilities

➽ 563,260 volumes & equivalents ➽ library hours: Mon.-Fri., 8:00 A.M.-11:00 P.M.; Sat., 9:00 A.M.-10:00 P.M.; Sun., 9:00 A.M.-11:00 P.M. ➽ LEXIS ➽ NEXIS ➽ WESTLAW ➽ DIALOG ➽ INFOTRAC ➽ DATATIMES ➽ LEGITECH ➽ FIRST SEARCH ➽ EPIC ➽ 9 full-time librarians ➽ library seats 1,295 ➽ computer lab

The Legal Information Center houses an extensive collection of federal and California documents for which Hastings is an official depository. The breadth and depth of the center's collection, and its state-of-the-art computer-assisted research capabilities, draw local attorneys, court personnel, and government agency employees to use the center's resources.

■ Curriculum

➽ Academic Support Program ➽ Clinical Instruction Program ➽ 6 scholarly publications ➽ 88 units/credits required to graduate ➽ 303 courses available; concentrations in civil litigation, international law, public interest law, and taxation ➽ selected concurrent masters degree programs with U.C. Berkeley ➽ full-time semesters, begin in Aug. ➽ range of first-year class size—16-85

The Hastings curriculum offers a broad spectrum of courses, from those that are fundamental to all forms of practice to those that reflect increased specialization. After three years of successful study, the student will receive a Juris Doctor degree, conferred by the Regents of the University of California.

Students must complete six semesters in residence, earn 88 semester units, pass all required courses, and earn a cumulative G.P.A. of at least C (2.00). The program is designed for full-time students; new students are admitted only at the beginning of the fall semester.

■ Special Programs

Legal Education Opportunity Program—Initiated in 1969, the Legal Education Opportunity Program (LEOP) was designed to assist each student in excelling academically at Hastings. Students admitted through LEOP are offered a number of academic support services throughout their three years of study, beginning with orientation for incoming students and ending with a supplemental bar review course.

To be eligible for LEOP, applicants must complete the LEOP application which includes questions regarding cultural, economic, educational, familial, geographic, linguistic, physical, or social issues/circumstances affecting preparation for law school.

Institutes and Exchanges Program—As part of the second- and third-year course of study, students at Hastings have the opportunity to participate in student-exchange programs involving Nihon University, Japan; Leiden University, Netherlands; the University of British Columbia; and Vermont Law School, as well as the Land Conservation Institute, the Public Law Research Institute, and the Public Interest Clearinghouse.

■ Admission

➽ B.A. or equivalent required ➽ application deadline—Feb. 15 ➽ admission decisions made early Dec. to mid-April ➽ LSAT, LSDAS required ➽ median GPA—3.52 ➽ median LSAT score—164 ➽ application fee—$40

Although the selection process is highly competitive, each application is read with care and deliberation. Therefore, candidates are encouraged to provide a complete and candid picture of themselves.

The admission committee assesses the relative strength of each applicant's academic achievements; LSAT score; professional experience; community, volunteer, and extracurricular activities; letters of recommendation; and writing ability. Residence is not a factor.

■ Co-curricular and Student Activities

Hastings publishes more journals that offer credit than most other U.S. law schools. Second- and third-year students may earn academic credit by working on one of six law journals: *Hastings Communications and Entertainment Law Journal*, *Hastings Constitutional Law Quarterly*, *Hastings International and Comparative Law Review*, *Hastings Law Journal*, *Hastings Women's Law Journal*, and *West-Northwest*.

Beyond the first-year moot court requirement, Hastings offers Appellate Advocacy as a second-year elective. Students write a brief and present oral arguments based on the record of an actual case pending in the California or the United States Supreme Court. Second- and third-year students represent Hastings in a number of state, national, and international competitions.

Civil Justice Clinic, Criminal Practice Clinic, Worker's Rights Clinic, Environmental Law Clinic, and Civil Practice Clinic offer students valuable experiences in criminal and civil practice under the supervision of practicing attorneys.

The governing organization of the student body is the Associated Students of Hastings. Additionally, students participate in approximately 40 different social and political groups.

■ Expenses and Financial Aid

➧ *full-time tuition & fees—residents, $9,588; nonresidents, $17,287* ➧ *limited number of scholarships available* ➧ *FAFSA and Entering Student Financial Aid Supplement required for financial aid; due by Feb. 1*

Typically, some 82 percent of Hastings students receive financial assistance from college-administered sources. Scholarship awards are made to recognize and encourage the achievement, service, and professional promise of students.

■ Housing

On-campus housing is available at McAllister Tower, a 24-story building. The 250 apartments include efficiencies, studios, one-bedroom, and a few two-bedroom apartments. Students with families are clustered together to provide mutual support and companionship. The Off-Campus Housing Office provides current listings in San Francisco and the Bay Area as well as sample leases and other helpful publications.

■ Career Services

As part of its commitment to students and alumni, Hastings offers one of the most comprehensive law career services offices in Northern California. Students are provided assistance with law-related résumés, job-search strategies, interviewing techniques, and salary-negotiation skills. A complete set of online resource aids, accessed via a dedicated Local Area Network (LAN), is available for summer, part-time, and full-time job searches in the legal field.

Hastings annually lists 1,400-1,500 part-time and summer jobs for current students.

Through the fall and spring, approximately 200 employers visit the campus to interview students for both second-year summer associate positions and permanent post-graduation employment. An additional 200-300 employers from throughout the nation participate in the recruit-by-mail program.

Applicant Group for the 1995-1996 Academic Year

University of California—Hastings College of the Law
This grid includes only applicants who earned 120-180 LSAT scores under standard administrations.

LSAT Score	GPA 3.75 +		3.50 - 3.74		3.25 - 3.49		3.00 - 3.24		2.75 - 2.99		2.50 - 2.74		2.25 - 2.49		2.00 - 2.24		Below 2.00		No GPA		Total	
	Apps	Adm	Apps	Adm	Apps	Adm	Apps	Adm	Apps	Adm	Apps	Adm	Apps	Adm	Apps	Adm	Apps	Adm	Apps	Adm	Apps	Adm
175 - 180	5	4	6	6	6	6	4	4	1	1	0	0	1	1	0	0	0	0	0	0	23	22
170 - 174	19	19	37	37	35	35	20	20	15	13	4	4	2	0	2	0	0	0	3	3	137	131
165 - 169	65	62	146	145	132	126	93	66	51	24	25	3	10	0	1	1	0	0	14	12	537	439
160 - 164	140	131	312	238	371	156	208	50	105	10	67	4	23	1	5	0	1	0	21	13	1253	603
155 - 159	123	55	301	93	335	30	257	20	152	8	61	1	17	0	6	0	3	0	24	5	1279	212
150 - 154	70	7	165	10	211	8	200	9	112	4	78	0	30	0	13	0	3	0	21	1	903	39
145 - 149	28	6	67	6	124	5	109	2	88	2	59	1	33	0	21	1	0	0	16	0	545	23
140 - 144	5	0	21	0	48	0	49	0	65	0	45	1	28	0	13	0	3	0	15	0	292	1
135 - 139	0	0	7	0	14	0	15	0	28	0	25	0	13	0	7	0	2	0	9	0	120	0
130 - 134	0	0	0	0	6	0	2	0	4	0	11	0	6	0	4	0	3	0	1	0	37	0
125 - 129	0	0	0	0	0	0	1	0	2	0	4	0	3	0	2	0	0	0	1	0	13	0
120 - 124	0	0	0	0	0	0	0	0	1	0	0	0	1	0	0	0	0	0	0	0	2	0
Total	455	284	1062	535	1282	366	958	171	624	62	379	14	167	2	74	2	15	0	125	34	5141	1470

Apps = Number of Applicants
Adm = Number Admitted
Reflects 98% of the total applicant pool.

School of Law, University of California, Los Angeles

Law Admissions Office, 71 Dodd Hall
Box 951445
Los Angeles, CA 90095-1445
Phone: 310.825.4041

■ Introduction

The School of Law of the University of California Los Angeles is located on the university campus in the foothills of the Santa Monica Mountains in the Westwood section of the city.

■ Enrollment/Student Body

➧ 4,553 applicants ➧ 989 admitted first-year class 1995 ➧ 266 enrolled first-year class 1995 ➧ 955 total full-time ➧ 45.1% minority ➧ 50% women ➧ over 100 undergraduate schools represented

The student body is a diverse group of whom approximately 25 percent come from outside California.

■ Faculty

➧ 96 total ➧ 74 full-time ➧ 22 part-time or adjunct ➧ 30 women ➧ 11 minority ➧ 9 emeritus professors recalled to teach

■ Library and Physical Facilities

➧ over 500,000 volumes & equivalents ➧ library hours: Mon.-Thurs., 8:00 A.M.-MIDNIGHT; Fri., 8:00 A.M.-9:00 P.M.; Sat., 9:00 A.M.-6:00 P.M.; Sun., 1:00 P.M.-MIDNIGHT ➧ LEXIS ➧ NEXIS ➧ WESTLAW ➧ 11 full-time librarians

Other computerized systems are available. Students also have access to the university library system of over three million volumes.

■ Curriculum

➧ Academic Support Program ➧ 87 credits required to graduate ➧ degrees available: J.D.; LL.M.; J.D./M.B.A.; J.D./M.A. (Urban Planning)

The law school awards the J.D. degree to students who satisfactorily complete their law study over three years of residence. Only a full-time day program is offered. Second- and third-year students choose from a wide variety of courses, seminars, clinical programs, and independent studies. Outstanding programs in the traditional fields of legal study as well as a broad range of imaginative clinical offerings are made possible because of the school's large, distinguished, innovative faculty, and a new clinical study facility.

■ Special Programs

UCLA offers a wide variety of innovative programs. Joint-degree programs may be undertaken with the Graduate School of Management (J.D./M.B.A.), and the Urban Planning Department (J.D./M.A.).

The law school offers a substantial number of clinical programs designed to provide students with experience in performing a wide range of lawyering tasks in a variety of substantive law settings. Students participate in simulated exercises, live client casework, and part-time work in local agencies. The law school also offers an externship program. Students learn matters that cannot be taught in the classroom, such as how agencies make policy, how judges make decisions, how to investigate facts, and how strategy is developed for dealing with legal issues.

As many as 100 students a year have participated in the externship program. Past placements have included, for example, federal district and appellate courts, and public interest and government agencies.

One of the most outstanding features of the curriculum is its flexibility. By careful selection, students are able to build their own course of study, which can lead to either a broad sample of the legal spectrum or a highly specialized and concentrated development of expertise within a particular field.

■ Admission

➧ Baccalaureate degree required ➧ application deadline—Jan. 16 ➧ LSAT, LSDAS required ➧ median GPA—3.58 ➧ median LSAT score—162 ➧ application fee—$40

All applicants must have a baccalaureate degree and take the LSAT no later than December 1996. Any LSAT taken prior to December 1992 is not valid. There are no specific undergraduate course or major requirements. Students are admitted in the fall term only.

Admission is based primarily on proven academic and intellectual ability measured largely by the LSAT and the quality of undergraduate education as determined by not only the GPA, but also by such factors as the breadth, depth, and rigor of the undergraduate educational program. In appropriate cases, the admissions committee may also consider additional factors such as substantial career achievements, ethnicity, disadvantages overcome, diverse backgrounds, and other information relevant to the successful study and practice of law. Because of the large applicant pool, applicants are strongly urged to apply early.

UCLA accepts transfer students. Transfer applications are available after June 1st.

■ Minority Recruitment

In recognition of the underrepresentation of minority members in the legal profession and to diversify the law school's educational program and outlook, the law school in 1967 initiated efforts to increase significantly its minority student enrollment. Since then well over 3,700 minority students have been admitted. UCLA remains committed to maintaining a student body that reflects the diversity of American society. For information, students should contact the Admissions Office.

■ Student Activities

Diverse student interests are represented through various student organizations. Students edit and publish the *UCLA Law Review*. The *National Black Law Journal*, the *Chicano/Latino Law Review*, and the *Asian Pacific American Law Journal* are also published at UCLA, as are the *Entertainment Law Review*, the *Pacific Basin Law Journal*, the *UCLA Journal of Environmental Law and Policy*, and the *UCLA Women's Law Journal*. The Moot Court Honors Program operates a large and effective program of mock appellate advocacy. There is a very active Student Bar Association. There is a wide variety of other social and political groups. Students publish a law school newspaper and present an annual student-faculty musical.

■ Expenses and Financial Aid

- *tuition & fees—resident, $8,782; nonresident, $16,481*
- *scholarships available*
- *financial aid available*
- *admitted applicants will be sent the required forms*

Loans and some grants are available to students.

■ Career Services

The Career Services Office provides opportunities for part-time, summer, and full-time legal positions. It arranges interviews with employers from many parts of the country and maintains extensive files on a wide variety of positions available all over the nation. It also provides excellent career counseling services. The staff conducts individual and group counseling. They also call upon alumni, faculty, and other members of the bar for career counseling, and regularly sponsor career-related programs.

Applicant Group for the 1995-1996 Academic Year

University of California Los Angeles, School of Law
This grid includes only applicants who earned 120-180 LSAT scores under standard administrations.

LSAT Score	GPA 3.75 +		3.50 - 3.74		3.25 - 3.49		3.00 - 3.24		2.75 - 2.99		2.50 - 2.74		2.25 - 2.49		2.00 - 2.24		Below 2.00		No GPA		Total	
	Apps	Adm	Apps	Adm	Apps	Adm	Apps	Adm	Apps	Adm	Apps	Adm	Apps	Adm	Apps	Adm	Apps	Adm	Apps	Adm	Apps	Adm
175 - 180	11	10	9	9	10	10	8	6	3	0	0	0	0	0	0	0	0	0	0	0	41	35
170 - 174	34	33	52	51	36	28	16	8	11	1	3	0	4	0	0	0	0	0	4	3	160	124
165 - 169	98	95	200	175	126	58	56	6	30	1	13	1	7	0	1	0	0	0	11	4	542	340
160 - 164	191	150	337	157	279	41	135	6	72	3	31	1	9	0	4	0	1	0	14	1	1073	359
155 - 159	132	23	242	23	239	20	179	17	79	4	40	1	8	1	1	0	0	0	16	1	936	90
150 - 154	63	5	151	13	177	18	134	14	93	8	50	0	25	0	11	0	3	0	25	1	732	59
145 - 149	27	0	54	0	93	5	103	2	79	0	49	0	38	0	15	0	1	0	22	0	481	7
140 - 144	6	0	17	0	44	0	57	0	57	0	48	0	25	0	10	0	3	0	19	0	286	0
135 - 139	0	0	6	0	9	0	26	0	26	0	30	0	19	0	9	0	3	0	11	0	139	0
130 - 134	0	0	0	0	4	0	5	0	6	0	7	0	8	0	4	0	1	0	4	0	39	0
125 - 129	0	0	1	0	0	0	1	0	3	0	5	0	1	0	0	0	0	0	0	0	11	0
120 - 124	0	0	0	0	0	0	1	0	0	0	0	0	1	0	0	0	0	0	1	0	3	0
Total	562	316	1069	428	1017	180	721	59	459	17	276	3	145	1	55	0	12	0	127	10	4443	1014

Apps = Number of Applicants
Adm = Number Admitted
Reflects 98% of the total applicant pool.

California Western School of Law

225 Cedar Street
San Diego, CA 92101

E-Mail: msurbeck@cwsl.edu
Phone: 619.239.0391, 800.255.4252 ext. 1401 (admissions); 619.525.7083 (bulletin requests); Fax: 619.685.2916

■ Introduction

California Western is the oldest fully accredited law school in San Diego. Located in one of the most beautiful cities in the world, the law school has a history of providing contemporary legal education. The school is located downtown in a historically designated building. The new campus center houses the bookstore, campus deli, conference rooms, and offices, allowing for expansion of current library and classroom facilities.

■ Enrollment/Student Body

➽ 2,262 applicants ➽ 1,199 admitted first-year class 1995 ➽ 283 enrolled first-year class 1995 ➽ 796 total full-time ➽ 21.5% minority ➽ 47% women ➽ 43 states & 4 foreign countries represented ➽ 241 undergraduate schools represented

■ Faculty

➽ 72 total ➽ 46 full-time ➽ 28 full-/part-time women ➽ 8 minority

A young vibrant faculty are leading contributors to innovative research and practical legal education. The quality of our faculty is evidenced by their legal training at some of the finest law schools in the country, significant scholarly writings, participation in professional associations, and involvement in public service.

"We teach people how to be lawyers as well as how to think like them," says Professor Bill Lynch. "Students learn the practical side of becoming an attorney so that when they graduate they can practice the profession immediately and competently."

■ Library and Physical Facilities

➽ 231,293 volumes & equivalents ➽ library hours: 7:00 A.M.-MIDNIGHT ➽ LEXIS ➽ NEXIS ➽ WESTLAW ➽ DIALOG ➽ 8 full-time librarians ➽ library seats 508 ➽ student computer center ➽ laptop computer room

■ Curriculum

➽ Academic Support Program ➽ 89 credits required to graduate ➽ 118 courses available ➽ degrees available: J.D. ➽ start in Aug. ➽ first-year class size—fall, 280; spring, 50 ➽ fall class divided into three sections ➽ mid-year class starts spring trimester (Jan.)

Under the flexible trimester system, students may choose to graduate in two, two-and-one-half, or three years.

■ International Legal Studies Program

Publishing the third oldest *International Law Journal* in the United States, California Western also has one of the best collections of international, comparative, and foreign law resource materials in the Southwest.

"Each year, attorneys from all over the world present papers at the law school," says International Legal Studies Director, Professor John Noyes. "Students have the opportunity to interact with outstanding scholars on an academic and social level."

■ Clinical Internship Program

Our nationally recognized program trains students in lawyering skills and provides the opportunity to put their academic skills into practice immediately. "Over 80 percent of our students participate in the program," according to Professor Janet Weinstein, director of the program. "Students consider their internship experience to be one of the highlights of their education."

■ Graduate Courses

Many students take advantage of our affiliation agreement with San Diego State University, choosing graduate-level courses from such areas as social work, psychology, or business to enhance their legal education.

■ Specialty Courses and Programs

Programs include the Telecommunications Law Institute, the Interdisciplinary Training Program in Child Abuse, and the Institute for Criminal Defense Advocacy. Specialty courses include biotechnology and the law, environmental natural resources, sports, and entertainment law.

■ Admission Standards

➽ Bachelor's degree required ➽ application deadline—fall class, April 1; spring class, Nov. 1 ➽ LSAT, LSDAS required ➽ median GPA—3.13 ➽ median LSAT score—155 ➽ application fee—$45

"Admission is competitive," according to Assistant Dean for Admissions Nancy Ramsayer, "but applicants receive full consideration by reviewing each file carefully." Performance on the LSAT and the academic record are the most important factors. However, substantial consideration is given to other factors such as work experience, personal achievements, and volunteer service.

■ Commitment to Ethnic and Cultural Diversity

California Western actively recruits students from current underrepresented groups in the legal profession. According to Assistant Dean for Minority Affairs Linda N. Dews, "Our institutional commitment to diversity resulted in 27 percent ethnic representation in the fall '95 class. "Student organizations include Black Law (BLSA), Pan-Asian Bar, and La Raza.

The academic support program includes (1) a two-week, skills-oriented class, (2) tutorials offered throughout the first year via small group and individual sessions, and (3) academic counseling.

■ Housing

"Our Housing Office works closely with students to locate attractive, convenient housing, assist with roommates, and offer information on services associated with relocation," states Housing Coordinator Jill Meade. "We provide a full range of assistance to the student and his/her family to make the transition to San Diego and law school a smooth one."

■ Student Activities

➽ *Publications include: Law Review (top 10%), International Law Journal, and Telecommunications Law Journal*

Specialty student organizations include Pacific Rim Law Society, Institute for Public Interest Law, Environmental Law Society, Family Law Society, International Law Society, Lambda Alpha International Student Association, and Sports, and Entertainment Law Society.

Students share a spirit of cooperation. Study groups, the center of academic and emotional support, are common. Students are actively involved in a wide variety of activities through many student organizations.

Students who relish the challenge of competition will find ample opportunity through appellate advocacy or trial competitions. Our teams consistently place in regional and national competitions.

■ Expenses and Financial Aid

➽ *tuition & fees—full-time, $18,250 (fees, $70)*
➽ *estimated additional expenses—books, $650; rent, utilities, food, $6,850; transportation, $1,880; personal/misc. $3,740*
➽ *scholarships available: Academic Scholars Program, Deans Scholarships for Ethnic & Cultural Diversity, Career Transition Scholarship, J.D. Scholarship for Librarians*
➽ *financial aid available* ➽ *FAFSA need form required*
➽ *FWS, Perkins, Stafford (subsidized or unsubsidized or unsubsidized), and private loans available*

"Being a free-standing law school is a real advantage for us," says Financial Aid Executive Director Kyle Poston. "Law students are our only priority."

■ Career Services

The Office of Career Services informs students about the many career options available to law graduates through individual counseling. Workshop programs include the Pro Bono, Minority Career Development, and Alumni Career Advisor Network, as well as on- and off-campus recruitment and a monthly newsletter.

The Executive Director of Career Services, Lisa Kellogg, states that "the practical training received by our students makes California Western very popular with a broad range of legal employers."

■ Alumni

California Western has over 5,000 alumni located throughout the world, including a former U.S. ambassador; lawyers in the American embassies in France, Germany, and Belgium; and scores of judges and senior attorneys throughout the United States.

Applicant Group for the 1995-1996 Academic Year

California Western School of Law

	GPA																			
LSAT Score	3.75 +		3.50 - 3.74		3.25 - 3.49		3.00 - 3.24		2.75 - 2.99		2.50 - 2.74		2.25 - 2.49		2.00 - 2.24		1.99 -		LSAT Totals	
	Apps	Adm	Apps	Adm	Apps	Adm	Apps	Adm	Apps	Adm	Apps	Adm	Apps	Adm	Apps	Adm	Apps	Adm	Apps	Adm
175 - 180	0	0	0	0	0	0	0	0	0	0	0	0	0	0	0	0	0	0	0	0
170 - 174	0	0	0	0	0	0	0	0	1	1	1	1	0	0	0	0	0	0	2	2
165 - 169	2	2	6	6	2	2	2	2	5	5	3	3	1	1	0	0	0	0	21	21
160 - 164	3	3	12	12	16	16	26	24	35	35	19	19	8	8	9	7	1	0	129	124
155 - 159	9	9	40	40	75	74	93	90	90	85	68	52	27	13	15	5	1	0	418	368
150 - 154	14	14	63	63	135	131	190	171	151	93	103	33	62	10	19	2	2	0	739	517
145 - 149	10	8	32	22	85	49	135	48	94	8	77	9	45	1	16	0	3	0	497	145
140 - 144	4	3	10	2	20	3	56	1	60	1	56	0	25	0	12	0	4	0	247	10
135 - 139	0	0	3	0	4	0	15	0	24	0	24	0	13	0	7	0	1	0	91	0
130 - 134	0	0	1	0	1	0	5	0	3	0	10	0	4	0	1	0	0	0	25	0
125 - 129	0	0	0	0	0	0	0	0	0	0	2	0	2	0	0	0	0	0	4	0
120 - 124	0	0	0	0	0	0	0	0	0	0	0	0	0	0	0	0	1	0	0	0
GPA Totals	42	39	167	145	388	275	522	336	463	228	363	117	187	33	79	14	13	0	2173	1187

Apps = Number of Applicants
Adm = Number Admitted

Applicants with 120-180 LSAT scores earned under standard administrations 2,173
Applicants with only 10-48 LSAT scores earned under standard administrations . . . . 31 (not in grid)
Miscellaneous applicants with no LSAT, nonstandard administration, transfers, or visiting . . 1 (not in grid)
TOTAL 2,206

Campbell University—Norman Adrian Wiggins School of Law

P.O. Box 158
Buies Creek, NC 27506
Phone: 910.893.1754 or 1.800.334.4111

■ Introduction

Campbell University, Norman Adrian Wiggins School of Law admitted its charter class in August 1976. The School of Law was accredited by the North Carolina State Bar in 1978 and the American Bar Association in 1979.

Campbell University is located in the rural village of Buies Creek, 30 miles south of Raleigh, the state capital, and 30 miles north of Fayetteville—two of the most rapidly growing urban areas in the nation. Founded in 1887, the university's 1,450-acre campus offers programs for approximately 1,800 undergraduate and 800 graduate students.

While Campbell is a Southern Baptist university and establishment of the School of Law was conceived as a Christian mission, neither the School of Law nor the university, which also maintains a campus in Kuala Lumpur, Malaysia, is sectarian in the narrow sense of the word.

■ Enrollment/Student Body

➧ 1,000 applicants ➧ 190 admitted first-year class 1995 ➧ 116 enrolled first-year class 1995 ➧ 316 total full-time ➧ 11% minority ➧ 40% women

■ Faculty

➧ 35 total ➧ 20 full-time ➧ 15 part-time or adjunct ➧ 5 women

■ Library and Physical Facilities

➧ 156,342 volumes & equivalents ➧ library hours: Mon.-Thurs., 7:00 A.M.-MIDNIGHT; Fri., 7:00 A.M.-11:00 P.M., Sat., 8:00 A.M.-6:00 P.M.; Sun., NOON-MIDNIGHT ➧ LEXIS ➧ NEXIS ➧ WESTLAW ➧ 1 full-time librarians ➧ library seats 414

The School of Law is located in historic Kivett Hall in the center of the Campbell campus.

■ Curriculum

➧ 90 credits required to graduate ➧ degrees available: J.D./M.B.A. ➧ semesters, start in Aug.

The law school conducts a seven-week summer session and does not operate a part-time program. A majority of the total hours of study consists of required courses. A broad range of electives, usually including several seminars of 10 or fewer students, is available. The curriculum has been carefully planned to coalesce the practical and theoretical. Jurisprudence is a required subject, and one-third of the third-year curriculum is devoted to an innovative advocacy and practice course designed to bridge the gap between law school and law practice. Fulfillment of an advanced writing requirement and completion of one of several planning courses are also prerequisites for graduation.

■ Special Programs

Campbell's first-year program is designed to maximize the opportunity for success in law school and law practice. Over one-half of the first-year classes are sectioned, insuring an average size of 45 to 50 students in most classes, with each student participating in one section of only 25 students. Legal research and writing clinics of nine or ten students each are directed by teaching assistants under the supervision of faculty members.

The North Carolina State Bar's rule allows Campbell's second-year students to prosecute misdemeanors in state courts in conjunction with required criminal procedure and introductory trial advocacy courses.

Students also have the option of pursuing a J.D. and M.B.A. degree concurrently through a special arrangement with the Lundy-Fetterman School of Business at Campbell University.

In 1986, Campbell won the American College of Trial Lawyer's Emil Gumpert Award for the most outstanding trial advocacy program in the nation.

■ Admission

➧ B.A./B.S. required ➧ rolling admission ➧ LSAT, LSDAS required ➧ median GPA—3.30 ➧ median LSAT score—156 ➧ application fee—$40

Admission to the School of Law is granted on the basis of the faculty Admission Committee's evaluation of the probable contributions of the applicant to society and the legal profession. In an attempt to select objectively those who most possess traits essential for success in the practice of law, Campbell utilizes a comprehensive application questionnaire, including the LSAT/LSDAS reports and writing sample, and requires a personal interview as a prerequisite to admission.

Although a baccalaureate degree is generally required, students who have completed three-fourths of the work acceptable for the baccalaureate are also eligible to apply.

Each year, approximately 300 of those in the pool of qualified applicants are granted personal interviews. About 80 percent of those invited for interviews are selected on the basis of grade-point averages and LSAT scores, the balance primarily because of nonquantifiable factors. In past years, from 40 to 54 percent of those interviewed have been extended invitations for admission. Factors considered by the Admission Committee include the applicant's GPA, LSAT score, work experience, maturity, intellectual honesty, innovativeness, leadership, self-reliance, ability to overcome obstacles, pleasantness of personality, demonstrated moral and physical courage, sophistication in the sense of being able to function in varied contexts, and potential for unusual contributions to society.

■ Performance-based Admission Program

Since 1977, the School of Law has conducted a performance-based admission program during its summer session. Approximately 70 applicants take two regular law school courses for a total of six credit hours in the seven-week session. Students making a superior grade in each of the two courses are guaranteed positions in the first-year class in the fall. Students not making superior grades, but achieving a satisfactory average, are placed on a waiting list with qualified applicants not participating in the program. Performance in the program is a factor considered by the Admission Committee in filling vacancies from the waiting list.

■ Minority Admissions

The School of Law actively recruits minority students. Campbell's personalized admission and educational programs, equally available to minority and nonminority applicants and students, have resulted in the admission of minority students whose academic achievements have far surpassed projected class standing based solely on the LSAT/GPA statistics.

■ Student Activities

A chief goal in structuring a small law school was to afford every student an opportunity for meaningful participation in cocurricular activities. The student-edited *Campbell Law Review* was established in 1978. Students also publish the *Campbell Law Observer*, the nation's only student-edited newspaper for the legal profession, the circulation of which includes 10,000 North Carolina lawyers. The school has a full program of moot court activities, and students participate in regional and national moot court and trial court competitions. Delta Theta Phi and Phi Alpha Delta legal fraternities have established chapters at Campbell, as have Women in Law, the Law Students Civil Rights Research Council, and the Christian Legal Society. The Student Bar Association maintains an extensive speakers program and coordinates student participation in law school activities. Law Partners is an organization composed of spouses of law students. The law school maintains an active intramural program, running its own basketball league and participating in university leagues in other sports. Golf tournaments are held on the campus at Keith Hills Golf Club, one of North Carolina's outstanding golf courses.

■ Expenses and Financial Aid

➽ full-time tuition & fees—$13,500 ➽ 10 full-tuition scholarships, partial scholarships, research and teaching assistantships available ➽ minority scholarships available ➽ extensive financial aid program, including work-study, Law Student Assured Access, and National Director Student Loans

The cost of living in Buies Creek and the surrounding communities is low by national and urban standards.

■ Career Services

The placement office corresponds with over 1,800 employers. About 98 percent of all Campbell Law School alumni have passed at least one state bar examination. Approximately 10 to 20 alumni are admitted to the U.S. Supreme Court Bar yearly.

Admission Profile Not Available

Capital University Law School

665 S. High Street
Columbus, OH 43215

Phone: 614.445.8836, fax: 614.445.7125

■ Introduction

Capital University Law School is located in the historic German village district adjacent to downtown Columbus, Ohio, a growing major metropolitan area of over one million inhabitants. Columbus is the capital of Ohio, and all of the state judicial, legal, and governmental offices are readily available to law students. The metropolitan location provides various cultural opportunities, including a symphony, ballet, numerous resident theaters, touring shows, and extensive collegiate athletics.

The law school is a member of AALS, is fully accredited by the ABA, and is a charter member of the League of Ohio Law Schools. The university is an institution of the Lutheran Church of America and includes three undergraduate colleges, a Graduate School of Administration, and the law school. Total student population is about 3,450.

■ Enrollment/Student Body

➽ 1,107 applicants ➽ 672 admitted first-year class 1995
➽ 276 enrolled first-year class 1995 ➽ 476 total full-time
➽ 336 total part-time ➽ 9% minority ➽ 43% women
➽ 40 states & foreign countries represented
➽ 150 undergraduate schools represented

The law school actively encourages applications from minority students, women, and students with disabilities, and admits without regard to race, creed, national origin, or gender. Approximately 55 percent of all incoming full-time students reside outside of Ohio.

■ Faculty

➽ 31 total ➽ 46 part-time or adjunct ➽ 8 women
➽ 4 minority

■ Library and Physical Facilities

➽ 225,000 volumes & equivalents
➽ 24-hour access to law library ➽ LEXIS ➽ NEXIS
➽ WESTLAW ➽ INFOTRAC ➽ 5 full-time librarians

■ Curriculum

➽ Academic Success Program ➽ 86 credits required to graduate ➽ approx. 150 courses available
➽ degrees available: J.D.; J.D./M.B.A.; J.D./M.S. in Nursing; J.D./Masters of Sports Administration; J.D./LL.M. in Taxation; LL.M. in Business & Taxation; M.T. in Taxation
➽ semesters, start in Aug. ➽ 170-180 first-year day students, 85-90 first-year evening students

The school's primary mission is to provide both day and evening division students with an excellent education—an educational experience that combines competency-based legal education with a commitment to service and leadership in the profession and broader community. Capital is a forward-looking school. It combines a theoretical education with a program that emphasizes the skills and values necessary to practice in the 21st century.

Capital University's J.D. program combines the best of a traditional legal education with innovative programs. Our professors are accomplished scholars, whose first and foremost duty is teaching. The law school has the only ABA-approved postgraduate tax law program for lawyers and accountants in Ohio.

For further details and specific course offerings, please consult the law school viewbook available upon request from the school.

■ Multicultural Affairs

Capital University makes a significant effort to recruit, admit, and enroll minority students. Capital has many programs to aid in the retention of minority students; these include the presence of minority faculty, a director of minority affairs, availability of financial resources, and academic and nonacademic support, as well as placement opportunities through the minority clerkship program. Capital is constantly striving to create a more culturally diverse academic environment within the law school community.

■ Special Programs

The law school's outstanding clinical program, under supervision of faculty members, gives the student hands-on experience working in the legal system.

Within the professional and graduate curricula, programs designed to enrich the experience of our students and faculty and to better serve the local and world communities have begun and flourished. The innovative work of these programs—the Study Abroad at Home Summer Program, the Center for Dispute Resolution Jamaica Project, and the Citizen Education Program—was recognized in the Summer 1992 issue of the *Syllabus*, the publication of the ABA Section of Legal Education and Admissions to the Bar.

The Capital University Law School Center for Dispute Resolution acts as a resource for the development of dispute resolution methods which serve as alternatives to litigation.

The "Study Abroad at Home" program, the only one of its kind in the United States, brings up to four international law professors to Capital each summer to teach courses and participate in special seminars for the law school community. Acclaimed worldwide, the summer-long program has presented visiting professors from Brazil, Israel, Lebanon, Venezuela, Denmark, Japan, Ireland, Hungary, Turkey, Nigeria, and the People's Republic of China.

The Ethics Institute of Capital University Law School was established in 1989 with a mission of furthering ethical awareness and understanding in the fields of legal, medical, and business ethics.

Capital University offers the four following joint-degree programs:

In order to offer a joint **J.D./Master of Sports Administration/Facility Management Degree**, Capital University has entered into agreement with Ohio University, one of the pioneers in the field of sports administration. This program allows a student to participate in one of the nation's most reputable sports administration programs while earning a law degree.

The law school and the Graduate School of Administration cooperatively offer a joint J.D./Master of Business Administration. The curriculum allows simultaneous enrollment in both schools, and reduces by 18 hours the total hours of credit required for separate J.D. and M.B.A. degrees.

Capital's School of Nursing, in conjunction with the law school, offers a joint J.D./Masters of Science in Nursing Degree. A graduate with a M.N.S./J.D. is exceptionally well prepared to address the needs of a health care system that is becoming increasingly complex in terms of the need for technical competence, compassionate care, and public accountability.

Under the combined **J.D./LL.M. in Taxation**, a student who has had Federal Personal Income Tax (FPIT) may take 12 hours in advanced tax courses while pursuing a J.D. degree. Upon graduation the student could matriculate into the LL.M. program and complete the LL.M. degree in one semester of full-time study (12 credit hours).

■ Admission

➽ *Bachelor's degree required for admission*
➽ *application deadline—May 1* ➽ *LSAT, LSDAS required*
➽ *median GPA—3.25* ➽ *median LSAT score—153*
➽ *application fee—$35*

The law school seeks applicants who ranked in the upper half of their undergraduate class and achieved an LSAT score above the 50th percentile. Other factors used in evaluation include the competitiveness and difficulty of the candidate's undergraduate school and course of study, any graduate coursework, employment history, writing ability, and general background.

■ Expenses and Financial Aid

➽ *tuition & fees—first-year full-time, $14,663; first-year part-time, $8,987* ➽ *estimated additional expenses—$9,500 (includes books and living expenses)* ➽ *merit-based scholarships; need- & merit-based grants available*
➽ *minority scholarships available (see viewbook)*
➽ *financial aid available; work-study, student loans, research assistants and teaching assistants*
➽ *FAFSA required; forms are available after Jan. 1*

■ Student Activities

Numerous cocurricular and extracurricular activities are offered by Capital. These include the Night Prosecutors Program, an award-winning project for resolving minor disputes.

Capital University Law Review is a student-edited, general review which publishes four journals annually on significant topics of current, social concern.

Extensive programs in appellate and trial advocacy and client counseling are available. In addition to offering courses in these subjects, the law school encourages students to participate in intra- and interscholastic counseling and advocacy competitions each year.

■ Career Services

Capital University Law School maintains a full-time career services staff which assists students in achieving their career goals by providing individual career counseling; serving as an information clearinghouse for job postings and resource materials; presenting a variety of workshops on career options, résumé writing, interviewing, and job search strategies; developing the on-campus interview program; and promoting off-campus interview conferences.

Applicant Group for the 1995-1996 Academic Year

Capital University Law School

LSAT Score	GPA								
	3.75 +	3.50 - 3.74	3.25 - 3.49	3.00 - 3.24	2.75 - 2.99	2.50 - 2.74	2.25 - 2.49	2.00 - 2.24	Below 2.00
175 - 180	Very Likely	Very Likely	Very Likely	Very Likely	Very Likely	Very Likely	Possible	Possible	Unlikely
170 - 174	Very Likely	Very Likely	Very Likely	Very Likely	Very Likely	Very Likely	Possible	Possible	Unlikely
165 - 169	Very Likely	Very Likely	Very Likely	Very Likely	Very Likely	Very Likely	Possible	Unlikely	Unlikely
160 - 164	Very Likely	Very Likely	Very Likely	Very Likely	Very Likely	Possible	Possible	Unlikely	Unlikely
155 - 159	Very Likely	Very Likely	Very Likely	Very Likely	Possible	Possible	Unlikely	Unlikely	Unlikely
150 - 154	Very Likely	Very Likely	Very Likely	Possible	Possible	Unlikely	Unlikely	Unlikely	Unlikely
145 - 149	Possible	Possible	Possible	Unlikely	Unlikely	Unlikely	Unlikely	Unlikely	Unlikely
140 - 144	Unlikely	Unlikely	Unlikely	Unlikely	Unlikely	Unlikely	Unlikely	Unlikely	Unlikely
135 - 139	Unlikely	Unlikely	Unlikely	Unlikely	Unlikely	Unlikely	Unlikely	Unlikely	Unlikely
130 - 134	Unlikely	Unlikely	Unlikely	Unlikely	Unlikely	Unlikely	Unlikely	Unlikely	Unlikely
125 - 129	Unlikely	Unlikely	Unlikely	Unlikely	Unlikely	Unlikely	Unlikely	Unlikely	Unlikely
120 - 124	Unlikely	Unlikely	Unlikely	Unlikely	Unlikely	Unlikely	Unlikely	Unlikely	Unlikely

Very Likely Possible Unlikely

Benjamin N. Cardozo School of Law Yeshiva University

55 Fifth Avenue
New York, NY 10003

E-Mail: lawinfo@yu1.yu.edu
URL: http://www.yu.edu/csl/law/
Phone: 212.790.0274

■ Introduction

The Benjamin N. Cardozo School of Law is highly regarded for its unique curriculum, which combines traditional coursework with other academic disciplines such as history, literature, and philosophy. Cardozo is also well known for the number of clinical, internship, and externship opportunities in the areas of public and corporate law. Students may begin legal studies with one of three classes entering each year in September, January, or May.

■ Enrollment/Student Body

➡ 2,194 applicants ➡ enrolled—Jan., 53; May, 44; Sept., 287 ➡ student population—975 ➡ 136 undergraduate schools represented in 1995 entering classes

September's entering class is a traditional three-year program; January and May classes are Accelerated Entry Plans (AEP), designed so students may complete six semesters of law school in two-and-one-half-years. AEP programs are particularly appealing to mid-year graduates and returning students who wish to begin legal studies in January or May.

The student body parallels the heterogeneous population unique to New York City. There is a broad geographical distribution, a strong ethnic focus, approximately equal gender representation, and a wide range in ages and backgrounds. Many "returning students," who comprise nearly one-fifth of the student body, have advance degrees and work experience in other fields before entering law school.

■ Faculty

➡ 122 total ➡ 46 full-time ➡ 76 part-time or adjunct ➡ 32% women

Drawn from the leading ranks of America's legal community, many of Cardozo's faculty hold advanced degrees in other disciplines, i.e., philosophy, political science, and comparative literature. Cardozo was named among the top 20 law schools nationwide in a recent survey on faculty scholarship.

■ Library and Physical Facilities

➡ 385,000 volumes & equivalents ➡ LEXIS ➡ NEXIS ➡ WESTLAW ➡ OCLC ➡ Integrated Automated Library System ➡ 7 full-time librarians ➡ library seats 500

■ Location

Located in Greenwich Village, Cardozo is easily accessible to Manhattan courts, Wall Street, Midtown, and the art and music centers on the upper east and west sides.

■ Curriculum

➡ 84 credits required to graduate ➡ 135 courses available ➡ degree available: J.D. ➡ range of first-year class size—40-55

The first-year curriculum is prescribed; upper-level courses are mostly elective.

■ Professional Development/Clinical Opportunities

Cardozo's newly created **Intellectual Property Program**, encompassing the worlds of entertainment, fine art, multimedia, patenting, and computer technology, combines a specialized curriculum with related externships in this burgeoning area of law. **The Jacob Burns Institute for Advanced Legal Studies** provides funding for academic research and major symposia and also underwrites a scholarship program. The **Samuel and Ronnie Heyman Center on Corporate Governance** sponsors conferences in the area of corporate law and society and provides summer fellowships. The **International Institute** features a summer program in Israel covering the Arab-Israeli conflict; Islamic law, and civil liberties in Israel and the United States.

Cardozo's extensive clinical programs, internship, and externship opportunities offer vital support to firms and agencies. In the **Criminal Law Clinic**, participants represent criminally accused clients in Manhattan Criminal Court. The **Criminal Appeals Clinic** allows students to help file appeals for convicted petitioners before the Appellate Division of the New York State Supreme Court. The **Innocence Project**, an off-shoot of this clinic, assists prisoners whose innocence may be proven through DNA testing. In the **Prosecutor Practicum**, students work directly with senior staff at the Manhattan District Attorney's Office. **The Intensive Trial Advocacy Program** provides training in advanced trial techniques.

The Alexander Judicial Fellow Program places 25 outstanding students in clerkships with prominent federal judges. The **Bet Tzedek Legal Services Clinic**, nationally recognized for progressive work in representing elderly and disabled individuals, provides legal assistance in matters involving issues such as entitlement programs and discrimination. The **Mediation Clinic**, one of the first of its kind in the nation, provides training in alternative conflict resolution, and practical experience in the Brooklyn Mediation Center where students serve as arbiters in a wide range of disputes involving personal and social conflict. **Tax Clinic** participants represent taxpayers in cases pending before the United States Tax Court.

The **Appellate Externship Program** provides experience in the Appeals Unit of the New York City Department of Law. The **Summer Institute for Placement and Career Development** offers intensive seminars linked to related placements in areas such as International Trade Law, Real Estate Law, Entertainment Law, Environmental Law, and Civil and Criminal Litigation Practice. Cardozo's **Public Interest Summer Stipend Program** funds students working in government and public interest internships. **Telford Taylor Fellowships** are awarded to students securing internships with public international organizations or in international human rights.

■ Admission

➻ Baccalaureate degree, LSAT and LSDAS registration required ➻ deadlines: January admission, Dec. 1; May & Sept. admission, April 1 ➻ median GPA—3.34 (admitted students) ➻ median LSAT score—159 (admitted students) ➻ application fee—$60

Each applicant's LSAT score; undergraduate and graduate records; letters of recommendation; and material reflecting character, academic achievement, and aptitude for law study are carefully considered. Transfer students may enter in September or January.

Cardozo law school is a nonsectarian school, operating in accordance with the laws of New York State and the United States. The Association of American Law Schools, which, along with the American Bar Association, accredits the school, has established as one of its standards for accreditation the following: "A member school shall provide equality of legal education for all persons, including faculty and employees, with respect to hiring, continuation, promotion and tenure, applicants for admission, enrolled students, and graduates, without discrimination or segregation on the grounds of race, color, religion, national origin, sex, age, handicap or disability, or sexual orientation."

■ Publications/Student Activities

Cardozo Law Review, Arts and Entertainment Law Journal, Cardozo Women's Law Journal, Journal of International and Comparative Law, and Moot Court Honor Society each select students on the basis of scholarship and writing ability.

Cardozo Studies in Law and Literature is a professional journal edited by a senior member of the faculty.

Student organizations include the Student Bar Association; the Black, Asian, and Latino Law Students Associations; Cardozo Law Women; and the Gay and Lesbian Law Society. In addition, there are many organizations devoted to particular areas of law, e.g., the Constitutional Law Society, Environmental Law Society, International Law Society, Arts and Entertainment Law Society, and Criminal Law Society.

■ Expenses And Financial Aid

➻ tuition & fees—$18,100 ➻ merit and need-based awards available ➻ FAFSA required

■ Placement

Cardozo's Center for Professional Development coordinates a full range of placement services including career counseling, workshops on resume writing and interviewing skills, and mock interviews.

Ninety percent of the 1994 graduates who reported were employed within several months of graduation. The average overall starting salary was $52,275. Students were employed in the following areas: private practice (62 percent); business and industry (16 percent); government (9 percent); judicial clerkships (5 percent); public service (2 percent); teaching (1 percent); and other (5 percent).

In 1994, 87 percent of Cardozo graduates passed the New York State bar examination on their first attempt.

Applicant Group for the 1995-1996 Academic Year

Benjamin N. Cardozo School of Law Yeshiva University
This grid includes only applicants who earned 120-180 LSAT scores under standard administrations.

LSAT Score	3.75 +		3.50 - 3.74		3.25 - 3.49		3.00 - 3.24		2.75 - 2.99		2.50 - 2.74		2.25 - 2.49		2.00 - 2.24		Below 2.00		No GPA		Total	
	Apps	Adm	Apps	Adm	Apps	Adm	Apps	Adm	Apps	Adm	Apps	Adm	Apps	Adm	Apps	Adm	Apps	Adm	Apps	Adm	Apps	Adm
175 - 180	2	2	1	1	1	1	0	0	0	0	0	0	0	0	0	0	0	0	0	0	4	4
170 - 174	3	3	1	1	0	0	2	2	2	2	1	1	1	1	0	0	0	0	0	0	10	10
165 - 169	8	7	20	19	17	16	20	19	12	12	8	8	1	1	3	2	0	0	0	0	89	84
160 - 164	24	23	51	51	73	71	52	51	31	30	22	21	12	11	4	2	2	2	3	1	274	263
155 - 159	42	39	101	99	108	95	102	79	81	65	26	19	17	11	6	3	0	0	6	5	489	415
150 - 154	27	19	62	37	117	52	113	28	77	25	40	7	24	6	3	0	1	0	7	3	471	177
145 - 149	9	4	49	14	56	16	80	19	76	12	50	8	31	4	12	0	3	0	8	3	374	80
140 - 144	6	1	13	2	32	2	43	2	49	2	43	4	33	0	9	0	2	0	9	0	239	13
135 - 139	0	0	3	0	6	0	21	0	28	1	19	0	17	0	15	0	0	0	5	0	114	1
130 - 134	0	0	3	0	2	0	1	0	7	0	5	0	14	0	3	0	4	0	1	0	40	0
125 - 129	0	0	0	0	1	0	0	0	1	0	1	0	3	0	1	0	1	0	0	0	8	0
120 - 124	0	0	0	0	0	0	0	0	0	0	0	0	1	0	0	0	0	0	0	0	1	0
Total	121	98	304	224	413	253	434	200	364	149	215	68	154	34	56	7	13	2	39	12	2113	1047

(GPA columns)

Apps = Number of Applicants
Adm = Number Admitted
Reflects 97% of the total applicant pool.

Case Western Reserve University School of Law

11075 East Boulevard
Cleveland, OH 44106

E-Mail: lawadmissions@po.cwru.edu
URL: http://lawwww.cwru.edu
Phone: 216.368.3600

■ Introduction

The law school, located in Cleveland's beautiful University Circle, offers a nationally recognized legal education at a major comprehensive university in a city that is one of the nation's leading law centers. Founded in 1892, the school became a charter member of the AALS and was among the first schools accredited by the ABA. Today we have about 724 students who come from all over the country for our J.D. and LL.M. programs, and about 7,000 alumni living in virtually every state.

■ 1995 Entering Class

➡ *1,655 applicants* ➡ *216 enrolled*
➡ *22% students of color* ➡ *46% women*
➡ *41 states & foreign countries represented*
➡ *130 undergraduate schools represented* ➡ *59% outside Ohio*

■ Faculty

Our student-to-faculty ratio, including all faculty, is 15 to 1.

■ Library and Physical Facilities

➡ *342,630 volumes & equivalents* ➡ *LEXIS* ➡ *NEXIS* ➡ *WESTLAW* ➡ *CD-ROMs available on campus network: CIS Masterfile, WilsonDisc Index, LEGAL Trac, West CD-ROMs* ➡ *access to 700 electronic services and library catalogs through DIALOG, CWRUnet, OCLC-EPIC, USENET CLARINET, FREENET, DATATIMES, Internet, RLIN, HOLLIS Can/Law, VU-TEXT, CLL CAT, Dow Jones, Hannah Legislative Svc., CUY CTY PL CAT, QL (Quiclaw), NEWSNET, CPL, OCLC, OHIOLINK*

The award-winning law school building is handsome, contemporary, and comfortable. The law school is located in the heart of University Circle, one of the largest and richest cultural and educational centers in the nation, just 20 minutes away from downtown. The library's collection includes an extensive British collection and special collections in taxation, labor law, foreign investments, law-medicine, and international law. The library's professional and support staff places a heavy emphasis on assisting those who use the facilities. If we don't have what students need, we will get it. We have focused on the integration of modern technology with traditional research methods. Students benefit from the exciting advances in our computer technology that have enabled students to dial into our computer lab from their homes.

■ Curriculum

➡ *147 courses available* ➡ *degrees available: J.D./M.B.A. (Management); J.D./M.S.S.A. (Social Work); J.D./M.N.O. (Nonprofit Management); J.D./M.A. (Legal History)*
➡ *range of first-year class size—28-90*

The first year consists of required courses, including the Research, Analysis, and Writing (RAW) program, which is staffed by full-time instructors, all experienced lawyers. Each RAW section meets in a small group. After the first year every student must take Professional Responsibility and a course with a substantial writing requirement. An array of elective courses allows students (if they wish) to concentrate in special areas.

■ The Law Medicine Center

Our long-established Law-Medicine Center focuses on the whole range of legal, social, economic, scientific, and ethical issues in which law and medicine are interrelated. The center also sponsors lectures, major conferences, and smaller forums, and is involved in the journal *Health Matrix* (see below).

■ International Law Program

We expect to prepare our students for a global practice in the 21st century. Our recently endowed Frederick K. Cox International Law Center has enabled us to strengthen even further our international law curriculum, sponsor visiting scholars from around the world, and provide study and work abroad opportunities for our students. The *Journal of International Law* is student-edited (see below). In addition, the Canada-U.S. Law Institute (sponsored with the law school of the University of Western Ontario) and Russian Legal Studies Program (affiliated with St. Petersburg University) offer courses, cocurricular programs, and student exchanges.

■ Professional Skills Programs

Besides the traditional classes in substantive law, our law school offers professional skills courses of which we are especially proud, such as Evidence for Litigators and Trial Tactics. We offer a simulation course, called The Lawyering Process, in which students practice interviewing, counseling, and negotiation. In addition, our Law School Clinic allows third-year students to represent actual clients in both civil and criminal cases, earning academic credit while providing a community service. Student interns have the guidance of our five full-time clinic faculty, all experienced practitioners. The student-faculty ratio in our clinic is 8 to 1.

■ Graduate Law Study

Our **LL.M. in United States Legal Studies** provides graduates from foreign law schools the opportunity to study the U.S. legal system and institutions. Students have weekly seminars on international business transactions with area practitioners and are paired with a student mentor and a practitioner mentor from a Cleveland firm or corporation.

The **LL.M. in Taxation** is designed as a part- or full-time program for practicing professionals who wish to gain a thorough understanding of the nation's increasingly complex tax laws and be better able to advise clients, particularly those involved in complicated transactions.

■ Student Activities

The school sponsors four student-edited scholarly journals— the *Case Western Reserve Law Review*; the *Journal of International Law*; the *Canada-U.S. Law Journal*; and *Health Matrix: The Journal of Law-Medicine*. Our student Moot Court Board sponsors an intramural competition and three interscholastic competitions—National, Niagara, and Craven. A fourth moot court competition, the Jessup Competition, is administered by the Society of International Law Students. Finally, we have an intramural/extramural mock trial program. Other activities include the Student Bar Association; Black Law Students Association; Women's Law Association; International Law Society; Law School Academy (a weekly speakers series); National Lawyers Guild; Student Public Interest Law Fellowship; Lesbian and Gay Law Alliance; Second Career Students; Student International Law Society; Environmental Law Society; Jewish Law Students Association; and several legal fraternities.

■ Admission

➧ *Bachelor's degree required* ➧ *application deadline—April 1* ➧ *LSAT, LSDAS required*
➧ *median GPA—3.36* ➧ *median LSAT score—158*
➧ *application fee—$40*

Our admission process is selective (and, as a result, the attrition rate is negligible). We weigh not only grade-point averages and LSAT scores, but also nonquantitative factors. Our standards are rigorous, but not rigid. We accept applications as early as October for admission in the following fall; our deadline is April 1, although early applicants have the best chance for admission and scholarships. As decisions are made, candidates are notified; most decisions are made between January 1 and May 15.

■ Expenses And Financial Aid

➧ *tuition & fees—full-time, $18,900; part-time/credit unit, $763*
➧ *estimated additional expenses—$4,405/semester (books, room & board, living expenses)* ➧ *scholarships available: merit-based scholarships & diversity grants*
➧ *financial aid loan programs available*

In addition to participating in government financial aid programs, we have our own scholarship funds. Around one-third of each entering class receives grants. Every year 10 exceptional entering students receive full-tuition scholarships. Every applicant with an outstanding record is automatically considered for scholarship award. In addition, we offer diversity grants.

■ Career Services

Our office offers a full range of services to students and alumni. Our graduates find placement throughout the country, including every major metropolitan area. Each year, employers from around the country visit our campus to interview students. We have an extremely effective network of alumni who live and practice across the United States. Hundreds serve as career counselors, meeting individually with students and hosting luncheons and receptions that help students form important connections.

Applicant Group for the 1995-1996 Academic Year

Case Western Reserve University School of Law
This grid includes only applicants who earned 120-180 LSAT scores.

	GPA																	
	3.75 +		3.50 - 3.74		3.25 - 3.49		3.00 - 3.24		2.75 - 2.99		2.50 - 2.74		Below 2.50		No GPA		Total	
LSAT Score	Apps	Adm	Apps	Adm	Apps	Adm	Apps	Adm	Apps	Adm	Apps	Adm	Apps	Adm	Apps	Adm	Apps	Adm
170 - 180	4	4	6	6	1	1	3	3	5	4	1	1	2	1	0	0	22	20
165 - 169	12	12	16	16	18	17	12	12	6	6	12	12	2	2	2	2	80	79
160 - 164	34	34	41	41	72	71	57	57	38	34	28	21	9	5	5	3	284	266
155 - 159	36	34	84	78	116	94	79	50	39	18	17	4	9	0	4	0	384	278
150 - 154	42	29	63	41	83	35	59	16	48	6	26	3	10	0	5	0	336	130
145 - 149	14	5	33	5	38	6	39	4	33	0	15	1	13	0	0	0	185	21
Below 145	3	1	13	3	21	1	26	1	16	0	15	0	26	0	5	0	125	6

Apps = Number of Applicants
Adm = Number Admitted
Reflects 86% of the total applicant pool.
This grid is to be used solely as a general guide in assessing the possibility of admission based on quantitative factors. Nonquantitative factors are evaluated in all admission decisions. Multiple LSAT scores are averaged.

The Catholic University of America—Columbus School of Law

Office of Admissions
Washington, DC 20064

E-Mail: sokatch@law.cua.edu
URL: http://www.law.cua.edu
Phone: 202.319.5151

■ Introduction

Founded in 1897, the Columbus School of Law is located on the 154-acre campus of the university. Students and faculty have access to unique legal resources: the Supreme Court, the Congress, the United States and District of Columbia courts, and federal, executive, and administrative departments. Yet, while offering the advantages of the nation's capital, the campus is located in a pleasant, non-commercial area, and offers the scenic atmosphere of a suburban school. Classes are small and personal.

Although Catholic has religious affiliation, the school welcomes students of all religious, racial, and ethnic backgrounds to a program that emphasizes a commitment to community service and the ethical practice of law. The school has been a member of the AALS since 1921, and approved by the ABA since 1925.

■ Enrollment/Student Body

➻ 2,800 applicants ➻ 1,164 admitted first-year class 1995 ➻ 309 enrolled first-year class 1995 ➻ 694 total full-time ➻ 251 total part-time ➻ 17% minority ➻ 45% women ➻ 50 states & foreign countries represented ➻ 276 undergraduate schools represented ➻ fewer than 50 percent of students enter directly from college

The first-year day and evening classes are sectioned in such a way that individual courses have 32 to 70 students. Upper-class courses range from 10 to 70 students. Individual faculty members are available for informal sessions, thus providing a personalized education.

■ Faculty

➻ 130 total ➻ 50 full-time ➻ 80 part-time or adjunct ➻ 15 women ➻ 6 minority

The faculty brings a broad range of interests and experience to the academic setting. The adjunct faculty and professorial lecturers are selected from among local judges and practitioners for their expertise in given areas of law.

■ Library and Physical Facilities

➻ 252,000 volumes & equivalents ➻ library hours: Mon.-Fri., 7:00 A.M.-11:45 P.M.; Sat. & Sun., 9:00 A.M.-11:45 P.M. ➻ LEXIS ➻ NEXIS ➻ WESTLAW ➻ DIALOG ➻ computer lab, computer-equipped carrels ➻ 3 VCR playback rooms ➻ 8 full-time librarians ➻ library seats 500

The Library of Congress and specialized law collections throughout the city complement the law school's legal collections. A new law school facility, completed in 1994, houses all components of the law school. It combines contemporary style with the rich architectural history of the campus. Law students have full access to other campus facilities, including a 40-acre athletic complex with pool, Nautilus equipment, sauna, tennis courts, and track.

■ Curriculum

➻ Academic Support Program ➻ Law and Public Policy Program ➻ 84 credits required to graduate ➻ 153 courses available ➻ degrees available: J.D.; J.D./M.L.S.; J.D./M.S.W.; J.D./M.A. ➻ semesters, start in Aug. ➻ range of first-year class size—32-70 ➻ Comparative and International Law Institute ➻ Institute for Communications Law Studies ➻ Corporate and Securities Law Concentration

The prescribed first-year curriculum and method of teaching are designed to develop the analytical skills that characterize the able lawyer and to give the student familiarity with the major substantive areas of law. While lawyers traditionally have been heavily involved with the commercial interests of private or corporate clients, law is becoming increasingly responsive to problems that affect the public interest. The law school curriculum is designed to provide students with the basic knowledge to become effective lawyers in a changing legal environment.

■ Special Programs

The Institute for Communications Law Studies offers unique specialized training in communications law. The Institute currently offers nine courses and related externships to students who will receive the J.D. degree and a certificate from the Institute.

The Comparative and International Law Institute offers a concentration of courses in the public and private areas of international law. Externships and paid employment are also available in these areas. The institute also offers a six-week Summer Abroad Program at the Jagiellonian University in Cracow, Poland.

The Law and Public Policy Program uniquely combines classroom studies in legislative and administrative processes with externships in government agencies and advocacy organizations that affect national public policy.

■ Clinical Programs

The law school offers nine clinical programs, including seven that emphasize client representation, case planning, and trial and administrative advocacy. The other two clinical offerings are: the Securities and Exchange Commission Training Program and the Legal Externship Program.

■ Admission

➻ Bachelor's degree from an accredited college or university required ➻ application deadline—March 1 ➻ LSAT, LSDAS required ➻ median GPA—3.20 ➻ median LSAT score—157 ➻ application fee—$55 ➻ admission decisions are made beginning in Dec., and continue until the class is filled

While heavy consideration is given to the applicant's grade-point average and LSAT scores, decisions are influenced by such other factors as leadership qualities, rank in class, improving performance, academic standards of the undergraduate school, the curriculum, potential for contributing to diversity, relevant work experience, and evidence of factors that adversely affected the student's grades. Special consideration is given to applicants from disadvantaged groups.

The Preface Program, a three-week summer program, is offered to entering students whose credentials indicate that an intensive introduction to law school would be especially beneficial.

■ Student Activities

The *Catholic University Law Review*, the *Journal of Contemporary Health Law*, and *COMMLAW CONSPECTUS: Journal of Communications Law and Policy* are scholarly law journals staffed by outstanding students. The Moot Court Board conducts five major competitions and a number of intraschool competitions each academic year. The Honor Board administers the student-created honor code of ethical standards of personal and professional conduct. The Student Bar Association provides a channel for student opinion and selects representatives to participate as voting members of faculty committees. Other activities include the Thurgood Marshall American Inn of Court, Black Law Students Association, Women's Organization, Latin American Law Students Association, Jewish Law Students Association, Asian-Pacific American Law Students Association, and many other student-interest groups.

■ Expenses and Financial Aid

➽ tuition & fees—full-time, $20,125; part-time, $15,135 ➽ estimated additional expenses—(room, board, books, transportation)—$12,458 ➽ performance and need-based scholarships are available ➽ performance and need-based minority scholarships are available ➽ financial aid available ➽ registration with Need Access and FAFSA is required

Financial aid decisions are made beginning in March.

■ Career Services

The Office of Legal Career Services actively supports students and graduates in their search for employment by providing counseling as well as activities that facilitate direct placement. On-campus interviews are provided. The school's small size permits individual counseling for each student desiring assistance. Our admissions brochure lists employment statistics, including distribution by type of practice and by geographic location.

■ Housing

A limited amount of graduate housing is available on campus. A variety of apartments and private rooms are within easy traveling distance. The Admissions Office assists students in locating apartments and roommates. Our location is convenient to public transportation, including the metrorail system.

Applicant Group for the 1995-1996 Academic Year

The Catholic University of America—Columbus School of Law
This grid includes only applicants who earned 120-180 LSAT scores under standard administrations.

LSAT Score	GPA 3.75 +		3.50 - 3.74		3.25 - 3.49		3.00 - 3.24		2.75 - 2.99		2.50 - 2.74		2.25 - 2.49		2.00 - 2.24		Below 2.00		No GPA	
	Apps	Adm	Apps	Adm	Apps	Adm	Apps	Adm	Apps	Adm	Apps	Adm	Apps	Adm	Apps	Adm	Apps	Adm	Apps	Adm
165 - 180	6	6	5	5	10	10	11	10	19	18	12	11	7	4	1	0	0	0	1	1
160 - 164	9	8	25	25	52	51	62	60	52	45	44	31	23	11	3	0	1	1	2	2
155 - 159	22	22	86	82	142	131	155	125	100	62	70	27	37	9	9	2	3	1	6	4
150 - 154	23	17	85	62	156	81	185	68	142	31	72	13	44	6	12	2	4	0	6	2
145 - 149	14	5	33	5	86	18	115	18	115	14	84	16	40	6	20	1	5	0	8	2
140 - 144	5	0	18	1	32	1	53	3	48	3	51	0	39	3	13	1	2	0	1	0
120 - 139	0	0	6	0	22	0	32	0	34	0	41	0	28	0	28	0	8	0	18	0

Apps = Number of Applicants
Adm = Number Admitted
Reflects 98% of the total applicant pool.
This grid should be used only as a general guide, as many nonnumerical factors are considered in admission decisions.

Chicago-Kent College of Law—Illinois Institute of Technology

Office of Admissions and Financial Aid
565 West Adams Street
Chicago, IL 60661-3691

E-Mail: admitq@kentlaw.edu
URL: http://www.kentlaw.edu
Phone: 312.906.5020

■ Introduction

Chicago-Kent College of Law, Illinois Institute of Technology is nationally acclaimed for its innovative approaches to traditional legal education and its specialized programs within the law school curriculum.

The law school's unique affiliation with the Illinois Institute of Technology, one of the nation's largest scientific research centers, provides support for interdisciplinary programs including the Center for Law and Computers, and the certificate programs in Environmental and Energy Law and Intellectual Property Law.

Chicago-Kent is located in downtown Chicago, the heart of the city's commercial and legal communities. The new law school building, completed in 1992, is equipped with the latest technology and includes a four-story library and a complete courtroom. The college is fully accredited by the ABA and the AALS and is a member of the Order of the Coif.

■ Enrollment and Student Body

➧ *2,550 applicants* ➧ *889 total full-time* ➧ *335 total part-time* ➧ *17.5% minority* ➧ *47% women*
➧ *54 states & foreign countries represented*
➧ *297 enrolled first-year class 1995, day division*
➧ *96 enrolled first-year class 1995, evening division*
➧ *45% out-of-state in most recent entering class*

■ Faculty

➧ *149 total* ➧ *75 full-time* ➧ *74 part-time or adjunct*
➧ *39 women* ➧ *15 minority*

■ Library and Physical Facilities

➧ *500,000 volumes & equivalents* ➧ *library hours: Mon.-Thurs., 7:45 A.M.-11:00 P.M.; Fri., 7:45 A.M.-7:00 P.M.; Sat., 9:00 A.M.-5:00 P.M.; Sun., 10:00 A.M.-11:00 P.M.*
➧ *LEXIS* ➧ *NEXIS* ➧ *WESTLAW* ➧ *DIALOG*
➧ *9 full-time librarians* ➧ *library seats 689*

The law library is among the largest national libraries. The collection includes the Library of International Relations and a wealth of material in environmental and energy law, intellectual property, international trade, and labor law.

An essential educational feature of the library and the classrooms is the extensive computer network in the building. Seats in the majority of classrooms, many library carrels and numerous locations throughout the building are tied to the computer network, enabling students with their own laptop computers to connect into the network and the many legal databases. There are three computer laboratories with more than 80 personal computers reserved for student use. Students have 24-hour access to the network and to LEXIS/NEXIS and WESTLAW through their home computers.

The new Marovitz Courtroom integrates design features from the best courtroom and trial advocacy training facilities in the nation.

■ Curriculum

➧ *Academic Support Program* ➧ *84 units/credits required to graduate* ➧ *over 100 courses offered each academic year*
➧ *degrees available: J.D.; J.D./M.B.A.; J.D./LL.M. in Taxation; J.D./LL.M. in Financial Services Law; J.D./M.S. in Financial Markets & Trading; J.D./M.S. in Environmental Management; LL.M. in Taxation; LL.M. in Financial Services Law; LL.M. in International and Comparative Law*
➧ *range of first-year class size—30-100*

Day students usually complete the J.D. degree in three years. Evening students usually finish in four years. Students can transfer between divisions after completing their required courses in the division in which they originally enrolled.

■ Special Programs

Notebook Computer Project—One-third of the students in the first-year class have color notebook computers with the electronic course materials for most of their classes. They can type notes directly into the materials, highlight crucial text in different colors and create course outlines that contain their notes along with the highlighted materials.

Legal Research and Writing—Chicago-Kent has the most comprehensive legal research and writing program in the country. The three-year, five-course curriculum teaches students to analyze a wide range of legal problems and to write about them persuasively.

Environmental and Energy Law—The certificate program's interdisciplinary approach to the problems of environmental regulation and natural resources allocation prepares students for practice through a series of courses in law, economic and public policy analysis, and in the scientific aspects of environmental problems.

Clinical Education—The Law Offices of Chicago-Kent, one of the largest in-house clinical education programs in the country, offers nine clinical education programs that include civil, criminal, health, immigration, mediation and tax law, and externships with government agencies and federal judges.

Trial Skills/Litigation and Alternative Dispute Resolution—The law school offers a two-semester sequence in trial advocacy and an intensive course. The courses are taught by skilled judges and experienced practitioners. There is a certificate program in Litigation and Alternative Dispute Resolution studies.

International and Comparative Law—The certificate program encompasses study in international business and trade, international and comparative law, and international human rights. The Library of International Relations is one of few official depositories for United Nations and European Community documents and the largest public research collection in the Midwest.

Intellectual Property Law—The certificate program focuses on issues relating to patent, trademark, copyright, trade secrets, and unfair competition. In addition to traditional coursework, students learn how to draft intellectual property documents in specialized legal writing courses and can develop their litigation skills by participating in intellectual property moot court and intensive trial advocacy teams.

■ Admission

➽ *B.A. or B.S. required for admission* ➽ *suggested application deadline—April 1* ➽ *LSAT, LSDAS required* ➽ *median GPA—3.20* ➽ *median LSAT score—156* ➽ *application fee—$40* ➽ *rolling admission; early application preferred*

Admission is highly selective. Decisions are based on a range of factors including quantitative and qualitative criteria. Each application is individually reviewed; there is no cut-off. Although the GPA and LSAT are important threshold criteria, consideration also is given to nonnumerical factors such as the nature and rigor of the undergraduate curriculum, writing ability, graduate work and professional experience, extracurricular activities, diversity, and the personal statement. The admission requirements for the full- and part-time divisions are the same. Entering classes begin only in the fall. The law school is committed to attracting and retaining students from a variety of racial, ethnic, economic, geographic, and educational backgrounds.

■ Student Activities

The *Chicago-Kent Law Review* is published in symposium format by student editors and staff, in association with a faculty editor. Moot Court and Trial Advocacy teams successfully compete in local, regional, and national competitions every year, providing numerous opportunities to develop litigation expertise. Diverse student interests are represented in a wide variety of social, political, and professional student groups.

■ Expenses and Financial Aid

➽ *tuition & fees—full-time, $18,030; part-time, $13,030* ➽ *estimated additional expenses (books, insurance, transportation, living expenses)—$9,640* ➽ *scholarships available* ➽ *FAFSA, Chicago-Kent Application for Financial Aid and financial Aid transcripts from previous schools required for financial aid; priority deadline—April 1*

The Kent Legal Scholars Program provides full-tuition, renewable scholarships, research assistantships, and special seminars to a select group of students who demonstrate exceptional academic and leadership ability, regardless of need. Substantial scholarship assistance is offered to entering and continuing students based on need and merit. Federal and other loans are available. A loan-repayment program helps graduates who choose public interest careers.

■ Career Services

More than 95 percent of recent graduates found professional employment within six months of being licensed to practice.

The Office of Career Services, with five full-time staff members and two part-time career strategists, sponsors fall and spring on-campus interview programs and offers individual counseling on résumé-writing, interview techniques, and job-search strategies.

■ Housing

Affordable on- and off-campus housing is available. The law school is close to all public transportation.

Applicant Group for the 1995-1996 Academic Year

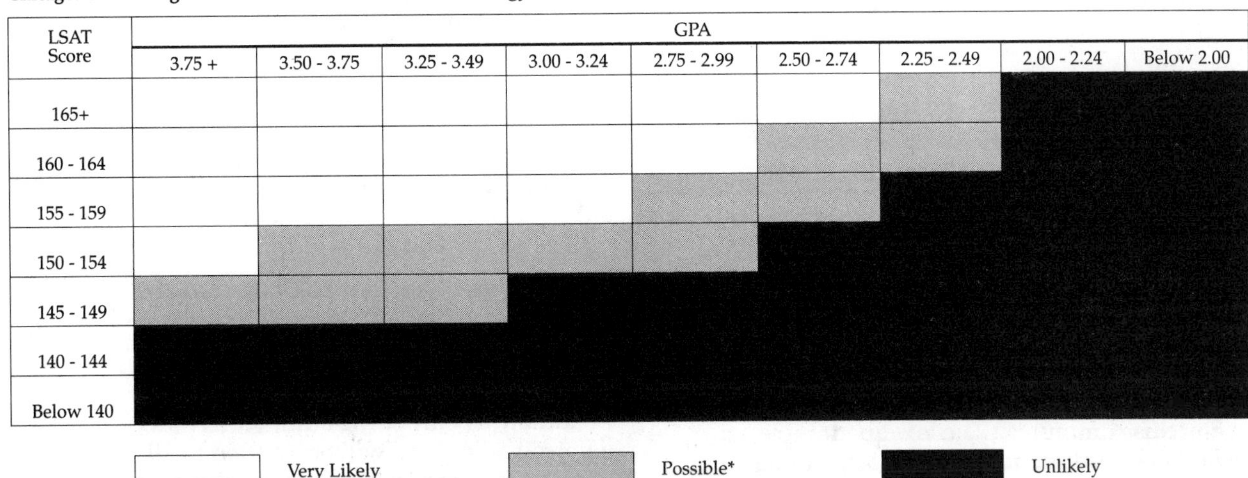

*Individual accomplishments are of particular importance.
The information in this grid is to be used only as a general guide. Each category represents numerous possible LSAT/GPA combinations so that a person with credentials at the upper limits of a category may have a better chance of admission than a person with credentials at the lower limits of the same category. This data does change from year to year and should be used as an approximate gauge of the likelihood of admission and **not** as a guarantee.

University of Chicago Law School

1111 E. 60th Street
Chicago, IL 60637

Phone: 312.702.9484

■ Introduction

Legal education at the University of Chicago has long stressed the interdependence of legal and social studies in the training of lawyers. The school's program combines an emphasis on technical legal knowledge and professional skills with a concern for illuminating the connections between law and the social forces with which it interacts. Contributing to the first objective are opportunities for the application of formal knowledge to specific professional tasks. The school's model court facility provides students the opportunity to take part in moot trials and appellate arguments and to observe actual court sessions. A significant fraction of the faculty represents disciplines other than law, including economics, history, sociology, philosophy, and political science. The curriculum also devotes substantial attention to relevant aspects of political theory, economics, legal history, comparative law, psychiatry, statistics, and other social science methodology. In addition to the student-edited University of Chicago *Law Review*, the University of Chicago *Legal Forum*, and the University of Chicago *Roundtable* the school is the home of four scholarly journals—Supreme Court Review; *Journal of Law and Economics*; *Journal of Legal Studies*; and *Crime and Justice: An Annual Review of Research*. It is also the home of the Center for Studies in Criminal Justice, the Legal History Program, the Law and Government Program, the Center for Constitutionalism in Eastern Europe, and the Law-Economics Program. The school is a charter member of the AALS and is on the approved list of the ABA.

■ Enrollment/Student Body

➽ 2,885 applicants ➽ 176 enrolled first-year class 1995 ➽ 545 total full-time J.D. ➽ 46 graduate students ➽ 21.3% minority ➽ 40% women ➽ 48 states & 29 foreign countries represented ➽ 177 undergraduate schools represented

■ Faculty

➽ 39 full-time ➽ 28 part-time or adjunct ➽ 4 minority

■ Library and Physical Facilities

➽ 575,000 volumes & equivalents
➽ 24 full-time library staff

The Law School is located on the 165-acre, tree-lined campus of the university in Hyde Park, a residential community on the shore of Lake Michigan 15 minutes south of Chicago's business and cultural center. Most of the university's faculty as well as its student body of 8,000 live in this community. The law quadrangle, designed by Eero Saarinen, consists of four connecting buildings surrounding an open court and reflecting pool. The six-story, glass-center structure contains the library, lounge, study areas, and offices. The library's collections of monographs, foreign law materials, and briefs and records in American appellate cases are outstanding. Offices and study areas are distributed around the library's open stacks, facilitating contact between students and faculty.

■ Curriculum

➽ 105 credits required to graduate ➽ joint degrees offered ➽ quarters, begin in Sept. ➽ 1994-1995 upper class curriculum: 82 courses (average size of 51 students) and 58 seminars (average size of 16 students).

The basic program of study involves three years (nine quarters) of full-time study leading to the J.D. degree. Recesses between quarters occur in mid-December and mid-March. In addition to coursework, first-year students perform individual assignments under the direction of a tutor. The tutorial work emphasizes training in research, preparation of legal documents, and oral argument. Second- and third-year students are encouraged to substitute seminar work and individual research under faculty supervision for courses. Students may take a limited number of relevant courses in other departments of the university for credit toward the J.D. degree.

■ Special Programs

In cooperation with the Graduate School of Business, the Law School offers a joint program leading to the J.D. and M.B.A. degrees in four years. Joint programs in history, international relations, and economics are also available. The university's School of Public Policy Studies, which includes several Law School faculty members, offers a one-year program leading to the Master of Arts degree in public policy.

■ Admission

➽ LSAT, LSDAS required ➽ application fee—$60
➽ use evaluative interviews

Admission to the Law School is based upon a careful review of each application by one or more members of the admissions committee. The committee considers all evidence that may indicate academic and professional promise. No automatic quantitative criteria are applied, although academic achievement as reflected in the college record and the evidence of intellectual ability provided by the LSAT are necessarily major determinants. The committee generally considers only a candidate's first LSAT score when multiple scores are presented unless a later score is substantially higher. Each year the Law School conducts evaluative interviews, by invitation, as part of the admissions process. One-year deferred admission will be granted to all admitted applicants who request it prior to June 15.

The admissions committee makes special efforts to ensure that each entering class contains students from a variety of geographic, educational, racial, and ethnic backgrounds, and is particularly interested in receiving applications from women and minority candidates, two groups that have traditionally been underrepresented in the profession.

■ Clinical Opportunities

The Mandel Legal Aid Clinic, located in the Law School, provides opportunities to learn litigation, lawyering, and other advocacy skills in five practice areas: criminal justice, employment discrimination, homeless assistance, mental health, and welfare work. The MacArthur Justice Center, part of the Clinic, focuses on constitutional impact litigation in such areas as the death penalty, parole board discretion, and state public defender resources. Every aspect of the Clinic's work is the responsibility of students under the supervision of the nine clinical faculty members.

■ Student Activities

About 40 percent of the members of the second- and third-year classes in the Law School serve on one of the three student journals. They are selected on the basis of either academic achievement in the first year or performance in a writing competition open to all students and conducted each year. The Hinton Moot Court Committee conducts a two-year program in appellate advocacy open to all second- and third-year students. Other student organizations include a local chapter of the Black Law Students Association, Environmental Law Society, the Law Women's Caucus, the Law School Film Society, the Federalist Society, International Comparative Law Society, National Lawyers Guild, the Law School Show, the Gay/Lesbian Law Students Association, Hispanic Law Students Association, and the Asian American Law Students Association.

■ Expenses and Financial Aid

➽ tuition & fees—$21,210 ➽ estimated additional expenses—$13,190 (living expenses)

Through scholarship and loan funds, the Law School provides assistance to students who demonstrate financial need. Applicants for need-based scholarships must register with Need Access. The Law School also offers a number of merit scholarships which provide up to full tuition to a limited number of exceptional students.

■ Housing

A graduate residence hall, located two blocks from the Law School, is available for 140 graduate students from all areas of the university. Every first-year law student who wishes to do so, usually between 80 to 100 students, will live in this facility, which has mostly single rooms with private baths. The university has sufficient single and married student housing in Hyde Park to meet the needs of all students who request it. Campus buses run frequently during the day and evening between these buildings and the Law School.

■ Career Services

A full-time placement office assists students in obtaining permanent, summer, and part-time employment. During the 1994-95 academic year, 350 employers scheduled interviews at the Law School. The distribution of employers by region was Midwest (31 percent), Northeast (36 percent), West (25 percent), and South (8 percent). At the time of graduation, 98 percent of the Class of 1995 was employed; 70 percent joined law firms, 26 percent obtained judicial clerkships, and the remainder were with government or legal services employers. Seven graduates of the Law School clerked for justices on the United States Supreme Court during the 1994-95 term. Ninety-nine percent of the Class of 1996 and 90 percent of the Class of 1997 had law-related positions during the summer of 1995.

Applicant Group for the 1995-1996 Academic Year

The median LSAT score of all applicants admitted for the 1995 entering class was 170. Of all the applicants who had LSAT scores at or above 170, 65 percent were offered admission. The comparable percentages of applicants offered admission with other LSAT scores: 169-167, 40 percent; 166-164, 14 percent; 163-161, 9 percent; below 161, 2 percent. The median GPA of all applicants admitted for the 1995 entering class was 3.75. Of all the applicants who had a GPA at or above 3.75, 42 percent were offered admission. The comparable percentages of applicants offered admission with other GPAs: 3.75-3.6, 31 percent; 3.59-3.4, 20 percent; 3.39-3.2; 6 percent; below 3.2, 4 percent.

University of Cincinnati College of Law

P.O. Box 210040
Office of Admissions and Financial Aid
Cincinnati, OH 45221-0040

E-Mail: admissions@law.uc.edu
URL: http://www.law.uc.edu
Phone: 513.556.6805

■ Introduction

The College of Law at the University of Cincinnati was established in 1833. America's fourth-oldest law school, the college today is a national public law school serving an enrollment of 400 students—approximately 135 per class. The College of Law is a cornerstone on the University of Cincinnati campus in historic Clifton. This central location approximately 10 minutes north of the city's downtown area provides easy access to state, county, and federal courts, including the U.S. Court of Appeals for the Sixth Circuit. A charter member of the AALS, the University of Cincinnati was one of the first law schools to have a chapter of the Order of the Coif and to be approved by the ABA.

■ Enrollment/Student Body

Report on first-year class 1995:
➻ 1,202 applicants ➻ 338 admitted ➻ 121 enrolled ➻ 11% minority ➻ 50% women ➻ 19 states & foreign countries represented ➻ 61 undergraduate schools represented ➻ 37 majors represented ➻ average age—26 ➻ 17% of class age 30+ upon entrance ➻ 73% state residents

■ Faculty

➻ 51 total ➻ 25 full-time ➻ 26 adjunct ➻ 7 women ➻ 2 minority

The law school has doubled the size of the faculty and constructed a new law building and library in the last 15 years. The resulting student-to-faculty ratio of 16:1 is one of the best nationally.

■ Library and Physical Facilities

➻ 354,562 volumes & equivalents ➻ library hours: Mon.-Fri., 7:45 A.M.-11:00 P.M.; Sat.-Sun., 10:00 A.M.-11:00 P.M. ➻ LEXIS ➻ NEXIS ➻ WESTLAW ➻ UCLIO ➻ OHIOLINK ➻ OCLC ➻ DIALOG ➻ EPIC ➻ DATATIMES ➻ 7 full-time librarians ➻ library seats 385

The College of Law is one of the few law libraries large enough to seat its entire student body, if necessary. Two new student computer labs offer an excellent array of computer-assisted research aids and laser printers.

The library has built two databases already via the Internet: DIANA, a database of human rights materials, supports the work of the Urban Morgan Institute for Human Rights; and the Securities Lawyer's Deskbook supports the work of the newly established Center for Corporate Law.

■ Curriculum

➻ 88 credits required to graduate ➻ 60-80 courses available ➻ degrees available: J.D./M.B.A.; J.D./M.C.P.; J.D./M.A. in Women's Studies ➻ semesters, Aug.-Dec., Jan.-May ➻ range of first-year class size—135

The College of Law has well developed academic traditions in all major areas of the law. Especially strong programs exist in the areas of corporate, environmental, intellectual property law, and human rights.

■ Special Programs

The College of Law recognizes that a lawyer needs both a firm grasp of subject matter and expertise in professional skills. The college has developed an extensive legal research and writing program that not only encompasses the first year, but upper-level courses as well. To involve students directly in the legal system, the Judge In Residence Program brings actual trials to the law school courtroom so that students can observe a visiting judge. The Extern Program provides students with client-representation experience and the opportunity to work with practicing attorneys in public agencies. Additionally, the College of Law has centers in the international human rights and corporate law areas. Each center offers a fellowship program, research opportunities, and in-depth study in their respective areas. Additional information on the Urban Morgan Institute for Human Rights and the Center for Corporate Law can be received by contacting the Admissions Office.

■ Admission Standards

➻ Bachelor's degree required ➻ application deadline—April 1 ➻ LSAT, LSDAS required ➻ median GPA—3.47 ➻ median LSAT score—160 ➻ application fee—$35

Applicants must have a baccalaureate degree from an accredited institution prior to enrollment. A valid LSAT score and the LSDAS subscription are required. Applications should be submitted before April 1. Admission to the college is based upon a selective review of each candidate's file. Although the admissions committee relies on the grade-point average and LSAT score to determine the applicant's academic potential, other nonquantitative factors believed to be relevant to success in law school are considered; i.e., the quality of the applicant's education, participation in community service, employment experience, graduate work, and letters of recommendation. The educational philosophy of the college reflects a belief that a quality legal education is enhanced by having a heterogeneous student body. The committee, therefore, also considers race, cultural background, unusual personal circumstances, and age. Admission decisions are made on a rolling basis. Special consideration is given to competitive applications from members of minority groups who have been economically and culturally disadvantaged. Particular effort is made to provide adequate financial assistance for all students admitted.

■ Student Activities

The University of Cincinnati Law Review was founded in 1927 and was the first law review published by an Ohio law school. Edited quarterly by student editors, *Law Review* members are selected on the basis of both scholastic achievement and writing ability. The College's Moot Court Program participates in all national intercollegiate competitions and annually hosts the National Product Liabilities Competition. The Student Bar Association and Student Legal Education Committee participate in governance of the college, providing student members for law school committees. Additionally, the Volunteer Lawyers for the Poor (VLP) organization was founded in 1991.

■ Expenses and Financial Aid

- *tuition & fees—resident, $6,570; nonresident, $12,768*
- *scholarships available*
- *FAFSA required, March 1 deadline*

Living expenses are estimated at $9,691 for independent students. Scholarships are awarded to approximately 60 percent of the entering class on the basis of academic merit alone or on the basis of merit and financial need. Deadline for receipt of the Scholarship Information Sheet form is March 1. The University Financial Aid Office assists students in obtaining Perkins Loans.

■ Placement

The college maintains an active Career Planning and Placement Center with a professional staff available to counsel students seeking permanent, summer, and part-time employment. The Career Planning and Placement Office provides an on-campus recruiting program with over 60 law firms and agencies, businesses, corporations, and financial institutions participating. In recent years, over 90 percent of each graduating class has accepted employment within six months of graduation. Typically, 55-60 percent of a graduating class will enter private practice; 10-15 percent, judicial clerkships; 10 percent, business/corporations; 10 percent, government; and 2-4 percent, public interest. While 75 percent of graduates accept employment in the Midwest, an increasing number have accepted positions nationally. Graduates are employed in 48 states, the District of Columbia, and numerous foreign countries. The average salary for the class of 1994 was $39,059.

Applicant Group for the 1995-1996 Academic Year

University of Cincinnati College of Law
This grid includes only applicants who earned 120-180 LSAT scores under standard administrations.

LSAT Score	GPA 3.75 +		3.50 - 3.74		3.25 - 3.49		3.00 - 3.24		2.75 - 2.99		2.50 - 2.74		2.25 - 2.49		2.00 - 2.24		Below 2.00		No GPA		Total	
	Apps	Adm	Apps	Adm	Apps	Adm	Apps	Adm	Apps	Adm	Apps	Adm	Apps	Adm	Apps	Adm	Apps	Adm	Apps	Adm	Apps	Adm
175 - 180	0	0	0	0	1	1	0	0	0	0	0	0	0	0	0	0	0	0	0	0	1	1
170 - 174	0	0	3	2	1	1	1	1	0	0	0	0	2	2	1	1	0	0	0	0	8	7
165 - 169	8	8	3	3	9	8	9	9	10	9	5	5	2	2	1	0	1	0	1	1	49	45
160 - 164	14	13	29	28	49	44	41	30	20	17	9	8	9	5	2	1	0	0	1	0	174	146
155 - 159	35	30	43	28	59	8	54	6	30	2	21	2	7	0	4	0	0	0	2	0	255	76
150 - 154	31	14	59	11	72	7	70	3	46	5	27	3	5	0	3	0	2	0	4	0	319	43
145 - 149	12	1	21	4	37	0	39	3	34	1	34	1	6	0	3	0	1	0	1	0	188	10
140 - 144	3	0	9	0	17	0	20	0	23	0	12	0	13	0	5	0	2	0	3	0	107	0
135 - 139	1	0	0	0	5	0	9	0	8	0	9	0	10	0	3	0	1	0	0	0	46	0
130 - 134	0	0	1	0	3	0	4	0	5	0	1	0	3	0	1	0	2	0	1	0	21	0
125 - 129	0	0	1	0	0	0	3	0	1	0	1	0	4	0	0	0	1	0	2	0	13	0
120 - 124	0	0	0	0	0	0	0	0	0	0	0	0	1	0	0	0	0	0	0	0	1	0
Total	104	66	169	76	253	69	250	52	177	34	119	19	62	9	23	2	10	0	15	1	1182	328

Apps = Number of Applicants
Adm = Number Admitted
Reflects 98% of the total applicant pool.

Cleveland State University—Cleveland-Marshall College of Law

1801 Euclid Ave.
Cleveland, OH 44115

E-Mail: mmcnally@trans.csuohio.edu
URL: http://www.csuohio.edu/law
Phone: 216.687.2304

■ Introduction

The Cleveland State University College of Law, located on the university's new urban campus in downtown Cleveland, is the largest law school in Ohio. It has been training lawyers since its forerunners, the Cleveland Law School and John Marshall Law School, were established in 1887 and 1916, respectively. Since becoming part of the state university system in 1969, the Cleveland-Marshall College of Law has maintained and enhanced its long-standing reputation for training attorneys dedicated to the service of their communities. The college operates a full-time day and part-time evening program, preparing students for practice in any jurisdiction. It is a member of AALS and the League of Ohio Law Schools and is approved by the ABA. Located on Lake Erie, Cleveland is an active cultural center, nationally renowned for its parks, libraries, and museums. The Cleveland Symphony Orchestra is one of the finest in the world. Cleveland is also a major industrial center and headquarters for many large corporations. An excellent rapid transportation system links downtown Cleveland and Cleveland State University to the eastern and western suburbs of the city.

■ Enrollment/Student Body

➽ *802 admitted first-year class 1995* ➽ *303 enrolled first-year class 1995* ➽ *571 total full-time* ➽ *339 total part-time*
➽ *13% minority* ➽ *43% women (first-year class)*
➽ *25 states & foreign countries represented*
➽ *150 undergraduate schools represented*

From 15 to 20 percent of each entering class is likely to be over 30 years old, with as many as 15 percent earning advanced degrees before beginning the study of law. From 20 to 25 percent of each class comes to Cleveland State from outside Ohio. Students of color and women are actively recruited and are encouraged to apply.

■ Faculty

➽ *65 total* ➽ *34 full-time* ➽ *31 part-time or adjunct*

■ Library and Physical Facilities

➽ *380,000 volumes & equivalents* ➽ *LEXIS*
➽ *NEXIS* ➽ *WESTLAW*

The university library, with over 800,000 volumes, is readily accessible to law students. Other university facilities, including a bookstore, cafeterias, and modern gymnasium, are also available to law students and are within walking distance.

■ Curriculum

➽ *87 credits required to graduate*
➽ *degrees available: J.D.; J.D./M.B.A.; J.D./M.P.A.*

In both day and evening programs, the core curriculum and most elective courses are taught by full-time faculty. The adjunct faculty, consisting of prominent judges and lawyers, teach in highly specialized areas. Typically, the J.D. program is completed by full-time day students in three academic years and by part-time evening students in four academic years and two summers. Full-time students may also attend summer sessions to accelerate their study.

■ Special Programs

The urban setting of the college offers unusual opportunities to bring challenging legal experiences to students. Externship programs take the student out of the classroom and into the courtroom. A Street Law Program allows students to earn course credit while teaching law in area high schools. A more specialized clinical opportunity is afforded the students who participate in these programs. The Fair Employment Practices Clinic provides credit for participation in litigation dealing with employment discrimination. The Judicial Externship Program offers upper-level students opportunities to work with state appellate and federal court judges. A joint program with the College of Business permits interested students to earn both the J.D. and M.B.A. degrees in four years. A new program, the J.D./M.P.A. degree program, has been introduced this year. This program is being offered jointly by the College of Urban Studies and the College of Law. Each year lawyers, judges, and legal scholars of national renown are invited to the College of Law as Cleveland-Marshall Fund lecturers. Each of these distinguished visitors delivers a major address and spends two days at the College of Law meeting informally with students and faculty and conducting class sessions.

■ Admission

➽ *fall admission only* ➽ *LSAT, LSDAS required*

Applicants are admitted by the Dean upon the recommendation of an Admissions Committee composed of faculty members and students. Criteria for admission are identical for the full-time and part-time programs. Each applicant must have received a bachelor's level degree from a college or university accredited at the time of the applicant's graduation. Applicants are urged to take the LSAT no later than December of the year in which application is made. Experience has shown that undergraduate grade-point averages and LSAT scores are generally the most reliable measures available for predicting success in law school. For this reason, most students are admitted primarily upon an index combining grades and test scores. However, under the Legal Careers Opportunity Program (LCOP), instituted by the law faculty in 1970, the admissions committee may consider many other factors in an effort to identify students who have faced adversity in the pursuit of their educational opportunities or who have accomplishments and experiences suggesting that they do have the ability to succeed in law school if given the opportunity.

These factors include length of time since graduation from college, achievement after college, racial and ethnic status, economic disadvantage, and extracurricular activity. LCOP applicants are required to submit a writing sample, three letters of recommendation, and a personal statement in addition to an LSDAS report. LCOP students are required to attend a summer program prior to fall admission. The application deadline is March 1.

■ Student Activities

The Cleveland State Law Review is edited and published by an editorial board consisting entirely of students of high academic standing and superior writing ability. The law review publishes articles by students and legal scholars for the practicing bar and for use in scholarly research. The Journal of Law and Health is an interdisciplinary publication that explores ideas in health law and policy. A Moot Court Program is offered to give students an understanding of the appellate process and of the work performed by lawyers at the appellate level. An extensive intramural competition is conducted each year, and outstanding students represent the college in nationwide competitions. All students are members of the Student Bar Association, an affiliate of the Law Student Division of the ABA. Phi Alpha Delta, Delta Theta Phi, and Tau Epsilon Rho, national legal fraternities, have active chapters on campus. Other student organizations include the Black Law Students Association, the National Lawyers Guild, and the Women's Caucus. In addition, students of the College of Law publish a student newspaper, *The Gavel.*

■ Expenses and Financial Aid

➽ tuition & fees—Ohio resident, $3,270 per semester ($252 per credit hour); nonresident, $6,540 per semester ($504 per credit hour) ➽ part-time students take 10 credits per semester ➽ financial aid available; GAPSFAS due March 1

The financial aid program at the college utilizes combinations of tuition grants, work-study employment awards, scholarships, and loans. Awards are made primarily on the basis of need, and the college is able to meet a high proportion of the need of all students applying for aid.

■ Career Services

A full-time placement director provides placement services for students and alumni. Each year employers from law firms, corporations, business, government, legal services, and public interest groups interview students at the Cleveland-Marshall College of Law for part-time, summer, and full-time employment. It is estimated that approximately 50 percent of the attorneys practicing in greater Cleveland are graduates of Cleveland State and its predecessors. Our graduates continue to be highly visible on the northern Ohio bench, in business and industry, public service, government, and private practice.

Applicant Group for the 1995-1996 Academic Year

Cleveland State University—Cleveland-Marshall College of Law
This grid includes only applicants who earned 120-180 LSAT scores under standard administrations.

LSAT Score	GPA 3.75 +		3.50 - 3.74		3.25 - 3.49		3.00 - 3.24		2.75 - 2.99		2.50 - 2.74		2.25 - 2.49		2.00 - 2.24		Below 2.00		No GPA		Total	
	Apps	Adm	Apps	Adm	Apps	Adm	Apps	Adm	Apps	Adm	Apps	Adm	Apps	Adm	Apps	Adm	Apps	Adm	Apps	Adm	Apps	Adm
175 - 180	0	0	0	0	0	0	0	0	0	0	0	0	0	0	0	0	0	0	0	0	0	0
170 - 174	0	0	0	0	0	0	0	0	0	0	0	0	0	0	0	0	0	0	0	0	0	0
165 - 169	2	1	0	0	0	0	1	1	0	0	3	1	2	2	0	0	0	0	0	0	8	5
160 - 164	3	2	6	3	10	2	14	10	8	3	8	3	5	1	2	1	0	0	2	0	58	25
155 - 159	11	6	25	14	34	20	36	25	34	22	41	22	11	5	4	1	0	0	3	0	199	115
150 - 154	14	10	38	26	67	46	89	62	60	41	51	18	22	0	11	0	6	0	5	1	363	204
145 - 149	22	17	42	31	66	43	118	50	105	22	74	6	30	0	17	0	3	0	2	1	479	170
140 - 144	3	2	13	7	27	3	41	12	51	5	51	2	46	0	15	0	6	0	6	0	259	31
135 - 139	1	0	7	1	14	1	22	1	33	2	42	2	33	0	22	0	3	0	4	0	181	7
130 - 134	0	0	0	0	7	0	5	0	5	0	6	0	13	0	12	0	5	0	4	0	57	0
125 - 129	0	0	0	0	1	0	1	0	3	0	2	0	4	0	5	0	1	0	0	0	17	0
120 - 124	0	0	0	0	0	0	0	0	0	0	0	0	2	0	0	0	0	0	0	0	2	0
Total	56	38	131	82	226	115	327	161	299	95	278	54	168	8	88	2	24	0	26	2	1623	557

Apps = Number of Applicants
Adm = Number Admitted
Represents 98% of applicant pool.

University of Colorado School of Law

Fleming Law Building
Campus Box 403
Boulder, CO 80309-0403

URL: http://stripe.colorado.edu/~lawlib/lawscinf.htm
Phone: 303.492.7203; Catalog Request: 303.493.5706

■ Introduction

The entire School of Law is contained within the Fleming Law Building located on the Boulder campus of the University of Colorado. High admission standards, combined with a relatively small student body and a favorable faculty-to-student ratio, assure a stimulating and challenging academic environment that encourages in-class participation and informal consultations with faculty. The school is a charter member of the AALS and is ABA approved.

■ Enrollment/Student Body—First-Year Class 1995

➽ 2,792 applicants ➽ 655 admitted ➽ 177 enrolled ➽ 498 total full-time ➽ 21% minority ➽ 51% women ➽ 97 undergraduate schools represented ➽ 30 states represented

■ Faculty

➽ 69 total ➽ 35 full-time ➽ 34 part-time or adjunct ➽ 12 women ➽ 9 minority

■ Library and Physical Facilities

➽ 325,000 volumes & equivalents ➽ LEXIS ➽ NEXIS ➽ WESTLAW ➽ LEGISLATE ➽ DIALOG ➽ First Search ➽ CALI ➽ Internet ➽ 7.5 full-time librarians ➽ library seats 360 (plus lounge seating)

Professional librarians are available to assist students between 9:00 A.M. and 7:00 P.M. The university maintains a computer lab in the library providing word processing applications, internet access, and CALR services. Students may elect to access computer services from their homes via modem. All computer resources are offered to law students at no charge.

■ Curriculum

➽ Academic Support Program ➽ 89 credits required to graduate ➽ 100 courses available ➽ degrees available: J.D.; J.D./M.B.A.; J.D./M.P.A. (plus other joint degrees) ➽ semesters, start in Aug. ➽ range of first-year class size—24-80

First semester runs from late August to mid-December and second semester from mid-January to mid-May. An eight-week summer session is offered in June and July for students with advanced standing at any accredited law school. With a limited number of additional hours, a certificate in tax or environmental policy is attainable. The first-year curriculum is required of all students. During the second and third years, coursework may emphasize such areas as natural resources, environmental law, criminal law, commercial law, constitutional law, taxation, public law, American Indian law, litigation, and jurisprudence.

■ Special Programs

The Natural Resources Law Center has three major areas of activity: research and publication, legal education, and the distinguished visitors and fellows program.

The National Wildlife Federation's Natural Resources Litigation Clinic involves students in complex administrative and judicial environmental litigation, most of which reaches the state supreme court or federal appellate court level. A number of student-assisted clinic cases have set precedents and have been published in environmental law texts.

The Legal Aid and Defender Program allows students to represent low-income clients in actual civil and criminal cases in Colorado courts under the supervision of full-time faculty who are experienced trial attorneys.

The Indian Law Clinic provides students the opportunity to work with native Americans on their unique legal problems.

The Appellate Advocacy Clinic is taught at the Law School by a member of the Appellate Division of the Colorado State Public Defender's Office. Each student, under direct supervision of the instructor, is responsible for completing an appellate brief and attending the oral argument in the Colorado Supreme Court or the Colorado Court of Appeals. In addition, students meet in formal classes to discuss appellate procedure, issue identification, appellate writing, and oral advocacy.

■ Admission

➽ Bachelor's degree from an accredited school required ➽ application deadline—Feb. 15 (earlier is recommended) ➽ rolling admission (first letters go out about Feb. 1; class is usually full about May/June; admission thereafter from the waiting list is limited) ➽ LSAT, LSDAS required ➽ median GPA—3.50 ➽ median LSAT score—162 ➽ application fee—$40 ➽ new students matriculate in Aug.

Offers of admission are heavily based on GPA and LSAT, but these scores are considered in the context of the entire application, with emphasis placed on special qualities such as motivation, undergraduate program, diversity in economic, social or cultural background, unusual employment or other experience, leadership, perseverance in overcoming personal handicaps or disadvantages, and the ability to contribute the perspectives of racial or ethnic minority or other distinctive minorities to the class. The CU Law School considers race affirmatively as a means of offering equal opportunity for obtaining a legal education. An introductory summer program, available by invitation only, is offered to admitted students whose qualifications suggest that additional academic support may be particularly helpful for successful law study. Several positions are offered each year to transfer and visiting students, based on space available in the second-and third-year classes. Criteria for these students are the same as for first-year students and include law school performance.

■ Housing

The university has dormitories for single students and apartments for married students. Inquiries should be sent to University Residence Halls, Room 80 Hallett, Boulder, CO 80310. Off-campus housing requests should be sent to University Memorial Center Room 336, CB 206, University of Colorado at Boulder, Boulder, CO 80309, or to Family Housing, 1350 20th Street, Boulder, CO 80302. Most law students live in private housing; students are advised to seek housing early.

■ Student Activities

The Rothgerber Moot Court Competition offers students an opportunity to develop skills in appellate brief writing and oral argument before panels of distinguished judges and lawyers. The Jessup International Law Moot Court Competition and two Trial Practice Competitions also provide students with valuable experience in written and oral advocacy.

The *University of Colorado Law Review*, a professional journal edited entirely by students, publishes scholarly articles and comments on matters of national and state concern. The *Colorado Journal of International Environmental Law* is one of only two such journals in the nation.

Over 20 student organizations invite participation in projects, programs, and social activities. New organizations are created as needs are identified.

■ Expenses and Financial Aid

➽ *tuition & fees—full-time resident, $4,394; full-time nonresident, $14,630* ➽ *estimated additional expenses—$10,100 (all living costs)* ➽ *scholarships available (limited state & private funds)* ➽ *minority scholarships available (some tuition assistance)*

Grants-in-aid are available on a limited basis to eligible resident students and are awarded on the basis of need. Nonresident students may not be awarded grants from state funds under present state policy but may be considered for scholarships from private funds. Nonresident students may establish Colorado residency by maintaining their legal residence in Colorado for 12 consecutive months. Once they have established Colorado residency, they qualify for the lower resident tuition rates. Students may not be employed during their first year, but limited outside employment may be compatible with second- and third-year schedules. Students applying for financial aid, including grants, must file the Free Application for Federal Student Aid. This form is available from all local high schools, colleges, and universities, and will be processed at no charge. For the best possible financial aid package, early filing (as soon after January 1 as the applicant's tax information is available) is strongly recommended.

■ Career Services

The CU Law School has an active Office of Career Services that provides a broad range of employment and career counseling services. Liaison is maintained with law firms, government agencies, courts, businesses, and other employers that seek the services of students and graduates. A survey of our 1994 graduates resulted in responses from 95.2 percent of the class. Data from that survey indicated that more than 74 percent of the respondents were employed within six months of graduation. The bar passage rate for first-time takers for the July 1995 Bar in Colorado was 94 percent.

Applicant Group for the 1995-1996 Academic Year

University of Colorado School of Law
This grid includes only applicants who earned 120-180 LSAT scores under standard administrations.

	GPA																					
LSAT Score	3.75 +		3.50 - 3.74		3.25 - 3.49		3.00 - 3.24		2.75 - 2.99		2.50 - 2.74		2.25 - 2.49		2.00 - 2.24		Below 2.00		No GPA		Total	
	Apps	Adm	Apps	Adm	Apps	Adm	Apps	Adm	Apps	Adm	Apps	Adm	Apps	Adm	Apps	Adm	Apps	Adm	Apps	Adm		
175 - 180	0	0	1	1	4	4	1	1	1	1	1	1	1	1	0	0	0	0	0	0	9	9
170 - 174	6	6	11	11	19	19	12	12	5	3	2	1	2	0	1	0	0	0	0	0	58	52
165 - 169	21	21	62	61	77	70	59	42	43	9	17	4	7	1	0	0	1	0	2	2	289	210
160 - 164	61	54	134	93	203	67	127	27	73	9	33	1	11	0	6	0	0	0	4	0	652	251
155 - 159	66	18	144	26	179	13	143	6	80	8	46	7	21	0	3	0	2	0	8	1	692	79
150 - 154	37	3	82	5	104	4	132	5	87	7	42	0	17	1	8	0	0	0	3	0	512	25
145 - 149	10	0	35	2	59	2	70	4	70	1	37	1	19	2	6	0	0	0	4	0	310	12
140 - 144	0	0	14	1	29	0	27	0	32	0	18	0	14	0	6	0	2	0	2	0	144	1
135 - 139	2	0	5	0	2	0	6	0	10	0	17	0	8	0	3	0	2	0	6	0	61	0
130 - 134	0	0	1	0	0	0	1	0	2	0	1	0	1	0	0	0	3	0	1	0	10	0
125 - 129	0	0	0	0	0	0	0	0	0	0	2	0	0	0	0	0	0	0	2	0	4	0
120 - 124	0	0	0	0	0	0	0	0	0	0	0	0	0	0	0	0	0	0	0	0	0	0
Total	203	102	489	200	676	179	578	97	403	38	216	15	101	5	33	0	10	0	32	3	2741	639

Apps = Number of Applicants
Adm = Number Admitted
Reflects 98% of the total applicant pool.

Columbia University School of Law

435 West 116th Street
New York, NY 10027

Phone: 212.854.2670 and 854.2678

Introduction

Columbia School of Law, in the City of New York, is distinguished, perhaps uniquely among leading American law schools, as an international center of legal education that stimulates its students to consider the full dimensions of the possibility of the law—as an intellectual pursuit, as a career, and as an instrument of human progress. The character of academic and social life at Columbia, like that of New York City, is fiercely democratic, dynamic, creative, and innovative. The law school is especially committed to educating students of differing perspectives, from diverse backgrounds, and with varied life experiences. Men and women choosing to study law at Columbia hail from the small towns, farms, and suburbs of the West, Midwest, and South; the industrial corridors and Ivy halls of the Northeast; the inner cities of every major American metropolis; and the international centers of Europe, Asia, Africa, and Latin America.

Through our admissions program, we seek to enroll an entering class that reflects the broad range of economic, ethnic, and cultural strains found in America. From around the world, we welcome students who will enrich learning at Columbia and thereafter advance the developing legal cultures of their homelands.

Professional prospects for Columbia law graduates are quite extraordinary. Not surprisingly, many of our graduates proceed to productive careers in every conceivable arena of private practice. But, it should be emphasized that while Columbia-trained attorneys are especially well-regarded for their work in corporate law and finance, an unusually high number also serve as state and federal judges, prosecutors, civil and human rights advocates, legal scholars, public defenders, business executives, elected officials, and national and international leaders. Noteworthy also is the fact that many Columbia law alumnae/i contribute significantly to the shaping of American culture at large. Currently, our graduates serve in leadership roles across the fields of art, music, film, publishing, science, professional athletics, philanthropy, and higher education. With an exceptionally talented student body and faculty, and a strong tradition of encouraging students with specialized interests to develop those interests in depth, Columbia School of Law provides a legal education that gives our students a singular capacity for imagination, originality, and high responsibility in their professional lives.

J.D. Enrollment/Student Body

➽ *5,761 applicants 1995* ➽ *342 enrolled first-year class*
➽ *1,060 total full-time students* ➽ *30% minority*
➽ *43% women* ➽ *46 states, 32 foreign countries, and 195 undergraduate schools represented in student body*
➽ *13% earned at least one other graduate or professional degree*

Faculty

➽ *104 total* ➽ *64 full-time (17 women, 8 minority)*
➽ *40 part-time or adjunct*

Library Resources and Research Facilities

➽ *935,357 library volumes & equivalents* ➽ *LEXIS*
➽ *NEXIS* ➽ *WESTLAW* ➽ *DIALOG*

The second largest law collection in this country, Columbia's library is especially rich in American law and legal history, international law, comparative law, Roman law, and the legal literature of the major European countries, China, and Japan. CD-ROMs are also used to support research, not just in American law, but in German, Argentine, and Australian law as well. In addition, the many libraries of the university, containing more than five million volumes, are available to law students.

The law library's online catalog provides access to the collection and acts as an index to the major legal serials, as well as providing access to the online catalogs of several other major law school libraries. Columbia provides its law students with one of the most extensive and sophisticated computer support systems of any law school in the nation. The law school's computer network includes a computer lab in the library which is used for instruction, research, and writing. The network is also available through modems to students working in their dorms or homes. The law library provides facilities for visually impaired students.

Curriculum

➽ *Academic Support Program* ➽ *83 total units required to graduate* ➽ *184 courses available* ➽ *joint programs with Columbia University's Arts and Sciences (M.A., M.Phil., Ph.D); Business (M.B.A.); International and Public Affairs (M.I.A.); Journalism (M.S.); Theatre Arts (M.F.A.); Social Work (M.S.W.); Architecture Planning and Preservation (M.S.); and with Princeton University's Woodrow Wilson School of Public and International Affairs (M.I.A.)*

The foundation of the Juris Doctor (J.D.) program consists of legal method, contracts, torts, constitutional law, civil procedure, property, criminal law, foundations of the regulatory state, and perspectives on legal thought. The upper-class program is entirely elective, except for three research and writing requirements, a course in professional responsibility, and a pro bono service requirement. There are approximately 100 seminars (normally limited to 18 students). In these small classes, students engage in intensive study and individualized instruction.

Columbia has a special commitment to clinical education, which places the student in the role of a lawyer doing a lawyer's actual work under intensive faculty supervision. Some examples of clinical opportunities are Family Advocacy, Fair Housing, Law and the Arts,

Non-Profit Organizations, and Alternative Dispute Resolution: Mediation Clinic. Also available is a summer program which places 60-70 students in Civil Rights and Human Rights Internships in law firms and organizations throughout this country and around the world.

Especially distinguished are Columbia's offerings in international, foreign, and comparative law; constitutional law and theory; corporate and securities law; and human rights.

■ Special Programs

The school is well situated for developing a broad urban affairs program, since New York City is the home of an extraordinary variety of private and government agencies concerned with urban problems, ranging from legal service agencies to community development projects. In all, some 30 courses and seminars are offered in urban law, civil rights and liberties, and criminal law. A variety of legal training opportunities include the Morningside Heights Legal Services, federal and criminal court clerkships, the student legal assistance committee, and placement with urban agencies.

In the fields of international, comparative, and foreign law, Columbia offers approximately 40 courses and specialized seminars. In addition, Columbia is the home of the Parker School of Foreign and Comparative Law, a center for scholarly activity in foreign and comparative law that sponsors courses, publications, conferences, and scholarships.

Columbia's longstanding leadership in international law has been strengthened greatly in the last decade by the establishment of its Center for Chinese Legal Studies, its Center for Japanese Legal Studies, its Center for Korean Legal Studies, and a joint degree program with the University of Paris I-Panthéon-Sorbonne.

Columbia is especially strong in the areas of constitutional law. Over 15 different members of the faculty teach at least one course or seminar in constitutional law or constitutional theory.

Other special Columbia programs, serving as catalysts for scholarly work, curricular development, and student enrichment include: the Center for Law and the Arts; the Center for Law and Economic Studies; the Human Rights Internship Program; the Jaffin Program in Law and Social Responsibility; the Legislative Drafting Research Fund; the Samuel Rubin Program, advancing civil rights and civil liberties; the Julius Silver program in Law, Science, and Technology; the Feminism and Legal Theory Project; and the Center for Public Interest Law.

■ Admission

➧ *LSAT, LSDAS required* ➧ *median GPA—3.60*
➧ *median LSAT score—168* ➧ *application fee—$65*

All first-year students enter in late August. Candidates applying for regular admission should apply after September 1 of the year preceding their desired matriculation, but before February 15, the application deadline. Early Decision candidates must complete their applications by December 1 and are notified in late December.

■ Expenses and Financial Aid

➧ *tuition & fees—$23,178/1995-96* ➧ *estimated room, board, and personal expenses—$12,340* ➧ *1995-96 average grant value—$9,395* ➧ *need-based scholarship program* ➧ *financial aid application deadline—March 1* ➧ *Public Interest Loan Forgiveness Program (LRAP) available*

Applicant Group for the 1995-1996 Academic Year

Columbia University School of Law
This grid includes only applicants who earned 120-180 LSAT scores under standard administrations.

LSAT Score	3.75 +		3.50 - 3.74		3.25 - 3.49		3.00 - 3.24		Below 3.00		No GPA		Total	
	Apps	Adm	Apps	Adm	Apps	Adm	Apps	Adm	Apps	Adm	Apps	Adm	Apps	Adm
175 - 180	60	59	48	45	41	29	12	6	6	0	0	0	167	139
170 - 174	148	139	155	124	131	80	29	12	22	1	9	6	494	362
165 - 169	355	165	477	143	263	55	93	9	50	9	22	11	1260	392
160 - 164	249	34	431	33	323	25	171	17	102	11	20	8	1296	128
155 - 159	167	17	279	28	243	22	136	16	98	4	27	4	950	91
Below 155	106	9	247	9	301	7	246	1	481	2	91	2	1472	30
Total	1085	423	1637	382	1302	218	687	61	759	27	169	31	5639	1142

(GPA spans the columns 3.75 + through Total.)

Apps = Number of Applicants
Adm = Number Admitted

University of Connecticut School of Law

55 Elizabeth Street
Hartford, CT 06105-2296

E-Mail: admit@brandeis.law.uconn.edu
URL: http://www.law.uconn.edu
Phone: 860.241.4696

■ Introduction

Through several decades of sustained intellectual growth, the University of Connecticut School of Law has emerged as one of the leading public law schools in the United States. Because of Connecticut's extraordinary ratio of 10:1 full-time students to full-time faculty, 40 percent of the first-year curriculum is offered in seminar format and 70 percent of the advanced courses have 20 or fewer students. An intensive first-year skills program, a rich and varied curriculum, three student-edited journals, student organizations active across the spectrum of legal and social concerns, a regular flow of visiting lecturers, and a committed body of graduates all combine to make Connecticut a school of exceptional strength.

■ Enrollment/Student Body

➽ *1122 day applicants* ➽ *505 evening applicants*
➽ *381 admitted first-year day class 1995*
➽ *163 admitted first-year evening class 1995*
➽ *126 enrolled first-year day class 1995*
➽ *65 enrolled first-year evening class 1995*
➽ *432 total full-time* ➽ *196 total part-time*
➽ *15.9% minority* ➽ *48% women*
➽ *18 states & foreign countries represented*
➽ *188 undergraduate schools represented*
➽ *41 undergraduate majors represented in first-year class*
➽ *10 foreign colleges & universities represented*

Our students constitute a culturally and intellectually diverse community. Their undergraduate majors include East Asian studies, math, and physics, in addition to the more usual fields such as history, economics, and philosophy.

■ Faculty

➽ *85 total* ➽ *44 full-time* ➽ *41 part-time or adjunct*
➽ *10 women* ➽ *6 part-time women* ➽ *4 full-time minority*

■ Library and Physical Facilities

➽ *416,819 volumes & equivalents* ➽ *library hours: Mon.-Fri., 8:30 A.M.-11:00 P.M.; Sat., 9:00 A.M.-7:00 P.M.; Sun., 10:00 A.M.-11:00 P.M.* ➽ *LEXIS* ➽ *NEXIS* ➽ *WESTLAW*
➽ *DIALOG* ➽ *17 professional library staff*
➽ *120,000-sq. ft., 600 seat library completed in 1995*
➽ *online catalog of all library holdings*
➽ *member of New England Law Libraries Consortium, RLG*

The campus, listed on the National Register of Historic Sites, is probably the most beautiful of any law school. The new library, completed in 1995 at a cost of over $20 million, will be the finest—and, at 120,000-square feet, one of the largest—in the country.

With its immediate neighbors—the Hartford Seminary, the Hartford College for Women, and the Connecticut Historical Society—the school is part of an academic enclave in a turn-of-the-century residential neighborhood.

Although the school has no dormitories, most students live within walking distance of the campus. Housing is plentiful and varied. The School maintains a comprehensive housing list, with information about accessibility for students with special physical requirements.

■ Curriculum

➽ *Academic Support Program* ➽ *86 credits required to graduate* ➽ *150 courses available* ➽ *degrees available: J.D.; J.D./M.P.H.; J.D./M.S.W.; J.D./M.B.A.; J.D./M.P.A.; J.D./M.A. in Public Policy (Trinity College); J.D./M.L.S. with Southern Connecticut State University*

■ Special Programs

Connecticut was a pioneer in clinical legal education, and our clinics continue to be a distinguishing strength of the school. Students interested in law and economics, feminist legal thought, and legal philosophy will find courses and specialists to meet their needs. Extensive offerings in environmental law are supplemented by a semester exchange program with the University of London and another with the Environmental Law Center at Vermont. International law occupies an increasingly prominent place in the curriculum, reinforced by the student-edited *Journal of International Law*. Student-faculty exchange programs with Leiden (Netherlands), Exeter (U.K.), the University of Puerto Rico, the University of International Business and Economics (China), Aix-en-Provence (France), and the Master's Program leading to the LL.M. for foreign lawyers all provide opportunities for our students to learn from and study with peers trained in different legal systems.

■ Services for Students With Disabilities

The Disabled Student Services Liaison (DSSL) at the School of Law works with students with disabilities in the development and implementation of reasonable accommodations to allow access to both its physical facilities and its educational and extracurricular programs. Associate Dean Laurie Werling serves as liaison. Her office hours are Mon.-Fri., 8:30 A.M.-4:30 P.M.

Students with mobility impairments considering applying or admitted to the School of Law are invited to tour the campus. If assistance is required, please contact the DSSL. Students with other disabilities may contact the DSSL for discussion of accommodations.

■ Academic Support Program

Each year, the School of Law offers an Academic Support Program to entering first-year students who requested special admissions consideration, or whose admissions files suggest that they would benefit from individual attention. The program is designed to promote the academic success of those who participate, as well as to demonstrate the School of Law's commitment to ensuring that all admitted students have a full opportunity to maximize their academic potential.

The program consists of a summer session and an academic-year tutorial program. The summer session is conducted during the week immediately prior to the beginning of classes.

■ Admission

➽ *Bachelor's degree required (or foreign equivalent)* ➽ *application deadline—March 1* ➽ *LSAT, LSDAS required* ➽ *median GPA—3.29* ➽ *median LSAT score—159* ➽ *application fee (day or evening)—$30; (day and evening)—$45*

■ Student Activities

The *Connecticut Law Review,* now in its twenty-eighth volume, publishes approximately 1,000 pages of critical legal discussion each year. The *Law Review* is managed entirely by a student Board of Editors.

The *Connecticut Journal of International Law,* now in its eleventh volume, publishes up to three issues per year on topics concerning both public and private international law. Circulated internationally, the *Journal* is wholly student-managed and edited. The *Journal* also sponsors an international legal symposium each year, and a number of campus lectures, panel discussions, and social events open to the entire law school community each semester.

There is also a new publication for those interested in insurance—the *Connecticut Insurance Law Journal*. It is now in its second year.

The **Connecticut Moot Court Board** provides students with the opportunity to practice oral advocacy in the challenging setting of intramural and interscholastic competitions.

The **Student Bar Association** is the representative student government of the school. It manages an annual budget consisting of funds derived from the Student Activities Fee and the university tuition to support the various student organizations, and to enhance generally the quality of student life.

In addition, a large number of organizations have active chapters on campus.

■ Expenses and Financial Aid

➽ *full-time tuition & fees—resident, $9,972; RI, MA, NH, or VT resident, $14,958; resident of any other state, $21,030* ➽ *part-time tuition & fees—resident, $348/credit hour; RI, MA, NH, or VT resident, $522/credit hour; resident of any other state, $734/credit hour* ➽ *financial aid available; Tuition Remission Grant, opportunity scholarship, Stafford Loan* ➽ *law school financial aid application required by March 1*

■ Career Services

Connecticut operates a comprehensive career services office for the benefit of students and alumni/ae. The school offers a large and geographically diverse on-campus interviewing program, extensive individual and group counseling, a resource library, job listings, mentor programs, employment information sessions, newsletters, and job bulletins. Also, the School participates in several off-site public interest, minority, and patent intellectual property job fairs.

Applicant Group for the 1995-1996 Academic Year

University of Connecticut School of Law
This grid includes only applicants with a 3-digit LSAT score and a GPA (approximately 97% of all full-time applicants).

	GPA																			
LSAT Score	3.75 - 4.00		3.50 - 3.74		3.25 - 3.49		3.00 - 3.24		2.75 - 2.99		2.50 - 2.74		2.25 - 2.49		2.00 - 2.24		Below 2.00		Total	
	Apps	Adm	Apps	Adm	Apps	Adm	Apps	Adm	Apps	Adm	Apps	Adm	Apps	Adm	Apps	Adm	Apps	Adm	Apps	Adm
175 - 180	0	0	1	1	0	0	0	0	0	0	0	0	0	0	0	0	0	0	1	1
170 - 174	0	0	4	4	4	4	2	2	1	0	0	0	2	1	1	0	0	0	14	11
165 - 169	1	1	13	12	13	13	20	20	10	7	9	4	3	1	0	0	0	0	69	58
160 - 164	13	13	32	32	45	44	42	36	24	13	11	3	4	1	2	0	0	0	173	142
155 - 159	14	12	44	36	55	31	68	22	33	4	26	2	7	0	3	0	0	0	250	107
150 - 154	13	6	31	6	62	5	63	6	52	4	28	1	17	3	1	1	2	0	269	32
145 - 149	2	1	16	1	19	1	46	6	30	0	23	2	14	0	8	0	1	0	159	11
140 - 144	2	1	8	2	12	2	25	1	13	1	17	2	8	0	7	0	1	0	93	9
135 - 139	0	0	2	1	6	0	11	1	5	0	10	0	4	0	6	0	1	0	45	2
130 - 134	0	0	1	0	2	0	1	0	2	0	2	1	0	0	3	0	3	0	14	1
125 - 129	0	0	0	0	0	0	0	0	3	0	0	0	0	0	0	0	0	0	3	0
120 - 124	0	0	0	0	0	0	0	0	0	0	0	0	0	0	0	0	0	0	0	0
Total	45	34	152	95	218	100	278	94	173	29	126	15	59	6	31	1	8	0	1090	374

Apps = Number of Applicants
Adm = Number Admitted

Cornell University Law School

Ithaca, NY 14853

E-Mail: lawadmit@law.mail.cornell.edu
URL: http://www.law.cornell.edu/admit/admit.htm

■ Introduction

Cornell is a national center of learning located in Ithaca, New York, the heart of the Finger Lakes region of New York State. The law school's small classes, broad curriculum and distinguished faculty, combined with the advantages of being part of one of the world's leading research universities, make it ideal for those who see legal study as a way to make meaningful contributions at all levels of society. Students find Ithaca to be a safe and nonstressful, yet culturally rich, environment in which to pursue legal studies.

■ Enrollment/Student Body

➻ 3,700 applicants ➻ 188 enrolled first-year class 1995 ➻ 568 total full-time ➻ 23% minority ➻ 40% women ➻ 58 states & foreign countries represented ➻ 250 undergraduate schools represented

Sixty percent of Cornell's entering students have taken one or more years between completion of their undergraduate degree and enrollment in law school. Selective admissions standards, combined with an emphasis on applicants' unique records and achievements, ensure that the student body is made up of people with wide-ranging interests, skills, concerns, and backgrounds.

■ Faculty

➻ 57 total ➻ 39 full-time ➻ 18 part-time or adjunct ➻ 10 women ➻ 4 minority

Cornell's faculty includes tenured and tenure-track faculty who teach and produce scholarship in their area of law; clinical faculty who run client-focused and simulation courses centered around legal aid and several specialty clinics; and a large number of visitors, associated faculty from other university divisions, and adjunct faculty who teach at the school each year. Many of the latter group are legal scholars and professors from other countries who teach in the law school's significant international program.

■ Library and Physical Facilities

➻ 550,000 volumes & microform equivalents ➻ library hours: Mon.-Thurs., 8:00 A.M.-11:00 P.M.; Fri., 8:00 A.M.-7:00 P.M.; Sat. 9:00 A.M.-5:00 P.M.; Sun., NOON-11:00 P.M. ➻ LEXIS ➻ NEXIS ➻ WESTLAW ➻ DIALOG ➻ 7 full-time librarians ➻ library seats 443

The law school is located in the renovated and expanded Myron Taylor Hall, at the heart of the scenic 740 acre Cornell University campus. Hughes Hall, the law school dormitory, is adjacent to the main law school building and contains single rooms for about 80 students and a dining facility for breakfast and lunch.

Cornell is one of the nation's leaders in the development and support of computer-assisted legal research and writing. Students have access to the full array of Internet services, including sophisticated electronic mail. The law school's multiple-node network and computer terminals are available to students for word processing, legal research, statistical analysis, and database management. Students also have access to any of the 17 satellite computer clusters and mainframe facilities located on the university campus.

■ Curriculum

➻ Academic Support Program ➻ 84 semester credit hours required to graduate ➻ degrees and joint/combined programs: J.D.; J.D. with specialization in international legal studies; J.D./LL.M. in International Law and Comparative Law; J.D./Maîtrise en Droit; LL.M.; J.S.D.; J.D./M.B.A.; J.D./M.P.A.; J.D./M.I.L.R.; J.D./M.R.P.; J.D./M.A.; J.D./Ph.D. ➻ semesters, start in late Aug. ➻ first-year section size—27; other class ranges—70-100; first-year intensive writing classes average—15

Cornell offers a national law curriculum leading to the J.D. degree. First-year students take a group of required courses and an intensive Practice Training course stressing a variety of legal research, writing, and advocacy techniques. After the first year, students may choose from a wide range of elective courses, including many seminars and problem courses. Optional concentrations are offered in four areas—advocacy, public law, business law and regulation, and general practice.

■ International Legal Studies

The Berger International Legal Studies Program is one of the country's oldest and most distinguished programs in international legal education. Cornell's comprehensive program features a unique J.D. specialization opportunity, a three-year J.D./LL.M. degree in International and Comparative Law, a four-year J.D./Maîtrise en Droit (French law degree) program, a Paris summer institute with the University of Paris I (Panthéon-Sorbonne), a comprehensive speaker series, a large number of visiting foreign professors and scholars, a weekly luncheon discussion series, and a leading journal of international and comparative law edited by students.

■ Clinical Studies

The Cornell Legal Aid Clinic, offering legal services to individuals financially unable to employ an attorney, provides students with the chance to engage in the supervised practice of law under the direction of experienced attorneys. Clinical faculty also conduct a variety of other specialized clinics and skills courses within the regular curriculum.

■ Admission

➻ Bachelor's degree from accredited college or university required ➻ application deadline—Feb. 1 ➻ LSAT, LSDAS required ➻ application fee—$65

Admission is highly competitive. The admissions committee bases its decisions on such nonquantifiable factors as extracurricular and community activities, life experience, and work background. They also consider factors such as the LSAT score, undergraduate grades, graduate work, and recommendations. Minority background may be considered a positive factor in an applicant's file and members of traditionally under-represented minority groups are encouraged to submit a separate statement describing their ethnic, cultural, and linguistic backgrounds.

■ Student Activities

Student-edited law journals include the *Cornell Law Review* (published continuously since 1916), the *Cornell International Law Journal* (established in 1967), and the newly established *Cornell Journal of Law and Public Policy.* Student organizations and activities include: American Indian Law Students Association; Asian American Law Students Association; Black Law Students Association; Herbert W. Briggs Society of International Law; Cornell Christian Legal Society; Cornell Criminal Justice Society; Cornell Law Community Volunteer Program; Cornell Law Student Association; Cornell Prison Project; Corporate Law Society; *Dicta*; Entertainment and Sports Law Union; Environmental Law Society; Federalist Society; James R. Withrow, Jr., Program on Legal Ethics; Jewish Law Student Association; Lambda Law Students; Latino American Law Students Association; Law Partners' Association; Moot Court Program; National Lawyer's Guild; Phi Alpha Delta; Phi Delta Phi; Public Interest Law Union; Women's Law Coalition.

■ Expenses and Financial Aid

➽ tuition & fees—$21,135 ➽ estimated additional expenses—$7,100, room & meals; $760, books & supplies; $3,905, personal expenses ➽ need-based scholarships offered ➽ Need Access Diskette required no later than March 15

Cornell offers a need-based financial aid program. About 40 percent of students receive scholarship aid, with a higher percentage receiving government-backed loans. Minority and/or economically disadvantaged students are eligible for enhanced scholarship awards.

A generous Public Interest Low Income Protection Plan assists those choosing qualifying public interest law jobs through the use of a moderated loan repayment plan and loan forgiveness.

■ Career Services

The Career Office provides employment counseling to students and serves as a liaison with legal employers, both public and private. Cornell's students continue to be among the most recruited in the country. Every fall, hundreds of employers from across the country visit the law school and conduct employment interviews. Employers also participate in law school-sponsored job fairs in cities such as Boston, Los Angeles, New York, San Francisco, and Washington, DC.

Applicant Group for the 1995-1996 Academic Year

Cornell University Law School
This grid includes only applicants who earned 120-180 LSAT scores under standard administrations and with reported GPAs.

LSAT Score	GPA 3.75 +		3.50 - 3.74		3.25 - 3.49		3.00 - 3.24		Below 3.00	
	Apps	Adm	Apps	Adm	Apps	Adm	Apps	Adm	Apps	Adm
175 - 180	16	16	6	6	12	11	6	3	3	1
170 - 174	36	35	54	51	55	34	20	4	13	3
165 - 169	132	115	233	191	175	102	79	13	37	5
160 - 164	205	93	319	105	242	38	113	14	72	9
155 - 159	119	15	187	17	178	23	103	16	80	8
Below 155	88	12	258	11	239	14	205	11	282	3

Apps = Number of Applicants
Adm = Number Admitted
Reflects 98% of the total applicant pool.

We provide this grid because it is a convenient way to give applicants important information about our admissions process. By doing so, we are not implying that LSAT scores and GPAs are the only factors considered. To the contrary, our process includes a careful review of many nonnumerical factors that are simply too complicated to represent in a two-dimensional grid.

Creighton University School of Law

2500 California Plaza
Omaha, NE 68178

URL: http://bluejay.creighton.edu/CULAW
Phone: 402.280.2872

■ Introduction

Creighton University, a privately endowed and supported Jesuit University, was founded in 1878. Creighton is the most diverse educational institution of its size in the nation. In addition to the School of Law, Creighton has a Medical School, Dental School, School of Pharmacy and Allied Health, School of Nursing, School of Business Administration, College of Arts and Sciences, and a Graduate School, making it the center of professional education in the Midwest. The university is located just blocks from downtown Omaha, a metropolitan area with a population of more than 600,000. Known as the River City, Omaha is the heart of the Midlands and the largest metroplex between Chicago and Denver.

■ The School of Law

The School of Law was established in 1904, has been a member of the AALS since 1907 and approved by the ABA for more than 55 years. Alumni from the law school are practicing in all 50 states and in more than 5 foreign countries. The law school's current enrollment is 504 students from over 38 states and more than 185 undergraduate institutions. Twenty-five full-time professors and a group of part-time specialists chosen from the bench and bar comprise the faculty.

■ Enrollment/Student Body

➽ 922 applicants ➽ 449 admitted first-year class 1995 ➽ 153 enrolled first-year class 1995 ➽ 484 total full-time ➽ 20 total part-time ➽ 8% minority ➽ 44% women ➽ 41 states & foreign countries represented ➽ 185 undergraduate schools represented

■ Faculty

➽ 64 total ➽ 25 full-time ➽ 39 part-time or adjunct ➽ 19 women ➽ 1 minority

■ Library and Physical Facilities

➽ 223,123 volumes & equivalents ➽ library hours: Mon.-Thurs., 7:00 A.M.-MIDNIGHT; Fri., 7:00 A.M.-8:00 P.M.; Sat., 9:00 A.M.-8:00 P.M.; Sun., NOON-MIDNIGHT ➽ LEXIS ➽ NEXIS ➽ WESTLAW ➽ 6 full-time librarians ➽ library seats 325

■ Curriculum

➽ Academic Support Program ➽ 94 credits required to graduate ➽ 135 courses available ➽ degrees available: J.D.; J.D./M.B.A. ➽ semesters, start in Aug. ➽ range of first-year class size—10-75

The first-year curriculum, required of all students, consists of Civil Procedure, Constitutional Law, Contracts, Legal Research, Legal Writing, Property, and Torts. Other than Professional Responsibility and advanced legal writing, required of all second-year students, second- and third-year students design their own program of studies from the numerous electives and seminars offered. The curriculum prepares students for the practice of law in any state.

■ Clinic and Internships

Third-year students selected to work in the Legal Clinic provide pro bono legal assistance to indigent citizens of Omaha. The School of Law also offers judicial and clinical internships in a number of city, county, federal, and Legal Aid offices.

■ Student Activities

The Student Bar Association is the student government of the law school. The purposes of the organization are to make law students aware of the obligations and opportunities existing for lawyers through Bar Association activities, promote a consciousness of professional responsibility, and provide a forum for student activities.

The school has chapters of the American Trial Lawyers Association and Phi Alpha Delta and Phi Delta Phi legal fraternities. Other student groups include the Black Law Students Association, the Latino Law Students Association, the Society of International Law, the Environmental Law Society, the Law Partners Association, Federalist Society, ACLU Chapter, Public Interest Forum, the Rutherford Institute, and the Women Law Students Association.

The *Creighton Law Review*, edited and managed by students, is a scholarly legal journal that is circulated nationally and internationally. The *Review* publishes articles contributed by prominent legal scholars, in addition to notes and comments written by students. Appellate brief writing and oral argument begins in the first-year Legal Writing program. During the second year, intraschool tournaments culminate in the selection of students for the domestic and international Moot Court Boards and the selection of teams to compete in regional and national moot court tournaments and the Philip C. Jessup International Law Moot Court program. The Client Counseling program promotes student knowledge and interest in the counseling and interviewing functions of law practice. An intraschool competition is held annually and culminates in students being selected for the Client Counseling Board and to represent Creighton in the national competition sponsored by the ABA's Law Student Division.

■ Admission

➽ Bachelor's degree from accredited college or university required ➽ application deadline—May 1, rolling admission, early application preferred ➽ LSAT, LSDAS required ➽ median GPA—3.21 ➽ median LSAT score—153 ➽ application fee—$40

The applicant's LSAT score and undergraduate GPA are the primary factors in determining acceptance. Applicants with an LSAT percentile of 82-99 and a GPA range of 2.8 or higher have a very good chance of being admitted. Applicants with an LSAT percentile of 56-81 and a GPA of 3.1 or higher have a good chance of being admitted. Applicants with an LSAT percentile of 45 to 55 and a GPA of 3.25 or higher are also considered. Other factors that are considered by the Admissions Committee include the personal statement, demonstrated leadership ability, employment and other experience, and graduate degrees. Two letters of reference are required.

■ Expenses and Financial Aid

- *tuition & fees—full-time, $13,610; part-time (per credit hour) $455*
- *estimated additional expenses—$11,030*
- *merit & merit/need-based scholarships available*
- *minority scholarships available*
- *financial aid available*
- *FAFSA form for need analysis*

Most scholarships are awarded on the basis of superior academic achievement, and LSAT scores. Continuation of scholarship aid after the first year is normally contingent upon academic achievement and participation in co-curricular activities of high academic worth. Once an applicant has been accepted, scholarship applications will be mailed to those applicants who meet merit guidelines. Long-term, low-interest loans under federal programs, as well as Law Access Loans and LAWLOANS through NORWEST Bank are available. Those seeking loans and scholarship aid must use the FAFSA form. Additional information about scholarships and financial aid is available through the law school's Admissions Office.

■ Minority Scholarship Program

The School of Law actively recruits minority students and has a substantial minority scholarship program. For the 1995-96 school year twenty-five students have minority scholarships ranging from one-quarter to full tuition.

■ Career Services

The law school's Office of Career Service is committed to providing professional placement services for students and alumni. In addition to seminars and personal counseling, the office hosts prospective employers for on-campus interviews and posts notices for job openings throughout the year.

Applicant Group for the 1995-1996 Academic Year

Creighton University School of Law
This grid includes only applicants who earned 120-180 LSAT scores under standard administrations in the 1994-1995 testing year.

GPA

LSAT Score	3.75 +		3.50 - 3.74		3.25 - 3.49		3.00 - 3.24		2.75 - 2.99		2.50 - 2.74		2.25 - 2.49		2.00 - 2.24		Below 2.00		No GPA		Total	
	Apps	Adm	Apps	Adm	Apps	Adm	Apps	Adm	Apps	Adm	Apps	Adm	Apps	Adm	Apps	Adm	Apps	Adm	Apps	Adm	Apps	Adm
175 - 180	0	0	0	0	0	0	0	0	0	0	0	0	0	0	0	0	0	0	0	0	0	0
170 - 174	0	0	0	0	0	0	0	0	0	0	0	0	0	0	0	0	0	0	0	0	0	0
165 - 169	2	2	0	0	0	0	0	0	3	3	1	1	0	0	0	0	0	0	1	1	7	7
160 - 164	6	6	5	5	6	6	5	5	5	5	7	7	2	2	2	1	0	0	0	0	38	37
155 - 159	13	13	23	22	18	18	28	25	13	12	17	14	9	5	3	2	1	0	2	1	127	112
150 - 154	15	15	30	27	50	42	56	48	67	41	35	16	19	6	2	1	1	0	1	0	276	196
145 - 149	14	13	35	26	48	25	61	17	52	5	37	7	13	0	6	0	1	0	0	0	267	93
140 - 144	2	1	12	5	19	1	21	0	23	0	20	0	18	1	1	0	2	0	1	0	119	8
Below 140	1	0	1	0	6	0	7	0	13	0	11	0	7	0	10	2	1	0	4	0	61	2
Total	53	50	106	85	147	92	178	95	176	66	128	45	68	14	24	6	6	0	9	2	895	455

Apps = Number of Applicants
Adm = Number Admitted
Reflects 98% of the total applicant pool.

Cumberland School of Law of Samford University

800 Lakeshore Drive
Birmingham, AL 35229

Phone: 205.870.2702, 800.888.7213

■ Introduction

The Cumberland School of Law, established in 1847 as a part of Cumberland University in Lebanon, Tennessee, is one of the oldest law schools in the country. The school was acquired by Samford University in 1961 and is now known as the Cumberland School of Law of Samford University. Today, Samford University is the largest privately supported and fully accredited institution of higher learning in Alabama. The beautiful campus is located in a suburban area of Birmingham, Alabama's largest city. Birmingham is the state's industrial, business, and cultural center. The Cumberland School of Law has been a member of the Association of American Law Schools (AALS) since 1952, and has been accredited by the American Bar Association (ABA) since 1949.

■ Enrollment/Student Body

➽ *1,220 applicants* ➽ *224 enrolled first-year class 1995* ➽ *full time only* ➽ *8.6% minority* ➽ *36% women* ➽ *28 states represented* ➽ *180 undergraduate schools represented* ➽ *55% of 1995 first-year class from outside Alabama* ➽ *fall semester enrollment only*

Since more than half of the entering class come from other states, the Student Bar Association (SBA) actively assists each student who desires help in relocating to Birmingham by providing a number of services. For example, students may join the Phoenix Organization for a one-time fee of $30, thereby relieving them of the need to pay deposits to local utility companies.

■ Faculty

➽ *58 total* ➽ *33 full-time* ➽ *25 part-time* ➽ *7 women (full-time)* ➽ *4 minority (full-time)*

A strength of the law school, the 33 full-time faculty members hail from 23 law schools. The academic credentials, scholarly achievements, and publications of each faculty member are highlighted in the *Admissions Prospectus*.

■ Library and Physical Facilities

➽ *210,000 volumes & equivalents* ➽ *library hours: Mon.-Fri., 7:30 A.M.-MIDNIGHT; Sat., 9:00 A.M.-10:00 P.M.; Sun., 1:00 P.M.-MIDNIGHT* ➽ *computer rooms providing 30 NEXIS and WESTLAW terminals* ➽ *2 personal computer labs* ➽ *LEGALTRAC CD-ROM* ➽ *13 full-time librarians* ➽ *library seats 450* ➽ *12 conference rooms* ➽ *laptop computers available for checkout*

The new Lucille Stewart Beeson Law Library, an $8.4 million, free-standing, Georgian structure, opened in March of 1995. The new library is visually stunning as well as superbly functional. This 61,000-square-foot, three-and-one-half story building is connected to the law school by a second-story breezeway. The building's design is intended to make all facilities easily accessible to students with disabilities.

Complete training on WESTLAW, LEXIS, and LEGALTRAC is a part of the first-year curriculum through the Legal Research and Writing Program. Many study carrels and conference rooms are wired for data transmission. In addition, law students have full access to the University's four campus libraries as well as six computer labs.

■ Curriculum

➽ *Academic Support Program* ➽ *90 credits required for J.D.* ➽ *145 courses offered (courses are 2-, 3-, or 4-hour courses)* ➽ *53 credit hours in prescribed courses required* ➽ *supervised analytical writing requirement* ➽ *7 joint degrees available: J.D./M.Acc.; J.D./M.A.E.; J.D./M.B.A.; J.D./M.P.A.; J.D./M.P.H.; J.D./M.Div.; J.D./M.S. (Environmental Management)* ➽ *semesters, start in Aug.* ➽ *range of first-year class size—5-80*

■ International Law

Cumberland conducts two ABA-approved international summer programs that are offered at the University of Durham, Durham, England and the University of Victoria, Victoria, British Columbia. The graduate degree of M.C.L., Master of Comparative Law, is offered to international law school graduates.

■ Special Programs

Cumberland has an exceptional record of recent trial-advocacy competition victories, winning both the ABA and ATLA national championships (including several national second- and third-place awards); winning 24 regional championships; and winning the coveted American College of Trial Lawyers' Emily Gumpert Award for Excellence in the Teaching of Trial Advocacy.

Cumberland students have the chance to get class credit, and a professional leg-up, working for Birmingham's major law firms, judges' offices, and corporate legal departments. The clinical curriculum offers second- and third-year students judicial and corporate externships, as well as externships in the offices of the I.R.S. and the U.S. Attorney. In addition, the Alabama Third-Year Practice Rule gives third-year students a chance to practice law under the supervision of a licensed attorney.

The law school also has an active intellectual life. Students may participate in the faculty-run Cumberland Colloquium on Law, Religion, and Culture and the student-run Ray Rushton Distinguished Lecturer Series, as well as many other student organizations. Students also may participate in the Partnership Between Alumni and Law Students Program (PALS), designed to pair up law students with practicing alumni in the Birmingham area.

■ Admission

➽ *Bachelor's degree from accredited college or university required* ➽ *LSAT, LSDAS required* ➽ *application fee—$40*

➡ Reactivation fee—$40 ➡ applications accepted between Oct. 1 and May 1 ➡ applicants admitted on a rolling admission basis ➡ priority application deadline—Feb. 28; final—May 1 ➡ 1995 matriculated class averages—LSAT, 154; GPA, 3.1

Cumberland School of Law of Samford University does not use a number index system or formula when choosing who will be admitted. Every applicant's file is thoroughly reviewed by the Faculty Admissions Committee. In addition to the LSAT score and undergraduate GPA, other important factors considered are: undergraduate school grade trend and difficulty of major; extracurricular activities and/or employment while in undergraduate school; graduate work; employment experience; personal statement; and letters of recommendation.

Admitted applicants are required to pay a nonrefundable $400 seat deposit that is credited toward tuition. The first installment of $150 is due April 1; the second installment of $250 is due June 1.

■ Student Activities

The Student Bar Association (SBA) is the foundation of student organization at the law school and functions as the first professional organization of a law student's career. Student Bar chapters keep students in touch with job opportunities and bar requirements. In addition to many outstanding organizations, students may also be invited to join one of three national legal fraternities and be inducted into two honorary societies, Order of the Barrister, and Curia Honoris. Student-run publications include *Cumberland Law Review*, *American Journal of Trial Advocacy*, and *Pro Confesso*.

■ Expenses and Financial Aid

➡ 1995-1996 tuition—$15,698 (flat rate) ➡ additional expenses—locker rental, $10; parking decal, $20; graduation fee, $37 ➡ Guaranteed Student Loan Program available through the Financial Aid Office ➡ financial aid filing deadline—March 1

All admitted applicants are automatically considered for merit and recruiting scholarship awards. Various other scholarships are available to outstanding students who distinguish themselves academically, or who make outstanding contributions through leadership in the law school's programs.

■ Career Services

Through the Career Services Office (a member of the National Association for Law Placement), the law school assists all law students in locating summer clerkships and part-time and permanent employment upon graduation. Students also receive individual counseling and take part in workshops on everything from career choices to interviewing techniques and networking. The office schedules on-campus interview programs during the fall and spring semesters. Off-campus recruiting programs also are available. Cumberland students and graduates are encouraged to attend well-known recruiting conferences in Chicago, Atlanta, Nashville, and Washington, D.C. The Career Services Office also surveys each graduating class six months after graduation, and based on data collected from the most recent graduates (Class of '94), 91 percent had successfully obtained law related employment.

Applicant Group for the 1995-1996 Academic Year

Cumberland School of Law—Samford University

LSAT Score	GPA								
	3.75 +	3.50 - 3.74	3.25 - 3.49	3.00 - 3.24	2.75 - 2.99	2.50 - 2.74	2.25 - 2.49	2.00 - 2.24	Below 2.00
175 - 180									
170 - 174									
165 - 169									
160 - 164									
155 - 159									
150 - 154									
145 - 149									
140 - 144									
135 - 139									
130 - 134									
125 - 129									
120 - 124									

Good Possibility   Possible   Unlikely

University of Dayton School of Law

300 College Park
Dayton, OH 45469-1320

E-Mail: lawinfo@odo.law.udayton.edu
URL: http://www.udayton.edu
Phone: 513.229.3555

■ Overview

The University of Dayton School of Law offers a single division, full-time program of studies in a supportive and value-centered environment. The curriculum combines both traditional and innovative teaching methods, and it is designed to prepare graduates for the practice of law or for law-related careers nationwide. A private law school of 485 students, the University of Dayton School of Law continues to build a national reputation as alumni of the law school find employment in a variety of settings throughout the country. The School of Law is approved by the ABA and is a member of the AALS.

■ Mission

The mission of the University of Dayton School of Law is to enroll a diverse group of men and women who are intellectually curious, who possess self-discipline, and who are well motivated, and to rigorously train them in the substantive and procedural principles of public and private law. Faculty expect that graduates will become highly qualified and competent practicing attorneys who will uphold the highest professional standards.

■ Enrollment/Student Body

➧ 165 enrolled first-year class 1995 ➧ 19% minority students in first-year class ➧ 122 undergraduate colleges represented in first-year class 1995 ➧ 38/62 female/male ratio in first-year class ➧ 55% of first-year class from 24 states other than Ohio ➧ 12% of the first-year class had undergraduate major in engineering and the sciences

■ Environment for Studying Law

Law School—The School of Law is currently located in Albert Emanuel Hall and includes class and seminar rooms, a courtroom complex, faculty and student organization offices, formal reception area, and student lounge. The law building and law library are located in the central part of the university campus, within a short walk of university facilities and services.

Keller Hall—Joseph E. Keller Hall will be dedicated in the fall of 1997 as the new center for legal education at the University of Dayton. With technology integrated throughout the building, this 122,500 square-foot complex will feature a dramatic atrium, state-of-the-art classrooms and spacious law library. Keller Hall will provide an outstanding environment for studying law and will enhance the school's tradition of preparing highly qualified legal professionals.

The University—Founded in 1850, the University of Dayton today is the largest private university in Ohio and the eighth-largest Catholic university in the nation. More than 6,500 undergraduate students and 3,500 graduate students are enrolled at the university. The 110-acre campus is located in a residential neighborhood minutes from the city's center and includes a variety of student services, such as health care, on-campus housing, child care, meal plans, and banking.

The City—Law students have special opportunities available because the metropolitan area (population of 942,000) is home to a sizable judicial and legal community. Municipal courts, the Montgomery County Court of Common Pleas, the Second Ohio District Court of Appeals, and the U.S. District Court for the Southern District of Ohio are all located nearby. In addition, law students may find part-time employment with a number of the area's several Fortune 500 companies and their divisions (NCR, Standard Register, Mead, and LEXIS/NEXIS).

■ Law Library

➧ 215,000 volumes & equivalents ➧ more than 5,500 legal serials ➧ LEXIS ➧ WESTLAW ➧ computer center for word processing and database management ➧ 11 full-time staff

■ Faculty

➧ 27 full-time ➧ 31 adjunct

Student and alumni evaluations consistently give high marks to faculty of the law school. Faculty members are noted for being accessible to students, and it is this commitment that creates an environment which fosters faculty-student interaction. Faculty members at the School of Law bring a breadth of experience and research interests to the classroom.

■ Special Programs

Program in Law and Technology—The Program in Law and Technology allows upper-level students the opportunity to enroll in a number of specialized courses covering computer law, patent law, copyright law, trademark law, trade secrets, and transfers of technology and licensing. Additionally, qualified students may be placed as interns with area legal departments and law firms.

Joint Degree Programs—The School of Law offers joint degrees in conjunction with two graduate programs at the University of Dayton. The joint-degree programs are: J.D./Master of Business Administration, and J.D./Master of Science in Educational Administration. Each program is an integrated program of study that results in the conferral of both degrees at the time of graduation.

Law Clinic—The School of Law operates a law clinic which functions as a "typical" small, general-practice law office. Located within the law building, the clinic provides third-year students with the opportunity to represent actual clients, usually in cases involving civil matters.

Judicial Externships—Second- and third-year law students may participate in the law school's externship program offering the opportunity to clerk with area municipal, county, and federal judges. Externs undertake research for case decisions, thereby further developing research and writing skills, as well as gaining more direct knowledge of the judicial system.

Professional Skills Courses—Development of professional skills is offered through a variety of courses at the University of Dayton. These courses emphasize roles, situations, and problems that are commonly encountered by practicing attorneys. Professional skills courses include the three-semester Legal Profession course series, Negotiation and Mediation, Civil Trial Practice and Criminal Trial Practice, Mock Trial, Complex Litigation, and Land Use Planning.

Academic Excellence Program—The Academic Excellence Program includes a five-day orientation program prior to the start of the academic year, and a weekly tutorial session during both the first and second semesters. Entering students who are from economically or educationally disadvantaged backgrounds are especially encouraged to take part in the Academic Excellence Program.

■ Alumni and Placement Information

Graduates of the School of Law find success in a variety of career endeavors across the United States. A full-time placement director assists students in career planning and employment search activities. Counseling, career reference materials, position postings for direct contacts, and coordination of on- and off-campus interviews are provided as appropriate for those seeking clerkships, part-time and summer employment, further legal education, or permanent positions. Alumni of the School of Law include 2,400 men and women who are using their legal training in a variety of settings throughout the United States.

■ Activities

Student activities include the *University of Dayton Law Review*, Moot Court Board, Volunteer Income Tax Assistance, Student Bar Association, Women's Caucus, Black Law Students Association, Delta Theta Phi, Phi Alpha Delta, Phi Delta Phi, Society of International Law, Association of Trial Lawyers of America, *Equitable Relief* newspaper, *Fiat Justia* yearbook, Law and Medicine Society, the Law and Technology Society, Christian Legal Society, the Jewish Student Union, St. Thomas More Society, and the Federalist Society.

■ Admission

➧ *candidates wishing to be considered for full or partial scholarships should submit admission materials by March 1* ➧ *Priority deadline for applications—May 1*

■ Expenses and Financial Aid

➧ *full-time tuition—$15,668* ➧ *35 scholarship awards per year available (based on past academic performance and performance on the LSAT—ranging from full tuition to $2,500)* ➧ *loan programs available* ➧ *part-time employment available for upper-level students*

■ Questions Regarding the School of Law

Prospective students are invited to contact the School of Law Office of Admission with questions and concerns. The Office of Admission hours are Monday through Friday, 8:30 A.M. to 4:30 P.M. (Phone requests for admission materials may be made anytime throughout the week.)

Requests for materials also may be made via the Internet: lawinfo@odo.law.udayton.edu

Applicant Group for the 1995-1996 Academic Year

University of Dayton School of Law
This grid provides a general sense of the admission decisions rendered by the Admission Committee. Candidates who have specific questions regarding admission criteria are welcome to phone the School of Law Admission Office.

	GPA															
LSAT Score	3.75 +		3.50 - 3.74		3.25 - 3.49		3.00 - 3.24		2.75 - 2.99		2.50 - 2.74		Below 2.50		Total	
	Apps	Adm	Apps	Adm	Apps	Adm	Apps	Adm	Apps	Adm	Apps	Adm	Apps	Adm	Apps	Adm
160 - 180	11	11	14	14	15	14	12	11	14	13	11	11	13	11	90	85
155 - 159	19	19	30	30	47	43	48	46	45	43	43	39	25	21	257	241
150 - 154	39	38	47	46	79	64	76	30	67	20	43	6	48	10	399	214
140 - 149	26	21	82	56	134	60	139	16	123	11	88	5	90	2	682	171
120 - 139	5	2	10	0	10	0	27	0	35	0	47	0	85	0	219	2
Total	100	91	183	146	285	181	302	103	284	87	232	61	261	44	1647	713

Apps = Number of Applicants
Adm = Number Admitted
Reflects 99% of the total applicant pool.

University of Denver College of Law

7039 E. 18th Avenue
Denver, CO 80220

Phone: 303.871.6135

■ Introduction

The University of Denver College of Law, a private institution, is located on a 33-acre site which is 15 minutes from downtown Denver. The Law Center, built in 1984, provides more than "state-of-the-art" library, classroom, and student facilities; it also reflects the tradition of the Inns of Court, where students learn the law in the company of members of the bench and bar. The campus is home to the National Center for Preventive Law, the Rocky Mountain Mineral Law Foundation, and other organizations which enhance the academic atmosphere.

■ Enrollment/Student Body

➻ 2,693 applicants ➻ 1,256 admitted first-year class 1995 ➻ 356 enrolled first-year class 1995 ➻ 800 total full-time ➻ 280 total part-time ➻ 13.6% minority ➻ 45% women ➻ 55 states & foreign countries represented ➻ 159 undergraduate schools represented

■ Faculty

➻ 83 total ➻ 49 full-time ➻ 38 part-time or adjunct ➻ 17 women ➻ 6 minority

■ Library and Physical Facilities

➻ 291,839 volumes & equivalents ➻ library hours: Mon.-Thurs., 7:30 A.M.-MIDNIGHT; Fri., 7:30 A.M.-10:00 P.M.; Sat., 8:00 A.M.-10:00 P.M.; Sun., 9:00 A.M.-MIDNIGHT ➻ LEXIS ➻ NEXIS ➻ WESTLAW ➻ DIALOG ➻ INFOTRAC ➻ 8 full-time librarians ➻ library seats 642

■ Curriculum

➻ Academic Support Program ➻ 90 credits required to graduate ➻ 117 courses available ➻ degrees available: J.D.; J.D./M.B.A.; J.D. dual degree in International Studies, International Management, Psychology, History, Social Work, Sociology, and Mineral Economics ➻ semesters, start in Aug. ➻ range of first-year class size—20-84

Lawyering Process Course—The first-year curriculum includes an innovative Lawyering Process Course which offers students, in small group law firm settings, experience with the standard operations and skills of the lawyer's craft in interviewing, counseling, negotiation, decision making, and litigation. The small groups replicate law firms and reinforce cooperative work. Coursework in legal research and writing is taught in the context of simulated client problems.

■ Special Programs

Drawing upon its location in one of the nation's natural resources and energy capitals, the University of Denver College of Law offers a rich program in natural resources and environmental law. Students can choose from a variety of courses. There are also abundant opportunities for independent research and internships in the local energy, environment, and natural resource community.

The International Legal Studies program is designed for students interested in international comparative law, international organization, or transnational business. Students in the program may work on the *Denver Journal of International Law and Policy* as staff members and editors. The International Law Society sponsors a rich schedule of outside speakers and an annual conference with invited guests from many organizations.

Denver University has the only comprehensive program in transportation law in the United States. The program offers a unique opportunity to study the legal, regulatory, economic, and political developments in transportation. The basic course in Transportational Law offers an overview of all aspects of economic regulation of each of the domestic transport modes and also provides a survey of liability issues of the government's role in providing transport services. Students concentrating in Transportation Law are eligible for special scholarships that are awarded separately from other law scholarships.

The Business and Commercial Law program not only trains students to work with business entities but also prepares them for the specific needs of the corporate attorney. The program culminates in specialized seminars in business and commercial law. Corporate internships, highly prized one-semester assignments with large local corporations, are a valuable supplement to the coursework.

The Lawyering Skills program focuses on "what lawyers do." Courses in the regular curriculum are supplemented by the practical experience gained through public service legal work in the Student Law Office or through several internships or externships. The capstone of the program is the Student Law Office (Basic Civil Representation, Basic Criminal Representation, Advanced Public Interest Clinic) where students represent needy clients at all levels of the dispute resolution process. If the case reaches the litigation phase, the student handles all aspects of pretrial, trial preparation, and the trial itself—under faculty supervision. Focusing on one-to-one teaching and student responsibility, the program offers a rare opportunity to acquire lawyering skills.

■ Admission

➻ Bachelor's degree required for admission ➻ application deadline—March 1 ➻ rolling admission, application preferred Nov.-Jan. ➻ LSAT, LSDAS required ➻ median GPA—3.20 ➻ median LSAT score—157 ➻ application fee—$45

Applications should reach the College of Law between November and February to receive maximum consideration for admission the following August. Students may begin law study only in August. Applicants must take the LSAT and subscribe to LSDAS. A baccalaureate degree from an approved college or university is required prior to registration. LSAT scores and records of academic performances are individually evaluated in the admission process. Of equal importance, however, are the applicant's work experience, significant personal accomplishments, interests, goals, and reasons for seeking admission to law school.

■ Student Activities

Student activities are sponsored by the Student Bar Association to which most students belong. The University of Denver's Moot Court program is designed to promote the necessary development of students' oral and written skills. D.U.'s law students have the opportunity to participate in six different Moot Court competitions. The Moot Court Board is comprised of students who have demonstrated merit in D.U.'s Moot Court program and have displayed a commitment to improving the oral and written skills of the student body. With faculty integrated support, the Moot Court Board organizes and runs D.U.'s Moot Court program.

Three scholarly journals are edited at the College of Law allowing students to participate in scholarly research in varied fields. Academic credit is awarded for work in the *Law Review*, *Journal of International Law and Policy*, and *Transportation Law Journal*. Many special interest organizations on campus are officially recognized by the Student Bar Association. Among those groups are the Asian American Law Students Association, the Black Law Students Association, the Entertainment Law Society, the Hispanic Law Students Association, the Native American Law Students Association, the Public Interest Law Group, the Student Trial Lawyers Association, and the Women's Law Caucus/Children's Legal Issues in Perspective.

■ Expenses and Financial Aid

➡ tuition & fees—full-time, $16,895; part-time, $10,900 ➡ estimated additional expenses—$10,000 (health insurance, books, room and board, transportation) ➡ merit- and need-based scholarships available ➡ minority scholarships available ➡ FAFSA and GAPSFAS form due Feb. 1

The Chancellor's Scholarship Program provides a unique educational experience to a limited number of motivated and qualified students committed to public service through law. These scholarships are awarded through open competition to entering first-year students. The annual scholarships are renewed for successive years based on satisfactory academic performance and full participation in all the activities of the program.

■ Career Services

The law school maintains a placement office staffed by a full-time director and a full-time assistant who aid both students and alumni in securing employment. The Placement Office offers direct referral to part-time, full-time, summer, and career positions; arrangement of on-campus interviews each fall for second- and third-year students with law firms, governmental agencies, and corporations; and career counseling. The Placement Office emphasizes its policy against discriminatory practices in the interviewing and hiring of its students and graduates.

Applicant Group for the 1995-1996 Academic Year

University of Denver College of Law
This grid includes only applicants who earned 120-180 LSAT scores under standard administrations.

	GPA																					
LSAT Score	3.75 +		3.50 - 3.74		3.25 - 3.49		3.00 - 3.24		2.75 - 2.99		2.50 - 2.74		2.25 - 2.49		2.00 - 2.24		Below 2.00		No GPA		Total	
	Apps	Adm	Apps	Adm	Apps	Adm	Apps	Adm	Apps	Adm	Apps	Adm	Apps	Adm	Apps	Adm	Apps	Adm	Apps	Adm	Apps	Adm
175 - 180	0	0	0	0	0	0	0	0	0	0	0	0	0	0	0	0	0	0	0	0	0	0
170 - 174	1	1	3	2	0	0	2	2	0	0	0	0	3	3	0	0	0	0	0	0	9	8
165 - 169	2	2	9	8	9	9	12	12	13	13	8	7	3	3	0	0	0	0	2	1	58	55
160 - 164	22	22	34	32	52	50	66	64	62	61	39	36	16	16	4	4	0	0	0	0	295	285
155 - 159	42	40	101	97	140	130	162	127	131	93	74	45	28	11	7	3	1	0	10	9	696	555
150 - 154	40	21	85	47	171	62	199	45	155	38	80	22	61	15	12	1	1	1	4	1	808	253
145 - 149	14	3	31	5	87	12	121	15	99	6	57	3	37	3	13	1	0	0	6	3	465	51
140 - 144	4	1	16	2	30	0	51	1	42	1	37	0	30	0	14	0	2	0	4	0	230	5
135 - 139	2	0	4	0	6	0	13	0	19	1	20	0	12	0	9	0	0	0	7	0	92	1
130 - 134	0	0	2	0	3	0	7	0	5	0	5	0	1	0	2	0	2	0	1	0	28	0
125 - 129	1	0	0	0	0	0	0	0	0	0	2	0	1	0	1	0	0	0	0	0	5	0
120 - 124	0	0	0	0	0	0	0	0	0	0	0	0	0	0	1	0	0	0	1	1	2	1
Total	128	90	285	193	498	263	633	266	526	213	322	113	192	51	63	9	6	1	35	15	2688	1214

Apps = Number of Applicants
Adm = Number Admitted
Reflects 98% of the total applicant pool.

DePaul University College of Law

25 East Jackson Boulevard
Chicago, IL 60604

E-Mail: lawinfo@wppost.depaul.edu
URL: http://www.depaul.edu/law
Phone: 312.362.6831, toll-free: 1.800.428.7453

■ Introduction

DePaul University is the second largest private university in Illinois and enjoys the advantages of education conducted in a vibrant urban setting. Located in the heart of Chicago's business and legal communities, the College of Law is just a short walk from the Harold Washington Library, the largest municipal library in the world. Proximity to courts, government offices, and many law firms affords extensive contact with Chicago's legal community. Alumni include the Mayor of Chicago, state and federal judges, and managing partners of several Chicago law firms. The college offers full-time, part-time, and summer programs. DePaul is fully accredited by the ABA, is a member of AALS, and has an Order of the Coif chapter. The College of Law has embarked on an ambitious $14 million fund-raising campaign to enhance its endowment and programs, including $6 million targeted for a complete renovation and expansion of its physical plant.

■ Enrollment/Student Body

➧ 2,688 applicants ➧ 396 enrolled first-year class 1995 (294 full-time, 102 part-time) ➧ 807 total full-time ➧ 322 total part-time ➧ 12.8% minority ➧ 46% women ➧ 35 states & foreign countries represented ➧ 130 undergraduate schools represented in 1995 class

The college has an increasingly national enrollment—48 percent of 1995 entering students were from out-of-state. Each entering class brings a rich diversity in age, ethnicity, education, and career experience. For example, 35 students in the 1995 entering class had earned graduate and professional degrees. The average age of full-time day students and part-time evening students is 24 and 27, respectively. DePaul's bar passage rate has consistently exceeded the state average.

■ Faculty

➧ 121 total ➧ 51 full-time ➧ 70 part-time ➧ 20 women ➧ 5 minority

DePaul faculty are recognized scholars who represent a variety of professional backgrounds and interests as diverse as the curriculum. Many have advanced degrees in fields such as biology, political science, business, psychology, archaeology, theatre, public health, and philosophy.

■ Expenses and Financial Aid

➧ tuition & fees—full-time, $16,195; part-time, $10,308
➧ additional expenses—approximately $10,000
➧ performance and need-based scholarships available
➧ Free Application for Federal Student Aid due March 1

■ Curriculum

➧ Academic Support Program ➧ 86 units required to graduate ➧ 144 courses available ➧ degrees available: J.D. & J.D./M.B.A. ➧ semesters, start in early Aug. ➧ range of first-year class size—18-85 students

■ Library and Physical Facilities

➧ 330,000 volumes & equivalents ➧ library hours: Mon.-Fri., 8:00 A.M.-11:00 P.M.; Sat., 8:00 A.M.-6:00 P.M.; Sun., NOON-10:00 P.M. ➧ LEXIS ➧ NEXIS ➧ WESTLAW ➧ DIALOG ➧ ILLINET Online ➧ 8 full-time librarians

Holding extensive tax, health, and human rights law collections, the library is designated as an official government depository. Fully networked word processing and data management facilities include 95 personal computers. The college occupies six floors in both the 17-story Lewis Center and adjoining 15-story O'Malley Place in Chicago's Loop. Expanded facilities include a new library, new lounge and student organization offices, and state-of-the-art Lawyering Skills Center. Completely video-equipped rooms enable faculty to record student performances and create simulated jury trials, mediation, negotiations, and appellate arguments.

■ Special Specific Programs

Legal Clinic—An in-house component of the college, the legal clinic has a full-time staff of eight, including three clinical professors. Students serve clients from the initial interview through trial, and acquire extensive experience.

Externships—Providing students with academic credit through supervised field work, externships are offered by federal and state judges, various municipal agencies, and a number of not-for-profit organizations.

International Human Rights Law Institute—This research institute offers exciting student-faculty collaboration. It sponsors conferences, engages in scholarly work, and cooperates with other human rights organizations and international bodies. The Institute hosts lawyers and judges from Eastern Europe and Central America, and housed the UN investigation of war crimes in the former Yugoslavia.

Center for Church/State Studies—An academic, non-denominational research institute, the center directs studies of the legal structures of American religious organizations.

Health Law Institute—This research institute sponsors national conferences on health law issues and works with community organizations on health policy and legislation. The centerpiece of the Institute is the monthly student-edited *Journal of Health and Hospital Law.*

Study Abroad—DePaul and the University College Dublin have a student-exchange program whereby a small number of second-year students from both law schools undertake legal studies abroad for a semester.

J.D./M.B.A.—DePaul grants the combined Juris Doctor and Master of Business Administration degree.

Graduate Studies—DePaul was the first United States law school to offer courses toward the LL.M. in Health Law. The college also offers the LL.M. in Taxation program, featuring leading tax practitioners from Chicago law firms. DePaul educates about 100 graduate students in Health Law and Tax Law each year.

Professional Skills—DePaul is committed to education in professional skills. Among courses offered in dispute resolution are Arbitration, Dispute Resolution, Mediation, Mediation Clinic, Advanced Mediation, Interviewing, Counseling, and Negotiation. Courses in litigation skills include Product Liability, Juvenile Law, Pretrial Civil and Criminal Strategies, Trial Advocacy, Advanced Trial Advocacy, Complex Litigation, Law Clinic, Extern and Appellate Technique.

■ Admission

➠ *Bachelor's degree from an accredited college of university required* ➠ *application deadline—April 1*
➠ *rolling admissions (first letters sent about March 1)*
➠ *LSAT, LSDAS required* ➠ *median GPA—3.27*
➠ *median LSAT score—156* ➠ *application fee—$40*

DePaul adheres to a policy of nondiscrimination and encourages applications from traditionally underrepresented minority groups. A faculty committee reviews applications. Undergraduate GPA and LSAT score are highly significant admission criteria. When the LSAT is repeated, the average score is used. For the 1995-96 academic year, 2,172 candidates applied for admission to the full-time (day) division; 516 candidates applied to the part-time (evening) division.

■ Student Activities

In addition to legal writing and research and senior research seminar courses, four student-edited law journals provide students with intensive legal research and writing training. The journals are *The DePaul Law Review*, the *Journal of Health and Hospital Law*, the *DePaul Business Law Journal*, and the *Journal of Art and Entertainment Law*. The Student Bar Association sponsors lectures and social functions. Through the Student Bar Association and student-faculty committees, students participate in the decision process of the college. Among student organizations are the Moot Court Society; Women's Law Caucus; the Black, Latino, and Asian law student associations; the student newspaper, *Cause of Action*; Public Interest Law Association; DePaul chapter of the ACLU; International Law Society; Decalogue Society; National Lawyers Guild; Computer Law Society; Federalist Society; and Environmental Law Society.

■ Career Services

Alumni, faculty, and students contribute to an active and aggressive career services network. The College of Law sponsors an extensive on-campus interviewing program and a series of career seminars for students. The teaching and publishing reputations of the faculty and the largest alumni/ae bench and bar network in the Chicago area complement three full-time DePaul career services officers.

Applicant Group for the 1995-1996 Academic Year

DePaul University College of Law
This grid includes all full-time applicants who earned LSAT scores on the new 120-180 scale under standard test administrations and whose submission files were complete and reviewed by the faculty admission committee.

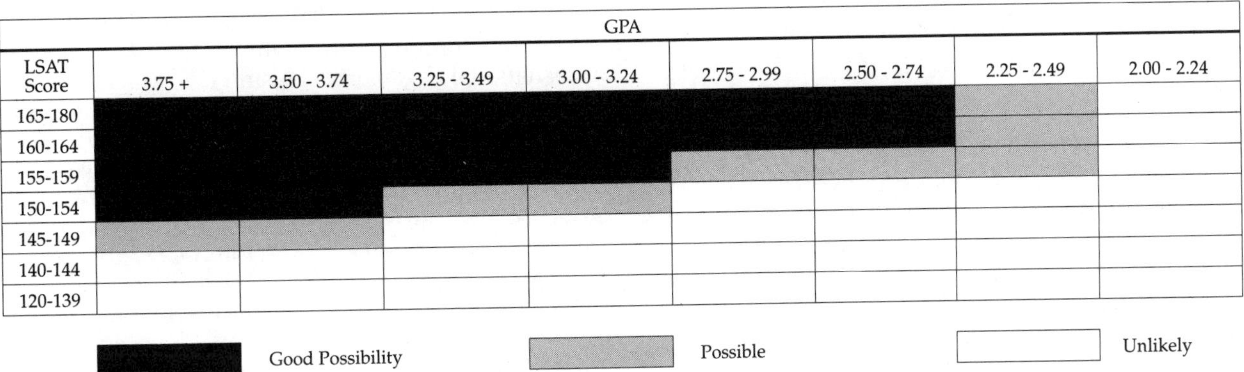

This chart is to be used as a general guide only.

Detroit College of Law at Michigan State University

N210 North Business Complex
East Lansing, MI 48824

Phone: 517.432.0222

■ Introduction

Founded in 1891, Detroit College of Law at Michigan State University was the first law school established in Detroit. The college is a privately controlled and endowed coeducational institution devoted exclusively to professional education in law. For over 100 years it has continued to provide superior educational opportunities to qualified and ambitious men and women. Many of the most eminent lawyers, judges, public officials, and business executives in Michigan are graduates of this famous law school; four of the last six federal judges appointed to the bench of the United States District Court for the Eastern District of Michigan are alumni of the college. One of these four federal judges was recently elevated to the bench of the United States Court of Appeals for the Eastern District of Michigan.

Detroit College of Law at Michigan State University offers students the best of both worlds: the quality of exceptional legal tradition; the strength of a great international university.

Detroit College of Law at Michigan State University is fully accredited and approved by the American Bar Association (ABA) and is a member of the Association of American Law Schools (AALS).

■ Enrollment/Student Body

➧ *1,029 applicants* ➧ *215 enrolled first-year class 1995* ➧ *409 total full-time* ➧ *306 total part-time* ➧ *12.3% minority* ➧ *36% women* ➧ *150 undergraduate schools represented*

The students of the Detroit College of Law at Michigan State University represent a wide diversity of educational backgrounds, experiences, and national origin. DCL/MSU students are undergoing a legal education in the theory and purpose of the law, along with its practical application, thus equipping them to fulfill unique and complicated demands in and outside of the legal profession.

■ Faculty

➧ *64 total* ➧ *29 full-time* ➧ *35 part-time or adjunct* ➧ *11 women* ➧ *9 minority*

The faculty is composed of resident professors who are devoted, on a full-time basis, to the teaching of law; legal research instructors; and a cadre of adjunct faculty members and practicing attorneys who are specialists with extensive experience in the field of law they teach. By utilizing the talents of both the professional teacher and the practicing attorney, the academic viewpoint of the former is blended with the practical approach of the latter into a sound, well-balanced education in both theory and practice of the legal system.

■ Library and Physical Facilities

➧ *over 200,000 volumes & equivalents* ➧ *LEXIS* ➧ *NEXIS* ➧ *WESTLAW* ➧ *OCLC* ➧ *Internet* ➧ *INFOTRAC* ➧ *6 full-time librarians*

The library collection is designed to meet the educational needs of law students. This major research collection includes the statutes of the 50 states, the United States, and Canada, as well as collections of numerous decisions, legal periodicals, and treatises. The recently opened computer lab is equipped with 24 new computers—18 Value Point IBM PCs and 6 Macintosh Quadra 610 computers—linked to a Novell Local Area Network. The network supports a variety of programs, including word processing, Computer Assisted Legal Instruction (CALI), and Microsoft Mail, an e-mail system. The college has recently become an Internet affiliate through MERIT.

■ Curriculum

➧ *85 units/credits required to graduate* ➧ *over 125 courses available* ➧ *J.D. degree* ➧ *first-year entry in Aug.* ➧ *3-year day and 4-year evening* ➧ *8-week summer session for both day and evening divisions* ➧ *curriculum-related programs offered: Law Review, Moot Court, Externships, International and Comparative Law, Taxation, Lawyering Skills, Dean King Honors Program*

■ Special Programs

International and Comparative Law—DCL/MSU students who wish to develop expertise in this field have the opportunity to study a wide variety of international legal issues. Some of the extensive course offerings include Admiralty, Chinese Law, Comparative Law, Immigration Law, International Business Transactions, International Criminal Law, Nuclear Weapons Doctrine: Arms Control and International Human Rights, International Litigation in U.S. Courts, International Taxation, International Wildlife and Environmental Law, Law of the European Community, Socialist Legal Systems, Transnational Legal Research, and U.S.-Canadian Taxation.

Center for Canadian-United States Law—The Center offers specific courses on Canadian law and Canadian-American legal relations within the Law School's already extensive international law program. The Center also sponsors the Canadian Summer Law Internship Program which is available to DCL/MSU students and guest students from other ABA-accredited law schools.

Taxation—The college has extensive offerings in taxation designed to provide interested students with the opportunity to develop an expertise in taxation. Some of the courses include Basic Income Taxation, Estate and Gift Taxation, Partnership Taxation, Business Income Taxation, U.S.-Canadian Taxation, and International Taxation.

Lawyering Skills—Every substantive course develops legal analysis and reasoning; most of them develop other skills as well. DCL/MSU offers the following courses that focus directly on the development of lawyering skills beyond legal analysis and reasoning: Advanced Problems in Environmental Law, Advocacy I & II, Arbitration, Business Securities and Tax Planning, Contract Drafting, Counseling, Discovery and Trial Preparation, Transnational Legal Research, and Trial Advocacy and Litigation Seminar.

■ Admission

➧ *Bachelor's degree from an accredited college or university required* ➧ *application deadline—Aug. entry, April 15* ➧ *rolling admissions* ➧ *LSAT, LSDAS required* ➧ *median GPA—2.93* ➧ *median LSAT score—151* ➧ *application fee—$50*

An admission decision is more complex than a mere ranking of applicants on the basis of a numerical formula. Detroit College of Law at Michigan State University is committed to a broad inquiry into the role and function of law in society and seeks a diverse student body as an integral part of its educational program. Accordingly, for purposes of discretionary admission, DCL/MSU will consider other subjective criteria in addition to an applicant's undergraduate grade-point average and LSAT score.

■ Curricular Activities

The *Detroit College of Law Review* is a legal periodical, published by law students, in which recognized legal scholars contribute book reviews and articles of keen interest to the legal community. The college also publishes the *Journal of International Law & Practice* and *Entertainment & Sports Law Forum.*

Moot Court at DCL/MSU is an extensive program of advocacy training in a competitive framework, permitting students to develop skills beyond those acquired in the first-year Research, Writing, and Advocacy course. The Moot Court Program participates in several national competitions, with teams researching a complex legal problem, writing and submitting a brief and then orally arguing before benches selected from judges and practitioners expert in the field.

Externship Programs are available in the Federal Defender's Office, County Circuit Courts, U.S. Attorney's Office, U.S. Department of Justice, U.S. District Court, U.S. Magistrate's Office, and County Prosecutor's Offices.

■ Student Activities

➧ *Student Senate* ➧ *Wolverine Student Bar Association* ➧ *Federalist Society* ➧ *Detroit Bar Association* ➧ *Women's Law Caucus* ➧ *International Law Society* ➧ *Environmental Law Society* ➧ *Phi Alpha Delta* ➧ *ABA Student Division* ➧ *Delta Theta Phi* ➧ *Hands on Detroit* ➧ *Entertainment & Sports Law Society* ➧ *National Lawyers Guild* ➧ *Christian Law Society* ➧ *DCL Tax & Estate Planning Society* ➧ *Triangle Bar*

Applicant Group for the 1995-1996 Academic Year

Detroit College of Law at Michigan State University

	GPA								
LSAT Score	3.75 +	3.50 - 3.74	3.25 - 3.49	3.00 - 3.24	2.75 - 2.99	2.50 - 2.74	2.25 - 2.49	2.00 - 2.24	Below 2.00
175-180									
170-174									
165-169									
160-164									
155-159									
150-154									
145-149									
140-144									
135-139									
130-134									
125-129									
120-124									

Good Possibility Possible Unlikely

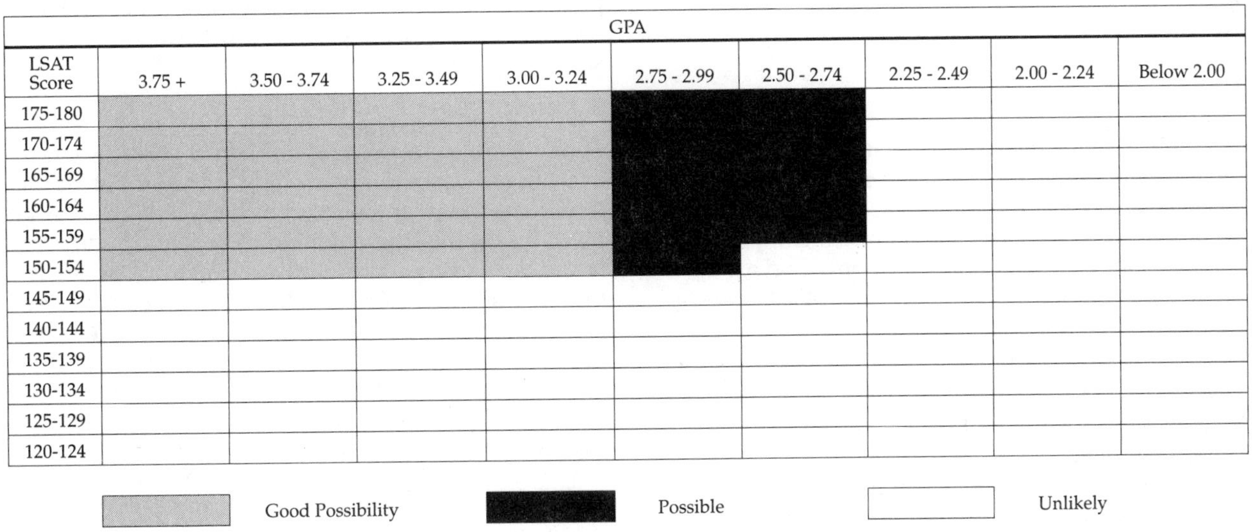

University of Detroit Mercy School of Law

Office of Admissions
651 E. Jefferson Avenue
Detroit, MI 48226

E-Mail: schmitda@udmercy.edu
Phone: 313.596.9849

■ Introduction

Founded in 1912, the University of Detroit Mercy School of Law is a well-established private school located opposite the Renaissance Center in a downtown Detroit riverfront complex of cultural, sports, convention, and residential facilities. The school is within walking distance of federal and state courts and downtown law firms. Windsor, Canada, is a five-minute drive across the river. A traditionally rich cultural center, with such renowned institutions as the Detroit Symphony and the Detroit Institute of Arts, the Detroit metropolitan area also provides a unique laboratory for the study of contemporary legal problems associated with urban and industrial redevelopment.

As a national law school, with a faculty drawn from throughout the country and abroad, the school offers a broad curriculum and seeks to attract a geographically diverse student body. The school is a member of the AALS and is accredited by the ABA.

■ Student Body

- *763 total students*
- *15% minority first-year class 1995*
- *49% women first-year class 1995*

The student body is drawn from diverse geographical, ethnic, and religious backgrounds. Two-thirds of the students in the entering class are in the full-time day program. Academic attrition among first-year students is traditionally about 11 percent.

■ Faculty

- *28 full-time*
- *29 part-time*

■ Library and Physical Facilities

- *190,000 volumes & equivalents*
- *NEXIS*
- *WESTLAW*

The law school campus includes an architectural-prize-winning library building and a striking three-story interior atrium that serves as an unusually spacious student lounge.

The library is air-conditioned, and contains comfortable reading areas, typing and audiovisual rooms, and group study rooms, as well as individual study carrels.

Dowling Hall, a Detroit landmark, contains attractive classrooms, offices, and a bookstore; the atrium and adjoining cafeteria provide a congenial setting for informal student-faculty discussions.

■ Curriculum

- *Academic Support Program*
- *90 credits required to graduate*
- *degrees available: J.D.; J.D./M.B.A.*
- *semesters system*

The school offers a three-year, full-time day program and a four-year, part-time evening program, both leading to the J.D. degree; academic standards in the two programs are identical. Basic courses in civil procedure, contracts, property, criminal law, torts, constitutional law, taxation, evidence, legal research and writing, and professional responsibility are required, and students must take at least one seminar in their final year. The remainder of the curriculum is elective. The academic year is divided into two semesters and a summer session. Students may accelerate by enrolling in the summer session.

■ Special Programs

The school's commitment to the concept of quality legal education as an approach to urban problems is reflected in opportunities to represent indigent clients under close faculty guidance and a variety of externship placements available through the Urban Law Clinic.

To refine research and writing skills, students may undertake independent research under the direction of a faculty member. The school also provides an opportunity for qualified students to pursue a four-year joint J.D./M.B.A. degree.

Additionally, the law school has a special J.D. degree program for Canadian lawyers, a cross-registration program with the University of Windsor, an exchange program with a French university (the University of Clermot—Ferrand), continuing legal education programs for lawyers and other professionals as well as a consortium of courses with other local law schools entitled the Intellectual Property Law Institute.

The school also offers a special summer program for disadvantaged applicants who do not meet minimum standards for the entering class but nevertheless show potential for the study of law. Successful completion of the summer program permits admission as a regular student in the fall semester.

■ London Law Programme

The program offers second- and third-year law students an exceptional opportunity to study abroad for an academic semester. An integral part of the law school, the program provides for the study of international and comparative law at one of the world's leading centers of these disciplines and enables students to better understand our Anglo-American common law system and its origins.

University of Detroit Mercy is the only American law school to operate a foreign-based academic-year program organized on a semester basis. Although the program is primarily for University of Detroit Mercy law students, a limited number of spaces are available for students from other American and Canadian schools. Occasionally, qualified students from other countries like France and Mexico participate.

The program has been approved by the Council of the Section of Legal Education and Admissions to the Bar of the American Bar Association.

■ Admission

➽ *undergraduate degree from accredited institution required*
➽ *application deadline—April 15* ➽ *fall admission only*
➽ *LSAT, LSDAS required* ➽ *median GPA—3.15*
➽ *median LSAT score—151* ➽ *application fee—$50*

The school does not require a specific prelaw curriculum and agrees with the recommendations set forth in the introduction to this guide.

While the admissions committee considers the LSAT and undergraduate grades as the most important determinants of admission, it also considers factors such as letters of recommendation, evidence of maturity and leadership, graduate work, and work experience. Two letters of recommendation are required.

Applications are reviewed on a continuous basis and decisions communicated as early as possible. Interviews, though not required, may be granted upon request. A $150 nonrefundable deposit is required of all admitted applicants and credited toward the first semester's tuition. A second deposit may be required. In general, transfer students must have a 3.0 GPA or be in the upper quarter of their law class.

The law school has nondiscrimination and affirmative action policies.

■ Activities

The *Law Review* is edited entirely by a student editorial board. Students edit and publish the *Michigan Business Law Journal* which is the quarterly newsletter of the Business Law Section of the Michigan State Bar. A student moot court board helps to supervise the required appellate advocacy program and administers the school's Gallagher and Professional Responsibility competitions, as well as participation by students in regional and national competitions.

The Student Bar Association, affiliated with the Law Student Division of the ABA, plays a significant role in student affairs and program development. A student newspaper, *In Brief*, is published for the law school community. Some of the other approximately 25 student organizations include the Black Law Students Alliance; the Latin American Students Organization; the Women's Law Caucus; the Justice Frank Murphy Honor Society; the International Law Society; and chapters of two coeducational legal fraternities.

■ Expenses and Financial Aid

➽ *tuition—$450/credit hour* ➽ *estimated additional expenses—$9,500 (room, board, personal expenses)*
➽ *academic scholarships available*

Students who are Michigan residents may apply to the Michigan Board of Higher Education for tuition grants. Loans are available through the Federal Perkins Loan (formerly NDSL) and Michigan Guaranteed Loan Programs and through the state of Michigan. Work-study positions are also available.

■ Placement

A Dean of Placement actively encourages law firms and other prospective employers to interview at the school and counsels and assists students in acquiring both temporary and full-time employment.

Applicant Group for the 1995-1996 Academic Year

University of Detroit Mercy School of Law

	GPA									
LSAT Score	3.75 +	3.50 - 3.74	3.25 - 3.49	3.00 - 3.24	2.75 - 2.99	2.50 - 2.74	2.25 - 2.49	2.00 - 2.24	Below 2.00	NoGPA
175-180	Good Possibility	Good Possibility	Good Possibility	Good Possibility	Good Possibility					
170-174	Good Possibility	Good Possibility	Good Possibility	Good Possibility	Good Possibility					
165-169	Good Possibility	Good Possibility	Good Possibility	Possible	Possible					
160-164	Good Possibility	Good Possibility	Good Possibility	Possible	Possible					
155-159	Good Possibility	Good Possibility	Good Possibility	Possible	Possible					
150-154	Possible	Possible	Possible	Possible	Possible					
145-149	Possible	Possible	Possible	Possible	Possible					
140-144										
135-139										
130-134										
125-129										
120-124										

■ Good Possibility ▒ Possible □ Unlikely

Dickinson School of Law

150 South College Street
Carlisle, PA 17013

E-Mail: admission@dsl.edu
Phone: 800.840.1122

■ Introduction

Founded in 1834, The Dickinson School of Law, oldest of the independent law schools, has been a pioneer in skills training and comparative law curricula and has been recognized nationally for the excellence of its advocacy program. In addition to providing small class sizes and easy accessibility of faculty, the Dickinson community fosters a magnanimous spirit in which students are quick to help one another. The academic atmosphere, while competitive, is friendly and cooperative. Our rigorous academic program includes many opportunities for real-life, hands-on experience in clinical settings and moot court competitions. Students also have the opportunity to work on three respected law journals and participate in a wide array of extracurricular activities which greatly enhance the law school experience. Our location in historic Carlisle, Pennsylvania enables students to pursue their education in a friendly, affordable environment with easy access to Pittsburgh, Philadelphia, New York, Washington, DC, and Baltimore. Located less than 20 miles from the state capital of Harrisburg, the school affords opportunities for part-time work in state government agencies and private law firms during the school year and in the summer.

■ Enrollment/Student Body

➽ *1,455 applicants* ➽ *175 enrolled first-year class 1995*
➽ *521 total full-time* ➽ *8% minority* ➽ *47% women*
➽ *32 states & foreign countries represented*
➽ *219 undergraduate schools represented*

■ Faculty

➽ *85 total* ➽ *27 full-time* ➽ *58 part-time or adjunct*
➽ *7 women* ➽ *3 minority*

■ Library and Physical Facilities

➽ *374,800 volumes & equivalents* ➽ *hours (public use): Mon.-Thurs., 8:00 A.M.-9:00 P.M.; Fri., 8:00 A.M.-5:00 P.M.; students have 24-hour access* ➽ *LEXIS* ➽ *NEXIS*
➽ *WESTLAW* ➽ *OCLC* ➽ *RLIN* ➽ *EPIC*
➽ *7 full-time librarians* ➽ *library seats 449*

LEXIS and WESTLAW computerized legal research terminals and IBM personal computers are available to students. Some accommodations for single students are available in the Levinson Curtilage, a dormitory quadrangle located next to the Trickett Hall complex. Reasonably priced off-campus housing is readily available.

Our campus is adjacent to Dickinson College, a separate, unrelated undergraduate school that offers law students access to its library, food service, and cultural activities.

The law school's Community Law Center in downtown Carlisle houses state-of-the-art clinic facilities similar to real law offices. It includes an 1,800-square-foot law library for use by student lawyers in the Disability and Family Law clinics and the Mediation Center.

■ Programs of Study/Degree Requirements

Dickinson School of Law graduates receive a broad-based theoretical and practical legal education that prepares them to practice law anywhere in the United States. With more than 100 courses in the J.D. program, Dickinson provides electives and seminars in developing areas of the law as the profession adjusts to meet the changing needs of society. Skills preparation in trial and appellate advocacy, client counseling, mediation, and legal writing complement the standard coursework. With several national interscholastic moot court championships to its credit, Dickinson's advocacy program has been recognized for excellence by the American College of Trial Lawyers. Since the mid-60s, almost 50 Dickinson teams have finished first or second or have otherwise distinguished themselves in interscholastic advocacy competitions.

Foreign lawyers with law degrees not founded substantially on the English Common Law curriculum may apply for admission to the Master of Laws in Comparative Law degree program, which requires successful completion of an academic year in residence. The foreign law school attended must have a standing comparable to AALS- and ABA-approved schools.

■ Summer Sessions Abroad

In the early 1980s, Dickinson became one of the first fully accredited law schools to establish an overseas comparative law program for American students. Dickinson offers two, four-week summer credit programs; one in Florence, Italy, the other in Vienna, Austria and Strasbourg, France. In Florence, Dickinson professors collaborate with University of Florence Law School faculty and distinguished lecturers from the Italian legal and business communities. The Vienna/Strasbourg program is held in cooperation with the Economic University of Vienna, the Universities of Vienna and Strasbourg law schools, and legal personnel from the United Nations Commission on International Trade Law and the Council of Europe.

■ Special Programs and Activities

Dickinson was also a pioneer in providing hands-on, clinical experiences to assist students in developing the skills necessary to counsel clients effectively. The school's internal clinics include the Family Law Clinic, which handles matters involving divorce, child custody, visitation, protection from abuse and other family-related cases; the Disability Law Clinic, which handles disability-related cases; and the Mediation Center, which specializes in helping to settle conflicts between neighbors, landlords and tenants, merchants and consumers, and other disputants. Students in the Prison Clinic represent inmates in two Pennsylvania correctional facilities. There are also many field placement opportunities in Legal Services, public defenders' and district attorneys' offices, judicial clerkships, and legal departments of state agencies.

■ Admission

➽ *Bachelor's degree required* ➽ *application deadline—March 1* ➽ *LSAT, LSDAS required* ➽ *median GPA—3.30* ➽ *median LSAT score—155* ➽ *application fee—$50*

Prior to enrollment, applicants must have completed work for an undergraduate degree from an accredited college or university, as required by accreditation rules of the AALS and the ABA, and must have submitted all college transcripts and scores on the LSAT. All relevant factors will be considered by the Admissions Committee to identify those applicants who are most likely to make a substantial and constructive contribution to the law school and to the legal profession. There are no automatic admissions or denials based on the numbers. Last year, Dickinson rejected 56 applicants who had LSAT scores above the previous year's median of 154.

Dickinson is a strong supporter of the Council on Legal Education Opportunity program, having hosted a CLEO summer institute six times during the past 11 years. Through participation in CLEO, implementation of a special minority visitation weekend and other aggressive recruiting efforts, Dickinson is working to increase minority enrollment and broaden the diversity of its student body.

Personal interviews are not part of the admissions process, but applicants are invited to visit campus and attend a class, preferably in the fall.

Students with an outstanding first-year performance at another AALS school may be considered for admission as second-year students. Transfer applications must be received on or before June 15. No action will be taken on these applications until first-year grades and class standing are received.

The Dickinson School of Law does not discriminate on the basis of race, religion, color, national origin, sex, age, sexual orientation, or disability in the administration of any of its educational programs or activities or with respect to admissions or employment.

■ Cocurricular Activities

Founded in 1897, the quarterly *Dickinson Law Review* ranks as one of the oldest law school publications in the country. The *Dickinson Journal of International Law* publishes articles on private and public international law. The *Dickinson Journal of Environmental Law & Policy* is a forum for articles that treat aspects of environmental law. The Student Bar Association promotes the interests of the school and the students. A wide variety of student organizations are also active at Dickinson.

■ Expenses and Financial Aid

Dickinson is one of the best buys in legal education. The current annual tuition is $13,800. The estimated annual cost for an unmarried student living in school housing, excluding personal expenses, is $19,600. Tuition and fees are subject to change. Grants and scholarships are awarded primarily on the basis of established need with due consideration for academic achievement and potential. Students seeking financial assistance must register with FAF by February 15.

Applicant Group for the 1995-1996 Academic Year

Dickinson School of Law

This grid includes only applicants who earned 120-180 LSAT scores under standard administrations.

LSAT Score	GPA 3.75 +		3.50 - 3.74		3.25 - 3.49		3.00 - 3.24		2.75 - 2.99		2.50 - 2.74		2.25 - 2.49		2.00 - 2.24		Below 2.00		No GPA		Total	
	Apps	Adm	Apps	Adm	Apps	Adm	Apps	Adm	Apps	Adm	Apps	Adm	Apps	Adm	Apps	Adm	Apps	Adm	Apps	Adm	Apps	Adm
175 - 180	0	0	0	0	1	1	0	0	0	0	0	0	0	0	0	0	0	0	0	0	1	1
170 - 174	0	0	1	1	1	1	0	0	0	0	1	1	0	0	0	0	0	0	0	0	3	3
165 - 169	4	4	2	2	4	4	7	6	5	5	3	3	2	0	0	0	1	1	0	0	28	25
160 - 164	7	7	24	24	24	24	29	28	25	24	15	13	6	4	2	0	1	0	1	1	134	125
155 - 159	31	31	66	61	114	105	70	59	35	22	30	14	12	5	2	0	0	0	0	0	360	297
150 - 154	31	15	99	47	107	35	84	17	57	6	25	5	17	1	5	0	0	0	4	2	429	128
145 - 149	7	1	40	7	55	3	65	8	46	5	31	3	14	0	7	0	1	0	4	0	270	27
140 - 144	4	1	9	3	29	5	24	5	25	2	20	2	10	0	6	1	1	0	1	0	129	19
135 - 139	1	0	4	1	3	0	9	0	9	1	9	0	8	1	8	0	1	0	0	0	52	3
130 - 134	0	0	1	0	2	0	2	0	2	1	4	0	6	0	2	0	0	0	1	1	20	2
125 - 129	0	0	0	0	0	0	0	0	2	0	1	0	1	0	1	0	0	0	1	0	6	0
120 - 124	0	0	0	0	0	0	0	0	0	0	0	0	1	0	0	0	0	0	0	0	1	0
Total	85	59	246	146	340	178	290	123	206	66	139	41	77	11	33	1	5	1	12	4	1433	630

Apps = Number of Applicants
Adm = Number Admitted
Reflects 99% of the total applicant pool.

District of Columbia School of Law

4250 Connecticut Avenue, N.W.
Washington, DC 20008

Phone: 202.274.7341

■ Introduction

In 1986, the City Council of the District of Columbia authorized the establishment of the District of Columbia School of Law. The founding class was admitted in 1988. The Council created a dual mission for the School of Law and charged its Board of Governors with a special mandate to recruit and enroll, to the degree feasible, students from ethnic, racial, or other population groups that in the past have been underrepresented among persons admitted to the bar. It also charged the Board with representing the legal needs of low-income persons, particularly those who reside in the District of Columbia.

The DC School of Law is the only publicly funded law school in Washington, DC. During the academic year 1995-96, DC School of Law will formally merge with the University of the District of Columbia (UDC), and become the University of the District of Columbia School of Law. The law school has full-time and part-time programs.

■ Enrollment/Student Body

➧ 109 full-time enrolled first-year class, 1995; 26 part-time enrolled first-year class, 1995 ➧ 60% full-time minority; 80% part-time minority ➧ 53% full-time women; 54% part-time women ➧ 30% full-time DC residents; 42% part-time DC residents ➧ full-time average age—29; part-time average age—33 ➧ 29 states represented ➧ 100 undergraduate schools represented

The School of Law prides itself in attracting an extraordinary student body now totaling about 264. Our student body is a culturally and ethnically diverse group.

■ Faculty

➧ 25 total ➧ 19 full-time ➧ 6 part-time ➧ 9 women ➧ 6 minority

■ Library and Physical Facilities

➧ 175,000 volumes & equivalents ➧ LEXIS ➧ WESTLAW ➧ CALI ➧ DIALOG ➧ 6 full-time librarians ➧ library seats 142

The School of Law temporarily occupies existing buildings at the University of the District of Columbia's Van Ness campus. The Law School is located in a section of northwest Washington, DC known for its harmonious blend of residential and business communities.

In addition to the regular law volumes and volume equivalents, the library supports the Clinical Program by maintaining a small collection of clinical practice material and other materials pertinent to each of the clinics.

The Computer Center features terminals for student research, word processing, and computer-assisted tutorials in core subjects.

The campus is conveniently located on the Metro's Red Line at the UDC/Van Ness subway stop.

■ Curriculum

➧ Academic Support Program ➧ 85 credits required to graduate ➧ 18 required courses ➧ 2 semesters of clinical work required for full-time; 1 semester of clinical work required for part-time ➧ 6 clinics available ➧ 49 total courses available ➧ J.D. degree ➧ semesters, start in mid-Aug.

Consistent with DC Law School's mission, the basic program is designed to equip students with the professional skills of practicing lawyers as well as the traditional substantive knowledge of law.

Orientation is a one-week program introducing first-year students to the study of law and the School of Law community. During orientation, students take Lawyering Process I to learn basic legal analysis, and they meet administration, faculty, and continuing students. There is a dean's reception for first-year students in the fall semester. There are also other events planned by student organizations.

In the first year, students take a prescribed program consisting of required courses and one elective course. After the first year, students must also take courses in Evidence, Constitutional Law I and II, Property and Professional Responsibility.

In the second year, full-time students begin their clinical experience by taking Clinic One. In the third year, they take Clinic Two. Part-time students take one clinic in the summer of their second or third year. The clinics offered in the 1995-96 academic year are Housing/Consumer, Public Entitlements, HIV/AIDS, Juvenile, Legislation, and Government Accountability Project (GAP).

The School of Law offers a limited number of summer courses; it does not allow early graduation. Students normally complete the program in three calendar years.

DCSL considers academic support to be an integral part of its course of study. Students in academic difficulty at the end of their first semester may apply to be in the enhanced program, which may involve adjusting courseloads, counseling, and group and individual tutoring. In addition, faculty members hold extra review sessions during the semester in required courses and provide sample examination questions with model answers. During the first two weeks at the law school, students are given two diagnostic tests, one in reading and one in writing. Test results may be used to help students improve their skills.

The emphasis of the school is on public interest law; the overall curriculum—clinic and classroom—is designed to support that orientation. In addition, DCSL's goals are consistent with the objectives of legal education proposed by the Long-Range Planning Committee of the American Bar Association. These objectives include "training for [lawyering] competence…[and]...training in professional responsibility."

■ Internship Program

- *one semester internship, 8 credits*
- *internship seminar, 2 credits*

In addition to the clinic program, students in the second semester, second year, or third year may elect to do an internship in which they work 30 hours a week outside the law school in judicial, legislative, or Congressional offices, or in public interest legal organizations. Faculty members monitor each placement and students must attend a weekly Internship Seminar at the school. The School of Law emphasizes the importance of supervision, educational merit, and public service in each internship.

■ The Writing Program

Each DCSL student is required to produce significant pieces of writing each of the three years of study. In the first year students satisfy the writing requirement in the Lawyering Process course. In the second and third years, students may satisfy the legal writing requirement as part of a seminar, elective course, clinical practice, or independent study.

■ Admission

- *Bachelor's degree from accredited college or university required*
- *application deadline—April 1*
- *rolling admission, early application preferred*
- *LSAT, LSDAS required*
- *application fee—$35*
- *fall admission, full-time, day & part-time, evening*

Admission is based upon academic and nonacademic achievements and professional promise. Because the LSAT does not measure the skills, determination, and personal commitment that are vital to competence and success as a legal practitioner, DCSL looks at an applicant's LSAT scores and grades in tandem with other criteria that we believe may provide a more accurate measure of a candidate's potential for success in the study of law. This approach means that our Admissions Committee considers all submitted application material. It reviews closely the application essays and other information supplied with the application, including support documents and recommendations.

■ Student Activities

The first issue of the biannual *The District of Columbia Law Review* was published in 1992. *The Side-Bar* is the student newspaper which is published quarterly. Students participate in many of the decision processes of the law school. Numerous student organizations are active at the law school.

■ Expenses and Financial Aid

- *tuition & fees—DC residents, $7,000; nonresidents, $14,000*
- *part-time—$250 per credit—DC residents*
- *part-time—$500 per credit—nonresidents*
- *additional expenses—$17,140 (room, board, books)*
- *need- & merit-based scholarships available*
- *FAFSA for need analysis due April 30.*

■ Career Services

The Career Services Office provides employment information and career services to the School of Law's student body and graduates. The office maintains listings of permanent job openings, fellowships, summer clerkships, and part-time opportunities. The office also coordinates potential internship sites and invites employers to conduct on-campus interviews. The office provides resources for career planning, counseling sessions to assist students in developing their career goals, résumé workshops, and other relevant seminars.

Admission Profile Not Available

Drake University Law School

2507 University Avenue
Des Moines, IA 50311

E-Mail: lawadmit@acad.drake.edu
URL: HTTP://www.drake.edu/public/lawlib/top.html
Phone: 800.44.DRAKE, ex. 2782 or 515.271.2782

■ Introduction

Drake University Law School, a charter member of the AALS, is one of the 25 oldest law schools in the nation, tracing its history to 1865. Accredited by the ABA, the Law School became affiliated with Drake University, a private, independent institution of higher learning, at its founding in 1881.

Drake Law School is located in Iowa's capital, Des Moines, providing law students the opportunity to get hands-on experience with the executive, judicial, and legislative branches of government, the federal courts, administrative agencies, and a wide array of law firms and businesses.

■ Enrollment/Student Body

➧ 1,190 applicants ➧ 587 admitted first-year class 1995 ➧ 152 enrolled first-year class 1995 ➧ 502 total full-time ➧ 17 total part-time ➧ 8% minority ➧ 38% women ➧ 42 states & 3 foreign countries represented ➧ 196 undergraduate schools represented

■ Faculty

➧ 47 total ➧ 23 full-time ➧ 24 part-time or adjunct ➧ 16 women ➧ 5 minority

■ Library and Physical Facilities

➧ 250,000 volumes & equivalents ➧ library hours: Mon.-Thurs., 7:00 A.M.-MIDNIGHT; Fri., 7:00 A.M.-10:30 P.M.; Sat., 9:00 A.M.-10:30 P.M.; Sun., NOON-MIDNIGHT ➧ LEXIS ➧ NEXIS ➧ WESTLAW ➧ 5 full-time librarians ➧ library seats 700

The Dwight D. Opperman Hall and Law Library, dedicated in 1993 by U.S. Supreme Court Justice Anthony Kennedy, has approximately 70,000 square feet and provides Drake Law students with a state-of-the-art facility for legal research, class seminars and studying. Opperman Hall is wired for computers and is equipped with both online legal research training centers.

■ Legal Clinic

The Neal and Bea Smith Law Center, built in 1987, houses the Drake Law School Legal Clinic. The center is a state-of-the-art law office, with each student having access to the latest in computer technology. The center was selected as the national training and resource institute for public service attorneys. The $1.75 million addition, dedicated in 1994 by U.S. Attorney General Janet Reno, includes a fully computerized courtroom and training facilities for Drake law students.

■ Curriculum

➧ Academic Support Program ➧ Tutorial Supplement Program of Instruction ➧ 90 credits required to graduate ➧ 96 courses available ➧ additional summer agricultural law and constitutional law program courses which vary annually are also offered ➧ degrees available: J.D.; J.D./Pharmacy D.; J.D./M.B.A.; J.D./M.P.A.; J.D./M.A. (Mass Comm.); J.D./M.S. (Economics/Iowa State); J.D./M.A. (Pol. Sci./Iowa State); J.D./M.S.W. (Social Work/Iowa) ➧ semesters, start in Aug. ➧ range of first-year class size—15-80

Educational excellence has long been achieved at Drake Law School through a balance of theory and practice that recognizes the need for both in a quality legal education. The J.D. curriculum at Drake is national in scope and emphasis.

Summer school is available for both incoming and continuing students, and may accelerate graduation.

■ Special Programs

Trial Practice and Advocacy Skills Programs—Drake students can refine their litigation and lawyering skills by participating in a variety of programs and courses. Students can render meaningful public service by providing lawyering services to low-income and elderly clients through Drake's client representation program. The Neal and Bea Smith Law Center houses the Law School's client representation and judicial clerkship programs, and serves as a center for other professional skills courses and programs.

Students receive academic credit for internships with state and federal judges at either the trial or appellate levels, with state or federal administrative agencies, the state legislature, and state prosecutors. Students may also develop lawyering skills and earn academic credit for participation on Drake's moot court, mock trial, or lawyering skills teams. Third-year students also participate as members in two American Inns of Court Chapters that have been formed by lawyers and judges in Des Moines.

Constitutional Law Programs—Drake is home to the Constitutional Law Resource Center, which was made possible through the United States Congress' selection of Drake Law School to receive one of four endowment appropriations awarded nationally. The center sponsors a lecture series and an annual symposium featuring nationally recognized constitutional scholars.

Another lecture, the Dwight D. Opperman Lecture in Constitutional Law, emphasizes the significance of constitutional study and the Law School's commitment to it. The Opperman Lecture has been given by Justices of the United States Supreme Court, who have also met with students and participated in the intellectual life of the Law School.

A Summer Institute in Constitutional Law is offered annually for entering first-year students.

Agricultural Law—Drake has one of the few programs in the nation addressing the timely and important issues in American and international agricultural law and policy. The Agricultural Law Center hosts an annual Summer Agricultural Law Institute and conference, and students write and edit an agricultural law reporter.

■ Admission

➽ Bachelor's degree required ➽ priority application deadline—March 1 ➽ rolling admission ➽ LSAT, LSDAS required ➽ median GPA—3.19 ➽ median LSAT score—153 ➽ application fee—$35

The Law School is committed to attracting, enrolling, retaining, and graduating an academically strong and diverse student body.

All applications are reviewed by a faculty admission committee. Admission to Drake Law School is based upon an evaluation of an applicant's LSAT scores, undergraduate GPA, undergraduate institution, coursework, grade trend, writing skills as demonstrated in the LSAT writing sample and personal statement, community and extracurricular involvement, graduate school record, relevant work experience, and letters of recommendation.

■ Student Activities

Law students participate in many student organizations and cocurricular activities. *The Drake Law Review*, a student edited journal, is published quarterly. Students also publish a law school newspaper. Drake moot court teams consistently win regional competitions and finish strong in national competitions. The Student Bar Association, Legal Research Service, and honorary societies provide students with leadership, public service, and learning opportunities. Drake students have also formed a variety of organizations around their special interests, including the Drake Law Women, Black Law Students Association, Latino Law Society, Asian-Pacific Islander Association, International Law Society, Christian Legal Society, Environmental Law Society, Federalist Society, National Lawyers Guild and the Law Student Division of the American Bar Association.

■ Expenses and Financial Aid

➽ tuition & fees—full-time, $15,200; part-time, $510/credit ➽ estimated additional expenses—$8,525 (room & board, $4,950; personal expenses, $2,400; books, $800; transportation, $375) ➽ scholarships available: Law General (need & merit); Law Opportunity (disadvantaged); Merit Awards ➽ minority scholarships available: Law Opportunity ➽ financial aid available; FAFSA, all other forms are accepted ➽ priority deadline for scholarships and financial aid—March 1

■ Career Services

The Law School Career Services Office offers career-planning and counseling services, assistance in résumé preparation, salary and geographical employment statistics, on-campus interviews, nationwide job postings, and state bar examination information. More than 93 percent of 1993 Drake Law School graduates were employed in legal positions within 6 months of graduation. Law School alumni practice in all 50 states and several foreign countries.

Applicant Group for the 1995-1996 Academic Year

Drake University Law School
This grid includes only applicants who earned 120-180 LSAT scores under standard administrations.

	GPA																				
LSAT Score	3.75 +		3.50 - 3.74		3.25 - 3.49		3.00 - 3.24		2.75 - 2.99		2.50 - 2.74		2.25 - 2.49		2.00 - 2.24		Below 2.00		No GPA		Total	
	Apps	Adm	Apps	Adm	Apps	Adm	Apps	Adm	Apps	Adm	Apps	Adm	Apps	Adm	Apps	Adm	Apps	Adm	Apps	Adm	Apps	Adm
175 - 180	0	0	0	0	0	0	0	0	0	0	0	0	0	0	0	0	0	0	0	0	0	0
170 - 174	0	0	1	1	1	1	0	0	0	0	0	0	0	0	0	0	0	0	1	0	3	2
165 - 169	1	1	0	0	0	0	1	1	3	3	1	1	1	1	0	0	0	0	0	0	7	7
160 - 164	3	3	9	9	8	7	13	12	6	6	4	4	4	3	5	4	2	1	1	0	55	49
155 - 159	12	12	16	16	39	37	41	40	36	35	34	30	12	6	10	8	1	1	1	0	202	185
150 - 154	26	26	47	47	69	65	68	59	58	30	36	9	20	5	9	0	4	2	1	1	338	244
145 - 149	12	11	31	27	51	19	66	18	56	11	47	1	24	1	14	1	1	0	5	3	307	92
Below 145	4	1	14	2	29	1	41	2	40	0	49	0	33	0	21	0	7	0	8	0	246	6
Total	60	54	118	102	197	130	230	132	198	85	170	45	94	16	59	13	15	4	17	4	1158	585

Apps = Number of Applicants
Adm = Number Admitted
Reflects 98% of the total applicant pool.

Duke University School of Law

Science Drive & Towerview Road
Box 90393
Durham, NC 27708-0393

E-Mail: admissions@faculty.law.duke.edu
URL: http://www.law.duke.edu
Phone: 919.613.7200

■ Introduction

Duke Law School is distinguished by a learning environment that is similar to the professional environment in which students will work as lawyers. The school has a high level of intellectual engagement and interaction between students and faculty, a small student body, and a first-year small section program. The learning environment is characterized by an emphasis on professional values such as integrity, teamwork, and intellectual risk taking. The law school has been a pioneer in forging interdisciplinary relationships with other departments of the university. Through coursework and joint-degree programs in wide-ranging fields, students are able to both broaden and specialize their legal education by utilizing the full intellectual resources of the university.

■ Enrollment/Student Body

➻ 3,014 applicants ➻ 895 admitted first-year class 1995 ➻ 205 enrolled first-year class 1995 ➻ 593 total full-time ➻ 14.5% minority students ➻ 40% women students ➻ 46 states and 28 foreign countries represented ➻ 212 undergraduate schools represented ➻ 48 foreign LL.M. students in 1995 entering class

The characteristic that most distinguishes the student body at Duke from that at other top law schools is the collegiality and collaborative spirit that consistently develops among its members.

■ Faculty

➻ 98 total faculty members ➻ 35 full-time ➻ 63 part-time or adjunct ➻ 30 women ➻ 6 minority

Faculty members' backgrounds and interests are as varied as they are distinguished. They bring to the classroom not only a love of teaching, but significant practical experience in both the public and private sectors. On the faculty are former Fulbright Scholars, Rhodes Scholars, and Marshall Scholars. A number of faculty members have served as Supreme Court clerks and one was the chief judge for the U.S. Court of Military Appeals. An exceptionally high number of our faculty members hold joint appointments with other departments within the university and have Ph.D.'s in a wide variety of subjects. The faculty also embodies a high degree of internationalization. Two faculty members were born and educated in other countries; a large number of visiting professors from abroad teach here each year; and many faculty members have extensive international ties and connections.

■ Library and Physical Facilities

➻ 477,000 volumes & equivalents ➻ library hours: 24 hours/day ➻ LEXIS ➻ NEXIS ➻ WESTLAW ➻ First Search ➻ Uncover ➻ DIALOG ➻ 9 full-time librarians ➻ library seats 451 ➻ Student Research Network

Duke Law Library's outstanding collection of materials is accessible to students through the law school's state-of-the-art computer network. Students have the use of over 85 student terminals in the library, 67 carrels which are wired to the network for students to plug in their own notebook computer, and network access from home. Using the network, students can browse the Internet, use word processing software, research legal databases, and view the online catalog of all library materials.

Law students are encouraged to take advantage of the extensive resources of Duke University, equally renowned for its excellence in undergraduate, professional and graduate schools, and research endeavors. With impressive Gothic architecture, 20 acres of formal and informal gardens, and 7,700 acres of undeveloped forest, the beauty of the Duke campus is unsurpassed.

■ Curriculum

➻ 84 units/credits required to graduate ➻ 96 courses available ➻ degrees available: J.D.; J.D./LL.M.; J.D./M.B.A.; J.D./M.E.M.; J.D./M.P.P.; J.D./Ph.D. (Pol. Sci.); J.D./M.A. (in 11 departments); J.D./M.D. ➻ semesters, start in Aug. with exception of joint-degree programs ➻ range of first-year class size—25-129

During the first year, students are divided into small sections of 25-35 students. Students have one substantive course in the small section and are in a small class for legal writing. With support from a grant by the Keck Foundation, Duke offers an innovative program in Ethics and the Legal Profession, including an intensive one-week course in professional responsibility during the first year. Classes in the second and third years are entirely elective.

■ Special Programs

J.D./LL.M. in International and Comparative Legal Studies. Duke Law School offers students enrolled in the J.D. program a unique opportunity to study concurrently for the Master of Laws (LL.M.) in Comparative and International Legal Studies. Students may earn these two degrees through extending legal study by only two summers. J.D./LL.M. students enroll at Duke during the summer preceding the first year of school, and spend four weeks during the following summer at one of Duke's Institutes of Transnational Law in Brussels or in Hong Kong.

J.D./M.A. or M.S. Programs. Based on the idea that society will be best served by lawyers with diverse education, training, and background, Duke offers accelerated joint-degree programs through which students may obtain a J.D. and a master's degree in any of the following disciplines—Public Policy, Environmental Studies, Political Science, Economics, History, English, Philosophy, Humanities, Cultural Anthropology, Romance Studies, or Mechanical Engineering. The only additional time necessary to obtain both degrees is the summer that precedes the first year of school. In addition to the accelerated programs, Duke offers four-year, joint-degree programs combining law and Public Policy, Environmental Management, or Business Administration.

■ Admission

➽ suggested application deadline—Jan. 15 ➽ early application preferred ➽ LSAT, LSDAS required ➽ median GPA—3.64 ➽ median LSAT score—166 ➽ application fee—$65 ➽ encourage students to take LSAT no later than Dec.

Admission to the law school is determined after careful consideration of all information presented in the application. Undergraduate grades, undergraduate institution, and LSAT scores are among the most important criteria in admission decisions. The committee also heavily weighs demonstrated leadership, community service, graduate study in another discipline, work experience, and other information indicating academic or professional potential. Letters of recommendation play a critical role in the decision-making process. Admission interviews are not granted, although students are encouraged to visit the school during the spring semester to see the campus, sit in on a class, and meet with students.

■ Cocurricular Activities

The law school publishes four scholarly journals—Duke *Law Journal, Law and Contemporary Problems, Alaska Law Review*, and the *Duke Journal of Comparative and International Law*, and two annuals, *Duke Journal of Gender Law & Policy* and the *Duke Environmental Law & Policy Forum*. Particularly popular with students is the Pro Bono Project, an organization through which over 200 students provide volunteer legal service in the public, private, and nonprofit sectors.

■ Expenses and Financial Aid

➽ full-time tuition & fees—$21,704 ➽ average additional expenses—$10,923 ➽ merit- and need-based scholarships available ➽ financial aid available; FAFSA need analysis form should by filed in Feb.

A generous loan forgiveness program assists students choosing to work in government and other public interest jobs after graduation.

■ Career Services

The full-time staff of the Office of Career Services works actively to assist students in obtaining summer and permanent employment. In the fall of 1995, almost 350 employers came to Duke from 30 states to interview second- and third-year students. Another 800 employers requested résumés of students. Six months after graduation, 97 percent of the Class of 1994 was employed; 69 percent in private practice, 24 percent in judicial clerkship (including one clerkship in the U.S. Supreme Court), and the remainder in public service, government, business, or academic study. Graduates found employment in 29 states, 34 percent of employed graduates went to the Northeast, 44 percent to the South, 12 percent to the Midwest, and 10 percent to the West.

Applicant Group for the 1995-1996 Academic Year

Duke University School of Law
This grid includes only applicants who earned 120-180 LSAT scores under standard administrations.

	GPA																					
LSAT Score	3.75 +		3.50 - 3.74		3.25 - 3.49		3.00 - 3.24		2.75 - 2.99		2.50 - 2.74		2.25 - 2.49		2.00 - 2.24		Below 2.00		No GPA		Total	
	Apps	Adm	Apps	Adm	Apps	Adm	Apps	Adm	Apps	Adm	Apps	Adm	Apps	Adm	Apps	Adm	Apps	Adm	Apps	Adm	Apps	Adm
175 - 180	29	28	24	23	22	20	9	3	1	0	0	0	1	0	0	0	0	0	0	0	86	74
170 - 174	67	66	93	88	72	55	26	8	11	3	1	1	4	1	0	0	0	0	3	2	277	224
165 - 169	189	172	232	140	143	51	62	3	16	2	4	0	3	1	0	0	0	0	6	1	657	370
160 - 164	184	87	247	49	170	11	88	9	38	1	14	0	5	0	3	0	0	0	7	1	754	158
155 - 159	84	10	122	14	125	11	63	5	26	0	18	1	4	0	2	0	0	0	11	1	457	42
150 - 154	44	1	75	6	83	4	54	6	30	0	21	0	7	0	2	0	0	0	6	0	322	17
145 - 149	22	1	39	0	45	0	35	0	34	0	18	0	9	0	2	0	0	0	7	0	213	1
140 - 144	6	0	9	0	12	0	20	0	16	0	12	0	7	0	2	0	1	0	6	0	89	0
135 - 139	0	0	3	0	9	0	9	0	11	0	7	0	3	0	2	0	1	0	6	0	49	0
130 - 134	1	0	0	0	2	0	4	0	4	0	1	0	0	0	2	0	0	0	1	0	15	0
125 - 129	0	0	1	0	0	0	0	0	0	0	4	0	3	0	0	0	0	0	1	0	9	0
120 - 124	0	0	1	0	0	0	0	0	0	0	1	0	0	0	0	0	0	0	0	0	2	0
Total	626	365	846	320	683	152	370	34	187	6	101	2	46	2	15	0	2	0	54	5	2930	886

Apps = Number of Applicants
Adm = Number Admitted
Reflects 98% of the total applicant pool.

Duquesne University School of Law

217 Hanley Hall
900 Locust Street
Pittsburgh, PA 15282

E-Mail: ricci@duq2.cc.duq.edu
Phone: 412.396.6296

■ Introduction

The Duquesne University School of Law has been in existence since 1911 and is the only multiple-division law school in Western Pennsylvania. Admission requirements, instruction, and the nature and scope of the work required of students are identical for both the full-time day division and the part-time evening division. The School of Law is approved by the ABA and is a member of the AALS.

Duquesne's 39-acre campus is uniquely situated, affording access, within walking distance, to the downtown legal, business, and government communities, and state and federal courts.

■ Enrollment/Student Body

➽ *first-year class enrollment—day, 116, evening, 91*
➽ *299 total full-time* ➽ *344 total part-time*
➽ *9.5% minority* ➽ *42% women*
➽ *28 states & foreign countries represented*
➽ *187 undergraduate schools represented*

The Duquesne University School of Law does not discriminate on the basis of race, creed, color, sex, national or ethnic origin, handicap, or age, nor in the administration of its admission and educational policies. The law school seeks diversity in the student body and encourages members of minority groups and others who have been underrepresented in the legal profession to apply. Out-of-state students typically comprise 30 percent of the full-time entering class.

■ Faculty

➽ *60 total* ➽ *24 full-time plus 5 research and writing professors* ➽ *44 part-time or adjunct* ➽ *7 women* ➽ *5 minority*

■ Library and Physical Facilities

➽ *200,000 volumes & equivalents* ➽ *library hours: Mon.-Thurs., 8:00 A.M.-MIDNIGHT; Fri., 8:00 A.M.-10:00 P.M.; Sat., 9:00 A.M.-9:00 P.M.; Sun., 1:00 P.M.-MIDNIGHT* ➽ *LEXIS* ➽ *WESTLAW* ➽ *5 full-time librarians* ➽ *library seats 325*

In 1982, the law school moved into the newly completed Edward J. Hanley Hall. This modern facility houses all classrooms, faculty offices, and study rooms for the Law School, including the James P. McArdle Moot Court Room and the John E. Laughlin Memorial Library. The library contains group-study rooms, individual study carrels, and the law school's computer lab. All first-year students are trained on computer-assisted legal research.

■ Curriculum

➽ *BLSA (student-run tutoring program) offered*
➽ *87 credits required to graduate* ➽ *112 courses available*
➽ *degrees available: J.D.; J.D./M.B.A.; J.D./M.Div; J.D./M.S. Env. Sc. and Mgt.* ➽ *semesters, start in Aug.*
➽ *range of first-year class size—20-100*

The course of study offered at the School of Law is sufficiently broad to prepare students for practice in all states. Three years are required for completion of the course of study in the day division, four years in the evening division.

Electives are offered after the first year of study in such developing areas as products and the consumer, environmental law, law and psychiatry, controlling medical therapy and experimentation, sex discrimination and the law, and legal medicine. An endowed chair in Law and Economics provides students with the opportunity to develop a knowledge of the application of economic principles to the study of law. These elective courses allow students to explore the more contemporary problems of law and society.

■ Special Programs

Students are afforded an opportunity to participate in numerous educational and professional activities, including moot court competitions and a wide variety of clinical programs.

■ Admission

➽ *Bachelor's degree required* ➽ *application deadlines—day, April 1; evening, May 1* ➽ *rolling admission*
➽ *LSAT, LSDAS required* ➽ *application fee—$50*

All candidates for admission must take the LSAT, subscribe to LSDAS, and be graduates of an accredited college or university before enrolling in the law school. Personal interviews by members of the Admissions Committee are not granted, but applicants are encouraged to schedule an appointment to visit the school for an information session and/or a tour of the facilities.

The large number of applications received makes the admission process very selective. Most applicants apply well in advance of the deadlines. Students are admitted only for the fall semester.

In evaluating applications, the complete academic record is reviewed with consideration given to the competitiveness of the undergraduate institution, the college major, rank in class, and the overall academic performance. The LSAT is considered to be an important factor in assessing an applicant's ability to succeed in legal study. Graduate study, extracurricular activities, and recommendations also contribute to the committee's assessment. Work experience is considered when an applicant has been employed full-time for a significant length of time.

■ Student Activities

The Student Bar Association maintains a liaison between students and faculty and sponsors social and professional activities for the student body.

Membership in the *Duquesne Law Review* is based on the demonstrated academic ability of the student as well as his or her interest in becoming active in this publication.

Juris, the law school news magazine, is an ABA-award-winning publication containing articles of current interest to the entire legal community. Students also publish the *Duquesne Business Law Journal*.

There are also active chapters of the following organizations available to law students: Phi Alpha Delta legal fraternity; the Women Law Association (WLA); Black Law Students Association (BLSA); ABA/LSD American Bar Association/Law Student Division; International Law Society; Sports and Entertainment Law, Association of Trial Lawyers of America, Environmental Law Association, Health Care Law Society, Association for Public Interest Law, and the Corporate Law Society.

■ Expenses and Financial Aid

➻ *tuition & fees—full-time, $12,215; part-time, $9,201; fee, $620/yr* ➻ *estimated additional expenses—$6,000 (books, room & board)* ➻ *need- and merit-based scholarships available*
➻ *minority scholarships available (need- and merit-based)*
➻ *financial aid available*
➻ *Duquesne Financial Aid application due May 31*
➻ *PHEAA, FAF, and GAPSFAS accepted*

By maintaining a very competitive tuition rate, Duquesne consistently strives to ensure that the outstanding private legal education provided by the law school is within the reach of all qualified students. A limited number of merit scholarships are awarded to the most outstanding day-division applicants each year. Law School grants-in-aid are awarded primarily on the basis of need. A number of loans sponsored by the state and federal government are available to law students. For further information write to the Financial Aid Office, Duquesne University, Pittsburgh, PA 15282.

■ Housing

Accommodations are not available for law students in the university dormitories. For off-campus residence information write to the Office of Commuter Affairs, Duquesne University, Pittsburgh, PA 15282. Off-campus accommodations are available nearby.

■ Career Services

The law school's Career Services Office staff offers assistance to students and alumni who are interested in obtaining full-time, part-time, and summer employment. The Career Services Office offers a fall and spring on-campus interview program in which law firms, government agencies, corporations, and accounting firms conduct individual interviews.

Duquesne University School of Law is a member of the National Association for Law Placement, the National Association for Public Interest Law Publication Network, and the Allegheny County Bar Association Minority Job Fair.

Graduates of the law school have consistently passed the Pennsylvania bar examination at a rate that well exceeds the statewide average. The law school has nearly 5,000 alumni throughout the United States and in several foreign countries, with the majority practicing in Pennsylvania and the northeastern United States.

Applicant Group for the 1995-1996 Academic Year

The law school recognizes the different strengths presented by our day and evening division students and acknowledges that the diversity in the groups cannot be accurately or completely represented in a single grid of average undergraduate GPA and LSAT scores. Graduate degrees and extensive employment experience predominate in the evening division and these factors are considered crucial to an individual assessment of admissibility. Day-division applications are also reviewed individually and factors such as leadership experience, community service, and other nonacademic experiences are considered. Applicants should contact the Admissions Office for specific information on the current year's class—Phone: 412.396.6296.

Emory University School of Law

Gambrell Hall
1301 Clifton Road
Atlanta, GA 30322
Phone: 404.727.6801

■ Introduction

Emory's location in Atlanta, a national business and legal center, gives Emory law students the opportunity to take advanced classes from, and work with, some of the leading judges and lawyers in the United States. Atlanta is one of America's most beautiful and most livable cities.

The law school also benefits from the strength of Emory University, which was founded in 1836. Emory University School of Law is accredited by the American Bar Association, is a member of the Association of American Law Schools, and has a chapter of Order of the Coif.

■ Enrollment/Student Body

➧ *3,254 applicants* ➧ *1,035 admitted first-year class 1995* ➧ *249 enrolled first-year class 1995* ➧ *742 total full-time* ➧ *18.5% minority* ➧ *38% women* ➧ *42 states & foreign countries represented* ➧ *over 110 undergraduate schools represented*

■ Faculty

➧ *78 total* ➧ *40 full-time* ➧ *38 part-time or adjunct* ➧ *9 women* ➧ *6 minority*

■ Library & Physical Facilities

➧ *300,000+ volumes & equivalents* ➧ *library hours: Mon.-Fri., 8:00 A.M.-MIDNIGHT; Sat., 9:00 A.M.-MIDNIGHT; Sun., 10:00 A.M.-MIDNIGHT* ➧ *LEXIS* ➧ *WESTLAW* ➧ *6 full-time librarians* ➧ *library seats over 400*

Our modern, air-conditioned building, Gambrell Hall, is a part of Emory's 630-acre campus in Druid Hills, six miles northeast of downtown Atlanta.

Gambrell Hall, constructed in 1972, contains the classrooms, faculty offices, administrative offices, student-organization offices, and a 450 seat auditorium. Gambrell Hall also houses a-state-of-the-art courtroom television studio equipped for four camera operation. The new Hugh F. McMillan Law Library sits adjacent to Gambrell Hall and is designed for easy student access. Students are trained on LEXIS and WESTLAW terminals and learn both the techniques of computer assisted legal research and traditional research methods. Students may also use the library's computer labs— which offer MacIntosh and DOS compatible computers.

■ Curriculum

➧ *88 credits required to graduate* ➧ *180 courses available* ➧ *degrees available: J.D.; J.D./M.B.A.; J.D./M.Div.; J.D./M.T.S.; J.D./M.P.H.* ➧ *semesters, start in Aug.* ➧ *range of first-year class size—30-60*

The basic program of study involves three years of full-time study leading to the J.D. degree. The fall semester runs from late August to mid-December; the spring semester begins in mid-January and ends in mid-May.

The program of courses for the first year is prescribed. The program of courses for the second and third years is primarily elective. Students can sample a broad spectrum of courses and/or concentrate on a particular area of law.

All first-year courses and the basic second- and third-year courses are taught by full-time faculty members. A distinguished group of judges and practicing attorneys offer specialized courses.

■ Special Programs

The law school believes that its program of trial training is special. Emory's program uses as instructors many lawyers and judges from around the United States. For a two-week period, each second-year student works full-time with these lawyers and judges on each stage of the litigation of a simulated case.

Emory's affiliation with the Carter Center for Public Policy and its location in a city that is fast becoming an international legal center provide some unique opportunities in international law. Visiting international law professors from the former Soviet Union, Yugoslavia, and South Africa greatly enrich course offerings in that area.

The law school offers joint-degree programs with Emory's School of Business Administration with the School of Theology, and with the School of Public Health.

■ Admission

➧ *Bachelor's degree from an accredited college or university required* ➧ *application deadline—March 1* ➧ *LSAT, LSDAS required* ➧ *median GPA—3.40* ➧ *median LSAT score—161* ➧ *application fee—$45* ➧ *modified rolling admission, early application preferred*

The law school accepts beginning students for the fall term only. Prior to enrollment, a student must have earned a bachelor's degree from an approved institution.

Applications for admission must be received by Emory no later than March 1. Early applications are both encouraged and appreciated.

Many factors are considered in making admissions decisions. Of particular importance are academic accomplishments and LSAT scores. Extracurricular activities, work experience, level of quality and difficulty of undergraduate courses, performance in graduate school, and letters of recommendation are also considered. Special consideration is given to members of minority groups, and members of such groups are encouraged to apply and to provide the Director of Admissions with any specific information about their background or accomplishments that would be of particular interest.

Applicants are encouraged to visit the law school. Upon acceptance, applicants are required to submit a nonrefundable $250 tuition deposit to reserve a space in the entering class.

■ Student Activities

A wide variety of organizations and activities are available to students. As there are three law reviews at Emory, *Emory Law Journal*, *Bankruptcy Developments Journal*, and *Emory International Law Review*, more than 30 percent of the second- and third-year students are involved in law review research, writing, and editing. Candidates for the reviews are selected from second- and third-year classes by the student editorial boards on the basis of scholarship and writing ability.

Students also participate in moot court. Each first-year student prepares a brief and presents an oral argument. In addition, many second- and third-year students compete in intramural and national moot court competitions.

There are numerous special interest and social groups and a very active Student Bar Association.

■ Expenses and Financial Aid

➽ *full-time tuition & fees—$19,600* ➽ *estimated additional expenses—$9,000 (room, board, & books)*
➽ *scholarships available: Robert W. Woodruff Fellowships (merit-based) & other merit/need*
➽ *FAF form and profile due to the College Scholarship Service in early Feb. for financial aid*

■ Career Services

The law school regards placement as a matter of highest priority. A full-time career services office assists students in obtaining permanent, summer, and part-time employment. It arranges interviews with employers from many parts of the country and maintains extensive files on a wide variety of professional opportunities all over the United States. The great majority of Emory graduates join private law firms after graduation. Others work as judicial clerks, enter government service, or work for banks, corporations, or legal aid agencies. Still others pursue a teaching career, but usually after working as a judicial clerk or engaging in the practice of law.

Emory School of Law provides a full range of career planning and placement services. The class of 1994 reported 91 percent employment within six months after graduation in the following fields: 57 percent in private practice; 12 percent in government; 9 percent in judicial clerkships; and 7 percent in legal services/public interest, academic, and other fields. The geographic distribution reflected by these figures was as follows: Atlanta 52 percent, Southeast (excluding Atlanta), 12 percent; Northeast, 23 percent; Midwest, 3 percent; West, 3 percent.

Applicant Group for the 1995-1996 Academic Year

Emory University School of Law
Graph reflects admission decisions as of 9/01/95.

LSAT Score	GPA								
	3.75 +	3.50 - 3.74	3.25 - 3.49	3.00 - 3.24	2.75 - 2.99	2.50 - 2.74	2.25 - 2.49	2.00 - 2.24	Below 2.00
175 - 180	Good Possibility	Good Possibility	Good Possibility	Good Possibility	Possible	Unlikely	Unlikely	Unlikely	Unlikely
170 - 174	Good Possibility	Good Possibility	Good Possibility	Good Possibility	Possible	Unlikely	Unlikely	Unlikely	Unlikely
165 - 169	Good Possibility	Good Possibility	Good Possibility	Good Possibility	Possible	Unlikely	Unlikely	Unlikely	Unlikely
160 - 164	Good Possibility	Good Possibility	Good Possibility	Good Possibility	Possible	Unlikely	Unlikely	Unlikely	Unlikely
155 - 159	Good Possibility	Good Possibility	Possible	Possible	Possible	Unlikely	Unlikely	Unlikely	Unlikely
150 - 154	Possible	Possible	Possible	Possible	Unlikely	Unlikely	Unlikely	Unlikely	Unlikely
145 - 149	Possible	Possible	Possible	Unlikely	Unlikely	Unlikely	Unlikely	Unlikely	Unlikely
140 - 144	Unlikely	Unlikely	Unlikely	Unlikely	Unlikely	Unlikely	Unlikely	Unlikely	Unlikely
135 - 139	Unlikely	Unlikely	Unlikely	Unlikely	Unlikely	Unlikely	Unlikely	Unlikely	Unlikely
130 - 134	Unlikely	Unlikely	Unlikely	Unlikely	Unlikely	Unlikely	Unlikely	Unlikely	Unlikely
125 - 129	Unlikely	Unlikely	Unlikely	Unlikely	Unlikely	Unlikely	Unlikely	Unlikely	Unlikely
120 - 124	Unlikely	Unlikely	Unlikely	Unlikely	Unlikely	Unlikely	Unlikely	Unlikely	Unlikely

Good Possibility Possible Unlikely

Note: This chart is to be used as a general guide in determining the chances for admittance.

University of Florida College of Law

Assistant Dean for Admissions
P.O. Box 117622, 325 Holland Hall
Gainesville, FL 32611-7622

URL: http://nervp.nerdc.ufl.edu/~lawinfo/college/
Phone: 904.392.2087, fax: 904.392.8727

■ Introduction

The University of Florida College of Law offers a three-year post-baccalaureate curriculum leading to the degree of Juris Doctor (J.D.), a number of joint-degree programs, and a post-J.D. program leading to the degree of Master of Laws in Taxation (LL.M.), and a Master of Laws in Comparative Law (LL.M.) for foreign lawyers. The study of law at the University of Florida prepares students for creative problem solving, dispute resolution, planning and counseling, and policy-making roles in contemporary society. With a student body consistently ranked among the nation's finest, the college is known for graduating leaders for Florida's legal, political, business, and educational sectors, and its faculty and alumni are recognized at the national and international level.

The University of Florida, occupying 2,000 acres mostly within Gainesville's 85,000-population urban area, is a member of the prestigious Association of American Universities and is recognized as one of the nation's leading research universities by the Carnegie Commission on Higher Education. Gainesville, with extensive educational, cultural, and recreational offerings, is consistently ranked among the best places to live in America.

■ History of the College of Law

➻ *founded in 1909* ➻ *Association of American Law Schools membership since 1920*
➻ *New York State Regents accreditation since 1917*
➻ *American Bar Association approval since 1925*

■ Enrollment/Student Body

➻ *2,443 applicants* ➻ *491 admitted first-year class 1995*
➻ *204 enrolled first-year class 1995* ➻ *1,170 total full-time*
➻ *22.2% minority* ➻ *42% women*
➻ *73 undergraduate schools represented*
➻ *286 admitted spring 1996* ➻ *200 enrolled spring 1996*

■ Faculty

➻ *78 full-time* ➻ *9 part-time* ➻ *26 women*
➻ *8 minority*

■ Library and Physical Facilities

➻ *558,000 volumes & equivalents* ➻ *library hours: Mon.-Fri., 7:30 A.M.-11:00 P.M.; Sat., 9:00 A.M.-5:00 P.M.; Sun., 11:00 A.M.-11:00 P.M.* ➻ *LEXIS* ➻ *WESTLAW*
➻ *DIALOG* ➻ *PLATO* ➻ *27 full-time librarians/staff*
➻ *library seats 800*

The College of Law is housed in two adjacent buildings on the University of Florida campus in North Central Florida. The Legal Information Center's extensive holdings rank it among the two largest law libraries in the Southeastern United States. The library long has been a national leader in audiovisual and microform services and computerized legal research. The library also offers IBM PCs for student use.

■ Curriculum

➻ *88 credits required to graduate* ➻ *over 100 courses & seminars available* ➻ *degrees available: J.D.; J.D./M.B.A.; J.D./M.A.; & J.D./Ph.D.* ➻ *semesters, start in Aug., Jan., and May (8-week term)*

The College of Law curriculum includes traditional courses on law and legal analysis, skills training courses, international law offerings, and seminars on contemporary legal issues. Students generally are required to complete the first-year curriculum in sequence, and spring entrants are required to attend the first summer term. All students must complete a major research and writing project in the senior year.

Joint-degree programs in accounting, business administration, mass communications, history, political science, psychology and public administration, sociology, and urban and regional planning are available to students who meet the requirements of both the College of Law and the Graduate School.

■ Special Programs

The college is home to a nationally acclaimed Graduate Tax Program, leading to the degree LL.M. in Taxation. The program publishes the *Florida Tax Review*, which utilizes LL.M. student assistants. The college also offers a Master of Laws degree in Comparative Law (LL.M.) for foreign lawyers seeking to improve their understanding of American law.

Clinical programs provide J.D. students with the opportunity to represent actual clients in civil and criminal court cases. The college's Center for Governmental Responsibility provides students with an opportunity to conduct public interest and environmental research with staff attorneys.

■ Admission

➻ *Bachelor's degree from accredited college or university required* ➻ *application deadline—fall, Feb. 1; spring, May 15*
➻ *rolling admissions, early application preferred*
➻ *LSAT, LSDAS required* ➻ *application fee—$20*
➻ *median GPA—fall, 3.50; spring, 3.40*
➻ *median LSAT score—fall, 158; spring, 156*

The College of Law enrolls only full-time students in the fall and spring. Approximately 95 percent of those entering successfully complete the first two semesters. The college subscribes to the suggestions on prelaw study included in this guide. In addition to the bulleted requirements above, the College of Law requests that each applicant provide a personal statement and three letters of evaluation. Admission standards are significantly higher for non-Florida residents.

Approximately 50 percent of admission decisions are based primarily on the undergraduate grade-point average and LSAT score. The remainder of each class is selected on the basis of both quantitative and nonquantitative criteria. Applications cannot be processed more than one year in advance of the intended month of entry. However, early completion of applications is strongly recommended. Applicants must take the LSAT prior to application deadlines.

Students may transfer in August, January, or May from ABA/AALS law schools, but the Admissions Committee accepts only those transfer applicants who will have completed their first year of law school before enrolling at the University of Florida. Candidates must be in the upper one-third of their class to be considered. A letter of good standing from the dean is required. No more than 28 semester hours will be transferred.

The University of Florida and the College of Law actively recruit minority students. Scholarships and grants are available for qualified minority students. Inquiries should be addressed to the Assistant Dean for Student and Minority Affairs, University of Florida College of Law, Gainesville, FL 32611-2038.

■ Student/Extracurricular Activities

Student activities include the *Florida Law Review*, *Florida Journal of International Law*, Moot Court and Trial Team. More than 20 extracurricular organizations provide additional opportunities for student involvement.

■ Expenses and Financial Aid

- *tuition & fees—Florida residents, $121 per semester hour; nonresidents $385 per semester hour*
- *estimated additional expenses—$9,100 room, board, books*
- *performance & need-based scholarships available*
- *deadlines—April 1 for fall applicants; July 1 for spring applicants (FAFSA required—see catalog)*

In addition to scholarships and awards, the College of Law provides short- and long-term loans to qualified students. Students applying for College of Law financial aid must have an undergraduate GPA of at least 3.2 and a single or average LSAT score of 158 or higher, and must submit the FAFSA. GPA and LSAT figures used are those reported by LSDAS. For information concerning federal, state, and Law Access loans, write to: Director of Financial Aid, College of Law, 164 Holland Hall, Gainesville, FL 32611-2038.

■ Housing

Housing is available for single students in university dormitories and for families in university apartments adjacent to the law school. Off-campus housing is also available. For more information, write to the Director of Housing, University of Florida, Gainesville, FL 32611.

■ Career Services

The Career Planning and Placement Office assists students in finding employment or clerkships. Approximately 250 employers recruit on campus each year. Approximately 85-90 percent of recent College of Law graduates seeking employment have jobs after taking the bar.

Applicant Group for the 1995-1996 Academic Year

University of Florida College of Law
This grid includes only applicants who earned 120-180 LSAT scores under standard administrations.

LSAT Score	GPA 3.75 +		3.50 - 3.74		3.25 - 3.49		3.00 - 3.24		2.75 - 2.99		2.50 - 2.74		2.25 - 2.49		2.00 - 2.24		Below 2.00		No GPA		Total	
	Apps	Adm	Apps	Adm	Apps	Adm	Apps	Adm	Apps	Adm	Apps	Adm	Apps	Adm	Apps	Adm	Apps	Adm	Apps	Adm	Apps	Adm
175 - 180	1	1	1	1	1	1	1	1	0	0	0	0	0	0	0	0	0	0	0	0	4	4
170 - 174	6	5	3	3	5	4	4	4	5	3	0	0	2	1	1	0	0	0	0	0	26	20
165 - 169	10	9	24	23	28	22	22	12	16	2	3	2	1	1	1	0	0	0	1	1	106	72
160 - 164	45	36	81	59	88	44	67	15	37	4	15	1	8	0	4	1	0	0	2	1	347	161
155 - 159	54	36	82	35	127	20	82	3	66	5	41	2	15	0	4	0	2	0	3	0	476	101
150 - 154	42	19	75	19	103	10	103	7	68	6	47	2	14	1	9	0	0	0	9	1	470	65
145 - 149	12	2	41	10	61	9	70	9	72	4	39	1	23	0	12	0	3	0	4	0	337	35
140 - 144	4	1	25	3	39	5	37	9	39	0	38	1	14	0	9	0	2	0	9	0	216	19
135 - 139	1	0	9	1	5	0	22	0	25	0	20	0	13	0	8	0	0	0	3	0	106	1
130 - 134	3	0	1	0	1	0	4	0	7	0	9	1	9	1	2	0	1	0	1	0	38	2
125 - 129	0	0	0	0	3	0	1	0	2	0	1	0	2	0	0	0	0	0	0	0	9	0
120 - 124	0	0	0	0	0	0	0	0	1	0	0	0	0	0	0	0	0	0	0	0	1	0
Total	178	109	342	154	461	115	413	60	338	24	213	10	101	4	50	1	8	0	32	3	2136	480

Apps = Number of Applicants
Adm = Number Admitted
Reflects 98% of the total applicant pool.

The Florida State University College of Law

College of Law
Tallahassee, FL 32306-1034

Phone: 904.644.3787

■ Introduction

The Florida State University College of Law is widely recognized for both its commitment to teaching and its cutting-edge scholarship. The college subscribes to the idea that the best legal education is the result of a lively dialogue in an intimate learning environment. Our low student-to-faculty ratio allows for a diversity of class offerings while emphasizing a personalized legal education. The college is situated blocks from the Florida Capitol, the First District Court of Appeal, the Florida Supreme Court, the United States District Court, and other centers of judicial and administrative activity. Proximity to these institutions offers students a unique opportunity to observe firsthand the workings of the state government and courts. The curriculum is continually evolving to reflect changes in the practice of law. Two current areas of emphasis are environmental and international law. The college is a member of the Association of American Law Schools (AALS) and is ABA-approved.

■ Enrollment/Student Body

➽ 2,317 applicants ➽ 603 admitted first-year class 1995 ➽ 205 enrolled first-year class 1995 ➽ 621 total full-time ➽ 24% minority ➽ 45% women ➽ 81 undergraduate schools represented

■ Faculty

➽ 48 total ➽ 41 full-time ➽ 7 adjunct ➽ 13 women ➽ 6 minority

■ Library and Physical Facilities

➽ 375,000 volumes & equivalents ➽ library hours: Mon.-Thurs., 7:30 A.M.-MIDNIGHT; Fri., 7:30 A.M.-10:00 P.M.; Sat., 9:00 A.M.-10:00 P.M.; Sun., 10:00 A.M.-MIDNIGHT ➽ LEXIS ➽ NEXIS ➽ WESTLAW ➽ 7 full-time librarians ➽ library seats 384

The physical facilities of the College of Law consist of B.K. Roberts Hall opened in 1971; a separate, connected law library building opened in 1983; and the Village Green, completed in 1988.

Roberts Hall houses faculty, staff and student offices, lounges, classrooms, seminar rooms, and a practice courtroom making extensive use of state-of-the-art video technology. The College of Law has been designated a downlink site by the American Law Institute-American Bar Association. Both Roberts Hall and the law library comply with all architectural regulations facilitating use for disabled students.

The law library's volumes and microform volume equivalents are all cataloged in the Florida State University libraries online database, accessible through computer terminals located throughout the library and also available for remote access using computers with modems. Serial subscriptions exceed 6,200; holdings include a wide range of audiovisual materials. Individual and group study, video viewing, microform reading, and computer use and instruction are accommodated within the law library.

■ Curriculum

➽ Academic Support Program ➽ 20-hour pro bono requirement ➽ 88 credits required to graduate ➽ 124 courses available plus clinics & internships ➽ degrees available: J.D.; J.D./M.B.A.; J.D./M.P.A.; J.D./International Affairs; J.D./Urban & Regional Planning; J.D./Economics ➽ range of first-year class size—30-70

The school operates on the semester basis. The first-year curriculum is mandatory. Current catalogs indicate the range of electives available. While the general curriculum is national in focus, some courses especially relevant to the Florida bar and Florida practice are offered.

■ Special Programs

The college's location in the state capital provides students with a variety of externship opportunities. Judicial externships are available with state trial and appellate courts, including the Florida Supreme Court and the federal courts. Externship opportunities with government agencies and commissions, the state attorney, the public defender and legal services offices are also provided. The college's Children's Advocacy Center offers law students an opportunity to represent children in a variety of legal areas under the supervision of clinical faculty. The Florida Dispute Resolution Center, a joint project of the college and the Florida Supreme Court, encourages the use of alternate dispute resolution methods, and provides law students opportunities to gain hands-on knowledge of a rapidly growing area of the law. The college sponsors two summer law programs abroad, one at Oxford University in England, and the other at the University of the West Indies in Barbados. Faculty from Florida State and the host institutions participate in the programs which are open to students who have completed the first year of law school. The college also coordinates a public service fellowship program which provides fellowships to students in return for a commitment to public service activities.

■ Admission Standards

➽ Bachelor's degree from accredited college or university required ➽ application deadline—Feb. 15 ➽ early application preferred ➽ LSAT, LSDAS required ➽ median GPA—3.30 ➽ median LSAT score—157 ➽ application fee—$20

More than 2,300 applications are expected this year for the 200 places in the entering class.

Files are reviewed by a faculty committee. The committee considers the LSAT, UGPA, and the pattern of undergraduate performance from year to year as well as the school and coursework pursued by the applicant. Also, it weighs a number of other factors, including institutional interest in maintaining a student body as diverse as possible in the categories of ethnicity, gender, and educational background.

Transfer applicants may be admitted to any term after completion of the first year. Transcripts showing a full year's work and a dean's letter indicating the student's class rank and stating that the student is in good academic standing and eligible to return must be provided. Applicants must be enrolled in an ABA-approved law school. Applicants must be in the top 25 percent of their first-year class to be eligible for transfer.

■ Student Activities

One of the most attractive aspects of Florida State University's academic climate is the wide variety of educational and professional opportunities available outside the traditional classroom. The College of Law sponsors *Law Review*, the *Journal of Land Use and Environmental Law*, the *Journal of Transnational Law*, a nationally recognized moot court and trial advocacy program, and a variety of social and professional organizations. The college boasts active ACLU, NLG, and STLA chapters; a Women's Law Society; a Black Law Students Association chapter; a Christian Legal Society; an Entertainment, Arts, and Sports Law Society; a Federalist Society; an International Law Society; a Lawyers for Animal Welfare chapter; an Environmental Law Society; a Spanish-American Law Students Association chapter; and Law Partners, a law students' spouse and significant others support group. Both Phi Delta Phi and Phi Alpha Deltalegal honoraries maintain a chapter on campus. F.S.U. was granted a chapter of Order of the Coif in 1979. The Student Bar Association serves an active student government role and coordinates such services as the roommate referral program, a co-op bookstore, and coordination of many law school-sponsored social activities.

■ Expenses and Financial Aid

➽ *tuition & fees—full-time, in-state, $3,608; full-time, out-of-state, $11,250* ➽ *scholarships available (academic and need-based)* ➽ *minority scholarships available* ➽ *financial aid available; Federal Free Form (FAFSA) analysis preferred by March 1*

■ Housing

Housing is available for single and married students in university dormitories. Three private apartment complexes are located across the street from the College of Law building. Information may be obtained from the Director of Housing, 106 Cawthon Hall, Florida State University, Tallahassee, FL 32306.

■ Career Services

The College of Law is staffed with a full-time director of Career Planning and Placement, who assists both students and alumni in obtaining positions and also helps students find part-time and summer jobs. Students have many opportunities to make their talents known before graduation in both clinical programs and part-time work for law offices, state agencies, and legislators.

Applicant Group for the 1995—1996 Academic Year

The Florida State University College of Law
This grid includes only applicants who earned 120-180 LSAT scores under standard administrations.

	GPA																					
LSAT Score	3.75 +		3.50 - 3.74		3.25 - 3.49		3.00 - 3.24		2.75 - 2.99		2.50 - 2.74		2.25 - 2.49		2.00 - 2.24		Below 2.00		No GPA		Total	
	Apps	Adm	Apps	Adm	Apps	Adm	Apps	Adm	Apps	Adm	Apps	Adm	Apps	Adm	Apps	Adm	Apps	Adm	Apps	Adm	Apps	Adm
175 - 180	0	0	0	0	0	0	0	0	0	0	0	0	0	0	0	0	0	0	0	0	0	0
170 - 174	1	1	0	0	2	2	0	0	2	2	0	0	1	1	1	0	0	0	0	0	7	6
165 - 169	3	3	7	7	13	13	12	12	13	9	7	2	1	1	1	0	0	0	1	1	58	48
160 - 164	15	15	38	38	42	42	52	45	32	15	16	7	11	3	3	0	0	0	0	0	209	165
155 - 159	41	39	84	75	123	76	97	33	96	14	50	7	22	0	3	0	2	0	3	1	521	245
150 - 154	35	17	82	25	126	17	126	11	102	9	75	2	27	1	8	0	3	0	5	1	589	83
145 - 149	16	5	42	14	77	6	95	9	83	5	54	1	31	0	11	0	2	0	5	0	416	40
140 - 144	1	0	26	2	46	1	52	2	45	0	52	0	24	0	11	0	1	0	6	0	264	5
135 - 139	2	0	11	0	12	1	24	0	33	0	25	0	13	0	7	0	2	0	8	0	137	1
130 - 134	2	0	2	0	1	0	1	0	10	0	11	0	13	0	2	0	3	0	3	0	48	0
125 - 129	0	0	0	0	1	0	1	0	2	0	1	0	4	0	2	0	0	0	0	0	11	0
120 - 124	0	0	0	0	0	0	1	0	0	0	0	0	1	0	1	0	0	0	0	0	3	0
Total	116	80	292	161	443	158	461	112	418	54	291	19	148	6	50	0	13	0	31	3	2263	593

Apps = Number of Applicants
Adm = Number Admitted
Reflects 99% of the total applicant pool.

Fordham University School of Law

140 West 62nd Street
New York, NY 10023
Phone: 212.636.6810

■ Introduction

Founded in 1841, Fordham University is a private institution, located in New York City, with an enrollment of some 13,000 students. The law school campus is immediately adjacent to Lincoln Center for the Performing Arts, in the heart of Manhattan. Fordham School of Law, founded in 1905, has been a member of the AALS since 1936 and is fully approved by the ABA.

■ Enrollment/Student Body

➽ 5,056 applicants ➽ 1,451 admitted first-year class 1995 ➽ 450 enrolled first-year class 1995 (335 full-time, 115 part-time) ➽ 1,129 total full-time ➽ 352 total part-time ➽ 26% minority (29% minority first-year class) ➽ 42% women (44% women first-year class) ➽ 39 states, the District of Columbia, & 6 foreign countries represented ➽ 259 colleges and universities represented

■ Faculty

➽ 206 total ➽ 61 full-time ➽ 145 part-time or adjunct ➽ 16 women full-time, 44 women part-time or adjunct ➽ 4 minority full-time, 14 minority part-time or adjunct

■ Library and Physical Facilities

➽ 450,000 volumes & equivalents ➽ library hours: Mon.-Fri., 7:00 A.M.-1:00 A.M.; Sat., 8:00 A.M.-1:00 A.M.; Sun., 8:00 A.M.-1:00 A.M. ➽ LEXIS ➽ NEXIS ➽ WESTLAW ➽ DIALOG ➽ 10 full-time librarians ➽ library seats 560

In addition to classroom, faculty, and administrative office space, the law school contains a large amphitheater, an atrium for special events and gatherings, a formal moot courtroom, a student lounge, a spacious cafeteria, and a library. The computer center contains 34 Windows-based Pentium PCs emulated to both LEXIS and WESTLAW, and supported by laser printers and various word processing packages. These PCs run on the law school's LAN and will eventually allow access, through the Internet, to global information resources, in addition to the law libraries of several New York area law schools. Law students also have access to the University Computing Center, located within steps of the law school building, which contains nearly 100 DOS-based and Apple PCs, in addition to VAX mainframe terminals which run SPSS statistical and other sophisticated mainframe software packages.

■ Curriculum

➽ Academic Support Program ➽ 83 credits required to graduate, of which 45 credits are required courses ➽ 190 courses available ➽ degrees available: J.D.; J.D./M.B.A.; LL.M. ➽ semesters, start in Aug. ➽ range of first-year class size—18-122

■ Special Programs

An extensive and growing clinical component is offered which includes a Trial Advocacy Program and clinics in litigation, mediation, prosecution, domestic violence, and tax. Externships in federal, state, and city judges' offices, prosecutors' offices, the Legal Aid Society, the ACLU, the Children's Defense Fund, and many other public service settings throughout the city are also offered. A pilot program on lawyering skills introduces first-year students to a broad range of law practice skills, including negotiating, dispute resolution, client counseling, and witness interviewing. The Moot Court Program, considered by faculty to be one of the more important aspects of the student's law training, provides students with opportunities to participate in several intramural competitions as well as a variety of interschool competitions throughout the country.

Fordham Public Service Programs—Fordham's commitment to producing graduates who will devote themselves to the public interest has resulted in the establishment of the Public Interest Resource Center, an administrative support base for the three public interest organizations in operation: The Fordham Law Community Service Project, The Fordham Student Sponsored Fellowship, and Fordham Pro Bono Students. The Stein Institute on Law and Ethics sponsors lectures and seminars throughout the year. The Stein Center for Ethics and Public Interest Law sponsors an annual symposium on current ethical issues; roundtable discussions among practitioners, scholars, and students engaged in public interest law; and the Stein Scholars Program, a three-year program for specially selected law students who will work in public interest law settings and undertake specialized academic work in legal ethics.

The Fordham Center on European Community Law and International Antitrust provides a teaching and resource facility devoted to two overlapping areas of international law: European Community and international antitrust.

■ Admission

➽ Bachelor's degree from accredited college or university required ➽ application deadline—March 1 ➽ LSAT, LSDAS required ➽ median GPA for full-time students—3.40 (overall day and evening not reported) ➽ median LSAT score for full-time students—163 (overall day and evening not reported

The selection of students is handled primarily by ten full-time faculty members, the Dean of Admissions, the Assistant Dean/Director of Admissions, and the Assistant Dean for Student Affairs, who together constitute the Admissions Committee. The Admissions Committee determines admissions criteria based on an evaluation of the applicant pool, comparison to the qualifications of recently admitted classes, and the first-year law school performance of the three most recently admitted classes as revealed in first-year performance validity/correlation studies. For the majority of applicants numeric indicators (LSAT score and UGPA) are the principal criteria relied upon, and the majority of admitted students present an LSAT score above the 91st percentile and a UGPA above a 3.30. Qualitative factors including prior employment, student activities, service to the community, leadership ability, propensity for public service, and communication skills are also considered in selecting the incoming class. The law school makes an aggressive effort to identify and enroll applicants from the African American, Asian American, Latino, and Native American communities, in addition to applicants who are culturally, socially, or economically disadvantaged. Over the past five years the law school has received an average of 5,000 applications annually for approximately 450 seats, and its acceptance rate has varied from 13.9 percent to 28.7 percent.

■ Student Activities

Students publish five scholarly journals: the *Fordham Law Review;* the *Fordham Urban Law Journal*; the *Fordham International Law Journal*; the *Fordham Environmental Law Journal;* and the *Fordham Intellectual Property, Media, & Entertainment Law Journal*. Each contains lead articles by distinguished members of the profession as well as student notes and comments. These journals are cited in appellate court opinions throughout the country. Fordham is a member of the Order of the Coif, the national honor society for law students. Students who are in the top 10 percent of their graduating class are eligible for membership. Other activities and organizations include the American Bar Association, Law Student Division; Amnesty International; Asian American Law Students Association; Black Law Students Association; Christian Law Students; the Crowley Labor Guild; Fordham Democratic Law Students Association; Fordham Federalist Society; Fordham Follies; Gay and Lesbian Law Association; Jewish Law Students; Fordham Law Women; Older Law Students Association; Fordham Republican Law Students Association; Latin American Law Students Association; National Lawyers Guild; Phi Alpha Delta Law Fraternity; the *Advocate;* and the yearbook.

■ Expenses and Financial Aid

- *tuition & fees—full-time, $20,499; part-time, $15,399*
- *almost all aid is need-based, though a small number of donor scholarships are awarded on the basis of merit*
- *Profile and FAFSA required; due in early Feb.*

A twenty-story dormitory, with several hundred beds (in two- and three-bedroom apartments) set aside for law students, and located on the Lincoln Center campus, opened in the summer of 1993. Rates for 1993-94 ranged from $5,685 to $6,900 per person, per academic year (single vs. double occupancy bedroom).

■ Career Services

The School of Law maintains a professionally staffed Career Planning Center which assists all students and alumni/ae in determining their career directions and opportunities and in developing effective employment search skills and strategies. Hundreds of law firms, governmental and public service agencies, and corporations interview at the law school each year. Applications are solicited by employers from almost every state. Employment trends for recent graduates have been about as follows: private practice, 68 percent; government and public interest, 11 percent; corporations, 11 percent; judicial clerkships, 9 percent; and academic, 1 percent.

Academic Group for the 1995-1996 Academic Year

Fordham University School of Law
This data reflects the applicant pool for the fall 1995 entering class.

LSAT Score	2.00 - 2.49		2.50 - 2.99		3.00 - 3.49		3.50 - 4.33		Totals	
	Adm	Apps	Adm	Apps	Adm	Apps	Adm	Apps	Adm	Apps
176 - 180	1	1	2	3	5	5	2	2	10	11
172 - 175	1	3	2	4	25	25	9	9	37	41
168 - 171	2	4	18	23	64	64	51	52	135	143
164 - 167	11	23	59	78	267	269	177	179	514	549
160 - 163	11	27	46	144	234	455	208	301	499	927
156 - 159	1	24	22	160	44	410	24	281	91	875
152 - 155	5	43	45	199	64	402	20	221	134	865
148 - 151	0	63	7	163	15	285	6	127	28	638
120 - 147	0	142	2	316	0	312	1	125	3	895
Applications Which Never Became Complete									0	112
Total	32	330	203	1090	718	2227	498	1297	1451	5056

(Column groups are Undergraduate GPA ranges.)

Apps = Applications Received
Adm = Applications Accepted

Franklin Pierce Law Center

Admissions Office
2 White Street
Concord, NH 03301

URL: http://www.fplc.edu
Phone: 603.228.9217

■ Introduction

Franklin Pierce Law Center is a private, ABA-approved national law school. Established in 1973 to encourage innovation in legal education, it remains the only law school in New Hampshire.

The Law Center's commitment to innovation in legal education is reflected in its emphasis on individually tailored legal education; a broad range of learning settings including lectures and seminars, real-client clinics, independent study, and externships with lawyers and judges; a community spirit of caring and compassion; and a close working relationship between students and faculty. Self-reliant students who know their own strengths and objectives thrive at Franklin Pierce and find the focus on personal pride and responsibility more motivating than fear, competition, or class rank.

The Law Center is one of the smallest private law schools in the United States. Each entering class numbers approximately 130 students. Classes tend to be small, especially after the first year. Thirty-five of the 50 elective courses enroll 35 or fewer students.

Located in New Hampshire's capital city of Concord (40,000 population), the Law Center is 25 minutes from Manchester, New Hampshire's largest city, and approximately one hour from Boston, the Atlantic seacoast, the state's lake region, and the White Mountains.

■ Enrollment/Student Body

➻ *1,343 applicants* ➻ *488 admitted first-year class 1995*
➻ *138 enrolled first-year class 1995* ➻ *398 total full-time*
➻ *8% minority* ➻ *36% women*
➻ *35 states & 4 foreign countries represented*
➻ *201 undergraduate schools represented*

■ Faculty

➻ *54 total* ➻ *26 full-time* ➻ *28 part-time or adjunct*
➻ *15 women*

■ Library and Physical Facilities

➻ *194,000 volumes & equivalents* ➻ *library hours: Mon.-Thurs., 8:00 A.M.-MIDNIGHT; Fri., 8:00 A.M.-10:00 P.M.; Sat., 10:00 A.M.-10:00 P.M.; Sun., 10:00 A.M.-MIDNIGHT*
➻ *LEXIS* ➻ *NEXIS* ➻ *WESTLAW* ➻ *DIALOG*
➻ *5 full-time librarians* ➻ *library seats 250*

It is the largest law library in the state with special strength in intellectual property.

■ Curriculum

➻ *84 credits required to graduate* ➻ *92 courses available*
➻ *degrees available: J.D.; J.D./Master of Intellectual Property*
➻ *semesters, start in Aug.*
➻ *range of first-year class size—27-138*

■ Special Programs

Intellectual Property—The internationally recognized intellectual and industrial property (patents, licensing, technology transfer, trade secrets, trademarks, and copyrights) specialization is supported by five full-time faculty members who are intellectual property lawyers. The patent specialty, for those with a technological degree or equivalent, exposes students to patent claim drafting, patent application preparation, and U.S. Patent and Trademark Office procedures. These students are prepared for patent practice immediately upon receiving their J.D. degree. Many will have passed the patent bar examination prior to graduation and gained practical intellectual property experience through externships as well as part-time and summer jobs with law firms, corporations, and the U.S. Court of Appeals for the Federal Circuit in Washington, D.C.

Public Interest—The public interest faculty work with students to tailor the curriculum (coursework, clinical work, and externships) to fit individual interests and assist students with finding summer and full-time employment.

Civil Practice Clinic—The clinic provides an opportunity within the Law Center to acquire skills in relating effectively with clients and advocating their interests in court. Each year approximately 35 second- and third-year students provide legal assistance to county residents who come to the clinic with problems such as divorce, neglect and abuse of children, child support, housing, and debt collection.

Criminal Law—The Appellate Defender Program, housed at the Law Center, gives students the opportunity to prepare briefs for the New Hampshire Supreme Court in criminal cases ranging from disorderly conduct to first-degree murder. Through the Criminal Practice Clinic students represent clients charged with misdemeanor and juvenile offenses in Concord District Court. In addition, many students work closely with trial attorneys in the statewide Public Defender Program as part of externships and summer jobs.

The Institute for Health, Law and Ethics— is a professional collaboration comprised of faculty members from Franklin Pierce Law Center, Dartmouth Medical School, and the University of New Hampshire. In its ongoing effort to encourage understanding and cooperation among the separate disciplines, the Institute provides students with externships, independent study and employment opportunities, working alongside policymakers in provider and legislative settings.

Current projects include: sponsorship of public forums dealing with family decision-making, a child's right to refuse medical treatment, medical futility, and experimentation with human subjects and preimplantation embryos; sponsorship of a regional conference about the ethics of patenting medical procedures; participation on local hospital ethics committees, medical societies and the New Hampshire Health Reform Task Force; and sponsorship of an expert conference to develop guidelines for guardians.

■ Admission

➽ *B.A. or B.S. degree required* ➽ *application deadline—April 1* ➽ *rolling admissions* ➽ *LSAT, LSDAS required* ➽ *median GPA—2.9* ➽ *median LSAT score—154* ➽ *application fee—$45*

While LSAT scores and grade-point average are, of course, factors that must be considered in the decision-making process, neither alone is determinative.

Our Admissions Committee is composed of members of the faculty, student body, and admissions staff. The committee utilizes the collective wisdom of affording each application a thorough and thoughtful review. The candidate's personal statement, letters of recommendation, and résumé are evaluated along with the "numbers." Community service, employment during college, and other nonacademic accomplishments are given weight to the extent that they reflect initiative, social responsibility, maturity, and other qualities. Franklin Pierce does not discriminate on the basis of age, sex, race, color, religion, national origin, marital status, sexual orientation, or disability, and encourages members of groups underrepresented in the legal profession to seek admission.

■ Student Activities

Students prepare notes and comments for *IDEA: the Journal of Law and Technology*, published by the Center's Patent, Trademark and Copyright Research Foundation; *Risk Issues in Health & Safety*; and *Annual Survey of New Hampshire Law*, an annual publication consisting of six articles focusing principally on recent NH Supreme Court opinions. Articles are written by second-year and edited by third-year students. Student organizations include: Minority Law Student Association, the Law Students Cooperative, Public Interest Coalition, Women's Law Caucus, the Environmental Law Society, the International Law Society, In-house Lawyering, BiGALLA (Bisexual, Gay, and Lesbian Alliance), and SIPLA (Student Intellectual Property Law Association), as well as chapters of the American Trial Lawyers Association, National Lawyers Guild, Phi Alpha Delta Fraternity, and the American Bar Association/Law Students Division.

■ Expenses and Financial Aid

➽ *tuition & fees—$14,200* ➽ *estimated additional expenses—books $500, living expenses $11,200*
➽ *scholarships available: Franklin Pierce Law Center Scholarships based on need* ➽ *merit scholarships available—four scholarships awarded based upon academic record*
➽ *diversity scholarships available—five full-time tuition scholarships for members of underrepresented groups*
➽ *FPLC Financial Aid Application and FAFSA required*
➽ *application deadline—April 1*
➽ *decisions made on a rolling basis*

■ Career Services

The Career Services Center works with students and alumni to find the best match between their skills and interests and changing legal markets. The center provides extensive individual counseling and guidance; brings attorneys to campus to provide first-hand information about the practice of law; advises students of all resources through weekly publications and job boards; coordinates the efforts of faculty, staff, and student groups to provide information about opportunities to gain experience; and conducts outreach to employers.

Applicant Group for the 1995-1996 Academic Year

Franklin Pierce Law Center

LSAT Score	GPA								
	3.75 +	3.50 - 3.74	3.25 - 3.49	3.00 - 3.24	2.75 - 2.99	2.50 - 2.74	2.25 - 2.49	2.00 - 2.24	Below 2.00
175 - 180	Good Possibility	Good Possibility	Good Possibility	Good Possibility	Good Possibility	Good Possibility	Good Possibility	Good Possibility	Unlikely
170 - 174	Good Possibility	Good Possibility	Good Possibility	Good Possibility	Good Possibility	Good Possibility	Good Possibility	Possible	Unlikely
165 - 169	Good Possibility	Good Possibility	Good Possibility	Good Possibility	Good Possibility	Possible	Possible	Possible	Unlikely
160 - 164	Good Possibility	Good Possibility	Good Possibility	Good Possibility	Possible	Possible	Possible	Possible	Unlikely
155 - 159	Good Possibility	Good Possibility	Good Possibility	Good Possibility	Possible	Possible	Possible	Unlikely	Unlikely
150 - 154	Possible	Possible	Possible	Possible	Unlikely	Unlikely	Unlikely	Unlikely	Unlikely
145 - 149	Unlikely	Unlikely	Unlikely	Unlikely	Unlikely	Unlikely	Unlikely	Unlikely	Unlikely
140 - 144	Unlikely	Unlikely	Unlikely	Unlikely	Unlikely	Unlikely	Unlikely	Unlikely	Unlikely
135 - 139	Unlikely	Unlikely	Unlikely	Unlikely	Unlikely	Unlikely	Unlikely	Unlikely	Unlikely
130 - 134	Unlikely	Unlikely	Unlikely	Unlikely	Unlikely	Unlikely	Unlikely	Unlikely	Unlikely
125 - 129	Unlikely	Unlikely	Unlikely	Unlikely	Unlikely	Unlikely	Unlikely	Unlikely	Unlikely
120 - 124	Unlikely	Unlikely	Unlikely	Unlikely	Unlikely	Unlikely	Unlikely	Unlikely	Unlikely

Good Possibility   Possible   Unlikely

Note: This chart is to be used as a general guide in determining the chances for admittance. Nonnumerical factors are strongly considered for applicants in all three categories.

George Mason University School of Law

3401 N. Fairfax Drive
Arlington, VA 22201-4498

Phone: 703.993.8010

■ Introduction

George Mason University School of Law was established by authority of the Virginia General Assembly in 1979. It is fully accredited by the ABA, and is a member of the AALS.

Recently, GMUSL has been recognized for its pioneering changes in legal education geared to the increasingly specialized and complex fields of practice that now characterize the legal profession.

■ Enrollment/Student Body

➧ 2,660 applicants ➧ 760 admitted first-year class 1995 ➧ 218 enrolled first-year class 1995 ➧ 375 total full-time ➧ 321 total part-time ➧ 9.6% minority ➧ 38% women ➧ 26 states & foreign countries represented ➧ 236 undergraduate schools represented

George Mason University is an Equal Opportunity/Affirmative Action institution.

■ Faculty

➧ 57 total ➧ 33 full-time ➧ 24 part-time or adjunct ➧ 10 women ➧ 8 minority

■ Library and Physical Facilities

➧ 300,000 volumes & equivalents ➧ library hours: Mon.-Fri., 7:00 A.M.-11:00 P.M.; Sat.-Sun., 8:00 A.M.-10:00 P.M. ➧ LEXIS ➧ NEXIS ➧ WESTLAW ➧ 10 full-time librarians ➧ library seats 600

The school is a member of the library network of the Consortium for Continuing Higher Education in Northern Virginia, affording access to general university and public library collections.

■ Curriculum

➧ Academic Support Program ➧ 90 credits required to graduate ➧ degrees available: J.D. ➧ semesters, start in Aug.

GMUSL has developed five specialized J.D. programs that give our graduates a competitive edge in today's job market. Four are offered in the three-year day division and one is offered in the four-year evening program. In addition, GMUSL offers a standard law school program in both the day and evening division. More than half the student body elects the standard program.

In each program, "Quantitative Methods for Lawyers" is required of all first-year students and provides the methodological and technical tools necessary to handle complex legal problems by offering a concise primer of economics, accounting, and finance needed for modern law practice.

The legal writing, research, and analysis program reflects the law school's emphasis on the development of legal writing skills. Three years of legal writing courses are required in small classes of 15 students.

■ Special Programs

The Corporate and Securities Law Track prepares students to work in a variety of fields related to corporate law and financial markets. By developing a thorough understanding of both law and underlying theory, students are prepared to deal with rapidly changing business and legal environments.

The Regulatory Law Track prepares students for practice in and before the numerous agencies that regulate business and other activities. Students are taught economics, the economic analysis of law, administrative law, legislation, lobbying, and negotiation, as well as several substantive areas of regulatory law.

The International Business Track prepares students for practice in the rapidly changing global business community, and provides them with a well-rounded legal education emphasizing analytical and writing skills.

The Litigation Law Track provides an academic program for students interested in litigation and other dispute-resolution processes. This is not a clinical training program. The track courses focus on the processes of dispute resolution and lawyers' roles from an analytical perspective.

The Patent Law Track is designed for students having a degree in engineering or one of the physical or biological sciences who may want to consider specializing in patent law. The track is a four-year evening division program. It is possible, however, to complete the requirements for the Patent track in three years as a full-time day student provided that you can take Patent Law courses during the evening.

■ Admission

➧ Bachelor's degree required ➧ application deadline—March 1 ➧ LSAT, LSDAS required ➧ median GPA—3.25 ➧ median LSAT score—161 ➧ application fee—$35

Admission selection is based primarily upon the applicant's academic background and LSAT score. Also given consideration are the LSAT writing sample, extracurricular activities, employment and professional experience, a personal statement, letters of recommendation, advanced degrees, and any other information in the file.

■ Student Activities

George Mason University provides many services to enhance the law school experience and enable students to take full advantage of the university's educational and personal enrichment opportunities.

Student activities include the *George Mason University Law Review*, *Civil Rights Law Journal*, a newspaper, a yearbook, and numerous law-related organizations.

Because of the location of the School of Law, students have an unparalleled opportunity to gain experience in such varied settings as the Office of the U.S. Attorney for both the District of Columbia and the Eastern District of Virginia, as well as federal courts and agencies, local governments, and private firms. GMU's Work-Study Program provides eligible students with on-campus jobs. Eligibility is based partly on need.

Minority Student Services, Disability Support Services, and the Office of Veterans Services provide specialized assistance, as does the Counseling Center, where a staff of professionals helps students to reach personal, social, and academic goals.

The Patriot Center, a 10,000-seat arena, is home to GMU sports events and community programs. The Harris Theater and Center for Performing Arts provide world-class dance, music, and theater performances. The Sports and Recreation Complex offers indoor and outdoor tracks and playing fields, weight room, sauna, and other facilities.

■ Expenses and Financial Aid

➽ *tuition & fees—full-time resident, $7,084; full-time nonresident, $17,920; part-time resident, $253/semester hour; part-time nonresident, $640/semester hour; resident total annual average part-time tuition and fees, $5,692; nonresident total annual average part-time tuition and fees, $14,400* ➽ *estimated additional expenses—$13,000* ➽ *merit-based scholarships available up to $6,500* ➽ *financial aid available; FAFSA and institutional forms required* ➽ *need analysis done on a one-to-one basis*

George Mason University participates in the Direct Lending Program.

A number of fellowships paying up to $6,500 per year are available for students entering the first year. These fellowships are awarded competitively to students with academic promise, and are aimed in part at encouraging law study by members of minority groups.

■ Career Services

The Office of Career Services aids students and alumni in finding permanent, part-time, and summer jobs by serving as a clearinghouse for information on available positions. It also advises on résumé and interview preparation, and coordinates on-campus interviews. The office focuses on providing resources for career planning and development. As many as 150 firms, businesses, and government agencies recruit on campus each year. Graduates find employment in the legal profession throughout the country.

Admission Profile Not Available

George Washington University Law School

Washington, DC 20052

URL: http://www.law.gwu.edu
Phone: 202.994.7230

■ Introduction

Four blocks from the White House and minutes away from Congress, the U.S. Supreme Court, and various federal departments and agencies, the law school offers its students a special opportunity to study and observe lawmaking at its primary source. The George Washington University Law School, established in 1865, is the oldest law school in the District of Columbia. It is a charter member of the AALS and is fully accredited.

The law school is part of George Washington University and is located on its campus in downtown Washington. The university, established in 1821, is a private, nonsectarian institution.

■ Enrollment/Student Body

➽ 6,471 applicants ➽ 1,934 admitted first-year class 1995 ➽ 504 enrolled first-year class 1995 ➽ 1,310 total full-time ➽ 26.4% minority ➽ 45% women ➽ 83 states & foreign countries represented ➽ 281 undergraduate schools represented

The student body of over 1,700 is a varied and interesting group. It represents 50 states and numerous foreign countries. In the last few years, the number of women and minorities seeking a law school education has increased greatly; in the 1995 entering class women constitute 48 percent and minorities 32 percent of the enrollment.

George Washington University does not discriminate against any person on the basis of race, color, religion, sex, national origin, age, disability, or veteran status. This policy covers all programs, services, policies, and procedures of the university, including admission to educational programs and employment. The university is subject to the District of Columbia Human Rights Law.

Inquiries concerning the application of this policy and federal laws and regulations concerning discrimination in education or employment programs and activities may be addressed to Susan B. Kaplan, Special Assistant to the President, George Washington University, Rice Hall, Washington, DC 20052, phone: 202.994.6500, or to the Assistant Secretary for Civil Rights of the Department of Education.

■ Faculty

➽ 252 total ➽ 67 full-time ➽ 185 part-time or adjunct ➽ 75 women ➽ 23 minority

The 61 full-time instructors teach all the basic courses in the law school. In addition, there are 138 adjunct instructors, many of whom are eminent government officials and highly regarded experienced practitioners.

■ Library and Physical Facilities

➽ 454,752 volumes & equivalents ➽ library hours: Mon.-Fri., 8:00 A.M.-11:45 P.M.; Sat.-Sun., 9:00 A.M.-11:45 P.M. ➽ LEXIS ➽ NEXIS ➽ WESTLAW ➽ DIALOG ➽ ALADIN ➽ 14 full-time librarians ➽ library seats 828

In the fall of 1984, the law school completed a $16.7 million expansion of its physical plant to substantially improve the facilities for future students. The development included an expansion of the Jacob Burns Law Library and the construction of a new classroom building. Its new facilities provide ample room for study, research, and offices. Stockton and Lerner Halls provide classrooms and offices.

■ Curriculum

➽ Academic Support Program ➽ 84 credits required to graduate ➽ 228 courses available ➽ degrees available: J.D.; J.D./M.A.; J.D./M.B.A.; J.D./M.P.H.; J.D./M.H.S.A.; J.D./M.P.A.; LL.M.; LL.M./M.P.H.; S.J.D. ➽ semesters, start in Aug. & Jan. ➽ range of first-year class size—85-110

The law school is one of the largest in the country and offers many courses and programs. A wide variety of courses are offered in public law as well as in the traditional fields of law. Normally, several sections are offered for all required and basic courses. In addition, a large number of advanced and specialized courses in areas of primary interest are scheduled.

The school awards the J.D. degree upon the satisfactory completion of 84 semester hours. This requirement is normally satisfied in three academic years of full-time study. In some cases, summer school offerings permit a student to accelerate by one semester. In addition to the full-time division, admitted applicants may choose to attend the law school in a part-time program which normally requires four academic years and one summer session to complete.

■ Special Programs

The George Washington University Law School offers an unusually strong program leading to the J.D. degree and also to the graduate degrees of Master of Law and Doctor of Juridical Science. A unique concentration of courses is available to students in the areas of patent, tax, and government procurement law; international and comparative law; economic regulation, labor, and corporate law; land-use management; and environmental law. All graduate courses are available to qualified J.D. candidates.

The law school also offers a number of courses structured around such contemporary problems as consumer protection and environmental policies. In many courses, students participate actively in the investigation and resolution of legal disputes in addition to reading about them. The Community Legal Clinic, Institute of Law and Aging, Legal Aid Bureau, and Law Students in Court are examples of these programs. In the Law Students in Court program, third-year students represent clients in both civil and criminal cases under the District of Columbia's third-year practice rule. Students may also take a number of credit hours of clinical work under the close supervision of a faculty member.

■ Admission

➽ *Bachelor's degree required for admission*
➽ *application deadline—March 1* ➽ *rolling admission*
➽ *LSAT, LSDAS required* ➽ *median GPA—3.50*
➽ *median LSAT score—162* ➽ *application fee—$55*

The George Washington University Law School receives approximately 6,500 applications per year for the entering class. The majority of these applicants are undoubtedly qualified for law study, but space limitations compel the Admissions Committee to be highly selective. No inflexible standards are set; rather, the committee seeks to choose those whose undergraduate records and LSAT scores indicate probable success in law study. Other factors considered include the undergraduate school and major, the personal statement of the applicant, and letters of recommendation, if submitted. In addition to the above, the Admissions Committee makes a positive effort to choose those applicants who will bring as broad a diversity of background as possible to the entering class. The committee begins to review completed applications in mid-January and makes decisions on a rolling basis. Decisions are reported to the applicants immediately, whether the decision is to admit, deny, or take no action and hold the applicant's file for later review.

All applicants must receive an undergraduate degree from an accredited school prior to registration. They must take the LSAT and subscribe to LSDAS. Beginning students are admitted only in September.

■ Student Activities

The *George Washington Law Review* is edited and managed by students of the law school. Published five times a year, the *Law Review* is devoted exclusively to state and federal public law. In addition, student boards publish the *Journal of International Law and Economics*, and the *Intellectual Property Law Journal and the Environmental Lawyer.*

The law school newspaper, *The Advocate*, is written and published by students. The Legal Aid Bureau, also student run, is particularly active in offering students opportunities to participate in investigation, research, and litigation.

The Student Bar Association, to which all students belong, is represented on committees overseeing the curriculum, library, and other areas. The association sponsors many activities such as the Van Vleck Case Club Competition, special lectures, a book exchange, and social events.

Applicant Group for the 1995-1996 Academic Year

George Washington University Law School
This grid includes only applicants who earned 120-180 LSAT scores under standard administrations.

LSAT Score	GPA 3.75 +		3.50 - 3.74		3.25 - 3.49		3.00 - 3.24		2.75 - 2.99		2.50 - 2.74		2.25 - 2.49		2.00 - 2.24		Below 2.00		No GPA		Total	
	Apps	Adm	Apps	Adm	Apps	Adm	Apps	Adm	Apps	Adm	Apps	Adm	Apps	Adm	Apps	Adm	Apps	Adm	Apps	Adm	Apps	Adm
175 - 180	4	4	1	1	9	9	4	4	1	1	1	1	0	0	1	0	0	0	1	1	22	21
170 - 174	12	12	22	22	33	33	22	18	11	3	4	0	2	0	2	0	0	0	1	1	109	89
165 - 169	51	50	132	124	140	130	114	60	57	8	21	3	10	0	2	0	1	0	3	2	531	377
160 - 164	153	149	400	369	456	308	283	72	121	14	67	5	28	1	6	0	0	0	16	3	1530	921
155 - 159	144	56	389	115	388	49	283	33	153	17	68	6	28	1	10	0	2	0	16	6	1481	283
150 - 154	64	9	169	20	286	32	254	52	161	23	84	10	45	2	13	0	5	0	20	2	1101	150
145 - 149	37	8	61	9	119	17	134	16	125	11	83	5	53	1	15	0	4	0	27	1	658	68
140 - 144	8	0	22	0	50	0	66	0	59	0	58	0	47	0	13	0	5	0	20	0	348	0
135 - 139	2	0	11	0	14	0	33	0	26	0	35	0	23	0	22	0	2	0	11	0	179	0
130 - 134	1	0	3	0	6	0	3	0	13	0	10	0	6	0	5	0	2	0	2	0	51	0
125 - 129	0	0	0	0	1	0	3	0	2	0	2	0	4	0	4	0	0	0	1	0	17	0
120 - 124	0	0	0	0	0	0	0	0	0	0	1	0	0	0	0	0	0	0	0	0	1	0
Total	476	288	1210	660	1502	578	1199	255	729	77	434	30	246	5	93	0	21	0	118	16	6028	1909

Apps = Number of Applicants
Adm = Number Admitted
Reflects 98% of the total applicant pool.

Georgetown University Law Center

600 New Jersey Avenue, N.W.
Washington, DC 20001

Phone: 202.662.9010

■ Introduction

The Law Center is ideally situated to take advantage of the extensive legal resources of Washington. Its proximity to the courts, Congress, government departments, and administrative agencies provides the Georgetown student with an atmosphere for creative thought and learning. The Supreme Court, the District of Columbia's Judiciary Square, the U.S. Capitol, and the House and Senate Office buildings are a short walk from the Law Center. The excellent research facilities of the Library of Congress are easily accessible. One of the nation's largest law schools, Georgetown has been a member of the AALS since 1902 and was approved by the ABA in 1924.

■ Enrollment/Student Body

➽ 8,000 applicants ➽ 2,074 admitted first-year class 1995 ➽ 667 enrolled first-year class 1995 ➽ 1,526 total full-time ➽ 498 total part-time ➽ 26% minority ➽ 46% women ➽ 47 states & 7 foreign countries represented ➽ 223 undergraduate schools represented

Georgetown is proud of the diversity of its student body and maintains that diversity by actively recruiting women and those from diverse ethnic, racial, economic, and educational backgrounds.

■ Faculty

➽ 253 total ➽ 87 full-time ➽ 166 part-time or adjunct ➽ 56 women ➽ 17 minority

■ Library and Physical Facilities

➽ 822,686 volumes & equivalents ➽ library hours: Mon.-Fri., 8:00 A.M.-MIDNIGHT; Sat., 9:00 A.M.-10:00 P.M.; Sun., 10:00 A.M.-MIDNIGHT; extended hours during exams; Reading Room open until 2:00 A.M.; 24-hours during exams ➽ LEXIS ➽ NEXIS ➽ WESTLAW ➽ DIALOG ➽ 22 full-time librarians ➽ library seats 1,270

The library combines modern information delivery systems with the book collection of a major research library. Among its volumes are the reported decisions of all federal and state courts as well as federal administrative tribunals, all federal and state statutes, subscriptions to over 8,000 serial titles, and a growing collection of treatises. Special collections of microforms with all available Congressional publications, records and briefs of the U.S. Supreme Court and several other courts, and United Nations documents.

McDonough Hall, with its lecture halls, seminar rooms, faculty offices, bookstore and student dining area and lounges is the academic center of the campus. The Law Center is accessible to students with disabilities.

■ Curriculum

➽ Academic Support Program ➽ 83 credits required to graduate ➽ 230 courses available ➽ degrees available: J.D.; J.D./M.B.A.; J.D./M.S.F.S.; J.D./M.P.H.; J.D./Phil.; J.D./Gov't ➽ range of first-year class size—20-130 ➽ 100+ graduate courses available to J.D. students

Day and evening programs are offered leading to the J.D. degree. Entry to both programs is in the fall. During the first year, students are enrolled in either the "A" or "B" curriculum. Students in the "A" curriculum begin their studies with eight courses, including one elective course in the spring semester. The "B" curriculum, available to one section of full-time students, requires eight different courses which emphasize the sources of law in history, philosophy, political theory, and economics. It also seeks to reflect the increasingly public nature of contemporary law. Electives satisfy the remaining degree requirements. A residency of six semesters is required for full-time students, eight semesters for part-time.

■ Tutorial Program

The tutorial program is structured to assist first-year students in analyzing fact patterns, identifying relevant legal issues, briefing cases, and taking class notes. First-year students who fall within guidelines for participation set by the faculty are invited to participate in the program. Other students may be admitted to the program for special reasons upon permission of the Dean. Tutorial groups are established for each of the five first-year sections. Each group is coordinated by an upperclass tutor who meets with participants at least once a week for two hours. Any unusual learning problem revealed by this process is then given individual attention.

■ The Writing Center

The Writing Center provides J.D. and graduate students with assistance on their written work. Senior Writing Fellows at the center provide feedback on making the transition from another field of expertise, approaching scholarly writing, using computer technology and word processing to improve legal research and writing, paying proper attention to legal citation form and footnotes, and mastering English grammar.

■ Special Programs

Georgetown Law Center, a pioneer in clinical legal education, offers an unmatched clinical program. Clinical programs are divided into two categories: (1) actual client representation programs that permit students to represent people in court or in administrative hearings and (2) other programs that allow students to participate in a nontrial context in federal and local agencies, schools, and other institutions. The Law Center also offers a Public Interest Law Scholars Program that gives special encouragement, in the form of enriched educational opportunities, career counseling, and a limited number of summer employment stipends to students who are committed to practice law in the public interest.

■ Admissions

➽ *B.A. or B.S. degree required* ➽ *application deadline—day, Feb. 1; eve., March 1* ➽ *rolling admission, early application encouraged* ➽ *LSAT, LSDAS required* ➽ *early action program—Nov. 1* ➽ *median GPA—3.51* ➽ *median LSAT score—166* ➽ *application fee—$60*

Graduation from an accredited college is generally a prerequisite to admission, but mature students with compelling personal circumstances may be admitted after three years of college. Candidates are evaluated on two scales, academic or objective criteria and personal or subjective criteria. Academic information includes undergraduate records and LSAT scores. Personal factors include extracurricular activities, recommendations, work experience, and diversity of background. Other information giving insight into a candidate's potential for successful performance is also considered. Although Georgetown does not use numerical cutoffs, only candidates with strong objective and subjective credentials are encouraged to apply. Upon acceptance, a prospective student must submit a nonrefundable deposit of $100 by April 15.

■ Student Housing

The Gewirz Student Center, opened in the fall of 1993, houses approximately 300 students. Priority for this housing is given to first-year students. The Gewirz Student Center offers a variety of apartment styles with one, two, and three private bedrooms. The apartments are air-conditioned and contain a kitchen and bathroom (the three-bedroom apartments have two bathrooms). Some apartments include a separate living room. Also available are apartments designed for students with disabilities.

For those who will not reside on campus, the Office of Student Affairs maintains a listing of available apartments, houses, and rooms to rent. During the summer, the office also offers an off-campus housing program.

■ Student Activities

The Law Center publishes eight student-edited scholarly journals. The *Law Weekly*, the school newspaper, is also printed under student direction. The Barristers' Council is responsible for the many appellate advocacy and trial practice programs, including intraschool and interschool competitions. Through the Student Bar Association and student/faculty committees, students participate in the decision processes of the Law Center. Over 55 student organizations and legal fraternities support personal and professional interests.

■ Financial Aid

➽ *tuition & fees—full-time, $21,280; part-time, $725/credit hour* ➽ *estimated additional expenses—$13,790 (room & board, books, transportation, and personal expenses)* ➽ *financial aid available; FAFSA and/or CSS Profile on Need Access Diskette and institutional application due March 1* ➽ *all GULC aid is need-based, awards combine federal & school loans & grant funds*

■ Career Services

Services include on-going consultation on job-search strategies, career decision-making and résumé writing assistance; interview skills training sessions; programs on law practice, opportunities in the legal profession, and trends in the legal job market; one of the largest on-campus interview programs in the country and off-campus interview opportunities; an extensive print and data resource center; and active current job listing resources. Intensive one-on-one counseling provided by professionals assigned as career advisors to entering class sections.

Admission Profile Not Available

University of Georgia School of Law

Athens, GA 30602-6012

URL: http://www.lawsch.uga.edu
Phone: 706.542.7060

■ Introduction

The University of Georgia School of Law, established in 1859, is on the campus of the nation's first state-chartered university (1785). It is an excellent setting for the study of law with outstanding libraries and academic, cultural, social, and recreational opportunities. Located in Athens, the commercial and legal center for northeast Georgia, the campus is less than an hour from Atlanta. This location enables students to live and study in a university setting yet be in close proximity to one of the nation's outstanding metropolitan areas.

The School of Law is approved by the American Bar Association, is a member of the Association of American Law Schools, and has a chapter of the Order of the Coif.

■ Enrollment/Student Body

➽ *2,315 applicants* ➽ *519 admitted first-year class 1995* ➽ *218 enrolled first-year class 1995* ➽ *641 total full-time* ➽ *13.6% minority* ➽ *43% women*

■ Faculty

➽ *56 total* ➽ *42 full-time* ➽ *18 part-time or adjunct* ➽ *12 women* ➽ *5 minority* ➽ *13 endowed chairs*

■ Library and Physical Facilities

➽ *457,672 volumes & equivalents* ➽ *library hours: Mon.-Fri., 7:30 A.M.-MIDNIGHT; Sat. & Sun., 8:00 A.M.-MIDNIGHT* ➽ *LEXIS* ➽ *NEXIS* ➽ *WESTLAW* ➽ *INFOTRAC* ➽ *INNOPAC* ➽ *9 full-time librarians* ➽ *library seats 469*

The Law Library is the only library in the Southeast designated as a Specialized European Documentation Center by the European Community.

The university's main library with over 3 million volumes is adjacent. The Institute of Continuing Judicial Education is located in the school; the Institute of Continuing Legal Education is located nearby. The shops, restaurants, and businesses of downtown Athens are about two blocks away.

■ Curriculum

➽ *Academic Support Program* ➽ *Legal Aid and Defender Clinic, Prosecutorial Clinic, Prisoner Legal Counseling Project, Public Interest Practicum* ➽ *88 credits required to graduate* ➽ *degrees available: J.D./M.B.A.; J.D./Masters of Historic Preservation* ➽ *semesters, start in Aug.* ➽ *range of first-year class size—43-73*

The required first-year courses provide a basic foundation and are followed by a diverse offering of elective courses during the second and third years of full-time, day study.

Students are offered an outstanding clinical education in criminal and civil procedure. Certified third-year students are permitted to try cases in the civil and criminal courts and to appear before governmental administrative authorities.

International and Comparative Law—While the overall curriculum of the University of Georgia School of Law has gained a national reputation for high quality, the school's reputation as a center for International Law goes beyond national boundaries. The Dean Rusk Center for International and Comparative Law conducts research and policy analyses relating to laws that affect international trade and development. Georgia law students edit and publish the *Georgia Journal of International and Comparative Law*. Summer clerkships with British law firms provide unique educational opportunities as does the annual Brussels Seminar at the University of Brussels.

The School of Law has formal exchange agreements with the University of Regensberg (Germany), Southhampton University (Great Britain), and the University of Brussels (Belgium).

Scholarly publications and Moot Court Activities—Georgia law students edit and publish three internationally circulated scholarly journals. The *Georgia Law Review*, the *Georgia Journal of International and Comparative Law*, and the *Journal of Intellectual Property Law*.

Moot Court teams successfully participate in numerous state, regional, and national events. In the last five years, Georgia moot court teams have won three national championships and one world championship.

■ Admission

➽ *Bachelor's degree required* ➽ *application deadline—March 1* ➽ *LSAT, LSDAS required* ➽ *median GPA—3.48* ➽ *median LSAT score—162* ➽ *application fee—$30*

The School of Law seeks to enroll a talented, diverse student body. The Admissions Committee considers admission test scores and grade-point averages significant measures upon which to base admission decisions, but it also recognizes the importance of other components of the applicant's record. In reviewing an applicant's file, the committee members may take into consideration whether the applicant might contribute to the academic, cultural, ethnic, geographical, racial or socio-economic diversity of the law school.

■ Expenses and Student Financial Aid

➽ *tuition & fees—full-time resident, $2,988; full-time nonresident, $8,270* ➽ *estimated additional expenses—$7,000 min. (room, board, books, supplies, etc.)* ➽ *scholarships available* ➽ *minority scholarships available* ➽ *financial aid available; FAFSA, Free Application for Federal Student Aid required*

Fees include charges for health services, transportation services, and most campus athletic and cultural activities.

School of Law scholarships include Academic Merit Scholarships, Tuition Equalization Scholarships which waive the nonresident portion of tuition for nonresident students, and Academic Merit/Financial Need Scholarships. Applications for scholarships are not required for merit-based scholarships awarded by the School of Law.

Candidates are encouraged to complete admission application files by January 31 to ensure full consideration for all merit awards.

Candidates who may demonstrate financial need are encouraged to contact the University Office of Student Financial Aid regarding student loans and other student financial aid programs. Applications for Regents Opportunity Scholarships for economically disadvantaged applicants are available in late spring.

The University of Georgia participates in the Federal Direct Student Lending Program.

Limited part-time employment may be available on- or off-campus; however, first-year law students are not encouraged to work.

■ Housing

Law students may reside in university residence halls and family housing units. Students desiring university housing are encouraged to make early application.

Most law students choose to live in nearby off-campus rental units. Ample housing opportunities are available in Athens at rates below those in typical metropolitan areas.

■ Student Activities

Students participate in School of Law governance through the Student Bar Association and by way of representation on faculty and administrative committees. Intramural sports are available through law school leagues.

Student interest organizations are active on campus. The Equal Justice Foundation provides financial assistance to University of Georgia law clerks serving the public interest.

■ Legal Career Services

The School of Law maintains a Legal Career Services Office to assist students and alumni with employment matters. Alumni and faculty members actively support the employment efforts of the students.

Services of the Legal Career Services Office range from coordinating on-campus interviews and career seminars to an outreach program including participation in one of the most successful off-campus interview consortium programs in the United States.

In the past five years, an average of greater than 92 percent of the graduates have reported successful placement within six months of graduation.

The average first-time bar passage rate for Georgia graduates exceeds 94 percent over the last several years.

Applicant Group for the 1995-1996 Academic Year

University of Georgia School of Law
This grid includes only applicants who earned 120-180 LSAT scores under standard administrations.

	GPA																				
LSAT Score	3.75 +		3.50 - 3.74		3.25 - 3.49		3.00 - 3.24		2.75 - 2.99		2.50 - 2.74		2.25 - 2.49		2.00 - 2.24		Below 2.00		No GPA		Total	
	Apps	Adm	Apps	Adm	Apps	Adm	Apps	Adm	Apps	Adm	Apps	Adm	Apps	Adm	Apps	Adm	Apps	Adm	Apps	Adm	Apps	Adm
175 - 180	0	0	1	1	1	1	1	1	1	1	0	0	0	0	0	0	0	0	0	0	4	4
170 - 174	4	4	8	8	2	2	8	8	3	1	1	1	0	0	1	0	0	0	0	0	27	24
165 - 169	17	16	31	31	36	36	31	30	16	5	9	5	4	0	0	0	0	0	2	2	146	125
160 - 164	52	39	79	51	110	60	91	36	60	8	20	1	7	0	2	0	1	0	1	0	423	195
155 - 159	50	24	102	30	144	19	102	5	62	2	32	2	19	0	6	0	0	0	1	0	518	82
150 - 154	38	8	77	17	107	6	105	9	66	5	53	1	27	1	7	0	2	0	3	0	485	47
145 - 149	14	1	42	9	67	9	77	9	66	1	44	0	24	0	9	0	2	0	4	0	349	29
140 - 144	3	2	17	2	25	0	33	2	28	0	39	0	19	0	9	0	2	0	8	0	183	6
135 - 139	0	0	3	0	13	1	21	0	16	0	18	0	10	0	5	0	3	0	3	0	92	1
130 - 134	0	0	2	0	3	0	4	0	11	0	4	0	4	0	6	0	2	0	2	0	38	0
125 - 129	0	0	0	0	0	0	0	0	1	0	1	0	1	0	0	0	0	0	1	0	4	0
120 - 124	0	0	0	0	0	0	0	0	0	0	0	0	1	0	0	0	0	0	0	0	1	0
Total	178	94	362	149	508	134	473	100	330	23	221	10	116	1	45	0	12	0	25	2	2270	513

Apps = Number of Applicants
Adm = Number Admitted
Reflects 99% of the total applicant pool.

Georgia State University College of Law

P.O. Box 4049
Atlanta, GA 30302-4049

E-Mail: lawhld@gsusgi2.gsu.edu
Phone: 404.651.2048

■ Introduction

Georgia State University College of Law is located in downtown Atlanta, the center of legal, financial, and governmental activities in the Southeast. This location provides easy access to federal, state, and local courts and agencies, the State Capitol, legislature, corporations, major law firms in the metropolitan area, and the library and other facilities of Georgia State University.

The College of Law began operation in 1982. The College of Law is accredited by the American Bar Association and is a member of the Association of American Law Schools.

■ Enrollment/Student Body

➧ 2,843 applicants ➧ 496 admitted first-year class 1995 ➧ 197 enrolled first-year class 1995 ➧ 401 total full-time ➧ 230 total part-time ➧ 26% minority ➧ 48% women

■ Faculty

➧ 67 total ➧ 40 full-time ➧ 27 part-time or adjunct ➧ 29 women ➧ 13 minority

■ Library and Physical Facilities

➧ 249,219 volumes & equivalents ➧ library hours: Mon.-Fri., 7:00 A.M.-11:00 P.M.; Sat., 9:00 A.M.-9:00 P.M.; Sun., 10:00 A.M.-11:00 P.M. ➧ LEXIS ➧ NEXIS ➧ WESTLAW ➧ DIALOG ➧ OLLI ➧ 6 full-time librarians ➧ library seats 335

Georgia State University College of Law is one of the leading law schools in the Southeast. Located on a 25-acre campus in the heart of downtown Atlanta, the College of Law building houses a moot courtroom equipped with state-of-the-art video technology and provides activities directed toward trial and appellate advocacy. Students have access to many other campus facilities including the athletic complex, which offers a variety of individual fitness opportunities and team sports.

■ Curriculum

➧ Academic Support Program ➧ Summer Skills Program ➧ 90 credits required to graduate ➧ 202 courses available ➧ degrees and combined degrees available: J.D.; J.D./M.B.A.; J.D./M.P.A. ➧ semesters, start in Aug. ➧ range of first-year class size—16-133

The College of Law offers both a full-time, six-semester program and a part-time, nine-semester program leading to the degree of Juris Doctor. In addition, speakers such as Supreme Court Justices Sandra Day O'Connor and Antonin Scalia, International Court Judge Stephen Schwebel, U.S. Court of Appeals Judge Leon Higgenbotham, Derrick Bell and others enrich our program. A six-day orientation program introduces first-year students to the study of law.

■ Special Programs

Tax Law Clinic—The Tax Law Clinic permits students to assist individual clients to prepare their cases for presentation before the Small Claims Division of U.S. Tax Court and before the Appeals Office of the Internal Revenue Service. Under appropriate supervision, students will provide advice in a wide range of matters arising in regard to the Internal Revenue Code. Students will interview clients, research legal issues, analyze facts, and prepare protests and petitions.

Externships—Externships are designed to tie theoretical knowledge to a practical base of experience in the profession. Externships involve actual participation in rendering legal services. Enrollment may be limited and may involve a selection process. Students interested in the externship program should contact the Lawyer Skills Development Office.

Trial Advocacy—Trial advocacy has several components. The first is the required second-year litigation course, which is offered in the spring semester. Second, after completing the second-year required course, students may take advanced advocacy seminars in the areas of civil and criminal litigation. Finally, students may become members of the Student Trial Lawyer Association (STLA) and the National Association of Criminal Defense Law Student Division (NACDL). The STLA annually sponsors student advocate teams in the ATLA Trial Competition and the Georgia Intrastate Trial Competition. As a result of the impressive performance of our trial advocacy teams, Georgia State University's College of Law was identified as having one of the top 16 trial advocacy programs in the country and was invited to the 1989, 1990, 1991, 1992, and 1993 National Invitational Trial Competition Tournament of Champions. In 1989 and 1993, a GSU College of Law student was selected Best Advocate at the NITT competition. In 1990 our team finished fourth, and in 1992 and 1993 we placed second in the nation. In 1994, GSU won the NADCL competition in Houston, Texas.

Moot Court—The Moot Court Society consists of second- and third-year students who have distinguished themselves in appellate advocacy and who are interested in achieving excellence in brief writing and oral advocacy. The society competes in numerous national and regional competitions. In addition, members prepare the case, problems, and trial briefs for the appellate, advocacy course competitions and serve as judges and brief graders in the Appellate Court competition. The College of Law has fielded teams that have won the Intrastate Competition, the regional NAAC and National Moot Court competitions, the 1988 National Championship in the National Moot Court Competition sponsored by the Association of the Bar of the City of New York, and the 1990 and 1992 Wagner Cup National Labor Law Competition.

■ Admission

➽ *Bachelor's degree from accredited college or university required* ➽ *application deadline—March 1, rolling admissions policy beginning in Jan., early application is encouraged* ➽ *LSAT, LSDAS required* ➽ *median GPA—3.13* ➽ *median LSAT score—157* ➽ *application fee—$10*

The College of Law of Georgia State University actively seeks to enroll a student body with diversity in educational, cultural, and racial backgrounds that will enrich the educational experience of the entire group.

Applicants are encouraged to visit the College of Law. Please make arrangements through the Admissions Office to tour the campus; talk with students, faculty and admissions staff; or attend a class.

■ Student Activities

The *Georgia State University Law Review* is published four times a year by students who have demonstrated outstanding writing and academic skills.

Student organizations include Asian-American Law Student Association, Association of Women Law Students, Black Law Students Association, Christian Legal Society, Delta Theta Phi Law Fraternity, Environmental Law Society, Federalist Society, International and Comparative Law Society, Jewish Student Association, National Association of Criminal Defense Lawyers, GSU Public Interest Law, Lesbian and Gay Law Student Association, Phi Delta Phi Law Fraternity, Phi Alpha Delta Law Fraternity, Sports and Entertainment Law Association, Student Trial Lawyers' Association, Student Bar Association, and Student Division of Federal Bar Association.

■ Expenses and Financial Aid

➽ *tuition & fees—full-time resident, $2,870/year; full-time nonresident, $8,502; part-time resident, $1,886; part-time nonresident, $5,406* ➽ *estimated additional expenses—$7,000 (room, board, books)* ➽ *performance- and need-based scholarships available* ➽ *minority scholarships available* ➽ *financial aid available; Fee Application for Federal Student Aid form preferred*

■ Career Services

The Career Planning Office offers a broad range of services including individual career counseling, educational programs about career options, workshops to assist in the development of job-search skills, networking programs, current job listing services, on-campus interviews, and job fairs. Students may begin using the Career Planning Office in November of the first year of law school, and may continue utilizing career planning services throughout their careers. Specific programs geared toward minority students are the Atlanta Bar Association Minority Clerkship Program and the Southeastern Minority Job Fair.

Applicant Group for the 1995-1996 Academic Year

Georgia State University College of Law
This grid includes only applicants who earned 120-180 LSAT scores under standard administrations.

	GPA																					
LSAT Score	3.75 +		3.50 - 3.74		3.25 - 3.49		3.00 - 3.24		2.75 - 2.99		2.50 - 2.74		2.25 - 2.49		2.00 - 2.24		Below 2.00		No GPA		Total	
	Apps	Adm	Apps	Adm	Apps	Adm	Apps	Adm	Apps	Adm	Apps	Adm	Apps	Adm	Apps	Adm	Apps	Adm	Apps	Adm	Apps	Adm
175 - 180	0	0	0	0	0	0	0	0	0	0	0	0	0	0	0	0	0	0	0	0	0	0
170 - 174	1	0	2	2	1	1	1	1	1	1	0	0	0	0	0	0	0	0	1	0	7	5
165 - 169	4	4	5	5	7	6	10	9	10	7	9	5	7	4	1	0	1	1	1	0	55	41
160 - 164	14	13	24	23	38	33	52	52	36	25	26	9	14	5	3	0	1	1	1	1	209	162
155 - 159	22	18	50	35	92	44	94	35	93	21	51	8	35	4	10	0	0	0	5	1	452	166
150 - 154	21	8	69	13	116	11	139	13	130	13	110	15	55	6	15	2	6	0	10	1	671	82
145 - 149	13	2	56	12	80	8	119	5	115	3	93	2	67	1	28	0	3	0	9	0	583	33
140 - 144	4	1	12	1	51	1	73	2	72	1	89	0	56	0	25	0	3	0	19	0	404	6
135 - 139	1	0	7	0	17	0	37	0	64	1	68	0	45	0	23	0	3	0	15	0	280	1
130 - 134	0	0	3	0	4	0	19	0	20	0	22	0	16	0	13	0	4	0	9	0	110	0
125 - 129	0	0	1	0	1	0	4	0	3	0	3	0	5	0	3	0	1	0	5	0	26	0
120 - 124	0	0	0	0	0	0	0	0	0	0	0	0	3	0	1	0	0	0	1	0	5	0
Total	80	46	229	91	407	104	548	117	544	72	471	39	303	20	122	2	22	2	76	3	2802	496

Apps = Number of Applicants
Adm = Number Admitted
Reflects 98% of the total applicant pool.

Golden Gate University School of Law

536 Mission Street
San Francisco, CA 94105

E-Mail: lawadmit@ggu.edu
URL: http://www.ggu.edu
Phone: 415.442.6630

■ Introduction

Founded in 1901, Golden Gate University School of Law is located in the heart of San Francisco's legal and financial district. The law school is noted for integrating practical skills training with legal theory. Golden Gate has a distinguished faculty who share a strong commitment to both excellence in teaching and accessibility to students.

The school is accredited by the ABA and is a member of the AALS.

■ Enrollment/Student Body

➧ 2,534 fall applicants ➧ 1,203 admitted first-year class 1995 ➧ 216 enrolled first-year class 1995 ➧ 469 total full-time ➧ 244 total part-time ➧ 28.1% minority ➧ 51% women ➧ 39 states & foreign countries represented ➧ 221 undergraduate schools represented

■ Faculty

➧ 135 total ➧ 35 full-time ➧ 100 part-time or adjunct ➧ 62 women ➧ 21 minority

■ Library Facilities

➧ 200,000 volumes & equivalents ➧ LEXIS ➧ WESTLAW ➧ CALI ➧ 12 full-time librarians ➧ library seats 350

■ Curriculum

➧ Academic Assistance Program ➧ 86 credits required to graduate ➧ 128 courses available

Golden Gate University School of Law affords students a "practical" legal education. The curriculum is designed to lay the foundations of modern legal theory, but also foster those lawyering skills necessary for a successful practice. Because writing is the lawyer's basic tool, the law school trains students to master the skills needed to draft a wide array of legal documents. Through its Academic Assistance Program, the law school provides all students with additional instruction in legal analysis and exam-writing skills.

■ Special Programs

Program Options—The law school offers both full-time and part-time programs. The full-time program normally involves three years of study; the part-time evening program takes four years. Golden Gate also offers mid-year admission, thus allowing students to begin law school in January.

Specialty Areas—The law school's curriculum offers students the opportunity to concentrate in one of many specialty areas, including corporate and commercial law, criminal law, entertainment law, environmental law, intellectual property law, labor and employment law, real estate development, or public interest law.

Students may also earn Certificates of Specialization in Litigation, Environmental, International and Public Interest law. Each certificate evidences completion of core courses and significant clinical or practical experience in the specialty area.

Each summer, Golden Gate offers courses focusing on Pacific Rim issues in Bangkok, Thailand, in cooperation with Chulalongkorn University. In the summer of 1996, the law school offered a new study abroad program at the University of Malta. Golden Gate graduates are eligible to participate in a student exchange program with the University of Paris at Nanterre.

Students who enroll in the Public Interest Law Program work with Public Interest Clearinghouse, which places students with the interest groups and agencies throughout the San Francisco Bay Area. The law school also offers a public interest loan forgiveness program for graduates who obtain employment in public interest law.

The Environmental Law program includes basic courses in Environmental Law, but also offers clinical opportunities and advanced seminars in such areas as Hazardous Site Liability, International Environmental Law, California Environmental Law, and Race, Poverty and the Environment.

The law school houses the Graduate Program in Taxation, which offers an LL.M. in Taxation. In 1994, Golden Gate instituted a new LL.M. program in International Legal Studies, which has attracted many international scholars and attorneys.

Advocacy Training—The law school offers an advocacy and dispute resolution curriculum that is one of the most comprehensive in the country. Its nationally recognized litigation program trains students in every aspect of litigation, from the pretrial thinking and planning stages, to the techniques of trial, to the appellate review of a case. Students with a serious interest in litigation may participate in trial advocacy and appellate advocacy competitions. Over the past several years, the law school's teams have won four regional championships in trial competitions and were semi-finalists in six others.

Besides learning courtroom tactics, Golden Gate may learn techniques of mediation and arbitration in Alternative Dispute Resolution. Students also receive training in the skills of client counseling and negotiating.

Clinics and Externships—Clinical programs, both on-site and field placement, are an integral part of the curriculum at Golden Gate. Through these programs, students may earn academic credit while working closely with practicing attorneys.

The law school houses three legal clinics. In the Women's Employment Rights Clinic, students represent low-income women with employment-related problems. Through the Environmental law and Justice Clinic, students assist Northern California communities in protecting their environmental interests. The Constitutional Law Clinic, established in 1976 as part of the Western Center for Constitutional Rights, enables students to work on civil rights cases focusing on health care issues of institutionalized persons.

Students may also receive credit for participating in the Judicial Externship Program, which places students with the judges on the California Supreme Court, federal district courts, and the California state appellate and superior courts.

Combined Degrees—The law school, in conjunction with the university's graduate programs in management, finance, taxation, accounting, and public administration, offers one of the most extensive combined-degree programs in the nation, which allow a student to pursue simultaneously a law degree and a master's degree in a related field.

■ Admission

➽ Bachelor's degree required ➽ April 15 deadline for fall; Nov. 15 for midyear ➽ median GPA—3.11 ➽ median LSAT score—155 ➽ application fee—$40

Admission is competitive. The Admission Committee considers applicants' undergraduate GPA, LSAT score, and information contained in their personal statement. The committee also weighs such factors as graduate work, social and economic background, and personal and employment accomplishments.

■ Minority Students

Applications from minority students and other underrepresented groups are encouraged and given special attention. Golden Gate participates in the CLEO Program and offers a summer Conditional Admissions Program designed to enhance the achievement of minority students. The law school works closely with minority student groups regarding issues such as admissions, academic assistance, and placement. In October 1993, the law school received the California Minority Counsel Program's Second Annual Law School Racial and Ethnic Diversity Commitment Award.

■ Student Activities and Scholarship

The law school has over fifteen student organizations, which range from groups representing minority students to groups focusing on specific areas of the law. In addition, a student editorial board publishes three issues of the *Golden Gate University Law Review* annually. In 1994, the law school began publishing the *Annual Survey of International and Comparative Law.*

■ Expenses and Financial Aid

➽ tuition & fees—full-time, $16,965; part-time, $11,115 ➽ estimated additional expenses—$13,500 (housing, transportation, insurance, books, food) ➽ financial aid available ➽ FAFSA, FAAP, Financial Aid Transcripts, and SAR due March 1 for priority

Approximately 85 percent of the student body receives some form of financial aid. Golden Gate awards merit scholarships to many highly-qualified entering students. Last year, Merit Scholarships ranged in amount from $6,000 to full tuition. In addition, the law school participates in federally subsidized and private loan programs.

■ Placement

The Career Services Office maintains listings of summer, part-time, and permanent positions and organizes on- and off-campus recruiting programs.

Applicant Group for the 1995-1996 Academic Year

Golden Gate University School of Law
This grid includes only applicants who earned 120-180 LSAT scores under standard administrations.

LSAT Score	3.75 +		3.50 - 3.74		3.25 - 3.49		3.00 - 3.24		2.75 - 2.99		2.50 - 2.74		2.25 - 2.49		2.00 - 2.24		Below 2.00		No GPA		Total	
	Apps	Adm	Apps	Adm	Apps	Adm	Apps	Adm	Apps	Adm	Apps	Adm	Apps	Adm	Apps	Adm	Apps	Adm	Apps	Adm	Apps	Adm
175 - 180	0	0	0	0	0	0	0	0	0	0	0	0	0	0	0	0	0	0	0	0	0	0
170 - 174	1	1	2	2	0	0	2	1	2	2	0	0	0	0	0	0	0	0	0	0	7	6
165 - 169	2	2	6	6	7	7	6	6	16	16	4	4	9	7	1	1	2	1	4	3	57	53
160 - 164	5	5	14	13	24	24	28	27	37	37	29	27	15	12	6	5	0	0	5	5	163	155
155 - 159	15	14	38	37	85	83	112	112	106	100	81	68	33	20	14	3	2	1	9	8	495	446
150 - 154	23	23	53	47	116	105	169	129	129	56	122	40	56	8	29	2	6	1	13	5	716	416
145 - 149	17	14	47	21	105	46	131	28	135	15	99	14	54	8	24	0	4	0	11	2	627	148
140 - 144	8	0	17	4	39	2	63	8	85	4	77	1	41	2	25	0	7	0	10	0	372	21
135 - 139	0	0	5	0	11	0	20	0	39	0	35	0	28	0	16	0	3	0	7	0	164	0
130 - 134	0	0	2	0	7	0	4	0	2	0	9	0	8	0	8	0	3	0	6	0	49	0
125 - 129	0	0	0	0	1	0	0	0	1	0	5	0	4	0	1	0	1	0	3	0	16	0
120 - 124	0	0	0	0	0	0	0	0	1	0	0	0	1	0	1	0	1	0	0	0	4	0
Total	71	59	184	130	395	267	535	311	553	230	461	154	249	57	125	11	29	3	68	23	2670	1245

Apps = Number of Applicants
Adm = Number Admitted
Reflects 97% of the total applicant pool.

Gonzaga University School of Law

Box 3528
Spokane, WA 99220

E-Mail: sharond@gulaw.gonzaga.edu
URL: http://law.wuacc.edu/gonzaga/libhome.html
Phone: 509.328.4220 Toll-free: 800.572.9658 WA residents, 800.523.9712 Continental US

■ Introduction

Gonzaga University School of Law belongs to a long and distinguished tradition of humanistic, Catholic, and Jesuit education. It is an integral part of Gonzaga University, which was founded in 1887 and continues to maintain the tradition of academic excellence in education that is at the heart of the mission of the 450-year-old Jesuit order. The School of Law was established in 1912. The campus is located in Spokane, a four-season city with the Spokane River flowing through its center. The city of 170,000 serves as the regional hub of the Inland Northwest, a large area running from the Cascade Mountains in the west to the Rockies in the east. Canada is a mere 100 miles to the north.

Spokane is not only an economic hub for manufacturing, agriculture, and light industry, but it is also a recreational sports area abundant with lakes, mountains, and forests. In minutes you can get away from the city's robust, rapidly growing business community to the surrounding pine-covered hills, where there is an evergreen splendor unlike any place in America.

■ Enrollment/Student Body

➧ *1,735 applicants* ➧ *993 admitted first-year class 1995* ➧ *239 enrolled first-year class 1995* ➧ *575 total full-time* ➧ *12 total part-time* ➧ *14% minority* ➧ *37% women* ➧ *40 states & foreign countries represented* ➧ *227 undergraduate schools represented* ➧ *average age—28*

■ Faculty

➧ *43 total* ➧ *33 full-time* ➧ *10 part-time or adjunct* ➧ *12 women*

The faculty are committed to teaching excellence and are eager to develop student abilities through classroom and personal instruction—and they are accessible and approachable.

■ Library and Physical Facilities

➧ *200,215 volumes & equivalents* ➧ *library hours: Mon.-Thurs., 8:00 A.M.-MIDNIGHT; Fri., 8:00 A.M.-10:00 P.M.; Sat., 10:00 A.M.-10:00 P.M.; Sun., NOON-MIDNIGHT* ➧ *LEXIS* ➧ *NEXIS* ➧ *WESTLAW* ➧ *DIALOG, CARL* ➧ *5 full-time librarians* ➧ *library seats 468*

Students also have access to campus facilities such as the Foley Center, a new 137,000-square-foot high-technology library; the University Health and Counseling Centers; the Student Union; and the Martin Athletic Center, complete with indoor running track, full-sized pool, state-of-the-art weight room, dance studio, basketball/volleyball courts, and racquetball courts.

■ Curriculum

➧ *Academic Support Program* ➧ *90 credits required to graduate* ➧ *75 courses available* ➧ *degrees available: J.D./M.B.A. and M.A.C.C./J.D.* ➧ *semesters, start in Aug.* ➧ *range of Legal Writing sections—15-20*

There is a deliberate and delicate balance to legal education at Gonzaga. The rigorous, full, and rounded curriculum focuses on legal analysis, problem solving, values, and ethics. Equally as important is the emphasis on practical experience to develop real-world lawyering skills. Beyond the required courses, students are free to tailor their studies to areas of interest.

The School of Law offers a favorable student-to-faculty ratio and an emphasis on positive rather than negative competition.

■ Special Programs

The first year of coursework is devoted to building a strong legal foundation for upper-division study. In order to ease the transition to the rigorous demands of law school, entering students may take advantage of the support offered through the student and attorney mentor programs, academic advisors, and special tutorials.

Joint programs leading to the J.D./M.B.A. and the M.A.C.C./J.D. degree are offered to prepare students who anticipate careers in other fields that require thorough knowledge of business, accountancy, and the law. Application must be made to the School of Business as well as to the School of Law.

An added dimension to the legal education for many Gonzaga law students is the opportunity to practice law while in school through the award-winning clinical law program.

■ Admission

➧ *Bachelor's degree required for admission* ➧ *application deadline—March 15* ➧ *LSAT, LSDAS required* ➧ *median GPA—3.09* ➧ *median LSAT score—153* ➧ *application fee—$40*

The School of Law endeavors to attract students with ambitious minds, professional motivation, and commitment to the highest ethics and values of the legal profession and to public service. A faculty committee reviews all applications. The consideration of applicants is not restricted to impersonal statistics. The enriching qualities of applicants such as work and life experiences, personal accomplishment, and opinions of others reflected in letters of recommendation will be considered.

The School of Law seeks to enroll a diverse student body to assure that the school and the legal profession are enriched through the participation of people from different cultural and ethnic backgrounds. Those individuals who desire diversity factors to be considered in their admission decision should include it in their application.

Students who have completed 45 semester credits or their equivalent or less and who are in good standing at another ABA law school may apply for admission to the School of Law with advanced standing.

Special Admission Program—The School of Law offers special acceptance to a limited number of applicants who do not meet regular admissions requirements, but whose application file suggests there may be potential for success beyond what the statistics would normally predict. There is no special application procedure for this program, and applicants will be considered auto-matically. Those accepted will be admitted to a special summer program, which will consist of 10 weeks commencing the summer before entrance into the first year. Students who are successful in the summer program will continue with their studies in the fall semester.

■ Student Activities

Students find it easy to become involved in a broad range of activities at the School of Law. Gonzaga is a major player in moot court competition through five moot court teams. The student-run *Gonzaga Law Review*, more than 29 years in existence, is circulated throughout the country. The award-winning Student Bar Association is a strong, active organization which encourages student involvement. There is also an opportunity to participate in intraschool moot court competition, two legal fraternities, and other numerous organizations and activities.

Law students, representing many cultural heritages, join together in the Multi-Cultural Law Caucus to provide a support network on campus and in the Spokane community for those students of diverse backgrounds.

■ Housing

The Gonzaga campus is in a residential area with housing within walking distance to the School of Law. Rental housing rates are reasonably priced compared to larger population centers. The University does provide one graduate/law housing complex.

■ Expenses and Financial Aid

➧ *tuition & fees—full-time, $16,120 (31 credits per year); part-time, $11,040 (20 credits per year)*
➧ *estimated additional expenses—$11,150 (books, $850; room and board, $6,400; personal, $2,950; transportation, $950)*
➧ *academic and need-based scholarships available*
➧ *minority scholarships available: full tuition minority waivers, $5,000 renewable scholarships, Thomas More scholarships*
➧ *financial aid available; FAF SA (needed for all types) due May 1* ➧ *loans available—Stafford, SLS, LAL*

Law school is a career investment. For the tuition, fees, and other costs incurred to attend Gonzaga University, each student is offered an opportunity for a quality legal education and a rewarding legal career. For those who need financial assistance to help fund this investment, Gonzaga University will assist in identifying and obtaining financial aid packages.

■ Career Services

The active Career Services Office is dedicated to assisting law students and alumni in planning careers and seeking employment throughout law school and in the course of their professional career. The size of the school allows the Career Services Director the opportunity to work individually with students and alumni in their job searches. Entering students are pleased to learn Gonzaga participates in federal and state work-study programs and provides interns to more than 200 Spokane law firms and numerous government agencies.

Applicant Group for the 1995-1996 Academic Year

Gonzaga University School of Law
This grid includes only applicants who earned 120-180 LSAT scores under standard administrations.

LSAT Score	GPA 3.75 +		3.50 - 3.74		3.25 - 3.49		3.00 - 3.24		2.75 - 2.99		2.50 - 2.74		2.25 - 2.49		2.00 - 2.24		Below 2.00		No GPA		Total	
	Apps	Adm	Apps	Adm	Apps	Adm	Apps	Adm	Apps	Adm	Apps	Adm	Apps	Adm	Apps	Adm	Apps	Adm	Apps	Adm	Apps	Adm
175 - 180	0	0	0	0	0	0	0	0	0	0	0	0	0	0	0	0	0	0	0	0	0	0
170 - 174	0	0	2	2	0	0	0	0	0	0	0	0	1	1	0	0	0	0	0	0	3	3
165 - 169	1	1	2	2	1	1	0	0	4	4	6	3	2	2	1	1	0	0	0	0	17	14
160 - 164	8	8	9	8	15	15	15	14	10	9	10	9	2	2	4	4	0	0	1	1	74	70
155 - 159	17	17	23	20	38	37	55	54	51	51	34	28	16	15	4	3	0	0	1	1	239	226
150 - 154	13	13	44	40	73	71	109	103	94	84	63	38	41	25	10	4	4	1	5	2	456	381
145 - 149	10	9	32	26	68	42	76	35	76	17	58	6	23	2	10	1	2	0	3	3	358	141
140 - 144	3	0	11	3	23	2	46	1	40	3	35	4	21	0	5	0	2	0	4	2	190	15
135 - 139	1	0	4	2	5	0	8	0	14	1	24	1	12	0	8	0	1	0	2	0	79	4
130 - 134	0	0	1	0	5	0	4	0	2	0	8	0	3	0	2	0	0	0	1	0	26	0
125 - 129	0	0	0	0	0	0	0	0	0	0	2	0	1	0	0	0	0	0	0	0	3	0
120 - 124	0	0	0	0	0	0	0	0	0	0	0	0	0	0	0	0	1	0	0	0	1	0
Total	53	48	128	103	228	168	313	207	291	169	240	89	122	47	44	13	10	1	17	9	1446	854

Apps = Number of Applicants
Adm = Number Admitted
Reflects 98% of the total applicant pool.

Hamline University School of Law

1536 Hewitt Avenue
St. Paul, MN 55104

E-Mail: lawadm@seq.hamline.edu
URL: http://www.hamline.edu
Phone: 612.641.2461 or 800.388.3688

■ Introduction

Hamline University School of Law is known for its strong commitment to social issues and comprehensive legal education. The school offers a curriculum in which analytical ability, lawyering skills and ethical sensitivity are carefully integrated. Law students are afforded the intellectual and social advantages of participation in the larger community of Hamline University with its rich heritage dating back to 1854. The School of Law is the only private, university-affiliated law school in the state, and is a member of the Association of American Law Schools. The beautiful 44-acre Hamline campus is located in a residential neighborhood midway between the downtowns of St. Paul and Minneapolis. The Twin Cities of St. Paul and Minneapolis are frequently cited as two of the nations "most livable" cities. Thirty-nine of the largest businesses in Fortune magazine are headquartered here, and the state capital is just minutes away from the campus.

■ Enrollment/Student Body

➽ 1,614 applicants ➽ 229 enrolled first-year class 1995 ➽ 590 total full-time ➽ 12% minority ➽ 50% women ➽ 48 states & foreign countries represented ➽ 188 undergraduate schools represented ➽ average age first-year class 1995—27

■ Faculty

➽ 29 full-time ➽ 44 part-time or adjunct ➽ 11 full-time women ➽ 2 full-time minority ➽ 6 legal writing instructors

88 practicum mentor-attorneys bring the experience of their day-to-day practice into the educational program.

■ Library and Physical Facilities

➽ 220,000 volumes & equivalents ➽ cooperative borrowing between local law libraries and local college libraries ➽ LEXIS ➽ NEXIS ➽ WESTLAW ➽ DIALOG ➽ 5 full-time librarians ➽ library seats 360 ➽ computerized catalog system which also searches the holdings of local university and reference libraries

The School of Law is accessible to persons with disabilities and housed in a modern, award-winning law center.

■ Curriculum

➽ Academic Support Program ➽ 120 courses available ➽ combined degrees available: J.D./M.A.P.A. (Master of Arts in Public Administration); J.D./M.B.A. with the University of St. Thomas ➽ full-time program only ➽ semesters, start in Aug. ➽ range of first-year class size—41-73 ➽ 3 daytime scheduling options first-year, 3-year program, 2-1/2 with summer school

First-year students may select a traditional all-day schedule or may elect to block their classes in either the morning or the afternoon. First-year students may also choose to reduce their courseload by dropping one course each semester, while continuing to be considered full-time students by ABA standards. These courses can be taken the following summer or in the next year.

■ General Practice Clinic

The School of Law operates a law clinic that functions as a typical small, general practice law office. Supervised by clinical instructors, students handle their own case load, from client counseling through the litigation, settlement, or mediation. Students represent clients in immigration, public interest, criminal defense, child advocacy, and family law mediation cases.

■ Practicum Program

Guided by a seasoned judge or attorney, students serve as interns in law offices, public agencies, and courtrooms in specialized areas such as child advocacy, criminal work, corporate practice, administrative law, and public interest practice.

■ Public Law

Extensive offerings in public law are available for those considering legislative, administrative, or public interest careers.

■ Alternative Dispute Resolution (ADR)

In addition to course offerings, Hamline sponsors a summer Dispute Resolution Institute, taught by nationally recognized scholars and practitioners in the ADR field.

■ Student Activities

The *Hamline Law Review* publishes articles by students, leading members of the academic community, and practicing attorneys.

The *Hamline Journal of Public Law and Policy* is a forum for public policy articles on state and federal legislative, executive, and administrative functions.

The faculty edited, *Journal of Law and Religion* has established an international reputation and publishes articles, colloquia, and essays of interest to the legal, ethical, and religious communities.

Participation in **Moot Court** offers students the opportunity to develop and refine writing and speaking skills for academic credit with the assistance of faculty members as well as members of the bench and bar. Hamline's teams have won numerous awards.

Student organizations are numerous and include organizations representing specialized areas of law.

■ Admission

➽ *Bachelor's degree required* ➽ *application deadline—May 15, rolling admission, early application preferred* ➽ *LSAT, LSDAS required* ➽ *median GPA—3.12* ➽ *median LSAT score—154* ➽ *application fee—$30* ➽ *summer conditional program, acceptance by performance*

All applications are reviewed by an admissions committee composed of faculty members, administrators, and students. Hamline's admissions policy is designed to maintain and enhance the diversity, vigor, social concern, professional dedication, and academic ability of the student body. Hamline is strongly committed to a student body diverse in its cultural, economic, racial, and ethnic composition and actively pursues such diversity.

The School of Law strives to maintain a selection process that emphasizes a fair examination of each person as an individual, not merely as a set of credentials. In addition to the LSAT and undergraduate GPA, the committee gives significant weight to motivation, personal experiences, employment history, graduate education, maturity, letters of recommendation, and the ability to articulate one's interest in and suitability for the study of law.

At the discretion of the Admissions Committee, a limited number of students whose objective factors qualify them for entrance directly into the fall program are given the opportunity to demonstrate their ability and earn a position in the fall entering class by successfully completing summer coursework. This Acceptance by Performance program serves as part of the admissions process, and participation in this program does not guarantee admission to Hamline as a degree candidate.

■ Expenses and Financial Aid

➽ *tuition & fees—$13,808* ➽ *estimated additional expenses—$3,322-$4,791 (on-campus housing and meal plan)* ➽ *merit-based scholarships* ➽ *minority scholarships*

■ Career Services

A wide variety of career-information programs and skills workshops are offered by our Career Services Office. Individualized counseling is also provided in areas such as interviewing, résumé writing, career assessment, and the development of job-search strategies. The office maintains extensive job listings for part-time, summer, and full-time employment. The 1994 Employment Survey showed 90 percent of those seeking employment employed in legally related positions six months after graduation.

Applicant Group for the 1995-1996 Academic Year

Hamline University School of Law
This grid includes only applicants who earned 120-180 LSAT scores under standard administrations.

LSAT Score	GPA 3.75 +		3.50 - 3.74		3.25 - 3.49		3.00 - 3.24		2.75 - 2.99		2.50 - 2.74		2.25 - 2.49		2.00 - 2.24		Below 2.00		No GPA		Total	
	Apps	Adm	Apps	Adm	Apps	Adm	Apps	Adm	Apps	Adm	Apps	Adm	Apps	Adm	Apps	Adm	Apps	Adm	Apps	Adm	Apps	Adm
175 - 180	0	0	1	1	0	0	0	0	0	0	0	0	0	0	0	0	0	0	0	0	1	1
170 - 174	2	2	1	1	0	0	0	0	0	0	0	0	1	1	0	0	0	0	0	0	4	4
165 - 169	1	1	5	5	2	1	8	8	5	4	1	1	2	1	2	1	0	0	0	0	26	22
160 - 164	6	6	10	10	15	13	20	20	17	16	9	6	5	4	4	1	1	1	1	1	88	78
155 - 159	12	12	25	24	32	32	49	46	42	36	37	22	22	11	4	2	3	1	2	1	228	187
150 - 154	21	19	37	37	77	67	96	71	75	38	58	22	35	10	15	5	4	0	9	3	427	272
145 - 149	8	5	30	18	59	19	84	22	82	13	76	10	30	4	15	2	3	1	6	2	393	96
140 - 144	4	1	12	1	26	5	56	11	56	3	45	3	32	1	12	0	5	0	2	0	250	25
135 - 139	2	0	6	0	10	1	16	0	24	2	24	1	26	1	13	0	2	0	4	1	127	6
130 - 134	1	0	2	0	3	0	2	0	8	0	8	1	6	0	4	0	0	0	3	0	37	1
125 - 129	0	0	0	0	0	0	1	0	3	0	3	0	0	0	1	0	0	0	0	0	8	0
120 - 124	0	0	0	0	0	0	0	0	0	0	1	0	0	0	0	0	0	0	0	0	1	0
Total	57	46	129	97	224	138	332	178	312	112	262	66	159	33	70	11	18	3	27	8	1590	692

Apps = Number of Applicants
Adm = Number Admitted
Reflects 98% of the total applicant pool.
This grid includes applicants admitted through our Acceptance By Performance summer conditional program.

Harvard University Law School

1563 Massachusetts Avenue
Cambridge, MA 02138

Phone: 617.495.3109

■ Introduction

Harvard Law School, established in 1817, is the oldest existing law school in the United States. It is located, along with most other parts of Harvard University, in Cambridge, Massachusetts. The school offers a diverse curriculum intended to provide comprehensive training for those who wish to become legal practitioners, as well as those interested in public service, law teaching, and legal scholarship. Through its faculty, students, and graduates, Harvard seeks to make substantial contributions toward solving the complex legal problems confronting our society.

■ Enrollment/Student Body

➽ 6,800 applicants ➽ 843 admitted first-year class 1995 ➽ 559 enrolled first-year class 1995 ➽ 1,658 total full-time J.D., 145 total LL.M. ➽ 27.1% minority ➽ 41% women ➽ 50 states & 20 foreign countries represented (J.D.) ➽ 53 foreign countries (LL.M.) ➽ 275 undergraduate schools represented

■ Faculty

➽ 158 total ➽ 105 full-time ➽ 53 part-time or adjunct ➽ 54 women ➽ 23 minority

■ Library & Physical Facilities

➽ 1,847,567 volumes & equivalents ➽ library hours: Mon.-Thurs., 8:30 A.M.-MIDNIGHT; Fri.-Sat., 8:30 A.M.-9:00 P.M.; Sun., NOON-MIDNIGHT ➽ LEXIS (home access avail.) ➽ NEXIS (home access avail.) ➽ WESTLAW (home access avail.) ➽ 32 full-time librarians ➽ library seats 901

The school occupies 21 buildings that include dormitories, dining facilities, classrooms, and offices. Through the public access catalog, many online research systems are available. Included are DIALOG, RLIN, Vu/Text, Dow-Jones News/Retrieval, Legi-Slate, and Legal Resources Index, among others.

■ Curriculum

➽ Academic Support Program ➽ 82 credits required to graduate ➽ 225 courses available ➽ degrees available: J.D.; LL.M.; S.J.D.; J.D./M.B.A.; J.D./M.A.L.D.; J.D./M.P.P.; J.D./Ph.D. and numerous other concurrent degrees ➽ cross-registration possibilities with other Harvard graduate schools ➽ range of first-year class size—45-135

Our basic aim is to train students to be lawyers. The emphasis is not on any particular type of law; the curriculum includes courses in civil liberties as well as corporate finance, international trade as well as criminal law, and taxation as well as legal services for the poor. Nor is the curriculum oriented toward mastering detail or teaching the law "as it is." Law reform, legal philosophy, the historical development of legal institutions—all of these subjects and many more are important fields of study for an educated member of the profession. Since the law changes often and the problems lawyers face vary endlessly, it is more important to master the enduring principles of law, its methods of reasoning, and its process of development and change rather than the law as it is currently written.

The first-year curriculum is designed to give each student a thorough grounding in the basic intellectual processes of legal reasoning and analysis. It consists of criminal law, contracts, civil procedure, torts, property, a legal methods course including Ames moot court work, and an elective course during the second semester. Except for a required paper and a course in professional responsibility, the second and third years of the J.D. degree program are entirely elective.

■ Special Programs

Special research and study programs of particular interest to students in the J.D. program include the Criminal Justice Institute, the East Asian Legal Studies Program, the Islamic Legal Studies Program, the Human Rights Program, the Program on International Financial Systems, the European Law Research Center, the Program in Law and Economics, the Program on the Legal Profession, and the Program on Negotiation.

■ Admission

➽ Bachelor's degree from accredited college or university required ➽ rolling admission, early application preferred ➽ LSAT, LSDAS required ➽ application fees—$50/$65/$75

A main goal of our selection process is to enroll the ablest student body possible. To do this, we try to understand each applicant's academic and personal achievements, and compare these achievements to those of all other applicants. In understanding these factors, we evaluate all information in each applicant's file including transcripts, extracurricular and community activities, work experience, personal background, letters of recommendation, personal statements, and LSAT scores. Background factors such as demonstrated societal, economic, educational, or personal disadvantage the candidate has overcome often help the committee to fully understand applicants' achievements.

Our admission standards are set only by the comparative quality of our applicants, not by an absolute minimum level of achievement. All completed applications receive full consideration for admission. We have no computational methods for making admissions decisions, no mechanical shortcuts, no substitutes for careful assessment and good judgment. We encourage all those who would like to study law at Harvard to apply. We actively encourage applications from minority groups, women, older candidates, and others who are well qualified, but who might not seek admission for financial, geographic, or other reasons.

Please see the applicant group section for further information about the selection process.

■ Student Activities

Law-related activities at Harvard Law School are diverse and numerous. They include 12 law student publications—*Harvard Law Review, Harvard Journal on Legislation, Negotiation Journal, Harvard International Law Journal, Harvard Civil Rights-Civil Liberties Law Review, Harvard Environmental Law Review, Harvard Women's Law Journal, Harvard Journal of Law and Public Policy, Harvard Human Rights Journal, Harvard Latino Law Review, Harvard Black-letter Journal,* and *Harvard Journal of Law and Technology—as* well as the Board of Student Advisers (which administers the Ames moot court and alternative programs), the Legislative Research Bureau, International Law Society, Civil Liberties Union, and Student Bar Association. Massachusetts allows law students to represent the indigent of the Commonwealth in the district courts. There are three curricular-based organizations that represent indigent clients under this provision. They include the Criminal Justice Institute, the Legal Services Clinic, and the Immigration Clinic. In addition, there are five extracurricular student-practice organizations which allow students similar opportunities—the Harvard Legal Aid Bureau, Harvard Defenders, Prison Legal Assistance Project, Students for Public Interest Law, and the Harvard Mediation Program. Other activities are the *Law School Record* (America's oldest law school newspaper); Law School Forum; Yearbook; Drama Society; Harvard Black Law Students Association; Harvard Environmental Law Society; Lambda; La Alianza; Native American Law Students Association; Asian American Law Students Association; Women's Law Association, and more than 35 other student organizations not mentioned above.

■ Expenses and Financial Aid

➽ *tuition & fees—full-time, $21,134* ➽ *estimated additional expenses—$12,446 (room, board, living expenses, books & supplies)* ➽ *scholarships and financial aid available*

All students who demonstrate financial need according to a combination of federal and institutional guidelines receive assistance. Our program includes the Low Income Protection Plan, which provides partial forgiveness of loans to graduates who pursue public interest and other low-paid law-related careers.

■ Career Services

Our placement office assists students in obtaining permanent, part-time, and summer positions. Recently the employment pattern at graduation has been—law firms, 60 percent; judicial clerkships, 26 percent; federal, state, and local government, 2 percent; legal services, 3 percent; and teaching, further education, corporations, and other positions, 9 percent. Sixty-seven percent of each year's class locates in New York; Washington, DC; Massachusetts; or California; the remainder locates in about 33 other states and several foreign countries. In the past few years, 97 percent of the graduates have accepted offers for employment or further education by the time of graduation.

Applicant Group for the 1995-1996 Academic Year

We do not provide a profile chart of applicants considered and admitted because it is based solely upon undergraduate GPA and LSAT scores. Our admissions process takes many factors besides college grades and LSAT scores into account, and is far too complex to be represented fairly or completely by a two-factor profile.

At no point on any objective scale of qualifications are the chances for admission to Harvard Law School 0 or 100 percent. A number of applicants with relatively low UGPAs or LSAT scores are offered admission each year while a significant proportion of candidates with very high grades and/or LSAT scores are not admitted.

University of Hawai'i at Mānoa—William S. Richardson School of Law

2515 Dole Street
Honolulu, HI 96822
Phone: 808.956.3000

■ Introduction

Established in 1973, the University of Hawai'i School of Law is located in Honolulu on the main campus of Hawai'i's nine-campus system. As the only law school in the state, its primary purpose is to equip degree candidates for active, effective, and creative participation as lawyers in both the private and public sectors. The school has ABA accreditation and membership in AALS.

Some unique and differentiating features of this law school are: its small size and close interaction among faculty, students, and the Hawai'i legal community; its emphasis on and resources for environmental/ocean law, Pacific-Asian legal systems, and elder law; its standing as perhaps the most racially and ethnically diverse law school in the country; and its graduation requirement of 60 hours of law-related community service.

■ Enrollment/Student Body

➠ 782 applicants ➠ 146 admitted first-year class 1995 ➠ 74 enrolled first-year class 1995 ➠ 241 total full-time ➠ 72.2% minority ➠ 49% women ➠ 24 states & foreign countries represented ➠ 95 undergraduate schools represented

The student body reflects Hawai'i's diversity. Students represent the following race/ethnic groups: African American, Caucasian, Chinese, Filipino, Hispanic, Japanese, Korean, native American, native Hawaiian, Micronesian, Samoan, Fijian, Laotian, and Vietnamese. A number of students come from Japan, China, Guam, Samoa, Yap, and Palau.

■ Curriculum

➠ 89 credits required to graduate, 42 of which are nonelective ➠ approximately 80 courses available ➠ degrees available: J.D.; J.D./M.B.A.; J.D./M.A. Asian Studies; J.D./Masters in Urban & Regional Planning ➠ semesters, start in Aug. (new students) and Jan. (transfers & visiting students) ➠ range of first-year class size—12-75 ➠ 6 semesters of full-time residency ➠ other dual degree programs can be arranged

The J.D. program is a three-year program of full-time day study. Full-time registration is defined as enrollment for a minimum of 12 credits each semester. First-year students begin with a one-week orientation; the first-year curriculum is entirely prescribed. All students must fulfill 60 hours of pro bono law-related community service in order to graduate.

■ Faculty

➠ 44 total ➠ 18 full-time ➠ 26 part-time or adjunct ➠ 7 women ➠ 13 minority

■ Library and Physical Facilities

➠ 234,551 volumes & equivalents ➠ library hours: Mon.-Thurs., 8:00 A.M.-9:00 P.M.; Fri., 8:00 A.M.-5:00 P.M.; Sat., 9:00 A.M.-5:00 P.M.; Sun., 1:00 P.M.-9:00 P.M. ➠ LEXIS ➠ NEXIS ➠ WESTLAW ➠ 5 full-time librarians ➠ library seats 392

The library contains a study carrel for each student and seminar/discussion rooms for study groups. Law students have full access to all facilities of the university, including the health, counseling and computing centers, and athletic facilities.

■ Pacific-Asian Legal Studies

Because of Hawai'i's location, population, culture, and economic relationships, the law school faculty is developing a program in Pacific-Asian Legal Studies (PALS). The program has the two-fold purpose of conducting new research and enriching the J.D. curriculum. A number of faculty have expertise in Pacific/Asian research, teaching, and consultation. Recent and occasional course offerings in PALS have included Chinese Business Law, Chinese Law and Society, Pacific Island Legal Systems, Korean Law, Japanese Criminal Law, and Japanese Trade Law. Law students have full access to all facilities of the university, including the health, counseling and computing centers, and athletic facilities. The Certificate in Pacific-Asian Legal Studies allows students to focus elective coursework and earn the certificate in addition to the J.D.

The program benefits from a faculty exchange with the Hiroshima, Japan, Law Faculty. A unique offering is the opportunity for selected students to do a full semester externship for academic credit with the court systems in certain Pacific Island nations. Students may also arrange a semester of study with certain law faculties in Asia with prior approval.

■ Environmental/Ocean Law Programs

Students may focus their elective courses in the area of environmental law and earn the Certificate in Environmental Law along with the J.D. degree. Emphasis is on fresh water resources, oceans, coastal waters, and land use—all areas of special interest to Hawai'i and the Pacific.

The University of Hawai'i has unusually extensive programs in different types of marine research, and the law faculty is equally interested in ocean law and policy. Law students may elect to combine their J.D. studies with a university certificate program in Ocean Policy. The university also offers a certificate in Resource Management.

■ Admission

➠ Bachelor's degree from an accredited college or university required ➠ application deadline—Feb. 16 (firm) ➠ LSAT, LSDAS required ➠ median GPA—3.55 ➠ median LSAT score—161 ➠ application fee—$30 pending Regent's approval

Admission is determined by an applicant's academic achievement, aptitude for the study of law, and professional promise. Preference is given to residents of Hawai'i and to those with strong ties to or special interest in

Hawai'i or the Asia-Pacific region. Besides LSAT and undergraduate GPA and major, other factors considered are: academic work beyond the bachelor's degree, work experience, writing ability, community service, class diversity, and unusual accomplishments.

Applications from students wishing to transfer, or from those wishing to visit for a semester or two, are considered on a space-available basis for both August and January admission.

■ Expenses and Financial Aid

➧ *1995-96 tuition & fees—resident, $2,500; nonresident, 8,280; significant increases are pending for 1996-97* ➧ *estimated minimum annual living expenses—$9,000* ➧ *financial aid administered by Central University of Hawai'i Financial Aid Office, deadline—March 1* ➧ *FAFSA required for financial aid* ➧ *1996-97 tuition & fees—resident, $5,000 (est.); nonresident, $12,000 (est.); both pending final Regent's action*

■ Student Activities

A student editorial board publishes the *University of Hawai'i Law Review* while other students participate in the moot court program, including national moot court competitions in international and environmental law. The 1993 Jessup International Moot Court Team placed first in the nation and second in international competition. The 1994 Jessup Team again won the Northwest Region and finished among the top teams in the national rounds while the 1995 Jessup Team captured the Pacific Regional championship and won first place honors for Best Memorial in the international competition. The 1995 Environmental Team placed among the top ten (of 80) in the nation.

Other students are active in a variety of organizations within the school and the Honolulu community including: Advocates for Public Interest Law (APIL), the American Bar Association Student Division, American Inns of Court, Student Bar Association, Phi Delta Phi and Delta Theta Phi International Legal Fraternities, the Pacific Islands and Pacific-Asian Legal Studies Organizations, Association of Women Law Students, and Environmental Law Society. Student affinity groups include the Filipino Law Students Association and the *'Ahahui 'O Hawai'i*, an organization of native Hawaiian law students.

■ Career Services

Career counseling and services are provided to students and alumni for part-time, summer clerk, or associate positions in both the public and private sectors. Placement emphasis is almost exclusively on Hawai'i and the Asia/Pacific region, since about 90 percent of our graduates remain here. On-campus facilities are available for interviews. All large firms in Honolulu and many medium and small firms participate in the fall on-campus interview season for second- and third-year students. Most recent graduating classes have had a 85-90 percent employment rate six months after graduation.

Applicant Group for the 1995-1996 Academic Year

University of Hawai'i at Mānoa—William S. Richardson School of Law
This grid includes only applicants who earned 120-180 LSAT scores under standard administrations in the 1992-1995 testing period.

LSAT Score	GPA 3.75 & Up		3.50 - 3.74		3.25 - 3.49		3.00 - 3.24		2.75 - 2.99		2.50 - 2.74		2.25 - 2.49		2.00 - 2.24		Below 2.00		No GPA		Totals	
	Apps	Adm	Apps	Adm	Apps	Adm	Apps	Adm	Apps	Adm	Apps	Adm	Apps	Adm	Apps	Adm	Apps	Adm	Apps	Adm	Apps	Adm
170- 180	2	1	2	2	3	3	2	0	2	0	0	0	0	0	0	0	0	0	0	0	11	6
165 - 169	5	5	8	7	8	7	8	2	3	2	1	0	4	2	0	0	0	0	1	1	38	26
160 - 164	15	12	26	20	22	9	20	9	14	6	7	0	2	0	0	0	0	0	1	1	107	57
155 - 159	17	8	27	9	33	6	28	4	16	2	8	1	2	0	2	0	0	0	3	1	136	31
150 - 154	17	5	37	9	40	7	27	0	38	0	18	0	6	0	2	0	0	0	3	2	188	23
145 - 149	4	0	12	1	24	0	25	0	21	0	13	0	8	0	3	0	1	0	3	0	114	1
140 - 144	1	0	6	0	10	0	7	0	14	0	10	0	8	0	4	0	2	0	2	0	64	0
Below 140	0	0	1	0	4	0	3	0	11	0	6	0	4	0	3	0	1	0	3	0	36	0
Total	61	31	119	48	144	32	120	15	119	10	63	1	34	2	14	0	4	0	16	5	694	144

Apps = Number of Applicants
Adm = Number Admitted
Figures reflect admission decisions as of 9/29/95. They do not include students admitted from the Pre-Admission Program nor those files that were left incomplete by applicants. Combined figures are for both residents and nonresidents.

Hofstra University School of Law

Hempstead, NY 11550

Phone: 516.463.5916

■ Introduction

The Hofstra University School of Law is accredited by the ABA and is a member of the AALS. As a national law school, Hofstra provides a legal education designed to give students fundamental professional training and to prepare them for practice in any jurisdiction. Hofstra promotes considerable faculty/student contact and a strong sense of community.

■ Enrollment/Student Body

➧ *2,557 applicants* ➧ *1,144 admitted first-year class 1995* ➧ *290 enrolled first-year class 1995* ➧ *850 total full-time* ➧ *16.7% minority* ➧ *41% women* ➧ *18 states & foreign countries represented* ➧ *112 undergraduate schools represented*

■ Faculty

➧ *66 total* ➧ *42 full-time* ➧ *24 part-time or adjunct* ➧ *18 women* ➧ *5 minority*

One of Hofstra's greatest strengths is its faculty. The faculty are persons of academic distinction, and many of them are recognized as national authorities in their fields. They make it a point to be accessible to students outside of the traditional classroom setting. There are frequent lectures and scholarly activities emanating from the 17 endowed chairs and distinguished professorships.

■ Library and Physical Facilities

➧ *440,000 volumes & equivalents* ➧ *library hours: Mon.-Thurs., 8:00 A.M.-MIDNIGHT; Fri., 8:00 A.M.-9:00 P.M.; Sat., 9:00 A.M.-6:00 P.M.; Sun., NOON-MIDNIGHT* ➧ *LEXIS* ➧ *NEXIS* ➧ *WESTLAW* ➧ *DIALOG* ➧ *8 full-time librarians* ➧ *library seats 682*

■ Curriculum

➧ *Academic Support Program* ➧ *87 credits required to graduate* ➧ *degrees and combined degrees available: J.D.; J.D./M.B.A.* ➧ *semesters, start in late Aug.* ➧ *range of first-year class size—28-30 (small section); 117-120 (large section)*

■ Special Programs

Each entering student at Hofstra is placed in one small section of fewer than 30 students in a substantive course during the first semester of their first year. This small section experience enables a closer relationship between students and faculty in a seminar-like environment.

During the spring semester of their first year, students receive intensive instruction in legal research and writing. During the fall semester of their second year, students participate in the Appellate Advocacy Program, in which they receive instruction in persuasive writing and oral advocacy.

Each January, Hofstra students are able to select a three-credit course on trial techniques that is patterned on the program of the National Institute for Trial Advocacy. A carefully orchestrated sequence of exercises, covering every aspect of a trial from jury selection to closing arguments, builds the students' abilities so that they are able to conduct a full jury trial at the end of the course.

A courthouse of the United States District Court for the Eastern District of New York is located on the Hofstra campus. The court cooperates with the law school in various academic programs and offers the students additional educational and practical experiences.

Civil Externship Program—The Civil Externship Program provides students with opportunities to learn lawyering skills through placements in a variety of non-profit organizations or government agencies.

Criminal Externship Program—The Criminal Externship Program provides an opportunity for students to learn about all phases of criminal law practice through placements in such agencies as Nassau, Queens, and Kings County District Attorneys' offices and New York City, Nassau County, and Suffolk Legal Aid offices. Students work approximately 15 hours per week.

Alternative Dispute Resolution Clinic—The goals of the Alternative Dispute Resolution Clinic are to teach mediation skills, provide clinically supervised mediation experience, and provide direction in the advanced study of theoretical, legal, ethical, and practical issues posed by the use of mediation as an alternative to litigation. The students, under direct faculty supervision, mediate disputes at the Queens Mediation Center concerning claims of property damage and personal injury, consumer and landlord-tenant disagreements, and noise and"lifestyle" disputes.

Criminal Justice Clinic—This program is a one-semester clinic in which students represent defendants in criminal cases in Nassau County District Court and in Hempstead and Mineola Village courts. Students represent clients in pretrial conferences, witness interviewing, motion and brief writing, case investigations, and trials—from jury selection through verdict.

Judicial Externship Program—The Judicial Externship Program provides an opportunity for students to serve as apprentices to state and federal judges for a semester. As judicial externs, for approximately 15 hours per week, students do research, write memoranda, observe court proceedings, and discuss cases with their judge.

Disabilities Law Clinic—The Disabilities Law Clinic is a new clinic that began handling cases in the fall of 1992. The clinic focuses principally on cases involving the Americans with Disabilities Act of 1990, transportation cases, public access cases, and employment discrimination cases.

Environmental Law Clinic—This program provides an opportunity to work on current environmental issues with public interest law firms, state or local environmental agencies, and private practitioners engaged in pro bono work in the field.

Housing Rights Clinic—Students handle a wide variety of housing cases for low-income clients, including defenses of eviction cases; actions by tenants against landlords challenging substandard conditions in their apartments; fair housing and exclusionary zoning cases; public utility shut-off cases; and work on behalf of community groups for housing rehabilitation. The course develops lawyering skills with special emphasis on litigation strategy, pretrial and trial preparation, and trial advocacy.

Pro Bono Student Lawyers Project— The Pro Bono Student Lawyers Project places students with a variety of existing agencies, service organizations, law firms, and private practitioners. Students in the program volunteer their time without compensation or credit to work on pro bono cases.

Unemployment Action Center—The Unemployment Action Center (UAC) is a nonprofit, student-run corporation that offers free advice and representation to persons denied unemployment benefits. The Unemployment Action Center received the New York State Bar Association Law Student Pro Bono Award for 1992.

■ Admission

- *Bachelor's degree required for admission*
- *application deadline—April 15*
- *modified rolling admission*
- *LSAT, LSDAS required*
- *median GPA—3.30*
- *median LSAT score—157*
- *application fee—$60*

■ Student Activities

Hofstra students publish three journals. The *Hofstra Law Review* enjoys national renown and an international circulation. The *Labor Law Journal* publishes scholarly articles on various aspects of labor and employment law. The *Law and Policy Symposium* focuses on an analysis of a single issue from various perspectives. The inaugural issue will cover state constitutions. Other student organizations include Asian Pacific American Law Students Association (APALSA); Black Law Students Association (BLSA); Coming Out For Civil Rights; *Conscience* (the law school's student newspaper); *Environmental Law Digest*; Environmental Law Society; Federalist Society; Gaelic Law Students Society; Hofstra Law Women; Italian Law Students Association (ILSA); International Law Society; Jewish Law Students Association (JLSA); Lambda Alpha International; Latino-Latina American Law Students Association (LALSA); Phi Alpha Delta (PAD); *Pocket Part* (the law school yearbook); Public Justice Foundation; Republican Law Students Association; Sports & Entertainment Law Group; Student Bar Association; Trial Advocacy Club; and Unemployment Action Center.

■ Expenses and Financial Aid

- *tuition & fees—$19,454*
- *financial aid and scholarships available*

■ Career Services

The Office of Career Services provides a wide range of services to facilitate job placement. The senior assistant dean for career services and the director organize recruitment programs, conduct job development campaigns, teach résumé writing and interviewing techniques, provide career counseling to students and alumni, and maintain employment statistics.

Admission Profile Not Available

University of Houston Law Center

Office of Admissions
4800 Calhoun
Houston, TX 77204-6391

URL: http://www.lawlib.uh.edu/
Phone: 713.743.1070

■ Introduction

The University of Houston Law Center is located at the University of Houston. Located three miles south of downtown, the campus extends over 550 acres of wooded terrain. The state-assisted Law Center, located in the nation's sixth largest legal market, is noted throughout the South and Southwest not only for its excellence, but for its progressive and innovative approach to the teaching of law. The College of Law, the academic branch of the Law Center, is fully accredited by the American Bar Association and the American Association of Law Schools and has a chapter of the Order of the Coif, the national legal honorary scholastic society. The Law Center confers a J.D. degree as a first degree in law and a Masters of Law (LL.M.) degree to students pursuing work beyond the J.D. degree.

■ Enrollment/Student Body

➽ *3,048 applicants* ➽ *861 admitted first-year class 1995* ➽ *302 enrolled first-year class 1995* ➽ *811 total full-time* ➽ *251 total first-year full-time* ➽ *207 total part-time* ➽ *61 total first-year part-time* ➽ *20% minority* ➽ *40% women* ➽ *142 undergraduate schools represented* ➽ *129 students enrolled in LL.M. program*

■ Faculty

➽ *143 total* ➽ *48 full-time* ➽ *95 part-time* ➽ *29 women* ➽ *7 minority*

■ Library and Physical Facilities

➽ *400,000 volumes & equivalents* ➽ *10 full-time librarians* ➽ *LEXIS* ➽ *WESTLAW* ➽ *full access to Internet and World Wide Web* ➽ *Special Collections in International Law with emphasis on Latin America, Admiralty, Tax, Labor, Oil & Gas, and Mexican Law*

■ Curriculum/Basic Program of Study

➽ *88 credits required to graduate* ➽ *Academic Enrichment Program* ➽ *215 courses available* ➽ *full-time class starts early fall* ➽ *part-time (evening) class starts early summer*

The first-year curriculum at the Law Center is prescribed. Students are also required to complete a course in professional responsibility and one major piece of legal research and writing before graduation. Emphasis is placed on legal theory and the varying approaches to the law.

■ Special Programs

➽ *concurrent degree programs: J.D./M.B.A.; J.D./M.A. in History; J.D./M.P.H.; J.D./Ph.D. in Medical Humanities* ➽ *LL.M. degrees offered in Health Law, International Law, Intellectual Property Law; Energy, Environmental, and Natural Resources Law; and Tax Law*

The University of Houston Law Center emphasizes current legal and administrative problems confronting the region and nation, including intellectual property law, environmental law, energy law, tax law, health law, and international law, with an emphasis on Latin America. The Law Center is home to the Health Law & Policy Institute, a research and instruction center on interdisciplinary issues. The Law Center is also host to the Intellectual Property Program, the Trial Advocacy Institute, the Environmental Liability Law Curriculum, the Institute for Higher Education Law and Governance, and the International Law Institute. The Law Center operates the Mexican Legal Studies Program, an annual summer school in Mexico for students interested in the Mexican legal system, particularly as it applies to foreign investors seeking to do business in Mexico. The Law Center also offers the broadest law curriculum of any law school in Texas.

■ Clinical Programs and Trial Advocacy

The Law Center offers a wide variety of clinical course offerings. Students can choose among different areas of concentration, such as agency or judicial internships; health or environmental law; and criminal prosecution or defense. The Law Center houses the Legal Aid Clinic, which gives students clinic opportunities in providing legal services to the indigent. The Law Center also offers skills training in both civil and criminal trial and appellate advocacy. The Trial Advocacy Institute oversees the design and implementation of trial advocacy courses at the Law Center.

■ Activities

The Student Bar Association has input into every facet of student life at the Law Center. The SBA participates in the first-year orientation, organizes the annual charity Fun-Run, aids in the selection of student representatives to sit on various faculty committees, and presents student attitudes and views of development both within and outside the Law Center.

The Law Center features an extensive moot court program, an active chapter of Phi Delta Phi, as well as the *Law Review* and the *Houston Journal of International Law*, two student-run scholarly publications.

Other student organizations include the Association of Women in Law, Black Law Students Association, Hispanic Law Students Association, Asian Law Students Association, Mandamus (Gay & Lesbian Student Organization), Lex Judaica (Jewish students), public interest law organizations, Health Law Organization, Intellectual Property Student Organization, and Environmental Law Society.

■ Student Body

The student body consists of approximately 1,100 persons from across the United States, although most students come from Texas and the Southwest. There is no provisional acceptance.

■ Admission

➽ *Bachelor's degree from an accredited university*
➽ *application deadline—Feb. 1* ➽ *LSAT, LSDAS required*
➽ *median GPA—3.28* ➽ *median LSAT score—159*
➽ *application fee—$50*

A completed application and LSDAS report must be furnished to the Law Center before February 1 to guarantee consideration for the following fall or summer semesters. Only new-scale LSAT scores will be accepted for consideration. Admission is based primarily on the applicant's test results and academic record. Multiple LSAT scores are averaged. Approximately 30 percent of students are admitted based on consideration of additional factors including background or career, graduate work, honors, ethnicity, extracurricular activities, employment, and a personal statement as requested on the application. The Law Center attempts to obtain broad diversity among students, and thus welcomes applications from those who will bring different perspectives to the Law Center.

■ Expenses and Financial Aid

➽ *tuition & fees—full-time resident, $4,959; nonresident, $8,836* ➽ *estimated additional expenses (room, board, and books)—$6,236* ➽ *merit scholarships available*
➽ *FAFSA for need analysis*

The Law Center forwards financial aid materials to applicants once they are accepted. The Financial Aid Counselor will assist accepted applicants with their questions. Once accepted, all applicants are automatically considered for merit scholarships.

■ Career Services

The Law Center's Career Services Office actively assists students and graduates in legal career planning. The office annually hosts prospective employers in on-campus interview and recruiting programs for second- and third-year students seeking summer clerkships and permanent positions. The Career Services Office receives notices of part-time and full-time positions available within the legal community, which are maintained for student review, and maintains a wide variety of resources such as legal directories, employers' résumés, and legal career planning publications.

Applicant Group for the 1995-1996 Academic Year

University of Houston Law Center
This grid includes only applicants who earned 120-180 LSAT scores under standard administrations.

	GPA																					
LSAT Score	3.75 +		3.50 - 3.74		3.25 - 3.49		3.00 - 3.24		2.75 - 2.99		2.50 - 2.74		2.25 - 2.49		2.00 - 2.24		Below 2.00		No GPA		Total	
	Apps	Adm	Apps	Adm	Apps	Adm	Apps	Adm	Apps	Adm	Apps	Adm	Apps	Adm	Apps	Adm	Apps	Adm	Apps	Adm	Apps	Adm
175 - 180	1	1	0	0	1	1	0	0	3	3	0	0	0	0	0	0	0	0	0	0	5	5
170 - 174	1	1	3	3	3	3	3	3	6	6	0	0	4	4	0	0	0	0	0	0	20	20
165 - 169	11	10	16	16	27	25	30	29	25	21	11	9	9	3	2	1	1	0	0	0	132	114
160 - 164	20	20	63	62	86	84	75	71	63	36	30	8	21	2	2	0	0	0	4	1	364	284
155 - 159	61	61	100	90	164	90	148	48	88	11	66	2	25	0	8	0	0	0	5	1	665	303
150 - 154	49	37	106	24	143	16	184	17	128	10	90	4	43	1	10	0	5	0	7	2	765	111
145 - 149	13	2	53	7	90	1	121	4	95	2	70	0	34	0	22	0	4	0	3	0	505	16
140 - 144	6	0	13	0	46	2	57	1	60	0	63	1	45	0	21	0	3	0	9	0	323	4
135 - 139	1	0	4	0	14	0	30	0	33	0	40	0	32	0	15	0	2	0	8	0	179	0
130 - 134	0	0	0	0	2	0	4	0	8	0	15	0	9	0	10	0	4	0	3	0	55	0
125 - 129	0	0	1	0	0	0	2	0	1	0	1	0	5	0	1	0	0	0	2	0	13	0
120 - 124	0	0	0	0	0	0	0	0	1	0	0	0	0	0	0	0	0	0	0	0	1	0
Total	163	132	359	202	576	222	654	173	511	89	386	24	227	10	91	1	19	0	41	4	3027	857

Apps = Number of Applicants
Adm = Number Admitted
Reflects 99% of the total applicant pool.

Howard University School of Law

2900 Van Ness Street, NW
Washington, DC 20006

Phone: 202.806.8008

■ Introduction

Howard University, a coeducational, private institution in Washington, DC, was chartered by the U.S. Congress in 1867. Howard is a historically black institution that offers an educational experience of exceptional quality and value to students with high academic potential. Particular emphasis is placed on providing educational opportunities for promising African Americans and other persons of color who have been underrepresented in the legal profession, and non-minority persons with a strong interest in civil and human rights, as well as public service. The law school has a diverse student body and faculty. The main campus of Howard is located in northwest Washington. The law school is located on a separate 22-acre campus, also in northwest Washington, approximately three miles from the main campus. Howard University School of Law is fully approved by the American Bar Association and the Association of American Law Schools, and certifies its graduates for bar examination in all jurisdictions of the United States.

■ Enrollment

➧ *1,591 applicants* ➧ *384 admitted first-year class 1995* ➧ *156 enrolled first-year class 1995* ➧ *443 total full-time* ➧ *93.2% minority* ➧ *56% women* ➧ *38 states & foreign countries represented* ➧ *81 undergraduate schools represented* ➧ *30 different undergraduate majors represented*

■ Student Body

There are 428 full-time students in the J.D. Program. Another 15 students participate full-time in the M.C.J. program. They come from all parts of the United States, as well as Asia, Africa, Canada, and the Caribbean. The academic attrition rate is six percent. Attrition for other reasons is approximately another four percent.

■ Faculty

➧ *46 total* ➧ *29 full-time* ➧ *17 part-time or adjunct* ➧ *13 women* ➧ *38 people of color* ➧ *5 legal writing*

■ Library & Physical Facilities

➧ *250,000 volumes & equivalents* ➧ *library hours: Mon.-Thurs., 8:00 A.M.-MIDNIGHT; Fri., 8:00 A.M.-9:00 P.M.; Sat., 9:00 A.M.-9:00 P.M.; Sun., 1:00 P.M.-MIDNIGHT; extended hours during reading and exam periods* ➧ *LEXIS* ➧ *NEXIS* ➧ *WESTLAW* ➧ *CALI* ➧ *DIALOG* ➧ OCLC ➧ *LEGALTRAC* ➧ *7 full-time librarians*

The Allen Mercer Daniel Law Library is both a working collection for law students and lawyers and a research institution for legal scholars. The civil rights archive contains briefs, working papers, and materials of the NAACP and other civil rights organizations. The library has a collection that emphasizes civil and political rights and literature to support study of the legal problems of the poor. The law library offers two computer labs containing both IBM and Macintosh personal computers with a 1:9 computer/student ratio. Howard University is a member of the Consortium of Universities of the Washington Metropolitan Area.

■ Curriculum

➧ *Academic Support Program* ➧ *Elder Law Clinic* ➧ *Public Service Program* ➧ *Criminal Justice Clinic* ➧ *Internship* ➧ *88 credits required to graduate, with a cumulative weighted average of not less than 70* ➧ *residence in the last full year is also a requirement for graduation* ➧ *degrees available: J.D.; J.D./M.B.A.; M.C.J.* ➧ *range of first-year class size—30-50*

The curriculum leading to the first degree in law covers three academic years of two semesters each. Howard has no summer or evening program; it is a full-time day program. Experience has shown that beginning students must devote their entire time to their studies. During the first two years, emphasis is on the fundamental analytical concepts and skills of the law and the system by which it is administered; the functions required of a lawyer within a legal system based upon the common law. These courses afford rigorous training in the recognition of essential facts, in analysis and synthesis, and in the presentation of legal materials. The curriculum in the third year provides diversified experience and a solid foundation for whatever specialization is desired. There is an emphasis on effective legal writing throughout the law school curriculum. Howard is firmly committed to producing lawyers who have mastered the art of effective written communication. Students wishing to participate in the Joint J.D./M.B.A program must be admitted both to the School of Law and the School of Business, one may use the law school application only to apply for the J.D./M.B.A. degree. Students interested in the M.C.J. program should make inquiry to the School of Law.

■ Special Programs

The School of Law has a strong commitment to public service and to human and civil rights. Many programs and activities in the school reflect that fact. The school also provides an opportunity for clinical experience in civil and criminal litigation and employment law. Other areas are either available or under active consideration.

■ Minority Programs

Howard University is a historically black institution, and has always had a strong, anti-discrimination policy. The School of Law, consistent with the mission and tradition of the university, believes in affirmative action both with regard to admissions and financial aid in order to ensure that all members of under-represented groups may have access to the legal profession.

■ Admission

➽ *Bachelor's degree from a college or university acceptable to the School of Law is required* ➽ *application deadline—April 30, rolling admissions used; early application preferred (Oct. 30)* ➽ *LSAT, LSDAS required* ➽ *median GPA—3.00* ➽ *median LSAT score—152* ➽ *application fee—$60* ➽ *letters of recommendation and undergraduate dean's survey should accompany application*

The large number of applications received for the available spaces in the first-year class has made the admissions process highly selective. The School of Law admits only full-time students for entrance in the fall. Applicants must take the LSAT, (and GMAT for the J.D./M.B.A.) and should arrange to take the LSAT no later than February of the year admission is sought to allow adequate processing time. Applicants must register with the LSDAS and must have obtained their college degrees before enrolling.

■ Student Activities

The *Howard Law Journal*, scheduled for publication three times a year, publishes legal materials of scholarly and professional interest. The national and international moot court teams, which sponsor intramural competitions and participate in competitions nationwide, have won numerous honors. The Student Bar Association (SBA) is the general student government organization. The *Barrister*, the student newspaper, publishes several issues a year. Other organizations represent students from diverse ethnic backgrounds, including, African Americans, Latinos, Africans, Caribbean Islanders, and Asian Pacific Islanders. Other activities include three legal fraternities and a legal sorority, as well as organizations that address a range of student needs and interests.

■ Expenses and Financial Aid

➽ *tuition & fees—full-time, $11,100* ➽ *additional expenses—$11,000 (room, board, & miscellaneous living expenses)* ➽ *merit scholarships are available*
➽ *need-based scholarships & grants are available*
➽ *financial aid available; financial aid form due April 1*
➽ *extensive list of loans available*

■ Career Services

The Career Services Office is an integral part of the law school. To assist students, the office offers workshops on job search techniques and résumé writing, and seminars on career development and practice specialties. The office also maintains an extensive resource library with online employer research systems, newsletters, and updated listings of career opportunities. Howard affords its students varied career opportunities. Each year, the Career Services Office sponsors two on-campus interview programs and more than 250 recruiters from law firms, government agencies, and corporations visit the law school with offers of employment for promising students and graduates. Graduates work for courts; large and small private firms; federal, state, and local government agencies; public interest organizations; and public and private corporations throughout the United States.

Applicant Group for the 1995-1996 Academic Year

Howard University School of Law
This grid includes only applicants who earned 120-180 LSAT scores under standard administrations (reflects 97% of the total applicant pool).

LSAT Score	GPA 3.75 +		3.50 - 3.74		3.25 - 3.49		3.00 - 3.24		2.75 - 2.99		2.50 - 2.74		2.25 - 2.49		2.00 - 2.24		Below 2.00		No GPA		Total	
	Apps	Adm	Apps	Adm	Apps	Adm	Apps	Adm	Apps	Adm	Apps	Adm	Apps	Adm	Apps	Adm	Apps	Adm	Apps	Adm	Apps	Adm
175 - 180	0	0	0	0	0	0	0	0	0	0	0	0	0	0	0	0	0	0	0	0	0	0
170 - 174	0	0	0	0	0	0	0	0	0	0	0	0	0	0	0	0	0	0	0	0	0	0
165 - 169	1	1	1	1	0	0	2	2	0	0	0	0	0	0	0	0	0	0	0	0	4	4
160 - 164	2	2	1	1	2	2	5	5	6	6	7	5	2	1	0	0	0	0	0	0	25	22
155 - 159	2	2	4	4	10	10	14	13	18	15	11	8	4	4	3	2	0	0	3	1	69	59
150 - 154	4	4	6	6	32	28	34	30	45	35	37	24	30	16	9	3	3	1	3	1	203	148
145 - 149	9	7	25	15	42	23	60	27	72	16	63	12	49	6	21	3	1	0	6	0	348	109
140 - 144	6	3	20	6	28	0	59	3	87	4	79	2	62	0	23	0	9	1	3	0	376	19
135 - 139	4	0	9	0	24	1	45	1	56	1	65	1	50	0	31	0	5	0	11	0	300	4
130 - 134	1	0	7	0	9	0	13	0	30	0	21	0	28	0	11	0	9	0	5	0	134	0
125 - 129	0	0	0	0	1	0	5	0	3	0	11	0	7	0	5	0	4	0	3	0	39	0
120 - 124	0	0	0	0	0	0	0	0	1	0	1	0	3	0	0	0	0	0	0	0	5	0
Total	29	19	73	33	148	64	237	81	318	77	295	52	235	27	103	8	31	2	34	2	1503	365

Apps = Number of Applicants
Adm = Number Admitted

University of Idaho College of Law

6th & Rayburn
Moscow, ID 83843

URL: http://www.uidaho.edu/law/lawcoll.html
Phone: 208.885.6422

■ Introduction

The College of Law is located on the main campus of the University of Idaho in the city of Moscow, about 90 miles southeast of Spokane, Washington, and about 8 miles east of Pullman, Washington. The Moscow-Pullman community is the cultural center of a vast inland area of the Northwest covering parts of Idaho, Washington, and Oregon. This area is renowned for outstanding opportunities for outdoor sports and activities. Washington State University and the University of Idaho are only eight miles apart, and the two universities make their resources jointly available in many fields. The College of Law was established in 1909. It has been a member of the AALS since 1915 and has been on the approved list of the ABA since 1925.

■ Enrollment/Student Body

➽ 703 applicants ➽ 234 admitted first-year class 1995 ➽ 96 enrolled first-year class 1995 ➽ 279 total full-time ➽ 10.8% minority ➽ 42% women ➽ 15 states & foreign countries represented ➽ 79 undergraduate schools represented

Students from Idaho constitute approximately 80 percent of the student body; the other 20 percent come from all regions of the United States. Although the total enrollment of the College of Law is relatively small (approximately 300), students typically represent over 70 different colleges and universities. Academic attrition is about 7 percent.

■ Faculty

➽ 30 total ➽ 27 full-time ➽ 3 part-time or adjunct ➽ 9 women ➽ 1 minority

■ Library and Physical Facilities

➽ 161,085 volumes & equivalents ➽ library hours: Mon.-Thurs., 7:30 A.M.-11:00 P.M.; Fri., 7:30 A.M.-8:30 P.M.; Sat., 9:30 A.M.-6:30 P.M.; Sun., 10:30 A.M.-11:00 P.M. ➽ LEXIS ➽ NEXIS ➽ WESTLAW ➽ DIALOG ➽ Online Legal Periodical Indices ➽ 34 full-time librarians ➽ library seats 369

The College of Law occupies an air-conditioned building designed for its use and completed in 1973. It contains a courtroom, classrooms, offices for the clinical training program, and the law library which houses two computer labs with access to the Internet, LEXIS/NEXIS, and WESTLAW/DIALOG. It is located across the street from the general library of the university.

The law library subscribes to CD-ROM libraries. Membership in the Western Library Network and the Inland Northwest Library Automation Network allows users to ascertain holdings of hundreds of libraries across the nation.

Law students have access to the other libraries of the University of Idaho, as well as to those of Washington State University.

■ Curriculum

➽ In-house Clinical Program ➽ 88 credits required to graduate ➽ 61 courses available ➽ degree available: J.D. ➽ semesters, start in Aug., Jan., & May (summer) ➽ externships

The school operates on a semester basis with six semesters and 88 semester credit hours required for the J.D. degree. A summer session is held for advanced students only, and the J.D. degree can be secured in five semesters and two summer sessions. The first-year curriculum is required and includes the traditional subjects of contracts, torts, procedure, property, and criminal law.

The focus is upon basic general principles widely applicable throughout the United States. Standard casebooks and other teaching materials are used, occasionally supplemented by references to the more localized problems of Idaho or the Northwest. No work is offered toward any degree other than the J.D.

■ Special Programs

The law school operates a variety of clinical programs. Law students in their third year may qualify as interns under the laws of Idaho and work in our in-house clinic. Interns are eligible to present cases in court under appropriate supervision. The in-house clinic includes a general practice unit, an appellate unit in which students practice in federal and state appellate courts, and a tribal court unit in which students serve as public defenders in the NezPerce and Coeur D'Alene Tribal Courts. In 1994-95 the UI College of Law and Idaho Legal Aid Services established a pilot project to provide civil representation to members of several Idaho Indian tribes.

Externships are available, for limited credit, with the Supreme Court and Court of Appeals of Idaho, the United States Court of Appeals for the Ninth Circuit, the United States District Court for the District of Idaho, the Attorney General of Idaho, and the United States Attorney for the District of Idaho. Interns may also receive limited credit for work performed in law offices and selected public agencies.

■ Admission

➽ Bachelor's degree required for admission ➽ application deadline—Feb. 1 ➽ LSAT, LSDAS required ➽ median GPA—3.22 ➽ median LSAT score—155 ➽ application fee—$30

Applications are accepted beginning in September preceding the year in which enrollment is desired. Entering students are admitted only at the beginning of the fall semester. Applicants must submit LSAT scores and college transcripts for evaluation through LSDAS. Late fall application is recommended, and the deadline for being considered in the first wave of acceptances is Feb. 1. In making decisions, the Admissions Committee relies on the LSAT and the college record, weighing scores slightly heavier.

■ Student Activities

Students publish the *Idaho Law Review*, which is devoted particularly to state and regional problems, although articles of general national interest do appear. An intramural moot court competition is held on a voluntary basis and, from winning teams, students are selected to participate in the National, International, and ABA Moot Court Teams. The Student Bar Association represents student interests, both educational and social, in many ways. From its ranks come elected student members who sit on various faculty/student committees. There are chapters of the Phi Alpha Delta, Delta Theta Phi, and Phi Delta Phi legal fraternities at the College of Law, as well as the American Bar Association Law Student Division, the Board of Student Advocates, the Christian Legal Society, the Environmental Law Society, the Federalist Society, the *Idaho Law Review*, the Idaho Women Lawyer's Student Chapter, the Idaho Trial Lawyers Association, the International Law Society, Law Students for Alternative Dispute Resolution, the Minority Law Student Association, the Student Bar Association, the Student Division of the Idaho State Bar's Corporate and Securities Section, the Public International Law Group, and the Law Student Spouse/Partner Association.

■ Expenses and Financial Aid

- *tuition & fees—resident, $3,260; nonresident, $8,640*
- *in-house & general achievement scholarships available*
- *outstanding achievement minority scholarships available*
- *financial aid available; University of Idaho Scholarship and Financial Aid Application required*
- *FAF due Feb. 15*

■ Career Services

The law school sponsors a variety of activities designed to facilitate students' career planning and assist in their employment search as summer clerks or for permanent positions. Facilities are available for on-campus interviews and the school is able to work with employers who cannot visit the school but have indicated a desire to recruit by mail. The majority of graduates find employment in Idaho, although Washington and Oregon continue to be popular locations. Graduates are also employed throughout the United States and several foreign countries. In recent years students have followed the national averages in finding employment in positions requiring bar membership or extensive legal training.

Applicant Group for the 1995-1996 Academic Year

University of Idaho College of Law
This grid includes only applicants who earned 120-180 LSAT scores under standard administrations.

GPA

LSAT Score	3.75 +		3.50 - 3.74		3.25 - 3.49		3.00 - 3.24		2.75 - 2.99		2.50 - 2.74		2.25 - 2.49		2.00 - 2.24		Below 2.00		No GPA		Total	
	Apps	Adm	Apps	Adm	Apps	Adm	Apps	Adm	Apps	Adm	Apps	Adm	Apps	Adm	Apps	Adm	Apps	Adm	Apps	Adm	Apps	Adm
175 - 180	0	0	0	0	0	0	0	0	1	1	0	0	0	0	0	0	0	0	0	0	1	1
170 - 174	0	0	0	0	0	0	0	0	0	0	0	0	0	0	0	0	0	0	0	0	0	0
165 - 169	3	2	1	1	3	3	2	2	2	2	4	3	0	0	1	1	0	0	1	1	17	15
160 - 164	3	3	7	7	4	4	12	11	15	9	6	4	5	2	0	0	1	0	0	0	53	40
155 - 159	7	7	20	20	24	20	35	20	24	8	15	3	3	2	4	0	0	0	0	0	132	80
150 - 154	11	9	22	14	39	15	47	15	32	4	30	4	14	4	5	0	2	0	2	1	204	66
145 - 149	6	2	12	3	32	1	32	3	35	1	16	1	8	0	4	0	1	0	4	2	150	13
140 - 144	1	0	4	1	15	3	18	3	19	0	14	2	4	0	4	1	0	0	2	0	81	10
135 - 139	0	0	3	0	4	0	4	0	3	0	6	0	4	0	5	0	2	0	3	0	34	0
130 - 134	0	0	0	0	1	0	1	0	1	0	3	0	0	0	2	0	0	0	1	0	9	0
125 - 129	1	0	0	0	0	0	0	0	0	0	0	0	0	0	0	0	0	0	0	0	1	0
120 - 124	0	0	0	0	0	0	0	0	0	0	1	0	0	0	0	0	0	0	0	0	1	0
Total	32	23	69	46	122	46	151	54	132	25	95	17	38	8	25	2	6	0	13	4	683	225

Apps = Number of Applicants
Adm = Number Admitted
Reflects 97% of the total applicant pool.

University of Illinois College of Law

504 East Pennsylvania Avenue
Champaign, IL 61820

E-Mail: admissions@law.uiuc.edu
URL: http://www.law.uiuc.edu
Phone: 217.244.6415

■ Introduction

Established nearly a century ago, the University of Illinois College of Law fosters excellence in legal education through a close community of faculty members and students, where teaching goes hand in hand with scholarship. The resources—intellectual, cultural, and recreational—of one of the world's largest and best universities are readily available to our law students, as is the appealing ambience of a university community. The college's comparatively low tuition costs, as well as the area's moderate living costs, make our program an outstanding value.

■ Enrollment/Student Body

➽ 1,951 applicants ➽ 212 enrolled first-year class 1995 ➽ 623 total full-time ➽ 27% minority ➽ 40% women ➽ 38 states & foreign countries represented ➽ 165 undergraduate schools represented

■ Faculty

➽ 74 total ➽ 39 full-time ➽ 35 part-time ➽ 8 women ➽ 4 minority

■ Library and Physical Facilities

➽ 643,058 volumes & equivalents ➽ LEXIS ➽ NEXIS ➽ WESTLAW ➽ 6 full-time librarians

In August 1993 the college completed a major addition and renovation which greatly increased the amount of space available for students.

The law library ranks sixth nationally in the number of titles held. The library has a substantial international collection and is one of the few American law libraries designated as a depository by the European Economic Community.

Directly across the street from the law school is one of the country's largest physical education buildings, with indoor and outdoor swimming pools, tennis courts, four gyms, weight and exercise equipment, archery, and ball courts of all kinds. The facility is free for students.

■ Curriculum

➽ Academic Support Program ➽ 90 credits required to graduate ➽ 110 courses available ➽ degrees and combined degrees available: J.D.; LL.M.; J.D./M.B.A.; J.D./M.D.; J.D./D.V.M.; J.D./M.A. in Labor & Industrial Relations; J.D./M.A. in Urban Planning; J.D./Master of Education; Doctor of Education ➽ semesters, start in Aug. ➽ range of first-year class size—65-70

In the second and third years, courses vary in size. Seminar enrollment is limited to 12 students, and trial advocacy sections are limited to 20 students each. Independent studies—in which students work individually with faculty on research topics of special interest—are also offered.

■ Special Programs

International Legal Studies—Students pursuing international legal studies can choose from 13 international and comparative law courses, ranging from European Community law to international human rights law. Faculty members have long-standing international connections, and some collaborate with international scholars and legal experts to teach these courses.

Trial Advocacy Program—The college's trial advocacy program is especially popular, enrolling about three-quarters of the third-year class. The year-long program teaches the art of courtroom litigation and concludes with students conducting a day-long mock trial.

Environmental Law—The college has an active program of environmental and planning studies. Beyond the first-year course in property, the college offers courses in environmental law, natural resources, and land-use planning.

An innovative computer-based course called Metro-Apex offers a semester-long simulation of environmental controversies and legal disputes. Students adopt and enforce regulations and conduct full-scale administrative and judicial proceedings.

Taxation—Illinois offers one of the strongest tax curricula in the country, with core courses that address all aspects of tax practice and advanced offerings that integrate tax problems with other fields of law.

Skills Training—The College offers a live-client Civil Clinic, as well as classes in legal drafting, business planning, advanced bankruptcy, environmental management, estate planning, and tax practice; all challenge students to solve concrete problems and draft legal documents in a variety of fields. Courses on computer applications in the law and quantitative methods in legal decision-making familiarize students with sophisticated techniques necessary in today's law practice; these include computerized methods of document preparation and information retrieval, statistical analysis, the use of computer simulations in litigation, and the calculation of damage awards.

Offerings on alternative dispute resolution, the lawyer as negotiator, and collective bargaining and labor arbitration engage students in mock negotiations, arbitrations, and alternatives to traditional trials.

■ Admission

➽ Bachelor's degree required ➽ application deadline—March 15 ➽rolling admissions, application by Jan. 15 ➽ LSAT, LSDAS required ➽ median GPA—3.41 ➽ median LSAT score—161 ➽ application fee—$30

In evaluating applications, the Admissions Committee places great weight on the undergraduate grade-point average and the Law School Admission Test score. Nevertheless, a thorough admissions process, including individual review of all files by a faculty committee, attempts to identify students whose grades or scores appear to underpredict their performance in law school, as well as students whose admission would contribute to diversity at the College of Law. The committee also considers graduate work in other fields, employment experience, and demonstrated leadership ability. Applicants are not judged on the basis of in-state residency.

■ Student Activities

Students can write for the *University of Illinois Law Review* or for the *Elder Law Journal*, the only law journal in the country to concentrate on the legal problems of the elderly. Illinois students also write analyses of recent court decisions for the monthly *Illinois Bar Journal*.

Students interested in appellate advocacy can compete in any of a number of moot court competitions and can gain practical experience through the client counseling and negotiation competitions.

The small size of the college allows students to become actively involved in the college's more than 30 student organizations.

■ Expenses and Financial Aid

➡ *tuition & fees—full-time resident, $5,958; full-time nonresident, $15,094* ➡ *estimated additional expenses—$8,244 average (room, board, books, transportation, personal)* ➡ *merit-based scholarships available* ➡ *FAFSA due by March 15*

Approximately 30 tuition waivers are available to African American, Latino, and native American first-year students. Numerous graduate assistantships are available on-campus to second- and third-year students. Graduate assistants receive a tuition waiver plus a monthly stipend.

■ Career Services

The Office of Career Services works individually with students to help them decide which career choices are most attractive. Staff members arrange mock interviews with attorneys, assist with writing résumés and cover letters, and offer dozens of programs throughout the year. Faculty members counsel students on career goals, and attorneys regularly visit the college to discuss such topics as how to prepare for an interview or succeed as a summer associate.

Students participate in an active on-campus interviewing program and respond to requests for résumés from hundreds of employers nationwide. On average over the last five years, 90 percent of our graduates accepted positions within six months of completing the J.D.

Applicant Group for the 1995-1996 Academic Year

University of Illinois College of Law
This grid includes only applicants who earned 120-180 LSAT scores under standard administrations.

	GPA																					
LSAT Score	3.75 +		3.50 - 3.74		3.25 - 3.49		3.00 - 3.24		2.75 - 2.99		2.50 - 2.74		2.25 - 2.49		2.00 - 2.24		Below 2.00		No GPA		Total	
	Apps	Adm	Apps	Adm	Apps	Adm	Apps	Adm	Apps	Adm	Apps	Adm	Apps	Adm	Apps	Adm	Apps	Adm	Apps	Adm	Apps	Adm
175 - 180	1	1	1	1	1	1	2	2	1	0	0	0	0	0	0	0	0	0	0	0	6	5
170 - 174	7	7	6	6	6	5	3	3	5	4	1	1	1	1	0	0	0	0	0	0	29	27
165 - 169	21	21	30	28	33	28	19	18	13	7	5	2	4	0	2	0	0	0	0	0	127	104
160 - 164	64	61	88	70	107	80	79	33	32	8	16	2	6	1	4	0	0	0	2	2	398	257
155 - 159	58	21	118	30	121	17	84	8	55	5	21	1	12	0	2	0	1	0	8	2	480	84
150 - 154	35	2	80	6	85	6	82	6	52	4	29	2	10	0	5	1	1	0	7	0	386	27
145 - 149	13	3	35	3	44	2	57	7	44	5	24	0	10	1	5	0	2	0	6	0	240	21
140 - 144	4	1	17	0	18	0	31	0	24	0	27	0	22	0	3	0	2	0	5	0	153	1
135 - 139	0	0	1	0	4	0	11	0	19	0	10	0	13	0	6	0	2	0	4	0	70	0
130 - 134	0	0	2	0	2	0	4	0	4	0	8	0	4	0	2	0	4	0	1	0	31	0
125 - 129	0	0	0	0	0	0	0	0	0	0	1	0	0	0	0	0	0	0	0	0	1	0
120 - 124	0	0	0	0	0	0	0	0	0	0	0	0	1	0	0	0	0	0	1	0	2	0
Total	203	117	378	144	421	139	372	77	249	33	142	8	83	3	29	1	12	0	34	4	1923	526

Apps = Number of Applicants
Adm = Number Admitted
Reflects 99% of the total applicant pool.

Note: This chart is to be used as a a general guide only. Nonnumerical factors are strongly considered for all applicants.

Indiana University School of Law—Bloomington

Admissions Office, Law Building, Room 230
Bloomington, IN 47405-1001

E-Mail: lawadmis@indiana.edu
URL: http://www.law.indiana.edu
Phone: 812.855.4765

■ Introduction

Founded in 1842, Indiana University School of Law—Bloomington, is located on the beautifully wooded campus of one of the nation's largest teaching and research universities. The presence of the university, including its world famous School of Music, offers students cultural opportunities available in few urban areas, while retaining the advantages of a small university town. The school is a charter member of the AALS and is approved by the ABA.

■ Enrollment/Student Body

➽ *1,773 applicants* ➽ *693 admitted first-year class 1995* ➽ *210 enrolled first-year class 1995* ➽ *620 total full-time* ➽ *6 total part-time* ➽ *20.8% minority* ➽ *44% women* ➽ *43 states & foreign countries represented* ➽ *193 undergraduate schools represented*

■ Faculty

➽ *53 total* ➽ *34 full-time* ➽ *19 part-time or adjunct* ➽ *13 women* ➽ *2 minority*

■ Library and Physical Facilities

➽ *560,000 volumes & equivalents* ➽ *library hours: Mon.-Fri., 7:30 A.M.-MIDNIGHT; Sat., 8:00 A.M.-10:00 P.M.; Sun., 11:00 A.M.-MIDNIGHT; extended hours during exams* ➽ *LEXIS* ➽ *NEXIS* ➽ *WESTLAW* ➽ *DIALOG* ➽ *WILSON-ONLINE* ➽ *9 full-time librarians* ➽ *library seats 659*

The law library's extensive collection is one of only ten in the nation to contain complete sets of records and briefs filed before the United States Supreme Court. It includes an exceptional collection in Anglo-American law and strong holdings in international and foreign law. Computer-assisted legal research systems and nonlaw databases, interactive video systems, and a computer center for student use are available.

■ Curriculum

➽ *Academic Support Program* ➽ *86 credits required to graduate* ➽ *134 courses available* ➽ *degrees and combined degrees available: J.D.; J.D./M.B.A.; J.D./M.P.A.; J.D./M.S.E.S.; J.D./M.L.S.; LL.M.; M.C.L.* ➽ *fall semesters start in Aug.* ➽ *range of first-year class size—26-100*

The curriculum does not emphasize the law of any state and its many offerings include traditional courses as well as specialized courses such as communications law, law and biomedical advance, immigration law, international business transactions, and environmental litigation. The school also offers intensive training in litigation. Students may also participate in clinics which enable them to deal with client problems under close faculty supervision.

The Legal Education Opportunity Program (LEOP) is a voluntary program designed to provide academic and peer support to selected law students through a series of voluntary workshops and classes. In addition, the School offers a Peer Advisor Program which pairs upper-class students with first-year students.

■ Joint-Degree Programs

Four formal joint J.D. and master's or doctoral degree programs are available with the School of Business, the School of Public and Environmental Affairs, and the School of Library and Information Science. Joint-degree programs in other disciplines may be individually designed.

■ London Law Consortium

The School of Law participates in a consortium with seven other law schools to offer a semester of study in London during the spring. Classes are held at the Florida State University London Study Center. Students are eligible to participate during their second or third year in law school, and, to date, all those wishing to participate have been able to do so.

■ Accelerated/Summer Program

By starting law school in the summer session and attending full summer sessions in the following two years, students may complete degree requirements in 27 months. Students who begin in the accelerated program are not required to continue with the program. Students who do not choose to begin their legal education in the accelerated program may enroll in summer-session courses following their first year.

■ Special Programs

The Center for the Study of Law and Society provides a forum for those students and faculty across the Bloomington campus interested in law-related research. Some of its research projects include transnational disputing, the role of courts, alternative dispute resolution, and the regulation of markets.

■ Admission

➽ *Bachelor's degree required for admission* ➽ *application deadline—March 1 priority, rolling admission* ➽ *LSAT, LSDAS required* ➽ *median GPA—3.39* ➽ *median LSAT score—159* ➽ *application fee—$35*

Generally, the quality and size of the applicant pool forces the Admissions Committee to rely heavily on the undergraduate grade-point average and the LSAT score. However, numerical indicators are not the only considerations used in evaluating applications. The committee considers the quality of the applicant's undergraduate institution, level and rigor of coursework, letters of recommendation (particularly from undergraduate or graduate faculty members), graduate work, employment during and after college, extracurricular activities, potential for service to the profession, educational diversity, and state of residence. Increasing the diversity of the student body, particularly with respect to minorities, is also important to the school.

■ Housing

Law students live both off campus and in graduate- or married-student campus housing. For information concerning campus housing contact Halls of Residence, 801 N. Jordan Ave., Bloomington, IN 47405-2107.

■ Student Activities

The *Indiana Law Journal* publishes articles by legal scholars, practitioners, jurists, and IU law students. Students edit the journal and publish it four times a year. Members are selected on the basis of academic achievement or through a writing competition. The *Federal Communications Law Journal* is the nation's oldest and largest communications law journal. A student-managed journal that publishes three times a year, the journal features articles of interest to those involved in federal communications law, telecommunications, intellectual property and information policy. The *Indiana Journal of Global Legal Studies* is a multidisciplinary journal that specializes in international and comparative law articles. The editorial board consists of practitioners and faculty from the law, business, and public policy schools.

■ Expenses and Financial Aid

➧ *tuition & fees—resident, $5,099; nonresident, $14,027*
➧ *estimated additional expenses—$9,814 includes room and board, books, supplies, and personal expenses*
➧ *fellowships available: scholastic and need-based*
➧ *minority fellowship available* ➧ *financial aid available; separate application for fellowship; FAFSA and FAC sheet for loan consideration*

■ Career Services

The Career Services Office actively assists with career planning and locating summer and permanent jobs. Typically, over 90 percent of each graduating class accepts employment within six months of graduation. Approximately one-half locate outside Indiana. Each year over 200 employers interview on-campus or at off-campus interview programs. Over 60 percent of each graduating class works in private law firms.

Applicant Group for the 1995-1996 Academic Year

Indiana University School of Law—Bloomington
This grid includes only applicants who earned 120-180 LSAT scores under standard administrations.

	GPA																					
LSAT Score	3.75 +		3.50 - 3.74		3.25 - 3.49		3.00 - 3.24		2.75 - 2.99		2.50 - 2.74		2.25 - 2.49		2.00 - 2.24		Below 2.00		No GPA		Total	
	Apps	Adm	Apps	Adm	Apps	Adm	Apps	Adm	Apps	Adm	Apps	Adm	Apps	Adm	Apps	Adm	Apps	Adm	Apps	Adm	Apps	Adm
175 - 180	1	1	1	1	0	0	1	1	0	0	1	1	0	0	0	0	0	0	0	0	4	4
170 - 174	5	5	2	2	2	2	5	5	4	4	0	0	0	0	0	0	0	0	1	1	19	19
165 - 169	19	19	16	16	24	24	14	14	17	15	3	3	3	3	1	0	0	0	1	1	98	95
160 - 164	32	32	73	73	101	97	60	53	27	23	16	10	7	3	1	0	1	0	4	1	322	292
155 - 159	62	50	99	40	109	35	75	11	42	7	27	4	13	2	2	0	1	0	4	0	434	149
150 - 154	37	16	79	17	93	11	80	6	50	6	23	3	13	0	6	1	0	0	4	0	385	60
145 - 149	15	3	30	4	49	8	46	11	59	7	27	2	16	2	4	0	6	0	6	0	258	37
140 - 144	1	0	10	4	21	4	26	4	22	2	28	2	21	2	2	0	2	0	4	0	137	18
135 - 139	1	0	2	1	3	1	9	2	14	0	7	0	11	0	4	0	2	0	3	0	56	4
130 - 134	0	0	0	0	1	0	2	0	3	0	3	0	5	0	2	0	3	0	0	0	19	0
125 - 129	0	0	0	0	0	0	0	0	0	0	0	0	0	0	0	0	0	0	0	0	0	0
120 - 124	0	0	0	0	0	0	0	0	0	0	0	0	0	0	0	0	0	0	0	0	0	0
Total	173	126	312	158	403	182	318	107	238	64	135	25	89	12	22	1	15	0	27	3	1732	678

Apps = Number of Applicants
Adm = Number Admitted
Reflects 98% of the total applicant pool.

Indiana University School of Law—Indianapolis

735 W. New York Street
Indianapolis, IN 46202

E-Mail: amespada@indyvax.iupui.edu
URL: http://www.iupui.edu/it/iuilaw/iuilaw.html
Phone: 317.274.2459

■ Introduction

The law school is located on the Indianapolis campus of Indiana University and Purdue University. This location is also home to most of the professional schools of Indiana University including the Schools of Medicine, Dentistry, Nursing, and Social Work. The law school is just minutes away from the state's courts, legislature, and major law firms, giving students opportunities not only to observe the legal process in action, but also to participate in that process as law clerks, judicial interns, and legislative staff assistants. With nearly 800 students, the school is the largest in the state of Indiana and one of the few Big Ten law schools to offer the cultural, recreational, and professional advantages of an urban educational environment.

■ Enrollment/Student Body

➽ 1,206 applicants ➽ 478 admitted ➽ 256 enrolled first-year class 1995 ➽ 574 total full-time ➽ 261 total part-time ➽ 46% women ➽ 39 states & foreign countries represented ➽ 167 undergraduate schools represented

■ Faculty

➽ 58 total ➽ 41 full-time ➽ 17 part-time or adjunct ➽ 15 women ➽ 6 minority

■ Library and Physical Facilities

➽ 410,000 volumes & equivalents ➽ library hours: Mon.-Thurs., 8:00 A.M.-MIDNIGHT; Fri., 8:00 A.M.-11:00 P.M.; Sat., 9:00 A.M.-7:00 P.M. ➽ LEXIS ➽ NEXIS ➽ WESTLAW ➽ 25 full-time librarians ➽ library seats 412

One of the largest in the nation, the library is a depository for the United States government and the United Nations publications. The library computer center features terminals from which students can conduct legal research.

■ Curriculum

➽ Academic Support Program ➽ 90 credits required to graduate, of the 90 hours, 53 are in prescribed courses ➽ 112 courses available plus internships ➽ degrees available: J.D./M.B.A.; J.D./M.P.A.; J.D./M.H.A. ➽ semesters, start in Aug. ➽ range of first-year class size varies with the class, some as few as 30, others 70-90

■ Academic Support Programs

Students are offered assistance through the Dean's Tutorial Society and the Tutorial Study Group. Supervised by a tenured faculty member, the tutorial society is staffed by academically distinguished students who offer assistance in case briefing, exam preparation, and through individual tutoring. The Tutorial Study Group meets for two hours each week under the direction of a faculty member and assists students with their legal writing and analytical skills.

■ Special Summer Program

Summer admission is offered to a select group of applicants who can benefit from a class emphasizing writing and analytical skills. Applicants who have either an LSAT score or GPA that is outside of the median range of accepted students, persons who are returning to school after several years outside of the classroom, and students for whom English is a second language may be considered for the summer program. Summer admittees earn two credits toward their J.D. degree, and continuation in the fall is not contingent upon performance in the summer program. There is no special application form for summer admission. All applicants who are not presumptively admitted and whose file is completed by February 1 are considered for the summer program.

■ Clinical Experiences

The law school offers several clinical programs: The Civil Practice Clinic allows students the opportunity to represent clients in a variety of cases, including housing, dissolution of marriage, support, consumer, and administrative matters. In the Civil Practice Disability Clinic, students represent school-age children with special needs, as well as persons who are afflicted with the HIV virus, Alzheimer's disease, and AIDS. In the Criminal Defense Clinic, students represent clients in criminal cases involving a variety of misdemeanors or class D felony charges in the state of Indiana. A Federal Court internship program in which students work with federal judges is also operated each semester.

The law school has a Center for Law and Health. The center provides an environment for the study of the critical issues relating to health care. The center interprets health care regulations and conducts research on law reform issues both nationally and locally.

■ International Law

The law school offers several courses and seminars in the area of international law. Students can further cultivate their interest through participation in the professional journal, the *Indiana International and Comparative Law Review* and the International Law Society. Practical experience also can be gained through involvement in an internship in international law. Each year, the school sponsors a month-long China Summer Program, offered cooperatively with the East China Institute of Politics and Law in Shanghai. The program includes daily lectures in all major areas of Chinese law, instruction in the Chinese language, and visits to local courts and institutions.

■ Admission

➽ *LSAT, LSDAS required* ➽ *median GPA—3.30*
➽ *median LSAT score—157*

The School of Law seeks to attain a culturally rich and diverse student body. To this end, admission decisions are based on a variety of factors. In addition to the LSAT and undergraduate GPA, the admissions committee considers, among other things, the undergraduate institution attended and its distribution of grades, the undergraduate major and grade performance from year to year, extracurricular activities and work responsibilities while in school, postgraduate experience, and proven ability to overcome adversity. Letters of recommendation and a short personal statement are also encouraged.

■ Student Activities

Students at the School of Law may participate in various activities, including the Student Bar Association, the Black Law Student Association, intramural and regional moot court, client counseling competitions, the student newspaper, legal fraternities, Women's Caucus, the *Indiana Law Review*, the *Indiana International and Comparative Law Review*, and the Dean's Tutorial Society. Students also serve as voting members on several faculty committees.

■ Expenses and Financial Aid

➽ *resident tuition & fees—full-time, $5,110; part-time, $3,791*
➽ *nonresident tuition & fees—full-time, $13,020; part-time, $9,660*

Forty-four percent of the school's students receive financial aid. Scholarships are awarded on the basis of need and merit. Awards range from $1,000 to full tuition, regardless of residency status. While the law school does not grant fee waivers for applications, it will consider fee waivers for the LSAT.

■ Career Services and Bar Passage

The Career Services Office serves students interested in part-time, summer, and permanent employment. Services include, but are not limited to, inviting prospective employers to campus, staging mock interviews, a résumé review service, workshops, brown bag lunches with attorneys, judges and persons in alternative careers, and individual counseling sessions. The law school's graduates have an outstanding record of achievement on the Indiana Bar Examination—better than a 91 percent passage rate since the early 1970s.

Applicant Group for the 1995-1996 Academic Year

Indiana University School of Law—Indianapolis
This grid includes only applicants who earned 120-180 LSAT scores under standard administrations.

LSAT Score	GPA 3.75 +		3.50 - 3.74		3.25 - 3.49		3.00 - 3.24		2.75 - 2.99		2.50 - 2.74		2.25 - 2.49		2.00 - 2.24		Below 2.00		No GPA		Total	
	Apps	Adm	Apps	Adm	Apps	Adm	Apps	Adm	Apps	Adm	Apps	Adm	Apps	Adm	Apps	Adm	Apps	Adm	Apps	Adm	Apps	Adm
175 - 180	0	0	0	0	0	0	0	0	0	0	1	1	0	0	0	0	0	0	0	0	1	1
170 - 174	2	2	1	1	0	0	1	1	0	0	0	0	0	0	0	0	0	0	0	0	4	4
165 - 169	5	5	3	3	3	3	1	1	3	3	2	1	1	1	1	0	0	0	0	0	19	17
160 - 164	9	9	10	10	22	21	12	12	10	10	9	3	4	2	1	0	1	0	0	0	78	67
155 - 159	32	31	34	33	51	47	59	46	35	22	21	9	14	2	3	0	1	0	1	1	251	191
150 - 154	17	14	52	37	60	31	56	15	58	9	47	8	23	1	7	0	2	0	5	4	327	119
145 - 149	10	1	24	4	49	14	47	8	53	10	36	2	16	2	12	1	6	0	5	1	258	43
140 - 144	2	0	10	3	23	1	22	4	27	2	27	4	9	0	6	0	3	0	6	0	135	14
135 - 139	0	0	6	0	4	0	8	0	15	0	11	0	14	0	14	0	1	0	4	0	77	0
130 - 134	0	0	2	0	2	0	5	0	5	0	3	0	3	0	2	0	0	0	3	0	25	0
125 - 129	0	0	1	0	0	0	1	0	1	0	0	0	0	0	1	0	0	0	0	0	4	0
120 - 124	0	0	0	0	0	0	0	0	0	0	0	0	0	0	0	0	0	0	0	0	0	0
Total	77	62	143	91	214	117	212	87	207	56	157	28	84	8	47	1	14	0	24	6	1179	456

Apps = Number of Applicants
Adm = Number Admitted
Reflects 98% of the total applicant pool.

Inter American University School of Law

P.O. Box 70351
San Juan, PR 00936-8351

Phone: 809.751.1912, exts. 2013, 2012

■ Introduction

The Inter American University School of Law is one of the 11 units of the Inter American University of Puerto Rico, a private nonprofit educational corporation accredited by the Middle States Association of Colleges and Secondary Schools, the Puerto Rico Council of Higher Education, and the Commonwealth of Puerto Rico Department of Education. The School of Law is approved by the ABA and is located in San Juan, the capital city of Puerto Rico. Since its founding, the School of Law has successfully strived to meet the needs of the legal profession in particular, and Puerto Rico's society in general.

■ Enrollment/Student Body

➽ 1,047 applicants ➽ 345 admitted first-year class 1995 ➽ 200 enrolled first-year class 1995 ➽ 354 total full-time ➽ 294 total part-time ➽ 323 total women

The student body comes mainly from Puerto Rico, although applicants from the mainland are encouraged to apply.

■ Faculty

➽ 46 total ➽ 30 full-time ➽ 16 part-time or adjunct ➽ 16 women

■ Library and Physical Facilities

➽ 167,995 volumes & equivalents ➽ 100 library hours per week: Mon.-Fri., 7:30 A.M.-11:00 P.M.; Sat.-Sun. & holidays, 9:00 A.M.-10:00 P.M. ➽ LEXIS ➽ NEXIS ➽ DIALOG ➽ DOBIS/LUVEN ➽ MICRO JURIS ➽ 9 full-time librarians ➽ library seats 329

The Domingo Toledo Alamo Law School Library is a fully developed learning resources and audiovisual center, and contains two laboratories for computer-assisted legal research and learning.

Acquisitions, circulation, and cataloging functions are fully automated, and an online union catalog contains the resources of all the libraries of the university system.

In January 1990, the library signed a collaboration agreement to establish a consortium with the law school library of the Catholic University of Puerto Rico and the library of the Supreme Court of Puerto Rico, with the purpose of coordinating collection development and sharing its resources through an automated bibliographic network, interlibrary loans, and telecommunication services.

■ Curriculum

➽ 92 credits required to graduate ➽ 158 + courses available for J.D. ➽ semesters, start in Aug. & Jan.

The J.D. program covers three years in the day division and four years in the evening division. Candidates must complete a minimum of 92 credit hours with a GPA of not less than 2.5 to qualify for graduation.

Inter American University School of Law offers a three-week preparation course to be taken during the summer on a compulsory basis by students admitted to the school.

Students who enter law school must be willing to make a heavy commitment of time and energy. For its part, Inter American University is willing to provide the best possible professional educational experience through the careful recruitment of a first-rate faculty, the development of a progressive curriculum, and a willingness to create new and exciting programs of clinical studies and research.

■ Admission

➽ Bachelor's degree required ➽ application deadline—March 31 ➽ LSAT required ➽ application fee—$25 ➽ median GPA—full-time, 3.24; part-time, 3.18 ➽ median LSAT score—full-time, 140; part-time, 140

Proficiency in Spanish is essential in the program. Applicants must have a minimum grade index of 2.5, a medical certificate for students 21 years or younger, a police department certificate of good conduct, and appear for a personal interview, if required.

Candidates are required to take the Prueba de Admision para Estudios Graduados (PAEG), The Aptitude Test for Graduate Education. Students should attain a 575 minimum score on this test. Application forms and other relevant information concerning the PAEG may be obtained from—Educational Testing Service, G.P.O. Box 1271, San Juan, PR 00936.

■ Housing

The university does not provide housing for law students. However, the areas surrounding the School of Law contain many private houses, apartments, and condominiums for rent.

■ Student Activities

The Inter American School of Law Review is the official publication of the School of Law. Leading articles are prepared by academicians, student members of *Law Review*, and practicing members of the profession. Its members work under the supervision of an editorial board of four students chosen on the basis of merit and dedication to the *Review*, and an academic advisor who is a faculty member appointed by the Dean.

Student organizations include the Student Council, an organization that represents the student body and participates in matters of administrative policy related to students' interests. Council representatives serve on various faculty committees, as well as the University Senate and the Board of Trustees; the Law Student Division of the American Bar Association; Phi Alpha Delta legal fraternity (composed not only of law students of the school, but also of distinguished, honorary members who are Supreme Court Justices, Federal District Court Judges, and other prominent attorneys); and the National

Association of Law Students (which represents the three law schools of Puerto Rico and provides needed services to students, the legal profession, and the general community).

Guest speakers are invited to speak on topics of current concern in law and the social and behavioral sciences. The law review, *Revista Juridica de la Universidad Interamericana*, is written principally in Spanish by students, professors, and legal scholars on areas of current importance in the development of the law.

The Legal Aid Clinic Program of the Faculty is integrated with the Community Law Office through a combined effort of the U.S. Legal Service Corporation and Inter American University. Law students are provided with the opportunity to learn skills such as interviewing, negotiation and counseling, fact gathering and analysis, legal research and drafting, decision-making about alternative strategies, and preparation for trial and field practice. They also represent clients before administrative agencies and courts with the close supervision of the program's staff attorneys-professors, pursuant to rules of the Supreme Court of Puerto Rico. Students also gain practical experience by serving with Puerto Rico Legal Services, Inc.; San Juan Community Law Office, Inc.; Legal Aid Society of Puerto Rico; the district attorney's offices; and the Environmental Quality Board.

■ Expenses and Financial Aid

➽ *tuition & fees—full-time, $8,480; part-time, $6,360*
➽ *additional expenses (room & board, personal, books & supplies, transportation, and loan fees) full-time and part-time, $7,403* ➽ *scholarships available: State Student Incentive Grant Program, Legislature Educational Fund and merit (merit application due Aug. & Jan.)*
➽ *financial aid available; applications due—March 31*

The general university fee is $20 per semester. Students pay $100 to reserve a place in the class (after admission approval), $5 for the *Law Review*, and $10 per semester for student activities. There is a deferred-payment plan, and financial aid options include Federal Guaranteed Loan Program; Perkins Loan; Stafford; LAL; the Commonwealth Education Fund; the Students Incentive Grant program, and the College Work-Study Program. The university also has an Honor Scholarship program for law students based on academic accomplishment and financial need.

■ Career Services

The placement program's main purpose is to locate job opportunities for students and alumni, to orient students and alumni with regard to those job opportunities, and to advise prospective employees of placement services offered by the school.

The Dean of Students Office gives orientation and provides information concerning available graduate programs in Puerto Rico, the United States, and foreign countries. A collection of catalogues of law school graduate programs in the United States, Europe, and Canada is kept.

The Continuing Legal Education Program offers advanced courses and seminars concerning different fields of the law of interest to practicing lawyers as well as to the community in general.

Admission Profile Not Available

University of Iowa College of Law

276 Boyd Law Building
Melrose at Byington Streets
Iowa City, IA 52242

E-Mail: law-admissions@uiowa.edu
Phone: 319.335.9071

■ Introduction

The College of Law was founded in 1865 and is the oldest law school west of the Mississippi River. It has been continuously approved by the ABA and is a charter member of the AALS. In 1967, the Iowa College of Law was among the first law schools to commit itself to take aggressive steps to encourage a stronger minority presence in legal education. Minority students constitute 22 percent of the student body of the College of Law. This is particularly noteworthy when it is considered that the state of Iowa has less than a 5 percent minority population. Iowa has hosted numerous summer institutes sponsored by the Council on Legal Education Opportunity (CLEO).

■ Student Body

➽ 1,564 applicants ➽ 497 admitted first-year class 1995 ➽ 225 enrolled first-year class 1995 ➽ 682 total full-time ➽ 22% minority ➽ 44% women ➽ 41 states & foreign countries represented ➽ 195 undergraduate schools represented

■ Faculty

➽ 53 total ➽ 49 full-time ➽ 4 part-time or adjunct ➽ 14 women ➽ 6 minority

■ Library and Physical Facilities

➽ 806,534 volumes & equivalents ➽ library open 104 hours per week ➽ LEXIS ➽ NEXIS ➽ WESTLAW ➽ ILP ➽ 12 full-time librarians ➽ library seats 672 ➽ 12 carrels in A/B room for audio/video playback & microfilm reading/printing ➽ 2 CD-ROM workstations with numerous databases ➽ 32-station LAN ➽ 381 individual study carrels

The law building's central location on a bluff overlooking the Iowa River provides a professional enclave well suited to the college's intensive style of education, but with easy access to the academic, cultural, social, and recreational resources of the university.

■ Curriculum

➽ Academic Support Program ➽ 90 semester hours required to graduate ➽ 190 courses available ➽ degrees available: J.D.; J.D./M.B.A., (joint-program students enrolled in law and 14 other departments) ➽ semesters, start in Aug. ➽ range of first-year class size—28-120 ➽ accelerated program begins in mid-May ➽ graduate (LL.M.) program in International and Comparative Law

■ Special Programs

Iowa is a leader among the nation's law schools in the development of a modern curriculum in which individual instruction in basic lawyer skills is integrated with the exploration of conceptual and institutional issues central to the legal process. The mainspring of this progressive curriculum is an ambitious writing program in which faculty-supervised writing exercises are provided in small classes each semester of a student's training. The lawyer-skills emphasis shifts from first-year concern with close analysis, research, precise expression, and advocacy to upper-class work on drafting, interviewing, counseling, negotiation, and litigation skills. The College of Law features a small-section program in the first year under which each student takes two courses in small sections of 30 or fewer. The first-year curriculum is required; thereafter, almost all courses are electives. The College of Law has a strong research orientation and students are encouraged to propose special projects in which they are interested.

■ Legal Clinic

Students who have completed the equivalent of three semesters (which may include a full summer session) toward their J.D. degrees (usually in excess of 37 credits) are eligible to participate in the College of Law's Legal Clinic Program. Students in the law school's in-house program work directly with faculty members on cases involving civil rights and liberties, statutory entitlements, criminal defense, and general representation in civil matters. The clinic also administers specialized programs in representing farmers in financial distress and persons with disabilities. Clinic interns participate fully in interviewing, fact investigation, negotiation, trials, and appellate proceedings.

■ International Law

The College of Law offers a strong program of study in international law. In this era of accelerating global interdependence, virtually any lawyer may find herself or himself confronted by problems that require knowledge and understanding of international law and foreign legal systems. The study of international and comparative law provides unique insight into the nature of law and legal process and helps to establish the necessary theoretical foundations upon which superior lawyering skills depend.

■ Admission

➽ Bachelor's degree from approved college or university required ➽ application deadline—Feb. 1 ➽ LSAT, LSDAS required ➽ median GPA—3.56 ➽ median LSAT score—160 ➽ application fee—$20 ➽ foreign application fee—$30

A faculty rule limits the college to no more than 30 percent nonresidents in the freshman class, so the resulting criteria for nonresidents are somewhat higher. Criteria other than the LSAT will be taken into account for applicants who demonstrate the inapplicability of the LSAT as a predictor of success for them. Included in this group are applicants from disadvantaged backgrounds as well as others.

■ Student Activities

Student-run cocurricular programs include the *Iowa Law Review*, the *Journal of Corporation Law*, the *Journal of Transnational Law and Contemporary Problems*, the Moot Court Board, Trial Advocacy, and Client Counseling. Other law student organizations are the American Bar Association Law Student Division, Equal Justice Foundation, National Lawyers Guild, Iowa Student Bar Association, International Law Society, Environmental Law Society, Phi Delta Phi and Phi Alpha Delta (national law fraternities open to both men and women), the Black Law Students Association, the Chicano Hispanic Association for Legal Education, Asian American Law Student Association, Native American Law Student Association, National Lesbian and Gay Law Association, Christian Law Students, and the Organization of Women Law Students and Staff.

■ Expenses and Financial Aid

➽ *tuition & fees—full-time resident, $4,660; nonresident, $12,876* ➽ *estimated additional expenses—$8,820 (health fee, books & supplies, room & board, personal, transportation)* ➽ *merit- & need-based scholarships available* ➽ *minority scholarships available* ➽ *financial aid available*

The Law Opportunity Fellowship program funds a limited number of three-year tuition and research assistant positions for traditionally underrepresented minority students. Eligibility for financial aid is based on need established by completion of the Free Application for Federal Student Aid (FAFSA). FAFSA forms are available after January 1 and should be completed as soon as possible.

■ Career Services

Each year the Placement Office brings a variety of employers to campus from across the United States to conduct job interviews. During the 1993-94 academic year (the most recent year for which we have complete statistics) just under 200 employers visited the campus. Of those graduates reporting, 94 percent were placed within six months of graduation. Nearly all of our second-year students (and a good number of our first-year students) seek and find law-related employment for the summer. While most work as clerks in law firms throughout the country, some work as prosecuting interns for county attorney's offices across the state and others serve as research assistants to faculty members here at the law school. The Placement Office actively encourages students' career growth by sponsoring weekly programs that explore the various employment options available, from small- and large-firm practice, judicial clerkships, and prosecution careers to the areas of public interest, government, and corporate legal counsel. The placement staff meets individually with all first-year students to make sure they get off to a good start.

Applicant Group for the 1995-1996 Academic Year

University of Iowa College of Law
This grid includes only applicants who earned 120-180 LSAT scores under standard administrations.

	GPA																					
LSAT Score	3.75 +		3.50 - 3.74		3.25 - 3.49		3.00 - 3.24		2.75 - 2.99		2.50 - 2.74		2.25 - 2.49		2.00 - 2.24		Below 2.00		No GPA		Total	
	Apps	Adm	Apps	Adm	Apps	Adm	Apps	Adm	Apps	Adm	Apps	Adm	Apps	Adm	Apps	Adm	Apps	Adm	Apps	Adm	Apps	Adm
175 - 180	1	1	0	0	0	0	0	0	1	1	0	0	0	0	0	0	0	0	0	0	2	2
170 - 174	4	4	4	4	1	1	4	4	4	4	0	0	3	2	0	0	0	0	0	0	20	19
165 - 169	18	18	10	10	22	19	10	7	13	7	5	1	1	0	1	0	0	0	2	1	82	63
160 - 164	40	39	64	55	51	25	44	19	24	9	15	6	7	3	2	1	1	0	1	1	249	158
155 - 159	62	44	82	35	77	27	70	19	27	2	15	1	13	3	3	0	0	0	5	3	354	134
150 - 154	46	12	87	25	67	11	57	7	45	1	22	2	10	0	9	0	3	2	6	2	352	62
145 - 149	19	4	24	4	55	9	34	4	30	3	31	5	13	1	5	0	1	0	7	0	219	30
140 - 144	2	0	12	2	20	0	21	0	33	0	18	1	10	0	7	0	2	0	5	0	130	3
135 - 139	2	1	5	0	7	0	16	0	9	0	12	0	10	0	9	0	1	0	3	0	74	1
130 - 134	0	0	0	0	1	0	3	0	4	0	5	0	7	0	2	0	3	0	1	0	26	0
125 - 129	0	0	0	0	0	0	1	0	1	0	0	0	0	0	1	0	0	0	0	0	3	0
120 - 124	0	0	0	0	0	0	0	0	0	0	1	0	1	0	0	0	0	0	0	0	2	0
Total	194	123	288	135	301	92	260	60	191	27	124	16	75	9	39	1	11	2	30	7	1513	472

Apps = Number of Applicants
Adm = Number Admitted
Reflects 98% of the total applicant pool.

The John Marshall School of Law

315 South Plymouth Court
Chicago, IL 60604

Phone: 800.537.4280; 312.987.1406

■ Introduction

The John Marshall law school is nationally respected for its intellectual property program, legal writing, and trial advocacy programs. Additionally, we offer a unique international program based on relationships with schools in Ireland, Yugoslavia, and China. Our long involvement in privacy issues means exciting courses in informatic law, and our fair housing and patent clinics provide unusual opportunities for students to put their learning to practice.

Located in the heart of Chicago's financial district, The John Marshall law school since 1899 has offered opportunities via a dynamic setting, stimulating classes, and an interactive faculty and staff to give our students a strong background in the law. JMLS is a member of AALS and is accredited by the ABA.

■ Enrollment/Student Body

➽ 1,862 applicants ➽ 242 enrolled first-year class 1995 ➽ 819 total full-time ➽ 342 total part-time ➽ 17.2% minority ➽ 41% women ➽ 33 states & foreign countries represented by first-year class ➽ 124 undergraduate schools represented by first-year class ➽ 41% out-of-state

■ Faculty

➽ 188 total ➽ 54 full-time ➽ 136 part-time or adjunct ➽ 14 women ➽ 4 minority

■ Library and Physical Facilities

➽ 280,000 volumes & equivalents ➽ 900 audiovisual tapes ➽ library hours: Mon.-Fri., 8:00 A.M.-11:00 P.M.; Sat.-Sun., 9:00 A.M.-9:00 P.M. ➽ LEXIS ➽ NEXIS ➽ WESTLAW ➽ CALI ➽ DIALOG ➽ 20 full-time librarians ➽ library seats 594

The library's Center for Computerized Legal Instruction includes eight LEXIS terminals, eight WESTLAW terminals, and 17 PCs with CALI (Computer Assisted Legal Instruction) software. Seventeen PCs with WordPerfect software are available in two word processing centers. Special arrangements with LEXIS and WESTLAW permit students to access these services from their home computers.

■ Curriculum

➽ 90 semester hours required to graduate ➽ degrees available: J.D.; J.D./M.B.A.; LL.M. ➽ semesters, start in Aug. & Jan. ➽ range of first-year class size—10-50

The school has day and evening divisions, both requiring 90 semester hours to earn the J.D. degree. The instruction, course content, and scholastic requirements are identical in each division. Summer-term courses are also offered. A joint J.D./M.B.A. degree program in cooperation with Rosary College is also offered.

■ Special Programs

The law school offers comprehensive professional skills training. Three interrelated programs comprise this training—the Lawyering Skills Program, the Center for Advocacy, and the Clinical Law Externship Program. The Legal Writing Program, formally known as Lawyering Skills, consists of a four-semester required sequence of courses taught in small sections, enabling faculty to work with students individually. The Center for Advocacy serves John Marshall students by providing a comprehensive and focused approach to attaining advocacy skills. The Clinical Law Externship Program places students with approved federal, state, and local agencies, law firms, the judiciary, and other legal organizations to gain practical experience outside the classroom.

The Center for Informatics Law was established in 1983 to carry on legal research and policy analysis regarding newly developing information and communications technology. Courses offered include Information Law and Policy, Computers and the Law, and Media Law and the Right of Privacy. Qualified students may apply after their first year of academic study to work for the center as research assistants. The Center for Intellectual Property Law offers extensive programs in this rapidly growing area of law. Courses in the J.D. program focus on patent and trade secrets; trademark, unfair competition, and copyright law; computer and franchising law; and entertainment law.

■ Admission

➽ B.A./B.S. required ➽ application deadline—March 1/ Oct. 1, rolling admission ➽ LSAT, LSDAS required ➽ median GPA—3.20 ➽ median LSAT score—152 ➽ application fee—$50

Students are admitted in August and January. Applications for August entrance may be filed between October 1 and March 1; for January entrance, between May 1 and October 1. The LSAT score is evaluated together with the cumulative grade-point average and other relevant factors including difficulty of undergraduate program, postgraduate experience, leadership potential, business and professional background, and letters of recommendation. Applicants from minority and disadvantaged groups will be given special consideration in cases where their overall records are competitive with other applicants. Applicants with a B average overall and an LSAT score in the 74th percentile may be presumed to be within the range for favorable consideration. A Summer Conditional Program is offered to a limited number of candidates whose qualifications do not meet the usual standards, but whose discrepant predictors may be persuasive of probable success in law school. A special minority program, the Legal Education Access Program, is also offered during the fall semester. No separate application form is used for either of these programs.

■ Student Activities

The *John Marshall Law Review*, edited exclusively by students, publishes works on a broad range of current legal topics written by legal scholars, practitioners, and John Marshall law students. The *Software Law Journal* is an international law review focusing on law and policy with regard to software, databases, and information networks. It is managed by a student editorial board. The John Marshall Moot Court Council and Executive Board are the student organizations that coordinate the various moot court activities, including participation in over 20 national and international competitions. The law school sponsors a nationally respected moot court competition, the John Marshall National Moot Court Competition in Information Technology and Privacy. A new, national trial advocacy competition, cosponsored with the American Bar Association and focusing on criminal justice problems, is also held each spring at the law school. Many fraternal, ethnic, and legal-interest organizations reflect the broad variety of interests among John Marshall students.

■ Expenses and Financial Aid

➧ *tuition & fees (1995-1996)—full-time, $15,820/year; part-time, $11,620* ➧ *estimated additional expenses (1995-1996)—$12,900/year (books, $650; living expenses, $12,250; registration, $60)* ➧ *academic scholarships available* ➧ *academic minority scholarships available* ➧ *need-based financial aid available; JMLS financial aid form due May 1* ➧ *participates in federal Stafford and Access Group loan programs*

Tuition for the 1995-96 academic year is $525 per semester-hour. The regular day-division courseload is 15 hours and the regular evening-division courseload is 9-11 hours. Dean's scholarships and grants are awarded to entering students based upon academic achievement. Renewal of these awards is based on academic performance. All applicants for financial aid must file the Graduate and Professional School Financial Aid Service Free Application for Federal Student Aid (FAFSA) form.

■ Career Services

The Career Services Office assists students and graduates in obtaining permanent employment and helps students find summer and part-time positions. The office also offers a two-semester program in professional/personal development. There is an active on-campus interviewing program throughout the year and many employers who do not interview on-campus do interview John Marshall students in their offices. Virtually all of the major Chicago law firms include John Marshall graduates among their associates and partners. In addition to private practice, John Marshall graduates can be found in government, corporate, and public interest sectors. Some of our most recent graduates have taken positions with the U.S. Department of Justice and other agencies of the federal government, in accounting firms, and as judicial clerks in federal courts of appeal, U.S. district courts, and state supreme and appellate courts.

Applicant Group for the 1995-1996 Academic Year

The John Marshall School of Law
This grid includes only applicants who earned 120-180 LSAT scores under standard administrations.

	GPA																					
LSAT Score	3.75 +		3.50 - 3.74		3.25 - 3.49		3.00 - 3.24		2.75 - 2.99		2.50 - 2.74		2.25 - 2.49		2.00 - 2.24		Below 2.00		No GPA		Total	
	Apps	Adm	Apps	Adm	Apps	Adm	Apps	Adm	Apps	Adm	Apps	Adm	Apps	Adm	Apps	Adm	Apps	Adm	Apps	Adm	Apps	Adm
175 - 180	0	0	0	0	0	0	0	0	0	0	0	0	0	0	0	0	0	0	0	0	0	0
170 - 174	0	0	0	0	0	0	0	0	0	0	0	0	1	1	0	0	0	0	0	0	1	1
165 - 169	0	0	0	0	1	1	5	5	2	2	2	1	2	2	0	0	0	0	0	0	12	11
160 - 164	5	4	15	11	6	6	12	12	27	21	21	19	6	5	7	6	1	0	3	3	103	87
155 - 159	13	8	16	14	35	27	63	49	75	65	54	40	30	16	6	5	1	1	2	0	295	225
150 - 154	12	12	39	31	82	68	101	84	116	73	88	33	47	10	25	8	2	0	4	3	516	322
145 - 149	11	8	34	21	67	41	101	48	114	31	87	11	54	6	15	0	11	0	6	0	500	166
140 - 144	0	0	7	2	24	12	63	10	62	8	59	5	60	5	17	0	11	0	6	2	309	44
135 - 139	0	0	4	0	4	1	25	2	22	1	28	0	33	0	13	0	3	0	5	2	137	6
130 - 134	0	0	1	1	0	0	5	0	6	2	13	0	11	0	9	1	5	0	6	0	56	4
125 - 129	0	0	0	0	3	0	0	0	2	0	5	0	2	0	1	0	2	0	2	0	17	0
120 - 124	0	0	0	0	0	0	0	0	0	0	0	0	2	0	0	0	0	0	0	0	2	0
Total	41	32	116	80	222	156	375	210	426	203	357	109	248	45	93	20	36	1	34	10	1948	866

Apps = Number of Applicants
Adm = Number Admitted
Reflects 99% of the total applicant pool.

University of Kansas School of Law

205 Green Hall
Lawrence, KS 66045

E-Mail: lindeman@law.wpo.ukans.edu
URL: http://lark.cc.ukans.edu/~kulaw/
Phone: 913.864.4378

■ Introduction

The University of Kansas School of Law was founded in 1891, replacing a Department of Law that had existed since 1878. The School of Law is located in Lawrence, Kansas, 40 miles west of Kansas City and 25 miles east of Topeka, the state capital. The school is a charter member of the AALS and is fully accredited by the ABA.

■ Enrollment/Student Body

➧ 803 applicants ➧ 347 admitted first-year class 1995 ➧ 178 enrolled first-year class 1995 ➧ 498 total full-time ➧ 13% minority ➧ 41% women ➧ 29 states & foreign countries represented ➧ 80 undergraduate schools represented

The student body consists of 82 percent Kansas residents. The nonresidents come from all parts of the country.

■ Faculty

➧ 38 total ➧ 29 full-time ➧ 9 part-time or adjunct ➧ 10 women ➧ 4 minority

■ Library and Physical Facilities

➧ 325,000 volumes & equivalents ➧ library hours: Mon.-Thurs., 7:30 A.M.-11:00 P.M.; Fri., 7:30 A.M.-5:00 P.M.; Sat., 10:00 A.M.-5:00 P.M.; Sun., 1:00 P.M.-11:00 P.M. ➧ LEXIS ➧ NEXIS ➧ WESTLAW ➧ DIALOG ➧ 3 full-time librarians ➧ library seats 353

The law library has ample reading areas and individual study carrels and maintains a microcomputer laboratory for student use.

■ Curriculum

➧ Academic Support Program ➧ 90 credits required to graduate ➧ 115 courses available ➧ degrees available: J.D.; J.D./M.B.A.; J.D./M.P.A.; J.D./M.A. in Economics; J.D./M.S. in Urban Planning; J.D./M.S.W.; J.D./M.S. Health Services Administration; J.D./M.A. in Philosophy ➧ fall semester starts in Aug. and summer semester starts in May ➧ range of first-year class size—20-100

Six semesters of full-time study are required for graduation. Two summer sessions of five weeks each are available. Students may begin their law studies in either the summer session or the fall semester. Students who begin in the summer and are continuously enrolled in summer sessions and regular semesters can graduate in 26 months. The summer program is also open to students with advanced standing at an accredited law school other than the University of Kansas.

The first-year curriculum is prescribed. All first-year students take one course in a small section of about 20 students. Second- and third-year students are required to take courses in commercial law, constitutional law, evidence, and legal profession. Each student must also complete a faculty-supervised writing project in the second or third year. Upper-class students can choose from a wide variety of elective courses, workshops, and clinical programs. Many third-year courses offer intensive training in planning and supervising legal transactions and drafting legal documents.

■ Special Programs

The Legal Aid Clinic is operated for the benefit of the Douglas County Legal Aid Society. Third-year law students represent low-income clients in actual civil cases under the supervision of clinical faculty and practicing attorneys in Lawrence. Students in the Criminal Justice Clinic assist prosecutors in virtually all phases of the criminal process, including criminal trials. Participants in the Defender Project counsel and perform legal services for indigent inmates of the U.S. Penitentiary at Leavenworth, the Kansas State Penitentiary, and Kansas Correctional Institution at Lansing.

The Judicial Clerkship Clinic provides an opportunity for students to serve as part-time law clerks for judges in a district court, the Kansas Court of Appeals, or a federal court. The Legislative Clinic sends a number of students to work as legislative interns to Kansas state legislators.

The Elderlaw Clinic enables students to represent elderly individuals primarily in consumer, housing, and public benefit matters.

The Public Policy Clinic gives students practical experience in applying analytical policy methods to public policy issues.

The school offers seven joint-degree programs. Each program allows a student to obtain two degrees in less time than it would normally take to earn them separately, generally four years.

■ Admission

➧ Bachelor's degree required for admission ➧ application deadline—March 15 ➧ LSAT, LSDAS required ➧ median GPA—3.41 ➧ median LSAT score—158 ➧ application fee—$40

The application deadline is March 15 for both the summer session and the fall semester. The school encourages students to apply by February 1.

The Admissions Committee seeks to admit highly qualified students with diverse backgrounds. Admissions decisions are based on a variety of criteria. The committee considers and compares applicants' undergraduate coursework and grades, and LSAT scores as well as other factors, including race, ethnic background, employment or professional experience, undergraduate and graduate program of study, leadership in university and civic activities, unique individual qualities and achievements, and demonstrated ability to overcome cultural, financial, or other disadvantages. The committee also considers the applicant's state of residence; preference is given to

Kansas residents. One letter of recommendation is required, two or three letters are encouraged. If possible, one letter should be from an academic reference. A personal statement is also required.

The School of Law is committed to the principle of providing access to the legal profession to men and women of all races, religions, ethnic backgrounds, and physical abilities. To that end, the School of Law engages in active recruitment of potential applicants with diverse backgrounds and characteristics, including those of minority race and ethnic background.

Admissions decisions are made from January through April. After the class is filled, a waiting list is established. Each applicant offered admission pays a $50 deposit which is refunded to the student at enrollment.

■ Student Activities

The *Kansas Law Review*, published four times annually, is edited by third-year students. The *Kansas Journal of Law and Public Policy* is edited by third-year students and is published twice annually. The Moot Court Council operates all phases of the Appellate Advocacy program and also has responsibility for the Moot Court competition. The Student Bar Association is responsible for most student activities. There are active chapters of Phi Alpha Delta and Phi Delta Phi legal fraternities, Black American Law Students Association, Hispanic American Law Students Association, Native American Law Student Association, Asian Pacific Islander Law Student Association, Women-in-Law, Christian Legal Society, Jewish Law Students Association, Catholic Law Students, International Law Society, American Trial Lawyers Association, Federalist Society, National Lawyer's Guild, Environmental Law Society, and Order of the Coif.

■ Expenses and Financial Aid

➽ *tuition & fees—full-time resident, $3,712; nonresident, $8,590* ➽ *estimated additional expenses—$10,000 (books, room and board, transportation, and misc. expenses)* ➽ *merit-based scholarships available (generally first year only)* ➽ *minority scholarships available* ➽ *financial aid available: FAFSA Form—priority deadline March 1*

For more information: Office of Student Financial Aid, University of Kansas, 50 Strong Hall, Lawrence, KS 66045.

■ Career Services

The school has a full-time career services director and an aggressive placement program involving career counseling, a wide variety of workshops, and resource facilities for extensive legal and nontraditional job hunting research. Of the numerous placement opportunities available to law school graduates, law firms of all sizes attracted the highest percentage (51 percent) of those placed. By November 1, 1994, 80 percent of the 1994 class was employed. Students were placed in 20 states across the nation and in two foreign countries. The greatest percentage (70 percent) of those placed chose to remain in Kansas and the Kansas City metropolitan area.

Applicant Group for the 1995-1996 Academic Year

University of Kansas School of Law
This grid includes only applicants who earned 120-180 LSAT scores under standard administrations.

	GPA																					
LSAT Score	3.75 +		3.50 - 3.74		3.25 - 3.49		3.00 - 3.24		2.75 - 2.99		2.50 - 2.74		2.25 - 2.49		2.00 - 2.24		Below 2.00		No GPA		Total	
	Apps	Adm	Apps	Adm	Apps	Adm	Apps	Adm	Apps	Adm	Apps	Adm	Apps	Adm	Apps	Adm	Apps	Adm	Apps	Adm	Apps	Adm
175 - 180	2	2	0	0	0	0	0	0	0	0	0	0	0	0	0	0	0	0	0	0	2	2
170 - 174	1	1	2	2	1	1	1	1	2	1	0	0	1	0	0	0	0	0	0	0	8	6
165 - 169	7	7	3	3	5	4	6	6	2	2	1	0	1	1	0	0	0	0	0	0	25	23
160 - 164	13	13	26	24	20	20	22	21	11	9	12	7	6	1	2	0	0	0	1	1	113	96
155 - 159	29	29	38	35	41	35	24	17	22	6	13	2	10	0	2	1	0	0	1	1	180	126
150 - 154	27	15	40	17	37	14	41	10	36	3	16	1	12	4	3	0	1	0	1	0	214	64
145 - 149	7	3	15	5	20	3	31	4	18	2	16	1	11	1	7	1	1	0	1	1	127	21
140 - 144	0	0	10	1	10	0	10	2	7	1	13	3	9	0	4	0	1	0	3	0	67	7
135 - 139	0	0	1	0	3	0	3	0	5	0	3	0	5	0	4	0	1	0	1	0	26	0
130 - 134	0	0	1	0	1	0	1	0	2	0	3	0	2	0	3	0	0	0	3	0	16	0
125 - 129	0	0	0	0	0	0	0	0	0	0	0	0	0	0	0	0	0	0	0	0	0	0
120 - 124	0	0	0	0	0	0	0	0	0	0	0	0	0	0	0	0	0	0	0	0	0	0
Total	86	70	136	87	138	77	139	61	105	24	77	14	57	7	25	2	4	0	11	3	778	345

Apps = Number of Applicants
Adm = Number Admitted
Reflects 99% of the total applicant pool.

University of Kentucky College of Law

Dean's Office, 209 Law Building
Lexington, KY 40506-0048

URL: http://www.uky.edu/Law
Phone: 606.257.7938 for catalogs; 606.257.1678 for other inquiries

■ Introduction

The University of Kentucky College of Law is a medium-sized, state-supported law school located on the main campus of the university at Lexington. Lexington, a city of approximately 220,000, is the center of the Bluegrass horse farm region of Kentucky. The college was founded in 1908, has held membership in the AALS since 1912, and has been approved by the ABA since 1925. The faculty has wide experience in teaching, research, law practice, and government service and provides a student-faculty ratio of 19 to 1. By long tradition, the educational mission of the school has been to prepare its graduates for a full range of professional interests in law throughout the nation.

■ Enrollment/Student Body

➧ *1,037 applicants* ➧ *150 enrolled first-year class 1995*
➧ *435 total full-time (376 residents, 59 nonresidents)*
➧ *8% minority* ➧ *34% women*
➧ *27 states & foreign countries represented*
➧ *116 undergraduate schools represented*

■ Faculty

➧ *52 total* ➧ *28 full-time* ➧ *24 part-time or adjunct*
➧ *13 women* ➧ *3 minority*

■ Library and Physical Facilities

➧ *350,000 volumes & equivalents* ➧ *LEXIS* ➧ *NEXIS*
➧ *WESTLAW* ➧ *DIALOG* ➧ *library seats 392*

The college is housed in a contemporary brick and marble building that provides all facilities for a complete program of legal education, including a large courtroom. The law library contains one of the major legal collections in the southeast. The newest acquisition, a state-of-the-art, 50-station computer laboratory for students, was completed in fall 1993 and is located on the main floor of the library.

■ Curriculum

➧ *Academic Support Program* ➧ *90 credits required to graduate* ➧ *64 courses available*
➧ *degrees available: J.D.; J.D./M.B.A.; J.D./M.P.A.*
➧ *range of first-year class size—10-75*

The college offers only a full-time program, designed to be completed over three academic years (six semesters) of residence. The first-year program is prescribed. In the second and third years, a full range of elective courses is offered in traditional and newly developing legal fields. After the first year, the only specific requirements are that each student take a course in professional ethics and complete a seminar that involves substantial writing.

■ Special Programs

The Mineral Law Center, established in 1983, concentrates on environmental and natural resource issues. It publishes the *Journal of Natural Resources and Environmental Law,* a journal devoted to these issues. The center is a resource for the state and nation in matters of coal extraction and use, natural resources, and environmental protection. The college provides second- and third-year students with opportunities for clinical experience in civil and criminal cases and for judicial clerkships. All students are offered a variety of academic support services by faculty members and are invited to participate in all seminars for the bench and bar sponsored by the college's Office of Continuing Legal Education. The college also hosts two lectureship series, bringing U.S. Supreme Court Justices and other national figures to speak to its students and the community.

■ Student Activities

The College of Law has a variety of cocurricular activities in which students may earn credit and which are an integral part of the instructional program. The *Kentucky Law Journal*, a quarterly publication containing articles by prominent national scholars, is the tenth oldest American law review and is edited entirely by a student editorial board.

Another journal, the *Journal of Natural Resources and Environmental Law,* focuses on articles about mineral, natural resources, and environmental law, and also offers its student staff an opportunity to work with lawyers of national stature.

The Moot Court Program consists of competitive appellate arguments by student teams; the successful team represents the college each year in the National Moot Court Competition. The college's teams have a history of excellence and have advanced to the national finals six times in the last decade.

The Trial Advocacy Board teaches effective trial level advocacy through student competition; its members also are members of the local chapter of Inns of Court.

The Student Bar Association, affiliated with the Law Student Division of the ABA, serves as the student governing body, produces a student newspaper, and arranges weekly professional, cultural, and social programs. It was recognized by the ABA as one of the nation's top SBA's in 1992, 1994, and again in 1995.

The college has long had an Order of the Coif. Other organizations include the Women's Law Caucus, Black Law Students Association, the Christian Legal Society, the International Law Society, National Lawyers' Guild, The Federalist Society, Student Public Interest Law Foundation, the Natural Resource and Environmental Law Society, and three legal fraternities.

■ Admission

➧ *Bachelor's degree from accredited college or university required* ➧ *application deadline—March 1; admission decisions begin in Nov., continue weekly through spring*
➧ *LSAT, LSDAS required* ➧ *median GPA—3.28*
➧ *median LSAT score—159* ➧ *application fee—$25*

Admission is considered and granted by the Faculty Admissions Committee. Each file is reviewed completely before any action is taken. The committee considers all the information in an applicant's file, including undergraduate-grade record, the LSAT score, and other quantitative and nonquantitative factors indicative of aptitude for law study. The committee examines with particular care the grade average for the most recent semesters of undergraduate study, recommendations of faculty, the nature and difficulty of coursework attempted, undergraduate extracurricular activities, work experience, and postbaccalaureate experiences. The committee reviews the file of each applicant to determine whether there is evidence of both the capability and motivation to do successful law school work. The committee also considers factors that bear on the provision of adequate legal services to all segments of Kentucky. Each applicant is urged to read the full description of the admissions process contained in the law school bulletin and to provide full information about his or her intellectual and non-academic achievements. The February LSAT is the last examination accepted by the Admissions Committee. Applicants are admitted for the fall term only.

■ Expenses and Financial Aid

➽ 1996-97 annual full-time tuition & fees—resident, $4,740; nonresident, $12,340 ➽ estimated additional expenses—$8,000 (books, room & board, misc.) ➽ minority scholarships available ➽ financial aid programs available; Federal Free Form due April 1 for all loan assistance and work-study

Scholarships for the first year of study are merit-based and usually awarded to students whose credentials are exceptional. The largest and most prestigious are the three-year, $20,000 awards to Bert Combs Scholars, two of whom are chosen each year by an application and competition process.

For all other first-year student scholarship awards, no additional application is necessary. All students admitted to the College of Law are considered automatically by the Scholarships and Honors Committee on the basis of their admission files. Second- and third-year students must submit applications on the basis of merit and/or need.

Law students are also eligible for loan assistance through the Federal Direct Student Loan Program, and two national private loan programs specifically for law students. Contact the university Student Financial Aid Office, 128 Funkhouser Building, University of Kentucky, Lexington, KY 40506-0054.

■ Career Services

UK Law students have access to hundreds of summer and permanent jobs nationwide through the College of Law's on-campus interviewing program and its participation in six off-campus interviewing conferences. The Southeastern Law Placement Consortium holds an annual conference in Atlanta that attracts government, corporate, and law firm employers from across the country. UK also participates in the Southeastern Law School's Minority Job Fair, the Mid-South Law Placement Consortium, the NAPIL Public Interest Job Fair, and the Sci-Law Job Fair. Many local legal employers hire UK law students to work part-time during the school year. The College's Career Planning Office, run by a Director of Career Services who formerly practiced law, also has initiated a computerized service to inform UK law students about employers and job openings in its region. UK's percentage of students placed six months after graduation exceeds 90 percent every year; 15 to 20 percent of the students from each graduating class are selected for state and federal judicial clerkships.

Applicant Group for the 1995-1996 Academic Year

University of Kentucky College of Law
Figures in the profile reflect admission decisions for all applicants with a 120-180 LSAT scale score who applied for the class which entered in the fall of 1995.

GPA

LSAT Score	3.75 - 4.00		3.50 - 3.74		3.25 - 3.49		3.00 - 3.24		2.75 - 2.99		2.50 - 2.74		2.25 - 2.49		Below 2.25		Total	
	Apps	Adm	Apps	Adm	Apps	Adm	Apps	Adm	Apps	Adm	Apps	Adm	Apps	Adm	Apps	Adm	Apps	Adm
165 & Above	9	9	7	7	8	8	12	12	6	6	7	7	3	3	5	3	57	55
160 - 164	13	13	37	37	32	32	34	35	29	28	12	8	9	4	3	2	169	158
155 - 159	26	20	42	26	44	22	50	23	37	9	22	8	12	1	6	0	239	109
150 - 154	18	4	36	5	53	4	45	1	43	3	38	1	16	2	5	0	254	20
145 - 149	10	0	15	0	25	0	32	1	36	5	36	3	10	2	7	0	171	11
140 - 144	3	0	4	0	16	0	19	0	17	2	16	0	17	0	5	0	97	2
Below 140	1	0	3	0	5	0	10	0	11	0	8	0	6	0	6	0	50	0
Total	80	46	144	75	183	66	202	71	179	53	139	27	73	12	37	5	1037	355

Apps = Number of Applicants
Adm = Number Admitted
The class enrolled was composed of 81% Kentucky residents. It had a median LSAT score of 159 for residents and 161 for nonresidents; its overall median GPA was 3.28.

Lewis and Clark, Northwestern School of Law

10015 S.W. Terwilliger Blvd.
Portland, OR 97219

E-Mail: spence@lclark.edu
URL: http://www.lclark.edu/law.html
Phone: 503.768.6613

■ Introduction

Northwestern School of Law of Lewis and Clark College believes in a balanced approach to legal education that assures a solid theoretical foundation along with hands-on experience in practice. The campus is one of the most beautiful in the nation. Situated next to a state park, students are only a moment away from an extensive trail system used by joggers, walkers, and bicyclists. The law school is accredited by the ABA and AALS.

■ Enrollment/Student Body

➽ 2,160 applicants ➽ 839 admitted first-year class 1995 ➽ 223 enrolled first-year class 1995 ➽ 514 total full-time ➽ 186 total part-time ➽ 15% minority ➽ 43% women ➽ approximately 34 states & foreign countries represented ➽ 251 undergraduate schools represented

The 680-700 students attending the law school represent a spectrum of ages, experiences, and priorities. Business executives, biologists interested in resources and environmental law, students of politics, musicians, school teachers—people from almost all of the analytical disciplines meet at the law school in a common pursuit. The atmosphere at the law school is one of mutual support during a time of academic challenge. Students and faculty can often be found discussing questions long after class has ended.

■ Faculty

➽ 81 total ➽ 29 full-time ➽ 52 part-time or adjunct ➽ 25 women ➽ 1 minority

The full-time faculty were educated at the nation's most distinguished law schools. The faculty reflects a breadth of experience and interests that give depth and creative energy to their teaching. A number of faculty members have spent sabbaticals in recent years teaching in other countries; several have been Fulbright professors in such places as China, Greece, and Venezuela.

■ Library/Physical Facilities

➽ 410,000 volumes & equivalents ➽ library hours: Mon.-Thurs., 7:00 A.M.-MIDNIGHT; Fri., 7:00 A.M.-10:00 P.M.; Sat.-Sun., 9:00 A.M.-MIDNIGHT ➽ LEXIS ➽ NEXIS ➽ WESTLAW ➽ INFOTRAC, Internet access, PORTALS, DIALOG, CALI, OCLC, WLN, INNOVATIVE, ORBIS, FIRSTSEARCH, QL SYSTEM ➽ 8 full-time librarians ➽ library seats 400

The materials and staff of the Paul Boley Law Library, the largest law library in the state, the second largest in the northwest, well exceed the standards set by the Association of American Law Schools.

Our collection of more than 410,000 volumes, and volume equivalents, includes extensive materials in Environmental Law, Federal Legislative History, Tax, Commercial, Intellectual Property, and Legal History. It is also the only academic law library in the country to be a Patent and Trademark Depository Library. Supporting our collection is a sophisticated computer infrastructure of instruction labs and local area networks.

Framed by majestic fir trees, the campus is composed of contemporary buildings with both classrooms and a large state park within a moment's walk from the library. Traditional student needs and those of individuals with disabilities are met through a variety of facilities.

■ Curriculum

➽ 86 units/credits required to graduate ➽ 142 courses available ➽ degrees available: J.D., LL.M. in Environmental & Natural Resources Law ➽ semesters, start in Aug. ➽ range of first-year class size—30-90 ➽ Academic Enhancement Program

The law school confers both the J.D. degree and a specialized LL.M. in Environmental and Natural Resources Law. To earn a J.D., a student must take a prescribed first-year set of courses. In the upper division, students must take a seminar, constitutional law, and professionalism and fulfill two writing requirements. Students choose between a three-year day program and a four-year evening program. Admission criteria, faculty, academic opportunities, and graduation requirements are the same for each. After the first year, students may select courses in either division as their scheduling requirements suggest.

■ Specific Special Programs

Environmental Law Certificate: The faculty has established a certificate program to acknowledge the law school's nationally renowned concentration in Environmental and Natural Resource Law. The specialty is grounded in a core curriculum broad enough to allow students to prepare for careers in numerous areas of law practice.

Tax Certificate: The faculty has approved an upper division set of courses in the business and tax curriculum that allow the student to develop an expertise in tax.

Practical Skills: Students have many opportunities to gain hands-on experience in the legal profession. Among them are the Legal Clinic, externships, moot courts, and trial advocacy.

The Legal Clinic is located in downtown Portland where students perform a variety of legal services under the tutelage of faculty members. Students interview and counsel clients, prepare cases, conduct trials, negotiate settlements, and prepare appeals.

Externships combine practical and scholarly components by placing the student in full-time work for a semester and then requiring a substantial research paper and attendance at a special seminar. Four types of externship are available—judicial, natural resources and environmental law, criminal, and general. Externs are placed in Oregon, throughout the United States, and in foreign countries.

Moot Court experience may be gained in mock trial, appellate advocacy, environmental law, international law, and client counseling. The school regularly competes at the regional and national levels.

Trial Advocacy provides students with the opportunity to try civil and criminal cases in front of local judges in the trial practice course offered each year. A criminal practice course deals solely with criminal trial work and is taught by a local trial judge.

■ Admission

➧ *Bachelor's degree required* ➧ *application deadline—March 15, rolling admission* ➧ *LSAT, LSDAS required* ➧ *median GPA—3.27* ➧ *median LSAT score—160* ➧ *application fee—$50*

Lewis and Clark affirmatively seeks a diverse student body. The Admission Committee makes a serious effort to consider each applicant as an individual. Factors such as college, program, length of time since the degree was obtained, experience, writing ability, and community activities are taken into consideration. Only those candidates with excellent professional promise are admitted. Academic attrition is low, averaging 2 to 4 percent.

First-year students may begin only in the fall; there is no provision for midyear admission.

■ Student Activities

These include the law review, *Environmental Law,* numerous speakers on campus, an endowed program that brings an outstanding legal scholar to campus for lectures and seminars, and many student organizations reflecting the diverse make-up of the student body.

■ Expenses and Financial Aid

➧ *tuition & fees—full-time, $15,625; part-time, $11,000* ➧ *estimated additional expenses—$7,500 (books, rent, transportation, living expenses)* ➧ *scholarships available* ➧ *financial aid available; FAF form application due Feb. 15*

Approximately 40 percent of the students at Lewis and Clark receive some scholarship support during their law school career. The school annually awards Dean's Fellowships, Natural Resources Scholarships, and Public Interest Fellowships for up to $10,000 apiece. In addition, loan money and work-study funds are available. There is no separate application procedure for scholarship funds. Scholarship consideration is part of the admission process. Students are considered on the basis of undergraduate record, LSAT score, activities, and writing ability.

Students interested in loans need to apply for financial aid as early as possible and should not wait for an admission decision to begin the process.

■ Career Services

The Career Services Office gives seminars, maintains an alumni network around the country to help with positions after graduation, and hosts panels of working attorneys who discuss with students specific areas of practice. There are on-campus interviews each fall, and the career services office assists students in finding clerking positions during law school. Recent graduates have been placed in a wide variety of desirable positions around the country.

Academic Group for the 1995-1996 Academic Year

Lewis and Clark, Northwestern School of Law
This grid includes only applicants who earned 120-180 LSAT scores under standard administrations.

	GPA																					
LSAT Score	3.75 +		3.50 - 3.74		3.25 - 3.49		3.00 - 3.24		2.75 - 2.99		2.50 - 2.74		2.25 - 2.49		2.00 - 2.24		Below 2.00		No GPA		Total	
	Apps	Adm	Apps	Adm	Apps	Adm	Apps	Adm	Apps	Adm	Apps	Adm	Apps	Adm	Apps	Adm	Apps	Adm	Apps	Adm	Apps	Adm
175 - 180	0	0	2	2	0	0	0	0	1	1	0	0	1	1	0	0	0	0	0	0	4	4
170 - 174	3	2	3	3	3	3	8	8	4	4	1	1	3	3	0	0	0	0	2	1	27	25
165 - 169	8	8	17	16	25	25	23	22	25	22	8	8	10	10	0	0	0	0	2	2	118	113
160 - 164	26	26	50	48	106	100	89	84	65	55	38	27	18	8	8	4	1	0	8	5	409	357
155 - 159	37	31	95	69	134	80	130	39	89	14	44	5	12	0	4	0	2	0	6	1	553	239
150 - 154	21	8	66	17	99	17	107	11	72	3	57	2	21	2	10	1	0	0	9	2	462	63
145 - 149	10	1	32	3	66	4	78	7	65	3	38	1	11	0	13	0	0	0	4	1	317	20
140 - 144	1	0	10	1	20	1	34	0	35	0	26	0	13	0	6	0	0	0	5	0	150	2
135 - 139	0	0	1	0	6	0	13	0	9	0	10	0	11	0	4	0	1	0	4	0	59	0
130 - 134	0	0	0	0	3	0	2	0	2	0	1	0	3	0	1	0	0	0	1	0	13	0
125 - 129	1	0	0	0	0	0	0	0	1	0	0	0	1	0	0	0	0	0	0	0	3	0
120 - 124	0	0	0	0	0	0	0	0	0	0	0	0	0	0	0	0	0	0	0	0	0	0
Total	107	76	276	159	462	230	484	171	368	102	223	44	104	24	46	5	4	0	41	12	2115	823

Apps = Number of Applicants
Adm = Number Admitted
Reflects 98% of the total applicant pool.

Louisiana State University Law Center

Baton Rouge, LA 70803

Phone: 504.388.8646

■ Introduction

The Louisiana State University Law Center was originally established as the Louisiana State University Law School in 1907, pursuant to an authorization contained in the university charter. In 1979, the Law Center was renamed the Paul M. Hebert Law Center of Louisiana State University. The Law Center holds membership in the AALS and is on the approved list of the ABA.

■ Enrollment/Student Body

➧ 1,071 applicants ➧ 539 admitted first-year class 1995 ➧ 280 enrolled first-year class 1995 ➧ 677 total full-time ➧ 8% minority ➧ 46% women

■ Faculty

➧ 44 total ➧ 33 full-time ➧ 11 part-time or adjunct ➧ 3 women ➧ 1 minority

■ Library and Physical Facilities

➧ 552,426 volumes & equivalents ➧ library hours: Mon.-Fri., 7:00 A.M.-11:00 P.M.; Sat., 9:00 A.M.-5:00 P.M.; Sun., NOON-11:00 P.M. ➧ LEXIS ➧ NEXIS ➧ WESTLAW ➧ DIALOG ➧ 8 full-time librarians ➧ library seats 565

The Law Center Building, completed in October 1969, adds extensive facilities to the original Law Center Building dedicated in 1938. This complex provides classroom areas, seminar rooms, discussion rooms, and meeting areas as well as a practice courtroom. Special offices for student research and student activities such as the *Louisiana Law Review*, Appellate Advocacy Board, and Student Bar Association are included in the facility. The law library, housed in the complex, provides one of the most complete collections of Roman and modern civil law reports and materials in the country. Library resources include reading rooms, discussion rooms, study carrels, personal computers, and audiovisual facilities. Students also have access to other campus facilities including the Student Health Center, residential housing, and the Sports Recreational Complex.

■ Curriculum

➧ 97 units required to graduate ➧ 87 courses available ➧ degrees available: J.D.; J.D./M.P.A.; LL.M; & M.C.L. ➧ semesters, start in Aug. ➧ range of first-year class size—75-80

First-year students have a prescribed curriculum and thereafter students may choose a wide variety of electives in addition to the core of civil law courses. An orientation program and library tour introduces the first-year class to the study of law. The Law Center's dedication to the study of both the civil and the common law prepares its graduates to practice in any state and in some foreign countries. Students receive a unique insight with the comparison of the two legal systems. Seven semesters of resident study are required for the degree. In addition to its full-time law faculty, the LSU Law Center each semester invites a number of special lecturers, including practicing attorneys and legal scholars, to teach courses in which they are particularly distinguished. A number of faculty have law degrees from foreign countries. This serves to promote the study of international law and an understanding of the policies of foreign law.

■ Summer Session Abroad

The Law Center conducts a summer program in France at the University of Aix-Marseille III Law School, Aix-en-Provence, France. All classes of the six-week summer program are conducted in English and are designed to meet the requirements of the ABA and AALS.

■ Special Programs

A wide variety of courses affords each student the opportunity to participate in the preparation and trial of mock cases, both civil and criminal, and also to develop skill in legal negotiations and counseling. LSU sponsors and encourages student participation in national trial and appellate competitions throughout the school year.

In cooperation with the Center of Continuing Professional Development, the Law Center presents several seminars, institutes, and conferences for practicing lawyers.

The LSU Law Center admits candidates for the degrees of Master of Laws (LL.M.) and Master of Civil Law (M.C.L.). The program is highly selective and admits students with exceptional ability.

■ Admission

➧ Bachelor's degree from accredited college or university required ➧ application deadline—Feb. 1, rolling admission, early applications preferred ➧ LSAT, LSDAS required ➧ median GPA—3.32 ➧ median LSAT score—153 ➧ application fee—$25

No specific prelaw curriculum is required for admission. Applicants are chosen mainly on the basis of the combination of their GPA and LSAT score. Applicants are advised to take the LSAT in October or no later than December prior to the year in which they seek admission to the Law Center. When the LSAT is repeated, the highest score received is used. The Law Center admits students only in the fall and only for full-time study. There are no night courses offered. Written recommendations are not required, and personal interviews are not encouraged. Because of the great number of applicants, only a few nonresidents are accepted. Transfer applications may be made, but only students who originally would be admissible to the Law Center and have excellent law school records are accepted.

Louisiana State University assures equal opportunity for all qualified persons without regard to race, color, religion, sex, national origin, age, disability, marital status, or veteran's status in the admission to, participation in, or employment in the programs and activities that the university operates.

■ Student Activities

The *Louisiana Law Review* was established to encourage high-quality legal scholarship in the student body, to contribute to the development of the law by scholarly criticism and analysis, and to serve the bar of Louisiana by comments and discussion of current cases and legal problems. It is edited by a board of student editors with faculty cooperation.

The Louisiana Chapter of the Order of the Coif, a national honorary law fraternity, was established in the Law Center in 1942. Election to the Order of the Coif is recognized as the highest honor a law student may receive.

Since a large number of graduates of the Law Center go directly into practice, the LSU Law Center has an extensive Trial Advocacy Program in which moot court training is offered both for trial work and in appellate argument.

All students in the Law Center are eligible to join the Student Bar Association. This association promotes and coordinates student activities within the Law Center and serves as an instructional medium for postgraduate bar association activities.

■ Expenses and Financial Aid

- *tuition & fees—full-time/semester resident students, $1,961; full-time/semester nonresident students, $4,271*
- *estimated additional expenses—$350/semester books*
- *performance & need-based scholarships available*
- *ACT form for need analysis due to financial aid office in March*

A number of loan funds are available to help deserving students who need financial assistance to continue their education. All such funds are subject to the policies and regulations authorized by the LSU Student Loan Fund Committee. Detailed information on all loan funds may be secured by contacting the Student Loan Section, LSU Office of Financial Aid and Scholarships, 202 Himes Hall, Baton Rouge, LA 70803.

■ Career Services

The Career Services Office of the Law Center provides job opportunities for students and graduates. It serves as a liaison between the numerous firms, businesses, and governmental agencies in providing on-campus interviews each year. This office offers a series of workshops and individual counseling to help meet the career needs of all students.

Applicant Group for the 1995-1996 Academic Year

Louisiana State University Law Center
This grid includes only applicants who earned 120-180 LSAT scores under standard administrations.

GPA

LSAT Score	3.75 +		3.50 - 3.74		3.25 - 3.49		3.00 - 3.24		2.75 - 2.99		2.50 - 2.74		2.25 - 2.49		2.00 - 2.24		Below 2.00		No GPA		Total	
	Apps	Adm	Apps	Adm	Apps	Adm	Apps	Adm	Apps	Adm	Apps	Adm	Apps	Adm	Apps	Adm	Apps	Adm	Apps	Adm	Apps	Adm
175 - 180	1	1	0	0	1	1	0	0	0	0	0	0	1	1	0	0	0	0	0	0	3	3
170 - 174	1	1	2	2	2	2	0	0	0	0	1	1	0	0	0	0	0	0	0	0	6	6
165 - 169	3	3	2	2	4	4	7	6	5	5	2	2	3	2	1	1	1	0	0	0	28	25
160 - 164	10	10	12	11	21	21	12	12	17	12	15	11	10	4	1	0	0	0	0	0	98	81
155 - 159	13	13	16	16	35	35	41	34	39	17	22	9	9	3	10	2	2	0	4	1	191	130
150 - 154	19	18	33	33	67	57	79	47	58	18	29	1	19	2	4	0	1	0	4	1	313	177
145 - 149	8	8	25	19	45	34	41	15	51	5	32	1	23	1	8	0	1	0	1	0	235	83
140 - 144	5	5	4	2	19	9	19	3	24	1	20	1	12	0	7	0	3	0	6	1	119	22
135 - 139	2	2	4	3	2	0	8	0	6	1	15	0	6	0	5	0	0	0	6	3	54	9
130 - 134	0	0	0	0	0	0	1	0	1	0	3	0	2	0	2	0	0	0	0	0	9	0
125 - 129	0	0	0	0	0	0	0	0	1	0	0	0	0	0	1	0	0	0	1	0	3	0
120 - 124	0	0	0	0	0	0	0	0	0	0	0	0	0	0	0	0	0	0	0	0	0	0
Total	62	61	98	88	196	163	208	117	202	59	139	26	85	13	39	3	8	0	22	6	1059	536

Apps = Number of Applicants
Adm = Number Admitted
Reflects 98% of the total applicant pool.

University of Louisville School of Law

E-Mail: jltorb01@ulkyvm.louisville.edu
URL: http://www.louisville.edu/groups/law-www/
Louisville, KY 40292
Phone: 502.852.6364

■ Introduction

Founded in 1846, the University of Louisville School of Law is Kentucky's oldest law school and America's fifth oldest in continuous operation. Heir to the legacy of Justice Louis D. Brandeis, the school is distinguished by a rich history, national outreach, and profound dedication to public service. It is an integral part of the University of Louisville, a public institution and major research center founded in 1798. The metropolitan area, with a population of approximately one million, combines a gracious ambience of southern hospitality with cultural, aesthetic, and recreational attractions that have put Louisville on the "Places Rated Almanac" top ten list of most livable American cities. Historic Churchill Downs, the acclaimed Kentucky Center for the Arts, the J.B. Speed Art Museum and the university's outstanding sports facilities are near the law school or within a few minutes drive.

■ Enrollment/Student Body

➽ 1,212 applicants ➽ 442 admitted first-year class 1995 ➽ 181 enrolled first-year class 1995 ➽ 51% women first-year class 1995 ➽ 366 total full-time ➽ 112 total part-time ➽ 7% minority ➽ 26 states & foreign countries represented and over 100 undergraduate schools represented

The School of Law promotes equal opportunity, geographical and cultural diversity, and a positive learning environment for all students.

■ Faculty

➽ 42 total ➽ 27 full-time ➽ 15 part-time or adjunct ➽ 13 women (including 5 adjunct faculty) ➽ 3 minority

Based on full-time equivalency standards, the law school has an attractive faculty-student ratio of 1 to 18. Law faculty recently have acted as consultants to the Kentucky General Assembly, the U.S. Securities and Exchange Commission, the State Justice Institute, the U.S. Administrative Office of the Courts, and the constitutional drafting commissions of the former Soviet republics of Belarus and Kyrghystan.

■ Library and Physical Facilities

➽ 244,678 volumes & equivalents (4,576 serials) ➽ library hours: Mon.-Thurs., 8:00 A.M.-11:00 P.M.; Fri., 8:00 A.M.-6:00 P.M.; Sat., 9:00 A.M.-5:00 P.M.; Sun., 1:00 P.M.-11:00 P.M. ➽ LEXIS ➽ WESTLAW ➽ OCLC ➽ 4 full-time librarians ➽ library seats 367

The modern law library contains two computer rooms; OCLC, LEXIS and WESTLAW services; CD-ROM and interactive instructional workstations. The library also houses the Brandeis Rare Book Room and, by direction of Justice Brandeis, a collection of original Supreme Court briefs.

■ Curriculum

➽ 90 units/credits and public service component required for J.D. degree (3 years full-time, 4 years part-time) ➽ 120 courses available, 5 internship programs; 9 moot court, mock trial, and other professional skill competitions; law reviews and individual studies ➽ degrees available: J.D. and two combined degree (M.B.A./J.D. and J.D./M.Div.) programs ➽ semesters, start in Aug. and Jan.; summer term in May ➽ range of first-year class size—40-65 (in 3 sections)

The law school full-time day division and part-time evening division share the same curriculum, faculty, and academic standards. After basic courses in the first year, students take "core" courses in doctrinal subjects, advanced research and writing, and professional responsibility. Students also may choose among a rich variety of specialized and interdisciplinary electives. The School of Law conducts an innovative summer enrichment program for selected, newly admitted students. A highly successful academic support office serves students throughout the year.

■ Special Programs

The School of Law contains a Center for Environmental Policy, which promotes interdisciplinary studies. National speakers present the annual Brandeis Lecture, Harlan Lecture, Petrilli Family Law Seminar, and the Carl A. Warns Labor/Employment Law Institute. The school operates clinical internship programs in which upperclass students, with supervision, represent clients and appear in court. The school has active faculty and/or student international exchanges with law schools in England, France, Germany, Japan, and Australia.

The M.B.A/J.D. program is offered jointly by the School of Law and the School of Business. Upon successful completion of the program, the student is awarded both the M.B.A. and J.D. degrees. The School of Law, in connection with the Louisville Presbyterian Theological Seminary, offers a double competency program leading to the degree of Master of Divinity (M.Div.) as well as the J.D.

■ Samuel L. Greenebaum Public Service Program

Reflecting the spirit of Justice Louis D. Brandeis, the School of Law was one of America's first five law schools to adopt public service as part of the prescribed course of study. Through this public service work, students develop lawyering skills, serve their communities and establish professional values.

■ Admission

➽ Baccalaureate degree (candidacy) required ➽ priority deadline—Feb. 15 ➽ rolling admission ➽ LSAT, LSDAS required ➽ median GPA—3.31 ➽ median LSAT score—158 ➽ application fee—$30

The School of Law has no specific prelaw requirements but agrees with the suggestions on prelaw study contained in the first section of this handbook. Applicants are encouraged to complete their files no later than February 15. Later applications ordinarily will be considered only if space becomes available. In truly exceptional circumstances, the School of Law may consider applicants who have taken the LSAT in June immediately preceding the fall semester of expected enrollment. Applicants with nontraditional credentials may be invited to a summer admission-by-performance program.

■ Expenses and Financial Aid

➽ *annual tuition & fees—full-time resident, $4,470; full-time nonresident, $11,820; part-time resident, $3,740; part-time nonresident, $9,860 (10 hours per semester)*
➽ *estimated additional expenses—$9,810 (includes full housing, board, books & supplies, transportation, and personal expenses)*
➽ *moderate cost housing available near university*
➽ *merit and need scholarships available* ➽ *financial aid approximately $340,000 in 1995-96* ➽ *FAFSA required*

■ Publications and Student Activities

The School of Law publishes three student-edited periodicals with national or international circulation. The *Journal of Family Law*, the school's law review, is published quarterly, including an international edition. The *Journal of Law and Education* is published jointly by the law schools of the University of Louisville and the University of South Carolina. *The Brandeis Brief* is a magazine-style publication containing interdisciplinary articles in the Brandeis tradition and news of the law school.

The School of Law emphasizes professional skill programs. It participates in nine different national moot court competitions including an international moot court program, a negotiations competition sponsored by the American Bar Association, a mock trial program sponsored by the American Bar Association, and a mock trial program sponsored by the Association of Trial Lawyers of America. All students are thoroughly trained in legal writing and oral argument in their first year, and they may participate in the intraschool Pirtle-Washer Competition.

Honor students are recognized by membership in the law school's Brandeis Society. The Society awards the prestigious Brandeis Medal to America's outstanding lawyers and jurists. Recipients have included Supreme Court Justices Sandra Day O'Connor and Harry Blackman, Judge Leon Higginbotham, Senator Christopher Dodd, and civil rights attorney Morris Dees.

The Student Bar Association, affiliated with the Law Student Division of the American Bar Association, plays an important role in law school governance.

■ Career Opportunities

Graduates have enjoyed a higher Kentucky bar passage rate than the overall average, and they have been successful in other states as well. The most recent (1994) national survey of law graduates showed University of Louisville law students above the national average in obtaining law employment within six months of graduation. Approximately three-quarters of our 1994 graduates are working in Kentucky. Job listings, various databases, informational sessions, hard copy resources, job fairs, and individual counseling are available to assist students in their job searches.

Applicant Group for the 1995-1996 Academic Year

University of Louisville School of Law
This grid includes only applicants who earned 120-180 LSAT scores under standard administrations.

GPA

LSAT Score	3.75 +		3.50 - 3.74		3.25 - 3.49		3.00 - 3.24		2.75 - 2.99		2.50 - 2.74		2.25 - 2.49		2.00 - 2.24		Below 2.00		No GPA		Total	
	Apps	Adm	Apps	Adm	Apps	Adm	Apps	Adm	Apps	Adm	Apps	Adm	Apps	Adm	Apps	Adm	Apps	Adm	Apps	Adm	Apps	Adm
175 - 180	0	0	0	0	0	0	0	0	0	0	0	0	0	0	0	0	0	0	0	0	0	0
170 - 174	2	2	0	0	1	1	0	0	0	0	0	0	2	2	0	0	0	0	0	0	5	5
165 - 169	0	0	2	2	3	3	3	3	2	1	2	2	5	3	2	2	1	0	1	1	21	17
160 - 164	4	4	15	15	11	10	10	10	19	18	11	8	8	5	0	0	0	0	1	1	79	71
155 - 159	21	21	27	26	45	41	60	44	48	35	32	20	14	4	3	1	0	0	2	1	252	193
150 - 154	16	11	44	29	86	28	79	22	76	16	49	10	18	7	3	2	1	0	5	0	377	125
145 - 149	12	4	33	2	33	1	53	3	58	4	31	2	15	3	5	0	2	0	4	2	246	21
140 - 144	3	1	3	0	18	0	25	1	17	0	30	1	21	0	8	0	1	0	1	0	127	3
135 - 139	1	0	0	0	6	0	8	0	8	0	9	0	12	0	1	0	0	0	3	0	48	0
130 - 134	1	0	3	0	0	0	2	0	2	0	3	0	4	0	3	0	0	0	0	0	18	0
125 - 129	0	0	0	0	0	0	0	0	2	0	2	0	0	0	0	0	0	0	0	0	4	0
120 - 124	0	0	0	0	0	0	0	0	0	0	0	0	0	0	0	0	0	0	1	0	1	0
Total	60	43	127	74	203	84	240	83	232	74	169	43	99	24	25	5	5	0	18	5	1178	435

Apps = Number of Applicants
Adm = Number Admitted
Reflects 98% of the total applicant pool. Students admitted through the summer admission-by-performance program are included.

Loyola University Chicago School of Law

One East Pearson Street
Chicago, IL 60611
Phone: 312.915.7170, 1.800.545.5744

■ Introduction

Loyola University Chicago is the second largest private institution of higher learning in Illinois. The School of Law is located on the Water Tower campus of the university, a few blocks north of the Chicago Loop. This campus adjoins Michigan Avenue at the historical Water Tower, a Chicago landmark, in approximately the center of the renowned "Magnificent Mile," a commercial center over which the John Hancock Center towers. This location provides ready access to the state and federal courts and to the offices of most other institutions of federal, state, and local government as well as the cultural centers of Chicago. The school is a member of the AALS and is approved by the ABA.

■ Enrollment/Student Body

➻ 2,553 applicants ➻ 896 admitted first-year class 1995 ➻ 230 enrolled first-year class 1995 ➻ 769 total J.D. students ➻ 580 total full-time J.D. students ➻ 189 total part-time J.D. students ➻ 22% minority J.D. students ➻ 51% women J.D. students ➻ 25 states & foreign countries represented in the student body ➻ 105 undergraduate schools represented in the student body

■ Faculty

➻ 154 total faculty members ➻ 34 full-time ➻ 120 part-time or adjunct ➻ 56 women ➻ 6 minority

■ Library and Physical Facilities

➻ over 300,000 volumes & equivalents ➻ library hours (including weekends & evenings): 99 hours/week ➻ LEXIS ➻ NEXIS ➻ WESTLAW ➻ 8.5 full-time librarians ➻ library seats 370

■ Curriculum

➻ Academic Support Program ➻ 86 units/credits required to graduate ➻ 101 courses available ➻ degrees available: J.D.; LL.M.; M.J.; J.D./M.B.A.; J.D./M.S.W.; J.D./M.A.; J.D./M.I.R. ➻ semesters, start in Aug. ➻ range of first-year class size—60-75 ➻ first-year legal writing sections of 16 maximum

■ Foreign Study Programs

Since 1983 the School of Law has offered a program of international and comparative law courses at the Rome Center for Liberal Arts, the university's campus in Rome, Italy. Each summer, for approximately five weeks, law students from the United States and elsewhere can take one or more of the courses offered in Rome by members of the full-time Loyola law faculty.

In January 1989, Loyola inaugurated its London Advocacy Program in which eight students travel to London for approximately 15 days to become immersed in the world of the British barrister. In addition to a series of lectures and tours, law students accompany British barristers to courts and observe them as they conduct trials at London's renowned "Old Bailey."

The Institute for Health Law sponsors a summer course on comparative health law in conjunction with the McGill University Center for Medicine, Ethics, and Law. In alternate summers, the program is conducted at McGill University in Montreal, Canada.

■ Dual Degree Programs

The School of Law has dual-degree programs with Loyola's School of Social Work, the Graduate Program of the Department of Political Science, the Graduate School of Business, and the Institute of Human Resources and Industrial Relations. The dual-degree programs are structured to allow completion after four years.

■ Civitas ChildLaw Center

The Civitas ChildLaw Center was created to prepare law students to represent abused and neglected children. Each year only ten Civitas Scholars are accepted into the program from among the law school's entering class. Each scholar selected receives a $3,000 grant, renewable for three years, as well as summer financial internship support. In addition to a regular course of legal study, the selected Civitas Scholars will have the opportunity to participate in a unique specialized curriculum, including extensive extern opportunities and "hands-on" internship experiences designed to create enhanced knowledge and practical skills needed for effective representation of children.

As an integral component of the law school, the center is able to draw on the full resources of Loyola University, including its schools of medicine, nursing, social work, and education, to educate students dedicated to using the law for children. The center is the first of its kind at any American law school and is being referred to as a model for other law school-based child advocacy programs. At the conclusion of the three-year J.D. program, students will have been trained thoroughly to serve as skilled litigators and advocates for children. An LL.M. is available.

■ Institute for Health Law

The Institute for Health Law was created in 1984, in recognition of the need for an academic forum to study the field of health law and to act as a vehicle to foster dialogue between the law and the health sciences. Based in a university with schools of medicine, dentistry, nursing, and social work, and a large urban medical center, the School of Law is in an ideal position to act as a catalyst to foster interdisciplinary evaluation of the expansive legal issues encountered by our health delivery systems.

In pursuing its mission to be a leading academic-based health law program, the institute is focusing on teaching and research activities. In teaching, the institute is the sponsor of the first Master of Jurisprudence in health law (M.J. and D.Law) degree programs in the country, designed to provide health professionals with an intensive overview of health-care law. In addition, the institute offers a health law LL.M. and S.J.D. for attorneys who wish to specialize in this field. In the J.D. curriculum, the institute works with law faculty to ensure that the school's health law offerings are both comprehensive and timely. There are currently 18 health law courses taught in the law school.

■ Admission

➻ B.A. degree required ➻ application deadline—April 1 ➻ rolling admission, early application preferred ➻ LSAT, LSDAS required ➻ median GPA—3.31 ➻ median LSAT score—160 ➻ application fee—$45

Factors other than LSAT scores and college grades are considered whenever the LSAT and the GPA are at or above acceptable levels. Such factors include work experience, specialized education, and other evidence of ability to contribute invaluable insight to law classes.

■ Cocurricular Activities

Students are encouraged to participate in cocurricular activities, especially after completion of the first year. *The Loyola Law Journal* is a quarterly professional journal edited by students who are selected on a competitive basis. Articles, comments, and notes on both state and federal developments in law are published. *The Loyola Consumer Law Reporter* is devoted to legal analyses of current issues affecting consumers. Students compete in approximately 12 interschool and intraschool moot court and mock trial competitions. All students are eligible to participate on the staff of the School of Law newspaper, *Blackacre*, which is published approximately eight times each year. All students are members of the Loyola Student Bar Association, the principal instrument of student government. There are over 25 student organizations, including a law fraternity (Phi Alpha Delta), groups devoted to particular areas of legal practice, and ethnic groups.

■ Expenses and Financial Aid

➻ full-time tuition & fees—$17,628 ➻ part-time tuition & fees—$13,216 ➻ estimated additional expenses—$9,400 (books, rent, food, clothing, and transportation) ➻ scholarships available: average $3,500, academic, public interest, ethnic, Law Journal, and Consumer Law Reporter ➻ minority scholarships available: black, Hispanic, and Italian ➻ financial aid available ➻ FAFSA required, priority deadline March 1

■ Career Services

The Career Services Office assists students and alumni with career planning and employment selection.

A year-round on-campus employer interview and recruitment program provides employment opportunities for students. In addition, there is daily posting of employment opportunities for legal and nonlegal positions.

Seminars by practicing attorneys and alumni; résumé preparation, review and critique; interviewing techniques and strategies; individual counseling sessions; and job-search strategies are just some of the many programs for students and alumni administered by the Career Services Office.

The School of Law is a member of the National Association for Law Placement (NALP) and participates in research projects applicable to law students and graduates such as the annual survey of graduates concerning their employment choices and salaries.

Applicant Group for the 1995-1996 Academic Year

Loyola University Chicago School of Law
This grid includes only applicants who earned 120-180 LSAT scores under standard administrations.

LSAT Score	GPA 3.75 +		3.50 - 3.74		3.25 - 3.49		3.00 - 3.24		2.75 - 2.99		2.50 - 2.74		2.25 - 2.49		2.00 - 2.24		Below 2.00		No GPA		Total	
	Apps	Adm	Apps	Adm	Apps	Adm	Apps	Adm	Apps	Adm	Apps	Adm	Apps	Adm	Apps	Adm	Apps	Adm	Apps	Adm	Apps	Adm
175 - 180	0	0	0	0	1	1	0	0	0	0	0	0	1	0	0	0	0	0	0	0	2	1
170 - 174	0	0	3	3	3	3	3	3	2	2	0	0	1	1	0	0	0	0	0	0	12	12
165 - 169	8	8	13	13	17	16	12	8	13	13	7	6	3	1	1	1	0	0	1	1	75	67
160 - 164	23	23	70	68	72	72	75	70	44	39	31	24	8	5	2	1	1	0	2	2	328	304
155 - 159	53	46	116	94	145	97	145	82	93	36	48	13	28	7	5	4	1	0	5	4	639	383
150 - 154	36	10	90	22	155	21	135	13	117	7	74	2	40	2	16	0	3	0	8	3	674	80
145 - 149	15	2	46	5	78	6	106	8	80	1	57	2	33	0	11	2	7	0	3	0	436	26
140 - 144	1	0	12	1	28	2	52	0	61	2	43	1	33	0	13	0	4	0	4	0	251	6
135 - 139	0	0	6	0	5	1	20	0	16	0	26	0	16	0	6	0	4	0	4	0	103	1
130 - 134	0	0	2	0	1	0	4	0	4	0	10	1	7	0	5	0	4	0	4	0	41	1
125 - 129	0	0	0	0	1	0	1	0	1	0	3	0	1	0	0	0	0	0	1	1	8	1
120 - 124	0	0	1	0	0	0	0	0	0	0	0	0	1	0	0	0	0	0	2	0	4	0
Total	136	89	359	206	506	219	553	184	431	100	299	49	172	16	59	8	24	0	34	11	2573	882

Apps = Number of Applicants
Adm = Number Admitted
Reflects 99% of the total applicant pool.

Loyola Law School, Los Angeles, Loyola Marymount University

1441 W. Olympic Blvd.
Los Angeles, CA 90015

E-Mail: lawadmis@lmulaw.lmu.edu
Phone: 213.736.1180

■ Introduction

Loyola Law School, established in 1920, is one of the oldest law schools in Southern California. The Law School has strong ties with the city of Los Angeles, one of the world's most important legal, political, and financial centers. Loyola is a member of the Order of the Coif and provides the highest standards of education and professional development in the context of the university's deeply held ethical and moral values. Recognized for the teaching excellence of its faculty, Loyola offers a comprehensive academic program with the opportunity for both in-depth scholarly development and intensive preparation for the practice of law.

■ Enrollment/Student Body

➻ 3,584 applicants ➻ 1,092 admitted first-year class 1995 ➻ 437 enrolled first-year class 1995 ➻ 982 total full-time ➻ 414 total part-time ➻ 37.2% minority ➻ 44% women ➻ over 40 states & foreign countries represented ➻ over 100 undergraduate schools represented

■ Library and Physical Facilities

➻ 393,083 volumes & equivalents ➻ library hours: Mon.-Thurs., 7:00 A.M.-MIDNIGHT; Fri., 7:00 A.M.-8:30 P.M.; Sat., 9:00 A.M.-8:30 P.M.; Sun., 9:00 A.M.-MIDNIGHT ➻ LEXIS ➻ NEXIS ➻ WESTLAW ➻ DIALOG ➻ C.CALI ➻ 12 full-time librarians ➻ library seats 683

Loyola's modern and dynamic campus was designed by the internationally renowned architect Frank Gehry. Encompassing an entire city block, the Law School occupies eight buildings, including a new parking structure, classrooms, courtrooms, advanced audio-visual and computer centers, dining facilities and offices. The "academical village" design with its many courtyards, plazas, rooftop terraces, and grassy knolls, has become the focal point for outdoor group study, social activities, and various participation sports. The William M. Rains Law Library features large reading areas, open stacks, individual study carrels, group-study areas, and extensive online and database resources. Large computer research and word processing centers equipped with personal computers and laser printers are designated solely for student use. With one of the largest budgets in the nation and an aggressive schedule for expansion, Loyola is committed to maintaining one of the country's finest law libraries.

■ Faculty

➻ 107 total ➻ 59 full-time ➻ 48 part-time or adjunct ➻ 23 women ➻ 13 minority

■ Curriculum

Loyola's curriculum is designed to provide the knowledge and skills that will enable students to become excellent practicing lawyers. The curriculum integrates traditional instruction in legal doctrine and theory with a special commitment to innovative skills education. The first-year curriculum includes a rigorous grounding in basic subjects and includes an intensive course in legal writing, taught by the full-time faculty. The required upper-division curriculum includes Ethics, Counseling, and Negotiation, in which simulated negotiation and counseling exercises provide students with an opportunity to apply the principles of legal ethics in a practical context.

Because of its large faculty, the Law School has a wide variety of course offerings, ranging from comprehensive offerings in the traditional subjects to a wide variety of advanced courses in many areas, including environmental law, entertainment law, international law, and the protection of civil and constitutional rights.

The 87-unit course of study for the J.D. can be completed in three years by full-time day students, and in four years by part-time evening students. The day and evening programs have identical admission standards and academic requirements.

■ Special Programs

Loyola's extensive clinical program offers students an opportunity to explore the nature of the attorney-client relationship, experience the operation of legal institutions, and, particularly, to refine and enhance lawyering skills. In addition to an extensive program of clinical placements in courts, government, and legal service agencies throughout the region, the Law School supports an on-campus clinic, the Western Center for Disability Rights, which is nationally recognized for excellence in the representation of disabled persons.

The Law School offers a summer program in Central America that enables students to take courses in Costa Rica on international environmental law and the protection of human rights. The Central American program includes a variety of study trips to neighboring countries.

■ Admission

➻ Baccalaureate degree required ➻ application deadline—day, Feb. 1; evening, April 17 ➻ LSAT, LSDAS required ➻ median GPA—3.34 ➻ median LSAT score—161 ➻ application fee—$50

The Law School is nonsectarian and is committed to maintaining the diversity of its student population. Members of all religious, ethnic, and cultural groups are actively recruited and encouraged to apply. All applications are reviewed in their entirety and many factors, both academic and nonacademic, are considered. Applicants are encouraged to provide information about extracurricular activities and awards, educational history, cultural background, and other life experiences. Applicants are strongly urged to take the LSAT no later than the December administration. At least one academic letter of evaluation is recommended. Decisions are made on a rolling basis.

■ Student Activities

Three journals are published by Loyola students: the *Loyola of Los Angeles Law Review*; the *International and Comparative Law Journal*; and the *Entertainment Law Journal*. Membership on intramural and intermural moot court and trial advocacy teams is highly sought. Students can participate in student bar associations and the monthly newspaper, as well as in a number of student organizations including the Black Law Students Association, Asian-Pacific American Law Students Association, La Raza de Loyola, Christian Legal Society, Jewish Law Students Association, Lesbian and Gay Law Union, St. Thomas More Legal Honor Society, Phi Alpha Delta Professional Legal Fraternity, Phi Delta Phi Honor Fraternity, and the Women's Law Association.

■ Expenses and Financial Aid

➽ *tuition & fees—full-time, $18,634; part-time, $12,532*
➽ *scholarships available* ➽ *financial aid available; FAFSA forms due March 2*

Loyola offers a number of full- and partial-tuition scholarships to entering students based on academic achievement. Additional scholarship funds are set aside for continuing students who are in approximately the top 10 percent of their class at the end of the first year. Applicants should complete the FAFSA by March 2.

■ Career Services

The Office of Career Services provides a professional staff to counsel students and graduates and to assist them in job searches in a variety of ways. Many major national and regional firms recruited in the On-Campus Interviewing Program in 1995, and students and graduates are employed by the nation's most prestigious private and public legal institutions.

■ Alumni

Loyola Law School has graduated more than 10,000 alumni since its founding. Many of these graduates play significant roles in major national and international law firms, government offices, public interest agencies, the entertainment industry, and the judiciary both in California and throughout the United States.

Some of Loyola's prominent alumni include Bob Miller '71, Governor of Nevada; Benjamin Cayetano '71, Governor of Hawaii; Mary Orozco '61, first Latina member of the California Bar; Johnnie Cochran '62, criminal defense attorney; Deidre Hill '85, first female African American president of the Los Angeles Police Commission; Robert Shapiro '68, defense attorney.

Applicant Group for the 1995-1996 Academic Year

Loyola Law School, Los Angeles, Loyola Marymount University
This grid includes only applicants who earned 120-180 LSAT scores under standard administrations.

	LSAT Score															
GPA	120 - 142		143 - 148		149 - 153		154 - 157		158 - 162		163 - 169		170 - 180		Total	
	Apps	Adm	Apps	Adm	Apps	Adm	Apps	Adm	Apps	Adm	Apps	Adm	Apps	Adm	Apps	Adm
3.75 & above	4	0	14	0	34	12	42	24	42	39	19	19	0	0	155	94
3.74-3.50	10	0	37	4	95	25	115	33	121	111	57	57	4	4	439	234
3.49-3.25	34	1	96	10	166	38	148	49	155	122	75	75	6	6	680	301
3.24-3.00	63	0	130	10	187	35	136	31	135	97	49	48	5	5	705	226
2.99-2.75	76	0	126	0	141	17	91	20	96	56	41	40	10	10	581	143
2.74-2.50	71	0	102	4	86	1	74	9	51	26	23	23	2	2	409	65
2.49-2.25	56	0	65	0	39	1	27	2	17	6	14	10	2	2	220	21
2.24-2.00	36	0	32	0	23	0	9	0	7	1	5	3	1	0	113	4
1.99 - 1.00	5	0	2	0	6	0	0	0	0	0	0	0	0	0	13	0
Pass/Fail CES	11	0	11	0	15	1	10	1	4	1	1	1	0	0	52	4
Total	366	1	615	28	792	130	652	109	628	459	284	276	30	29	3367	1092

Apps = Number of Applicants (Grid represents 94% of applicant pool)
Adm = Number Admitted (Grid represents 100% of admit pool)

Loyola University New Orleans School of Law

7214 St. Charles Avenue
New Orleans, LA 70118

Phone: 504.861.5575

■ Introduction

The School of Law was established at Loyola University in 1914. It has been approved by the ABA since 1931 and has been a member of the AALS since 1934. The university is a member of the Southern Association of Colleges and Schools and is operated by the Jesuits of the Southern Province. The campus is located in uptown New Orleans approximately five miles from the historic French Quarter and the Central Business District.

■ Enrollment/Student Body

➽ 1,996 applicants ➽ 995 admitted first-year class 1995 ➽ 297 enrolled first-year class 1995 ➽ 553 total full-time ➽ 212 total part-time ➽ 24.3% minority ➽ 48% women ➽ 30 states & foreign countries represented ➽ 158 undergraduate schools represented in first year class

■ Faculty

➽ 77 total ➽ 36 full-time ➽ 41 part-time or adjunct ➽ 14 women ➽ 6 minority

■ Library and Physical Facilities

➽ 244,315 volumes & equivalents ➽ library hours: Mon.-Thurs., 7:30 A.M.-MIDNIGHT; Fri., 7:30 A.M.-9:00 P.M.; Sat., 10:00 A.M.-10:00 P.M.; Sun., 11:00 A.M.-11:00 P.M. ➽ LEXIS ➽ NEXIS ➽ WESTLAW ➽ DIALOG ➽ 7 full-time librarians ➽ library seats 529

In 1986, the School of Law moved to a new and larger facility on the Broadway Campus of Loyola University. Located approximately six blocks from the main campus, the facility houses all academic and research components of the School of Law, including the Gillis W. Long Law Poverty Center. The law school is designed to accommodate the needs of people with disabilities. Law students also have complete access to the facilities located on the main campus.

The library's collection of over 235,000 volumes supports the curriculum and research needs of the law school faculty and students. Its working collection contains legal authorities of international law, comparative law, and laws of individual foreign countries, as well as materials dealing with law-related subjects. In addition to conventional resources, the library has extensive computer facilities for students' use.

■ Curriculum

➽ Academic Support Program ➽ 90 credits required to graduate ➽ 124 courses available ➽ degrees available: J.D./M.B.A.; J.D./M.A.—Religious Studies; Administration; J.D./Master of Urban and Regional Planning; J.D. ➽ semesters, start in Aug. ➽ range of first-year class size—40-100

■ Special Programs

The State of Louisiana is governed in the area of private (property) law by the civil law tradition as found in the provisions of the Louisiana Civil Code. The common law tradition, however, is predominant throughout most of the United States. The School of Law offers both traditions. The full-time student may select either tradition while still maintaining sufficient flexibility to elect courses in the other. Such a system allows the student to study the private law by the comparative method. The part-time (evening) program offers the civil law tradition as found in the State of Louisiana.

In addition to the regular curriculum, each student entering the School of Law must accumulate a number of lawyering-skills points in order to graduate. Lawyering-skills points, including trial practice, client counseling, and negotiation and document drafting, may be earned by taking certain skills courses for which normal academic credit is given; by participating in other skills-related activities such as moot court and trial competitions; and by participating in short extracurricular courses that will be offered by the School of Law from time to time.

Full-time students are required to be in residence for a minimum of six full semesters. The normal time frame for part-time students is eight semesters and two summer sessions.

Loyola offers three summer-abroad programs. Courses are taught in five-week sessions in Cuernavaca, Mexico, Kyoto, Japan and Eastern Europe. All students, after completion of their freshman year, are permitted to enroll in summer school classes.

The Law Clinic, celebrating over twenty-five years of service to the community, is a vital component to the law school. Students chosen to participate in the senior-year program will be assigned cases, civil and criminal, and will be expected to prepare them for trial. Thereafter, they will actually participate in the trial process. Upper-division students also have an opportunity to serve as judicial clerks in the federal extern program sponsored in conjunction with the U. S. District Court for the Eastern District of Louisiana.

The Public Law Center represents a new departure in American legal education. The center takes legislative initiatives from the conceptual stage through research and drafting into the actual legislative process, then beyond into administrative rulemaking following the enactment of new statutes. In addition, the center offers a vital program of legislative and administrative assistance to community and public interest groups, thereby providing access to two nonlitigation advocacy methodologies traditionally underutilized by the poor and disadvantaged interests of society.

■ Admission

➽ *Bachelor's degree required* ➽ *rolling admission, priority given to applications completed by April 1*
➽ *LSAT, LSDAS required* ➽ *median GPA—3.00*
➽ *median LSAT score—152* ➽ *application fee—$20*

■ Student Activities

The *Loyola Law Review* is published by a student editorial board and includes student work and articles written by specialists from the practicing bar, as well as from the academic community. Staff membership is based on scholarship and interest in legal writing.

The *Poverty Law Journal* is open to qualified students and is devoted to issues faced by the poor, children, the elderly, and all others who are unable to afford legal representation. The Moot Court Board, selected from prior years' competitions, is responsible for the Moot Court Program. Teams are entered each year in competitions.

The Student Bar Association is comprised of all students enrolled in the day and evening divisions of the law school. It provides a professional program for students and appoints members to attend faculty meetings and to sit on the student-faculty relations committee. The law school newspaper, *The Code*, is published by a student editorial board. Three legal fraternities, Delta Theta Phi, Phi Alpha Delta, and Phi Delta Phi have active chapters within the school. Other organizations include BLSA, SALSA, Association of Women Law Students, Native American Law Society, Cajun American Law Society, Maritime Law Association, St. Thomas More Law Club, the Trial Advocacy Club, the Association of Trial Lawyers of America (ATLA), and the National Lawyers Guild.

■ Expenses and Financial Aid

➽ *tuition & fees—full-time, $16,905; part-time, $11,455*
➽ *estimated additional expenses—$10,200 (books, room and board, transportation, misc.)*
➽ *scholarships available: based on academic merit only*
➽ *minority scholarships available: based on academic merit only*
➽ *financial aid available; FAFSA analysis, no deadline, priority given to those applications completed by May 1*

■ Career Services

The School of Law Career Services Office offers a variety of services to both students and alumni. Staffed by the director and an assistant, the office maintains and operates a career-planning center, assists students in preparing résumés, videotapes mock interviews, and conducts seminars on career planning, employment opportunities, and interviewing techniques. The office actively solicits job opportunities for summer and school-term clerkships, as well as employment options for each year's graduating class.

Applicant Group for the 1995-1996 Academic Year

Loyola University New Orleans School of Law
This grid includes only applicants who earned 120-180 LSAT scores under standard administrations.

	GPA																					
LSAT Score	3.75 +		3.50 - 3.74		3.25 - 3.49		3.00 - 3.24		2.75 - 2.99		2.50 - 2.74		2.25 - 2.49		2.00 - 2.24		Below 2.00		No GPA		Total	
	Apps	Adm	Apps	Adm	Apps	Adm	Apps	Adm	Apps	Adm	Apps	Adm	Apps	Adm	Apps	Adm	Apps	Adm	Apps	Adm	Apps	Adm
175 - 180	0	0	0	0	0	0	0	0	0	0	0	0	0	0	0	0	0	0	0	0	0	0
170 - 174	0	0	2	2	0	0	0	0	0	0	0	0	1	1	0	0	0	0	0	0	3	3
165 - 169	1	1	0	0	2	2	4	4	3	3	2	1	1	0	0	0	2	1	0	0	15	12
160 - 164	7	7	2	2	12	11	10	9	17	17	13	13	6	5	1	0	1	1	1	1	70	66
155 - 159	13	12	16	16	29	29	39	39	57	52	50	40	24	7	12	3	0	0	3	1	243	199
150 - 154	12	11	27	25	75	75	127	125	116	96	76	35	46	8	11	3	4	0	2	0	496	378
145 - 149	7	6	39	36	67	49	136	74	142	56	115	35	50	2	24	0	3	0	7	1	590	259
140 - 144	0	0	7	4	43	14	58	15	65	14	64	5	55	0	16	0	3	0	6	1	317	53
135 - 139	1	0	5	0	11	3	18	1	25	0	27	0	17	0	24	0	3	0	5	1	136	5
130 - 134	0	0	3	0	2	0	1	0	6	0	10	0	7	0	7	0	1	0	2	0	39	0
125 - 129	0	0	0	0	0	0	0	0	1	0	2	0	1	0	0	0	0	0	0	0	4	0
120 - 124	0	0	0	0	0	0	0	0	1	0	0	0	0	0	0	0	0	0	0	0	1	0
Total	41	37	101	85	241	183	393	267	433	238	359	129	208	23	95	6	17	2	26	5	1914	975

Apps = Number of Applicants
Adm = Number Admitted
Reflects 98% of the total applicant pool.

University of Maine School of Law

246 Deering Ave.
Portland, ME 04102

URL: http://www.law.usm.maine.edu
Phone: 207.780.4341

■ Introduction

The University of Maine School of Law is an administrative unit of the University of Southern Maine, a part of the University of Maine System. The law school is located in Portland, which, though the largest metropolitan area in northern New England, is a "livable" city that retains many elements of an attractive seacoast community. A distinctive feature of the school is its small size, which engenders close working relationships between students and faculty and a strong sense of community among students. The school is a charter member of the AALS and is fully approved by the ABA.

■ Enrollment/Student Body

➽ *862 applicants* ➽ *338 admitted first-year class 1995*
➽ *94 enrolled first-year class 1995* ➽ *280 total full-time*
➽ *7% minority* ➽ *46% women*
➽ *30 states & foreign countries represented*
➽ *111 undergraduate schools represented*

■ Faculty

➽ *23 total* ➽ *16 full-time* ➽ *7 part-time or adjunct*
➽ *7 women*

■ Library and Physical Facilities

➽ *280,000 volumes & equivalents* ➽ *library hours: Sun.-Thurs., 8:00 A.M.-11:00 P.M.; Fri., 8:00 A.M.-9:00 P.M.; Sat., 9:00 A.M.-8:00 P.M.* ➽ *LEXIS* ➽ *NEXIS*
➽ *WESTLAW* ➽ *6 full-time librarians*

■ Curriculum

➽ *89 credits required to graduate* ➽ *98 courses available*
➽ *degrees available: J.D.; joint degrees program with USM in Public Policy and Management*
➽ *semesters, start in Aug.*

The first-year curriculum is a structured program of courses prescribed for all first-year students. A primary objective of the first-year curriculum is the development of students' legal analytical skills and their ability to read and understand cases and statutory material. The program also provides an introduction to legal research and writing. Most courses after the first year are elective. However, all students are required successfully to complete Professional Responsibility, Constitutional Law II, and one of the upper-level courses designated by the faculty as a "perspective" course—one which places the law in a broader philosophical, historical, or comparative context. In addition, each student must fulfill the Independent Writing Requirement, which may be done in several ways: through an Independent Writing Project (a substantial research project under the direction of a faculty member), or through membership on the *Maine Law Review, Ocean and Coastal Law Journal*, or the Moot Court Board.

■ Special Programs

The University of Maine School of Law has initiated an Integrated Clinical Education Program through the Cumberland Legal Aid Clinic. Third-year law students represent clients under faculty supervision in this approved legal assistance office. A number of clinical courses are offered, including the General Practice Clinic, Criminal Law Practicum, Family Law Practicum, Estate Planning Practicum, and the Rural Access Clinic, offered in the summer session. Clinic students also participate in the Domestic Violence Project and the Forensic Psychiatry Project. The practicum courses include, in addition to client representation, a classroom component emphasizing direct application of substantive and procedural law to a specific area of practice.

The School's Marine Law Institute conducts research on laws and policies affecting ocean and coastal resources. Law students have an opportunity to participate as research assistants in this work.

The law school sponsors a statewide law-related education program which provides resources for teachers who use the law in their classroom teaching. The Teachers/Law Students Project trains up to twenty law students and pairs them with middle and high school teachers.

The school coordinates *pro bono* opportunities for law students in various public interest endeavors, such as CASA (Court Appointed Special Advocates), Volunteer Lawyers Project, Maine Pre-Trial Services, and the Family Law Project.

■ Admission

➽ *Bachelor's degree from an accredited college or university required* ➽ *application deadline—Feb. 15*
➽ *LSAT, LSDAS required* ➽ *median GPA—3.24*
➽ *median LSAT score—156* ➽ *application fee—$25*

■ Student Activities

The *Maine Law Review*, published twice a year, concerns itself with national, regional, and state legal problems, with emphasis on matters of current interest. The *Ocean and Coastal Law Journal*, published by the law school's Marine Law Institute, includes student articles on marine resource, environmental, and ocean legal issues. The moot court board represents the school at regional and national competitions with other law schools.

Law students participate as voting members on many law school and university committees. The Student Bar Association performs the varied functions of student government, and acts as an umbrella organization, coordinating the activities of a number of student organizations: the Black Law Students Association, La Cofradía Environmental Law Society, Federalist Society, International Law Society, Lesbian/Gay/Bisexual Law Caucus, Maine Association for Public Interest Law, Maine Law and Technology Association, National Lawyers Guild, Native American Law Students Association, Phi Alpha Delta, and Women's Law Association.

■ Expenses and Financial Aid

➽ *tuition—residents, $264/credit hour; nonresident $524/credit hour* ➽ *annual fees—$300*
➽ *estimated additional expenses (room, board, books)—$7,450* ➽ *need-based scholarships available*
➽ *minority scholarships available* ➽ *financial aid available*
➽ *FAFSA due at processing center by Feb. 1*
➽ *New England Board of Higher Education Compact Tuition—$396/credit hour*

■ Career Services

➽ 1994 placement rate (six months after graduation)—85%
➽ 1994 first-time bar passage rate—87%

The Career Services Office provides a full range of services including counseling; career resource materials; specific summer, full-time, part-time, and work/study job listings; and extensive on-campus recruiting. The small enrollment of the law school ensures services tailored to meet the specific needs of students. In addition to individual counseling, a series of workshops and panel discussions with practitioners is held each year. Graduates practice from Alaska to Florida, although most remain in New England and many choose to stay in Maine. The full-time Career Services Director is happy to provide further information to interested applicants.

Applicant Group for the 1995-1996 Academic Year

University of Maine School of Law
This grid includes only applicants who earned 120-180 LSAT scores under standard administrations.

LSAT Score	3.75 +		3.50 - 3.74		3.25 - 3.49		3.00 - 3.24		2.75 - 2.99		2.50 - 2.74		2.25 - 2.49		2.00 - 2.24		Below 2.00		No GPA		Total	
	Apps	Adm	Apps	Adm	Apps	Adm	Apps	Adm	Apps	Adm	Apps	Adm	Apps	Adm	Apps	Adm	Apps	Adm	Apps	Adm	Apps	Adm
175 - 180	0	0	0	0	0	0	1	1	0	0	0	0	0	0	0	0	0	0	0	0	1	1
170 - 174	1	1	1	1	1	1	0	0	0	0	1	1	0	0	0	0	0	0	0	0	4	4
165 - 169	1	1	5	5	4	4	8	7	1	0	9	6	1	0	0	0	0	0	0	0	29	23
160 - 164	6	5	12	12	23	22	31	25	20	8	9	3	7	1	1	0	1	0	0	0	110	76
155 - 159	13	12	38	38	51	45	59	29	28	9	24	1	8	0	2	0	0	0	1	1	224	135
150 - 154	9	7	22	16	44	19	52	14	41	4	24	5	12	0	2	0	0	0	2	0	208	65
145 - 149	4	3	14	6	43	13	25	3	32	3	19	2	11	1	11	0	1	0	1	1	161	32
140 - 144	1	0	5	2	6	0	13	0	18	1	6	1	8	0	6	0	2	0	0	0	65	4
135 - 139	0	0	2	0	3	0	7	0	4	0	6	0	5	0	2	0	2	0	1	1	32	1
130 - 134	0	0	0	0	0	0	2	0	2	0	1	0	1	0	1	0	1	0	1	0	9	0
125 - 129	0	0	0	0	0	0	0	0	0	0	0	0	0	0	0	0	0	0	0	0	0	0
120 - 124	0	0	0	0	0	0	0	0	0	0	0	0	0	0	0	0	0	0	0	0	0	0
Total	35	29	99	80	175	104	198	79	146	25	99	19	53	2	25	0	7	0	6	3	843	341

Apps = Number of Applicants
Adm = Number Admitted
Reflects 98% of the total applicant pool.

Marquette University Law School

Office of Admissions, Sensenbrenner Hall
1103 W. Wisconsin Avenue, P.O. Box 1881
Milwaukee, WI 53201-1881

Phone: 414.288.6767

■ Introduction

For more than a century, Marquette University Law School has been committed to training men and women to serve the public interest by becoming highly skilled, ethical, and moral attorneys. Traditionally, the Law School's curriculum has emphasized the practical aspects of legal practice. In recent years that emphasis has expanded to include particular excellence in the areas of intellectual property, international law, business law, criminal law and procedure, children and the law, and litigation related courses. The National Sports Law Institute, the premiere sports law program in the U.S., is part of the Law School. Our alumni of over 5,500 serve in a broad range of legal, public, and corporate positions throughout the United States.

The Law School is located on the University campus—within two blocks of the state courthouse, and a short walk to the federal courthouse, and to the legal center of the State of Wisconsin. Marquette is the only Law School in the city of Milwaukee and in southeast Wisconsin. Marquette University—a Catholic, Jesuit, urban, and national university—the largest private university in Wisconsin is located in downtown Milwaukee, two miles west of Lake Michigan. The Catholic and Jesuit nature of the institution means a specific concern for the well-being of the individual, whether that be the law student, the lawyer's client, or the victim of crime. Persons of all religious backgrounds attend Marquette, serve on the faculty, and are valued within the Law School community. The Law School is committed to academic freedom and the broadest possible inquiry and examination of all subjects.

Milwaukee is a vibrant city. It is the largest city in Wisconsin (pop. 630,000) yet has the appeal of small town living. It is remarkably clean, well-run, and known for its ethnic festivals and cosmopolitan cuisine.

■ Enrollment/Student Body

➽ 1,086 applicants ➽ 430 admitted first-year class 1995 ➽ 140 enrolled first-year class 1995 ➽ 469 total full-time ➽ 6 total part-time ➽ 14.7% minority ➽ 41% women ➽ 34 states & 3 foreign countries represented ➽ 162 U.S. and 3 foreign undergraduate schools represented in student body

The Law School is actively committed to increasing diversity and encourages applications from members of groups historically disadvantaged in the U.S. and underrepresented in the legal profession.

■ Faculty

➽ 58 total ➽ 23 full-time ➽ 35 part-time or adjunct ➽ 14 women faculty ➽ 3 minority faculty

■ Library and Physical Facility

➽ 238,148 volumes & equivalents ➽ library hours: Mon.-Thurs., 7:00 A.M.-MIDNIGHT; Fri., 7:00 A.M.-8:00 P.M.; Sat., 9:00 A.M.-8:00 P.M.; Sun., 10:00 A.M.-MIDNIGHT ➽ LEXIS ➽ NEXIS ➽ WESTLAW ➽ DIALOG ➽ MARQCAT ➽ LEGALTRAC ➽ CALI ➽ WISCAT ➽ OCLC ➽ 9 full-time librarians ➽ library seats 410

The Law School is located in Sensenbrenner Hall, an attractive, comfortable, four-story, air-conditioned building that houses faculty offices, classrooms, two courtrooms, and administrative offices. The Legal Research Center, a four-level facility of contemporary design houses the library and is connected to the Law School. The law library has two computer labs and provides students access to computer-assisted legal research systems, and computer-assisted legal instruction exercises. The law library is a federal document depository and is the largest legal research facility in southeastern Wisconsin. Law students have access to all Marquette University campus facilities, including both fitness and recreation centers.

■ Curriculum

➽ Academic Support Program ➽ 90 credits required to graduate ➽ 102 courses available ➽ degrees available: J.D.; J.D./M.B.A.; J.D./M.A. Pol. Sci.; J.D./M.A. International Affairs ➽ semesters, start in Aug. ➽ range of first-year class size—21-84

The Law School Curriculum is designed to prepare students to practice law in the twenty-first century. This means an explicit emphasis on a strong core curriculum that includes consideration of the theoretical underpinnings of the law, as well as the practical application of substantive legal concepts. The Law School's curriculum is national in focus and scope, and emphasizes the skills and values necessary to be a competent and ethical lawyer, as well as a contributing citizen and community leader. The Law School takes advantage of its location to include on its adjunct faculty many of the state's outstanding practitioners who supplement required and core courses with a broad range of elective and specialty courses. Beginning in the 1996-97 academic year, the Law School will offer an expanded part-time program during the day. It is anticipated that beginning in the 1997-98 academic year the Law School will admit its first part-time evening classes.

■ Special Programs

Our comprehensive trial-practice courses are an excellent complement to the curriculum and provide an exceptional opportunity for students to develop trial skills. Distinctive programs include the Small Business Assistance Project, Prosecutor and Defender Clinics, Judicial Internships (Appellate and Trial), Municipal Ordinance Defense Clinic, Children with Special Health Needs Project, and supervised fieldwork opportunities in specialized areas.

■ Admission

➽ *Bachelor's degree from an accredited college or university required* ➽ *application deadline—April 1; rolling admission, early application preferred* ➽ *LSAT, LSDAS required* ➽ *median GPA—3.10* ➽ *median LSAT score—156* ➽ *application fee—$35*

Review of completed applications begins in January and continues through the spring. All applications are read. Although the applicant's overall academic performance and LSAT score are principal considerations in the selection process, non-numeric factors play a part in the review. Personal accomplishments are highly valued by the Admissions Committee as are characteristics of diversity which contribute to the enrichment of the student community and the profession. Accepted applicants are required to submit an initial tuition deposit after April 1; a second deposit is required in June. Tuition deposits are applied to the fall semester's tuition. Applicants are welcome to visit the Law School (arrangements should be made through the Admission Office) or to contact the Office of Admissions with inquiries, but interviews are not part of the application process.

■ Diploma Admission

Since 1933, graduates of the Law School who otherwise qualify have been admitted to practice in all courts of Wisconsin without being required to take the Wisconsin Bar Examination. Marquette graduates are entitled to sit for bar examinations in any American jurisdiction.

■ Student Activities

The Law School publishes the *Marquette Law Review*, a scholarly legal journal, founded in 1916, edited and substantially written by law students, and the *Marquette Sports Law Journal*. All students have the opportunity to develop advocacy skills during the first year of law school. Law School Moot Court teams have won regional titles or championships in National Moot Court and National Labor Law competitions. A diverse selection of law student organizations are active at Marquette.

■ Expenses and Financial Aid

➽ *tuition & fees—full-time, $15,310; part-time, $581/hr.* ➽ *estimated additional expenses—$9,000 (room & board, personal, medical)* ➽ *renewable scholarships available (performance & diversity tuition-based awards)* ➽ *renewable minority scholarships available (tuition-based awards, amounts vary)* ➽ *financial aid available; FAFSA required— Federal Stafford Loan, Federal Perkins.*

■ Career Services

The Office of Career Planning processes hundreds of listings of employment opportunities, coordinates campus interviews, and provides counseling assistance to students. Marquette law alumni are engaged in the practice of law in virtually every state and U.S. territory. In recent years over 90 percent of graduates have secured employment.

■ Housing

University apartments are located within two blocks of the Law School. In addition to campus housing, ample and affordable housing is available throughout the city of Milwaukee and its suburbs. Applications for university apartments may be obtained from the Law School Office of Admissions or the Office of Residence Life, Tower Hall, Marquette University, Milwaukee WI 53201-1881, Phone: 414.288.7208.

Applicant Group for the 1995-1996 Academic Year

Marquette University Law School
This grid includes only applicants who earned 120-180 LSAT scores under standard administrations.

	GPA																	
LSAT Score	3.75 +		3.50 - 3.74		3.25 - 3.49		3.00 - 3.24		2.75 - 2.99		2.50 - 2.74		Below 2.49		No GPA		Total	
	Apps	Adm	Apps	Adm	Apps	Adm	Apps	Adm	Apps	Adm	Apps	Adm	Apps	Adm	Apps	Adm	Apps	Adm
165 - 180	1	1	4	4	1	1	3	2	3	2	0	0	2	2	0	0	14	12
160 - 164	7	7	13	11	14	13	10	9	19	15	11	6	5	3	0	0	79	64
155 - 159	7	7	39	37	46	44	42	39	46	40	32	22	15	6	5	4	232	199
150 - 154	13	6	49	27	75	39	63	23	60	23	33	8	28	6	4	0	325	132
145 - 149	7	2	17	0	48	9	48	7	57	7	34	3	29	5	1	0	241	33
120 - 144	1	0	10	2	19	1	27	0	39	2	35	0	45	0	7	0	183	5
Total	36	23	132	81	203	107	193	80	224	89	145	39	124	22	17	4	1074	445

Apps = Number of Applicants
Adm = Number Admitted
Reflects 99% of the total applicant pool.

University of Maryland School of Law

500 West Baltimore Street
Baltimore, MD 21201

E-Mail: admissions@law.ab.umd.edu
URL: http://www.law.ab.umd.edu
Phone: 410.706.3492

■ Introduction

Providing a legal education comprising an exciting mix of theory and practice, the University of Maryland Law School is an integral part of downtown Baltimore's legal and business community. Just a few blocks from the famous Inner Harbor and Oriole Park at Camden Yards, the law school is one of six professional schools of the University of Maryland at Baltimore. Our location within the Baltimore-Washington-Annapolis triangle affords students the full advantages of proximity to local, state, and national governments, as well as many law firms, agencies, and organizations of prominence. Maryland is a member of AALS and has a chapter of the Order of the Coif. Maryland maintains strong ties to its alumni; 39 percent of the alumni contribute to the school each year, placing it in the top 10 percent of law schools in the country, public or private, in overall participation.

■ Enrollment/Student Body

➧ 3,484 applicants, 964 admitted, 277 enrolled first-year class 1995 ➧ 863 total enrollment—611 day, 252 evening, 30% minority, 49% women, 278 undergraduate schools, 37 states and foreign countries

■ Faculty

➧ 111 total ➧ 54 full-time (18 women, 9 minority) ➧ 57 adjunct ➧ faculty/student ratio—1:16

■ Library and Physical Facilities

➧ 360,000 volumes & equivalents ➧ 4,017 serials, periodicals, and looseleaf services ➧ LEXIS ➧ WESTLAW ➧ CARL ➧ UNCOVER ➧ Legal Resource Index available through online catalog ➧ OCLC First Search ➧ access to numerous databases and library catalogs through DIALOG and Internet ➧ 8 full-time librarians

The School of Law comprises an unusual, attractive, and functional series of buildings surrounding two inner courtyards, one of which is the famous Westminster Burial Ground. Westminster Hall, adjacent to the law library, is designed to accommodate a variety of school and community activities, including receptions, formal lectures, and a variety of university and community functions. The Thurgood Marshall Law Library, the largest law library in the state of Maryland, occupies an attractive four-story facility adjacent to the School of Law.

■ Curriculum

➧ Juris Doctor (J.D.) program ➧ 3-year day, 4-year part-time day and evening programs ➧ 85 credits required to graduate ➧ fall and spring semesters, summer session (evening classes only) open to students in good standing at any ABA-approved law school ➧ 160 elective courses ➧ Academic Support Program ➧ range of first-year class size—23-100

Each first-semester student is assigned to a fall-semester course with enrollment of approximately 25, combining an introduction to legal institutions and processes, an understanding of the skills necessary in the professional use of case law and legislation, and one of the traditional substantive courses. In addition to promoting close contact between professor and student and allowing for substantial research and writing experience, it also serves as a precursor to the live-client Legal Theory and Practice course required of full-time students in their second or third semester. Second- and third-year students take constitutional law and legal profession, and select a program of study from a wide range of courses, seminars, independent studies, simulations, clinics, and internships. Specialization in a number of subject areas is available but not required. Each student must produce at least one substantial paper based on extensive research.

■ Legal Theory and Practice

Maryland integrates traditional classroom study of legal theory with experiential learning through our Legal Theory and Practice courses. In connection with one of the traditional law school courses, day students undertake a number of carefully selected clinical practice experiences under close faculty supervision. Students meet regularly with their instructors to review the substantive, professional, ethical, and craft issues raised by their work and to explore the connections between what is taught in the classroom and the practice of law as they are experiencing it. As a student explained it, "Legal Theory and Practice represents an institutional commitment to help students figure out what a lawyer can be, and what roles in society a lawyer can and should play."

■ Clinical Law Program

Building on Legal Theory and Practice, students electing to enroll in the nationally recognized Clinical Law Program undertake primary responsibility for direct client service and begin the transition from law school to law practice; from learning to be a lawyer to being one. Maryland has made a significant commitment to clinical education and has one of the nation's finest programs for clinical practice.

Practice in the clinic includes civil and criminal law matters and may include appearances before courts, administrative agencies, legislatures, and other officials. Through personal experience, supervision, and coursework, students think reflectively about the legal profession, about their work as lawyers, and about the role of lawyers in a just society.

■ Dual Degrees and Interdisciplinary Study

➧ dual degrees with Business Administration, Criminal Justice, Liberal Education, Marine/Environmental Sciences, Policy Sciences, Public Management, Social Work

Maryland's interdisciplinary programs, including the Environmental Law Program, the Law and Health Care

Program, and the Entrepreneurship Program, offer students the opportunity to work with lawyers and professionals in related disciplines toward the resolution of problems that transcend traditional disciplinary boundaries. Supplementing the dual-degree programs, students are encouraged to explore the connection between law and other disciplines by enrolling in as many as nine credits in related graduate level programs.

■ Admission

➽ *application deadline—Feb. 15, rolling admissions*
➽ *median GPA—3.35* ➽ *median LSAT score—159*
➽ *application fee—$40*

First-year students are admitted only for the fall. Applicants should file applications as early as possible after September 1 of the year preceding enrollment and prior to February 15. Later receipt of the application, the LSAT score, or LSDAS report may seriously prejudice the applicant's chances of acceptance. February 1996 LSAT scores will be considered on time for August 1996 admission. Applicants are welcome to visit the school, but interviews are not part of the admission process.

Admission decisions are made by a faculty committee. Although the undergraduate record and LSAT score(s) are determinative in many cases, the entire file of each applicant is reviewed and supplemental information is considered. Multiple test scores normally are averaged.

We expect applicants to come from different backgrounds, have different experiences, and have many reasons for wanting to study law. We do not seek to cast students into any particular acceptable mold. In addition to academic ability, the qualities of the students we seek may be reflected in their personal background as reflected in such characteristics as race and ethnicity, gender, geographic origin and cultural and language background; racial, disability, social, and economic barriers overcome; interpersonal skills, as demonstrated by extracurricular pursuits, work or service experience, and leadership activities; potential for intellectual and social growth, as demonstrated by personal talents and skills, maturity, and compassion; and other special circumstances and characteristics which, when combined with academic skills necessary for sound legal education, promises to make a special contribution to the community.

■ Student Activities

Students at the University of Maryland School of Law have the opportunity to participate in a variety of activities, including several journals and dozens of social, political, and professional student groups.

■ Expenses and Financial Aid

➽ *full-time tuition & fees—resident, $8,987; nonresident, $15,722* ➽ *evening tuition & fees—resident, $6,590; nonresident, $11,639* ➽ *FAFSA and financial aid transcripts required* ➽ *State of Maryland Loan Repayment Assistance for some public interest employment*

■ Career Services

Preparation for the legal profession requires a dual approach—academic accomplishment and professional development. Career Services supports the latter by mediating between the classroom and the professional world. As of this writing, the class of 1994 was employed as follows—36 percent, private firms; 15 percent, judicial clerkships; 15 percent, public sector; 16 percent, not responding/not employed; 16 percent, business/corporations; 1 percent, military; and 1 percent, academe.

Applicant Group for the 1995-1996 Academic Year

University of Maryland School of Law
Approximately 3,500 candidates applied for admission to Maryland's 1995 entering class. Figures in the chart below reflect 1995 admission decisions as of 6/1/95.

	LSAT Score											
	151 & Below		152 - 154		155 - 157		158 - 160		161 - 163		164 & Above	
GPA	Apps	Adm	Apps	Adm	Apps	Adm	Apps	Adm	Apps	Adm	Apps	Adm
3.75 - 4.00	46	14	29	10	41	30	32	29	20	20	24	24
3.50 - 3.74	113	17	83	10	86	40	82	61	50	50	31	30
3.25 - 3.49	227	22	107	15	138	23	105	54	76	70	46	45
3.00 - 3.24	307	33	92	16	101	13	70	15	57	33	51	46
2.75 - 2.99	331	29	79	12	68	12	64	11	37	9	42	27
2.74 & Below	492	15	86	11	69	9	57	8	49	15	34	16
Total	1516	130	476	74	503	127	410	178	289	197	228	188

Apps = Number of Applicants
Adm = Number Admitted

McGeorge School of Law, University of the Pacific

3200 Fifth Avenue
Sacramento, CA 95817

Phone: 916.739.7105

■ Introduction

McGeorge School of Law of the University of the Pacific is located in Sacramento, California, the capital of the nation's most populous state. Established in 1924, the school offers both full-time day and part-time evening programs as well as graduate law programs and a Summer Prelaw Program. McGeorge is a member of the AALS, is accredited by the ABA and the State Bar of California, and has a chapter of the Order of the Coif.

■ Enrollment/Student Body

➡ *2,257 applicants* ➡ *1,197 admitted first-year class 1995*
➡ *405 enrolled first-year class 1995 (334 day, 71 evening)*
➡ *886 total full-time* ➡ *334 total part-time*
➡ *23% minority* ➡ *45% women*
➡ *35 states & 10 foreign countries represented*
➡ *210 U.S. & 3 foreign undergraduate schools represented*

■ Faculty

➡ *113 total* ➡ *53 full-time* ➡ *60 visiting or adjunct*
➡ *30 women* ➡ *10 minority*

■ Library and Physical Facilities

➡ *400,000 volumes & equivalents* ➡ *library hours: Sun.-Thurs., 8:00 A.M.-MIDNIGHT; Fri. & Sat., 8:00 A.M.-11:00 P.M.*
➡ *LEXIS* ➡ *NEXIS* ➡ *WESTLAW* ➡ *DIALOG*
➡ *21 full-time librarians* ➡ *library seats 550*

McGeorge's unique 21-acre law school campus in Sacramento is separate from the university's main campus in Stockton. The McGeorge campus includes a variety of classroom settings, the law library, the Courtroom of the Future, the Center for Advanced Study of Law and Policy, the Institute for Administrative Justice, model law offices and clinical facilities, the Student Center, student apartments, and recreational facilities.

McGeorge's law library provides spacious and well-lighted reading rooms with a variety of study carrels, tables, and group study rooms. Terminals for access to LEXIS and WESTLAW as well as CD ROM stations are located throughout the library. The LawLab provides terminals for access to Internet and intracampus communications, computer-assisted legal instruction, and word processing.

■ Curriculum

➡ *Minority Student Program; Student Bar Association Tutorial Program* ➡ *88 credits required to graduate*
➡ *136 courses available* ➡ *46 clinical offerings*
➡ *degrees available: J.D.; J.D./M.B.A.; J.D./M.P.P.A.; LL.M. (Taxation, Business & Taxation, Transnational Business Practice)*
➡ *semesters, start in Aug.* ➡ *range of first-year class size—28-115*

Completion of the J.D. program requires six semesters for day division students. Evening division students normally require eight semesters although an accelerated program is available through attendance at summer sessions. Special areas of curricular strength, in addition to those listed below, are business and taxation; criminal justice; family, juvenile justice, and child protection law; trial advocacy and practice skills; and alternative dispute resolution mechanisms.

■ Special Programs

Governmental Affairs—A specialized curriculum leads to a J.D. degree with a separate certificate in Governmental Affairs. Legislation and administrative rule-making at the federal, state, and local levels affect issues ranging from the environment and land use to education, civil rights, and business structuring. Sacramento is home for the California legislature, the governor's office, and many state and federal administrative agencies. A broad range of student externships complement foundational and advanced elective courses in the areas of legislative policy-making and governmental affairs.

Clinical and Internship Opportunities—The importance McGeorge places on clinical experiences is evidenced by the number and breadth of on- and off-campus clinics and externships. Legal employers value realistic practice experience which enables a recent graduate to begin work with a firm or agency as an effective participant. The *McGeorge Admissions Bulletin* provides an overview of the school's extensive clinical offerings in civil and criminal practice settings.

Environmental, Natural Resources, and Land Use Planning—California's environmental statutes have served as models for other states and, in some respects, for the federal government as well. More than any other state, California is the forum in which the major environmental policy disputes of the era are being heard. McGeorge offers an integrated classroom and externship curriculum which takes advantage of the school's location in the state's capital.

International Business Transactions—For over twenty years, McGeorge has been training lawyers capable of practicing in the international sphere. In addition to offering a solid core of business law courses, there is an extensive array of international courses. The unique LL.M. program in Transnational Business Practice combines advanced international business coursework with an internship period in a foreign law firm or agency.

■ Admission

➡ *Bachelor's degree or senior standing from accredited college or university required* ➡ *application deadline—day division, May 1* ➡ *LSAT, LSDAS required*
➡ *median GPA—3.13* ➡ *median LSAT score—155*
➡ *application fee—$40*

An applicant's undergraduate record and LSAT results are important factors in the decision process. When there are multiple LSAT scores, the highest is accorded significant weight. Other factors considered are grade patterns or trends, employment and career accomplishments, graduate work, and extracurricular or community activities. Ethnic, cultural, and experiential backgrounds that contribute to student body diversity are valued.

■ Student Activities

➽ *Pacific Law Journal* ➽ *The Transnational Lawyer Journal* ➽ *student moot court, international moot court, and community legal services boards* ➽ *over 35 professional, social, and academic student organizations*

■ Expenses and Financial Aid

➽ *first-year tuition & fees—full-time, $16,400; part-time, $9,714* ➽ *estimated additional expenses—$13,910 (housing, food, books, utilities, transportation, personal expenses)* ➽ *merit-based scholarships and diversity grants* ➽ *financial aid office provides individual counseling*

■ Housing

McGeorge has 165 on-campus apartments, including efficiencies and one or two-bedroom units. Early application is advised. The Housing Office assists in locating off-campus accommodations which are readily available in Sacramento.

■ Career Services

The well-staffed Career Development Office offers a full range of counseling and resource services for students and alumni. Fall and spring interview seasons bring employers to campus, and other employers from throughout the country use the CDO facilities to solicit applications from McGeorge students. Among the services provided by CDO are résumé, job search, and interview workshops, a program of speakers with first-hand information about traditional and nontraditional law careers, and individual counseling about career paths.

Applicant Group for the 1995-1996 Academic Year

McGeorge School of Law, University of the Pacific
This grid includes only applicants who earned 120-180 LSAT scores under standard administrations.

GPA																		
LSAT Score	3.50 +		3.25 - 3.49		3.00 - 3.24		2.75 - 2.99		2.50 - 2.74		2.25 - 2.49		Below 2.25		No GPA		Total	
	Apps	Adm	Apps	Adm	Apps	Adm	Apps	Adm	Apps	Adm	Apps	Adm	Apps	Adm	Apps	Adm	Apps	Adm
165 - 180	8	8	3	3	7	6	9	9	6	6	6	6	0	0	1	1	40	39
155 - 164	73	72	125	120	156	148	137	122	80	65	28	21	13	4	7	4	619	556
150 - 154	82	76	117	106	148	118	138	95	94	42	43	17	22	7	7	4	651	465
145 - 149	45	21	71	23	106	24	90	7	69	3	36	4	19	1	4	0	440	83
140 - 144	14	1	32	1	48	0	51	0	51	0	29	0	17	0	6	0	248	2
120 - 139	6	0	10	0	21	0	26	0	30	0	18	0	17	0	3	0	131	0
Total	228	178	358	253	486	296	451	233	330	116	160	48	88	12	28	9	2129	1145

Apps = Number of Applicants
Adm = Number Admitted
Reflects 97% of the total applicant pool.

The University of Memphis—Cecil C. Humphreys School of Law

Law School Admissions Office
Memphis, TN 38152

Phone: 901.678.2073

■ Introduction

The School of Law, located on the University of Memphis campus, was established in 1962 and was accredited by the ABA in 1965. The school is conveniently located east of the downtown area of Memphis. With a population of over 900,000, Memphis provides an excellent location for local, state, and federal courts, and the various judicial administrative offices associated with them.

■ Enrollment/Student Body: 1995-96

➻ 1,213 applicants ➻ 449 admitted first-year class 1995 ➻ 185 enrolled first-year class 1995 ➻ 171 first-year, full-time ➻ 14 first-year, part-time ➻ 17% minority, first-year class ➻ 43% women, first-year class ➻ 80 undergraduate schools represented, first-year class ➻ 20% nonresidents, first-year class ➻ average age, first-year class—26

Preference in admission is given to resident applicants because of the school's primary responsibility to provide adequate opportunities for citizens of Tennessee to pursue a legal education.

■ Faculty

➻ 43 total ➻ 22 full-time ➻ 22 part-time or adjunct ➻ 14 women ➻ 4 minority

■ Library and Physical Facilities

➻ 258,242 volumes & equivalents ➻ library hours: Mon.-Thurs., 7:00 A.M.-MIDNIGHT; Fri., 7:00 A.M.-10:30 P.M.; Sat., 9:00 A.M.-10:00 P.M.; Sun., 11:00 A.M.-MIDNIGHT ➻ LEXIS ➻ NEXIS ➻ WESTLAW ➻ DIALOG ➻ 6 full-time librarians ➻ library seats 307 ➻ library designated as a federal depository—2,686 serials

■ Curriculum

➻ Academic Support Program ➻ 90 credits required to graduate ➻ 80 courses available ➻ degrees available: J.D.; J.D./M.B.A. ➻ range of first-year class size—165-185

The school offers a full-time day program on the semester system. Students normally graduate in three years, although summer classes are available and some students graduate after five semesters plus two summers. A total of 90 semester hours are required for graduation; 56 are required, and 34 are electives that may be chosen from a wide selection of elective courses, seminars, externships, law review or moot court participation, and independent research.

A part-time day program is available for up to 10 percent of the entering class. This program, unlike the full-time program, permits students to be employed more than 20 hours per week while attending law school.

The faculty-to-student ratio of 1:20 enables the faculty to take a personal interest in the welfare and education of our students. In addition, approximately 20 distinguished practicing attorneys offer upper-level elective courses and participate in the first-year legal research and writing program.

■ Special Programs

In cooperation with the College of Business and Economics, a joint J.D./M.B.A. program is available.

Upper-class law students are eligible to enroll in practice skills courses which are under the supervision of the full-time faculty. Several clinics provide students with the opportunity to represent clients under the supervision of an attorney.

The school has an externship program in conjunction with four federal agencies: the United States Attorney's Office for the Western District of Tennessee, the Equal Employment Opportunity Commission, the National Labor Relations Board, and the U.S. Bankruptcy Court. These programs allow a limited number of students to earn two credit-hours by working in one of these agencies 10 hours a week for one semester.

■ Admission

➻ Bachelor's degree required for admission ➻ application deadline—Feb. 15 ➻ LSAT, LSDAS required ➻ median GPA—3.16 ➻ median LSAT score—154 ➻ application fee—$10 ➻ fall entrance only for first-year class

A completed file includes application form, domicile certificate, application matching form, LSDAS report, dean's certification form, recommendation with waiver form, and personal statement. An applicant must have taken the LSAT within three years prior to enrollment, and must have utilized LSDAS. Students are admitted only in the fall semester.

Approximately 85 percent of admissions are based on a weighted combination of the LSAT score and the cumulative undergraduate GPA. Approximately 15 percent of the entering class will be selected by the Faculty Admission Committee through the subjective admission process. In this process, the committee takes into consideration non-quantifiable subjective factors, such as undergraduate institution, performance in "core" and "major" curriculum, public or community service, personal background, employment history, and performance in graduate school. Offers of acceptance are then extended to those applicants in the subjective pool whom the committee feels have the best chance of successfully competing in law school.

In an effort to increase the number of blacks admitted to law school in Tennessee, the Tennessee Prelaw Fellowship Program (TPFP) is offered. TPFP is a preparatory and developmental effort available to black Tennessee residents only. Students participate for two consecutive summers in an eight-week intensive development program. Students who successfully complete both summers, and who meet minimum requirements for admission, will be offered admission to the law school.

Aside from TPFP, the law school encourages applications from members of racial and ethnic groups who have been underrepresented in the legal profession. A student who has done acceptable work at a law school on the approved list of the ABA may be admitted to advanced standing under a transfer student program.

■ Student Activities

The University of Memphis Law Review is written, edited, and published quarterly by a student staff with contributions made by legal specialists in various fields. Students also participate in national, regional, and intraschool moot court and mock trial activities. All students are members of the Student Bar Association, which organizes many social and law-related activities. There are also active chapters of the Black Law Students Association, legal fraternities, and other special-interest organizations.

■ Expenses and Financial Aid

➽ *full-time tuition & fees—resident, $3,582; nonresident, $8,978* ➽. *part-time tuition & fees—resident, $152/credit hour; nonresident, $386/credit hour*
➽ *estimated additional expenses—$4,370, room & board; $700, books and supplies* ➽ *scholarships available*
➽ *minority scholarships available: Black Law Student Scholarships available to enrolled black students who are Tennessee residents* ➽ *financial aid available; Free Application for Federal Student Aid (FAFSA) required, priority deadline—April 1*

Financial aid is available in the form of scholarships, loans, and on-campus jobs. During 1994-95, 76 students received approximately $325,000 in scholarship awards. Scholarships may range from $500 to $8,000 for the academic year.

■ Career Services

The School of Law maintains the Career Services Office to assist students seeking part-time and summer employment, and alumni and graduates searching for full-time positions. The office provides students with information on employment searches, résumé writing, and interviewing skills.

The School of Law is a member of the Southeastern Law Placement Consortium, a group of 11 Southeastern law schools that sponsors a recruiting conference in Atlanta each October. The recruiting conferences provide second- and third-year students and judicial law clerks with the opportunity to interview with law firms from cities throughout the country, as well as with government agencies and corporations.

The law school is a founding member of the Southeastern Law Schools Minority Job Fair. The purpose of this Job Fair is to provide minority students with an additional opportunity to interview with law firms, public interest and governmental employers, and corporations.

According to the 1994 graduating class employment survey, more than 90 percent of those graduates responding reported employment within nine months of graduation.

Applicant Group for the 1995-1996 Academic Year

The University of Memphis—Cecil C. Humphreys School of Law
This grid includes only applicants who earned 120-180 LSAT scores under standard administrations.

LSAT Score	GPA 3.75 +		3.50 - 3.74		3.25 - 3.49		3.00 - 3.24		2.75 - 2.99		2.50 - 2.74		2.25 - 2.49		2.00 - 2.24		Below 2.00		No GPA		Total	
	Apps	Adm	Apps	Adm	Apps	Adm	Apps	Adm	Apps	Adm	Apps	Adm	Apps	Adm	Apps	Adm	Apps	Adm	Apps	Adm	Apps	Adm
175 - 180	0	0	0	0	0	0	0	0	0	0	0	0	0	0	0	0	0	0	0	0	0	0
170 - 174	0	0	1	1	1	1	0	0	0	0	1	1	1	1	0	0	0	0	0	0	4	4
165 - 169	2	1	1	1	0	0	1	1	1	1	3	3	2	2	1	1	0	0	0	0	11	10
160 - 164	7	7	5	5	8	6	12	12	9	8	11	10	5	5	2	1	0	0	1	1	60	55
155 - 159	15	13	15	15	20	18	46	40	30	26	26	19	13	5	5	0	0	0	1	0	171	136
150 - 154	8	8	30	30	62	48	86	47	72	15	51	6	25	1	8	1	1	0	3	1	346	157
145 - 149	8	7	33	19	45	8	53	5	77	4	43	1	21	4	8	0	3	0	1	0	292	48
140 - 144	6	3	8	0	15	1	31	5	42	2	24	2	23	0	12	0	3	0	0	0	164	13
135 - 139	2	0	2	1	9	1	12	0	24	0	15	0	9	0	4	0	2	0	3	0	82	2
130 - 134	1	0	0	0	1	0	4	0	4	0	4	0	4	0	2	0	1	0	0	0	21	0
125 - 129	0	0	0	0	0	0	4	0	1	0	3	0	0	0	1	0	1	0	0	0	10	0
120 - 124	0	0	0	0	0	0	0	0	0	0	0	0	0	0	0	0	0	0	1	0	1	0
Total	49	39	95	72	161	83	249	110	260	56	181	42	103	18	43	3	11	0	10	2	1162	425

Apps = Number of Applicants
Adm = Number Admitted
Reflects 99% of the total applicant pool.

Mercer University—Walter F. George School of Law

Office of Admissions
Macon, GA 31207
Phone: (toll-free) out-of-state, 800.MERCER-U, ext. 2605; in-state 800.342.0841, ext. 2605

■ Introduction

The Walter F. George School of Law of Mercer University is located in Macon, about 80 miles south of Atlanta. Founded in 1873, it is one of the oldest private law schools in the South. Named for a distinguished alumnus who served as a United States Senator for 36 years, the school became a member of AALS in 1923 and has been ABA-approved since 1925. In 1987, George Woodruff bequeathed the school $15 million, making possible the curricular and programmatic renaissance now enjoyed by Mercer law students. Two major initiatives were pursued as a result of Mr. Woodruff's beneficence: enrollment was reduced to approximately 400 students, and a new curriculum was put in place. The new curriculum emphasizes small classes, a progression in the course of study, and a unique sixth semester designed to facilitate the transition from student to lawyer.

■ Enrollment/Student Body

➽ 1,413 applicants ➽ 128 enrolled first-year class 1995 ➽ 408 total full-time ➽ 15.9% minority ➽ 40% women ➽ 28 states & foreign countries represented ➽ 138 undergraduate schools represented

■ Faculty

➽ 53 total ➽ 29 full-time ➽ 24 part-time or adjunct ➽ 8 women ➽ 2 minority

■ Library and Physical Facilities

➽ 265,000 volumes & equivalents ➽ library hours: Mon.-Thurs., 8:00 A.M.-9:00 P.M.; Fri., 8:00 A.M.-6:00 P.M.; Sat., 9:00 A.M.-5:30 P.M.; Sun., 1:00 P.M.-8:00 P.M. ➽ LEXIS ➽ WESTLAW ➽ NEXIS—On line ➽ DIALOG ➽ 5 full-time librarians ➽ library seats 320 ➽ library keys provide 24-hour access

Mercer School of Law enjoys the use of one of the finest law buildings in the country. The library contains a computer learning center. The computer learning center offers 24-hour access to all legal research databases and the new computer lab offers Internet access along with CALI, word processing, LEXIS/NEXIS, and WESTLAW/DIALOG.

■ Admission

➽ Bachelor's degree required for admission ➽ application deadline—March 1 ➽ rolling admissions, early application preferred ➽ LSAT, LSDAS required ➽ median GPA—3.23 ➽ median LSAT score—156 ➽ application fee—$45

The Admissions Committee weighs a wide range of factors, including LSAT score and undergraduate GPA. Letters of recommendation are required and are considered along with other evidence of nonacademic experiences. Other factors that influence the admission decision include (1) undergraduate activities and honors; (2) work/military experience; (3) quality of the applicant's undergraduate institution; (4) postgraduate work; (5) factors that indicate an unusual degree of motivation or maturity; and, (6) factors that would contribute to the overall diversity of the entering class.

■ Student Activities

The Mercer Law Review is the oldest and most widely circulated student-staffed legal journal in the state of Georgia.

In addition to the Student Bar Association, the law school has chapters of Phi Alpha Delta and Phi Delta Phi legal fraternities, Black Law Students Association, Hispanic Bar Association, Environmental Law Society, International Law Society, Christian Legal Society, Jewish Legal Society, Mercer Sportsman, Law Spouses, Legal Eagle, and the Public Interest Society, as well as student chapters of the American Trial Lawyers Association and National Association of Criminal Defense Lawyers.

■ Curriculum

➽ Academic Support Program ➽ 90 credits required to graduate ➽ 106 courses available ➽ degrees and combined degrees available: J.D.; J.D./M.B.A. ➽ range of first-year class size—25-75

Mercer School of Law offers an innovative curriculum, known as the Woodruff Program, leading in an orderly fashion toward the practice of law. Each year begins with an introductory week-long course exploring one role of the practicing lawyer. The first-year course Introduction to Law Study focuses on the lawyer as legal analyst and initiates the student into the law school routine of briefing and analyzing appellate case options. Introduction to Counseling, featuring the lawyer as problem-solver for the client, kicks off the second year. Introduction to Dispute Resolution launches the final year by teaching the lawyering skills of negotiation and mediation in the lawyer's roles as an advocate representing the client.

First-semester courses immerse the student in case-method study of the classic subjects of the common law. The focus broadens from case analysis to include constitutional and statutory analysis in the second semester. The middle semesters of legal study offer a wide array of electives along with required courses that ensure a thorough grounding in the core elements of the general practice of law. Students are required to select electives from three blocks of courses so that every Mercer graduate has the breadth of legal background to adapt to the changing demands of modern practice. Mercer offers enough small sections of a very popular Trial Practice Course, which enables each student to learn trial techniques through individual videotaped performances and one-on-one tape reviews with the professor.

One pervasive skill needed for law practice is the ability to write clearly and convincingly. In each year of law study students sharpen their powers of written persuasion. In the spring semester of the first year, students take the basic course in Legal Writing, followed by a Legal Writing II in the second year, and a writing seminar on a topic of current interest in the final year.

The last semester of study offers students a unique opportunity to make the transition from law school to law practice. An intensive session features advanced courses in a variety of practical lawyering skills such as negotiation, business planning, and advanced criminal trial techniques. Also during this session, a number of outstanding judges and lawyers offer Mercer students a variety of "Practice Electives," courses exploring particular areas of specialized practice. Noted lawyers are called upon to provide the benefit of their experience and perspective in a special pre-practice course titled Perspectives on Lawyering. The course of study at Mercer is a logical progression of preparation for the practice of law.

■ Special Programs

The Woodruff Program is one of the most innovative and exciting education programs available, and unlike special programs at other schools, it is offered to every Mercer student. A more complete description of the program is available from the Office of Admissions. The National Criminal Defense College sponsors summer practice institutes that bring several hundred criminal defense attorneys to Mercer from across the United States. Selected students are given the opportunity to meet, observe, and work with some of the most prominent criminal defense attorneys in the nation.

■ Expenses and Financial Aid

- *full-time tuition & fees—$16,443*
- *merit scholarships available*
- *minority scholarships available*
- *financial aid available; FAF due March 1*

The tuition rate is guaranteed to remain the same for students in good standing for three consecutive years. Tuition for the 1996 entering class will be set in May. For entering students, scholarships and loans are available to applicants with strong admissions credentials and demonstrated need. The school has its own scholarships and loan funds.

■ Career Services

Mercer Law School has an active placement office headed by the Assistant Dean for Career Services. Alumni and faculty members support students in their efforts to find satisfying employment. The office assists students in obtaining permanent, summer, and part-time employment.

Services of the office include arranging on-campus interviews with employers, career planning seminars, and off-campus interviewing consortia. Individual career counseling and résumé and cover letter writing workshops also comprise much of the work of the office. There is an extensive library of career resources available for student use.

The Class of 1994 reported 98.6 percent employed within six months of graduation. Members of the Class of 1994 who took the February Georgia Bar Examination passed the exam at a rate of over 98 percent.

Applicant Group for the 1995-1996 Academic Year

Mercer University—Walter F. George School of Law
This grid includes only applicants who earned 120-180 LSAT scores under standard administrations.

	GPA																					
LSAT Score	3.75 +		3.50 - 3.74		3.25 - 3.49		3.00 - 3.24		2.75 - 2.99		2.50 - 2.74		2.25 - 2.49		2.00 - 2.24		Below 2.00		No GPA		Total	
	Apps	Adm	Apps	Adm	Apps	Adm	Apps	Adm	Apps	Adm	Apps	Adm	Apps	Adm	Apps	Adm	Apps	Adm	Apps	Adm	Apps	Adm
175 - 180	0	0	0	0	0	0	0	0	0	0	0	0	0	0	0	0	0	0	0	0	0	0
170 - 174	0	0	0	0	0	0	0	0	0	0	0	0	1	1	0	0	0	0	0	0	1	1
165 - 169	2	2	2	2	6	6	2	2	5	4	2	1	3	3	0	0	0	0	0	0	22	20
160 - 164	8	8	15	15	12	10	14	13	19	19	11	7	11	4	1	1	0	0	0	0	91	77
155 - 159	11	11	29	28	47	46	66	49	45	19	39	12	25	5	5	1	1	0	0	0	268	171
150 - 154	10	8	38	28	76	21	85	3	69	5	58	6	28	3	9	3	6	0	2	0	381	77
145 - 149	7	2	25	4	47	10	62	4	59	6	50	1	28	1	10	0	1	0	0	0	289	28
140 - 144	4	1	12	3	21	1	29	3	29	0	26	1	19	0	12	0	2	0	5	1	159	10
135 - 139	5	0	4	1	8	1	14	0	23	0	24	0	20	0	9	1	1	0	1	0	109	3
130 - 134	0	0	0	0	0	0	2	0	7	0	9	0	4	0	5	0	1	0	1	0	29	0
125 - 129	0	0	0	0	0	0	1	0	1	0	3	0	1	0	0	0	0	0	1	0	7	0
120 - 124	0	0	0	0	0	0	0	0	0	0	0	0	0	0	0	0	0	0	0	0	0	0
Total	47	32	125	81	217	95	275	74	257	53	222	28	140	17	51	6	12	0	10	1	1356	387

Apps = Number of Applicants
Adm = Number Admitted
Reflects 98% of the total applicant pool.

University of Miami School of Law

P.O. Box 248087
Coral Gables, FL 33124-8087
Phone: 305.284.2523

■ Introduction

Established in 1926 in Coral Gables, Florida, the University of Miami School of Law is part of one of the largest private research universities in the United States. The school's location, in a city of 40,000 south of Miami, allows students to attend law school in a tranquil subtropical setting while gaining legal experience in the nearby international business center of Miami. The school is accredited by the American Bar Association and is a member of the Association of American Law Schools. The school has a chapter of the Order of the Coif, the legal profession's most prestigious scholastic honor society.

■ Enrollment/Student Body

➽ 2,714 applicants ➽ 1,337 admitted first-year class 1995 ➽ 471 enrolled first-year class 1995 ➽ 1,093 total full-time ➽ 248 total part-time ➽ 32% minority ➽ 43% women ➽ 69 states & foreign countries represented ➽ over 300 undergraduate schools represented ➽ 43% out-of-state residents

■ Faculty

➽ 130 total ➽ 54 full-time ➽ 76 part-time or adjunct ➽ 13 full-time women ➽ 6 full-time minority

The quality of a University of Miami legal education is directly attributable to the faculty, whose expertise covers the wide spectrum of the law, from jurisprudence to the law of the sea, from labor law to land use, from legal ethics to the law of international sales, and from Latin American legal systems to British legal history.

■ Library and Physical Facilities

➽ 425,783 volumes & equivalents ➽ library hours: Mon.-Thurs., 7:00 A.M.-12:30 A.M.; Fri., 7:00 A.M.-MIDNIGHT; Sat., 8:30 A.M.-MIDNIGHT; Sun., 8:30 A.M.-12:30 A.M. ➽ LEXIS ➽ NEXIS ➽ WESTLAW ➽ LEGAL-TRAC ➽ CCH Access ➽ DIALOG ➽ 13 full-time librarians ➽ 25 full-time staff ➽ library seats 640

The library is a 128,000-square-foot state-of-the-art research facility featuring a 600-node LAN.

■ Curriculum

➽ 88 units required to graduate ➽ 170+ courses, workshops, and seminars ➽ degrees available: J.D. & LL.M. ➽ semesters, start in Aug. ➽ range of first-year class size—120 day/80 evening divisions; one first-year class will be approximately 40 students; tutorial will be approximately 25-30 students

Students ordinarily satisfy the requirements for the J.D. degree in three academic years of full-time study. An evening program and summer sessions are also available. A joint J.D./M.B.A. program is planned for the summer of 1996.

The school offers a graduate curriculum through which the degree of Master of Laws (LL.M.) is conferred, and offers specialization in inter-American law, international law, ocean and coastal law, taxation, estate planning, or real property development.

Applicants to the LL.M. Program must have earned a J.D. degree or its equivalent from an accredited law school and demonstrated the capacity for graduate law work. The school also offers an LL.M. for foreign students.

■ Special Programs

Studies in law and economics, law and the behavioral sciences, empirical research methods, and legal history, provide centers for interdisciplinary as well as traditional research in law.

The school offers one of the most comprehensive and sophisticated skills-training programs in the nation. This unique model of clinical legal education integrates trial, pretrial, and clinical experiences into one program, enabling students to more quickly develop the full range of effective trial advocacy skills. Directed by a full-time faculty member, more than 50 distinguished trial attorneys and judges, from both state and federal courts, assist with the trial and pretrial courses and help to supervise the clinical placements.

The school also offers the London Summer Program, a seven-week course of study at University College London.

The school is committed to increasing the representation of minorities in the legal profession and offers several innovative programs for admitted minority students. The James Weldon Johnson Summer Institute, held for five weeks before the fall semester, acquaints students with the discipline necessary to succeed in law school. The Professional Opportunities Program for Black Law Students, a coalition of local bar organizations, established attorneys, law firms, and the school, assists students in securing federal or judicial clerkships, summer associate positions, and internships, and provides a mentor program with attorneys.

■ Admission

➽ Bachelor's degree from a regionally accredited college or university required ➽ application deadline—March 8 (priority) ➽ LSAT, LSDAS required ➽ median GPA—3.22 ➽ median LSAT score—69-70th percentile ➽ nonrefundable application fee—$45 ➽ rolling admissions, early application preferred

Admission to the school is highly competitive. LSAT scores and undergraduate averages are used in the selection process. Letters of recommendation are required. Also considered are the applicant's work and extracurricular history, special skills, and background. The school encourages members of minority groups to apply. Entering students are admitted only in the fall semester. Applicants are urged to apply for admission as early as possible after September 1. Applications received after March 8 will be considered on a space-available basis. Applications will be accepted until July 31. Transfer applications will be considered for students with excellent records who have completed at least, but no more than, one full year of work at an ABA-accredited law school.

■ Student Activities

The school's many student activities include an active Student Bar Association and a student-run Honor Council; publications such as the *University of Miami Law Review*, *Inter-American Law Review*, *Yearbook of International Law*, *Entertainment and Sports Law Review*, and *Business Law Journal*; and about 40 diverse student organizations.

The school runs one of the nation's largest mock trial competitions, involving over 200 experienced lawyers who coach some 100 students. The school is distinguished by winning state, regional, and national competitions in moot court, negotiation, and client counseling.

■ Expenses and Financial Aid

➻ *Yearly tuition & fees—full-time, $19,928; part-time, $14,706*
➻ *estimated additional expenses—$9,075 min. (room, board, books) plus $4,900 (personal and transportation)*
➻ *merit and need-based scholarships available*
➻ *financial aid available; FAFSA form for need analysis due in Jan. or early Feb.*

Scholarship aid available through the school normally does not exceed the cost of tuition. Most scholarships are awarded on the basis of merit, although need is sometimes considered. All admitted applicants are automatically considered for scholarship awards. Those admitted by February 1 are considered for the Harvey T. Reid and Soia Mentschikoff Scholarships. Loan funds are available through the Law School Financial Aid Office. The priority deadline for all financial assistance is March 1.

Scholarships are also available through the Florida Minority Participation in Legal Education Program (Florida MPLE). Recipients receive substantial tuition grants and a stipend. Eligible applicants are U.S. citizens who are Florida residents, members of a historically disadvantaged minority group, and who have been accepted for full-time admission to a participating Florida law school. Recipients agree to apply for the Florida Bar and practice a minimum of three years in the state of Florida. For further information contact: The Florida Education Fund, MPLE Offices, 18350 NW 2nd Avenue, 3rd Floor, Miami, FL 33169.

On-campus, furnished three-bedroom apartments are available for law students. The approximate annual cost of $4,824 includes utilities, local phone service, and television cable. Off-campus housing information is available from the Office of Student Recruiting.

■ Career Services

The Career Planning Center provides opportunities for students to interview with more than 300 employers in Florida and nationwide. The Career Planning Center's fall On-campus Interviewing Program attracts local and national employers, providing interview opportunities with firms, corporations, government, the courts, and public interest and public service organizations. Students may also pursue summer and permanent positions at numerous job fairs in which the Center participates. Students and alumni are invited to meet with career counselors and participate in résumé writing programs, interviewing skills workshops, and firm networking events. The Center offers access to a resource library, state-of-the-art computer research, and a 24-hour job hotline listing several hundred clerkship and associate positions annually.

Admission to the school is based upon all aspects of an applicant's background, and not limited to only the LSAT and undergraduate grade-point average; therefore, a grid has not been included with this profile.

University of Michigan Law School

Hutchins Hall
Ann Arbor, MI 48109-1215

E-Mail: http://www.law.umich.edu
Phone: 313.764.0537

■ Introduction

The University of Michigan Law School is located in Ann Arbor, a cosmopolitan city rich in cultural offerings and recreational opportunities. Established in 1859, the school is housed in magnificent Gothic buildings on the university's main campus. The school's faculty includes a diverse group of scholars, practitioners, judges, and educators, many of whom enjoy distinguished reputations in fields outside the law. Michigan's graduates are found in every state, in every major American city, and on every continent. Michigan is one of a few law schools whose graduates regularly go on to careers as law professors and legal scholars.

■ Enrollment/Student Body

➧ 4,147 applicants ➧ 340 enrolled first-year class 1995
➧ 1,159 total full-time ➧ 37 full-time graduate students
➧ 20.8% students of color ➧ 43% women
➧ 88 states & foreign countries represented
➧ 214 undergraduate schools represented

The first-year class includes approximately 340 J.D. candidates who are joined each year by about 30 new graduate students, most of them young law faculty from a score of foreign countries. Students routinely come from all 50 states. In 1995, 35 percent of the first-year students were classified as Michigan residents.

■ Faculty

➧ 104 total ➧ 61 full-time ➧ 44 part-time or adjunct
➧ 21 women ➧ 7 minority

Michigan is the home of interdisciplinary legal scholarship and teaching. Even our clinical programs benefit from an interdisciplinary emphasis. For example, the legal work of the Child Advocacy Clinic utilizes the work of psychiatrists, social workers, and physicians; the Great Lakes Natural Resources Clinic coordinates its classes with the School of Natural Resources; and the Legal Assistance for Urban Communities clinical program makes use of business organizational theories.

■ Library and Physical Facilities

➧ 750,000 volumes & equivalents ➧ library hours: 8:00 A.M.-MIDNIGHT daily ➧ LEXIS ➧ NEXIS
➧ WESTLAW ➧ LEXCALIBUR
➧ 11 full-time librarians ➧ library seats 856

■ Curriculum

➧ Academic Support Program ➧ Minority Affairs Program
➧ 83 credits required to graduate ➧ 97 courses available
➧ 71 seminars ➧ 9 clinical offerings ➧ degrees available: J.D.; LL.M.; M.C.L.; S.J.D.; J.D./M.B.A.; J.D./M.H.S.A.; J.D./M.A.; Modern Middle Eastern & North African Studies; Natural Resources; World Politics; Public Policy Studies; Russian & East European Studies; J.D./Ph.D. in Economics

The first-year program is designed to give all students mastery of the basic methods of legal analysis, and of the processes of reasoning used by lawyers, while introducing major areas of legal specialization. A small-section program emphasizes the importance of collegiality between faculty and students, as does the unusually large number of students hired as research assistants with the help of the William Cook endowment. The first-year curriculum is presented to four sections of first-year students. One section begins work in late May, and three start in the fall. One of these, the New Section, employs team teaching and looks at selected topics through an interdisciplinary approach. The Legal Practice Skills Program affords another opportunity for small-group work. Every student has the option of taking at least one elective course during the first year. The second and third years are entirely elective, the only requirements being that each student elect before graduation one seminar and a course meeting the professional responsibility requirement.

In addition to the joint J.D. programs with other disciplines, other concurrent programs may be arranged. The Belfield-Bates Overseas Travel Fellowships provide funds for legal studies abroad or professional internships with international or governmental agencies or law firms. Externships provide individual students with advanced training in their areas of interest.

■ Clinical Opportunities

The Law School offers an extensive range of clinical opportunities to its students—two general clinical courses; the Child Advocacy Clinic; Criminal Appellate Practice; the Environmental Law Clinic; Women and the Law; the interdisciplinary Legal Assistance for Urban Communities Clinic; Public Interest Legal Practice; and Law in a Public Health Crisis: The Response to AIDS. The Family Law Project, the Haitian Law Project, the Immigration Law Project, and the Unemployment Benefits Clinic are student-run organizations offering additional opportunities for counseling, courtroom experience, and some course credit.

■ Admission

➧ Bachelor's degree required ➧ application deadline—Feb. 15, modified rolling (strongest applications evaluated earliest)
➧ LSAT, LSDAS required ➧ median GPA—3.56
➧ median LSAT score—167 ➧ application fee—$70

Michigan seeks to form a class which comprises an exciting and productive mix of students who will enhance the educational experience for each other. Law School Admission Test scores and the quality of the applicant's educational experience (particularly the nature of and performance in course work) are relied on heavily. Serious regard also is given to one's promise of making a notable contribution to the class by way of a particular strength in one or more of the many attainments and characteristics examined in the application process. Selections among applicants are guided by the purpose of making the school a better and livelier place in which to learn, and improving its service to the profession and the public.

■ Student Activities

The *Michigan Law Review* covers significant research in all areas of law. The *Journal of Law Reform* focuses on the law as it has changed and as it ought to be, while the *Michigan Journal of International Law* concentrates on international and comparative law. The *Michigan Journal of Gender and Law* publishes feminist perspectives on gender issues in the law. The *Michigan Telecommunication and Technology Law Review* is among the first solely electronic, online legal journals, dedicated to exploring complex issues surrounding regulation of communication technology. Two new journals, the *Michigan Law and Policy Review*, and the *Michigan Journal of Race and Law*, will begin publication soon. Students interested in combining oral argument with experience as writers of briefs may choose to enter the Campbell Moot Court Competition or the Philip C. Jessup International Moot Court Competition. The Law School Student Senate funds over 50 student organizations. Students enjoy speakers and social support through groups defined by religion, ethnicity, sexual orientation, age, or gender.

■ Expenses and Financial Aid

➧ *tuition & fees—resident, $15,814; nonresident, $22,026* ➧ *estimated additional expenses—$12,000* ➧ *financial aid available; Need Access and FAFSA forms required*

Nearly all financial aid is need-based and consists of a combination of loans and grants. The school's Financial Aid program is very substantial, drawing on a variety of Law School Scholarship and Loan Funds, as well as funds from the federal government and other external sources. Parental information is necessary in order to be considered for grant aid. We endeavor to provide financial assistance to all full-time students seeking the J.D. degree who would be unable to meet the costs of their law school education if drawing only on their own and family resources. Merit scholarships are also available. They are awarded to outstanding candidates remarkable for their anticipated contribution to the Law School and the legal profession. They vary in amount from several thousand dollars per year to full tuition plus a stipend for three years. A few merit-based awards are made each year. A post-graduate Debt Management Program enhances law graduates' freedom to pursue public interest or other positions in which salaries are lower than many alternatives.

■ Career Services

The Law School Career Services Office at Michigan schedules more than 11,000 interviews each year with over 700 potential employers from all over the country. It also informs students of announcements of some 2,000 other employment opportunities with employers who do not visit the school. The Director of the Office of Public Service works with students interested in employment in the public sector. The majority of Michigan graduates accept positions with private law firms. A substantial proportion accept judicial clerkships. Michigan graduates last year were offered positions in 47 states and the District of Columbia, as well as several foreign countries.

Admission Profile Not Available

University of Minnesota Law School

229 19th Avenue South
Minneapolis, MN 55455

URL: http://www.law.umn.edu
Phone: 612.625.5005

■ Introduction

The University of Minnesota Law School has entered its 107th year in vigorous health. The quality of Minnesota's faculty, the academic credentials of its students, and the caliber of its library collection and physical facilities are the strongest in the history of the school. This vitality is a result of thoughtful and forward-looking development of the school's century-old tradition of excellence in legal education. The law school provides a personal, collegial environment for the study of law; at the same time, students have access to the academic, professional, and cultural resources of the larger university, and the Twin Cities of St. Paul and Minneapolis, one of the most progressive and livable metropolitan communities in the country.

■ Enrollment/Student Body

➧ 2,120 applicants ➧ 260 enrolled first-year class 1995 ➧ 810 total full-time ➧ 16% minority ➧ 45% women ➧ 36 states & foreign countries represented ➧ 219 undergraduate schools represented

■ Faculty

➧ 115 total ➧ 43 full-time ➧ 72 part-time or adjunct ➧ 14 women ➧ 5 minority

The faculty's wide-ranging expertise allows students to choose from a curriculum that offers traditional legal training as well as innovative clinical and computer-assisted programs.

■ Library and Physical Facilities

➧ 800,000 volumes & equivalents ➧ library hours: open 365 days/year, 24 hours/day; staffed, Mon.-Fri., 8:00 A.M.-10:00 P.M.; Sat., 9:00 A.M.-6:00 P.M.; Sun., NOON-6:00 P.M. ➧ LEXIS ➧ NEXIS ➧ WESTLAW ➧ LUMINA ➧ 28 full-time librarians ➧ library seats 900

The award-winning Law Center on the west bank of the university's Minneapolis Campus, dedicated in 1978, remains a model for new law school complexes. The Law Library is the sixth largest academic law library in the United States and offers an exceptional international collection, comprehensive primary and secondary legal materials, and computerized connections to WESTLAW, LEXIS, and the entire University of Minnesota library system.

■ Curriculum

➧ Academic Support Program ➧ 88 credits required to graduate ➧ 130 courses available ➧ degrees available: J.D.; J.D./M.B.A.; J.D./M.P.A. (Public Affairs), joint degrees are available with most graduate programs ➧ semesters, start in late Aug. ➧ range of first-year class size—18-108

The traditional Socratic teaching method appears in all three years of the J.D. curriculum. Tutorial seminars, computer-assisted instruction, and clinical and simulated skills training are offered in various forms throughout a student's law school career. Students must fulfill a legal writing requirement in each of their three years and take one class in professional responsibility, but otherwise their second and third years are entirely elective. The first-year writing class and the various moot courts, journals, and writing seminars all provide students with small-group instruction, editing, and supervision.

■ Clinical Legal Education

The Law School has developed one of the country's largest and most active clinical programs. Each year, over 160 students receive academic credit for participating in negotiations, client interviews, court appearances, and other casework supervised by clinic faculty. Clinic course offerings include domestic abuse, bankruptcy, appellate practice, civil litigation, federal taxation, criminal prosecution and defense, asylum law, public interest law, worker's compensation, and child advocacy, social security disability, gender and the law, family law, and prisoner assistance in civil matters.

■ International Law

International programs are supported by a broad comparative and international law curriculum taught by Minnesota's own faculty experts on GATT, Public and Private International Law, and International Human Rights, and by visiting international scholars. This year, law professors and students from the People's Republic of China, Mexico, Poland, France, Germany, and Sweden are engaged in research, J.D., and graduate studies, and scholars from many other countries will visit for special programs. Summer sessions abroad in alternate years offer the study of comparative law at Lyon, France or Uppsala, Sweden. School-year study is possible in several countries for students possessing fluency in the language of the host institution.

■ Computer-Assisted Study and Research

The Law School is home to and a founding member of CCALI, the Center for Computer-Assisted Legal Instruction, a consortium of more than 116 law schools, which develops computer-assisted exercises for legal education. Students complete these tutorials, drills, and simulation exercises as assignments or supplements for classroom instruction. The Law School computer lab provides student access to personal computers for CCALI exercises, computer-based legal research, and word processing.

■ Admission

➧ Bachelor's degree required ➧ application deadline—March 1; rolling admissions, early application preferred ➧ LSAT, LSDAS required ➧ median GPA—3.61 ➧ median LSAT score—162 ➧ application fee—$30

The Admissions Committee seeks to enroll 270 highly qualified, widely talented full-time students each fall. Roughly half of the class is selected on the basis of numerical indicators of potential success in law school. The other half of the class is drawn from a pool of similarly well-qualified applicants for whom numerical predictors, while high, are less determinative of the committee's decision. For this second group of applicants, the committee considers individual scholastic honors, extracurricular activities, personal statements, recommendations, work experience, unusual life experiences, and other factors that indicate a potential for success as a law student and lawyer. Minnesota is committed to equal educational opportunities for women and minorities and strongly encourages their applications. Applicants are encouraged to visit the Law School. Arrangements can be made through the Office of Admissions to sit in on a class, tour the Law Center, and meet with an admissions representative.

■ Student Activities

Members of the *Minnesota Law Review*, founded in 1917, *The Journal of Law and Inequality*, established in 1982, *The Minnesota Journal of Global Trade*, established in 1991, and *The Journal of Technology, Law and Business*, established in 1994, analyze scholarly legal articles, refining their writing skills under close editorial supervision. Minnesota's moot court teams have built a strong record of success in regional and national competition. Extracurricular organizations focus on international human rights, minority concerns, public interest law internships, environmental law, law and religion, and other areas.

■ Expenses and Financial Aid

➧ *tuition & fees—full-time resident, $8,228; nonresident, $14,124* ➧ *estimated additional expenses—$8,900*
➧ *scholarships available (performance and need-based)*
➧ *minority scholarships available (performance and need-based)*
➧ *financial aid available* ➧ *FAFSA form for need analysis should be filed before Feb. 15*

In recent years more than 85 percent of the student body has received financial aid, primarily in loans, but including scholarships, grants, and work-study programs. Forms are available from the Office of Student Financial Aid, 210 Fraser Hall, 106 Pleasant Street, S.E., University of Minnesota, Minneapolis, MN 55455.

■ Career Services

Our graduates are leaders in federal and state judiciary and government, academics, law practice, legal services, and business. In 1995-96, approximately 125 law firms, corporations, and governmental agencies from around the United States will interview on campus. In addition, more than 900 employers send notices for posting in the Career Services Office. While a majority of graduates accept positions in the Midwest, the national composition of our student body is attractive to employees across the country. The Career Services Office provides numerous career-planning seminars and services, and maintains a resource library.

Applicant Group for the 1995-1996 Academic Year

University of Minnesota Law School
This grid includes only applicants who earned 120-180 LSAT scores under standard administrations.

LSAT Score	GPA 3.75 +		3.50 - 3.74		3.25 - 3.49		3.00 - 3.24		2.75 - 2.99		Below 2.75		No GPA		Total	
	Apps	Adm	Apps	Adm	Apps	Adm	Apps	Adm	Apps	Adm	Apps	Adm	Apps	Adm	Apps	Adm
175 - 180	2	2	4	4	3	3	0	0	1	1	0	0	0	0	10	10
170 - 174	14	13	13	13	8	8	11	11	9	7	5	2	0	0	60	54
165 - 169	49	48	64	63	44	38	42	31	19	5	8	1	4	2	230	188
160 - 164	84	81	145	111	125	35	69	7	41	5	17	1	5	2	486	242
155 - 159	90	44	125	22	111	23	75	6	38	4	25	1	7	1	471	101
Below 155	61	6	125	11	168	15	166	14	124	5	171	2	31	2	846	55
Total	300	194	476	224	459	122	363	69	232	27	226	7	47	7	2103	650

Apps = Number of Applicants
Adm = Number Admitted
Reflects 98% of the total applicant pool.

The University of Mississippi School of Law

University, MS 38677

E-Mail: lawmiss@sunset.backbone.olemiss.edu
URL: http://www.olemiss.edu/depts/law_school/law-hom.html
Phone: 601.232.7361

■ Introduction

Recognizing the need for formal law instruction in the state of Mississippi, the legislature in 1854 established the Department of Law at The University of Mississippi. Over the years, the law department has evolved into today's modern Law Center. Located in Oxford, Mississippi, on the main campus of the University of Mississippi, the Law Center is housed in Lamar Hall, named in honor of the late Mississippian, L.Q.C. Lamar, former Associate Justice of the United States Supreme Court and first law professor at the university. Oxford, a small town of approximately 10,000 people, lies nestled in the quiet hills of North Mississippi, just 75 miles southeast of bustling Memphis, Tennessee, and 180 miles north of the state capital of Jackson.

The University of Mississippi is the fourth oldest state-supported law school in the nation. The School of Law is fully approved by the American Bar Association and is a long-standing member of the Association of American Law Schools.

■ Enrollment/Student Body

➽ 1,349 applicants ➽ 362 admitted first-year class 1995 ➽ 178 enrolled first-year class 1995 ➽ 465 total full-time ➽ 2 total part-time ➽ 14% minority ➽ 36% women ➽ 19 states represented ➽ 98 undergraduate schools represented

■ Faculty

➽ 30 total ➽ 25 full-time ➽ 5 part-time or adjunct ➽ 5 women ➽ 4 minority

■ Library and Physical Facilities

➽ 263,000 volumes & equivalents ➽ library hours: 115 ➽ LEXIS ➽ NEXIS ➽ WESTLAW ➽ DIALOG ➽ 6 full-time librarians ➽ library seats 402

In August 1978, the law school moved into a new and modern five-story structure which contains, among many other features, five large classrooms with tiered seating and video capabilities, two fully-equipped Moot Court Rooms, office space for several auxiliary law programs and their staff, and individual faculty offices.

The law library collection consists of nearly 263,000 volumes, 122,000 of which are in microform equivalents. During 1989-90, the law library installed an online system, replacing the card catalog and other manual record-keeping systems. The law library also expanded onto an additional floor of the building, adding a microcomputer lab, additional seating at study carrels for students, and growth space for the library's collection.

■ Special Programs

The law school actively recruits minority students and has on staff an Assistant to the Dean for Minority Affairs, who provides counseling and support programs for minority students both before and after enrollment. At present, 56 minority students are pursuing a law degree.

■ Curriculum

➽ Academic Support Program ➽ 90 credits required to graduate ➽ 93 courses available ➽ degrees available: J.D.; J.D./M.B.A. ➽ semesters, start in June and August

■ Housing Intern Program

The University of Mississippi Housing Law Clinic is a vital part of the School of Law. The second- and third-year students enrolled in the clinic receive training in negotiation, drafting, counseling, and advocacy. They spend approximately 10 hours each week on the projects of the clinic and attending the classroom component of the program.

■ Admission

➽ Bachelor's degree required for admission ➽ application deadline—March 1 ➽ LSAT, LSDAS required ➽ median GPA—3.31 ➽ median LSAT score—151 ➽ application fee—$20

Admission to law school is gained by committee approval based upon an applicant's credentials. These credentials include a satisfactory Law School Admission Test (LSAT) score and an acceptable academic record at the undergraduate level. A bachelor's degree from an accredited school is required before an applicant can register for law school.

There are no prelaw requisites. Every applicant must take the LSAT and subscribe to the LSDAS. An LSAT score obtained more than three years before application is not valid, and the applicant will be required to retake the test. Applications are available the September preceding admission, with the application deadline for both summer and fall enrollment being March 1. However, early application is encouraged. Applicants who file late risk being placed on a waiting list.

Although the LSAT and GPA are obviously the most important factors in the admissions process, other considerations are: (1) grade patterns and progression; (2) quality of undergraduate institution; (3) difficulty of major field of study; (4) number of years since bachelor's degree was earned; (5) job experience; (6) social, personal, or economic circumstances that may have affected college grades or performance on the LSAT or academic record; (7) nonacademic achievements; (8) letters of recommendation; and (9) residency.

■ Student Activities

The *Mississippi Law Journal* is edited and published by law students. Students also administer the Moot Court program. Membership in each is competitive with grade and writing requirements.

■ Expenses and Financial Aid

➽ *tuition & fees—full-time resident, $3,096; full-time non-resident, $7,018* ➽ *estimated additional expenses—$7,000 (books and living expenses)* ➽ *scholarships available* ➽ *minority scholarships available* ➽ *financial aid available; FAF due—March 1*

■ Career Services

A full-time Director of Career Services assists students in finding permanent, summer, or part-time employment. Seventy-five to 100 law firms and other prospective employers interview at the law school each year. The majority of graduating seniors are employed prior to graduation, with the remaining few being placed within six months of graduation. The law school is an active member of the National Association of Law Placement (NALP) and annually participates in the Mid-South Placement Consortium (Nashville), the Southeastern Public Interest Job Fair (Washington, DC), the National Public Interest Law Career Fair (Atlanta), and the Minority Job Fair (Atlanta).

Applicant Group for the 1995-1996 Academic Year

The University of Mississippi School of Law
This grid includes only applicants who earned 120-180 LSAT scores under standard administrations.

	GPA																					
LSAT Score	3.75 +		3.50 - 3.74		3.25 - 3.49		3.00 - 3.24		2.75 - 2.99		2.50 - 2.74		2.25 - 2.49		2.00 - 2.24		Below 2.00		No GPA		Total	
	Apps	Adm	Apps	Adm	Apps	Adm	Apps	Adm	Apps	Adm	Apps	Adm	Apps	Adm	Apps	Adm	Apps	Adm	Apps	Adm	Apps	Adm
175 - 180	0	0	0	0	0	0	0	0	0	0	0	0	0	0	0	0	0	0	0	0	0	0
170 - 174	1	1	1	1	0	0	1	1	0	0	1	1	0	0	0	0	0	0	0	0	4	4
165 - 169	3	3	2	2	2	2	2	2	3	2	1	0	2	0	0	0	1	0	0	0	16	11
160 - 164	7	6	9	8	13	12	12	10	16	13	4	1	6	0	0	0	0	0	0	0	67	50
155 - 159	21	20	17	15	50	43	41	19	33	8	27	4	16	3	5	1	1	0	0	0	211	113
150 - 154	17	12	45	28	68	16	84	14	81	11	55	7	23	1	6	0	3	0	4	0	386	89
145 - 149	23	14	51	13	49	18	76	18	74	8	50	2	27	0	10	0	1	0	1	0	362	73
140 - 144	3	2	11	3	28	5	34	5	30	1	25	0	14	0	8	0	3	0	5	0	161	16
135 - 139	4	1	3	1	11	1	16	0	20	1	10	0	9	0	7	0	1	0	2	0	83	4
130 - 134	0	0	2	0	4	0	1	0	5	0	3	0	2	0	4	0	1	0	2	0	24	0
125 - 129	0	0	0	0	0	0	3	0	2	0	5	0	0	0	0	0	0	0	0	0	10	0
120 - 124	0	0	0	0	0	0	0	0	0	0	0	0	0	0	0	0	0	0	0	0	0	0
Total	79	59	141	71	225	97	270	69	264	44	181	15	99	4	40	1	11	0	15	0	1324	360

Apps = Number of Applicants
Adm = Number Admitted
Reflects 98% of the total applicant pool.

Mississippi College School of Law

151 E. Griffith St.
Jackson, MS 39201
Phone: 601.353.3907

■ Introduction

Mississippi College School of Law is conveniently located in downtown Jackson, the state capital, and is within walking distance of the legislature, as well as all federal and state administrative agencies and courts. Jackson is the legal and commercial center of the state and has a metropolitan population of approximately 400,000. The main campus of Mississippi College, with an enrollment of more than 3,000 students, is located in Clinton, a suburb 12 miles west of Jackson. Mississippi College School of Law is fully accredited by the American Bar Association and is a member of the Association of American Law Schools.

■ Enrollment/Student Body

➽ 891 applicants ➽ 465 admitted first-year class 1995 ➽ 153 enrolled first-year class 1995 ➽ 385 total full-time ➽ 9% minority ➽ 36% women ➽ 28 states & foreign countries represented ➽ 110 undergraduate schools represented

■ Faculty

➽ 37 total ➽ 16 full-time ➽ 21 part-time or adjunct ➽ 7 women ➽ 2 minority

■ Library and Physical Facilities

➽ 220,000 volumes & equivalents ➽ library hours: Mon.-Thurs., 8:00 A.M.-MIDNIGHT; Fri., 8:00 A.M.-9:00 P.M.; Sat., 9:00 A.M.-9:00 P.M.; Sun., 2:00 P.M.-10:00 P.M. ➽ LEXIS ➽ NEXIS ➽ WESTLAW ➽ DIALOG ➽ 4 full-time librarians ➽ library seats 207

The Law Library is housed on the second and third floors of the facility in attractive space that makes generous use of natural light and affords pleasing views of the park-like law school grounds. Carpeted throughout, the library has separate rooms for individual and group study, typing, audiovisual equipment, microform use, and photocopying. A chief feature is the modern computer lab that provides computer-assisted legal instruction and word processing using both WordPerfect and Microsoft Word software. The library is a government depository and serves bench and bar, along with its students, by providing access to primary and secondary authority for legal research in federal and state law, in addition to selective foreign and international materials.

■ Curriculum

➽ Academic Support Program ➽ 88 credits required to graduate ➽ 81 courses available ➽ degree available: J.D. ➽ semesters, start in Aug. ➽ range of first-year class size—12-75

Mississippi College School of Law is an institution that provides superior academic instruction with a curriculum that is national in focus. The school is operated on a semester basis. A beginning student must enter in the fall semester. A summer term is available to second- and third-year students who wish to accelerate and/or enrich their studies.

■ Special Programs

In order to assist students in choosing elective courses, four areas of concentration have been developed. These areas consist of general practice, commercial and corporate practice, government-related practice, and litigation practice. These groupings, however, are not intended to provide specialization during a student's first degree in law. Recognizing the importance of developing lawyering skills, Mississippi College School of Law has a curriculum that includes instruction in both theoretical and practical skills. Students have an opportunity to put into practice what they have learned in courses such as Pretrial Practice, Trial Practice, Counseling and Negotiation, Appellate Advocacy I and II, Legal Drafting, and Real Estate Transactions.

■ Minority Program

The law school offers a variety of programs to assist minority students: dedicated scholarships/stipends; Academic Support Program; Minority Interaction Placement in conjunction with the state bar; and CLEO participation. Minority students are strongly encouraged to apply and each applicant's entire record will be carefully considered.

■ Admission

➽ Bachelor's degree required ➽ application deadline—May 1 ➽ LSAT, LSDAS required ➽ median GPA—3.10 ➽ median LSAT score—152 ➽ application fee—$25

The admissions standards are set annually by the faculty. They are based on the college undergraduate grade-point average, the LSAT score, and personal and/or academic achievements or honors. A degree from an accredited four-year college or university is a prerequisite to admission. Every applicant must take the LSAT and subscribe to the LSDAS prior to being considered for admission. The school makes admissions decisions without discrimination against any person on the basis of race, religion, sex, or national origin. A $25 application fee must accompany the application. The LSAT scores should reach the Admissions Office by May 1 for fall admission. When an applicant is accepted, a deposit of $100 is required to reserve a seat in the entering class. A second deposit of $200 must be received by July 1. Upon enrollment, these nonrefundable payments are credited to the applicant's tuition.

■ Student Activities

The *Mississippi College Law Review* is a legal journal edited and published by law students selected on the basis of scholarship and the ability to do creative, scholarly research and writing. The students write comments and notes on legal developments and significant cases and edit lead articles and book reviews written by professors, lawyers, judges, legislators, and other scholars. Membership on the *Law Review* staff is recognized as both an honor and a unique educational experience. Mississippi College School of Law also provides an appellate advocacy program administered by the Moot Court Board, composed of second- and third-year students. This required program provides students with instruction and practice in both brief writing and oral argument. The Law Student Bar Association (LSBA) is the organized student government of the law school. All students are members and are eligible to hold office in the association. Other student activities include: three national legal fraternity chapters, Phi Alpha Delta, Delta Theta Phi, and Phi Delta Phi; a student chapter of the Mississippi Trial Lawyers Association; the Women's Student Bar; Christian Legal Society; Black Law Students Association; the Law School Speakers Program; and Environmental Law Club.

■ Expenses and Financial Aid

- *tuition & fees—full-time, $11,650*
- *estimated additional expenses—$13,790 (room & board, $7,200; books, $850; travel, $2,500; personal, $3,240)*
- *performance-based scholarships available*
- *performance-based minority scholarships available*
- *financial aid available*
- *FAFSA financial aid form due May 1*
- *MS College financial aid application*

■ Career Services

The Dean of Student Services coordinates and assists in placement activities. In addition to the traditional on-campus interviews, the law school also sponsors regional interviews that enable students to interview in the employers' home city. Graduates are finding employment with major law firms, corporations, and government agencies throughout the United States, with a primary focus in the Southeast. Students have received clerkships with the United States Circuit Court of Appeals, United States District Courts, and the Supreme Courts of various states.

Applicant Group for the 1995-1996 Academic Year

Mississippi College School of Law

Highest LSAT	GPA 3.75 +		3.50 - 3.74		3.25 - 3.49		3.00 - 3.24		2.75 - 2.99		2.50 -2.74		Below 2.50		No GPA		Total	
	Apps	Adm	Apps	Adm	Apps	Adm	Apps	Adm	Apps	Adm	Apps	Adm	Apps	Adm	Apps	Adm	Apps	Adm
175 - 180	0	0	0	0	0	0	0	0	0	0	0	0	0	0	0	0	0	0
170 - 174	0	0	0	0	0	0	0	0	0	0	0	0	1	1	0	0	1	1
165 - 169	1	1	0	0	0	0	2	2	1	1	0	0	0	0	0	0	4	4
160 - 164	2	2	3	3	1	1	4	4	3	3	6	6	1	1	0	0	20	20
155 - 159	7	7	2	2	8	8	12	11	21	21	21	21	26	16	0	0	97	86
150 - 154	6	6	18	18	46	45	52	51	50	45	46	30	44	3	1	1	263	199
145 - 149	9	9	18	18	27	24	66	49	56	19	32	5	28	1	1	1	237	126
140 - 144	2	0	5	2	5	0	13	0	20	0	28	0	22	0	0	0	95	2
Below 140	0	0	4	0	8	0	9	0	15	0	11	0	20	0	0	0	67	0
Total	27	25	50	43	95	78	158	117	166	89	144	62	142	22	2	2	784	438

Apps = Number of Applicants
Adm = Number Admitted
Reflects 88% of the total applicant pool.

University of Missouri—Columbia School of Law

103 Hulston Hall
Columbia, MO 65211
Phone: 314.882.6042, fax: 314.882.9625

■ Introduction

The University of Missouri (now called the University of Missouri—Columbia or Mizzou) was founded in 1839 and was the first state university established west of the Mississippi. The School of Law in Columbia was established in 1872. The faculty consists almost entirely of full-time teachers with prior experience in the practice of law. The school has an enviable history of service to the state and the nation. It is a charter member of the AALS and is fully accredited.

The new law building, completed in the fall of 1988, has tripled the space available to the law school and serves as a focal point of the Mizzou campus.

■ Enrollment/Student Body

➻ 890 applicants ➻ 363 admitted first-year class 1995 ➻ 146 enrolled first-year class 1995 ➻ 462 total full-time ➻ 9.5% minority ➻ 38% women ➻ 34 states & foreign countries represented ➻ 121 undergraduate schools represented

■ Faculty

➻ 33 total ➻ 23 full-time ➻ 10 part-time or adjunct ➻ 11 women ➻ 2 minority

■ Library and Physical Facilities

➻ 295,000 volumes & equivalents ➻ library hours: Mon.-Thurs., 8:00 A.M.-10:00 P.M.; (building hours 7:30 A.M.-MIDNIGHT); Fri.-Sat., 8:00 A.M.-6:00 P.M.; Sun., 10:00 A.M.-10:00 P.M. ➻ LEXIS ➻ NEXIS ➻ WESTLAW ➻ INFOTRAC ➻ LUMIN/OCLC ➻ 6 full-time librarians ➻ library seats 465 ➻ 22 private 3L study rooms

The law library is a focal point to the new law building, with windows overlooking most of the campus. The library also includes a state-of-the-art computer lab with 20 individual work stations for word processing, database searching, and other uses.

■ Curriculum

➻ 89 credits required to graduate ➻ 90 courses available ➻ degree available: J.D. ➻ semesters, start in Aug. ➻ usually admit 3-5 second-year transfer students

The program of study leading to the J.D. degree consists of six semesters of study. There is one seven-week semester each summer.

The first-year curriculum is prescribed. A substantial portion of the second-year curriculum is also prescribed. There is writing instruction in each year of study. A student must complete the 89 semester hours with a minimum average of 70 on a 55 to 100 scale for graduation.

■ Special Programs

The School of Law and the College of Business and Public Administration will offer a dual-degree program beginning in 1995. Students completing the designated coursework in both schools will be eligible to receive J.D. and M.B.A. degrees in four years, rather than five years customarily required. Interested students must meet admission requirements, and submit an application for each school.

The School of Law recognizes the importance of providing students with experiences to enhance lawyering skills and promote awareness of ethical issues. Two clinical programs and an externship program have been developed to meet this need. The Family Violence Clinic allows students to represent indigent victims of domestic abuse. The Criminal Prosecution Clinic allows students to represent the state at felony preliminary hearings and misdemeanor trials. Both clinics provide intensive faculty supervision and emphasize client contact and courtroom experience. Additionally, the School of Law offers student internships that place students with public and not-for-profit agencies, as well as with judges.

The School of Law participates in the London Law Consortium. A semester in London, each January through May, is available to second-and third-year law students in good standing. The courses are taught by regular faculty from the participating American universities. Students also may enroll in classes taught by British professors.

The Center for the Study of Dispute Resolution is a unique feature of the law school created to respond to the needs of lawyers and others to understand various methods of preventing and resolving disputes. The Center sponsors interdisciplinary research and conferences, and, through its own student editorial board, publishes the *Journal of Dispute Resolution*. The Center provides national leadership in this rapidly developing area of the law.

■ Admission

➻ Bachelor's degree required for admission ➻ rolling admission ➻ preference given to applications before March 1 ➻ LSAT, LSDAS required ➻ median GPA—3.46 ➻ median LSAT score—157 ➻ application fee—$40 ➻ nonrefundable deposit to hold seat—$150

A faculty committee reviews all applications. No one is automatically accepted or rejected. In many cases, factors other than GPA or LSAT score prove to be determinative. When the LSAT is repeated, the school will use an average of those scores for its evaluation. Qualifications of applicants with a disadvantaged background (cultural or economic) are specially evaluated.

Students should apply very early in the year. Applicants are encouraged to visit the School of Law. Arrangements can be made through the Admissions Office to attend a law class, meet with an admissions counselor, or tour the facilities.

■ Student Activities

The School of Law publishes the *Missouri Law Review*, a respected periodical, four times each year. The review contains articles written by legal specialists and by students. It is edited by a student editorial board. Law students become eligible to participate in the review after their first year in law school.

The School of Law also maintains a very active appellate advocacy program under the supervision of a specially selected student Board of Advocates. These programs are open to all law students. Students are involved in a wide variety of advocacy competitions.

The school has chapters of the Order of the Coif; the Order of Barristers; Student Bar Association; BLSA; Women's Law Association; and Phi Delta Phi, Phi Alpha Delta, and Delta Theta Phi legal fraternities. There are numerous other student organizations that encompass almost every aspect of social and academic life at the law school.

■ Expenses and Financial Aid

- *tuition & fees—residents, $7,368; nonresidents, $14,538*
- *estimated additional expenses—$9,100 (books/supplies, room & board, personal expenses, and transportation)*
- *scholarships available: mostly academic, some need-based—usually range from $500\yr. to full tuition*
- *minority scholarships available: academic and need-based—usually range from $500\yr. to full tuition*
- *financial aid available: Stafford, Supplemental, Law Access, and university loan programs*
- *highly recommended that Free Application Form for Student Aid (FAFSA) be submitted by March 1*

Although it is necessary to apply for scholarships on an annual basis, scholarships are normally renewed each year for those students who have need and maintain academic achievement.

■ Career Services

The Career Services Office serves as a liaison between students and prospective employers. As many as 85 firms, businesses, government agencies, and judges interview on campus each year. Graduates find employment in the legal profession in Missouri and throughout the country, and the world.

The office focuses on providing resources for career planning and development. A series of workshops, seminars, and individual counseling sessions help students develop their career goals and locate employment.

Applicant Group for the 1995-1996 Academic Year

University of Missouri—Columbia School of Law
This grid includes only applicants who earned 120-180 LSAT scores under standard administrations.

LSAT Score	GPA 3.75 +		3.50 - 3.74		3.25 - 3.49		3.00 - 3.24		2.75 - 2.99		2.50 - 2.74		2.25 - 2.49		2.00 - 2.24		Below 2.00		No GPA		Total	
	Apps	Adm	Apps	Adm	Apps	Adm	Apps	Adm	Apps	Adm	Apps	Adm	Apps	Adm	Apps	Adm	Apps	Adm	Apps	Adm	Apps	Adm
175 - 180	0	0	0	0	1	1	1	1	1	1	0	0	0	0	0	0	0	0	0	0	3	3
170 - 174	2	2	2	2	0	0	0	0	1	1	0	0	0	0	0	0	0	0	0	0	5	5
165 - 169	6	6	8	8	3	3	3	3	4	3	3	2	1	1	0	0	0	0	1	1	29	27
160 - 164	13	13	18	18	17	16	15	15	8	6	9	4	1	0	1	0	0	0	4	4	86	76
155 - 159	22	22	39	38	56	50	38	19	32	5	16	3	10	0	1	0	1	0	11	9	226	146
150 - 154	37	36	32	22	47	13	42	4	39	2	20	2	14	0	3	0	2	0	8	3	244	82
145 - 149	6	1	20	1	30	0	39	2	28	1	17	4	4	1	4	0	0	0	6	3	154	13
140 - 144	2	0	8	1	7	1	12	2	17	2	17	0	7	0	3	0	0	0	4	0	77	6
135 - 139	0	0	1	0	4	0	4	0	2	0	6	1	9	0	8	0	0	0	2	1	36	2
130 - 134	0	0	0	0	0	0	1	0	1	0	2	0	2	0	0	0	0	0	1	0	7	0
125 - 129	0	0	0	0	0	0	0	0	2	0	1	0	0	0	0	0	0	0	0	0	3	0
120 - 124	0	0	0	0	0	0	0	0	0	0	1	0	0	0	0	0	0	0	0	0	1	0
Total	88	80	128	90	165	84	155	46	135	21	92	16	48	2	20	0	3	0	37	21	871	360

Apps = Number of Applicants
Adm = Number Admitted
Reflects 99% of the total applicant pool.
This chart is to be used as a general guide only. Nonnumerical factors are strongly considered for all applicants.

University of Missouri—Kansas City School of Law

5100 Rockhill Road
Kansas City, MO 64110

E-Mail: klosterj@smtpgate.umkc.edu
URL: http://www.law.umkc.edu
Phone: 816.235.1657

■ Introduction

The University of Missouri—Kansas City (UMKC) School of Law was founded in 1895 as the Kansas City School of Law. It merged with the University of Kansas City in 1938 and affiliated with the University of Missouri in 1963. It is fully accredited by the ABA and the AALS.

■ Enrollment/Student Body

➼ 931 applicants ➼ 177 enrolled first-year
➼ 471 full-time ➼ 13 part-time ➼ 10% minority
➼ 45% women ➼ 25 states & foreign countries represented
➼ 139 undergraduate schools represented

■ Faculty

➼ 61 total ➼ 29 full-time ➼ 32 part-time or adjunct
➼ 10 women ➼ 3 minority

■ Library and Physical Facilities

➼ 255,000 volumes & equivalents ➼ LEXIS/NEXIS
➼ WESTLAW/DIALOG ➼ Internet
➼ Virtual Classroom ➼ Extensive CD-ROM and electronic database collection ➼ Interactive Video
➼ 7 full-time librarians/tech support ➼ library seats 400

The School of Law is housed on the UMKC campus, in the center of a metroplex that is, itself, in the center of the nation. Its location offers convenient access to downtown law offices, courts, and government agencies. The law building contains modern classrooms equipped with audiovisual aids, a large student lounge, and offices for student organizations. A fully equipped Computer Media Center houses LEXIS and WESTLAW terminals, a student computer lab, and a virtual classroom for use in training students in the use of the Internet and other technologies applicable to law.

A unique feature of the building is the placement of student study stations in office suites shared by faculty. These student stations include study carrels and private or double-occupancy student offices available to all second- and third-year students. This suite arrangement provides considerable study space and facilitates student-student and student-faculty interaction.

■ Curriculum

➼ Academic Support Programs ➼ full-time and flex (part-time day) programs ➼ 91 credits required to graduate
➼ large selection of courses available
➼ degrees available: J.D.; J.D./M.B.A.; LL.M. (Tax and General); and J.D./LL.M. (Tax) ➼ semesters, start in Aug.
➼ range of first-year class size—15-60

The first-year J.D. program is prescribed. First-year courses are taught in classes of fewer than 60 students each. Students take a year-long intensive course in Introduction to Law and Lawyering Processes that includes instruction in legal analysis, research, writing, and advocacy. Classes in this course are taught in groups of fewer than 30, with workshops of 15. The upper-level program includes seven required courses, as well as familiarity requirements in federal agency law and jurisprudence. Students must also complete an intensive research and writing project. Students may elect from a broad selection of elective courses, including approved nonlaw courses in other UMKC divisions. No class offered is larger than 80 students, and most are significantly smaller.

Courses at UMKC are taught in a variety of formats, but all have in common high-quality teaching and student-faculty interaction. Many of the substantive required and elective courses include problem-solving and skills components, and there are many smaller skills courses offered as well.

The School is committed to the success of its students. An academic enrichment program in the form of supervised, structured study groups and periodic lectures is offered to all first-year students. Additional opportunities include a week-long summer program and weekly enrichment sessions made available on a more limited basis.

Students may graduate in two-and-one-half years by attending two summer sessions. An LL.M. degree is available, including a degree with a concentration in taxation. Courses in the LL.M. program are available to J.D. candidates as electives.

■ J.D./M.B.A. Dual-Degree Program

The School of Law has a dual-degree program with the School of Business and Public Administration. The program allows students to earn a J.D. degree and a Master of Business Administration degree on an accelerated basis through cross-acceptance of credit hours. Applicants must satisfy the admission requirements of each school and, if admitted, may enroll in the first year of law school either before or after beginning M.B.A. courses.

■ J.D./LL.M. (Tax) Combined-Degree Program

The School of Law has a combined degree program that allows qualified J.D. students to apply up to twelve hours of approved J.D. tax courses toward an LL.M. degree. This will allow the student to earn the LL.M. on an accelerated basis, generally requiring only one additional semester (or two summers) beyond that required for the J.D.

■ Student Activities

UMKC's location in a metropolitan area provides many opportunities for student participation in clinical programs, including judicial clerkships, Legal Aid, Public Defender, and death penalty clinics. Missouri and Kansas Supreme Court rules permit senior law students to appear in court on behalf of indigent persons. Students write and edit a substantial portion of the UMKC Law Review, a scholarly legal journal, and also serve as assistant editors of the Urban Lawyer, published by the ABA Section of Local

Government Law, and of the *Journal of the American Academy of Matrimonial Lawyers*.

All students develop skills in appellate advocacy through Introduction to Law, with further opportunity to participate in a sequenced upper-level program. UMKC also has an extensive trial advocacy program. Both offer opportunities for participation in national competition. UMKC also participates in the ABA Negotiation and Client Counseling competitions, as well as several specialized moot court competitions. UMKC competition teams have won regional or national honors in each of the past several years.

The law school has an active Student Bar Association affiliated with the Law Student Division of the ABA. Students are represented at faculty and committee meetings and play an important role in establishing school policy. Three national fraternities, Delta Theta Phi, Phi Alpha Delta, and Phi Delta Phi, have chapters at the school, as do BLSA, Association of Women Law Students, and other organizations that specialize in particular areas of interest.

■ Admission

➽ Bachelor's degree from accredited school required; combined degree admission without undergrad degree possible ➽ rolling admissions, early application preferred ➽ LSAT, LSDAS required ➽ median GPA—3.12 ➽ median LSAT score—154 ➽ application fee—$25

Some students are chosen based primarily on an index formula determined by combining an applicant's cumulative undergraduate grade-point average with the LSAT score. Other candidates are admitted based on a combination of factors designed to ensure that the entering class contains persons of diverse background whose index scores and other achievements qualify them for law study.

Students may be admitted with a bachelor's degree from an approved institution or, in appropriate cases, with 90 hours of acceptable academic work. A $100 seat deposit is payable by April 1, or within 20 days of admission, whichever comes later. Applicants are encouraged to visit the school. Arrangements can be made through the Admissions Office to meet with students and faculty, visit a class or tour the law school.

■ Expenses and Financial Aid

➽ full-time tuition & fees (1995-96)—resident, $7,606; nonresident, $14,747 ➽ estimated additional expenses—$8,900 (room & board, transportation, medical and personal expenses) ➽ merit and need-based scholarships available ➽ merit and need-based diversity scholarships available ➽ government loan program available through UMKC Financial Aid Office ➽ FFS, UMKC financial aid form and financial aid transcripts required

■ Career Services

The Career Services Office assists law students and graduates in exploring and defining career options through individual counseling, workshops, and seminars. Law firms, businesses, and government agencies interview students on campus for summer clerkships and post-graduate employment. Additionally, area law firms list available clerk and attorney positions with the office. In cooperation with area bar associations, a mentor program pairs first-year students with practicing attorneys. The Career Services Office also provides resources for career planning and development.

Applicant Group for the 1995-1996 Academic Year

University of Missouri—Kansas City (UMKC) School of Law

	GPA								
LSAT Score	3.75 +	3.50 - 3.74	3.25 - 3.49	3.00 - 3.24	2.75 - 2.99	2.50 - 2.74	2.25 - 2.49	2.00 - 2.24	Below 2.00
165 & above	Good Possibility	Good Possibility	Good Possibility	Good Possibility	Good Possibility	Good Possibility	Good Possibility	Unlikely	Unlikely
160 - 164	Good Possibility	Good Possibility	Good Possibility	Good Possibility	Good Possibility	Good Possibility	Good Possibility	Unlikely	Unlikely
155 - 159	Good Possibility	Good Possibility	Good Possibility	Good Possibility	Possible	Possible	Unlikely	Unlikely	Unlikely
150 -154	Good Possibility	Good Possibility	Good Possibility	Possible	Possible	Unlikely	Unlikely	Unlikely	Unlikely
145 - 149	Possible	Possible	Possible	Unlikely	Unlikely	Unlikely	Unlikely	Unlikely	Unlikely
140 - 144	Unlikely	Unlikely	Unlikely	Unlikely	Unlikely	Unlikely	Unlikely	Unlikely	Unlikely
Below 140	Unlikely	Unlikely	Unlikely	Unlikely	Unlikely	Unlikely	Unlikely	Unlikely	Unlikely

Good Possibility — Possible — Unlikely

The school of law considers many factors beyond LSAT score and GPA. This chart should be used only as a general guide.

University of Montana School of Law

Missoula, MT 59812

Phone: 406.243.4311

■ Introduction

The University of Montana is located in Missoula, on the west slopes of the Rocky Mountains. Missoula is situated halfway between Yellowstone and Glacier National Parks and is surrounded by several of the largest designated wilderness areas in the continental United States. The city is known for its outdoor opportunities and quality of life.

The University of Montana School of Law was established in 1911. It has been accredited by the AALS since 1914 and by the ABA since 1923. As one of the smallest law schools in the nation, students enjoy a congenial academic, intellectual, and social environment. The law school serves as a legal center for the state.

■ Enrollment: First-Year Class

➽ *614 applicants* ➽ *185 admitted first-year class 1995* ➽ *79 enrolled first-year class 1995* ➽ *6.8% minority* ➽ *40% women* ➽ *17 states,countries, and Indian tribes represented* ➽ *44 undergraduate schools represented*

■ Faculty

➽ *28 total* ➽ *17 full-time* ➽ *11 part-time* ➽ *11 women*

■ Library and Physical Facilities

➽ *127,352 volumes & equivalents* ➽ *LEXIS* ➽ *WESTLAW* ➽ *two computer labs* ➽ *computer research integrated with class assignments*

■ Curriculum

➽ *90 semester hours required to graduate* ➽ *65 courses available* ➽ *degrees available: J.D.; J.D./M.P.A.; J.D./M.S.* ➽ *semesters, start in late Aug. or early September*

The University of Montana School of Law integrates theory and practice throughout its curriculum to instill entry level practice competence in its graduates. The law school's curriculum, teaching methodology, and assessment techniques are designed to address the following components of a lawyer's work: (1) knowledge of the law; (2) the ability to apply legal rules to resolve problems; (3) ability to use lawyer skills (e.g., negotiation, client counseling); (4) perspective on the societal role and responsibility of lawyers; and (5) sensitivity to the dynamics of social and interpersonal interaction.

The school has created three distinctive programs to acquaint first-year students with the ways lawyers think and work: (1) the Introductory Program, (2) the Lawyer Skills Program, and (3) the Law Firm Program. In the introductory program, students are initiated into the legal culture by surveying legal history, the American legal system, the litigation process, legal writing, and legal analysis and jurisprudence. The law school is one of the few to introduce first-year students to the skills involved in dispute resolution, including client counseling, legal drafting, and oral argument. The innovative "law firm" program encourages students to cooperate and collaborate rather than compete as they begin to think and work as lawyers. From the beginning of law school, entering students belong to "law firms," groups of six students, called associates, directed by specially trained upper-class students.

The school has long emphasized performance in its curriculum. The school's four-semester legal writing program and three-year dispute resolution program represent a coherent and comprehensive approach to lawyer skills. Students master specific transactional skills such as planning an estate, drafting a contract, and creating a small business.

The upper-division clinical training program provides students with a wide range of opportunities to earn required academic credit by working on actual cases under the supervision of faculty and practicing attorneys in Missoula. The clinical offerings include the Montana Defender Project, Natural Resource Clinic, Indian Law Clinic, Montana Legal Services Association, ASUM Legal Services, Missoula County Attorney's Office, Forest Service Clinic, University of Montana Legal Counsel's Office, Missoula City Attorney's Office, and Disability Law Clinic.

■ Special Programs

The law school also offers students wishing to specialize several clusters of courses. Because of Montana's natural setting, many students enroll in the natural resource and environmental law courses. The school offers basic and advanced courses in resource and environmental law, as well as natural resource clinics and the opportunity to participate on the *Public Land Law Review*.

Montana is home to seven Indian reservations. The law school's Indian Law courses, Indian Law Clinic, and Native American Law Student Association provide opportunities for students to learn about and participate in the administration of justice for Montana's native Americans.

The school also offers clusters of courses in the areas of business and tax (with emphasis on the problems of small businesses), public law, and individual and property rights.

The school offers two joint-degree programs. A joint program in law and environmental studies allows students to earn both their J.D. and an M.S. in as little as four years. A joint program in law and public administration leads to both the J.D. and M.P.A. degrees in four years.

■ Admission

➽ *application deadline—March 15, rolling admissions, early application preferred* ➽ *LSAT, LSDAS required* ➽ *median GPA—3.27* ➽ *median LSAT score—158* ➽ *application fee—$60*

A committee of the law faculty passes on all applications. Candidates must be of good moral character, have intellectual promise, and have a baccalaureate degree from an approved college or university prior to matriculation. As a state-assisted institution, the School of Law gives some preference in admissions to residents. The school seeks a diverse student body and welcomes applications from members of groups historically underrepresented in the legal profession.

The most important admissions criteria are the cumulative undergraduate GPA and the LSAT score. The admissions committee weighs such factors as writing ability; experience prior to application to law school, including graduate study, college attended, trend in grades, quality of work in difficult courses, ability to overcome economic or other disadvantage, and change in performance after an absence from college.

The school recognizes a commitment to providing full opportunities for the study of law and entry into the legal profession of qualified members of groups (notably racial and ethnic minorities) which have been victims of discrimination in various forms. This commitment is implemented by special recruitment and retention efforts.

If the LSAT is repeated, the average of the scores will be used in computing the applicant's prediction index. No test score achieved later than the February administration of the LSAT can be considered in decisions for the subsequent September.

■ Student Activities

All students are members of the Student Bar Association. Its programs contribute to the professional development and the social life of the student body. Clayberg Inn of Phi Delta Phi national law fraternity encourages scholarship, promotes fellowship, and fosters the ideals of the profession. The Women's Law Caucus is part of the SBA, and other organizations include a Christian Legal Society, a student chapter of the American Trial Lawyers—Montana Trial Lawyers Association, the Environmental Law Group, the Native American Law Student Association, the Federalist Society, the University of Montana Public Interest Law Coalition, Edna Rankin Law Society, and Montana Defense Trial Lawyers Association. The *Montana Law Review* and the *Public Land Law Review* afford supplementary training in analyzing legal problems precisely and presenting legal issues cogently. The UMLS team placed first in the nation in the 1991-1992 American Trial Lawyers Association trial competition and first in the 1990-1991 American Bar Association Client Counseling Competition. The UMLS National Moot Court Competition teams have advanced from regional to the national finals nine times in the last 14 years.

■ Expenses and Financial Aid

- *tuition & fees—residents, $5,090; nonresidents, $10,252*
- *estimated additional expenses—$7,000 (room, board, books)*
- *performance and need-based scholarships available (primarily to second- and third-year students)*
- *file FAFSA financial aid applications by March 1*

■ Career Services

The School of Law maintains a career service to assist students in finding part-time and summer employment, and attorney positions upon graduation. The job placement rate for the 1992 class for the period not less than 18 months after graduation was 86 percent.

Applicant Group for the 1995-1996 Academic Year

University of Montana School of Law
This grid includes only applicants who earned 120-180 LSAT scores under standard administrations.

LSAT Score	3.75 +		3.50 - 3.74		3.25 - 3.49		3.00 - 3.24		2.75 - 2.99		2.50 - 2.74		2.25 - 2.49		2.00 - 2.24		Below 2.00		No GPA		Total	
	Apps	Adm	Apps	Adm	Apps	Adm	Apps	Adm	Apps	Adm	Apps	Adm	Apps	Adm	Apps	Adm	Apps	Adm	Apps	Adm	Apps	Adm
175 - 180	0	0	0	0	0	0	0	0	0	0	0	0	0	0	0	0	0	0	0	0	0	0
170 - 174	0	0	1	1	0	0	0	0	0	0	1	1	1	1	0	0	0	0	0	0	3	3
165 - 169	2	2	3	3	3	3	3	3	1	1	1	1	0	0	0	0	0	0	1	1	14	14
160 - 164	7	7	12	12	7	6	20	18	9	8	6	2	1	0	1	1	0	0	0	0	63	54
155 - 159	12	11	24	20	17	11	27	10	26	7	16	2	11	0	5	1	0	0	3	0	141	62
150 - 154	4	2	26	13	22	4	39	6	32	2	20	3	14	3	2	0	1	0	3	1	163	34
145 - 149	6	1	14	2	23	2	22	2	17	0	15	1	6	0	4	0	2	0	3	0	112	8
140 - 144	2	0	2	0	14	1	16	0	16	1	7	1	7	0	4	0	0	0	2	1	70	4
135 - 139	1	0	2	0	4	0	4	0	4	0	1	0	2	0	8	1	1	0	1	0	28	1
130 - 134	0	0	1	0	1	0	0	0	0	0	0	0	2	0	1	0	0	0	2	0	7	0
125 - 129	0	0	0	0	0	0	0	0	0	0	0	0	0	0	0	0	0	0	0	0	0	0
120 - 124	0	0	0	0	0	0	0	0	0	0	0	0	0	0	0	0	0	0	1	0	1	0
Total	34	23	85	51	91	27	131	39	105	19	67	11	44	4	25	3	4	0	16	3	602	180

Apps = Number of Applicants
Adm = Number Admitted
Reflects 98% of the total applicant pool.

University of Nebraska College of Law

P.O. Box 830902
Lincoln, NE 68583-0902
Phone: 402.472.2161

■ Introduction

The University of Nebraska College of Law is large enough to provide students with a diverse curriculum, yet small enough to ensure that students are not lost in a faceless crowd. The college was founded in 1888 and is accredited by both the AALS and the ABA. It is located on the East Campus of the University of Nebraska in Lincoln, a city of approximately 200,000, and the state capital.

■ Enrollment/Student Body

➧ 777 applicants ➧ 388 admitted first-year class 1995 ➧ 137 enrolled first-year class 1995 ➧ 415 total full-time ➧ 10% minority ➧ 40% women ➧ 19 states & foreign countries represented ➧ 59 undergraduate schools represented

■ Faculty

➧ 45 total ➧ 26 full-time ➧ 19 part-time ➧ 5 women ➧ 2 minority

■ Library and Physical Facilities

➧ 323,969 volumes & equivalents ➧ library hours: Mon.-Fri., 7:30 A.M.-12:30 A.M.; Sat., 9:00 A.M.-10:00 P.M.; Sun., NOON-12:30 A.M. ➧ LEXIS ➧ NEXIS ➧ WESTLAW ➧ DIALOG ➧ 5 full-time librarians ➧ library seats 301

The law college building offers the best in modern facilities, all of which are accessible to the physically disabled. The college's courtroom addition features a fully equipped teaching courtroom and expanded facilities for the civil clinical program.

The law library provides an excellent study atmosphere. Students have access to microform materials, audio and video materials, CD-ROM network, and the LEXIS and WESTLAW computerized research systems. The law library has a student computer laboratory with personal computers and printers.

■ Curriculum

➧ Academic Support Program ➧ 96 credits required to graduate ➧ 90 courses available ➧ degrees available: J.D.; M.L.S.; J.D/M.B.A.; J.D./M.P.A. (Accounting); J.D./Ph.D. (Psychology); J.D./Econ.; J.D./Poli.Sci.; J.D./M.C.R.P. (Community and Regional Planning); J.D./Ph.D. (Ed. Admin); J.D./individually designed programs ➧ semesters, start in Aug. ➧ range of first-year class size—25-70

The academic year runs from late August to early May. A two-day orientation before the beginning of the fall semester introduces first-year students to the law school and the study of law. Although completing the requirements for a J.D. degree normally takes three years, it is possible to graduate in two and one-half years by attending summer school during two summers. The college offers no night classes and only rarely accepts part-time students. Students receiving the J.D. degree are qualified to practice law in any state upon passage of that state's bar examination.

The first-year curriculum is 18 hours per semester and includes civil procedure, contracts, criminal law, legal process, legal writing, property, and torts. Courses in the second and third years are elective, with the exception of required courses in constitutional law, professional responsibility, and a research seminar. The curriculum encompasses a broad range of areas, from taxation and securities to Native American law, legal control of discrimination, and international transactions. The college offers many courses in the environmental and natural resource law areas including environmental law I and II, international and environmental law, water law, oil and gas law and agricultural law. The average upper-class student takes 15 hours per semester.

■ Special Programs

Skills and Clinical Education. The college offers professional skills courses in pretrial litigation, trial advocacy, advanced trial advocacy, negotiations, alternative dispute resolution, client interviewing and counseling, business planning, and civil and criminal clinic to allow second- and third-year students to develop lawyering skills and to learn strategic and practical skills in simulated settings or in the handling of real cases for actual clients. In civil clinic, third-year students represent clients in and out of court in a wide range of civil matters including bankruptcy, tax audits, litigation, domestic relations, immigration, adoption, and landlord-tenant disputes. Students in criminal clinic prosecute misdemeanor cases in Lancaster County, including drug possession, assault, trespass, forgery, escape, arson, and extortion.

Joint degree programs. The college's interdisciplinary program in Law and Psychology is recognized as one of the finest in the nation. Students can receive either a Ph.D. and J.D. after six years of study or an M.A. and J.D. after four years of study. The college also participates in six other joint degree programs and will work with students to individually design programs in disciplines not covered by a formal program. In each program, students will earn two degrees with fewer credit hours and in less time than if the degrees were pursued separately.

■ Admission

➧ Bachelor's degree from accredited institution required ➧ application deadline—March 1 ➧ rolling admission, early application preferred ➧ LSAT, LSDAS required ➧ median GPA—3.34 ➧ median LSAT score—155 ➧ application fee—$25

The college starts reviewing applications in early January. Although an applicant's undergraduate GPA and LSAT score weigh heavily in the admission decision, substantial weight is also given to the quality of the applicant's undergraduate institution, course of study, personal statement, work experience, extracurricular activities, recommendations, and other background information supplied by the applicant. The college will waive the application fee upon demonstration of financial need. To visit a law class, meet with admission personnel, or tour the Law College, call the Admissions Office. The College of Law has an annual open house in February.

The college takes special care in evaluating applications from members of minority groups that have been underrepresented in the legal profession. The college also participates in the CLEO program and looks favorably upon candidates for admission who have successfully completed the program.

The college provides an Academic Resource Program to assist first-year students in developing and improving fundamental skills such as note-taking, case briefing, outlining, analyzing, and exam-taking. The college also offers a skills seminar to focus on these skills. Participation in the seminar is by invitation.

■ Student Activities

The *Nebraska Law Review*, published by a student editorial board, publishes leading articles from well-known authorities in their fields, as well as student notes and comments. The *Nebraska Transcript*, published by students three times a year, provides information about the college to students, faculty, and alumni. Other student activities and organizations include the National Moot Court Competition, Client Counseling Competition, National Trial Competition, Student Bar Association, Women's Law Caucus, Community Legal Education Project, Black Law Students Association, Civil Liberties Group, Equal Justice Foundation, Multi-Cultural Legal Society, Natural Resources Law Society, Christian Legal Society, Federalist Society, Association of Trial Lawyers of America, International Law Society, Law Student Research Service, The Rutherford Institute, Volunteer Income Tax Assistance Program, and three national legal fraternities.

■ Expenses and Financial Aid

➽ *tuition & fees—resident, $4,374; nonresident, $9,720* ➽ *estimated additional expenses—$8,520 (books, living expenses, transportation, personal)* ➽ *academic scholarships, need-based grants, and opportunity grants available* ➽ *FAFSA forms and College of Law need-based grant application forms for financial aid due March 1*

For the 1995-1996 academic year, resident tuition is $94.50 per hour, and nonresident tuition is $243 per hour. Fees total $486 per semester.

■ Career Services

The college operates its own career services office for students seeking full-time employment or summer clerkships. The office provides students with a variety of placement-related services and also organizes on-campus interviews by private law firms, governmental agencies, corporations, and other potential employers. As of December 1994, approximately 90 percent of the members of the class of 1994 were employed or were enrolled in advanced degree programs.

Applicant Group for the 1995-1996 Academic Year

University of Nebraska College of Law
This grid includes only applicants who earned 120-180 LSAT scores under standard administrations.

LSAT Score	3.75 +		3.50 - 3.74		3.25 - 3.49		3.00 - 3.24		2.75 - 2.99		2.50 - 2.74		2.25 - 2.49		2.00 - 2.24		Below 2.00		No GPA		Total	
	Apps	Adm	Apps	Adm	Apps	Adm	Apps	Adm	Apps	Adm	Apps	Adm	Apps	Adm	Apps	Adm	Apps	Adm	Apps	Adm	Apps	Adm
175 - 180	1	1	0	0	0	0	0	0	0	0	0	0	0	0	0	0	0	0	0	0	1	1
170 - 174	3	3	0	0	0	0	0	0	1	1	1	0	1	1	0	0	0	0	0	0	6	5
165 - 169	5	5	2	2	7	7	2	2	3	3	0	0	0	0	0	0	0	0	0	0	19	19
160 - 164	11	10	15	15	14	14	11	11	12	10	9	6	2	2	1	1	0	0	0	0	75	69
155 - 159	14	13	27	26	33	33	34	28	26	16	18	6	7	0	0	0	0	0	2	1	161	123
150 - 154	21	19	50	39	56	33	45	16	30	8	23	3	8	1	1	0	0	0	1	1	235	120
145 - 149	13	8	23	7	29	7	35	5	15	1	20	1	9	0	4	0	1	0	2	0	151	29
140 - 144	2	0	11	2	17	1	8	1	13	1	8	0	5	0	3	0	1	0	2	0	70	5
135 - 139	1	0	2	0	3	0	3	0	9	0	8	0	3	0	3	0	0	0	2	0	34	0
130 - 134	0	0	0	0	1	0	3	0	2	0	0	0	2	0	1	0	1	0	2	0	12	0
125 - 129	0	0	0	0	0	0	0	0	0	0	2	0	0	0	0	0	0	0	0	0	2	0
120 - 124	0	0	0	0	0	0	0	0	0	0	0	0	0	0	0	0	0	0	0	0	0	0
Total	71	59	130	91	160	95	141	63	111	40	89	16	37	4	13	1	3	0	11	2	766	371

Apps = Number of Applicants
Adm = Number Admitted
Reflects 99% of the total applicant pool.

New England School of Law

154 Stuart Street
Boston, MA 02116

Phone: 617.422.7210

■ Introduction

New England School of Law was founded in 1908 as Portia Law School, the only school in the nation dedicated exclusively to the legal education of women. The institution became coeducational in 1934, but it has remained sensitive to the needs of those underrepresented in the legal profession. New England is fully accredited by the American Bar Association (ABA).

Boston is an ideal city in which to study law. Our school occupies two completely modern, downtown facilities near Boston's government, business, and theater districts.

New England capitalizes on its advantageous location by providing an extensive clinical program and by utilizing members of the city's legal community as adjunct faculty and lecturers. The school has attracted a number of distinguished speakers through its Speakers Series and other events. Most notably, we welcomed United States Supreme Court Justice Sandra Day O'Connor on September 20, 1991, and United States Supreme Court Justice Harry A. Blackmun on March 11, 1993.

■ Enrollment/Student Body

➥ 3,422 applicants ➥ 1,464 admitted first-year class 1995 ➥ 360 enrolled first-year class 1995 ➥ 651 total full-time ➥ 446 total part-time ➥ 12.1% minority ➥ 46% women ➥ 42 states & foreign countries represented ➥ 316 undergraduate schools represented

■ Faculty

➥ 102 total members ➥ 40 full-time ➥ 62 part-time or adjunct ➥ 10 women ➥ 4 minority

■ Library and Physical Facilities

➥ 260,000 volumes & equivalents ➥ library hours: Mon.-Fri., 8:00 A.M.-11:00 P.M.; Sat., 9:00 A.M.-10:00 P.M.; Sun., 10:00 A.M.-11:00 P.M. ➥ LEXIS ➥ NEXIS ➥ WESTLAW ➥ DIALOG ➥ OCLC ➥ CALI ➥ 8 full-time librarians ➥ library seats 415

The tri-level law library incorporates computerized legal research equipment, study carrels, typing space, and consultation and lounge areas. Offering the latest in technology, the library has an extensive audio and video collection, several trials presented on Interactive Videodisc, and a significant number of CD-ROM indexes to legal research tools.

■ Curriculum

➥ Academic Support Program ➥ 84 units/credits required to graduate ➥ 98 courses available ➥ J.D. degree offered ➥ semesters, start in Aug. ➥ range of first-year class size—15-115

As a national law school, New England's curriculum is designed to prepare graduates to practice in any jurisdiction in the United States. The school has both a day and evening division, each offering the J.D. degree. The day program requires 84 credit hours over three academic years. The work of the first year is prescribed. Second-year students are required to take criminal law and procedure, evidence, and professional responsibility. Remaining courses are elective.

The evening program requires 84 credit hours over four academic years. The evening program curriculum is prescribed for the first and second years; the third and fourth years are elective.

In addition to its day and evening programs, New England offers a third program of study for persons whose child-care responsibilities permit only part-time study with more flexibility.

■ Special Programs

New England prides itself on the great variety of high quality clinical programs available to its students. The school offers 15 clinics and maintains its own fully equipped Clinical Law Office, in which supervised students handle actual cases. Besides its civil and criminal practice clinics, the school offers clinical programs in such diverse areas of law, as: health, mental health, immigration, tax, employment, land use, environmental, administrative, prisoners' rights, government lawyer, and domestic violence.

■ Admission

➥ Bachelor's degree required for admission ➥ application deadline—March 15 ➥ LSAT, LSDAS required ➥ median GPA—2.92 ➥ median LSAT score—151 ➥ application fee—$50

New England requires the LSAT, use of the LSDAS, and two letters of recommendation. This information, together with a completed application, must be received by the Admissions Office by March 15 (and preferably much earlier, since decisions are made on a rolling basis).

Like most law schools in desirable urban locations, New England receives applications from many more qualified individuals than it can accommodate. The Admissions Committee makes decisions to provide stability and diversity in the entering class. Factors that reflect stability are the GPA and the LSAT score. Factors weighted heavily for diversity include, but are not limited to, undergraduate major and institution, extracurricular activities and/or work experience, geographic distribution, minority status, gender, and exceptional characteristics.

■ Student Activities

Upper-class students are selected for membership on the *New England Law Review* on the basis of academic achievement or success in a writing competition. Our other scholarly journal, *The New England Journal of Criminal and Civil Confinement*, is the only student publication in the country devoted solely to this field. Other student publications include an *Environmental and International Law*

Annual. Our school participates in several moot court programs, including the National Moot Court, the Jessup (international law), the National Environmental Law, the F. Lee Bailey Moot Court, and National Tax Moot Court. In 1991 and 1992, New England teams won the Northeast Regional round of the National Trial Competition.

The Student Bar Association (SBA) is the school's student government, with members serving as student representatives on most faculty and law school committees. The SBA also sponsors a variety of social events, athletic competitions, community participation including a partnership with Boston High School, and a Speaker's Forum. Other student organizations include the Computer Law Society, Environmental Law Society, International Law Society, Lesbian and Gay Caucus, Minority Students' Association, the Women's Law Caucus, and others.

■ Minority Programs

As part of fulfilling its continued pledge to those underrepresented in the legal profession, New England has developed a new recruitment program, funded additional allocations of financial aid, and established the Charles Hamilton Houston Enrichment Program (CHHEP). The CHHEP has three components that involve first-year students: the speaker series, the first-year discussion groups, and the academic support program.

■ Housing

New England does not operate student housing facilities. Numerous privately owned apartment buildings are within walking and commuting distance of the school, and roommate referral listings are available in the admissions office.

■ Expenses and Financial Aid

➽ *tuition & fees—full-time, $12,650; part-time, $9,526* ➽ *estimated additional expenses—books, $450; health insurance, $585; living expenses, $10,550* ➽ *scholarships available: NESL grant, Maclean grant, Arthur Getchell grants, Jacqueline Lloyd grants, Trustee Scholars* ➽ *minority scholarships available: Jacqueline Lloyd grant* ➽ *financial aid available* ➽ *Free Application for Federal Student Aid (FAFSA) and New England School of Law Financial Aid Application required, due April 15*

The school participates in the Federal Perkins Loan and Federal Work-Study programs. Limited institutional employment, grants, and scholarships are also available to needy applicants, including the MacLean Grant for students from extremely disadvantaged backgrounds and the Jacqueline Lloyd grant for students from minority backgrounds.

■ Placement

The Law School maintains a Career Services Office to assist students and alumni in securing law-related employment both prior to and after graduation. The services provided by the office include individual and group career counseling, résumé preparation, maintenance of a career-resource library, and specific job listings for students and graduates. In addition, information is disseminated concerning summer internships, part-time and full-time employment, judicial clerkships, and graduate programs.

Respondents to the employment survey of the Class of 1994 indicated an overall employment rate of 83 percent. Of the employed graduates, 44 percent were working in private law practice.

Applicant Group for the 1995-1996 Academic Year

New England School of Law
This grid includes only applicants who earned 120-180 LSAT scores under standard administrations.

LSAT Score	3.75 +		3.50 - 3.74		3.25 - 3.49		3.00 - 3.24		2.75 - 2.99		2.50 - 2.74		2.25 - 2.49		2.00 - 2.24		Below 2.00		No GPA		Total	
	Apps	Adm	Apps	Adm	Apps	Adm	Apps	Adm	Apps	Adm	Apps	Adm	Apps	Adm	Apps	Adm	Apps	Adm	Apps	Adm	Apps	Adm
175 - 180	0	0	0	0	0	0	0	0	1	1	1	1	0	0	0	0	0	0	0	0	2	2
170 - 174	1	1	0	0	0	0	2	2	1	1	0	0	0	0	0	0	0	0	1	1	5	5
165 - 169	0	0	1	1	3	3	3	2	3	3	4	4	2	1	1	0	0	0	2	1	19	15
160 - 164	1	1	9	8	16	15	24	22	36	33	19	18	12	6	4	2	1	0	1	0	123	105
155 - 159	8	6	31	31	62	60	97	92	97	91	72	58	26	14	12	7	0	0	2	2	407	361
150 - 154	18	14	56	50	155	142	219	160	246	126	153	60	81	17	28	4	5	0	10	4	971	577
145 - 149	13	11	69	38	160	57	247	66	247	52	164	20	81	15	24	3	6	0	6	1	1017	263
140 - 144	6	4	33	8	65	8	116	17	117	5	85	4	50	4	34	0	6	0	11	0	523	50
135 - 139	1	0	12	0	20	1	46	2	36	1	45	0	28	1	16	1	5	0	12	2	221	8
130 - 134	0	0	2	0	1	0	5	0	8	0	13	0	13	0	5	0	3	0	2	0	52	0
125 - 129	0	0	1	0	0	0	1	0	2	0	4	0	2	0	3	0	1	0	2	0	16	0
120 - 124	0	0	0	0	0	0	1	0	1	0	1	0	0	0	0	0	1	0	0	0	4	0
Total	48	37	214	136	482	286	761	363	795	313	561	165	295	58	127	17	28	0	49	11	3360	1386

Apps = Number of Applicants
Adm = Number Admitted
Reflects 98% of the total applicant pool.

University of New Mexico School of Law

1117 Stanford N.E.
Albuquerque, NM 87131-1431

Phone: 505.277.0572

■ Introduction

The University of New Mexico is the state's major university with over 24,000 students. The law school, located on the north campus of the university in Albuquerque, is just minutes from the downtown area and 60 miles from Santa Fe, the state's capital. This proximity to local, state, and federal courts, key government offices, and law firms allows students opportunities to observe and participate in the practice of law. In their leisure, students have access to symphony, theater, the Santa Fe Opera, galleries, museums, and the beauty of outdoor New Mexico. The combination of Indian, Spanish, and Anglo cultures reflected in food, music, art, architecture, and local customs heightens Albuquerque's appeal.

The University of New Mexico School of Law is known for its small classes, easy student-faculty interaction, and innovative education and research. The School of Law has an 11:1 student-faculty ratio, one of the best in the country. This ratio allows the school to offer more courses with smaller enrollments.

The school offers a comprehensive curriculum and has special programs in natural resources law, American Indian law, and international transboundary law. It also has a legal education equal opportunity program that recruits and assists minority students and is a member of the Southwest CLEO consortium. It is a member of the AALS and is fully approved by the ABA.

■ Enrollment/Student Body

➽ *1,136 applicants* ➽ *209 admitted first-year class 1995* ➽ *107 enrolled first-year class 1995* ➽ *335 total full-time* ➽ *45% minority* ➽ *52% women* ➽ *57 undergraduate schools represented in first-year class*

■ Faculty

➽ *59 total* ➽ *32 full-time* ➽ *28 adjunct* ➽ *16 women* ➽ *8 minority*

■ Library and Physical Facilities

➽ *346,000 volumes & equivalents* ➽ *library hours: Mon.-Thurs., 7:30 A.M.-MIDNIGHT; Fri., 7:30 A.M.-8:00 P.M.; Sat., 9:00 A.M.-8:00 P.M.; Sun., NOON-MIDNIGHT* ➽ *LEXIS* ➽ *NEXIS* ➽ *WESTLAW* ➽ *Q/L* ➽ *DIALOG* ➽ *4 full-time librarians* ➽ *library seats 380*

The law school is housed in Bratton Hall. In addition to classrooms, seminar rooms, the moot courtroom, the library, and faculty and student organization offices, Bratton Hall also houses the Natural Resources Center, the American Indian Law Center, and the Law Practice Clinic.

The UNM Law Library is the primary New Mexico legal research center. The library includes comprehensive collections of British, federal, and state court reports, and annotations, session laws, current state and federal statutes, legal treatises, periodicals, encyclopedias, digests, administrative reports, and other classes of legal materials. Special collections are being developed in American Indian law, Mexican and Latin American law, community land grant law, and natural resources law.

Over 100 carrels are available to students and faculty engaged in ongoing research. Pocket lounges and browsing areas, audiovisual carrels, group study rooms, a photocopy facility, and a computer lab are available for students' use.

■ Curriculum

➽ *Academic Support Program* ➽ *programs offered: Orientation, Mentor, Summer Academic Support/Academic Year Tutorials* ➽ *86 credits required to graduate* ➽ *over 120 courses available* ➽ *degrees available: J.D.; J.D./M.B.A.; J.D./M.P.A.; J.D./M.A. (Latin American Studies)* ➽ *semesters, start in Aug. & Jan. (15 weeks), May (clinic)* ➽ *range of first-year class size—16-55*

First-year students must take a full first-year curriculum, including basic courses in torts, contracts, civil procedure, property, and criminal law. Emphasis is also placed on the skills of advocacy; legal writing, oral argument, litigation, counseling, and negotiation. Second- and third-year courses are elective except for Ethics, Introduction to Constitutional Law, and a clinical program. Students normally complete the requirements for the J.D. degree in three academic years (six semesters).

Unlike most other law schools, UNM requires six credit hours of clinical work for graduation. In 1970, the New Mexico Supreme Court adopted a rule permitting students to practice before state courts. Today, the UNM Program in Clinical Law is regarded as one of the finest practical-lawyering programs in the country. The program is based at the school, but also has a branch in the Bernalillo County District Attorney's office. In the fall 1993, the Southwest Indian Law Clinic was established. It allows students to gain practical experience by working directly with New Mexico's different tribal governments. The clinical program also operates an extern placement program. Students may elect assignment to a judge's office, the Public Defender's Office, federal and state administrative offices, and private practitioners.

■ Special Programs

Four research and training institutes are a part of the law school—the American Indian Law Center; the Institute of Public Law; the Natural Resources Center; and the International Transboundary Center. The American Indian Law Center is an independent institute devoted to strengthening Indian tribal government. It has worked closely with the Navajo, Pueblo, and other tribes to assist them in improving their judicial systems. The Institute of Public Law serves New Mexico and the Southwest in an advisory capacity and provides training programs and research for state and local governments. Recent activities by its centers include projects in bioethics, environmental clean-up, wildlife law, and mediation.

The Natural Resources Center plans and administers special academic programs in natural resources and policy and coordinates research activities and grant programs. Since 1961, the law school has published the *Natural Resources Journal*. The journal has led to the development of a special program at the law school. Students may earn a certificate showing concentration in this area of law. The International Transboundary Center is research-oriented and concerns itself with the management of natural resources complicated by political divisions.

UNM law students may earn an Indian Law Certificate. Students must complete 21 hours of coursework in Indian law and fulfill the J.D. writing requirement in a study focused on an Indian law subject. The School of Law is a member of a consortium which offers six weeks of summer law study in Guanajuato.

■ Admission

➻ Bachelor's degree from an accredited college or university required ➻ application deadline—Feb. 1 ➻ LSAT, LSDAS required ➻ median GPA—3.24 ➻ median LSAT score—155 ➻ application fee—$40 ➻ admittance fall semester only ➻ no deposit required of accepted applicants

Applicants should take the LSAT no later than December before the year in which they wish to enroll.

A five-member committee reviews all applications from residents and all competitive applications from nonresidents. Substantial weight is given to the applicant's personal statement, prior work experience, extracurricular activities, recommendations, and to other background information supplied by the applicant.

The profile printed below does not make any distinction between residents and nonresidents, but applications from New Mexico residents are given very decided preference.

■ Student Activities

Extracurricular activities include the *Natural Resources Journal*, the *New Mexico Law Review*, and several moot court and mock trial competitions. All law students are members of the university's Graduate/Professional Student Association and the Student Bar Association. Students may participate in more than 15 law-student organizations.

■ Expenses and Financial Aid

➻ full-time tuition & fees—resident, $2,984/year; nonresident, $10,012/year ➻ estimated additional expenses—room & board, $5,558; books & supplies, $668; transportation, $1,020; personal expenses, $1,926; childcare supplement for any number of dependents age 12 or under, $2,550 ➻ grants available ➻ Native American grants available ➻ financial aid available ➻ UNM FAFSA Addendum due March 1 or ASAP after admission

The law school awards a significant number of need-based grants to full-time students each year.

Applicant Group for the 1995-1996 Academic Year

University of New Mexico School of Law
This grid includes only applicants who earned 120-180 LSAT scores under standard administrations.

LSAT Score	3.75 +		3.50 - 3.74		3.25 - 3.49		3.00 - 3.24		2.75 - 2.99		2.50 - 2.74		2.25 - 2.49		2.00 - 2.24		Below 2.00		No GPA		Total	
	Apps	Adm	Apps	Adm	Apps	Adm	Apps	Adm	Apps	Adm	Apps	Adm	Apps	Adm	Apps	Adm	Apps	Adm	Apps	Adm	Apps	Adm
175 - 180	0	0	0	0	1	1	0	0	0	0	0	0	0	0	0	0	0	0	0	0	1	1
170 - 174	0	0	0	0	3	3	1	0	3	2	0	0	0	0	0	0	0	0	0	0	7	5
165 - 169	5	5	2	2	8	4	7	4	10	5	3	0	1	0	0	0	0	0	0	0	36	20
160 - 164	10	7	23	9	29	15	21	10	18	3	18	7	7	0	0	0	1	0	3	1	130	52
155 - 159	15	6	36	11	51	16	51	11	42	9	11	2	9	0	6	1	2	0	0	0	223	56
150 - 154	17	2	35	12	55	6	70	7	48	3	24	1	18	4	6	0	3	0	6	0	282	35
145 - 149	9	2	23	2	34	4	55	4	38	5	26	6	12	0	9	1	5	0	4	0	215	24
140 - 144	5	0	5	1	17	1	23	2	20	2	13	2	19	2	8	0	2	0	2	0	114	10
135 - 139	0	0	3	0	11	0	8	0	14	0	15	0	15	0	5	0	4	0	3	0	78	0
130 - 134	0	0	0	0	1	0	3	0	3	0	2	0	0	0	3	0	2	0	0	0	14	0
125 - 129	0	0	0	0	0	0	0	0	2	0	1	0	0	0	0	0	1	0	0	0	4	0
120 - 124	0	0	0	0	0	0	0	0	1	0	0	0	0	0	0	0	0	0	0	0	1	0
Total	61	22	127	37	210	50	239	38	199	29	113	18	81	6	37	2	20	0	18	1	1105	203

Apps = Number of Applicants
Adm = Number Admitted
Reflects 97% of the total applicant pool.

City University of New York School of Law at Queens College

65-21 Main Street
Flushing, NY 11367

Phone: 718.575.4210

■ Introduction

CUNY School of Law at Queens College has a special emphasis on public service and public interest law. The school is fully accredited by the American Bar Association. It is the only publicly funded law school in New York City.

The School of Law is a unit of the City University of New York, one of the largest and most distinguished university systems in the nation. Queens College, on whose campus the Law School is situated, is one of nine four-year colleges in the CUNY system.

■ Enrollment/Student Body

➡ 1,997 applicants ➡ 446 admitted first-year class 1995 ➡ 160 enrolled first-year class 1995 ➡ 456 total full-time ➡ 2 total part-time ➡ 33% minority ➡ 52% women ➡ 29 states & foreign countries represented ➡ 195 undergraduate schools represented

The law school has been remarkably successful in recruiting the diverse, committed, and richly experienced student body that it has sought. The median age of matriculated students during 1994-95 was 29. Approximately 80 percent of enrolled students in 1994-95 were residents of New York State, and approximately one-third have attended one or more of the City University schools for undergraduate or graduate work. The academic credentials of our students run the full range of possible grades and scores. Where the traditional indicators are low, the applicants can demonstrate academic potential through nonstandard indicia and very strong work or life experiences that are relevant to the school's mission.

■ Faculty

➡ 58 total ➡ 40 full-time ➡ 18 part-time or adjunct ➡ 36 women ➡ 23 minority

■ Library and Physical Facilities

➡ 221,692 volumes & equivalents ➡ library hours: open to public: Mon.-Thurs., 8:00 A.M.-8:00 P.M.; Fri., 8:00 A.M.-5:00 P.M. ➡ library hours to students: 7:00 A.M.-MIDNIGHT, 7 days per week ➡ WESTLAW ➡ DIALOG ➡ 8 full-time librarians ➡ library seats 397

The law school's permanent facility is unique in that it allocates space—offices—for student use. Each pair of offices, called a Section, comprises a suite of rooms. Two of these rooms are student work areas, with a desk, bookshelves, and locking file drawers for each student. In addition, there are three faculty offices, a Section Library (with access to computer-assisted legal research databases), a secretarial/reception area, and photocopy and word processing equipment.

The library combines a substantial print collection with extensive microform holdings and widely accessible computer databases.

■ Curriculum

➡ Academic Support Program ➡ 91 credits required to graduate ➡ J.D. degrees available ➡ semesters, start in Aug. ➡ range of first-year class size—20-160

Our purpose is to create an educational program that honors students' aspirations toward a legal career built on a commitment to justice, fairness, and equality.

The overall theme of an integrated curriculum is especially reflected in our treatment of three areas that are given much heavier emphasis than has been traditional. These areas are legal theory, clinical education, and professional responsibility. The first three semesters consist almost entirely of required courses. The final three semesters allow the student to select from a number of elective courses, in a variety of doctrinal areas. In addition, in the final two semesters, the student is enrolled either in a concentration area (with classroom work and practice placement combined) or in a clinic (with virtually full-time live-client practice).

The school offers only a full-time day program.

■ Lawyering Seminars

Clinical work is comprehensively integrated into the course of study. Throughout the program students are organized into work units called Lawyering Seminars. These offices of 20 students provide a context for a series of simulated practice situations related to the substantive courses. Each Lawyering Seminar is affiliated with a faculty member. Through the simulations, the students engage in a wide range of lawyering tasks; they draft documents, interview and counsel clients, engage in negotiations, and make arguments before trial and appellate courts, often reviewing their work with the Lawyering Seminar teachers and other faculty.

We believe that grappling with issues of professional responsibility is at the heart of public interest practice, and that an awareness of personal and professional responsibility therefore should be integral to students' lawyering work.

■ Admission

➡ Bachelor's degree from accredited college or university required ➡ application deadline—March 15 ➡ LSAT, LSDAS required ➡ application fee—$40 ➡ early application preferred

We actively seek to recruit, retain, promote, and train students of all races, national origins, classes, and belief systems, without regard to gender or sexual preference.

We admit people based on several criteria. We look at academic performance and scores on the LSAT, and beyond these to other demonstrations of academic promise.

Assessment of academic ability alone does not dominate the admissions process. We try to assess some of the less tangible qualities that make an outstanding lawyer, including judgment, energy, initiative, and the ability to work both collaboratively and independently. We look for indications that the candidate has a special affinity for our particular program; people with a demonstrated commitment to the principles of justice, fairness, and equality in the legal process; people with a sensitivity to the diversity of society and the equal worth of each of its members; and people who manifest a regard for providing all groups the broadest participation in our public life.

Finally, we try to select a diverse group of students, genuinely representative of the remarkable diversity of the city the school serves.

The school's admissions process is described in detail in its application materials. In brief, all applications are read closely. The detailed personal statement that we require forms the core of most applications. Two recommendations, are required and are also often a decisive part of the applicant's file. Applicants may be invited to come in and meet with members of the committee. Students who have questions about our program or who want to visit the law school are of course welcome to contact the Admissions Office for an informational interview with a member of the Admissions Office staff.

■ Expenses and Financial Aid

➽ full-time tuition & fees—resident, $3225.85/semester; nonresident, $4840.85/semester ➽ estimated additional expenses—$9,000 (room & board, transportation, personal expenses, insurance) ➽ Law School Tuition Waivers available ➽ special CUNY form only (no cost to process) required for financial aid

Federal Perkins Loans (formerly NDSL) and federal work-study funds are available, as are a limited number of tuition waivers. During 1993-94, approximately 68 percent of our students received tuition waivers ranging from $100 to $2,500 for the year or other financial assistance.

■ Career Services

The law school views the placement function as part of its academic program. Our placement program begins in the first year. We encourage students to reflect on the choices they make as they seek work and decide among employment opportunities. We also work actively to develop job opportunities during the year, during the summer, and after graduation.

Applicant Group for the 1995-1996 Academic Year

City University of New York School of Law at Queens College
This grid includes only applicants who earned 120-180 LSAT scores under standard administrations.

LSAT Score	GPA 3.75 +		3.50 - 3.74		3.25 - 3.49		3.00 - 3.24		2.75 - 2.99		2.50 - 2.74		2.25 - 2.49		2.00 - 2.24		Below 2.00		No GPA		Total	
	Apps	Adm	Apps	Adm	Apps	Adm	Apps	Adm	Apps	Adm	Apps	Adm	Apps	Adm	Apps	Adm	Apps	Adm	Apps	Adm	Apps	Adm
175 - 180	0	0	0	0	0	0	0	0	0	0	0	0	0	0	0	0	0	0	0	0	0	0
170 - 174	0	0	1	1	1	1	0	0	1	0	0	0	0	0	0	0	0	0	0	0	3	2
165 - 169	0	0	4	4	2	1	1	1	3	1	1	1	1	1	1	1	0	0	1	1	14	11
160 - 164	2	2	3	2	10	7	22	14	8	4	5	2	5	1	1	0	0	0	2	2	58	34
155 - 159	10	6	17	15	17	15	34	21	27	8	15	6	11	1	6	0	2	0	2	1	141	73
150 - 154	6	4	19	9	47	31	68	18	74	24	54	11	31	6	15	2	3	0	7	4	324	109
145 - 149	10	8	24	10	71	25	105	29	103	18	113	18	64	9	32	2	9	1	11	2	542	122
140 - 144	8	3	18	7	42	8	76	14	88	12	90	9	50	7	19	1	3	0	13	1	407	62
135 - 139	3	0	9	1	15	1	45	3	51	3	61	4	32	2	29	1	6	0	16	0	267	15
130 - 134	0	0	4	0	10	1	16	0	22	1	20	0	29	0	15	0	6	0	7	0	129	2
125 - 129	0	0	0	0	0	0	0	0	3	0	3	0	5	0	4	0	2	0	2	0	19	0
120 - 124	0	0	0	0	0	0	0	0	0	0	0	0	3	0	0	0	1	0	1	0	5	0
Total	39	23	99	49	215	90	367	100	380	71	362	51	231	27	122	7	32	1	62	11	1909	430

Apps = Number of Applicants
Adm = Number Admitted
Reflects 97% of the total applicant pool.

New York Law School

57 Worth Street
New York, NY 10013-2960

Phone: 212.431.2888

■ Introduction

New York Law School has been an integral part of New York's legal community for over 100 years. Founded in 1891, the school's approach to law study combines practical perspective with theoretical analysis to produce a "lawyer-centered" legal education. The school's central location and proximity to courts, government agencies, major law firms, corporations, and financial institutions provides invaluable educational and practical experiences for students. The Law School offers clerkship and externship opportunities in numerous law offices and government agencies within walking distance. The Law School is located in TriBeCa, one of the city's most colorful and dynamic communities and the home of film studios, art galleries, fine restaurants, and numerous other cultural and entertainment resources.

The school's success is reflected in the many leaders of the legal and business community who are New York Law School graduates. It offers a full-time day program, a part-time day program, and a part-time evening program. New York Law School is a member of the Association of American Law Schools, is fully approved by the ABA, and is chartered by the New York State Board of Regents.

■ Enrollment/Student Body

➧ 4,542 applicants ➧ 2,076 admitted first-year class 1995 ➧ 468 enrolled first-year class 1995 ➧ 911 total full-time ➧ 490 total part-time ➧ 23% minority ➧ 43% women ➧ 31 states & foreign countries represented ➧ 192 undergraduate schools represented ➧ 39 first-year students hold advanced degrees

New York Law School has a long-standing and continuing interest in enrolling students from varied backgrounds, including older students, minority students, women, career changers, and public servants. Students range in age from 21 to 65, with the average age of 26.

■ Faculty

➧ 126 total ➧ 52 full-time ➧ 74 part-time or adjunct ➧ 42 women ➧ 15 minority

The school's broad curriculum of more than 200 elective courses and seminars is taught by a distinguished faculty. Leading jurists and attorneys who work in nearby offices are members of the adjunct faculty and teach courses in their areas of practice and expertise. Collectively, the faculty offers exceptional breadth and depth in their backgrounds and professional interests.

■ Library and Physical Facilities

➧ 395,000 volumes & equivalents ➧ library hours: Mon.-Thurs., 8:00 A.M.-11:00 P.M.; Fri., 8:00 A.M.-10:00 P.M.; Sat. and Sun., 10:00 A.M.-10:00 P.M. ➧ LEXIS ➧ NEXIS ➧ Law Schools Online ➧ WESTLAW ➧ OCLC ➧ RLIN ➧ LegalTrac ➧ Wilsondisc ➧ CD-ROM Tower ➧ 13 full-time librarians ➧ library seats 616

The Mendik Library houses the collection and reflects the latest developments in information technology. Designed to be a functional, comfortable environment in which to study, it features separate rooms for computer terminals, spacious study areas, and informal lounges. Of particular interest is the Communications Library, devoted to material related to the school's Media Law program.

The Law School's facilities occupy a group of four connected buildings in Lower Manhattan near the courts, city, state, and federal offices, and the financial district. A new Student Center includes a cafeteria situated in a sky-lit atrium, student organization offices, bookstore, art gallery, and a spacious lounge area.

■ Curriculum and Special Programs

➧ Academic Support Program ➧ 86 units/credits required to graduate ➧ 225 courses available ➧ degrees available: J.D./M.B.A. with Baruch College (City University of New York); and Bachelor's/J.D. with Stevens Institute of Technology ➧ range of first-year class size—15-120

The curriculum is designed to prepare students to be effective, productive, and responsible members of the legal profession. The required curriculum, comprising the entire first year and part of the second year, provides a foundation in legal reasoning and in areas of law that are considered indispensable building blocks of a legal education. In the second year and thereafter, students may design their programs with elective courses chosen from an extraordinarily rich array.

The Lawyering Skills Program—Elements such as legal analysis and legal writing, counseling, interviewing, negotiating, advocacy, planning, and strategizing form the core subject areas of the school's Lawyering Skills Program. This program integrates skills-related courses as part of the required first-year sequence and thereafter. The key elements of the Lawyering Skills Program include simulation courses such as Negotiating, Counseling, and Interviewing, Trial Advocacy, externships and judicial internships, practice workshops, and clinics.

The Externship and Judicial Internship Programs—These programs permit students to do actual lawyering work at placements in law offices.

Communications Media Center—In response to the explosive growth of new communication technologies, the Law School established a Communications Media Center in 1977. The center promotes education, discussion, research, and writing about mass communications law.

■ Clinical Program

The school has a tradition of a strong clinical program that permits students to do actual lawyering work, representing clients in clinics supervised by Law School faculty.

■ Admission

➽ *Bachelor's degree from accredited college or university required for admission* ➽ *application deadline—April 1* ➽ *rolling admissions, early application preferred* ➽ *LSAT, LSDAS required* ➽ *median GPA—3.00* ➽ *median LSAT score—154* ➽ *application fee—$50*

In the admission process a range of factors is taken into account, including the applicant's academic record and Law School Admission Test scores. The school seeks to admit students who, in addition to possessing strong academic credentials, also have demonstrated leadership ability, motivation, and a sense of service and responsibility to society. In evaluating applicants, excellence in a particular field of study, motivation, progression of grades, strength of undergraduate curriculum, work and community-service experience, graduate study in other disciplines, and extracurricular activities all are considered. Writing ability receives particular attention.

The school seeks to enroll a diverse student body made up of individuals who, through their backgrounds, experiences, perspectives, and ambitions, promise to enrich the law school community and, ultimately, the larger society.

■ Student Activities

There is a Moot Court Board with active and successful participation in intermural competitions, as well as three scholarly publications, edited and staffed by students, that are integral parts of the Law School's program—*New York Law School Law Review, New York Law School Journal of International and Comparative Law*, and *New York Law School Journal of Human Rights*. Students have established some 32 interest organizations as well.

■ Expenses and Financial Aid

➽ *tuition & fees—full-time, $18,570; part-time, $13,930* ➽ *average additional expenses—$7,000 (room, board, books)* ➽ *merit and need-based scholarships available* ➽ *minority scholarships available* ➽ *financial aid available*

New York Law School has established a program of financial aid to assist students in meeting the costs of a legal education. Financial assistance is available in the form of grants, scholarships, work-study awards, and loans. New York Law School awards scholarships on the basis of academic merit and financial need. Complete information may be obtained from the Office of Financial Aid.

■ Career Services

The Career Services Office provides an array of services, including individual career counseling; On-Campus Interview Programs; numerous career panels and workshops; alumni services and network/mentoring programs; law firm lists categorized by specialty areas and size; computerized legal employer databases; and information on summer, full-time, and part-time positions and alternative career opportunities.

Applicant Group for the 1995-1996 Academic Year

New York Law School
This grid includes only applicants who earned 120-180 LSAT scores under standard administrations.

LSAT Score	GPA 3.75 +		3.50 - 3.74		3.25 - 3.49		3.00 - 3.24		2.75 - 2.99		2.50 - 2.74		2.25 - 2.49		2.00 - 2.24		Below 2.00		No GPA		Total	
	Apps	Adm	Apps	Adm	Apps	Adm	Apps	Adm	Apps	Adm	Apps	Adm	Apps	Adm	Apps	Adm	Apps	Adm	Apps	Adm	Apps	Adm
175 - 180	0	0	1	1	0	0	1	1	0	0	0	0	1	1	0	0	0	0	0	0	3	3
170 - 174	0	0	0	0	2	1	1	1	1	1	0	0	0	0	1	1	0	0	0	0	5	4
165 - 169	6	6	9	9	11	11	12	12	7	7	3	3	3	3	1	1	0	0	0	0	52	52
160 - 164	13	11	27	25	43	43	42	40	35	34	35	34	15	15	7	6	4	2	8	5	229	215
155 - 159	23	23	47	46	94	89	140	139	127	119	71	69	34	26	12	9	2	1	5	3	555	524
150 - 154	26	25	111	102	189	175	244	221	259	216	158	100	84	39	39	14	7	0	19	4	1136	896
145 - 149	19	12	89	53	137	58	241	87	246	55	191	36	94	10	58	2	10	1	32	4	1117	318
140 - 144	14	4	36	4	76	8	134	2	184	7	142	5	102	1	29	0	8	0	29	1	754	32
135 - 139	3	0	15	0	24	0	51	0	83	0	89	0	64	0	38	0	5	0	23	0	395	0
130 - 134	0	0	2	0	8	0	19	0	25	0	33	0	29	0	15	0	8	0	11	0	150	0
125 - 129	0	0	0	0	1	0	0	0	3	0	7	0	5	0	3	0	3	0	1	0	23	0
120 - 124	0	0	0	0	0	0	1	0	0	0	0	0	2	0	0	0	0	0	1	0	4	0
Total	104	81	337	240	585	385	886	503	970	439	729	247	433	95	203	33	47	4	129	17	4423	2044

Apps = Number of Applicants
Adm = Number Admitted
Reflects 97% of the total applicant pool.

New York University School of Law

110 West Third Street
New York, NY 10012

Phone: 212.998.6060; Fax: 212.995.4527

■ Introduction

Founded in 1835, New York University School of Law has a record of academic excellence and national scholarly influence extending back into the nineteenth century. More than 100 years ago it became one of the first law schools routinely to admit women and those from groups discriminated against by many other institutions.

NYU has been a pioneer in such widely diverse areas as the clinical education programs for all interested students, programs to train lawyers for public service, and interdisciplinary colloquia in fields including jurisprudence, criminal law and criminology, legal history, and international legal studies.

These traditions remain vibrant today as the School of Law, located on the university's campus in Greenwich Village—a residential neighborhood with its own rich history—continues to use its position in New York City to create a twenty-first century legal education in global justice, grounded in solid sociological and jurisprudential training and reflected in sensitive professional service to the world's peoples.

■ Enrollment/Student Body

➧ 6,623 applicants ➧ 422 enrolled first-year class 1995 ➧ 1,275 total full-time ➧ 24% minority ➧ 46% women ➧ 69 states & foreign countries represented ➧ 219 undergraduate schools represented ➧ 15% hold advanced or professional degrees

■ Faculty

➧ 95 full-time faculty (34 women, 5 minority) ➧ 97 part-time or adjunct faculty (13 women, 4 minority)

■ Library and Physical Facilities

➧ 912,000 volumes & equivalents ➧ 100 library hours per week ➧ LEXIS ➧ NEXIS ➧ WESTLAW ➧ DIALOG ➧ 17 full-time librarians

In addition to its classroom and clinical buildings, the School of Law owns two modern apartment buildings which provide housing for more than 900 people, including law students, their spouses, their partners, and their children.

■ Curriculum

➧ 82 credits required to graduate ➧ 187 courses available beyond first year ➧ degrees available: J.D./LL.M. in Taxation; J.D./M.A. (sociology, politics, history, philosophy, economics, French); J.D./M.B.A.; J.D./M/P.A. with Princeton or NYU; J.D./M.S.W.; J.D./M.U.P.; LL.M.; M.C.J.; J.S.D. ➧ semesters, start in Aug. ➧ range of first-year class size—18-105

NYU School of Law's Law Center includes the J.D. and graduate divisions, the Global Law Program, the Center for International Studies, the Center for Research in Crime and Justice, the Arthur Garfield Hays Civil Liberties Program, the Program for the Study of Law, Philosophy and Social Theory, the Program on Philanthropy and the Law, the Public Interest Center, and the Institute for Judicial Administration.

NYU's curriculum is distinguished by its strength in traditional areas of legal study, interdisciplinary study, and clinical education, and has long been committed to educating lawyers who will use their degrees to serve the public. The **Root-Tilden-Snow Program** and the **Public Interest Center**, with seven full-time staff members, sponsor speakers, offer academic and career counseling, and administer summer internship, volunteer, and mentoring programs.

The interdisciplinary programs combine a resident faculty, distinguished visitors, and courses at entry through advanced levels.

The J.D. Program is enriched by the graduate program, which offers advanced degrees. Attorneys, law teachers, and judges from over 30 countries enroll each year in degree programs in corporations, international, tax, trade regulation, and individual specialties.

■ Admission

➧ baccalaureate degree or its foreign equivalent required ➧ application deadline—early action, Oct. 15; regular Feb. 1 ➧ LSAT, LSDAS required ➧ median GPA—3.65 ➧ median LSAT score—168 ➧ application fee—$65

The admissions process is highly selective. The Committee on Admissions selects candidates with the strongest combination of qualifications and the greatest potential to contribute to NYU and to the legal profession. The committee bases its decisions on intellectual potential, academic achievement, character, community involvement, and work experience.

New York University has one of the largest and most competitive applicant pools in the country; only about one in six of those who apply is admitted. An applicant's undergraduate record and LSAT, while important, are not the sole determinants for admission. No index or cut-off is used in reviewing applications. An applicant's transcripts are analyzed for breadth and depth of coursework, trend in grades, and rank; the competitiveness of the school and major are taken into account, as are special honors and awards.

A strong undergraduate record and LSAT are most important for those applying to law school directly after graduating from college. In all cases, however, other aspects of the application significantly influence the decision. Letters of recommendation, activities, and work experience are reviewed for evidence of significant nonacademic or professional achievement, and for qualities including rigor of thought, maturity, judgment, motivation, leadership, imagination, and social commitment. Factors beyond the undergraduate record are particularly important for older applicants, for international students, for those who have experienced educational or socioeconomic disadvantage, and for those who have racial or ethnic identities that are underrepresented in the student body and the legal profession.

In making its decisions the committee aims to enroll an entering class of students with diverse experience, backgrounds, and points of view. Applicants are encouraged to provide information to help the committee reach thoughtful, informed decisions on their applications.

■ Student Activities

Student-edited publications are *New York University Law Review, Annual Survey of American Law, Environmental Law Journal, Journal of International Law and Politics,* and *New York University Review of Law and Social Change. The Commentator* is the law school newspaper. There are more than 50 active student organizations in 1995-96, and in most years.

■ Expenses and Financial Aid

➽ *full-time tuition—$22,144* ➽ *an average amount of additional expenses—$14,485 (rent, food, utilities, personal expenses, books, and course expenses)* ➽ *scholarships available* ➽ *FAFSA form required for federal aid*

NYU will award 22 Root-Tilden-Snow and up to 20 Public Service Scholarships to entering students who will spend their careers in low-paying public service jobs. Other financial aid is provided on the basis of need. Aid awarded to first-year students is automatically renewable depending on student's summer earnings. Federal and private loans provide the majority of funding. Eighty percent of the class entering in 1995 received NYU or federal aid.

Loan Forgiveness Program—Graduates who pursue careers in public service or other low-paying sectors of the legal profession will receive post-graduation benefits through NYU's Loan Repayment Assistance Program. The program will pay benefits based on salary to assist our graduates in the repayment of Law School educational debt. Low income is currently defined as $52,020 in determining LRAP eligibility.

■ Career Services

NYU has an extensive placement program. Career planning for first-year students includes personal career counseling; workshops on all aspects of the search, specialty panels featuring speakers from all areas of practice, and a videotape mock interview program. In 1994-95, more than 800 private law firms, public interest organizations, government agencies, corporations, and public accounting firms came to NYU to interview students. Two-thirds of these employers were from outside New York.

In summer 1994, the most recent year for which information is available, 94 percent of first-year students and almost 100 percent of second-year students reported law-related employment. Each summer more than 100 first- and second-year students receive grants from the School of Law to work in public interest positions.

Ninety percent of the 1995 graduating class reporting indicated that they secured their first choice of employment. An additional eight percent reported securing their second choice.

The Career Services Office sponsors recruitment programs in several cities, and, with area law schools, a public service symposium and a recruiting conference for students of color.

Admission Profile Not Available

University of North Carolina School of Law

Campus Box 3380, 101 Van Hecke-Wettach Hall
Chapel Hill, NC 27599-3380

E-Mail: law_admission@unc.edu
Phone: 919.962.5109

■ Introduction

The University of North Carolina, the first state university chartered in the United States, has offered degrees in law since 1845. The School of Law has been a member of the AALS since 1920 and has been an approved school since the ABA began its accreditation activities in 1923. The School of Law is one of the outstanding institutions in the United States, and the University of North Carolina is recognized as being among the nation's leaders in graduate and professional education. The school aims to provide quality legal education that will prepare students to practice successfully in any jurisdiction. Chapel Hill is a university community close to the metropolitan and industrial centers of Greensboro and Durham, the Research Triangle Park, and the state capital, Raleigh. The immediate area offers an attractive blend of an academic atmosphere in a cosmopolitan setting.

■ Enrollment/Student Body

➻ *2,767 applicants* ➻ *579 admitted first-year class 1995* ➻ *234 enrolled first-year class 1995* ➻ *696 total full-time* ➻ *18.7% minority* ➻ *46% women* ➻ *27 states plus Washington D.C. represented in entering class 1995* ➻ *98 undergraduate schools represented in entering class 1995* ➻ *12.8% 30 years or older in first-year class 1995*

■ Faculty

➻ *90 total* ➻ *43 full-time* ➻ *47 part-time* ➻ *31 women* ➻ *4 minority*

■ Library and Physical Facilities

➻ *408,000 volumes & equivalents* ➻ *library hours: Mon.-Fri., 7:30 A.M.-MIDNIGHT; Sat., 9:00 A.M.-9:00 P.M.; Sun., 10:00 A.M.-MIDNIGHT* ➻ *LEXIS* ➻ *NEXIS* ➻ *WESTLAW* ➻ *21 full-time library staff* ➻ *library seats 513*

The school occupies a contemporary complex within walking distance of residence halls, dining halls, athletic facilities, student union, and the main libraries. The law library, wholly contained within the complex, includes microforms, CD-ROM, interactive video, and other specialized items. Also included within the library wing is a microcomputer laboratory with 17 workstations, and an electronic resources learning center with 10 workstations to access computer-assisted legal research systems and CD-ROM libraries.

■ Admission

➻ *Bachelor's degree from accredited college or university required* ➻ *application deadline—Feb. 1* ➻ *LSAT, LSDAS required* ➻ *median GPA—3.50* ➻ *median LSAT score—162* ➻ *application fee—$55*

Admission is a competitive process, and applicants with the strongest records are given priority. A substantial majority of admission decisions are made on the basis of combining LSAT scores with undergraduate grades, with 50 percent weight placed on the undergraduate grade-point average. Other relevant factors also are considered in order to assure meaningful diversity in the entering class. Graduate school grades are not incorporated with undergraduate grades but are considered among the other factors. Letters of recommendation are required for all applicants. Admission decisions are made progressively from December into the late spring, and are controlled to ensure that all applications submitted by February 1 are given equal consideration.

Applicants are encouraged to visit the law school to attend a class and then tour the campus. Guided tours and self-guided tours are both available. Regular group sessions are conducted throughout the year. Personal meetings are also available typically in the fall.

■ Student Activities

The *North Carolina Law Review*, a professional journal edited by students, publishes articles, comments, and notes on national and local legal problems; the *N.C. Journal of International Law*, edited by students, performs a similar function in international matters. The Student Bar Association sponsors a full range of professional, athletic, and social events, a speakers program, minority recruitment, a legal research service for practicing lawyers, and participation in school governance. There is a complete Moot Court Program that is student operated and privately endowed. The school sponsors teams that compete nationally in moot court, client counseling, and international law. Students serve on most faculty committees. Other student organizations include the American Indian Law Students Association, Black Law Students Association, Christian Legal Society, Hispanic Law Students Association, Phi Alpha Delta, Women in Law, Second Careers in Law, and Public Interest Law Fellowships.

■ Expenses and Financial Aid

➻ *full-time tuition & fees—resident, $2,243; nonresident, $12,396* ➻ *estimated additional expenses—$5,824* ➻ *Chancellors Scholars Program scholarship available* ➻ *Minority Presence Scholarship available* ➻ *need-based scholarships available (FAFSA due March 1)*

Most scholarships are awarded based on a combination of need and merit. Admitted applicants are automatically considered for merit-based scholarships. A significant amount of scholarship funds are awarded to students who are members of a minority group.

Recipients of the Chancellors Scholars awards benefit from substantial financial support which generally includes full tuition and fees and a stipend toward living expenses. Awards are made only on a merit basis.

Financial aid sources available to law students include need-based sources. Some research assistance grants are available for second- and third-year students. Applications for scholarships and loans must be completed by March 1.

■ Housing

There are graduate dormitories near the law school for single students. University student family housing and private apartments are available. Information may be obtained by writing to the University Housing Office, Carr Building CB 5500, Chapel Hill, NC 27599-3380.

■ Placement

The Career Development and Services Office, with a full-time director and staff, assists students and alumni with summer and permanent positions. Interviews are held in the law school, and contact is maintained with law offices and agencies throughout the country.

In 1994-95, over 220 employers from throughout the United States and the District of Columbia interviewed on campus;

1994 graduates are employed in 20 states, the District of Columbia, Puerto Rico, U.S. Virgin Islands, and two foreign countries. Of those 1994 graduates reporting to the Placement Office, 94 percent had accepted employment by December 1994; 30 percent accepted employment outside of North Carolina. Sixty percent of 1994 graduates entered private practice, 7 percent accepted judicial clerkships, 8 percent entered business-related fields, 12 percent entered government practice, and 4 percent entered public interest work.

■ Correspondence

Admissions Office, University of North Carolina, School of Law, Van Hecke-Wettach Hall CB 3380, Chapel Hill, NC 27599-3380. Phone: 919.962.5106.

Applicant Group for the 1995-1996 Academic Year

University of North Carolina School of Law
This grid includes only applicants who earned 120-180 LSAT scores under standard administrations.

LSAT Score	GPA 3.75 +		3.50 - 3.74		3.25 - 3.49		3.00 - 3.24		2.75 - 2.99		2.50 - 2.74		2.25 - 2.49		2.00 - 2.24		Below 2.00		No GPA		Total	
	Apps	Adm	Apps	Adm	Apps	Adm	Apps	Adm	Apps	Adm	Apps	Adm	Apps	Adm	Apps	Adm	Apps	Adm	Apps	Adm	Apps	Adm
175 - 180	3	3	3	3	6	6	0	0	2	2	0	0	0	0	0	0	0	0	0	0	14	14
170 - 174	11	11	14	14	14	13	12	10	10	3	1	0	1	0	0	0	0	0	0	0	63	51
165 - 169	51	51	85	75	63	36	59	17	25	4	8	1	3	0	2	0	0	0	1	0	297	184
160 - 164	104	82	172	66	170	43	111	12	50	6	32	2	6	1	4	1	0	0	2	1	651	214
155 - 159	79	31	160	17	171	25	127	8	54	8	27	3	15	0	5	0	1	0	3	0	642	92
150 - 154	38	4	94	10	109	5	88	10	58	8	45	1	29	1	8	0	0	0	9	0	478	39
145 - 149	26	3	46	2	61	5	66	11	64	3	36	0	14	0	12	0	1	0	7	1	333	25
140 - 144	3	0	18	0	28	0	29	0	32	0	26	0	25	0	5	0	1	0	2	0	169	0
135 - 139	2	0	3	0	16	0	19	0	21	0	12	0	9	0	8	0	1	0	4	0	95	0
130 - 134	1	0	1	0	2	0	4	0	4	0	3	0	3	0	3	0	2	0	0	0	23	0
125 - 129	0	0	1	0	0	0	1	0	1	0	3	0	0	0	0	0	0	0	0	0	6	0
120 - 124	0	0	1	0	0	0	0	0	0	0	0	0	0	0	0	0	0	0	0	0	1	0
Total	318	185	598	187	640	133	516	68	321	34	193	7	105	2	47	1	6	0	28	2	2772	619

Apps = Number of Applicants
Adm = Number Admitted
Reflects 98% of the total applicant pool.

North Carolina Central University School of Law

1512 South Alston Avenue
Durham, NC 27707

Phone: 919.560.6333

■ Introduction

The North Carolina Central University School of Law was established in 1939. The School of Law is located in Durham, which, along with Raleigh and Chapel Hill, forms North Carolina's thriving "Research Triangle." The school has been accredited by the American Bar Association since 1950.

North Carolina Central University (NCCU) was chartered in 1909 as a private institution and opened to students in July of 1910. In 1923, when the General Assembly of North Carolina appropriated funds for the purchase and maintenance of the school, the institution became the first state-supported liberal arts college for African Americans in the United States. In July 1972, NCCU became one of the constituent institutions of the University of North Carolina system. Today, the School of Law is one of the most diverse in the country.

■ Enrollment/Student Body

➻ *1,433 applicants* ➻ *218 admitted first-year class 1995* ➻ *86 enrolled first-year class 1995* ➻ *239 total full-time* ➻ *90 total part-time* ➻ *52.6% minority* ➻ *54% women*

■ Faculty

➻ *25 total* ➻ *20 full-time* ➻ *5 part-time or adjunct* ➻ *10 women* ➻ *14 minority*

■ Library and Physical Facilities

➻ *101,649 volumes & 493,453 pieces* ➻ *library hours: Mon.-Thurs., 8:00 A.M.-MIDNIGHT; Fri., 8:00 A.M.-9:00 P.M.; Sat., 10:00 A.M.-9:00 P.M.; Sun., 1:00 P.M.-10:00 P.M.* ➻ *LEXIS* ➻ *NEXIS* ➻ *WESTLAW* ➻ *DIALOG* ➻ *5 full-time librarians*

■ Curriculum

➻ *Academic Support Program* ➻ *88 credits required to graduate* ➻ *degrees available: J.D.; J.D./M.L.S.; J.D./M.B.A.* ➻ *semesters, start in Aug.* ➻ *range of first-year class size—20-45*

■ Special Programs

The joint degree J.D./M.L.S. program allows students interested in a career in law librarianship to simultaneously pursue the J.D. degree and a masters degree in library and information sciences. Application to and acceptance by both the School of Law and the School of Library and Information Sciences are required.

The School of Law and the NCCU Business School offers a J.D./M.B.A. program enabling a student to receive the J.D. and M.B.A. degrees in four years rather than the usual five. Students must be accepted into both programs.

The Clinical Program consists of courses in evidence and trial practice with mock trials and oral arguments involving outstanding trial lawyers, appellate lawyers, and jurists. Third-year students represent indigent clients in civil matters and misdemeanor criminal cases under the supervision of practicing attorneys connected with local legal service or district attorney offices.

The School of Law offers the only part-time evening law program in North Carolina. This four-year program offers a unique opportunity for motivated professionals to pursue a legal education while maintaining their current careers.

■ Admission

➻ *Bachelor's degree required for admission* ➻ *application deadline—April 15* ➻ *rolling admission* ➻ *LSAT, LSDAS required* ➻ *median GPA—full-time program, 3.00; part-time program, 3.23* ➻ *median LSAT score—full-time program, 149; part-time program, 155* ➻ *application fee—$30*

North Carolina Central University School of Law welcomes students of all races to contribute to its diversity as it continues to pursue with vigor its historic mission of producing a substantial percentage of minority attorneys for the state and nation. The school gives considerable weight to the traditional criteria of the LSAT score and UGPA, but it also considers evidence that an applicant has demonstrated in other ways a likelihood of succeeding in the legal profession.

The School of Law seeks students who are more likely to contribute affirmatively to the learning of others by reason of their intellectual attainments, demonstrated emotional maturity and self-discipline, social background, or exceptional capacity to benefit from the school's educational program. For this reason, applicants are asked to provide full information about their intellectual attainments, their personal achievements, employment experience, and social background.

■ Student Activities

The *North Carolina Central Law Journal*, published semiannually, is devoted to articles by legal scholars and to case notes and comments by students. Invitations to join the *Law Journal* are extended to students on the basis of academic achievement and writing ability.

The School of Law has a complete moot court and trial advocacy program. Intra- and interscholastic competitions provide students with an opportunity to write appellate briefs, participate in mock trials and appellate oral arguments, and counsel clients.

Student organizations at the School of Law include the Student Bar Association, Moot Court Board, American Bar Association/Law Students Division, Black Law Students Association, Entertainment and Sports Law Association, Intellectual Property Society, Women's Caucus, National Lawyers Guild and F.A.C.E.S. (Future Attorneys Challenging Elementary Students). There are chapters of three legal fraternities— Delta Theta Phi; Phi Alpha Delta; and Phi Delta Phi.

■ Expenses and Financial Aid

➽ tuition & fees—resident, $1,825; nonresident, $10,439; part-time tuition and fees—resident $1,825; nonresident, $10,439 ➽ estimated additional expenses—$13,438 (books, supplies, and living expenses) ➽ merit- and need-based scholarships available ➽ merit- and need-based minority scholarships available ➽ financial aid available ➽ application for Federal Student Aid (FAFSA) form for need analysis due by Feb. 1

■ Housing

There is a graduate dormitory near the law school for single students. Information may be obtained by writing to the University Housing Director, North Carolina Central University, P.O. Box 19382, Durham, N.C., 27707.

■ Career Services

The Placement Office offers a range of services to students and prospective employers. These services include career counseling, interview preparation and résumé writing workshops, firm and résumé referral banks, a placement information booklet and resource library, and an on-campus interview program. Graduates typically find employment in judicial clerkships, government agencies, law firms, legal service organizations, and the Judge Advocate General's Corps.

Admission Profile Not Available
Applicants should feel free to contact the Admission Office for additional information.

University of North Dakota School of Law

Office of the Dean
Grand Forks, ND 58202

URL: http://www.law.und.nodak.edu
Phone: 701.777.2260

■ Introduction

The University of North Dakota School of Law was established in 1899, and has been a member of the AALS since 1910. In 1923, it was approved by the ABA; it is a fully accredited graduate professional school of the university awarding the J.D. degree. The School of Law is located on the main campus of the university in Grand Forks, a city of approximately 50,000, in the northeastern part of the state. The third largest city in the state, Grand Forks is a center of commerce for the Upper Great Plains, as well as a large legal community, including county, state, and federal trial courts.

■ Enrollment/Student Body

➽ *217 total full-time*

While a large percentage of the entering students are North Dakota residents, the School of Law enrolls students from all parts of the country.

■ Library and Physical Facilities

➽ *230,000 volumes & equivalents*

The Thormodsgard Law Library, constructed in 1973 as an addition to the classroom and office building, offers generous seating and study space on its four levels. The Baker Moot Court Room, completed in 1973, provides facilities for trial and appellate arguments, and is occasionally used by the North Dakota Supreme Court, United States Court of Appeals for the Eighth Circuit, United States District Court for the District of North Dakota, and other state and federal courts.

■ Curriculum

➽ *90 credits required to graduate*

The curriculum of the School of Law covers a period of three full academic years. All the work of the first year is prescribed. Courses in the second and third years are elective, except for the course in Professional Responsibility.

■ Special Programs

The size of the student body is ideally suited for close professional contact with the faculty. Students are given ample opportunity to participate in the governance of the school. Elected members of the Student Bar Association attend regularly scheduled faculty meetings and are active voting participants in most law school committees. Participation by students in the State Bar Association of North Dakota is encouraged, and students are eligible to serve on selected state bar committees.

The School of Law is committed to the principle that all students should have an opportunity to elect, as a portion of their educational development, clinical legal education. This is not intended to diminish the law school's responsibility for education in legal analysis and legal principles, but adds an additional responsibility, providing experience in the application of analysis and theory.

The clinical program provides training in practical skills through simulation training and client representation. Under supervision, law students work with clients in cases, as permitted under the rule of the North Dakota Supreme Court. Training is received in such skills as interviewing, counseling, negotiating, fact gathering, and advocacy.

The school has an extensive Trial Advocacy Program, in which students learn trial skills in a simulated advocacy setting under the close supervision of experienced trial lawyers. Each student in this course is responsible, with one student advocate cocounsel, for the trial of at least one full civil or criminal case during the semester. This program has received the Emil Gumpert Award of the American College of Trial Lawyers for excellence in the teaching of trial advocacy.

During sessions of the state legislature, selected students serve as legislative interns at the state capital in Bismarck.

Central Legal Research, directed by an attorney under the supervision of the Dean, is housed in the School of Law. This bureau is the research arm for the criminal justice system of the State of North Dakota. Competitively hired students perform original legal research upon request for judges, prosecutors, court-appointed defense counsel, police, and others.

In 1982 the law school initiated a new foreign exchange program, the UND-University of Oslo Program. The Norwegian program provides for exchange of students and faculty between these two fine law schools.

■ Admission

➽ *undergraduate degree from accredited college or university required* ➽ *application deadline—April 1*
➽ *LSAT, LSDAS required* ➽ *median GPA—3.27*
➽ *median LSAT score—151*

The School of Law has no specific undergraduate course prerequisites and agrees with the observations in the introduction to this guide. The school admits students only in August, and only for full-time study. Applications are available upon request. The policy of the faculty of the School of Law is to admit those applicants who, in the determination of the faculty, will be able to satisfactorily complete the law school program. The admissions committee utilizes the following criteria to achieve this goal: (1) LSAT score; (2) undergraduate GPA; (3) past performance in an academic environment; (4) past performance in activities that would tend to predict the applicant's ability to complete successfully the law school program; and, (5) other evidence relevant to predicted success and prospective professional responsibility. The total number of students admitted is, of course, limited by considerations involving space and faculty courseload.

The law school does not have a nonresident quota; however, preference is given to residents.

Students who have begun the study of law in other accredited law schools may be admitted in exceptional circumstances to advanced standing, provided they have fulfilled the requirements for admission to the University of North Dakota School of Law. Ordinarily, no transfer credit will be allowed for more than two semesters of work completed elsewhere, nor will transfer credit be given for any courses in which an unsatisfactory or failing grade has been received. Moreover, admission may be conditioned upon meeting such additional requirements as the faculty may prescribe. No student will be admitted as a transfer student with advanced standing who is not eligible to continue as a student at his or her present law school.

■ Student Activities

The *North Dakota Law Review* and Agricultural Law Research program provide research and writing opportunities. Students also participate in various moot court activities, including regional and national competitions. Student organizations include the Law Women's Caucus and an active Student Bar Association. The School of Law also has chapters of the Order of the Coif and Phi Alpha Delta and Phi Delta Phi legal fraternities.

■ Expenses and Financial Aid

➽ *full-time tuition & fees—resident, $1,924/semester; nonresident, $4,037/semester (1995-96)*
➽ *scholarships available* ➽ *financial aid available*

The semester fees include student activity and university fees totaling $159 per semester and a $500 per semester professional fee. The student activity and university fees cover payment for health services, the university center, campus publications, and drama and athletic events. The professional fee is a fee assessed by the School of Law and is used to support and improve the law school program. Fees are subject to change without notice. Loan funds for all qualified students are available through the university Student Financial Aids Office, Twamley Hall.

■ Housing

The university's family housing facilities are open to law students. University residence halls are open to single law students. Inquiries should be directed to the Housing Office, Post Office Box 9029, University Station, Grand Forks, ND 58202.

Applicant Group for the 1995-1996 Academic Year

University of North Dakota School of Law
This grid includes only applicants who earned 120-180 LSAT scores under standard administrations.

LSAT Score	GPA 3.75 +		3.50 - 3.74		3.25 - 3.49		3.00 - 3.24		2.75 - 2.99		2.50 - 2.74		2.25 - 2.49		2.00 - 2.24		Below 2.00		No GPA		Total	
	Apps	Adm	Apps	Adm	Apps	Adm	Apps	Adm	Apps	Adm	Apps	Adm	Apps	Adm	Apps	Adm	Apps	Adm	Apps	Adm	Apps	Adm
175 - 180	0	0	0	0	0	0	0	0	0	0	0	0	0	0	0	0	0	0	0	0	0	0
170 - 174	0	0	0	0	0	0	0	0	0	0	0	0	0	0	0	0	0	0	0	0	0	0
165 - 169	0	0	0	0	0	0	0	0	0	0	1	0	0	0	0	0	0	0	0	0	1	0
160 - 164	0	0	2	2	5	3	3	3	4	3	0	0	1	0	0	0	0	0	0	0	15	11
155 - 159	1	1	9	7	9	9	15	14	11	7	7	2	4	1	0	0	0	0	0	0	56	41
150 - 154	4	3	17	16	20	17	19	15	25	16	21	9	8	2	2	0	3	1	2	2	121	81
145 - 149	6	5	11	4	15	7	18	5	14	5	17	1	9	0	7	0	3	0	0	0	100	27
140 - 144	1	0	7	2	10	1	10	1	14	2	13	0	6	0	6	0	2	0	0	0	69	6
135 - 139	1	0	1	0	2	0	5	0	4	0	3	0	3	0	3	0	0	0	1	0	23	0
130 - 134	0	0	0	0	1	0	0	0	1	0	1	0	1	0	3	0	0	0	0	0	7	0
125 - 129	0	0	0	0	0	0	0	0	1	0	0	0	0	0	0	0	0	0	0	0	1	0
120 - 124	0	0	0	0	0	0	0	0	0	0	0	0	0	0	0	0	0	0	0	0	0	0
Total	13	9	47	31	62	37	70	38	74	33	63	12	32	3	21	0	8	1	3	2	393	166

Apps = Number of Applicants
Adm = Number Admitted
Reflects 98% of the total applicant pool.

Northeastern University School of Law

P.O. Box 728
Boston, MA 02117-0728

Phone: 617.373.2395

■ Introduction

Located in Boston, Massachusetts, Northeastern is a small law school with a unique program combining rigorous academic study with practical legal work experience and a strong tradition of public service. While maintaining the highest academic standards, it enables students to learn the skills of actual practice across a broad spectrum of the law. The cooperative legal education program ensures that no graduate will enter the practice of law without having first spent half of his or her second and third years as a full-time apprentice or legal assistant to cooperating employers, generally in several diverse areas of legal practice. Through this program, students have an unusual opportunity to learn an array of practical skills, to observe various approaches to the practice of law, and to determine which areas of the law interest them most. The law school is accredited by the ABA and is a member of the AALS.

■ Enrollment/Student Body

➽ 2,811 applicants ➽ 757 admitted first-year class 1995 ➽ 193 enrolled first-year class 1995 ➽ 617 total full-time ➽ 24% minority ➽ 64% women ➽ 43 states & foreign countries represented ➽ 219 undergraduate schools represented

■ Faculty

➽ 61 total ➽ 32 full-time ➽ 29 part-time or adjunct ➽ 24 women ➽ 12 minority

■ Library and Physical Facilities

➽ 260,496 volumes & equivalents ➽ library hours: Mon.-Thurs., 8:00 A.M.-11:00 P.M.; Fri., 8:00 A.M.-9:00 P.M.; Sat., 9:00 A.M.-9:00 P.M.; Sun., NOON-10:00 P.M. ➽ LEXIS ➽ NEXIS ➽ WESTLAW ➽ DIALOG ➽ 7 full-time librarians and 2 paraprofessional staff ➽ library seats 291

■ Curriculum

➽ Academic Success Program ➽ Legal Writing, Legal Analysis, and Analytical Skills workshops ➽ 99 credits required to graduate ➽ public interest graduation requirement ➽ 85-95 total courses available ➽ degrees available: J.D.; J.D./M.B.A.; J.D./M.S. in Accounting ➽ first-year class starts late Aug. ➽ range of first-year class size—50-100

■ Special Programs

The **Cooperative Legal Education Program** is an integral part of each student's experience at Northeastern: academic credit is awarded for successful completion of four quarters of legal "co-op" work. Students earn their J.D. degree in the same time as their counterparts at other law schools.

First-year students begin in late August and follow a traditional full-time academic program for nine months until the end of May. The second year starts in June. Half the class undertakes work as full-time clerks for the summer quarter; the other half undertakes the first academic period of the second year. At the end of the summer, the sections exchange places. They continue this process of alternating work and academic periods through the 24 months of the second and third years.

Students work for large and small firms, judges, government agencies, legal assistance and public defender organizations, corporate law departments, unions, and practically every type of legal practitioner. There are over 750 participating employers throughout the United States, including Alaska and Hawaii, and students occasionally work in foreign nations.

The cooperative program is not a way to "work your way through law school." However, earnings from cooperative employment may somewhat reduce the net cost of attending school during the second and third years. Salaries range from a nominal amount to in excess of $1,000 per week. Recent statistics show average earnings of just over $375 per week. Each year the school provides roughly $250,000 in funding to students engaged in public interest work and judicial internships.

The school offers clinical courses including the Certiorari/Criminal Appeals Clinic, the Domestic Violence Clinic, the Poverty Law and Practice Program, the Criminal Advocacy Program, and the Prisoner's Rights Program.

The **Domestic Violence Clinic**, which combines classroom instruction with supervised clinical practice, is offered each quarter. There are openings for eight students; places are allocated based on responses to a questionnaire. The class meets for an average of three hours each week. In addition, each student must commit a minimum of 16 hours per week to advocating for battered women.

The course integrates theory, substantive law, and skills training. The substantive law focus is on the Massachusetts Abuse Prevention Act, related areas of family law, benefits, and the criminal process as it relates to domestic violence. Skills training focuses on interviewing, counseling, and preparation and presentation of cases.

The **Poverty Law and Practice Program** combines classroom instruction with clinical practice under the supervision of experienced clinical instructors. All course and clinical work takes place at the new clinical offices on campus.

The clinic supports community organizations struggling with issues of urban poverty. The focus of the clinic concentrates on the intersection of work and welfare and involves both individual and group representation.

■ Admission

➽ Bachelor's degree required ➽ application deadline—March 1 ➽ LSAT, LSDAS required ➽ median GPA—3.29 ➽ median LSAT score—157 ➽ application fee—$55

Northeastern operates a full-time day program only. Students are enrolled only in late August.

An applicant should ordinarily have undergraduate grades and LSAT scores in the 80th percentile or better. The Admission Committee recognizes that some very successful students are not adept at taking standardized multiple-choice tests, that the grading standards among undergraduate schools vary, and that all courses of undergraduate study are not equally demanding. In addition to attempting to assess a candidate's academic achievement to date, the committee considers other factors that indicate his or her potential. These include professional or work experience, extracurricular or community activities, and clear indications of unusual determination, motivation, and accomplishment.

■ Student Activities

Students are elected to serve as representatives on all standing committees within the school. Through the Black Law Students Association, Asian American Law Students Association, and the Latina/o American Law Students Association, students work closely with the school in an effort to recruit minority students. Other student groups include the Environmental Law Forum; Critical Legal Theory Study Group; Women's Caucus; Lesbian, Gay, and Bisexual Caucus; the National Lawyers Guild; the Business Law Forum; the Arts and Entertainment Law Committee; Christian Legal Society; Jewish Law Student Association; Older/Non-Traditional and Re-Entry Law Student Caucus; the International Law Society; the Cooperative Income Sharing Program; the Coalition for the Public Interest; Moot Court Society; the Student of Color Coalition; Parents in Law School Group; and the Student Bar Association.

■ Expenses and Financial Aid

➽ full-time tuition & fees—$18,825 ➽ estimated additional expenses—$14,900 (living expenses and books)
➽ limited merit- and need-based scholarships available
➽ FAFSA, Northeastern Graduate/Law Financial Aid Form, and Financial Aid Transcript (FAT) due March 1

■ Career Services

The Office of Career Services assists students with all phases of the job-search process. Northeastern graduates are employed throughout the United States and abroad with private firms, government agencies, legal services and public defender organizations, the judiciary, labor unions and corporate law departments. An average 35 percent of NUSL graduates accept post-graduate positions with their former co-op employers. In recent years, approximately 23 percent of NUSL graduates, almost twice the national average, began their legal careers as judicial clerks. Graduates of the School of Law have entered public interest work at a rate nearly five times the national average. In addition, for the last seven years, NUSL graduates have been among the 25 recipients nationwide to be awarded the prestigious Skadden Fellowship, enabling them to pursue careers in public interest law.

Applicant Group for the 1995-1996 Academic Year

Northeastern University School of Law
This grid includes only applicants who earned 120-180 LSAT scores under standard administrations.

	GPA																				
LSAT Score	3.75 +		3.50 - 3.74		3.25 - 3.49		3.00 - 3.24		2.75 - 2.99		2.50 - 2.74		2.25 - 2.49		2.00 - 2.24		Below 2.00		No GPA		Total	
	Apps	Adm	Apps	Adm	Apps	Adm	Apps	Adm	Apps	Adm	Apps	Adm	Apps	Adm	Apps	Adm	Apps	Adm	Apps	Adm	Apps	Adm
175 - 180	2	2	1	1	0	0	1	1	0	0	1	1	0	0	0	0	0	0	0	0	5	5
170 - 174	0	0	4	4	8	7	5	5	2	2	2	2	1	0	0	0	0	0	1	1	23	21
165 - 169	8	8	20	20	28	25	24	17	13	6	11	2	3	0	3	0	0	0	3	3	113	81
160 - 164	24	24	60	53	91	72	112	63	63	18	26	8	7	2	6	0	2	1	2	2	393	243
155 - 159	44	34	116	63	170	61	161	39	102	13	66	6	14	0	7	0	2	1	9	4	691	221
150 - 154	26	9	82	29	156	35	153	25	122	13	81	3	36	0	10	1	1	0	8	4	675	119
145 - 149	12	3	42	3	100	8	108	11	97	7	59	1	26	0	9	0	5	0	6	1	464	34
140 - 144	5	0	17	0	32	1	61	5	41	1	43	0	25	2	8	0	3	0	2	0	237	9
135 - 139	0	0	6	0	11	0	28	0	14	0	24	0	9	0	6	0	3	0	7	0	108	0
130 - 134	0	0	0	0	1	0	8	0	5	0	5	0	3	0	2	0	3	0	4	0	31	0
125 - 129	0	0	0	0	0	0	1	0	1	0	1	0	5	0	0	0	0	0	1	0	9	0
120 - 124	0	0	0	0	0	0	0	0	1	0	0	0	2	0	0	0	0	0	0	0	3	0
Total	121	80	348	173	597	209	662	166	461	60	319	23	131	4	51	1	19	2	43	15	2752	733

Apps = Number of Applicants
Adm = Number Admitted
Reflects 98% of the total applicant pool.

Northern Illinois University College of Law

DeKalb, IL 60115

E-Mail: lawadm@niu.edu
Phone: 815.753.1420 or 815.753.8595

■ Introduction

The College of Law is located on the 546-acre main campus of NIU in DeKalb. The community of DeKalb, known as the "Barb City" because barbed wire was invented here, is conveniently located approximately 60 miles west of Chicago and 25 miles outside of the suburban area on the Illinois Research and Development Corridor. It is close enough to the Chicago metropolitan area to draw on its resources, yet retain its own college-town flavor—a safe and low-cost environment with a high quality of life.

The College of Law seeks to prepare its graduates not only for the traditional role of lawyers, but for the tasks we can now only speculate will be assumed by the law-trained.

■ Enrollment/Student Body

➧ 1,295 applicants ➧ 351 admitted first-year class 1995 ➧ 97 enrolled first-year class 1995 ➧ 291 total full-time ➧ 8 total part-time ➧ 20.4% minority ➧ 44% women ➧ 14 states & foreign countries represented ➧ 113 undergraduate schools represented

The current student body reflects broad geographic, cultural, and economic diversity. Though over 24,000 students currently attend NIU, the law school limits its enrollment to approximately 100 students per class.

■ Faculty

➧ 43 total ➧ 29 full-time ➧ 14 part-time or adjunct ➧ 8 women ➧ 4 minority

The school has a diverse and professionally distinguished faculty dedicated to teaching and scholarship.

■ Library and Physical Facilities

➧ 225,000 volumes & equivalents ➧ LEXIS ➧ WESTLAW ➧ Illinois State Legislative Information System (LIS)

The College of Law is located at the center of campus in Swen Parson Hall, an impressive gothic building that combines the distinction of the traditional with the sleek lines of the modern in its architectural design. The classrooms are designed to maximize interaction between students and their professors. The law school provides an atmosphere of shared goals and achievement and a genuine sense of community. The David C. Shapiro Memorial Law Library provides one of the best ratios of library resources to students. The Founders Memorial Library, adjacent to the College of Law, contains more than 1.2 million volumes and an additional one million federal, state, and international governmental documents.

■ Curriculum

➧ Academic Support Program ➧ 85 units/credits required to graduate ➧ 77 courses available ➧ degrees available: J.D.; J.D./M.B.A. ➧ semesters, start in Aug.

The College of Law provides its students with the type of curriculum that will make them well-rounded legal professionals. The first year consists of required courses in civil procedure, constitutional law, contracts, criminal law, legal research, legal writing and advocacy, property, and torts. A second course in constitutional law in the second year and a course in legal ethics in the third year are required. Students select the remainder of the 85 hours required for graduation from a wide range of electives.

The law school recognizes that a rigorous analytical legal education taught from traditional materials can be enriched by a breadth of exposure, in all areas of the curriculum, to supervised training in the skills of law practice. Clinical lawyering skills programs offer students the opportunity to acquire essential techniques needed in pretrial and trial work through structured simulations in the classroom and professional experiences in a variety of legal settings. The Externship Program provides students with sound educational experience under the supervision of a practicing attorney, or as a law clerk for a judge.

■ Student Activities

The College of Law affords its students a wide variety of educationally and professionally oriented activities. Among these are the *Law Review*, a forum for the expression of serious legal scholarship, and *The Advocate*, a newspaper published by law students. Members of the Moot Court Society compete in the National, ABA, the all-Illinois, and the Chicago Bar Association Moot Courts; and the International Law Society participates in the Philip C. Jessup International Moot Court competition. Student organizations include the Student Bar Association, the Black Law Students Association, the Hispanic Law Students Association, the Women's Law Caucus, the Law Students Civil Rights Research Council, the Christian Legal Society, the Business Law Club, the Federalist Society, Delta Theta Phi, a chapter of the National Association for Public Interest Law, and Phi Alpha Delta. Many of these organizations provide peer-support programs.

■ Admission

➧ B.S./B.A. required for admission ➧ application deadline—May 15 ➧ rolling admission; early application preferred ➧ LSAT, LSDAS required ➧ median GPA—3.00 ➧ median LSAT score—156 ➧ application fee—$35 ➧ separate part-time application

The College of Law grants admission strictly on a competitive basis through an evaluation of an applicant's aptitude and professional promise. Prospective students are encouraged to visit. Such visits, however, will not play a role in the evaluation process.

Two letters of recommendation and a personal statement must be included with the other necessary application materials. To be considered for the part-time option, an additional application—obtainable from the Admissions

Office—must be submitted. The applicant's undergraduate record and LSAT score are of principal importance to the Admissions Committee, but the committee is also interested in other factors such as an applicant's reasons for seeking admission, the applicant's school or community activities and accomplishments, employment background, and the applicant's ability to add diversity to the law school community.

■ Expenses and Financial Aid

➽ *full-time tuition & fees—resident; $5,057; nonresident $9,329* ➽ *Dean's scholarships, Dean's grants, and Rhoten Smith Scholarship available* ➽ *work-study and loan programs available* ➽ *FAFSA for financial aid due March 1*

Persons who enter as nonresidents usually qualify as Illinois residents for their second and third years. After the first year, law students qualify for research assistantships. Admitted students are sent financial aid information.

■ Housing

Moderately priced housing is available both on campus and off campus. Neptune Hall, one block from the law school, designates its first floor just for law students. Married and handicapped housing is also available on campus. The law school floor is $3,516 per academic year depending on the meal plan chosen. Housing information is sent to admitted students.

■ Career Services

The College of Law Career Services Office provides a service for law students to improve awareness and provide assistance in the selection of suitable employment opportunities. The office refers qualified applicants to prospective employers and conducts on-campus interviews. The Career Services Office maintains listings of opportunities in the legal profession as well as information on judicial clerkships and fellowships.

The director of career services counsels and advises students on all phases of career and placement activity and provides assistance with résumé preparation, job-search strategy, and interviewing skills. A library of placement resources is maintained for both students and alumni.

■ Correspondence

Northern Illinois University, College of Law, DeKalb, IL 60115. Phone: 815.753.1420 or 800.892.3050 (Illinois Only).

Applicant Group for the 1995-1996 Academic Year

Northern Illinois University College of Law
This grid includes only applicants who earned 120-180 LSAT scores under standard administrations (reflects 90% of all applicants).

LSAT Score	3.75 +		3.50 - 3.74		3.25 - 3.49		3.00 - 3.24		2.75 - 2.99		2.50 - 2.74		2.25 - 2.49		2.00 - 2.24		Below 2.00		Total	
	Apps	Adm	Apps	Adm	Apps	Adm	Apps	Adm	Apps	Adm	Apps	Adm	Apps	Adm	Apps	Adm	Apps	Adm	Apps	Adm
175 - 180	0	0	0	0	0	0	0	0	0	0	0	0	0	0	0	0	0	0	0	0
170 - 174	0	0	1	1	0	0	0	0	0	0	1	1	2	2	0	0	0	0	4	4
165 - 169	0	0	1	1	0	0	5	4	3	3	1	1	1	1	1	1	1	0	13	11
160 - 164	0	0	8	8	8	8	14	14	12	12	16	16	7	6	5	4	2	2	72	70
155 - 159	7	7	17	15	34	33	47	43	37	30	42	29	23	16	8	5	4	3	219	181
150 - 154	9	7	25	11	45	14	53	7	77	9	51	3	26	1	12	0	2	0	300	52
145 - 149	9	1	19	2	49	5	67	7	61	4	55	3	39	1	14	1	4	0	317	24
140 - 144	3	1	9	2	18	2	29	0	38	1	42	0	28	0	15	0	8	0	190	6
135 - 139	0	0	3	0	4	0	18	0	21	1	26	1	18	0	11	0	7	0	108	2
130 - 134	0	0	1	0	0	0	1	0	2	0	5	0	8	0	2	0	5	0	24	0
125 - 129	0	0	0	0	2	0	0	0	1	0	1	0	1	0	1	0	1	0	7	0
120 - 124	0	0	0	0	0	0	0	0	0	0	0	0	0	0	0	0	0	0	0	0
Total	28	16	84	40	160	62	234	75	252	60	240	54	153	27	69	11	34	5	1254	350

Apps = Number of Applicants
Adm = Number Admitted

	App	Adm
Applicants with 120-180 LSAT scores earned under standard administrations	1,254	350
Applicants with only 10-48 LSAT scores earned under standard administrations	2	0
Applicants with no LSAT or Nonstandard Administration LSAT	39	1
Total	1,295	351

Northern Kentucky University—Salmon P. Chase College of Law

Office of Admissions
Nunn Dr.
Highland Heights, KY 41099
Phone: 606.572.6476

■ Introduction

The Salmon P. Chase College of Law of Northern Kentucky University, founded in 1893 in Cincinnati, Ohio, is located in Highland Heights, Kentucky, eight miles southeast of Cincinnati. The campus is situated on 300 acres of rolling countryside in the largest metropolitan area of any state university in Kentucky. The curriculum not only provides instruction aimed at developing competent legal practitioners, but also includes courses that will enable students to become especially proficient in certain areas of the law. Day and evening programs are offered. Apartment and traditional student housing is available on campus.

■ Enrollment/Student Body

➧ 1,027 applicants ➧ 237 admitted first-year class 1995 ➧ 111 enrolled first-year class 1995 ➧ 224 total full-time ➧ 187 total part-time ➧ 9.2% minority ➧ 39.9% women ➧ 14 states & foreign countries represented ➧ 48 undergraduate schools represented in first year class

The College of Law is operated under the auspices of the Commonwealth of Kentucky; thus, some preference is given to Kentucky residents.

■ Faculty

➧ 59 total ➧ 19 full-time ➧ 40 part-time or adjunct ➧ 7 full-time women ➧ 2 full-time minority

The Chase College Foundation brings in outstanding legal scholars, judges, and practitioners to enrich the education of the student body.

■ Library and Physical Facilities

➧ 238,027 volumes & equivalents ➧ library hours: Mon.-Thurs., 8:00 A.M.-MIDNIGHT; Fri., 8:00 A.M.-10:00 P.M.; Sat., 9:00 A.M.-9:00 P.M.; Sun., NOON-10:00 P.M. ➧ extended hours during exams, shortened hours during academic breaks ➧ LEXIS ➧ NEXIS ➧ WESTLAW ➧ DIALOG ➧ 5 full-time librarians ➧ library seats 230

The extensive law library has a liberal borrowing policy and participates in interlibrary lending programs.

Students also have access to excellent recreational facilities at A.D. Albright Health Center on campus, including basketball and racquetball courts, Nautilus and other exercise equipment, indoor running track and pool, and sauna. University Center, including a cafeteria, snack bar, and bookstore, is near the College of Law.

■ Curriculum

➧ 90 credits required to graduate ➧ 85 courses available ➧ degrees available: J.D.; J.D./M.B.A. ➧ semesters, start in Aug. ➧ range of first-year class size—12-62

The program of study may be completed in three years for full-time students and four years for part-time students. A week-long course introduces first-year students to the study of law. Forty-one semester hours of coursework are prescribed. Students must also select 19 hours from a list of core courses. Two additional courses developing legal research and drafting skills are required. The remaining hours may be chosen from a broad offering of electives.

Informal academic support is available to all students. Students may earn credit for work as law clerks in federal courts.

■ Special Programs

The J.D./M.B.A. degree is designed for students who seek to expand their expertise in the increasingly dynamic and complex business area. Selected courses in the College of Law serve as electives for 9 of the 36 hours required for the M.B.A. degree while M.B.A. courses count for 14 of the 90 hours required in the J.D. program. Thus, the number of hours required to obtain the joint degree is less than the number required if each degree were pursued independently.

The College of Law operates a prestigious Moot Court Program, entering teams in the National Moot Court, Tri-School Moot Court, and other competitions. Degree credit may be earned for participation in this program.

The College of Law has established the Ohio Valley Environmental and Natural Resources Law Institute which will sponsor annually both a national environmental law moot court competition and an environmental law symposium.

A course in Trial Advocacy based upon a national model allows students to practice and participate in every part of a trial. The course ends with its students conducting an entire civil and criminal trial including jury selection and jury deliberation.

Students may participate in the Children's Law Clinic representing clients under attorney supervision.

■ Admission

➧ Bachelor's degree from accredited college or university required ➧ application deadline—May 15 ➧ priority application deadline—Feb. 1 ➧ LSAT, LSDAS required ➧ median GPA—3.19 ➧ median LSAT score—155 ➧ application fee—$25 ➧ financial aid deadline—Feb. 1 ➧ rolling admission, early application preferred

First-year students are admitted for the fall semester only. In measuring academic potential for admission, the Admissions Committee relies primarily on the applicant's undergraduate GPA and the applicant's performance on the LSAT. Each file is reviewed for motivational factors, which include rising trend in academic performance, college and/or course selection, graduate study, employment pressures, competence in another profession or vocation, significant changes in the LSAT, leadership ability, cultural or educational deprivation, and evidence of oral or written linguistic ability. The committee seeks diversity in the student body by considering, in no particular order, sex, age, minority status, and cultural or geographic background.

Persons in good academic standing at another ABA-accredited school may apply for admission as transfer students. Transfer determinations are based upon the quality of the applicant's performance at the other law school and the reason for the applicant's desire to transfer.

■ Student Activities

The Northern Kentucky Law Review, published by the students of the College of Law, devotes space to national and regional law problems. The Student Bar Association (SBA) sponsors many activities, including a student mentor program, as well as student-faculty mixers and other social events. The SBA also selects students to participate on several faculty committees. There are chapters of the Black American Law Students Association, Delta Theta Phi Law Fraternity, Phi Alpha Delta Law Fraternity, and the Law Student Division of the American Bar Association. Other groups at the College of Law include the Chase Trial Lawyers Association, Christian Legal Society, Environmental Law Society, International Law Society, and Women's Law Caucus. Additionally, the Kentucky Municipal Law Center, the Academy of Criminal Justice Sciences, and the Ohio Valley Environmental and Natural Resources Law Institute are housed in Nunn Hall.

■ Expenses and Financial Aid

➡ tuition & fees—resident, $191/sem. hr (not to exceed $2,270/sem.); nonresident, $497/sem. hr. (not to exceed $5,947/sem.) ➡ estimated additional expenses—$1,800-$5,396/sem. (books & supplies, room & board, transportation, personal) ➡ one-year & multiyear performance and need-based scholarships available ➡ one-year and multiyear performance and need-based minority scholarships available ➡ appropriate form for need analysis due to national processing organization in Jan.; form required may vary from year to year

Northern Kentucky University financial aid application forms are due February 1. The latter forms are available from the Financial Aid Office, Northern Kentucky University at 606.572.5144. Certain scholarships and stipends have been established specifically to aid students from Kentucky or designated counties in Ohio.

All tuition and fees are due and payable prior to the first day of classes.

■ Career Services

With the support of a Placement Advisory Board, made up of practitioners in Ohio and Kentucky, and a Student Placement Board, Chase has a strong program to assist students in planning their legal careers. This includes scheduling on-campus interviews, posting job notices from law firms throughout Kentucky and greater Cincinnati, holding career seminars and publishing a placement newsletter. Students participate in the All-Kentucky Legal Job Fair, a public interest job fair, a federal job options program and the Minority Access Program. Reciprocal agreements with career services offices at other law schools assist those students who are looking for opportunities in different parts of the country. Chase alumni are employed in 45 states and throughout the world. Further, the Career Development Office houses a career opportunity library and provides access to several employment databases.

Applicant Group for the 1995-1996 Academic Year

Northern Kentucky University—Salmon P. Chase College of Law
This grid includes only applicants who earned 120-180 LSAT scores under standard administrations.

	GPA																					
LSAT Score	3.75 +		3.50 - 3.74		3.25 - 3.49		3.00 - 3.24		2.75 - 2.99		2.50 - 2.74		2.25 - 2.49		2.00 - 2.24		Below 2.00		No GPA		Total	
	Apps	Adm	Apps	Adm	Apps	Adm	Apps	Adm	Apps	Adm	Apps	Adm	Apps	Adm	Apps	Adm	Apps	Adm	Apps	Adm	Apps	Adm
175 - 180	0	0	0	0	0	0	0	0	0	0	0	0	0	0	0	0	0	0	0	0	0	0
170 - 174	0	0	1	1	0	0	0	0	0	0	0	0	0	0	0	0	0	0	0	0	1	1
165 - 169	1	1	2	2	1	1	2	2	1	1	0	0	2	2	1	1	1	0	0	0	11	10
160 - 164	3	3	8	8	4	3	4	4	7	4	1	1	4	1	1	1	0	0	0	0	32	25
155 - 159	8	7	20	19	13	11	26	17	23	15	22	17	11	6	5	2	0	0	0	0	128	94
150 - 154	12	8	33	8	64	20	70	19	57	6	47	6	21	2	5	1	3	1	4	1	316	72
145 - 149	12	1	36	2	45	2	45	1	58	5	38	0	22	1	9	0	1	0	5	0	271	12
140 - 144	5	0	5	0	30	0	26	1	26	1	31	0	17	0	6	0	1	0	4	0	151	2
135 - 139	1	0	1	0	9	0	11	0	14	0	13	0	11	0	5	1	2	0	4	0	71	1
130 - 134	0	0	0	0	1	0	3	0	3	0	2	0	2	0	6	0	0	0	2	0	19	0
125 - 129	0	0	0	0	0	0	1	0	1	0	1	0	1	0	0	0	1	0	0	0	5	0
120 - 124	0	0	0	0	0	0	0	0	0	0	0	0	0	0	0	0	0	0	1	0	1	0
Total	42	20	106	40	167	37	188	44	190	32	155	24	91	12	38	6	9	1	20	1	1006	217

Apps = Number of Applicants
Adm = Number Admitted
Reflects 99% of the total applicant pool.

Northwestern University School of Law

357 East Chicago Avenue
Chicago, IL 60611

E-Mail: nulawadm@harold.law.nwu.edu
Phone: 312.503.8465

■ Introduction

Northwestern University School of Law offers students an outstanding education, magnificent lakefront facilities in the heart of one of the nation's most interesting cities, and membership in a scholarly community enriched by the accomplishments of its faculty and the achievements of its graduates.

Northwestern was founded in 1859 as a small law department and between 1873 and 1891 was called Union College of Law. In 1893 John Henry Wigmore joined the faculty, serving as dean for 28 years and setting the intellectual standard for the school that remains to this day.

■ Enrollment/Student Body

➡ 3,586 applicants ➡ 717 admitted first-year class 1995 ➡ 203 enrolled first-year class 1995 ➡ 606 total full-time ➡ no part-time program ➡ 21.3% minority ➡ 45% women ➡ 40 states & 10 foreign countries represented ➡ 178 colleges and universities represented

■ Faculty

➡ 168 total ➡ 54 full-time ➡ 114 part-time or adjunct ➡ 43 women, (16 full-time, 27 part-time/adjunct) ➡ 14 minority, (5 full-time, 9 part-time/adjunct)

The activities and varied academic interests of Northwestern's faculty complement and enrich their instruction and contribute to a high degree of innovation in both teaching and scholarship.

The faculty includes scholars with advanced degrees in economics, history, philosophy, and political science as well as law; it includes a former chairman of the United States Securities and Exchange Commission, a former deputy solicitor general of the United States, and individuals who have argued before the European Court of Human Rights. Among the faculty are men and women who began their law careers as judicial clerks in state supreme courts, U.S. district courts, courts of appeals, and the Supreme Court of the United States, and they have devoted their energies since then to many different areas of the law in this country and abroad.

■ Library and Physical Facilities

➡ 604,300 volumes & equivalents ➡ library hours: Mon.-Thurs., 7:30 A.M.-MIDNIGHT; Fri., 7:30 A.M.-8:00 P.M.; Sat., 9:00 A.M.-8:00 P.M.; Sun., 9:00 A.M.-MIDNIGHT ➡ LEXIS ➡ NEXIS ➡ WESTLAW ➡ CCH Access ➡ DIALOG ➡ 12 full-time librarians ➡ library seats 750

Northwestern consists of a complex of three connected buildings. The original buildings, Levy Mayer Hall and the Elbert H. Gary Library, both completed in 1926, and Robert R. McCormick Hall and the Owen L. Coon Library, both completed in 1960, form a quadrangle around a garden area. An addition, the Arthur Rubloff Building, was dedicated in 1984 and has doubled library space and greatly expanded student study and activity areas. It includes classrooms, a moot courtroom, offices, and an 800-seat university auditorium. The Rubloff Building also houses the national headquarters of the American Bar Association and the American Bar Foundation.

The current law library collection is known as one of the finest in the nation and includes outstanding collections in international, foreign, and Anglo-American law and rare books. An open-stack policy encourages student use of the collections.

■ Curriculum

➡ 86 credits required to graduate ➡ more than 130 courses available ➡ degrees available: J.D.; J.D./M.M.; J.D./Ph.D.; LL.M.; S.J.D. ➡ semesters, start in Aug. ➡ range of first-year class size—25-100 ➡ senior writing requirements for graduation ➡ clinical program available ➡ senior research program available

Northwestern offers a curriculum designed to develop fundamental legal skills rather than to merely impart knowledge of the legal rules applicable to one jurisdiction or region. The Senior Research Program enables third-year students to do individual research under the supervision of a professor, using library, field, and interdisciplinary research methods. Students may receive up to 12 hours of credit during two semesters. Northwestern has made a firm commitment to quality clinical education by maintaining a fully funded clinical program with five full-time professors and eight staff attorneys. Clinic attorneys and students handle both civil and criminal cases and are intensively involved in juvenile court work.

■ Special Programs

The school offers two combined-degree programs in cooperation with other schools in the university—the J.D./Master of Management program with J.L. Kellogg Graduate School of Management and the J.D./Ph.D. in one of the social sciences with the Graduate School.

Law students may be able to work with the university-based Center for Urban Affairs and Policy Research, designed to bring together the work of various disciplines related to urban affairs and to apply research efforts to problems of urban society. A limited number of fellowships are awarded to second- and third-year law students for work with the center.

■ Student Activities

Northwestern offers a number of student activities that provide students with opportunities to practice their skills and gain experience in legal analysis, writing and research, and oral and written argument. Students at Northwestern are fortunate to have several scholarly journals available for research, writing, and editing—the *Northwestern University Law Review*, *Journal of Criminal Law and Criminology*, and *Northwestern Journal of International Law & Business*. The First-year Moot Court Program, participation in which is required of all first-year students, trains students in preparing briefs and delivering oral arguments. The annual Julius Miner Moot Court competition, a voluntary second-year program, provides excellent practice in appellate advocacy. Each year law schools throughout the United States and in more than 30 foreign countries participate in the Philip C. Jessup International Law Moot Court competition. Northwestern teams have been among the most successful at the regional, national, and international level tournaments.

The Student Bar Association is the basic student governing group in which all students belong and whose activities and programs range from educational to recreational. The SBA voices the concerns of the student body in matters of curriculum and administration. Student groups and activities, most established under the aegis of the SBA, have grown out of student's concerns and interests and represent diverse political ideologies; multiple ethnic, minority, and religious affiliations; and far-ranging career focuses and public issues. There are more than 32 student organizations.

■ Admission

➧ *Bachelor's degree or its equivalent from accredited college or university required* ➧ *application deadline—Feb. 1* ➧ *rolling admissions; early completion of application encouraged* ➧ *LSAT, LSDAS required* ➧ *application fee—$60 ($75 after Jan. 1)* ➧ *two letters of recommendation required* ➧ *personal statement required*

Competition for admission is intense, but each application is reviewed regardless of the LSAT score and the GPA, and a decision is made based on a broad range of factors.

■ Expenses and Financial Aid

➧ *tuition & fees—$20,128* ➧ *estimated additional expenses—$12,532 (room, board, books, transportation, personal)* ➧ *merit- and need-based scholarships available* ➧ *minority scholarships available* ➧ *FAFSA required* ➧ *University Application required* ➧ *Loan Repayment Assistance Program available* ➧ *deadline for financial aid application—March 15*

■ Housing

Two dormitories with dining and recreational facilities are close to the law school and are available to all students. Off-campus housing is easily accessible by public transportation.

■ Placement

Northwestern operates a full-range career counseling and placement service. The office schedules student interviews with employers, offers useful workshops, individual counseling, and other services to help students pursue their professional goals. Responding to increased student interest in international law, the school recently established a summer internship program that attempts to match students with law firms, international corporations, and government and public agencies abroad.

Admission Profile Not Available

University of Notre Dame Law School

P.O. Box 959
Notre Dame, IN 46556-0959

E-Mail: law.bulletin.l@nd.edu
URL: http://www.nd.edu
Phone: 219.631.6626, Fax: 219.631.6371

■ Introduction

Notre Dame Law School is located on the university campus near South Bend, Indiana. Founded in 1869, it is the oldest law school under Catholic auspices in the United States. It is accredited by the AALS and the ABA.

Notre Dame is proud of its Christian tradition and of its prominent place as a national forum for debate and exploration in human values. Its law school stands in that tradition and in a tradition of academic excellence and humanistic legal education that has placed practicing lawyers throughout the nation and abroad—on the bench, in government, in business, and in service to the poor and disadvantaged. Its student body includes men and women of all races and creeds, from 200 colleges and universities, about half of whom are non-Catholic. The Law School is particularly conscious of its tradition of close faculty-student relationships and of the implications this has for the humanistic practice of law and for legal service to the community.

■ Enrollment/Student Body

➧ *164 enrolled first-year class 1995* ➧ *597 total full-time* ➧ *16% minority* ➧ *38% women* ➧ *103 undergraduate schools represented*

■ Faculty

➧ *28 full-time* ➧ *25 part-time or adjunct*

Faculty members have extensive experience in private practice and government service, and represent a broad spectrum of law schools and state bars.

■ Library and Physical Facilities

➧ *354,000 volumes & equivalents* ➧ *library hours: 24 hours/day, 7 days/week* ➧ *LEXIS* ➧ *NEXIS* ➧ *WESTLAW* ➧ *VUTEXT* ➧ *DIALOG* ➧ *7 full-time librarians*

The Law School is a handsome building with traditional Tudor Gothic exterior on the Notre Dame Campus. The collections and services of the recently refurbished Kresge Law Library are designed to support student learning and research through acquisition of information technologies and continuous implementation of new services. With permanent learning centers contributed by the major national legal databases, the library is a national leader in legal research techniques using automated technology.

■ Curriculum

➧ *Academic Support Program* ➧ *90 credits required to graduate* ➧ *degrees available: J.D.; J.D./M.B.A.; LL.M.; J.D./M.S.E.G.; J.S.D., and other joint degrees* ➧ *semesters, start in Aug.*

The school awards the J.D. degree after three years (six semesters) of full-time residential day study. The Law School curriculum has been revised to make it completely attuned to the needs of the competent and compassionate lawyer of today. A broad range of electives offers extensive interdisciplinary and specialized programs and clinical work that places students in supervised practice throughout northern Indiana and southern Michigan.

■ London Programs

The Notre Dame London Law Center (Concannon Program of International Law) is an integral part of the University of Notre Dame Law School. Founded in 1968, it provides the opportunity for American students to study law in the country that gave birth to common law. By providing an extensive array of international and comparative law courses, some taught by prominent British professors, the program serves the student with the strong interest in comparative and international law. But the program is not limited to those with such an interest. The course of studies is designed to further the education of all law students by availing them of an opportunity to observe the American legal system against the background of its common law origins, the laws and practices of other nations, and the law of nations.

All courses offered by the center are in strict conformity with the recommended standards of the Association of American Law Schools and the American Bar Association. The academic standards are fully equal to those of the home campus.

The Law School also offers a summer program in London. It is the oldest American summer law program conducted in London, with more than 100 students from over 50 different law schools. The curriculum emphasizes courses in the comparative and international law field taught largely by British faculty.

An LL.M. program in comparative and international law also is offered.

■ Admission

➧ *Bachelor's degree required for admission* ➧ *application deadline—March 1* ➧ *LSAT, LSDAS required* ➧ *application fee—$45*

Admissions result from recommendations by a faculty committee that considers each application individually. The faculty members and the Dean make their decisions based on the whole-person concept, including academic performance, work experiences, recommendations, extracurricular activities, activities evidencing concern for charitable and social improvements, and leadership qualities, as well as LSAT scores.

Special consideration is given to disadvantaged students, resulting in a significant representation of ethnic minority groups.

■ Student Activities

The school publishes *The Notre Dame Law Review*, *The Journal of Law, Ethics & Public Policy*; *The Journal of Legislation*, the only journal of legal philosophy in the nation, *The American Journal of Jurisprudence*, and *The Journal of College & University Law*. The school has a three-year moot court program; a mock trial program; a legal clinic, including mediation and immigration clinics; a student bar association; and chapters of the Women's Legal Forum, Hispanic American Law Association, the Christian Legal Society, the Black Law Students Association, and the Social Justice Forum and Asian Law Students Association.

The Legal Clinic operates civil and criminal legal aid programs in northern Indiana and southern Michigan. The Notre Dame Center for Civil and Human Rights operates an LL.M. and J.S.D. Program with emphasis on international human rights. It maintains an extensive library of civil rights-related materials. The Thomas J. White Center on Law and Government prepares students to serve as government lawyers. It publishes the *Journal of Law, Ethics and Public Policy*. The National Institute for Trial Advocacy, whose purpose is to contribute to the development of a competent, effective, and professionally responsible trial bar, is headquartered in the Law School. The Moot Court Program provides training and practice in appellate advocacy. Notre Dame Law School is a regular participant in The Philip C. Jessup International Moot Court Competition. The Trial Advocacy Program, offered as courses in the third year, involves students in the preparation and trial of a jury case.

■ Expenses and Financial Aid

- *tuition & fees—$18,420*
- *scholarships available (need- and merit-based)*
- *financial aid available; FAFSA form required*
- *work-study available*

The Law School awards grants to disadvantaged students on the basis of need and demonstrated ability to perform satisfactorily in the Law School. The Judge Roger Kiley Fellowships, highly prestigious awards of national renown, are reserved for exceptional academic leaders.

■ Housing

Both men and women may live on the university campus, and the university provides apartments for married students with children. Single students interested in serving as resident assistants in the university dorms should contact the director of student affairs at the university.

■ Career Services

The Career Services Office is an integral part of the Law School. Many interviewers representing the full spectrum of lawyer job opportunities actively recruit at the office each year. A national network of Law School alumni assisting in job opportunities is coordinated through the Career Services Office.

Admission Profile Not Available

Nova Southeastern University—Shepard Broad Law Center

3305 College Avenue
Fort Lauderdale, FL 33314 Phone: 954.452.6117

■ Introduction

Nova Southeastern Law Center opened in 1974 as part of Nova Southeastern University, a private, nonsectarian institution. The Law Center is accredited by the American Bar Association and is a member of the AALS. Goodwin Hall, our new building, is located just west of Fort Lauderdale. It is easily accessible from the airport and from all areas of Dade, Broward, and Palm Beach counties.

■ Faculty

➽ 92 total ➽ 41 full-time ➽ 51 part-time or adjunct ➽ 18 women ➽ 9 minority

Our faculty is committed to excellence in teaching and maintains an open-door policy for students. By limiting first-year courses to sections of 50 or fewer students, they can offer each student individualized attention. Our faculty is relatively young and represents numerous practice fields. Their expertise is reflected in scholarly articles and texts as well as in their public service activities. Distinguished practicing attorneys join our full-time faculty, particularly for courses in our skills curriculum.

■ Library and Physical Facilities

➽ 278,789 volumes & equivalents ➽ library hours: Mon.-Thurs., 7:45 A.M.-MIDNIGHT; Fri., 7:45 A.M.-10:00 P.M.; Sat., 9:00 A.M.-9:00 P.M.; Sun., 10:00 A.M.-MIDNIGHT ➽ LEXIS ➽ NEXIS ➽ WESTLAW ➽ DIALOG ➽ 9 full-time librarians ➽ library seats 549

The Law Center moved into a new building in July 1992. Surrounded by palm trees and adjoining a small campus lake, Goodwin Hall is within walking distance of university cafeteria, bookstore, dormitory, and apartment facilities.

Goodwin Hall is divided into two wings, which are connected by a spacious atrium. The atrium functions as a town hall—a place where students relax between classes, assemble for speakers, or listen to lunch-hour musical performances by students attending the university's high school.

The classroom/student activities wing includes the Civil Clinic, Disability Law Institute, and the Center for the Study of Youth Policy. There are 9 classroom and seminar rooms. Our courtrooms are used by students in trial advocacy classes, by National Institute for Trial Advocacy programs, and by state appellate court judges. All faculty offices are on the second floor of this wing.

The library's extensive holdings include special collections in tax, criminal law, law and popular culture, and international law. There are several LEXIS and WESTLAW computerized legal research terminals, and Computer Assisted Instruction is available for student use. Several publications are available on CD-ROM. The library is a depository for state, federal, and United Nations documents.

■ Curriculum

➽ Academic Support Program ➽ 87 units/credits required to graduate ➽ 100 courses available ➽ degrees available: J.D.; J.D./M.B.A.; J.D./M.S. (Psych.); J.D./M.U.R.P. ➽ range of first-year class size—22-45

First-year students begin their studies in an intensive orientation taught by members of the full-time faculty. Three upper-class offerings—Legal Research and Writing III, Professional Responsibility, and Constitutional Law II—and all first-year courses are required. Upper-class students can select from numerous electives, which include extensive skills offerings.

We have applied for ABA approval to add a part-time evening division. Evening classes should commence in August 1995.

■ Special Programs

Our clinical programs are constantly augmented and expanded to include additional areas of the law. An in-house civil clinic allows students to represent indigent clients. Projects funded by external grants include representation for persons with AIDS and representation of children needing advocacy. External placements are available with agencies such as the SEC and IRS as well as with Legal Aid offices. Criminal clinic internships are available with state attorneys' and public defenders' offices throughout Florida.

Many Nova Southeastern students participate in our highly acclaimed Judicial Internship Program. Our Legislative Internship Program, Guardian Ad Litem Program, Corporate Internship Program, and Individuals with Disabilities Project provide valuable academic experiences, and students in our Street Law Program introduce middle and high school students to the legal system.

A limited number of first-year students are accepted for admission into the Children's/Family Law concentration. Other students pursue joint degrees in business, psychology, and urban planning.

Students who attend two eight-week summer sessions can accelerate their graduation by one semester. As many as 20 courses are offered during the typical summer term.

Students may also enroll in summer courses in Caracas, Venezuala.

■ Admissions

➽ Bachelor's degree from accredited college or university required for admission ➽ application deadline—March 1, applications after March 1 at extreme disadvantage ➽ LSAT, LSDAS required ➽ median GPA—2.88 ➽ median LSAT score—150 ➽ application fee—$45

Each application is read by at least one member of the admissions committee. In passing upon applications, the committee reviews undergraduate grades, the LSAT score, and the writing sample. However, committee members also consider the applicant's personal statement, work experience, and letters of recommendation. While no single factor is determinative, applicants who fail to demonstrate academic promise on both the LSAT score and the GPA are unlikely to be offered admission.

Selected students who otherwise would be rejected may receive an opportunity to compete for admission by taking two three-credit courses during June and July. Summer Conditional Acceptance Program courses are taught by experienced full-time faculty members. Students earning at least a 2.5 average for the summer are admitted to the entering class.

The Law Center is committed to diversity in its student body. Approximately 39 percent of the entering class is female; over 26 percent are members of minority groups. The average age is 27.

Applicants are encouraged to visit the campus, either for an Admissions Open House or for a classroom visit. Alumni in many regions are available to answer applicant questions about the Nova Southeastern experience.

■ Student Activities

The top 5 percent of the first-year class is invited to join the *Nova Southeastern Law Review*, which is published three times each year. Symposium topics have dealt with issues as varied as Drug Testing, Hurricane Andrew, and Legal Humor. Other students write for the *Journal of International & Comparative Law*.

The Moot Court Society sponsors the F. Lee Bailey Moot Court Competition. Mr. Bailey, an adjunct faculty member, works with teams from throughout the United States during this competition.

Students participate on faculty committees and with organizations such as ATLA, BLSA, JLSA, HLSA, Lambda, and Florida Association for Women Lawyers. The Student Bar Association is particularly active, and there are several legal fraternities and Inns of Court chapters. Ad hoc groups are formed for various sports activities.

■ Expenses and Financial Aid

➽ tuition & fees—full-time, $17,990; part-time, $14,500 ➽ estimated additional expenses—$8,000-$14,000 (room, board, books, transportation) ➽ merit and need-based scholarships available ➽ minority merit and need-based scholarships available ➽ financial aid available (FAF form and Nova Southeastern financial aid application required)

A number of partial tuition waivers are available. These waivers are awarded on the basis of demonstrated financial need and academic merit. In addition to work-study opportunities, upper-class students are able to work as faculty research assistants at salaries that approximate those for law clerks.

■ Career Services

Our Career Services Office assists students and alumni with career counseling and the employment process. In addition to facilitating on-campus interviews and résumé distribution, the director coordinates career-option seminars and interviewing workshops. Although opportunities are available throughout the country, most alumni choose employment in Florida firms and government agencies.

Applicant Group for the 1995-1996 Academic Year

Nova Southeastern University—Shepard Broad Law Center
This grid includes only applicants who earned 120-180 LSAT scores under standard administrations.

LSAT Score	GPA 3.75 +		3.50 - 3.74		3.25 - 3.49		3.00 - 3.24		2.75 - 2.99		2.50 - 2.74		2.25 - 2.49		2.00 - 2.24		Below 2.00		No GPA		Total	
	Apps	Adm	Apps	Adm	Apps	Adm	Apps	Adm	Apps	Adm	Apps	Adm	Apps	Adm	Apps	Adm	Apps	Adm	Apps	Adm	Apps	Adm
175 - 180	0	0	0	0	0	0	0	0	0	0	0	0	0	0	0	0	0	0	0	0	0	0
170 - 174	0	0	0	0	0	0	0	0	0	0	0	0	0	0	0	0	0	0	0	0	0	0
165 - 169	0	0	1	1	3	3	0	0	2	2	3	3	0	0	2	2	0	0	0	0	11	11
160 - 164	4	4	7	7	5	5	9	9	19	19	11	11	6	6	3	2	0	0	1	1	65	64
155 - 159	6	6	12	12	21	21	29	29	54	53	41	33	19	9	11	4	1	1	5	2	199	170
150 - 154	15	15	32	31	71	70	101	92	140	104	110	54	63	18	24	4	5	1	7	4	568	393
145 - 149	12	12	31	22	95	46	145	44	163	23	131	19	81	9	36	6	5	0	4	2	703	183
140 - 144	4	1	26	11	58	15	67	18	99	7	105	11	59	4	31	2	5	0	13	2	467	71
135 - 139	5	1	11	2	13	1	38	1	46	0	57	1	40	0	28	1	7	0	8	1	253	8
130 - 134	1	0	4	0	4	0	5	0	14	0	19	0	24	1	14	0	6	0	8	0	99	1
125 - 129	0	0	0	0	2	0	1	0	5	0	6	0	8	0	2	0	1	0	2	0	27	0
120 - 124	0	0	0	0	0	0	1	0	1	0	1	0	0	0	0	0	0	0	1	0	4	0
Total	47	39	124	86	272	161	396	193	543	208	484	132	300	47	151	21	30	2	49	12	2396	901

Apps = Number of Applicants
Adm = Number Admitted
Reflects 97% of the total applicant pool.

Ohio Northern University—Claude W. Pettit College of Law

525 S. Main Street
Ada, OH 45810

URL: http://www.law.onu.edu
Phone: 419.772.2211

■ Introduction

Founded in 1885, the Claude W. Pettit College of Law of Ohio Northern University is fully accredited by the American Bar Association and is a member of both the Association of American Law Schools and the League of Ohio Law Schools.

The university of 3,000 students is small enough to provide individual attention to student needs, yet large enough to provide the amenities of a major research institution. The 280-acre campus is located in Ada, a small and picturesque college town in the midwest. Ada is approximately 70 to 90 miles from the Ohio cities of Dayton, Toledo, and Columbus, as well as Fort Wayne, Indiana.

■ Enrollment/Student Body

➽ 1,164 applicants ➽ 620 admitted first-year class 1995 ➽ 127 enrolled first-year class 1995 ➽ 355 total full-time ➽ 9.6% minority ➽ 34% women ➽ 34 states & foreign countries represented ➽ 212 undergraduate schools represented

■ Faculty

➽ 38 total ➽ 19 full-time ➽ 19 part-time or adjunct ➽ 8 women

The faculty strives for excellence in both teaching and scholarship. All faculty members have practiced law, bringing a wealth of practical experience gained from law firms, corporate law departments, and government to the classroom. The faculty also maintains a high level of scholarly productivity and professional service.

Small classes and individual attention are the hallmarks of the college. First-year classes are generally limited to 45 or fewer students. Faculty maintain open-door policies to foster good communication with students.

■ Library and Physical Facilities

➽ 240,000 volumes & equivalents ➽ library hours: Mon.-Fri., 8:00 A.M.-MIDNIGHT; Sat., 9:00 A.M.-MIDNIGHT; Sun., 11:00 A.M.-MIDNIGHT ➽ LEXIS ➽ NEXIS ➽ WESTLAW ➽ 5 full-time librarians ➽ library seats 300

The College of Law is housed in Tilton Hall, a modern building containing classrooms, faculty and administrative offices, student organization offices, moot courtrooms, a student lounge, and the law library. The Taggart Law Library, a federal government depository, houses online card cataloguing and an excellent computer lab.

Law students also have access to the other campus facilities, including a wide variety of entertainment programs at the Freed Center for the Performing Arts and the athletic facilities in the recently expanded Sports Center.

■ Curriculum

➽ Academic Support Program ➽ full-time program ➽ 87 credits required to graduate ➽ 80 courses available ➽ degrees available: J.D.; B.S./Pharmacy/J.D. ➽ semesters, start in Aug. ➽ range of first-year class size—41

First-year courses include contracts, torts, property, civil procedure, criminal law, and legal writing and research. Courses required in the second and third years include Constitutional law, federal income taxation, evidence, business associations, corporations, legal profession, and trial advocacy.

Students may choose from over 67 elective courses, including advanced courses and seminars. Each student must complete a research paper in the second or third year under the supervision of a faculty member.

■ Special Programs

Pharmacy and Law—This cooperative venture involving the Colleges of Law and Pharmacy provides students with the opportunity to earn a joint degree and utilize the services of the Pharmacy-Law Institute. The Institute publishes *The Journal of Pharmacy & Law*; sponsors research and instructional programs; and conducts workshops, conferences, and seminars.

Clinical Education—The College of Law offers a variety of opportunities for experiential learning in its clinical education program. Clinics focusing on the problems of the economically disadvantaged and elderly are offered at its offices in Ada and nearby Lima. Students also participate in extern programs with judges' offices, legal aid societies, public defender offices, and prosecutors' offices.

Icelandic Exchange Program—The college shares an exchange program with the law school at the University of Iceland. Participating students travel to Iceland to experience its culture and legal system.

■ Admission

➽ Bachelor's degree from accredited college or university required ➽ no application deadline ➽ rolling admission, early application preferred ➽ LSAT, LSDAS required ➽ median GPA—3.00 ➽ median LSAT score—152 ➽ application fee—$40

While Ohio Northern gives significant weight to the LSAT and undergraduate GPA, the Admissions Committee may consider other nonquantifiable factors such as candidates' undergraduate program and grade trends, completion of other graduate degrees, professional accomplishments, and socioeconomic or cultural barriers faced by the applicant. Letters of recommendation are not required, but letters from persons who have a basis to assess the candidate's intellectual ability, such as former professors or employers, will be considered by the committee.

Ohio Northern University is committed to a culturally and socially diverse student body. Applications from women, minority group members, and persons with disabilities are strongly encouraged. The College of Law is a contributing supporter of the Council on Legal Education

Opportunity (CLEO) Program. The facilities of the College of Law are accessible to physically handicapped students.

■ Student Activities

Students can choose from a variety of extracurricular activities. The College of Law publishes the *Ohio Northern University Law Review*, a student-edited commentary on legal issues. Students also serve on the staff of *The Journal of Pharmacy and Law*, published by the Pharmacy-Law Institute.

Intraschool, regional, and national moot court competitions are open to all students. Ohio Northern University students participate in at least 10 national and regional moot court competitions each year.

Through the Student Bar Association, students participate in a variety of extracurricular activities such as the Environmental Law and International Law societies. Students volunteer their services through the Volunteer Income Tax Assistance program. Ohio Northern also has active chapters of BLSA (Black Law Students Association), LAW (Legal Association of Women), Christian Legal Society, and the Cardozo Law Student Association. Ohio Northern also offers membership in Phi Kappa Phi (national honorary society), the Willis Society (honorary society), Phi Alpha Delta, Delta Theta Phi, and Phi Delta Phi.

■ Expenses and Financial Aid

➽ full-time tuition & fees—$19,290 ➽ average additional expenses—$5,000 (books, living expenses, transportation) ➽ merit-based scholarships and need-based grants are available, renewable for second and third years ➽ financial aid available ➽ FAFSA required, FAF accepted for financial aid ➽ students who apply after March 15 may be disadvantaged in consideration for scholarship or grant aid

Our Legal Scholar Program provides scholarship awards for students whose undergraduate records demonstrate academic excellence. The scholarship amounts range from $7,000 to $14,000 and are renewable provided the student remains in good academic standing. Additionally, substantial scholarships are awarded to students who excel in their first year of law school. Diversity awards, subject to the availability of funds, are also made available to selected students.

■ Career Services

Through individualized counseling, students and graduates obtain valuable guidance in obtaining summer jobs and permanent positions. The Office of Career Services assists in the application and interviewing processes; provides current listings of positions in law firms, governmental agencies, and corporations; and hosts on-campus interviews.

Applicant Group for the 1995-1996 Academic Year

Ohio Northern University—Claude W. Pettit College of Law

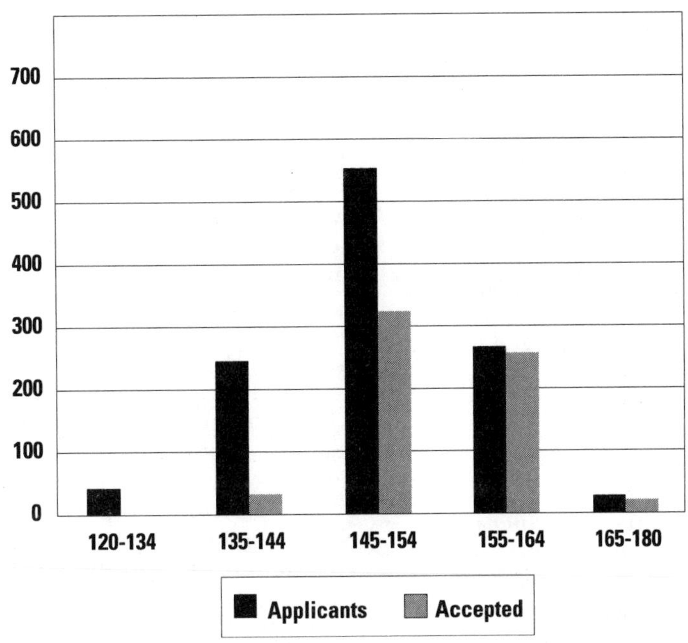

This chart is to be used as a general guide only. Nonnumerical factors are strongly considered for all applicants.

The Ohio State University College of Law

John Deaver Drinko Hall
55 West 12th Avenue
Columbus, OH 43210
Phone: 614.292.8810

■ Introduction

Founded in 1891, the College of Law is located on the main campus of The Ohio State University, one of the largest comprehensive institutions of higher education in the world. In addition to being the state capital, Columbus is a commercial and cultural center which has expanded dramatically in the past decade. The curriculum and experiences of law students are enriched by the opportunities presented by interaction with the university, state government, the bar, the bench, and community organizations.

■ Enrollment/Student Body

- *enrollment: first-year class, 220; total, 660*
- *16% minority*
- *43% women*
- *33 states & over 180 colleges and universities represented*

■ Faculty

- *35 full-time faculty*
- *20 part-time faculty*
- *10 women full-time faculty*
- *7 minority full-time faculty*
- *student/full-time faculty ratio: 19:1*

■ Library and Physical Facilities

- *615,000 volumes & equivalents*
- *LEXIS*
- *WESTLAW*
- *12 other databases*
- *8.5 full-time professional librarians*
- *10 support staff*
- *carrels for 350*
- *computer lab for student use*

Construction of a new addition and renovation of the existing building were completed in 1993. The result is a state-of-the-art teaching and research facility that includes three comfortably furnished lounges for students. The building has an abundance of natural light which creates a bright and cheerful environment. Attractive landscaping and a covered colonnade invite students to spend time outdoors in good weather studying or just relaxing.

The law library, the largest in the state and the 14th largest in the nation, has an extensive research collection. The collection of foreign law materials is very strong, containing titles from over 100 jurisdictions, with particular strengths in legal literature from the Commonwealth countries, France, and Germany. The library is a partial government depository for federal documents.

The new library has a computer laboratory for students and comfortable study and seating space for all students. Students also have immediate access to the vast collections housed in the university libraries.

■ Curriculum

- *summer program at Oxford University*
- *joint degrees: J.D./M.B.A.; J.D./M.P.A.; J.D./M.H.A., and others*
- *91 semester hours required*
- *clinical programs*
- *legal writing*
- *dispute resolution courses and journal*

After the first-year, the curriculum is largely elective. Class size in most first-year courses is between 50 and 70 students; first-year students also take two substantive law courses in which there are only 30-35 students. The curriculum offers great depth in specialized areas such as tax, commercial, administrative, international, and criminal law. In addition, offerings extend beyond the traditional curriculum into areas such as legislation, legal history, natural resources, law and social sciences, alternative dispute resolution, and international trade relations.

■ Special Programs

The college offers a summer program at the Oxford University for upper-level students. In addition, the College has been designated a Comprehensive National Resources Center by the U.S. Department of Education. This designation provides funding for fellowships for law students to study foreign languages, study-abroad opportunities, and electronic linkages with foreign universities. The college also offers certificate programs in International Business and Environmental Law.

Ohio State has one of the oldest clinical programs in the country. Second-year students can enroll in courses that simulate litigation practice and procedure. Third-year students can enroll in civil, criminal, or dispute resolution clinics to represent clients under the close supervision of an attorney and a faculty member.

The college offers joint degree programs in business administration, public administration, and health administration. In addition, students may earn joint degrees in individually designed programs.

During their second year, all students participate in the moot court program. Following that course, students may compete for positions on teams the college places in national interschool competitions.

■ Activities

Students have played a major role in shaping the law school. The College of Law was established in 1891 in response to requests from Columbus law clerks for formal legal training. Students organized the *Ohio State Law Journal* and were instrumental in establishing the Legal Clinic, the *Ohio State Journal on Dispute Resolution*, and the Student Funded Fellowship Program. Students serve on all standing faculty committees. The Student Bar Association serves as the students' governing body, hosts social events and various speakers throughout the year, and runs the bookstore for law students.

There are many student organizations, including three legal fraternities, Asian American Law Students Association, Black Law Students Association, Christian Legal Society, Environmental Law Association, Federalist Society, Feminist Law Caucus, Gay and Lesbian Caucus, Health Care Organization, Hispanic Law Students Association, International Law Society, Law and Technology Association, Sports and Entertainment Law Association, a student newspaper, a Street Law Program, and a Volunteer Income Tax Assistance Program.

■ Admission

➽ *Bachelor's degree required* ➽ *application deadline—March 15* ➽ *LSAT, LSDAS required*
➽ *median GPA—3.48* ➽ *median LSAT score—159*
➽ *application fee—$30* ➽ *rolling admission*

Each candidate's file is carefully reviewed. The most important factor is the candidate's academic potential which is usually best evidenced by the LSAT score and undergraduate transcript. Some factors believed relevant to success in law school may also be considered, such as trend in academic performance; letters of recommendation which address the candidate's intellectual potential; achievement in graduate school; caliber of the undergraduate college or university; unusually time-consuming extracurricular activities or work experience; and rigor of coursework selected. The college desires to enroll a diverse student body and, consistent with that objective, those from disadvantaged backgrounds, who have unusual or extensive work experience, or who have overcome severe or unusual obstacles to obtain an education are thought by the Admissions Committee to add diversity. For the same reason, the college has an affirmative action program. Applicants are encouraged to visit the college.

■ Expenses and Financial Aid

➽ *1995-96 tuition & fees—residents, $5,860; nonresidents, $13,980* ➽ *estimated additional expenses—$7,800*
➽ *financial aid—mostly need-based; competition for merit-based awards is strong* ➽ *Free Application for Federal Student Aid (FAFSA) required; March 1 deadline*
➽ *65 percent of the entering class receive grants*

■ Housing

The university has dormitories for single graduate and professional students as well as married student housing units. The college provides assistance in locating off-campus housing. Columbus, a major metropolitan area, offers a wide variety of housing.

■ Placement

The placement office helps all students secure summer and permanent positions, and also helps second-and third-year students find part-time employment during the academic year. Under the supervision of a full-time director, the program provides a wide range of services including individual counseling in career selection, resume preparation, and interviewing techniques. The office runs the largest on-campus interview program in the state and posts hundreds of openings from employers who cannot visit the campus. Although national law firms constitute the largest category of employers in the on-campus interviewing program, opportunities to interview with employers from all levels of government and corporate legal departments are also available. Typically, more than 90 percent of each graduating class accept law-related employment within nine months of graduation. Generally, 65 percent go into private practice and 15 percent into government work, 10-15 percent into judicial clerkships, with the remainder divided among corporate law positions, and public interest organizations. Graduates are currently practicing in all 50 states, the District of Columbia, and more than a dozen foreign countries.

Applicant Group for the 1995-1996 Academic Year

The Ohio State University College of Law
This grid includes only applicants who earned 120-180 LSAT scores under standard administrations.

	GPA																					
LSAT Score	3.75 +		3.50 - 3.74		3.25 - 3.49		3.00 - 3.24		2.75 - 2.99		2.50 - 2.74		2.25 - 2.49		2.00 - 2.24		Below 2.00		No GPA		Total	
	Apps	Adm	Apps	Adm	Apps	Adm	Apps	Adm	Apps	Adm	Apps	Adm	Apps	Adm	Apps	Adm	Apps	Adm	Apps	Adm	Apps	Adm
175 - 180	1	1	0	0	0	0	0	0	0	0	0	0	0	0	0	0	0	0	0	0	1	1
170 - 174	2	2	2	2	0	0	1	1	2	1	0	0	0	0	1	1	0	0	0	0	8	7
165 - 169	10	10	13	13	22	21	15	14	7	7	1	1	3	1	0	0	1	1	0	0	72	68
160 - 164	30	29	44	42	58	49	40	34	19	14	12	4	4	1	0	0	0	0	0	0	207	173
155 - 159	53	51	88	79	87	55	61	22	30	6	18	4	5	1	5	2	1	0	2	2	350	222
150 - 154	41	28	72	26	65	11	68	3	43	4	29	5	11	1	6	0	1	0	5	1	341	79
145 - 149	20	8	32	5	35	6	59	9	42	7	35	3	14	0	6	0	1	0	4	0	248	38
140 - 144	2	1	10	1	18	0	28	5	22	0	23	0	21	0	4	0	1	0	3	0	132	7
135 - 139	2	1	3	0	12	0	11	0	9	0	11	0	14	0	9	0	2	0	9	0	82	1
130 - 134	1	0	1	0	2	0	2	0	3	0	2	0	5	0	0	0	3	0	2	0	21	0
125 - 129	0	0	0	0	0	0	4	0	2	0	0	0	1	1	0	0	2	0	0	0	9	1
120 - 124	0	0	0	0	0	0	0	0	0	0	0	0	0	0	0	0	0	0	0	0	0	0
Total	162	131	265	168	299	142	289	88	179	39	131	17	78	5	31	3	12	1	25	3	1471	597

Apps = Number of Applicants
Adm = Number Admitted
Reflects 98% of the total applicant pool.

University of Oklahoma College of Law

300 Timberdell Road
Norman, OK 73019

E-Mail: srichard@hamilton.law.uoknor.edu
Phone: 405.325.4726

■ Introduction

The University of Oklahoma College of Law is located on the main campus of the university in Norman, a city of 89,000 in the Oklahoma City metropolitan area. The college was founded in 1909. The only state-supported law school in Oklahoma, it has been a member of the AALS since 1911 and ABA-approved since that list was first published in 1923. The Law Center, on the south campus of the University of Oklahoma, is within walking distance of dormitories, apartments, book exchange, and recreational facilities.

■ Enrollment/Student Body

➧ *960 applicants* ➧ *278 admitted first-year class 1995* ➧ *175 enrolled first-year class 1995* ➧ *600 total full-time* ➧ *12% minority* ➧ *40% women* ➧ *24 states & foreign countries represented* ➧ *68 undergraduate schools represented*

■ Faculty

➧ *54 total* ➧ *35 full-time* ➧ *19 visiting or adjunct* ➧ *11 women* ➧ *5 minority*

■ Library and Physical Facilities

➧ *296,358 volumes & equivalents* ➧ *library hours: Mon.-Thurs., 7:30 A.M.-11:00 P.M.; Fri., 7:30 A.M.-8:00 P.M.; Sat., 8:00 A.M.-8:00 P.M.; Sun., 1:00 P.M.-11:00 P.M.* ➧ *LEXIS* ➧ *WESTLAW* ➧ *7 full-time librarians* ➧ *Native Peoples Collection*

The law library features three computer labs (one for LEXIS and WESTLAW and two for word processing and other computer activities), as well as a variety of automated indexes and CD ROMs. Records for all materials in the law library are contained in OLIN (Oklahoma Library Information Network) which serves as the online catalog for the entire University of Oklahoma campus.

■ Curriculum

➧ *Academic Support Program* ➧ *Summer Abroad Program, Oxford, England* ➧ *90 credits required to graduate* ➧ *125 courses available* ➧ *degrees available: J.D.; J.D./M.B.A.; J.D./Master of Public Health; J.D./ M.S. in Environmental Mgmt.; J.D./M.S. in Occupational Health* ➧ *semesters, start in Aug. & Jan.* ➧ *summer session, starts mid-May*

Each fall, first-year students attend a two-day required orientation conducted on the Thursday and Friday before classes begin on Monday. The first-year curriculum is prescribed. Students are assigned all of their first-year classes in one of four sections. Students are assigned a faculty advisor for their first year of law study.

■ Special Programs

The American Indian Law and Policy Center of the College of Law provides a resource on historic and contemporary matters relating to Native Americans. The center supports the work of the *American Indian Law Review* and the Native American Law Students Association.

The Oxford Summer Program in Law is cosponsored by the College of Law and the Department for Continuing Education of Oxford University. The program affords students an opportunity to live and study in stimulating and beautiful surroundings under the guidance of American and English legal educators.

The Enrichment Program brings outstanding individuals in law and public service to the school to speak on a variety of subjects.

The Jurist-in-Residence Program brings distinguished justices and judges to the College of Law as resident scholars providing instruction in the areas of criminal law, constitutional law, and trial techniques.

The International Law Professor-in-Residence appoints distinguished international visiting scholars.

The Clinical Legal Education Program is designed to provide law students an opportunity to prepare for the practice of law by working with actual clients with real legal problems. Clinical opportunities include the Cleveland County Legal Aid Office, the Criminal Defense Clinic, the Externship Clinic, and the Judicial Clinic.

Students may receive course credit for participation in all clinical programs. Supervision of students is provided by the director and assistant director of the clinical legal education program.

■ Admission

➧ *Bachelor's degree required* ➧ *application deadline—March 15* ➧ *rolling admission, fall semester only* ➧ *LSAT, LSDAS required* ➧ *median GPA—3.35* ➧ *median LSAT score—154* ➧ *application fee—$50*

A faculty committee reviews all applications. In evaluating an applicant, undergraduate grade-point average and the LSAT score are each given great weight. Consideration is also given to employment experience, achievements in graduate study, extracurricular activities, and other relevant factors. In evaluating grade-point averages, consideration is given to distinct trends or discrepancies among the applicant's grades, time commitments while attending, and other relevant factors.

The College of Law conducts a special admission program each summer. Admission to this program is offered to a select group of about 20 students whose grade-point averages and LSAT scores do not meet the current standards for regular admission, but whose records reveal past performance affected by adverse circumstances or disadvantage and other factors, and whose records indicate possible future success. Factors considered by the Admissions Committee include, but are not limited to, social, cultural, or physical handicaps. Students in the program are required to complete six hours of summer coursework beginning in mid-May.

■ Student Activities

The *Oklahoma Law Review*, a quarterly publication, is a student publication that is scholarly in tone and gives expression to legal scholarship. Each issue has major articles by authorities in the field and sections written by the student members of the *Review* on significant topics and recent developments in the law.

The *American Indian Law Review*, published biannually, includes articles by authorities in the field; student-written sections; and addresses by noted speakers on Indian law, special recent developments in the area of Indian law, and recent federal developments of interest to tribal attorneys.

The Student Bar Association, affiliated with the Law Student Division of the American Bar Association, elects the Board of Governors to supervise activities and to present the students' viewpoints to the faculty and administration. Students sit as voting members on most of the College of Law faculty-administration committees. There are two legal fraternities and numerous student organizations.

The College of Law participates in several competitions including the National Moot Court, National Appellate Advocacy, National Trial Advocacy, American Client Counseling, Jessup International Law, and Thomas Tang. Course credit may be earned for participation in these teams.

■ Expenses and Financial Aid

- *full-time tuition—resident, $3,274; nonresident, $10,216*
- *estimated additional expenses—$7,800 (room & board, books)*
- *performance and need-based scholarships available*
- *Oklahoma State Regents Professional Study Grants*
- *financial aid available; FAFSA requested by March 1*

■ Career Services

The Office of Legal Career Services is involved in a variety of activities designed to assist students seeking employment as summer clerks and attorneys. While the most visible activity sponsored by the college is its fall on-campus interview program, many students benefit from the office's collection of materials about legal employers and legal careers, available positions, and bar membership requirements.

Typically 93 percent of our graduating students accept positions within twelve months of graduation.

The College of Law participates in two Minority Job Fairs each year. They are held in Dallas and Atlanta. We also participate in the National Association of Public Interest Law job fair held annually in Washington, DC.

Applicant Group for the 1995-1996 Academic Year

University of Oklahoma College of Law
This grid includes only applicants who earned 120-180 LSAT scores under standard administrations.

LSAT Score	3.75 +		3.50 - 3.74		3.25 - 3.49		3.00 - 3.24		2.75 - 2.99		2.50 - 2.74		2.25 - 2.49		2.00 - 2.24		Below 2.00		No GPA		Total	
	Apps	Adm	Apps	Adm	Apps	Adm	Apps	Adm	Apps	Adm	Apps	Adm	Apps	Adm	Apps	Adm	Apps	Adm	Apps	Adm	Apps	Adm
175 - 180	0	0	0	0	0	0	0	0	0	0	0	0	0	0	0	0	0	0	0	0	0	0
170 - 174	0	0	1	1	1	1	0	0	0	0	0	0	0	0	0	0	0	0	0	0	2	2
165 - 169	3	3	0	0	2	2	4	3	2	2	3	2	2	2	0	0	0	0	0	0	16	14
160 - 164	8	8	14	14	7	7	9	9	7	7	6	1	5	3	0	0	0	0	1	1	57	50
155 - 159	10	9	25	25	32	31	34	28	27	16	11	2	11	1	2	0	0	0	1	1	153	113
150 - 154	13	11	32	28	56	28	67	27	48	11	25	2	17	3	6	0	3	0	2	0	269	110
145 - 149	10	7	22	11	48	15	64	4	39	4	31	4	12	1	9	0	0	0	2	0	237	46
140 - 144	2	1	7	4	17	0	25	4	20	0	12	0	18	1	6	0	1	0	5	0	113	10
135 - 139	2	1	4	1	4	0	6	0	12	0	14	0	10	0	9	0	0	0	6	0	67	2
130 - 134	0	0	0	0	1	0	2	0	3	0	2	0	6	0	2	0	1	0	3	0	20	0
125 - 129	0	0	1	0	0	0	1	0	1	0	1	0	1	0	0	0	0	0	1	0	6	0
120 - 124	0	0	0	0	0	0	0	0	0	0	0	0	0	0	1	0	0	0	0	0	1	0
Total	48	40	106	84	168	84	212	75	159	40	105	11	82	11	35	0	5	0	21	2	941	347

Apps = Number of Applicants
Adm = Number Admitted
Reflects 98% of the total applicant pool.

Oklahoma City University School of Law

P.O. Box 61310
Oklahoma City, OK 73146-1310
Phone: 1.800.633.7242 or 405.521.5354

■ Introduction

Oklahoma City University School of Law is located within a metropolitan area of over 950,000, only minutes from several of Oklahoma's largest law firms, corporations, banks, city and state government agencies, and the federal courts. As part of Epworth University, it was the first law school founded in Oklahoma.

The School of Law is fully accredited by the American Bar Association, the Supreme Court of Oklahoma, and the Oklahoma Board of Bar Examiners.

■ Enrollment/Student Body

➡ 1,316 applicants ➡ 623 admitted first-year class 1995 ➡ 233 enrolled first-year class 1995 ➡ 425 total full-time ➡ 215 total part-time ➡ 10.8% minority ➡ 37% women ➡ 46 states & foreign countries represented ➡ 242 undergraduate schools represented

■ Faculty

➡ 32 full-time ➡ 33 part-time or adjunct ➡ 12 women ➡ 5 minority

■ Library and Physical Facilities

➡ 230,000 volumes & equivalents ➡ LEXIS ➡ NEXIS ➡ WESTLAW ➡ Internet ➡ 5 full-time librarians

The law library is a member of CALI and subscribes to the Varalex Interactive Video Library. The law library subscribes to some of the West CD-ROM libraries and has four workstations. In addition, the law library offers student training and access to WESTLAW and LEXIS in the permanent learning center, plus access to the word processing computer lab.

■ Curriculum

➡ 90 credits required to graduate ➡ 99 courses available ➡ degrees available: J.D.; J.D./M.B.A.; J.D./M. Div. ➡ semesters, start in Aug. ➡ range of first-year class size—20-83

The School of Law has full J.D. programs during both the day and evening hours, requiring the completion of 90 semester hours. The school operates two 16-week semesters and one eight-week summer term. Day students may complete their degree requirements in two-and-a-half years, and evening students in four years by attending summer sessions.

All students take Civil Procedure, Constitutional Law, Contracts, Criminal Law, Criminal Procedure, Legal Research and Writing, Legal Profession, Property, Torts, and Evidence. The remaining 47 hours of work may be selected from electives and seminars. All upper-class students are required to complete a substantial written project.

The law school faculty consists of full-time and adjunct professors and seven to nine writing instructors. Full-time faculty members hail from many states and hold degrees from 27 different graduate or professional schools. Law degrees among faculty members represent a diversity of law schools, including the nation's most prestigious.

■ Special Programs

Three times each year, the student-edited *Law Review* is published. The School of Law also enters student teams in such interscholastic competitions as the National Moot Court Competition, the Philip C. Jessup International Moot Court Competition, the Benton Moot Court Competition, and the American Trial Lawyers Association Student Trial Advocacy Competition. OCU is gaining a national reputation for its performance in these competitions.

Most of the students selected for these teams are members of the Moot Court Board, an honors organization comprised of students selected for their skills in oral advocacy. The board sponsors an annual Intramural Moot Court Competition judged by 80 to 90 judges and lawyers from the Oklahoma City area.

Oklahoma has one of the most liberal policies toward limited licenses for legal interns. Students who have completed at least 50 hours are eligible, and those who qualify may appear in court under certain circumstances. In the fall of 1988, the School of Law opened the Native American Legal Resource Center, an institution which seeks to improve the quality of legal representation for individuals with problems in the field of Native American law. The center is designed to provide high quality basic and advanced training and resource support in varied areas of Native American law. It is also active in providing direct services to tribal court personnel and practitioners through its sponsorship of training seminars for judges, clerks, and other personnel of the Courts of Indian Offenses (CFR Courts), and continuing legal education programs for attorneys and others with an interest in this area of the law.

As a corollary to the center, the School of Law has also opened the Native American Legal Assistance Clinic, a for-credit clinical program currently operated in conjunction with Legal Aid of Western Oklahoma and Oklahoma Indian Legal Services. This clinic provides students with the opportunity for supervised hands-on experience in dealing with real-life problems in the field while receiving training for which academic credit is awarded.

■ Admission

➡ Bachelor's degree required ➡ application deadline—Aug. 1 ➡ LSAT, LSDAS required ➡ median GPA—3.06 ➡ median LSAT score—149 ➡ application fee—$35

Admission decisions are determined by a faculty committee that considers each application separately. Many factors are considered, including academic performance, undergraduate institution and curriculum, advanced degrees, work experiences, background, activities, recommendations, and LSAT scores.

Regular students are admitted only in the fall term. Transcript evaluation by LSDAS is required, as are standard law school recommendation forms supplied by the School of Law.

The summer Alternate Admissions Program offers approximately 60 students who cannot meet ordinary admissions requirements for law school an opportunity to earn their way academically into regular fall admission.

■ Student Activities

Active student organizations include the *Law Review*, Moot Court Board, Federalist Society, Black American Law Students Association, Phi Alpha Delta, Phi Delta Phi, Iota Tau Tau, Native American Law Students Association, American Inns of Court, Merit Scholars, and the Trial Lawyers Association. The social year culminates in the annual spring dance and Gridiron (the Gridiron is a student roast of faculty and administrators).

■ Expenses and Financial Aid

➽ *tuition & fees—full-time, $12,245; part-time, $7,900* ➽ *estimated additional expenses—$3,830 (on-campus housing, $875/semester; meal plan, $1,040)* ➽ *scholarships available: Hatton Sumners & University Merit* ➽ *minority scholarships available* ➽ *financial aid available; FAF & ACT forms*

In addition to the nonrefundable $35 application fee, when accepted a student is required to pay a $250 nonrefundable tuition deposit, credited toward the first semester's tuition.

A number of scholarships for first-year and upper-class students are available. Both financial need and academic promise/performance are considered in awards. For example, the Hatton W. Sumners Scholarship Foundation offers up to five full scholarships each year to outstanding beginning students. These scholarships cover full tuition, books, fees, and a stipend for room and board. Minority applications are encouraged. The Kerr Foundation Scholarship Program provides scholarship assistance to upper-class students on the basis of academic performance, participation in school activities, exemplary character, and need. Other scholarships and various loan funds are also available. Students with need who are seeking financial aid should contact the Office of Financial Aid. The school accepts the Financial Aid Form (FAF) of the College Scholarship Service.

■ Career Services

The School of Law operates an Office of Career Services. The service assists students seeking employment or legal internship positions and graduates seeking positions.

All students have access to notices of job opportunities, campus interviews, and general placement information issued by Career Services. Registration with the office affords them individual attention and notification of opportunities available in their fields of interest.

Applicant Group for the 1995-1996 Academic Year

Oklahoma City University School of Law

LSAT Score	GPA								
	3.75 +	3.50 - 3.74	3.25 - 3.49	3.00 - 3.24	2.75 - 2.99	2.50 - 2.74	2.25 - 2.49	2.00 - 2.24	Below 2.00
175 - 180									
170 - 174									
165 - 169									
160 - 164									
155 - 159									
150 - 154									
145 - 149									
140 - 144									
135 - 139									
130 - 134									
125 - 129									
120 - 124									

Good Possibility   Possible   Unlikely

Apps = Number of Applicants
Adm = Number Admitted
Reflects 98% of the total applicant pool.

University of Oregon School of Law

Office of Admissions, Room 201
1221 University of Oregon
Eugene, OR 97403-1221

URL: http://www.law.uoregon.edu
Phone: 541.346.3846

■ Introduction

Eugene, Oregon is nestled in the southern Willamette Valley which is outlined by the Coast Range and the Pacific Ocean to the west and the Cascade mountain range to the east. Named by Sunset Magazine (October 1992) as one of the top five college towns in the west, Eugene is the home of an internationally-ranked research institution—the University of Oregon. The University of Oregon School of Law was founded in 1884 and continues to promote the joy of learning, creative scholarship, public service, ethics, and commitment to human diversity as well as providing a broad level of legal training for a wide variety of professional interests. The university, the surrounding community and the state offer students a wealth of cultural, social, and athletic opportunities as well as the tools to prepare their lives for the future.

■ Enrollment/Student Body

➽ 1,380 applicants ➽ 546 admitted first-year class 1995 ➽ 181 enrolled first-year class 1995 ➽ 478 total full-time ➽ 16% minority ➽ 49% women ➽ 95 undergraduate schools represented in first-year class 1995

■ Faculty

➽ 38 total ➽ 32 full-time ➽ 6 part-time ➽ 12 women ➽ 5 minority ➽ 4 endowed professorships

■ Library and Physical Facilities

➽ 340,000 volumes & equivalents ➽ LEXIS ➽ NEXIS ➽ WESTLAW ➽ Janus ➽ 6 full-time librarians ➽ library seats 297

The library's collection is accessed through Janus, an on-line catalog that is an important tool for researchers. The online Legal Resource Room in the law library contains 21 computer workstations which can be used to access information, information management, electronic communication, and word processing.

The Law Center's facilities include spacious classrooms, seminar rooms, a courtroom with videotape facilities, Student Bar Association office, student organization offices, *Oregon Law Review* and *Journal of Environmental Law and Litigation* (JELL) offices, offices for clinical programs, and a student lounge and courtyard.

■ Curriculum

➽ Academic Support Program ➽ 85 credits required to graduate ➽ degrees available: J.D.; J.D./M.B.A.; J.D./M.S, ➽ semesters, start in Aug.

The School of Law core curriculum emphasizes rigorous courses in all traditional legal subjects: civil procedure, contracts, criminal law, legal research and writing, legislative and administrative processes, property, and torts. The elective curriculum allows students to concentrate their studies in particular areas such as business and corporate law, international law, estate planning, taxation, litigation, constitutional law, intellectual property law, and administrative law.

■ Academic Programs

The Business Law Program offers second- and third-year students an opportunity to receive a Business Law Statement of Completion or an Estate Planning Statement of Completion upon successfully completing a number of specific courses.

The School of Law and the Graduate School of Management offer a concurrent J.D./M.B.A. degree program; the School of Law and the Graduate School's Interdisciplinary Studies Program offer a concurrent J.D./M.S. with a specialty in environmental studies.

An intensive year-long research and writing program is required of all first-year students. Students present final oral arguments at the end of the second semester in a courtroom setting.

The location of the school in the natural resource laden Pacific Northwest has led to a strong emphasis in environmental law and ocean and coastal law offerings. Courses in water resources law, land use law, environment and pollution, ocean and coastal law, law of the sea, public land law, Indian law, and wildlife law give students insight into legal problems involved in these specific areas. Statements of completion offered in Environmental and Natural Resources and Ocean and Coastal Law give the school the distinction of being one of only a few schools in the nation to offer such programs.

The School of Law offers six clinical programs: Civil Practice, Criminal Defense, Prosecution, Environmental Law, Health Law, and Mediation.

The Academic Support Program is a voluntary program designed to address the academic needs of nontraditional law students. This nationally recognized program includes a two-week summer orientation and an academic year program designed to teach the principles that underlie first-year coursework, to develop research and writing skills, and to clarify the law school examination process. Particular emphasis is given to cross-cultural analysis of legal issues.

■ Admission

➽ Bachelor's degree required ➽ application deadline—April 1 ➽ LSAT, LSDAS required ➽ median GPA—3.50 ➽ median LSAT score—159 ➽ application fee—$50

Over 1,350 applications were received for the 155 openings in the fall 1995 entering class. While the applicant's entire background is considered, numerical credentials are given considerable weight. Written recommendations and personal statements are highly encouraged. Entering students are accepted for admission in the fall only.

The school does not discriminate on the basis of race, color, religion, sex, age, disability, national origin, marital status, veteran status, or sexual orientation.

■ Student Activities

The *Oregon Law Review* is published by a student editorial board and has been in continuous publication since 1921. The *Journal of Environmental Law and Litigation* (JELL) is published by students and focuses on current issues in environmental law. The Moot Court Board sponsors five in-house school competitions each year from which teams are selected to represent the school in regional and national competitions. The Student Bar Association represents the student body by serving on faculty committees and sponsoring numerous activities. Other organizations include Black Law Students Association; Christian Legal Society; FACT; Federalist Society; International Law Society; Jewish Law Students Association; Journal of Environmental Law & Litigation; Land Air Water; Lesbian & Gay Law Student Association; Minority Law Students Association; *Monitor*; National Lawyers Guild; Oregon Law Students' Public Interest Fund; Oregon Women Lawyers; Partners in Law, Lovers & Relatives Support; Peer Advising Board; People's Law School; Phi Alpha Delta; Phi Delta Phi; Sports Club; *The Weekly Dissent*, Entertainment Law Club; and the Women's Law Forum.

■ Expenses and Financial Aid

- *full-time tuition & fees—resident, $8,000/yr; nonresident, $13,190/yr*
- *estimated additional expenses—$6,800 (books, room & board, personal)*
- *academic and need-based scholarships available*
- *academic and need-based minority scholarships available*
- *financial aid available; FAFSA due March 1*

■ Career Services

The Career Services Office provides counseling, assistance with résumé preparation, job search strategy, and interviewing skills. It offers a library of career planning resources for use by student and alumni. Law firms, corporations, government organizations, and public interest agencies visit the campus for on-site interviews each year. Graduates have risen to prominent positions in the state and federal court systems, have served with distinction in state and national legislative and executive offices, and have distinguished themselves in private practice and in business.

Applicant Group for the 1995-1996 Academic Year

University of Oregon School of Law

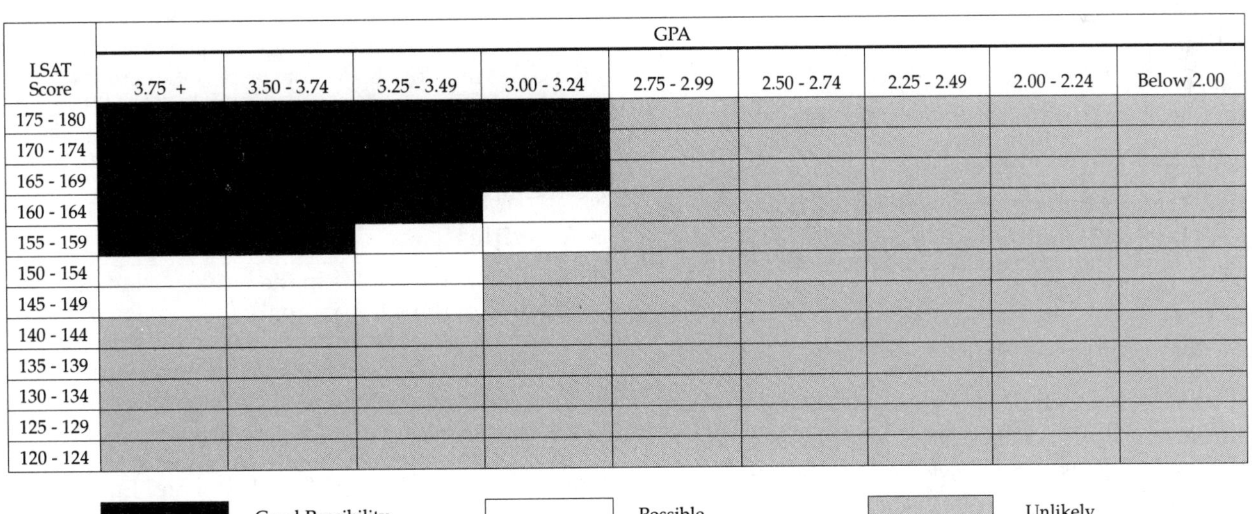

Pace University School of Law

78 North Broadway
White Plains, NY 10603
Phone: 914.422.4210

■ Introduction

The Pace University School of Law, a division of a multi-campus university, is fully accredited by the ABA and is a member of the AALS. Located in White Plains, NY, the law school provides convenient access to metropolitan New York, Connecticut, and New Jersey. In the area are the headquarters of some of the nation's largest corporations, as well as a large legal community and county, state, and federal courts. This concentration and the law school's proximity to New York City have enabled Pace to attract highly qualified professors, speakers, and advisors.

The programs of the law school, including the J.D., LL.M., and S.J.D. in Environmental Law, are national in perspective and are based on the concept that rigorous standards and high quality teaching can coexist with an atmosphere congenial to learning and enjoyment. The aspirations of the students and faculty are high: to achieve national recognition and to reflect the range and level of varied resources of the metropolitan New York City area.

The law school has just expanded into new buildings on its verdant campus setting. The school is noted for its community atmosphere and closeness of students, faculty, and alumni.

■ Enrollment/Student Body

➡ 2,751 applicants ➡ 970 admitted first-year class 1995 ➡ 281 enrolled first-year class 1995 ➡ 474 total full-time ➡ 329 total part-time ➡ 47% women

■ Faculty

➡ 91 total ➡ 51 full-time ➡ 40 part-time or adjunct ➡ 2 emeritus in residence ➡ 15 women ➡ 3 minority

■ Library and Physical Facilities

➡ 300,000 volumes & equivalents ➡ library hours: Mon.-Thurs., 8:00 A.M.-MIDNIGHT; Fri., 8:00 A.M.-10:00 P.M.; Sat., 9:00 A.M.-9:00 P.M.; Sun., 11:00 A.M.-11:00 P.M. ➡ LEXIS ➡ NEXIS ➡ WESTLAW ➡ DIALOG ➡ VUTEXT ➡ EPIC ➡ RLIN ➡ OCLC ➡ PALS ➡ 10 full-time librarians ➡ library seats 346

■ Curriculum

➡ Academic Support Program ➡ 90 total credits required to graduate ➡ 134 courses available ➡ degrees available: J.D.; J.D./M.B.A.; J.D./M.P.A.; LL.M.; S.J.D. in Environmental Law ➡ semesters, first-year begin mid-Aug. ➡ range of first-year class size—270

■ Special Programs

Certificates in Environmental Law, Health Law, and International Law are awarded when students complete a sequence of courses with specified GPAs in the applicable area. Clinics are available in appellate and civil (health) litigation, criminal prosecution (domestic violence) and criminal defense as well as trial courses and externships. The environmental litigation clinic run by Robert F. Kennedy, Jr., has achieved national recognition. Pace has the unique London Program largely taught by the Faculty of Law, University College, London. The program includes the opportunity for clinical internships with members of Parliament, law firms, and corporations.

Pace offers the opportunity to pursue the joint J.D./M.B.A. or joint J.D./M.P.A. degree programs. The programs are typically completed in four years of full-time study; evening study is also possible.

■ Admission

➡ Bachelor's degree required ➡ application deadline—March 15 ➡ rolling admission ➡ LSAT, LSDAS required ➡ median GPA—3.20 ➡ median LSAT score—155 ➡ application fee—$55 ➡ 2 letters of recommendation and a personal statement

The law school received over 2,751 applications for 1995 admission. It enrolls approximately 170 day and 90 evening students annually. Admission is very competitive. The GPAs of the admitted classes average 3.20, and the mean LSAT score is around the 70th percentile. The GPA and LSAT are the most important criteria for admission. However, many additional factors (e.g., schools attended, grade progression, courses, experiences) are also considered.

Minority students are encouraged to apply and identify themselves as such on the application. Pace encourages representation in the school and profession.

A number of students who show academic promise (e.g., high GPAs and low LSATs or the reverse) are invited to enroll in the Summer Conditional Admission Program. If a student, upon completion of the two courses, receives a C+ (2.33) GPA with neither grade below a C, he/she is guaranteed admission to the entering fall class.

■ Activities

Students may participate in the writing, running, and production of three law journals: the *Pace Law Review*; the *Pace Environmental Law Review*; and the *Pace Journal of International and Comparative Law*. Other law student organizations at Pace include *Hearsay*, the student newspaper, moot court board, Student Bar Association, Women's Association of Law Students, Minority Student Association, Entertainment and Sports Law, Labor and Employment Law, Environmental Law, and International Law Clubs, and other special-interest groups. Special activities such as workshops and speakers sponsored by these groups, as well as social events, enrich Pace's offerings.

In addition, Pace students compete in the Philip C. Jessup International Moot Court, the National Moot Court, the National Client Counseling Competitions, and the National Trial Competition. Pace hosts the annual National Environmental Law Moot Court Competition and an international commercial law arbitration moot in Vienna. Students may also attend programs by our Continuing Legal Education (CLE) programs.

■ Expenses and Financial Aid

➻ *tuition & fees—full-time, $18,210; part-time, $13,710* ➻ *estimated additional expenses—$9,395 (off-campus living allowance)* ➻ *merit- and need-based scholarships available* ➻ *financial aid available* ➻ *FAFSA required completed by March 15, Profile Form or the Need Access Application*

■ Career Services

The school's reputation continues to grow and, over the course of the past 19 years, Pace has succeeded in firmly establishing itself in the legal marketplace. That success is due largely to the achievements of our graduates and continued employer satisfaction. Pace graduates typically go on to careers with national, regional, and local law firms; government agencies; county prosecutors; and public interest organizations. Pace students are awarded federal and state judicial clerkships each year.

The Office of Career Development provides guidance and assistance to students as they engage in the search for legal employment. The office serves as a liaison between law students and legal employers. It solicits and identifies employment opportunities; develops and maintains resources for student use in their job search; and encourages employers to accept student résumés and to interview on campus. The office provides counseling on résumé and cover letter preparation, interviewing techniques and career options as well as advice on how best to conduct a job search.

Admission Profile Not Available

University of Pennsylvania Law School

3400 Chestnut Street
Philadelphia, PA 19104

E-Mail: admis@oyez.law.upenn.edu
URL: http://www.law.upenn.edu
Phone: 215.898.7400

■ Introduction

The study of law at the University of Pennsylvania began in 1790 and the Law School was formally organized in 1852. The Law School is a charter member of the AALS and is on the approved list of the ABA. The university is a private institution. The Law School, located on the university campus, is convenient to the many places of cultural and historical interest in Philadelphia.

■ Enrollment/Student Body

➽ 4,135 applicants ➽ 1,215 admitted first-year class 1995
➽ 232 enrolled first-year class 1995 ➽ 741 total full-time
➽ 23.5% minority ➽ 40% women
➽ 42 states & foreign countries represented
➽ 162 undergraduate schools represented

The student body is a diverse group of J.D. candidates plus a number of full-time graduate students from the United States and abroad. In recent years, 47 percent of the J.D. candidates did not matriculate directly from undergraduate study; 12 percent possess other graduate or professional degrees.

■ Faculty

➽ 91 total ➽ 41 full-time ➽ 50 part-time or adjunct
➽ 8 women ➽ 4 minority

■ Libraries and Physical Facilities

➽ 560,000 volumes & equivalents ➽ library hours: Mon.-Thurs., 7:30 A.M.-MIDNIGHT; Fri., 7:30 A.M.-11:00 P.M.; Sat., 9:00 A.M.-11:00 P.M.; Sun., 9:00 A.M.-MIDNIGHT ➽ LEXIS ➽ NEXIS ➽ WESTLAW ➽ DIALOG ➽ BRS ➽ VUTEXT ➽ Dow Jones ➽ 14 full-time librarians ➽ library seats 525 ➽ 657 computer ports

The Law School is a modern, self-contained complex of buildings. A new library adjacent to the Law School was completed in 1993. Law students also have ready access to the university's other libraries, which contain an additional three million books.

■ Curriculum

➽ degrees available: J.D.; J.D./M.B.A.; J.D./M.S.W.; J.D./M.C.P.; J.D./M.A. Economics; J.D./M.A. Middle Eastern Studies; J.D./M.A. Public Policy; J.D./Ph.D. Philosophy; LL.M.; S.J.D.

The Law School awards the J.D. degree upon the successful completion of three academic years. There are no summer or night classes. The school operates on the semester basis.

The prescribed program of the first year includes courses based on statutory and administrative law, as well as the traditional common law courses. In a small group, each student receives individualized instruction in legal research and writing. In the second and third years the work is elective, with opportunity for in-depth work in particular areas, including nonclassroom study. Additionally, second- and third-year students are required to perform 35 hours of unpaid professional service each year. This public service is a graduation requirement. Under rules on the practice of law in the Commonwealth, students in the Law School's clinical programs are permitted to represent clients in a variety of judicial and administrative tribunals. All third-year students write a major senior research paper. The program of graduate study leads to the degree of Master of Laws (LL.M.) and Doctor of Juridical Science of Law (S.J.D.).

■ Special Programs

The Law School's sensitivity to the problems confronting contemporary society is reflected in its programs. Among these are four-year programs with the Department of City Planning, leading to the J.D. and Master of City Planning degrees; the Wharton School of Business Administration, leading to the J.D. and M.B.A. or J.D. and M.A./Ph.D. in Public Policy and Management; the Department of Economics leading to the J.D. and M.A. or, through a very rigorous program, a combined J.D./Ph.D.; the School of Social Work leading to the J.D. and Master of Social Work; and the Department of Philosophy leading to a J.D./Ph.D. in Philosophy. In conjunction with the university's Middle East Center, the Law School offers a program designed for law students who wish to focus their attention on legal issues arising in the Islamic Middle East. Through arrangements with the graduate faculty, well-qualified J.D. candidates may pursue a joint program in other law-related graduate disciplines. Selected students may spend one semester working and studying in externship programs away from the Law School. The Law School maintains a Legal Assistance Office where students represent clients under the supervision of experienced attorneys. A small-business clinic has been established in conjunction with the Wharton School.

■ Admission

➽ Bachelor's degree from accredited institution required
➽ application deadline—Feb. 1 ➽ LSAT, LSDAS required
➽ median GPA—3.60 ➽ mean LSAT score—166
➽ application fee—$60

Admission is highly selective. The school lays prime emphasis upon overall undergraduate performance and LSAT score. It may also take into account maturity, extracurricular records, and other personal qualifications. Recommendations, preferably from former instructors, are required. Personal interviews are not required, but students contemplating law study are encouraged to visit the school. For the class that entered in August 1995, the average LSAT score was in the 94th percentile. The Law School strongly encourages applications from members of minority groups. The deadline for admission and financial aid applications is February 1. The school admits students only in the fall and only for full-time study. The school accepts a number of transfer students each year from applicants with superior undergraduate and law school records.

■ Housing

Facilities for single and married students are available in the Graduate Towers and International House, which are adjacent to the Law School. A wide range of off-campus facilities is also available. For information students may write to the Office of Graduate Housing, 3901 Locust Walk, Philadelphia, PA 19104.

■ Student Activities

The *University of Pennsylvania Law Review* is edited by a board of student editors. It dates from 1896 and is a lineal successor to the *American Law Register,* which originated in 1852. The Law School also publishes a *Journal of International Business Law* and the *Comparative Labor Law Journal*. There is a chapter of the Order of the Coif. Student representatives participate in the governance of the Law School by participating in committee and faculty meetings. There is a full program of moot court activities. Other activities include the National Lawyer's Guild, the Federalist Society, and the Environmental Law Group. There are organizations for women, black, Asian-American, Latino, and gay and lesbian students, and various professional interests.

■ Expenses and Financial Aid

➧ *tuition & fees—full-time, $22,097* ➧ *estimated additional expenses—$11,353* ➧ *scholarships available (Public Interest Scholarships)* ➧ *need-based grants available* ➧ *minority scholarships available* ➧ *financial aid available* ➧ *FAFSA required for need-based scholarships, as well as institutional application*

The school maintains a substantial program of both scholarship and loan aid based entirely on need. Over 75 percent of the student body receives some type of financial aid.

Entering students may apply for several Public Interest Scholarships. These cover two-thirds of tuition and fees for three years. Applicants are selected on the basis of previous work experience in the public sector and commitment to employment in the public sector after graduation. Applications for the scholarships are contained in our admission material.

The Law School has a loan forgiveness program to assist graduates in repaying law school debts if they choose to work in the public sector.

■ Career Services

The Career Planning and Placement Office is staffed by four professionals who assist law students in finding employment and counsel students and alumni on employment opportunities. We offer specialized counseling for public interest work, first-year job searches, minority students' concerns, and judicial clerkships. About 70 percent of the Class of 1994 entered private practice and 20 percent held judicial clerkships, and 10 percent in government and public interest positions.

Applicant Group for the 1995-1996 Academic Year

University of Pennsylvania Law School
This grid includes only applicants who earned 120-180 LSAT scores under standard administrations.

	GPA																					
LSAT Score	3.75 +		3.50 - 3.74		3.25 - 3.49		3.00 - 3.24		2.75 - 2.99		2.50 - 2.74		2.25 - 2.49		2.00 - 2.24		Below 2.00		No GPA		Total	
	Apps	Adm	Apps	Adm	Apps	Adm	Apps	Adm	Apps	Adm	Apps	Adm	Apps	Adm	Apps	Adm	Apps	Adm	Apps	Adm	Apps	Adm
175 - 180	24	24	22	21	22	18	8	2	1	0	0	0	1	0	0	0	0	0	0	0	78	65
170 - 174	67	65	85	77	79	50	24	5	12	3	2	1	1	0	2	0	0	0	5	3	277	204
165 - 169	206	190	307	262	195	103	77	13	40	6	9	1	6	0	0	0	0	0	14	12	854	587
160 - 164	264	95	422	68	274	13	135	12	50	5	26	2	7	0	0	0	1	0	10	3	1189	198
155 - 159	138	17	227	15	195	17	92	11	47	2	21	1	11	0	0	0	0	0	12	1	743	64
150 - 154	56	4	90	13	111	9	92	5	53	0	33	0	11	0	3	0	1	0	15	1	465	32
145 - 149	23	1	46	2	50	1	43	0	48	1	21	0	11	0	6	0	1	0	7	0	256	5
140 - 144	5	1	18	0	25	0	27	0	24	0	17	0	10	0	4	0	0	0	10	0	140	1
135 - 139	0	0	4	0	6	1	9	0	11	0	5	0	4	0	4	0	0	0	2	0	45	1
130 - 134	1	0	2	0	1	0	3	0	5	0	3	0	0	0	1	0	2	0	0	0	18	0
125 - 129	0	0	0	0	0	0	0	0	2	0	1	0	0	0	2	0	1	0	0	0	6	0
120 - 124	0	0	1	0	0	0	0	0	0	0	0	0	0	0	0	0	0	0	0	0	1	0
Total	784	397	1224	458	958	212	510	48	293	17	138	5	62	0	22	0	6	0	75	20	4072	1157

Apps = Number of Applicants
Adm = Number Admitted
Reflects 98% of the total applicant pool.

Pepperdine University School of Law

24255 Pacific Coast Highway
Malibu, CA 90263

URL: HTTP://law-www.pepperdine.edu
Phone: 310.456.4631

■ Introduction

Pepperdine University School of Law is located in the Odell McConnell Law Center on the university's 830-acre Malibu campus in Los Angeles County. This campus is the site of Seaver College, the university's undergraduate school, and the School of Business and Management's Residential M.B.A. program. The natural beauty of the Malibu campus combines the majesty of the rugged Santa Monica Mountains with a breathtaking view of the Pacific Ocean. Known for its clean air and almost rural setting, Malibu is less than a half hour's drive from the heavily populated San Fernando Valley; the business and legal communities of Santa Monica, Westwood, and Century City, and the fast-growing Thousand Oaks/Conejo Valley areas in nearby Ventura County. It is less than a 45-minute drive from downtown Los Angeles.

The School of Law is approved by the ABA and is a member of the AALS. With 35 percent of its students coming from states other than California, the school has a national reputation for excellence. Pepperdine offers a unique opportunity for the student who wishes to pursue a legal education in an institution that stresses academic excellence while supporting Christian values. Pepperdine is an independent, private university with a long-standing relationship with churches of Christ.

■ Enrollment/Student Body

➧ *2,970 applicants* ➧ *1,010 admitted first-year class 1995*
➧ *240 enrolled first-year class 1995* ➧ *702 total full-time*
➧ *24.8% minority* ➧ *48% women*
➧ *40 states & foreign countries represented*
➧ *200 undergraduate schools represented*

The school actively recruits minority students.

■ Faculty

➧ *56 total* ➧ *33 full-time* ➧ *49 part-time or adjunct*
➧ *7 women* ➧ *4 minority* ➧ *16 women part-time*

The full-time opportunity for a personal relationship between faculty and students increases the effectiveness of the entire educational experience.

■ Library and Physical Facilities

➧ *252,000 volumes & equivalents* ➧ *library hours: Mon.-Fri., 7:00 A.M.-MIDNIGHT; Sat., 10:00 A.M.-10:00 P.M.; Sun., NOON-MIDNIGHT* ➧ *LEXIS* ➧ *NEXIS* ➧ *WESTLAW*
➧ *5 full-time librarians* ➧ *library seats 500*

The Jerene Appleby Harnish Law Library maintains an online public catalog as well as online, CD-ROM, and book indexes to provide access to the monograph and serials collections. All first-year students receive extensive training in both the LEXIS/NEXIS and the WESTLAW/DIALOG computer-assisted legal research systems, administered through the library.

■ Curriculum

➧ *Academic Support Program*
➧ *88 credits required to graduate* ➧ *131 courses available*
➧ *degrees available: J.D.; J.D./M.B.A.; M.D.R.*
➧ *semesters, start in Aug., Jan., May*

An eight-week summer session is available for interested continuing students. It is possible to accelerate graduation one semester by taking appropriate courseloads for two summer sessions. During the summer session, classes are offered in the evenings to allow students employment opportunities during the day.

■ Special Programs

Through extensive clinical programs and the California State Bar Legal Intern Program, students engage in a wide variety of practical legal activities under the supervision of experienced attorneys. The faculties of the School of Law and the Pepperdine University School of Business and Management offer a four-year, combined-degree program in business administration, J.D./M.B.A.

■ Institute for Dispute Resolution

In 1986, the School of Law established the Institute for Dispute Resolution, recognizing the needs for effective, timely, and affordable justice. The most comprehensive dispute resolution program in the country, the institute's activities include academic programs, research, publications, national training and actual dispute resolution activities. In 1988, the institute began its unique certificate program, which recognizes students who complete special coursework in the dispute-resolution field. (In 1995, the institute expanded its program to offer a Masters in Dispute Resolution.) Through the institute, the School of Law has received national recognition as a leader in the field of dispute resolution.

■ London Program

The School of Law offers a limited selection of courses in London, England, with an emphasis on international law in each semester, as well as the summer. Second- and third-year students are given the opportunity to take courses in London under the direction of Pepperdine faculty and London adjunct professors. Several students from other law schools also participate.

■ Student Activities

Students are involved in a number of challenging activities, such as publication of the *Pepperdine Law Review*. The school operates one of the finest moot court programs in the country, with Pepperdine students excelling in statewide and national competitions. There are also successful trial advocacy and client-counseling competitions. Student organizations and legal fraternities offer additional opportunities for activities centered around the profession of law.

■ Admission

- ➽ *four-year undergraduate degree required*
- ➽ *application deadline—March 1* ➽ *rolling admission*
- ➽ *LSAT, LSDAS required* ➽ *median GPA—3.20*
- ➽ *median LSAT score—158* ➽ *application fee—$50*

No specific prelaw curriculum is required. First-year students are admitted only in the fall. Applications should be received by March 1.

Pepperdine University does not discriminate on the basis of race, color, national or ethnic origin, religion, age, sex, disability, or prior military service. Evaluation is based on GPA, LSAT score, personal references, and extracurricular activities. The GPA and LSAT scores provide the objective factors in the selection process. In addition, intangible and personal factors are weighed to ensure diversity among the student body and to meet institutional objectives. Admission is limited to those who show substantial promise of successfully completing the study of law.

A limited number of transfer students may be accepted each year. Transfer applicants must be in good academic standing (top 15 percent of class) at a law school approved by the ABA and holding membership in the AALS, and must complete their last 58 units in residence at Pepperdine.

■ Housing

A limited number of law students can be housed in the on-campus School of Law apartment complex, which is located directly across the street from the Law Center.

■ Expenses and Financial Aid

- ➽ *tuition & fees—$19,870 full-time; $735/unit part-time*
- ➽ *estimated additional expenses—$15,732 (room & board, $8,856; books, $700; travel, $1,944; personal, $3,492*
- ➽ *merit and need-based scholarships available*
- ➽ *diversity scholarships available*
- ➽ *financial aid available; FAFSA*

An active financial aid program provides over 85 percent of the student body with some type of financial assistance. Scholarship grants are available to students with outstanding academic credentials and to those with demonstrated financial need. The school's catalog contains loan and scholarship information. The deadline for students to complete applications for financial aid is May 1 of the entering year. Financial aid application packages are available January 15.

■ Career Services

Career planning services are available to students and alumni of the School of Law, which is a member of the National Association for Law Placement and participates in its annual employment survey of law graduates. The law school currently has alumni located in 49 states and 12 foreign countries; the largest concentration of 1994 alumni was located in California. Graduates have become affiliated with prestigious law firms, government agencies, and corporations in Southern California and throughout the country.

Applicant Group for the 1995-1996 Academic Year

Pepperdine University School of Law
This grid includes only applicants who earned 120-180 LSAT scores under standard administrations.

LSAT Score	3.75 +		3.50 - 3.74		3.25 - 3.49		3.00 - 3.24		2.75 - 2.99		2.50 - 2.74		2.25 - 2.49		2.00 - 2.24		Below 2.00		No GPA		Total	
	Apps	Adm	Apps	Adm	Apps	Adm	Apps	Adm	Apps	Adm	Apps	Adm	Apps	Adm	Apps	Adm	Apps	Adm	Apps	Adm	Apps	Adm
175 - 180	0	0	0	0	1	1	0	0	0	0	0	0	0	0	0	0	0	0	0	0	1	1
170 - 174	0	0	0	0	0	0	2	2	1	1	0	0	1	1	1	0	0	0	0	0	5	4
165 - 169	10	10	9	9	12	11	8	7	9	7	9	9	7	4	0	0	0	0	3	2	67	59
160 - 164	28	25	54	53	68	64	55	51	57	53	33	31	13	5	6	1	1	0	0	0	315	283
155 - 159	49	47	93	88	162	145	162	145	111	73	62	19	24	1	11	2	1	0	8	1	683	521
150 - 154	29	13	101	28	166	40	204	21	152	9	78	3	40	2	16	1	5	0	12	2	803	119
145 - 149	14	0	37	1	95	2	122	3	112	2	77	2	53	3	23	0	3	0	9	0	545	13
140 - 144	3	0	19	1	38	1	59	0	67	3	66	2	40	0	12	0	1	0	8	0	313	7
135 - 139	0	0	6	0	10	0	25	0	37	0	35	0	27	0	16	0	2	0	5	0	163	0
130 - 134	0	0	0	0	1	0	7	0	4	0	8	0	6	0	6	0	2	0	2	0	36	0
125 - 129	0	0	1	0	0	0	0	0	1	0	3	0	1	0	1	0	2	0	0	0	9	0
120 - 124	0	0	0	0	0	0	0	0	1	0	0	0	2	0	0	0	1	0	0	0	4	0
Total	133	95	320	180	553	264	644	229	552	148	371	66	214	16	92	4	18	0	47	5	2944	1007

Apps = Number of Applicants
Adm = Number Admitted
Reflects 97% of the total applicant pool.

University of Pittsburgh School of Law

3900 Forbes Avenue
Pittsburgh, PA 15260

URL: http://www.law.pitt.edu
Phone: 412.648.1412

■ Introduction

Tradition: Law teaching at the University of Pittsburgh began in 1843, making Pittsburgh one of the first universities in the United States to offer a legal education. **Reputation:** The University of Pittsburgh remains one of the finest law schools in the country, featuring a broad and varied curriculum, an internationally renowned, enthusiastic faculty, first-rate physical facilities, and a talented and heterogeneous student body. **Venue**: The School of Law is located in its own modern building on the university campus in Oakland, the cultural and educational center of the city of Pittsburgh. State and federal courts, major corporate headquarters, and hundreds of large and small law firms are located nearby in downtown Pittsburgh, minutes from the campus. The Oakland area is home to four colleges and universities, the seven-hospital University Health Center, scientific and high-tech research centers, museums, art galleries, and libraries. The university campus abuts a safe and attractive city park, and desirable and affordable residential areas are less than a mile away.

■ Enrollment/Student Body

➧ *1,655 applicants* ➧ *842 admitted first-year class 1995* ➧ *243 enrolled first-year class 1995* ➧ *697 total full-time* ➧ *6 total flex-time* ➧ *14% minority* ➧ *41% women* ➧ *38 states & foreign countries represented* ➧ *198 undergraduate schools represented*

■ Faculty

➧ *74 total* ➧ *44 full-time* ➧ *30 part-time or adjunct* ➧ *18 women* ➧ *7 minority*

■ Library and Physical Facilities

➧ *300,000+ volumes & equivalents* ➧ *library hours: Mon.-Thurs., 8:00 A.M.-MIDNIGHT; Fri., 8:00 A.M.-11:00 P.M.; Sat., 9:00 A.M.-8:00 P.M.; Sun., NOON-MIDNIGHT* ➧ *LEXIS* ➧ *NEXIS* ➧ *WESTLAW* ➧ *6 full-time librarians* ➧ *library seats 442*

Faculty offices ring the perimeter of the library. This encourages ease of interaction between students and faculty.

■ Curriculum

➧ *Academic Support Program* ➧ *88 credits required to graduate* ➧ *128 courses available* ➧ *21 are seminars with limited enrollment (15 students)* ➧ *degrees available: J.D./M.P.A., Law and Urban and Public Administration; J.D./M.P.I.A., Law and International Affairs; J.D./M.U.R.P., Law and Urban and Regional Planning; J.D./M.B.A., Law and Business Administration; J.D./M.P.H., Law and Public Health; J.D./M.A., Law and Medical Ethics; J.D./M.S.I.A., Law and Industrial Management; J.D./M.S., Law and Public Management, Law and Arts Management* ➧ *range of first-year class size—10-80*

The first-year class is divided into three sections. For each section, one course is taught in a small class of fewer than 30 students. Upper-level students may enroll in seminars, limited to 15 students, where they complete a faculty-supervised writing project. The upper-level curriculum is extremely varied, and the courses have been grouped into 19 practice areas, permitting students to develop a specialization, if they choose.

■ Special Programs

Clinical Programs—Six specialized legal clinics and a wide range of externship positions offer students the opportunity to learn by handling actual cases under the supervision of experienced lawyers and the law faculty. In the interdisciplinary Child Welfare Law Clinic, students represent parents and children involved in proceedings before the Pennsylvania juvenile courts. Participants receive training from members of the law faculty, as well as teachers from the School of Social Work, and the departments of Psychiatry, Psychology, and Pediatric Medicine. In the Criminal and Appellate Practice Clinic, students work with the local public defender.

The Corporate Counsel Clinic allows students to gain practical experience representing business clients by serving as legal advisers in the Management Game course at Carnegie Mellon University's Graduate School of Industrial Administration. Students in the Elder Law/Guardianship Clinic represent older individuals in guardianship proceedings before Pennsylvania courts.

The Health Law Clinic focuses on litigation techniques and skills. If these cases go on to the federal district court in Western Pennsylvania, students also represent their clients in these proceedings.

The new Community Development Clinic focuses on the lawyer's role in community development, assisting with housing, finance, family support and business acquisitions.

The law school's externship program permits students to earn academic credit while working in public law offices, as clerks for one of the 25 federal and state judges, or with one of many institutions associated with the program.

Mellon Legal Writing Program—The Mellon Legal Writing Program provides academic support to minority students through intensive training in legal analysis and writing. The program has been so successful in enhancing the performance of minority students that it was expanded to include other underrepresented groups, including older students and students with disabilities.

Students in the Mellon program participate in a week-long orientation prior to the start of classes. Throughout the academic year, students receive close, individual attention in class meetings of only 10 to 12 people.

Receptions, class parties, and group projects are held to provide opportunities for Mellon Program students to develop friendships and mentoring relationships with minority attorneys.

International Law—In the law school's dynamic program in international law, 21 courses are offered by internationally respected faculty. Students participate in two annual international law moot court competitions, and the very active International Law Society sponsors a range of speakers and programs. Summer internships with international organizations in Geneva are available, as are opportunities to earn joint degrees with graduate programs in business and international studies. Students also have participated in internships with the international corporations headquartered in Pittsburgh, including Alcoa, Mellon Bank, PPG Industries, and Westinghouse.

The study of international law at the University of Pittsburgh is enhanced by active faculty exchange programs with the University of Augsburg (Germany) and by visiting faculty from various other non-U.S. law faculties. It also benefits from other respected international programs at the University of Pittsburgh, such as the Center for International Studies, identified by the Council on Learning as one of the exemplary programs in the country. In addition, the school offers courses in French, Chinese, German, and Spanish for lawyers.

■ Admission

➻ *Bachelor's degree from accredited college or university required* ➻ *application deadline—March 1* ➻ *LSAT, LSDAS required* ➻ *median GPA—3.28* ➻ *median LSAT score—156* ➻ *application fee—$40*

This School of Law is committed to providing opportunities for individuals in all segments of society: minorities, women, older students, and students with disabilities.

Since some individuals do not score well on standardized tests, in accepting students we look at all factors and all information submitted to see if an individual has the potential and capacity to study law.

■ Student Activities

The *Law Review* is a quarterly legal periodical published by second- and third-year law students. The *Journal of Law and Commerce* is a semiannual legal periodical focusing on commercial law.

There are many organizations at the law school that provide rewarding social and intellectual experiences.

■ Expenses and Financial Aid

➻ *full-time tuition & fees—resident, $10,883; nonresident, $16,633* ➻ *additional expenses (room, board, other living expenses)—$9,120* ➻ *scholarships available: need-based and academic* ➻ *minority scholarships available* ➻ *financial aid available; FAFSA required for loans, law school financial aid form required for scholarships*

■ Career Services

The Placement Office provides year-round assistance to the school's students and graduates. The office serves as a clearinghouse for information on summer, part-time, and permanent work with law firms, corporations, accounting firms, government agencies, judges, and other legal employers. Placement rate for the class of 1995 was 75 percent.

Applicant Group for the 1995-1996 Academic Year

University of Pittsburgh School of Law
This grid includes only applicants who earned 120-180 LSAT scores under standard administrations.

LSAT Score	3.75 +		3.50 - 3.74		3.25 - 3.49		3.00 - 3.24		2.75 - 2.99		2.50 - 2.74		2.25 - 2.49		2.00 - 2.24		Below 2.00		No GPA		Total	
	Apps	Adm	Apps	Adm	Apps	Adm	Apps	Adm	Apps	Adm	Apps	Adm	Apps	Adm	Apps	Adm	Apps	Adm	Apps	Adm	Apps	Adm
175 - 180	0	0	0	0	0	0	1	1	0	0	0	0	0	0	0	0	0	0	0	0	1	1
170 - 174	0	0	2	2	4	4	5	3	3	3	3	3	2	2	1	0	0	0	0	0	20	17
165 - 169	3	3	12	12	8	7	11	11	5	5	7	4	3	1	1	0	0	0	1	1	51	44
160 - 164	17	17	19	19	45	45	38	37	36	33	16	15	6	4	3	0	0	0	3	2	183	172
155 - 159	32	32	80	78	96	90	79	66	73	57	33	20	8	1	2	0	1	0	3	2	407	346
150 - 154	23	22	59	39	87	52	94	28	57	15	36	3	8	2	4	0	4	0	7	2	379	163
145 - 149	13	6	27	14	47	9	73	13	67	20	45	8	19	1	10	0	2	0	2	0	305	71
140 - 144	1	1	12	3	15	2	32	4	42	2	24	4	28	3	9	0	1	0	5	0	169	19
135 - 139	1	0	6	0	6	0	14	0	9	0	20	0	20	0	10	0	5	0	3	0	94	0
130 - 134	0	0	0	0	1	0	3	0	3	0	1	0	9	0	6	0	6	0	0	0	29	0
125 - 129	0	0	0	0	0	0	0	0	3	0	0	0	2	0	1	0	0	0	0	0	6	0
120 - 124	0	0	0	0	0	0	0	0	0	0	0	0	0	0	0	0	0	0	0	0	0	0
Total	90	81	217	167	309	209	350	163	298	135	185	57	105	14	47	0	19	0	24	7	1644	833

Apps = Number of Applicants
Adm = Number Admitted
Reflects 99% of the total applicant pool.

Pontifical Catholic University of Puerto Rico, School of Law

Ponce, PR 00732

Phone: 787.841.2000 ext. 339 or 340

■ Introduction

The School of Law of the Pontifical Catholic University of Puerto Rico was founded in 1961. It is located within the main campus of the Pontifical Catholic University of Puerto Rico, on the southern part of the island in the historical city of Ponce, one of the most beautiful places in Puerto Rico.

The primary objective of the Pontifical Catholic University of Puerto Rico School of Law is the formation of lawyers imbued with a deep love and concern for their Catholic faith and steeped in the redeeming truths of Christian philosophy and ethics. The law school of the Pontifical Catholic University of Puerto Rico hopes to contribute to upholding the high ethical, cultural, and literary accomplishments of the Puerto Rican bar, which historically represents a tradition of moral austerity, intellectual achievement, and professional competence.

■ Enrollment/Student Body

➽ *460 total part-time & full-time students*
➽ *most students are from Puerto Rico*

■ Library and Physical Facilities

➽ *168,387 volumes of Puerto Rican, Hispanic, Anglo American, and foreign legal publications* ➽ *LEXIS* ➽ *NEXIS* ➽ *WESTLAW* ➽ *DIALOG*

The School of Law occupies the Spellman Building. Its location on the campus of Pontifical Catholic University of Puerto Rico enables the students to study related academic disciplines, to participate in the intellectual life, and to enjoy many other facilities of the university.

Among the materials in the library is a comprehensive and growing collection of legal treatises, tests, monographs, and periodicals, including the most important and recent publications in civil, common, and comparative law. Modern audiovisual equipment and computerized services are also available. The library is an authorized depository for United Nations documents as well as for United States documents. In addition, it offers the services of the computerized WESTLAW and LEXIS/NEXIS systems, which permit computer-assisted legal research.

■ Curriculum

➽ *94 credits required to graduate* ➽ *degrees available: J.D.; J.D./M.B.A.* ➽ *semesters system*

The required subjects are Introduction to Law, Constitutional Law, Torts, Property Law, Legal Ethics and Professional Responsibility, Theology, Family Law, Successions and Donations, Penal Law, Criminal Procedure, Administrative Law, Obligations, Contracts, Notary Law, Civil Procedure, Evidence, Mortgages, Trial Practice, Legal Aid Clinic, Corporations, Mercantile Law, Negotiable Instruments, Federal Jurisdiction, Special Legal Proceedings, Computers and the Legal Profession, Analysis of Jurisprudence, Legal Document Workshop, and Legal Bibliography. The basic program covers three years in the day division or four years in the evening division.

The school curriculum includes a clinical program for third-year students. Pursuant to a rule approved by the Supreme Court of the Commonwealth of Puerto Rico in 1974, students practice trial advocacy under the supervision of law school professors in the superior and district courts and in administrative agencies.

The required credits for the joint degree are as follows: J.D. degree, 88 credits (82 required credits and 6 elective credits) and an additional 6 approved elective credits in the Graduate Program of the School of Business Administration, for a total of 94 credits; M.B.A. degree, 37 credits (31 required credits and 6 elective credits) and an additional 6 approved elective credits in J.D., for a total of 43 credits, plus four hours of Theology.

■ Admission

➽ *Bachelor's degree required for admission*
➽ *application deadline—April 15* ➽ *LSAT and PAEG required* ➽ *beginning students admitted in Aug.*

Application for admission is open to men and women of good character who have received a bachelor's degree from a qualified institution with substantive content or training and a 2.5 grade-point average. Students without a bachelor's degree are not admitted.

The required forms of application and all other information may be obtained upon request from the registrar of the law school and should be filed with all supporting documents before May 15 in order to ensure consideration. The School of Law admits beginning students in August for both the full-time and part-time programs.

Applicants are required to take both the LSAT and the Prueba de Admision para Estudios Graduados (PAEG).

Test scores are not the only factor considered. Besides the objective factors, there are many intangible and personal considerations, such as strong motivation, disadvantaged circumstances, evidence of improving performance, and relevant work experience. A personal interview of the applicant by a committee is essential before a decision is made. Applicants of both sexes and from all religious, racial, social, and ethnic backgrounds are encouraged to apply.

All courses are offered only in Spanish. Consequently, students are required to be proficient in Spanish.

■ Student Activities

The law review, *Revista de Derecho Puertorriqueño*, is devoted to scholarly analysis and discussion of development of the law. It publishes student notes, comments, and surveys, as well as articles of outstanding quality submitted by attorneys, judges, and other members of the legal profession. We have a student council, a chapter of the National Association of Law Students of Puerto Rico, and an Association Pro Women's Rights. Local chapters of Phi Alpha Delta international law fraternity, the Delta Theta Phi law fraternity, and the Law Student Division of the ABA are also active and well organized in the law school.

■ Housing

Students live either in the university residences or in private housing. Inquiries concerning housing facilities should be addressed to the Housing Office, Pontifical Catholic University of Puerto Rico, Ponce, Puerto Rico 00732.

■ Expenses and Financial Aid

- *tuition—$210/credit hour, $241.50 fees*
- *estimated additional expenses—$3,570/semester*
- *scholarships available*
- *financial aid available*

There is a deferred plan for students who have financial difficulties at the time of registration. The university has made available for law students several full-tuition scholarships to be awarded on the basis of scholastic excellence and financial need. The university also has an office for loans and other types of financial aid for students.

Admission Profile Not Available

University of Puerto Rico School of Law

P.O. Box 23349, UPR Station
Rio Piedras, PR 00931-3349

Phone: 809.764.1655

■ Introduction

The University of Puerto Rico School of Law was founded in 1913 at its present site on the University Campus at Rio Piedras, within the metropolitan area of San Juan. The School of Law has been accredited by the American Bar Association since 1945 and the University of Puerto Rico is accredited by the Middle States Colleges Association. In 1948, the school was approved by the Association of American Law Schools. It is also accredited by the Council on Higher Education and the Puerto Rico Supreme Court.

■ Enrollment/Student Body

➻ 746 applicants ➻ 179 admitted first-year class 1995 ➻ 154 enrolled first-year class 1995 ➻ 317 total full-time ➻ 208 total part-time ➻ 57% women ➻ 3 states & foreign countries represented ➻ more than 20 undergraduate schools represented

■ Faculty

➻ 56 total ➻ 33 full-time ➻ 23 part-time or adjunct ➻ 7 women

■ Library and Physical Facilities

➻ 275,064 volumes & equivalents ➻ library hours: Mon.-Fri., 7:30 A.M.-11:45 P.M.; Sat. & Sun., 8:00 A.M.-10:15 P.M. ➻ LEXIS ➻ NEXIS ➻ WESTLAW ➻ DIALOG ➻ COMPUCLERK ➻ CUMPULEY ➻ LEGALTRAC ➻ INFOTRAC ➻ MICROJURIS ➻ PRONLINX ➻ 10 full-time librarians ➻ library seats 400

The law library is the largest law library in the Caribbean. Its collection reflects both the Romano-Germanic civil law and Anglo-American common law traditions. The law library is in the process of developing a comprehensive collection of legal materials from the Caribbean Basin including resources from Mexico, Central America, Venezuela, and Colombia, as well as the island jurisdictions. In addition to hard-copy and microform materials, the law library subscribes to a variety of computerized legal research services. The law library has been designated as a European Documentation Centre by the European Communities and is also a selective depository for U.S. government documents.

■ Curriculum

➻ 92 credits required to graduate ➻ 124 courses available ➻ J.D. degree available ➻ semesters, start in Aug. ➻ range of first-year class size—10-50

The basic program covers three years in the day division and four years in the evening division. Seventy credits consist of required courses and 22 are elective. Students are required to take two seminars (two credit-hours each).

■ Special Programs

The curriculum includes a clinical program for third-year students. The Legal Aid Clinic handles upwards of 1,300 cases per year. Rules for the participation of students before the local courts were approved by the Puerto Rico Supreme Court in March 1974 and by the U.S. District Court in 1991.

The clinical program also includes the Project for the Legal Representation of Handicapped Persons, where second- and third-year students participate in administrative and judicial proceedings on behalf of clients with disabilities.

■ Student Exchange Programs

The law school has Student Exchange Programs with the University of Arizona College of Law and the University of Connecticut School of Law. Under these programs, the students will register at their home institution but will take a full course load at the host institution. The credits and grades earned during a single semester will be awarded by the home institution according to the standard procedure of the home law school.

The law school also sponsors the UPR Summer Law Program at the University of Barcelona, Spain (June 23 to July 31, 1995).

There is a second program with the University of Barcelona. It is a four year program. Three years will be studied at the University of Puerto Rico, School of Law and one year will be abroad at the University of Barcelona. At the end of the four years, the students will receive the Juris Doctor and a degree of law from Barcelona.

■ Admission

➻ Bachelor's degree from accredited college or university required ➻ application deadline—Feb. 16 ➻ LSAT, LSDAS required ➻ median GPA—3.42 ➻ median LSAT score—147 ➻ application fee—$15 ➻ median PAEG—668

The admissions procedure is absolutely nondiscriminating. There is no preference toward undergraduates from the University of Puerto Rico, nor toward men or women.

The University of Puerto Rico School of Law does not have a minority group breakdown since approximately 98 percent of our students are Puerto Rican, which would be considered a minority in stateside institutions, but certainly not in Puerto Rico. Racial composition is highly mixed due to the historical circumstances of the island.

Applicants must take the LSAT and the Prueba de Admision para Estudios Graduados (PAEG) no later than the year of application, and must complete their undergraduate degree before enrolling in the law school. The LSAT, the PAEG, and the graduating index are given the same weight.

The cases of applicants with disabilities, who, by reason of their disability cannot take the required aptitude tests, are considered individually by the Admissions Committee.

■ Expenses and Financial Aid

➽ *tuition & fees—full-time, $2,623; part-time, $1,713* ➽ *estimated additional expenses—$5,000 (books, room & board, and transportation)* ➽ *performance and need-based scholarships available* ➽ *financial aid available* ➽ *FAF due April 15*

Resident law students pay tuition and fees amounting to $75 per credit each semester. Nonresident students who are American citizens pay the same amount that would be required from Puerto Rican students if they were to study in the state from which the nonresidents come, thus establishing a reciprocity principle.

Regular fees for medical services amount to $130 for the first semester and $165 for the second semester, which includes summer. The medical fee for the summer session only is $46.

Nonresident students—Nonresident students who are not American citizens pay tuition and fees amounting to $1,750 for eight or more credits for each semester. Regular fees for basic medical services amount to $115 for the first semester and $161 for the second semester, which includes summer.

All financial aid for the University of Puerto Rico is administered by the Office of Financial Aid, Dean of Students, Rio Piedras Campus, University of Puerto Rico, San Juan, PR 00931. Each student is considered on his or her own merit and need. Awards are made only after an applicant has been admitted.

■ Career Services

Since 1981, the school has had an Office of Student Affairs under an assistant dean that offers a variety of services, including placement. The Placement Officer, with the aid of the Puerto Rico Bar Association, the Department of Justice, and other government agencies, helps students obtain part-time jobs, regular jobs, or scholarships.

The Office of Student Affairs has initiated a series of statistical studies on the school's graduates and will continue to do so. Among the school's alumni are the Governor of Puerto Rico, the Secretary of Justice, most cabinet members, and Puerto Rico Supreme Court justices, judges, and legislators.

Applicant Group for the 1995-1996 Academic Year

University of Puerto Rico School of Law
This grid includes only applicants who earned 120-180 LSAT scores under standard administrations.

	GPA																					
LSAT Score	3.75 +		3.50 - 3.74		3.25 - 3.49		3.00 - 3.24		2.75 - 2.99		2.50 - 2.74		2.25 - 2.49		2.00 - 2.24		Below 2.00		No GPA		Total	
	Apps	Adm	Apps	Adm	Apps	Adm	Apps	Adm	Apps	Adm	Apps	Adm	Apps	Adm	Apps	Adm	Apps	Adm	Apps	Adm	Apps	Adm
175 - 180	0	0	0	0	0	0	0	0	0	0	0	0	0	0	0	0	0	0	0	0	0	0
170 - 174	0	0	0	0	0	0	0	0	0	0	0	0	0	0	0	0	0	0	0	0	0	0
165 - 169	0	0	0	0	0	0	0	0	0	0	0	0	0	0	0	0	0	0	0	0	0	0
160 - 164	0	0	0	0	0	0	0	0	0	0	0	0	1	1	0	0	0	0	0	0	1	1
155 - 159	1	1	4	3	1	1	3	3	4	4	0	0	1	1	0	0	0	0	0	0	14	13
150 - 154	5	4	5	5	13	12	12	12	13	9	6	6	3	2	0	0	0	0	1	0	58	50
145 - 149	7	7	12	12	14	13	13	6	13	7	7	1	1	0	1	0	0	0	0	0	68	46
140 - 144	13	11	16	14	18	8	31	9	24	0	22	1	9	0	1	0	3	0	1	0	138	43
135 - 139	7	4	29	6	27	5	40	2	24	0	17	0	13	0	3	0	1	0	8	0	169	17
130 - 134	6	0	15	0	20	0	31	0	21	0	11	0	14	0	3	0	2	0	5	1	128	1
125 - 129	2	0	5	0	13	0	8	0	9	0	11	0	5	0	3	0	0	0	2	0	58	0
120 - 124	0	0	3	0	1	0	3	0	0	0	4	0	4	0	0	0	1	0	1	0	17	0
Total	41	27	89	40	107	39	141	32	108	20	78	8	51	4	11	0	7	0	18	1	651	171

Apps = Number of Applicants
Adm = Number Admitted
Reflects 100% of the total applicant pool.

Quinnipiac College School of Law

275 Mt. Carmel Avenue
Hamden, CT 06518-1948

E-Mail: ladm@quinnipiac.edu
Phone: 203.287.3400

■ Introduction

Dedicated in the fall of 1995, the new, award winning Quinnipiac College School of Law Center is located on the idyllic Hamden Campus of Quinnipiac College. Adjacent to a beautiful pond and across the road from Sleeping Giant State Park, the Law Center complex provides a modern, relaxed, and secure environment in which to study. The new Law Center is designed to provide a 21st century facility for students and faculty.

The center completes a Quinnipiac College quadrangle, which includes all of the major academic buildings on campus.

Quinnipiac is considered one of the most beautiful college campuses in New England. It offers a spacious 180-acre campus, yet, it is only 90 minutes from New York and two-and-one half-hours from Boston. Eight miles from metropolitan New Haven, students will continue to have easy access to the area's diverse resources. The area offers many excellent employment and residential opportunities as well as extensive cultural and recreational facilities.

■ Enrollment/Student Body

➽ 2,404 applicants ➽ 961 admitted first-year class 1995 ➽ 256 enrolled first-year class 1995 ➽ 565 total full-time ➽ 230 total part-time ➽ 13% minority ➽ 36% women ➽ 27 states & foreign countries represented ➽ 134 undergraduate schools represented

Traditionally, the fall class is taught in four sections, three day and one evening. The law school seeks to enroll 225 students in the fall and 40 students in January.

■ Faculty

➽ 65 total ➽ 40 full-time ➽ 21 part-time or adjunct ➽ 20 women ➽ 3 minority

Although the fundamental strength of the law school lies in the faculty's dedication to academic excellence, the rigors of its programs are tempered by the personal attention and individual regard that students receive. Indeed, the care with which members of the faculty demonstrate their interest in each student's progress and success is a distinguishing characteristic of Quinnipiac College School of Law.

In addition to teaching, members of the faculty devote considerable attention to scholarly research. Before joining the faculty, many enjoyed successful legal careers in a variety of areas including corporate, governmental, tax, and general practice.

■ Library and Physical Facilities

➽ 293,309 volumes & equivalents ➽ library hours: Mon.-Thurs., 8:30 A.M.-11:00 P.M.; Fri.-Sat., 8:30 A.M.-9:00 P.M.; Sun., 1:00 P.M.-11:00 P.M. ➽ LEXIS ➽ NEXIS ➽ WESTLAW ➽ DIALOG ➽ 6 full-time librarians ➽ library seats 400

■ Curriculum

➽ 86 total units/credits required to graduate ➽ 115 courses available ➽ J.D. degree available (upon completion of 6 full-time or 8 part-time semesters) ➽ semesters, start in Aug. & Jan. ➽ range of first-year class size—15-65

Full-time students are admitted in the fall (day only), while part-time students are admitted in the fall and in the spring.

The first- and second-year curriculum is traditional and prescribed. There is flexibility within the electives scheme to allow students to fashion their own programs of concentration. A flex-time program is also possible.

A Quinnipiac Law education offers the opportunity to be either a generalist or specialist. Concentrations include business and tax law, health care law, public interest law, and litigation. The J.D./M.B.A. and J.D./M.H.A. (Master in Health Care Administration) degree programs are also available.

■ Special Programs

A total of nine clinical and externship programs are available to full-time day students after completion of their second semester. These programs represent tangible work experience to employers and often provide an important service to the community.

The five clinical programs are appellate, health care, civil, tax, and criminal justice. The four externship programs are Corporate Counsel, Public Interest, Legislative, and Judicial.

An Academic Support Program and a writing program are made available to students of the law school.

■ Admission

➽ Bachelor's degree required ➽ LSAT, LSDAS required ➽ median GPA—2.86 ➽ median LSAT score—152 ➽ application fee—$40 ➽ rolling admission, early application preferred ➽ Pre-Admission Summer Program

Admission is based on a variety of factors—undergraduate scholastic record, scores on the Law School Admission Test, and other evidence such as advanced degrees, employment, experience, and extracurricular activities. Although the best indicator for performance in law school is past performance, this may be rebutted in certain cases when factors in the background of an individual, such as economic, cultural, and physical considerations, indicate that past performance may not be a reliable guide.

In the Pre-Admission Summer Program, students not admitted through the regular admissions process attend a small seven-week session taught by a full-time faculty member, applying normal standards to assess students' performance. Students who attain the acceptable grade are admitted to the regular part-time program. The offering of the Pre-Admission Summer Program is determined on a year-to-year basis. The law school also participates in CLEO.

Admission decisions are made by a faculty admissions committee which reviews every application. The law school places special emphasis on minority recruitment. Application fee waivers are available.

■ Student Activities

The Law School publishes *QLR (the Law Review)* two to four times a year. The journal is organized and edited by a board of student editors under the guidance of faculty advisors.

The *Connecticut Probate Law Journal* is the result of a cooperative effort with the Connecticut Probate Assembly that chose Quinnipiac, from the three law schools in the state, to produce it.

The Moot Court Board organizes an annual intramural moot court competition for entry onto the Board. The Moot Court Board edits briefs and supervises its own members as they participate in regional and national competitions. In the past, the Mock Trial Society competed in the National Association of Criminal Defense Lawyers Cathy G. Bennett Criminal Trial Competition, and won two of three Best Advocate awards.

Quinnipiac has a very active Student Bar Association, and students publish their own newspaper titled the *Quinnipiac Legal Times*. The law school has local chapters of three international professional law fraternities—Delta Theta Phi; Phi Delta Phi, and Phi Alpha Delta. In addition, it has chapters of BLSA, LALSA, Jewish Law Students' Association, and Law Women's Association.

■ Expenses and Financial Aid

- *tuition & fees—full-time, $15,960; part-time, $665/credit*
- *estimated additional expenses—campus identification fee, $25; Student Bar Association fee, $75; student fee, $290*
- *academic and need-based scholarships available*
- *diversity scholarships available*
- *FAFSA & Quinnipiac Financial Aid application required*
- *work/study program*

In 1995-96, approximately 80 percent of the student body receives some form of financial aid. Total scholarship funding exceeded $1 million.

■ Housing

There is ample, affordable housing available throughout Fairfield and New Haven counties. The School of Law Admissions Office and the Quinnipiac College Office of Residential Life assist in securing off-campus accommodations.

■ Career Services

The office assists students in writing résumés and letters of application, in interviewing techniques, and in other employment-related questions. It sponsors an extensive on-campus recruitment program for summer internships as well as for permanent jobs, and career symposia to expose students to more diverse areas of work and to apprise them of employment trends.

Placement statistics attest to the success of the law school's students in the contemporary job market. A number of the law school's alumni/ae are judicial clerks, Justice Department attorneys, and associates in prestigious metropolitan firms.

Applicant Group for the 1995-1996 Academic Year

Quinnipiac College School of Law
This grid includes only applicants who earned 120-180 LSAT scores under standard administrations.

LSAT Score	3.75 +		3.50 - 3.74		3.25 - 3.49		3.00 - 3.24		2.75 - 2.99		2.50 - 2.74		2.25 - 2.49		2.00 - 2.24		Below 2.00		No GPA		Total	
	Apps	Adm	Apps	Adm	Apps	Adm	Apps	Adm	Apps	Adm	Apps	Adm	Apps	Adm	Apps	Adm	Apps	Adm	Apps	Adm	Apps	Adm
175 - 180	0	0	0	0	0	0	1	1	0	0	0	0	0	0	0	0	0	0	0	0	1	1
170 - 174	0	0	0	0	0	0	0	0	1	1	1	1	0	0	0	0	0	0	0	0	2	2
165 - 169	0	0	0	0	1	1	3	3	2	2	1	1	2	2	1	1	0	0	0	0	10	10
160 - 164	6	6	8	8	12	12	3	3	21	20	9	8	7	7	1	1	1	0	0	0	68	65
155 - 159	7	7	16	16	31	31	42	40	47	46	39	39	19	18	12	9	3	1	3	2	219	209
150 - 154	8	8	31	31	69	67	96	90	142	127	118	107	65	52	19	10	7	1	6	2	561	495
145 - 149	6	5	40	13	74	30	170	47	212	56	160	33	78	14	33	3	10	0	9	4	792	205
140 - 144	5	1	22	1	48	3	103	4	95	3	100	2	60	2	24	1	7	0	10	0	474	17
135 - 139	0	0	4	0	16	0	41	0	43	1	40	0	32	1	21	1	4	0	8	0	209	3
130 - 134	0	0	1	0	6	0	8	0	6	0	19	0	15	0	9	1	4	0	4	1	72	2
125 - 129	0	0	0	0	0	0	0	0	0	0	5	0	4	0	1	0	0	0	3	1	13	1
120 - 124	0	0	0	0	0	0	0	0	0	0	1	0	0	0	1	0	0	0	1	0	3	0
Total	32	27	122	69	257	144	467	188	569	256	493	191	282	96	122	27	36	2	44	10	2424	1010

Apps = Number of Applicants
Adm = Number Admitted
Reflects 97% of the total applicant pool.

Regent University School of Law

1000 Regent University Drive
Virginia Beach, VA 23464-9832

URL: http://www.regent.edu/acad/schlaw
Phone: 804.579.4584

■ Introduction

The School of Law at Regent University, formerly CBN University, opened in 1986 and is the successor to the O. W. Coburn School of Law at Oral Roberts University. Regent University is a graduate-level institution affiliated with the Christian Broadcasting Network, Inc., a multifaceted television ministry that broadcasts Christian and family-oriented programming in the United States and in 58 foreign countries.

Regent University is located on a beautiful campus in Virginia Beach, which is famed for its 28 miles of ocean and bay beaches. It is within an hour's drive from historic Yorktown, Jamestown, and Colonial Williamsburg and within four hours of Washington, DC, the Blue Ridge Mountains, and North Carolina's Outer Banks.

The foremost objective of the School of Law at Regent University is to train professional lawyers to participate effectively in the private and public sectors of this nation. The School of Law is unique, however, in that its curriculum is taught in the context of a historical and Biblical foundation and framework. Students learn not only the current status and trends of the law, but they also learn the historical and Biblical foundations for our Anglo-American legal system.

Regent University School of Law has been approved by the American Bar Association since 1989. Graduates are eligible to take the bar examination in all 50 states and the District of Columbia.

■ Enrollment/Student Body

➽ 590 applicants ➽ 267 admitted first-year class 1995 ➽ 139 enrolled first-year class 1995 ➽ 348 total full-time ➽ 8% minority ➽ 29% women ➽ 35 states & foreign countries represented ➽ 118 undergraduate schools represented

■ Faculty

➽ 31 total ➽ 16 full-time ➽ 15 part-time or adjunct ➽ 5 women ➽ 2 minority

Adjunct faculty includes judges, private practitioners, and public prosecutors.

■ Library and Physical Facilities

➽ 290,000 volumes & equivalents ➽ library hours: Mon.-Fri., 7:30 A.M.-MIDNIGHT; Sat., 8:00 A.M.-MIDNIGHT ➽ LEXIS ➽ NEXIS ➽ WESTLAW ➽ DIALOG ➽ INFOTRAC ➽ LEGALTRAC ➽ CALI ➽ 4 full-time librarians ➽ library seats 200

The law school is located in the newly constructed Robertson Hall. Completed in 1993, this four-story, 143,000-square-foot, building has been acclaimed as "one of the preeminent law school facilities in the country." Equipped with the latest technological equipment, this magnificent structure will easily accommodate the anticipated growth to 500 students by the year 2000.

Robertson Hall is adjacent to the 150,000-square-foot university library which houses the law library on the third floor. The law library contains all the materials necessary for training students for the practice of law plus significant materials for advanced research in public policy and law.

■ Curriculum

➽ 90 units/credits required to graduate ➽ 75 courses available ➽ degrees available: J.D.; J.D./M.B.A.; J.D./M.A. in Public Policy; J.D./M.A. in Management; J.D./M.A. in Communications ➽ semesters, start in Aug. ➽ range of first-year class size—50-75

■ Externship Opportunities

In addition to the regular course offerings, students have the opportunity to receive academic credit through legal externships. A standing extern program has been established with the local U.S. Attorney's Office and The American Center for Law and Justice, a not-for-profit public interest law firm dedicated to defending the religious and civil liberties of Americans. Students may also seek approval for externships with judges, prosecutors, and public defenders.

■ Admission

➽ Bachelor's degree required for admission ➽ application deadline—April 1 ➽ LSAT, LSDAS required ➽ median GPA—3.00 ➽ median LSAT score—152 ➽ application fee—$40

The law school admission committee assesses the qualifications of each applicant by examining his or her undergraduate record, LSAT score, any graduate study or work experience, the applicant's statement of goals, three recommendations and, in most cases, one personal interview. The committee further determines if the educational experience at Regent University will meet a mutually shared goal discerned by the committee and the student. A student must be willing to receive a legal education in accordance with the university's Statement of Faith.

The law school admits a limited number of second-year transfer students who are in good academic standing at their current law school. All transfer students are required to take The Common Law and Constitutional Law at Regent University.

■ Student Activities

The *Regent University Law Review* provides a forum for a Christian perspective on law in a traditional legal periodical. Student editors and staff members, chosen on the basis of academic achievement and writing ability, gain valuable experience by writing and editing the *Law Review* under the guidance of the law faculty.

Both the Moot Court Board and the Dispute Resolution and Client Counseling Board involve students in the professional skills program. These student-managed boards plan and prepare for intramural and national competitions.

Each year students do volunteer work with the Volunteer Income Tax Assistance (VITA) program sponsored by the student division of the American Bar Association.

In addition to an active student bar association, law students are involved in other organizations including student chapters in the Grotius International Law Society, the Christian Legal Society, the Federalist Society, the American Center for Law and Justice, the Black Law Students Association (BLSA), the Rutherford Institute, the American Trial Lawyers Association (ATLA), and the American Bar Association. Other student-initiated groups include the Women's Legal Society and Law Wives. Law students also are involved in the university-wide Council of Graduate Students.

■ Expenses and Financial Aid

➽ *full-time tuition & fees—$13,800* ➽ *estimated additional expenses—$550 (books and supplies)* ➽ *scholarships available: performance- and need-based, as well as several institutionally funded scholarships and grants, and several named and endowed scholarships* ➽ *minority scholarships available* ➽ *financial aid application due July 15*

■ Career Services

The law school at Regent University has developed a three-year placement strategy. The program includes self-assessment, a general investigation of career opportunities, and a specific career search. Workshops are conducted to assist students with résumé writing, interviews, and career selection.

The Law Career Services Department offers both on-campus interviewing and a Non-Visiting Employers Program. Regent law students also participate in the Virginia law schools public interest and spring recruitment job fairs. For 1995-96, selected students will receive grants from the Virginia Law Foundation for summer clerkships with public-interest organizations. The career services program has a national focus, with its graduates employed in the legal profession in a variety of capacities including judicial clerks, criminal prosecutors, public-interest attorneys, corporate counsel, and as partners and associates in firms across the nation.

Applicant Group for the 1995-1996 Academic Year

Regent University School of Law
This grid includes only applicants who earned 120-180 LSAT scores under standard administrations (95% of all applicants).

	GPA																					
LSAT Score	3.75 +		3.50 - 3.74		3.25 - 3.49		3.00 - 3.24		2.75 - 2.99		2.50 - 2.74		2.25 - 2.49		2.00 - 2.24		Below 2.00		No GPA		Total	
	Apps	Adm	Apps	Adm	Apps	Adm	Apps	Adm	Apps	Adm	Apps	Adm	Apps	Adm	Apps	Adm	Apps	Adm	Apps	Adm	Apps	Adm
175 - 180	0	0	0	0	0	0	0	0	0	0	1	1	0	0	0	0	0	0	0	0	1	1
170 - 174	1	1	0	0	1	1	0	0	0	0	0	0	0	0	0	0	0	0	0	0	2	2
165 - 169	0	0	0	0	1	1	0	0	0	0	0	0	0	0	0	0	0	0	0	0	1	1
160 - 164	4	4	2	2	4	4	1	1	3	3	2	2	3	3	1	1	0	0	0	0	20	20
155 - 159	2	2	15	15	11	11	12	12	6	6	12	10	7	6	2	1	0	0	0	0	67	63
150 - 154	5	4	12	11	18	18	25	25	26	26	19	14	12	6	3	1	4	1	1	1	125	107
145 - 149	4	4	10	5	23	16	24	10	31	8	20	8	17	7	7	2	3	1	0	0	139	61
140 - 144	1	0	12	1	7	0	12	1	18	0	17	0	11	1	10	0	3	0	1	1	92	4
135 - 139	0	0	0	0	6	0	13	0	6	0	12	0	11	0	7	0	2	0	0	0	57	0
130 - 134	0	0	1	0	5	0	0	0	1	0	1	0	3	0	4	0	0	0	0	0	15	0
125 - 129	0	0	0	0	1	0	0	0	0	0	0	0	2	0	1	0	0	0	0	0	4	0
120 - 124	0	0	0	0	0	0	0	0	0	0	0	0	0	0	1	0	0	0	0	0	1	0
Total	17	15	52	34	77	51	87	49	91	43	84	35	66	23	36	5	12	2	2	2	524	259

Apps = Number of Applicants
Adm = Number Admitted

University of Richmond—T.C. Williams School of Law

E-Mail: rahman@uofrlaw.urich.edu
URL: http://www.urich.edu/~law/
University of Richmond, VA 23173
Phone: 804.289.8189

Introduction

The University of Richmond School of Law, founded in 1870, enjoys an established reputation for preparing its graduates for legal careers throughout the U.S. Accredited by the ABA and a member of the AALS, its J.D. qualifies graduates to seek admission to the bar of all 50 states and the District of Columbia.

Situated on the university's beautiful suburban campus, the law school community thrives on the stimulation found only in such an academic setting. Yet, the campus is within a 20-minute drive of Richmond's pulsating legal community.

Enrollment/Student Body

➧ 1,631 applicants ➧ 556 admitted first-year class 1995 ➧ 172 enrolled first-year class 1995 ➧ 476 total full-time ➧ 5 total part-time ➧ 25% minority ➧ 48% women ➧ 44 states & foreign countries represented ➧ 175 undergraduate schools represented

Faculty

➧ 90 total ➧ 25 full-time ➧ 65 part-time or adjunct ➧ 41 women ➧ 10 minority

Library and Physical Facilities

➧ 230,000 volumes & equivalents ➧ library hours: 105.5 per week—Mon.-Thurs., 7:30 A.M.-MIDNIGHT; Fri., 7:30 A.M.-9:00 P.M.; Sat., 9:00 A.M.-9:00 P.M.; Sun., 10:00 A.M.-MIDNIGHT ➧ LEXIS ➧ NEXIS ➧ WESTLAW ➧ DIALOG ➧ VuText ➧ VA Legislative Bill Service ➧ 6 full-time librarians ➧ library seats 601

The law school building provides technically equipped classrooms, seminar rooms, a state-of-the-art law library, a magnificent courtroom, faculty offices, administrative offices, lounges, and offices for student organizations.

University of Richmond is the first law school in the country to require that entering first-year students own a laptop computer.

Every student is assigned to a study carrel in our expansive law library. Each carrel consists of a desk with a sliding tray for a laptop computer and a secure storage area allowing students ready access to books and notes.

These carrels are linked via students' personal computers to a school-wide computer system giving instant access to the electronic age in law.

Curriculum

➧ clinical programs offered ➧ 86 units/credits required to graduate ➧ 111 courses available ➧ degrees available: J.D.; J.D./M.B.A.; J.D./M.U.R.P.; J.D./M.H.A.; J.D./M.S.W. ➧ range of first-year class size—80-85

Courses in environmental law, contracts, torts, criminal law, procedure, property, and constitutional law comprise the first-year curriculum. Required upper-level courses include professional responsibility and a third-year writing seminar. Elective courses in a variety of areas are available to satisfy each student's interests.

In addition, all students complete a program in legal reasoning, writing, research, and fundamental lawyering skills and values. In mock law offices, students interview and counsel clients, negotiate simulated transactions, and resolve legal disputes through trial and appeal.

International Program

In addition to the on-campus curriculum, students may participate in our popular Summer Programs in Cambridge, England and Caracas, Venezuela. For over 20 years students participating in these programs have, under the guidance of world prominent lecturers, gained valuable perspectives on the international legal system and international trade.

Special Programs

Several dual-degree programs are offered that allow students to earn the J.D. degree as well as a master's degree in a related discipline. Students can reduce the time and cost associated with obtaining two degrees while enjoying the study of two fields of interest. Dual-degree programs are available in Business Administration, Health Administration, Social Work, and Urban Studies and Planning.

The law school operates the Youth Advocacy, Worker's Protection and Advocacy, and Mental Disabilities Clinics in which qualified third-year law students represent clients. These clinics are staffed by teaching, practicing attorneys who work together with students to represent clients in civil, criminal, and administrative proceedings. Students receive assistance in developing trial strategies and guidance in courtroom procedure while handling several court cases each semester.

The law school also arranges exciting clinical placements for academic credit in the nearby courts and law offices. Among the opportunities available are positions in various Commonwealth, city, and county attorneys' offices; the Virginia Attorney General's Office; the U.S. Attorney's Office; the ACLU; environmental organizations; and the Alternative Dispute Resolution Center.

Student Activities

A student board publishes *The University of Richmond Law Review* on a quarterly basis. The *Law Review* presents scholarly articles by professors, judges, attorneys, and students on matters of current interest in the law.

The *Richmond Journal of Law and Technology*, the first student edited scholarly journal to be published exclusively in electronic form, went online April 10, 1995.

Richmond's moot court activities allow students to test their research, brief-writing, trial, and appellate advocacy skills. Students participate in intraschool tournaments that lead to membership on the Moot Court Board and on teams that represent the law school in regional and national competitions.

The Client Counseling and Negotiation Board organizes intra- and interschool competitions. It most recently hosted the National Environmental Negotiation Competition, which was attended by teams from schools throughout the country.

Other student organizations playing a vital role in the law school community include the Student Bar Association, the Law Student Division of the ABA, the Public Interest Law Association, the Black Law Students Association, the Women's Law Association, and the Multi-Ethnic Law Students Association.

■ Admission

- *B.S./B.A. degree required for admission*
- *application deadline—Jan. 15*
- *LSAT, LSDAS required*
- *median GPA—3.02*
- *median LSAT score—159*
- *application fee—$35*

Applications are reviewed beginning in late January. All decisions are released by May 15. The undergraduate GPA and LSAT are two important items considered by the admissions committee, although the committee is also interested in extracurricular and community-service activities and employment experience. The law school provides an equal educational opportunity without regard to race, color, national origin, age, sex, sexual orientation, handicap, or religion.

Applicants who apply and complete their admissions files with our office before January 1 (including all support documentation) will be eligible to participate in the Richmond Applicant Video Essay (RAVE) program. RAVE allows selected applicants to personalize their files by providing a videotaped interview to be viewed by the admissions committee. Applicants will be selected in early January and will receive detailed instructions at that time. Admission conferences are available in November, December, and January. Although these conferences do not impact on the committee's decision, they are invaluable in providing information and answering questions.

■ Expenses and Financial Aid

- *tuition & fees—full-time, $16,100; part-time, $800/credit hour*
- *estimated additional expenses—books, $800; room & board, $5,220; personal expenses, $1,350*
- *merit and need-based scholarships available*
- *minority scholarships available*
- *financial aid available; FAFSA form due Feb. 25*

■ Career Services

Our Career Services Office is responsible for bringing students and legal employers together. Over 85 percent of our recent classes were employed within nine months after receiving their diplomas.

In addition to reviewing résumés, counseling students, and arranging for on-campus interviews, our office conducts many innovative marketing campaigns. We were the first law school in the country to send videotaped interviews to law firms. Students identify geographic areas in which they are most interested; we then contact employers from these areas with information about the law school, its curriculum, and student résumés.

Applicant Group for the 1995-1996 Academic Year

University of Richmond—T.C. Williams School of Law
This grid includes only applicants who earned 120-180 LSAT scores under standard administrations.

	GPA																					
LSAT Score	3.75 +		3.50 - 3.74		3.25 - 3.49		3.00 - 3.24		2.75 - 2.99		2.50 - 2.74		2.25 - 2.49		2.00 - 2.24		Below 2.00		No GPA		Total	
	Apps	Adm	Apps	Adm	Apps	Adm	Apps	Adm	Apps	Adm	Apps	Adm	Apps	Adm	Apps	Adm	Apps	Adm	Apps	Adm	Apps	Adm
175 - 180	0	0	0	0	0	0	0	0	0	0	0	0	0	0	0	0	0	0	0	0	0	0
170 - 174	1	1	3	3	3	3	3	3	1	1	1	1	1	0	1	1	0	0	0	0	14	13
165 - 169	4	3	10	9	14	14	11	10	9	8	3	2	7	3	1	0	1	1	0	0	60	50
160 - 164	9	9	31	31	44	43	64	63	41	36	30	26	14	6	0	0	2	0	0	0	235	214
155 - 159	14	11	45	28	111	50	114	43	67	13	40	7	14	2	6	1	3	0	1	0	415	155
150 - 154	20	2	48	8	81	8	100	24	63	12	50	13	26	6	5	0	4	1	6	2	403	76
145 - 149	11	1	25	5	55	5	57	9	50	5	34	10	16	2	10	2	3	0	3	1	264	40
140 - 144	3	0	8	0	14	0	33	0	22	1	19	0	15	0	8	0	0	0	2	0	124	1
135 - 139	1	0	0	0	4	0	9	0	12	0	16	0	6	0	10	0	1	0	2	0	61	0
130 - 134	0	0	0	0	1	0	1	0	1	0	6	0	5	0	4	0	1	0	3	0	22	0
125 - 129	1	0	0	0	0	0	1	0	0	0	1	0	1	0	0	0	0	0	0	0	4	0
120 - 124	0	0	0	0	0	0	0	0	0	0	0	0	0	0	0	0	0	0	0	0	0	0
Total	64	27	170	84	327	123	393	152	266	76	200	59	105	19	45	4	15	2	17	3	1602	549

Apps = Number of Applicants
Adm = Number Admitted
Reflects 98% of the total applicant pool.

Roger Williams University School of Law

Ten Metacom Avenue
Bristol, RI 02809
Phone: 800.633.2727 or 401.254.4555

■ Introduction

Roger Williams University School of Law is located on a peninsula in the historic seacoast community of Bristol, Rhode Island, which is a quaint small town providing an ideal place to study law. The School of Law is a private entity and the only law school in the state of Rhode Island. While the academic environment is challenging, a collegial atmosphere exists. As a small school, there is a strong sense of camaraderie among the students, and the faculty is both accessible and approachable.

■ Enrollment/Student Body

➽ 700 applicants ➽ 176 matriculated first-year class 1995 ➽ 104 enrolled first-year full-time ➽ 72 enrolled first-year part-time ➽ 6.6% minority ➽ 39% women ➽ 17 states represented ➽ 134 undergraduate schools represented

The Roger Williams student body is diverse in age range: average in full-time—24; average in part-time—33.

■ Faculty

➽ 26 full-time ➽ 4 adjunct ➽ 9 women ➽ 17 men ➽ 3 minority

■ Library

➽ 165,000 volumes & equivalents ➽ library hours: Mon.-Thur., 7:30 A.M.-MIDNIGHT; Fri., 7:30 A.M.-10:00 P.M.; Sat., 9:00 A.M.-10:00 P.M.; Sun., 9:00 A.M.-MIDNIGHT ➽ LEXIS ➽ NEXIS ➽ WESTLAW ➽ DIALOG ➽ 6 full-time librarians ➽ library seats 380 ➽ member, CRIARL (Consortium of RI Academic and Research Libraries)

■ Physical Facilities

A new School of Law building, at a cost of $12 million, was opened in 1993. The state-of-the-art law school building features both an appellate and trial moot courtroom; law practice center including a mock law firm; class and seminar rooms, faculty offices, administrative suites; student services offices, cafe, post office, bookstore, xerography center, and student organization offices. The school is conveniently located in the center of Rhode Island. Providence, the state's capital and legal center, is only 20 minutes away and offers employment and externship opportunities. The resort town of Newport is located close by and is the hub of significant cultural, sporting, and recreational events. Boston, Cape Cod, and the seasonal activities of New England are all in close proximity to Bristol.

■ Curriculum

➽ 90 credits required to graduate ➽ degrees available: J.D.; J.D./M.C.P. ➽ range of first-year class size—20-60 ➽ evening program available ➽ summer session available ➽ Academic Advising Program

The study of law at Roger Williams University School of Law features a combination of a rigorous core curriculum designed to instill in students fundamental lawyering knowledge and a comprehensive practical-skills training program.

Skills Training Curriculum—A significant aspect of Roger Williams University School of Law's curriculum is its comprehensive skills training program. To satisfy a complex society and ever-changing legal profession, practitioners must master not only traditional legal analysis but also the ability to elicit and convey information. The School of Law has carefully planned a legal skills program which is designed to give the student, in a small-group setting, intensive training in the practical skills critical to lawyering.

The Legal Methods Program enables all students to develop, over their entire course of study, the lawyering skills necessary to solve problems and communicate both orally and in writing. The required courses of this program range from the basic legal research and writing course (Legal Methods I) of the first semester of the first year to the simulation courses of the second and subsequent semesters. A basic discussion of the American legal system is included. The simulation courses provide practical training in appellate advocacy (Legal Methods II), interviewing and client counseling (Legal Methods III), and trial advocacy (Legal Methods IV). These courses are taught in our Law Practice Center, which is comprised of a mini-law firm and trial courtroom.

■ Special Programs

Clinics and Student Clerkships—Following the four required Legal Method courses, students may elect to enroll in a live client clinic, or alternative dispute resolution, negotiation, or advanced trial practice courses. The Family Law and the Criminal Defense clinics, located in downtown Providence, RI, provide a semester-long opportunity for students to represent low-income clients before various state agencies and courts in a range of matters under the supervision of a full-time member of the faculty. Also, students can choose to engage in a semester-long supervised clerkship experience in a judge's chambers or in a public interest or governmental law office for academic credit.

■ Admission

➽ Bachelor's degree required for admission ➽ application deadline—May 15 ➽ LSAT, LSDAS required ➽ median GPA—3.20 ➽ median LSAT score—153 ➽ application fee—$60 ➽ admission to fall term only

Admission is competitive at Roger Williams University School of Law and is based on the undergraduate grade-point average and the Law School Admission Test (LSAT) score as well as other indicators of probable success in the study of law such as: graduate degree, work experience, undergraduate extracurricular activities, and community service. All applicants must register with the Law School Data Assembly Service (LSDAS). Code: #3081.

Students are admitted only in the fall. Admission is offered on a rolling basis. Applicants improve their opportunity for favorable decisions by applying early. The deadline for admission is May 15. A personal statement and the $60 fee must accompany all applications. Letters of recommendation are not required but will certainly be considered by the admission committee if submitted. Personal interviews are not part of the regular admission process. Multiple LSAT scores are averaged. Admission criteria are identical for both the regular and extended divisions.

■ Student Activities

Cocurricular Activities—*Law Review*—Membership on *Law Review* is considered one of the most valuable and prestigious of the student activities. *Roger Williams University Law Review* is staffed and primarily administered by students who are selected by their academic achievement and superior writing ability. This group publishes annual editions which consist of scholarly papers written by both students and members of the legal academic community.

Moot Court Honor Society—Moot Court Honor Society is comprised of students possessing superior appellate advocacy and writing ability. This prestigious organization sponsors speakers and programs on appellate advocacy, organizes an intraschool competition, and sends moot court teams to interschool competitions.

Extracurricular Activities—The School of Law recognizes the importance of extracurricular activities in law school life. Participation in such organizations enhances the curriculum and affords students valuable opportunities to refine skills and access information.

Although participation in extracurricular activities is voluntary, Roger Williams University School of Law students have chosen to become very involved. The students have formed many organizations, concentrating on both social and academic activities. The student governing body is the Student Bar Association (SBA) which is run by an executive board selected through schoolwide elections. The SBA has instituted several events including: mentor/mentee program (between upperclass students and incoming first-year students); annual golf tournament and Barrister's Ball; Volunteer Income Tax Assistance Program; awards banquet; and an annual Spring Fling. Additionally, the SBA supports *The Docket*, which is the student newspaper. Students are eligible to become a student member of the American Bar Association—Law Schools Division.

■ Expenses and Financial Aid

➽ full-time tuition—$16,050 ➽ part-time tuition—$12,305 ➽ $535 per credit ➽ Roger Williams University Law School Financial Aid Form and FAFSA required by April 30 for full consideration

■ Career Services

Roger Williams University School of Law provides students with the most comprehensive career services available. The objective of the Career Services Office is to aid students in making career decisions and assist them in reaching their goals. Knowledgeable professionals help match the students' educational and experiential skills with employment opportunities on a national level.

Admission Profile Not Available

Rutgers—The State University—School of Law—Camden

406 Penn Street
Camden, NJ 08102

URL: http://www-CamLaw.Rutgers.Edu
Phone: 609.225.6102

Introduction

Set against a center-city Philadelphia backdrop, Rutgers University's thriving urban campus in Camden is a handsome blend of converted Victorian buildings and newly constructed facilities. The School of Law shares the spacious campus mall with two undergraduate colleges, the Graduate School, and the School of Business. A member of the Association of American Law Schools, the school is included on the list of approved schools of the American Bar Association.

Enrollment/Student Body

➥ 2,111 applicants ➥ 743 admitted first-year class 1995 ➥ 224 enrolled first-year class 1995 ➥ 621 total full-time ➥ 155 total part-time ➥ 23% minority ➥ 42% women ➥ 34 states & foreign countries represented ➥ 230 undergraduate schools represented

Faculty

➥ 39 full-time ➥ 56 part-time or adjunct ➥ 19 women ➥ 8 minority

The law school faculty is engaged in a dynamic program of scholarship, teaching, and service to the bar and community. The faculty is ranked among the 20 most accomplished producers of scholarly articles in eminent journals. Faculty scholarship has been cited by numerous courts, including the New Jersey and United States Supreme Courts. Faculty members also serve as consultants and reporters for the American Bar Association, the American Law Institute, and several federal and state commissions, and are counsel in important public-interest litigation.

Library and Physical Facilities

➥ 380,000 volumes & equivalents ➥ library hours: Mon.-Thurs., 8:00 A.M.-MIDNIGHT; Fri., 8:00 A.M.-10:00 P.M.; Sat., 9:00 A.M.-5:00 P.M.; Sun., 10:00 A.M.-MIDNIGHT ➥ LEXIS ➥ NEXIS ➥ WESTLAW ➥ 7 full-time librarians ➥ library seats over 400

Noted for its extensive collection of East European legal materials, the law library, with its especially broad holdings in government documents and legal periodicals, provides comprehensive research support for students and faculty. Students receive extensive training in the use of computers in legal research. A major renovation to the building for additional library space has been completed.

Curriculum

➥ Academic Support Program ➥ Concentrations in Tax Law and International and Comparative Law ➥ 84 credits required to graduate ➥ 160 courses available ➥ degrees available: J.D./M.B.A.; J.D./M.A. (Pol. Sci.); J.D./M.C.R.P. (Urban Planning); J.D./M.P.A. ➥ semesters, start in Aug. & Jan.

The full-time program requires six semesters; the part-time evening program is completed in eight semesters, plus one summer session (a limited number of part-time day spaces are available). Both programs are subject to the same admission and academic standards, and are taught by the same faculty. After the core curriculum is completed, students select their own courses. Courses in both Professional Responsibility and Introduction to Federal Income Taxation and the completion of three courses with significant writing components are required for graduation. The general curriculum prepares students for work in any jurisdiction of the United States.

Special Programs

Concentrations in taxation and international law are available and a broad range of courses in business, commercial, public interest, criminal, and family law are also offered. The law school, in conjunction with the Society for the Reform of Criminal Law, also publishes a refereed scholarly journal devoted to international and comparative criminal law, *The Criminal Law Forum*. The international and comparative law program also encompasses a faculty and student exchange program with the University of Graz, Austria.

Central to the curriculum is the lawyering program that engages students in various issues that arise in the practice of law. Simulated lawyering activities are incorporated throughout the curriculum.

The Externship Program furnishes third-year students an opportunity to work 12 to 15 hours a week in various federal and state judicial chambers, public agencies, or public-interest organizations. Students in the clinical program represent low income elderly clients and small businesses.

The active pro bono program provides opportunities for students to represent clients in such areas as domestic violence cases. Students may also serve as mediators in the alternative dispute resolution program of Camden Municipal Court.

The student-directed *Rutgers Law Journal* offers in-depth training in independent research and analysis of current legal problems. One issue of the journal each year is devoted to a symposium on state constitutional law.

The extensive Moot Court Programs provide trial experience before panels of judges and practicing attorneys.

Admission

➥ Baccalaureate degree required for admission ➥ application deadline—March 1 ➥ LSAT, LSDAS required ➥ median GPA—3.30 ➥ median LSAT score—156 ➥ application fee—$40

Entering class size ranges between 200 and 250. Those students who matriculated in fall 1995, under the regular admissions process, had a median LSAT of 157, with a 3.38 undergraduate average. The school also has a special admissions program that applies a greater range of criteria. A few places are available for applicants for advanced standing; transfer students may be admitted at the beginning of either semester only upon completion of one full year of law study.

■ Student Activities

Among the numerous student organizations are the Hispanic Students Association, Asian/Pacific American Law Students Association, Association for Public Interest Law, Black Law Students Association, Christian Legal Society, Community Outreach Group, Environmental Law Students Association, Francis Deak International Law Society, Gay-Bar, Human Rights Group, Italian-American Law Students Organization, Jewish Law Students Association, Law Journal (publishes the *Rutgers Law Journal*), Phi Alpha Delta law fraternity, Pro Bono/Public Interest Steering Committee, and the Women's Law Caucus.

In addition, there are active intramural programs in various sports for men and women. The gymnasium offers recreational swimming, tennis, racquetball, squash, and basketball.

■ Expenses and Financial Aid

➽ full-time tuition & fees—resident, $8,550; nonresident, $12,305 ➽ part-time tuition—resident, $313 per credit; nonresident, $471.25 per credit ➽ student fee—$193.75 per semester ➽ scholarships available ➽ minority scholarships available ➽ financial aid available; FAFSA form due March 1 for full consideration

In the 1994-1995 academic year, over $6.3 million was distributed to students in the law school through fellowships, grants, loans, and employment. The average financial aid package was about $14,500, with 75 percent of all law students receiving some form of assistance. The largest program was the Stafford Loan Program, providing over $7.2 million to some 550 students.

■ Housing

An air-conditioned and carpeted residence hall, with 12 two-bedroom and 50 four-bedroom apartments, opened in 1986. There also are abundant housing opportunities in the nearby suburbs or in Philadelphia, made more convenient by an excellent transportation system. In addition, first-year students are invited to attend a Housing Opportunity Day sponsored by the Student Bar Association.

■ Career Services

The Career Services office has five staff members, as well as computer databases and numerous publications available to assist students in achieving their career goals. Each year, nearly 200 national and regional law firms and agencies interview second- and third-year students for summer and permanent employment through on-campus recruiting programs, job fairs, and a consortium of Delaware Valley law schools. In recent years, over 90 percent of each graduating class has been employed within nine months after commencement. Members of the recent graduating classes have accepted employment in many states—from the East Coast to California and abroad.

Applicant Group for the 1995-1996 Academic Year

Rutgers—The State University—School of Law—Camden
This grid includes only applicants who earned 120-180 LSAT scores under standard administrations.

	GPA																					
LSAT Score	3.75 +		3.50 - 3.74		3.25 - 3.49		3.00 - 3.24		2.75 - 2.99		2.50 - 2.74		2.25 - 2.49		2.00 - 2.24		Below 2.00		No GPA		Total	
	Apps	Adm	Apps	Adm	Apps	Adm	Apps	Adm	Apps	Adm	Apps	Adm	Apps	Adm	Apps	Adm	Apps	Adm	Apps	Adm	Apps	Adm
175 - 180	0	0	0	0	0	0	1	1	0	0	0	0	0	0	0	0	0	0	0	0	1	1
170 - 174	1	1	1	1	1	1	2	2	0	0	0	0	0	0	0	0	0	0	0	0	5	5
165 - 169	9	9	0	0	7	7	4	4	12	11	2	2	2	1	2	2	0	0	0	0	38	36
160 - 164	9	9	27	27	34	34	34	33	27	26	19	13	13	5	4	0	1	1	3	2	171	150
155 - 159	33	33	63	62	101	97	89	74	72	23	44	13	25	6	8	0	2	0	3	2	440	310
150 - 154	28	24	56	47	101	45	120	20	111	18	56	5	36	2	15	1	3	0	10	2	536	164
145 - 149	7	4	45	14	79	14	97	10	100	10	50	4	29	0	12	1	4	0	4	0	427	57
140 - 144	8	2	15	2	41	2	47	0	56	1	53	1	33	0	13	1	2	0	8	2	276	11
135 - 139	0	0	6	1	11	0	21	0	24	0	25	0	17	0	12	0	3	0	6	1	125	2
130 - 134	0	0	0	0	3	0	11	0	11	0	11	0	8	0	2	0	6	0	2	0	54	0
125 - 129	0	0	0	0	0	0	1	0	3	0	0	0	1	0	0	0	0	0	1	0	6	0
120 - 124	0	0	0	0	0	0	0	0	0	0	2	0	0	0	1	0	0	0	0	0	3	0
Total	95	82	213	154	378	200	427	144	416	89	262	38	164	14	69	5	21	1	37	9	2082	736

Apps = Number of Applicants
Adm = Number Admitted
Reflects 99% of the total applicant pool.

Rutgers University School of Law—Newark

S.I. Newhouse Center for Law & Justice
15 Washington Street
Newark, NJ 07102
Phone: 201.648.5557

■ Introduction

The Rutgers School of Law—Newark is the oldest law school in New Jersey. The School of Law is accredited by the American Bar Association and registered by the Board of Regents of New York. It has a chapter of the Order of the Coif.

The School of Law is located on the urban campus of Rutgers University in Newark. The social, cultural, vocational, and educational opportunities of the New York-Newark area combine to provide a fitting location for the study of law.

Qualities that typify the Rutgers School of Law—Newark include its informal atmosphere, its nationally recognized faculty, a comparatively favorable tuition, a public-interest focus, and a very diverse student body. Almost 80 percent of the students are New Jersey residents, but all parts of the country are represented.

■ Enrollment/Student Body

➠ 2,835 applicants ➠ 645 admitted first-year class 1995 ➠ 249 enrolled first-year class 1995 ➠ 549 total full-time ➠ 243 total part-time ➠ 32.2% minority ➠ 44% women ➠ 16 states & foreign countries represented ➠ 140 undergraduate schools represented

New Jersey residents receive no preference except in admission from the waiting list.

■ Faculty

➠ 39 full-time ➠ 45 part-time or adjunct ➠ 11 women ➠ 7 minority ➠ 9 full-time clinical staff

■ Library and Physical Facilities

➠ 404,424 volumes & 140,000 microform equivalents ➠ library hours: Mon.-Fri., 8:00 A.M.-MIDNIGHT; Sat., 9:00 A.M.-MIDNIGHT; Sun., NOON-MIDNIGHT ➠ LEXIS ➠ NEXIS ➠ CALI WESTLAW ➠ DIALOG ➠ 9 full-time librarians ➠ 13 support staff ➠ library seats 394

The Justice Henry Ackerson Library has an extensive collection of primary and secondary legal materials and associated finding tools for the federal law of the United States and the law of all fifty states, international law, and the law of England. The library is a depository for federal and New Jersey government publications. A training program in WESTLAW and LEXIS automated legal research programs is offered to each student as part of the course in Legal Research and Writing I & II. Library includes student computer lab with 22 work stations.

■ Curriculum

➠ Academic Support Program ➠ 84 credits required to graduate ➠ research and teaching assistantships ➠ 120 courses available ➠ degrees available: J.D./M.A., Criminal Justice; J.D./M.C.R.P.; J.D./M.A. Pol. Sci. ➠ semester available in U. of Leiden, Holland ➠ semesters, start in Aug.

Following the required courses, the law school allows the student substantial freedom in the selection of courses and seminars. During the four upper-class terms, approximately 200 class and seminar hours are available to satisfy the 53 credit-hours required.

Second- and third-year clinics include the Urban Legal Clinic, Constitutional Litigation Clinic, Women's Rights Clinic, Environmental Law Clinic, Animal Rights Clinic, Tax Law Clinic, and Special Ed Clinic.

Only limited summer courses are available. The first-year curriculum is prescribed except for one enrichment elective; the second and third years are fully elective.

A part-time program permits students to earn a J.D. degree in the evening over a four or four-and-one-half year period. Evening summer classes are available and are necessary for those students who wish to complete their program in four years. The summer after the first year is required.

The law school permits limited cross-registration with other Rutgers graduate programs, such as business, social work, sociology, economics, and political science. Law students may enroll in certain courses in these graduate schools and receive up to nine credits toward the law degree.

With permission, upper-class students may engage in independent research projects under the supervision of a member of the faculty and may earn credit for work in the chambers of federal and state judges.

■ Admission

➠ B.A. required for admission—in exceptional cases, 3/4 of B.A. acceptable ➠ application deadline—March 1 ➠ LSAT, LSDAS required ➠ median GPA—3.36 ➠ median LSAT score—161 ➠ application fee—$40

While factors other than undergraduate GPAs and LSAT scores are given significant weight in admissions decisions, applicants should be aware that approximately 11 applications are received for each seat. The mean scores of the classes entering in the last five years under the regular admissions program have been around a 3.4 GPA and the 86th percentile LSAT ranges.

There is a Minority Student Admission Program for minority and disadvantaged applicants. Minorities include Black/African, Asian, Hispanic, and Native Americans. Disadvantaged applicants include nonminorities who grew up as members of low-income families with a history of poverty or who can demonstrate that for other reasons they are educationally disadvantaged. The mean scores of persons entering under the Minority Student Program were around the 42nd percentile range (LSAT), and 3.10 (GPA). Inquiries concerning this program should be directed to the Dean of the Minority Student Program.

LSAT scores older than three years from date of application to law school are not accepted. Applications received after March 1 have little prospect of favorable action. Applicants whose files do not contain all required documentation by June 1 will be denied admission. First-year students are accepted for classes commencing in the fall only. Transfer and visiting student applications are also accepted for the spring term, but only students with excellent law school records are accepted at any time.

Personal interviews are not a part of the admissions process, and applicants are requested not to seek them. Periodically during the academic year, the Director of Admissions conducts group meetings to answer questions of general interest and to explain admissions procedures. Any interested person should call the Office of Admissions to make an appointment for one of these meetings.

■ Student Activities

Publications—Students contribute to the *Rutgers Law Review*, the *Rutgers Journal of Computers, Technology and the Law*, and the *Women's Rights Law Reporter*.

Organizations—The variety of student-run organizations reflects the varied professional, political, social, and community interests of the student body. There are approximately 24 such organizations.

■ Expenses and Financial Aid

- *full-time tuition & fees—resident, $8,488; nonresident, $12,243*
- *part-time tuition & fees—resident, $313 per credit hour, plus student fee of $345 per year; nonresident, $471 per credit hour, plus student fee of $345 per year*
- *estimated additional expenses—$15,000-$18,000 (living expenses, books, travel, miscellaneous)*
- *need-based scholarships available*
- *Graduate Law Fellowship (1-year tuition)*
- *merit scholarships*
- *minority scholarships*
- *Clyde Ferguson Scholarship (full tuition)*
- *Ralph Bunche Fellowships (full tuition and stipend)*
- *financial aid available; FAFSA and Rutgers Institutional Form (FA005) due March 1*

The school administers an aid program for students in the school that integrates scholarships, loans, and college work-study into a total program based upon the student's financial needs within the limits of the funds available. In most cases, students are expected to provide for most of their personal living expenses.

■ Housing

An eight-story university apartment complex offers 22 two-bedroom units and 66 four-bedroom units, as well as 10 apartments for married students of the graduate schools of Rutgers University in Newark. Other accommodations are available in the vicinity of the school, as well as in nearby suburban areas and New York City. Public transportation is readily available.

■ Career Services

The Office of Career Services provides information, job hunting, strategy training (including interview workshops and résumé review), and contacts, both direct (through on-campus interviews, résumé collection and job postings), and indirect (through lists, directories and alumnae/i records).

In the past several years, over 85 percent of the graduates seeking law placement have obtained law-related jobs within six months of graduation.

Applicant Group for the 1995-1996 Academic Year

Rutgers University School of Law—Newark
This grid includes only applicants who earned 120-180 LSAT scores under standard administrations.

	GPA																					
LSAT Score	3.75 +		3.50 - 3.74		3.25 - 3.49		3.00 - 3.24		2.75 - 2.99		2.50 - 2.74		2.25 - 2.49		2.00 - 2.24		Below 2.00		No GPA		Total	
	Apps	Adm	Apps	Adm	Apps	Adm	Apps	Adm	Apps	Adm	Apps	Adm	Apps	Adm	Apps	Adm	Apps	Adm	Apps	Adm	Apps	Adm
175 - 180	0	0	2	2	1	1	1	1	1	1	0	0	1	1	0	0	0	0	0	0	6	6
170 - 174	0	0	0	0	0	0	4	4	3	3	1	1	1	1	1	1	0	0	0	0	10	10
165 - 169	15	15	14	13	26	26	17	16	16	14	7	7	2	2	3	2	0	0	1	1	101	96
160 - 164	26	24	44	42	69	63	51	43	30	22	38	23	9	1	2	0	1	1	6	4	276	223
155 - 159	50	40	94	44	114	34	91	18	74	9	35	9	12	0	6	0	3	0	5	0	484	154
150 - 154	29	8	80	16	120	15	120	15	109	16	55	4	20	2	15	1	2	0	16	2	566	79
145 - 149	15	1	54	11	76	9	98	15	103	7	69	6	28	1	21	0	5	0	6	1	475	51
140 - 144	13	0	26	3	53	2	72	1	80	5	77	3	46	1	19	1	9	0	11	0	406	16
135 - 139	5	0	13	1	16	0	39	0	39	0	51	0	39	0	24	1	2	0	10	0	238	2
130 - 134	1	0	2	0	8	0	13	0	18	1	16	0	13	0	13	0	6	0	5	0	95	1
125 - 129	0	0	0	0	2	0	1	0	1	0	4	0	3	0	1	0	3	0	5	0	20	0
120 - 124	0	0	0	0	0	0	0	0	0	0	1	0	3	0	0	0	0	0	2	0	6	0
Total	154	88	329	132	485	150	507	113	474	78	354	53	177	9	105	6	31	1	67	8	2683	638

Apps = Number of Applicants
Adm = Number Admitted
Reflects 99% of the total applicant pool.

St. John's University School of Law

8000 Utopia Parkway
Jamaica, NY 11439

Phone: 718.990.6611

■ Introduction

St. John's University School of Law is a forceful presence and an integral part of the New York metropolitan area. It imparts to its students training and competency in the basic skills and techniques of the legal profession, a grasp of the history and the system of common law, and a familiarity with important statutes and decisions in federal and state jurisdictions, including the state of New York.

The recently-completed expansion of the law school produced a state-of-the-art facility with a gross total square footage of 179,400, one of the highest space per student ratios in the country. Some highlights of the new addition include expanded facilities for student activities, new alumni function areas, a student lounge, faculty offices, and classrooms for teaching clinical and lawyering skills.

The School of Law is located on the Queens Campus of St. John's University. Situated on almost 100 rolling acres in a residential area of New York City, the campus boasts a spectacular view of the Manhattan skyline. St. John's School of Law is approved by the ABA and is a member of the AALS.

■ Enrollment/Student Body

➧ 2,974 applicants ➧ 1,027 admitted first-year class 1995 ➧ 262 enrolled first-year class 1995 ➧ 827 total full-time ➧ 291 total part-time ➧ 25% minority ➧ 38% women ➧ 112 undergraduate schools represented in 1995 entering class

■ Faculty

➧ 79 total ➧ 59 full-time ➧ 20 part-time or adjunct ➧ 16 full-time women ➧ 10 full-time minority

■ Library and Physical Facilities

➧ 440,000 volumes and equivalents ➧ library hours: Mon.,-Fri., 8:30 A.M.-MIDNIGHT; Sat.,-Sun., 10:00 A.M.-MIDNIGHT ➧ LEXIS ➧ NEXIS ➧ WESTLAW ➧ DIALOG ➧ 8 full-time librarians ➧ library seats 607

The showpiece of the law school building is its beautiful new library which incorporates the most recent advances in law library science and technology. It contains a 22-terminal computer classroom, a 30-terminal computer laboratory, and eight study rooms for student conferences. The library occupies approximately 60,000-square feet on five of the seven building levels. It has been designated a depository library for U.S. government documents.

■ Curriculum

➧ Academic Support Program ➧ 85 credits required to graduate ➧ 123 courses available ➧ degrees available: J.D.; B.A./B.S. & J.D.; J.D./M.A. Gov't & Politics; M.B.A./J.D. ➧ semesters, start in Aug. & Jan.

■ Special Programs

An elective clinical program is available to second- and third-year full-time students.

In the Civil Clinical Seminar, students work 12 hours per week in (1) a legal services office assisting lawyers who provide legal representation to the poor in a variety of civil matters; or (2) a public service or governmental agency such as the United States Attorney's Office, the Securities and Exchange Commission, and the New York Legal Aid Society.

In the Criminal Clinical Seminar, students work 12 hours per week in a District Attorney's office, a Legal Aid office, or in the law department of the Supreme Court or Criminal Court.

In the Judicial Clinical Seminar, students work 12 hours per week in the federal, state, or city court system.

The Estate Administration Clinical Component is offered in conjunction with the elective Estate Administration. Participants assist the Surrogate in nearby counties and receive practical insight into the functioning of the Surrogate's Court, which is responsible for the judicial administering of decedent's estates.

■ Elder Law Clinic

This in-school, live client clinic allows students to represent actual clients in real cases under the close supervision of a faculty member. Students interview clients, draft pleadings and litigation papers, perform legal research, participate in discovery proceedings, prepare for trial, engage in settlement negotiations and try cases, while honing skills such as decision-making and office management. The three-credit per semester clinic is open to second- and third-year students who must enroll for a full academic year and devote a minimum of 15 hours per week.

■ Special Diversity Admissions Program

The law school sponsors a special educational program for individuals who have suffered the effects of discrimination, chronic financial hardship, and/or other social, educational, or physical disadvantages to such an extent that their undergraduate performance or LSAT score would not otherwise warrant unconditional acceptance into the entering class. This program, which is available at no charge to the participants, consists of a substantial course taught and graded according to the same qualitative standard applied to all first-year courses, as well as a legal writing course. The program enables individuals whose LSAT score and/or grade-point average are not reliable predictors of their success to demonstrate that they have the ability to succeed in the study of law.

■ Admission Standards

➧ Bachelor's degree required ➧ application deadline—March 1 & Nov. 1 ➧ LSAT, LSDAS required

➻ *median GPA—3.00* ➻ *median LSAT score—156*
➻ *application fee—$50*

■ Student Activities

Publications—*St. John's Law Review, The Catholic Lawyer, Journal of Legal Commentary, International Law Review of the New York State Bar Association, American Bankruptcy Institute Law Review.*

Mock Trial and Appellate Activities—Moot Court, Criminal Law Institute, Civil Trial Institute.

Specialized Legal Activities—The Student Bar Association, Admiralty Law Society, Women's Law Association, Bankruptcy Law Society, Environmental Law Club, Entertainment and Sports Club, International Law Society, Intellectual Property, Labor and Employment Club, Real Property Club, and Client Counseling Competition. The School also maintains chapters in two legal societies, Phi Delta Phi and Phi Alpha Delta and the Black, Asian, and Latino Law Students Association.

■ Expenses and Financial Aid

➻ *tuition & fees—full-time, $19,000; part-time, $14,250* ➻ *scholarships available: St. Thomas More, University Scholarships and Law School Scholarships* ➻ *diversity minority scholarships available* ➻ *financial aid available; FAFSA by April 1*

Although there are no dormitory facilities at St. John's, many students find suitable living accommodations in the vicinity of the university. A housing service for all St. John's students is provided by the university's Office of Student Life. In addition, the law school Admissions Office coordinates a housing network for law school students. Students with housing needs are invited to contact the housing network coordinator in the law school Admissions Office for assistance and information. Average housing costs run approximately $500 per month.

■ Career Services

Career Services provides an array of services to students and alumni, including résumé and cover letter critiquing, mock interview coaching, career and job opening newsletters, lists of prospective employers, interview programs, and career education panels. Recent graduates have obtained employment in many areas of the legal profession, including the largest New York law firms and smaller firms throughout the metropolitan area and elsewhere, corporations, and government agencies and other public service employers. Annually, 5-8 percent accept federal and state judicial clerkships.

Alumni of the School of Law are currently practicing throughout the United States and its territories. Many have achieved positions of prominence in executive and legislative branches of the government, as members of the judiciary, and in both private and corporate practice. The governors of New York and the U.S. Virgin Islands, a former governor of California, and the U.S. Secretary of Commerce are graduates of St. John's.

Applicant Group for the 1995-1996 Academic Year

St. John's University School of Law
This grid includes only applicants who earned 120-180 LSAT scores under standard administrations.

	GPA																				
LSAT Score	3.75 +		3.50 - 3.74		3.25 - 3.49		3.00 - 3.24		2.75 - 2.99		2.50 - 2.74		2.25 - 2.49		2.00 - 2.24		Below 2.00		No GPA		Total	
	Apps	Adm	Apps	Adm	Apps	Adm	Apps	Adm	Apps	Adm	Apps	Adm	Apps	Adm	Apps	Adm	Apps	Adm	Apps	Adm	Apps	Adm
175 - 180	0	0	0	0	0	0	1	1	0	0	0	0	0	0	0	0	0	0	0	0	1	1
170 - 174	1	1	0	0	3	3	2	2	3	3	0	0	1	1	1	1	0	0	0	0	11	11
165 - 169	6	6	6	6	9	8	11	11	7	6	11	11	3	3	4	4	0	0	1	1	58	56
160 - 164	13	12	29	29	33	33	50	50	50	50	30	30	11	11	5	5	1	0	1	1	223	221
155 - 159	32	26	81	63	108	91	129	102	107	87	63	48	16	10	8	2	3	2	2	2	549	433
150 - 154	31	10	101	23	174	42	194	51	163	43	107	34	52	9	21	7	3	0	18	5	864	224
149 - 120	33	2	102	3	204	8	297	11	323	13	232	5	180	3	74	1	22	1	48	2	1515	49
Total	116	57	319	124	531	185	684	228	653	202	443	128	263	37	113	20	29	3	70	11	3221	995

Apps = Number of Applicants
Adm = Number Admitted
Reflects 97% of the total applicant pool.

Saint Louis University School of Law

3700 Lindell Blvd.
St. Louis, MO 63108

URL: http://lawlib.slu.edu/home.htm
Phone: 314.977.2800

■ Introduction

At Saint Louis University School of Law, you will find a unique character and atmosphere that are the result of a number of factors, including Jesuit institutional traditions and goals, the law faculty and students, and the quality of life in a thriving midwestern city. The School of Law is known for its open and friendly atmosphere, for the rapport among students and between students and faculty, and for its inviting physical plant. It is located on the main campus of Saint Louis University in midtown. The campus is just a block from the Fox Theatre and Powell Symphony Hall, just minutes from St. Louis Union Station, the Arch, the riverfront, and downtown. There is a wide choice of affordable rental housing for students in the neighborhoods around the university. St. Louis offers the amenities of urban living without the inconveniences and high costs normally associated with living in a major metropolitan area.

■ Enrollment/Student Body

➽ *1,361 applicants* ➽ *608 admitted first-year class 1995* ➽ *268 enrolled first-year class 1995* ➽ *561 total full-time* ➽ *282 total part-time* ➽ *18.2% minority first-year class 1995* ➽ *42% women* ➽ *43 states & foreign countries represented* ➽ *125 undergraduate schools represented*

■ Faculty

➽ *59 total* ➽ *44 full-time* ➽ *15 part-time or adjunct* ➽ *11 women* ➽ *3 minority*

The offices of individual faculty members are located in the law library, and all classrooms, administrative offices, and clinical facilities are housed within this same building complex for convenience and collegiality.

■ Library and Physical Facilities

➽ *450,000 volumes & equivalents* ➽ *library hours: Mon.-Thurs., 9:00 A.M.-MIDNIGHT; Fri., 8:00 A.M.-11:00 P.M.; Sat., 9:00 A.M.-8:00 P.M.; Sun., 10:00 A.M.-MIDNIGHT* ➽ *LEXIS* ➽ *NEXIS* ➽ *WESTLAW* ➽ *DIALOG* ➽ *9 full-time librarians* ➽ *library seats 437*

■ Curriculum

➽ *Academic Support Program* ➽ *88 credits required to graduate* ➽ *100+ courses available* ➽ *degrees available: J.D.; J.D./M.B.A.; J.D./M.H.A.; J.D./M.U.A.; J.D./M.S.W.; others as requested* ➽ *semesters, start in Aug.* ➽ *range of first-year class size—30-90*

A cumulative grade-point average (GPA) of 2.0 is required to earn the J.D. degree. The part-time program of legal education involves the same degree of academic quality and rigor, and the same admissions standards in evaluating applicants, as the full-time program. The same faculty members are involved in teaching both the full- and part-time programs.

The school has gained national recognition in the areas of health law, lawyering skills, employment law, and international law.

■ Special Programs

The Center for Health Law Studies—The Center's faculty work closely with Saint Louis University's School of Medicine, School of Nursing, School of Allied Health Professions, Graduate Department of Hospital and Health Care Administration, and the Medical Center.

The school's health law program is unique in that there are eight full-time faculty members teaching in the health law area. Its endowed library collection in health law provides an outstanding research facility. Many special programs are offered throughout the year to bring students information about the many opportunities in health law. Saint Louis University health law alumni are particularly helpful in this area.

The Center for International and Comparative Law—The strength of the international law program at Saint Louis University School of Law is a result of the combination of curricular and extracurricular offerings, permanent and visiting faculty, and a strong library collection.

The school also has developed cooperative agreements with Sichuan University in Chengdu, People's Republic of China, and the University of Warsaw.

To complement the course offerings in international law, the school has a number of special study opportunities in European countries. Through the Brussels Seminar and the Ruhr University Exchange Program, the school offers its qualified students four to five weeks of high quality instruction in Europe, at no charge for tuition and accommodations.

The Center for Employment Law—The center offers interested students an opportunity to specialize in the subject of the employment relationship as a unifying thread for their study of law.

■ Admission

➽ *Bachelor's degree required* ➽ *preferential application deadline—March 1* ➽ *LSAT, LSDAS required* ➽ *median GPA—3.23* ➽ *median LSAT score—155* ➽ *application fee—$40*

Factors considered by the committee in addition to the GPA and LSAT score are strength of the undergraduate program, work experience, any extraordinary circumstances that may have affected a student's performance in college, and motivation.

There are 175 spaces available for full-time students and 75 spaces available for part-time students in the fall entering class.

The admissions committee is composed of the Assistant Dean for Admissions, four faculty members, and three law students. The committee uses an admission index in preliminary evaluations of applicants. With the exception of those applications whose index falls in a clearly defined upper or lower percentile and whose application is reviewed by the Assistant Dean and the faculty committee chair, the committee reviews the entire application of each applicant. No action is taken without the consensus of the committee.

The School of Law is committed to increasing the number of minorities in the legal profession. Accordingly, the School of Law actively seeks applications from qualified minorities.

A special admissions program is conducted each summer at the School of Law. The Summer Institute is designed to identify students who have suffered the effects of cultural or racial discrimination, cultural deprivation, or economic or other disadvantages to such an extent that their undergraduate work or performance on standardized tests is affected.

■ Student Activities

Student organizations play a vital role in meeting the many special interests of the student body. Programs and publications sponsored by these organizations add considerable depth to the overall program.

■ Expenses and Financial Aid

- *tuition & fees—full-time, $16,000; part-time, $11,950/$735*
- *estimated additional expenses—$7,500 (includes room & board)*
- *academic merit scholarships available*
- *minority scholarships available: merit & need-based*
- *financial aid available; FAFSA required*

The majority of law students receive some form of financial assistance. Most awards are need-based, with the exception of the academic scholarships and grants administered directly by the School of Law.

■ Career Services

The Career Planning and Placement Office is designed to assist students, alumni, and employers. Students and alumni are welcome to utilize the services of the office throughout their academic and legal careers. These services include career counseling, assistance in developing résumés and letters, access to job postings, an alumni job bulletin, assistance in the job search in other geographic areas, and on-campus interviews for current students. The office houses a career library which has information on a wide range of employers and career choices, including government job bulletins, books and brochures on a variety of practice areas and placement bulletins from law schools throughout the United States. The office lists positions for student clerks, summer positions, full-time positions for recent graduates, and positions for attorneys with experience. In order to assist students in finding additional information about employers, the LEXIS, NEXIS, and WESTLAW computer research services are also available in the Career Library.

The distribution of graduates by types of employment is comparable to that of many law schools. Approximately 70 percent of the graduates enter private practice. Within six months of graduation, 95 percent of the class is employed, with salaries ranging from $20,000 to $70,000. Although there are alumni practicing in all 50 states and several foreign countries, the majority are practicing in the midwest region, especially in the states of Illinois and Missouri.

Applicant Group for the 1995-1996 Academic Year

Saint Louis University School of Law

LSAT Score	GPA						
	3.75 +	3.50 - 3.74	3.25 - 3.49	3.00 - 3.24	2.75 - 2.99	2.50 - 2.74	Below 2.50
175 - 180	Likely	Likely	Likely	Likely	Likely	Likely	Likely
170 - 174	Likely	Likely	Likely	Likely	Likely	Likely	Likely
165 - 169	Likely	Likely	Likely	Likely	Likely	Likely	Likely
160 - 164	Likely	Likely	Likely	Likely	Possible	Possible	Possible
155 - 159	Likely	Likely	Possible	Possible	Possible	Possible	Possible
150 - 154	Possible	Possible	Possible	Possible	Possible	Unlikely	Unlikely
145 - 149	Possible	Possible	Possible	Unlikely	Unlikely	Unlikely	Unlikely
140 - 144	Possible	Unlikely	Unlikely	Unlikely	Unlikely	Unlikely	Unlikely
135 - 139	Unlikely	Unlikely	Unlikely	Unlikely	Unlikely	Unlikely	Unlikely
130 - 134	Unlikely	Unlikely	Unlikely	Unlikely	Unlikely	Unlikely	Unlikely
125 - 129	Unlikely	Unlikely	Unlikely	Unlikely	Unlikely	Unlikely	Unlikely
120 - 124	Unlikely	Unlikely	Unlikely	Unlikely	Unlikely	Unlikely	Unlikely

Likely / Possible / Unlikely

St. Mary's University School of Law

One Camino Santa Maria
San Antonio, TX 78228-8601
Phone: 210.436.3523

■ Introduction

St. Mary's University School of Law, founded in San Antonio, Texas in 1927, is maintaining its strength as an institution that offers a solid curriculum of traditional legal studies and teaches its students the practical skills and habits of mind that enable them to become effective advocates. As part of a Catholic institution founded by the Society of Mary (Marianists), the mission of the law school is to give its students the knowledge and attributes of mind and character essential to the effective rendition of public service, while developing new methodologies to prepare students for the practice of law in a changing world.

■ Enrollment/Student Body

➽ 1,927 applicants ➽ 833 admitted first-year class 1995 ➽ 270 enrolled first-year class 1995 ➽ 770 total full-time ➽ 33% minority ➽ 47% women ➽ 25 states & foreign countries represented ➽ 101 undergraduate schools represented

■ Faculty

➽ 82 total ➽ 33 full-time ➽ 49 part-time or adjunct ➽ 25 women ➽ 14 minority

■ Library and Physical Facilities

➽ 267,600 volumes & equivalents ➽ library hours: Mon.-Thurs., 7:00 A.M.-MIDNIGHT; Fri., 7:00 A.M.-10:00 P.M.; Sat., 9:00 A.M.-10:00 P.M.; Sun., 10:00 A.M.-MIDNIGHT ➽ LEXIS ➽ NEXIS ➽ WESTLAW ➽ DIALOG ➽ 8 full-time librarians ➽ library seats 446

The Sarita Kennedy East Law Library is a modern, recently constructed, award-winning building. The collection includes legal documents from the United Nations that provide access to American, British, Canadian, and International law.

■ Curriculum

➽ Academic Support Program ➽ 90 credits required to graduate ➽ 145 courses available ➽ degrees available: J.D.; J.D./M.B.A.; J.D./M.P.A.; J.D./EC.; J.D./IR.; J.D./TH.; J.D./ Engineering ➽ semesters, start in Aug. ➽ range of first-year class size—85

Required first-year courses are Constitutional Law, Contracts, Criminal Law, Legal Research and Writing, Procedure I, Property, and Torts. In addition to other electives, all students must take the following required courses: Professional Responsibility; Evidence; Texas Civil Procedure; and one course chosen from Jurisprudence, American Legal History, Legal Philosophy, or Law and Economics, and complete one research paper. Texas Civil Procedure is only required of those planning to take the Texas bar examination.

■ Clinical Legal Education

The Civil Justice Clinic introduces students to the skills and responsibilities of lawyering through supervised representation of low-income, including homeless, clients in four areas of civil law cases: family law, public benefits, landlord-tenant disputes, and wills and probate.

The Criminal Justice Clinic provides legal services to indigents of all ages who are charged with crimes ranging from misdemeanors to capital offenses.

The Immigration and Human Rights Clinic engages students in the representation of indigent foreign nationals in a variety of immigration cases, and in the advocacy of human rights.

The Community Development Clinic involves students in capacity-building economic development activities in San Antonio and the *colonias* of South Texas.

■ International Law

The St. Mary's Institute on World Legal Problems is conducted at the University of Innsbruck in Austria during July and August. The program is designed to provide law students with a broader understanding of global issues and the role that law can play in their peaceful resolution.

Other international programs include: Centre for Conciliation and Arbitration; Institute on International Human Rights; *Abogados de las Américas;* Center for International Legal Studies; Inter-American Legal Studies Program; and two LL.M. programs: international and comparative law and American legal studies for foreign students are scheduled to begin in fall of 1996.

Visiting lecturers have included the Hon. William H. Rehnquist, Chief Justice of the United States, during the 1991 and 1994 Institutes, and the Hon. Ruth Bader Ginsburg, Distinguished Visiting Lecturer, (1995).

■ Judicial Internships

St. Mary's students are eligible to apply for an internship with the Supreme Court of Texas, where they work under the supervision of a justice, preparing memoranda and making oral presentations in conferences with the Court. Similar programs exist with the Texas Court of Criminal Appeals and with the Texas Court of Appeals, both located in Austin, Texas.

■ Center for International Legal Studies

The Center for International Legal Studies was established as part of the law school's strategic plan for the development of a strong concentration in international and comparative law, particularly the law of the Americas. The center's Foreign Visiting Scholars program has attracted legal scholars from several other nations, including Nigeria, Russia, and Mexico.

■ Admission Standards

➽ *Bachelor's degree required* ➽ *application deadline—March 1* ➽ *LSAT, LSDAS required* ➽ *median GPA—3.00* ➽ *median LSAT score—154* ➽ *application fee—$45*

St. Mary's goal is to create an intellectually stimulating student body comprised of persons with diverse backgrounds who share a desire for academic excellence and accomplishment in the practice of law. In addition to academic ability, we seek evidence of qualities such as leadership ability, maturity, community organization skills, knowledge of other languages and cultures, a history of overcoming disadvantage, public interest accomplishments, or success in a previous career. Participants in the CLEO program are especially encouraged to apply. A faculty committee reviews all applications. No one is automatically rejected. All files are read.

■ Student Activities

Student organizations include the American Civil Liberties Union; Asian-Pacific American Law Student Association; Black Allied Law Students Association; Board of Advocates; Christian Legal Society; Criminal Law Association; Delta Alpha Delta; Delta Theta Phi; Environmental Law Society; Family Law Association; Federalist Society; Harlan Society; Hispanic Law Students Association; International Law Association; Jewish Law Students Association; Law Student Division, San Antonio Bar Association; Phi Alpha Delta; Phi Delta Phi; Public Interest Law Association; Republican Law Students Association; Society of Legal Entrepreneurs; Sports and Entertainment and Arts Law; *St. Mary's Law Journal*; St. Thomas More Society; Student Aggie Bar Association; Student Bar Association; William Sessions American Inn of Court; Women's Law Association; Legal Education Association for Gay & Lesbian Issues.

■ Expenses and Financial Aid

➽ *tuition & fees—$470/credit hr.* ➽ *student service fee—$70* ➽ *University Center fee—$20* ➽ *parking fee—$30* ➽ *performance and need-based scholarships available* ➽ *donated funds may be earmarked for minority scholarships* ➽ *financial aid available; financial aid forms must be filed with the University Office of Financial Assistance between Jan. 1 and April 1 of the year for which student is enrolling*

■ Career Services

The Office of Career Services is under the direction of an associate dean with 10 years of recruiting experience on a hiring committee in a major law firm. The mission of the office is to provide personal, individualized assistance to all students as they seek employment during and after law school. Confidential strategy sessions provide a unique opportunity for students to develop a personal plan to assess and meet their career goals. The office publishes a weekly job newsletter for students, and a monthly job newsletter for graduates. The office's Student Résumé Center offers an extensive and up-to-date library of career resources and directories of attorneys, as well as computer terminals with employer databases to help students direct and begin their careers in legal and nontraditional positions. A diverse and active alumni association offers mentors and career programs throughout the year.

Ninety-two percent of the class of 1994 reported employment within six months following graduation, a figure slightly better than national statistics.

Applicant Group for the 1995-1996 Academic Year

St. Mary's University School of Law
This grid includes only applicants who earned 120-180 LSAT scores under standard administrations.

LSAT Score	GPA 3.75 +		3.50 - 3.74		3.25 - 3.49		3.00 - 3.24		2.75 - 2.99		2.50 - 2.74		2.25 - 2.49		2.00 - 2.24		Below 2.00		No GPA		Total	
	Apps	Adm	Apps	Adm	Apps	Adm	Apps	Adm	Apps	Adm	Apps	Adm	Apps	Adm	Apps	Adm	Apps	Adm	Apps	Adm	Apps	Adm
175 - 180	0	0	0	0	0	0	0	0	0	0	0	0	0	0	0	0	0	0	0	0	0	0
170 - 174	0	0	0	0	1	1	0	0	0	0	0	0	0	0	0	0	0	0	0	0	1	1
165 - 169	0	0	0	0	3	3	6	6	1	1	1	1	3	3	0	0	1	0	0	0	15	14
160 - 164	6	6	10	10	11	11	13	13	17	17	7	7	10	9	2	1	1	1	0	0	77	75
155 - 159	11	11	19	19	45	43	59	58	58	53	38	30	28	16	10	3	0	0	1	0	269	233
150 - 154	12	12	42	35	63	57	97	80	107	65	99	55	49	18	12	0	5	1	3	1	489	324
145 - 149	9	9	29	16	73	34	104	40	98	28	93	22	55	8	28	4	4	0	6	1	499	162
140 - 144	4	2	7	0	38	1	45	3	59	4	66	1	44	0	26	2	7	0	2	0	298	13
135 - 139	1	0	3	0	13	0	22	0	33	0	42	1	39	0	14	0	13	1	4	0	184	2
130 - 134	0	0	0	0	4	0	1	0	7	0	14	0	8	0	9	0	5	0	3	0	51	0
125 - 129	0	0	0	0	0	0	1	0	1	0	2	0	5	0	1	0	2	0	0	0	12	0
120 - 124	0	0	0	0	0	0	1	0	1	0	0	0	0	0	0	0	0	0	0	0	2	0
Total	43	40	110	80	251	150	349	200	382	168	362	117	241	54	102	10	38	3	19	2	1897	824

Apps = Number of Applicants (Reflects 98% of the total applicant pool.)
Adm = Number Admitted

St. Thomas University School of Law

16400 NW 32 Avenue
Miami, FL 33054

Phone: 305.623.2310

■ Introduction

St. Thomas University School of Law, one of the newest and most technologically-oriented law schools in the country, was granted full approval by the American Bar Association in 1995. The only Catholic law school in the Southeastern United States, St. Thomas emphasizes professional ethics throughout its programs, provides intensive academic support on an individual and small-group basis, and offers a broad curriculum, including an array of clinical experiences.

St. Thomas University is located on a 140-acre campus in northwest suburban Miami. Fifteen miles southeast in downtown Miami stands the new federal courthouse, the location of the United States District Court for the Southern District of Florida. State trial and appellate courts are several blocks away. Approximately 20 miles to the north of the law school is the city of Ft. Lauderdale, another venue for state trial and appellate courts.

■ Enrollment/Student Body

➡ *1,736 applicants* ➡ *740 admitted first-year class 1995* ➡ *201 enrolled first-year class 1995* ➡ *521 total full-time* ➡ *33% minority* ➡ *37% women* ➡ *24 states & foreign countries represented* ➡ *105 undergraduate schools represented*

■ Faculty

➡ *61 total* ➡ *34 full-time* ➡ *27 part-time or adjunct* ➡ *23 women* ➡ *12 minority*

■ Library and Physical Facilities

➡ *233,834 volumes & equivalents* ➡ *library hours: Mon.-Thurs., 8:00 A.M.-MIDNIGHT; Fri., 8:00 A.M.-10:00 P.M.; Sat., 9:00 A.M.-10:00 P.M.; Sun., 9:00 A.M.-MIDNIGHT*
➡ *LEXIS* ➡ *NEXIS* ➡ *WESTLAW* ➡ *DIALOG*
➡ *7 full-time librarians, 9 full-time support staff*
➡ *library seats 300—study rooms available*
➡ *computer lab and other locations with 65+ PCs & printers*

Students are provided with unlimited opportunities to use online full-text computer-assisted legal retrieval systems. Personal computers are available for student use and the library has over 200 software packages, including word processing, database management, and spreadsheet programs.

■ Curriculum

➡ *Academic Support Program* ➡ *90 credits required to graduate* ➡ *over 100 courses available*
➡ *J.D. degree available* ➡ *semesters, start in Aug.*

The curriculum of the School of Law covers a period of three academic years. The first-year curriculum is fully prescribed, while the second-year curriculum is partially prescribed, with third-year courses being electives.

■ Clinical Legal Education Programs

St. Thomas University School of Law has three clinical legal education programs—the Field Placement Clinic, the Immigration Clinic, and the Appellate Litigation Clinic. Each clinic is a year-long program for which third-year students receive eight hours of credits. The classroom component for each clinic is two hours per week.

The Field Placement Clinic involves 20 students working as interns in public defender, states attorneys, city and county attorneys, and Legal Services offices. Supervising attorneys are assigned by the offices involved and general supervision, including a classroom component, is provided by a full-time, tenure-track professor. Many students in this clinic try cases or participate in trials conducted by the supervising attorneys.

In the **Immigration Clinic**, third-year law students, under the supervision of an experienced faculty member, represent indigent immigrants detained at a nearby federal facility in deportation and exclusion hearings and other immigration matters before immigration judges. Immigration Clinic is a year-long course.

In the **Appellate Litigation Clinic**, which also has offices at the law school, students represent indigents in appellate cases before courts of appeals under the supervision of a tenure-track faculty member. The students brief and argue the cases on appeal.

In the **Peter T. Fay American Inn of Court at St. Thomas**, the first of its kind in South Florida, students are able to interact professionally with distinguished members of the local bench and bar.

Street Law is a two-hour-per-week course in which law students teach local high school students in areas of the law of practical importance in the daily lives of community members. Selected topics include consumer, housing, and constitutional law, as well as criminal law and procedure.

The **St. Thomas Public Service Fellowship Program**, sponsored by the Florida Bar Foundation Interest on Trust Accounts program, places selected law students in various public service agencies where they provide legal assistance to indigents under the supervision and direction of attorneys working in the agencies involved. The fellows are paid for their work and receive no course credit.

Legal Assistance Wednesday, L.A.W., is a pro bono program sponsored by St. Thomas University School of Law and Greater Bethel A.M.E. Church, with additional support from the Florida Bar Foundation. Every Wednesday, students and attorneys volunteer their time to provide legal assistance and representation to the poor.

■ Admission

➡ *Bachelor's degree required* ➡ *application deadline—April 30, early application preferred*
➡ *LSAT, LSDAS required* ➡ *median GPA—2.86*
➡ *median LSAT score—151* ➡ *application fee—$40*

Applicants must possess a bachelor's degree from a regionally accredited college or university. While no particular program of prelaw study is required, the undergraduate transcript should reflect a strong aptitude for study in a challenging academic field. The School of Law does not discriminate on the basis of sex, age, race, color, disability, religion, or national origin in its educational programs, admission policies, employment policies, financial aid, or other school-administered programs. The School of Law is committed to a policy of enhancing the diversity of its student body and encouraging applications for admission from members of all minority groups.

In determining which applicants will be accepted for admission, the Admissions Committee will look for both demonstrated academic ability and diversity of background. Consideration will be given to a variety of factors beyond the Law School Admission Test score and the undergraduate grade-point average. Those factors include work experience, honors or awards, extracurricular activities, strong letters of recommendation from instructors or others familiar with the applicant's academic abilities, and ethnic diversity.

■ Student Activities

The *St. Thomas Law Review* is a scholarly journal edited and managed by students of the School of Law. The *St. Thomas Law Review* publishes articles submitted by students, faculty, and members of the Bench and Bar. Membership is based on superior academic credentials and writing abilities.

The Student Bar Association is active in matters concerning law students and in selecting representative student members to serve on faculty committees. Numerous student organizations are active on campus, and students publish the newspaper, *Opinio Juris*.

■ Expenses and Financial Aid

➧ *full-time tuition & fees—$16,930* ➧ *estimated additional expenses—$13,800 (books & supplies, $1,400; room & board, $7,200; transportation, $2,200; personal expenses, $3,000)* ➧ *scholarships available* ➧ *minority scholarships available (diversity, among other criteria, determines eligibility)* ➧ *financial aid available; FAFSA due March 1 (priority)*

The awarding of financial aid is administered by the University Financial Aid Office. Inquiries regarding financial aid programs should be directed to the University Financial Aid Office, St. Thomas University, 16400 N.W. 32nd Avenue, Miami, FL 33054, or call 305.628.6547.

■ Career Services

The Career Services Office is dedicated to assisting law students in articulating, developing, and eventually attaining their professional goals. It offers a range of traditional and innovative services and programs to facilitate the career planning efforts of our students and to maximize their potential for employment.

Career and personal development workshops are scheduled regularly and the office maintains a Career Services Library for students' use. Employers from the legal, government, and corporate sectors are invited on campus during the fall semester to conduct a recruitment interview with students. Contact the Assistant Dean for Career Services for more information, 305.623.2351.

Admission Profile Not Available

University of San Diego School of Law

5998 Alcala Park
San Diego, CA 92110-2492

E-Mail: jdinfo@acusd.edu
URL: http://acusd.edu/~usdlaw
Phone: 619.260.4528

Introduction

Only 40 years old, USD School of Law is already recognized as a leading center of legal education. Set in a landmark location overlooking San Diego's spectacular shoreline, the School of Law fosters a climate of stimulating and rigorous intellectual exchange between professors and students. The university and the San Diego community offer a wealth of cultural, social, and athletic activities. The graceful Spanish Renaissance architecture and year-round mild weather make this an attractive place to live and study. Centrally located to downtown San Diego, the School of Law has strong ties in the Southern California legal community—one in four lawyers practicing in the San Diego area is a USD graduate. The curriculum and student experience is enhanced by eminent visitors, specialized clinical programs, and research institutes. As part of a private, values-based university, the educational environment supports the broader personal and ethical development of students and concern for issues of social justice. USD School of Law is accredited by the ABA and a member of the AALS.

Enrollment/Student Body

➻ *3,320 applicants* ➻ *330 enrolled first-year class 1995* ➻ *763 total full-time* ➻ *347 total part-time* ➻ *21% minority first-year; 19.5% minority all years* ➻ *43% women* ➻ *30 states & foreign countries represented first-year class 1995* ➻ *116 undergraduate schools represented first-year class 1995* ➻ *age range first-year class 1995—20-51*

Faculty

➻ *60 full-time* ➻ *40 part-time or adjunct* ➻ *35 women* ➻ *12 minority*

The School of Law offers a large faculty with experts in virtually every major field of law. They bring diverse personal, professional, and academic backgrounds, including judicial clerks, practitioners from the private and public sector, and sitting and former judges. The faculty includes authors of leading casebooks and treatises, scholarly monographs published by the finest university presses, and influential articles in the nation's leading law reviews.

Library and Physical Facilities

➻ *over 375,000 volumes & equivalents* ➻ *library hours: Sun.-Thurs., 8:00 A.M.-MIDNIGHT; Fri.-Sat., 8:00 A.M.-10:00 P.M.* ➻ *CALI (Computer Assisted Legal Instruction)* ➻ *10 librarians* ➻ *library seats 600*

Newly opened in 1990, the Pardee Legal Research Center was custom designed for law student use and provides state-of-the-art technology and services. It is regarded as one of the top 20 academic law libraries in the country. The collection is expanding in international law and business.

Curriculum

➻ *Academic Support Program* ➻ *85 credits required to graduate* ➻ *over 150 total courses available* ➻ *semesters, start in Aug.* ➻ *degrees available: J.D.; J.D./M.B.A.; J.D./M.I.B.; J.D./M.A.; LL.M. in Comparative Law for Foreign Lawyers; LL.M. General, Tax and International Law* ➻ *range of first-year class size—20-85*

Students in the day division normally require six semesters to complete the J.D., while evening-division students normally complete it in eight semesters plus one summer session. Attendance at two summer sessions may accelerate graduation by one semester. The first-year curriculum is prescribed. There are many small classes, including a legal research and writing program with a student faculty ratio of 20:1. Legal writing instructors work with students to develop research and writing, computer, and oral advocacy skills.

Special Programs

Institute on International and Comparative Law—The School of Law, in cooperation with five foreign schools, sponsors the Institute on International and Comparative Law. Continuing law students can take law classes in Barcelona, Dublin, Florence, London, Oxford, and Paris. The programs introduce law students to international law and legal institutions and place emphasis on both study and traveling during four- to six-week sessions.

Clinical Education Program—The Clinical Education Program is recognized as one of the most extensive and successful in the nation. The law school received the Emil Gumpert Award from the American College of Trial Lawyers for excellence in trial advocacy training. Clinics handle cases in the areas of civil, criminal, immigration, mental health, and environmental law. The Center for Public Interest Law and Children's Advocacy Institute offer unique research and clinical opportunities. Law student interns attend the state regulatory hearings and learn public interest advocacy. Other programs for practical experience include judicial internships and Pro Bono Legal Advocates. Students can take courses in mediation and negotiation enhancing their skills in a variety of programs connected with the USD.

Distinguished Visitors and Speakers—The School of Law attracts an outstanding array of speakers and senior "Distinguished Professors," drawn from the nation's elite law schools, including Columbia, Chicago, NYU, and Northwestern, and "Practitioners-in-Residence," drawn from the nation's outstanding law firms and internationally renowned visiting scholars from Oxford, the European Union, and Russia. Lecturers and speakers enriching student experience recently included Supreme Court Justices O'Connor, Blackmun, Scalia, Nobel Laureate Milton Friedman; consumer advocate Ralph Nader; civil rights attorney Morris Dees; and Elaine Jones,

Director—Counsel of the NAACP Legal Defense and Educational Fund.

■ Admission

➽ Bachelor's degree from an approved college or university required for admission ➽ priority application deadline—Feb. 1 ➽ rolling admission, early application preferred ➽ LSAT, LSDAS required ➽ median accepted GPA—3.24 ➽ median accepted LSAT score—160 ➽ application fee—$35

While the applicant's LSAT score and undergraduate GPA are important elements in the admission process, other factors are considered. The School of Law has been successful both in admitting minority and other non-traditional students and in retaining them to graduation. An outstanding Academic Support Program is available.

■ Student Activities

Student activities range from writing for a legal publication and doing scholarly research to participating in the law school student/faculty intramural sports activities. National publications include the *San Diego Law Review* and the *California Regulatory Law Reporter*, which covers the activities of 70 state agencies and 25 public interest organizations, and is the only journal of its kind nationwide. The USD Moot Court Board coordinates appellate advocacy competitions where students argue cases regarding contemporary legal disputes at the local, regional, and national levels. The USD Moot Court team is considered one of the best in the nation. The USD team was best in the nation in the 1995 Jessup International Law Competition.

The 1994 Jessup International Law Team came home with best brief and best oralist in the world. The USD Mock Trial Team competes in the ABA's National Trial Competitions and has placed first in the Western Regionals for the past six years. A broad range of student organizations have active chapters on campus.

■ Expenses and Financial Aid

➽ tuition & fees—full-time, $18,120; part-time, $12,860 ➽ over 225 scholarships available—entering merit awards, academic achievement scholarships, Dean's Outstanding Scholar awards, diversity scholarships, and activity grants ➽ financial aid available; FAFSA form for need analysis due March 2; institutional financial aid application required after acceptance

■ Career Services

Each year the USD School of Law Career Services Office lists approximately 850 law clerking, intern, and attorney positions with law firm, public interest, government, corporate, and academic employers. In addition to these position listings received directly from employers, Career Services subscribes to 25 legal job bulletins that provide detailed application and hiring criteria on thousands of nationwide employment opportunities. USD's fall interviewing program includes approximately 250 affiliated and on-campus interviewers from 27 states and 66 cities. In conducting their job search, students will also have access to many other programs and resources that serve their diverse career interests, goals, and objectives. USD students and graduates work in 50 states and 15 countries with prestigious law firms and with government, public interest, corporate, and academic employers.

Academic Group for the 1995-1996 Academic Year

University of San Diego School of Law

LSAT Score	GPA								
	3.75 +	3.50 - 3.74	3.25 - 3.49	3.00 - 3.24	2.75 - 2.99	2.50 - 2.74	2.25 - 2.49	2.00 - 2.24	Below 2.00
175 - 180	Very Likely	Very Likely	Very Likely	Very Likely	Very Likely	Very Likely	Very Likely	Very Likely	Unlikely
170 - 174	Very Likely	Very Likely	Very Likely	Very Likely	Very Likely	Very Likely	Very Likely	Possible	Unlikely
165 - 169	Very Likely	Very Likely	Very Likely	Very Likely	Very Likely	Very Likely	Very Likely	Possible	Unlikely
160 - 164	Very Likely	Very Likely	Very Likely	Very Likely	Very Likely	Very Likely	Possible	Unlikely	Unlikely
155 - 159	Very Likely	Very Likely	Very Likely	Possible	Possible	Possible	Unlikely	Unlikely	Unlikely
150 - 154	Possible	Possible	Possible	Possible	Unlikely	Unlikely	Unlikely	Unlikely	Unlikely
145 - 149	Unlikely	Unlikely	Unlikely	Unlikely	Unlikely	Unlikely	Unlikely	Unlikely	Unlikely
140 - 144	Unlikely	Unlikely	Unlikely	Unlikely	Unlikely	Unlikely	Unlikely	Unlikely	Unlikely
135 - 139	Unlikely	Unlikely	Unlikely	Unlikely	Unlikely	Unlikely	Unlikely	Unlikely	Unlikely
130 - 134	Unlikely	Unlikely	Unlikely	Unlikely	Unlikely	Unlikely	Unlikely	Unlikely	Unlikely
125 - 129	Unlikely	Unlikely	Unlikely	Unlikely	Unlikely	Unlikely	Unlikely	Unlikely	Unlikely
120 - 124	Unlikely	Unlikely	Unlikely	Unlikely	Unlikely	Unlikely	Unlikely	Unlikely	Unlikely

Very Likely Possible Unlikely

University of San Francisco School of Law

2130 Fulton Street
San Francisco, CA 94117-1080

Phone: 415.666.6586

■ Introduction

The University of San Francisco School of Law is situated on a 51-acre residential campus adjacent to Golden Gate Park and a short distance from downtown San Francisco. Its graduates play leading roles on the bench and in the bar of the San Francisco Bay Area and in over 40 states and 20 foreign countries. The university was founded by the Jesuit fathers in 1855. The law school dates from 1912 and is located in its own modern building, which was constructed in 1962.

The school's close proximity to the San Francisco Civic Center makes it convenient for students to engage in clerkships with the federal and state courts. San Francisco, the concentrated center for legal activity in the western United States, includes numerous administrative clerking opportunities. The school is fully accredited by the ABA and is a member of the AALS.

■ Enrollment/Student Body

➽ 3,497 applicants ➽ 1,046 admitted first-year class 1995 ➽ 221 enrolled first-year class 1995 ➽ 567 total full-time ➽ 120 total part-time ➽ 24.7% minority ➽ 51% women ➽ 25 states & foreign countries represented ➽ 95 undergraduate schools represented

At the time of admission the median age of the day and evening students is 25. Students in the two divisions merge into an integral unit of organizations for mutual activities.

■ Faculty

➽ 85 total ➽ 27 full-time ➽ 58 part-time or adjunct ➽ 24 women ➽ 13 minority

The school draws from the best of the Bay Area and from the finest lawyers in the area to their area of expertise. The faculty is further supplemented by visiting faculty from throughout the United States, Europe, and China.

Upper-class moot court teams participate in major national, regional, and state competitions.

The Student Bar Association is responsible for student activities and liaison with the faculty and administration. Students participate directly in the school's governance through voting representation at faculty meetings and on faculty committees.

■ Library and Physical Facilities

➽ approximately 264,797 volumes & equivalents ➽ 100 library hours per week ➽ LEXIS ➽ NEXIS ➽ WESTLAW ➽ DIALOG ➽ INNOPAC automated library system ➽ 6 full-time librarians ➽ 6 library support staff ➽ library seats 293 ➽ student computer lab ➽ CD-ROM

The law school and law library are self-contained in a modern three-story structure. The library's collection includes approximately 264,797 volumes of Anglo American legal materials in print and microformat. A student computer center, group-study conference rooms, and copier facilities are also located in the law library. CD-ROM titles and workstations are available to students.

■ Admission

➽ B.A./B.S. required for admission ➽ application deadline—Feb. 1 (priority) ➽ LSAT, LSDAS required ➽ median GPA—3.20 ➽ median LSAT score—157 ➽ application fee—$40

The School of Law does not discriminate on the basis of sex, race, color, creed, age, handicap, or national origin. Beginning students are admitted only in the fall semester, and applicants must present a baccalaureate degree prior to registration. No application is considered until all supporting documents have been received. The admission committee employs a rolling admissions procedure. The committee strives to bring together an entering class that represents a variety of social, educational, geographical, and cultural backgrounds. Students from economically disadvantaged backgrounds are encouraged to apply through the Special Admission Program.

■ Curriculum

➽ 86 units/credits required to graduate ➽ degrees available: J.D.; J.D./M.B.A. ➽ semesters, start in Aug. & Jan. ➽ summer session starts in June ➽ range of first-year class size—day, 85; evening, 60

The first-year program begins with a four-day orientation program featuring a "minicourse," seminars, and a practice exam. The first-year curriculum includes the traditional curriculum plus Moot Court. The upper-class curriculum permits students to pursue their particular areas of interest.

■ Clinical Education—Law Clinic

The in-house Law Clinic gives students an alternative to learning law in a classroom. The clinic accepts cases in the following areas—criminal, and civil (with an emphasis on civil rights issues). Students are supervised by four full-time professors and work closely with them while meeting with clients, taking depositions, writing briefs, and making court appearances. In addition, all clinic participants meet in a weekly briefing session where they discuss current cases and share ideas, strategies, and "war stories."

■ Additional Clinical Opportunities

Consistent with its commitment to practical training, the School of Law offers opportunities for students to experience actual law practice while in law school. Students may obtain practical experience outside the law school. Many students earn a semester's academic credit by clerking for the courts. Students may also receive academic credit by clerking for governmental agencies, state and federal courts, public interest law firms, corporate legal departments, and private firms.

The School of Law pioneered and now directs a program in "Street Law." Under the program, students from five Bay Area law schools receive academic credit for teaching a course on the basics of our legal system to pupils in local high schools.

■ Student Activities

- *University of San Francisco Law Review*
- *University of San Francisco Maritime Law Journal*
- *The FORUM, student newspaper*
- *over 20 professional, social, and academic student organizations under the auspices of the Student Bar Association*

■ Intensive Advocacy Program

A two-week Intensive Advocacy Program is offered each summer. This unique program provides outstanding training in both pretrial and trial skills. The program features over 80 hours of lecture, demonstration, and practice workshops. At the conclusion of the program each student will conduct a jury trial. The faculty for the program will be made up of over 100 distinguished judges, practitioners, and professors from around the United States.

■ International Law and Study Abroad

The school offers an extensive list of courses in International Law. The faculty exchange program offers students the opportunity to study with faculty visiting USF from Irish, Czech, and Chinese universities. Summer study abroad programs are available in both Ireland, the Czech Republic, and Indonesia.

The Asian Pacific Legal Studies program at the University of San Francisco School of Law is unique among Bay Area Law Schools and is one of only a few Asian law programs currently offered in the United States. The program has four components—curriculum, research and publication, academic exchange, and community outreach.

■ Expenses and Financial Aid

tuition & fees—full-time, $17,810; part-time, $635/unit · *$9,300 average additional expenses (housing, board, books, misc. for 9 months)* · *scholarships available* · *financial aid available (grants and low-interest subsidized loans)*

■ Career Services

The Career Services Office facilitates the job search process for law school students and alumni. The office features a complete resource library, including in-depth dossiers on legal employers, and an aggressive placement program. Workshops, individual counseling, and panel presentations enable students to discern which areas of practice and types of employers best suit their individual career goals. In addition to listings for externships, part-time, permanent, and summer employment with law firms, corporations, accounting firms, governmental agencies, the judiciary, and other legal employers, USF also features fall and spring on-campus interview programs. Students are encouraged to consider employment in public interest law and may join the Public Interest Law Program sponsored by the Public Interest Clearinghouse. The law school is a member of the National Association for Law Placement.

Applicant Group for the 1995-1996 Academic Year

University of San Francisco School of Law

GPA	LSAT Percentile Rank									
	1 - 10	11 - 20	21 - 30	31 - 40	41 - 50	51 - 60	61 - 70	71 - 80	81 - 90	91 - 99
3.75 +										
3.74 - 3.50										
3.49 - 3.25										
3.24 - 3.00										
2.99 - 2.75										
2.74 - 2.50										
2.49 - 2.25										
2.24 - 2.00										
Below 2.00										
No GPA										

Unlikely · Possible · Highly Probable

Santa Clara University School of Law

500 El Camino Real
Santa Clara, CA 95053

URL: http://www.scu.edu/scu/Departments/Law
Phone: 408.554.4800

■ Introduction

Santa Clara University School of Law is located 46 miles from San Francisco, near the southern tip of San Francisco Bay. It is situated on the university campus, which was founded by the Jesuit fathers in 1851 and which surrounds the Mission of Santa Clara de Asis, the eighth of California's original 21 missions. The School of Law was added to the Santa Clara College in 1912 when the college became a university. The school is approved by the ABA and is a member of the AALS.

For more than 140 years, Santa Clara has fostered an exceptional academic program based on the Jesuit tradition. Located adjacent to San Jose and situated in the midst of one of the nation's greatest concentrations of high technology industry, internationally known as Silicon Valley, the law school has established a curriculum that addresses the fundamental demands of law practice and the evolving needs of society.

■ Enrollment/Student Body

➻ 3,414 applicants first-year class 1995 ➻ 1,158 admitted first-year class 1995 ➻ 285 enrolled first-year class 1995 ➻ 660 total full-time ➻ 222 total part-time ➻ 37% minority ➻ 50% women ➻ 99 undergraduate schools represented in entering class

Santa Clara is consistently among the top 20 law schools nationwide in terms of ethnic diversity.

■ Faculty

➻ 75 total ➻ 35 full-time ➻ 40 part-time ➻ 15 women ➻ 5 minority

■ Library and Physical Facilities

➻ 234,893 volumes & equivalents ➻ library hours: Mon.-Fri., 8:00 A.M.-MIDNIGHT; Sat., 9:00 A.M.-8:00 P.M.; Sun., 10:00 A.M.-MIDNIGHT ➻ hours extended during exam periods ➻ LEXIS ➻ NEXIS ➻ WESTLAW ➻ OSCAR ➻ online catalog ➻ 18 full-time librarians and staff ➻ library seats 446

The School of Law is on the 103-acre university campus. Towering palm trees, spacious lawns, and extensive flower gardens surround the Heafey Law Library. A traditional moot courtroom provides the setting for advocacy training and activities of the Edwin A. Heafey, Jr. Center for Trial and Appellate Advocacy. Other facilities include Bergin Hall faculty office building, Bannan Hall classroom building and Law House where law career services and alumni offices are located. Students also have access to other campus facilities including computer laboratories, Cowell Student Health Center, Benson Memorial Center, and Leavey Activities Center with its pool, basketball, volleyball and racquetball courts, steam room and sauna.

■ Curriculum

➻ full-time and part-time programs ➻ Academic Success Program ➻ 86 semester units required to graduate ➻ 138 courses available ➻ degrees available: J.D. and J.D./M.B.A. ➻ semesters, start in Aug.

An academic orientation introduces first-year students to the study of law. The first-year curriculum is prescribed. The legal research and writing course includes a unique full-month program in the middle of the first year. The Academic Success Program has been used as a model academic assistance program by Law School Admission Council. All students of color are encouraged to participate in a special Pre-Law Orientation, a First-Year Program, an Upper-Division Program, and an Introduction to the Bar Program.

The J.D./M.B.A. Combined Degree Program offers students the opportunity to earn both degrees in three-and-one-half to four years. This means a savings in both time and tuition fees.

■ International Law Certificate

A specialized curriculum allows students to earn a Certificate in International Law. The Institute of International and Comparative Law sponsors summer law study programs in Budapest, Hungary; Strasbourg, France; Geneva, Switzerland; Oxford, England; Hong Kong; Singapore; Seoul, Korea; Bangkok, Thailand; Ho Chi Minh City, People's Republic of Vietnam; Beijing, People's Republic of China; Kuala Lumpur, Malaysia; and Tokyo, Japan. All of the programs, with the exception of Oxford, offer internships with law offices, corporations or groups particularly suited to give students on-site observation and participation in areas of international law.

■ Computer and High-Technology Law Certificate

Santa Clara has capitalized on its Silicon Valley location by establishing a specialized curriculum that emphasizes computer and high-technology law. Students seeking an emphasis on high technology issues can enroll in courses such as patent law, copyright, biotechnology law, and technology licensing and may earn a Certificate in High Technology Law.

■ Public Interest Law Certificate

Students concerned with social issues and public service can receive a Certificate in Public Interest Law through the Public Interest Law Program. The Public Interest Endowment funds a limited number of scholarships, summer work fellowships, and income supplement grants for graduates. Students may also enroll in selected graduate counseling courses for credit.

■ Clinical Programs

The Santa Clara University Law Clinic allows students to practice law under the supervision of an experienced attorney. Students participate in all phases of a case from the initial client interview through the trial.

Students have the opportunity to earn credit for work as law clerks with public agencies such as the district attorney or public defender, with legal aid offices, or with private law offices. Students may also work as judges' clerks in appellate courts including the California Supreme Court, or trial courts including the United States District Court and local superior and municipal courts.

■ Student Activities

The school's quarterly, *Santa Clara Law Review*, is published by a student editorial board. It includes comments contributed by students as well as experts in various legal fields. The *Computer and High Technology Law Journal* provides a practical resource for high technology industry and the corresponding legal community.

Through the Student Bar Association and student-faculty committees, students participate in the decision processes of the law school.

■ Admissions

➽ Baccalaureate degree from accredited college or university required ➽ application deadline—March 1
➽ rolling admissions, early application preferred
➽ LSAT, LSDAS required ➽ median GPA—3.30
➽ median LSAT score—157 ➽ application fee—$40 ($60 international)

A faculty committee reviews all applications. No one is automatically accepted or rejected. When the LSAT is repeated, the highest score received is used.

Recognizing the critical need for persons from underrepresented groups to gain access to the legal profession, the School of Law has adopted a policy for special admission. Applicants may request a special consideration because of race, disadvantaged background, or other factors. Over 35 percent of the entering class is composed of students of color and 50 percent are women.

Applicants are encouraged to visit the School of Law. Arrangements can be made through the Admissions Office to attend a law class, meet with an admission counselor, or tour the campus.

■ Expenses and Financial Aid

➽ tuition & fees—$18,482, full-time; $13,503, part-time
➽ additional expenses—$8,000 min. (room, board, books)
➽ academic and need-based scholarships available
➽ public interest scholarships, summer fellowships, and income supplement grants ➽ FAFSA form for needs analysis should be completed in Jan. or early Feb.
➽ financial aid counselor available for individual counseling

■ Career Services

The Career Services Office serves as a liaison between students and prospective employers. Firms, businesses, and government agencies interview on campus each year. Graduates find employment in the legal profession throughout the 50 states. Office services include individual career counseling and a series of workshops in job-search strategies. Strong alumni support assists students in all stages of their career exploration and development.

Applicant Group for the 1995-1996 Academic Year

Santa Clara University School of Law
This grid includes only applicants who earned 120-180 LSAT scores under standard administrations.

LSAT Score	GPA 3.75 +		3.50 - 3.74		3.25 - 3.49		3.00 - 3.24		2.75 - 2.99		2.50 - 2.74		2.25 - 2.49		2.00 - 2.24		Below 2.00		No GPA		Total	
	Apps	Adm	Apps	Adm	Apps	Adm	Apps	Adm	Apps	Adm	Apps	Adm	Apps	Adm	Apps	Adm	Apps	Adm	Apps	Adm	Apps	Adm
175 - 180	0	0	1	1	2	2	1	1	2	2	0	0	0	0	0	0	0	0	0	0	6	6
170 - 174	5	4	7	6	2	2	2	1	5	3	2	2	0	0	0	0	0	0	0	0	23	18
165 - 169	7	7	18	16	23	22	19	17	31	16	7	3	6	2	0	0	0	0	5	4	116	87
160 - 164	32	32	81	76	105	97	78	68	58	27	34	11	15	3	2	0	1	0	7	5	413	319
155 - 159	60	51	154	140	196	154	177	99	131	25	59	9	21	4	5	1	2	0	22	13	827	496
150 - 154	49	32	125	55	185	53	204	34	137	8	92	8	24	0	14	0	4	0	22	2	856	192
145 - 149	28	8	73	8	106	7	141	7	120	2	77	2	44	0	16	0	2	0	17	0	624	34
140 - 144	6	0	21	2	36	1	66	2	67	0	51	0	22	0	13	0	1	0	16	0	299	5
135 - 139	0	0	6	0	11	0	20	0	29	0	22	0	19	0	8	0	1	0	7	0	123	0
130 - 134	0	0	3	0	7	0	3	0	4	0	9	0	4	0	3	0	0	0	1	0	34	0
125 - 129	0	0	0	0	0	0	3	0	1	0	3	0	3	0	2	0	1	0	0	0	13	0
120 - 124	0	0	0	0	0	0	0	0	2	0	1	0	0	0	0	0	1	0	0	0	4	0
Total	187	134	489	304	673	338	714	229	587	83	357	35	158	9	63	1	13	0	97	24	3338	1157

Apps = Number of Applicants
Adm = Number Admitted
Reflects 98% of the total applicant pool.

Seattle University School of Law

950 Broadway Plaza
Tacoma, WA 98402

E-Mail: lawadmis@seattleu.edu
URL: http://www.law.seattleu.edu
Phone: 206.591.2252

■ Introduction

In the Pacific Northwest, midway between Seattle, Washington's largest city, and its state capital, Olympia, sits a three-building complex in downtown Tacoma. This is the home of the Seattle University School of Law. Housed with the law school are the Washington State Court of Appeals, the Pierce County Office of Assigned Counsel, the Federal Public Defender, and a number of private law firms.

Tacoma, a major port city and part of the "gateway to Asia," offers students a lively urban environment that represents an ideal setting for our brand of legal education—a student body from throughout the nation; a blend of traditional textbook and innovative hands-on legal education; the school that former Supreme Court Chief Justice Warren Burger over a decade ago termed "a remarkable experiment in legal education." The experiment is working.

■ Enrollment/Student Body

➻ 1,609 applicants ➻ 751 admitted first-year class 1995 ➻ 279 enrolled first-year class 1995 ➻ 721 total full-time ➻ 166 total part-time ➻ 20.3% minority ➻ 46% women ➻ 45 states & foreign countries represented ➻ 245 undergraduate schools represented

Seattle University law students range in age from 21 to 54. While their average age at entry is 29, about 30 percent choose to pursue legal studies directly after undergraduate school. The remainder come to us from an impressive array of professional careers. On average, they rank in the top quarter of their graduating class and their performance on the LSAT is solidly in the 80th percentile.

■ Faculty

➻ 65 total ➻ 41 full-time ➻ 24 adjunct ➻ 25 women ➻ 6 minority

When the law faculty meet to decide on faculty selection, promotion, and tenure, they first consider teaching aptitude and performance. Against this backdrop, the professors' production of significant scholarship is impressive, earning them a place among the "top 50" law faculties in the nation (1st/1989 and 2nd/1992 Editions, *Faculty Scholarship Survey*).

■ Library

➻ 320,776 volumes & equivalents ➻ library hours: 7:00 A.M.-MIDNIGHT, daily ➻ LEXIS ➻ NEXIS ➻ WESTLAW ➻ DIALOG ➻ BRS ➻ VUTEXT ➻ WILSONLINE ➻ 10 other CD-ROM databases ➻ DATATIMES ➻ 8 full-time librarians ➻ library seats 600

The Law Library houses one of the largest law collections in the Northwest. Ranked among the top law libraries in the West, the SU Law Library offers students superb resources for legal research.

■ Curriculum

➻ 90 credits required to graduate ➻ 125 courses offered each year ➻ J.D. degree ➻ semesters, start in late Aug. ➻ optional early start in June ➻ range of first-year class size—15-80

In the first intensive year, the curriculum concentrates on the highly traditional and prescribed basic courses, and on an intensive, year-long course refining legal analysis and writing skills which the ABA has called "among the finest legal writing programs in the nation." The upper-level courses allow for choice, innovation, and diversity. Students may choose either a broad, balanced program of study, or focus on a particular area such as Business, Corporate, and Tax Law (20 related courses plus clerkship opportunities with over 100 law firms, government agencies, and corporations in Western Washington); Law in the Public Sector (40 course offerings); or Environmental Law (12 courses plus internships with the Port of Seattle, Sierra Club Legal Defense Fund, U.S. Environmental Protection Agency, and Washington Environmental Council, among others). An innovative clinic program allows students to integrate a live client component with a substantive course.

■ Academic Resource Center

The law school's Academic Resource Center offers a range of academic support services designed to maximize every student's success. Workshops and seminars for new students emphasize self-evaluation techniques and support-group strategies. Representative programs include the following workshops—Effective Study Techniques; How To Outline; Preparing For Exams; and Organizing Your Time. The center is staffed by a full-time director (a J.D. graduate) and second- and third-year law students who serve as advisors and teaching assistants.

■ Expanded Scheduling

One of the most distinctive and popular features of the academic program is what we term "expanded scheduling." Seattle University, unlike any other school in the region, offers courses from 8:00 A.M. to 10:00 P.M., all year, for all students. At entry, students have the option of completing first-year studies over nine, twelve, or fifteen months. They may commence their studies in the summer or in the fall.

■ Admission

➻ Bachelor's degree from an accredited college or university ➻ application deadline—April 1 ➻ rolling admissions, early application preferred ➻ LSAT, LSDAS required ➻ application fee—$50 ➻ typed personal statement and two letters of recommendation required ➻ median GPA—3.24 ➻ median LSAT score—158

The Faculty Admission Committee places primary emphasis on three factors: (1) LSAT scores; (2) undergraduate academic performance; and (3) personal accomplishments.

Each applicant file is reviewed individually by a minimum of two evaluators. Personal achievements weigh heavily in each admission decision.

Candidates for admission are advised to apply as early as possible and complete their files no later than April 1. A very few spaces in the class are held for persons taking the February and June LSATs.

The law school is committed to a wholly nondiscriminatory admission policy and philosophy.

■ Alternative Admission

A select group of applicants is admitted each year through an alternative-admission program established by the law school based on recognition that traditional admission criteria are, in some cases, inadequate predictors of success in law school and the legal profession. The majority of individuals considered for this program are members of historically disadvantaged groups. Enrollment is strictly limited to 10 percent of the entering class.

■ Student Activities

A partial listing of student organizations illustrates the scope of interests held by law students—Alaska Student Bar Association; Asian/Pacific Islander Law Student Association; Black Law Student Association; Christian Legal Fellowship; Entertainment/Sports Law Association; Environmental Law Society; Hispanic Organization for Legal Advancement; Inn of Court; International Law Society; Jewish Law Society; Law Review; Native American Student Bar Association; Lesbian & Gay Legal Society; Moot Court; Public Interest Law Foundation; Student Bar Association; and Women's Law Caucus.

■ Expenses and Financial Aid

➽ *tuition & fees—$15,380* ➽ *estimated additional expenses—$10,025 (books, room, board, and living expenses)*
➽ *performance and/or need-based scholarships available*
➽ *minority scholarships available*

Well over 80 percent of the student body receives some form of financial assistance. A full 30 percent of students receive law school-funded scholarships which total over $1 million per year. Information on scholarships, grants, loans, and employment opportunities is mailed to all applicants.

■ Career Services

More than 90 percent of law students have been employed in at least one law firm, legal agency, or other law-related position prior to graduation. Many have held two or three such jobs in order to strengthen and diversify their resumes. Our alumni/ae are employed throughout the U.S. and in 19 foreign countries. Recently compiled employment statistics reveal that our graduates are engaged in: private practice/55 percent; government service/15 percent; business & industry/11 percent; judicial service/10 percent; public interest law/3 percent; academics/3 percent; and advanced studies/3 percent. Eighty-six percent of 1994 graduates passed the Washington bar exam on their first attempt (11 points higher than the statewide average).

Applicant Group for the 1995-1996 Academic Year

Seattle University School of Law

LSAT Score	GPA									
	3.75 +	3.50 - 3.74	3.25 - 3.49	3.00 - 3.24	2.75 - 2.99	2.50 - 2.74	2.25 - 2.49	2.00 - 2.24	Below 2.00	No GPA
175 - 180	Likely	Likely	Likely	Likely	Likely	Possible	Unlikely	Unlikely	Unlikely	Likely
170 - 174	Likely	Likely	Likely	Likely	Likely	Possible	Unlikely	Unlikely	Unlikely	Likely
165 - 169	Likely	Likely	Likely	Likely	Likely	Possible	Unlikely	Unlikely	Unlikely	Likely
160 - 164	Likely	Likely	Likely	Likely	Likely	Possible	Unlikely	Unlikely	Unlikely	Likely
155 - 159	Likely	Likely	Likely	Likely	Possible	Unlikely	Unlikely	Unlikely	Unlikely	Likely
150 - 154	Possible	Possible	Possible	Possible	Unlikely	Unlikely	Unlikely	Unlikely	Unlikely	Possible
145 - 149	Unlikely	Unlikely	Unlikely	Unlikely	Unlikely	Unlikely	Unlikely	Unlikely	Unlikely	Unlikely
140 - 144	Unlikely	Unlikely	Unlikely	Unlikely	Unlikely	Unlikely	Unlikely	Unlikely	Unlikely	Unlikely
135 - 139	Unlikely	Unlikely	Unlikely	Unlikely	Unlikely	Unlikely	Unlikely	Unlikely	Unlikely	Unlikely
130 - 134	Unlikely	Unlikely	Unlikely	Unlikely	Unlikely	Unlikely	Unlikely	Unlikely	Unlikely	Unlikely
125 - 129	Unlikely	Unlikely	Unlikely	Unlikely	Unlikely	Unlikely	Unlikely	Unlikely	Unlikely	Unlikely
120 - 124	Unlikely	Unlikely	Unlikely	Unlikely	Unlikely	Unlikely	Unlikely	Unlikely	Unlikely	Unlikely

Likely · Possible · Unlikely

Of applicants in the Unlikely category, about one in 20 candidates was admitted to the Alternative Admission Program.

Seton Hall University School of Law

Office of Admissions
1 Newark Center
Newark, NJ 07102-5210

E-Mail: admitme@lanmail.shu.edu
URL: http://www.shu.edu/law/
Phone: 201.642.8747

■ Introduction

Founded in 1951, Seton Hall University School of Law is the only private law school in the state of New Jersey. While it values its Catholic identity as a division of the university, the law school is a pluralistic community representing a diversity of racial, cultural, religious, and socioeconomic backgrounds. The school was recently recognized for its high level of student satisfaction and its high rate of judicial clerkship placement. The law school building is architecturally dynamic fostering a congenial atmosphere and incorporating technological sophistication for the study of law. Our Gateway Center location puts our students in the midst of federal, appellate, state and county courts, the Legal Center, and hundreds of law firms and legal agencies.

■ Enrollment/Student Body

➽ 3,176 applicants ➽ 1,390 admitted first-year class 1995 ➽ 445 enrolled first-year class 1995 ➽ 992 total full-time ➽ 375 total part-time ➽ 20% minority ➽ 45% women ➽ 25 states represented in first-year class ➽ 191 undergraduate schools represented in first-year class

Day-division applications numbered 2,650 for 320 seats, and evening-division applications numbered 526 for 90 seats. Women comprise 49 percent of the 1995 first-year class, while minority matriculants comprise 19 percent.

■ Faculty

➽ 148 total ➽ 51 full-time ➽ 97 part-time or adjunct ➽ 46 women ➽ 16 minority

■ Library and Physical Facilities

➽ 315,595 volumes & equivalents ➽ library hours: Mon.-Fri., 8:00 A.M.-11:45 P.M.; Sat., 9:00 A.M.-10:00 P.M.; Sun. 10:00 A.M.-10:00 P.M. ➽ LEXIS ➽ NEXIS ➽ WESTLAW ➽ DIALOG ➽ 11 professional librarians ➽ 15 library assistants ➽ library seats 600

■ Curriculum

➽ Academic Support Program ➽ 85 credits required to graduate ➽ 176 courses available ➽ degrees available: J.D.; J.D./M.B.A. ➽ semesters, start in Sept.

The program emphasizes humanistic principles and encourages their synthesis with knowledge of the law and professional responsibility. The law school is committed to in-depth training in legal writing and research.

The school year is conducted on a two-semester basis. The day division requires three years; the evening division normally requires four.

■ Special Programs

Clinics—Seton Hall Law School is committed to clinical education and is at its forefront. The 23 years of service performed by the law school's clinics was recognized by Congress and the President in the form of a $5.4 million grant. With this grant, the school has created the Center for Social Justice, a clinical legal education center that serves as a national model. The school's litigation clinics presently represent more than 3,000 disadvantaged and underrepresented clients each year in a wide range of litigation such as housing and shelter, consumer protection, family law, public entitlement, juvenile justice, disability law, immigration, inmate advocacy, and gun control.

Judicial Internships—The law school also offers judicial internships with justices of the New Jersey Supreme Court; judges of the New Jersey Appellate Division, Chancery and Law Courts, the Third Circuit Court of Appeals, the U.S. District Courts, and the U.S. Bankruptcy Courts. There are internship programs with the Environmental Protection Agency, the Office of the U.S. Trustee for Bankruptcy, and the Internal Revenue Service.

Journals—The law school offers students an opportunity to advance legal scholarship through four student journals—*The Seton Hall Law Review, Seton Hall Legislative Journal, Seton Hall Constitutional Law Journal*, and the *Seton Hall Sports Law Journal*.

Foreign Study—Each summer the law school cosponsors, with the Universities of Parma and Milan, a course of international studies for American law students in Milan, Genoa, and Parma, Italy. The law school hosts students from the University of Milan Law School.

M.B.A./J.D. Program—Students may be admitted to the joint M.B.A./J.D. program during the first year of their law school career. The M.B.A. degree consists of 60 credits, and a maximum of 12 credits may be applied to both degree requirements. The LSAT and GMAT examinations are both required.

LEO Institute—The Monsignor Thomas Fahy Legal Education Opportunities (LEO) Institute provides an intense, summer-long classroom experience for educationally disadvantaged students.

Moot Court Program—Students represent the law school in the National Moot Court Competition as well as in 14 interschool competitions focusing on specific areas of law.

■ Admission

➽ B.A./B.S. required ➽ application deadline—April 1 ➽ LSAT, LSDAS required ➽ median GPA—3.13 ➽ median LSAT score—154 ➽ application fee—$50

All applicants for admission as beginning law students are required to hold a bachelor's degree from a regionally accredited four-year institution by the time of matriculation. The LSAT is also required for all prospective applicants. TOEFL is required of applicants whose pre-college education was not in English, if they present an LSAT score below 150.

The law school recognizes the desirability of bringing together an entering class of diverse cultural, social, and educational backgrounds. Candidates are expected to demonstrate sufficient academic achievement in a rigorous undergraduate and/or graduate major and communicate that they possess the aptitude for the successful pursuit of the demanding three- or four-year professional degree program. Nonquantifiable indicators of success in law school may surface in one's demonstrated skills. These skills can be reflected in things such as the employment record, meaningful community endeavors, and unusual cocurricular service projects of a candidate.

Applicants from disadvantaged groups, regardless of race, religion, age, sex, sexual orientation, or national origin, may wish to inquire into the Monsignor Thomas Fahy Legal Education Opportunities Institute (LEO Institute).

Acceptances are processed for candidates as early as December. Subsequent decisions are processed regularly through June. A $500 tuition deposit is required by April 1. A second tuition deposit of $1,000 is due in June.

■ Student Activities

Student organizations flourish at Seton Hall. Many are related to specific areas of practice; others related to student governance and student representation on faculty standing committees. International law fraternities have chapters here. Several organizations, including the St. Thomas More Society, are committed to community service. Many other groups represent a wide range of professional interests, religious commitments, and cultural identities found among an enormously diverse student population.

The law school is also very involved in encouraging the study of law and the pursuit of legal careers among college and high school students, through the Mentor and Pre-Legal programs.

■ Expenses and Financial Aid

➽ *tuition & fees—full-time, $17,160; part-time, $13,100 ($571/credit hour)* ➽ *recommended budget including tuition—full-time, $33,800; part-time, $28,900*
➽ *merit and need-based scholarships available*
➽ *merit, need-based, and geography-specific minority scholarships available* ➽ *FAFSA due May 15th*

In 1995-96, over $2 million was allocated from the law center's financial resources to approximately 55 percent of the student body. The average student loan was approximately $15,000. From all sources, approximately 1,000 students received over $20 million in aid and loans.

■ Career Services

Seton Hall School of Law maintains a Career Services Office staffed by three full-time counselors who assist students in defining their career objectives and goals and establishing contact with employers. Every fall, law firm, corporate, public interest, and government employers conduct interviews through the school's On-Campus Interview Program. The placement ratio for 1994 graduates was 92 percent.

Applicant Group for the 1995-1996 Academic Year

Seton Hall University School of Law
This grid includes only applicants who earned 120-180 LSAT scores under standard administrations.

LSAT Score	3.75 +		3.50 - 3.74		3.25 - 3.49		3.00 - 3.24		2.75 - 2.99		2.50 - 2.74		2.25 - 2.49		2.00 - 2.24		Below 2.00		No GPA		Total	
	Apps	Adm	Apps	Adm	Apps	Adm	Apps	Adm	Apps	Adm	Apps	Adm	Apps	Adm	Apps	Adm	Apps	Adm	Apps	Adm	Apps	Adm
175 - 180	0	0	0	0	0	0	0	0	0	0	0	0	0	0	0	0	0	0	0	0	0	0
170 - 174	1	1	1	1	1	1	0	0	2	2	0	0	0	0	0	0	0	0	0	0	5	5
165 - 169	3	3	6	6	4	4	6	6	7	7	5	5	4	2	2	2	0	0	1	1	38	36
160 - 164	8	8	24	23	24	23	41	41	27	27	35	29	12	8	5	1	3	0	3	2	182	162
155 - 159	26	26	68	68	101	100	121	120	110	101	60	38	27	5	12	2	1	0	2	1	528	461
150 - 154	33	30	105	83	165	131	187	132	175	106	96	25	58	5	20	1	5	0	10	6	854	519
145 - 149	11	3	65	22	111	27	157	26	153	27	101	10	56	2	25	1	10	1	9	2	698	121
140 - 144	16	0	27	2	53	1	75	7	93	4	77	6	56	0	24	0	5	0	6	1	432	21
135 - 139	2	0	13	1	13	0	34	1	48	2	44	1	35	0	29	0	5	0	8	0	231	5
130 - 134	1	0	0	0	5	0	9	0	9	0	22	0	16	0	9	0	5	0	3	0	79	0
125 - 129	0	0	0	0	1	0	0	0	2	0	5	0	1	0	0	0	2	0	1	0	12	0
120 - 124	0	0	0	0	0	0	0	0	0	0	1	0	1	0	1	0	0	0	0	0	3	0
Total	101	71	309	206	478	287	630	333	626	276	446	114	266	22	127	7	36	1	43	13	3062	1330

Apps = Number of Applicants
Adm = Number Admitted
Reflects 98% of the total applicant pool.

University of South Carolina School of Law

Columbia, SC 29208

Phone: 803.777.6605

■ Introduction

The University of South Carolina School of Law, established in 1867, is located in Columbia, South Carolina. Situated in the state capital in the center of the state, there is easy access to the mountains and to the coast. The school is within close proximity of state and federal courts, government agencies, the State Capitol, and large law firms. The School of Law is fully accredited by the American Bar Association and has been a member of the Association of American Law Schools since 1924.

■ Enrollment/Student Body

➧ 1,538 applicants ➧ 446 admitted first-year class 1995 ➧ 250 enrolled first-year class 1995 ➧ 765 total full-time ➧ 10% minority ➧ 39% women ➧ 13 states & foreign countries represented ➧ 81 undergraduate schools represented ➧ 87% residents of South Carolina

■ Faculty

➧ 69 total ➧ 44 full-time ➧ 25 part-time or adjunct ➧ 9 women ➧ 3 minority

■ Library and Physical Facilities

➧ 326,000 volumes & equivalents ➧ library hours: open 111 hours per week under regular schedule; Mon.-Thurs., 7:00 A.M.-MIDNIGHT; Fri., 7:00 A.M.-10:00 P.M.; Sat., 9:00 A.M.-10:00 P.M.; Sun., 9:00 A.M.-MIDNIGHT ➧ LEXIS ➧ NEXIS ➧ WESTLAW ➧ DIALOG ➧ RLIN ➧ OCLC ➧ USCAN (online card catalog) ➧ 5.5 full-time librarians ➧ library seats 645 ➧ South Carolina Legal History Collection is housed in the School of Law Library

Closed carrels are available for assignment to students for year-long use.

■ Curriculum

➧ Academic Support Program ➧ 90 total units/credits required to graduate ➧ 121 courses available ➧ joint degrees programs: J.D./Masters Business Administration; J.D./Masters Criminal Justice; J.D./Masters Public Administration; J.D./Masters International Business; J.D./Masters Employee Personnel Relations; J.D./Master of Accountancy; J.D./Master of Arts in Economics ➧ two semesters, begin in Aug. and Jan. ➧ one summer session ➧ beginning students admitted for fall semester only ➧ range of first-year class size—20-80

Transfer students are accepted in limited numbers.

■ Special Programs

Clinical Legal Education Program. Under special court rule, third-year law students in South Carolina may represent clients and appear in court when enrolled in a clinical legal education course. The clinical education program offers courses designed to develop lawyering skills. The program, through the use of simulation techniques, offers training in trial advocacy, negotiation, settlement, interviewing, and counseling. Clinics include domestic relations, criminal defense, appellate practice, employment discrimination, social security, and bankruptcy.

■ Admissions

➧ Bachelor's degree from an accredited college or university required for admission ➧ application deadline—Feb. 15 ➧ fall admission only ➧ transfer application deadline—May 15 ➧ LSAT, LSDAS required ➧ median GPA—3.30 ➧ median LSAT score—157 ➧ application fee—SC resident, $25; non-SC resident, $35 ➧ state-supported institution, admission standards are higher for nonresidents of South Carolina ➧ candidates who want to be considered for merit scholarships must complete their applications by Feb. 1

The Faculty Committee on Admissions reviews applications to the School of Law. Factors considered include LSAT, GPA, degree-granting institution, major, work and/or military experience, extracurricular activities, letters of recommendation, and the personal statement. When multiple LSAT scores are presented, the average of the scores is used.

The fall 1995 entering class was 8 percent minority, 41 percent women, and 91 percent South Carolina residents.

Visits to the Office of Admissions and the School of Law to discuss specific questions and concerns are welcomed.

■ Student Activities

Order of the Coif—National legal honorary society which recognizes outstanding student academic achievement.

Order of Wig and Robe—Local legal scholastic organization organized in 1935.

South Carolina Law Review—Published quarterly and contains articles by distinguished scholars, members of the bar, and students.

South Carolina Environmental Law Journal—Published regularly by students of the School of Law. Each issue, containing articles written by attorneys, professors, and professionals in the field, provides updates on current developments in environmental law.

Real Property, Probate, and Trust Journal—The School of Law serves as the host affiliate for this ABA journal.

Pro Bono Program—Directed by a student board, the Pro Bono Program offers students an opportunity to be involved in activities such as income tax assistance, legal research, and teaching law-related courses to juveniles. On May 1, 1991, former President Bush named the Pro Bono Program the 444th "Daily Point of Light" for its outstanding contribution to community service through volunteer action.

Moot Court—Teams are sponsored in the National, International, American Bar Association, and Labor Law Moot Court competitions and National Trial Competition.

Other student organizations include the Student Bar Association, which is the student government for the School of Law, the Black Law Student Association, the Association of Women Law Students, the Christian Legal Society, and the Environmental Law Society.

■ Expenses and Financial Aid

➽ *full-time tuition & fees—SC resident, $6,168 per year; non- SC resident, $12,224* ➽ *average amount of additional expenses—$9,000 (rent, transportation, utilities, books, food, misc.)* ➽ *scholarships available (merit-based full- and half-tuition scholarships, need-based scholarships)* ➽ *minority scholarships available (merit-based full- and half-tuition scholarships)* ➽ *financial aid available* ➽ *priority deadline for applications for federal student loan programs—April 15* ➽ *Application for Federal Student Aid (AFSA) required*

Candidates who want to be considered for merit scholarships should complete their application to the School of Law by February 1.

■ Office of Career Services

The Office of Career Services serves as liaison between students and legal employers and offers services to equip students with the skills and information necessary for a successful employment search. Services available include individual counseling, résumé writing, and interviewing seminars, on-campus interviews, participation in job fairs including the Southeastern Law Placement Consortium in Atlanta, GA; the South Atlantic Recruiting Conference in Washington, DC; the Southeastern Minority Job Fair; and the Southeastern Public Interest Job Fair.

Applicant Group for the 1995-1996 Academic Year

University of South Carolina School of Law
This grid includes only applicants who earned 120-180 LSAT scores under standard administrations.

LSAT Score	GPA 3.75 +		3.50 - 3.74		3.25 - 3.49		3.00 - 3.24		2.75 - 2.99		2.50 - 2.74		2.25 - 2.49		2.00 - 2.24		Below 2.00		No GPA		Total	
	Apps	Adm	Apps	Adm	Apps	Adm	Apps	Adm	Apps	Adm	Apps	Adm	Apps	Adm	Apps	Adm	Apps	Adm	Apps	Adm	Apps	Adm
175 - 180	0	0	0	0	0	0	0	0	1	1	0	0	0	0	0	0	0	0	0	0	1	1
170 - 174	0	0	1	1	0	0	1	1	1	1	0	0	0	0	0	0	0	0	0	0	3	3
165 - 169	7	7	6	6	5	5	7	6	5	4	3	3	3	1	0	0	1	0	0	0	37	32
160 - 164	13	13	16	16	20	19	44	37	28	23	12	7	11	6	2	1	0	0	2	2	148	124
155 - 159	28	21	45	23	88	53	73	29	59	19	28	9	21	5	8	3	0	0	4	2	354	164
150 - 154	31	15	59	17	84	16	88	15	72	10	39	1	25	5	7	0	3	0	6	2	414	81
145 - 149	15	1	30	5	42	5	65	5	53	5	44	2	18	0	14	0	1	0	3	0	285	23
140 - 144	2	1	11	5	25	0	28	0	33	1	21	3	14	0	6	0	3	0	4	1	147	11
135 - 139	1	0	5	0	9	0	11	0	13	0	18	0	6	0	7	0	2	0	7	1	79	1
130 - 134	0	0	1	0	1	0	3	0	2	0	3	0	2	0	5	0	2	0	3	0	22	0
125 - 129	0	0	0	0	0	0	2	0	1	0	2	0	1	0	1	0	0	0	0	0	7	0
120 - 124	0	0	0	0	0	0	0	0	0	0	0	0	0	0	0	0	0	0	0	0	0	0
Total	97	58	174	73	274	98	322	93	268	64	170	25	101	17	50	4	12	0	29	8	1497	440

Apps = Number of Applicants
Adm = Number Admitted
Reflects 98% of the total applicant pool.

University of South Dakota School of Law

Admissions/Office of the Dean
414 E. Clark
Vermillion, SD 57069-2390

URL: http://www.usd.edu/law/legal.html
Phone: 605.677.5443

■ Introduction

The School of Law, located on the university campus in Vermillion, is noted for its contributions in training distinguished leaders for the bench, the bar, and the law-making bodies of the state and region. Founded in 1901, the school is accredited by both the ABA and the AALS.

Approximately 223 students are enrolled at USD School of Law, with a total university population of approximately 7,300. The city of Vermillion, with a population of just over 10,000, provides a small-town atmosphere for students, faculty, and staff.

■ Enrollment/Student Body

➻ 529 applicants ➻ 188 admitted first-year class 1995 ➻ 80 enrolled first-year class 1995 ➻ 223 total full-time ➻ 4% minority ➻ 35% women ➻ 15 states represented ➻ 36 undergraduate schools represented

■ Faculty

➻ 17 total ➻ 15 full-time ➻ 2 part-time or adjunct ➻ 3 women

Excellent student-faculty ratio fosters a close relationship between students and teaching faculty.

■ Library and Physical Facilities

➻ 171,833 volumes & equivalents ➻ library hours: Mon.-Thurs., 7:30 A.M.-MIDNIGHT; Fri., 7:30 A.M.-6:00 P.M.; Sat., 10:00 A.M.-5:00 P.M.; Sun., NOON-MIDNIGHT ➻ LEXIS ➻ NEXIS ➻ WESTLAW ➻ DIALOG ➻ SDLN ➻ 5 full-time librarians ➻ library seats 223 ➻ approx. 85 computer-assisted legal instruction exercises

The law school has been housed in its present facility since 1981. It contains three classrooms, three seminar rooms, a student computer room, a spacious student lounge, offices for faculty, administration, and student organizations, and a teaching courtroom with judges' chambers and an audiovisual control room. The courtroom doubles as an assembly hall.

The library occupies a substantial portion of all three floors of the facility, and provides study carrels for students and group study space. Many library functions are automated providing easy access to the library's own collection and to the collection of more than 30 other libraries in South Dakota and 18 other law libraries in the region.

■ Curriculum

➻ 90 credits required to graduate ➻ 70 courses available ➻ degrees available: J.D.; J.D./Masters offered in 10 areas including Bus., Educ., Arts & Science, Agriculture ➻ semesters, start in Aug. ➻ range of first-year class size—75

There is a three-semester core curriculum and three semesters of advanced studies. Ninety semester credits are required for the J.D. degree. The first-year curriculum is required of all students. In the second and third years, electives are available in addition to required courses. An optional clinical externship/academic course semester is available for 15 credit hours during the spring semester. Also, during the summer a clinical externship program is offered for 7 credit hours. Clinical interns learn by doing under the close supervision of an attorney and the clinical law director. Skills training is also available to second- and third-year students in the trial techniques course, negotiations, and other courses, each of which utilizes to the fullest extent the audiovisual capabilities of the law school.

The excellent student-to-faculty ratio fosters a close relationship between students and a teaching faculty of 16 full-time and two part-time teachers.

■ Special Programs

The school has joint programs with other departments of the graduate school, with joint degrees available in accounting, business administration, history, English, psychology, education, political science/public administration, and economics. Students may transfer nine hours of approved interdisciplinary coursework for J.D. credit. For students not enrolled in a joint-degree program, up to six interdisciplinary credits may be applied toward the 90-credit J.D. requirement.

Various paid, summer legal internships both within and outside of South Dakota are available in both private firms and public agencies. The South Dakota Supreme Court has adopted a student-practice rule that allows students who have completed their second year to represent clients in court under the supervision of a member of the bar.

■ Admission Standards

➻ Bachelor's degree required ➻ preferred application deadline—March 1 ➻ rolling admission, early application preferred ➻ LSAT, LSDAS required ➻ median GPA—3.28 ➻ median LSAT score—156 ➻ application fee—(first time applications only) ➻ application form, 2 letters of recommendation, personal statement required

Accepted students are required to pay a $50 nonrefundable deposit to reserve a position in the entering first-year class, and to submit two photographs and an official transcript reflecting their undergraduate degree.

Students who do not meet regular admission criteria may be invited to participate in the Summer Screening Program. Program participants are enrolled in two noncredit law school courses during a five-week summer session. Up to 10 students who receive the highest cumulative grade-point average while maintaining a grade of 70 or better in both courses are offered admission to the entering first-year class. The program provides a valuable proving ground for applicants whose abilities are not accurately reflected in past undergraduate or LSAT performance.

USD School of Law is committed to providing full opportunity for the study of law and entry into the profession by qualified members or groups (notably racial and ethnic minorities, including Native Americans) that have been victims of discrimination in various forms.

Transfer students may apply for admission with advanced standing only if they are in good standing and eligible to return to the transferor law school.

Foreign students who attended undergraduate programs in which English was not the dominant language must also submit a TOEFL score as part of their application package.

■ Student Activities

The *South Dakota Law Review* presents articles by second- and third-year students, lawyers, judges, and professors. Cocurricular activities include a Moot Court Board and Clinical Counseling and Negotiations Board. Competitions in all activities are held at the intramural, regional, and national levels.

The school is active in the Law Student Division of the ABA. Two legal fraternities—Delta Theta Phi and Phi Alpha Delta—are active at the school. Other organizations with chapters at the school include Women in Law, the Native American Law Students Association, the Christian Legal Society, the Environmental Law Society, and the International Law Students Association.

■ Expenses and Financial Aid

- *tuition & fees—full-time resident, $4,421*
- *estimated additional expenses—$3,500 (books, room & board)*
- *academic performance and need-based scholarships available*
- *financial aid available; FAFSA needs analysis must be submitted through central University Financial Aid Office*

Scholarships are awarded to more than 42 percent of the student body.

A limited number of teaching and research assistantships are available for academically qualified second- and third-year students. A research service provided by the McKusick Law Library for practicing attorneys also provides employment opportunities for several law students during the academic year.

Student loans are available through the university's Office of Student Financial Aids (605.677.5446). For information about minority scholarship programs, applicants should contact Minority Student Financial Aids Coordinator, 14 Slagle Hall, USD, 414 E. Clark St., Vermillion, SD 57069-2390 (605.677.5446).

■ Career Services

The placement opportunities for third-year law students have been excellent both in South Dakota, the surrounding areas, and throughout the United States. Approximately one-third of the graduates of the school practice law outside of South Dakota. The law school also has an active program to place first- and second-year students in summer internship programs with law firms.

Applicant Group for the 1995-1996 Academic Year

University of South Dakota School of Law
This grid does **not** include 11 students admitted through the Summer Screening Program.

LSAT Score	GPA 3.75 +		3.50 - 3.74		3.25 - 3.49		3.00 - 3.24		2.75 - 2.99		2.50 - 2.74		2.25 - 2.49		2.00 - 2.24		Below 2.00		No GPA	Total	
	Apps	Adm	Apps	Adm	Apps	Adm	Apps	Adm	Apps	Adm	Apps	Adm	Apps	Adm	Apps	Adm	Apps	Adm	Apps	Apps	Adm
170-175	0	0	0	0	0	0	1	1	0	0	0	0	0	0	0	0	0	0	0	1	1
165 - 169	2	2	1	1	0	0	2	2	3	2	1	1	0	0	2	1	0	0	0	11	9
160 - 164	2	2	5	5	7	7	5	5	5	5	8	6	1	1	2	2	2	1	0	37	34
155 - 159	9	8	15	15	12	11	24	22	20	11	9	2	7	3	3	1	0	0	0	99	73
150 - 154	15	14	16	12	36	20	38	16	32	6	16	1	11	1	5	0	2	0	0	171	70
145 - 149	8	0	14	0	19	1	25	0	17	0	9	0	6	0	8	0	1	0	0	107	1
140 - 144	3	0	5	0	11	0	6	0	10	0	13	0	4	0	2	0	0	0	0	54	0
135 - 139	0	0	1	0	6	0	5	0	6	0	5	0	3	0	4	0	1	0	0	31	0
130 - 134	0	0	0	0	0	0	0	0	3	0	1	0	2	0	1	0	0	0	0	7	0
125 - 129	0	0	0	0	0	0	0	0	0	0	1	0	1	0	0	0	0	0	1	3	0
120 - 124	0	0	0	0	0	0	0	0	0	0	0	0	0	0	0	0	0	0	0	0	0
No LSAT	0	0	0	0	0	0	0	0	0	0	0	0	0	0	0	0	0	0	8	8	0
Total	39	26	57	33	91	39	106	46	96	24	63	10	35	5	27	4	6	1	9	529	188

Apps = Number of Applicants
Adm = Number Admitted

Average LSAT for Accepted Applicants: 156
Average GPA for Accepted Applicants; 3.28

Total Number of Applicants: 529
Total Number Accepted: 188
Average Class Size: 75

South Texas College of Law

1303 San Jacinto Street
Houston, TX 77002-7000

Phone: 713.646.1810

■ Introduction

South Texas College of Law is a private, nonprofit, independent educational institution located in downtown Houston. Founded in 1923, South Texas is the oldest law school in the metropolitan area and one of the larger private law schools in the nation. South Texas offers both full-time and part-time study leading to the Doctor of Jurisprudence degree, and is accredited by the ABA.

■ Enrollment/Student Body

➽ *2,658 applicants* ➽ *913 admitted first-year class 1995* ➽ *423 enrolled first-year class 1995* ➽ *853 total full-time* ➽ *396 total part-time* ➽ *21% minority* ➽ *40% women* ➽ *35 states & foreign countries represented* ➽ *262 undergraduate schools represented*

The student-to-faculty ratio at South Texas is approximately 22 to 1. The approximate median age of students is 29. Many South Texas students are pursuing law as a second career or to complement their current employment.

■ Faculty

➽ *96 total* ➽ *56 full-time* ➽ *40 part-time or adjunct* ➽ *25 women* ➽ *5 minority*

■ Library and Physical Facilities

➽ *317,000 volumes & equivalents* ➽ *library hours: Mon.-Thurs., 7:30 A.M.-MIDNIGHT; Fri., 7:30 A.M.-10:00 P.M.; Sat., 8:30 A.M.-7:00 P.M.; Sun., 10:00 A.M.-10:00 P.M.* ➽ *LEXIS* ➽ *NEXIS* ➽ *WESTLAW* ➽ *DIALOG* ➽ *Epic* ➽ *Internet* ➽ *11 full-time librarians* ➽ *library seats 594*

Located in the law school complex are the hearing rooms and chambers of the First and Fourteenth Texas Courts of Appeals (intermediate appellate tribunals with both civil and criminal jurisdiction), making South Texas the only American law school to house two appellate courts on a permanent basis.

Also housed in the complex is the law library, which is committed to new information technology. Library users enjoy access to a variety of online databases; interactive video; CD-ROM and laserdisc databases; a modern computer center; and one of the most advanced multimedia departments in the country.

■ Curriculum

➽ *Academic Support Program* ➽ *90 credits required to graduate* ➽ *150 courses available* ➽ *J.D. degree available* ➽ *semesters, start in Aug. and Jan.* ➽ *range of first-year class size—20-80*

The curriculum at South Texas College of Law combines classroom instruction with simulated and clinical courses and cocurricular activities. The full-time program requires a minimum of 90 weeks of study and the part-time program requires a minimum of 120 weeks of study.

South Texas operates a unified class scheduling system, whereby students may select convenient class times rather than having to choose between day and evening divisions. To accommodate part-time working students, a complete curriculum of classes is scheduled after 5:30 P.M. A few classes also are scheduled on Saturday.

■ Special Programs

South Texas administers an academic assistance program, assisting eligible students in their first 30 hours of coursework through individual and small-group tutorial sessions and weekly reviews of study techniques, such as taking class notes, outlining, briefing cases, and reviewing for examinations. The program is augmented by periodic seminars covering similar topics, which are open to all interested students.

South Texas sponsors a Center for Legal Responsibility to promote conflict resolution outside the traditional judicial system, providing programs for elementary schools, youth villages, and similar organizations. These programs are taught by participating students in cooperation with pro bono activities of members of the legal community.

South Texas provides students with practical legal experience through on-campus clinics in disability entitlement, mediation, and capital-punishment appeals. In each of these clinics, students work on actual cases under the direction of a faculty member. Externships provide practical hands-on experience through placements in prosecutors' offices, state and federal government agencies, and with members of the state and federal judiciary, both at the trial and appellate level.

■ Admission Standards

➽ *Bachelor's degree required* ➽ *application deadline—fall, March 1; spring, Oct. 1* ➽ *LSAT, LSDAS required* ➽ *median GPA—3.00* ➽ *median LSAT score—154* ➽ *application fee—$40*

Beginning and transfer students are admitted for the fall and spring terms, and early application is encouraged. Students are admitted primarily on the basis of their LSAT score and undergraduate grade-point average. A significant percentage of each class, however, is selected on the basis of other additional factors, such as exceptional personal or academic achievement (not necessarily demonstrated in academic or testing assessments); letters of recommendation; work, community service, or life experiences; leadership potential; a history of overcoming adversity and hardship; and a talent for communicating effectively. Every attempt is made to evaluate each applicant as an individual, a prospective student, and a future professional.

South Texas College of Law does not discriminate on the basis of sex, sexual orientation, age, race, color, religion, national or ethnic origin, or disability in administration of its educational policies, admission policies, scholarship and loan programs, and other school-administered programs. South Texas gives special consideration to applications from members of minority groups to help ensure a diverse student body.

■ Student Activities

The *South Texas Law Review* is a scholarly periodical published and edited by a staff of law school students selected for membership on the basis of outstanding scholarship or writing ability. In addition, South Texas students edit and publish the *Corporate Counsel Review* on behalf of the Corporate Counsel Section of the State Bar of Texas, and *Currents*, a journal of international trade law, which focuses on the latest legislation, treaties, cases, and trends affecting international trade.

Each year, South Texas is represented by student teams at various state, national, and international moot court competitions, as well as mock trial, client counseling, and negotiation and settlement competitions. Since 1980, South Texas teams have earned an unmatched record, winning various national and state championships and numerous individual honors.

The Student Bar Association is the general organization for all students. The college has a local honor society, the Order of the Lytae; a chapter of the National Order of Barristers; three legal fraternities; and numerous special-interest student organizations.

■ Expenses and Financial Aid

- *tuition & fees—full-time, $13,800; part-time, $9,400*
- *estimated additional expenses—$11,708 (room and board, books, transportation, and other personal expenses)*
- *academic merit and financial need scholarships available*
- *financial aid available; FAFSA form for need analysis due to central processor in Feb. or early March for fall, and July or early Aug. for spring*

The college offers a deferred tuition payment program. In addition, various financial aid programs are available. Depending on the circumstances, students at South Texas may be eligible for Tuition Equalization Grants and State Student Incentive Grants for Texas residents, Stafford Loans, the Law Access Loan, and Federal work-study. South Texas also offers an expanding variety of merit and need-based scholarships, tuition waivers, grants, and emergency loans. A number of scholarships and grants are targeted toward members of minority groups. Deadlines for these assistance programs vary. Interested applicants may contact the Office of Scholarships and Financial Aid at the college.

■ Career Services

The Career Services Office at South Texas assists students in obtaining full-time or part-time employment and aids graduating seniors and alumni in obtaining permanent employment. While no law school can assure students or graduates of employment, the Career Services Office has expanded its activities each year on behalf of South Texas constituents, with favorable results. The Career Services Office provides professional seminars, counseling, and referrals to assist students and graduates in marketing themselves to potential employers. In addition, the Career Services Office sponsors a mentor program, whereby students can meet informally with alumni to network and learn more about the legal profession.

Applicant Group for the 1995-1996 Academic Year

South Texas College of Law

	Highest LSAT Score																									
GPA	120 - 124		125 - 129		130 - 134		135 - 139		140 - 144		145 - 149		150 - 154		155 - 159		160 - 164		165 - 169		170 - 174		175 - 180		Total	
	Apps	Adm	Apps	Adm	Apps	Adm	Apps	Adm	Apps	Adm	Apps	Adm	Apps	Adm	Apps	Adm	Apps	Adm	Apps	Adm	Apps	Adm	Apps	Adm	Apps	Adm
3.75 - 4.00	0	0	0	0	0	0	1	0	3	2	4	2	13	13	12	12	4	4	0	0	0	0	0	0	37	33
3.50 - 3.74	0	0	1	0	1	0	4	0	14	1	28	17	42	41	25	25	12	12	3	3	0	0	0	0	130	99
3.25 - 3.49	0	0	0	0	2	0	11	1	36	0	73	15	91	77	47	44	18	18	3	3	0	0	0	0	281	158
3.00 - 3.24	0	0	2	0	6	0	18	0	55	0	111	17	142	109	64	62	23	22	6	6	1	1	0	0	428	217
2.75 - 2.99	0	0	0	0	4	1	35	0	57	0	114	13	134	89	66	65	27	27	3	3	0	0	0	0	440	198
2.50 - 2.74	0	0	1	0	12	0	37	0	69	1	100	9	108	42	65	61	16	15	2	2	1	1	0	0	411	131
2.25 - 2.49	0	0	1	0	11	0	33	0	53	1	58	4	67	11	21	13	17	16	7	6	2	2	0	0	270	53
2.00 - 2.24	0	0	2	0	8	0	15	0	33	0	22	1	22	3	6	1	4	1	3	2	0	0	0	0	115	8
No GPA	0	0	0	0	7	0	5	0	12	1	5	1	10	3	6	3	0	0	0	0	0	0	0	0	45	8
Total	0	0	7	0	51	1	159	1	332	6	515	79	629	388	312	286	121	115	27	25	4	4	0	0	2157	905

Apps = Number of Applicants
Adm = Number Admitted

University of Southern California Law School

USC Law School
University Park
Los Angeles, CA 90089-0071

URL: http://www.usc.edu/dept/law-lib/index.html
Phone: 213.740.7331

■ Introduction

The University of Southern California Law School is a nationally oriented, private institution offering an innovative program focusing on the law as an expression of social values and as an instrument for implementing social goals. The Law School is small and informal, boasting an unusually advantageous student/faculty ratio of better than 15:1. Instruction is both highly theoretical and highly practical, emphasizing in various courses both a critical understanding of how law functions in society and a practical knowledge of how lawyers function within the legal system. The school has achieved national recognition both for its innovative, interdisciplinary-oriented young faculty and for its leadership in clinical education.

The Law School's location on the main campus of the University of Southern California, University Park, facilitates access to instruction in law-related disciplines. University Park is located five miles from the center of Los Angeles, a dynamic city which itself is the core of an internationally important region.

Fully accredited nationwide, the USC Law School has been a member of the AALS since 1907, and was included in the first group of schools to be accredited by the ABA.

■ Enrollment/Student Body

➻ *3,650 applicants* ➻ *205 enrolled first-year class 1995*
➻ *610 total full-time* ➻ *39% minority*
➻ *45% women* ➻ *40 states represented*
➻ *125 undergraduate schools represented*

Typically, the size of the entering class is between 195 and 200 students, divided for first-year instructional purposes into two, three, or four sections.

■ Faculty

➻ *49 full-time* ➻ *32 part-time or adjunct*

■ Library and Physical Facilities

➻ *340,000 volumes & equivalents* ➻ *LEXIS*
➻ *WESTLAW* ➻ *21 full-time librarians*

The law library has an excellent, service-oriented professional staff. Study carrels and tables throughout the library are wired so that students can attach their own laptop computers to the network. The library collection includes a substantial number of interdisciplinary materials, reflecting the Law School's commitment to this aspect of legal education.

■ Curriculum

➻ *Academic Support Program* ➻ *88 credits required to graduate* ➻ *joint degrees offered*

The USC Law School operates on a semester basis, and admits only full-time students. The first-year curriculum consists of required courses; the remaining two years are elective, enabling students to concentrate on subjects of special interest. Numerous courses are offered by faculty experts in international law, corporations and business-government relationships, bioethics, civil rights and liberties, and judicial administration. The curriculum draws upon several related disciplines such as philosophy, linguistics, economics, psychology, sociology, international relations, and urban planning to provide an integrated approach to legal study.

■ Special Programs

Dual Degrees—The Law School maintains dual-degree programs with the Graduate School of Business Administration, the Department of Economics, the School of Philosophy, the School of Public Administration, the School of Urban and Regional Planning, the School of Social Work, the School of Religion, the Annenberg School of Communications, and the School of International Relations. These programs enable qualified students to earn a law degree and the appropriate Master's degree. The Law School also maintains a dual-degree program with the California Institute of Technology, enabling students to receive a J.D. from USC and a Ph.D. in Social Science from Cal Tech, or to complete the requirements for the Graduate Certificate in the USC Program for the Study of Women and Men in Society.

Legal Clinics—The Post-Conviction Justice Project and Children's Legal Issues, taught by faculty members with substantial practical experience, enable students to gain valuable advocacy skills and learn first-hand about access to justice and children's rights by representing real clients. In addition, the school arranges placements for academic credit with federal and state court judges, and numerous government and public interest law offices.

■ Admission

➻ *Bachelor's degree from an accredited college required*
➻ *application deadline—Feb. 1; early application encouraged*
➻ *median GPA—3.50* ➻ *median LSAT score—164 (92nd percentile)* ➻ *application fee—$60*

Students applying for admission should take the LSAT no later than the December administration. Admissions decisions are made on the basis of the student's academic record, LSAT score, personal statement, and letters of recommendation. The Admissions Committee gives primary consideration to outstanding academic and professional promise and to qualities which will enhance the diversity of the student body, or will enrich the Law School educational environment. Applicants are strongly urged to submit at least one academic recommendation letter.

The committee focuses on the student's college grades, academic major, selection of courses, and significant scholarly achievements. The Law School does not require applicants to take any specific college courses of study.

Whatever the discipline, the student should concentrate on developing strong writing and analytic skills.

■ Student Activities

The school's *Law Review* has one of the largest circulations in the nation. Students also publish the *Southern California Interdisciplinary Law Journal*, and the *Review of Law and Women's Studies*. The Moot Court competition sends participants to national and state competitions; recently the final rounds at the Law School have been judged by justices of the U.S. Supreme Court. The Order of the Coif, the national legal scholastic honor society, has a local chapter at the school.

Public service activities abound. The Public Interest Law Foundation provides financial assistance for summer and postgraduate public-service employment and volunteer opportunities. The school provides annual awards to students who excel in public and community service, and who author the best essay on a social-justice topic.

Asian, African American, and Latino law students are represented by associations. Other student organizations include international and entertainment law societies, chapters of major legal fraternities, a Women's Law Association, Gay and Lesbian Law Union, Christian Legal Society, Jewish Law Students, and chapters of the ACLU and Federalist Society.

■ Expenses and Financial Aid

➨ *1995-96 tuition—$10,600/semester*

A significant financial commitment is made each year to assist worthy applicants so that they may attend. No student should refrain from applying because of financial need.

To assist in the partial payment of educational loans, the Law School offers funds to graduates who accept employment with low-paying public interest organizations.

For more information, please call Mary Bingham, Director of Financial Aid at 213.740.7331.

■ Housing

University housing is available for law students in various university dormitories and apartments.

■ Career Services

The Law School maintains a career services office to assist students and alumni in securing professional employment. The office provides a variety of services including arranging on-campus interviews by legal employers, assisting students in summer and part-time job searches, and maintaining a file and monthly newsletter for alumni seeking a change of employment. In addition, programs designed to provide guidance concerning career selection are offered during the year. The career services office maintains a public interest and government employment directory listing all available positions. Each year, several hundred private firms, government agencies, public interest agencies, and corporations from throughout the country come to USC Law School to interview students for summer and permanent employment. Historically, approximately 90 percent of each graduating class has found employment.

Applicant Group for the 1995-1996 Academic Year

University of Southern California Law School
This grid includes only applicants who earned 120-180 LSAT scores under standard administrations.

GPA

LSAT Score	3.75 +		3.50 - 3.74		3.25 - 3.49		3.00 - 3.24		2.75 - 2.99		Below 2.75		No GPA		Total	
	Apps	Adm	Apps	Adm	Apps	Adm	Apps	Adm	Apps	Adm	Apps	Adm	Apps	Adm	Apps	Adm
175 - 180	1	1	0	0	5	4	1	0	2	0	1	0	0	0	10	5
170 - 174	9	7	18	17	22	19	7	2	12	7	6	1	0	0	74	53
165 - 169	44	41	84	79	82	77	55	30	31	8	23	5	7	4	326	244
160 - 164	83	68	220	149	239	62	125	15	72	5	48	3	5	0	792	302
155 - 159	90	25	184	21	230	15	158	17	97	9	57	3	10	0	826	90
150 - 154	45	4	119	8	150	17	132	16	100	4	100	0	13	0	659	49
Below 150	21	0	63	2	136	4	311	1	155	0	268	1	37	0	855	8
Total	293	146	688	276	864	198	653	81	469	33	503	13	72	4	3542	751

Apps = Number of Applicants
Adm = Number Admitted
Reflects 97% of the total applicant pool.

Southern Illinois University School of Law

Lesar Law Building
Carbondale, IL 62901-6804
Phone: 618.453.8767

■ Introduction

Southern Illinois University School of Law is located in Carbondale, a community of 27,000 people in the hilly, wooded Ozark area of Illinois. Carbondale's quality of life has recently been rated as number one among all small cities in Illinois. The School of Law is one of nine colleges of Southern Illinois University-Carbondale, a comprehensive state university with a total student enrollment of 24,000. The school is fully accredited by the ABA and is a member of the Association of American Law Schools.

■ Enrollment/Student Body

➧ 848 applicants ➧ 369 admitted first-year class 1995
➧ 131 enrolled first-year class 1995 ➧ 354 total full-time
➧ 17.8% minority ➧ 41% women
➧ 16 states & foreign countries represented
➧ 52 undergraduate schools represented

■ Faculty

➧ 32 total ➧ 24 full-time ➧ 8 part-time or adjunct
➧ 9 women ➧ 3 minority

■ Library and Physical Facilities

➧ 320,000 volumes & equivalents ➧ library hours: Mon.-Fri., 8:00 A.M.-10:00 P.M.; Sat., 9:00 A.M.-5:00 P.M.; Sun., 2:00 P.M.-10:00 P.M. ➧ LEXIS ➧ NEXIS
➧ WESTLAW ➧ LEGALTRAC
➧ 7 full-time librarians ➧ library seats 407

The law library's professional staff provides a wide range of services to patrons. The online public catalog provides immediate and detailed information about the monographs and journals available in the library collection. A LAN-based computer lab provides access to computer-assisted research systems, both legal (e.g., WESTLAW, LEXIS) and nonlegal, as well as computer-aided instruction, word processing, and other applications software. Ample seating in a variety of settings, including tables, unreserved carrels, and locked carrels for research assistants and seminar students, help make the library an activity center of the law school. All facilities are fully accessible to individuals with disabilities. Students have 24-hour keyed access to the library and other facilities.

■ Curriculum

➧ Academic Support Program ➧ 90 credits required to graduate ➧ 83 courses available
➧ degrees available: J.D.; J.D./M.D.; J.D./M.B.A.; J.D./M. Acct.; J.D./M.P.A. ➧ semesters, start in Aug.
➧ range of first-year class size—20-65

All students have a uniform first-year curriculum. A broad range of courses and seminars is offered in the second and third years. Throughout the curriculum the faculty emphasize the inculcation of professional skills such as writing, oral argumentation, drafting documents, interviewing, negotiating, and counseling.

■ Special Programs

The school's clinical program enables senior law students to have various "real-life" experiences with clients and the legal system under the supervision of clinical faculty members, judges, and licensed attorneys. The Elderly Clinic provides direct legal assistance to persons over 60 years of age in the 13 southernmost counties of Illinois. Students may participate in an externship program in which they obtain academic credit while working with the state's attorney, public defender, Illinois Attorney General's office, and other approved legal offices as well as federal and state judges. The ADR Clinic allows students to learn more about alternative dispute resolution techniques and participate with clients in some of the processes. An elderly mediation service is one of the practical applications for the ADR Clinic student.

Concurrent J.D./Masters Degree programs (M.B.A., M.P.A., M. Acct.) are offered in conjunction with the Graduate School. An innovative six-year program offered in cooperation with the School of Medicine permits selected students to concurrently obtain J.D. and M.D. degrees.

The school has a very strong health law curriculum, featuring five courses in this specialty.

The school provides a comprehensive legal argumentation program, sponsoring teams that compete in the National Moot Court, ABA Moot Court, all-Illinois Moot Court, and Philip C. Jessup International Moot Court competitions. SIU law students have enjoyed success in these competitions.

Environmental law is a prominent subject in the law school's curriculum, with six elective courses as well as a National Environment Law Moot Court team.

As part of its mission to emphasize leadership skills, the law school sponsors an active public speakers' program focusing on important national and regional issues. In addition, the school sponsors a major symposium each year bringing a large number of prominent legal educators to Carbondale. Recent symposia have addressed the legal ramifications of the Persian Gulf Crisis (1990), the Bill of Rights (1991), Justice Oliver Wendell Holmes (1993), and Brown v. Board of Education (1994).

■ Admission

➧ Bachelor's degree required ➧ rolling admission, early application (before Feb. 1) recommended
➧ LSAT, LSDAS required ➧ median GPA—3.20
➧ median LSAT score—155 ➧ application fee—$25

Admission decisions are based on a number of factors, the LSAT score and undergraduate GPA being most prominent. Multiple LSAT scores are averaged. There is no formal cutoff for either the LSAT score or GPAs.

Other factors considered by the admissions committee include trends in academic performance, writing ability, leadership and maturity, letters of recommendation, employment or community service experience, and obstacles imposed by racial, religious, ethnic, gender, or disability discrimination. The admissions committee actively recruits minority students.

■ Student Activities

The school publishes the *SIU Law Journal*, which provides editorial and writing experience for a number of upper-class students. Students with a particular interest in health law can also publish articles in *The Journal of Legal Medicine*.

All students automatically belong to the Student Bar Association. The SBA schedules lectures and social affairs, provides services to its members, and serves as a channel of communication between students and faculty. Students play an active role in law school governance, serving on most faculty committees. Other student organizations include Phi Alpha Delta, the International Law Society, the Women's Law Forum, the Environmental Law Society, the Black Law Student Association, Lesbian and Gay Law Students, the Rutherford Institute, Phi Delta Phi, the Law School Democrats, the Law School Republicans, the Nontraditional Students, the Law and Medicine Society, the Christian Legal Society, the Peer Support Network, and law student divisions of the Illinois State Bar Association and the ABA.

■ Expenses and Financial Aid

➽ *full-time tuition & fees—resident, $4,934/yr.; nonresident, $12,942/yr.* ➽ *estimated additional expenses—$7,686 (books & supplies, room & board, transportation & misc.)*
➽ *partial tuition-waiver scholarships available*
➽ *financial aid available; Free Application for Federal Student Aid (FAFSA) need form is preferred*

Student loans, work-study opportunities, and most other forms of financial aid are administered by the university's Financial Aid Office. Information concerning loans and financial aid procedures may be obtained from the Financial Aid Office, Woody Hall, Southern Illinois University-Carbondale.

A relatively large number of research assistantships are available to qualified upper-class students. Approximately one quarter of the upper-class students hold research assistantships.

■ Career Services

Under the direction of an assistant dean, the Career Development Office provides services for both enrolled students and alumni. Students have the opportunity to participate in a variety of regional and national job fairs and career conferences throughout the year. Other programs and services provided include individual career counseling, an on-campus interview program, a research pool service, and career workshops. Special panel presentations that cover a variety of career and employment topics are offered during Law Week in February.

The Career Development Office provides a job listing service, subscribes to a variety of job newsletters, publishes a biweekly job vacancy bulletin, and exchanges job bulletins with other law schools. The career library contains diverse career materials including firm résumés, corporate brochures, and directories.

Applicant Group for the 1995-1996 Academic Year

Southern Illinois University School of Law
This grid includes only applicants who earned 120-180 LSAT scores under standard administrations.

	GPA																					
LSAT Score	3.75 +		3.50 - 3.74		3.25 - 3.49		3.00 - 3.24		2.75 - 2.99		2.50 - 2.74		2.25 - 2.49		2.00 - 2.24		Below 2.00		No GPA		Total	
	Apps	Adm	Apps	Adm	Apps	Adm	Apps	Adm	Apps	Adm	Apps	Adm	Apps	Adm	Apps	Adm	Apps	Adm	Apps	Adm	Apps	Adm
175 - 180	0	0	0	0	0	0	0	0	0	0	0	0	0	0	0	0	0	0	0	0	0	0
170 - 174	1	1	0	0	0	0	0	0	0	0	0	0	1	1	0	0	0	0	0	0	2	2
165 - 169	0	0	1	1	0	0	1	1	3	3	2	2	0	0	0	0	0	0	0	0	7	7
160 - 164	3	3	6	6	11	11	12	12	12	12	8	8	5	5	3	2	1	1	2	1	63	61
155 - 159	4	3	18	17	28	28	38	36	22	20	19	14	10	5	6	2	1	1	3	1	149	127
150 - 154	16	14	33	30	41	15	49	15	39	8	23	2	18	3	6	0	2	0	1	0	228	87
145 - 149	9	4	32	13	32	6	34	8	38	6	21	2	13	2	3	0	1	1	5	1	188	43
140 - 144	5	2	7	2	14	2	19	3	18	1	22	2	12	1	5	0	2	0	4	1	108	14
135 - 139	1	1	0	0	2	0	9	1	9	0	8	0	10	0	6	0	1	0	2	0	48	2
130 - 134	0	0	0	0	0	0	3	0	5	0	11	0	4	0	3	0	2	0	0	0	28	0
125 - 129	0	0	0	0	0	0	1	0	0	0	2	0	1	0	1	0	0	0	0	0	5	0
120 - 124	0	0	0	0	0	0	0	0	0	0	0	0	1	0	0	0	0	0	2	0	3	0
Total	39	28	97	69	128	62	166	76	146	50	116	30	75	17	33	4	10	3	19	4	829	343

Apps = Number of Applicants
Adm = Number Admitted
Reflects 98% of the total applicant pool.

Southern Methodist University School of Law

Director of Admissions
P.O. Box 750110
Dallas, TX 75275-0110

E-Mail: acooper@sun.cis.smu.edu
URL: http://www.smu.edu/~law
Phone: 214.768.2550

■ Introduction

SMU law school, located just five miles north of the central business district of Dallas and situated in a beautiful, residential neighborhood, is an intimate learning community within a vibrant urban center.

Consistently recognized as one of the top 40 law schools in the country by the practicing bar, SMU law school provides its graduates the opportunity to become part of a professional community of 8,000 graduates practicing in all 50 states and 60 foreign countries.

■ Enrollment/Student Body

➠ 2,082 applicants ➠ 261 enrolled first-year class 1995 ➠ 22.7% minority ➠ 43% women ➠ 39 states, 20 foreign countries, and the District of Columbia represented ➠ 151 undergraduate schools represented

Each year, SMU attracts students from the top 25 percent of the national applicant pool. This small and selective student body is the core of our close-knit learning community.

■ Faculty

➠ 90 total ➠ 41 full-time ➠ 49 part-time or adjunct ➠ 13 women (full-time) ➠ 8 minority (full-time)

At SMU, students receive individual attention from nationally-recognized faculty who have practical experience as attorneys in addition to experience in the classroom.

■ Library and Physical Facilities

➠ 467,503 volumes & equivalents ➠ computer center with WESTLAW and LEXIS ➠ 9 full-time librarians ➠ library seats 700

The Law School Quadrangle, a six acre self-contained corner of campus, offers students easy and convenient access to all law school facilities. The four buildings in the quad house state-of-the-art classrooms, student lounges, faculty offices, expansive student affairs and career services offices, and a library where students have open-stack access to holdings ranked in the top 25 in the nation. The larger SMU campus offers law students a variety of housing options, a child-care facility, a health center, and a fitness/wellness center.

■ Curriculum

➠ Tutorial Services and Academic Support Program ➠ 90 credits required to graduate ➠ 160 courses available ➠ degrees available: J.D.; J.D./M.B.A.; J.D./M.A. in Economics; LL.M.; LL.M. (Taxation); LL.M. (International and Comparative Law—for foreign attorneys only)

Students find a sophisticated curriculum at the SMU School of Law that complements its wide breadth of offerings with extensive depth of focus.

The classroom requirements consist of 90 hours of course study completed over three years. In the first year students study a prescribed set of courses that lay a solid foundation for advanced study and for development of essential lawyering skills, including an innovative hands-on course designed to develop students' interviewing and negotiating skills. In the second and third years, students have limited requirements.

The classroom requirements are complemented by the public service requirement. Following completion of the first year, students are required to complete 30 hours of law-related public service prior to graduation. Students may choose from a wide variety of pre-approved public service placements or design one of their own.

During the three years, students have a mix of lecture and seminar courses. In the first year, the entering class is divided into sections of 75-80 students. All of the substantive law courses are taken with the section; all of the skills courses are taken with a subgroup of 15-18 students from the section. In the second and third years, the lecture courses have an average of 40 students and the seminar courses have an average of 15 students.

Externships and Clinics—Externships offer students opportunity to work at a government agency for up to two hours of course credit. Popular externships include those with the U.S. Attorney, the SEC, and the EPA.

Clinics offer students an opportunity to engage in the practice of law for up to five hours of course credit. Currently SMU has four clinical programs: civil, criminal, immigration, and tax.

Overseas Study—SMU offers students an opportunity to study law for six weeks at University College at Oxford University in England.

■ Admission Standards

➠ Bachelor's degree required ➠ application deadline: Dec. 15—early decision; Feb. 15—regular decision; April 15—late decision ➠ LSAT, LSDAS required ➠ application fee—$45 ➠ median LSAT—157 ➠ median UGPA—3.18

The goal of the admissions process is to identify applicants who have the ability to handle a rigorous intellectual challenge, a capacity to acquire lawyering skills and the potential for success as a law student and a lawyer. In the admission process, the Admission Committee wants to know about each applicant's unique abilities, accomplishments, and personality. To that end, each application is considered in its entirety: LSAT scores, undergraduate performance, graduate studies, work experience, activities, a personal statement, and letters of recommendation are all read and evaluated.

■ Student Activities

SMU offers selected students opportunities to write and research for five legal publications: *SMU Law Review, Journal of Air Law & Commerce, International Lawyer, Computer Section Reporter*, and *NAFTA: Law and Business Review of the Americas*.

SMU students who are aspiring advocates develop and showcase their lawyering skills in 10 regional, national, and international competitions annually, including mock trial, client counseling, negotiation, and moot court competitions. As team members, students are coached by faculty members and local lawyers.

Student organizations offer students opportunities to develop friendships, to find support and advice, and to learn about legal topics. The following student organizations are active at SMU: Student Bar Association; Asian Law Students Association; Black Law Students Association; Hispanic Law Students Association; Women in Law; Law Students with Families; Jewish Law Students Association; Christian Legal Society; Environmental Law Society; International Law Society; Intellectual Property Society; and three legal fraternities.

■ Expenses and Financial Aid

- *full-time tuition & fees—$18,848*
- *estimated additional expenses—$7,372 (room & board, $4,508; books, $930; misc., $1,942)*

A legal education at SMU should be considered an investment in the future. Recognizing that most students do not have sufficient personal resources to pay for this investment, SMU provides $1.2 million scholarships annually and access to loans.

The scholarships are awarded on the basis of merit and diversity.

■ Career Services

SMU provides students with job placement assistance throughout their legal careers. The Career Services Office helps students develop their job search and career development skills and partner with students in locating summer and permanent job opportunities.

SMU graduates fare well in the legal job market. During the last five years, an average of 90 percent of our graduates have been employed within six months following graduation. Graduates' average starting salary in the private section was $51,458 and their average starting salary in the public sector was $31,376. Graduates who accept jobs in the public sector may be eligible to receive assistance repaying their law school debts.

Applicant Group for the 1995-1996 Academic Year

Southern Methodist University School of Law
This grid includes only applicants who earned 120-180 LSAT scores under standard administrations.

LSAT Score	GPA 3.75 +		3.50 - 3.74		3.25 - 3.49		3.00 - 3.24		2.75 - 2.99		2.50 - 2.74		2.25 - 2.49		2.00 - 2.24		Below 2.00		No GPA		Total	
	Apps	Adm	Apps	Adm	Apps	Adm	Apps	Adm	Apps	Adm	Apps	Adm	Apps	Adm	Apps	Adm	Apps	Adm	Apps	Adm	Apps	Adm
175 - 180	0	0	0	0	1	1	0	0	0	0	1	1	0	0	0	0	0	0	0	0	2	2
170 - 174	2	2	2	2	3	2	0	0	4	3	0	0	2	1	0	0	0	0	0	0	13	10
165 - 169	10	10	11	11	11	11	16	16	17	17	7	5	5	2	0	0	1	0	0	0	78	72
160 - 164	24	24	55	52	55	54	58	56	39	30	22	19	17	11	0	0	2	0	1	1	273	247
155 - 159	37	33	86	72	129	100	113	77	81	40	40	21	14	5	7	2	2	0	5	3	514	353
150 - 154	35	14	87	34	105	24	151	33	91	11	65	8	21	4	5	1	1	0	4	1	565	130
145 - 149	12	3	35	6	68	5	81	10	72	9	49	4	28	2	8	0	2	0	3	1	358	40
140 - 144	2	1	6	1	17	0	29	2	32	0	26	1	28	1	7	0	2	0	5	1	154	7
135 - 139	1	0	1	0	7	0	15	0	14	1	10	0	16	0	2	0	4	0	5	1	75	2
130 - 134	0	0	3	0	0	0	2	0	2	0	3	0	2	0	1	0	2	0	4	1	19	1
125 - 129	0	0	1	0	0	0	0	0	1	0	1	0	2	0	1	0	0	0	0	0	6	0
120 - 124	0	0	0	0	0	0	0	0	0	0	0	0	0	0	0	0	0	0	0	0	0	0
Total	123	87	287	178	396	197	465	194	353	111	224	59	135	26	31	3	16	0	27	9	2057	864

Apps = Number of Applicants
Adm = Number Admitted
Reflects 98% of the total applicant pool.

Southern University Law Center

Admissions Office
P.O. Box 9294, Southern Branch Post Office
Baton Rouge, LA 70813
Phone: 504.771.5340 or 800.537.1135

■ Introduction

In September 1947, the Southern University School of Law was officially opened. Accredited by the American Bar Association, the Supreme Court of Louisiana, and the Southern Association of Colleges and Secondary Schools, the Law Center maintains a high standard of professional education. It is fully approved by the Veterans Administration for the training of eligible veterans. The Southern University Law Center adheres to the principle of equal opportunity without regard to race, sex, color, creed, national origin, age, handicap, or marital status.

■ Enrollment/Student Body

➽ *1,405 applicants* ➽ *205 admitted first-year class 1995*
➽ *125 enrolled first-year class 1995* ➽ *324 total full-time*
➽ *63% minority* ➽ *43% women*
➽ *22 states & foreign countries represented*
➽ *59 undergraduate schools represented*

■ Faculty

➽ *38 total* ➽ *28 full-time* ➽ *10 part-time or adjunct*
➽ *10 women* ➽ *25 minority*

■ Library and Physical Facilities

➽ *366,085 volumes & equivalents* ➽ *library hours: Mon.-Thurs., 7:30 A.M.-MIDNIGHT; Fri., 7:30 A.M.-5:00 P.M.; Sat., 9:00 A.M.-5:00 P.M.; Sun., 2:00 P.M.-10:00 P.M.* ➽ *LEXIS*
➽ *NEXIS* ➽ *WESTLAW* ➽ *DIALOG* ➽ *Legal Trac*
➽ *6 full-time librarians* ➽ *library seats 284*

The Law Center building is located on the parent campus of the Southern University system. A $4 million expansion and improvement program has been completed. The new facility gives the Law Center a total area of approximately 80,000 square feet.

Special arrangements have been made with the Louisiana State University Library, which has one of the largest collections of Anglo-American and civil law materials in the South, to make its resources available for research purposes through the Southern University Law Library.

Training sessions are conducted each semester by library staff to assist students in the proper utilization of the WESTLAW system.

■ Curriculum

➽ *Academic Support Program* ➽ *Pre-Law Success offered*
➽ *96 credits required to graduate* ➽ *81 courses available*
➽ *fall semester—Aug.-Dec.* ➽ *spring semester—Jan.-May*
➽ *summer session—June-July*

The program of study is designed to give students a comprehensive knowledge of both the civil law and common law. While emphasis is given to the substantive and procedural law of Louisiana with its French and Spanish origins, Anglo-American law is strongly integrated into the curriculum. Fundamental differences in method and approach and the results reached in the two systems are analyzed.

The civil law system of Louisiana offers the law student a unique educational opportunity. The program of instruction examines the historical background of the civil law system and its development in the Anglo-American setting.

Students are trained in the art of advocacy, legal research, and the sources and social purposes of legal principles. Techniques to discipline the students' minds in legal reasoning are an integral part of the educational objectives of the Law Center. Students are instructed in the ethics of the legal profession and the professional responsibility of the lawyer to society.

The three-year curriculum is based upon the standard professional courses usually given in ABA-approved member schools. The curriculum requires a full six semesters of residence. Any study undertaken in a summer session shall not count toward residence requirements. Electives have been integrated as part of the curriculum, and students are required to take courses specified for the respective years.

■ Admission

➽ *Bachelor's degree required* ➽ *application deadline—March 31* ➽ *LSAT, LSDAS required*
➽ *median GPA—2.62* ➽ *median LSAT score—145*
➽ *no application fee*

The Law Center does not prescribe any prelegal courses but strongly recommends a foundation in such courses as English, Speech, Political Science, History, Economics, Psychology, Logic, Mathematics and Analytical Courses, and Science.

Students beginning the study of law are admitted only in the fall semester. The Law Center operates a full-time day program. Applicants are advised to take the LSAT prior to the February test date of the expected year of enrollment. Under no circumstances will a score received on the test administered more than three years prior to the anticipated date of acceptance be considered. All applications for admission are reviewed by a special committee. Though many variables are taken into consideration for admission, primary emphasis is given to the undergraduate grade-point average and scores from the LSAT. Work experience and past pursuits are also reviewed.

Completed application forms, in addition to two letters of recommendation and one copy of official transcript, should be filed with the Admissions Office during the fall semester prior to the year in which admission is sought.

■ Housing

Dormitory accommodations are available for law students. All students desiring to live in campus housing are required to submit an application to the Housing Office, in addition to a security deposit of $50. Applications should be made to the Director of Housing, Southern University, as early as possible.

■ Student Activities

Students with advanced standing are eligible to enroll in the Clinical Education Program, which allows students to handle cases under the direct supervision of a full-time faculty member of the Law Center.

The *Southern University Law Review* is a scholarly periodical published under the auspices of the Southern University Law Center. Editorial administration and managerial responsibilities are handled by the student members of the *Law Review* staff with guidance from a faculty advisor. Membership is conditional on the submissions by each candidate, or other interested students, of a manuscript deemed by the editorial board to be publishable. *Law Review* membership provides eligible students with a wealth of experience in legal research and writing.

■ Other Student Organizations

- *Moot Court board* ➧ *Student Bar Association*
- *Law Student Division, ABA*
- *Black Law Students Association*
- *Delta Theta Phi Law Fraternity*
- *Phi Alpha Delta Law Fraternity, International*
- *Women in Law* ➧ *Environmental Law Society*
- *Sports & Entertainment Legal Association*
- *Student Trial Lawyers Association*

The purposes of the Student Bar Association are to promote the general welfare of the Law Center, encourage among its members high scholarship, and cultivate rapport and cooperation among the students, faculty, and members of the legal profession.

■ Expenses and Financial Aid

➧ *full-time tuition & fees—resident, $3,088; nonresident, $3,088 + $3,200* ➧ *estimated additional expenses—$6,900 (books, lodging, food, transportation, misc.)*
➧ *merit and need-based scholarships available*
➧ *limited merit and need-based scholarships available*
➧ *financial aid available; financial aid transcripts from other schools, copy of previous signed tax return, and financial aid verification data required Student Aid Report (SAR)*
➧ *all forms due April 15*

A limited number of direct stipends and jobs are available. Direct stipends are awarded on the basis of the applicant's academic standing and demonstrated financial need. Applications for stipends should be directed to the Scholarship Committee, Southern University Law Center. Short-term loans to meet emergency needs are available from the Law Center loan fund. All students are expected to pay the required fees on the day of registration.

■ Career Services

The placement office assists students and alumni in obtaining meaningful employment opportunities. Information on part-time employment before graduation is available through this office. Assistance is also given in job-seeking skills and interviewing techniques.

Admission Profile Not Available

Southwestern University School of Law

675 South Westmoreland Avenue
Los Angeles, CA 90005-3992
Phone: 213.738.6717

■ Introduction

The only law school with four courses of study leading to the J.D. degree, Southwestern University School of Law offers traditional full-time and part-time programs as well as a unique two-year alternative curriculum. Located among Los Angeles' major law firms and corporate headquarters, the campus is just a short distance from the courts and government offices in the downtown district. Many public officials and members of the California judiciary are among the outstanding Southwestern graduates who practice law throughout the U.S. and abroad. Southwestern was founded in 1911 as an independent, nonprofit, nonsectarian institution, is approved by the ABA, and holds membership in the AALS.

■ Enrollment/Student Body

➧ 3,100 applicants ➧ 423 enrolled first-year class 1995 ➧ 838 total full-time ➧ 369 total part-time ➧ 29.7% minority ➧ 49% women ➧ over 260 undergraduate schools represented

Southwestern students come from virtually every state as well as from a dozen foreign countries. More than two-thirds have prior work experience or have already completed advanced degrees in such diverse disciplines as accounting, business, chemistry, engineering, international relations, medicine, and urban planning.

■ Faculty

➧ 87 total ➧ 48 full-time ➧ 39 part-time or adjunct ➧ 19 women ➧ 20 minority

The full-time faculty brings to the classroom an average of seven years of law practice and over a dozen years of law teaching experience, and includes several nationally recognized experts on the law. Distinguished judicial officers and practicing attorneys on the adjunct faculty offer courses in a number of legal specialties.

■ Library and Physical Facilities

➧ 364,000 volumes & equivalents ➧ over 100 weekly library hours include: Mon.-Thurs., 7:00 A.M.-MIDNIGHT; Fri., 7:00 A.M.-9:00 P.M.; Sat., 9:00 A.M.-8:00 P.M.; Sun., 9:00 A.M. -11:00 P.M. ➧ LEXIS ➧ NEXIS ➧ WESTLAW ➧ RLIN ➧ WILSONLINE ➧ LEGALTRAC ➧ 8 full-time librarians ➧ library seats 547 ➧ one of the most extensive multimedia legal collections in Southern California ➧ state and federal government depository

The library also features computer labs, group-study rooms, and CALI stations, as well as enhanced collections on constitutional law, entertainment law, environmental law, international law, and taxation. The campus includes the historic five-story Bullocks Wilshire building that is currently being adapted primarily to accommodate the law library by the 1996-97 academic year.

■ Curriculum

➧ Academic Support Program ➧ 87 units/credits required to graduate ➧ more than 140 courses available ➧ J.D. degree ➧ semesters, begin mid-Aug. (July for SCALE program) ➧ range of first-year class size—25-100 ➧ 8-week on-campus summer session ➧ Foreign Summer Law Program in Argentina, Canada, & Mexico

Southwestern's four courses of study include a three-year, full-time day division; a four-year, part-time evening division; a four-year, part-time day division known as PLEAS (Part-time Legal Education Alternative at Southwestern), designed to accommodate students with child-care responsibilities; and an intensive, two-calendar-year alternative program known as SCALE (Southwestern's Conceptual Approach to Legal Education; see below).

The required curriculum for students in the day, evening, and PLEAS divisions includes 19 courses ranging from Business Associations to Torts. More than 120 elective courses and over 100 different externships are offered.

Legal Research and Writing is required of all first-year students. Students must also fulfill an advanced writing requirement later in their course of studies.

■ SCALE Program

SCALE, introduced in 1974, is an alternative, innovative legal education course of study offered exclusively at Southwestern. Its two calendar years of instruction are equivalent to three full academic years in the traditional J.D. curriculum. The program design presents the law as an integrated whole rather than as a series of discrete courses, incorporating instruction in lawyering skills throughout. In the second year, the classroom functions as a "teaching law office" using simulated client files as the primary instructional vehicle. SCALE students also undertake off-campus externships to acquaint them with the working life of the lawyer and judge.

■ Student Support Network

An extensive network of faculty, administrators, students, and alumni provides individual counseling and guidance through the Academic Support Program, Helpnet, the Tutorial Program, the Student Mentor Program, and the Alumni Mentor Program.

■ Public Interest Involvement

A member school of the National Association for Public Interest Law, Southwestern encourages students to pursue public interest service through special scholarship funds, a Loan Forgiveness Program for new graduates involved in public interest careers, several summer grants for students working with public-service agencies, student volunteer work with local schools and community organizations, and a variety of externships.

■ Expenses and Financial Aid

➽ tuition & fees—$18,220 (SCALE program, $23,723); part-time, $11,576 ➽ estimated additional expenses—housing, food, transportation, $1,400/month; books and supplies, $425-$625/year ➽ financial aid available ➽ financial aid application, FAFSA, financial aid transcripts, due June 3 ➽ Federal Work/Study funds available

Among the more than 40 institutional scholarship funds are the Paul W. Wildman Scholarship Program and the John J. Schumacher Minority Leadership Scholarship Program, which have been established to provide up to full-tuition renewable scholarships to members of the entering class who demonstrate exceptional academic and leadership potential.

■ Career Services

The career planning and placement program at Southwestern helps prepare students to succeed in a changing legal job market. The office helps students identify and evaluate their career options and goals, learn about available practice areas, and prepare for and conduct a successful job search. Individual and small-group sessions on résumé writing, interview techniques, and job-search strategies are conducted. Special panel presentations, seminars, and individual mock interview sessions featuring alumni and other attorneys representing a variety of law practice and legal specialization options are also offered. In addition, the Placement Office sponsors intensive on- and off-campus interview programs with prospective employers and maintains comprehensive job listings from around the U.S. and several foreign countries.

■ Admission

➽ Bachelor's degree required for admission ➽ application deadline—June 30 (May 30 for SCALE) ➽ LSAT, LSDAS required ➽ application fee—$50 ➽ rolling admissions, early application advised

Southwestern does not require a particular prelaw major or curriculum. Primary emphasis is placed upon GPA and LSAT scores earned within the past three-year period. Applicants with GPAs of 3.15 and LSAT scores in the 70th percentile have a good chance of acceptance, although these are not minimum standards for all cases. Factors considered in the assessment of each applicant's file include nonacademic work, community involvement, motivation, recommendations, and diversity.

■ Student Activities

Southwestern has one of the most active and successful interscholastic Moot Court Honors programs in the country, with teams participating in 14 competitions a year. Teams also compete through the Interscholastic Trial Advocacy Program. The *Southwestern University Law Review* and the *Southwestern Journal of Law and Trade in the Americas* feature scholarly articles and commentary on current legal issues contributed by noted jurists, attorneys, academicians, and students, and sponsor Distinguished Lecture Series and symposia on campus.

A five-time ABA regional award winner and National Student Bar Association award winner, Southwestern's Student Bar Association sponsors student welfare programs and community outreach projects. There are also over 35 on-campus student organizations including three legal fraternities; minority, cultural, and religious groups; and a variety of associations concerned with specific areas of law.

Applicant Group for the 1995-1996 Academic Year

Southwestern University School of Law

GPA	LSAT Score									
	120 - 124	125 - 129	130 - 134	135 - 139	140 - 144	145 - 149	150 - 154	155 - 159	160 - 169	170 - 180
3.75+						Possible	Very Likely	Very Likely	Very Likely	Very Likely
3.50 - 3.74						Possible	Very Likely	Very Likely	Very Likely	Very Likely
3.25 - 3.49						Possible	Possible	Very Likely	Very Likely	Very Likely
3.00 - 3.24							Possible	Very Likely	Very Likely	Very Likely
2.75 - 2.99							Possible	Possible	Possible	Very Likely
2.50 - 2.74								Possible	Possible	Possible
2.25 - 2.49									Possible	Possible
2.00 - 2.24										
Below 2.00										
No GPA										

Very Likely ■ Possible ■ Unlikely □

Note: This chart is to be used as a a general guide only in determining chances for admittance. Nonnumerical factors are strongly considered for all applicants.

Stanford University Law School

Office of Admissions
Stanford, CA 94305-8610

URL: http://www-leland.STANFORD.edu/group/law
Phone: 415.723.4985

■ Introduction

Stanford Law School is a privately funded institution dedicated to professional and graduate education and to the advancement of legal knowledge. Part of world-renowned Stanford University, it is located on Stanford's 6,109-acre campus, 35 miles south of San Francisco, California. The Law School admitted its first students in 1893 and granted its first LL.B. degree in 1901.

The school is small and intimate, enabling students to pursue personalized courses of study. In addition to providing a top-flight education, Stanford strives to maintain an environment in which diverse students feel welcome and respect one another's backgrounds and views.

■ Enrollment/Student Body

➻ 4,298 applicants ➻ 496 admitted first-year class 1995 ➻ 176 enrolled first-year class 1995 ➻ 574 total full-time ➻ 31% minority ➻ 45% women ➻ 44 states & 10 foreign countries represented ➻ 153 undergraduate schools represented

■ Faculty

➻ 45 total ➻ 39 full-time faculty; includes 6 emeriti ➻ 53 visiting and lecturers ➻ 10 women ➻ 5 minority

■ Library and Physical Facilities

➻ 436,000 volumes & equivalents ➻ library hours: Mon.-Thurs., 8:00 A.M.-MIDNIGHT; Fri., 8:00 A.M.-6:00 P.M.; Sat., 9:00 A.M.-5:00 P.M.; Sun., 10:00 A.M.-MIDNIGHT ➻ LEXIS ➻ NEXIS ➻ WESTLAW ➻ numerous other online research systems available ➻ 9 full-time librarians ➻ assignable library carrels

Robert Crown Law Library is one of this nation's most efficient and comfortable legal-research facilities. Features include a computer-assisted research center, online catalogs, open stacks, and rooms for conferences and joint work. The law library resources are augmented by the interdisciplinary 6.6-million volume Stanford University collections.

■ Curriculum

➻ 86 units/credits required to graduate ➻ course listings available in current school bulletin ➻ semesters, start in Sept. ➻ range of first-year class size—10-60

Stanford Law School offers a day curriculum leading to the Doctor of Jurisprudence (J.D.), or one of three other degrees. The J.D., the basic professional degree, normally requires three years of full-time study. The first-year curriculum allows two to four elective courses. Each first-year student also participates in a small section class in research and legal writing. The second and third years are fully elective.

The Law School has special strengths in business law, high technology law, intellectual property, environmental and natural resources law, constitutional law, public policy, law and economics, problem solving, dispute resolution, legal history and theory, international law, and certain areas of public interest practice. Law students may also take relevant courses in other university departments.

■ Special Programs

Stanford Law School is a participant in a number of interdisciplinary programs, including: joint degree programs with Stanford's Graduate School of Business and other departments including economics, history, and political science, and a program leading to a J.D. and masters degree in International Policy Studies (J.D./I.P.S.); joint degree programs with the Woodrow Wilson School of Public and International Affairs at Princeton University (J.D./M.P.A.) and with the Johns Hopkins School of Advanced Studies (J.D./M.A.); graduate level research and policy -oriented work at the Stanford Center on Conflict and Negotiation, John M. Olin Program in Law and Economics Law & Technology Policy Center, and Cyberspace Law Institute (a joint venture with Georgetown University Law Center); and supervised practice with clients at the East Palo Alto Community Law Project and other legal service entities in the Bay Area.

■ Admission

➻ B.A. required for admission ➻ application deadline—Feb. 15 ➻ rolling admissions ➻ LSAT, LSDAS required ➻ median GPA—3.77 ➻ median LSAT score—168 ➻ application fee—$65

Admission to Stanford Law School is based primarily upon superior academic achievement and potential to contribute to the development of the law. Competition is severe: the 176 members of the Class of 1998 were selected from among 4,298 applicants. The largest part of each class is drawn from the upper 4 percent of their undergraduate colleges and the upper 4 percent of the LSAT pool.

In evaluating individual files, the faculty considers both the record of undergraduate and graduate education and the applicant's nonacademic experience, talents, and aspirations.

Recent classes included many persons who have chosen to study law in order to enhance their contribution to fields like finance, academics, computer and natural sciences, medicine, the arts, and government. Because of its strong belief in the value of diversity, the school especially encourages applications from African Americans, Mexican Americans, American Indians, and Puerto Ricans, as well as others whose ethnic and social background provide additional dimensions that will enhance the school's program.

Applications must be postmarked after September 15 and before February 15 to meet the application deadline.

■ Student Activities

Thirty student organizations enrich the law school experience. Opportunities for scholarly work are provided through *Stanford Law Review; Stanford Journal of International Law; Stanford Journal of Law, Business and Finance; Stanford Law & Policy Review;* and *Stanford Environmental Law Journal.* Courtroom skills are developed in moot court. Other student-run activities include the newspaper (*Stanford Law Journal*), conferences, and Stanford Law Students Association.

Students who are female, Asian, Black, Latino, native American, Christian, Jewish, older, bisexual, gay, or lesbian will all find groups with their particular concerns. Other organizations focus on criminal law, environmental law, international law, the J.D./M.B.A. program, law and technology, and public interest law. Local affiliates of the Federalist Society and National Lawyers Guild are also present.

■ Expenses and Financial Aid

- *1995-96 full-time tuition & fees—$22,350*
- *estimated additional expenses (housing and misc.)—single students, $10,500; married students, $19,300*
- *scholarships awarded on the basis of financial need*
- *financial aid available; Need Access diskette and FAFSA forms required*

The purpose of student financial aid is to assist students who would otherwise be unable to pursue a legal education at Stanford. Approximately 74 percent of the student body receives tuition fellowship or loan assistance.

Stanford law students planning public service careers may obtain Public Service Fellowships for their second and third years of school. The school also offers grants to students who dedicate a law school summer to qualified public-service work. And for graduates who take low-paying public interest jobs and have substantial educational debt, the school has a loan relief program—Public Interest Loan Repayment Assistance Program (LRAP).

■ Career Services

The Office of Career Services helps students find both permanent employment following graduation and part-time and summer employment during law school. Over 265 employers representing 450 offices from throughout the country participate in the spring and fall on-campus interview programs. The office also offers counseling and information on traditional and nontraditional careers and employers. The school encourages students to consider public interest and public-sector employment, and assists students to secure such positions.

A survey of students graduating in the Class of 1995 showed the following employment patterns: law firm associates, 49 percent; judicial clerks, 29 percent; nonlaw, public interest, government, or law teaching, 10 percent; business firms, 6 percent.

Applicant Group for the 1995-1996 Academic Year

Stanford University Law School
This grid includes only applicants who earned 120-180 LSAT scores under standard administrations.

LSAT Score	GPA 3.75 +		3.50 - 3.74		3.25 - 3.49		3.00 - 3.24		2.75 - 2.99		2.50 - 2.74		2.25 - 2.49		2.00 - 2.24		Below 2.00		No GPA		Total	
	Apps	Adm	Apps	Adm	Apps	Adm	Apps	Adm	Apps	Adm	Apps	Adm	Apps	Adm	Apps	Adm	Apps	Adm	Apps	Adm	Apps	Adm
175 - 180	86	60	55	10	34	2	11	0	2	0	0	0	1	0	0	0	0	0	0	0	189	72
170 - 174	163	104	160	20	86	7	19	2	10	1	5	1	2	0	0	0	0	0	8	4	453	139
165 - 169	322	124	365	35	176	20	80	7	22	1	13	0	5	0	2	0	0	0	22	5	1007	192
160 - 164	260	16	371	22	217	15	94	5	52	1	26	0	6	0	3	0	2	0	20	2	1051	61
155 - 159	145	6	178	3	149	3	83	2	36	0	27	0	6	0	3	0	0	0	25	1	652	15
150 - 154	48	1	65	0	76	0	63	0	38	0	32	0	11	0	6	0	2	0	15	0	356	1
145 - 149	14	0	42	0	49	0	35	0	33	0	26	0	12	0	5	0	2	0	14	0	232	0
140 - 144	3	0	8	0	19	0	23	0	27	0	18	0	11	0	4	0	0	0	14	0	127	0
135 - 139	0	0	8	0	13	0	7	0	13	0	15	0	8	0	2	0	1	0	8	0	75	0
130 - 134	0	0	0	0	5	0	4	0	3	0	3	0	2	0	2	0	0	0	1	0	20	0
125 - 129	0	0	0	0	0	0	0	0	3	0	1	0	0	0	1	0	0	0	0	0	5	0
120 - 124	0	0	0	0	0	0	0	0	2	0	0	0	0	0	0	0	0	0	0	0	2	0
Total	1041	311	1252	90	824	47	419	16	241	3	166	1	64	0	28	0	7	0	127	12	4169	480

Apps = Number of Applicants
Adm = Number Admitted
Reflects 97% of the total applicant pool.

Stetson University College of Law

1401 61st Street South
St. Petersburg, FL 33707

E-Mail: lawadmit@hermes.law.stetson.edu
URL: http://www.law.stetson.edu
Phone: 813.562.7800, ext. 7911

■ Introduction

Stetson University College of Law, founded in 1900, is Florida's first law school. For more than half a century it was located in DeLand, Florida, on the main campus of Stetson University. In 1954, it was relocated on its own campus in St. Petersburg, Florida. The present campus is only a few miles from downtown St. Petersburg, Tampa, and Clearwater, a metropolitan area in which many educational opportunities are afforded because of the heavy concentration of law firms and courts. The College of Law is approved by the ABA and became a member of the AALS in 1931.

It is the policy of the Stetson University College of Law not to discriminate on the basis of sex, age, disability, race, color, religion, or national or ethnic origin in its admissions policies. The school is particularly proud of its long history of providing an education to people with disabilities.

■ Enrollment/Student Body

➧ 2,022 applicants ➧ 783 admitted first-year class 1995-96
➧ 303 enrolled first-year class 1995-96
➧ 680 total full-time ➧ 16.8% minority
➧ 53% women ➧ 44 states & foreign countries represented
➧ 191 undergraduate schools represented

The number of applicants, admitted and enrolled in the 1995-96 first-year class represent the spring, summer, and fall entering classes.

■ Faculty

➧ 67 total ➧ 33 full-time ➧ 34 part-time or adjunct
➧ 8 women ➧ 5 minority

■ Library and Physical Facilities

➧ 325,000 volumes & equivalents ➧ library hours: Mon.-Thurs., 7:00 A.M.-MIDNIGHT; Fri., 7:00 A.M.-10:00 P.M.; Sat., 9:00 A.M.-10:00 P.M.; Sun., 9:00 A.M.- MIDNIGHT
➧ LEXIS ➧ NEXIS ➧ WESTLAW
➧ 7 full-time librarians ➧ library seats 304

The physical plant of the college is located on an 18-acre campus. Adapted from an early type of Spanish architecture featuring a central plaza with palm trees, fountains, and massive arcades after the plan of ancient monasteries, it is nevertheless utilitarian in every educational particular. The college has three model courtroom/classrooms, two of which are used by state courts and administrative boards for periodic sessions which students are usually invited to attend.

■ Curriculum

➧ Academic Support Program ➧ 88 credits required to graduate ➧ 125 courses available ➧ degrees available: J.D.; J.D./M.B.A. ➧ semester system, new classes enroll in Jan., May, and Aug., curriculum for first 3 semesters is prescribed ➧ range of first-year class size—30-70

The academic program at Stetson devotes significant attention to the lawyering process. The Stetson faculty believes that the teaching of substantive law is enhanced by extensive training in criminal and civil procedure, and by coursework or related experiences in client counseling, drafting legal papers, trial practice, and actual representation of clients—all under close faculty supervision. Stetson is a pioneer and a national leader in the development of trial practice, in which students perform the functions of a lawyer in close collaboration with a faculty member. The College of Law's courtrooms, equipped with closed-circuit video systems, allow students to observe and evaluate their own performances.

■ Special Programs

Clinical Programs—Members of the second- and third-year classes may become eligible to participate in the Civil Government Law Clinic, the Civil Poverty Law Clinic, the Elderlaw Clinic, the Labor Law Clinic, the Prosecution Clinic, and the Public Defender Clinic. These individualized practical experiences give students an opportunity to acquire a measure of self-confidence and a sense of the professional responsibility that is indispensable to successful law practice.

Trial Advocacy—The growth and development of Stetson's trial program continues unabated. Stetson is the first law school in the nation to win every national trial competition in one academic year (1993-94).Throughout its history, Stetson has excelled in both regional and national competitions, including most recently:

- 1995—First and Second Place, Chester Bedell Memorial Trial Competition
- 1995—First Place, Southeast Regional, ABA Trial Competition
- 1995—Final Four, Regional ATLA Mock Trial Competition
- 1995—First and Second Place, Academy of Florida Trial Lawyers Intra State Trial Competition
- 1995—Second Place, ABA National Trial Competition
- 1995—First Place, National Invitational Trial Competition, Tournament of Champions
- 1994—First Place, National Invitational Trial Competition, Tournament of Champions
- 1994—First Place, National Association of Criminal Defense Lawyers "Cathy E. Bennett" Memorial Trial Competition
- 1994—First Place, National American Bar Association Trial Competition
- 1994—First Place, American Bar Association National Criminal Justice Trial Competition
- 1994—First and Second Place, American Trial Lawyers Association National Competition

■ Expenses and Financial Aid

➽ *full-time tuition and fees—$18,175* ➽ *estimated additional expenses—$10,000 (room, board, and expenses of a single student living on campus)* ➽ *academic merit awards available for entering students and currently enrolled students* ➽ *diversity-based scholarships in varying amounts available for minority students* ➽ *financial aid available; FAFSA forms, deadlines are the same as application deadlines*

■ Career Services

Stetson is firmly dedicated to helping students reach their ultimate goals and become successful attorneys. The Career Services Office assists students and graduates in securing all types of legal employment and provides group seminars and individual counseling on subjects ranging from interviewing techniques and strategies for obtaining various types of jobs to letter and resume writing.

Career Services, a liaison between students and legal employers, brings numerous legal organizations to the campus to interview second- and third-year students. The office posts numerous other legal employment opportunities for associate, part-time, and summer positions throughout the year. For other job-related opportunities, the office's reference library consists of materials and information on graduate programs, government agencies, law firms, judicial clerkships, career options, and teaching opportunities.

Stetson also participates in regional job fairs, where a diverse pool of legal employers grant on-the-spot interviews. Stetson students have experienced an impressive employment success rate through such job fairs.

■ Florida Bar Exam

Stetson is best known for its rigorous, demanding academic program. Our students work very hard and their dedication is rewarded when they take the bar exam. Over the past ten years, Stetson graduates have maintained the overall highest bar passage rate of any Florida law school, approximately 90 percent.

Applicant Group for the 1995-1996 Academic Year

Stetson University College of Law
This grid includes only applicants who earned 120-180 LSAT scores under standard administrations.

LSAT Score	GPA 3.75 +		3.50 - 3.74		3.25 - 3.49		3.00 - 3.24		2.75 - 2.99		2.50 - 2.74		2.25 - 2.49		2.00 - 2.24		Below 2.00		No GPA		Total	
	Apps	Adm	Apps	Adm	Apps	Adm	Apps	Adm	Apps	Adm	Apps	Adm	Apps	Adm	Apps	Adm	Apps	Adm	Apps	Adm	Apps	Adm
175 - 180	0	0	0	0	0	0	0	0	0	0	0	0	0	0	0	0	0	0	0	0	0	0
170 - 174	0	0	1	1	1	0	0	0	0	0	0	0	0	0	0	0	0	0	0	0	2	1
165 - 169	1	1	4	4	5	4	2	1	6	6	2	1	3	2	1	1	0	0	1	1	25	21
160 - 164	8	7	14	14	19	19	18	18	17	13	9	6	8	1	3	0	0	0	1	0	97	78
155 - 159	10	9	38	34	74	64	65	52	66	37	49	19	25	6	6	1	0	0	5	2	338	224
150 - 154	22	17	66	48	97	69	138	63	114	31	78	11	39	4	10	0	3	0	4	0	571	243
145 - 149	12	5	39	18	78	18	116	19	91	7	74	6	29	1	14	1	5	0	7	3	465	78
140 - 144	3	0	23	3	41	3	46	1	51	3	59	5	23	0	14	0	2	0	3	1	265	16
135 - 139	1	1	8	1	11	1	22	1	33	0	22	0	15	0	8	0	4	0	8	2	132	6
130 - 134	2	0	1	0	1	0	6	0	12	0	12	0	13	0	4	0	2	0	4	0	57	0
125 - 129	0	0	0	0	2	0	1	0	1	0	0	0	4	0	1	0	0	0	1	0	10	0
120 - 124	0	0	0	0	0	0	1	0	0	0	0	0	1	0	1	0	0	0	0	0	3	0
Total	59	40	194	123	329	178	415	155	391	97	305	48	160	14	62	3	16	0	34	9	1965	667

Apps = Number of Applicants
Adm = Number Admitted
Reflects 97% of the total applicant pool.

Suffolk University Law School

41 Temple Street
Boston, MA 02114

E-Mail: lawadm@admin.suffolk.edu
Phone: 617.573.8144

■ Introduction

Established in 1906, the Law School is located in the heart of historic Boston and is a short distance from New England's largest legal center. The Law School is approved by the American Bar Association and is a member of the Association of American Law Schools.

At Suffolk University Law School, you will find a consistent emphasis on academic excellence in educating lawyers and advancing the legal profession. The curriculum builds upon a strong core of substantive courses that provide extensive exposure to all fundamental areas of the law.

The school's downtown Boston location allows it to draw upon outstanding leaders from the legal community as distinguished lecturers and adjunct faculty.

■ Enrollment/Student Body

➽ 2,700 applicants ➽ 1,000 admitted first-year class 1995, day division ➽ 300 admitted first year class 1995, evening division ➽ 375 enrolled first-year class 1995, day division ➽ 200 enrolled first year class 1995, evening division ➽ 1,023 total full-time ➽ 709 total part-time ➽ 12% minority ➽ 51.5% women ➽ 50 states & foreign countries represented ➽ 322 undergraduate schools represented

■ Faculty

➽ 137 total ➽ 61 full-time ➽ 76 part-time or adjunct ➽ 10 full-time writing instructors ➽ 16 clinical supervisors ➽ 2 legal practice skills specialists ➽ 33 women ➽ 10 minority

■ Library and Physical Facilities

➽ 300,000 volumes & equivalents ➽ library hours: Mon.-Fri., 8:00 A.M.-11:00 P.M.; Sat. & Sun., 9:00 A.M.-11:00 P.M. ➽ LEXIS ➽ NEXIS ➽ WESTLAW ➽ DIALOG ➽ 10 full-time librarians ➽ library seats 655

■ Curriculum

➽ Academic Support Program ➽ 84 credits required to graduate ➽ 170 courses available ➽ degrees available: J.D.; J.D./M.B.A.; J.D./M.P.A.; J.D./M.S.F.; J.D./M.S.I.E.

■ Special Programs

One of the key components of Suffolk's first-year curriculum is the Legal Practice Skills Program (LPS). Each year, 10 full-time, highly qualified instructors teach small (18-20) groups of first-year students the basics of legal research and writing.

Clinical legal education is an area of primary interest at Suffolk University Law School.

Suffolk Voluntary Defenders—This program consists of a field and classroom component. Students receive thorough training in trial practice skills in their second year, and represent indigent adult and juvenile criminal defendants in the Massachusetts District Courts in their third year.

The Prosecutor Program—Students in their final year are assigned to a court in proximity to Suffolk Law School where they work under the supervision of an assistant district attorney. In this court they appear weekly, are assigned cases, and handle all aspects of prosecution. They learn how a criminal case progresses through the judicial system from the arrest stage through the trial and appeal to a six-person jury session. Court appearances are supplemented by weekly classes in the law school.

Suffolk University Legal Assistance Bureau (SULAB)—This civil clinical program is designed for students in their final year. It has two components, the Family Unit and the Housing Unit, both located in a law office setting. In the Family Unit, students generally represent clients seeking a divorce in the probate courts of Suffolk and Middlesex counties. Students in the Housing Unit typically represent tenants in summary process proceedings in the Boston Housing Court.

S.U. Clinica Legal—This program provides legal assistance in housing cases to indigent tenants in Chelsea, Massachusetts. The program is staffed by second- and third-year students fluent in either Spanish or an Asian language, who can provide legal representation to the growing Latino and Asian populations. The students assume full responsibility for their cases. Their representation includes interviewing and counseling, drafting pleadings, negotiating with counsel, and trying cases.

Battered Women's Advocacy Program (BWAP)—Similar to other clinical programs, BWAP combines classroom lectures/discussions with actual client representation under the supervision of an attorney working in the area. The majority of clients are women who seek protection from abusive spouses or partners, but all victims of domestic violence are represented. Students staff a "crisis line" at the Law School, giving legal advice to domestic violence victims in an effort to help them understand and pursue their civil and criminal remedies. Students appear in court under Supreme Judicial Court Rule 3:03, which allows them to represent clients without compensation in both civil and criminal cases.

Legal Internship Program—Students are provided opportunities to work for government or nonprofit agencies and must perform 90 hours of uncompensated legal service for the agency in addition to satisfying a classroom component. Students may make unsolicited inquiries to agencies that have not sought student assistance or may refer to listings of placement opportunities provided by the Suffolk Career Services Office.

Simulation and Trial Advocacy Programs—Suffolk University Law School has long been known for graduating outstanding trial lawyers. The new trial classroom was designed as a modern trial courtroom housed with the latest video equipment that enables students to review their performance as trial counsel.

■ Admission

➽ *B.A./B.S. required for admission* ➽ *modified rolling admission, early application encouraged; application deadline—March 1* ➽ *LSAT, LSDAS required* ➽ *median GPA—3.20* ➽ *median LSAT score—156* ➽ *application fee—$50*

Admission to the Law School is highly competitive. Applicants must submit both a dean's certification of good standing and a letter of recommendation.

Candidates applying for admission must take the LSAT no later than February. The admission committee does not use a minimum cut-off system in its evaluation of an applicant's LSAT score or GPA. The subjective review includes analysis of class rank, grade trends, year of graduation, range as well as depth of courses, and extracurricular activities. Work experience since graduation is evaluated on the basis of achievement since college, maturity, and responsibility. Applicants are required to submit a personal statement discussing any subjective factors they feel are particularly important to a review of their application.

The review of completed files begins in early November. While the application deadline is March 1, it is clearly to the applicant's advantage to complete his or her file early.

A student who has maintained a satisfactory academic record at another accredited law school and who meets the admission requirements of Suffolk University Law School may apply for admission as a transfer student. Students applying for transfer must do so by June 4.

Admitted applicants reserve a place by paying a two-part deposit totaling $500. No payment is required before April 15.

■ Student Activities

Law students edit and publish the *Suffolk University Law Review* and *Transnational Law Journal*. Each year the law review boards select new students who have academically distinguished themselves. Other publications include *The Advocate*, an alumni/ae-student magazine, and *Dicta*, the Law School newspaper.

Participation in the Moot Court Program is compulsory for first-year students; upper-class students may participate in a voluntary Moot Court Program or on the school's national or international moot court teams.

Over 30 student organizations are active on campus and play a vital role in meeting the many special interests of students.

■ Expenses and Financial Aid

➽ *1995-96 tuition & fees—full-time, $16,580; part-time, $12,436* ➽ *estimated additional expenses—books and supplies, $921; health insurance, $600* ➽ *scholarships available* ➽ *David J. Sargent Fellowship available (full-time)* ➽ *need and merit-based financial aid available* ➽ *FAFSA, Profile, Suffolk Financial Aid Application, financial aid transcripts, tax returns, & W2 forms (students and parents, if applicable) required by March 1*

■ Career Services

A professional staff of 6 assists students and alumni/ae in securing part-time, summer, and permanent employment. Assistance is also provided for students seeking volunteer and work-study positions. A special feature of the service is an alumni network of over 13,000 Suffolk University Law School graduates.

Applicant Group for the 1995-1996 Academic Year

Suffolk University Law School
This grid includes only applicants who earned 120-180 LSAT scores under standard administrations.

LSAT Score	3.75 +		3.50 - 3.74		3.25 - 3.49		3.00 - 3.24		2.75 - 2.99		2.50 - 2.74		2.25 - 2.49		2.00 - 2.24		Below 2.00		No GPA		Total	
	Apps	Adm	Apps	Adm	Apps	Adm	Apps	Adm	Apps	Adm	Apps	Adm	Apps	Adm	Apps	Adm	Apps	Adm	Apps	Adm	Apps	Adm
175 - 180	0	0	0	0	0	0	1	1	1	1	0	0	0	0	0	0	0	0	0	0	2	2
170 - 174	1	1	2	2	1	1	1	1	0	0	0	0	1	1	0	0	0	0	1	1	7	7
165 - 169	1	1	8	8	6	6	9	9	5	3	7	6	3	0	1	0	0	0	1	1	41	34
160 - 164	10	10	34	34	47	46	50	49	37	30	17	12	15	5	4	1	2	0	5	3	221	190
155 - 159	14	14	52	51	109	103	119	111	78	53	67	22	16	2	9	0	2	0	5	3	471	359
150 - 154	22	21	69	67	144	134	160	130	144	62	86	18	47	7	14	2	4	0	11	5	701	446
145 - 149	9	8	54	36	117	70	137	57	117	30	75	21	53	8	14	2	2	0	7	6	585	238
140 - 144	3	3	25	6	37	8	72	24	64	14	50	8	33	3	15	0	4	2	6	1	309	69
135 - 139	1	0	6	2	13	2	37	4	27	0	26	2	19	1	8	0	4	0	8	0	149	11
130 - 134	0	0	1	0	1	0	2	0	2	0	7	0	6	0	1	0	3	0	3	2	26	2
125 - 129	0	0	1	0	0	0	1	0	1	0	2	0	3	0	3	0	0	0	2	0	13	0
120 - 124	0	0	0	0	0	0	0	0	1	0	0	0	0	0	0	0	1	0	0	0	2	0
Total	61	58	252	206	475	370	589	386	477	193	337	89	196	27	69	5	22	2	49	22	2527	1358

Apps = Number of Applicants
Adm = Number Admitted
Reflects 98% of the total applicant pool.

Syracuse University College of Law

Office of Admissions and Financial Aid
Suite 212
Syracuse, NY 13244-1030

E-Mail: admissions@law.syr.edu
URL: http://www.law.syr.edu
Phone: 315.443.1962

■ Introduction

Syracuse University College of Law was established in 1895 and celebrated its centennial in 1995-96. The college is a charter member of the AALS and is fully approved by the ABA. It is one of the oldest of the 15 academic units comprising Syracuse University, a major teaching and research institution. The College of Law is located on the 200-acre Syracuse University campus, which overlooks the scenic upstate city of Syracuse, New York.

■ Enrollment/Student Body

➽ 2,518 applicants first-year class 1995 ➽ 1,149 admitted ➽ 271 enrolled ➽ 787 total full-time ➽ 7 total part-time ➽ 23.6% minority ➽ 43% women ➽ 43 states & 7 foreign countries represented ➽ 311 undergraduate schools represented ➽ 25—average age ➽ 9% possess advanced degrees

■ Faculty

➽ 81 total ➽ 41 full-time ➽ 40 part-time or adjunct ➽ 24 women ➽ 7 minority

■ Library and Physical Facilities

➽ 346,246 volumes & equivalents ➽ LEXIS ➽ NEXIS ➽ WESTLAW ➽ DIALOG ➽ 11 full-time librarians & staff ➽ library seats 531 ➽ computer cluster with 35 IBM PCs ➽ 42-title CD-ROM network

■ Curriculum

➽ Academic Support Program ➽ Legal Education Opportunity Program ➽ 87 credits required for J.D. degree ➽ degrees available: J.D.; J.D./M.B.A.; J.D./M.P.A.; J.D./M.S.; J.D./M.A.; J.D./Ph.D.

The Applied Learning Program at Syracuse provides educational settings that integrate opportunities for students to acquire an understanding of legal theory and doctrine, develop professional skills, and get exposure to the values and ethics of the legal profession. Throughout the curriculum students have the opportunity to work closely with faculty members and other students in small learning settings on simulated or actual legal problems.

■ Special Programs

Law Firm—Each first-year student is assigned to a law firm, a small class where students develop legal writing, research, problem-solving, counseling, negotiation and advocacy skills in connection with simulated problems.

■ Applied Learning Centers

Business Law Center—Students take foundation courses in business associations, commercial transactions, and federal income taxation, followed by advanced business law courses, and participate in a skills seminar or a clinic or externship related to business practice. Additional options include seminars such as Law and Economics or one of the year-long Applied Learning Seminars.

Family Law and Social Policy Center—Students study family law and courses examining major public law social welfare programs. Applied learning opportunities include clinics, externships, and the Family Issues course, which provides experience in areas such as domestic violence and international adoption.

Law, Technology, and Management Center—Emphasizes interdisciplinary and applied approaches to the study of commercial development of new technologies. Coursework involves the study of intellectual property, licensing, patents and copyrights, tax consequences of technology, and business management. Law students work with management and engineering graduate students on projects that involve development and distribution of new technologies.

■ Concentration Programs

Law and Economics Program—Provides training in basic economics and a special field known as Law and Economics. Furthers understanding in related areas such as commercial law, real estate development, administrative law, public law, international trade, environmental law, tort law, and technology law.

International Legal Studies—Course offerings include public international law, commercial transactions, comparative law, and international and comparative tax. Co-curricular activities include moot court competitions, the International Law Society, and the *Syracuse Journal of International Law and Commerce*. Summer programs are offered in Hong Kong, London, and Zimbabwe.

Clinical Programs—Students enrolled in a clinic represent clients in actual legal matters in a supervised setting. Diverse clinical opportunities at the College of Law include: the Civil Law Clinic, the Children's Rights Clinic, the Criminal Law Clinic, the Housing and Finance Clinic, and the Public Interest Law Firm. The College of Law also offers two popular externship programs in which students get hands-on experience by working in the offices of local judges and lawyers.

Joint Degree Programs—Formal joint degree options are offered with many graduate programs of Syracuse University. Other joint degrees may be designed to fit special career objectives.

Advocacy Skills Training—Students participate in intraschool programs throughout the year and are actively involved and highly successful in national moot court competitions.

■ Admission

➽ Bachelor's degree required ➽ application deadline—April 1 ➽ rolling admissions, early application encouraged ➽ LSAT, LSDAS required ➽ median GPA—3.30 ➽ median LSAT score—153 ➽ application fee—$40

The experience of Syracuse reveals that undergraduate grades and LSAT scores are reliable measures, in most cases, for predicting probable success in law study. Thus, an index combining grades and test scores becomes a factor in most admission decisions. However, recognizing that numerical indicators are not always the best predictors of success in law school—even when considered in combination with other factors—the college admits a limited number of students each year through its Legal Education Opportunity (LEO) Program. A goal of the LEO program is the admission of persons who may have been deprived of equal education opportunities for reasons of race, gender, poverty, or other factors beyond their control.

■ Expenses and Financial Aid

➽ *tuition & fees—$18,720* ➽ *estimated additional expenses—$11,000 (room, board, and personal)* ➽ *need-based grants and merit scholarships available* ➽ *forms required: FAFSA, Syracuse internal application and applicant & parent federal tax returns* ➽ *FAFSA due to processor by January 31; internal application and applicant & parent federal tax returns due by March 1*

The College of Law offers a financial aid program that awards combinations of tuition grants, work-study, and loans, primarily on the basis of financial need. Scholarships and fellowships are also awarded to students of outstanding academic promise. Approximately 80 percent of the student body receives some form of financial aid.

■ Career Services

Syracuse graduates are employed throughout the United States. The Office of Career Services administers a comprehensive program that utilizes the most current resources available to assist students in developing a career plan and employment search strategy. A broad mix of innovative and traditional support, provided by the professional staff, empowers students with the confidence and skills necessary to conduct an effective job search in a competitive marketplace.

Applicant Group for the 1995-1996 Academic Year

Syracuse University College of Law
This grid includes only applicants who earned 120-180 LSAT scores under standard administrations.

	GPA																					
LSAT Score	3.75 +		3.50 - 3.74		3.25 - 3.49		3.00 - 3.24		2.75 - 2.99		2.50 - 2.74		2.25 - 2.49		2.00 - 2.24		Below 2.00		No GPA		Total	
	Apps	Adm	Apps	Adm	Apps	Adm	Apps	Adm	Apps	Adm	Apps	Adm	Apps	Adm	Apps	Adm	Apps	Adm	Apps	Adm	Apps	Adm
170 - 180	0	0	0	0	1	1	1	1	2	2	1	1	1	1	0	0	0	0	0	0	6	6
165 - 169	3	3	0	0	6	6	8	8	3	3	5	5	1	0	1	1	0	0	1	1	28	27
160 - 164	9	9	19	19	28	28	33	33	27	24	24	20	4	1	4	2	1	1	3	2	152	139
155 - 159	18	17	50	48	91	88	111	107	86	60	42	13	13	1	7	1	1	0	1	1	420	336
150 - 154	35	35	95	93	153	130	168	75	114	34	94	17	32	6	11	1	1	0	7	5	710	396
145 - 149	15	13	68	45	97	36	145	25	118	19	76	4	36	2	23	1	2	0	3	2	583	147
Below 145	8	3	38	13	67	25	114	11	118	5	92	3	72	0	31	0	8	0	21	2	569	62
Total	88	80	270	218	443	314	580	260	468	147	334	63	159	11	77	6	13	1	36	13	2468	1113

Apps = Number of Applicants
Adm = Number Admitted
Reflects 98% of the total applicant pool.
This chart is provided as a general guide in assessing an applicant's possibility of admission based solely on quantitative factors. It should be noted that nonquantitative factors are also considered in all admission decisions.

Temple University School of Law

1719 North Broad Street
Philadelphia, PA 19122

E-Mail: law@astro.ocis.temple.edu
URL: http://astro.ocis.temple.edu/~law/index.html
Phone: 215.204.8925

■ Introduction

Established in 1895, Temple University School of Law is an urban law school with a national reputation for excellence in academics and clinical education. The law school is situated in Philadelphia on the 90-acre main campus of Temple University, a state-related university. Philadelphia offers something for everyone—history, music, art, theater, sports, and entertainment. For the legal scholar, Philadelphia is also home to the U.S. Court of Appeals for the Third Circuit, the U.S. District Court for the Eastern District of Pennsylvania, the Pennsylvania Supreme Court, state appellate and trial courts, and federal, state, and municipal agencies.

■ Student Body

➻ *3,572 applicants* ➻ *1,063 admitted first-year class 1995* ➻ *360 enrolled first-year class 1995* ➻ *802 total full-time* ➻ *383 total part-time* ➻ *25% minority* ➻ *46% women* ➻ *61 states & foreign countries represented* ➻ *331 undergraduate schools represented*

■ Faculty

➻ *207 total* ➻ *55 full-time (14 women, 12 minority)* ➻ *152 part-time or adjunct*

■ Curriculum

➻ *83 credits required to graduate* ➻ *196 courses available* ➻ *degrees available: J.D.; J.D./M.B.A.; J.D./LL.M. in Taxation* ➻ *semesters, start in Aug. only* ➻ *range of first-year class size—8-91*

Temple's extensive clinical program and our innovative skills courses for both prospective trial lawyers and transactional lawyers are evidence of Temple's philosophy that a legal education must provide both practical and theoretical knowledge.

Temple Law School has a national reputation for its prize-winning **trial advocacy** programs. Temple's National Trial Team beat 234 teams from 119 law schools to win the 1995 National Trial Championship Competition. In 1993, Temple was awarded the prestigious E. Smythe Gambrell Professionalism Award by the American Bar Association for its innovative advocacy course, known as the "Integrated Program," which combines the teaching of trial advocacy, evidence, and professional responsibility.

Temple's reputation for superior training in **business and tax law** is bolstered by an innovative program which combines the teaching of professional responsibility, substantive law courses, and business skills, such as interviewing , negotiating, and drafting. Students use these skills in several clinicals, including the Nonprofit Associations Clinical, the Federal Estate and Gift Tax Clinical, and the Business Law Clinical. Prospective business lawyers can also pursue the J.D./M.B.A. dual degree program, offered in conjunction with the School of Business and Management, or the J.D./LL.M. in Taxation.

For students interested in **international law**, Temple offers a unique semester abroad program in Tokyo, Japan (see below). The Japan program capitalizes on Temple's strengths in international law—a distinguished international law faculty; a diverse curriculum in international and comparative law; the opportunity for summer study in Rome, Athens, and Tel Aviv; a Master of Laws (LL.M.) program for international students holding foreign law degrees; and active student organizations, such as the *International Law Journal* and the International Law Society.

Public service is a Temple tradition. Students provide much-needed legal services in the Philadelphia area through the clinical program, the Temple Legal Aid Office, located in the law school building, and the Temple Law, Education and Participation Program (LEAP), which offers programs designed to teach children about the law. Public Interest careers are supported by the Student Public Interest Network which provides grants for summer internships, and the Barrack Public Interest Fellowships, a loan forgiveness program for Temple graduates in public interest jobs.

Students interested in environmental law, health care law, criminal law, family law, or civil rights law, can also explore these specialties at Temple.

■ Japan Program

Recognizing that an international experience is best gained by actually living, learning, and working abroad, the law school has established a semester-abroad program in Tokyo, Japan. No other law school in the country presently offers a semester-abroad program outside of London. The curriculum, taught by U.S. and Japanese law professors to U.S. and Japanese students, includes a mix of standard law courses and specialty courses focusing on comparative, Japanese, and Asian legal studies. Internships in Japanese law firms and corporations are also available.

■ Library and Physical Facilities

➻ *468,178 volumes & equivalents* ➻ *library hours: Mon.-Thurs., 8:00 A.M.-11:00 P.M.; Fri., 8:00 A.M.-10:00 P.M.; Sat., 9:00 A.M.-5:00 P.M.; Sun., 1:00 P.M.-10:00 P.M.* ➻ *LEXIS* ➻ *NEXIS* ➻ *WESTLAW* ➻ *RLN* ➻ *INNOVAC* ➻ *DIALOG* ➻ *CALI* ➻ *10 full-time librarians* ➻ *library seats 569*

The law library features a unique group of 17th, 18th, and 19th century law books called the William Rawle collection. Computer research laboratories provide access to legal research databases, the library card catalog and serials system, the Internet, word processing, career planning, and general student information. In addition, library carrels are wired for computer usage and the law school offers an affordable PC loaner program. Two mock trial practice rooms are furnished with judicial benches, jury boxes, and video equipment. A large moot courtroom, recently refurbished in the federal style, houses the original bench from the Third Circuit Court of Appeals.

■ Activities

Students are an integral part of policy-making and governance at the law school. The Student Bar Association is the umbrella organization that oversees over 30 student groups. Student publications include the *Temple Law Review*, the *Temple Environmental Law & Technology Journal*, the *Temple International and Comparative Law Journal*, and the *Temple Political & Civil Rights Law Review*. Students who excel in trial advocacy may participate in the National Trial Team, the Moot Court Honor Society, and the Barrister's Society. Each year, the Asian American Law Student Association, the Black Law Students Association, and the Latino Law Students Association sponsor Law Day for People of Color for prospective minority law students.

■ Career Planning

The Career Planning Office provides one-on-one counseling, administers several on-campus and off-campus interview programs, publishes a weekly newsletter, sponsors workshops and programs on job search skills, and maintains the Career Planning Resources Center. According to the responses of 95 percent of its members, the 1994 graduating class had a placement rate of 93 percent.

■ Admission

➽ Bachelor's degree from accredited college or university required ➽ application deadline—March 1 ➽ LSAT, LSDAS required ➽ median GPA—3.27 ➽ median LSAT score—156 ➽ application fee—$50 ➽ rolling admissions, early application preferred

At the discretion of the faculty Admissions Committee, applications may be considered under Temple's discretionary admissions process, called the Sp.A.C.E. Program. The Sp.A.C.E. Program was established by the faculty over 20 years ago in fulfillment of Temple's mission of offering opportunities to students who might otherwise be foreclosed from pursuing a high quality legal education. Under the Sp.A.C.E. Program, the faculty carefully and individually selects applicants who have outstanding performance records and exceptional aptitudes for the study and practice of law, not necessarily reflected by grades and LSAT scores. Applicants reviewed under the Sp.A.C.E. Program include: members of minority groups; applicants who have overcome serious economic deprivation or who come from families historically foreclosed from higher education; applicants who have demonstrated exceptional leadership ability; and applicants with serious physical disabilities.

■ Expenses and Financial Aid

➽ tuition—$7,800 full-time, resident; $14,314 full-time, nonresident; $6,240 part-time, resident; $11,452 part-time, nonresident ➽ merit scholarships and need-based grants available ➽ FAFSA need analysis form due March 1

Applicant Group for the 1995-1996 Academic Year

Temple University School of Law
This grid includes only applicants who earned 120-180 LSAT scores under standard administrations.

LSAT Score	GPA 3.75 +		3.50 - 3.74		3.25 - 3.49		3.00 - 3.24		2.75 - 2.99		2.50 - 2.74		2.25 - 2.49		2.00 - 2.24		Below 2.00		No GPA		Total	
	Apps	Adm	Apps	Adm	Apps	Adm	Apps	Adm	Apps	Adm	Apps	Adm	Apps	Adm	Apps	Adm	Apps	Adm	Apps	Adm	Apps	Adm
170 +	0	0	1	1	2	2	4	4	4	3	1	1	1	1	0	0	0	0	0	0	13	12
165 - 169	9	9	4	4	11	10	11	11	17	16	5	3	4	2	2	1	1	1	2	0	66	57
160 - 164	20	20	29	28	45	43	69	51	44	28	23	12	10	7	4	1	0	0	4	2	248	192
155 - 159	33	32	100	92	150	94	147	64	100	40	75	31	37	10	8	2	2	1	1	0	653	366
150 - 154	38	24	123	63	185	50	229	54	166	36	95	12	45	7	12	2	5	0	10	1	908	249
145 - 149	21	8	88	26	123	31	180	29	145	27	102	21	59	4	23	0	4	0	8	1	753	147
140 - 144	11	3	35	4	69	6	92	7	105	6	89	3	60	0	19	0	0	0	9	0	489	29
Below 140	6	0	15	0	26	0	52	0	73	0	79	0	48	0	35	0	12	0	16	0	362	0
Total	138	96	395	218	611	236	784	220	654	156	469	83	264	31	103	6	24	2	50	4	3492	1052

Apps = Number of Applicants
Adm = Number Admitted
Reflects 99% of the total applicant pool.

University of Tennessee College of Law

Admissions Office
Knoxville, TN 37996-4070

Phone: 423.974.4131

■ Introduction

For more than a century, the University of Tennessee College of Law has offered a strong combination of practical and theoretical legal training. Established in 1890, the College of Law is a charter member of the AALS and is ABA approved.

■ Enrollment/Student Body

➻ 1,141 applicants 1995 ➻ 322 admitted first-year class 1995 ➻ 167 enrolled first-year class 1995 ➻ 480 total enrollment ➻ 11.7% minority enrollment 1995 ➻ 48.3% women enrollment 1995 ➻ 71 undergraduate schools represented

Traditionally, Tennessee residents account for approximately 80 percent of the student body; however, our students are from every region of the United States.

■ Faculty

➻ 36 full-time ➻ 17 adjunct faculty of prominent area attorneys

The quality of our faculty is evidenced by their legal training at some of the finest law schools in the United States, the significance of their scholarly writings, their activity in professional associations, and their involvement in public service.

■ Library and Physical Facilities

➻ over 365,000 volumes & equivalents ➻ LEXIS ➻ NEXIS ➻ WESTLAW ➻ INFOTRAC legal data retrieval systems ➻ 18 full-time library staff, 1 part-time ➻ ready access to vast collection at the University of Tennessee main library system

Ground was broken in the fall of 1994 for a $21.5 million expansion and renovation of the College of Law building. The new complex will be nearly double the size of the existing building and will contain a greater number and variety of teaching, research, and organizational activity areas. Until the new facility is complete in early 1997, law classes will be held in various academic buildings on campus.

■ Location

The University of Tennessee College of Law is located on the main campus of the University of Tennessee at Knoxville, the largest city in east Tennessee and the third largest in the state. More than 25,000 students attend UTK. On any game Saturday in the fall, Neyland Stadium is home to nearly 100,000 Vol fans. Knoxville has the natural advantage of being located in the foothills of the Great Smokey Mountains, making hiking, biking, golf, and fishing popular and accessible activities. Members of the law school community enjoy access to campus facilities for sports and recreation, leisure, the performing arts, entertainment, and other activities and services.

■ Curriculum

➻ Academic Support Program ➻ 89 credits required to graduate ➻ degrees available: J.D.; J.D./M.B.A.; J.D./M.P.A. ➻ semesters, start in Aug. only

First-year students begin law school with a week-long Introductory Period, a series of minicourses to introduce students to the study of law. Second- and third-year students may choose from over 75 elective courses.

The College of Law is preparing two optional programs for students in the near future. Since much of the future growth in law jobs, in Tennessee and nationwide, appears likely to occur in a business practice, the **Center for Entrepreneurial Law** will allow second-and third-year students to focus on the legal aspects of the conduct of public and private enterprise, emphasizing the needs of small and intermediate sized business concerns.

The **Center for Advocacy and Dispute Resolution** will allow interested students to focus their second- and third-year experience toward preparation for a career in advocacy, commonly thought of as litigation or trial practice.

Applicants interested in these two programs should contact the admissions office for more information and for specific dates when these programs will be available.

■ Special Programs

The Civil and Criminal Advocacy Clinic—Established in 1947 as only the second such legal law school clinic, this is one of the oldest continually operating clinical programs in the United States. It provides an ideal opportunity for third-year students to examine the parameters and demands of law practice while working cooperatively with other students and teachers in a supportive environment.

Moot Court Program—Twice in recent years, University of Tennessee teams have distinguished themselves by winning the National Moot Court Competition. The National Trial Team won the National Association of Criminal Defense Lawyers Trial Competition in 1991. The 1993 Jerome Prince Evidence team was unbeaten in taking first place in the national competition. The Environmental Law Moot Court team placed second in the U.S. in the National Environmental Competition in 1992 and 1993. The Advocates' Prize Moot Court Competition offers intracollege competition in written and oral advocacy.

Mediation Clinic—participants work in teams to mediate real civil and misdemeanor cases in the lower courts. Students gain valuable first-hand experience in this emerging form of conflict resolution.

■ Student Activities

The *Tennessee Law Review*, a legal periodical published quarterly by students of the College of Law, offers participants an excellent opportunity to conduct legal research and writing of a scholarly and practical nature. The Student Bar Association and various other student organizations offer numerous programs, services, and special events. The national honor fraternity, Order of the Coif, and two leading professional fraternities, Phi Delta Phi and Phi Alpha Delta, have local chapters here.

■ Admission

➽ *Bachelor's degree from accredited four-year institution required* ➽ *apply between October 1 but before February 1* ➽ *application fee—$15* ➽ *median GPA entering class 1995 —3.46* ➽ *median LSAT entering class 1995—156*

Admission to the College of Law is competitive. The Admissions Committee places substantial emphasis on traditional indicators of performance—the undergraduate GPA and the LSAT score. The committee also considers factors such as improvement in undergraduate grades and graduate school performance; strength of undergraduate institution and major course of study; extracurricular activities; community service; and employment and professional experience. Also considered are circumstances that may have affected an applicant's grades or LSAT score, and economic, social, or cultural background or success in overcoming social or economic disadvantages. Applicants are required to submit two letters of recommendation and write a personal statement and an essay to complete the application file.

The College of Law also recognizes its obligation to assure meaningful access to legal education to qualified applicants who are members of groups that have been historically underrepresented in the legal profession. Members of historically underrepresented minority groups are encouraged to apply. The College of Law encourages applications from such students. Successful completion of the Council on Legal Education Opportunity (CLEO) summer institute and the Tennessee Pre-Professional Program may also be considered by the Admissions Committee.

■ Expenses, Financial Aid, and Housing

➽ *annual full-time tuition & fees—residents, $3,564; nonresidents, $8,958* ➽ *scholarships available (merit and/or need-based)* ➽ *minority scholarships available* ➽ *financial aid available: Perkins Loans, Stafford Loans, Law Access, Law Loans, work-study*

Students who wish to receive priority consideration for need-based scholarships must complete the Free Application for Federal Student Aid (FAFSA) by February 14. There is no application form to complete for merit-based scholarships. Eligible students are automatically considered.

Campus apartment and residence hall housing is open to law students. Knoxville also has ample private apartment housing available.

■ Career Services

Through Career Services, our students and alumni can acquire the skills and knowledge necessary for their first job search and for long-term career planning, as well as useful information about the many professional arenas in which a law degree can be used. These efforts have contributed to the consistently high employment rate for College of Law graduates, above the national average in recent years. There are approximately 6,000 alumni of the College of Law in 49 states, the District of Columbia, and a dozen foreign countries.

Applicant Group for the 1995-1996 Academic Year

University of Tennessee College of Law
This grid includes only applicants who earned 120-180 LSAT scores under standard administrations.

LSAT Score	GPA: 3.75 +		3.50 - 3.74		3.25 - 3.49		3.00 - 3.24		2.75 - 2.99		2.50 - 2.74		2.25 - 2.49		2.00 - 2.24		Below 2.00		No GPA		Total	
	Apps	Adm	Apps	Adm	Apps	Adm	Apps	Adm	Apps	Adm	Apps	Adm	Apps	Adm	Apps	Adm	Apps	Adm	Apps	Adm	Apps	Adm
175-180	0	0	0	0	0	0	0	0	0	0	0	0	0	0	0	0	0	0	0	0	0	0
170-174	1	1	1	1	1	1	1	1	1	0	1	1	0	0	0	0	0	0	0	0	6	5
165-169	6	6	5	5	5	5	6	3	3	2	3	1	2	0	2	1	1	0	0	0	33	23
160-164	14	14	21	18	26	23	24	17	13	8	12	1	2	0	2	0	0	0	0	0	114	81
155-159	30	28	57	40	65	28	56	17	42	3	18	1	7	1	6	0	0	0	0	0	281	118
150-154	28	18	54	14	76	10	66	5	54	3	36	6	12	1	4	0	0	0	0	0	330	57
145-149	5	1	35	8	37	1	45	4	36	2	18	4	12	1	7	0	1	0	0	0	196	21
140-144	6	0	6	1	12	2	18	3	21	4	21	1	8	0	3	0	1	0	0	0	96	11
135-139	2	0	1	0	12	1	10	0	8	1	3	0	3	0	5	0	1	0	0	0	45	2
130-134	1	0	0	0	1	0	4	0	2	0	2	0	5	0	1	0	0	0	0	0	16	0
125-129	0	0	0	0	0	0	2	0	2	0	2	0	1	0	1	0	0	0	0	0	8	0
120-124	0	0	0	0	0	0	0	0	0	0	0	0	0	0	0	0	0	0	0	0	0	0
Total	93	68	180	87	235	70	232	50	182	23	116	15	52	3	31	1	4	0	0	0	1125	318

Apps = Number of Applicants
Adm = Number Admitted
Reflects 99% of the total applicant pool.

The University of Texas School of Law

Post Office Box 149105
Austin, TX 78714-9105

E-Mail: admissions@mail.law.utexas.edu
URL: http://www.law.utexas.edu
Phone: 512.471.8268

■ Introduction

The School of Law is located on the University of Texas campus in Austin, the state capital. This location provides ready access to the state legislature, the Supreme Court of Texas, federal trial and appellate courts, offices of state and federal agencies, and the libraries and other facilities of the University of Texas campus. Long recognized as having a distinguished faculty and educational program, the law school has been a member of the AALS since 1907, and is fully accredited.

Austin is situated in the hill country of Texas, allowing for easy access to lakes and wilderness areas. The University of Texas plays an important role in this metropolitan area of over one million, and many of the entertainment and cultural activities cater to the student population.

■ Enrollment/Student Body

➻ *4,100 applicants* ➻ *512 enrolled first-year class 1995* ➻ *1,468 total full-time* ➻ *25% minority* ➻ *41% women* ➻ *over 250 undergraduate schools represented* ➻ *nonresident enrollment limited to 20 %*

■ Library and Physical Facilities

➻ *880,000+ volumes & equivalents* ➻ *20 full-time librarians*

Recent additions and alterations to the law school complex have made it one of the most attractive and spacious educational facilities of any law school in the nation. Eight large classrooms, numerous seminar rooms, and spacious student lounge areas provide an attractive setting for law study. Federal and state courts hold trial and appellate cases in the moot courtroom on a regular basis. The Tarlton Law Library is the fifth largest in the nation. Open stacks and the most modern computer and audiovisual equipment available make the library facilities accessible to students, scholars, and practicing lawyers.

■ Curriculum

➻ *86 credits required to graduate* ➻ *various joint-degree programs offered* ➻ *semesters, start the last week of Aug.*

All first-year students (except those in the Extended First-Year Program for parents of small children and disabled students) are required to take a full courseload of 15 hours per week in contracts, property, torts, civil procedure, criminal law, constitutional law, brief writing and oral advocacy, and legal research and writing. After the first year, the only required courses are professional responsibility, advanced constitutional law, and a writing and research seminar. The student may design his or her course of study from an array of course offerings in many fields of law. These offerings include interdisciplinary and advanced public and private law courses. There is also a large summer program enabling the student to complete degree requirements in less than three years.

The school offers a Master of Laws (LL.M.) program for foreign law school graduates. The law school offers three joint-degree programs: J.D./Master of Public Administration with the LBJ School of Public Affairs; J.D./Master in Business Administration with the Graduate School of Business; and J.D./Master of Arts in Latin American Studies. Each of the joint-degree programs can be completed within four years.

■ Special Programs

The school offers clinical education courses for credit in such fields as capital punishment, children's rights, criminal defense, elder law, fair housing, juvenile justice, and mental health. Internships are available to qualified students with the Texas Supreme Court, the Texas Court of Criminal Appeals, and the Third Court of Appeals. The law school also has an extensive trial advocacy program.

■ Admission

➻ *early decision deadline—Nov. 1* ➻ *regular decision deadline—Feb. 1* ➻ *median LSAT score—161* ➻ *median GPA—3.55* ➻ *application fee—$65 (applicants presenting foreign credentials—$75)*

To be eligible for admission, an applicant must hold a baccalaureate degree from an accredited college or university and must have a competitive grade-point average and LSAT score. In 1995, only one of every three resident applicants was offered admission, and one of five nonresident applicants was offered admission. Minority students are actively recruited, and financial aid is available to support their attendance. Special facilities are available for students who have disabilities. A $200 seat deposit is required from an applicant who is offered admission. This application fee is subject to change without notice.

The law school accepts a limited number of transfer students who have completed the first year curriculum at an accredited law school and who have compiled a superior academic record at their original law school.

■ Student Activities

The School of Law offers many student-administered, cocurricular activities that enhance the law students' regular studies. Student-edited journals include *American Journal of Criminal Law; Hispanic Law Journal; The Review of Litigation; Texas Environmental Law Journal; Texas Forum on Civil Liberties and Civil Rights; Texas Intellectual Property Law Journal; Texas International Law Journal; Texas Journal of Business Law; Texas Journal of Women and the Law;* and *Texas Law Review.* Other activities include the Legal Research Board, whose members research actual legal problems for practicing attorneys; the Student Bar Association, which includes the entire student body and promotes student social and professional activities; the Women's Law Caucus; the Chicano Law Students Association; the Thurgood Marshall

Legal Society; the Teaching Quizmaster Program, in which qualified second- and third-year students teach the first-year courses in legal research and writing; the Board of Advocates, which administers the mock trial and moot court programs; and chapters of legal fraternities. The Mock Trial and Moot Court Program consists of 11 voluntary intramural competitions involving both trial and appellate advocacy and 17 interscholastic competitions. The following competitions are also offered—Alternative Dispute Resolution; Client Counseling; Negotiations; and Voir Dire. Interscholastic teams consistently achieve a high degree of success in competition and have won several national championships.

■ Expenses and Financial Aid

➡ *tuition & fees—resident, $5,500/yr.; nonresident, $12,000/yr.* ➡ *scholarships available (up to 3 years)*

A limited number of scholarships are awarded to first-year students on the basis of performance in undergraduate studies, academic promise in the study of law, and financial need. The prestigious Rice Scholarship is designed to support eight outstanding law students with full tuition and fees for all three years of law school. Scholarships and research assistantships are available for second- and third-year students. The law school administers several short- and long-term loan funds for students with financial need, and the university offers substantial federally funded loan programs. Information on these programs is given in the Law School Application/Bulletin.

■ Housing

The large majority of our students select off-campus housing. The law school is within 25 minutes by car of almost any point in Austin, and good housing is available within walking distance. Arrangements must be made by the student. For information concerning university dormitories, write to: The University of Texas Housing Division, Kinsolving Dormitory, Austin, TX 78712, or call 512.471.3136.

■ Career Services

Each year, the law school's active placement service arranges interviews with over 300 employers throughout the country, including law firms, judges, corporations, government agencies, and public interest organizations. The service is available to students and alumni seeking part-time jobs, summer clerkships, and full-time employment. Within six months after graduation, 94 percent of the 1994 graduates were employed.

Applicant Group for the 1995-1996 Academic Year

The University of Texas School of Law
This grid includes only applicants who earned 120-180 LSAT scores under standard administrations.

	GPA																					
LSAT Score	3.75 +		3.50 - 3.74		3.25 - 3.49		3.00 - 3.24		2.75 - 2.99		2.50 - 2.74		2.25 - 2.49		2.00 - 2.24		Below 2.00		No GPA		Total	
	Apps	Adm	Apps	Adm	Apps	Adm	Apps	Adm	Apps	Adm	Apps	Adm	Apps	Adm	Apps	Adm	Apps	Adm	Apps	Adm	Apps	Adm
175-180	11	10	5	5	9	9	2	0	5	2	0	0	0	0	0	0	0	0	0	0	32	26
170-174	34	34	38	36	33	21	20	4	11	4	2	0	4	0	1	0	0	0	0	0	143	99
165-169	92	78	140	108	121	61	88	23	45	3	15	2	12	0	2	0	0	0	3	3	518	278
160-164	174	111	255	107	229	70	141	17	89	8	36	1	16	0	3	0	0	0	7	2	950	316
155-159	142	68	227	72	220	37	148	17	90	10	45	2	15	0	2	0	0	0	7	2	896	208
150-154	81	21	146	32	142	22	161	20	94	5	52	1	29	0	8	0	2	0	9	0	724	101
145-149	27	7	49	5	85	3	84	2	73	0	50	0	19	0	7	0	0	0	8	0	402	17
140-144	5	0	14	0	38	1	43	0	47	0	33	0	29	0	11	0	4	0	4	0	228	1
135-139	0	0	3	0	7	0	21	0	23	0	25	0	16	0	12	0	4	0	7	0	118	0
130-134	0	0	2	0	0	0	2	0	9	0	7	0	3	0	3	0	3	0	2	0	31	0
125-129	0	0	1	0	1	0	0	0	0	0	1	0	1	0	0	0	0	0	0	0	4	0
120-124	0	0	0	0	0	0	0	0	0	0	0	0	2	0	0	0	0	0	1	0	3	0
Total	566	329	880	365	885	224	710	83	486	32	266	6	146	0	49	0	13	0	48	7	4049	1046

Apps = Number of Applicants
Adm = Number Admitted
Reflects 98% of the total applicant pool.

Texas Southern University—Thurgood Marshall School of Law

Office of Admissions
3100 Cleburne Avenue
Houston, TX 77004

Phone: 713.313.7114

■ Introduction

The Thurgood Marshall School of Law, a state institution founded in 1947, seeks to provide a legal education and an opportunity to excel to students from a wide range of backgrounds, including those who otherwise would not have an opportunity for legal training. The law school is accredited by the ABA. The student body is truly multi-ethnic and multicultural. The law school is housed in a tri-level structure and is located just outside downtown Houston. Campus housing is available in the form of modern apartments for single and married students. The school makes extensive use of legal facilities in Houston through its clinical programs.

■ Enrollment/Student Body

➡ 1,360 applicants ➡ 530 admitted first-year class 1995
➡ 255 enrolled first-year class 1995 ➡ 550 total full-time
➡ 80% minority ➡ 46% women
➡ 31 states & foreign countries represented
➡ 136 undergraduate schools represented

A majority of the students are from Texas, but all parts of the country are represented. Approximately 52 percent of the students are black, 22 percent Chicano, 20 percent Caucasian, and 4 percent Asian and Native American. The median age range is about 25 to 35 years.

■ Faculty

➡ 48 total ➡ 29 full-time ➡ 19 part-time or adjunct
➡ 9 women ➡ 24 minority

■ Library and Physical Facilities

➡ 300,000 volumes & equivalents ➡ library hours: Mon.-Thurs., 7:00 A.M.-MIDNIGHT; Fri., 7:00 A.M.-10:00 P.M.; Sat., 9:00 A.M.-10:00 P.M.; Sun., NOON-MIDNIGHT
➡ LEXIS ➡ NEXIS ➡ WESTLAW ➡ DIALOG
➡ 5 full-time librarians ➡ library seats 335

Students receive individual and/or group orientation and intensive training in the use of the library. The law school has recently undergone approximately $3 million in renovations, expanding the available space from 16,000 to 32,000 square feet.

■ Curriculum

➡ Academic Support Program ➡ Moot Court, Law Review & Legal Clinics offered ➡ 90 credits required to graduate
➡ 74 courses available ➡ J.D. degree available
➡ semesters, start in Aug.
➡ range of first-year class size—230-260

Upon entry to the School of Law, all students in the first-year class are required to attend a week-long orientation program. Attention is given to examanship, briefing cases, outlining, and an overview of law school life and expectations.

The law school offers a three-year, full-time J.D. program. The minimum courseload is 12 hours. Required courses for the first year are Case Analysis and Legal Writing, Civil Procedure, Property, Contracts, Torts, Appellate Litigation, and Criminal Law. Second-year students must take Constitutional Law, Evidence, Criminal Procedure, Trial Simulation, Business Associations, Commercial Law, Basic Federal Taxation, Professional Responsibility, and Wills and Trusts. Third-year students are required to take Federal Jurisdiction and Procedure, a seminar/independent research project, and Texas Practice. The remaining hours required to complete the degree may be selected from a number of areas of interest.

The law school operates a full-time, in-house clinic in which students work under the supervision of faculty and adjunct faculty members. Internships are available with the Harris County District Attorney's Office, the Federal Magistrates, Gulf Coast Legal Foundation, the Federal Bankruptcy Court, the Harris County Attorney's Office, the Internal Revenue Service, and the U.S. District Court. The school operates a number of clinics, including Homeless Advocacy, Immigration, Aids, and Elderly. A judicial externship with state and federal judges is available to academically outstanding third-year students. The summer session offers a different series of related courses each year. A six-week summer pre-enrollment (L.E.A.P) program, by invitation, and a tutorial program for all first-year classes are provided.

■ Admission

➡ Baccalaureate degree required ➡ LSAT, LSDAS required
➡ median GPA—2.66 ➡ median LSAT score—145
➡ application fee—$40

The GPA and LSAT (or average LSAT if attempted more than once on same scale) are factored into a formula which places more weight on the LSAT. The number derived, the index, is used to determine an applicant's initial competitiveness.

No particular undergraduate major is preferred, but the school looks for applicants with broad backgrounds in the social sciences, natural sciences, humanities, and business sciences. Admission decisions are based primarily on the applicant's motivation and intellectual capacity, undergraduate GPA, and LSAT scores. Newly admitted students must send two seat deposits ($150 upon acceptance and $100 in June), which are refundable upon matriculation. The law school makes special efforts to recruit members of minority groups. Transfer applications are accepted; students must submit a transcript and letter from the dean of their former law school stating that they are in good standing. All newly admitted students must submit an official transcript from the baccalaureate degree-granting institution as well as all law schools attended. No application will be evaluated by the Admissions Committee until the LSDAS report has been received. In order to ensure complete review, applications must be received by the Office of Admissions no later than April 1, although there is no official deadline. Entering students are admitted only in August (fall semester). Students are notified of acceptance after the Admissions Committee has reviewed the complete file. Early completion of applications is encouraged. Admission decisions are made on a rolling basis.

■ Student Activities

Numerous law school organizations are active on campus. A student board edits the *Thurgood Marshall Law Review*. Moot court competitions are held in trial and appellate work, labor law, and client counseling.

■ Expenses and Financial Aid

➧ *full-time tuition—resident, $130/sem. hr.; nonresident, $250/sem. hr.* ➧ *estimated additional expenses per semester—fees, $350; books & supplies, $275; parking $25*
➧ *law school & university scholarships available*
➧ *numerous minority scholarships available*
➧ *financial aid available; forms due May 1*

About 90 percent of the students receive some form of aid. The law school administers its own scholarship program, which is competitive. Scholarships are awarded on the basis of both need and merit, and may range up to full tuition. The university also offers additional scholarship aid, and the law school and the university offer loan assistance. Ten to fifteen percent of the students hold assistantships. The aid application deadline is May 1.

The scholarship program makes several awards (approximately 40) each year. The awards have enabled out-of-state residents to qualify for resident-tuition rates. In addition, a number of law students each year qualify for the federal work study and loan programs. Additional limited scholarship aid is available to students after they have completed a year of law study. An applicant in need of other financial assistance should make arrangements for financial aid through the Director of Financial Aid, Thurgood Marshall School of Law, Texas Southern University, 3100 Cleburne Ave., Houston, TX 77004.

■ Career Services

The law school employs a full-time placement officer. Graduates are placed primarily with law firms, federal and state agencies, legal services, judges, and businesses. The Office of Placement and Career Development also conducts a major national effort to encourage legal employers in every major city in the United States to recruit Texas Southern University Thurgood Marshall School of Law graduates.

Applicant Group for the 1995-1996 Academic Year

Texas Southern University—Thurgood Marshall School of Law
This grid includes only applicants who earned 120-180 LSAT scores under standard administrations.

LSAT Score	GPA 3.75 +		3.50 - 3.74		3.25 - 3.49		3.00 - 3.24		2.75 - 2.99		2.50 - 2.74		2.25 - 2.49		2.00 - 2.24		Below 2.00		No GPA		Total	
	Apps	Adm	Apps	Adm	Apps	Adm	Apps	Adm	Apps	Adm	Apps	Adm	Apps	Adm	Apps	Adm	Apps	Adm	Apps	Adm	Apps	Adm
175-180	0	0	0	0	0	0	0	0	0	0	0	0	0	0	0	0	0	0	0	0	0	0
170-174	0	0	0	0	0	0	0	0	0	0	0	0	0	0	0	0	0	0	0	0	0	0
165-169	0	0	0	0	0	0	0	0	0	0	0	0	1	1	0	0	0	0	0	0	1	1
160-164	0	0	0	0	1	1	2	2	0	0	4	4	2	2	0	0	0	0	0	0	9	9
155-159	1	1	2	2	0	0	3	2	2	2	3	3	2	2	2	2	0	0	0	0	15	14
150-154	1	1	5	5	6	5	11	10	25	22	20	19	29	28	8	8	5	5	2	0	112	103
145-149	2	2	15	15	21	19	41	39	46	35	65	54	42	31	29	22	5	2	3	0	269	219
140-144	3	2	8	6	25	15	47	27	57	30	84	28	72	18	39	4	9	0	11	1	355	131
135-139	3	2	10	2	16	5	42	4	52	4	57	9	63	3	54	1	12	4	14	0	323	34
130-134	0	0	3	0	5	0	11	0	30	2	31	1	36	2	21	0	15	0	11	0	163	5
125-129	0	0	0	0	2	0	3	0	5	0	8	0	8	0	7	1	0	0	2	0	35	1
120-124	0	0	0	0	1	0	0	0	0	0	0	0	1	0	1	0	0	0	0	0	3	0
Total	10	8	43	30	77	45	160	84	217	95	272	118	256	87	161	38	46	11	43	1	1285	517

Apps = Number of Applicants
Adm = Number Admitted
Reflects 98% of the total applicant pool.

Texas Tech University School of Law

Box 40004
Lubbock, TX 79409

Phone: 806.742.3791

■ Introduction

The School of Law, which accepted its first class in 1967, is located on the main campus of Texas Tech University in Lubbock. It is fully accredited, having received approval from the Supreme Court of Texas and the ABA and membership in the AALS at the earliest dates possible under the rules of those organizations. As a result, its graduates are eligible for admission to practice in any state in the nation, and many are engaged in practice throughout the United States. In 1974, a chapter of the Order of the Coif, the national legal honorary society, was established at the School of Law.

■ Enrollment/Student Body

➽ *1,544 applicants* ➽ *580 accepted first-year class 1995* ➽ *236 enrolled first-year class 1995* ➽ *628 total full-time* ➽ *15% minority* ➽ *37% women* ➽ *73 undergraduate schools represented*

■ Faculty

➽ *34 total* ➽ *22 full-time* ➽ *11 part-time or adjunct* ➽ *9 women* ➽ *4 minority*

■ Library and Physical Facilities

➽ *250,000 volumes & equivalents* ➽ *library hours: Mon.-Thurs., 7:30 A.M.-MIDNIGHT; Fri., 7:30 A.M.-6:00 P.M.; Sat., NOON-6:00 P.M.; Sun., 2:00 P.M.-MIDNIGHT* ➽ *LEXIS* ➽ *NEXIS* ➽ *WESTLAW* ➽ *5 full-time librarians* ➽ *library seats 475*

The law school is housed in a beautiful and functional building designed to comfortably accommodate a student body of about 600 and a full-time faculty of 29. The recent renovation of the law library added 12,000-square-feet of stack and study space. Two hundred fifty study carrels housing 500 students are equipped with 250 PCs offering access to WESTLAW and LEXIS, as well as to the library's online catalog. Word processing capabilities are also provided. Student organizations occupy spacious offices on the third floor. Two other notable features of the building are the beautiful and functional courtroom where the Texas Court of Appeals sits each year, and the Forum which serves as a student lounge and the site of various law school social functions. As a result of the remodeling, the building now complies with ADA standards.

■ Curriculum

➽ *Academic Support Program* ➽ *90 semester hours required to graduate* ➽ *degrees available: J.D.; J.D./M.B.A.; J.D./M.P.A.; J.D./AG. ECON.; J.D. Master of Finance* ➽ *semesters, start in Aug. & Jan.* ➽ *range of first-year class size—60-70* ➽ *summer sessions available*

The program of study is planned to equip the student to practice law as advocate, counselor, judge, or law teacher. At the same time, recognition is given to the use of law training as a stepping-stone to a career in government, politics, or business. All of the courses in the first year and some of the courses in the advanced years are required. The remainder of the courses are electives.

■ Special Programs

In addition to the basic program of study for the J.D. degree, qualified students may elect to pursue one of three joint-degree programs: the J.D./Master of Business Administration; the J.D./Master of Public Administration; and the J.D./Master of Science in Agricultural Economics. The joint-degree programs allow a student to complete the requirements for both degrees in less than four academic years instead of the five required if both degrees were pursued separately.

The School of Law offers opportunities to practice various lawyering skills in courses such as trial advocacy, appellate advocacy, arbitration, skills development, and others.

In recognition of the lack of representation of minority groups in the legal profession, the School of Law participates actively in programs designed to increase the number of minority group lawyers.

■ Admission

➽ *Bachelor's degree from accredited college or university required* ➽ *application deadline—Feb. 1* ➽ *LSAT, LSDAS required* ➽ *median GPA—3.38* ➽ *median LSAT score—156* ➽ *application fee—$50* ➽ *rolling admissions, early application preferred*

Written recommendations are not required, but in borderline cases may prove helpful. Anyone filing an application after February 1 will be at a disadvantage in competing for the limited number of places available. Accepted applicants must pay a $200 deposit to hold a place in the entering class. This acceptance deposit will be refunded to the applicants upon matriculation at the law school. One-half of the deposit is refundable upon timely written notice of a change in plans. Such notice is due April 1 for summer admission and May 1 for fall admission. In June, accepted applicants must pay one-half of their tuition and fees for the fall semester.

Admissions decisions are made by the Admissions Committee and are based on an evaluation of the LSAT score, the quality of the undergraduate coursework and performance, and other criteria including background and employment experience, graduate work, and evidence of leadership qualities in campus and community activities. The LSAT score and the undergraduate GPA are weighted about equally.

Applicants are admitted for entrance in the fall with the exception of 20 to 25 who are admitted to commence their studies in June. The summer admittees are selected from a group of applicants whose LSAT scores are below the 50th percentile and who are residents of Texas. By carrying a limited number of hours of law courses during the nine-week summer program, the students are able to take a reduced courseload over the remainder of the first year. All students admitted, however, including those admitted for summer entrance, are admitted for full-time study only.

■ Student Activities

In addition to activities available to all students of the university, there are many extracurricular activities provided for the law student.

The *Texas Tech Law Review*, published four times a year, consists of articles written by students and leading jurists, practitioners, and faculty. Membership is based on academic qualification.

The Board of Barristers supervises and conducts an extensive moot court program, in which the student develops skills in brief writing and in the art of oral advocacy. The school enters teams in interschool competition in mock trial, moot court, client counseling, and negotiation.

The Legal Research Board is a student organization that offers attorneys a service similar to that of a briefing staff. The board methodically researches requested legal topics and then compiles the information in a memorandum of law.

The Student Bar Association is the focal point for many student activities, both professional and social. The SBA cooperates closely with the faculty in bringing speakers and programs to the law school. In addition, the SBA sponsors numerous student social events.

The legal fraternities at the school sponsor professional and social functions. They admit both men and women to membership.

■ Expenses and Financial Aid

➽ tuition & fees—$5,298 ➽ average additional expenses—$8,902 (room and board, books, transportation, personal expenses) ➽ merit, minority, and need-based scholarships available ➽ FAFSA, financial aid transcripts, and loan applications required for financial aid

More than 80 scholarships are available, ranging in value from $1,000 to a full scholarship. Long-term educational loan funds are available through the Office of the Director of Financial Aid, and short-term loans are available through the Law School Foundation.

■ Housing

A variety of housing convenient to the campus is available for single and married students. Information on campus housing may be obtained from the Housing Office, Texas Tech University.

■ Career Services

The Placement Office of the School of Law is under the direction of the assistant dean. Graduates of the law school find employment in every area of practice in the public and private sectors. Historically, a significant majority of graduates are employed within six months of graduation. The law school is a member of the National Association of Law Placement, which provides information on opportunities for placement nationally to students.

Applicant Group for the 1995-1996 Academic Year

Texas Tech University School of Law
This grid includes only applicants who earned 120-180 LSAT scores under standard administrations.

LSAT Score	GPA 3.75 +		3.50 - 3.74		3.25 - 3.49		3.00 - 3.24		2.75 - 2.99		2.50 - 2.74		2.25 - 2.49		2.00 - 2.24		Below 2.00		No GPA		Total	
	Apps	Adm	Apps	Adm	Apps	Adm	Apps	Adm	Apps	Adm	Apps	Adm	Apps	Adm	Apps	Adm	Apps	Adm	Apps	Adm	Apps	Adm
175-180	0	0	0	0	0	0	0	0	1	1	0	0	0	0	0	0	0	0	0	0	1	1
170-174	2	2	1	1	2	2	0	0	3	3	0	0	0	0	0	0	0	0	0	0	8	8
165-169	3	3	3	2	9	9	10	9	5	5	3	2	3	2	0	0	0	0	0	0	36	32
160-164	7	7	17	17	27	27	23	21	18	18	7	5	15	5	2	0	0	0	2	0	118	100
155-159	32	31	58	57	74	67	66	46	45	22	31	1	13	1	5	0	1	0	2	1	327	226
150-154	22	21	63	52	74	43	107	34	71	8	56	2	17	0	6	0	4	0	7	0	427	160
145-149	10	7	23	8	50	9	66	11	60	0	49	1	20	0	9	0	1	0	7	1	295	37
140-144	4	0	8	0	28	0	32	0	38	0	28	0	27	1	9	0	4	0	4	0	182	1
135-139	0	0	1	0	10	0	15	0	16	0	18	0	18	0	8	0	4	0	4	0	94	0
130-134	0	0	0	0	1	0	1	0	4	0	3	0	5	0	5	0	1	0	1	0	21	0
125-129	0	0	1	0	0	0	0	0	1	0	0	0	1	0	1	0	0	0	1	0	5	0
120-124	0	0	0	0	0	0	0	0	1	0	0	0	0	0	0	0	0	0	0	0	1	0
Total	80	71	175	137	275	157	320	121	263	57	195	11	119	9	45	0	15	0	28	2	1515	565

Apps = Number of Applicants
Adm = Number Admitted

Texas Wesleyan University School of Law

2535 East Grauwyler
Irving, TX 75061

Phone: 800.733.9529; 214.579.5751

■ Introduction

Established in 1989, the law school became part of Texas Wesleyan University in 1992. The university recently celebrated its 100th anniversary, having been founded in 1890. A comprehensive university, Texas Wesleyan offers degrees in business, education, fine arts, humanities, and sciences. The university is accredited by the Southern Association of Colleges and Schools. In August 1994, the law school received provisional accreditation by the American Bar Association, which entitles students to the same recognition as students of fully approved ABA law schools. Texas Wesleyan University School of Law offers both full-time and part-time study leading to the Juris Doctor degree.

Many Wesleyan students are nontraditional, seeking a legal education at a later stage in their lives. For the entering class of fall 1995, the median age was 31. Students range in age from 21 to 68. A substantial proportion of students have engaged in a variety of positions in business, health sciences, education, and public service.

■ Enrollment/Student Body

➽ 904 applicants ➽ 502 admitted first-year class 1995 ➽ 263 enrolled first-year class 1995 ➽ 349 total full-time ➽ 322 total part-time ➽ 18% minority first-year class ➽ 42% women (287 women) ➽ 86 undergraduate schools represented in student body

■ Faculty

➽ 38 total ➽ 23 full-time ➽ 15 part-time or adjunct ➽ 7 women ➽ 2 minority

The 23 members of the full-time faculty hold 68 degrees from 42 educational institutions. Law schools represented by the faculty's degrees include Columbia, Chicago, George Washington, Texas, Utah and Yale, with graduate law degrees from such schools as Columbia, Harvard, New York University, Pennsylvania, and Virginia. Nonlaw doctoral and master's degrees include Stanford, Michigan, Chicago, Harvard, Texas, and Wisconsin. Faculty members have contributed numerous articles, essays, and other material for legal publishers and law journals around the country. Adjunct professors provide a considerable range of academic and professional experience as well.

■ Library and Physical Facilities

➽ 137,000 volumes & equivalents ➽ library hours: Mon.-Fri., 7:30 A.M.-MIDNIGHT; Sat., 9:00 A.M.-MIDNIGHT; Sun., 10:00 A.M.-MIDNIGHT ➽ LEXIS ➽ NEXIS ➽ WESTLAW ➽ 5 full-time librarians ➽ library seats 218

The law library's mission is to provide student access to the legal information resources needed to practice law in the digital age. In addition to its law book collection, the law library subscribes to major online electronic legal information services and several CD-ROM research tools. Students are furnished software and passwords for use on home computers to provide them access to online legal information beyond the law library walls. Complementing book and electronic sources, an extensive collection of U.S. Congressional documents, including full transcripts of all Congressional hearings, is available on microfiche. The law library is open more than 100 hours a week, during 65 of which at least one professional reference librarian is on duty.

Texas Wesleyan School of Law is located in a large contemporary facility in the Dallas/Fort Worth Metroplex. Plans are underway for the creation of a Law Center to be located in the Metroplex area. The Metroplex, with a population of 3.8 million, offers a relatively low cost of living and a growing economy and has rapidly grown to be one of the largest and most diversified metropolitan areas in the country.

■ Curriculum

➽ Academic Support Program ➽ 88 credits required to graduate ➽ 150 courses available ➽ degree available: J.D.

Eighty-eight hours of academic instruction are required for completion of the three-year full-time, or four-year part-time program leading to the Juris Doctor degree. The part-time program is offered in the evening for students who wish to work full-time while pursuing their legal education.

■ Skills Training

Wesleyan considers skills training to be a significant component of legal education. By participation in such skills courses as trial advocacy, moot court, pretrial practice, appellate practice, dispute resolution, mediation, negotiations, commercial arbitration, family mediation and crisis management, and estate planning, students develop strengths in oral advocacy, writing, and drafting. Additionally, the Externship Program enables students to work with practicing attorneys for academic credit and provides a supervised context in which students will be exposed to front-line practice before the bar and governmental agencies.

■ Admission

➽ Bachelor's degree from an accredited college or university required ➽ application deadline—preferably by March 1, later applications may be considered ➽ LSAT, LSDAS required ➽ median GPA—2.90 ➽ median LSAT score—150 ➽ application fee—$50

In addition to addressing academic achievements and aptitude, the Admissions Committee will endeavor, on the basis of the applicant's education and other experiences, to determine the professional promise of the applicant. In this connection, the committee will look for evidence of high achievement in various endeavors, prior employment, military experience, graduate study, community service, and other factors. To further our effort toward diversification, special attention is given to members of minority groups who traditionally have not been well represented in the legal profession. The diversity of the student body is also an important consideration with respect to the variety of undergraduate institutions and geographic areas represented in an entering class. Inquiries as to credentials and timing should be directed to the law school's Admission Office 214.579.5751. Wesleyan may admit students with advanced standing who are in good standing at a law school approved by the American Bar Association.

■ Activities

Student activities, complementing traditional academic programs, include the *Texas Wesleyan Law Review*, a scholarly periodical published by a staff of law students with membership based on outstanding grades and writing ability, Moot Court, the Order of Barristers, Mediation Clinics, and the Pro Bono Board. Cocurricular activities such as the Student Bar Association, the Criminal Justice Society, International Law Society, Intellectual Property Society, the Christian Legal Society, Black Law Students Association, Hispanic Law Students Association, Asian & Pacific American Law Students Association, Organization of Women Law Students, and two legal fraternities also serve to broaden the student experience.

■ Expenses and Financial Aid

➧ 1995-96 tuition & fees—$370/credit hour, plus $174 fees per semester ➧ approximate additional expenses—$500/semester (books and study guides) ➧ scholarships available ➧ financial aid available

FAFSA, financial aid transcripts, and loan applications required for financial aid. Loan information is available through the Office of Financial Aid, 214.579.5738.

■ Career Services

The Wesleyan Law School Career Services Office assists students, graduates, and employers in their mutual efforts to link those seeking legal positions with those providing employment opportunities. In addition to assisting with full-time employment opportunities, Career Services supports students securing part-time or temporary employment while attending law school. A range of services, such as career counseling, résumé writing, and on-campus interviewing are available. The law school also offers a career planning library. The school is a member of the National Association of Law Placement.

Admission Profile Not Available

Thomas M. Cooley Law School

217 S. Capital Avenue
Post Office Box 13038
Lansing, MI 48901

Phone: 517.371.5140

■ Introduction

America's leader in part-time, year-round legal education, Thomas M. Cooley Law School was established in 1972 in Lansing, Michigan by former Supreme Court Chief Justice Thomas E. Brennan and a group of dedicated lawyers and judges.

Named for Michigan's renowned Judge Cooley, the school is committed to open admissions, practical scholarship, and uncompromising professionalism. The American Bar Association approved Thomas Cooley Law School in 1975.

As an independent, graduate college, Thomas Cooley enjoys the reputation of a tough law school, run by experienced lawyers and judges. Its faculty, students, and alumni take pride in the school's close contacts with the bench and bar.

The *Thomas M. Cooley Law Review* has received national recognition for promoting the use of plain English lawsuit papers.

■ Enrollment/Student Body

➽ 2,200 applicants for all 1995 classes ➽ 1,794 accepted
➽ 932 matriculated first-year class 1995
➽ 55 total full-time ➽ 1,685 total part-time
➽ 11% minority ➽ 32% women

Of Thomas Cooley's diverse student body, 72 percent hail from out-of-state and 10 percent hold advanced degrees. The median age of entering students is 26.

■ Faculty

➽ 49 full-time ➽ 100 part-time or adjunct
➽ 14 women ➽ 3 minority

■ Library and Physical Facilities

➽ 341,000 volumes & equivalents ➽ library is open 111 hours per week including weekends ➽ LEXIS
➽ NEXIS ➽ WESTLAW ➽ 11.5 full-time librarians
➽ library seats 500

Cooley's research facility is designed to meet the research needs of today's law student. The library features a large computer lab, two electronic classrooms for computer-assisted legal instruction and Innopac, a state-of-the-art integrated automated library system.

Occupying nearly 65,000-square-feet and five levels, the library collection includes standard state and federal legal materials. Primary research materials from every state are maintained and updated. Nearby, the State Law Library and the general libraries of the city of Lansing, state of Michigan, Lansing Community College, and Michigan State University are available to Thomas Cooley students.

■ Curriculum

➽ 90 credits required to graduate ➽ J.D. degree
➽ three terms per year, beginning Jan., May, and Sept.

Thomas Cooley Law School is organized on a 12-month academic year, consisting of three full 15-week terms of school. Each term meets the definition of a full semester. Like the terms of the English Courts of Common Law, Thomas Cooley's three academic terms are designated Hilary Term (January to April), Trinity Term (May to August), and Michaelmas Term (September to December).

Thomas Cooley students typically attend classes only 10 hours per week. Many are employed full-time. Still, they graduate in three years or less. Some prefer to be full-time students and graduate in as little as 28 months. Classes are offered in the morning, afternoon, and evening.

Thomas Cooley's catalog lists 26 required and over 100 elective courses. Before graduating, every Thomas Cooley student argues a case before a real judge in a real courtroom.

■ Special Programs

The Sixty-Plus Law Center, Thomas Cooley's award-winning clinic for elderly citizens, permits students to earn academic credit while representing real clients.

Directed studies, trial workshops, law review, and moot court programs enrich the curriculum. Because Thomas Cooley has a national student body, civil and criminal practice courses for New York, New Jersey, Pennsylvania, Florida, Indiana, Arizona, Texas, Wisconsin, and Illinois are offered.

■ Admission

➽ Bachelor's degree required ➽ rolling admissions
➽ LSAT, LSDAS required ➽ application fee—$100
➽ median LSAT score—148 (30 old scale)
➽ $25 nonrefundable fee upon acceptance

The admissions office uses a simple index (15 times undergraduate grade-point average [UGPA] + LSAT) to determine admissibility. All applicants with an index of 180 or more are virtually assured of acceptance.

Candidates otherwise qualified may be rejected for specific negative factors by the Faculty Admissions Committee. Morning, afternoon, and evening divisions are organized in September, January, and May, respectively. There are 300 seats available in each new class. New students who cannot be accommodated in the class of their choice are carried forward to the next available class. Students with index scores below 180 are usually urged to retake the LSAT.

■ Student Activities

All students are members of the Student Bar Association, and chapters of two national legal fraternities have been established. In addition, students publish a newspaper, operate the Scholastic Review Board for student grade appeals, supervise the Student Tutorial Service, edit and publish *The Thomas M. Cooley Law Review*, and conduct an active intramural sports program.

The Thomas M. Cooley Law Review focuses upon legal questions of significance to state governments, state court jurists, and state public policy matters. The *Review* prepares and publishes three issues per year. Each issue features articles written by practicing attorneys, judges, and professors; casenotes and comments written by Thomas Cooley students; and distinguished briefs argued before the Michigan Supreme Court.

The school has an internship program with various state administrative agencies under which students are compensated to work a maximum of 20 hours per week. There are 32 clubs and organizations for students. They include the International Law Society, Women's Law Alliance, Black Law Students Association, Christian Legal Society, the Environmental Law Society, Jewish Law Caucus, Hispanic Law Society, and Asian Pacific American Law Students Association.

■ Expenses and Financial Aid

➽ tuition & fees—full-time/part-time, $465/per credit hour ➽ estimated additional expenses—$15,571 (room and board, books, personal, transportation) ➽ honors, need-based, academic standing, and special-factor scholarships available ➽ Martin Luther King and Rosa Parks minority scholarships available ➽ financial aid available

Because Thomas Cooley Law School seeks to attract top students and reward academic excellence, the Board of Directors has established a unique Honors Scholarship Program, based entirely on a student's entering credentials and his/her academic performance in law school. The chart below shows the percent of Thomas Cooley tuition awarded to first- and second-term honors scholars based on their admission index (multiply UGPA by 15 and add LSAT score to determine the index):

Index	Scholarship
219 or above	100 percent
218	90 percent
217	80 percent
216	70 percent
215	60 percent
213 & 214	50 percent
211 & 212	40 percent
209 & 210	30 percent
207 & 208	20 percent
205 & 206	10 percent

In the third and subsequent terms, all Thomas Cooley students who maintain a cumulative GPA of 3.0 or better are eligible for tuition scholarships ranging from 10 percent for a GPA of 3.0 to 100 percent for a GPA of 3.9.

Honors scholarships are applicable only to offset future tuition at Thomas Cooley Law School and are not redeemable in money. Many Cooley students qualify for State of Michigan tuition grants. More than 80 percent receive guaranteed student loans. Five to 10 percent are awarded work-study funds.

■ Housing

The law school does not operate residence facilities. There is an ample supply of living accommodations available nearby in all price ranges.

■ Career Services

The Career and Student Services Office provides a wide variety of services to students and graduates of the law school. Job postings (updated weekly) provide listings for full-time positions in both in and out of state, as well as listings for legally related part-time work in the greater Lansing area. Reciprocal agreements with law school placement offices in other parts of the country are maintained for those students and graduates who wish to practice in other states. Workshops and seminars, focusing on topics ranging from interviewing skills to business etiquette, are open to all students. Services for students and alumni include the Thomas Cooley Placement Hotline, a 24-hour recording of the most recent week's listings. The office also maintains a credential file system for graduates, utilized by employers who wish the Career and Student Services Office to supply résumés of interested candidates.

Acceptance and Scholarship Range

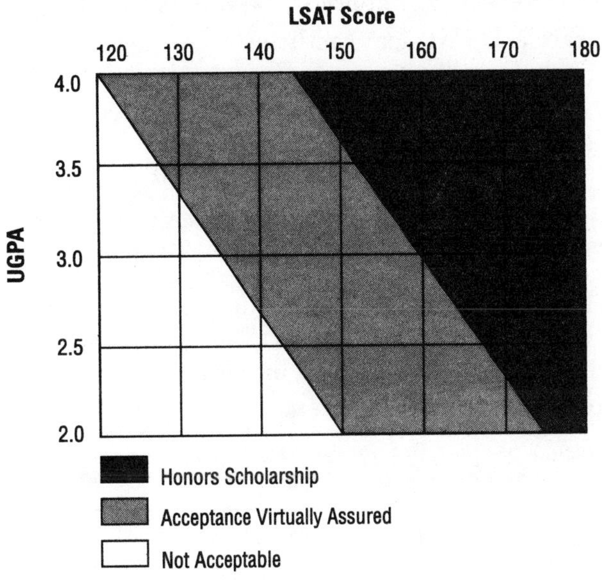

The University of Toledo College of Law

2801 West Bancroft Street
Toledo, OH 43606

Phone: 419.530.4131

■ Introduction

The University of Toledo is a state university of 24,000 students, conveniently located on the western edge of Toledo, Ohio, in one of the city's nicest residential areas.

The College of Law, located on the main campus of the University of Toledo, is accredited by the ABA and is a member of the AALS and the League of Ohio Law Schools. It has been training lawyers since 1906 and in 1984 was awarded a chapter of the Order of the Coif. Toledo, at the western end of Lake Erie, is conveniently located to Ann Arbor, Detroit, Cincinnati, Cleveland, Columbus, and Chicago.

■ Enrollment/Student Body

➻ *926 applicants* ➻ *509 admitted first-year class 1995* ➻ *213 enrolled first-year class 1995* ➻ *455 total full-time* ➻ *215 total part-time* ➻ *12% minority* ➻ *41% women* ➻ *25 states & foreign countries represented* ➻ *200 undergraduate schools represented*

The college seeks a diverse student body. Approximately 35 percent of the entering students come from outside Ohio. The day-division entering class ranges from 160 to 170; evening, from 50 to 60.

■ Faculty

➻ *52 total* ➻ *37 full-time* ➻ *15 part-time or adjunct* ➻ *12 women* ➻ *2 minority*

The full-time faculty hold law degrees from some of the most outstanding universities in the country. Many have advanced law degrees.

While legal scholarship is important and many faculty members have national reputations for scholarship, the College of Law places a high priority on effective teaching and accessibility to students.

■ Library and Physical Facilities

➻ *285,000 volumes & equivalents* ➻ *library hours: Mon.-Fri., 7:30 A.M.-MIDNIGHT; Sat.-Sun., 9:00 A.M.-MIDNIGHT* ➻ LEXIS ➻ NEXIS ➻ WESTLAW ➻ *14 full-time librarians* ➻ *library seats 540*

The spacious, modern Law Center includes tiered classrooms, a striking student lounge, moot courtroom, law office classroom, and amphitheater auditorium.

The law library contains eight group study rooms, videotaping facilities, and several microcomputers and printers for use by law students.

■ Curriculum

➻ *Academic Support Program* ➻ *87 credits required to graduate* ➻ *150 courses available* ➻ *degrees available: J.D.; J.D./M.B.A.* ➻ *semesters, start in Aug.* ➻ *range of first-year class size—20-55*

Both a full-time and a part-time program are available. The first-year curriculum is prescribed. Prior to graduation, all students are required to complete the course in Legal Ethics and a perspective course, as well as a scholarly paper within the context of a seminar.

■ Special Programs

The college was a pioneer in clinical legal education. Under a rule of the Ohio Supreme Court, upper-class students appear in court under close faculty supervision in both civil and criminal cases. Through the Dispute Resolution Clinic, mediation experience also is available in a variety of matters, including unruly child complaints and custody and visitation issues in parentage cases in juvenile court.

The college has a long-standing interest in international legal studies.

■ The Legal Institute of the Great Lakes

The Institute supports research, special studies, and conferences on legal issues of greater than ordinary import to the Great Lakes Region of the United States and Canada. The Institute sponsors a course of study on Law and the Great Lakes which integrates major topical areas including environmental law, natural resources law, transportation law, agricultural law, commercial and corporate law, and international and comparative Canadian law. It publishes a newsletter and an online electronic journal with student assistance.

■ Admission

➻ *Bachelor's degree from an accredited college or university required* ➻ *application deadline—full-time, March 15; part-time, May 15* ➻ *LSAT, LSDAS required* ➻ *median GPA—3.11* ➻ *median LSAT score—155* ➻ *application fee—$30*

Grades and LSAT scores are the most important determinants of admission. Evidence showing that the GPA and LSAT score understate an applicant's ability is carefully considered. Letters of recommendation are important.

Prospective students are encouraged to visit the College of Law and sit in on classes. Appointments can be made through the Admission Office.

■ Student Activities

The *University of Toledo Law Review* is published four times a year by students selected on the basis of scholarship. Students may also qualify by submitting a publishable article. Training and practice in brief writing and oral argument beyond the required appellate advocacy course are obtained in the Charles Fornoff Intramural Moot Court Competition and in several national and regional competitions. Client counseling and trial practice programs are also stressed. All students are members of the Student Bar Association. The Black Law Students Association, Business Law Society,

Environmental Law Society, Federalist Society, Health Care Law Association, Hispanic Law Student Association, International Law Society, Sports Law Association, and the Women Law Students Association are active student organizations.

■ Expenses and Financial Aid

➻ *full-time tuition & fees—$6,158, resident; $11,672, nonresident* ➻ *part-time tuition & fees—$4,362, resident; $8,268, nonresident* ➻ *per semester hour tuition and fees—$256.55, resident; $486.30, nonresident*
➻ *estimated additional expenses—$10,250 (room, board, books, personal expenses, transportation)*
➻ *merit and merit/need-based scholarships available*
➻ *financial aid available; need analysis form due to Financial Aid Office by April 1*

Under the terms of an agreement entered into by the states of Ohio and Michigan, residents of Monroe County, Michigan, who are attending the University of Toledo are treated as in-state residents for tuition purposes. Although the university has no housing for law students, housing near the university is plentiful. Newly admitted students desiring assistance in obtaining housing receive help from the Student Bar Association and the University's Off-Campus Living Office.

■ Career Services

The College places top priority on providing comprehensive career planning and placement for its students and graduates. The office assists students through workshops, videotapes, and counseling, and provides guest speakers on legal career options.

As a result of both on- and off-campus interviews, second- and third-year students in 1994-95 accepted summer or attorney positions in all major cities of Ohio and Michigan as well as other locations throughout the U.S.

The College's Judicial Clerkship Program places graduates as clerks with federal courts of appeals and district courts, and with state trial and appellate courts around the country. Second- and third-year students have the opportunity to participate in internships in federal and Ohio appellate courts.

College of Law graduates take the bar examination in many states. The college's first-time takers of the Ohio Bar Examination consistently pass the exam with scores above the state's average.

Applicant Group for the 1995-1996 Academic Year

The University of Toledo College of Law
Graph reflects admission decisions as of 9/1/95.

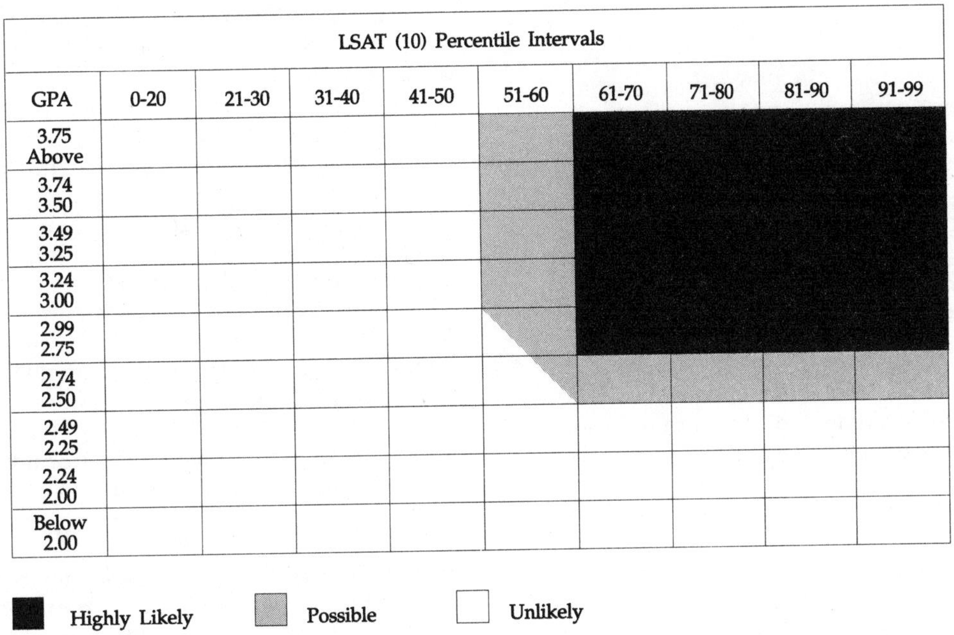

	LSAT (10) Percentile Intervals								
GPA	0-20	21-30	31-40	41-50	51-60	61-70	71-80	81-90	91-99
3.75 Above									
3.74 3.50									
3.49 3.25									
3.24 3.00									
2.99 2.75									
2.74 2.50									
2.49 2.25									
2.24 2.00									
Below 2.00									

■ Highly Likely ▨ Possible □ Unlikely

Touro College—Jacob D. Fuchsberg Law Center

300 Nassau Road
Huntington, NY 11743

E-Mail: stephend@tourolaw.edu
URL: http://law.touro.edu
Phone: 516.421.2244, ext. 313

■ Introduction

The Jacob D. Fuchsberg Law Center is a component of Touro College, which was established under Jewish auspices. The college derives its name from Judah and Isaac Touro, leaders of Colonial America, whose commitment to academic excellence and to the Jewish heritage represent the ideals upon which Touro College bases its mission.

Touro College is fully approved by the Middle States Association of Colleges and Schools. The Law Center is fully accredited by the American Bar Association and is a member of the Association of American Law Schools.

The Law Center is located in Huntington, Long Island, a residential community near the western boundary of Suffolk County, one of the most rapidly expanding and developing areas of New York State. The school enjoys the many benefits of a suburban campus in close proximity to New York City.

■ Enrollment/Student Body

➽ 2,142 applicants ➽ 881 admitted first-year class 1995 ➽ 246 enrolled first-year class 1995 ➽ 464 total full-time ➽ 330 total part-time ➽ 27.8% minority ➽ 40.7% women ➽ 17 states & 2 foreign countries represented in first-year class 1995 ➽ 105 undergraduate schools represented in first-year class 1995 ➽ average age in the full-time class is 26; part-time is 31

The law school has a diverse student body. Students range in age from 21 to 71.

■ Faculty

➽ 55 total ➽ 43 full-time ➽ 12 part-time or adjunct (varies by year) ➽ 16 women ➽ 3 minority

■ Library & Physical Facilities

➽ 338,000 volumes & equivalents ➽ library hours: Mon.-Thurs., 8:00 A.M.-11:45 P.M.; Fri., 8:00 A.M.-2:45 P.M.; Sat., closed; Sun., 9:00 A.M.-11:45 P.M. ➽ LEXIS ➽ NEXIS ➽ WESTLAW ➽ DIALOG ➽ DOWJONES NEWS ➽ RETRIEVAL ➽ OCLC ➽ AUTO-CITE ➽ 6 full-time librarians ➽ library seats 580

In observance of the Jewish Sabbath, the law library closes early on Friday, and remains closed on Saturday. Resource-sharing arrangements are available with nearby law libraries.

■ Curriculum

➽ Academic Support Program ➽ Professional Development Program ➽ Writing Clinic ➽ 87 credits required to graduate ➽ 107 courses available (not offered every semester) ➽ J.D. degree available ➽ fall semester begins mid-Aug.; spring semester begins early Jan. ➽ range of first-year class size—17-80

J.D. students may study full-time for three years or part-time in the day or evening for four years. The first-year curriculum is required. A number of required courses extend into the second year for full-time students and into the third year for part-time students. In addition, every student must, before graduation, satisfy a series of upper-division requirements as outlined in the Law Center bulletin. The upper-class curriculum includes specialties in commercial/corporate law, constitutional law, criminal law, employment/labor law, family law, government regulations, health law, intellectual property, international law, jurisprudence and legal history practice, property (estates and real estate), public interest law, torts, and a full range of clinical offerings.

■ Special Programs

The Institute of Local and Suburban Law—The Institute of Local and Suburban Law is dedicated to the research of local and suburban problems and education in the areas of municipal law, environmental law, and their interrelationship with state and federal law.

Legal Education Access Program—The Legal Education Access Program represents a committed effort by the Law Center to offset barriers to success that often are experienced by students of color at a predominately white law school. LEAP is comprised of several key components, including a three-week summer program; group discussions; a mentor program; and individual counseling and assistance for all participants.

The Housing Rights Project—The Housing Rights Project is an on-campus legal services program designed to offer students the opportunity to obtain hands-on experience by volunteering their time to provide representation for low-income clients in housing-related proceedings.

Institute of Jewish Law—The Institute of Jewish Law is concerned with research, scholarship, publication, and courses in Jewish Law.

Moscow Summer Program—A four-week program focuses on Russia's legal system in transition. Coursework is enhanced by supplemental lectures and tours.

The New India—A four-week summer program in Shimla, India, in the foothills of the Himalayas, focusing on India's legal system and international law in general.

LL.M. for Foreign Law Graduates—A Master's in U.S. Legal Studies serving the needs of both U.S. residents who hope to practice here and attorneys from abroad who wish to be familiar with U.S. laws and institutions.

■ Admission

➽ Bachelor's degree from accredited college/university required ➽ application deadline—May 1 ➽ early application preferred, rolling admission ➽ LSAT, LSDAS required ➽ median GPA—2.80 ➽ median LSAT score—151 ➽ application fee—$50 ➽ personal statement required

Students are admitted to the first-year full-time and part-time day and evening class for the fall semester of each academic year. Transfer students may be admitted to either fall or spring semesters. The admissions process is selective. It seeks to identify those applicants who evidence an ability to pursue the study of law successfully and to make a significant contribution to the educational program and diversity of the law school.

The principal criteria used in the admissions process are the cumulative grade-point average and the LSAT score. The selection process, however, recognizes that other factors, such as major and course selection, graduate study, personal qualities of character, integrity and good citizenship, and professional experience after college, may also be indicators of potential.

The effect of a long delay between college and proposed entry to law school is, of course, taken into consideration. Letters of recommendation from those with direct personal knowledge of the intellectual capacity of an applicant can contribute to the admission decision.

The Law Center does not and will not discriminate against any applicant for admission because of race, color, religion, sex, national origin, age, marital status, financial status, or physical disability.

Applicants are always welcome to visit the campus. The Admissions Office is open weekdays throughout the year. Visitors should make advance arrangements by contacting the Admissions Office. Inquiries may be addressed to the Director of Admissions.

■ Student Activities

Students may participate in various activities outside the classroom that offer opportunities for academic and social growth. Key among these are the *Touro Law Review*, the *Environmental Law Journal*, the *Touro Journal of International Law*, the *Journal of the Suffolk Academy of Law*, and the Moot Court Board. In addition to the Student Bar Association—which supports social and academic activities for all Touro students—there are 22 professional and social organizations open to students.

■ Expenses and Financial Aid

➽ *tuition & fees—full-time, $17,350; part-time, $13,600* ➽ *estimated additional expenses—(approximate cost of books and supplies in the first year)—$500* ➽ *scholarships available: Dean's Fellow Award, Merit Scholarship, Siben Fellowship, Incentive Award* ➽ *financial aid available; FAFSA and GAPSFAS due May 1, March 1 strongly preferred*

The Law Center provides access to federal and private loans, and the New York Tuition Assistance Program. Institutional aid includes the College Work-Study Program, the Touro Grant Program, Merit Scholarships, Tuition Incentive Awards, and Full-Tuition Scholarships through the Dean's Fellow Program. Financial need does not affect, in any way, admission decisions.

■ Career Services

The Office of Career Planning and Counseling functions as a career center, offering a variety of services to students and employers. Workshops and individual counseling on résumé preparation, interviewing techniques, job searching, and career options are provided. Employers participate in on-campus interviews, information seminars, and career panels. The resources of the placement library assist students in their efforts to secure employment upon graduation, and part-time and full-time employment during the school year and summer.

Admission Profile Not Available

Tulane University Law School

John Giffen Weinmann Hall
6329 Freret Street
New Orleans, LA 70118

E-Mail: admissions@law.tulane.edu
URL: http://www.law.tulane.edu
Phone: 504.865.5930, Fax: 504.865.6710

■ Introduction

Tulane Law School, established in 1847, provides comprehensive legal training in the common law, in all federal subjects, and in the civil law. Students have the opportunity, if they choose, to pursue comparative education in two legal systems. Tulane's location in a picturesque residential neighborhood of New Orleans provides ready access to the downtown activities of the U.S. Court of Appeals for the Fifth Circuit, the Louisiana Supreme Court, and lower federal and state civil and criminal courts. In addition to cultural events at Tulane University, students enjoy the advantages of city life and many aspects of traditional New Orleans including the annual Mardi Gras celebration.

■ Enrollment/Student Body

➻ 4,051 applicants ➻ 1,755 admitted first-year class 1995 ➻ 341 enrolled first-year class 1995 ➻ 1,014 total full-time ➻ 25% minority ➻ 43.3% women ➻ 52 states & foreign countries represented ➻ 225 undergraduate schools represented

■ Faculty

➻ 96 total ➻ 58 full-time ➻ 58 part-time or adjunct ➻ 17 women ➻ 6 minority

Assistant or associate deans oversee admission and financial aid, student life, minority student concerns, continuing legal education, community service, and the full-service Office of Career Services.

■ Library and Physical Facilities

➻ 501,000 volumes & equivalents ➻ library hours: Mon.-Fri., 7:30 A.M.-MIDNIGHT; Sat.-Sun., 9:00 A.M.-MIDNIGHT ➻ LEXIS ➻ NEXIS ➻ WESTLAW ➻ DIALOG ➻ EELS ➻ ORBIT ➻ QUICKLAW ➻ VUTEXT ➻ DATATIMES ➻ Internet ➻ MARC ➻ WILSONDISC ➻ INFOTRAC ➻ CALI ➻ several cataloging systems ➻ 10 full-time librarians ➻ library seats 596 ➻ 23 CD-ROM Players

The law library has both national and international collections. Located near the Law School is the university's Howard-Tilton Library, housing over one million volumes.

The Law School's new 160,000-square-foot building, John Giffen Weinmann Hall, opened in the spring of 1995. Designed to integrate classrooms, other student spaces, and faculty offices with a state-of-the-art library and computer facilities, the building is centrally located on campus.

On-campus housing is available. Off-campus housing is also plentiful and nearby.

■ Curriculum

➻ Academic Support Program 88 credits required to graduate ➻ 175 courses available ➻ degrees available: J.D.; J.D./M.B.A.; J.D./M.H.A.; J.D./M.A.; J.D./M.S.P.H.; LL.M.; M.C.L.; S.J.D. ➻ semesters, start in Aug. ➻ range of first-year class size—40-100

Six semesters in residence, at least a C average, and fulfillment of a 20-hour community service obligation are required for graduation from the J.D. degree program. The first-year curriculum, including a moot court argument, is required. Thereafter, all courses are elective. Many courses are taught in multiple sections to allow for smaller classes, and faculty members teach seminars in their fields of specialty.

The Legal Analysis course is a voluntary, invitational program during the first semester in which students work closely with faculty and senior fellows on writing and analysis skills.

■ Special Programs

Among the strengths for which the school is known are international and comparative law, admiralty and maritime law, and environmental law. The school offers four "concentration" programs which allow J.D. students to receive a certificate of completion of successful studies in (a) European Legal Practice, (b) Environmental Law, (c) Maritime Law, or (d) Sports Law. Tulane's Eason-Weinmann Center for Comparative Law, its Maritime Law Center, and its Institute for Enviromental Law and Policy add depth to the curriculum.

The annual Tulane Tax Institute and Corporate Law Institute, and the biennial Admiralty Law Institute, are recognized for their excellence. Tulane conducts a summer school in New Orleans and offers summer-study programs abroad in: England, Israel, The Netherlands, Canada, France, Italy, Germany, and Greece. All summer programs are open to law students enrolled at Tulane or other law schools.

■ Clinical Programs

The school offers eight different live clinical programs—civil, criminal, juvenile, immigration, environmental, appellate, legislative advocacy, and administrative advocacy. In addition, there is a very active simulated Trial Advocacy program, and selected third-year students may do externships with federal and state judges. The school was the first to institute a mandatory pro bono program, requiring that each student complete at least 20 hours of community-service work prior to graduation.

■ Joint-Degree and Graduate Programs

Joint-degree programs are offered in conjunction with Tulane's Freeman School of Business, (J.D./M.B.A.), School of Public Health and Tropical Medicine, (J.D./M.H.A. or M.P.H.), and Graduate School (J.D./M.A.), in a variety of fields including Latin American Studies and International Affairs. At the graduate level, the Law School offers a general LL.M. program, LL.M. programs in Admiralty and in Energy and Environmental Law, the M.C.L., and the S.J.D.

■ Admission

➽ Bachelor's degree from accredited university or college required; strong candidates who have completed 3/4 of work toward undergraduate degree are also considered ➽ application deadline—May 1; application by end of Feb. strongly recommended ➽ rolling admission, early application preferred ➽ LSAT, LSDAS required ➽ median GPA—3.30 ➽ median LSAT score—160 ➽ application fee—$45

Competition is keen, and a combination of the objective factors, the LSAT score and the UGPA, is relied upon heavily. In the case of multiple LSAT scores, the school looks at the highest score. However, Tulane seeks to individualize the admissions process by also considering subjective factors such as grade trends, courseload, undergraduate school, nonacademic activities, the student's background and experience, and the personal statement. A special admission program exists for students from disadvantaged backgrounds.

The Law School receives applications for admission starting October 1 and begins to announce decisions after December 1.

■ Student Activities

Credit may be earned for work on the student-edited *Tulane Law Review*, *Tulane Maritime Law Journal*, or for participation in the several moot court appellate and trial competitions. Other journals include the *Tulane Environmental Law Journal*, the *Journal of Law & Sexuality*, the *Tulane European and Civil Law Forum*, *Sports Lawyers' Journal*, and the *Tulane Journal of International and Comparative Law*. The Law School has a chapter of the Order of the Coif.

Over 20 student organizations are represented at Tulane including Tulane Law Women, Black Law Students Association, La Alianza, Asian Law Student Organization, Environmental Law Society, and several legal fraternities. The Tulane Public Interest Law Foundation raises funds, matched by the Law School, to support as many as 45 students each summer in public interest fellowships with a variety of organizations.

■ Expenses and Financial Aid

➽ 1995-96 full-time tuition & fees $21,286 ➽ estimated additional expenses—$10,120 (room, board, health, books, transportation, misc.) ➽ scholarships available; student must demonstrate need, after which scholarship size is indexed according to merit ➽ financial aid available; FAFSA due Feb. 15, preliminary financial aid form due at time of application for admission

■ Career Services

The Office of Career Services at the Law School assists both students and alumni in finding employment in the legal profession. The office is staffed by a full-time assistant dean, director, counselor, and support staff. A large career services library is available to students, as well as a full range of counseling services. Tulane offers both on- and off-campus interview programs.

The office has taken a proactive stance in assisting students with their job searches, with the result that Tulane graduates find law-related employment throughout the United States.

Applicant Group for the 1995-1996 Academic Year

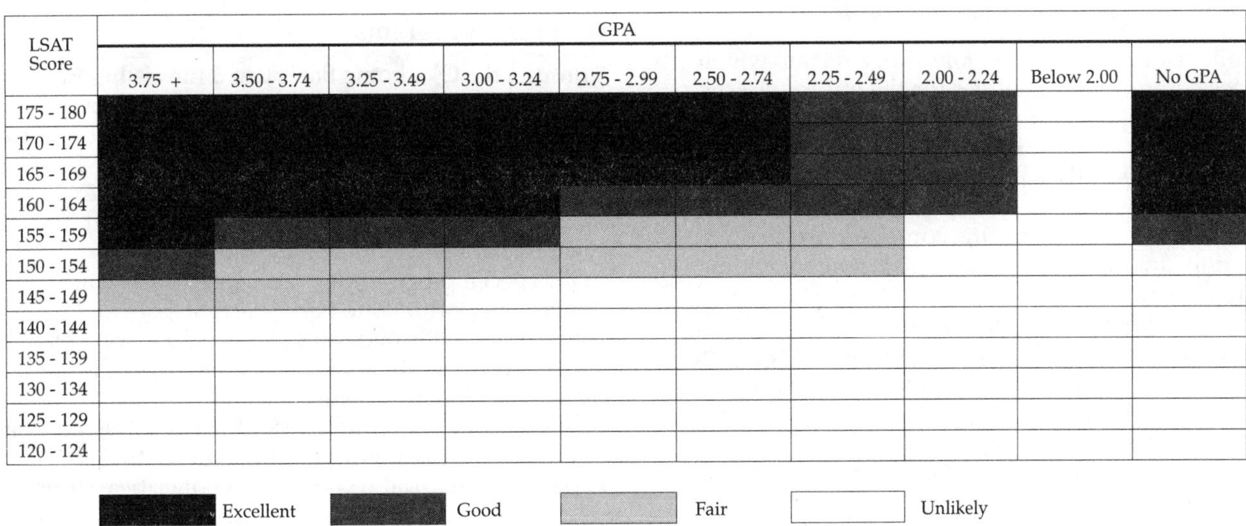

Tulane University Law School

LSAT Score	GPA 3.75 +	3.50 - 3.74	3.25 - 3.49	3.00 - 3.24	2.75 - 2.99	2.50 - 2.74	2.25 - 2.49	2.00 - 2.24	Below 2.00	No GPA
175 - 180	Excellent	Excellent	Excellent	Excellent	Excellent	Excellent	Good	Good	Unlikely	Excellent
170 - 174	Excellent	Excellent	Excellent	Excellent	Excellent	Excellent	Good	Good	Unlikely	Excellent
165 - 169	Excellent	Excellent	Excellent	Excellent	Excellent	Excellent	Good	Good	Unlikely	Excellent
160 - 164	Excellent	Excellent	Excellent	Excellent	Good	Good	Good	Good	Unlikely	Excellent
155 - 159	Excellent	Good	Good	Good	Fair	Fair	Fair	Unlikely	Unlikely	Good
150 - 154	Good	Fair	Fair	Fair	Fair	Fair	Fair	Unlikely	Unlikely	Unlikely
145 - 149	Fair	Fair	Fair	Unlikely	Unlikely	Unlikely	Unlikely	Unlikely	Unlikely	Unlikely
140 - 144	Unlikely	Unlikely	Unlikely	Unlikely	Unlikely	Unlikely	Unlikely	Unlikely	Unlikely	Unlikely
135 - 139	Unlikely	Unlikely	Unlikely	Unlikely	Unlikely	Unlikely	Unlikely	Unlikely	Unlikely	Unlikely
130 - 134	Unlikely	Unlikely	Unlikely	Unlikely	Unlikely	Unlikely	Unlikely	Unlikely	Unlikely	Unlikely
125 - 129	Unlikely	Unlikely	Unlikely	Unlikely	Unlikely	Unlikely	Unlikely	Unlikely	Unlikely	Unlikely
120 - 124	Unlikely	Unlikely	Unlikely	Unlikely	Unlikely	Unlikely	Unlikely	Unlikely	Unlikely	Unlikely

Excellent — Good — Fair — Unlikely

Reflects 98% of the total applicant pool.

University of Tulsa College of Law

3120 East Fourth Place
Tulsa, OK 74104

E-Mail: law_vls@utulsa.edu
URL: http://www.utulsa.edu/AcademicColleges/CollegeofLaw.html
Phone: 918.631.2709

■ Introduction

The College of Law, a private, nonsectarian institution, with an enrollment of about 655 students, is located on the main campus of the University of Tulsa about two miles from downtown Tulsa, providing the benefits of a quiet, residential campus and an active urban center. Tulsa is a flourishing city of approximately 725,000 located in the northeast quarter in the green country of Oklahoma, with lakes and hills nearby. The college is accredited by the ABA and the AALS. The university is accredited through the doctoral level and consists of five colleges and a graduate school.

■ Enrollment/Student Body

➠ *1,461 applicants* ➠ *660 admitted first-year class 1995* ➠ *216 enrolled first-year class 1995* ➠ *473 total full-time* ➠ *150 total part-time* ➠ *12.4% minority* ➠ *36% women* ➠ *45 states & foreign countries represented* ➠ *175 undergraduate schools represented*

Approximately 60 percent of the first-year class is from out-of-state. Typically, an entering class represents students from about 35 states and 130 colleges and universities.

■ Faculty

➠ *59 total* ➠ *36 full-time (includes one full-time chair)* ➠ *23 part-time or adjunct* ➠ *15 women* ➠ *5 minority*

■ Library and Physical Facilities

➠ *265,000 volumes & equivalents* ➠ *library hours: Mon.-Fri., 7:30 A.M.-MIDNIGHT; Sat., 9:00 A.M.-10:00 P.M.; Sun., 9:00 A.M.-MIDNIGHT* ➠ *LEXIS* ➠ *NEXIS* ➠ *WESTLAW* ➠ *DIALOG* ➠ *Legal Track (periodical index)* ➠ *Wilson Disk (periodical index)* ➠ *8 full-time librarians* ➠ *7 full-time support staff* ➠ *library seats 497*

The College of Law occupies John Rogers Hall, which provides commodious facilities for the library, classes, seminars, model courtroom, faculty, admissions, placement, and other support services.

The library presently contains specialized collections in energy law and policy and Native American law. Computer labs for word processing, computer-assisted legal instruction, and other law-related database searching also are available.

A library addition at TU will enable the College of Law to better serve not only its students, but also Tulsa's professional community, which uses the library extensively. The addition will permit the College of Law to double its collection, increase seating capacity, introduce expanded library technologies, and meet programmatic needs.

■ Curriculum

➠ *Academic Support Program* ➠ *minority support group* ➠ *88 credits required to graduate* ➠ *75 courses available* ➠ *degrees available: J.D.; J.D./M.A. in History, Modern Letters, Industrial/Organizational Psychology; J.D./M.S. in Geosciences, Biological Sciences, Anthropology; J.D./M.B.A.; J.D./Master of Accountancy; J.D./Master of Taxation*

The college is on a semester system. The full-time program typically takes three academic years. The first two semesters are devoted to required courses; thereafter, although some required, sequential courses are in the curriculum, a student is relatively free to select courses in areas of interest.

A part-time program is also available. Completion of this program generally takes four academic years. Both programs require successful completion of 88 credit hours.

Classes are offered during the summer in both divisions. The summer program consists of one eight-week and two four-week sessions. The first-year curriculum is required. Legal Authorities is taught in concentrated form to entering students during the week preceding the beginning of other courses.

To assist in curriculum planning, the faculty has defined the following three areas of concentration:

Corporate Practice—This area covers courses which are basic to a corporate or corporate-related practice, including those courses concerning business structures, governmental control of business, taxes, financing, and planning.

Energy Law and Policy—Energy, natural resources, and environmental law subjects are integrated into a comprehensive area of concentration designed to give students both theoretical and practical exposure to the field of energy and environmental law.

General Practice—These courses cover a wide range of subjects including procedure (both civil and criminal), basic corporate law, commercial law, evidence, federal income taxation, administrative law, and decedents' estates and trusts.

■ Special Programs

Through the Oklahoma Bar's Legal Internship Program, students who have completed 50 hours and certain prerequisites may be granted a limited license to practice law under the supervision of a practicing attorney. The College of Law, in cooperation with both state and federal courts located in Tulsa, also offers a Judicial Internship Program wherein students work in the court system.

Our special programs are our legal clinics which give students an opportunity to handle actual cases and develop professional skills under the close supervision of faculty supervisors, and the ADR Center for Dispute Resolution due to the growing interest in conflict management.

The National Environmental/Energy Law and Policy Institute offers students an opportunity to develop expertise in natural resource areas of critical importance.

The College of Law also offers **four certificate programs** that include coursework, research, and same practical experience in the following areas: **Native American Certificate; International and Comparative Law**

Certificate; **Resources, Energy, and Environmental Law Certificate**; and an alternative **Dispute Resolution Certificate**.

Since the summer of 1994, we have sponsored a summer institute which took faculty and students from the University of Tulsa College of Law to Comenius University in Bratislava, Slovakia to engage in a four-week program of classes and seminars.

■ Admission

➽ B.A. or B.S. degree required ➽ application deadline—Jan. 15 (for full consideration on scholarship awards) ➽ LSAT, LSDAS required ➽ median GPA—2.90 ➽ median LSAT score—153 ➽ application fee—$30

Application may be made by anyone who will be, by the time of enrollment, a graduate of a regionally accredited college. No applicant will be required to make a final decision on an offer prior to April 1. There is no firm application cutoff date; however, early applications are preferable. Tulsa is committed to an affirmative action program. Special care is taken in evaluating applications from members of minority groups traditionally not well represented in the profession.

■ Student Activities

The *Tulsa Law Journal*, edited by students, is published four times per year. The *Energy Law Journal*, the *Tulsa Journal of Comparative and International Law*, and the *Natural Resources Law Monograph Series* are also produced. Student competitions include national and international moot court, national trial advocacy, negotiations, and client counseling. The University of Tulsa's Student Bar Association has consistently been named an outstanding chapter by the American Bar Association. The student newspaper, *Baculus*, has achieved national recognition also for the efforts of its law school journalists. Student groups include ABA/LSD; American-Slovak Law Society; Asian-American Law Society; Black Law Student Association; Board of Advocates; Christian Legal Society; Delta Theta Phi; *Energy Law Journal*; Entertainment & Natural Resources Society; Federalist Society; Hispanic Law Society; International Law Society; Jewish Law Student Association; Korean Law Society; Law & Medicine Society; Moot Court Board; Native American Law Student Association; The NEXUS Society; Oklahoma Intercollegiate Legislature; Phi Alpha Delta; Phi Delta Phi; Public Interest Law Society; Rutherford Institute; Significant Others Society; Student Bar Association; Tulsa Law & Technology Association; Tulsa University Trial Lawyers Association; Volunteer Income Tax Assistance; and Women's Law Caucus.

■ Housing

Housing is available both in dormitories and university apartments. Accommodations are available in nonuniversity facilities at reasonable cost.

■ Expenses and Financial Aid

➽ tuition & fees—full-time, $14,100; part-time, $9,400 ➽ estimated additional expenses—on-campus, $7,710; off-campus, $9,050 (room & board, transportation, books & supplies) ➽ merit scholarships available ➽ financial aid available ➽ FAF, FFS, GAPSFAS, or USAF accepted

Tuition and fees are the same for resident and nonresident students.

■ Career Services

The University of Tulsa College of Law class of 1994 had an employment rate of approximately 74 percent six months after graduation. Approximately 5.8 percent of the class entered an advanced degree program.

Of the approximately 74 percent employed, the types of employment were as follows: private practice, 66.43 percent; business & industry, 12.14; government, 16.43 percent; judicial clerkships, 2.14 percent; public interest, 1.43 percent; and type unknown, 1.43 percent.

Prospects for Admission

University of Tulsa College of Law

GPA	LSAT Score						
	120-147	147-151	151-153	153-157	157-163	163-170	170-180
3.75 + Above	Unlikely	Unlikely	Possible	Likely	Likely	Likely	Likely
3.74 3.50	Unlikely	Unlikely	Possible	Likely	Likely	Likely	Likely
3.49 3.25	Unlikely	Unlikely	Possible	Likely	Likely	Likely	Likely
3.24 3.00	Unlikely	Unlikely	Possible	Possible	Likely	Likely	Likely
2.99 2.75	Unlikely	Unlikely	Possible	Possible	Likely	Likely	Likely
2.74 2.50	Unlikely	Unlikely	Unlikely	Possible	Possible	Likely	Likely
2.49 2.25	Unlikely	Unlikely	Unlikely	Unlikely	Possible	Possible	Likely
2.24 2.00	Unlikely	Unlikely	Unlikely	Unlikely	Unlikely	Possible	Possible

Unlikely* Possible Likely

* Individual accomplishments crucial

This chart is to be used as a general guide in determining the chances for admittance.

University of Utah College of Law

Admissions Office
Salt Lake City, UT 84112

E-Mail: admissions@law.utah.edu
Phone: 801.581.7479

■ Introduction

The University of Utah College of Law, approved by the ABA and a member of AALS, is situated in the foothills of the picturesque Wasatch Mountain Range of the Rocky Mountains, and is a five-minute drive from downtown Salt Lake City, the seat of federal, state, and local governmental bodies. The College of Law is nationally recognized for its academic reputation, innovative curriculum and favorable faculty/student ratio. There is a prevailing sense of community among students fostered by a faculty and administration that is friendly, open, and service oriented. An ABA accreditation review conducted recently, confirmed student responses to a survey which showed our students have a high level of satisfaction with virtually every facet of their law school experience.

■ Enrollment/Student Body

➧ 925 applicants ➧ 296 admitted first-year class 1995 ➧ 133 enrolled first-year class 1995 ➧ 366 total full-time ➧ 16% minority ➧ 43% women ➧ 44 states & 15 foreign countries represented ➧ 134 undergraduate & graduate schools represented

■ Faculty

➧ 65 total ➧ 28 full-time ➧ 37 part-time or adjunct ➧ 9 women ➧ 5 minority

■ Library and Physical Facilities

➧ 271,000 volumes & equivalents ➧ library hours: Mon.-Thurs., 7:00 A.M.-11:00 P.M.; Fri., 7:00 A.M.-8:00 P.M.; Sat., 9:00 A.M.-8:00 P.M.; Sun., 11:00 A.M.-11:00 P.M. ➧ LEXIS ➧ NEXIS ➧ WESTLAW ➧ VuText ➧ Internet ➧ Utah Capitol Hill Services ➧ Utah Courts Information Xchange ➧ PACER ➧ 7 full-time librarians; 5 of the full-time librarians hold law degrees ➧ library seats 381

The law center is located in the lower portion of the beautifully landscaped 1,500-acre University of Utah campus, which also serves as the site of the official state arboretum. The recently remodeled law building provides first-year students with their own study hall and personal carrels. It also houses two student computing labs, other computer support, and classrooms equipped with state-of-the-art video-computer projection equipment. Advanced students are provided a personal study carrel in the adjacent law library building—a modern, spacious facility with functional compact shelving to house its collection and the latest technological equipment and library research services.

■ Curriculum

➧ Academic Support Program ➧ 88 credits required to graduate ➧ 111 courses available ➧ degrees available: J.D.; J.D./M.B.A.; J.D./M.P.A.; LL.M. (Environmental Law) ➧ semesters, start in Aug. ➧ full-time, day program; 10-week summer term ➧ range of first-year class size—10-65

The innovative curriculum is designed to allow more efficient and rational sequencing of legal education that responds to the evolving legal, social, and ethical needs of our society. The entering students are first offered an intensive four-day Introduction to Law course before they begin the required first-year curriculum. Second-year students select from a variety of foundational Cornerstone courses. In the third year, students may take year-long intensive Capstone courses that provide the opportunity for in-depth study, research, and practicum in a focused area of law. In addition, students may select from more than 50 advanced courses and seminars, a variety of clinical and skills courses, and numerous cocurricular opportunities. The curriculum is geared to prepare students to practice in any state.

■ Special Programs

The Wallace Stegner Center for Land, Resources, and the Environment provides opportunities for J.D. candidates, while at Utah, to engage in academic courses and related law activities focusing on public lands, environment, natural resources, and energy. Regular courses offered include Natural Resource Law, Oil & Gas, Mining & Minerals, Water Law, Public Land Use, and Environmental Law. The law school offers a specialized LL.M. degree in natural resource and environmental law.

The clinical programs offer both live and simulated opportunities for students to assume the lawyering role. In the Civil Clinic and the Criminal Clinic, students directly represent clients, investigate cases, and appear in court. In the Judicial Clinic students act as clerks to judges, researching issues and drafting opinions in pending cases. The Judicial Extern Program allows students to spend a semester away from the school working as full-time clerks for certain courts.

■ Admission Standards

➧ Bachelor's degree required ➧ application deadline—Feb. 1 ➧ rolling admission, early application (Nov. 15-Jan. 15) preferred ➧ LSAT, LSDAS required ➧ median GPA—3.56 ➧ median LSAT score—161 ➧ application fee—$25-40 ➧ begin fall only

No applicant is accepted or rejected without a member of the Admission Committee having first fully considered the entire application. The Personal Statement should expand on the applicant's biographic and academic background and motivations for seeking a legal education. The College of Law makes a special effort to attract nontraditional students from diverse cultural, educational, economic, and ethnic backgrounds. Each applicant is evaluated for the contribution that person can make to the student body or the legal profession, in addition to evidence of demonstrated high academic ability. Qualified candidates may be invited to participate in the Academic Support Program.

■ Student Activities

The *Utah Law Review*, the *Journal of Contemporary Law*, and *Journal of Energy, Natural Resources, and Environmental Law* are professional journals edited and published by students.

Student organizations include the Student Bar Association, the Women's Law Caucus, Natural Resources Law Forum, the Moot Court Society, the Minority Law Caucus, the International Law Society, Health Law Coalition, Christian Legal Society, Intramural Sports, the Federalist Society, the Gay & Lesbian Law Student Alliance, Native American Law Student Association, and the Public Interest Law Organization.

■ Expenses and Financial Aid

- *tuition & fees—$4,516/yr., resident; $10,116/yr., nonresident*
- *need-based & merit scholarships available*
- *minority scholarships available: Minority Law Caucus Scholarship, Immigration & refugee Scholarship, need- & merit-based scholarships, diversity intern stipends*
- *financial aid available; Free Application for Federal Student Aid (FAFSA) due Feb. 15, may submit after Jan. 1*

Students who wish to apply for need-based scholarships or long-term loans such as Perkins Loans (formerly NDSL), Stafford Loans (formerly GSL), or others, must submit a FAFSA and should contact the Financial Aid Office, 105 SSB, University of Utah, Salt Lake City, UT 84112, (801) 581-6211. The deadline for submitting a FAFSA to begin the application process for financial aid is February 15. The law school also has an endowed Loan Forgiveness Program for qualified graduates who practice in the public sector.

■ Career Services

The College of Law and its graduates have access to one of the most technologically advanced Legal Career Services programs in the country. The LCS office transmits information to prospective employers, both on and off campus. The LCS office also offers personal counseling, maintains a resource library, and sponsors numerous seminars throughout the year.

Applicant Group for the 1995-1996 Academic Year

University of Utah College of Law
This grid includes only applicants who earned 120-180 LSAT scores under standard administrations.

	GPA																					
LSAT Score	3.75 +		3.50 - 3.74		3.25 - 3.49		3.00 - 3.24		2.75 - 2.99		2.50 - 2.74		2.25 - 2.49		2.00 - 2.24		Below 2.00		No GPA		Total	
	Apps	Adm	Apps	Adm	Apps	Adm	Apps	Adm	Apps	Adm	Apps	Adm	Apps	Adm	Apps	Adm	Apps	Adm	Apps	Adm	Apps	Adm
175-180	1	1	0	0	0	0	0	0	0	0	0	0	0	0	0	0	0	0	0	0	1	1
170-174	1	1	1	1	2	1	3	3	3	3	1	1	1	0	0	0	0	0	0	0	12	10
165-169	9	7	14	14	11	11	5	4	6	6	2	1	2	1	0	0	0	0	1	1	50	45
160-164	23	22	31	28	24	16	28	17	21	4	13	3	6	0	2	0	1	0	0	0	149	90
155-159	31	24	52	25	68	32	44	7	21	3	10	1	5	0	2	0	0	0	1	0	234	92
150-154	24	13	40	10	49	9	51	3	27	0	16	0	8	1	2	0	1	0	3	1	221	37
145-149	6	0	27	3	17	2	30	4	23	1	15	0	7	1	3	0	0	0	2	1	130	12
140-144	1	0	6	0	4	0	14	1	16	2	8	0	6	0	3	0	0	0	4	0	62	3
135-139	0	0	1	0	2	0	5	0	10	0	6	0	6	0	1	0	1	0	2	1	34	1
130-134	1	0	1	0	0	0	3	0	0	0	1	0	0	0	2	0	0	0	0	0	8	0
125-129	0	0	0	0	0	0	1	0	0	0	1	0	0	0	0	0	0	0	1	0	3	0
120-124	0	0	0	0	0	0	0	0	0	0	0	0	0	0	0	0	0	0	0	0	0	0
Total	97	68	173	81	177	71	184	39	127	19	73	6	41	3	15	0	3	0	14	4	904	291

Apps = Number of Applicants
Adm = Number Admitted
Reflects 98% of the total applicant pool.

Valparaiso University School of Law

Wesemann Hall
Valparaiso, IN 46383

E-Mail: valpolaw.valpo.edu
URL: http://www.law.valpoedu/default.htm
Phone: 800.262.0656 or 219.465.7829

■ Introduction

Founded in 1879, Valparaiso University School of Law is accredited by the American Bar Association and the Association of American Law Schools. Located in Valparaiso, Indiana, 55 miles southeast of Chicago and 15 miles from the Indiana Dunes National Lakeshore, Valparaiso University is a private university affiliated with the Lutheran Church. The School of Law seeks to challenge students intellectually and assist them in realizing their abilities and talents. The diversity and scholarship of the faculty offer students traditional lectures in the Socratic method and a strong skills-oriented clinical program.

■ Enrollment/Student Body

➥ *883 applicants* ➥ *447 admitted first-year class 1995* ➥ *142 enrolled first-year class 1995* ➥ *432 total full-time* ➥ *50 total part-time* ➥ *14% minority* ➥ *47% women* ➥ *40 states & foreign countries represented* ➥ *168 undergraduate schools represented*

■ Faculty

➥ *41 total* ➥ *21 full-time* ➥ *20 part-time or adjunct* ➥ *6 women* ➥ *2 minority*

Faculty members have completed graduate and professional studies at institutions throughout the world. While teaching is the primary and most important function of faculty members, they continuously engage in scholarly research and writing, as reflected in their numerous publications in professional law reviews, journals, and texts. Several faculty members maintain an active role in the practice of law.

■ Library and Physical Facilities

➥ *245,699 volumes & equivalents* ➥ *library hours: Mon.-Fri., 8:00 A.M.-MIDNIGHT; Sat.-Sun., 9:00 A.M.-MIDNIGHT* ➥ *LEXIS* ➥ *NEXIS* ➥ *WESTLAW* ➥ *DIALOG* ➥ *Datatimes* ➥ *QLSystems* ➥ *5 full-time librarians* ➥ *library seats 347*

Included in the law library collection are both hard book and microfilm format. Individual and group study carrels are available for student use.

■ Curriculum

➥ *90 credits atttempted, 85 earned, required to graduate* ➥ *85 courses available* ➥ *J.D. degree available* ➥ *semesters, start in Aug.* ➥ *range of first-year class size—45-90*

Five distinct elements of legal education make up the curriculum: legal analysis, practical training, legal theory, writing and research, and professional responsibility. Designed with a national scope preparing students for practice in any part of the country, the first-year curriculum is enhanced with three main objectives: to provide a solid foundation in the substantive areas of the law; to assist with the mastery of the basic methods of legal analysis and of the processes of reasoning used by lawyers; and to introduce students to the major areas of specialization, including civil or criminal litigation, taxation, international law, environmental law, comparative law, business and commercial law, and public law.

A 20-hour commitment of pro bono legal service is required of all students for graduation. Students help meet the need for legal service to the poor and gain valuable practical experience and contacts within the legal community.

A part-time day program allows students to extend their legal education from the normal three-year period to five years, enrolling in five to eleven credit-hours per semester.

■ Special Programs

Legal Internship Programs—These allow students to develop and enhance professional skills by working closely with faculty, attorneys, and judges on actual cases, client representation, and legal proceedings. Indiana court rules allow third-year students to represent indigent clients or state or local governmental agencies in court. Legal Services Clinic students participate in all stages of representation from interview to trial/hearings on issues of divorce, landlord/tenant, and public entitlements. Civil Criminal Law Clinic students represent indigents involved in the criminal justice system; the nature of the caseload varies but may include trial-level cases, appeals, and postconviction proceedings. With Current Representation, faculty members invite students to perform work in connection with legal representation provided by the faculty member. Seven extern programs are available to third-year students: Federal Judge Externship, U.S. Attorney Externship, Bankruptcy Externship, U.S. Environmental Protection Agency, Region V Externship, the County Prosecutors Externship, the Local Rules Externship, and the State Judge Externship.

Summer Study Abroad—Valparaiso's interests in international and comparative law are enhanced with its Summer Study Abroad Program in Cambridge, England. Participating law students attend classes led by Valparaiso's professors, distinguished alumni, visiting or guest faculty (which have included Supreme Court Justices), and guest lecturers from the host communities.

■ Admission Standards

➥ *Bachelor's degree from accredited college or university required* ➥ *application deadline—April 15* ➥ *rolling admission* ➥ *LSAT, LSDAS required* ➥ *median GPA—3.17* ➥ *median LSAT score—152* ➥ *application fee—$30*

The commitment to student-centered education is expressed in the admission policy. While the LSAT and

GPA weigh heavily in determining the applicant's academic ability, the Admissions Committee also considers nonquantifiable factors.

Valparaiso values diversity in its student body, and minorities are strongly encouraged to apply.

Valparaiso offers a voluntary Academic Support Program for select students identified by the Admission Committee; this includes a summer preparatory program and tutorial sessions during the semester.

■ Student Activities

The *Valparaiso University Law Review* is published four times per year by a student editorial board selected on the basis of academic achievement and quality of writing skills. The *Review* covers significant research in all areas of law. Students interested in enhancing advocacy skills may join the National Moot Court Competition, Client Counseling Competition, Mock Trial Competition, Negotiation Competition, Philip C. Jessup International Moot Court Competition, or the Giles Sutherland Rich Patent Law Competition.

The Student Bar Association conducts professional programs and social activities, and funds more than 20 student organizations, including the American Association of Trial Lawyers, Black Law Students Association, Hispanic Law Students Association, Christian Legal Society, Jewish Law Student Association, International Law Society, Midwest Environmental Law Caucus, Women Law Students Association, Patent Law Student Association, Law Spouses Association, and the *Forum* (student newspaper). Students participate in academic, literary, musical, social, and athletic events including intramural sports.

■ Expenses and Financial Aid

- *tuition & fees—full-time, $14,360; part-time, $7,220*
- *estimated additional expenses—$7,350 (room, board, & books)*
- *scholarships available*
- *minority scholarships available*
- *public-service grants & financial aid available*

Approximately one-quarter of the first-year students were awarded scholarships and about two-thirds received assistance through university law grants and loan programs. To assist students to pursue careers in public service, Valparaiso established a Loan Repayment Assistance Program; students may receive scholarships for summer employment and grants for securing positions with public-service employers upon graduation.

■ Career Services

The Career Services Office offers career planning and counseling including résumé/cover-letter preparation and state bar examination information as well as placement assistance; maintains an extensive resource library and coordinates an on-campus interview program; and participates in regional and national job fairs. For the class of 1994, 92 percent of graduates found law-related employment within six months of passing a bar. Alumni practice in 48 states and abroad.

Applicant Group for the 1995-1996 Academic Year

Valparaiso University School of Law

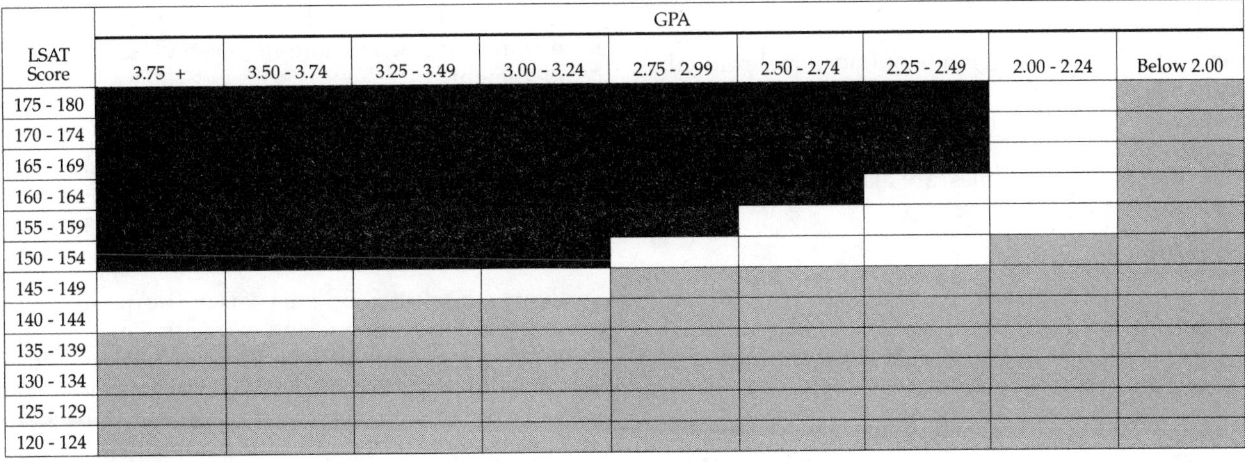

Acceptance Likely | Acceptance Possible | Acceptance Unlikely

Vanderbilt University School of Law

Admissions Office
Nashville, TN 37240
Phone: 615.322.6452

■ Introduction

Vanderbilt is an independent, privately endowed university founded in Nashville in 1873 by Commodore Cornelius Vanderbilt. The School of Law occupies a corner of the university's 305-acre campus. About 540 of Vanderbilt University's 8,600 students attend the law school, which is one of the 10 schools of the university. In its students, faculty, and educational approach, Vanderbilt is a nationally oriented law school with a reputation for excellence. It is a member of the AALS and is approved by the ABA.

Nashville, the state capital of Tennessee, has a metropolitan population of about one million, and is the location of the executive and legislative branches of the state government. State trial and appellate courts and the U.S. District Court, Middle Tennessee District, are located here.

■ Enrollment/Student Body

➧ 2,600 applicants ➧ 600 admitted first-year class 1995 ➧ 187 enrolled first-year class 1995 ➧ 550 total full-time ➧ 17% minority ➧ 38% women ➧ 48 states & foreign countries represented ➧ 203 undergraduate schools represented

■ Faculty

➧ 75 total ➧ 32 full-time ➧ 33 part-time or adjunct ➧ 18 women ➧ 5 minority

■ Library and Physical Facilities

➧ 329,060 volumes & equivalents ➧ library hours: Mon.-Sun., 7:30 A.M.-MIDNIGHT ➧ LEXIS ➧ NEXIS ➧ WESTLAW ➧ INFOTRAC ➧ CD-based systems ➧ 8 full-time librarians ➧ library seats 431

The School of Law and law library are housed in a well-designed modern building located near university activity centers, and are accessible to people who are disabled. In addition to the full range of traditional printed, microform, and online legal materials, the library performs extensive reference services and trains students in legal bibliography. All other university libraries, containing more than one million volumes, are also available to law students.

■ Curriculum

➧ 88 credits required to graduate ➧ 123 courses available ➧ degrees available: J.D./M.Div.; J.D./M.B.A.; J.D./M.P.P.; J.D./M.T.S.; J.D./M.A.; J.D./Ph.D. ➧ semesters, start in Aug. ➧ range of first-year class size—30-90

A student may take up to six credit-hours of work toward the J.D. degree in nonlaw courses offered by other departments of the university. All work is done under the honor system. The faculty-to-student ratio, 1 to 17, is excellent. The open-door policy and extensive faculty-student contact are traditions at Vanderbilt. First-year students are assigned in groups of 30 to an instructor who supervises a legal-writing and research program throughout the year.

■ Special Programs

Clinical programs offer law students the opportunity to obtain academic credit while actively participating in aspects of the actual practice of law. Through cooperative arrangements with Legal Services of Nashville, Inc., the District Attorney's Office, the Public Defender's Office of Nashville-Davidson County, and the juvenile court, students perform a number of legal services under the supervision of licensed attorneys.

Transnational Legal Studies Program—The Transnational Legal Studies Program coordinates courses and extracurricular activities to serve two general purposes. First, it provides an opportunity for those interested in specializing in either public or private international legal work to prepare effectively for such a career. Second, it permits students who do not have a career interest in international legal practice to gain some contact with the field as part of their broader legal endeavors, either by means of selected coursework or by participation in one or more of the extracurricular activities associated with the program.

Courses in the transnational program include Admiralty, Comparative Law, Conflict of Law, Foreign Relations Law of the United States, Immigration Law and Policy, Intellectual Property in International Trade, International Civil Litigation, International Commercial Transactions, International Law, Latin American Legal Systems, Law of Developing Countries, United States Taxation of Transnational Operations, and seminars in selected international problems.

Students interested in concentration in transnational studies should also examine offerings in the areas of economics, international business, and political science in the Graduate School and in Owen Graduate School of Management.

■ Admission

➧ Bachelor's degree from and accredited college or university required ➧ application deadline—Feb. 1 ➧ LSAT, LSDAS required ➧ median GPA—3.62 ➧ median LSAT score—163 ➧ application fee—$50

Students are selected on the basis of the quality of their undergraduate academic and extracurricular records, considered together with the LSAT results and letters of recommendation. The selection committee also takes into account any elements in the applicant's background that are likely to add depth and perspective to the law school student body or which indicate promise of leadership in the legal profession.

The faculty places great emphasis on the development during the college years of the abilities to read and comprehend accurately, thoroughly, and rapidly; to speak and write clearly and correctly; to think precisely; and to analyze complex situations and weigh and appraise their several elements. A broad cultural background is also important. Since law touches life at every point, every subject in the college curriculum may bear on a lawyer's work.

The entering class is limited to approximately 180 students. The school strictly adheres to a racially nondiscriminatory policy in its admissions process. Each application is reviewed on an individual basis, and no applicant is rejected solely because of a single quantitative predictor.

■ Student Activities

Extracurricular activities constitute an integral part of the instruction program. The school publishes two nationally recognized legal periodicals, the *Vanderbilt Law Review* and the *Vanderbilt Journal of Transnational Law*. In addition, the Vanderbilt Moot Court Board administers a moot court program of brief writing and oral argument available to students in both the first and second years. Vanderbilt enters teams in two national appellate advocacy competitions. The Vanderbilt Bar Association (VBA), official student organization of the law school, is affiliated with the Law Student Division of the ABA. The VBA publishes a newspaper and involves itself in a variety of activities, both professional and social. Active student organizations welcome members interested in the legal issues of health care, intellectual property, the environment, labor, crime, and litigation. Special interest groups include BLSA, ALSA, women students, Amnesty International, Christians, Jews, gays and lesbians, and legal fraternities.

■ Expenses and Financial Aid

➽ *full-time tuition & fees—$19,750* ➽ *estimated additional expenses—$12,400 (housing, food, books, travel, misc.)*
➽ *need-based & merit scholarships available*
➽ *need-based minority scholarships available*
➽ *financial aid available; CSS and FAFSA due March 1*

A substantial amount of scholarship aid is available for entering students. Most scholarships are awarded on the basis of need, and a significant amount of scholarship funds have been awarded to minority group students.

■ Career Services

The school maintains its own career services office with a full-time director and staff. In addition to working with students, the office also assists alumni with relocation. Over the past two years graduates have located in 35 states. Approximately 330 employers visit the campus each year to conduct interviews.

Admission Profile Not Available

Vermont Law School

Chelsea Street
South Royalton, VT 05068

E-Mail: admiss@vermontlaw.edu
URL: http://www.vermontlaw.edu
Phone: 800.227.1395 or 802.763.8303

■ Introduction

Five features distinguish legal education at Vermont Law School—a core J.D. curriculum that emphasizes the broader social context of the law in addition to focusing on legal doctrine and analysis; experiential programs that complement traditional classroom instruction; the internationally recognized Environmental Law Center; the informal atmosphere of a beautiful rural setting; and a real sense of community and commitment to public service that underlie the learning environment.

■ Enrollment/Student Body

➧ 1,670 applicants ➧ 847 admitted first-year class 1995 ➧ 164 enrolled first-year class 1995 ➧ 470 total full-time ➧ 10% minority ➧ 45% women ➧ 48 states & foreign countries represented ➧ 235 undergraduate schools represented

Vermont Law School is one of the most geographically diverse law schools in the country. Students come from 48 states and bring a remarkable range of experience and backgrounds. Their ages range from 21 to over 50, with the average being 26.

Diversity Information—Vermont Law School is committed to enrolling a diverse student body. Forty-five percent of students are women and 10 percent minorities. Diversity organizations include the Lesbian, Gay, Bisexual, Transgender, and Straight Alliance; Asian Pacific American Law Students Association; Black Law Students Association; National Latino Law Students Association; Native American Law Society; Women's Law Group.

■ Faculty

➧ 57 total ➧ 35 full-time ➧ 22 part-time or adjunct ➧ 18 women ➧ 2 minority

Vermont Law School attracts faculty who are committed to teaching and scholarship. Their professional involvement extends beyond teaching to include writing, research (frequently with student assistance), and service to the community.

■ Library and Physical Facilities

➧ 200,000 volumes & equivalents ➧ library hours: Mon.-Fri., 8:00 A.M.-MIDNIGHT; Sat.-Sun., 9:00 A.M.-MIDNIGHT ➧ LEXIS ➧ NEXIS ➧ WESTLAW ➧ DIALOG ➧ 5 full-time librarians ➧ library seats 350 ➧ member, New England Law Library Consortium ➧ access to Dartmouth College Library

Opened in 1991, the 33,000 square-foot Cornell Library houses all primary sources needed for student research. The library subscribes to some 2,650 periodicals and serials, and features an exceptionally fine environmental law collection. It also serves as a selective depository for United States government documents. Situated in a National Historic District along Vermont's scenic White River, the school's eight-acre campus is an integrated complex of renovated turn-of-the-century buildings, a new computer center, and a modern library and community center. Nearby Dartmouth College complements the law school's social and cultural offerings. School-owned housing is limited, but ample private accommodations are available in the surrounding community.

■ Curriculum

➧ Academic Support Program ➧ 84 credits required to graduate ➧ 100 courses available ➧ degrees available: J.D.; M.S.E.L.; J.D./M.S.E.L. ➧ summer session available (36 courses) ➧ range of first-year class size—20-82

Vermont Law School educates students in the understanding, skills, and values needed for private practice and public service. A wide variety of clinical programs, electives, seminars, and opportunities for supervised independent research are important adjuncts to a strong core curriculum.

Environmental Law Center—Vermont Law School's Environmental Law Center is recognized internationally as a preeminent center for the study of environmental law and policy. The Environmental Law Center offers a one-year program leading to a Master of Studies in Environmental Law (M.S.E.L.) degree based upon a multidisciplinary curriculum of law, science, policy, and economics, and a joint J.D.-M.S.E.L. degree program that can be completed in three academic years and two summers. The center offers over 50 environmental courses and an Environmental Semester in Washington, DC, and sponsors conferences and research.

General Practice Program—The optional General Practice Program has classes structured to operate as a law firm, with professors in the role of senior partners. Because it teaches the range of skills generally required of new associates in most types of legal environments, the program is also valuable to students who ultimately plan to specialize.

Special Programs—The **Semester in Practice Program** allows students to participate in a full-credit, supervised clinical program in a legal environment outside the law school. Students currently work throughout the Northeast, including New York, Boston, and Washington, DC. In the **Legislation Clinic**, students work under the direction of a legislative committee chair on research and drafting projects directly related to legislation pending before the Vermont General Assembly. Students working with the **South Royalton Legal Clinic** develop legal skills while providing legal assistance to low-income clients. The **Dispute Resolution Project** introduces students to nonlitigious approaches to dispute resolution, such as arbitration, mediation, and negotiation. Through the **Law School Exchange Program** students may spend a semester at another participating law school.

■ Admission

➡ *Bachelor's degree or equivalent required for admission* ➡ *application deadline—Feb. 15* ➡ *LSAT, LSDAS required* ➡ *median GPA—3.20* ➡ *median LSAT score—158* ➡ *application fee—$60* ➡ *admission to fall term only*

The school seeks candidates who will bring diverse perspectives and talents to the law school community and the community-at-large. Successful applicants demonstrate substantial ability, motivation, life experience, and unique personal attributes. The two most important admission criteria are the undergraduate record and the LSAT score. The LSAT score is normally weighted more than the GPA. A high LSAT score might offset a weak academic record if the academic work was undertaken some time ago. However, even a strong LSAT score will not compensate for recent marginal academic performance in college. Although there are no minimum scores or grades required, performance well below average is rarely competitive. Multiple LSAT scores are averaged. The LSAT writing sample is used in borderline cases. For a significant number of applicants, the application essay is decisive in determining admissibility. The school responds favorably to community and college involvement and work experience, and is committed to attracting people traditionally underrepresented in the legal profession.

■ Student Activities

A community-oriented and active student body supports more than 30 official organizations. A few are: *Vermont Law Review*; Vermont Legal Research Group; Environmental Law Society; Association of Trial Lawyers of America; *Forum* (student newspaper); Federalist Society; National Lawyers Guild; Jazz Ensemble; several minority student groups; and Women's Group. Student organizations and the law school sponsor a full range of social, cultural, and academic events. Students also field several intercollegiate and intramural athletic teams.

■ Expenses and Financial Aid

➡ *full-time tuition & fees—$17,325* ➡ *$12,000 average additional expenses* ➡ *merit scholarships, grants, and fellowships (primarily need-based)* ➡ *need-based diversity scholarships* ➡ *private, government, and school-funded loans* ➡ *Vermont Law School Financial Aid Application and FAFSA required by Feb. 15 for full consideration*

Combinations of loans, tuition grants, and work-study employment are used to meet demonstrated financial need. About 80 percent of the student body receives some form of assistance.

■ Career Services

Graduates work in the full range of legal and nonlegal positions throughout the U.S. The school aggressively pursues employment opportunities nationwide and provides a broad range of counseling and placement services. A Cooperative Legal Education program facilitates the transition from academics to legal practice.

Applicant Group for the 1995-1996 Academic Year

Vermont Law School
This grid includes only applicants who earned 120-180 LSAT scores under standard administrations.

LSAT Score	GPA 3.75 +		3.50 - 3.74		3.25 - 3.49		3.00 - 3.24		2.75 - 2.99		2.50 - 2.74		2.25 - 2.49		2.00 - 2.24		Below 2.00		No GPA		Total	
	Apps	Adm	Apps	Adm	Apps	Adm	Apps	Adm	Apps	Adm	Apps	Adm	Apps	Adm	Apps	Adm	Apps	Adm	Apps	Adm	Apps	Adm
175-180	0	0	1	1	0	0	1	1	0	0	0	0	0	0	0	0	0	0	0	0	2	2
170-174	0	0	1	1	1	1	3	3	1	1	2	2	0	0	0	0	0	0	1	1	9	9
165-169	5	5	4	3	13	12	18	15	9	8	4	4	6	2	1	0	0	0	2	1	62	50
160-164	17	17	26	26	63	60	50	44	46	41	34	25	13	11	8	3	1	1	6	4	264	232
155-159	27	26	47	43	106	93	120	94	86	60	65	38	15	9	9	4	0	0	5	2	480	369
150-154	16	7	44	27	73	32	107	36	80	15	52	8	27	4	7	1	2	0	8	2	416	132
145-149	2	1	27	4	55	7	59	2	66	3	44	1	13	0	10	1	1	0	1	0	278	19
140-144	1	0	7	1	14	0	21	0	34	0	20	0	14	0	3	0	2	0	1	0	117	1
135-139	0	0	1	0	2	0	7	0	3	0	11	1	9	0	4	0	1	0	1	0	39	1
130-134	1	0	1	0	1	0	3	0	0	0	4	0	2	0	1	0	0	0	0	0	13	0
125-129	0	0	0	0	0	0	0	0	0	0	2	0	1	0	1	0	0	0	0	0	4	0
120-124	0	0	0	0	0	0	0	0	0	0	0	0	0	0	0	0	0	0	0	0	0	0
Total	69	56	159	106	328	205	389	195	325	128	238	79	100	26	44	9	7	1	25	10	1684	815

Apps = Number of Applicants
Adm = Number Admitted
Reflects 98% of the total applicant pool.
Vermont Law School does not use cutoff LSAT scores or GPAs.

Villanova University School of Law

299 North Spring Mill Road
Villanova, PA 19085

E-Mail: carver@law.vill.edu
Phone: 610.519.7010

■ Introduction

The School of Law, opened in 1953, is approved by the American Bar Association and is a member of the Association of American Law Schools. Students are graduates of more then 200 colleges and universities; many have significant work experience outside of law.

The curriculum is responsive to the needs of modern law practice on local, regional, national, and global bases. Courses are designed to teach the rules of law and their application; to demonstrate how lawyers analyze legal issues and express arguments and conclusions; to inculcate the skills of the counselor, advocate, and decision maker; and to explore the ethical and moral dimensions of law practice and professional conduct.

Few law schools are located in a more beautiful and convenient environment. Although the school is in a tranquil suburban setting, the advantages of Philadelphia are 20 minutes by railroad with frequent commuter service.

■ Enrollment/Student Body for Incoming Class

➠ *1,358 applicants* ➠ *665 admitted* ➠ *238 enrolled*
➠ *690 total full-time* ➠ *16% minority* ➠ *45% women*
➠ *35 states & foreign countries represented*
➠ *195 undergraduate schools represented*

■ Faculty

➠ *75 total* ➠ *41 full-time* ➠ *34 part-time or adjunct*
➠ *10 women* ➠ *6 minority*

■ Library and Physical Facilities

➠ *432,000 volumes & equivalents* ➠ *library hours: 110 hours/wk., including 24 hour access for VU law students*
➠ *LEXIS* ➠ *NEXIS* ➠ *WESTLAW* ➠ *DIALOG*
➠ *10 full-time librarians* ➠ *library seats 368*

The library contains microform materials and readers, reading rooms, group study rooms, a computer laboratory, personal computers, photocopying equipment, and numerous individual study carrels. The library is an officially designated depository for United States government documents. Students also have access to the other university libraries and the many excellent libraries in the Philadelphia area.

A total of 150 computers and 10 Hewlett Packard Laser printers are available for student use in the library, computer lab, and the "computer-assisted learning" classroom.

The law school building also contains classrooms, including one equipped for study of law and computers; a moot courtroom; student lounges; faculty and administrative offices; and dining facilities.

■ Curriculum

➠ *Academic Support Program* ➠ *87 credits required to graduate* ➠ *151 courses available*
➠ *degrees available: J.D.; LL.M.; J.D./M.B.A.; J.D./Ph.D.*
➠ *semesters, start in Aug.*

■ Joint J.D./M.B.A. Program

The Villanova University School of Law and College of Commerce and Finance offer a joint program permitting simultaneous study for both the Law and the Master of Business Administration degrees. The College of Commerce and Finance is one of the few colleges of business in the United States whose Department of Accountancy and Master of Business Administration program have been approved by the American Assembly of Collegiate Schools of Business.

Credit is given in the program for certain courses by both the School of Law and the College of Commerce and Finance. Business courses may be taken in far less time, perhaps as little as three years, than it would take to obtain the degrees separately.

■ Joint J.D./Ph.D. Program in Law & Psychology

Villanova Law School, in cooperation with Hahnemann University Graduate School, offers an integrated program in Law and Psychology leading to a Juris Doctor from Villanova and a Ph.D. in clinical psychology from Hahnemann. The clinical psychology component is fully accredited by the American Psychological Association.

The program has three major purposes—(1) to produce lawyer-psychologists who can participate in the development of more databased mental health policy in the legislature and the courts; (2) to develop scientist-practitioners who will produce legally sophisticated social science research to assist the legal system in making better, more empirically based decisions; and (3) to educate highly trained clinicians who can contribute to the advancement of forensic psychology in such areas as criminal law, domestic relations, and civil commitment.

■ Special Programs

The clinical program in juvenile justice involves third-year students in the representation of indigent juvenile defendants in the Delaware County juvenile court. Clinical experience also is available through Delaware County Community Legal Services, and in the law school's Tax and Information Law clinics. Additional clinical experiences are available in some seminars.

In addition to traditional courses, students may represent actual clients and receive training in practical lawyers' skills such as trial practice, pretrial practice, appellate advocacy, drafting, interviewing, counseling, and negotiation. Directed research and seminar opportunities enable students to learn research and writing skills under the close supervision of a faculty member. Many of these courses are in small classes.

■ Admission

➽ Bachelor's degree required ➽ application deadline—Jan. 31 ➽ rolling admissions, most decisions made after application deadline ➽ LSAT, LSDAS required ➽ median GPA—3.45 ➽ median LSAT score—158 ➽ application fee—$75

■ Student Activities

The *Villanova Law Review* is a scholarly journal prepared and edited by law students. Members of the *Review* are selected on the basis of academic rank at the end of the first or second year of law studies. Students not selected on the basis of academic rank can enter an open writing competition. Successful competitors earn positions on the *Review* equivalent to those achieved by academic rank selection.

The *Villanova Environmental Law Journal* is a scholarly journal prepared and edited by law students. The *Journal* publishes both student and outside articles dealing with environmental issues. Students are selected for membership on the *Journal* by an open writing competition.

The Villanova *Sports and Entertainment Law Forum* is the newest scholarly journal prepared and edited by Villanova Law students.

The Moot Court Board recognizes students with outstanding writing and advocacy skills. Members participate in at least one Moot Court competition each year and assist in administering the Reimel Moot Court Competition.

Other student organizations include Asian-Pacific American Law Students, Black Law Students Association, Catholic Law Students, Christian Legal Society, Civil Rights Law Society, Corporate Law Society, Court Jesters, Criminal Law Society, *The Docket*, Environmental Law Society, Family Law Society, Health Law Society, Intellectual Property Protection Society, International Law Society, Jewish Law Students Association, Latin American Law Student Association, National Italian-American Bar Association Justian Society, Phi Delta Phi, Public Interest Law Society, Rugby Club, Sports and Entertainment Law Society, Tax Law Society, Women's Law Caucus.

■ Expenses and Financial Aid

➽ full-time tuition & fees—$17,200
➽ estimated additional expenses—$12,590 (room, board, books, and living expenses for off-campus students)
➽ scholarships and fellowships available
➽ financial aid available; FAFSA priority deadline is March 1

■ Career Services

An active, full-time career services office is available for career reference, research, counseling, communication instruction, and employment information. On-campus interviews with prospective legal employers are scheduled for second- and third-year students. Part-time jobs are also listed for second- and third-year students seeking employment during the school year. Graduates are employed in private law firms, corporations, public services, governmental agencies, judicial clerkships, and other law-related occupations.

Admission Profile Not Available

University of Virginia School of Law

Admissions Office
Charlottesville, VA 22901

Phone: 804.924.7351

■ Introduction

The University of Virginia School of Law is a public law school located in Charlottesville, 120 miles southwest of Washington, DC. Among the original schools contemplated in Mr. Jefferson's plan for the organization of the University of Virginia, the law school was established upon the opening of the University in 1825, and has been an integral part of the University since that date.

■ Enrollment/Student Body

➽ 4,101 applicants ➽ 966 admitted first-year class 1995 ➽ 380 enrolled first-year class 1995 ➽ 1,152 total full-time ➽ 15% minority ➽ 39% women ➽ 44 states, District of Columbia, & 6 foreign countries represented ➽ 227 undergraduate schools represented ➽ 56% residents ➽ 44% nonresidents

■ Faculty

➽ 114 total ➽ 59 full-time ➽ 55 part-time or adjunct ➽ 21 women ➽ 7 minority

■ Library and Physical Facilities

➽ 734,500 volumes & equivalents ➽ library hours: Mon.-Sat., 8 A.M.-MIDNIGHT; Sun., 10:00 A.M.-MIDNIGHT ➽ LEXIS ➽ NEXIS ➽ WESTLAW ➽ 10 full-time librarians ➽ library seats 662

The law building, completed in 1979, is a modern facility that houses library, classrooms, faculty and student organization offices, an auditorium, and research centers. Expansion, now in progress, will create 3 new moot courtrooms, more seminar rooms, additional student journal and organization space, a larger library, and a 100-seat computer lab.

■ Curriculum

➽ Academic Support Program ➽ 86 credits required to graduate ➽ 165 courses available ➽ degrees available: J.D.; LL.M.; S.J.D.; J.D./M.B.A.; J.D./M.A.; J.D./M.P.; J.D./M.S. ➽ semesters, start in Aug. ➽ range of first-year class size—32-128

The first-year curriculum is arranged so that each entering student takes one of five courses in the first semester in a class of only 32 students. This "small section" concept, plus numerous second- and third-year electives, seminars, and individual research projects, assures the student a great deal of contact and interaction with the faculty.

The first-semester curriculum of torts, contracts, civil procedure, criminal law, and legal writing is required of all students. Property, constitutional law, and also legal writing are required in the spring semester of the first year. The only other required course is Professional Responsibility. More than 150 electives are offered each year; these are outlined in the law school catalog. The Principles and Practice Program offers a unique blend of substantive and practical learning by pairing full-time faculty with full-time practitioners in semester long courses in a variety of topic areas.

■ Special Programs

The law school offers combined degree programs with the Department of Economics, the Department of History, the Department of English, the Department of Sociology, the Graduate School of Business Administration, the School of Architecture in Urban and Environmental Planning, the School of Commerce in Accounting, the Department of Philosophy, and the Department of Government and Foreign Affairs. A student not enrolled in one of these programs may take up to six credit hours of graduate courses in other schools and departments of the university.

In addition, the school offers opportunities for clinical experience under the direction of a clinical director and also offers interdisciplinary courses in law and medicine, law and economics, and law and social science.

■ Admission

➽ Bachelor's degree from accredited college or university required ➽ application deadline—Jan. 15 ➽ LSAT, LSDAS required ➽ median GPA—3.60 ➽ median LSAT score—164 ➽ application fee—$40

The Admissions Committee believes that absolute standards based on a combination of LSAT score and grade-point average (GPA) cannot be the sole criteria for selection. The committee recognizes that the real meaning of GPA will vary with such factors as quality of the institution attended, rigor of courses selected, and degree of grade inflation. The committee considers an array of elements in addition to the essential LSAT and GPA, with a view toward assembling a diverse class while arriving at a fair appraisal of the individual applicant.

Although it is difficult to predict the action on an individual application, the LSAT and GPA are the primary determinants for the committee; usually about 80 percent total weight is accorded these two factors. However, there are other elements taken into account: for example, the maturing effect of some years away from formal education; trends in academic performance versus solid but unexceptional work; employment during the undergraduate years; significant personal achievement in extracurricular work at college or in a work or military situation; and/or unusual prior training, background, or ethnicity, which promises a contribution to the law school community. Economic, social, or educational obstacles successfully overcome by an applicant have contributed to favorable consideration.

It is clear, though, that unless an applicant has a high LSAT score and strong GPA, the chances of admission are severely reduced. Each year, the committee chooses a few applicants whose GPA and LSAT are lower than the prevailing averages, but who present other impressive credentials for admission, and rejects some whose performance on these two predictors is quite high.

The charts provided below track the selection process during the 1995 admissions year. In reviewing these charts, it is important to note that, since the new 120-180 LSAT score scale replaced the old 10-48 scale as of June, 1991, most 1995 applicants to Virginia (99 percent) presented scores and Admission Indices based on the 120-180 scale. Consequently, these charts project actions taken on approximately 99 percent of our 1995 applicant pool. It is also important to keep in mind that students admitted under the affirmative action minority program described below are included in the analysis. To interpret the charts, one must understand the Admission Index. This number results from combining LSAT score(s) with the undergraduate GPA for each applicant, using weights for each chosen by this school. The formula used at Virginia for applicants with test scores on the 120-180 scale is (4.1590 X UGPA) + (.240 X LSAT) + (2.0) = Index. Thus, an applicant with a 3.62 UGPA and a 168 LSAT would receive a 57 Admissions Index, while a 3.17 UGPA and a 158 LSAT would produce a 53 Admissions Index. The index provides the law school with a convenient method for simultaneously reviewing LSAT score(s) and undergraduate GPAs.

The primary focus of minority recruitment at the University of Virginia is on black applicants. Members of other minority groups are given special attention by the Admissions Committee.

Student Activities

Popular student activities include Black Law Student Association, Environmental Law Forum, Federalist Society, First Year Council, *Journal of Law and Politics*, Legal Assistance Society, Libel Show, moot court competitions, Post-Conviction Assistance Project, Student Bar Association, Student Peer Advisors, Students United to Promote Racial Awareness, Virginia Health Law Forum, *Virginia Journal of International Law*, *Virginia Environmental Law Journal*, *Virginia Journal of Social Policy & the Law*, Virginia Law Women, *Virginia Law Review*, and *Virginia Tax Review*.

Expenses and Financial Aid

- *full-time tuition & fees—residents, $10,290; nonresidents, $18,694*
- *estimated additional expenses—$10,135 (room, board, books)*
- *need-based scholarships available*
- *financial aid available*
- *FAFSA form for need analysis due to Federal Student Aid Center in Feb.*

Career Services

The School of Law actively assists students seeking employment. Almost 90 percent of the Class of 1995 reported to the Office of Career Planning and Placement at graduation that they had obtained permanent employment, and well over 95 percent of the class will be employed within 6 months of graduation. More than 97 percent of the second-year class obtained internships during the summer of 1994, primarily through Career Planning and Placement Office services. Jobs obtained by Virginia students are remarkably diverse in both geography and type of employment. For example, in the graduating class of 1995, the graduates reporting jobs were employed in 38 states and the District of Columbia.

Profile of the Entering Class—Fall 1995

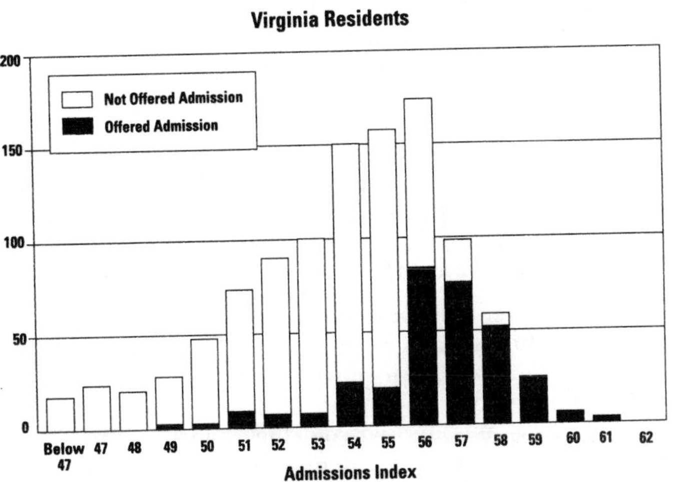

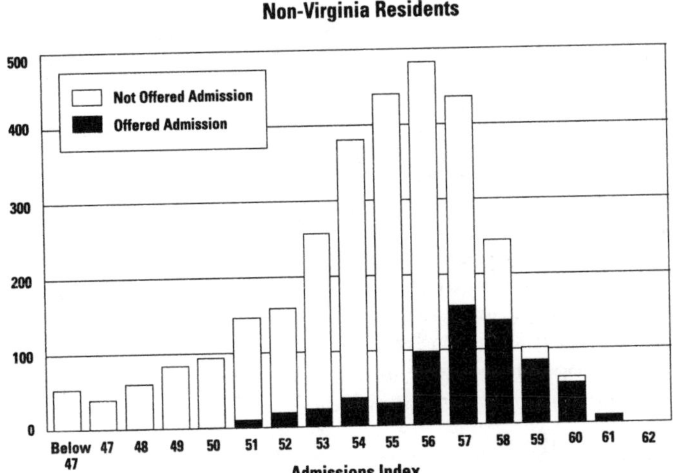

Wake Forest University School of Law

P.O. Box 7206
Reynolda Station
Winston-Salem, NC 27109

E-Mail: admissions@law.wfu.edu

■ Introduction

The Wake Forest University School of Law, established in 1894, is a member of AALS and is ABA-approved. Wake Forest is located in Winston-Salem, North Carolina, a city of 150,000 and a center for recreation, education, and the arts.

The philosophy at Wake Forest law school embodies meaningful promises for the future. The school's undertaking embraces seven principal commitments. They are—(1) To maintain a school of the right size that begins with a first-year class of 160 students comprised of four sections of 40 students each. (2) To develop and retain a faculty strong in teaching, strong in experience, and strong in current scholarly writing. (3) To assure that students are taught substantive law and research skills through maximum use of leading-edge technology. (4) To continue the school's emphasis on dispute resolution and the development of litigation skills through instruction, competition, and comprehensive clinical practice. (5) To build a bridge between law and management communities by an enhanced curriculum, the sharing of resources, and collaborative instruction. (6) To seek to provide placement opportunities for our students and graduates that match their potential. (7) To teach the transcendence of ethics and to inculcate in graduates the importance of doing good while doing well throughout their professional lives.

Our goal is to graduate students who are not only eligible to practice law but qualified as well.

■ Enrollment/Student Body

➽ 1,676 applicants ➽ 525 admitted first-year class 1995 ➽ 160 enrolled first-year class 1995 ➽ 470 total full-time ➽ 9.9% minority ➽ 40% women ➽ 39 states & foreign countries represented ➽ 177 undergraduate schools represented

■ Faculty

➽ 63 total ➽ 33 full-time ➽ 30 adjunct ➽ 15 women ➽ 4 minority ➽ 30 supervising clinical attorneys

■ Library and Physical Facilities

➽ 250,000 volumes & equivalents ➽ 108 library hours per week ➽ LEXIS ➽ NEXIS ➽ WESTLAW ➽ DIALOG ➽ EPIC ➽ ACES ➽ Dow Jones ➽ 6 full-time librarians ➽ library seats 568

The law school occupies the Worrell Professional Center for Law and Management which was dedicated on April 3, 1993, by Justice Sandra Day O'Connor. This 178,000-square-foot, state-of-the-art facility houses the law school and the School of Management.

■ Curriculum

➽ 89 units/credits required to graduate ➽ 100 courses available ➽ degrees available: J.D. & J.D./M.B.A. ➽ semesters, start in Aug. & Jan. ➽ first-year class size—approx. 40

Three academic years are divided into two semesters of 15 weeks each. A solid core of first-year courses is required, with strong emphasis on legal research and writing. Advanced elective courses are offered in specialty areas such as securities regulation, taxation, corporations, and environmental law.

■ Special Programs

The law school offers two clinical programs. The first is a third-year program of academic instruction, skills training, and live client representation, and is a cooperative venture of the bench, bar, and law school. Clinical students participate in an integrated program of both civil and criminal law practice. They are placed with supervising attorneys in the following areas—private practice, legal aid, the United States Attorney, district attorney, public defender, National Labor Relations Board, or corporate general counsel. The classroom component includes interviewing, counseling, negotiation, and discovery. The second clinical program is an in-house legal clinic for the elderly operating as an interdisciplinary element in the Sticht Center for the Aging.

The joint J.D./M.B.A. degree program permits the student to obtain both degrees in four years.

The School of Law will begin an LL.M. Program in American Law for foreign law graduates in the fall of 1996. Students who have received their law degrees in countries other than the United States are eligible for admission. A TOEFL (Test of English as a Foreign Language) is required. For more information write to the Director of Admissions.

■ Computer Instruction and Services

Wake Forest provides a wide range of computer services to students, faculty, and staff, and ranks among the top five law schools nationally for computers per student.

The Computerized Legal Research and Instruction Center contains 53 microcomputers, laser printers, and programs that allow students to access WESTLAW and LEXIS, use word processing and other legal software, and access computer-assisted legal research instruction programs.

■ Admission

➽ Bachelor's degree from accredited college or university required ➽ application deadline—March 15 ➽ rolling admission, early application preferred (particularly for scholarship consideration) ➽ LSAT, LSDAS required ➽ median GPA—3.33 ➽ median LSAT score—160 ➽ application fee—$50

First-year students are admitted in the fall semester and only for full-time study. One academic recommendation and a Dean's certification are required in addition to the other application materials, and the file must be completed by April 15. Applicants are advised of their status by May 15.

The LSAT score and the undergraduate GPA are combined into an index computed by LSDAS. For multiple LSAT scores, the higher test score will be used. The applicant should explain disparate scores. All files are reviewed on a case-by-case basis. The school considers a number of subjective factors indicating intellectual capacity, character, motivation, and maturity with the objective of selecting those most likely to succeed in law study and in the legal profession and also those who would contribute to the diversity essential to a rich educational experience.

The School of Law is committed to providing access to men and women of all races, religions, ethnic backgrounds, and physical abilities. Special scholarships and grants are available to qualified minority applicants. Inquiries should be addressed to the Director of Admissions and Financial Aid of the Law School.

Applicants admitted for the entering class in 1996 are required to pay a $300 nonrefundable deposit by April 1, and an interim tuition deposit on July 1 (both fees are applicable toward tuition and fee charges).

Personal interviews are not required, but may be arranged upon request. Individual applicants or groups are encouraged to visit the campus.

Transfer students who meet law school admission requirements are accepted on a space-available basis after the successful completion of one year at an AALS or ABA-approved law school.

■ Student Activities

All students are members of the Student Bar Association, which has an important place in the life of the law school. A number of other organizations allow students to pursue a variety of interests.

The *Wake Forest Law Review* is a recognized scholastic journal. Selection to the *Law Review* is based on academic performance or demonstrated writing and academic ability.

The Moot Court Board and Student Trial Bar assist in the administration of the school's strong trial and appellate advocacy program through various intramural and intercollegiate competitions.

■ Expenses and Financial Aid

➽ tuition & fees—$16,600 ➽ estimated living expenses—$5,000-7,000 ➽ merit and need-based scholarships available ➽ minority scholarships available ➽ FAF, Federal Needs Analysis, due May 1

Approximately 78 percent of the students receive financial assistance from scholarships, loans, work-study funds, and assistantships.

■ Placement

The Placement Program increases graduates' opportunities to reach their full professional potential, opportunities the law school believes it owes to its students.

The Office of Placement Services conducts workshops in résumé preparation, interviewing techniques, and career planning to help prepare students to find employment.

Firms and corporations who cannot send a representative to the campus may request résumés and invite students to interview. These services are provided for those seeking permanent employment, and for summer work, clerkships, and part-time employment.

The Office of Placement Services encourages employers to notify the director of openings for experienced attorneys. Placement maintains a list of Law School graduates seeking a change in employment. A listing of opportunities is mailed to these graduates each month.

Applicant Group for the 1995-1996 Academic Year

Wake Forest University School of Law
This grid includes only applicants who earned 120-180 LSAT scores.

	GPA																	
LSAT Score	3.75 +		3.50 - 3.74		3.25 - 3.49		3.00 - 3.24		2.75 - 2.99		2.50 - 2.74		2.00 - 2.49		Below 2.00		Total	
	Apps	Adm	Apps	Adm	Apps	Adm	Apps	Adm	Apps	Adm	Apps	Adm	Apps	Adm	Apps	Adm	Apps	Adm
175 - 180	1	1	0	0	0	0	0	0	0	0	0	0	0	0	0	0	1	1
170 - 174	4	4	5	5	5	5	6	6	5	4	1	1	3	3	0	0	29	28
165 - 169	9	9	14	14	18	18	24	20	12	12	7	5	3	2	0	0	87	80
160 - 164	32	32	61	59	98	82	76	60	38	25	29	6	12	1	0	0	346	265
155 - 159	55	43	90	42	140	22	108	5	52	1	29	3	14	0	0	0	488	116
150 - 154	19	2	53	4	77	4	74	6	35	3	39	2	19	0	0	0	316	21
145 - 149	8	3	18	0	43	4	40	6	38	1	25	4	18	0	1	0	191	18
140 - 144	1	0	11	2	12	0	13	0	17	1	15	0	17	0	1	0	87	3
135 - 139	1	0	0	0	5	0	12	0	6	0	5	0	11	0	0	0	40	0
130 - 134	0	0	1	0	1	0	4	0	2	0	1	0	1	0	0	0	10	0
125 - 129	0	0	1	0	0	0	0	0	2	0	1	0	2	0	1	0	7	0
120 - 124	0	0	0	0	0	0	1	0	0	0	0	0	0	0	0	0	1	0
Total	130	94	254	126	399	135	358	103	207	47	152	21	100	6	3	0	1603	532

Apps = Number of Applicants
Adm = Number Admitted
Reflects 96% of the total applicant pool.

Washburn University School of Law

1700 College
Topeka, KS 66621

E-Mail: washburn.admissions@law.wuacc.edu
URL: http://lawlib.wuacc.edu/washburn/school.law/welcome.html
Phone: 913.231.1185 (out-of-state), 800.332.0291 (in-state)

■ Introduction

Washburn University began as Lincoln College in 1865 and became Washburn College in 1868. The School of Law opened its doors in 1903, and in 1905 became one of the early members of the Association of American Law Schools. In 1923, Washburn was among the first law schools to be fully accredited by the American Bar Association. Washburn University today is an urban university serving 6,500 students. It is located in Topeka, the capital city of Kansas, about 60 miles west of Kansas City.

■ Enrollment/Student Body

➽ 991 applicants ➽ 440 admitted first-year class 1995 ➽ 150 enrolled first-year class 1995 ➽ 417 total full-time ➽ 18.5% minority ➽ 42% women ➽ 42 states & foreign countries represented ➽ 172 undergraduate schools represented

■ Faculty

➽ 27 full-time ➽ 9 women ➽ 7 minority ➽ 32 part-time or adjunct

■ Library and Physical Facilities

➽ 280,000 volumes & equivalents ➽ library hours: Mon.-Thurs., 7:30 A.M.-11:00 P.M.; Fri., 7:30 A.M.-9:00 P.M.; Sat., 8:00 A.M.-8:00 P.M.; Sun., NOON-11:00 P.M. ➽ LEXIS ➽ NEXIS ➽ WESTLAW ➽ Internet ➽ DIALOG ➽ Dow Jones ➽ 7 full-time librarians ➽ library seats 346 ➽ 30-station computer lab

Library highlights include a 30-station microcomputer lab, addition of 75 individual study carrels equipped for laptop microcomputer use, group study rooms, lounge seating areas, and a richly furbished special collections room. The law building has a barrier-free design. Washburn's clinical program, one of the first in the nation, is housed in an attached model law office. A beautiful moot courtroom is regularly used for administrative law hearings and occasional sittings by the Kansas Supreme Court and the U.S. Tenth Circuit Court of Appeals.

The law library has a national reputation for leadership in the use of new information technologies. The July, 1995 update of Don MacLeod's *The Internet Guide for the Legal Researcher* describes Washlaw, created by the Washburn law library staff, as "perhaps the most comprehensive law-related site on the Internet." The author advises that if you could "connect to only one Internet law site, pick this one." Washburn also hosts over 65 law-related listservs (online discussion groups), more than any other law school worldwide. Each law student receives a password for accessing LEXIS, WESTLAW, Internet, and E-mail from home or school. A local area network provides convenient access to one of the largest networked CD-ROM collections in the nation, computer-assisted learning exercises, and computer software.

The library collection has had over a decade of vigorous growth, ranking in the top quarter of all law school libraries for new titles added since 1979. A strong law-related videotape collection is used to supplement classroom instruction. Specialized research facilities include U.S. and Kansas government document depositories, a local public document room for the U.S. Nuclear Regulatory Commission, and a satellite reference center for the Kansas Patent Depository Library. Law students have access to the 200,000-volume Kansas Supreme Court Law Library.

■ Curriculum

➽ Academic Support Program ➽ 90 credits required to graduate ➽ 122 courses available ➽ semesters, start in Aug. and Jan. ➽ range of first-year class size—25-80 ➽ two six-week summer sessions

Students may begin their study in either the fall or spring semester. The first-year curriculum is prescribed. To complete the upper-level program, students must meet distributional requirements in six areas of study plus writing and oral presentational requirements.

■ Certificate Programs

A Certificate in Law and Mental Health is awarded jointly by Washburn and the world-renowned Menninger Foundation psychiatric center to students who graduate with 96 credit hours and receive a B average in at least 15 hours of credit in the Mental Health Law area. Students participate in a colloquium with psychiatric residents at Menninger and represent clients in mental disability cases in the Washburn Law Clinic.

Certificates in Tax Law, Family Law, and Agricultural Law are awarded to students graduating with 96 credit hours who achieve a B average in at least 15 hours of credit in the Tax, Family, or Agricultural Law area.

■ Special Programs

Washburn has gained national recognition through its Law Clinic, a general practice firm of senior law students representing indigent clients. The clinic experience includes direct client representation in a wide range of civil and criminal litigation.

Valuable academic and work opportunities are provided by the state legislature, state executive offices, state and federal district courts, state supreme court, court of appeals, bankruptcy court, and state and federal agencies.

Washburn sponsors a six-credit-hour, six-week program abroad each summer. Washburn faculty team teach classes with faculty members from the host school.

The Rural Law Center focuses teaching and research on aspects of the law affecting the rural environment.

■ Admission

➾ *Bachelor's degree from accredited college or university* ➾ *application deadline—fall, March 15; spring, Sept. 15* ➾ *LSAT, LSDAS required* ➾ *median GPA—3.27* ➾ *median LSAT score—154* ➾ *application fee—$30*

Significant factors that the Admissions Committee considers are the LSAT score and grade-point average. There is no automatic cutoff for LSAT score or GPA. Other factors which are evaluated are work experience, graduate work, cultural background, extracurricular activities, and the need for diversity in the student body. Late applications are accepted but applicants may be at a disadvantage. Admitted applicants pay a $100 admission deposit which applies toward tuition when the student enrolls. Applicants are encouraged to visit the school and attend a law class.

■ Student Activities

Students are selected to membership on the Board of Editors of the *Washburn Law Journal* on the basis of class rank or performance in a writing competition.

Washburn has assumed editorial responsibility for publication of the Family Law Quarterly of the American Bar Association's Family Law Section. The Quarterly provides a second editorial experience for Washburn students.

The Washburn Student Bar Association directs student affairs, sponsoring a wide variety of educational and social activities. Students participate in Moot Court, Client Counseling, Negotiations, and Trial Advocacy competitions. There are more than 20 active student organizations, including four law fraternities, Asian, Hispanic American, Native American, and Black Law Student Associations, Women's Legal Forum, and societies for students interested in Environmental, International, Public-Interest, Tax, and Sports Law.

■ Expenses and Financial Aid

➾ *full-time tuition—residents, $5,712 ($204 per credit hour); nonresidents, $8,624 ($308 per credit hour)* ➾ *books and supplies—$600* ➾ *performance and need-based scholarships available* ➾ *College Scholarship Service PROFILE required for need-based scholarships, Free Application for Federal Student Aid (FAFSA) required for loans* ➾ *financial aid forms due with admission applications*

Scholarships may be awarded on a combination of academic performance and need. Diversity is considered as a factor in making scholarship awards. Second- and third-year students appreciate the availability of research-assistant positions within the law school and the abundance of law-related jobs in Topeka.

Housing costs vary, but are quite reasonable: dormitory room and board from $3,110 per year; university apartments for families, 1 bedroom—$180. Most students live in apartments in the residential areas surrounding the campus.

■ Career Services

Washburn provides students and alumni with professional career-planning services. Programs emphasize assessment of career goals, exploration of varied applications of a legal education, and support for the transition into the professional marketplace. Extensive resources are available regarding local, regional, national, and international legal employment in the public and private sectors, graduate and foreign study, and judicial clerkships.

Washburn graduates' employment experiences are consistent with national law placement averages within one year of graduation. Alumni are located in every state in the nation and several foreign countries.

Applicant Group for the 1995-1996 Academic Year

Washburn University School of Law

LSAT Score	GPA 3.75 +		3.50 - 3.74		3.25 - 3.49		3.00 - 3.24		2.75 - 2.99		2.50 - 2.74		2.25 - 2.49		Below 2.25		Total	
	Apps	Adm	Apps	Adm	Apps	Adm	Apps	Adm	Apps	Adm	Apps	Adm	Apps	Adm	Apps	Adm	Apps	Adm
175 - 180	0	0	0	0	0	0	0	0	0	0	0	0	0	0	0	0	0	0
170 - 174	0	0	0	0	0	0	0	0	1	1	0	0	0	0	0	0	1	1
165 - 169	2	2	0	0	2	2	5	4	2	2	1	1	0	0	1	1	13	12
160 - 164	6	6	4	4	11	11	8	8	5	5	8	8	7	4	1	0	50	46
155 - 159	8	8	21	20	26	26	39	37	35	32	14	8	13	3	2	0	158	134
150 - 154	23	23	42	39	62	50	67	43	54	7	31	6	27	4	7	1	313	173
145 - 149	15	8	35	10	40	18	63	11	31	5	29	3	12	0	12	2	237	57
140 - 144	2	1	13	3	23	1	15	1	23	1	16	1	17	1	14	2	123	11
Below 140	1	0	3	0	3	0	6	1	7	0	8	0	15	0	12	0	55	1
Total	57	48	118	76	167	108	203	105	158	53	107	27	91	12	49	6	950	435

Apps = Number of Applicants
Adm = Number Admitted
This chart is to be used for general purposes only. Nonnumerical factors are weighed heavily in all admission decisions.

University of Washington School of Law

316 Condon Hall
1100 N.E. Campus Parkway
Seattle, WA 98105-6617

E-Mail: admit@law.washington.edu
URL: http://www.law.washington.edu
Phone: 206.543.4078

■ Introduction

Established in 1899, the School of Law is part of the main campus of the University of Washington, approximately four miles from downtown Seattle. The university, the largest single campus institution in the western United States, with an enrollment of 33,500 students, offers nearly every discipline for study. The School of Law has 44 full-time faculty members and about 500 J.D. students. Because of the favorable student-to-faculty ratio, classes are generally small, with frequent opportunities for student-teacher contacts. Each first-year student is usually in at least one class of 30 or fewer students, in addition to the Basic Legal Skills course. The school is a member of the AALS, is approved by the ABA, and has a chapter of the Order of the Coif.

■ Enrollment/Student Body

➧ *2,400 applicants* ➧ *469 admitted first-year class 1995*
➧ *169 enrolled first-year class 1995*
➧ *495 total full-time J.D.* ➧ *37.8% minority*
➧ *48% women* ➧ *23 states represented*
➧ *80 undergraduate schools represented*

■ Faculty

➧ *70 total* ➧ *45 full-time* ➧ *25 part-time or adjunct*
➧ *16 women* ➧ *3 minority*

■ Library and Physical Facilities

➧ *450,000 volumes & equivalents* ➧ *library hours: Mon.,-Thurs., 8:00 A.M.-10:00 P.M.; Fri., 8:00 A.M.-6:00 P.M.; Sat., 10:00 A.M.-6:00 P.M.; Sun., NOON-10:00 P.M.* ➧ *LEXIS*
➧ *NEXIS* ➧ *CD-ROM & full Internet accessibility*
➧ *11.5 full-time librarians* ➧ *library seats 454*

■ Curriculum

➧ *135 quarter credits required to graduate*
➧ *115 courses available; full-time day program only*
➧ *degrees available: J.D./M.B.A.; J.D./International Studies; LL.M. in Asian Law, Law and Marine Affairs, International Environmental Law, Law of Sustainable International Development, and Taxation* ➧ *quarters, begin in Oct.*
➧ *range of first-year class size—30-120*

The first-year curriculum is prescribed. After that, except for an analytical writing requirement and a class in professional responsibility, all courses in the second and third years are elective. In addition to traditional courses and seminars, advanced students may participate in a criminal, mediation, family and employment law, immigration, affordable housing or refugee advocacy clinic, or in courses in trial advocacy. Judicial, legislative, agency, and public interest externships are available. Students must also perform 60 hours of public service legal work.

Students are encouraged to rely on their initiative and to develop their own powers of perception. Classroom discussion in which students participate fully is one means used to assist this development. Independent research projects, either in the context of a seminar or through individualized study under faculty supervision, are also emphasized. Although it is a state law school, Washington state law is not emphasized unduly. Graduates of the school are prepared to practice law anywhere in the United States or in other common law countries.

■ Special Programs

Students studying for the J.D. program may take courses in any of the LL.M. programs during the second and third years. The UW also offers a master's degree in Law Librarianship.

■ Admission Standards

➧ *Bachelor's degree required*
➧ *application deadline—Jan. 15; applicants must take the LSAT no later that Dec.*
➧ *decisions made from Jan. 15 to April 1*
➧ *LSAT, LSDAS required* ➧ *median GPA—3.55*
➧ *application fee—$50* ➧ *median LSAT score—162; multiple LSAT scores are averaged*

In selecting the entering class, the law school does not make all of its admission decisions solely on the basis of predicted academic performance. Important academic objectives are furthered by classes comprised of students having talents and skills derived from diverse backgrounds believed to be relevant to a rich and effective study of law.

33 percent of the incoming class consists of students of color, for whom the school provides student, faculty, and professional mentoring programs.

■ Student Activities

The *Washington Law Review* and *Pacific Rim Law and Policy Journal* are edited and published by students. The University of Washington is consistently among the top scoring Moot Court teams in the nation.

Through the Student Bar Association and student/faculty committees, students participate in the decision processes of the law school. Student organizations include the Law Women's Caucus; Minority Law Students Association; Asian Pacific American Law Students; Coalition of Black Law Students; Filipino Law Students Association; Latino/Latina Law Students Association; Native American Law Students Association; Environmental Law Society; International Law Society; Christian Legal Society; National Lawyer's Guild; Law, Science, and Technology Group; Lesbian and Gay Legal Society; Phi Alpha Delta; ABA Student Division; Federalist Society, and Public Interest Project.

■ Expenses and Financial Aid

- *full-time tuition & fees—resident, $4,800; nonresident, $12,000*
- *estimated additional expenses—$11,000 (books, $850; room & board, $7,250; transportation, $750; insurance, $370; personal, $1,850)*
- *need-based scholarships available*
- *financial aid available; FAFSA due Feb. 28*

■ Career Services

The Career Services Office serves as a liaison between students and prospective employers. Firms, agencies, and other potential employers are invited to interview at the school and to list job openings in the regularly published placement bulletin. About 90 percent of the graduates choose to remain in Washington state.

Applicant Group for the 1995-1996 Academic Year

University of Washington School of Law
This grid includes 100% of all applications reviewed with scores on the 180 score scale.

Average LSAT Score

GPA Range	120 - 153		154 - 156		157 - 159		160 - 162		163 - 165		166 - 168		169 - 180		Total	
	Adm	Apps	Adm	Apps	Adm	Apps	Adm	Apps	Adm	Apps	Adm	Apps	Adm	Apps	Adm	Apps
3.75 & Above	8	40	8	37	12	62	20	51	36	42	34	35	25	26	143	293
3.50 - 3.74	8	108	5	74	15	92	20	102	33	82	45	61	36	36	162	555
3.25 - 3.49	7	162	7	67	6	80	19	118	15	88	11	55	24	31	89	601
3.00 - 3.24	3	149	5	64	7	65	7	58	4	41	4	25	10	22	40	424
2.75 - 2.99	1	101	2	30	4	34	4	26	4	26	1	18	7	14	23	249
2.50 - 2.74	0	66	0	12	2	9	3	13	0	7	0	5	1	3	6	115
Below 2.50	0	45	0	8	0	5	0	4	0	3	0	4	0	3	0	72
LSAT only	0	30	1	8	0	9	0	4	1	4	2	6	1	3	5	64
Total	27	701	28	300	46	356	73	376	93	293	97	209	104	138	468	2373

Apps = Number of Applicants
Adm = Number Admitted
In cases where an applicant presented multiple LSAT scores, the average score was used.

This information is presented to give applicants some idea of the likelihood of admission. It should be noted, however, that these data can and do change from year to year. In addition, there is some latitude within each category, so that a person presenting credentials at the upper limits of one cell might have an excellent chance for admission, while another applicant at the lower limits might only have a marginal chance. For these reasons, this chart should be used as an approximate gauge of the likelihood of admission and **NOT** as a guarantee.

Washington and Lee University School of Law

Lewis Hall
Lexington, VA 24450

E-Mail: lawadm@wlu.edu
URL: http://www.wlu.edu/law
Phone: 540.463.8504

■ Introduction

Washington and Lee University School of Law is a private institution located in Lexington, Virginia, approximately 175 miles southwest of Washington, DC, in the Blue Ridge Mountains. Founded in 1849, the school is a member of the AALS and is fully accredited by the ABA.

As a small, selective private law school, Washington and Lee takes pride in offering a nationally oriented legal education that is professionally rigorous and intellectually challenging. The size of the school is carefully controlled to achieve a generous faculty-to-student ratio and a closely-knit community of students and faculty, in which the opportunity for informal contact and collaboration in ongoing research enhances the educational process. The school seeks to limit its total enrollment to 360 students; there are 35 regular faculty members and 11 adjunct members.

■ Enrollment/Student Body

➡ *2,139 applicants* ➡ *474 admitted first-year class 1995* ➡ *130 enrolled first-year class 1995* ➡ *374 total full-time* ➡ *15% minority* ➡ *40% women* ➡ *42 states & foreign countries represented* ➡ *189 undergraduate schools represented*

■ Faculty

➡ *47 total* ➡ *35 full-time* ➡ *11 part-time or adjunct* ➡ *10 women* ➡ *3 minority*

■ Library and Physical Facilities

➡ *317,500 volumes & equivalents* ➡ *library open 24 hours a day, 7 days a week, year-round* ➡ *LEXIS* ➡ *NEXIS* ➡ *WESTLAW* ➡ *7 full-time librarians* ➡ *library seats 400*

The School of Law is located on the campus of Washington and Lee University in Lewis Hall, originally built in 1976 and expanded in 1991 with the addition of the Lewis F. Powell, Jr. Archives, which house the Supreme Court and professional papers of retired Supreme Court Justice Powell, a graduate of the University's college and law school. Each student is provided his or her own study carrel or office space in Lewis Hall. Training in the use of all online research services is provided to all first-year students. Students have access to the library collection on an open-stack basis. The school makes extensive use of state-of-the-art video and computer technology in classroom settings and in trial advocacy training.

■ Curriculum

➡ *Academic Support Program* ➡ *85 credits required to graduate* ➡ *102 courses available (excluding all clinical programs and journals, which do carry academic credit)* ➡ *J.D. degree available* ➡ *range of first-year class size—19-60* ➡ *average class size after first-year—23*

■ Special Programs

Second- and third-year law students may elect to participate in a number of clinical or specialized practice programs offered by the School of Law, including the Legal Aid Society, providing legal services to indigent civil clients; the Western State Hospital Legal Aid Society, providing legal services to residents of a state mental hospital; the Alderson Legal Assistance Program, providing legal services to inmates of a major federal institution for female offenders; and the Public Defender Program, providing legal services to indigent persons charged with crimes. In the U.S. Attorney's Program, students participate in prosecutorial trial work in the federal court system. The Judicial Clerkship Program provides opportunities to clerk for trial or appellate judges in the Virginia court system.

The International Environmental Law Program was founded with a grant from the Creswell Foundation, and provides students with an opportunity to participate in a year-long program of seminars, directed research, and summer internships in the field of international environmental law. Governmental organizations, corporations, or public interest entities submit project proposals; program participants select the project and entity of their choice. Last year, students worked for the Natural Resources Defense Council, the government of Hungary, the Community Nutrition Institute, for public interest groups concerned with development in the Arctic, and in environmental issues dealing with human rights, among others.

The Virginia Capital Case Clearinghouse was established to provide research and litigation support to attorneys appointed to represent persons charged with capital crimes, or who are pursuing appeals of cases in which the death penalty has been imposed. Students pursue in-depth research into developments in current death-penalty law and assist with the preparation of pleadings, legal memoranda, and briefs in ongoing cases. Students write and edit the *Capital Case Digest*, a journal dealing with the complex and important area of capital sentencing.

■ Admission

➡ *undergraduate degree required for admission* ➡ *application deadline—Feb. 1* ➡ *applications received after Feb. 1 will be considered but cannot be guaranteed a response by April 1* ➡ *LSAT, LSDAS required* ➡ *median GPA—3.57* ➡ *median LSAT score—163* ➡ *application fee—$40*

Students enter the School of Law only in the fall semester, which begins in late August. There is no part-time program.

Although the LSAT score and undergraduate grade-point average are important factors considered by the Admissions Committee, other, more subjective factors, such as trends in grades, the rigor of an applicant's academic program, achievement in extracurricular or community service activities, work experience, and evaluations from professors are a significant part of an admissions decision. An applicant may request an interview with a member of the Admissions Committee. Applicants are encouraged to visit the school to sit in on classes, tour the facility, and talk with students and faculty if it is convenient for them to do so.

The School of Law actively seeks a diversified student body whose members are of different religious, racial, ethnic, economic, and geographic backgrounds. Applications from persons considering a change in career are encouraged.

■ Student Activities

The *Washington and Lee Law Review*, managed and published by students, is a quarterly journal for scholarly discussion of important legal problems. A variety of moot court and advocacy competitions, both intra- and interschool, provide students with opportunities to hone advocacy, counseling, negotiation, and trial skills.

All students are members of the Student Bar Association, which represents students in the ongoing affairs of the school and sponsors professional programs and social activities. Law students also participate in university intramural sports, drama, music, and political programs. The Black Law Student Association, Women Law Student Association, the National Lawyers Guild, the Federalist Society, the Environmental Law Forum, the International Law Society, and three national professional fraternities all present programs addressing matters of special concern to their members.

■ Expenses and Financial Aid

➧ tuition—$15,250 ➧ full-time fees—$221 ➧ estimated additional expenses—$6,500 (room, board, books, misc. expenses) ➧ need- and merit-based scholarships available ➧ merit-based fellowships available ➧ FAFSA required for financial aid

■ Housing Opportunities

On-campus housing is available in the Woods Creek Apartments, adjacent to the law school. The law school provides an off-campus housing referral service to interested students.

■ Career Services

The Placement Office acts as a liaison between law students and legal employers. Workshops, brown-bag lunches, and panel presentations focus on special topics or skills, but individual counseling with personal attention to each student is the hallmark of the placement effort. An active alumni network is in place to assist students. In recent years, approximately 65 percent of graduates have entered the private practice of law immediately following graduation. Twenty percent serve judicial clerkships. Other graduates go into business-related employment, including corporate law staffs, banks, and accounting firms; take positions in various federal, state, or local governmental agencies; serve in public interest law, or in the JAG Corps; and some pursue advanced law degrees. Graduates are employed throughout the country; in the last three years, students have accepted employment in 44 states and seven foreign countries. About 95 percent report employment within six months of graduation.

Applicant Group for the 1995-1996 Academic Year

Washington and Lee University School of Law
This grid includes only applicants who earned 120-180 LSAT scores under standard administrations.

LSAT Score	GPA: 3.75 +		3.50 - 3.74		3.25 - 3.49		3.00 - 3.24		2.75 - 2.99		2.50 - 2.74		2.25 - 2.49		2.00 - 2.24		Below 2.00		No GPA		Total	
	Apps	Adm	Apps	Adm	Apps	Adm	Apps	Adm	Apps	Adm	Apps	Adm	Apps	Adm	Apps	Adm	Apps	Adm	Apps	Adm	Apps	Adm
175 - 180	1	1	0	0	1	1	0	0	1	0	0	0	0	0	0	0	0	0	0	0	3	2
170 - 174	5	5	12	12	13	11	9	5	7	4	0	0	2	1	1	1	0	0	0	0	49	39
165 - 169	29	29	42	41	49	41	38	20	29	9	6	2	8	2	0	0	1	1	1	1	203	146
160 - 164	77	66	149	63	167	33	99	12	48	3	26	3	11	1	2	0	1	0	2	0	582	181
155 - 159	83	31	124	10	125	2	83	1	51	2	19	0	11	1	1	0	0	0	2	0	499	47
150 - 154	48	12	87	13	76	2	77	6	40	2	24	1	13	0	6	0	4	0	7	0	382	36
145 - 149	8	1	28	2	38	2	46	2	42	1	21	2	19	1	9	0	2	0	3	0	216	11
140 - 144	1	0	14	1	22	1	20	1	23	0	18	1	14	0	9	0	0	0	2	0	123	4
135 - 139	1	0	2	0	2	0	7	0	5	0	8	0	5	0	3	0	1	0	0	0	34	0
130 - 134	0	0	1	0	1	0	1	0	3	0	2	0	1	0	1	0	0	0	0	0	10	0
125 - 129	0	0	0	0	0	0	0	0	0	0	0	0	1	0	0	0	0	0	0	0	1	0
120 - 124	0	0	0	0	0	0	0	0	0	0	0	0	0	0	0	0	0	0	0	0	0	0
Total	253	145	459	142	494	93	380	47	249	21	124	9	85	6	32	1	9	1	17	1	2102	466

Apps = Number of Applicants
Adm = Number Admitted
Reflects 98% of the total applicant pool.

Washington University School of Law

Box 1120
One Brookings Drive
St. Louis, MO 63130

E-Mail: admiss@wulaw.wustl.edu
URL: http://www.wulaw.wustl.edu
Phone: 314.935.4525

■ Introduction

Founded in 1867, Washington University School of Law is the oldest private law school in continuous operation west of the Mississippi River. A charter member of the AALS and approved by the ABA, the school was one of the first accredited law schools to graduate women. The law school is located on the beautiful and serene 169-acre Hilltop Campus bordered by Forest Park, the site of the 1904 World's Fair, and the lovely suburban communities of Clayton and University City.

■ Enrollment/Student Body

➽ *1,770 applicants* ➽ *947 admitted first-year class 1995*
➽ *206 enrolled first-year class 1995* ➽ *622 total full-time*
➽ *18% minority* ➽ *40% women*
➽ *36 states & foreign countries represented*
➽ *110 undergraduate schools represented*

The law school has a national approach to legal education and attracts students from throughout the United States and several foreign countries. The wide variety of undergraduate academic disciplines enriches the Socratic method of teaching.

■ Faculty

➽ *112 total* ➽ *44 full-time* ➽ *68 part-time or adjunct*
➽ *31 women* ➽ *11 minority*

Our student-to-faculty ratio (including only full-time faculty) is 15 to 1.

■ Library and Physical Facilities

➽ *518,694 volumes & equivalents* ➽ *library hours: Mon.-Thurs., 7:00 A.M.-1:00 A.M.; Fri., 7:00 A.M.-MIDNIGHT; Sat., 9:00 A.M.-MIDNIGHT; Sun., 9:00 A.M.-1:00 A.M.*
➽ *LEXIS* ➽ *NEXIS* ➽ *WESTLAW*
➽ *Congressional Information System* ➽ *LEGI-SLATE*
➽ *assorted CD-ROMs* ➽ *8 full-time librarians*
➽ *library seats 310*

■ Curriculum

➽ *85 credits to graduate* ➽ *82 courses available*
➽ *degree available: J.D./Asian studies; J.D./M.B.A.; J.D./M.A.-Econ.; J.D./M.A.-Pol. Sci.; J.D./M.H.A.; J.D./M.S.W.; J.D./M.A. or M.S.-Environmental Policy; J.D./M.A.-European studies*

A three-year, full-time course of study leads to the J.D. degree. The prescribed first-year courses are sectioned to ensure individualized instruction. In addition, all first-year students participate in a year-long legal research and writing program. Coursework in the second and third years is chosen by the student. A Congressional Clinic and a Federal Administrative Agency Clinic offered in the spring semester of the third year allow a small group of students to work in Washington, DC, with individual members of Congress, congressional committees, and federal agencies. Other areas of strength include environmental, international, corporate, clinical education, urban studies, taxation, criminal, labor, and Asian.

■ Special Programs

➽ *Congressional Clinic (Washington DC)—spring sem., 3rd yr.*
➽ 7 joint-degree programs available

The School of Law offers a Masters degree (LL.M.) in Taxation. Combined-study programs exist between the Law School and School of Social Work (J.D./M.S.W.), the Health Administration Department of the School of Medicine (J.D./M.H.A.), the School of Business (J.D./M.B.A.), and the Department of Economics (J.D./M.S.Ec.), Political Science (J.D./M.A.), the Asian Studies department (J.D./M.A.), the European Studies department, and the Department of Engineering and Policy of the School of Engineering and Applied Science. This degree (J.D./M.S. or M.A.) places an emphasis on environmental law and policy.

Additional combined-degree programs are available by arrangement with other departments.

■ Admission

➽ *Bachelor's degree required* ➽ *application deadline—March 1* ➽ *LSAT, LSDAS required*
➽ *median GPA—3.40* ➽ *median LSAT score—160*
➽ *application fee—$50*

While there is no formal deadline for applying to the school of law, applications received after March 1 may not receive full consideration. The Admissions Committee informs applicants of their status by April 15. Decisions on transfer applications are made in mid-summer and considered only if the student has an outstanding record at another AALS-ABA approved school.

Admission decisions are based on a wide range of factors, including undergraduate record, the Law School Admissions Test score, and personal statement. Letters of recommendation are encouraged but not required, and should be limited to no more than three. Applicants are also advised to visit the law school; arrangements can be made by contacting the Admissions Office.

The committee makes a conscientious effort to examine the more personal variables which have a real impact on the quality of life and the quality of education in this institution, such as energy, motivation, self-discipline, and character. Insight into these variables is derived from careful examination of the undergraduate record, personal statement, résumé, and/or letters of recommendation, and other items in the applicant's file.

■ Housing

A wide range of affordable private housing is available near the School of Law. For housing information, students should contact the University Housing Office (314.935.5050).

■ Student Activities

The School of Law publishes two student-edited law review periodicals, the *Law Quarterly* and the *Journal of Urban and Contemporary Law*. A very active moot court program, mock trial competition, and competitions in negotiation and client counseling are available. Law students participate in a variety of other programs, including the Women's Law Caucus, the Pro Bono Law Association, the Black Law Students Association, the Asian American Law Student Association, and the Student Bar Association. The student body is self-regulated through the Law School Honor Council. Students are eligible for election to the Order of the Coif. Students also serve on many joint committees with faculty members.

■ Opportunities for Minority and Women Students

The environment for minority law students is excellent at Washington University. Minority students have been actively involved in law review publications, moot court, mock trial competitions, legal fraternities, student government, and other academic and extracurricular activities. Minorities with strong academic records will automatically be considered for the Minority Students in Law Program.

One of the first women to receive a degree from an American law school graduated from Washington University in 1871. The school successfully continues to recruit outstanding women, although admission decisions are made on a nondiscriminatory basis. Women with exceptional academic records are encouraged to apply for an Olin Fellowship, which provides full tuition and some stipends for eight women pursuing graduate degrees at Washington University. Application deadline for this award is February 1.

■ Expenses and Financial Aid

- *tuition & fees—$19,380 (1995-96)*
- *estimated additional expenses—$8,000 (housing, food, etc)*
- *scholarships available: Scholars in Law, Minority Scholars in Law, Olin Fellowship (for women), Buder Scholarship (for Native Americans), Farmer Scholarship (for African Americans), Fisse Scholarship, Chancellor's Fellowship*
- *financial aid available; FAFSA due March 1*

The school offers merit scholarships that are awarded to entering students with exceptional credentials without regard to financial need.

Most student aid is in the form of government and privately sponsored loans. One-half of the students receive some scholarship assistance; two-thirds receive loans. (Virtually all those receiving scholarships also receive loans).

■ Career Services

An aggressive and efficient Career Services Office serves both students and employers. For the class of 1994, 95% of the graduating class found employment within six months of graduation. Over half accepted positions outside metropolitan St. Louis, 49 percent entered private practice, and 32 percent found positions in the public sector. Others are employed in corporate legal departments, accounting firms, banks, and commercial businesses.

Applicant Group for the 1995-1996 Academic Year

Washington University School of Law
This grid includes only applicants who earned 120-180 LSAT scores under standard administrations.

LSAT Score	3.75 +		3.50 - 3.74		3.25 - 3.49		3.00 - 3.24		2.75 - 2.99		2.50 - 2.74		2.25 - 2.49		2.00 - 2.24		Below 2.00		No GPA		Total	
	Apps	Adm	Apps	Adm	Apps	Adm	Apps	Adm	Apps	Adm	Apps	Adm	Apps	Adm	Apps	Adm	Apps	Adm	Apps	Adm	Apps	Adm
175 - 180	1	1	0	0	1	1	0	0	1	1	0	0	0	0	0	0	0	0	0	0	3	3
170 - 174	9	8	8	7	4	4	4	2	5	4	0	0	3	2	1	1	0	0	0	0	34	28
165 - 169	35	31	37	36	42	39	30	29	19	18	8	8	2	2	0	0	0	0	1	1	174	164
160 - 164	69	67	99	94	121	114	64	58	40	30	16	12	5	3	2	1	1	1	0	0	417	380
155 - 159	38	27	82	61	111	59	90	24	51	7	24	4	10	1	0	0	1	0	8	3	415	186
150 - 154	26	9	52	15	80	19	77	13	60	18	36	6	11	0	4	0	0	0	8	2	354	82
145 - 149	7	4	17	4	39	10	46	10	39	9	17	7	12	0	3	0	1	0	4	1	185	45
140 - 144	1	1	9	6	12	2	18	1	14	0	15	0	8	0	5	0	2	0	3	0	87	10
135 - 139	1	0	1	0	3	0	5	0	7	0	5	0	7	0	4	0	2	0	3	0	38	0
130 - 134	0	0	0	0	3	0	1	0	0	0	3	0	3	0	2	0	0	0	0	0	12	0
125 - 129	0	0	0	0	0	0	0	0	0	0	1	0	1	0	2	0	0	0	0	0	4	0
120 - 124	0	0	0	0	0	0	0	0	0	0	0	0	0	0	0	0	0	0	0	0	0	0
Total	187	148	305	223	416	248	335	137	236	87	125	37	62	8	23	2	7	1	27	7	1723	898

Apps = Number of Applicants
Adm = Number Admitted
Reflects 99% of the total applicant pool.

Wayne State University Law School

Admissions Office
468 W. Ferry Mall
Detroit, MI 48202

E-Mail: inquire@novell.law.wayne.edu
URL: http://www.science.wayne.edu/~law/
Phone: 313.577.3937

■ Introduction

Wayne State University Law School was established in 1927, is accredited by the ABA, is a member of the AALS, and has a chapter of the Order of the Coif, the national honor society of the legal profession.

The Law School is a flagship unit of Wayne State University, a major metropolitan research university, located in the Detroit Cultural Center. The Law School's three-building complex is situated at the north end of the university's campus, which covers 185 beautifully landscaped acres and is highlighted by famous Yamasaki-designed buildings.

■ Enrollment/Student Body

➽ 1,288 applicants ➽ 493 admitted first-year class 1995 ➽ 227 enrolled first-year class 1995 ➽ 548 total full-time ➽ 199 total part-time ➽ 15.3% minority ➽ 46% women ➽ 13 states & foreign countries represented ➽ 99 undergraduate schools represented ➽ age range—21-54

Approximately 750 students are enrolled in the J.D. program, including individuals from diverse racial, ethnic and socioeconomic backgrounds. Student life, both social and academic, is unusually friendly.

When compared with graduates of other law schools, Wayne State law graduates consistently have the highest or the second highest passing rate on the Michigan Bar Examination.

■ Faculty

➽ 67 total ➽ 33 full-time ➽ 34 part-time or adjunct ➽ 9 women ➽ 3 minority

The members of the full-time faculty are committed to teaching, research, and publishing yet remain accessible to students. One-fourth of the faculty are elected members of the American Law Institute. Many are nationally or internationally recognized experts in their fields of specialization.

Judges and attorneys prominent in specific areas of law, and professors from the United States and other countries serve as adjunct faculty and visiting professors.

■ The Arthur Neef Law Library

➽ 500,000 volumes & equivalents ➽ library hours: Mon.-Thurs., 8:00 A.M.-11:00 P.M.; Fri., 8:00 A.M.-9:00 P.M.; Sat., 9:00 A.M.-9:00 P.M.; Sun., 11:00 A.M.-11:00 P.M.; exam periods until MIDNIGHT ➽ 24 hours a day off-site access ➽ LEXIS ➽ NEXIS ➽ WESTLAW ➽ 4 full-time librarians (3 hold J.D. degrees) ➽ library seats 456 ➽ 32-station computer lab ➽ 31st largest accredited law library

■ Curriculum

➽ Academic Support Program (Summer Institute) ➽ 86 credits required to graduate ➽ 103 total courses available ➽ degrees available: J.D.; J.D./M.A. History; J.D./M.A. Public Policy; J.D./M.B.A.—other disciplines by special arrangement ➽ semesters, start in Aug. ➽ range of first-year class size—25-80

The first-year curriculum includes the required basic courses: civil procedure, contracts, criminal law, property, torts, and legal research and writing.

The legal research and writing course is one of the best in the nation. The research and writing proficiency of Wayne State law students is highly valued by law firms and other employers. The course is taught by full-time instructors, who are attorneys with experience in the courts, legal practice, and teaching.

Upper-class students are required to take a semester each of constitutional law and professional responsibility. Other courses may be chosen from a broad and diverse range of elective courses, seminars, and skills training classes.

The Law School offers LL.M. programs in the areas of taxation, labor law, and corporate planning.

■ Admission

➽ Bachelor's degree required ➽ application deadline—March 15 ➽ rolling admission ➽ LSAT, LSDAS required ➽ median GPA—3.30 ➽ median LSAT score—156 ➽ application fee—$20

Most of the class is admitted strictly on the basis of superior undergraduate GPA and LSAT scores. Others are admitted on the basis of academic credentials and other discretionary factors.

Transfer applications may be made, but only students from ABA-approved law schools with excellent academic credentials will be accepted.

■ Minority Students and Other Special Programs

Wayne State Law School has a commitment to enroll a diverse student body and maintains an affirmative action admissions policy for minority group members. Our goal is to assure that every individual we admit has the potential to be successful at our law school.

Minority students admitted to Wayne State Law School have a high graduation and bar passage rate. Qualified minority students are considered for the Kenneth Cockrel, Wade McCree, and Law Alumni Scholarships/Fellowship.

The Supportive Services Program, under the full-time supervision of an Assistant Dean, offers academic and related support to all students. The Summer Institute Program allows entering students to complete Torts, a first-year required course, prior to the beginning of the regular academic year.

■ Student Activities

The *Wayne Law Review*, a scholarly legal journal with nationwide circulation, is published by upper-class law students selected on the basis of their superior academic achievement and/or writing ability.

The Wayne Moot Court Program enjoys national recognition and is affiliated with the Order of the Barristers, a national honorary organization.

The Student Trial Advocacy Program (STAP) provides basic instruction in evidence and the techniques of trial advocacy.

Many students work in the Free Legal Aid Clinic representing indigent clients in court under attorney supervision. Students in the Criminal Appellate Practice Program, in cooperation with the Michigan State Appellate Defender Office, prepare briefs and other pleadings for indigent clients with pending felony appeals.

Second- and third-year students may intern on a part-time basis for distinguished judges and in a variety of governmental and nonprofit agencies.

The Student Board of Governors plays a significant role in the decision-making process of the school and also sponsors social activities for law students. Other student organizations include the Black Law Students Association, Hispanic Law Student Association, Jewish Law Students Association, Federalist Society, Women's Law Caucus, National Lawyers Guild, Environmental Law Society, International Law Society, Student Recruiters organization, ABA Law Student Division, and legal fraternities.

■ Study Abroad

Each year a Wayne State Law Student is selected for the Freeman Fellowship to support study during a summer session at the Academy of International Law at the Hague, The Netherlands.

The Law School has a student exchange program with the School of Law of the University of Warwick, England for six weeks of study during the summer.

Wayne State Law students may also study one semester abroad through participation in the London Law Programme.

■ Intellectual Property Law Institute (I.P.L.I.)

The I.P.L.I. offers an exceptional and rich curriculum for law students and lawyers in such areas of intellectual property as patents, copyrights, trademarks, trade secrets, computers and related technology, communications and media, entertainment, technology transfer, trade regulation, and the arts.

■ Expenses and Financial Aid

➧ full-time tuition & fees—resident, $6,290; nonresident, $13,580 ➧ part-time tuition and fees—resident, $3,420; nonresident, $7,308 ➧ estimated additional expenses—$15,080 (books, room $ board, transportation, miscellaneous expenses) ➧ merit- and need-based scholarships available ➧ merit- and need-based minority scholarships available ➧ financial aid available ➧ FAFSA priority date—April 23

Applicant Group for the 1995-1996 Academic Year

Wayne State University Law School
This grid includes only applicants who earned 120-180 LSAT scores under standard administrations.

LSAT Score	GPA 3.75 +		3.50 - 3.74		3.25 - 3.49		3.00 - 3.24		2.75 - 2.99		2.50 - 2.74		2.25 - 2.49		2.00 - 2.24		Below 2.00		No GPA		Total	
	Apps	Adm	Apps	Adm	Apps	Adm	Apps	Adm	Apps	Adm	Apps	Adm	Apps	Adm	Apps	Adm	Apps	Adm	Apps	Adm	Apps	Adm
175 - 180	0	0	1	1	0	0	0	0	0	0	0	0	0	0	0	0	0	0	0	0	1	1
170 - 174	0	0	0	0	3	3	2	1	1	1	0	0	0	0	0	0	0	0	0	0	6	5
165 - 169	6	6	3	3	4	4	10	10	5	4	4	4	1	0	0	0	0	0	1	0	34	31
160 - 164	13	12	25	24	31	31	24	24	17	13	11	2	5	1	0	0	0	0	4	1	130	108
155 - 159	22	22	36	35	57	56	55	51	31	17	19	2	9	0	4	0	0	0	1	1	234	184
150 - 154	19	13	43	31	49	32	83	27	47	11	22	5	13	0	9	0	0	0	7	2	292	121
145 - 149	5	0	20	1	36	1	59	10	54	11	32	2	15	0	5	0	3	0	7	0	236	25
140 - 144	6	0	13	4	16	2	25	2	35	1	32	1	19	1	1	0	2	0	9	0	158	11
135 - 139	1	0	5	0	6	0	14	0	18	0	28	0	13	0	9	0	3	0	10	0	107	0
130 - 134	0	0	1	0	2	0	2	0	7	0	9	0	10	0	2	0	2	0	3	0	38	0
125 - 129	0	0	0	0	1	0	0	0	2	0	2	0	0	0	1	0	0	0	0	0	6	0
120 - 124	0	0	0	0	0	0	2	0	0	0	0	0	1	0	0	0	0	0	1	0	4	0
Total	72	53	147	99	205	129	276	125	217	58	159	16	86	2	31	0	10	0	43	4	1246	486

Apps = Number of Applicants
Adm = Number Admitted
Reflects 98% of the total applicant pool.

West Virginia University College of Law

P.O. Box 6130
Morgantown, WV 26506-6130

E-Mail: barnetc@wvnvm.wvnet.edu,
or devince@wvnvm.wvnet.edu
Phone: 304.293.5304

■ Introduction

The College of Law was established in 1878 and is the oldest professional school at West Virginia University. The university is located in Morgantown, West Virginia, a community of 50,000, and is easily accessible by interstate highways, commercial airlines, and bus services. The College of Law has been a member of the AALS since 1914 and was fully accredited by the ABA in 1923. The college has had a chapter of the Order of the Coif since 1925.

Since its founding in 1867, West Virginia University has become the center of graduate and professional education, research, and extension programs in West Virginia. The university's rural setting makes for an ideal learning environment for its 20,000 full-time students.

The College of Law has established itself as a national leader in legal issues relating to the development and production of energy resources. The college is the host institution for the Eastern Mineral Law Foundation, Inc., which annually publishes the National Coal Issue of the *West Virginia Law Review* and sponsors conferences and continuing legal education seminars on legal issues in mineral law.

West Virginia University provides a full range of both athletic and cultural facilities. The Personal Rapid Transit System (PRT) provides convenient, modern transportation among the university's three campuses.

■ Enrollment/Student Body

➽ *418 total full-time* ➽ *9 total part-time* ➽ *31 minority*
➽ *208 women*

■ Faculty

➽ *28 full-time* ➽ *12 part-time or adjunct*

■ Library and Physical Facilities

➽ *215,000 volumes & equivalents* ➽ *LEXIS*
➽ *WESTLAW* ➽ *CALI* ➽ *3 full-time librarians*
➽ *library seats 296*

The three-floor library features open stacks, group study rooms, study carrels, a rare book room, labs for word processing and computer-assisted legal instruction, and terminals to access legal research databases and the campus-wide, online catalog. A Co-op Day Care Center is located at the Law Center.

■ Curriculum

➽ *93 credits required to graduate*
➽ *degrees available: J.D.; J.D./M.B.A.; J.D./M.P.A.*

The first-year curriculum is required. The second- and third-year programs offer a number of course options and possibilities for concentration. No summer programs are regularly scheduled. The college does accept a limited number of transfer students only after the first year. The college has long stressed advocacy training, and each student completes the trial of a mock suit before a jury prior to graduation.

Students have the option of attending the College of Law on a part-time basis during the day along with full-time students. There is not a separate nighttime track.

■ Student Activities

Candidates for the *West Virginia Law Review* are selected on the basis of performance during their first year in law school and a writing competition.

An active Moot Court Program is conducted at the law school under the supervision of the Moot Court Board. Members competed in five interscholastic regional and national moot court competitions last year.

The Student Bar Association is the student government of the school. It is administered by elected representatives from each class, along with officers elected by the entire student body. All law school organizations have a representative on the council in order to foster a greater feeling of community among all law students.

The college hosts several other organizations representing the varied interests of students.

■ Opportunities for Minority Students

The opportunities available to minority students at the College of Law evolve from our institution's commitment to promote an academic environment comprised of student representation from all segments of society.

This commitment is furthered by the financial aid that is made available to our minority students. First of all, the Board of Trustees makes available full tuition and fees scholarships. Second, there is the W.E.B. Dubois Fellowship that provides full tuition, fees, and a yearly living stipend to qualified African American professional or graduate students. Third, the Mountain State Bar Association, an African American–founded professional association, provides available funds in the form of fellowships to African American students. Finally, the contributions from our alumni have contributed significantly to the total amount of money made available to minority students so they may finance their education.

Additional opportunities for minority students involve the academic support provided by our student-initiated Student/Faculty Academic Assistance Program and the social and professional support provided by our Black Law Students Association (BLSA).

Our Book Loan Program, which provides free textbooks and other materials for all of our members, is a popular feature of BLSA's support to our students. It cuts down on expenditures that would ordinarily be between $200 and $300 a semester.

The academic assistance program offers students an opportunity to become paired with a member of our faculty during their entire law school experience.

The most recent feature available to minority students who are considering law as a career is our **Pre Law**

Academy. The program involves seminars on the LSAT; information on joint-degree programs, financial aid, career planning, and legal research and writing; mock law school classes, and opportunities to speak with minority attorneys about issues and concerns.

■ Placement

The Meredith Career Services Center actively assists students and alumni in securing employment, including employment in nontraditional legal careers such as legal aid societies, business, insurance companies, and government agencies.

■ Admission

➽ *Baccalaureate degree from regionally accredited college or university required* ➽ *application deadline—Feb. 1*
➽ *LSAT required* ➽ *application fee—$45*

No specific prelaw curriculum is required for admission. The college subscribes to the suggestions on prelaw study in this handbook with an additional admonition that at least one year of accounting may be helpful.

In addition, undergraduate grades and performance on the LSAT are carefully and objectively evaluated and compared against that of all other applicants. Applicants must arrange for the timely submission of at least one recommendation from a college professor. Preference is given to West Virginia residents. The College of Law receives many more applications for admission than it has been able to accommodate.

Applications are accepted beginning in September of each year for the class to be admitted in the following August. As soon as applicant files can be completed, they will be notified of the final decision. Those accepted are required to make a deposit of $100 against tuition and fees within a designated period, but not before April 1.

■ Expenses and Financial Aid

➽ *full-time tuition & fees—residents, $4,122; nonresidents, $10,634* ➽ *estimated additional expenses for books and supplies—$800* ➽ *living allowance for 9 months—$6,740*
➽ *estimated budget: residents, $11,264; nonresident, $17,524*
➽ *Free Application for Federal Student Aid (FAFSA), Law School Datasheet due by March 1*
➽ *Scholarship application due by April 1*

Applicants for admission can seek financial assistance by contacting Joanna Hastings, Financial Aid Counselor, P.O. Box 6130, Morgantown, WV 26506-6130, phone: 304.293.5302.

Note: It is suggested that students apply for financial aid assistance before being accepted.

■ Housing

The University Housing Office (304.293.3621) provides information concerning university-owned housing, including dormitories and apartments. Off-campus privately owned housing information may be obtained by calling the main campus (304.293.5613). The university maintains 361 furnished and unfurnished apartments for graduate students, married students, faculty, and staff. There is usually a waiting list for apartments, so application should be made as early as possible. Listings for privately owned rentals change daily.

Admitted students are urged to visit Morgantown during the summer prior to registration to secure housing.

Applicant Group for the 1995-1996 Academic Year

West Virginia University College of Law
This grid includes only applicants who earned 120-180 LSAT scores under standard administrations.

	GPA																					
LSAT Score	3.75 +		3.50 - 3.74		3.25 - 3.49		3.00 - 3.24		2.75 - 2.99		2.50 - 2.74		2.25 - 2.49		2.00 - 2.24		Below 2.00		No GPA		Total	
	Apps	Adm	Apps	Adm	Apps	Adm	Apps	Adm	Apps	Adm	Apps	Adm	Apps	Adm	Apps	Adm	Apps	Adm	Apps	Adm	Apps	Adm
175 - 180	0	0	0	0	0	0	0	0	0	0	0	0	0	0	0	0	0	0	0	0	0	0
170 - 174	0	0	0	0	0	0	0	0	0	0	0	0	0	0	1	0	0	0	0	0	1	0
165 - 169	1	1	3	3	2	2	3	1	0	0	3	3	0	0	1	1	0	0	0	0	13	11
160 - 164	4	4	7	7	3	3	7	5	8	8	2	2	2	1	0	0	0	0	0	0	33	30
155 - 159	9	9	19	18	31	28	25	22	21	14	17	10	12	4	4	1	1	0	0	0	139	106
150 - 154	21	19	35	23	49	28	46	22	33	10	31	8	12	1	0	0	2	0	5	2	234	113
145 - 149	12	4	26	11	37	5	46	9	38	1	18	0	17	1	7	0	1	0	1	1	203	32
140 - 144	4	0	8	0	11	0	16	0	20	0	18	0	8	0	4	0	1	0	3	0	93	0
135 - 139	0	0	0	0	3	0	7	0	7	0	7	0	3	0	8	0	2	0	1	0	38	0
130 - 134	0	0	0	0	2	0	5	0	2	0	2	0	2	0	1	0	0	0	0	0	14	0
125 - 129	0	0	0	0	0	0	0	0	0	0	0	0	0	0	0	0	0	0	0	0	0	0
120 - 124	0	0	0	0	0	0	0	0	0	0	0	0	0	0	0	0	0	0	0	0	0	0
Total	51	37	98	62	138	66	155	59	129	33	98	23	56	7	26	2	7	0	10	3	768	292

Apps = Number of Applicants
Adm = Number Admitted
Reflects 98% of the total applicant pool.

Western New England College School of Law

Office of Admissions
1215 Wilbraham Road
Springfield, MA 01119-2689

E-Mail: lawadmis@wnec.edu
URL: http://www.law.wnec.edu
Phone: 413.782.1406

Introduction

Western New England College School of Law is centrally located in the Northeast. Springfield offers distinguished museums, a symphony, major recreational activities, and the Basketball Hall of Fame. Springfield is a city of approximately 157,000 residents, 19 percent of whom are African American, and 17 percent of whom are Hispanic. Along with the cultural opportunities available in Springfield, the nearby five colleges —Amherst, Hampshire, Mount Holyoke, Smith Colleges, and the University of Massachusetts—contribute to the recreational and cultural activities in the Pioneer Valley.

Enrollment/Student Body

➽ 1,681 applicants ➽ 943 admitted first-year class 1994 ➽ 225 enrolled first-year class 1994 ➽ 461 total full-time ➽ 280 total part-time ➽ 10% students of color ➽ 48% women

Faculty

➽ 57 total ➽ 28 full-time ➽ 29 part-time or adjunct ➽ 6 women ➽ 3 minority

Our faculty members come from varied backgrounds and all share a love of teaching. They take pride in their ability to engage students in rigorous law study without the rancor and bitter competitiveness that may characterize other legal educations. Our faculty encourages cooperation among students in the learning process and among each other.

Library and Physical Facilities

➽ 317,000 volumes & equivalents ➽ library hours: Mon.-Thurs., 8:00 A.M.-MIDNIGHT; Fri., 8:00 A.M.-10:00 P.M.; Sat., 9:00 A.M.-9:00 P.M.; Sun., 10:00 A.M.-11:00 P.M. ➽ Extended hours during exams ➽ LEXIS ➽ NEXIS ➽ WESTLAW ➽ MEDIS ➽ DIALOG ➽ OCLC ➽ 7 full-time library administrators ➽ library seats 397 ➽ We participate in the New England Law Library Consortium, so students have access to 13 academic and 2 private law libraries in New England.

The law school building was designed and constructed in 1978 and houses the law library, classrooms, a moot courtroom, faculty and administrative offices. The law school building is located on Western New England College's 94-acre campus and is in a residential section of Springfield.

The college recently opened the Alumni Healthful Living Center which includes a basketball court; an all-purpose room for aerobics and dance; an indoor track; two weight rooms; and four indoor tennis courts. The building will also include an 8-lane "stretch" swimming pool and two racquetball/handball courts and two squash courts.

Curriculum

➽ 88 units/credits required to graduate ➽ 83 courses available in 1994-95 and 6 clinics ➽ 75-90 students in full-time first-year classes; 60-75 students in part-time, first-year classes

The Legal Education Assistance Program (LEAP) is an optional program developed to provide academic support for first-year students who might benefit from extra assistance. Weekly hour-long classes are taught by instructors in the Lawyering Process program. Classes offer in-class writing exercises and practice examinations. Members of the Lawyering Process Department and the Admissions Office determine who will be invited to enroll in LEAP, and participation is voluntary.

Our first-year courses are taught using the Socratic Method. All required courses, both day and evening, are taught by full-time, tenure-track faculty members. Some upper-level courses are taught through classroom discussion of judicial decisions and statutes. Others are taught through simulations in which students perform the roles of lawyers in life-like situations and through clinics where students represent actual clients.

Special Programs

Clinical Courses—Clinics allow students to work with actual clients under the supervision of faculty and members of the legal community; students can choose from six clinical courses. Students in the Criminal Law Clinic represent indigent persons charged with misdemeanors in the Massachusetts District Court and handle all aspects of client representation. The Civil Clinic allows students to work with discrimination cases. Clinic students also meet regularly to discuss their cases and increase their understanding of their professional and ethical obligations.

Other clinical programs include the Disability Law Clinic, the Consumer Protection Clinic, and the Legal Services Clinic, where students work with Western Massachusetts Legal Services to interview and counsel clients. Finally, clinical internships allow students to work in the office of an attorney, judge, or magistrate to acquire substantive legal knowledge and practical skills.

Part-time Day and Evening Programs—Western New England College has a long-standing commitment to educating the part-time, evening law student. Evening students come to the law school mostly from the Springfield, Hartford, and Albany areas. The average age for the part-time evening division is 33, and students range in age 23 to 55. Evening law students spend approximately 30 hours per week studying and attending classes. First-year classes meet on Monday, Wednesday, and Thursday from 6:30 P.M.-9:30 P.M., with an additional hour either before or after Wednesday classes. The program takes four years including one or two summers, or four and one-half years without summer courses. Our part-time day program is similar to our part-time evening program, but is limited to students who have primary care responsibilities for children or other dependents. Classes are offered between 9 A.M. and 3 P.M. Monday though Friday; students will spend approximately 30 hours per week in class and preparation time.

■ Admission

➽ B.A., B.S. required for admission ➽ March 1 preferred deadline; rolling admission ➽ LSAT, LSDAS required ➽ median GPA—3.01 ➽ median LSAT score—151 ➽ application fee—$35 ➽ TOEFL preferred for foreign-educated applicants

All facets of the application are carefully considered, including racial, gender, physical, language, educational, social, and economic obstacles overcome in the applicant's pursuit of higher education.

■ Co-curricular Activities

The law school's *Law Review* is published by a student editorial board with faculty supervision. Students sit on faculty committees such as the Admissions Committee and the Academic Standards Committee, and two students attend regular faculty meetings. Student organizations include the Multi-Cultural Law Students Association, which incorporates all students of color and organizes a mentorship program for current students with the Springfield-based Concerned Lawyers of Color; the Environmental Law Coalition; the Jewish Law Students Association; the Law Rugby Club; and the Women's Law Association. Other groups include the Phi Alpha Delta fraternity, the Federalist Society, the Christian Law Students Association, a chapter of the American Bar Association's Law Student Division, the newspaper *Lex Brevis*, and a yearbook.

■ Expenses and Financial Aid

➽ 1995-96 tuition—full-time, $13,890; part-time, $10,416 ➽ estimated additional first-year educational expenses—books, $525; fees, $560 ➽ Dean's Scholarships, Connell, O'Connor, Sullivan, and Sheehan scholarships available ➽ Free Application for Federal Student Aid (FAFSA) required

Application fee waivers are granted upon completion of the law school's fee waiver application form and demonstration that payment of the $35 fee would constitute a heavy burden. Fee waiver forms may be obtained by calling the Office of Admissions, 413.782.1406.

■ Career Services

Individual attention to each student is of great importance at Western New England College School of Law, and counseling is an important function of Career Services. Students discuss potential career paths, employment application strategies, and review their résumés, cover letters, and other application materials with a professional counselor.

During the on-campus interview program, students interview with some of the most prestigious employers in Western Massachusetts and Connecticut. Students have additional opportunities throughout the academic year to interview with various employers. There are over 5,000 alumni employed in 46 states, U.S. Territories, Canada, Europe, and Asia. They are employed in diverse occupations, including top law firms in New York and Boston, Hartford insurance companies, state and district court judgeships, and many public defender's and district attorney's offices, and numerous small firms.

Applicant Group for the 1995-1996 Academic Year

Western New England College School of Law
This grid includes only applicants who earned 120-180 LSAT scores under standard administrations.

	GPA																					
LSAT Score	3.75 +		3.50 - 3.74		3.25 - 3.49		3.00 - 3.24		2.75 - 2.99		2.50 - 2.74		2.25 - 2.49		2.00 - 2.24		Below 2.00		No GPA		Total	
	Apps	Adm	Apps	Adm	Apps	Adm	Apps	Adm	Apps	Adm	Apps	Adm	Apps	Adm	Apps	Adm	Apps	Adm	Apps	Adm	Apps	Adm
175 - 180	0	0	0	0	0	0	0	0	0	0	0	0	0	0	0	0	0	0	0	0	0	0
170 - 174	0	0	0	0	0	0	1	1	0	0	0	0	0	0	0	0	0	0	0	0	1	1
165 - 169	1	1	1	1	1	1	3	3	2	2	4	3	0	0	0	0	0	0	0	0	12	11
160 - 164	3	3	7	6	5	4	19	18	13	12	8	7	4	3	6	4	0	0	1	1	66	58
155 - 159	2	2	14	14	25	23	38	35	45	42	36	34	17	15	12	8	0	0	3	2	192	175
150 - 154	10	8	35	33	74	71	94	87	95	81	78	53	47	29	16	8	9	5	7	1	465	376
145 - 149	6	6	42	37	80	68	132	88	118	38	77	17	57	8	15	3	5	0	5	2	537	267
140 - 144	5	3	19	7	29	7	67	14	72	10	67	1	37	2	15	0	4	0	4	1	319	45
135 - 139	0	0	7	0	8	1	32	2	26	0	23	0	17	0	10	0	4	0	3	0	130	3
130 - 134	0	0	0	0	6	0	6	0	5	0	9	0	9	0	3	0	1	0	4	0	43	0
125 - 129	0	0	1	0	0	0	0	0	1	0	1	0	4	0	0	0	1	0	2	0	10	0
120 - 124	0	0	0	0	0	0	1	0	0	0	1	0	0	0	0	0	0	0	0	0	2	0
Total	27	23	126	98	228	175	393	248	377	185	304	115	192	57	77	23	24	5	29	7	1777	936

Apps = Number of Applicants
Adm = Number Admitted
Reflects 98% of the total applicant pool.

Whittier Law School

5353 West Third Street
Los Angeles, CA 90020

Phone: 213.938.3621, ext. 123, 128

■ Introduction

Whittier College is a nationally recognized, independent college of arts and sciences founded in 1887 in Whittier, California. The Law School, located in Los Angeles, was established in 1975.

The Whittier tradition of concern for students as individuals is reflected in admissions practices, a close student-to-faculty ratio (approximately 23 to 1), small classes, and continuous student counseling and placement services.

Located in the residential Hollywood-Wilshire area of Los Angeles on a spacious five-acre site, the gracious Tudor-style building with its sweeping lawns and central open courtyard is a local landmark. Proximity to state and federal courts, law offices from downtown Los Angeles to Century City, libraries, and the cultural activities of metropolitan Los Angeles enrich the experiences and opportunities of law students. Affiliation with Whittier College ensures a continuing commitment to academic excellence and individual attention.

Whittier Law School is fully accredited by the ABA and is a member of the AALS.

■ Enrollment/Student Body

➽ 2,339 applicants ➽ 227 enrolled first-year class 1995 ➽ 451 total full-time ➽ 204 total part-time ➽ 35% minority ➽ 51% women ➽ 42 states & 2 foreign countries represented ➽ 107 undergraduate schools represented ➽ 40% nonresident

■ Faculty

➽ 46 total ➽ 34 full-time ➽ 12 part-time or adjunct ➽ 16 women ➽ 4 minority

The full-time faculty is drawn from law schools throughout the country so that the school's perspective will be a national one, preparing students to pursue legal careers anywhere in the United States.

Faculty members recognize that their teaching obligation includes considerable interaction with students. The unique building provides a noninstitutional atmosphere conducive to this interaction.

■ Library and Physical Facilities

➽ 230,000 volumes & equivalents ➽ library hours: Mon.-Fri., 7:30 A.M.-11:30 P.M.; Sat.-Sun., 10:00 A.M.-1:30 P.M. ➽ LEXIS ➽ NEXIS ➽ WESTLAW ➽ DIALOG ➽ 11 full-time librarians ➽ library seats 270

The library is a rapidly growing legal research collection and serves as a state and federal depository. The Student Computer Center, located in the Law School Library, is available to students free of charge. The center houses computer hardware and a variety of software to aid students with computer-assisted instruction and legal research.

The Law School also offers free, on-site parking.

■ Curriculum

➽ Academic Support Program ➽ 87 credits required to graduate ➽ 73 courses available ➽ J.D. degree available ➽ semesters, start in Aug., Jan., & June ➽ range of first-year class size—70-90

Typically, the J.D. will be completed in three years of full-time study; for evening students, four years, including three summer sessions, will be necessary.

First- and second-year evening students generally attend classes three evenings a week. Standards for admission and retention are identical for all students, and the full-time faculty serve both day and evening programs.

Required courses total 38 of the 87 units needed to graduate. The remainder of the requirement is met from a wide variety of elective courses reflecting the diversity of careers and activities of modern lawyers.

■ Special Programs

Whittier Law School offers a variety of externships with trial and appellate judges and government agencies. Students perform lawyering tasks and apply their academic studies to real client cases, gaining valuable insights into the operation of legal institutions.

The externship program is coordinated by a full-time, tenured professor who assures that students receive significant legal experience in interviewing and counseling clients, negotiating, participation in alternative dispute resolutions, drafting documents, or litigating in administrative hearings and trials.

The Center for Children's Rights enrolls 25 students yearly who receive fellowships and summer stipends to prepare for careers in children's rights advocacy. In addition to the regular curriculum, special classes, symposia, and extern opportunities are offered.

■ Admission

➽ Bachelor's degree required ➽ application deadline—March 15 ➽ rolling admissions, early application preferred ➽ LSAT, LSDAS required ➽ median GPA—3.00 ➽ median LSAT score—151 ➽ application fee—$50 ➽ Summer Performance Program

In rare instances, an applicant will be admitted as a special student without a baccalaureate degree upon showing an unusually high LSAT score, excellence in college work completed, a statement of personal factors indicating maturity, and capacity for legal studies and professional achievement.

Consistent with Whittier Law School's tradition of concern for students as individuals, no magic numbers are used to determine admissions decisions. In addition to the objective criteria of the LSAT score and the undergraduate GPA, subjective factors such as undergraduate school, course of study, graduate work, social and economic background, and personal accomplishments are considered.

Thus, objective criteria are balanced with subjective factors. Applicants are encouraged to discuss these factors in their written personal statements.

Summer Performance—Whittier permits a select group of applicants to be admitted based upon their performance during an eight-week, full-time Summer Performance Admission Program. Applicants are chosen from those individuals who have not demonstrated aptitude for the study of law according to the traditional criteria, but whom the faculty believes should be given an opportunity to perform based on other factors. Successful completion of this summer work will result in regular admission for the fall semester.

■ Student Activities

The law school's location in the center of one of America's busiest and most diverse legal communities affords many opportunities for law-related experiences as students pursue their legal education.

The *Whittier Law Review*, published by a board of student editors selected from among those with superior academic records in the law school, is open to all students on the basis of a writing competition. The *Review* stresses the highest standards of legal scholarship.

Moot court competition develops skills in written and oral advocacy. Students who perform well are invited to the Moot Court Honors Board. Members compete in school, regional, state, and national competitions.

The Student Bar Association is an independent student organization with officers elected by fellow students. Its activities include a speakers' program, publication of the student newspaper, various social functions, and participation in student-faculty committees for school governance.

Other student organizations represent the numerous and varied interests of Whittier law students.

■ Expenses and Financial Aid

- *tuition & fees—full-time, $18,000; part-time, $10,800*
- *estimated additional expenses—$12,425 (books & supplies, room & board, personal & transportation)*
- *scholarships available: need-based and merit-based*
- *minority scholarships available: diversity*
- *financial aid available; FAFSA required*

The law school offers several alternatives for financial assistance, including loan programs, scholarships, and employment opportunities.

After notification of admission, applicants will receive detailed information and instructions on applying for financial aid.

■ Career Services

Whittier Law School provides assistance to students and alumni in obtaining clerkships and attorney positions. The Office of Placement and Career Planning offers seminars and individual counseling on résumé writing, interviewing techniques, and career planning. Services are provided to help locate and place students in clerkship positions with private attorneys and companies, judges, and governmental agencies. The office hosts on-campus interviews for permanent attorney positions by firms and agencies. Individual guidance is given which is tailored to the student's and graduate's special needs and areas of legal interest.

Applicant Group for the 1995-1996 Academic Year

Whittier Law School
This grid includes only applicants who earned 120-180 LSAT scores under standard administrations.

LSAT Score	GPA 3.75 +		3.50 - 3.74		3.25 - 3.49		3.00 - 3.24		2.75 - 2.99		2.50 - 2.74		2.25 - 2.49		2.00 - 2.24		Below 2.00		No GPA		Total	
	Apps	Adm	Apps	Adm	Apps	Adm	Apps	Adm	Apps	Adm	Apps	Adm	Apps	Adm	Apps	Adm	Apps	Adm	Apps	Adm	Apps	Adm
175 - 180	0	0	0	0	0	0	0	0	0	0	0	0	0	0	0	0	0	0	0	0	0	0
170 - 174	0	0	0	0	0	0	0	0	3	3	0	0	0	0	0	0	0	0	0	0	3	3
165 - 169	2	2	1	1	3	3	2	1	3	3	6	6	3	2	0	0	1	0	0	0	21	18
160 - 164	4	4	7	7	9	9	12	12	14	14	12	12	9	9	7	7	1	0	1	1	76	75
155 - 159	8	8	19	19	41	38	47	47	73	73	45	42	25	21	7	5	2	1	8	5	275	259
150 - 154	7	7	46	44	78	76	99	97	121	109	117	77	48	30	32	12	4	0	13	4	565	456
145 - 149	8	6	32	28	86	55	145	75	155	39	127	18	76	8	43	4	7	0	15	4	694	237
140 - 144	3	0	11	4	46	5	77	9	100	3	95	1	55	0	23	1	4	0	19	0	433	23
135 - 139	0	0	5	0	11	0	36	0	36	2	51	0	40	1	26	0	4	0	8	0	217	3
130 - 134	0	0	0	0	3	0	3	0	9	0	16	0	11	0	14	0	5	0	4	0	65	0
125 - 129	0	0	1	0	2	0	0	0	2	0	3	0	4	0	1	0	1	0	3	0	17	0
120 - 124	0	0	0	0	0	0	0	0	0	0	1	0	0	0	1	0	1	0	0	0	3	0
Total	32	27	122	103	279	186	421	241	516	246	473	156	271	71	154	29	30	1	71	14	2369	1074

Apps = Number of Applicants
Adm = Number Admitted
Reflects 98% of the total applicant pool.

Widener University School of Law

P.O. Box 7474, Wilmington, DE 19803-0474
3800 Vartan Way, Harrisburg, PA 17110-9450

E-Mail: law.admissions@law.widener.edu
Phone: 302.477.2162
Phone: 717.541.3903

■ Introduction

Widener University School of Law is unique among American law schools. Widener has two campuses—one in Wilmington, Delaware, the corporate and banking center of the United States, and the other in Harrisburg, Pennsylvania, the state capital and a major center of commerce. Each campus offers a comprehensive curriculum of basic and advanced courses complemented by one of the most extensive clinical and skills programs in the country.

Widener has recently revised the first-year curriculum to provide greater emphasis on individual work in legal writing and more concentrated study in courses essential to current developments in legal practice. The intensity of study in the first year and throughout the curriculum is balanced by the strong commitment of faculty members to personal attention and individual counseling so that all students will be encouraged to fulfill their potential.

■ Enrollment/Student Body

➠ *3,137 applicants* ➠ *1,477 admitted first-year class 1995* ➠ *614 enrolled first-year class 1995* ➠ *1,383 total full-time* ➠ *608 total part-time* ➠ *5.9% minority* ➠ *42% women* ➠ *33 states & foreign countries represented* ➠ *210 undergraduate schools represented*

■ Faculty

➠ *193 total* ➠ *104 full-time* ➠ *89 part-time or adjunct* ➠ *73 women* ➠ *13 minority*

The full-time faculty possesses the broadest possible range of interests, expertise, and accomplishments. Many have served as clerks to notable judges and justices, and most have substantial legal practice experience. Many faculty members are actively engaged in professional activities that enhance the educational environment. Forty-four percent of the full-time faculty are women.

■ Library and Physical Facilities

➠ *530,000 volumes & equivalents* ➠ *LEXIS* ➠ *NEXIS* ➠ *WESTLAW* ➠ *DIALOG* ➠ *CIS Masterfile* ➠ *LEGALTRAC* ➠ *INFOTRAC* ➠ *17 full-time librarians*

The combined libraries of the two campuses house one of the most significant legal collections in the region and incorporate new technologies to enhance our information resources. The libraries' collection is rich in Anglo-American law with special collections in corporate, tax, environmental, health, administrative, legislative, constitutional, and regulatory law. The library is a selective depository for United States government documents. The library also has numerous nonbook resources, including legal and nonlegal databases, a growing collection of audio and videotapes, and a sizable microform collection.

Both campuses have personal computer laboratories available to students. All students receive instruction in LEXIS and WESTLAW. Classrooms and moot courtrooms are linked to videotaping equipment. Advanced telecommunications, utilizing videoconferencing equipment, permit total linkage between our two campuses.

A knowledgeable and service-oriented staff assists students with accessing the collection.

■ Curriculum

➠ *Academic Support Program* ➠ *87 credits required to graduate* ➠ *229 courses available* ➠ *degrees available: J.D.; J.D./M.B.A.; J.D./Psy.D.; LL.M.* ➠ *summer school* ➠ *range of first-year class size—25-110* ➠ *day and evening programs*

The law school offers two programs leading to the J.D. degree: a three-year day program and an evening program of four years. Each program requires the completion of 87 hours of credit. Day and evening programs are available on both campuses.

■ Special Programs and Institutes

Widener was a leader in developing professional skills courses and curricula in the early 1980s. The law school operates in-house clinics in the following areas: bankruptcy, civil (elder law, family law, and landlord-tenant), child advocacy, criminal defense, immigration, environmental, public interest, and energy law. In these clinics, students represent clients in a supervised setting.

A large number of supervised externships and judicial clerkships permit students to work as neophyte lawyers in nonprofit corporations and with state government agencies. Judicial externs are placed with state and federal courts in Washington, D.C., Maryland, Delaware, Pennsylvania, and New Jersey.

A second part of the Professional Skills Program is the Trial Advocacy Institute. That institute promotes and develops student trial practice skills through development of numerous courses and programs that focus on teaching trial advocacy.

An extensive moot court program that prepares students to compete in regional and national interschool competitions exists on both campuses. Moot court teams from Widener reached the ABA National Appellate Advocacy final round in past academic years.

The school's Health Law Institute provides research, policy analysis, specialty education, and service to law students, health lawyers, and health-care professionals. The institute's program takes advantage of the considerable expertise of the school's faculty in such areas as the rights of the elderly, professional liability, regulation of the health-care industry, and long-term care.

The School of Law's graduate program grants LL.M. degrees in Corporate Law and Finance, and in Health Law. A joint J.D./M.B.A. degree is offered in cooperation with the Widener School of Management and Applied Economics. The J.D./Psy.D. Program is offered in cooperation with the Widener University Institute for Graduate Clinical Psychology, and requires six years of study.

■ International Law Programs

Widener offers the opportunity to study international and comparative law courses while living abroad in Geneva, Paris, or Nairobi. Widener intends to start a foreign summer internship program in Sydney, Australia in Summer 1996. A student exchange program will also be available. The law school conducts summer programs in Switzerland and Kenya. The Geneva International Law Institute, held at the University of Geneva, provides a range of courses including International Trade Law. The Nairobi International Law Institute at the University of Nairobi offers courses in International Environmental Law and other areas. Widener can arrange for its students to spend a full semester at the University of Paris—Nanterre studying European Community Law and international law.

■ Student Activities

The students at the Delaware campus publish the *Delaware Journal of Corporate Law*, and *The Widener Law Symposium Journal*. The students at the Harrisburg campus publish the *Widener Journal of Public Law*.

Numerous cocurricular and extracurricular activities provide opportunities designed to enrich the law school experience on both campuses.

■ Admission

➧ baccalaureate degree required ➧ application deadline—May 15 ➧ rolling admissions ➧ LSAT, LSDAS required ➧ median GPA—3.10 ➧ application fee—$60 ➧ median LSAT score for standard admission—152

While there are no fixed admission criteria, great weight is given to the applicant's LSAT score and undergraduate grade-point average. Other materials considered for admission include graduate degrees, writing sample, extracurricular activities, and community activities.

The law school actively seeks to diversify the student body.

Widener conducts a summer Trial Admission Program (TAP) for a small number of carefully selected applicants who show promise of success in law studies despite a relatively low score on one of the two principal measures used for admission.

Interested persons are invited to visit either branch of the school.

■ Expenses and Financial Aid

➧ tuition & fees—full-time, $15,950; part-time, $11,975 ➧ estimated additional expenses—$11,227 (living expenses and books) ➧ Widener Achievement Scholarships available for qualified majority and minority applicants ➧ Loan Repayment Assistance Program available to selected graduates pursuing a career in public service ➧ financial aid available; FAFSA required for need analysis ➧ on-campus housing available in Delaware ➧ housing available adjacent to campus in both locations

■ Career Planning and Placement

The Career Planning and Placement Office actively provides career counseling and placement opportunities on both campuses. The office's programs, services, and guidance assist students as they formulate and realize professional, educational, and career goals. This office conducts on-campus interviewing programs at both campuses. Graduates are employed by large, medium, and small law firms; corporations; nonprofit corporations; governmental agencies; and the judiciary.

Admission Profile Not Available

Willamette University College of Law

Truman Wesley Collins Legal Center
900 State Street
Salem, OR 97301

URL: http://www.willamette.edu
Phone: 503.370.6282

■ Introduction

In 1883, Willamette University established the first law school in the Pacific Northwest, Willamette University College of Law. Today, it remains one of the smallest and most intellectually intimate law schools in the West. In its 113-year history, more than 4,500 alumni have benefited from a program of legal education that is traditional in content and approach.

Willamette University is located in Salem, Oregon's capital city, 45 minutes from metropolitan Portland. The peaceful 57-acre campus is situated adjacent to the state capitol and courts. A city of 117,000, Salem is "small town" in feel. It is bordered by pastures, farmland, and vineyards. The Cascade Mountains and Pacific Ocean are about a one-hour drive.

The College of Law has long been accredited by the American Bar Association and is a member of the Association of American Law Schools.

■ Enrollment/Student Body

➧ *1,186 applicants* ➧ *562 admitted first-year class 1995* ➧ *144 enrolled first-year class 1995* ➧ *458 total full-time* ➧ *11.8% minority* ➧ *39% women*

Students are drawn to Willamette principally from the West. The average age of the entering class is 26. About 15 percent of the class is 30 years of age or older.

■ Faculty

➧ *44 total* ➧ *27 full-time* ➧ *17 part-time or adjunct* ➧ *13 women* ➧ *2 minority*

Praised for their professional experience and commitment to teaching, Willamette's faculty includes three Fulbright Scholars, the "Thomas B. Stoel Professor of Law" endowed chair, a former chief justice and associate justice of the state supreme court, currently "Scholars-in-Residence," and the past president of the Oregon state bar, this year's "Practitioner-in-Residence."

■ Library and Physical Facilities

➧ *261,200 volumes & equivalents* ➧ *library hours: 24-hour access to library* ➧ *LEXIS* ➧ *NEXIS* ➧ *WESTLAW* ➧ *DIALOG* ➧ *Internet* ➧ *CALI* ➧ *6 full-time librarians, 2 half-time* ➧ *library seats 500*

The award-winning Truman Wesley Collins Legal Center is a technologically advanced and student-oriented facility. It houses the courtroom, classrooms, offices, and the spacious J.W. Long Library, the only 24-hour law library in the Pacific Northwest.

■ Admission

➧ *B.A. required for admission* ➧ *application deadline—April 1* ➧ *LSAT, LSDAS required* ➧ *median GPA—3.15* ➧ *median LSAT score—156* ➧ *application fee—$40*

Willamette's Committee on Admission gives each application a careful and thoughtful examination. Those candidates ideally positioned for admission to the College of Law will present a record of strong, consistent academic achievement. It is expected that this caliber of achievement will also be reflected in the strength of the candidate's LSAT score. The required personal statement and the two references are helpful in providing some insight into the candidate's preparedness for law school, but are not alone a basis for admission. The Committee does invite candidates with professional experience to include a résumé with their application.

■ Ethnic Student Programs

Willamette encourages applications from students interested in building a diverse community of attorneys to help meet the future needs of our region. Trustee scholarships are available to those demonstrating academic success and leadership in their college or community.

The Oregon State Bar Affirmative Action Program provides ethnic law students with opportunities for support and professional development. For more information, contact the Office of Admission or the Oregon State Bar, 503.620.0222.

■ Curriculum

➧ *Academic Support Program* ➧ *88 units/credits required to graduate* ➧ *100 courses available* ➧ *degrees available: J.D.; J.D./M.M.* ➧ *semesters, start in Aug.* ➧ *range of first-year class size—30-120*

Though one of the smallest law schools in the West, Willamette's curriculum is unusually comprehensive. Interest areas include international law, labor and employment law, tax law, environmental and natural resources law, commercial and business law, civil litigation, estate planning, criminal law, civil and constitutional rights, real estate, and dispute resolution.

■ Law in Government Program

The Law in Government Program at Willamette takes full advantage of the rich opportunities available in Salem, center of the state, county, and municipal government. Students may be court-certified after their second-year according to provisions established by the Oregon State Bar and the ABA.

■ Special Programs

Since 1973, with the Geo. H. Atkinson Graduate School of Management, Willamette has offered a joint-degree program leading to the awarding of two degrees in four years, the J.D. and the Master's of Management. To contact the Atkinson School, call 503.370.6167.

Since 1984, Willamette has lead the China Program, conducted at the East China Institute of Politics and Law in Shanghai. Willamette law students, with ABA approval and on an individual basis, may elect to spend a semester studying law in Quito, Ecuador.

Annually, 16 students are selected through a separate admission process to be candidates for a specialized certificate program in dispute resolution.

■ Placement and Bar Passage

In 1995, Willamette graduates continued the school's long history of success on the bar by passing the Oregon State Bar examination with a 91 percent pass rate for first-time test takers. Graduates taking the Washington State Bar for the first time achieved equal distinction passing that bar with a 90 percent pass rate. This reputation for success continues to well-position Willamette students for clerkship, externship, and full-time employment opportunities. To contact Career Services, call 503.370.6057.

■ Expenses, Financial Aid, and Scholarships

➽ *full-time tuition & fees—$15,400* ➽ *average additional expenses—books, $1,200; room & board, $6,930; misc., $1,890* ➽ *merit scholarships available* ➽ *FAFSA due Feb. 1*

Willamette's reputation as one of the best educational values in the West is well-deserved. Its facilities are among the finest and its tuition ranks among the lowest of any private law school on the West Coast. Despite this lower cost, Willamette maintains a strong, vital program of financial aid comprised of scholarships and federal and private loan options. Trustee scholarships are awarded at admission to a wide-range of first-year students who demonstrate a combination of strong academic achievement, outstanding professional promise, and a potential to make a noteworthy contribution to the character of the Willamette community. In 1995, trustee scholarships ranged from $5,000 to $15,000. Scholarships are renewed for the remaining two years so long as the student remains in good academic standing (2.00/4.00 scale). This scholarship renewal policy is among the most liberal.

In addition to scholarships, the first-year class also receives assistance in the form of student loans. Federal and private loans are administered through the Willamette University Office of Financial Aid. Students are eligible for work-study positions in the second and third year. To contact the Office of Financial Aid, call 503.370.6273.

■ Housing

Housing options in Salem and in the neighboring community of Keizer are many and range from older historic homes to modern apartment complexes. First-year students report securing rental housing in less than three days. The average rental for a one-bedroom apartment is about $450 a month. A three-bedroom house is approximately $700 a month.

Shared one-bedroom apartments are open to single law students in the University Apartment complex which opened in 1995. The apartments are one block from the College of Law. Several second- and third-year law students are employed each year by Residential Life as fraternity house directors. For more information, call the Office of Residential Life, 503.370.6212.

■ Interviews and Tours

Candidates desiring an informational interview and tour of the Truman Wesley Collins Legal Center should make arrangements to meet with the Director of Admission. Please call 503.370.6282.

Admission Profile Not Available

College of William and Mary School of Law

Law Admission
P.O. Box 8795
Williamsburg, VA 23187-8795

E-Mail: lawadm@facstaff.wm.edu
URL: http://www.wm.edu
Phone: 804.221.3785, Fax: 804.221.3261

■ Introduction

The College of William and Mary School of Law is located in historic Williamsburg in the tidewater area of Virginia, within easy reach of the metropolitan areas of Norfolk, Richmond, and Washington, D.C. A small, selective public law school, William and Mary offers a nationally recognized legal education program. Its origin dates from 1779, when George Wythe was appointed professor of law, making the College of William and Mary America's first educational institution to offer instruction in law. It is accredited by the ABA, is a member of the AALS, is registered by the New York State Department of Education, and has a chapter of the Order of the Coif.

■ Enrollment/Student Body

➧ 3,057 applicants ➧ 706 admitted first-year class 1995 ➧ 185 enrolled first-year class 1995 ➧ 524 total full-time ➧ 17% minority ➧ 49% women ➧ 36 states, D.C. & foreign countries represented ➧ 159 undergraduate schools represented

■ Faculty

➧ 64 total ➧ 30 full-time ➧ 34 part-time or adjunct ➧ 15 women ➧ 7 minority

■ Library and Physical Facilities

➧ 325,000 volumes & equivalents ➧ library hours: Mon.-Thurs., 7:30 A.M.-1:30 A.M.; Fri., 7:30 A.M.-12:30 A.M.; Sat., 9:00 A.M.-11:00 P.M.; Sun., 10:00 A.M.-1:30 A.M. ➧ LEXIS ➧ NEXIS ➧ WESTLAW ➧ DIALOG ➧ Virginia Legislative Service ➧ 7 full-time librarians ➧ library seats 430

The law school's modern barrier-free facility is located adjacent to the National Center for State Courts. The law school houses Courtroom 21, the world's most technologically advanced courtroom. The university's new apartment complex for graduate students is located adjacent to the law school. The law library contains a comprehensive collection of over 325,000 volumes and several legal and nonlegal computer-generated databases, as well as other CD-ROM information sources. Students may access LEXIS and WESTLAW from 34 terminals and use 25 additional personal computers in the library's computer lab. Law students also have access to the other university libraries.

■ Curriculum

➧ Academic Support Program ➧ 90 credits required to graduate ➧ 123 courses available ➧ degrees available: J.D.; J.D./M.B.A.; J.D./M.P.P.; J.D./M.A. (American Studies); LL.M. ➧ semesters, start in Aug. and Jan.

■ Special Programs

Successful completion of 90 semester credit hours of law studies and 90 weeks of residence is required. Required first-year courses include studies in constitutional law, contracts, torts, civil procedure, property, criminal law, legal skills, and statutory law. Prior to graduation, students must take a second year of legal skills, which includes professional ethics. Through simulated law firms, students in the Legal Skills Program experience and refine many lawyering skills such as interviewing, negotiation, legal briefing, and trial techniques. The school's Legal Skills Program was the winner of the 1991 American Bar Association's Gambrell Award for excellence in professional training. Fully accredited summer sessions are offered at the University of Exeter in Devonshire, England, the University of Madrid in Spain, and the University of Adelaide in Australia. The Law School also offers an LL.M. in the American Legal System for foreign attorneys. The law school provides a wide variety of externships, including: the Legal Aid Clinic and the Corporate Practice, Employee Relations, Attorney General Practice, and the Virginia Court of Appeals Externships. In addition, second- and third-year students are encouraged to work in a variety of legal settings, such as private firms and public law offices and legal clinics. The curriculum is enriched by the Institute of Bill of Rights Law, a privately funded organization. The Institute's central focus is scholarship and education on freedom of speech and of the press, with interests also in legal history, legal writing, and professional responsibility.

■ Admission

➧ Bachelor's degree from accredited college or university ➧ application deadline—March 1 ➧ LSAT, LSDAS required ➧ median GPA—3.39 ➧ median LSAT score—163 ➧ application fee—$35

The William and Mary School of Law is committed to providing opportunities for the study of law and entry into the legal profession to qualified racial and ethnic minority students, and students who, because of economic circumstances, may have been denied access to advantageous educational experiences. This commitment includes a special concern for determining the potential of these applicants through the admission process and special recruitment efforts. Applicants must take the LSAT and complete their college degree prior to enrolling in the law school. Transcript evaluation by LSDAS is required. Two written recommendations are required, one of which should be from a college professor or dean. Applications, which will be processed upon completion of three years of academic work, are available the September preceding admission. Personal interviews are not required; however, they will be granted upon request. Group meetings to answer questions of general interest, to explain admission procedures, and to introduce the College of William and Mary School of Law are conducted several times in the fall and winter months. Interested persons should contact the Office of Admission to reserve a seat. February 1 is the deadline for completing the registration process with LSDAS. Admission to the College of William and Mary School of Law is offered to those applicants who, in the opinion of the faculty admission committee, will make the most significant contribution to society as members of the legal profession. Factors such as general academic ability based on undergraduate work, capacity for the study of law based on the LSAT, work experience, and other personal qualities are considered.

■ Student Activities

William and Mary law students may participate in over 30 student organizations and writing experiences. Our student-managed law reviews and journals include: *The Administrative Law Review, William & Mary Bill of Rights Journal, William and Mary Environmental Law and Policy Review, William and Mary Journal of Women and the Law,* and the *William and Mary Law Review*. William and Mary students' diverse interests are illustrated by the following example list of student organizations: the Eastern State Hospital Legal Clinic, Law Students Involved in the Community, Public Service Fund, Student Legal Services, Black Law Students Association, Law Partners, Lesbian and Gay Law Association, Christian Law Fellowship, Mary and William Feminist Law Society, Federalist Society, Marshall-Wythe Democrats, Republican Graduate/Professional Students, the William and Mary School of Law Speakers Forum, the Phi Delta Phi and Phi Alpha Delta Legal Fraternities, and the Environmental Law, International Law, and William and Mary Sports and Entertainment Law Societies. The Law School curriculum is additionally enhanced by the extracurricular activities such as the National Trial Team and the Moot Court Program. Both programs involve students in intraschool, intramural, and national competitions. William and Mary Moot Court teams are extremely competitive on all levels. Our students have often placed and won Best Brief and Best Oral Argument at the Annual National Moot Court Competition, sponsored by the Association of the Bar of the City of New York, the profession's oldest and most prestigious moot court competition. Most recently, in 1995, the team placed second overall and again won Best Brief.

■ Expenses and Financial Aid

➽ *full-time tuition & fees—resident, $6,076; nonresident, $16,324* ➽ *estimated additional expenses—living allowance, $9,330; books, $800* ➽ *merit and need-based scholarships available* ➽ *financial aid available; FAFSA due Feb. 1*

■ Career Services

Employers from 17 states conducted on-campus interviews during 1994. Over 1,000 additional nonvisiting employers from all 50 states and the District of Columbia contacted the law school to recruit students. William and Mary students participate in 12 off-campus job fairs with a national employer base, including specialized programs for intellectual property law, public interest and government positions, and small regional firms. The Law School offers a variety of funding programs to assist students working in low-paying or nonpaying public-service positions during the summer. The class of 1994 reported employment in virtually all areas of the country. Approximately 39 percent remained in Virginia, the other 61 percent accepted positions in 24 states, the District of Columbia, and four foreign countries.

Applicant Group for the 1995-1996 Academic Year

College of William and Mary School of Law
This grid includes only applicants who earned 120-180 LSAT scores under standard administrations.

	GPA																					
LSAT Score	3.75 +		3.50 - 3.74		3.25 - 3.49		3.00 - 3.24		2.75 - 2.99		2.50 - 2.74		2.25 - 2.49		2.00 - 2.24		Below 2.00		No GPA		Total	
	Apps	Adm	Apps	Adm	Apps	Adm	Apps	Adm	Apps	Adm	Apps	Adm	Apps	Adm	Apps	Adm	Apps	Adm	Apps	Adm	Apps	Adm
175 - 180	0	0	1	1	4	4	1	1	1	1	0	0	0	0	0	0	0	0	0	0	7	7
170 - 174	5	5	12	12	18	17	9	9	3	3	4	2	1	1	1	0	0	0	0	0	53	49
165 - 169	25	24	65	65	73	73	58	56	32	21	10	2	2	0	2	1	1	0	2	2	270	244
160 - 164	76	53	184	101	217	66	130	24	53	4	24	1	14	2	5	0	1	0	5	1	709	252
155 - 159	88	16	150	21	205	11	126	6	77	4	40	6	18	1	4	1	1	0	1	1	710	67
150 - 154	47	5	82	7	130	11	139	22	76	11	58	4	23	1	5	0	2	0	8	0	570	61
145 - 149	16	1	45	2	69	1	88	4	76	0	53	1	23	0	10	0	1	0	7	0	388	9
140 - 144	2	0	23	0	25	0	45	0	39	0	25	0	18	0	8	0	1	0	3	0	189	0
135 - 139	0	0	2	0	5	0	10	0	14	0	12	0	9	0	6	0	2	0	2	0	62	0
130 - 134	0	0	0	0	2	0	4	0	6	0	7	0	4	0	2	0	0	0	1	0	26	0
125 - 129	1	0	0	0	0	0	3	0	0	0	0	0	2	0	1	0	0	0	1	0	8	0
120 - 124	0	0	0	0	0	0	0	0	0	0	0	0	0	0	0	0	0	0	0	0	0	0
Total	260	104	564	209	748	183	613	122	377	44	233	16	114	5	44	2	9	0	30	4	2992	689

Apps = Number of Applicants
Adm = Number Admitted
Reflects 98% of the total applicant pool.

William Mitchell College of Law

Admissions Office
875 Summit Avenue
St. Paul, MN 55105
Phone: 612.290.6329

■ Introduction

William Mitchell College of Law is the largest law school in Minnesota. It focuses on practical and theoretical skills in addition to its strong traditional academic curriculum. It is the only flexible program in the upper Midwest for law students who choose to work full- or part-time while pursuing a law degree. We also offer a full-time program. Among the college's 6,500 alumni/ae are these distinguished members of the judiciary: the late Warren E. Burger, '31, retired Chief Justice of the United States; Douglas K. Amdahl, '51, retired Chief Justice of the Minnesota Supreme Court; Peter Popovich, '47, retired Chief Justice of the Minnesota Supreme Court; Rosalie Wahl, '67, recently-retired justice on the Minnesota Supreme Court; and Esther Tomljanovich, '55, a justice on the Minnesota Supreme Court.

The college is accredited by the ABA, is a member of the Association of American Law Schools, and is approved by the U.S. Veterans Administration.

■ Enrollment/Student Body

➧ 338 enrolled first-year class 1995 ➧ 578 total full-time ➧ 490 total part-time ➧ 12.8% minority ➧ 49.2% women

William Mitchell is committed to correcting the historical problem of too few minority persons in the legal profession. We work to facilitate the admission of minority students and have minority-oriented organizations, curriculum, and academic support.

■ Faculty

➧ 36 full-time faculty ➧ 85 part-time or adjunct

The excellent full-time and part-time faculty bring their experience to the classroom in areas of special interest. Their expertise is particularly valuable in the areas of instruction relating to practical application of law such as legal writing and trial practice skills.

■ Library and Physical Facilities

➧ 200,000 volumes & equivalents ➧ LEXIS ➧ WESTLAW ➧ 17 full-time librarians

Our campus, located in St. Paul, Minnesota, provides space for classrooms, seminar rooms, moot courtrooms, the Law Clinic, library and study areas, a student lounge, and offices for student organizations. Students also have access to materials from other law libraries in the Twin Cities and, through the MINITEX interlibrary loan network, to libraries throughout the United States and Canada. Students are trained to use online computer terminals for legal research.

■ Curriculum

➧ Academic Support Program ➧ 86 credits required to graduate

William Mitchell offers 3, 3-1/2, and 4-year programs of afternoon and evening classes leading to a J.D. degree.

Students in the full-time program take 12 to 15 hours of classroom instruction per week over a three-year period. Students in the four-year part-time program take a maximum of 11 hours of classroom instruction per week over a period of four years, allowing them to work up to full time while attending school. The required courses and number of electives that can be taken are the same under all of the programs. All students must complete their degree requirements within six academic years of their original matriculation.

The college is not committed to any single system or method of instruction. The case method involves the study and analysis of selected cases, as well as classroom discussion of the rules of law established or illustrated by the cases. The problem method, seminars, written assignments, and simulated exercises are employed in certain courses. The use of videotapes and computers adds another learning dimension.

The curriculum has a broad national focus, and elective courses enable advanced students to specialize.

■ Special Programs

The William Mitchell Law Clinic results in a graduate who is ready to immediately begin to practice law. This is distinguished from one who needs to learn how to practice. Since its beginning in 1972, the Law Clinic has become a nationally recognized leader in trial advocacy teaching methods and clinical education. In 1981, the college received the prestigious Emil Gumpert Award for excellence in the teaching of trial advocacy. Students are eligible to participate in any of a broad range of clinical courses. The clinics are taught by full-time professors and supervisory attorneys.

The Legal Writing Program has been singled out for praise by the American Bar Association and the Association of American Law Schools as an excellent legal writing program. One of the strengths of the program is the 13 to 1 student-faculty ratio.

The Child Care Center meets the needs of our students who must have child care available at more flexible times than traditional child care facilities. The center is on campus.

■ Admission

➧ Bachelor's degree required for admission ➧ application deadline—April 15 ➧ LSAT required ➧ application fee—$35

Admission decisions are based upon academic factors such as the applicant's LSAT score and undergraduate GPA, as well as nonacademic factors such as work record, writing ability, economic or educational disadvantage, and handicap. The college does not require any particular area of undergraduate study, but does prefer applicants with strong written communication and analytical skills. William Mitchell College of Law admits students of either sex and of any race, color, religion, national or ethnic origin, and sexual preference.

■ Expenses and Financial Aid

➻ *tuition & fees—four year program, $10,500; three-year program, $14,460* ➻ *estimated additional expenses—books, $500 per year* ➻ *need-based scholarships available* ➻ *financial aid available—Stafford loans, Perkins loans, LAL, SLS, and SELF loans*

The Warren E. Burger Entrance Scholarship is awarded annually.

■ Housing

The college maintains no dormitories or housing facilities, but the college's location in an urban residential area assures students of the availability of private apartment housing. A monthly Housing Bulletin is published by the Student Service Office.

■ Career Services

William Mitchell graduates are highly employable. We attract a special kind of student: motivated, industrious, mature, and serious about a legal education. Many William Mitchell students hold full- or part-time jobs while in school and have valuable work experience to offer the employer. Also, because we combine practical skills with actual legal experience, our students have related experience to offer the employer. We provide a complete career services office with a full-time Assistant Dean and staff, on-campus interviews, a computerized résumé search service, career counseling, programs, publications, and job postings.

According to recent surveys of our graduates, 88 percent of those responding were satisfactorily employed within six to nine months after graduation; 45 percent of those were in private practice; 24 percent were in business and corporations; 25 percent were in government, including judicial clerkships; and the rest were in graduate school, teaching, or the military.

Applicant Group for the 1995-1996 Academic Year

William Mitchell College of Law
This grid includes only applicants who earned 120-180 LSAT scores under standard administrations.

LSAT Score	3.75 +		3.50 - 3.74		3.25 - 3.49		3.00 - 3.24		2.75 - 2.99		2.50 - 2.74		2.25 - 2.49		2.00 - 2.24		Below 2.00		No GPA		Total	
	Apps	Adm	Apps	Adm	Apps	Adm	Apps	Adm	Apps	Adm	Apps	Adm	Apps	Adm	Apps	Adm	Apps	Adm	Apps	Adm	Apps	Adm
175 - 180	0	0	0	0	0	0	0	0	0	0	0	0	0	0	0	0	0	0	0	0	0	0
170 - 174	2	2	1	1	0	0	0	0	1	1	0	0	0	0	0	0	0	0	0	0	4	4
165 - 169	4	4	3	3	1	1	3	3	7	7	3	3	1	1	2	1	0	0	0	0	24	23
160 - 164	3	3	11	11	22	22	16	16	20	20	10	9	6	6	1	1	1	0	1	1	91	89
155 - 159	18	18	32	32	42	42	45	45	42	39	38	33	21	17	8	8	0	0	2	2	248	236
150 - 154	17	17	32	32	76	70	94	60	81	28	49	13	32	10	15	3	5	1	1	1	402	235
145 - 149	12	11	28	25	56	37	77	30	71	21	62	15	23	2	15	1	4	0	1	0	349	142
140 - 144	4	3	8	6	29	12	43	16	46	5	36	3	27	1	7	0	2	0	5	2	207	48
135 - 139	1	1	5	3	5	1	11	0	9	1	18	0	9	0	5	0	3	0	1	0	67	6
130 - 134	0	0	0	0	2	0	1	0	2	0	4	0	2	0	4	0	0	0	0	0	15	0
125 - 129	0	0	0	0	0	0	0	0	0	0	2	0	2	0	1	0	0	0	0	0	5	0
120 - 124	0	0	0	0	0	0	0	0	0	0	0	0	0	0	0	0	0	0	0	0	0	0
Total	61	59	120	113	233	185	290	170	279	122	222	76	123	37	58	14	15	1	11	6	1412	783

Apps = Number of Applicants
Adm = Number Admitted
Reflects 95% of the total applicant pool.

University of Wisconsin Law School

975 Bascom Mall
Madison, WI 53706

Phone: 608.262.5914

■ Introduction

The University of Wisconsin Law School is a part of one of the world's largest, most honored, and most diversified universities. In Madison, a particularly interesting and livable city of just under 200,000, the school is located in the center of the main campus, close to downtown and the state capital. The school pioneered the belief that the law must be studied in action, as it relates to society, not as a self-contained system. Close connections with other departments and facilities of the university and research and service projects with state and federal governments have given concrete meaning to this law-in-action emphasis and have enriched the school's whole program. The school has a national reputation, is a charter member of the AALS, and is ABA-approved.

■ Enrollment/Student Body

➠ *2,220 applicants* ➠ *720 admitted first-year class 1995* ➠ *285 enrolled first-year class 1995* ➠ *816 total full-time* ➠ *68 total part-time* ➠ *21% minority* ➠ *45% women* ➠ *27 states & foreign countries represented* ➠ *119 undergraduate schools represented in first-year class* ➠ *loss of first-year students due to academic failure runs less than 2%*

■ Faculty

➠ *49 total, all full time* ➠ *11 women* ➠ *6 minority*

■ Library and Physical Facilities

➠ *400,000 volumes & equivalents* ➠ *library hours: Mon.-Thurs., 7:45 A.M.-MIDNIGHT; Fri., 7:45 A.M.-11:00 P.M.; Sat., 9:00 A.M.-9:00 P.M.; Sun., 9:00 A.M.-MIDNIGHT* ➠ *LEXIS* ➠ *NEXIS* ➠ *WESTLAW* ➠ *DIALOG* ➠ *10+ full-time librarians* ➠ *library seats 700*

The library's print collections are strong in all areas of U.S. state and federal law, international law, and the law of select foreign jurisdictions and support research and document requests from practitioners and legal scholars throughout the world. These print collections are complemented with distributed access to online legal information from virtually anywhere in the library through a combination of LANs, computer labs, and an innovative computer lap-top check-out program. Additionally, the library's online catalog ties into a campus rich in library resources, including the 5 million volumes located in the nearby main campus library and Historical Society Library.

■ Curriculum

➠ *Academic Support Program* ➠ *90 credits required to graduate* ➠ *semesters, start in Aug.* ➠ *range of first-year class size—20-89*

The first semester runs from late August to shortly before Christmas; the second, from January to May. A total of 13 weeks of summer school is available each year, making it possible for a student to complete credit and residence requirements in roughly two and one half years, including summers. Summer school is available for advanced students only, including students in good standing at other law schools. The first-year curriculum consists of required courses plus one limited elective choice. A broad selection of elective courses and seminars is available in the second and third years. Students who wish admission to the state bar of Wisconsin without bar examination must elect some advanced courses in traditional areas. In addition to the J.D., research-oriented LL.M. and S.J.D. programs are available on an individual basis. There are formalized dual-degree programs in Law and Public Administration, Law and Library Service, Law and Ibero-American Studies, Law and Environmental Studies, Law and Industrial Relations, Law and Business Masters Degree, Ph.D. in Philosophy, and Ph.D. in Sociology.

■ Special Programs

Eight clinical programs provide a variety of opportunities including public interest work, administrative and environmental law practices, judicial clerkships, legal services to institutionalized persons, representation of indigent defendants, and advocacy for disadvantaged persons.

■ Admission

➠ *Bachelor's degree from accredited college or university required* ➠ *application deadline—Feb. 1* ➠ *LSAT, LSDAS required* ➠ *median GPA—3.40* ➠ *median LSAT score—159* ➠ *application fee—$38*

The Law School has no specific undergraduate course prerequisites and agrees with the suggestions in the introduction of this handbook. Although most students attend on a full time basis, part-time attendance opportunities are available to those admitted students who cannot or do not wish to attend full time. It is faculty policy to encourage women and members of minority and disadvantaged groups to apply for admission. An active program for recruitment, admission, and financial aid for minority and disadvantaged students is important to the school. Applications are available the September preceding admission. Written recommendations are welcomed but not required; interviews are not part of the admissions process. A carefully prepared personal statement reflecting consideration of our admissions criteria is often very helpful to the Admissions Committee. An application deadline of February 1 is enforced. No statement of intention to enroll is required until after April 1. College grades and LSAT score are significant, but many other factors are considered. Large numbers of applications from highly qualified Wisconsin residents have forced Wisconsin's only state-supported law school to reserve approximately 70 to 80 percent of the available places for Wisconsin residents, with the result that criteria are somewhat higher for nonresidents. In recent years, the Law School has been able eventually to offer acceptance to about one of every three Wisconsin residents who apply and about one of every five nonresidents.

Transfer applications may be made, but only students with excellent law school records can be accepted. The deadline for transfer applicants for fall admission is June 1, but a decision cannot be expected until the full year's law school record is available.

■ Student Activities

In addition to the myriad of university activities, there are many activities especially for law students. The *Wisconsin Law Review*, edited by students, devotes substantial space to national and international problems and Wisconsin law. Written by both professionals in the field and law students, the student-edited *Wisconsin International Law Journal*, *Women's Law Journal*, and *Environmental Law Journal* offer articles of scholarly and practical interest in various areas of law. The Student Bar Association sponsors activities and nominates students for such student/faculty committees as curriculum, tenure, and admissions.

■ Expenses and Financial Aid

➧ *full-time tuition & fees—residents, $5,211; nonresidents, $13,488*

Scholarship grants are awarded to students on the basis of need, as determined through application to the Campus Office of Student Financial Services. Scholarship money is limited, and will not meet the student's total needs. Entering students must apply for financial aid no later than March 1, and, therefore, should not wait until acceptance to apply. The Law School participates in Free Application for Federal Student Aid and will not accept GAPSFAS applications. Loan funds from government and private sources to law students in 1995-96 amounted to approximately $5,000,000. The Law School has an emergency short-term loan fund available for qualified students.

■ Career Services

The school operates a full-time Career Services Office to assist students and alumni seeking summer, part-time, or permanent employment. Most graduates have found employment within a few months of graduation. About 65 percent remain in Wisconsin. Approximately 60 percent of the graduates enter private practice, and 20 percent enter government service. The average annual starting salary for the class of 1994 was over $41,000.

Applicant Group for the 1995-1996 Academic Year

University of Wisconsin Law School
This grid includes only applicants who earned 120-180 LSAT scores under standard administrations.

LSAT Score	GPA 3.75 +		3.50 - 3.74		3.25 - 3.49		3.00 - 3.24		2.75 - 2.99		2.50 - 2.74		2.25 - 2.49		2.00 - 2.24		Below 2.00		No GPA		Total	
	Apps	Adm	Apps	Adm	Apps	Adm	Apps	Adm	Apps	Adm	Apps	Adm	Apps	Adm	Apps	Adm	Apps	Adm	Apps	Adm	Apps	Adm
175 - 180	1	1	1	1	0	0	1	1	0	0	0	0	0	0	0	0	0	0	0	0	3	3
170 - 174	8	8	10	10	7	7	6	6	2	2	3	1	4	1	0	0	0	0	0	0	40	35
165 - 169	20	20	42	40	42	38	35	22	19	9	6	1	3	0	0	0	0	0	1	1	168	131
160 - 164	56	55	107	89	112	62	74	29	49	11	27	2	6	1	1	0	0	0	2	2	434	251
155 - 159	68	42	134	62	134	29	117	8	59	9	35	5	10	1	2	0	1	0	9	1	569	157
150 - 154	32	7	89	9	106	10	103	8	53	7	27	7	14	0	6	0	0	0	13	0	443	48
145 - 149	15	3	29	2	59	11	50	19	38	10	36	12	16	2	8	1	1	0	2	0	254	60
140 - 144	4	1	14	4	17	8	30	5	33	3	24	2	15	0	8	2	1	0	5	0	151	25
135 - 139	0	0	2	0	7	0	14	0	14	1	13	0	13	0	9	0	2	0	6	0	80	1
130 - 134	0	0	2	0	2	0	6	0	0	0	6	0	3	0	3	0	1	0	3	0	26	0
125 - 129	0	0	0	0	0	0	0	0	1	0	0	0	3	0	1	0	0	0	0	0	5	0
120 - 124	0	0	0	0	0	0	0	0	0	0	0	0	1	0	0	0	0	0	0	0	1	0
Total	204	137	430	217	486	165	436	98	268	52	177	30	88	5	38	3	6	0	41	4	2174	711

Apps = Number of Applicants
Adm = Number Admitted
Reflects 98% of the total applicant pool.

University of Wyoming College of Law

Post Office Box 3035
Laramie, WY 82071-3035

Phone: 307.766.6416

■ Introduction

The College of Law is located on the campus of the University of Wyoming in Laramie. The university, the only four-year institution of higher learning in Wyoming, comprises eight colleges, a graduate school, and several organized research units. The university has a student body of 11,000 in Laramie.

The College of Law, founded in 1920, is a member of the AALS and is accredited by the ABA. The college has approximately 230 students, a faculty of 14 full-time teachers, and several lecturers. The small student body and the excellent student-to-faculty ratio make possible a congenial atmosphere and a great amount of informal communication between students and faculty.

Laramie is a town of 25,000 located in the southeastern part of Wyoming at an altitude of 7,200 feet, on the high plains between two mountain ranges. Laramie's proximity to the mountains provides a variety of recreational activities including skiing, backpacking, rock climbing, hiking, camping, fishing, and hunting.

■ Enrollment/Student Body

➧ *602 applicants* ➧ *218 admitted first-year class 1995* ➧ *79 enrolled first-year class 1995* ➧ *226 total full-time* ➧ *6% minority* ➧ *42% women* ➧ *29 states & foreign countries represented* ➧ *70 undergraduate schools represented*

■ Faculty

➧ *17 total* ➧ *14 full-time* ➧ *3 part-time or adjunct* ➧ *5 women*

■ Library and Physical Facilities

➧ *174,000 volumes & equivalents* ➧ *library hours: Mon.-Thurs., 7:30 A.M.-MIDNIGHT; Fri., 7:30 A.M.-9:00 P.M.; Sat., 9:00 A.M.-9:00 P.M.; Sun., 10:00 A.M.-MIDNIGHT* ➧ *LEXIS* ➧ *NEXIS* ➧ *WESTLAW* ➧ *INFOTRAC* ➧ *3 full-time librarians* ➧ *library seats 181*

The College of Law first occupied its new building in 1977. The facility provides ample classroom, library, and student study space, and furnishes a pleasant environment for study. A new three-story library addition was completed in the fall of 1993. This addition doubled the existing square footage of the law library. All law students are trained in computerized legal research, as well as in traditional research methods.

■ Curriculum

➧ *Academic Support Program* ➧ *88 credits required to graduate* ➧ *60 courses available* ➧ *degrees available: J.D.; J.D./M.B.A.; J.D./M.P.A.* ➧ *semesters, start in Aug.* ➧ *range of first-year class size—20-80*

The first year consists entirely of required courses. During the second year, students must take additional required courses including evidence, professional responsibility, and a second semester of constitutional law and civil procedure. Students must also complete an advanced writing requirement prior to graduation. As a condition of graduation from the College of Law, all students must successfully complete at least two of the following three courses—administrative law, business organizations, and trusts and estates. In addition, all students must successfully complete at least one of the following three courses—creditors' rights, income taxation, or secured transactions.

In both the second and third years, practical legal training is available through courses in legal research, legal skills and problems, trial practice, and clinical work. The college has no summer session; however, graduation may be accelerated one semester by summer work at other accredited law schools.

■ Special Programs

The College of Law has a strong program of elective courses in natural resources law. Courses are regularly offered in environmental law, hazardous waste and water pollution, oil and gas, mining law, public land resources, water rights, and mineral taxation. Other electives include coverage of trial and appellate practice, corporate taxation, estate planning, corporate and commercial law, administrative and regulatory law, consumer law, and Indian law.

Students may obtain practical experience and receive academic credit for work in three clinical programs: (1) a defender aid program in which students brief and argue criminal appeals on behalf of indigent persons and assist penitentiary inmates in postconviction cases; (2) a prosecution assistance program in which students work directly with prosecuting attorneys and the United States Attorney in criminal cases; and, (3) a legal services program in which students provide legal assistance to economically disadvantaged persons. All clinical programs operate under faculty supervision.

■ Admission Standards

➧ *Bachelor's degree from accredited college or university required* ➧ *application deadline—April 1* ➧ *early application preferred* ➧ *early review of applications begins in late February* ➧ *LSAT, LSDAS required* ➧ *median GPA—3.30* ➧ *median LSAT score—154* ➧ *application fee—$35*

The College of Law restricts the entering class to 80. Approximately 55 of these students are Wyoming residents, and 25 are nonresidents. In recent years, about 85 percent of the entering class have successfully completed law study and received the J.D. degree. The school does not discriminate on the basis of race, sex, or age in making admissions decisions.

Students are admitted only for the fall semester. The college begins to accept applications in October for the class entering the following August. The entering class is selected from applications completed and on file by

April 1. Applications are accepted after April 1, but only to fill vacancies that occur in the class initially selected. To meet the April 1 deadline, applicants should take the LSAT no later than February and should subscribe to LSDAS and arrange for forwarding of official transcripts no later than mid-January.

As a general rule, applicants must have received an undergraduate degree prior to registration. In very exceptional cases, a candidate without an undergraduate degree who possesses extraordinary experience and training may be admitted.

Written recommendations are not required. Selection of the entering class is based primarily on LSAT score and undergraduate grade-point average. As a limited number of places are assigned to nonresidents, out-of-state applicants who do not have a 3.25 grade average on a 4.0 scale and an LSAT score in the 60th percentile have little chance of serious consideration. However, a lower grade-point average or LSAT score may be offset by a higher LSAT score or grade average.

■ Student Activities

The College of Law publishes the *Land and Water Law Review*, a student-edited journal devoted to legal problems of natural resources, environmental issues, questions of Wyoming jurisprudence, and legal topics of general interest.

Student professional organizations include Potter Law Club, which provides student government and social activities and affiliation with the Law Student Division of the ABA, three legal fraternities, Christian Legal Society, Minority Law Student Association, Natural Resources Law Forum, Women's Law Forum, and the Wyoming Trial Lawyers Association. Students represent the college each year in the National Moot Court Competition, National Environmental Law Moot Court Competition, National Client Counseling Competition, ATLA National Student Trial Advocacy Competition, and the Natural Resources Law Moot Court Competition. Student organizations include two law school honoraries: the Order of the Coif, and the Order of the Barrister.

■ Expenses and Financial Aid

- *tuition & fees—resident, $3,427, nonresident, $7,819*
- *estimated additional expenses—$6,500 (room, board, books)*
- *academic and need-based scholarships available*
- *Minority Graduate Assistantship Program*
- *financial aid available; FAF for need analysis due to College Board in Jan. or early Feb.*
- *College of Law Scholarship Application due June 1*

■ Career Services

The placement service, under the direction of the Career Services Director, coordinates job placement for law students and recent graduates who seek permanent or summer employment; disseminates information to potential employers; collects résumés and employer information; and arranges interviews and conferences. Advice is given on the various opportunities for legal employment, résumé preparation, job interview dynamics, and techniques for obtaining employment.

Applicant Group for the 1995-1996 Academic Year

University of Wyoming College of Law
This grid includes only applicants who earned 120-180 LSAT scores under standard administrations.

	GPA																					
LSAT Score	3.75 +		3.50 - 3.74		3.25 - 3.49		3.00 - 3.24		2.75 - 2.99		2.50 - 2.74		2.25 - 2.49		2.00 - 2.24		Below 2.00		No GPA		Total	
	Apps	Adm	Apps	Adm	Apps	Adm	Apps	Adm	Apps	Adm	Apps	Adm	Apps	Adm	Apps	Adm	Apps	Adm	Apps	Adm	Apps	Adm
175 - 180	0	0	0	0	0	0	0	0	0	0	0	0	0	0	0	0	0	0	0	0	0	0
170 - 174	0	0	0	0	0	0	0	0	0	0	0	0	0	0	0	0	0	0	0	0	0	0
165 - 169	1	1	1	1	2	1	2	2	2	2	2	2	1	1	0	0	0	0	0	0	11	10
160 - 164	5	4	10	10	6	5	17	15	11	9	11	6	4	1	1	0	0	0	2	0	67	50
155 - 159	5	3	22	22	18	17	30	20	18	3	9	1	9	2	4	0	0	0	1	0	116	68
150 - 154	11	9	21	21	26	17	35	8	35	4	20	3	15	4	4	0	2	0	1	0	170	66
145 - 149	2	1	13	1	22	6	28	2	18	2	14	0	11	1	4	0	0	0	4	1	116	14
140 - 144	2	0	5	0	14	0	13	0	17	0	4	0	5	0	7	1	1	0	1	0	69	1
135 - 139	0	0	2	0	5	0	3	0	1	0	6	0	3	0	2	0	2	0	3	0	27	0
130 - 134	0	0	0	0	0	0	0	0	0	0	0	0	1	0	3	0	0	0	0	0	4	0
125 - 129	1	0	0	0	0	0	0	0	0	0	1	0	0	0	0	0	0	0	0	0	2	0
120 - 124	0	0	0	0	0	0	0	0	0	0	0	0	0	0	0	0	0	0	0	0	0	0
Total	27	18	74	55	93	46	128	47	102	20	67	12	49	9	25	1	5	0	12	1	582	209

Apps = Number of Applicants
Adm = Number Admitted
Reflects 98% of the total applicant pool.

Yale Law School

P.O. Box 208329
New Haven, CT 06520-8329

URL: http://elsinore.cis.yale.edu/lawweb/lawschool/ylsfd.htm

■ Introduction

Yale Law School is an extraordinary community in which to study law. Our unmatched faculty-to-student ratio allows us to offer a vast array of courses, an average class size of under 20 students, and countless opportunities for independent research, writing, and student-organized seminars. Easy student-faculty interaction and institutional flexibility are hallmarks of the school. Law students have access to scholars in all of Yale's departments, to the university's nine-million-volume library system, and to its cultural, social, intellectual, and athletic activities. At the same time, Yale Law School has ties to the city of New Haven, a small, lively urban center with the attractions and problems of an American city. New Haven has two of the finest repertory theaters in the country, commercial theaters that bring in touring shows and performers, several first-rate museums, and the best pizza in America. Students are involved with New Haven's less prosperous side through the legal services organization.

■ Enrollment/Student Body

➧ 3,846 applicants ➧ 306 admitted first-year class 1995 (including previously deferred) ➧ 180 enrolled first-year class 1995 ➧ 573 total full-time ➧ 29.7% minority ➧ 45% women ➧ 71 states & foreign countries represented (1994-1995) ➧ 184 undergraduate schools represented (1994-1995)

The vitality of Yale Law School depends as much on the knowledge, experience, and expertise of the students as it does on the faculty, the library, the university, or the alumni. The school selects its students from applicants with the highest academic qualifications in the country; within this group, it seeks diversity of background and experience. Most of the international students in the school are enrolled in the LL.M program. The Law School welcomes older students and students with disabilities.

■ Faculty

➧ 105 total ➧ 48 full-time ➧ 57 part-time or adjunct ➧ 10 women full-time ➧ 6 minority full-time

The law school faculty is as broad-ranging in its interests and expertise as it is distinguished. It includes prominent scholars of economics, philosophy, and psychoanalysis, as well as leading specialists in every area of law. Approximately 50 full-time professors are joined each year by visiting lecturers, adjunct professors from other parts of the university, and practicing lawyers who assist the full-time clinical faculty as tutors in the clinical program. In addition, dozens of guest lecturers from around the world help to make Yale Law School a vibrant intellectual community.

■ Library and Physical Facilities

➧ 800,000 volumes & equivalents ➧ library hours: 24 hours a day, 7 days a week during academic year ➧ LEXIS ➧ NEXIS ➧ WESTLAW ➧ DIALOG ➧ 16 full-time librarians ➧ library seats 380

The Sterling Law Buildings occupy one city block at the heart of Yale University and close to downtown New Haven. Constructed in 1929-31, they were modeled on the idea of the English Inns of Court. Classrooms, offices, the law library and the international law library, two student computer labs, dormitory rooms for about 100 law students, and the dining hall surround a pleasant courtyard. A day-care center is located off-site.

■ Curriculum

➧ 82 credits required to graduate ➧ 142 courses available ➧ degrees available: J.D./M.P.A.; M.S.L.; LL.M.; J.S.D.; J.D.; J.D./M.P.P.M.; J.D./M.A.; J.D./Ph.D.; J.D./M.D.; J.D./M.E.S.; J.D./M.F.S.; J.D./M. DIV. ➧ semesters, start in Aug. ➧ range of first-year class size—15-90

In the fall semester, all first-year students take classes in constitutional law, contracts, procedure, and torts. After the first term, the only required course is criminal law. A supervised analytic paper, a substantial paper, and attendance at a series of lectures on professional responsibility are also required. For the first term, all grades are credit/fail. After that, grades are honors, pass, low pass, and fail, with credit/fail options.

■ Special Programs

Yale Law School sees the study of law as interrelated with other intellectual disciplines and with practical experience. The Law School encourages special programs, including joint-degree opportunities with many other departments at Yale and with some other universities, intensive semester experiences outside the law school, work with state legislative committees drafting legislation and preparing reports, and work with local organizations such as schools, human rights, and civil rights agencies under the aegis of student-run programs.

■ Transfer Students and Advanced Degrees

Yale Law School welcomes applications for transfer. Students who wish to transfer may be granted residence and academic credit for up to two semesters of study. Transfer students must do at least two years of work at Yale Law School.

In addition to the J.D., Yale Law School offers an LL.M degree, for those who are interested in teaching law. The Master of Studies in Law degree (M.S.L.) is a one-year program designed for professionals in other fields who desire an intensive introduction to the law.

■ Admission

➽ *Bachelor's degree from accredited college or university required* ➽ *application deadline—Feb. 15* ➽ *LSAT, LSDAS required* ➽ *median GPA—3.84* ➽ *median LSAT score—171* ➽ *application fee—$60*

The admissions process at Yale Law School is an intensely competitive one in which the totality of available information about the applicant is taken into account. No one element is decisive. The competition is stiff; nevertheless, we encourage all those who desire to be a part of the Yale Law School community to submit applications. Each application file is first read by the Dean or Director of Admissions. A group of the most highly rated files is then considered by faculty file readers. On the basis of the faculty ratings we admit candidates and establish a waiting list. Use of the waiting list varies from year to year; the list is not ranked until offers are to be made from the list. A number of waiting-list candidates are held for consideration through registration day. Faculty file readers' ratings are based on their own criteria, and the relative weight to be given to experience versus academic achievement is within each file reader's discretion. A 250-word essay, on a subject of your choice, is required. Personal statements of any length are welcome. Two letters of recommendation are required; additional letters are welcome. The Law School begins to issue decisions in late February. Minority applicants are evaluated in the same fashion as and along with nonminority applicants. Applicants are encouraged to bring to our attention aspects of their personal background and other special characteristics that they believe to be pertinent.

■ Student Activities

Yale Law students are very active outside the classroom. In any given year, as many as 40-50 student organizations may be active. Included in that group are six student-run journals.

■ Expenses and Financial Aid

➽ *$21,660 full-time tuition & fees* ➽ *average amount additional expenses—$10,550 (room & board, books, and personal expenses)* ➽ *need-based scholarships available for all eligible students* ➽ *financial aid available* ➽ *Loan Forgiveness Program (COAP)* ➽ *Need Access required* ➽ *FAFSA required*

Financial aid is awarded solely on the basis of need. Admissions decisions are made before and independently of financial aid decisions. Approximately 70 percent of the student body now receives some form of financial assistance; about 40 percent receive loans only. A financial aid award consists of a portion in gift and a portion in loan; typically the higher the total financial need, the higher the proportion of gift.

■ Career Services

Yale Law School graduates occupy positions of leadership in a tremendous range of endeavors. The Career Development Office, staffed by six full-time employees including three attorney counselors, helps students explore the unparalleled diversity of opportunities they face.

Applicant Group for the 1995-1996 Academic Year

Yale Law School

Average LSAT Score on the 120-180* Scale

Undergraduate GPA	Below 154		155 - 159		160 - 164		165 - 169		170 - 174		175 - 180		Total	
	Apps	Adm	Apps	Adm	Apps	Adm	Apps	Adm	Apps	Adm	Apps	Adm	Apps	Adm
3.75+	102	1	130	3	265	18	360	50	228	87	114	59	1199	218
3.50 - 3.74	134	0	151	1	265	14	312	6	162	17	72	19	1096	57
3.25 - 3.49	115	0	102	1	153	1	137	3	80	3	33	2	620	10
3.00 - 3.24	126	0	51	0	56	2	50	1	9	0	11	0	303	3
Below 3.00	235	0	48	0	60	0	30	0	14	1	2	0	389	1
No GPA	58	0	17	0	20	1	24	1	11	4	2	1	132	7
Total	770	1	499	5	819	36	913	61	504	111	234	81	3739	296*

Apps = Number of Applicants
Adm = Number Admitted
* Because only applicants with scores on the 120-180 scale are included above, the grid includes only 97% of applicants and 96% of admitted applicants. Total applicants for the fall of 1995 were 3843; total admitted applicants, 306.

Appendix A: Canadian Member Law Schools

University of Alberta
Faculty of Law
Room 484B, Admissions Office
Edmonton, Alberta
CANADA T6G 2H5

University of British Columbia
Faculty of Law
1822 East Mall
Vancouver, British Columbia
CANADA V6T 1Z1

University of Calgary
Faculty of Law
Calgary, Alberta
CANADA T2N 1N4

Dalhousie Law School
6061 University Avenue
Halifax, Nova Scotia
CANADA B3H 4H9

University of Manitoba
Faculty of Law
Robson Hall
Winnipeg, Manitoba
CANADA R3T 2N2

McGill University
Faculty of Law
3644 Peel
Montreal, Quebec
CANADA H3A 1W9

University of New Brunswick
Faculty of Law
P.O. Box 4400
Fredericton, New Brunswick
CANADA E3B 5A3

University of Ottawa
Faculty of Law
57 Louis Pasteur
P.O. Box 450
Station A
Ottawa, Ontario
CANADA K1N 6N5

Queen's University
Faculty of Law
Registrar of Law, Macdonald Hall
Kingston, Ontario
CANADA K7L 3N6

University of Saskatchewan
College of Law
Admissions Committee
15 Campus Drive
Saskatoon, Saskatchewan
CANADA S7N 5A6

University of Toronto
Faculty of Law
78 Queen's Park
Toronto, Ontario
CANADA M5S 2C5

University of Victoria
Faculty of Law
P.O. Box 2400
Victoria, British Columbia
CANADA V8W 3H7

University of Western Ontario
Faculty of Law
London, Ontario
CANADA N6A 3K7

University of Windsor
Faculty of Law
401 Sunset
Windsor, Ontario
CANADA N9B 3P4

York University
Osgoode Hall Law School
4700 Keele Street
North York, Ontario
CANADA M3J 1P3

Appendix B: U.S. Law Schools Not Approved by the ABA

Alabama

Birmingham School of Law
823 Frank Nelson Bldg.
205 North 20th Street
Birmingham, AL 35203

Jones School of Law
5345 Atlanta Highway
Montgomery, AL 36109

Miles Law School
P. O. Box 3800
Birmingham, AL 35208

California

American College of Law
1717 S. State College Blvd.
Suite 100
Anaheim, Ca 92806

CAL Northern School of Law
2525 Dominic Drive
Chico, CA 95928

California Pacific School of Law
1600 Truxton Avenue
Suite 100
Bakersfield, CA 93301

California Southern Law School
3775 Elizabeth Street
Riverside, CA 92506

Chapman University School of Law
1240 S. State College Road
Suite 200
Anaheim, CA 92806

Empire College
3033 Cleveland Avenue
Suite 102
Santa Rosa, CA 95401-2185

Glendale University
College of Law
220 North Glendale Avenue
Glendale, CA 91206

Humphreys College—School of Law
6650 Inglewood Avenue
Stockton, CA 95207

John F. Kennedy University School of Law
12 Altarinda Road
Orinda, CA 95207

University of LaVerne
College of Law at San Fernando Valley
5445 Balboa Boulevard
Encino, CA 91316

University of LaVerne
College of Law
1950 3rd Street
LaVerne, CA 91750

Lincoln Law School of Sacramento
3140 J Street
Sacramento, CA 95816

Lincoln Law School
of San Jose
2160 Lundy Avenue
San Jose, CA 95131

Monterey College of Law
404 West Franklin Street
Monterey, CA 93940

New College of California
School of Law
50 Fell Street
San Francisco, CA 94102

University of Northern California
Lorenzo Patino School of Law
727½ J Street
Sacramento, CA 95814

Oakland College of Law
436 14th Street
Suite 411
Oakland, CA 94612-2703

Peninsula University Law School
436 Dell Avenue
Mountain View, CA 94043

San Francisco Law School
20 Haight Street
San Francisco, CA 94102

San Joaquin College of Law
3385 East Shields Avenue
Fresno, CA 93726

Santa Barbara College of Law
911 Tremonto Road
Santa Barbara, CA 93103

Simon Greenleaf School of Law
3855 East LaPalma Avenue
Anaheim, CA 92807

Southern California University
for Professional Studies
202 Fashion Lane
Tustin, CA 92680-3328

Ventura College of Law
4475 Market Street
Ventura, CA 93003

University of West Los Angeles
School of Law
1155 W. Arbor Vitae Street
Inglewood, CA 90301-2902

Western State University
College of Law, Irvine
16485 Laguna Canyon Road
Irvine, CA 92718

Western State University—Fullerton
College of Law
1111 North State College Boulevard
Fullerton, CA 92631

Thomas Jefferson School of Law
2121 San Diego Avenue
San Diego, CA 92110

Florida

Florida Coastal School of Law
7555 Beach Boulevard
Jacksonville, FL 32216

University of Orlando School of Law
6441 E. Colonial Avenue
Orlando, FL 32807

Georgia

John Marshall Law School, Atlanta
805 Peachtree Street, N.E.
Suite 400
Atlanta, GA 30308

Massachusetts

Massachusetts School of Law
at Andover
500 Federal Street
Andover, MA 01810

Southern New England School of Law
333 Faunce Corner Road
North Dartmouth, MA 02747

Puerto Rico

Eugenio Maria De Hostos School of Law
GPO Box 1900
Mayaguez, Puerto Rico 00681

Tennessee

Nashville School of Law
2934 Sidco Drive
Nashville, TN 37204

Appendix C: LSAC Statement of Good Admission Practices

Introduction

This Statement of Good Admission Practices is designed to focus attention on principles that should guide law school admission programs. No attempt has been made to develop "legislative" guidelines, because no absolute rules apply to every situation. The statement is intended to improve the admission process in law schools and to promote fairness for all participants.

General Principles

1. The primary purpose of the law school admission process is to serve law school applicants, law schools, and the legal profession by making informed judgments about those who seek legal education. The responsibility that role carries with it demands the highest standards of professional conduct.

2. Law school admission professionals should avoid impropriety and the appearance of impropriety, as well as any conflict of interest or the appearance of conflict. They should not accept anything for themselves or the law school or pursue any activity that might compromise or seem to compromise their integrity or that of the admission process.

3. Law schools should strive to achieve and maintain the highest standards of accuracy and candor in the development and publication of print and other materials designed to inform or influence applicants. A law school should provide any applicant or potential applicant with information and data that will enable the applicant to assess his or her prospects for successfully (1) seeking admission to that school, (2) financing his or her education at that school, (3) completing the educational program at that school, and (4) seeking employment with degree from that school. If statistics are provided regarding admissions, financial aid, and placement, law schools should provide the most current information and should present it in an easily understood form. Significant errors of fact, as well as errors of omission, should be corrected promptly and prominently.

4. Law schools should establish application procedures that inform applicants of relevant criteria, processes, and deadlines, respect the confidentiality of student records and admission data, and provide for timely notification of admission decisions. Law schools should also ensure that all parties concerned with the admission process are familiar with and observe relevant laws, accreditation standards, and institutional guidelines, including the *Cautionary Policies Concerning LSAT Scores and Related Services* developed by Law School Admission Council (Law Services).

5. In making admission decisions, law schools should give special consideration to applicants who are members of cultural, ethnic, or racial groups that have not had adequate opportunities to develop and demonstrate potential for academic achievement and would not otherwise be meaningfully represented in the entering class. Schools should also make reasonable accommodations to the special needs of disabled applicants. Law schools should make a special effort to provide the information noted in Number 3 above to those applicants who are members of minority groups or who are disabled.

Admission Policy

1. Law schools should develop coherent and consistent admission policies. The admission policies should serve law school applicants by clearly setting forth the criteria on which admission decisions are made and the manner in which the criteria will be applied.

Law schools should develop and promulgate concise and coherent admission policies designed both to regularize the admission process and to inform fully prospective applicants and prelaw advisors of the means used to select new law students. The policies should include consideration of the various criteria and processes used to make admission decisions, such as the Law School Admission Test (LSAT), prior academic performance, professional and other work experiences, equal opportunity considerations, disabled status, geographical diversity, letters of recommendation, personal statements, and personal interviews, if required. These and other considerations related to a law school's institutional mission or objectives may result in a preference for certain applicants. Each law school's admission policies should be adequately disclosed to all prospective applicants at the outset of the admission process.

Scores obtained on the LSAT and undergraduate grade-point averages are factors by which applicants are judged by virtually all law schools. Law schools should ensure that all application materials accurately describe the manner in which LSAT scores, prior academic performance, and other factors are used in the admission process.

The LSAT is designed to measure some, but certainly not all, of the mental and academic abilities that are needed for successful law study. Within limits, it provides a reasonable assessment of these factors. LSAT scores provide at best a partial measure of an applicant's ability and should be considered in relation to the total range of information available about a prospective law student. Thus, the LSAT score should be used as only one of several criteria for evaluation and should not be given undue weight.

Use of cut-off LSAT scores below which no candidate will be considered is explicitly discouraged in the Law Services Cautionary Policies. However, a particular law school may discover evidence that applicants scoring below a certain point have substantial difficulty in performing satisfactorily in its program of studies. Based on that evidence, the law school may rationally choose to implement a policy of discouraging applications with LSAT scores below a certain point. Should a law school make that determination, applicants should be informed of that fact.

Similar considerations govern the evaluation of the applicant's prior academic record. Undergraduate grades are a significant indicator of potential success in law school. In addition to being one measure of academic ability, a strong scholastic record may indicate perseverance, organization, and motivation, all important factors which have few direct measures. There are, of course, measures of intellectual ability other than the cumulative grade point average. Unusual creativity, exceptional research skills, analytical prowess, and other factors may not be reflected on a candidate's college transcript.

In evaluating the academic record, law schools may choose to consider factors such as grade inflation, the age of the grades, discrepancies among the applicant's grades, the quality of the college attended, difficulty of course work, and time commitments while attending college.

Law schools may also take into consideration additional factors when choosing among various law school candidates. Letters of recommendation often have a significant impact on admission decisions. Some schools believe that letters of recommendation are usually more candid when the subject of the letter waives access to them and recommend that applicants limit their rights to inspect this portion of their admission files. However, waiver of access to letters of recommendation or of any part of the student's record should not be made a mandatory prerequisite to admission. The Buckley Amendment specifically mandates that U.S. law schools must not require such a waiver.

As with members of cultural, ethnic, and racial groups, law schools should also recognize the importance of providing equal educational opportunity for disabled individuals. Sometimes the applicant's disability may prevent the assembly of a complete admission file. For example, some applicants can take the LSAT only under special conditions, making it difficult to interpret their test scores. Others may seek to have certain admission requirements waived entirely. In these circumstances, law schools can properly give weight to the disabled applicant's demonstrated ability to overcome obstacles in building a record of academic and professional performance.

Admission of applicants from a wide variety of academic, cultural, ethnic, and racial backgrounds, and the resulting diversity, enhances and enriches the educational experience of all students and faculty.

It is proper to prefer students who have taken courses such as those that develop skills in both written and oral communications, develop analytical and problem-solving skills, or promote familiarity with the humanities and social sciences to understand the human condition and the social context in which legal problems arise. The decision to prefer either a classical liberal arts education or a more narrowly focused one should rest within the sound discretion of the law school.

2. Law schools that accept transfer applications should state clearly the application procedures for transfer applicants and inform them of all relevant deadlines, necessary documents and records, courses accepted for credit, and, to the extent possible, course equivalency.

Recruitment and Promotion

1. Law schools are responsible for all people they involve in admission, promotional, and recruitment activities (including graduates, students, and faculty), and for educating them about the principles of good practice outlined in this Statement, as well as all relevant laws, accreditation standards, and institutional policies. Law schools that use admission management firms or consulting firms are responsible for assuring that these firms adhere to sound admission practices.

The oversight role entrusted to law schools includes supervision of all personnel involved in the admission process. Law school personnel, students, and graduates who represent the law school at recruitment and other promotional activities should be informed of current law school programs and activities. They should be knowledgeable about the academic and financial requirements of attending the law school, and they should honestly and forthrightly respond to inquiries.

Professional recruiting organizations, though not formally affiliated with law schools, nonetheless are part of the admission process when they are engaged by law schools. Law schools engaging outside services are responsible for ensuring the integrity and the accuracy of the work performed for them. For example, errors or misleading statements appearing in recruitment brochures and law school catalogs may not be ascribed to the company performing the service. Law schools cannot abdicate the responsibility for accuracy by shifting blame to third parties.

2. Admissions publications should contain an accurate and current admission calendar and information about financial aid opportunities and requirements.

In addition to containing a complete listing of all relevant admission and financial aid deadlines, admission material should also convey accurate information about optimum dates, if any, for submitting admission materials. Among the items that might usefully be included are: dates for taking the Law School Admission Test; dates for submission of financial aid applications, including the best time for submission of materials to a financial aid need analysis service, if used; and the most useful date for submission of letters of recommendation. This information is particularly useful when law schools begin to make admission decisions prior to the deadline date for receipt of application materials under a "rolling" admission system.

Law schools should notify applicants about deadlines for financial aid applications and the criteria used in awarding aid. To the extent reasonably practicable, law schools should disclose how parental income will affect the financial aid determination. Similarly, the availability of need-based and of merit-based aid should be disclosed.

3. Law school admission professionals should be forthright and accurate in providing information about their institutions. Law school publications and any statements submitted for publication should contain current and accurate descriptions and representations of law school programs, campus life, and the surrounding community. Law schools should provide accurate, candid, and comprehensive information with respect to the law school opportunities sought by students and available to them.

Law school recruitment activities, e.g., law school forums, prelaw days, caravans, and law school fairs, provide an opportunity for law school representatives to engage in personal contact with applicants. In many instances, these activities are not only the first, but often the only direct contact applicants have with law schools until registration. In all of these instances, law school representatives should conduct themselves in a professional manner. Representatives attending these activities have an obligation to familiarize themselves with all aspects of the admission process at their respective schools. Recruitment activities should not include unreasonable and unfounded comparisons with other law schools.

4. Law schools should provide prelaw advisors and other educational and career counselors with accurate and appropriate information to assist them in counseling applicants about law school opportunities.

Issues of law school recruitment and enrollment require the cooperative efforts of college and university personnel working with law school admission counselors. Prelaw colleagues and other college counselors daily encounter students who are or may be interested in pursuing legal education. To serve the undergraduate population effectively, law schools should keep interested prelaw advisors, minority and other counselors informed of their admission requirements and institutional programs.

Application Procedures

1. Law schools should promptly notify applicants of admission decisions.

2. Law schools should respect the confidential nature of information received about applicants.

While a policy of openness and accessibility should form the basis for all communications with law school applicants, law schools should be scrupulous in maintaining the privacy of applicants. Without the expressed consent of the applicant involved and the author of the material in question, admission information relating to an applicant, such as LSAT scores, prior academic record, letters of recommendation, and dean's reports, should not be released to persons other than admission decision makers, the candidate and others with a legitimate interest in the admission process. This restriction would not prevent schools from sharing information that is not in a personally identifiable form, but even in this case, law schools should take care that the information is released with appropriate discretion.

From time to time, information about law school applicants at a particular law school is provided by Law Services. Information contained in many of these periodic reports is also confidential and should not be released to persons outside of the admission process, except as required by law.

3. A law school application should state clearly what information is being sought. The application should also state the applicant's obligation to provide accurate, current, and complete information. Further, the application should define the consequences of providing false, misleading, or incomplete information.

If the law school believes that false or misleading information has been provided by an applicant, that allegation should be submitted to the LSAC Misconduct and Irregularities in the Admission Process Subcommittee for investigation. Then, if misconduct is found, all law schools to which the applicant has applied, or may apply, will be notified.

4. Except under early decision plans, law schools should not require applicants or other persons to indicate the order of applicants' law school preferences.

Law schools should allow applicants the freedom to explore as many opportunities to pursue legal education as possible. To preserve applicant options, law schools should not base admission decisions on the order of applicants' law school preferences, unless the school has established an early decision plan. An early decision plan is one under which an applicant and a law school mutually agree at the point of application that the applicant will be given an admission decision at a date earlier than usual in return for the applicant's commitment, at that date, to attend the school and withdraw all applications pending at other law schools, and not initiate new applications.

5. Except under early decision plans, law schools should permit applicants to choose among offers of admission as well as offers of scholarships, grants, and loans without penalty until April 1. Admitted applicants who have submitted a timely financial aid application should not be required to commit to enroll until notified of financial aid awards that are within the control of the law school.

6. No law school has an obligation to maintain an offer of admission if it discovers that the applicant has accepted an offer at another institution. Except under early decision plans, law schools should not suggest that acceptance of their offer of admission creates a moral or legal obligation to register at that school. Every accepted applicant should be free to deal with all law schools and to accept an offer from one of them even though a deposit has been paid to another school. To provide applicants with an uncoerced choice among various law schools, no excessive fee should be required solely to maintain a place in the class. Law schools should give applicants sufficient warning and ample time before withdrawing offers.

7. Law schools should maintain a waiting list of reasonable length and only for a reasonable length of time.

Law schools using waiting lists should ensure that the lists are of reasonable length and that final decisions about applicants placed on the waiting lists are made and communicated to the applicant as soon as possible.

Index

These cards are for your convenience in writing to law schools for information. They are not applications for admission. At the beginning of each institution's *Official Guide* description, you will find the name and address of the office to which the card should be addressed.

If you wish to request information or application materials from more than six law schools, please use the postcards found in the *LSAT/LSDAS Registration and Information Book,* or prepare your own postcards in a similar format. You may also copy these cards and mail them in envelopes if you wish to request information from additional schools.

Notes

Notes